LONDON NIGHTMEN.

[*From a Daguerreotype by* BEARD.]

LONDON LABOUR
AND THE LONDON POOR

BY
HENRY MAYHEW

WITH A NEW INTRODUCTION BY
JOHN D. ROSENBERG
Professor of English, Columbia University

IN FOUR VOLUMES
VOLUME II
The London Street-Folk (continued)

DOVER PUBLICATIONS, INC.
NEW YORK

Copyright © 1968 by DOVER PUBLICATIONS, INC.
All rights reserved under Pan American and
International Copyright Conventions.

Published in Canada by General Publishing Company, Ltd.,
30 Lesmill Road, Don Mills, Toronto, Ontario.

Published in the United Kingdom by Constable and Company, Ltd.,
10 Orange Street, London WC 2.

This Dover edition, first published in 1968, is an unabridged republication of the work as published by Griffin, Bohn, and Company in 1861–1862, to which has been added a new Introduction by John D. Rosenberg.

Standard Book Number: 486-21935-6
Library of Congress Catalog Card Number: 68-19549

MANUFACTURED IN THE UNITED STATES OF AMERICA
DOVER PUBLICATIONS, INC.
180 VARICK STREET
NEW YORK, N. Y. 10014

CONTENTS

OF

VOLUME II.

THE STREET-FOLK.

	PAGE
INTRODUCTION	1
STREET-SELLERS OF SECOND-HAND ARTICLES	5
STREET-SELLERS OF LIVE ANIMALS	47
STREET-SELLERS OF MINERAL PRODUCTIONS AND NATURAL CURIOSITIES	81
THE STREET-BUYERS	103
THE STREET-JEWS	115
STREET-FINDERS OR COLLECTORS	136
THE STREETS OF LONDON	181
CHIMNEY-SWEEPERS	338
CROSSING-SWEEPERS	465

LIST OF ILLUSTRATIONS

LONDON NIGHTMEN	Frontispiece
A VIEW IN PETTICOAT-LANE	Facing page 36
A VIEW IN ROSEMARY-LANE	37
THE STREET DOG-SELLER	54
THE CRIPPLED STREET BIRD-SELLER	55
STREET-SELLER OF BIRDS'-NESTS	72
THE JEW OLD-CLOTHES MAN	73
THE BONE-GRUBBER	138
THE MUD-LARK	139
THE LONDON DUSTMAN	172
VIEW OF A DUST-YARD	173
THE LONDON SCAVENGER	226
STREET ORDERLIES	227
THE ABLE-BODIED PAUPER STREET-SWEEPER	262
THE RUBBISH-CARTER	263
THE LONDON SWEEP	346
ONE OF THE FEW REMAINING CLIMBING-SWEEPS	347
THE MILKMAID'S GARLAND	370
THE SWEEP'S HOME	371
THE SEWER-HUNTER	388
MODE OF CLEANSING CESSPOOLS	389
FLUSHING THE SEWERS	424
THE RAT-CATCHERS OF THE SEWERS	425
THE BEARDED CROSSING-SWEEPER AT THE EXCHANGE	470
THE CROSSING-SWEEPER THAT HAS BEEN A MAID-SERVANT	471
THE IRISH CROSSING-SWEEPER	480
THE ONE-LEGGED CROSSING-SWEEPER AT CHANCERY-LANE	481
THE BOY CROSSING-SWEEPERS	on page 507

LONDON LABOUR
AND
THE LONDON POOR.
VOL. II.

THE STREET-FOLK.
BOOK THE SECOND.

INTRODUCTION.

IN commencing a new volume I would devote a few pages to the consideration of the import of the facts already collected concerning the London Street-Folk, not only as regards the street-people themselves, but also in connection with the general society of which they form so large a proportion.

The precise extent of the proportion which the Street-Traders bear to the rest of the Metropolitan Population is the first point to be evolved; for the want, the ignorance, and the vice of a street-life being in a direct ratio to the numbers, it becomes of capital importance that we should know how many are seeking to pick up a livelihood in the public thoroughfares. This is the more essential because the Government returns never *have* given us, and probably never *will* give us, any correct information respecting it. The Census of 1841 set down the "Hawkers, Hucksters, and Pedlars" of the Metropolis as numbering 2045; and from the inquiries I have made among the street-sellers as to the means taken to obtain a full account of their numbers for the next population return, the Census of 1851 appears likely to be about as correct in its statements concerning the Street-Traders and Performers as the one which preceded it.

According to the accounts which have been collected during the progress of this work, the number of the London Street-People, so far as the inquiry has gone, is upwards of 40,000. This sum is made up of 30,000 Costermongers; 2000 Street-Sellers of "Green-Stuff," as Watercresses, Chickweed, and Groundsell, Turf, &c.; 4000 Street-Sellers of Eatables and Drinkables; 1000 selling Stationery, Books, Papers, and Engravings in the streets; and 4000 other street-sellers vending manufactured articles, either of metal, crockery, textile, chemical, or miscellaneous substances, making altogether 41,000, or in round numbers say 40,000 individuals. The 30,000 costermongers may be said to include 12,000 men, 6000 women, and 12,000 children.

The above numbers comprise the main body of people selling in the London streets; hence if we assert that, with the vendors of second-hand articles, as old metal, glass, linen, clothes, &c., and mineral productions, such as coke, salt, and sand, there are about 45,000 street-traders in the Metropolis, we shall not, I am satisfied, be very far from the truth.

The value of the Capital, or Stock in Trade, of these people, though individually trifling, amounts, collectively, to a considerable sum of money—indeed, to very nearly 40,000*l.*; or at the rate of about 1*l.* per head. Under the term Capital are included the donkeys, barrows, baskets, stalls, trays, boards, and goods belonging to the several street-traders; and though the stock of the watercress, the small-ware, the lucifer, the flower, or the chickweed and groundsell seller may not exceed in value 1*s.*, and the basket or tray upon which it is carried barely half that sum, that of the more prosperous costermonger, possessed of his barrow and donkey; or of the Cheap John, with his cart filled with hardware; or the Packman, with his bale of soft wares at his back, may be worth almost as many pounds as the others are pence.

The gross amount of trade done by the London Street-Sellers in the course of the year is so large that the mind is at first unable to comprehend how, without reckless extravagance, want can be in any way associated with the class. After the most cautious calculation, the results having been checked and re-checked in a variety of ways, so that the conclusion arrived at might be somewhat near and certainly not beyond the truth, it appears that the "*takings*" of the London Street-Sellers cannot be said to be less than 2,500,000*l.* per annum. But vast as this sum may seem, and especially when considered as only a portion of the annual expenditure of the Metropolitan Poor, still, when we come to spread the gross yearly receipts over 40,000 people, we find that the individual takings are but 62*l.* per annum, which (allowing the rate of profit to be in all cases even 50 per cent., though I am convinced it is often much less) gives to each street-trader an annual income of 20*l.* 13*s.* 4*d.*, or within a fraction of 8*s.* a week, all the year round. And when we come to deduct from this the loss by perishable articles, the keep of donkeys, the wear and tear, or hire, of barrows—the cost of stalls and baskets, together with the interest on stock-money (generally at the rate of 4*s.* a week—and often 1*s.* a day—for 1*l.*, or 1040*l.* per cent. per annum), we may with safety assert that the average gain or clear income of the Metropolitan Street-Sellers is rather under than over 7*s.* 6*d.* a week. Some of the more expert street-traders may clear 10*s.* or even 15*s.* weekly throughout the year, while the weekly profit of the less expert, the old people, and the children, may be said to be 3s. 6d. These incomes, however, are the average of the gross yearly profits rather than the regular weekly gains; the consequence is, that though they might be sufficient to keep the majority of the street-sellers in comparative comfort, were they constant and capable of being relied upon, from week to week—but being variable and uncertain, and rising sometimes from nothing in the winter to 1l. a week in the summer, when street commodities are plentiful and cheap, and the poorer classes have money wherewith to purchase them — and fluctuating moreover, even at the best of times, according as the weather is wet or fine, and the traffic of the streets consequently diminished or augmented—it is but natural that the people subject to such alternations should lack the prudence and temperance of those whose incomes are more regular and uniform.

To place the above facts clearly before the reader the following table has been prepared. The first column states the titles of the several classes of street-sellers; the second, the number of individuals belonging to each of these classes; the third, the value of their respective capitals or stock in trade; the fourth, the gross amount of trade done by them respectively every year; the fifth, the average yearly takings of each class; and the sixth, their average weekly gains. This gives us, as it were, a bird's-eye view of the earnings and pecuniary condition of the various kinds of street-sellers already treated of. It is here cited, as indeed all the statistics in this work are, as an approximation to the truth rather than a definite and accurate result.

DESCRIPTION OF CLASS.	Number of Persons in each Class.	Gross amount of capital, or stock in trade belonging to each class.	Gross amount of trade annually done by each class.	Average yearly receipts per head.	Average weekly gains.
COSTERMONGERS [a].			£		
Street-Sellers of Wet Fish			1,177,200		
,, ,, Dry fish			127,000		
,, ,, Shell Fish			156,600		
			1,460,800		
,, ,, Green Fruit			332,400		
,, ,, Dry Fruit	30,000 [b]	£25,000	1,000	£60	8s.
,, ,, Vegetables			292,200		
			625,600		
,, ,, Game, Poultry, Rabbits, &c.			80,000		
,, ,, Flowers, Roots, &c.			14,800		
			2,181,200		
STREET-SELLERS OF GREEN STUFF.					
Watercresses [c]	1,000	87	13,900	13	3s. 6d.
Chickweed, Groundsell, and Plantain [d]	1,000	42	14,000	14	5s.
Turf-Cutters and Sellers	40	20	570	14	5s. 6d.
STREET-SELLERS OF EATABLES AND DRINKABLES	4,000	9,000	203,100	50	10s.
STREET-SELLERS OF STATIONERY, LITERATURE, AND THE FINE ARTS	1,000	400	33,400	30	8s.
STREET-SELLERS OF MANUFACTURED ARTICLES of Metal, Crockery and Glass, Textile, Chemical, or Miscellaneous Substances	4,000	2,800	188,200	47	10s.
	41,040	£37,529	£2,634,370	£60	8s.

[a] The definition of a Costermonger strictly includes only such individuals as confine themselves to the sale of the produce of the Green and Fruit Markets: the term is here restricted to that signification.

[b] This number includes Men, Women, and Children.

[c] The Watercress trade is carried on in the streets, principally by old people and children. The chief mart to which the street-sellers of cresses resort is Farringdon-market, a place which but few or none of the regular Costermongers attend.

[d] The Chickweed and Groundsell Sellers and the Turf-Cutters' traffic has but little expense connected with it, and their trade is therefore nearly all profit.

Now, according to the above estimate, it would appear that the gross annual receipts of the entire body of street-sellers (for there are many besides those above specified—as for instance, the vendors of second-hand articles, &c.) may be estimated in round numbers at 3,000,000*l.* sterling, and their clear income at about 1,000,000*l.* per annum. Hence, we are enabled to perceive the importance of the apparently insignificant traffic of the streets; for were the street-traders to be prohibited from pursuing their calling, and so forced to apply for relief at the several metropolitan unions, the poor-rates would be at the least doubled. The total sum expended in the relief of the London poor, during 1848, was 725,000*l.*, but this we see is hardly three-fourths of the income of the street-traders. Those, therefore, who would put an end to the commerce of our streets, should reflect whether they would like to do so at the cost of doubling the present poor-rates and of reducing one-fortieth part of the entire metropolitan population from a state of comparative independence to absolute pauperism.

However unsatisfactory it may be to the aristocratic pride of the wealthy commercial classes, it cannot be denied that a very important element of the trade of this vast capital—this marvellous centre of the commerce of the world—I cite the stereotype phrases of civic eloquence, for they are at least truths—it is still undeniable, I say, that a large proportion of the commerce of the capital of Great Britain is in the hands of the Street-Folk. This simple enunciation might appear a mere platitude were it not that the street-sellers are a *proscribed class*. They are driven from stations to which long possession might have been thought to give them a quasi legal right; driven from them at the capricious desire of the shopkeepers, some of whom have had bitter reason, by the diminution of their own business, to repent their interference. They are bandied about at the will of a police-officer. They must "move on" and not obstruct a thoroughfare which may be crammed and blocked with the carriages of the wealthy until to cross the road on foot is a danger. They are, in fine, a body numbering thousands, who are allowed to live in the prosecution of the most ancient of all trades, sale or barter in the open air, *by sufferance alone.* They are classed as unauthorized or illegal and intrusive traders, though they "*turn over*" *millions in a year.*

The authorities, it is true, do not sanction any general arbitrary enforcement of the legal proscription of the Street-Folk, but they have no option if a section of shopkeepers choose to say to them, "Drive away from our doors these street-people." It appears to be sufficient for an inferior class of tradesmen—for such the meddlers with the street-folk generally seem to be—merely to desire such a removal in order to accomplish it. It is not necessary for them to say in excuse, "We pay heavy rents, and rates, and taxes, and are forced to let our lodgings accordingly; we pay for licences, and some of us as well pay fines for giving short weight to poor people, and that, too, when it is hardly safe to give short weight to our richer patrons; but what rates, taxes, or licences do these street-traders pay? Their lodgings may be dear enough, but their rates are nominally nothing" (being charged in the rent of their rooms). "From taxes they are blessedly exempt. They are called upon to pay no imposts on their property or income; they defray merely the trifling duties on their tobacco, beer, tea, sugar, coffee" (though these by the way—the chief articles in the excise and customs returns—make up one-half of the revenue of the country). "They ought to be put down. We can supply all that is wanting. What may become of *them* is simply their own concern."

The Act 50 Geo. III., c. 41, requires that every person "carrying to sell or exposing to sale any goods, wares, or merchandize," shall pay a yearly duty. But according to s. 23, "nothing in this Act shall extend to prohibit any person or persons from selling (by hawking in the streets) any printed papers licensed by authority; or any fish, fruit, or victuals." Among the privileged articles are also included barm or yeast, and coals. The same Act, moreover, contains nothing to prohibit the maker of any home-manufacture from exposing his goods to sale in any town-market or fair, nor any tinker, cooper, glazier, or other artizan, from going about and carrying the materials of his business. The unlicensed itinerant vendors of such things however as lucifer-matches, boot-laces, braces, fuzees, or any wares indeed, not of their own manufacture, are violators of the law, and subject to a penalty of 10*l.*, or three months' imprisonment for each offence. It is in practice, however, only in the hawking of such articles as those on which the duty is heavy and of considerable value to the revenue (such as tea, tobacco, or cigars), that there is any actual check in the London streets.

Nevertheless, a large proportion of the street-trading without a licence is contrary to law, and the people seeking to obtain a living by such means are strictly liable to fine or imprisonment, while even those street-traders whom the Act specially exempts—as for instance the street-sellers of fish, fruit, and vegetables, and of eatables and drinkables, as well as the street artizans, and who are said to have the right of "exposing their goods to sale in any market or fair in every city, borough, town-corporate, and market-town"—even these, I say, are liable to be punished for obstructing the highway whenever they attempt to do so.

Now these are surely anomalies which it is high time, in these free-trade days, should cease. *The endeavour to obtain an honest and independent livelihood should subject no man to fine or imprisonment;* nor should the poor hawker—the neediest perhaps of all tradesmen—be required to pay 4*l.* a year for the liberty to carry on his business when the wealthy shopkeeper can do so "scot-free." Moreover, it is a glaring iniquity that the rich tradesman should have it in his power, by complaining to the police, to deprive his poorer rival of the right to dispose of his goods in the streets. It is often said, in justification, that as the shopkeepers pay the principal portion of the rates and taxes, *they* must be protected in the exercise of their business. But this, in the first place, is far from the truth. As regards the taxes, the poorer classes pay nearly half of the national imposts: they pay the chief portion of the malt duty, and that is in round numbers 5,000,000*l.* a year; the greater part of the spirit duty, which is 4,350,000*l.*; the tobacco duty, 4,250,000*l.*; the sugar duty, 4,500,000*l.*; and the duty on tea, 5,330,000*l.*; making altogether 23,430,000*l.*, out of about 50,000,000*l.* Concerning the rates, however, it is not so easy to estimate what proportion the poor people contribute towards the local burdens of the country; but if they are householders, they have to pay quota of the parish and county expenses directly, and, if lodgers, indirectly in the rent of their apartments. Hence it is evident, that to consider the street-sellers unworthy of being protected in the exercise of their calling because they pay neither rates nor taxes, is to commit a gross injustice, not only to the street-sellers themselves by forcing them to contribute in their tea and sugar, their beer, gin, and tobacco, towards the expenses of a Government which exerts itself rather to injure than benefit them, but likewise to the ratepayers of the parish; for it is a necessary consequence, if the shopkeepers have the power to deprive the street-dealers of their living whenever the out-of-door tradesmen are thought to interfere with the business of those indoors (perhaps by underselling them), that the street-dealers, being unable to live by their own labour, must betake themselves to the union and live upon the labour of the parishioners, and thus the shopkeepers may be said to enrich themselves at the expense, not only of the poor street-people, but likewise of their brother ratepayers.

Nor can it be said that the *Street-Sellers* are interlopers upon these occasions, for if ancient custom be referred to, it will be found that the Shopkeepers are the real intruders, they having succeeded the Hawkers, who were, in truth, the original distributors of the produce of the country.

But though no body of Shopkeepers, nor, indeed, any other class of people *individually*, should possess the power to deprive the Hawkers of what is often the last shift of struggling independence—the sale of a few goods in the street—still it is evident that the *general* convenience of the public must be consulted, and that, were the Street-Traders to be allowed the right of pitching in any thoroughfare they pleased, many of our principal streets would be blocked up with costers' barrows, and the kerb of Regent-street possibly crowded like that of the New Cut, with the hawkers and hucksters that would be sure to resort thither; while those thoroughfares which, like Fleet-street and Cheapside, are now almost impassable at certain times of the day, from the increased traffic of the City, would be rendered still more impervious by the throngs of street-sellers that the crowd alone would be sure to attract to the spot.

Under the circumstances, therefore, it becomes necessary that we should provide for the vast body of Street-Sellers some authorized place of resort, where they might be both entitled and permitted to obtain an honest living according to Act of Parliament. To think for a moment of "putting down" street-trading is to be at once ignorant of the numbers and character of the people pursuing it. To pass an Act declaring 50,000 individuals rogues and vagabonds, would be to fill our prisons or our workhouses with men who would willingly earn their own living. Besides, the poor *will* buy of the poor. Subject the petty trader to fine and imprisonment as you please, still the very sympathy and patronage of the petty purchaser will in this country always call into existence a large body of purveyors to the poorer classes. I would suggest, therefore, and I do so after much consideration, and an earnest desire to meet all the difficulties of the case, that a number of "poor men's markets" be established throughout London, by the purchase or rental of plots of ground in the neighbourhood of the present street-markets; that a small toll be paid by each of the Street-Sellers attending such markets, for the right to vend their goods there— that the keeper or beadle of each market be likewise an Inspector of Weights and Measures, and that any hawker found using "slangs" of any kind, or resorting to any imposition whatever, be prohibited entering the market for the future—that the conduct and regulation of the markets be under the direction of a committee consisting of an equal number of shareholders, sellers, and working men—the latter as representatives of the buyers—and that the surplus funds (if any, after paying all expenses, together with a fair interest to the shareholders of the market) should be devoted to the education of the children of the hawkers before and after the hours of sale. There might also be a penny savings'-bank in connection with each of the markets, and a person stationed at the gates on the conclusion of the day's business, to collect all he could from the hawkers as they left.

There are already a sufficient number of poor-markets established at the East end of the town—though of a different character, such as the Old Clothes Exchange—to prove the practicability of the proposed plan among even the pettiest traders. And I am convinced, after long deliberation, that such institutions could not but tend to produce a rapid and marked improvement in the character of the London Hawkers.

This is the only way evident to me of meeting the evil of our present street-life—an evil which is increasing every day, and which threatens, ere long, almost to overwhelm us with its abominations. To revile the street-people is stark folly. Their ignorance is no demerit to them, even as it is no merit to us to know the little that we do. If we really wish the people better, let us, I say again, do for them what others have done for us, and without which (humiliating as it may be to our pride) we should most assuredly have been as they are. It is the continued forgetfulness of this truth—a truth which our wretched self-conceit is constantly driving from our minds—that prevents our stirring to improve the condition of these poor people; though, if we knew but the whole of the facts concerning them, and their sufferings and feelings, our very fears alone for the safety of the state would be sufficient to make us do something in their behalf. I am quite satisfied, from all I have seen, that there are thousands in this great metropolis ready to rush forth, on the least evidence of a rising of the people, to commit the most savage and revolting excesses—men who have no knowledge of the government of the country but as an armed despotism, preventing their earning their living, and who hate all law, because it is made to appear to them merely as an organised tyranny—men, too, who have neither religious nor moral principles to restrain the exercise of their grossest passions when once roused, and men who, from our very neglect of them, are necessarily and essentially the dangerous classes, whose existence we either rail at or deplore.

The rate of increase among the street-traders it is almost impossible to arrive at. The population returns afford us no data for the calculation, and the street-people themselves are unable to supply the least information on the subject; all they can tell us is, that about 20 years ago they took a guinea for every shilling that they get now. This heavy reduction of their receipts they attribute to the cheapness of commodities, and the necessity to carry and sell a greater quantity of goods in order to get the same profit, as well as to the increase in the number of street-traders; but when questioned as to the extent of such increase, their answers are of the vaguest possible kind. Arranging the street-people, however, as we have done, into three distinct classes, according to the causes which have led to their induction into a street-life, viz., those who are *born* and *bred* to the streets—those who *take* to the streets—and those who are *driven* to the streets, it is evident that the main elements of any extraordinary increase of the street-folk must be sought for among the two latter classes. Among the first the increase will, at the utmost, be at the same rate as the ordinary increase of the population—viz., 1½ per cent. per annum; for the English costermongers and street-traders in general appear to be remarkable rather for the small than the large number of their children, so that, even supposing all the boys and girls of the street-sellers to be brought up to the same mode of life as their father, we could not thus account for any *enormous* increase among the street-folk. With those, however, who *take* to the streets from the love of a "roving life," or the desire to "shake a free leg"—to quote the phrases of the men themselves—or are *driven* to the streets from an inability to obtain employment at the pursuit to which they have been accustomed, the case is far different.

That there is every day a greater difficulty for working men to live by their labour—either from the paucity of work, or from the scanty remuneration given for it—surely no one will be disposed to question when every one is crying out that the country is over-populated. Such being the case, it is evident that the number of mechanics in the streets must be daily augmenting, for, as I have before said, street-trading is the last shift of an unemployed artizan to keep himself and his family from the "Union." The workman out of work, sooner than starve or go to the parish for relief, takes to making up and vending on his own account the articles of his craft, whilst the underpaid workman, sooner than continue toiling from morning till midnight for a bare subsistence, resorts to the easier trade of buying and selling. Again, even among the less industrious of the working classes, the general decline in wages has tended, and is continually tending, to make their labour more and more irksome to them. There is a cant abroad at the present day, that there is a special pleasure in industry, and hence we are taught to regard all those who object to work as appertaining to the class of natural vagabonds; but where is the man among us that loves labour? for work or labour is merely that which is irksome to perform, and which every man requires a certain amount of remuneration to induce him to perform. If men really loved work they would pay to be allowed to do it rather than require to be paid for doing it. That occupation which is agreeable to us we call amusement, and that and that only which is disagreeable we term labour, or drudgery, according to the intensity of its irksomeness. Hence as the amount of remuneration given by way of inducement to a man to go through a certain amount of work becomes reduced, so does the stimulus to work become weakened, and this, through the decline of wages, is what is daily taking place among us. Our operatives are continually ceasing to be producers, and passing from the creators of wealth into the exchangers or distributors of it; becoming mere tradesmen, subsisting on the labour of other people rather than their own, and so adding to the very non-producers, the great number of whom is the main cause of the poverty of those who make all our riches. To teach a people the difficulty of living by labour is to inculcate the most dangerous of all lessons, and this is what we are daily doing. Our trading classes are increasing at a most enormous rate, and so giving rise to that exceeding competition, and consequently, to that continual reduction of prices—all of which must ultimately fall upon the working man. This appears to me to be the main cause of the increase of the London street people, and one for which I candidly confess I see no remedy.

OF THE STREET-SELLERS OF SECOND-HAND ARTICLES.

I HAVE already treated of the street-commerce in such things as are presented to the public in the form in which they are to be cooked, eaten, drank, or used. They have comprised the necessaries, delicacies, or luxuries of the street; they have been either the raw food or preparations ready cooked or mixed for immediate consumption, as in the case of the street eatables and drinkables; or else they were the proceeds of taste (or its substitute) in art or literature, or of usefulness or ingenuity in manufacture.

All these many objects of street-commerce may be classified in one well-known word: they are bought and sold *first-hand*. I have next to deal with the *second-hand* sellers of our streets; and in this division perhaps will be found more that is novel, curious, and interesting, than in that just completed.

Mr. Babbage, in his "Economy of Machinery and Manufactures," says, concerning the employment of materials of little value: "The worn-out saucepan and tin-ware of our kitchens, when beyond the reach of the tinker's art, are not utterly worthless. We sometimes meet carts loaded with old tin kettles and worn-out iron coal-skuttles traversing our streets. These have not yet completed their useful course; the less corroded parts are cut into strips, punched with small holes, and varnished with a coarse black varnish for the use of the trunk-maker, who protects the edges and angles of his boxes with them; the remainder are conveyed to the manufacturing chemists in the outskirts, who employ them in combination with pyroligneous acid, in making a black dye for the use of calico-printers."

Mr. Babbage has here indicated one portion of the nature of the street-trade in second-hand articles—the application of worn-out materials to a new purpose. But this second-hand commerce of the streets—for a street-commerce it mainly is, both in selling and buying—has a far greater extent than that above indicated, and many ramifications. Under the present head I shall treat only of street *sellers*, unless when a street *purchase* may be so intimately connected with a street *sale* that for the better understanding of the subject it may be necessary to sketch both. Of the STREET-BUYERS and the STREET-FINDERS, or COLLECTORS, both connected with the second-hand trade, I shall treat separately.

In London, where many, in order to live, struggle to extract a meal from the possession of an article which seems utterly worthless, nothing must be wasted. Many a thing which in a country town is kicked by the penniless out of their path even, or examined and left as meet only for the scavenger's cart, will in London be snatched up as a prize; it is money's worth. A crushed and torn bonnet, for instance, or, better still, an old hat, napless, shapeless, crownless, and brimless, will be picked up in the street, and carefully placed in a bag with similar things by one class of street-folk—the STREET-FINDERS. And to tempt the well-to-do to *sell* their second-hand goods, the street-trader offers the barter of shapely china or shining glass vessels; or blooming fuchsias or fragrant geraniums for "the rubbish," or else, in the spirit of the hero of the fairy tale, he exchanges, "new lamps for old."

Of the street sale of second-hand articles, with all the collateral or incidental matter bearing immediately on the subject, I shall treat under the following heads, or under such heads as really constitute the staple of the business, dismissing such as may be trifling or exceptional. Of these traffickers, then, there are five classes, the mere enumeration of the objects of their traffic being curious enough:—

1. *The Street-Sellers of Old Metal Articles,* such as knives, forks, and butchers' steels; saws, hammers, pincers, files, screw-drivers, planes, chisels, and other tools (more frequently those of the workers in wood than of other artisans); old scissors and shears; locks, keys, and hinges; shovels, fire-irons, trivets, chimney-cranes, fenders, and fire-guards; warming-pans (but rarely now); flat and Italian irons, curling-tongs; rings, horse-shoes, and nails; coffee and tea-pots, urns, trays, and canisters; pewter measures; scales and weights; bed-screws and keys; candlesticks and snuffers; niggards, generally called niggers (*i. e.,* false bottoms for grates); tobacco and snuff-boxes and spittoons; door-plates, numbers, knockers, and escutcheons; dog-collars and dog-chains (and other chains); gridirons; razors; coffee-mills; lamps; swords and daggers; gun and pistol-barrels and locks (and occasionally the entire weapon); bronze and cast metal figures; table, chair, and sofa castors; bell-pulls and bells; the larger buckles and other metal (most frequently brass) articles of harness furniture; compositors' sticks (the depositories of the type in the first instance); the multifarious kinds of tin-wares; stamps; cork-screws; barrel-taps; ink-stands; a multiplicity of culinary vessels and of old metal lids; footmen, broken machinery, and parts of machinery, as odd wheels, and screws of all sizes, &c., &c.

2. *The Street-Sellers of Old Linen, Cotton, and Woollen Articles,* such as old sheeting for towels; old curtains of dimity, muslin, cotton, or moreen; carpeting; blanketing for house-scouring cloths; ticking for beds and pillows; sacking for different purposes, according to its substance and quality; fringes; and stocking-legs for the supply of "jobbing worsted," and for re-footing.

I may here observe that in the street-trade, second-hand linen or cotton is often made to pay a double debt. The shirt-collars sold, sometimes to a considerable extent and very cheap, in the street-markets, are made out of linen which has previously been used in some other form; so is it with white waistcoats and other habiliments. Of the street-folk who vend such wares I shall speak chiefly in the fourth division of this subject, viz. the second-hand street-sellers of miscellaneous articles.

3. *The Street-Sellers of Old Glass and Crockery,* including the variety of bottles, odd, or in sets, or in broken sets; pans, pitchers, wash-hand basins, and other crockery utensils; china ornaments; pier, convex, and toilet glasses (often without the frames); pocket ink-bottles; wine, beer, and liqueur glasses; decanters; glass fish-bowls (occasionally); salt-cellars; sugar-basins; and lamp and gas glasses.

4. *The Street-Sellers of Miscellaneous Articles.* These are such as cannot properly be classed under any of the three preceding heads, and include a mass of miscellaneous commodities: Accordions and other musical instruments; brushes of all

descriptions; shaving-boxes and razor-strops; baskets of many kinds; stuffed birds, with and without frames; pictures, with and without frames; desks, work-boxes, tea-caddies, and many articles of old furniture; boot-jacks and hooks; shoe-horns; cartouche-boxes; pocket and opera glasses; rules, and measures in frames; backgammon, and chess or draught boards and men, and dice; boxes of dominoes; cribbage-boards and boxes, sometimes with old packs of cards; pope-boards (boards used in playing the game of "Pope," or "Pope Joan," though rarely seen now); "fish," or card counters of bone, ivory, or mother of pearl (an equal rarity); microscopes (occasionally); an extensive variety of broken or faded things, new or long kept, such as magic-lanterns, dissected maps or histories, &c., from the toy warehouses and shops; Dutch clocks; barometers; wooden trays; shells; music and books (the latter being often odd volumes of old novels); tee-totums, and similar playthings; ladies' head-combs; umbrellas and parasols; fishing-rods and nets; reins, and other parts of cart, gig, and "two-horse" harness; boxes full of "odds and ends" of old leather, such as water-pipes; and a mass of imperfect metal things, which had "better be described," said an old dealer, "as from a needle to an anchor."

5. *The Street-Sellers of Old Apparel*, including the body habiliments, constituting alike men's, women's, boys', girls', and infants' attire: as well as hats, caps, gloves, belts, and stockings; shirts and shirt-fronts ("dickeys"); handkerchiefs, stocks, and neck-ties; furs, such as victorines, boas, tippets, and edgings; beavers and bonnets; and the other several, and sometimes not easily describable, articles which constitute female fashionable or ordinary wear.

I may here observe, that of the wares which once formed a portion of the stock of the street-sellers of the fourth and fifth divisions, but which are now no longer objects of street sale, were, till within the last few years, fans; back and shoulder boards (to make girls grow straight!); several things at one time thought indispensable to every well-nurtured child, such as a coral and bells; belts, sashes, scabbards, epaulettes, feathers or plumes, hard leather stocks, and other indications of the volunteer, militia, and general military spirit of the early part of the present century.

Before proceeding immediately with my subject, I may say a few words concerning what is, in the estimation of some, a *second-hand* matter. I allude to the many uses to which that which is regarded, and indeed termed, "offal," or "refuse," or "waste," is put in a populous city. This may be evidenced in the multiform uses to which the "offal" of the animals which are slaughtered for our use are put. It is still more curiously shown in the uses of the offal of the animals which are killed, not for our use, but for that of our dogs and cats; and to this part of the subject I shall more especially confine the remarks I have to make. My observations on the uses of other waste articles will be found in another place.

What in the butcher's trade is considered the offal of a bullock, was explained by Mr. Deputy Hicks, before the last Select Committee of the House of Commons on Smithfield Market: "The carcass," he said, "as it hangs clear of everything else, is the carcass, and all else constitutes the offal."

The carcass may be briefly termed the four quarters, whereas the offal then comprises the hide, which in the average-sized bullock that is slaughtered in London is worth 12s.; but with the hide are sold the horns, which are worth about 10d. to the comb-makers, who use them to make their "tortoise-shell" articles, and for similar purposes. The hoofs are worth 2d. to the glue-makers, or prussiate of potash manufacturers. What "comes out of a bullock," to use the trade term, is the liver, the lights (or lungs), the stomach, the intestinal canal (sometimes 36 yards when extended), and the gall duct. These portions, with the legs (called "feet" in the trade), form what is styled the tripe-man's portion, and are disposed of to him by the butcher for 5s. 6d. Separately, the value of the liver is 8d., of the lights, 6d. (both for dogs'-meat), and of the legs which are worked into tooth-brush handles, dominoes, &c., 1s. The remaining 3s. 4d. is the worth of the other portion. The heart averages rather more than 1s.; the kidneys the same; the head, 1s. 9d.; the blood (which is "let down the drain" in all but the larger slaughtering houses) 1½d. (being 3d. for 9 gallons); the tallow (7 stone) 14s.; and the tail, I was told, "from nothing to 2s.," averaging about 6d.; the tongue, 2s. 6d. Thus the offal sells, altogether, first hand, for 1l. 18s. 6d.

I will now show the uses to which what is far more decidedly pronounced "offal," and what is much more "second-hand" in popular estimation, viz., a dead horse, is put, and even a dead horse's offal, and I will then show the difference in this curious trade between the Parisian and London horse offal.

The greatest horse-slaughtering establishments in France are at Montfaucon, a short distance from the capital. When the animal has been killed, it is "cut up," and the choicer portions of the flesh are eaten by the work-people of the establishment, and by the hangers-on and jobbers who haunt the locality of such places, and are often men of a desperate character. The rest of the carcass is sold for the feeding of dogs, cats, pigs, and poultry, a portion being also devoted to purposes of manure. The flesh on a horse of average size and fatness is 350 lbs.; which sells for 1l. 12s. 6d. But this is only one of the uses of the dead animal.

The skin is sold to a tanner for 10s. 6d. The hoofs to a manufacturer of sal ammonia, or similar preparations, or of Prussian blue, or to a comb or toy-maker, for 1s. 4d. The old shoes and the shoe-nails are worth 2½d. The hair of the mane and tail realizes 1½d. The tendons are disposed of, either fresh or dried, to glue-makers for 3d.— a pound of dried tendons (separated from the muscles) being about the average per horse. The bones are bought by the turners, cutlers, fan-makers, and the makers of ivory black and sal ammoniac, 90 lbs. being an average weight of the animal's bones, and realizing 2s. The intestines wrought into the different preparations required of the gut-makers, or for manure, are worth 2d.

The blood is used by the sugar-refiners, and by the fatteners of poultry, pigeons, and turkeys (which devour it greedily), or else for manure. When required for manure it is dried—20 lbs. of dried blood, which is the average weight, being worth 1s. 9d. The fat is removed from the carcass and melted down. It is in demand for the making of gas, of soap, and (when very fine) of—bear's grease; also for the dubbing or grease applied to harness and to shoe-leather. This fat when consumed in lamps communicates a greater portion of heat than does oil, and is therefore preferred by the makers of glass toys, and by enamellers and polishers. A horse at Montfaucon has been known to yield 60 lbs. of fat, but this is an extreme case; a yield of 12 lbs. is the produce of a horse in fair condition, but at these slaughter-houses there are so many lean and sorry jades that 8 lbs. may be taken as an average of fat, and at a value of 6d. per lb. Nor does the list end here; the dead and putrid flesh is made to teem with life, and to produce food for other living creatures. A pile of pieces of flesh, six inches in height, layer on layer, is slightly covered with hay or straw; the flies soon deposit their eggs in the attractive matter, and thus maggots are bred, the most of which are used as food for pheasants, and in a smaller degree of domestic fowls, and as baits for fish. These maggots give, or are supposed to give, a "game flavour" to poultry, and a very "high" flavour to pheasants. One horse's flesh thus produces maggots worth 1s. 5d. The total amount, then, realized on the dead horse, which may cost 10s. 6d., is as follows:—

	£	s.	d.
The flesh	1	12	6
The skin	0	10	6
The hoofs	0	1	4
The shoes and nails	0	0	2½
The mane and tail	0	0	1½
The tendons	0	0	3
The bones	0	2	0
The intestines	0	0	2
The blood	0	1	9
The fat	0	4	0
The maggots	0	1	5
	£2	14	3

The carcass of a French horse is also made available in another way, and which relates to a subject I have lately treated of—the destruction of rats; but this is not a regularly-accruing emolument. Montfaucon swarms with rats, and to kill them the carcass of a horse is placed in a room, into which the rats gain access through openings in the floor contrived for the purpose. At night the rats are lured by their keenness of scent to the room, and lured in numbers; the openings are then closed, and they are prisoners. In one room 16,000 were killed in four weeks. The Paris furriers gave from three to four francs for 100 skins, so that, taking the average at 3s. of our money, 16,000 rat-skins would return 24l.

In London the uses of the dead horse's flesh, bones, blood, &c., are different.

Horse-flesh is not—as yet—a portion of human food in this country. In a recent parliamentary inquiry, witnesses were examined as to whether horse-flesh was used by the sausage-makers. There was some presumption that such might be the case, but no direct evidence. I found, however, among butchers who had the best means of knowing, a strong conviction that such *was* the case. One highly-respectable tradesman told me he was as certain of it as that it was the month of June, though, if called upon to produce legal evidence proving either that such was the sausage-makers' practice, or that this *was* the month of June, he might fail in both instances.

I found among street-people who dealt in provisions a strong, or, at any rate, a strongly-expressed, opinion that the tongues, kidneys, and hearts of horses were sold as those of oxen. One man told me, somewhat triumphantly, as a result of his ingenuity in deduction, that he had thoughts at one time of trying to establish himself in a cats'-meat walk, and made inquiries into the nature of the calling: "I'm satisfied the 'osses' arts," he said, "is sold for beastesses'; 'cause you see, sir, there's nothing as 'ud be better liked for favourite cats and pet dogs, than a nice piece of 'art, but ven do you see the 'osses' 'arts on a barrow? If they don't go to the cats, vere does they go to? Vy, to the Christians."

I am assured, however, by tradesmen whose interest (to say nothing of other considerations) would probably make them glad to expose such practices, that this substitution of the equine for the bovine heart is not attempted, and is hardly possible. The bullock's heart, kidneys, and tongue, are so different in shape (the heart, more especially), and in the colour of the fat, while the rough tip of the ox's tongue is not found in that of the horse, that this second-hand, or offal kind of animal food could not be palmed off upon any one who had ever purchased the heart, kidneys, or tongue of an ox. "If the horse's tongue be used as a substitute for that of any other," said one butcher to me, "it is for the dried reindeer's—a savoury dish for the breakfast table!" Since writing the above, I have had convincing proof given me that the horses' tongues are cured and sold as "neats." The heart and kidneys are also palmed, I find, for those of oxen!! Thus, in one respect, there is a material difference between the usages, in respect of this food, between Paris and London.

One tradesman, in a large way of business—with many injunctions that I should make no allusion that might lead to his being known, as he said it might be his ruin, even though he never slaughtered the meat he sold, but was, in fact, a dead salesman or a vendor of meat consigned to him—one tradesman, I say, told me that he fancied there was an *unreasonable* objection to the eating of horse-flesh among us. The horse was quite as dainty in his food as the ox, he was quite as graminivorous, and shrunk more, from a nicer sense of smell, from anything pertaining to a contact with animal food than did the ox. The principal objection lies in the number of diseased horses sold at the knackers. My informant reasoned only from analogy, as he had never tasted horse-flesh; but a great-uncle of his, he told me, had relished it highly in the peninsular war.

The uses to which a horse's carcass are put in London are these:—The skin, for tanning, sells for 6s. as a low average; the hoofs, for glue, are worth 2d.; the shoes and nails, 1½d.; the mane and tail, 1½d.; the bones, which in London (as it was described to me) are "cracked up" for manure, bring 1s. 6d.; the fat is melted down and used for cart-grease and common harness oil; one person acquainted with the trade thought that the average yield of fat was 10 lbs. per horse ("taking it low"), another that it was 12 lbs. ("taking it square"), so that if 11 lbs. be accepted as an average, the fat, at 2d. per lb., would realize 1s. 10d. Of the tendons no use is made; of the blood none; and no maggots are reared upon putrid horse-flesh, but a butcher, who had been twenty years a farmer also, told me that he knew from experience that there was nothing so good as maggots for the fattening of poultry, and he thought, from what I told him of maggot-breeding in Montfaucon, that we were *behind* the French in this respect.

Thus the English dead horse—the vendor receiving on an average 1*l*. from the knacker,—realizes the following amount, without including the knacker's profit in disposing of the flesh to the cats'-meat man; but computing it merely at 2*l*. we have the subjoined receipts:—

	£	s.	d.
The flesh (averaging 2 cwt., sold at 2½d. per lb.	2	0	0
The skin	0	6	0
The hoofs	0	0	2
The shoes and nails	0	0	1½
The bones	0	1	6
The fat	0	1	10
The tendons	0	0	0
The tongue, &c.		—	?
The blood	0	0	0
The intestines	0	0	0
	£2	9	7½

The French dead horse, then, is made a source of nearly 5s. higher receipt than the English. On my inquiring the reason of this difference, and why the blood, &c., were not made available, I was told that the demand by the Prussian blue manufacturers and the sugar refiners was so fully supplied, and over-supplied, from the great cattle slaughter-houses, that the private butchers, for the trifling sum to be gained, let the blood be wasted. One bullock slaughterer in Fox and Knot-yard, who kills 180 cattle in a week, receives only 1*l*. for the blood of the whole number, which is received in a well in the slaughter-house. The amount paid for blood a few year's back was more than double its present rate. Under these circumstances, I was told, it would be useless trying to turn the wasted offal of a horse to any profitable purpose. There is, I am told, on an average, 1000 horses slaughtered every week in London, and this, at 2*l*. 10s. each animal, would make the value of the dead horses of the metropolis amount to 130,000*l*. per annum.

Were it not that I might be dwelling too long on the subject, I might point out how the offal of the skins was made to subserve other purposes from the Bermondsey tan-yards; and how the parings and scrapings went to the makers of glue and size, and the hair to the builders to mix with lime, &c., &c.

I may instance another thing in which the worth of what in many places is valueless refuse is exemplified, in the matter of "waste," as waste paper is always called in the trade. Paper in all its glossiest freshness is but a reproduction of what had become in some measure "waste," viz. the rags of the cotton or linen fabric after serving their original purpose. There is a body of men in London who occupy themselves entirely in collecting waste paper. It is no matter of what kind; a small prayer-book, a once perfumed and welcome love-note, lawyers' or tailors' bills, acts of parliament, and double sheets of the *Times*, form portions of the waste dealer's stock. Tons upon tons are thus consumed yearly. Books of every description are ingredients of this waste, and in every language; modern poems or pamphlets and old romances (perfect or imperfect), Shakespeare, Molière, Bibles, music, histories, stories, magazines, tracts to convert the heathen or to prove how easily and how immensely our national and individual wealth might be enhanced, the prospectuses of a thousand companies, each certain to prove a mine of wealth, schemes to pay off the national debt, or recommendations to wipe it off, auctioneers' catalogues and long-kept letters, children's copy-books and last century ledgers, printed effusions which have progressed no further than the unfolded sheets, uncut works and books mouldy from age—all these things are found in the insatiate bag of the waste collector, who of late has been worried because he could not supply enough! "I don't know how it is, sir," said one waste collector, with whom I had some conversation on the subject of street-sold books, with which business he was also connected, "I can't make it out, but paper gets scarcer or else I'm out of luck. Just at this time my family and me really couldn't live on my waste if we had to depend entirely upon it."

I am assured that in no place in the world is this traffic carried on to anything approaching the extent that it is in London. When I treat of the street-buyers I shall have some curious information to publish on the subject. I do but allude to it here as one strongly illustrative of "second-hand" appliances.

OF THE STREET-SELLERS OF SECOND-HAND METAL ARTICLES.

I HAVE in the preceding remarks specified the wares sold by the vendors of the second-hand articles of metal manufacture, or (as they are called in the streets) the "old metal" men. The several articles I have specified may never be all found at one time upon one stall, but they are all found on the respective stalls. "Aye, sir," said one old man whom I conversed with, "and there's more things every now and then comes to the stalls, and there used to be still more when I were young, but I can't call them all to mind, for times is worse with me, and so my memory fails. But there used to be a good many bayonets, and iron tinder-boxes, and steels for striking lights; I can remember them."

Some of the sellers have strong heavy barrows, which they wheel from street to street. As this requires a considerable exertion of strength, such part of the trade is carried on by strong men, generally of the costermongering class. The weight to be propelled is about 300 lbs. Of this class there are now a few, rarely more than half-a-dozen, who sell on commission in the way I have described concerning the swag-barrowmen.

These are the "old metal swags" of street classification, but their remuneration is less fixed than that of the other swag-barrowmen. It is sometimes a quarter, sometimes a third, and sometimes even a half of the amount taken. The men carrying on this traffic are the servants of the marine-store dealers, or vendors of old metal articles, who keep shops. If one of these people be "lumbered up," that is, if he find his stock increase too rapidly, he furnishes a barrow, and sends a man into the streets with it, to sell what the shopkeeper may find to be excessive. Sometimes if the tradesman can gain only the merest trifle more than he could gain from the people who buy for the melting-pot, he is satisfied.

There is, or perhaps was, an opinion prevalent that the street "old metals" in this way of business got rid of stolen goods in such a manner as the readiest mode of sale, some of which were purposely rusted, and sold at almost any price, so that they brought but a profit to the "fence," whose payment to the thief was little more than the price of old metal at the foundry. I understand, however, that this course is not now pursued, nor is it likely that it ever was pursued to any extent. The street-seller is directly under the eye of the police, and when there is a search for stolen goods, it is not very likely that they would be paraded, however battered or rusted for the purpose, before men who possessed descriptions of all goods stolen. Until the establishment of the present system of police, this might have been an occasional practice. One street-seller had even heard, and he "had it from the man what did it," that a last-maker's shop was some years back broken into in the expectation that money would be met with, but none was found; and as the thieves could not bring away such heavy lumbering things as lasts, they cursed their ill-luck, and brought away such tools as they could stow about their persons, and cover with their loose great coats. These were the large knives, fixed to swivels, and resembling a small scythe, used by the artizan to rough hew the block of beech-wood; and a variety of excellent rasps and files (for they must be of the best), necessary for the completion of the last. These very tools were, in ten days after the robbery, sold from a street-barrow.

The second-hand metal goods are sold from stalls as well as from barrows, and these stalls are often tended by women whose husbands may be in some other branch of street-commerce. One of these stalls I saw in the care of a stout elderly Jewess, who was fast asleep, nodding over her locks and keys. She was awakened by the passing policeman, lest her stock should be pilfered by the boys: "Come, wake up, mother, and shake yourself," he said, "I shall catch a weazel asleep next."

Some of these barrows and stalls are heaped with the goods, and some are very scantily supplied, but the barrows are by far the best stocked. Many of them (especially the swag) look like collections of the different stages of rust, from its incipient spots to its full possession of the entire metal. But amongst these seemingly useless things there is a gleam of brass or plated ware. On one barrow I saw an old brass door-plate, on which was engraven the name of a late learned judge, Baron B——; another had formerly announced the residence of a dignitary of the church, the Rev. Mr. ——.

The second-hand metal-sellers are to be seen in all the street-markets, especially on the Saturday nights; also in Poplar, Limehouse, and the Commercial-road, in Golden-lane, and in Old-street and Old-street-road, St. Luke's, in Hoxton and Shoreditch, in the Westminster Broadway, and the Whitechapel-road, in Rosemary-lane, and in the district where perhaps every street calling is pursued, but where some special street-trades seem peculiar to the genius of the place, in Petticoat-lane. A person unacquainted with the last-named locality may have formed an opinion that Petticoat-lane is merely a lane or street. But Petticoat-lane gives its name to a little district. It embraces Sandys-row, Artillery-passage, Artillery-lane, Frying-pan-alley, Catherine Wheel-alley, Tripe-yard, Fisher's-alley, Wentworth-street, Harper's-alley, Marlborough-court, Broad-place, Providence-place, Ellison-street, Swan-court, Little Love-court, Hutchinson-street, Little Middlesex-street, Hebrew-place, Boar's-head-yard, Black-horse-yard, Middlesex-street, Stoney-lane, Meeting-house-yard, Gravel-lane, White-street, Cutler-street, and Borer's-lane, until the wayfarer emerges into what appears the repose and spaciousness of Devonshire-square, Bishopsgate-street, up Borer's-lane, or into what in the contrast really looks like the aristocratic thoroughfare of the Aldgate High-street, down Middlesex-street; or into Houndsditch through the halls of the Old Clothes Exchange.

All these narrow streets, lanes, rows, passages, alleys, yards, courts, and places, are the sites of the street-trade carried on in this quarter. The whole neighbourhood rings with street cries, many uttered in those strange east-end Jewish tones which do not sound like English. Mixed with the incessant invitations to buy Hebrew dainties, or the "sheepest pargains," is occasionally heard the guttural utterance of the Erse tongue, for the "native Irish," as they are sometimes called, are in possession of some portion of the street-traffic of Petticoat-lane, the original Rag Fair. The savour of the place is moreover peculiar. There is fresh fish, and dried fish, and fish being fried in a style peculiar to the Jews; there is the fustiness of old clothes; there is the odour from the pans on which (still in the Jewish fashion) frizzle and hiss pieces of meat and onions; puddings are boiling and enveloped in steam; cakes with strange names are hot from the oven; tubs of big pickled cucumbers or of onions give a sort of acidity to the atmosphere; lemons and oranges abound; and altogether the scene is not only such as can only be seen in London, but only such as can be seen in this one part of the metropolis.

When I treat of the street-Jews, I shall have information highly curious to communicate, and when I come to the fifth division of my present subject, I shall more particularly describe Petticoat-lane, as the head-quarters of the second-hand clothes business.

I have here alluded to the character of this quarter as being one much resorted to formerly, and still largely used by the sellers of second-hand metal goods. Here I was informed that a strong-built man, known as Jack, or (appropriately enough) as Iron Jack, had, until his death six or seven years ago, one of the best-stocked barrows in London. This, in spite of remonstrances, and by a powerful exercise of his strength, the man lifted, as it were, on to the narrow foot-path, and every passer-by had his attention directed almost perforce to the contents of the barrow, for he must make a "*detour*" to advance on his way. One of this man's favourite pitches was close to the lofty walls of what, before the change in their charter, was one of the East India Company's vast warehouses. The contrast to any one who indulged a thought on the subject—and there is great food for thought in Petticoat-lane—was striking enough. Here towered the store-house of costly teas, and silks, and spices, and indigo; while at its foot was carried on the most minute, and apparently worthless of all street-trades, rusty screws and nails, such as only few would care to pick up in the street, being objects of earnest bargaining!

An experienced man in the business, who thought he was "turned 50, or somewhere about that," gave me the following account of his trade, his customers, &c.

"I've been in most street-trades," he said, "and was born to it, like, for my mother was a rag-gatherer—not a bad business once—and I helped her. I never saw my father, but he was a soldier, and it's supposed lost his life in foreign parts. No, I don't remember ever having heard what foreign parts, and it don't matter. Well, perhaps, this is about as tidy a trade for a bit of bread as any that's going now. Perhaps selling fish may be better, but that's to a man what knows fish well. I can't say I ever did. I'm more a dab at cooking it (with a laugh). I like a bloater best on what's an Irish gridiron. Do you know what that is, sir? I know, though I'm not Irish, but I married an Irish wife, and as good a woman as ever was a wife. It's done on the tongs, sir, laid across the fire, and the bloater's laid across the tongs. Some says it's best turned and turned very quick on the coals themselves, but the tongs is best, for you can raise or lower." [My informant seemed interested in his account of this and other modes of cookery, which I need not detail.] "This is really a very trying trade. O, I mean it tries a man's patience so. Why, it was in Easter week a man dressed like a gentleman—but I don't think he was a real gentleman—looked out some bolts, and a hammer head, and other things, odds and ends, and they came to $10\frac{1}{2}d$. He said he'd give 6d. 'Sixpence!' says I; 'why d' you think I stole 'em?' 'Well,' says he, 'if I didn't think you'd stole 'em, I shouldn't have come to *you*.' I don't think he was joking. Well, sir, we got to high words, and I said, ' Then I'm d——d if you have them for less than 1s.' And a bit of a crowd began to gather, they was most boys, but the p'liceman came up, as slow as you please, and so my friend flings down 1s., and puts the things in his pocket and marches off, with a few boys to keep him company. That's the way one's temper's tried. Well, it's hard to say what sells best. A latch-lock and keys goes off quick. I've had them from 2d. to 6d.; but it's only the lower-priced things as sells now in any trade. Bolts is a fairish stock, and so is all sorts of tools. Well, not saws so much as such things as screwdrivers, or hammers, or choppers, or tools that if they're rusty people can clean up theirselves. Saws ain't so easy to manage; bedkeys is good. No, I don't clean the metal up unless it's very bad; I think things don't sell so well that way. People's jealous that they're just done up on purpose to deceive, though they may cost only 1d. or 2d. There's that cheese-cutter now, it's getting rustier and there'll be very likely a better chance to sell it. This is how it is, sir, I know. You see if a man's going to buy old metal, and he sees it all rough and rusty, he says to himself, ' Well, there's no gammon about it; I can just see what it is.' Then folks like to clean up a thing theirselves, and it's as if it was something made from their own cleverness. That was just my feeling, sir, when I bought old metals for my own use, before I was in the trade, and I goes by that. O, working people's by far my best customers. Many of 'em's very fond of jobbing about their rooms or their houses, and they come to such as me. Then a many has fancies for pigeons, or rabbits, or poultry, or dogs, and they mostly make up the places for them theirselves, and as money's an object, why them sort of fancy people buys hinges, and locks, and screws, and hammers, and what they want of me. A clever mechanic can turn his hand to most things that he wants for his own use. I know a shoemaker that makes beautiful rabbit-hutches and sells them along with his prize cattle, as I calls his great big long-eared rabbits. Perhaps I take 2s. 6d. or 3s. a day, and it's about half profit.

Yes, this time of the year I make good 10s. 6d. a week, but in winter not 1s. a day. That would be very poor pickings for two people to live on, and I can't do without my drop of beer, but my wife has constant work with a first-rate laundress at Mile End, and so we rub on, for we've no family living."

This informant told me further of the way in which the old metal stocks sold in the streets were provided; but that branch of the subject relates to street-buying. Some of the street-sellers, however, buy their stocks of the shopkeepers.

I find a difficulty in estimating the number of the second-hand metal-ware street-sellers. Many of the stalls or barrows are the property of the marine-store shopkeepers, or old metal dealers (marine stores being about the only things the marine-store men do not sell), and these are generally placed near the shop, being indeed a portion of its contents out of doors. Some of the marine-store men (a class of traders, by the by, not superior to street-sellers, making no "odious" comparison as to the honesty of the two), when they have purchased largely—the refuse iron for instance after a house has been pulled down—establish two or three pitches in the street, confiding the stalls or barrows to their wives and children. I was told by several in the trade that there were 200 old metal sellers in the streets, but from the best information at my command not more than 50 appear to be strictly *street*-sellers, unconnected with shop-keeping. Estimating a weekly receipt, per individual, of 15s. (half being profit), the yearly street outlay among this body alone amounts to 1950l.

OF THE STREET-SELLERS OF SECOND-HAND METAL TRAYS, &c.

THERE are still some few portions of the old metal trade in the streets which require specific mention.

Among these is the sale of second-hand trays, occasionally with such things as bread-baskets. Instead of these wares, however, being matters of daily traffic, they are offered in the streets only at intervals, and generally on the Saturday and Monday evenings, while a few are hawked to public-houses. An Irishman, a rather melancholy looking man, but possessed of some humour, gave me the following account. His dress was a worn suit, such as masons work in; but I have seldom seen so coarse, and never on an Irishman of his class, except on a Sunday, so clean a shirt, and he made as free a display of it as if it were the choicest cambric. He washed it, he told me, with his own hands, as he had neither wife, nor mother, nor sister. "I was a cow-keeper's man, your honour," he said, "and he sent milk to Dublin. I thought I might do betthur, and I got to Liverpool, and walked here. Have I done betthur, is it? Sorry a betthur. Would I like to returren to Dublin? Well, perhaps, plaze God, I'll do betthur here yit. I've sould a power of different things in the sthreets, but I'm off for counthry work now. I have a few therrays left if your honour wants such a thing. I first sould a few for a man I lodged along wid in Kent-street, when he was sick, and so I got to know the therrade. He tould me to say, and it's the therruth, if anybody said, 'They're only secondhand,' that they was all the betthur for that, for if they hadn't been real good therrays at first, they would niver have lived to be second-hand ones. I calls the bigghur therrays butlers, and the smhaller, waithers. It's a poor therrade. One woman 'll say, 'Pooh! ould-fashioned things.' 'Will, thin, ma'am,' I'll say, 'a good thing like this is niver ould-fashioned, no more than the bhutiful mate and berrid, and the bhutiful new praties a coming in, that you'll be atin off of it, and thratin' your husband to, God save him. No lady iver goes to supper widout her therray.' Yes, indeed, thin, and it is a poor therrade. It's the bhutiful therrays I've sould for 6d. I buys them of a shop which dales in sich things. The perrofit! Sorry a perrofit is there in it at all at all; but I thries to make 4d. out of 1s. If I makes 6d. of a night it's good worruk."

These trays are usually carried under the arm, and are sometimes piled on a stool or small stand, in a street market. The prices are from 2d. to 10d., sometimes 1s. The stronger descriptions are sold to street-sellers to display their goods upon, as much as to any other class. Women and children occasionally sell them, but it is one of the callings which seems to be disappearing from the streets. From two men, who were familiar with this and other second-hand trades, I heard the following reasons assigned for the decadence. One man thought it was owing to "swag-trays" being got up so common and so cheap, but to look "stunning well," at least as long as the shininess lasted. The other contended that poor working people had enough to do now-a-days to get something to eat, without thinking of a tray to put it on.

If 20 persons, and that I am told is about the number of sellers, take in the one or two nights' sale 4s. a week each, on second-hand trays (33 per cent. being the rate of profit), the street expenditure is 208l. in a year.

In other second-hand metal articles there is now and then a separate trade. Two or three sets of small *fire-irons* may be offered in a street-market on a Saturday night; or a small stock of *flat and Italian irons* for the laundresses, who work cheap and must buy second-hand; or a *collection of tools* in the same way; but these are accidental sales, and are but ramifications from the general "old metal" trade that I have described. Perhaps, in the sale of these second-hand articles, 20 people may be regularly employed, and 300l. yearly may be taken.

In Petticoat-lane, Rosemary-lane, Whitecross-street, Ratcliff-highway, and in the street-markets generally, are to be seen men, women, and children selling *dinner knives and forks, razors, pocket-knives, and scissors*. The pocket-knives and scissors are kept well oiled, so that the weather does not rust them. These goods have been mostly repaired, ground, and polished for street-commerce. The women and children selling these articles are the wives and families of the men who repair, grind, and polish them, and who belong, correctly speaking, to the class of street-artizans, under which head they will be more particularly treated of. It is the same also with the street-vendors of second-hand tin saucepans and other vessels (a trade, by the way, which is rapidly decreasing), for these are generally made of the old drums of machines retinned, or are old saucepans and pots mended for use by the vendors, who are mostly working tinmen, and appertain to the artizan class.

OF THE STREET-SELLERS OF SECOND-HAND LINEN, &c.

I NOW come to the second variety of the several kinds of street-sellers of second-hand articles. The accounts of the street-trade in second-hand linens, however, need be but brief; for none of the callings I have now to notice supply a mode of subsistence to the street-sellers independently of other pursuits. They are resorted to whenever an opportunity or a prospect of remuneration presents itself by the class of general street-sellers, women as well as men—the women being the most numerous. The sale of these articles is on the Saturday and Monday nights, in the street-markets, and daily in Petticoat and Rosemary lanes.

One of the most saleable of all the second-hand textile commodities of the streets, is an article the demand for which is certainly creditable to the poorer and the working-classes of London—*towels*. The principal supply of this street-towelling is obtained from the several barracks in and near London. They are a portion of what were the sheets (of strong linen) of the soldiers' beds, which are periodically renewed, and the old sheeting is then sold to a contractor, of whom the street-folk buy it, and wash and prepare it for market. It is sold to the street-traders at 4*d*. per pound, 1 lb. making eight penny towels; some (inferior) is as low as 2*d*. The principal demand is by the working-classes.

"Why, for one time, sir," said a street-seller to me, "there wasn't much towelling in the streets, and I got a tidy lot, just when I knew it would go off, like a thief round a corner. I pitched in Whitecross-street, and not far from a woman that was making a great noise, and had a good lot of people about her, for cheap mackarel weren't so very plenty then as they are now. 'Here's your cheap mack'rel,' shouts she, 'cheap, cheap, cheap mac-mac-mac-*muck*'rel. Then *I* begins: 'Here's your cheap towelling; cheap, cheap, cheap, tow-tow-tow-*tow*-ellings. Here's towels a penny a piece, and two for twopence, or a double family towel for twopence.' I soon had a greater crowd than she had. O, yes! I gives 'em a good history of what I has to sell; patters, as you call it; a man that can't isn't fit for the streets. 'Here's what every wife should buy for her husband, and every husband for his wife,' I goes on. 'Domestic happiness is then secured. If a husband licks his wife, or a wife licks her husband, a towel is the handiest and most innocent thing it can be done with, and if it's wet it gives you a strong clipper on the cheek, as every respectable married person knows as well as I do. A clipper that way always does me good, and I'm satisfied it does more good to a gentleman than a lady.' Always patter for the women, sir, if you wants to sell. Yes, towels is good sale in London, but I prefer country business. I'm three times as much in the country as in town, and I'm just off to Ascot to sell cards, and do a little singing, and then I'll perhaps take a round to Bath and Bristol, but Bath's not what it was once."

Another street-seller told me that, as far as his experience went, Monday night was a better time for the sale of second-hand sheetings, &c., than Saturday, as on Monday the wives of the working-classes who sought to buy cheaply what was needed for household use, usually went out to make their purchases. The Saturday-night's mart is more one for immediate necessities, either for the Sunday's dinner or the Sunday's wear. It appears to me that in all these little distinctions—of which street-folk tell you, quite unconscious that they tell anything new—there is something of the history of the character of a people.

"Wrappers," or "bale-stuff," as it is sometimes styled, are also sold in the streets as second-hand goods. These are what have formed the covers of the packages of manufactures, and are bought (most frequently by the Jews) at the wholesale warehouses or the larger retail shops, and re-sold to the street-people, usually at $1\frac{1}{2}d.$ and 2*d*. per pound. These goods are sometimes sold entire, but are far more often cut into suitable sizes for towels, strong aprons, &c. They soon get "bleached," I was told, by washing and wear.

"*Burnt*" linen or calico is also sold in the streets as a second-hand article. On the occasion of a fire at any tradesman's, whose stock of drapery had been injured, the damaged wares are bought by the Jewish or other keepers of the haberdashery swag-shops. Some of these are sold by the second-hand street dealers, but the traffic for such articles is greater among the hawkers. Of this I have already given an account. The street-sale of these burnt (and sometimes *designedly* burnt) wares is in pieces, generally from 6*d*. to 1*s*. 6*d*. each, or in yards, frequently at 6*d*. per yard, but of course the price varies with the quality.

I believe that no *second-hand sheets* are sold in the streets as sheets, for when tolerably good they are received at the pawn-shops, and if indifferent, at the dolly-shops, or illegal pawn-shops. Street folk have told me of sheets being sold in the street-markets, but so rarely as merely to supply an exception. In Petticoat-lane, indeed, they are sold, but it is mostly by the Jew shopkeepers, who also expose their goods in the streets, and they are sold by them very often to street-traders, who convert them into other purposes.

The statistics of this trade present great difficulties. The second-hand linen, &c., is not a regular street traffic. It may be offered to the public 20 days or nights in a month, or not one. If a "job-lot" have been secured, the second-hand street-seller may confine himself to that especial stock. If his means compel him to offer only a paucity of second-hand goods, he may sell but one kind. Generally, however, the same man or woman trades in two, three, or more of the second-hand textile productions which I have specified, and it is hardly one street-seller out of 20, who if he have cleared his 10s. in a given time, by vending different articles, can tell the relative amount he cleared on each. The trade is, therefore, irregular, and is but a consequence, or—as one street-seller very well expressed it—a "tail" of other trades. For instance, if there has been a great auction of any corn-merchant's effects, there will be more sacking than usual in the street-markets; if there have been sales, beyond the average extent, of old household furniture, there will be a more ample street stock of curtains, carpeting, fringes, &c. Of the articles I have enumerated the sale of second-hand linen, more especially that from the barrack-stores, is the largest of any.

The most intelligent man whom I met with in this trade calculated that there were 80 of these second-hand street-folk plying their trade two nights in the week; that they took 8s. each weekly, about half of it being profit; thus the street expenditure would be 1664l. per annum.

Of the Street-Sellers of Second-hand Curtains.

SECOND-HAND Curtains, but only good ones, I was assured, can now be sold in the streets. "because common new ones can be had so cheap." The "good second-hands," however, sell readily. The most saleable of all second-hand curtains are those of chintz, especially old-fashioned chintz, now a scarce article; the next in demand are what were described to me as "good check," or the blue and white cotton curtains. White dimity curtains, though now rarely seen in a street-market, are not bought to be re-used as curtains —"there's too much washing about them for London"—but for petticoats, the covering of large pincushions, dressing-table covers, &c., and for the last-mentioned purpose they are bought by the householders of a small tenement who let a "well-furnished" bed-room or two.

The uses to which the second-hand chintz or check curtains are put, are often for "Waterloo" or "tent" beds. It is common for a single woman, struggling to "get a decent roof over her head," or for a young couple wishing to improve their comforts in furniture, to do so piece-meal. An old bedstead of a better sort may first be purchased, and so on to the concluding "decency," or, in the estimation of some poor persons, "dignity" of curtains. These persons are customers of the street-sellers — the second-hand curtains costing them from 8d. to 1s. 6d.

Moreen curtains have also a good sale. They are bought by working people (and by some of the dealers in second-hand furniture) for the re-covering of sofas, which had become ragged, the deficiency of stuffing being supplied with hay (which is likewise the "stuffing" of the new sofas sold by the "linen-drapers," or "slaughter-houses." Moreen curtains, too, are sometimes cut into pieces, for the re-covering of old horse-hair chairs, for which purpose they are sold at 3d. each piece.

Second-hand curtains are moreover cut into portions and sold for the hanging of the testers of bedsteads, but almost entirely for what the street-sellers call "half-teesters." These are required for the Waterloo bedsteads, "and if it's a nice thing, sir," said one woman, "and perticler if it's a chintz, and to be had for 6d., the women'll fight for it."

The second-hand curtains, when sold entire, are from 6d. to 2s. 6d. One man had lately sold a pair of "good moreens, only faded, but dyeing's cheap," for 3s. 6d.

Of the Street-Sellers of Second-hand Carpeting, Flannels, Stocking-legs, &c., &c.

I CLASS these second-hand wares together, as they are all of woollen materials.

Carpeting has a fair sale, and in the streets is vended not as an entire floor or stair-carpet, but in pieces. The floor-carpet pieces are from 2d. to 1s. each; the stair-carpet pieces are from 1d. to 4d. a yard. Hearth-rugs are very rarely offered to street-customers, but when offered are sold from 4d. to 1s. Drugget is also sold in the same way as the floor-carpeting, and sometimes for house-scouring cloths.

"I've sold carpet, sir," said a woman street-seller, who called all descriptions — rugs and drugget too—by that title; "and I would like to sell it regular, but my old man—he buys everything—says it can't be had regular. I've sold many things in the streets, but I'd rather sell good second-hand in carpet or curtains, or fur in winter, than anything else. They're nicer people as buys them. It would be a good business if it was regular. Ah! indeed, in my time, and before I was married, I have sold different things in a different way; but I'd rather not talk about that, and I make no complaints, for seeing what I see. I'm not so badly off. Them as buys carpet are very particular—I've known them take a tape out of their pockets and measure—but they're honourable customers. If they're satisfied they buy, most of them does, at once; without any of your 'is that the lowest?' as ladies asks in shops, and that when they don't think of buying, either. Carpet is bought by working people, and they use it for hearth-rugs, and for bed-sides, and such like. I know it by what I've heard them say when I've been selling. One Monday evening, five or six years back, I took 10s. 9d. in carpet; there had been some great sales at old houses, and a good quantity of carpet and curtains was sold in the streets. Perhaps I cleared 3s. 6d. on that 10s. 9d. But to take 4s. or 5s. is good work now, and often not more than 3d. in the 1s. profit. Still, it's a pretty good business, when you can get a stock of second-hands of different kinds to keep you going constantly."

What in the street-trade is known as *"Flannels,"* is for the most part second-hand blankets, which having been worn as bed furniture, and then very probably, or at the same time, used for ironing cloths, are found in the street-markets, where they are purchased for flannel petticoats for the children of the poor, or when not good enough for such use, for house cloths, at 1*d.* each.

The trade in *stocking legs* is considerable. In these legs the feet have been cut off, further darning being impossible, and the fragment of the stocking which is worth preserving is sold to the careful housewives who attach to it a new foot. Sometimes for winter wear a new cheap sock is attached to the footless hose. These legs sell from ½*d.* to 3*d.* the pair, but very rarely 3*d.*, and only when of the best quality, though the legs would not be saleable in the streets at all, had they not been of a good manufacture originally. Men's hose are sold in this way more largely than women's.

The trade in second-hand stockings is very considerable, but they form a part of the second-hand apparel of street-commerce, and I shall notice them under that head.

OF THE STREET-SELLERS OF SECOND-HAND BED-TICKING, SACKING, FRINGE, &c.

FOR *bed-ticking* there is generally a ready sale, but I was told "not near so ready as it was a dozen year or more back." One reason which I heard assigned for this was, that new ticking was made so cheap (being a thin common cotton, for the lining of common carpet-bags, portmanteaus, &c., that poor persons scrupled to give any equivalent price for good sound second-hand linen bed-ticking, "though," said a dealer, "it'll still wear out half a dozen of their new slop rigs. I should like a few of them there slop-masters, that's making fortins out of foolish or greedy folks, to have to live a few weeks in the streets by this sort of second-hand trade; they'd hear what was thought of them then by all sensible people, which aren't so many as they should be by a precious long sight."

The ticking sold in the street is bought for the patching of beds and for the making of pillows and bolsters, and for these purposes is sold in pieces at from 2*d.* to 4*d.* as the most frequent price. One woman who used to sell bed-ticking, but not lately, told me that she knew poor women who cared nothing for such convenience themselves, buy ticking to make pillows for their children.

Second-hand Sacking is sold without much difficulty in the street-markets, and usually in pieces at from 2*d.* to 6*d.* This sacking has been part of a corn sack, or of the strong package in which some kinds of goods are dispatched by sea or railway. It is bought for the mending of bedstead sacking, and for the making of porters' knots, &c.

Second-hand Fringe is still in fair demand, but though cheaper than ever, does not, I am assured, "sell so well as when it was dearer." Many of my readers will have remarked, when they have been passing the apartments occupied by the working class, that the valance fixed from the top of the window has its adornment of fringe; a blind is sometimes adorned in a similar manner, and so is the valance from the tester of a bedstead. For such uses the second-hand fringe is bought in the street-markets in pieces, sometimes called "quantities," of from 1*d.* to 1*s.*

Second-hand Table-cloths used to be an article of street-traffic to some extent. If offered at all now—and one man, though he was a regular street-seller, thought he had not seen one offered in a market this year—they are worn things such as will not be taken by the pawnbrokers, while the dolly-shop people would advance no more than the table-cloth might be worth for the rag-bag. *The glazed table-covers*, now in such general use, are not as yet sold second-hand in the streets.

I was told by a street-seller that he had heard an old man (since dead), who was a buyer of second-hand goods, say that in the old times, after a great sale by auction—as at Wanstead-house (Mr. Wellesley Pole's), about 30 years ago—the open-air trade was very brisk, as the street-sellers, like the shop-traders, proclaimed all their second-hand wares as having been bought at "the great sale." For some years no such "*ruse*" has been practised by street-folk.

OF THE STREET-SELLERS OF SECOND-HAND GLASS AND CROCKERY.

THESE sellers are another class who are fast disappearing from the streets of London. Before glass and crockery, but more especially glass, became so low-priced when new, the second-hand glass-man was one of the most prosperous of the open-air traders; he is now so much the reverse that he must generally mix up some other calling with his original business. One man, whose address was given to me as an experienced glass-man, I found selling mackarel and "pound crabs," and complaining bitterly that mackarel were high, and that he could make nothing out of them that week at 2*d.* each, for poor persons, he told me, would not give more. "Yes, sir," he said, "I've been in most trades, besides having been a pot-boy, both boy and man, and I don't like this fish-trade at all. I could get a pot-boy's place again, but I'm not so strong as I were, and it's slavish work in the place I could get; and a man that's not so young as he was once is chaffed so by the young lads and fellows in the tap-room and the skittle-ground. For this last three year or more I had to do something in addition to my glass for a crust. Before I dropped it as a bad consarn, I sold old shoes as well as old glass, and made both ends meet that way, a leather end and a glass end. I sold off my glass to a rag and bottle shop for 9*s.*, far less than it were worth, and I swopped my shoes for my fish-stall, and water-tub, and 3*s.* in money. I'll be out of this trade before long. The glass was good once; I've made my 15*s.* and 20*s.* a week at it: I don't know how long that is ago, but it's a good long time. Latterly I could do no business at all in it, or hardly any. The old shoes was middling, because they're a free-selling thing, but somehow it seems awkward mixing up any other trade with your glass."

The stall or barrow of a "second-hand glass-man" presented, and still, in a smaller degree, presents, a variety of articles, and a variety of colours, but over the whole prevails that haziness which seems to be considered proper to this trade. Even in the largest rag and bottle shops, the second-hand bottles always look dingy. "It wouldn't pay to wash them all," said one shopkeeper to me, "so we washes none; indeed, I b'lieve people would rather buy them as they is, and clean them themselves."

The street-assortment of second-hand glass may be described as one of "odds and ends"—odd goblets, odd wine-glasses, odd decanters, odd cruet-bottles, salt-cellars, and mustard-pots; together with a variety of "tops" to fit mustard-pots or butter-glasses, and of "stoppers" to fit any sized bottle, the latter articles being generally the most profitable. Occasionally may still be seen a blue spirit-decanter, one of a set of three, with "brandy," in faded gold letters, upon it, or a brass or plated label, as dingy as the bottle, hung by a fine wire-chain round the neck. Blue finger-glasses sold very well for use as sugar-basins to the wives of the better-off working-people or small tradesmen. One man, apparently about 40, who had been in this trade in his youth, and whom I questioned as to what was the quality of his stock, told me of the demand for "blue sugars," and pointed out to me one which happened to be on a stand by the door of a rag and bottle shop. When I mentioned its original use, he asked further about it, and after my answers seemed sceptical on the subject. "People that's quality," he said, "that's my notion on it, that hasn't neither to yarn their dinner, nor to cook it, but just open their mouths and eat it, can't dirty their hands so at dinner as to have glasses to wash 'em in arterards. But there's queer ways everywhere."

At one time what were called "doctors' bottles" formed a portion of the second-hand stock I am describing. These were phials bought by the poorer people, in which to obtain some physician's gratuitous prescription from the chemist's shop, or the time-honoured nostrum of some wonderful old woman. For a very long period, it must be borne in mind, all kinds of glass wares were dear. Small glass frames, to cover flower-roots, were also sold at these stalls, as were fragments of looking-glass. Beneath his stall or barrow, the "old glass-man" often had a few old wine or beer-bottles for sale.

At the period before cast-glass was so common, and, indeed, subsequently, until glass became cheap, it was not unusual to see at the second-hand stalls, rich cut-glass vessels which had been broken and cemented, for sale at a low figure, the glass-man being often a mender. It was the same with China punch-bowls, and the costlier kind of dishes, but this part of the trade is now unknown.

There is one curious sort of ornament still to be met with at these stalls—wide-mouthed bottles, embellished with coloured patterns of flowers, birds, &c., generally cut from "furniture prints," and kept close against the sides of the interior by the salt with which the bottles are filled. A few second-hand pitchers, tea-pots, &c., are still sold at from 1*d.* to 6*d.*

There are now not above six men (of the ordinary street-selling class) who carry on this trade regularly. Sometimes twelve stalls or barrows may be seen; sometimes one, and sometimes none. Calculating that each of the six dealers takes 12*s.* weekly, with a profit of 6*s.* or 7*s.*, we find 187*l.* 4*s.* expended in this department of street-commerce. The principal place for the trade is in High-street, Whitechapel.

OF THE STREET-SELLERS OF SECOND-HAND MISCELLANEOUS ARTICLES.

I HAVE in a former page specified some of the goods which make up the sum of the second-hand miscellaneous commerce of the streets of London.

I may premise that the trader of this class is a sort of street broker; and it is no more possible minutely to detail his especial traffic in the several articles of his stock, than it would be to give a specific account of each and several of the "sundries" to be found in the closets or corners of an old-furniture broker's or marine-store seller's premises, in describing his general business.

The members of this trade (as will be shown in the subsequent statements) are also "miscellaneous" in their character. A few have known liberal educations, and have been established in liberal professions; others have been artisans or shopkeepers, but the mass are of the general class of street-sellers.

I will first treat of the *Second-Hand Street-Sellers of Articles for Amusement,* giving a wide interpretation to the word "amusement."

The backgammon, chess, draught, and cribbage-boards of the second-hand trade have originally been of good quality—some indeed of a very superior manufacture; otherwise the "cheap Germans" (as I heard the low-priced foreign goods from the swag-shops called) would by their superior cheapness have rendered the business a nullity. The backgammon-boards are bought of brokers, when they are often in a worn, unhinged, and what may be called ragged condition. The street-seller "trims them up," but in this there is nothing of artisanship, although it requires some little taste and some dexterity of finger. A new hinge or two, or old hinges re-screwed, and a little pasting of leather and sometimes the application of strips of bookbinder's gold, is all that is required. The backgammon-boards are sometimes offered in the streets by an itinerant; sometimes (and more frequently than otherwise in a deplorable state, the points of the table being hardly distinguishable) they are part of the furniture of a second-hand stall. I have seen one at an old book-stall, but most usually they are vended by being hawked to the better sort of public-houses, and there they are more frequently disposed of by raffle than by sale. It is not once in a thousand times, I am informed, that second-hand "men" are sold with the board. Before the board has gone through its series of hands to the street-seller, the men have been lost or scattered. New men are sometimes sold or raffled with the backgammon-boards (as with the draught) at from 6*d.* to 2*s.* 6*d.* the set, the best being of box-wood.

Chess-boards and men—for without the men of

course a draught, or the top of a backgammon-board suffices for chess — are a commodity now rarely at the disposal of the street-sellers; and, as these means of a leisurely and abstruse amusement are not of a ready sale, the second-hand dealers do not "look out" for them, but merely speculate in them when the article "falls in their way" and seems a palpable bargain. Occasionally, a second-hand chess apparatus is still sold by the street-folk. One man—upon whose veracity I have every reason to rely—told me that he once sold a beautiful set of ivory men and a handsome "leather board" (second-hand) to a gentleman who accosted him as he saw him carry them along the street for sale, inviting him to step in doors, when the gentleman's residence was reached. The chess-men were then arranged and examined, and the seller asked 3*l*. 3*s*. for them, at once closing with the offer of 3*l*.; "for I found, sir," he said, "I had a gentleman to do with, for he told me he thought they were really cheap at 3*l*., and he would give me that." Another dealer in second-hand articles, when I asked him if he had ever sold chess-boards and men, replied, "Only twice, sir, and then at 4*s*. and 5*s*. the set; they was poor. I've seen chess played, and I should say it's a rum game; but I know nothing about it. I once had a old gent for a customer, and he was as nice and quiet a old gent as could be, and I always called on him when I thought I had a curus old tea-caddy, or knife-box, or anything that way. He didn't buy once in twenty calls, but he always gave me something for my trouble. He used to play at chess with another old gent, and if, after his servant had told him I'd come, I waited 'til I could wait no longer, and then knocked at his room door, he swore like a trooper.

Draught-boards are sold at from 3*d*. to 1*s*. second-hand. Cribbage-boards, also second-hand, and sometimes with cards, are only sold, I am informed, when they are very bad, at from 1*d*. to 3*d*., or very good, at from 2*s*. 6*d*. to 5*s*. One street-seller told me that he once sold a "Chinee" cribbage-board for 18*s*., which cost him 10*s*. "It was a most beautiful thing," he stated, "and was very high-worked, and was inlaid with ivory, and with green ivory too."

The Dice required for the playing of backgammon, or for any purpose, are bought of the waiters at the club-houses, generally at 2*l*. the dozen sets. They are retailed at about 25 per cent. profit. Dice in this way are readily disposed of by the street-people, as they are looked upon as "true," and are only about a sixth of the price they could be obtained for new ones in the duly-stamped covers. A few dice are sold at 6*d*. to 1*s*. the set, but they are old and battered.

There are but two men who support themselves wholly by the street-sale and the hawking of the different boards, &c., I have described. There are two, three, or sometimes four occasional participants in the trade. Of these one held a commission in Her Majesty's service, but was ruined by gaming, and when unable to live by any other means, he sells the implements with which he had been but too familiar. "He lost everything in Jermyn-street," a man who was sometimes his comrade in the sale of these articles said to me, "but he is a very gentlemanly and respectable man."

The profits in this trade are very uncertain. A man who was engaged in it told me that one week he had cleared 2*l*., and the next, with greater pains-taking, did not sell a single thing.

The other articles which are a portion of the second-hand miscellaneous trade of this nature are sold as often, or more often, at stalls than elsewhere. Dominoes, for instance, may be seen in the winter, and they are offered only in the winter, on perhaps 20 stalls. They are sold at from 4*d*. a set, and I heard of one superior set which were described to me as "brass-pinned," being sold in a handsome box for 5*s*., the shop price having been 15*s*. The great sale of dominoes is at Christmas.

Pope-Joan boards, which, I was told, were fifteen years ago sold readily in the streets, and were examined closely by the purchasers (who were mostly the wives of tradesmen), to see that the print or paint announcing the partitions for "intrigue," "matrimony," "friendship," "Pope," &c., were perfect, are now never, or rarely, seen. Formerly the price was 1*s*. to 1*s*. 9*d*. In the present year I could hear of but one man who had even offered a Pope-board for sale in the street, and he sold it, though almost new, for 3*d*.

"Fish," or the bone, ivory, or mother-o'-pearl card counters in the shape of fish, or sometimes in a circular form, used to be sold second-hand as freely as the Pope-boards, and are now as rarely to be seen.

Until about 20 years ago, as well as I can fix upon a term from the information I received, the apparatus for a game known as the "Devil among the tailors" was a portion of the miscellaneous second-hand trade or hawking of the streets. In it a top was set spinning on a long board, and the result depended upon the number of men, or "tailors," knocked down by the "devil" (top) of each player, these tailors being stationed, numbered, and scored (when knocked down) in the same way as when the balls are propelled into the numbered sockets in a bagatelle-board. I am moreover told that in the same second-hand calling were boards known as "solitaire-boards." These were round boards, with a certain number of holes, in each of which was a peg. One peg was removed at the selection of the player, and the game consisted in taking each remaining peg, by advancing another over its head into any vacant hole, and if at the end of the game only one peg remained in the board, the player won; if winning it could be called when the game could only be played by one person, and was for "solitary" amusement. Chinese puzzles, sometimes on a large scale, were then also a part of the second-hand traffic of the streets. These are a series of thin woods in geometrical shapes, which may be fitted into certain forms or patterns contained in a book, or on a sheet. These puzzles are sold in the streets still, but in smaller quantity and diminished size. Different games played with the teetotum were also a part of second-hand street-sale, but none of these bygone pastimes were vended to any extent.

From the best data I have been able to obtain it appears that the amount received by the street-sellers or street-hawkers in the sale of these second-hand articles of amusement is 10*l*. weekly, about half being profit, divided in the proportions I have intimated, as respects the number of street-sellers and the periods of sale; or 520*l*. expended yearly.

I should have stated that the principal customers of this branch of second-hand traders are found in the public-houses and at the cigar-shops, where the goods are carried by street-sellers, who hawk from place to place.

These dealers also attend the neighbouring, and, frequently in the summer, the more distant races, where for dice and the better quality of their "boards," &c., they generally find a prompt market. The sale at the fairs consists only of the lowest-priced goods, and in a very scant proportion compared to the races.

Of the Street-Sellers of Second-hand Musical Instruments.

Of this trade there are two branches; the sale of instruments which are really second-hand, and the sale of those which are pretendedly so; in other words, an honest and a dishonest business. As in street estimation the whole is a second-hand calling, I shall so deal with it.

At this season of the year, when fairs are frequent and the river steamers with their bands of music run oft and regularly, and out-door music may be played until late, the calling of the street-musician is "at its best." In the winter he is not unfrequently starving, especially if he be what is called "a chance hand," and have not the privilege of playing in public-houses when the weather renders it impossible to collect a street audience. Such persons are often compelled to part with their instruments, which they offer in the streets or the public-houses, for the pawnbrokers have been so often "stuck" (taken in) with inferior instruments, that it is difficult to pledge even a really good violin. With some of these musical men it goes hard to part with their instruments, as they have their full share of the pride of art. Some, however, sell them recklessly and at almost any price, to obtain the means of prolonging a drunken carouse.

From a man who is now a dealer in second-hand musical instruments, and is also a musician, I had the following account of his start in the second-hand trade, and of his feelings when he first had to part with his fiddle.

"I was a gentleman's footboy," he said, "when I was young, but I was always very fond of music, and so was my father before me. He was a tailor in a village in Suffolk and used to play the bass-fiddle at church. I hardly know how or when I learned to play, but I seemed to grow up to it. There was two neighbours used to call at my father's and practise, and one or other was always showing me something, and so I learned to play very well. Everybody said so. Before I was twelve, I've played nearly all night at a dance in a farm-house. I never played on anything but the violin. You must stick to one instrument, or you're not up to the mark on any if you keep changing. When I got a place as footboy it was in a gentleman's family in the country, and I never was so happy as when master and mistress was out dining, and I could play to the servants in the kitchen or the servants' hall. Sometimes they got up a bit of a dance to my violin. If there was a dance at Christmas at any of the tenants', they often got leave for me to go and play. It was very little money I got given, but too much drink. At last master said, he hired me to be his servant and not for a parish fiddler, so I must drop it. I left him not long after—he got so cross and snappish. In my next place—no, the next but one—I was on board wages, in London, a goodish bit, as the family were travelling, and I had time on my hands, and used to go and play at public-houses of a night, just for the amusement of the company at first, but I soon got to know other musicians and made a little money. Yes, indeed, I could have saved money easily then, but I didn't; I got too fond of a public-house life for that, and was never easy at home."

I need not very closely pursue this man's course to the streets, but merely intimate it. He had several places, remaining in some a year or more, in others two, three, or six months, but always unsettled. On leaving his last place he married a fellow-servant, older than himself, who had saved "a goodish bit of money," and they took a beer-shop in Bermondsey. A "free and easy" (concert), both vocal and instrumental, was held in the house, the man playing regularly, and the business went on, not unprosperously, until the wife died in child-bed, the child surviving. After this everything went wrong, and at last the man was "sold up," and was penniless. For three or four years he lived precariously on what he could earn as a musician, until about six or seven years ago, when one bitter winter's night he was without a farthing, and had laboured all day in the vain endeavour to earn a meal. His son, a boy then of five, had been sent home to him, and an old woman with whom he had placed the lad was incessantly dunning for 12*s*. due for the child's maintenance. The landlord clamoured for 15*s*. arrear of rent for a furnished room, and the hapless musician did not possess one thing which he could convert into money except his fiddle. He must leave his room next day. He had held no intercourse with his friends in the country since he heard of his father's death some years before, and was, indeed, resourceless. After dwelling on the many excellences of his violin, which he had purchased, "a dead bargain," for 3*l*. 15*s*., he said: "Well, sir, I sat down by the last bit of coal in the place, and sat a long time thinking, and didn't know what to do. There was nothing to hinder me going out in the morning, and working the streets with a mate, as I'd done before, but then there was little James that was sleeping there in his bed. He was very delicate then, and to drag him about and let him sleep in lodging-houses would have killed him, I knew. But then I couldn't think of parting with my violin. I felt I should never again have such another. I felt as if to part with it was parting with my last prop, for what was I to do? I sat a long time thinking, with my instrument on my knees, 'til—I'm sure I don't know how to describe it—I felt as if I was drunk, though I hadn't even tasted beer. So I went out boldly, just as if I *was* drunk, and with a deal of trouble persuaded a landlord I knew to lend me 1*l.* on my instrument, and keep it by him for three months, 'til I could redeem it. I have it now, sir. Next day I satisfied my two creditors by paying each half, and a week's rent in advance, and I walked off to a shop in Soho, where I bought a dirty old instrument, broken in parts, for 2*s.* 3*d.* I was great part of the day in doing it up, and in the evening earned 7*d.* by playing solos by Watchorn's door, and the Crown and Cushion, and the Lord Rodney, which are all in the Westminster-road. I lodged in Stangate-street. There was a young man—he looked like a respectable mechanic—gave me 1*d.*, and said: 'I wonder how you can use your fingers at all such a freezing night. It seems a good fiddle.' I assure you, sir, I was surprised myself to find what I could do with my instrument. 'There's a beer-shop over the way,' says the young man, 'step in, and I'll pay for a pint, and try my hand at it.' And so it was done, and I sold him my fiddle for 7*s.* 6*d.* No, sir, there was no take in; it was worth the money. I'd have sold it now that I've got a connection for half a guinea. Next day I bought such another instrument at the same shop for 3*s.*, and sold it after a while for 6*s.*, having done it up, in course. This it was that first put it into my head to start selling second-hand instruments, and so I began. Now I'm known as a man to be depended on, and with my second-hand business, and engagements every now and then as a musician, I do middling."

In this manner is the honest second-hand street-business in musical instruments carried on. It is usually done by hawking. A few, however, are sold at miscellaneous stalls, but they are generally such as require repair, and are often without the bow, &c. The persons carrying on the trade have all, as far as I could ascertain, been musicians.

Of the street-sale of musical instruments by drunken members of the "profession" I need say little, as it is exceptional, though it is certainly a branch of the trade, for so numerous is the body of street-musicians, and of so many classes is it composed, that this description of second-hand business is being constantly transacted, and often to the profit of the more wary dealers in these goods. The statistics I shall show at the close of my remarks on this subject.

Of the Music "Duffers."

SECOND-HAND GUITARS are vended by the street-sellers. The price varies from 7*s.* 6*d.* to 15*s.* *Harps* form no portion of the second-hand business of the streets. A *drum* is occasionally, and only occasionally, sold to a showman, but the chief second-hand traffic is in violins. *Accordions,* both new and old, used to sell readily in the streets, either from stalls or in hawking, "but," said a man who had formerly sold them, "they have been regularly 'duffed' out of the streets, so much cheap rubbish is made to sell. There's next to nothing done in them now. If one's offered to a man that's no judge of it, he'll be sure you want to cheat him, and perhaps abuse you; if he be a judge, of course it's no go, unless with a really good article."

Among the purchasers of second-hand musical instruments are those of the working-classes who wish to "practise," and the great number of street-musicians, street-showmen, and the indifferently paid members of the orchestras of minor (and not always of minor) theatres. Few of this class ever buy new instruments. There are sometimes, I am informed, as many as 50 persons, one-fourth being women, engaged in this second-hand sale. Sometimes, as at present, there are not above half the number. A broker who was engaged in the traffic estimated—and an intelligent street-seller agreed in the computation—that, take the year through, at least 25 individuals were regularly, but few of them fully, occupied with this traffic, and that their weekly takings averaged 30*s.* each, or an aggregate yearly amount of 190*l.* The weekly profits run from 10*s.* to 15*s.*, and sometimes the well-known dealers clear 40*s.* or 50*s.* a week, while others do not take 5*s.* Of this amount about two-thirds is expended on violins, and one-tenth of the whole, or nearly a tenth, on "duffing" instruments sold as second-hand, in which department of the business the amount "turned over" used to be twice, and even thrice as much. The sellers have nearly all been musicians in some capacity, the women being the wives or connections of the men.

What I have called the "dishonest trade" is known among the street-folk as "music-duffing." Among the swag-shopkeepers, at one place in Houndsditch more especially, are dealers in " duffing fiddles." These are German-made instruments, and are sold to the street-folk at 2*s.* 6*d.* or 3*s.* each, bow and all. When purchased by the music-duffers, they are discoloured so as to be made to look old. A music-duffer, assuming the way of a man half-drunk, will enter a public-house or accost any party in the street, saying: " Here, I must have money, for I won't go home 'til morning, 'til morning, 'til morning, I won't go home 'til morning, 'til daylight does appear. And so I may as well sell my old fiddle myself as take it to a rogue of a broker. Try it anybody, it's a fine old tone, equal to any Cremonar. It cost me two guineas and another fiddle, and a good 'un too, in exchange, but I may as well be my own broker, for I must have money any how, and I'll sell it for 10*s.*"

Possibly a bargain is struck for 5*s.*; for the duffing violin is perhaps purposely damaged in some slight way, so as to appear easily reparable, and any deficiency in tone may be attributed to that defect, which was of course occasioned by the drunkenness of the possessor. Or possibly the tone of the instrument may not be bad, but it may be made of such unsound materials, and in such a slop-way, though looking well to a little-practised eye, that it will soon fall to pieces. One man told me that he had often done the music-duffing, and had sold trash violins for 10s., 15s., and even 20s., "according," he said, "to the thickness of the buyer's head," but that was ten or twelve years ago.

It appears that when an impetus was given to the musical taste of the country by the establishment of cheap singing schools, or of music classes, (called at one time "singing for the million"), or by the prevalence of cheap concerts, where good music was heard, this duffing trade flourished, but now, I am assured, it is not more than a quarter of what it was. "There'll always be something done in it," said the informant I have before quoted, "as long as you can find young men that's conceited about their musical talents, fond of taking their medicine (drinking). If I've gone into a public-house room where I've seen a young gent that's bought a duffing fiddle of me, it don't happen once in twenty times that he complains and blows up about it, and only then, perhaps, if he happens to be drunkish, when people don't much mind what's said, and so it does me no harm. People's too proud to confess that they're ever 'done' at any time or in anything. Why, such gents has pretended, when I've sold 'em a duffer, and seen them afterwards, that they've done *me!*"

Nor is it to violins that this duffing or sham second-hand trade is confined. At the swag-shops *duffing cornopeans, French horns,* and *clarionets* are vended to the street-folk. One of these cornopeans may be bought for 14s.; a French horn for 10s.; and a clarionet for 7s. 6d.; or as a general rule at one-fourth of the price of a properly-made instrument sold as reasonably as possible. These things are also made to look old, and are disposed of in the same manner as the duffing violins. The sale, however, is and was always limited, for "if there be one working man," I was told, "or a man of any sort not professional in music, that tries his wind and his fingers on a clarionet, there's a dozen trying their touch and execution on a violin."

Another way in which the duffing music trade at one time was made available as a second-hand business was this:—A band would play before a pawnbroker's door, and the duffing German brass instruments might be well-toned enough, the inferiority consisting chiefly in the materials, but which were so polished up as to appear of the best. Some member of the band would then offer his brass instrument in pledge, and often obtain an advance of more than he had paid for it.

One man who had been himself engaged in what he called this "artful" business, told me that when two pawnbrokers, whom he knew, found that they had been tricked into advancing 15s. on cornopeans, which they could buy new in Houndsditch for 14s., they got him to drop the tickets of the pledge, which they drew out for the purpose, in the streets. These were picked up by some passer-by—and as there is a very common feeling that there is no harm, or indeed rather a merit, in cheating a pawnbroker or a tax-gatherer—the instruments were soon redeemed by the fortunate finder, or the person to whom he had disposed of his prize. Nor did the roguery end here. The same man told me that he had, in collusion with a pawnbroker, dropped tickets of (sham) second-hand musical instruments, which he had bought new at a swag-shop for the very purpose, the amount on the duplicate being double the cost, and as it is known that the pawnbrokers do not advance the value of any article, the finders were gulled into redeeming the pledge, as an advantageous bargain. "But I've left off all that dodging now, sir," said the man with a sort of a grunt, which seemed half a sigh and half a laugh; "I've left it off entirely, for I found I was getting into trouble."

The derivation of the term "duffing" I am unable to discover. The Rev. Mr. Dixon says, in his "Dovecote and Aviary," that the term "*Duffer,*" applied to pigeons, is a corruption of *Dovehouse,*—but *query?* In the slang dictionaries a "*Duffer*" is explained as "a man who hawks things;" hence it would be equivalent to *Pedlar,* which means strictly beggar—being from the Dutch *Bedelaar,* and the German *Bettler.*

Of the Street-Sellers of Second-Hand Weapons.

The sale of second-hand pistols, for to that weapon the street-sellers' or hawkers' trade in arms seems confined, is larger than might be cursorily imagined.

There must be something seductive about the possession of a pistol, for I am assured by persons familiar with the trade, that they have sold them to men who were ignorant, when first invited to purchase, how the weapon was loaded or discharged, and seemed half afraid to handle it. Perhaps the possession imparts a sense of security.

The pistols which are sometimes seen on the street-stalls are almost always old, rusted, or battered, and are useless to any one except to those who can repair and clean them for sale.

There are three men now selling new or second-hand pistols, I am told, who have been gunmakers.

This trade is carried on almost entirely by hawking to public-houses. I heard of no one who depended solely upon it, "but this is the way," one intelligent man stated to me, "if I am buying second-hand things at a broker's, or in Petticoat-lane, or anywhere, and there's a pistol that seems cheap, I'll buy it as readily as anything I know, and I'll soon sell it at a public-house, or I'll get it raffled for. Second-hand pistols sell better than new by such as me. If I was to offer a new one I should be told it was some Brummagem slop rubbish. If there's a little silver-plate let into the wood of the pistol, and a crest or initials engraved on it—I've got it done sometimes—there's a better chance of sale, for people think it's been made for somebody of consequence that wouldn't be fobbed off with an inferior thing. I don't think I've often sold pistols to working-men, but I've known them join in raffles for them, and the winner has often wanted to sell it back to me, and has sold it to somebody. It's tradesmen that buy, or gentlefolks, if you can get at them. A pistol's a sort of a plaything with them."

On my talking with a street-dealer concerning the street-trade in second-hand pistols, he produced a handsome pistol from his pocket. I inquired if it was customary for men in his way of life to carry pistols, and he expressed his conviction that it was, but only when travelling in the country, and in possession of money or valuable stock. "I gave only 7s. 6d. for this pistol," he said, "and have refused 10s. 6d. for it, for I shall get a better price, as it's an excellent article, on some of my rounds in town. I bought it to take to Ascot races with me, and have it with me now, but it's not loaded, for I'm going to Moulsey Hurst, where Hampton races are held. You're not safe if you travel after a great muster at a race by yourself without a pistol. Many a poor fellow like me has been robbed, and the public hear nothing about it, or say it's all gammon. At Ascot, sir, I trusted my money to a booth-keeper I knew, as a few men slept in his booth, and he put my bit of tin with his own under his head where he slept, for safe keeping. There's a little doing in second-hand pistols to such as me, but we generally sell them again."

Of *second-hand guns*, or other offensive weapons, there is no street sale. A few "*life-preservers*," some of gutta percha, are hawked, but they are generally new. Bullets and powder are not sold by the pistol-hawkers, but a *mould* for the casting of bullets is frequently sold along with the weapon.

Of these second-hand pistol-sellers there are now, I am told, more than there were last year. "I really believe," said one man, laughing, but I heard a similar account from others, "people were afraid the foreigners coming to the Great Exhibition had some mischief in their noddles, and so a pistol was wanted for protection. In my opinion, a pistol's just one of the things that people don't think of buying, 'til it's shown to them, and then they're tempted to have it."

The principal street-sale, independently of the hawking to public-houses, is in such places as Ratcliffe-highway, where the mates and petty officers of ships are accosted and invited to buy a good second-hand pistol. The wares thus vended are generally of a well-made kind.

In this traffic, which is known as a "straggling" trade, pursued by men who are at the same time pursuing other street-callings, it may be estimated, I am assured, that there are 20 men engaged, each taking as an average 1l. a week. In some weeks a man may take 5l.; in the next month he may sell no weapons at all. From 30 to 50 per cent. is the usual rate of profit, and the yearly street outlay on these second-hand offensive or defensive weapons is 1040l.

One man who "did a little in pistols" told me, "that 25 or 30 years ago, when he was a boy, his father sometimes cleared 2l. a week in the street-sale and hawking of second-hand *boxing-gloves*, and that he himself had sometimes carried the 'gloves' in his hand, and pistols in his pocket for sale, but that now boxing-gloves were in no demand whatever among street-buyers, and were 'a complete drug.' He used to sell them at 3s. the set, which is four gloves."

Of the Street-Sellers of Second-hand Curiosities.

SEVERAL of the things known in the street-trade as "curiosities" can hardly be styled second-hand with any propriety, but they are so styled in the streets, and are usually vended by street-merchants who trade in second-hand wares.

Curiosities are displayed, I cannot say temptingly (except perhaps to a sanguine antiquarian), for there is a great dinginess in the display, on stalls. One man whom I met wheeling his barrow in High-street, Camden-town, gave me an account of his trade. He was dirtily rather than meanly clad, and had a very self-satisfied expression of face. The principal things on his barrow were *coins, shells,* and *old buckles,* with a pair of the very high and wooden-heeled *shoes,* worn in the earlier part of the last century.

The coins were all of copper, and certainly did not lack variety. Among them were tokens, but none very old. There was the head of "Charles Marquis Cornwallis" looking fierce in a cocked hat, while on the reverse was Fame with her trumpet and a wreath, and banners at her feet, with the superscription: "His fame resounds from east to west." There was a head of Wellington with the date 1811, and the legend of "Vincit amor patriæ." Also "The R. Hon. W. Pitt, Lord Warden Cinque Ports," looking courtly in a bag wig, with his hair brushed from his brow into what the curiosity-seller called a "topping." This was announced as a "Cinque Ports token payable at Dover," and was dated 1794. "Wellingtons," said the man, "is cheap; that one's only a halfpenny, but here's one here, sir, as you seem to understand coins, as I hope to get 2d. for, and will take no less. It's 'J. Lackington, 1794,' you see, and on the back there's a Fame, and round her is written—and it's a good speciment of a coin—'Halfpenny of Lackington, Allen & Co., cheapest booksellers in the world.' That's scarcer and more vallyballer than Wellingtons or Nelsons either." Of the current coin of the realm, I saw none older than Charles II., and but one of his reign, and little legible. Indeed the reverse had been ground quite smooth, and some one had engraved upon it "Charles Dryland Tunbridg." A small "e" over the "g" of Tunbridg perfected the orthography. This, the street-seller said, was a "love-token" as well as an old coin, and "them love-tokens was getting scarce." Of foreign and colonial coins there were perhaps 60. The oldest I saw was one of Louis XV. of France and Navarre, 1774. There was one also of the "Republique Francaise" when Napoleon was First Consul. The colonial coins were more numerous than the foreign. There was the "One Penny token" of Lower Canada; the "one quarter anna" of the East India Company; the "half stiver of the colonies of Essequibo and Demarara;" the "halfpenny token of the province of Nova Scotia," &c. &c. There were also counterfeit halfcrowns and bank tokens worn from their simulated silver to rank copper. The principle on which this man "priced" his coins, as he called it, was simple enough. What was the size of a halfpenny he asked a penny for; the size of a penny coin was 2d. "It's a difficult trade is mine, sir," he said, "to carry on properly, for you may be so easily taken in, if you're not a judge of coins and other curiosities."

The shells of this man's stock in trade he called "conks" and "king conks." He had no "clamps" then, he told me, but they sold pretty well; he described them as "two shells together, one fitting inside the other." He also had sold what he called "African cowries," which were as "big as a pint pot," and the smaller cowries, which were "money in India, for his father was a soldier and had been there and saw it." The shells are sold from 1d. to 2s. 6d.

The old buckles were such as used to be worn on shoes, but the plate was all worn off, and "such like curiosities," the man told me, "got scarcer and scarcer."

Many of the stalls which are seen in the streets are the property of adjacent shop or storekeepers, and there are not now, I am informed, more than six men who carry on this trade apart from other commerce. Their average takings are 15s. weekly each man, about two-thirds being profit, or 234l. in a year. Some of the stands are in Great Wyld-street, but they are chiefly the property of the second-hand furniture brokers.

Of the Street-Sellers of Second-hand Telescopes and Pocket Glasses.

In the sale of second-hand telescopes only one man is now engaged in any extensive way, except on mere chance occasions. Fourteen or fifteen years ago, I was informed, there was a considerable street sale in small telescopes at 1s. each. They were made at Birmingham, my informant believed, but were sold as second-hand goods in London. Of this trade there is now no remains.

The principal seller of second-hand telescopes takes a stand on Tower Hill or by the Coal Exchange, and his customers, as he sells excellent "glasses," are mostly sea-faring men. He has sold, and still sells, telescopes from 2l. 10s. to 5l. each, the purchasers generally "trying" them, with strict examination, from Tower Hill, or on the Custom-House Quay. There are, in addition to this street-seller, six and sometimes eight others, who offer telescopes to persons about the docks or wharfs, who may be going some voyage. These are as often new as second-hand, but the second-hand articles are preferred. This, however, is a Jewish trade which will be treated of under another head.

An old opera-glass, or the smaller articles best known as "pocket-glasses," are occasionally hawked to public-houses and offered in the streets, but so little is done in them that I can obtain no statistics. A spectacle seller told me that he had once tried to sell two second-hand opera-glasses at 2s. 6d. each, in the street, and then in the public-houses, but was laughed at by the people who were usually his customers. "Opera-glasses!" they said, "why, what did they want with opera-glasses? wait until they had opera-boxes." He sold the glasses at last to a shopkeeper.

Of the Street-Sellers of other Miscellaneous Second-Hand Articles.

The other second-hand articles sold in the streets I will give under one head, specifying the different characteristics of the trade, when any striking peculiarities exist. To give a detail of the whole trade, or rather of the several kinds of articles in the whole trade, is impossible. I shall therefore select only such as are sold the more extensively, or present any novel or curious features of second-hand street-commerce.

Writing-desks, tea-caddies, dressing-cases, and *knife-boxes* used to be a ready sale, I was informed, when "good second-hand;" but they are "got up" now so cheaply by the poor fancy cabinet-makers who work for the "slaughterers," or furniture warehouses, and for some of the general-dealing swag-shops, that the sale of anything second-hand is greatly diminished. In fact I was told that as regards second-hand writing-desks and dressing-cases, it might be said there was "no trade at all now." A few, however, are still to be seen at miscellaneous stalls, and are occasionally, but very rarely, offered at a public-house "used" by artisans who may be considered "judges" of work. The tea-caddies are the things which are in best demand. "Working people buy them," I was informed, and "working people's wives. When women are the customers they look closely at the lock and key, as they keep 'my uncle's cards' there" (pawnbroker's duplicates).

One man had lately sold second-hand tea-caddies at 9d., 1s., and 1s. 3d. each, and cleared 2s. in a day when he had stock and devoted his time to this sale. He could not persevere in it if he wished, he told me, as he might lose a day in looking out for the caddies; he might go to fifty brokers and not find one caddy cheap enough for his purpose.

Brushes are sold second-hand in considerable quantities in the streets, and are usually vended at stalls. Shoe-brushes are in the best demand, and are generally sold, when in good condition, at 1s. the set, the cost to the street-seller being 8d. They are bought, I was told, by the people who clean their own shoes, or have to clean other people's. Clothes' brushes are not sold to any extent, as the "hard brush" of the shoe set is used by working people for a clothes' brush. Of late, I am told, second-hand brushes have sold more freely than ever. They were hardly to be had just when wanted, in a sufficient quantity, for the demand by persons going to Epsom and Ascot races, who carry a brush of little value with them, to brush the dust gathered on the road from their coats. The coster-girls buy very hard brushes, indeed mere stumps, with which they brush radishes; these brushes are vended at the street-stalls at 1*d.* each.

In *Stuffed Birds* for the embellishment of the walls of a room, there is still a small second-hand street sale, but none now in images or chimney-piece ornaments. "Why," said one dealer, "I can now buy new figures for 9*d.*, such as not many years ago cost 7*s.*, so what chance of a second-hand sale is there?" The stuffed birds which sell the best are starlings. They are all sold as second-hand, but are often "made up" for street-traffic; an old bird or two, I was told, in a new case, or a new bird in an old case. Last Saturday evening one man told me he had sold two "long cases" of starlings and small birds for 2*s.* 6*d.* each. There are no stuffed parrots or foreign birds in this sale, and no pheasants or other game, except sometimes wretched old things which are sold because they happen to be in a case.

The street-trade in second-hand *Lasts* is confined principally to Petticoat and Rosemary lanes, where they are bought by the "garret-masters" in the shoemaking trade who supply the large wholesale warehouses; that is to say, by small masters who find their own materials and sell the boots and shoes by the dozen pairs. The lasts are bought also by mechanics, street-sellers, and other poor persons who cobble their own shoes. A shoemaker told me that he occasionally bought a last at a street stall, or rather from street hampers in Petticoat and Rosemary lanes, and it seemed to him that second-hand stores of street lasts got neither bigger nor smaller: "I suppose it's this way," he reasoned; "the garret-master buys lasts to do the slop-snobbing cheap, mostly women's lasts, and he dies or is done up and goes to the "great house," and his lasts find their way back to the streets. You notice, sir, the first time you're in Rosemary-lane, how little a great many of the lasts have been used, and that shows what a terrible necessity there was to part with them. In some there's hardly any peg-marks at all." The lasts are sold from 1*d.* to 3*d.* each, or twice that amount in pairs, "rights and lefts," according to the size and the condition. There are about 20 street last-sellers in the second-hand trade of London—"at least 20," one man said, after he seemed to have been making a mental calculation on the subject.

Second-hand harness is sold largely, and when good is sold very readily. There is, I am told, far less slop-work in harness-making than in shoemaking or in the other trades, such as tailoring, and "many a lady's pony harness," it was said to me by a second-hand dealer, "goes next to a tradesman, and next to a costermonger's donkey, and if it's been good leather to begin with—as it will if it was made for a lady—why the traces 'll stand clouting, and patching, and piecing, and mending for a long time, and they'll do to cobble old boots last of all, for old leather 'll wear just in treading, when it might snap at a pull. Give me a good quality to begin with, sir, and it's serviceable to the end." In my inquiries among the costermongers I ascertained that if one of that body started his donkey, or rose from that to his pony, he never bought new harness, unless it were a new collar if he had a regard for the comfort of his beast, but bought old harness, and "did it up" himself, often using iron rivets, or clenched nails, to reunite the broken parts, where, of course, a harness-maker would apply a patch. Nor is it the costermongers alone who buy all their harness second-hand. The sweep, whose stock of soot is large enough to require the help of an ass and a cart in its transport; the collector of bones and offal from the butchers' slaughter-houses or shops; and the many who may be considered as co-traders with the costermonger class—the greengrocer, the street coal-seller by retail, the salt-sellers, the gravel and sand dealer (a few have small carts)—all, indeed, of that class of traders, buy their harness second-hand, and generally in the streets. The chief sale of second-hand harness is on the Friday afternoons, in Smithfield. The more especial street-sale is in Petticoat and Rosemary lanes, and in the many off-streets and alleys which may be called the tributaries to those great second-hand marts. There is no sale of these wares in the Saturday night markets, for in the crush and bustle generally prevailing there at such times, no room could be found for things requiring so much space as sets of second-hand harness, and no time sufficiently to examine them. "There's so much to look at, you understand, sir," said one second-hand street-trader, who did a little in harness as well as in barrows, "if you wants a decent set, and don't grudge a shilling or two—and I never grudges them myself when I has 'em—so that it takes a little time. You must see that the buckles has good tongues—and it's a sort of joke in the trade that a bad tongue's a d——d bad thing—and that the pannel of the pad ain't as hard as a board (flocks is the best stuffing, sir), and that the bit, if it's rusty, can be polished up, for a animal no more likes a rusty bit in his mouth than we likes a musty bit of bread in our'n. O, a man as treats his ass as a ass ought to be treated—and it's just the same if he has a pony—can't be too perticler. If I had my way I'd 'act a law making people perticler about 'osses' and asses' shoes. If your boot pinches you, sir, you can sing out to your bootmaker, but a ass can't blow up a farrier." It seems to me that in these homely remarks of my informant, there is, so to speak, a sound practical kindliness. There can be little doubt that a fellow who maltreats his ass or his dog, maltreats his wife and children when he dares.

Clocks are sold second-hand, but only by three or four foreigners, Dutchmen or Germans, who hawk them and sell them at 2*s.* 6*d.* or 3*s.* each, Dutch clocks only been disposed of in this way. These traders, therefore, come under the head of STREET-FOREIGNERS. "Ay," one street-seller remarked to me, "it's only Dutch now as is second-handed in the streets, but it'll soon be Americans. The swags is some of them hung up with Slick's;" [so he called the American clocks, meaning the "Sam *Slicks*," in reference to Mr. Justice Hallyburton's work of that title;] "they're hung up with 'em, sir, and no relation whatsoever (pawnbroker) 'll give a printed character of 'em (a duplicate), and so they must come to the streets, and jolly cheap they'll be." The foreigners who sell the second-hand Dutch clocks sell also new clocks of the same manufacture, and often on tally, 1s. a week being the usual payment.

Cartouche-boxes are sold at the miscellaneous stalls, but only after there has been what I heard called a "Tower sale" (sale of military stores). When bought of the street-sellers, the use of these boxes is far more peaceful than that for which they were manufactured. Instead of the receptacles of cartridges, the divisions are converted into nail boxes, each with its different assortment, or contain the smaller kinds of tools, such as awl-blades. These boxes are sold in the streets at ½d. or 1d. each, and are bought by jobbing shoe-makers more than by any other class.

Of the other second-hand commodities of the streets, I may observe that in *Trinkets* the trade is altogether Jewish; in *Maps*, with frames, it is now a nonentity, and so it is with *Fishing-rods, Cricket-bats, &c.*

In *Umbrellas* and *Parasols* the second-hand traffic is large, but those vended in the streets are nearly all "done up" for street-sale by the class known as "Mush," or more properly "Mushroom Fakers," that is to say, the makers or *fakers* (*facere*—the slang *fakement* being simply a corruption of the Latin *facimentum*) of those articles which are similar in shape to *mushrooms*. I shall treat of this class and the goods they sell under the head of Street-Artisans. The collectors of Old Umbrellas and Parasols are the same persons as collect the second-hand habiliments of male and female attire.

The men and women engaged in the street-commerce carried on in second-hand articles are, in all respects, a more mixed class than the generality of street-sellers. Some hawk in the streets goods which they also display in their shops, or in the windowless apartments known as their shops. Some are not in possession of shops, but often buy their wares of those who are. Some collect or purchase the articles they vend; others collect them by barter. The itinerant crock-man, the root-seller, the glazed table-cover seller, the hawker of spars and worked stone, and even the costermonger of the morning, is the dealer in second-hand articles of the afternoon and evening. The costermonger is, moreover, often the buyer and seller of second-hand harness in Smithfield. I may point out again, also, what a multifariousness of wares passes in the course of a month through the hands of a general street-seller; at one time new goods, at another second-hand; sometimes he is stationary at a pitch vending "lots," or "swag toys;" at others itinerant, selling braces, belts, and hose.

I found no miscellaneous dealer who could tell me of the proportionate receipts from the various articles he dealt in even for the last month. He "did well" in this, and badly in the other trade, but beyond such vague statements there is no precise information to be had. It should be recollected that the street-sellers do not keep accounts, or those documents would supply references. "It's all headwork with us," a street-seller said, somewhat boastingly, to me, as if the ignorance of book-keeping was rather commendable.

Of Second-hand Store Shops.

Perhaps it may add to the completeness of the information here given concerning the trading in old refuse articles, and especially those of a miscellaneous character, the manner in which, and the parties by whom the business is carried on, if I conclude this branch of the subject by an account of the shops of the second-hand dealers. The distance between the class of these shop-keepers and of the stall and barrow-keepers I have described is not great. It may be said to be merely from the street to within doors. Marine-store dealers have often in their start in life been street-sellers, not unfrequently coster-mongers, and street-sellers they again become if their ventures be unsuccessful. Some of them, however, make a good deal of money in what may be best understood as a "hugger-mugger way."

On this subject I cannot do better than quote Mr. Dickens, one of the most minute and truthful of observers:—

"The reader must often have perceived in some by-street, in a poor neighbourhood, a small dirty shop, exposing for sale the most extraordinary and confused jumble of old, worn-out, wretched articles, that can well be imagined. Our wonder at their ever having been bought, is only to be equalled by our astonishment at the idea of their ever being sold again. On a board, at the side of the door, are placed about twenty books—all odd volumes; and as many wine-glasses—all different patterns; several locks, an old earthenware pan, full of rusty keys; two or three gaudy chimney ornaments—cracked, of course; the remains of a lustre, without any drops; a round frame like a capital O, which has once held a mirror; a flute, complete with the exception of the middle joint; a pair of curling-irons; and a tinder-box. In front of the shop-window, are ranged some half-dozen high-backed chairs, with spinal complaints and wasted legs; a corner cupboard; two or three very dark mahogany tables with flaps like mathematical problems; some pickle-bottles, some surgeons' ditto, with gilt labels and without stoppers; an unframed portrait of some lady who flourished about the beginning of the thirteenth century, by an artist who never flourished at all; an incalculable host of miscellanies of every description, including armour and cabinets, rags and bones, fenders and street-door knockers, fire-irons, wearing-apparel and bedding, a hall-lamp, and a room-door. Imagine, in addition to this incongruous mass, a black doll in a white frock, with two faces—one looking up the street, and the other looking down, swinging over the door; a board with the squeezed-up inscription 'Dealer in marine stores,' in lanky white letters, whose height is strangely out of proportion to their width; and you have before you precisely the kind of shop to which we wish to direct your attention.

"Although the same heterogeneous mixture of things will be found at all these places, it is curious to observe how truly and accurately some of the minor articles which are exposed for sale— articles of wearing-apparel, for instance—mark the character of the neighbourhood. Take Drury-lane and Covent-garden for example.

"This is essentially a theatrical neighbourhood. There is not a potboy in the vicinity who is not, to a greater or less extent, a dramatic character. The errand-boys and chandlers'-shop-keepers' sons, are all stage-struck: they 'get up' plays in back kitchens hired for the purpose, and will stand before a shop-window for hours, contemplating a great staring portrait of Mr. somebody or other, of the Royal Coburg Theatre, 'as he appeared in the character of Tongo the Denounced.' The consequence is, that there is not a marine-store shop in the neighbourhood, which does not exhibit for sale some faded articles of dramatic finery, such as three or four pairs of soiled buff boots with turn-over red tops, heretofore worn by a 'fourth robber,' or 'fifth mob;' a pair of rusty broad-swords, a few gauntlets, and certain resplendent ornaments, which, if they were yellow instead of white, might be taken for insurance plates of the Sun Fire-office. There are several of these shops in the narrow streets and dirty courts, of which there are so many near the national theatres, and they all have tempting goods of this description, with the addition, perhaps, of a lady's pink dress covered with spangles; white wreaths, stage shoes, and a tiara like a tin lamp reflector. They have been purchased of some wretched supernumeraries, or sixth-rate actors, and are now offered for the benefit of the rising generation, who, on condition of making certain weekly payments, amounting in the whole to about ten times their value, may avail themselves of such desirable bargains.

"Let us take a very different quarter, and apply it to the same test. Look at a marine-store dealer's, in that reservoir of dirt, drunkenness, and drabs: thieves, oysters, baked potatoes, and pickled salmon — Ratcliff-highway. Here, the wearing-apparel is all nautical. Rough blue jackets, with mother-of-pearl buttons, oil-skin hats, coarse checked shirts, and large canvass trousers that look as if they were made for a pair of bodies instead of a pair of legs, are the staple commodities. Then, there are large bunches of cotton pocket-handkerchiefs, in colour and pattern unlike any one ever saw before, with the exception of those on the backs of the three young ladies without bonnets who passed just now. The furniture is much the same as elsewhere, with the addition of one or two models of ships, and some old prints of naval engagements in still older frames. In the window are a few compasses, a small tray containing silver watches in clumsy thick cases; and tobacco-boxes, the lid of each ornamented with a ship, or an anchor, or some such trophy. A sailor generally pawns or sells all he has before he has been long ashore, and if he does not, some favoured companion kindly saves him the trouble. In either case, it is an even chance that he afterwards unconsciously repurchases the same things at a higher price than he gave for them at first.

"Again: pay a visit, with a similar object, to a part of London, as unlike both of these as they are to each other. Cross over to the Surry side, and look at such shops of this description as are to be found near the King's Bench prison, and in 'the Rules.' How different, and how strikingly illustrative of the decay of some of the unfortunate residents in this part of the metropolis! Imprisonment and neglect have done their work. There is contamination in the profligate denizens of a debtors' prison; old friends have fallen off; the recollection of former prosperity has passed away; and with it all thoughts for the past, all care for the future. First, watches and rings, then cloaks, coats, and all the more expensive articles of dress, have found their way to the pawnbroker's. That miserable resource has failed at last, and the sale of some trifling article at one of these shops, has been the only mode left of raising a shilling or two, to meet the urgent demands of the moment. Dressing-cases and writing-desks, too old to pawn but too good to keep; guns, fishing-rods, musical instruments, all in the same condition; have first been sold, and the sacrifice has been but slightly felt. But hunger must be allayed, and what has already become a habit, is easily resorted to, when an emergency arises. Light articles of clothing, first of the ruined man, then of his wife, at last of their children, even of the youngest, have been parted with, piecemeal. There they are, thrown carelessly together until a purchaser presents himself, old, and patched and repaired, it is true; but the make and materials tell of better days: and the older they are, the greater the misery and destitution of those whom they once adorned."

Of the Street-sellers of Second-hand Apparel.

The multifariousness of the articles of this trade is limited only by what the uncertainty of the climate, the caprices of fashion, or the established styles of apparel in the kingdom, have caused to be worn, flung aside, and reworn as a revival of an obsolete style. It is to be remarked, however, that of the old-fashioned styles none that are costly have been revived. Laced coats, and embroidered and lappeted waistcoats, have long disappeared from second-hand traffic—the last stage of fashions—and indeed from all places but court or fancy balls and the theatre.

The great mart for second-hand apparel was, in the last century, in Monmouth-street; now, by one of those arbitrary, and almost always inappropriate, changes in the nomenclature of streets, termed Dudley-street, Seven Dials. "Monmouth-street finery" was a common term to express tawdriness and pretence. Now Monmouth-street, for its new name is hardly legitimated, has no finery. Its second-hand wares are almost wholly confined to old boots and shoes, which are vamped up with a good deal of trickery; so much so that a shoemaker, himself in the poorer practice of the "gentle craft," told me that blacking and brown paper were the materials of Monmouth-street cobbling. Almost every master in Monmouth-street now is, I am told, an Irishman; and the great majority of the workmen are Irishmen also. There were a few Jews and a few cockneys in this well-known street a year or two back, but now this branch of the second-hand trade is really in the hands of what may be called a clan. A little business is carried on in second-hand apparel, as well as boots and shoes, but it is insignificant.

The head-quarters of this second-hand trade are now in Petticoat and Rosemary lanes, especially in Petticoat-lane, and the traffic there carried on may be called enormous. As in other departments of commerce, both in our own capital, in many of our older cities, and in the cities of the Continent, the locality appropriated to this traffic is one of narrow streets, dark alleys, and most oppressive crowding. The traders seem to judge of a Rag-fair garment, whether a cotton frock or a ducal coachman's great-coat, by the touch, more reliably than by the sight; they inspect, so to speak, with their fingers more than their eyes. But the business in Petticoat and Rosemary lanes is mostly of a retail character. The wholesale mart—for the trade in old clothes has both a wholesale and retail form—is in a place of especial curiosity, and one of which, as being little known, I shall first speak.

Of the Old Clothes Exchange.

The trade in second-hand apparel is one of the most ancient of callings, and is known in almost every country, but anything like the Old Clothes Exchange of the Jewish quarter of London, in the extent and order of its business, is unequalled in the world. There is indeed no other such place, and it is rather remarkable that a business occupying so many persons, and requiring such facilities for examination and arrangement, should not until the year 1843 have had its regulated proceedings. The Old Clothes Exchange is the latest of the central marts, established in the metropolis.

Smithfield, or the Cattle Exchange, is the oldest of all the markets; it is mentioned as a place for the sale of horses in the time of Henry II. Billingsgate, or the Fish Exchange, is of ancient, but uncertain era. Covent Garden—the largest Fruit, Vegetable, and Flower Exchange—first became established as the centre of such commerce in the reign of Charles II.; the establishment of the Borough and Spitalfields markets, as other marts for the sale of fruits, vegetables, and flowers, being nearly as ancient. The Royal Exchange dates from the days of Queen Elizabeth, and the Bank of England and the Stock-Exchange from those of William III., while the present premises for the Corn and Coal Exchanges are modern.

Were it possible to obtain the statistics of the last quarter of a century, it would, perhaps, be found that in none of the important interests I have mentioned has there been a greater increase of business than in the trade in old clothes. Whether this purports a high degree of national prosperity or not, it is not my business at present to inquire, and be it as it may, it is certain that, until the last few years, the trade in old clothes used to be carried on entirely in the open air, and this in the localities which I have pointed out in my account of the trade in old metal (p. 10, vol. ii.) as comprising the Petticoat-lane district. The old clothes trade was also pursued in Rosemary-lane, but then—and so indeed it is now—this was but a branch of the more centralized commerce of Petticoat-lane. The head-quarters of the traffic at that time were confined to a space not more than ten square yards, adjoining Cutler-street. The chief traffic elsewhere was originally in Cutler-street, White-street, Carter-street, and in Harrow-alley—the districts of the celebrated Rag-fair.

The confusion and clamour before the institution of the present arrangements were extreme. Great as was the extent of the business transacted, people wondered how it could be accomplished, for it always appeared to a stranger, that there could be no order whatever in all the disorder. The wrangling was incessant, nor were the trade-contests always confined to wrangling alone. The passions of the Irish often drove them to resort to cuffs, kicks, and blows, which the Jews, although with a better command over their tempers, were not slack in returning. The East India Company, some of whose warehouses adjoined the market, frequently complained to the city authorities of the nuisance. Complaints from other quarters were also frequent, and sometimes as many as 200 constables were necessary to restore or enforce order. The nuisance, however, like many a public nuisance, was left to remedy itself, or rather it was left to be remedied by individual enterprise. Mr. L. Isaac, the present proprietor, purchased the houses which then filled up the back of Phil's-buildings, and formed the present Old Clothes Exchange. This was eight years ago; now there are no more policemen in the locality than in other equally populous parts.

Of Old Clothes Exchanges there are now two, both adjacent, the one first opened by Mr. Isaac being the most important. This is 100 feet by 70, and is the mart to which the collectors of the cast-off apparel of the metropolis bring their goods for sale. The goods are sold wholesale and retail, for an old clothes merchant will buy either a single hat, or an entire wardrobe, or a sackful of shoes,—I need not say *pairs*, for odd shoes are not rejected. In one department of "Isaac's Exchange," however, the goods are not sold to parties who buy for their own wearing, but to the old clothes merchant, who buys to sell again. In this portion of the mart are 90 stalls, averaging about six square feet each.

In another department, which communicates with the first, and is two-thirds of the size, are assembled such traders as buy the old garments to dispose of them, either after a process of cleaning, or when they have been repaired and renovated. These buyers are generally shopkeepers, residing in the old clothes districts of Marylebone-lane, Holywell-street, Monmouth-street, Union-street (Borough), Saffron-hill (Field-lane), Drury-lane, Shoreditch, the Waterloo-road, and other places of which I shall have to speak hereafter.

The difference between the first and second class of buyers above mentioned, is really that of the merchant and the retail shopkeeper. The one buys literally anything presented to him which is vendible, and in any quantity, for the supply of the wholesale dealers from distant parts, or for exportation, or for the general trade of London. The other purchases what suits his individual trade, and is likely to suit regular or promiscuous customers.

In another part of the same market is carried on the *retail* old clothes trade to any one—shopkeeper, artisan, clerk, costermonger, or gentlemen. This indeed, is partially the case in the other parts. "Yesh, inteet," said a Hebrew trader, whom I conversed with on the subject, "I shall be clad to shell you one coat, sir. Dish von is shust your shize; it is verra sheep, and vosh made by one tip-top shnip." Indeed, the keenness and anxiety to trade—whenever trade seems possible—causes many of the frequenters of these marts to infringe the arrangements as to the manner of the traffic, though the proprietors endeavour to cause the regulations to be strictly adhered to.

The second Exchange, which is a few yards apart from the other is known as Simmons and Levy's Clothes Exchange, and is unemployed, for its more especial business purposes, except in the mornings. The commerce is then wholesale, for here are sold collections of unredeemed pledges in wearing apparel, consigned there by the pawnbrokers, or the buyers at the auctions of unredeemed goods; as well as draughts from the stocks of the wardrobe dealers; a quantity of military or naval stores, and such like articles. In the afternoon the stalls are occupied by retail dealers. The ground is about as large as the first-mentioned exchange, but is longer and narrower.

In neither of these places is there even an attempt at architectural elegance, or even neatness. The stalls and partitions are of unpainted wood, the walls are bare, the only care that seems to be manifested is that the places should be dry. In the first instance the plainness was no doubt a necessity from motives of prudence, as the establishments were merely speculations, and now everything but *business* seems to be disregarded. The Old Clothes Exchanges have assuredly one recommendation as they are now seen—their appropriateness. They have a threadbare, patched, and *second-hand* look. The dresses worn by the dealers, and the dresses they deal in, are all in accordance with the genius of the place. But the eagerness, crowding, and energy, are the grand features of the scene; and of all the many curious sights in London there is none so picturesque (from the various costumes of the buyers and sellers), none so novel, and none so animated as that of the Old Clothes Exchange.

Business is carried on in the wholesale department of the Old Clothes Exchanges every day during the week; and in the retail on each day except the Hebrew Sabbath (Saturday). The Jews in the old clothes trade observe strictly the command that on their Sabbath day they shall do no manner of work, for on a visit I paid to the Exchange last Saturday, not a single Jew could I see engaged in any business. But though the Hebrew Sabbath is observed by the Jews and disregarded by the Christians, the Christian Sabbath, on the other hand, is disregarded by Jew and Christian alike, some few of the Irish excepted, who may occasionally go to early mass, and attend at the Exchange afterwards. Sunday, therefore, in "Rag-fair," is like the other days of the week (Saturday excepted); business closes on the Sunday, however, at 2 instead of 6.

On the Saturday the keen Jew-traders in the neighbourhood of the Exchanges may be seen standing at their doors—after the synagogue hours —or looking out of their windows, dressed in their best. The dress of the men is for the most part not distinguishable from that of the English on the Sunday, except that there may be a greater glitter of rings and watch-guards. The dress of the women is of every kind; becoming, handsome, rich, tawdry, but seldom neat.

OF THE WHOLESALE BUSINESS AT THE OLD CLOTHES EXCHANGE.

A CONSIDERABLE quantity of the old clothes disposed of at the Exchange are bought by merchants from Ireland. They are then packed in bales by porters, regularly employed for the purpose, and who literally *build* them up square and compact. These bales are each worth from 50*l.* to 300*l.*, though seldom 300*l.*, and it is curious to reflect from how many classes the pile of old garments has been collected —how many privations have been endured before some of these habiliments found their way into the possession of the old clothes-man—what besotted debauchery put others in his possession—with what cool calculation others were disposed of—how many were procured for money, and how many by the tempting offers of flowers, glass, crockery, spars, table-covers, lace, or millinery—what was the clothing which could first be spared when rent was to be defrayed or bread to be bought, and what was treasured until the last—in what scenes of gaiety or gravity, in the opera-house or the senate, had the perhaps departed wearers of some of that heap of old clothes figured—through how many possessors, and again through what new scenes of middle-class or artizan comfort had these dresses passed, or through what accidents of "genteel" privation and destitution—and lastly through what necessities of squalid wretchedness and low debauchery.

Every kind of old attire, from the highest to the *very lowest*, I was emphatically told, was sent to Ireland.

Some of the bales are composed of garments

originally made for the labouring classes. These are made up of every description of colour and material—cloth, corduroy, woollen cords, fustian, moleskin, flannel, velveteen, plaids, and the several varieties of those substances. In them are to be seen coats, great-coats, jackets, trousers, and breeches, but no other habiliments, such as boots, shirts, or stockings. I was told by a gentleman, who between 40 and 50 years ago was familiar with the liberty and poorer parts of Dublin, that the most coveted and the most saleable of all second-hand apparel was that of leather breeches, worn commonly in some of the country parts of England half a century back, and sent in considerable quantities at that time from London to Ireland. These nether habiliments were coveted because, as the Dublin sellers would say, they "would wear for ever, and look illigant after that." Buck-skin breeches are now never worn except by grooms in their liveries, and gentlemen when hunting, so that the trade in them in the Old Clothes Exchange, and their exportation to Ireland, are at an end. The next most saleable thing—I may mention, incidentally—vended cheap and second-hand in Dublin, to the poor Irishmen of the period I speak of, was a wig! And happy was the man who could wear two, one over the other.

Some of the Irish buyers who are regular frequenters of the London Old Clothes Exchange, take a small apartment, often a garret or a cellar, in Petticoat-lane or its vicinity, and to this room they convey their purchases until a sufficient stock has been collected. Among these old clothes the Irish possessors cook, or at any rate eat, their meals, and upon them they sleep. I did not hear that such dealers were more than ordinarily unhealthy; though it may, perhaps, be assumed that such habits are fatal to health. What may be the average duration of life among old clothes sellers who live in the midst of their wares, I do not know, and believe that no facts have been collected on the subject; but I certainly saw among them some very old men.

Other wholesale buyers from Ireland occupy decent lodgings in the neighbourhood—decent considering the locality. In Phil's-buildings, a kind of wide alley which forms one of the approaches to the Exchange, are eight respectable apartments, almost always let to the Irish old clothes merchants.

Tradesmen of the same class come also from the large towns of England and Scotland to buy for their customers some of the left-off clothes of London.

Nor is this the extent of the wholesale trade. Bales of old clothes are exported to Belgium and Holland, but principally to Holland. Of the quantity of goods thus exported to the Continent not above one-half, perhaps, can be called old *clothes*, while among these the old livery suits are in the best demand. The other goods of this foreign trade are old serges, duffles, carpeting, drugget, and heavy woollen goods generally, of all the descriptions which I have before enumerated as parcel of the second-hand trade of the streets.

Old merino curtains, and any second-hand decorations of fringes, woollen lace, &c., are in demand for Holland.

Twelve bales, averaging somewhere about 100*l.* each in value, but not fully 100*l.*, are sent direct every week of the year from the Old Clothes Exchange to distant places, and this is not the whole of the traffic, apart from what is done retail. I am informed on the best authority, that the average trade may be stated at 1500*l.* a week all the year round. When I come to the conclusion of the subject, however, I shall be able to present statistics of the amount turned over in the respective branches of the old clothes trade, as well as of the number of the traffickers, only one-fourth of whom are now Jews.

The conversation which goes on in the Old Clothes Exchange during business hours, apart from the "larking" of the young sweet-stuff and orange or cake-sellers, is all concerning business, but there is, even while business is being transacted, a frequent interchange of jokes, and even of practical jokes. The business talk—I was told by an old clothes collector, and I heard similar remarks—is often to the following effect:—

"How much is this here?" says the man who comes to buy. "One pound five," replies the Jew seller. "I won't give you above half the money." "Half de money," cries the salesman, "I can't take dat. Vat above the 16*s.* dat you offer now vill you give for it? Vill you give me eighteen? Vell, come, give ush your money, I've got ma rent to pay." But the man says, "I only bid you 12*s.* 6*d.*, and I shan't give no more." And then, if the seller finds he can get him to "spring" or advance no further, he says, " I shupposh I musht take your money even if I loosh by it. You'll be a better cushtomer anoder time." [This is still a common "deal," I am assured by one who began the business at 13 years old, and is now upwards of 60 years of age. The Petticoat-laner will always ask at least twice as much as he means to take.]

For a more detailed account of the mode of business as conducted at the Old Clothes Exchange I refer the reader to p. 368, vol. i. Subsequent visits have shown me nothing to alter in that description, although written (in one of my letters in the *Morning Chronicle*), nearly two years ago. I have merely to add that I have there mentioned the receipt of a halfpenny toll; but this, I find, is not levied on Saturdays and Sundays.

I ought not to omit stating that pilfering one from another by the poor persons who have collected the second-hand garments, and have carried them to the Old Clothes Exchange to dispose of, is of very rare occurrence. This is the more commendable, for many of the wares could not be identified by their owner, as he had procured them only that morning. If, as happens often enough, a man carried a dozen pairs of old shoes to the Exchange, and one pair were stolen, he might have some difficulty in swearing to the identity of the pair purloined. It is true that the Jews, and crock-men, and others, who collect, by sale or barter, masses of old clothes, note all their defects very minutely, and might have no moral doubt as to identity, nevertheless the magistrate would probably conclude that the legal evidence—were it only circumstantial—was insufficient. The young thieves, however, who flock from the low lodging-houses in the neighbourhood, are an especial trouble in Petticoat-lane, where the people robbed are generally too busy, and the article stolen of too little value, to induce a prosecution—a knowledge which the juvenile pilferer is not slow in acquiring. Sometimes when these boys are caught pilfering, they are severely beaten, especially by the women, who are aided by the men, if the thief offers any formidable resistance, or struggles to return the blows.

Of the Uses of Second-hand Garments.

I HAVE now to describe the uses to which the several kinds of garments which constitute the commerce of the Old Clothes Exchange are devoted, whether it be merely in the re-sale of the apparel, to be worn in its original form or in a repaired or renovated form; or whether it be "worked up" into other habiliments, or be useful for the making of other descriptions of woollen fabrics; or else whether it be fit merely for its last stages—the rag-bag for the paper-maker, or the manure heap for the hop-grower.

Each "left-off" garment has its peculiar after *uses*, according to its material and condition. The practised eye of the old clothes man at once embraces every capability of the apparel, and the amount which these capabilities will realize; whether they be woollen, linen, cotton, leathern, or silken goods; or whether they be articles which cannot be classed under any of those designations, such as macintoshes and furs.

A *surtout* coat is the most serviceable of any second-hand clothing, originally good. It can be re-cuffed, re-collared, or the skirts re-lined with new or old silk, or with a substitute for silk. It can be "restored" if the seams be white and the general appearance what is best understood by the expressive word "seedy." This restoration is a sort of re-dyeing, or rather re-colouring, by the application of gall and logwood with a small portion of copperas. If the under sleeve be worn, as it often is by those whose avocations are sedentary, it is renewed, and frequently with a second-hand piece of cloth "to match," so that there is no perceptible difference between the renewal and the other parts. Many an honest artisan in this way becomes possessed of his Sunday frock-coat, as does many a smarter clerk or shopman, impressed with a regard to his personal appearance.

In the last century, I may here observe, and perhaps in the early part of the present, when woollen cloth was much dearer, much more substantial, and therefore much more durable, it was common for economists to have a good coat "turned." It was taken to pieces by the tailor and re-made, the inner part becoming the outer. This mode prevailed alike in France and England; for Molière makes his miser, *Harpagon*, magnanimously resolve to incur the cost of his many-years'-old coat being "turned," for the celebration of his expected marriage with a young and wealthy bride. This way of dealing with a second-hand garment is not so general now as it was formerly in London, nor is it in the country.

If the surtout be incapable of restoration to the appearance of a "respectable" garment, the skirts are sold for the making of cloth caps; or for the material of boys' or "youths'" waistcoats; or for "poor country curates' gaiters;" but not so much now as they once were. The poor journeymen parsons," I was told, "now goes for the new slops; they're often green, and is had by 'vertisements, and bills, and them books about fashions which is all over both country and town. Do you know, sir, why them there books is always made so small? The leaves is about four inches square. That's to prevent their being any use as waste paper. I'll back a coat such as is sometimes sold by a gentleman's servant to wear out two new slops."

Cloaks are things of as ready sale as any kind of old garments. If good, or even reparable, they are in demand both for the home and foreign trades, as cloaks; if too far gone, which is but rarely the case, they are especially available for the same purposes as the surtout. The same may be said of the great-coat.

Dress-coats are far less useful, as if cleaned up and repaired they are not in demand among the working classes, and the clerks and shopmen on small salaries are often tempted by the price, I was told, to buy some wretched new slop thing rather than a superior coat second-hand. The dress-coats, however, are used for caps. Sometimes a coat, for which the collector may have given 9*d.*, is cut up for the repairs of better garments.

Trousers are re-seated and repaired where the material is strong enough; and they are, I am informed, now about the only habiliment which is ever "turned," and that but exceptionally. The repairs to trousers are more readily effected than those to coats, and trousers are freely bought by the collectors, and as freely re-bought by the public.

Waistcoats—I still speak of woollen fabrics—are sometimes used in cap-making, and were used in gaiter-making. But generally, at the present time, the worn edges are cut away, the buttons renewed or replaced by a new set, sometimes of glittering glass, the button-holes repaired or their jaggedness gummed down, and so the waistcoat is reproduced as a waistcoat, a size smaller. Sometimes a "vest," as waistcoats are occasionally called, is used by the cheap boot-makers for the "legs" of a woman's cloth boots, either laced or buttoned, but not a quarter as much as they would be, I was told, if the buttons and button-holes of the waistcoat would "do again" in the boot.

Nor is the woollen garment, if too thin, too worn, or too rotten to be devoted to any of the uses I have specified, flung away as worthless. To the traders in second-hand apparel, or in the remains of second-hand apparel, a dust-hole is an unknown receptacle. The woollen rag, for so it is then considered, when unravelled can be made available for the manufacture of cheap yarns, being mixed with new wool. It is more probable, however, that the piece of woollen fabric which has been rejected by those who make or mend, and who must make or mend so cheaply that the veriest vagrant may be their customer, is formed not only into a new material, but into a material which sometimes is made into a new garment. These garments are inferior to those woven of new wool, both in look and wear; but in some articles the re-manufacture is beautiful. The fabric thus snatched, as it were, from the ruins of cloth, is known as shoddy, the chief seat of manufacture being in Dewsbury, a small town in Yorkshire. The old material, when duly prepared, is torn into wool again by means of fine machinery, but the recovered wool is shorter in its fibre and more brittle in its nature; it is, indeed, more a woollen pulp than a wool.

Touching this peculiar branch of manufacture, I will here cite from the *Morning Chronicle* a brief description of a Shoddy Mill, so that the reader may have as comprehensive a knowledge as possible of the several uses to which his left-off clothes may be put.

" The small town of Dewsbury holds, in the woollen district, very much the same position which Oldham does in the cotton country—the spinning and preparing of waste and refuse materials. To this stuff the name of "shoddy" is given, but the real and orthodox " shoddy " is a production of the woollen districts, and consists of the second-hand wool manufactured by the tearing up, or rather the grinding, of woollen rags by means of coarse willows, called devils; the operation of which sends forth choking clouds of dry pungent dirt and floating fibres—the real and original " devil's dust." Having been, by the agency of the machinery in question, reduced to something like the original raw material, fresh wool is added to the pulp in different proportions, according to the quality of the stuff to be manufactured, and the mingled material is at length reworked in the usual way into a little serviceable cloth.

" There are some shoddy mills in the neighbourhood of Huddersfield, but the mean little town of Dewsbury may be taken as the metropolis of the manufacture. Some mills are devoted solely to the sorting, preparing, and grinding of rags, which are worked up in the neighbouring factories. Here great bales, choke full of filthy tatters, lie scattered about the yard, while the continual arrival of loaded waggons keeps adding to the heap. A glance at the exterior of these mills shows their character. The walls and part of the roof are covered with the thick clinging dust and fibre, which ascends in choky volumes from the open doors and glassless windows of the ground floor, and which also pours forth from a chimney, constructed for the purpose, exactly like smoke. The mill is covered as with a mildewy fungus, and upon the gray slates of the roof the frowzy deposit is often not less than two inches in depth.

In the upper story of these mills the rags are stored. A great ware-room is piled in many places from the floor to the ceiling with bales of woollen rags, torn strips and tatters of every colour peeping out from the bursting depositories. There is hardly a country in Europe which does not contribute its quota of material to the shoddy manufacturer. Rags are brought from France, Germany, and in great quantities from Belgium. Denmark, I understand, is favourably looked upon by the tatter merchants, being fertile in morsels of clothing, of fair quality. Of domestic rags, the Scotch bear off the palm; and possibly no one will be surprised to hear, that of all rags Irish rags are the most worn, the filthiest, and generally the most unprofitable. The gradations of value in the world of rags are indeed remarkable. I was shown rags worth 50*l*. per ton, and rags worth only 30*s*. The best class is formed of the remains of fine cloth, the produce of which, eked out with a few bundles of fresh wool, is destined to go forth to the world again as broad cloth, or at all events as pilot cloth. Fragments of damask and skirts of merino dresses form the staple of middle-class rags; and even the very worst bales —they appear unmitigated mashes of frowzy filth—afford here and there some fragments of calico, which are wrought up into brown paper. The refuse of all, mixed with the stuff which even the shoddy-making devil rejects, is packed off to the agricultural districts for use as manure, to fertilize the hop-gardens of Kent.

" Under the rag ware-room is the sorting and picking room. Here the bales are opened, and their contents piled in close, poverty-smelling masses, upon the floor. The operatives are entirely women. They sit upon low stools, or half sunk and half enthroned amid heaps of the filthy goods, busily employed in arranging them according to the colour and the quality of the morsels, and from the more pretending quality of rags carefully ripping out every particle of cotton which they can detect. Piles of rags of different sorts, dozens of feet high, are the obvious fruits of their labour. All these women are over eighteen years of age, and the wages which they are paid for ten hours' work are 6*s*. per week. They look squalid and dirty enough; but all of them chatter and several sing over their noisome labour. The atmosphere of the room is close and oppressive; and although no particularly offensive smell is perceptible, there is a choky, mildewy sort of odour—a hot, moist exhalation—arising from the sodden smouldering piles, as the workwomen toss armfuls of rags from one heap to another. This species of work is the lowest and foulest which any phase of the factory system can show.

" The devils are upon the ground floor. The choking dust bursts out from door and window, and it is not until a minute or so that the visitor can see the workmen moving amid the clouds, catching up armfuls of the sorted rags and tossing them into the machine to be torn into fibry fragments by the whirling revolutions of its teeth. The place in which this is done is a large bare room—the uncovered beams above, the rough stone walls, and the woodwork of the unglazed windows being as it were furred over with clinging woolly matter. On the floor, the dust and coarse filaments lie as if 'it had been snowing snuff.' The workmen are coated with the flying powder. They wear bandages over their mouths, so as to prevent as much as possible the inhalation of the dust, and seem loath to remove the protection for a moment. The rag grinders, with their squalid, dust-strewn garments, powdered to a dull grayish hue, and with their bandages tied over the greater part of their faces, move about like reanimated mummies in their swathings, looking most ghastly. The wages of these poor creatures do not exceed 7s. or 8s. a week. The men are much better paid, none of them making less than 18s. a week, and many earning as much as 22s. Not one of them, however, will admit that he found the trade injurious. The dust tickles them a little, they say, that is all. They feel it most of a Monday morning, after being all Sunday in the fresh air. When they first take to the work it hurts their throats a little, but they drink mint tea, and that soon cures them. They are all more or less subject to 'shoddy fever,' they confess, especially after tenting the grinding of the very dusty sorts of stuff—worsted stockings, for example. The shoddy fever is a sort of stuffing of the head and nose, with sore throat, and it sometimes forces them to give over work for two or three days, or at most a week; but the disorder, the workmen say, is not fatal, and leaves no particularly bad effects.

"In spite of all this, however, it is manifestly impossible for human lungs to breathe under such circumstances without suffering. The visitor exposed to the atmosphere for ten minutes experiences an unpleasant choky sensation in the throat, which lasts all the remainder of the day. The rag grinders, moreover, according to the best accounts, are very subject to asthmatic complaints, particularly when the air is dull and warm. The shoddy fever is said to be like a bad cold, with constant acrid running from the nose, and a great deal of expectoration. It is when there is a particularly dirty lot of rags to be ground that the people are usually attacked in this way, but the fever seldom keeps them more than two or three days from their work.

"In other mills the rags are not only ground, but the shoddy is worked up into coarse bad cloth, a great proportion of which is sent to America for slave clothing (and much now sold to the slop-shops).

"After the rags have been devilled into shoddy, the remaining processes are much the same, although conducted in a coarser way, as those performed in the manufacture of woollen cloth. The weaving is, for the most part, carried on at the homes of the workpeople. The domestic arrangements consist, in every case, of two tolerably large rooms, one above the other, with a cellar beneath—a plan of construction called in Yorkshire a "house and a chamber." The chamber has generally a bed amid the looms. The weavers complain of irregular work and diminished wages. Their average pay, one week with another, with their wives to wind for them—*i. e.*, to place the thread upon the bobbin which goes into the shuttle —is hardly so much as 10s. a week. They work long hours, often fourteen per day. Sometimes the weaver is a small capitalist with perhaps half a dozen looms, and a hand-jenny for spinning thread, the workpeople being within his own family as regular apprentices and journeymen."

Dr. Hemingway, a gentleman who has a large practice in the shoddy district, has given the following information touching the "shoddy fever":—

"The disease popularly known as 'shoddy fever,' and which is of frequent occurrence, is a species of bronchitis, caused by the irritating effect of the floating particles of dust upon the mucous membrane of the trachea and its ramifications. In general, the attack is easily cured—particularly if the patient has not been for any length of time exposed to the exciting cause—by effervescing saline draughts to allay the symptomatic febrile action, followed by expectorants to relieve the mucous membrane of the irritating dust; but a long continuance of employment in the contaminated atmosphere, bringing on as it does repeated attacks of the disease, is too apt, in the end, to undermine the constitution, and produce a train of pectoral diseases, often closing with pulmonary consumption. Ophthalmic attacks are by no means uncommon among the shoddy-grinders, some of whom, however, wear wire-gauze spectacles to protect the eyes. As regards the effect of the occupation upon health, it may shorten life by about five years on a rough average, taking, of course, as the point of comparison, the average longevity of the district in which the manufacture is carried on."

"Shoddy fever" is, in fact, a modification of the very fatal disease induced by what is called "dry grinding" at Sheffield; but of course the particles of woollen filament are less fatal in their influence than the floating steel dust produced by the operation in question.

At one time shoddy cloth was not good and firm enough to be used for other purposes than such as padding by tailors, and in the inner linings of carriages, by coach-builders. It was not used for purposes which would expose it to stress, but only to a moderate wear or friction. Now shoddy, which modern improvements have made susceptible of receiving a fine dye (it always looked a dead colour at one period), is made into cloth for soldiers' and sailors' uniforms and for pilot-coats; into blanketing, drugget, stair and other carpeting, and into those beautiful table-covers, with their rich woollen look, on which elegantly drawn and elaborately coloured designs are printed through the application of aquafortis. Thus the rags which the beggar could no longer hang about him to cover his nakedness, may be a component of the soldier's or sailor's uniform, the carpet of a palace, or the library table-cover of a prime-minister.

There is yet another use for old woollen clothes

What is not good for shoddy is good for manure, and more especially for the manure prepared by the agriculturists in Kent, Sussex, and Herefordshire, for the culture of a difficult plant—hops. It is good also for corn land (judiciously used), so that we again have the remains of the old garment in our beer or our bread.

I have hitherto spoken of *woollen* fabrics. The garments of other materials are seldom diverted from their original use, for as long as they will hold together they can be sold for exportation to Ireland, though of course for very trifling amounts.

The black *Velvet* and *Satin Waistcoats*—the latter now so commonly worn—are almost always resold as waistcoats, and oft enough, when rebound and rebuttoned, make a very respectable looking garment. Nothing sells better to the working-classes than a *good* second-hand vest of the two materials of satin or velvet. If the satin, however, be so worn and frayed that mending is impossible, the back, if not in the same plight, is removed for rebacking of any waistcoat, and the satin thrown away, one of the few things which in its last stage is utterly valueless. It is the same with silk waistcoats, and for the most part with velvet, but a velvet waistcoat may be thrown in the refuse heap with the woollen rags for manure. The coloured waistcoats of silk or velvet are dealt with in the same way. At one time, when under-waistcoats were worn, the edges being just discernible, quantities were made out of the full waistcoats where a sufficiency of the stuff was unworn. This fashion is now becoming less and less followed, and is principally in vogue in the matter of white under-waistcoats. For the jean and other vests—even if a mixture of materials—there is the same use as what I have described of the black satin, and failing that, they are generally transferable to the rag-bag.

Hats have become in greater demand than ever among the street-buyers since the introduction into the London trade, and to so great an extent, of the silk, velvet, French, or Parisian hats. The construction of these hats is the same, and the easy way in which the hat-bodies are made, has caused a number of poor persons, with no previous knowledge of hat-making, to enter into the trade. "There's hundreds starving at it," said a hat-manufacturer to me, "in Bermondsey, Lock's-fields, and the Borough; ay, hundreds." This facility in the making of the bodies of the new silk hats is quite as available in the restoration of the bodies of the old hats, as I shall show from the information of a highly-intelligent artisan, who told me that of all people he disliked rich slop-sellers; but there was another class which he disliked more, and that was rich slop-buyers.

The bodies of the stuff or beaver hats of the best quality are made of a firm felt, wrought up of fine wool, rabbits' hair, &c., and at once elastic, firm, and light. Over this is placed the nap, prepared from the hair of the beaver. The bodies of the silk hats are made of calico, which is blocked (as indeed is the felt) and stiffened and pasted up until "only a hat-maker can tell," as it was expressed to me, "good sound bodies from bad; and the slop-masters go for the cheap and bad." The covering is not a nap of any hair, but is of silk or velvet (the words are used indifferently in the trade) manufactured for the purpose. Thus if an old hat be broken, or rather crushed out of all shape, the body can be glazed and sized up again so as to suit the slop hatter, if sold to him as a body, and that whether it be of felt or calico. If, however, the silk cover of the hat be not worn utterly away, the body, without stripping off the cover, can be re-blocked and re-set, and the silk-velvet trimmed up and " set," or re-dyed, and a decent hat is sometimes produced by these means. More frequently, however, a steeping shower of rain destroys the whole fabric.

Second-hand Caps are rarely brought into this trade.

Such things as *drawers, flannel waistcoats*, and what is sometimes called "inner wear," sell very well when washed up, patched—for patches do not matter in a garment hidden from the eye when worn—or mended in any manner. Flannel waistcoats and drawers are often in demand by the street-sellers and the street-labourers, as they are considered " good against the rheumatics." These habiliments are often sold unrepaired, having been merely washed, as the poor men's wives may be competent to execute an easy bit of tailoring; or perhaps the men themselves, if they have been reared as mechanics; and they believe (perhaps erroneously) that so they obtain a better bargain. *Shirts* are repaired and sold as shirts, or for old linen; the trade is not large.

Men's Stockings are darned up, but only when there is little to be done in darning, as they are retailed at 2*d*. the pair. The sale is not very great, for the supply is not. "Lots might be sold," I was informed, "if they was to be had, for them flash coves never cares what they wears under their Wellingtons."

The Women's Apparel is sold to be re-worn in its original form quite as frequently, or more frequently, than it is mended up by the sellers; the purchasers often preferring to make the alterations themselves. A gown of stuff, cotton, or any material, if full-sized, is frequently bought and altered to fit a smaller person or a child, and so the worn parts may be cut away. It is very rarely also that the apparel of the middle-classes is made into any other article, with the sole exception, perhaps, of *silk gowns*. If a silk gown be not too much frayed, it is easily cleaned and polished up, so as to present a new gloss, and is sold readily enough; but if it be too far gone for this process, the old clothes renovator is often puzzled as to what uses to put it. A portion of a black silk dress may be serviceable to re-line the cuffs of the better kind of coats. There is seldom enough, I was told, to re-line the two skirts of a surtout, and it is difficult to match old silk; a man used to buying a good second-hand surtout, I was assured, would soon detect a difference in the shade of the silk, if the skirts were re-lined from the remains of different gowns, and say, " I'll not give any such money for that piebald thing."

Skirts may be sometimes re-lined this way on the getting up of frock coats, but very rarely. There is the same difficulty in using a coloured silk gown for the re-covering of a parasol. The quantity may not be enough for the gores, and cannot be matched to satisfy the eye, for the buyer of a silk parasol even in Rosemary-lane may be expected to be critical. When there is enough of good silk for the purposes I have mentioned, then, it must be borne in mind, the gown may be more valuable, because saleable to be re-worn as a gown. It is the same with satin dresses, but only a few of them, in comparison with the silk, are to be seen at the Old Clothes' Exchange.

Among the purposes to which portions of worn silk gowns are put are the making of spencers for little girls (usually by the purchasers, or by the dress-maker, who goes out to work for 1s. a day), of children's bonnets, for the lining of women's bonnets, the re-lining of muffs and fur-tippets, the patching of quilts (once a rather fashionable thing), the inner lining or curtains to a book-case, and other household appliances of a like kind. This kind of silk, too, no matter in how minute pieces, is bought by the fancy cabinet-makers (the small masters) for the lining of their dressing-cases and work-boxes supplied to the warehouses, but these poor artisans have neither means nor leisure to buy such articles of those connected with the traffic of the Old Clothes' Exchange, but must purchase it, of course at an enhanced price, of a broker who has bought it at the Exchange, or in some establishment connected with it. The second-hand silk is bought also for the dressing of dolls for the toy-shops, and for the lining of some toys. The hat-manufacturers of the cheaper sort, at one time, used second-hand silk for the padded lining of hats, but such is rarely the practice now. It was once used in the same manner by the bookbinders for lining the inner part of the back of a book. If there be any part of silk in a dress not suitable for any of these purposes it is wasted, or what is accounted wasted, although it may have been in wear for years. It is somewhat remarkable, that while woollen and even cotton goods can be "shoddied"—and if they are too rotten for that, they are made available for manure, or in the manufacture of paper—no use is made of the refuse of silk. Though one of the most beautiful and costly of textile fabrics, its "remains" are thrown aside, when a beggar's rags are preserved and made profitable. There can be little doubt that silk, like cotton, could be shoddied, but whether such a speculation would be remunerative or not is no part of my present inquiry.

There is not, as I shall subsequently show, so great an exportation of female attire as might be expected in comparison with male apparel; the poorer classes of the metropolis being too anxious to get any decent gown when within their slender means.

Stays, unless of superior make and in good condition, are little bought by the classes who are the chief customers of the old-clothes' men in London. I did not hear any reason for this from any of the old-clothes' people. One man thought, if there was a family of daughters, the stays which had became too small for the elder girl were altered for the younger, and that poor women liked to mend their old stays as long as they would stick together. Perhaps, there may be some repugnance —especially among the class of servant-maids who have not had "to rough it"—to wear street-collected stays; a repugnance not, perhaps, felt in the wearing of a gown which probably can be washed, and is not worn so near the person. The stays that are collected are for the most part exported, a great portion being sent to Ireland. If they are "worn to rags," the bones are taken out; but in the slop-made stays, it is not whalebone, but wood that is used to give, or preserve the due shape of the corset, and then the stays are valueless.

Old Stockings are of great sale both for home wear and foreign trade. In the trade of women's stockings there has been in the last 20 or 25 years a considerable change. Before that period black stockings were worn by servant girls, and the families of working people and small tradesmen; they "saved washing." Now, even in Petticoat-lane, women's stockings are white, or "mottled," or some light-coloured, very rarely black. I have heard this change attributed to what is rather vaguely called "pride." May it not be owing to a more cultivated sense of cleanliness? The women's stockings are sold darned and undarned, and at (retail) prices from 1d. to 4d.; 1d. or 2d. being the most frequent prices.

The *petticoats* and other under clothing are not much bought second-hand by the poor women of London, and are exported.

Women's caps used to be sold second-hand, I was told, both in the streets and the shops, but long ago, and before muslin and needlework were so cheap.

I heard of one article which formerly supplied considerable "stuff" (the word used) for second-hand purposes, and was a part, but never a considerable part, of the trade at Rag-fair. These were the "*pillions*," or large, firm, solid cushions which were attached to a saddle, so that a horse "carried double." Fifty years ago the farmer and his wife, of the more prosperous order, went regularly to church and market on one horse, a pillion sustaining the good dame. To the best sort of these pillions was appended what was called the "pillion cloth," often of a fine, but thin quality, which being really a sort of housing to the horse, cut straight and with few if any seams, was an excellent material for what I am informed was formerly called "making and mending." The colour was almost exclusively drab or blue. The pillion on which the squire's lady rode—and Sheridan makes his *Lady Teazle* deny "the pillion and the coach-horse," the butler being her cavalier—was a perfect piece of upholstery, set off with lace and fringes, which again were excellent for second-hand sale. Such a means of conveyance may still linger in some secluded country parts, but it is generally speaking obsolete.

Boots and *Shoes* are not to be had, I am told, in sufficient quantity for the demand from the slop-shops, the "translators," and the second-hand dealers. Great quantities of second-hand boots and shoes are sent to Ireland to be "translated" there. Of all the wares in this traffic, the clothing for the feet is what is most easily prepared to cheat the eye of the inexperienced, the imposition having the aids of heel-ball, &c., to fill up crevices, and of blacking to hide defects. Even when the boots or shoes are so worn out that no one will put a pair on his feet, though purchaseable for about 1*d*., the insoles are ripped out; the soles, if there be a sufficiency of leather, are shaped into insoles for children's shoes, and these insoles are sold in bundles of two dozen pairs at 2*d*. the bundle. So long as the boot or shoe be not in many holes, it can be cobblered up in Monmouth-street or elsewhere. Of the "translating" business transacted in those localities I had the following interesting account from a man who was lately engaged in it.

"Translation, as I understand it (said my informant), is this—to take a worn, old pair of shoes or boots, and by repairing them make them appear as if left off with hardly any wear—as if they were only soiled. I'll tell you the way they manage in Monmouth-street. There are in the trade 'horses' heads'—a 'horse's head' is the foot of a boot with sole and heel, and part of a front— the back and the remainder of the front having been used for refooting boots. There are also 'stand-bottoms' and 'lick-ups.' A 'stand-bottom' is where the shoe appears to be only soiled, and a 'lick-up' is a boot or shoe re-lasted to take the wrinkles out, the edges of the soles having been rasped and squared, and then blacked up to hide blemishes, and the bottom covered with a 'smother,' which I will describe. There is another article called a 'flyer,' that is, a shoe soled without having been welted. In Monmouth-street a 'horse's head' is generally retailed at 2*s*. 6*d*., but some fetch 4*s*. 6*d*.—that's the extreme price. They cost the translator from 1*s*. a dozen pair to 8*s*., but those at 8*s*. are good, and are used for the making up of Wellington boots. Some 'horses' heads'—such as are cut off that the boots may be re-footed on account of old fashion, or a misfit, when hardly worn—fetch 2*s*. 6*d*. a pair, and they are made up as new-footed boots, and sell from 10*s*. to 15*s*. The average price of feet (that is, for the 'horse's head,' as we call it) is 4*d*., and a pair of backs say 2*d*.; the back is attached loosely by chair stitching, as it is called, to the heel, instead of being stitched to the insole, as in a new boot. The wages for all this is 1*s*. 4*d*. in Monmouth-street (in Union-street, Borough, 1*s*. 6*d*.); but I was told by a master that he had got the work done in Gray's-inn-lane at 9*d*. Put it, however, at 1*s*. 4*d*. wages—then, with 4*d*. and 2*d*. for the feet and back, we have 1*s*. 10*d*. outlay (the workman finds his own grindery), and 8*d*. profit on each pair sold at a rate of 2*s*. 6*d*. Some masters will sell from 70 to 80 pairs per week: that's under the mark; and that's in 'horses' heads' alone. One man employs, or did lately employ, seven men on 'horses' heads' solely. The profit generally, in fair shops, in 'stand-bottoms,' is from 1*s*. 6*d*. to 2*s*. per pair, as they sell generally at 3*s*. 6*d*. One man takes, or did take, 100*l*. in a day (it was calculated as an average) over the counter, and all for the sort of shoes I have described. The profit of a 'lick-up' is the same as that of a 'stand-bottom.' To show the villanous way the 'stand-bottoms' are got up, I will tell you this. You have seen a broken upper-leather; well, we place a piece of leather, waxed, underneath the broken part, on which we set a few stitches through and through. When dry and finished, we take what is called a 'soft-heel-ball' and 'smother' it over, so that it sometimes would deceive a currier, as it appears like the upper leather. With regard to the bottoms, the worn part of the sole is opened from the edge, a piece of leather is made to fit exactly into the hole or worn part, and it is then nailed and filed until level. Paste is then applied, and 'smother' put over the part, and that imitates the dust of the road. This 'smother' is obtained from the dust of the room. It is placed in a silk stocking, tied at both ends, and then shook through, just like a powder-puff, only we shake at both ends. It is powdered out into our leather apron, and mixed with a certain preparation which I will describe to you (he did so), but I would rather not have it published, as it would lead others to practise similar deceptions. I believe there are about 2000 translators, so you may judge of the extent of the trade; and translators are more constantly employed than any other branch of the business. Many make a great deal of money. A journeyman translator can earn from 3*s*. to 4*s*. a day. You can give the average at 20*s*. a week, as the wages are good. It must be good, for we have 2*s*. for soling, heeling, and welting a pair of boots; and some men don't get more for making them. Monmouth-street is nothing like what it was; as to curious old garments, that's all gone. There's not one English master in the translating business in Monmouth-street—they are all Irish; and there is now hardly an English workman there— perhaps not one. I believe that all the tradesmen in Monmouth-street make their workmen lodge with them. I was lodging with one before I married a little while ago, and I know the system to be the same now as it was then, unless, indeed, it be altered for the worse. To show how disgusting these lodgings must be, I will state this:—I knew a Roman Catholic, who was attentive to his religious duties, but when pronounced on the point of death, and believing firmly that he was dying, he would not have his priest administer extreme unction, for the room was in such a filthy and revolting state he would not allow him to see it. Five men worked and slept in that room, and they were working and sleeping there in the man's illness— all the time that his life was despaired of. He was ill nine weeks. Unless the working shoemaker lodged there he would not be employed. Each man pays 2*s*. a week. I was there once, but I couldn't sleep in such a den; and five nights out of the seven I slept at my mother's, but my lodging had to be paid all the same. These men (myself excepted) were all Irish, and all teetotallers, as was the master. How often was the room cleaned out, do you say? Never, sir, never. The refuse of the men's labour was generally burnt, smudged away in the grate, smelling terribly. It would stifle you, though it didn't me, because I got used to it. I lodged in Union-street once. My employer had a room known as the 'barracks;' every lodger paid him 2s. 6d. a week. Five men worked and slept there, and three were *sitters*—that is, men who paid 1s. a week to sit there and work, lodging elsewhere. A little before that there were six sitters. The furniture was one table, one chair, and two beds. There was no place for purposes of decency: it fell to bits from decay, and was never repaired. This barrack man always stopped the 2s. 6d. for lodging, if he gave you only that amount of work in the week. The beds were decent enough; but as to Monmouth-street! you don't see a clean sheet there for nine weeks; and, recollect, such snobs are dirty fellows. There was no chair in the Monmouth-street room that I have spoken of, the men having only their seats used at work; but when the beds were let down for the night, the seats had to be placed in the fire-place because there was no space for them in the room. In many houses in Monmouth-street there is a system of sub-letting among the journeymen. In one room lodged a man and his wife (a laundress worked there), four children, and two single young men. The wife was actually delivered in this room whilst the men kept at their work—they never lost an hour's work; nor is this an unusual case—it's not an isolated case at all. I could instance ten or twelve cases of two or three married people living in one room in that street. The rats have scampered over the beds that lay huddled together in the kitchen. The husband of the wife confined as I have described paid 4s. a week, and the two single men paid 2s. a week each, so the master was rent free; and he received from each man 1s. 6d. a week for tea (without sugar), and no bread and butter, and 2d. a day for potatoes—that's the regular charge."

In connection with the translation of old boots and shoes, I have obtained the following statistics. There are—

In Drury-lane and streets adjacent, about....	50	shops.
Seven-dials do. do.	100	do.
Monmouth-street do. do.	40	do.
Hanway-court, Oxford-street do.	4	do.
Lisson-grove do. do.	100	do.
Paddington do. do.	30	do.
Petticoat-lane (shops, stands, &c.) do.	200	do.
Somers'-town do. do.	50	do.
Field-lane, Saffron-hill do.	40	do.
Clerkenwell do.	30	do.
Bethnal-green, Spitalfields do.	100	do.
Rosemary-lane, &c. do.	30	do.
	774	shops,

employing upwards of 2000 men in making-up and repairing old boots and shoes; besides hundreds of poor men and women who strive for a crust by buying and selling the old material, previously to translating it, and by mending up what will mend. They or their children stand in the street and try to sell them.

Monmouth-street, now the great old shoe district, has been "sketched" by Mr. Dickens, not as regards its connection with the subject of street-sale or of any particular trade, but as to its general character and appearance. I first cite Mr. Dickens' description of the Seven Dials, of which Monmouth-street is a seventh:—

"The stranger who finds himself in 'The Dials' for the first time, and stands, Belzoni-like, at the entrance of seven obscure passages, uncertain which to take, will see enough around him to keep his curiosity and attention awake for no inconsiderable time. From the irregular square into which he has plunged, the streets and courts dart in all directions, until they are lost in the unwholesome vapour which hangs over the house-tops, and renders the dirty perspective uncertain and confined; and, lounging at every corner, as if they came there to take a few gasps of such fresh air as has found its way so far, but is too much exhausted already, to be enabled to force itself into the narrow alleys around, are groups of people, whose appearance and dwellings would fill any mind but a regular Londoner's with astonishment.

"In addition to the numerous groups who are idling about the gin-shops and squabbling in the centre of the road, every post in the open space has its occupant, who leans against it for hours, with listless perseverance. It is odd enough that one class of men in London appear to have no enjoyment beyond leaning against posts. We never saw a regular bricklayer's labourer take any other recreation, fighting excepted. Pass through St. Giles's in the evening of a week-day, there they are in their fustian dresses, spotted with brick-dust and whitewash, leaning against posts. Walk through Seven Dials on Sunday morning: there they are again, drab or light corduroy trowsers, Blucher boots, blue coats, and great yellow waistcoats, leaning against posts. The idea of a man dressing himself in his best clothes, to lean against a post all day!

"The peculiar character of these streets, and the close resemblance each one bears to its neighbour, by no means tends to decrease the bewilderment in which the unexperienced wayfarer through 'the Dials' finds himself involved. He traverses streets of dirty, straggling houses, with now and then an unexpected court, composed of buildings as ill-proportioned and deformed as the half-naked children that wallow in the kennels. Here and there, a little dark chandler's shop, with a cracked bell hung up behind the door to announce the entrance of a customer, or betray the presence of some young gentleman in whom a passion for shop tills has developed itself at an early age; others, as if for support, against some handsome lofty building, which usurps the place of a low dingy public-house; long rows of broken and patched windows expose plants that may have flourished when 'The Dials' were built, in vessels as dirty as 'The Dials' themselves; and shops for the purchase of rags, bones, old iron, and kitchen-stuff, vie in cleanliness with the bird-fanciers and rabbit-dealers, which one might fancy so many arks, but for the irresistible conviction that no bird in its proper senses, who was permitted to leave one of them would ever come back again. Brokers' shops, which would seem to have been established by humane individuals, as refuges for destitute bugs, interspersed with announcements of day-schools, penny theatres, petition-writers, mangles, and music for balls or routs, complete the 'still-life' of the subject; and dirty men, filthy women, squalid children, fluttering shuttlecocks, noisy battledores, reeking pipes, bad fruit, more than doubtful oysters, attenuated cats, depressed dogs, and anatomical fowls, are its cheerful accompaniments.

"If the external appearance of the houses, or a glance at their inhabitants, present but few attractions, a closer acquaintance with either is little calculated to alter one's first impression. Every room has its separate tenant, and every tenant is, by the same mysterious dispensation which causes a country curate to 'increase and multiply' most marvellously, generally the head of a numerous family.

"The man in the shop, perhaps, is in the baked 'jemmy' line, or the fire-wood and hearth-stone line, or any other line which requires a floating capital of eighteen pence or thereabouts: and he and his family live in the shop, and the small back parlour behind it. Then there is an Irish labourer and *his* family in the back kitchen, and a jobbing-man — carpet-beater and so forth — with *his* family, in the front one. In the front one pair there's another man with another wife and family, and in the back one-pair there's 'a young 'oman as takes in tambour-work, and dresses quite genteel,' who talks a good deal about 'my friend,' and can't 'abear anything low.' The second floor front, and the rest of the lodgers, are just a second edition of the people below, except a shabby-genteel man in the back attic, who has his half-pint of coffee every morning from the coffee-shop next door but one, which boasts a little front den called a coffee-room, with a fire-place, over which is an inscription, politely requesting that, 'to prevent mistakes,' customers will 'please to pay on delivery.' The shabby-genteel man is an object of some mystery, but as he leads a life of seclusion, and never was known to buy anything beyond an occasional pen, except half-pints of coffee, penny loaves, and ha'porths of ink, his fellow-lodgers very naturally suppose him to be an author; and rumours are current in the Dials, that he writes poems for Mr. Warren.

"Now any body who passed through the Dials on a hot summer's evening, and saw the different women of the house gossiping on the steps, would be apt to think that all was harmony among them, and that a more primitive set of people than the native Diallers could not be imagined. Alas! the man in the shop illtreats his family; the carpet-beater extends his professional pursuits to his wife; the one-pair front has an undying feud with the two-pair front, in consequence of the two-pair front persisting in dancing over his (the one-pair front's) head, when he and his family have retired for the night; the two-pair back *will* interfere with the front kitchen's children; the Irishman comes home drunk every other night, and attacks every body; and the one-pair back screams at everything. Animosities spring up between floor and floor; the very cellar asserts his equality. Mrs. A. 'smacks' Mrs. B.'s child for 'making faces.' Mrs. B. forthwith throws cold water over Mrs. A.'s child for 'calling names.' The husbands are embroiled — the quarrel becomes general — an assault is the consequence, and a police-officer the result."

Of Monmouth-street the same author says:—

"We have always entertained a particular attachment towards Monmouth-street, as the only true and real emporium for second-hand wearing apparel. Monmouth-street is venerable from its antiquity, and respectable from its usefulness. Holywell-street we despise; the red-headed and red-whiskered Jews who forcibly haul you into their squalid houses, and thrust you into a suit of clothes whether you will or not, we detest.

"The inhabitants of Monmouth-street are a distinct class; a peaceable and retiring race, who immure themselves for the most part in deep cellars, or small back parlours, and who seldom come forth into the world, except in the dusk and coolness of evening, when they may be seen seated, in chairs on the pavement, smoking their pipes, or watching the gambols of their engaging children as they revel in the gutter, a happy troop of infantine scavengers. Their countenances bear a thoughtful and a dirty cast, certain indications of their love of traffic; and their habitations are distinguished by that disregard of outward appearance, and neglect of personal comfort, so common among people who are constantly immersed in profound speculations, and deeply engaged in sedentary pursuits.

"Through every alteration and every change Monmouth-street has still remained the burial-place of the fashions; and such, to judge from all present appearances, it will remain until there are no more fashions to bury."

Of the Street-Sellers of Petticoat and Rosemary-Lanes.

IMMEDIATELY connected with the trade of the central mart for old clothes are the adjoining streets of Petticoat-lane, and those of the not very distant Rosemary-lane. In these localities is a second-hand garment-seller at almost every step, but the whole stock of these traders, decent, frowsy, half-rotten, or smart and good habiliments, has first passed through the channel of the Exchange. The men who sell these goods have all bought them at the Exchange — the exceptions being insignificant — so that this street-sale is but an extension of the trade of the central mart, with the addition that the wares have been made ready for use.

A cursory observation might lead an inexperienced person to the conclusion, that these old clothes traders who are standing by the bundles of gowns, or lines of coats, hanging from their door-posts, or in the place from which the window has been removed, or at the sides of their houses, or

SCENE IN PETTICOAT-LANE.

A VIEW IN ROSEMARY-LANE.

piled in the street before them, are drowsy people, for they seem to sit among their property, lost in thought, or caring only for the fumes of a pipe. But let any one indicate, even by an approving glance, the likelihood of his becoming a customer, and see if there be any lack of diligence in business. Some, indeed, pertinaciously invite attention to their wares; some (and often well-dressed women) leave their premises a few yards to accost a stranger pointing to a " good dress-coat" or " an excellent frock" (coat). I am told that this practice is less pursued than it was, and it seems that the solicitations are now addressed chiefly to strangers. These strangers, persons happening to be passing, or visitors from curiosity, are at once recognised; for as in all not very extended localities, where the inhabitants pursue a similar calling, they are, as regards their knowledge of one another, as the members of one family. Thus a stranger is as easily recognised as he would be in a little rustic hamlet where a strange face is not seen once a quarter. Indeed so narrow are some of the streets and alleys in this quarter, and so little is there of privacy, owing to the removal, in warm weather, even of the casements, that the room is commanded in all its domestic details; and as among these details there is generally a further display of goods similar to the articles outside, the jammed-up places really look like a great family house with merely a sort of channel, dignified by the name of a street, between the right and left suites of apartments.

In one off-street, where on a Sunday there is a considerable demand for Jewish sweet-meats by Christian boys, and a little sly, and perhaps not very successful gambling on the part of the ingenuous youth to possess themselves of these confectionaries at the easiest rate, there are some mounds of builders' rubbish upon which, if an inquisitive person ascended, he could command the details of the upper rooms, probably the bed chambers—if in their crowded apartments these traders can find spaces for beds.

It must not be supposed that old clothes are more than the great staple of the traffic of this district. Wherever persons are assembled there are certain to be purveyors of provisions and of cool or hot drinks for warm or cold weather. The interior of the Old Clothes Exchange has its oyster-stall, its fountain of ginger-beer, its coffee-house, and ale-house, and a troop of peripatetic traders, boys principally, carrying trays. Outside the walls of the Exchange this trade is still thicker. A Jew boy thrusts a tin of highly-glazed cakes and pastry under the people's noses here; and on the other side a basket of oranges regales the same sense by its proximity. At the next step the thoroughfare is interrupted by a gaudy-looking ginger-beer, lemonade, raspberryade, and nectar fountain; " a halfpenny a glass, a halfpenny a glass, sparkling lemonade!" shouts the vendor as you pass. The fountain and the glasses glitter in the sun, the varnish of the wood-work shines, the lemonade really does sparkle, and all looks clean—except the owner. Close by is a brawny young Irishman, his red beard unshorn for perhaps ten days, and his neck, where it had been exposed to the weather, a far deeper red than his beard, and he is carrying a small basket of nuts, and selling them as gravely as if they were articles suited to his strength. A little lower is the cry, in a woman's voice, " Fish, fried fish! Ha'penny; fish, fried fish!" and so monotonously and mechanically is it ejaculated that one might think the seller's life was passed in uttering these few words, even as a rook's is in crying " Caw, caw." Here I saw a poor Irishwoman who had a child on her back buy a piece of this fish (which may be had " hot " or " cold "), and tear out a piece with her teeth, and this with all the eagerness and relish of appetite or hunger; first eating the brown outside and then *sucking* the bone. I never saw fish look firmer or whiter. That fried fish is to be procured is manifest to more senses than one, for you can hear the sound of its being fried, and smell the fumes from the oil. In an open window opposite frizzle on an old tray, small pieces of thinly-cut meat, with a mixture of onions, kept hot by being placed over an old pan containing charcoal. In another room a mess of batter is smoking over a grate. " Penny a lot, oysters," resounds from different parts. Some of the sellers command two streets by establishing their stalls or tubs at a corner. Lads pass, carrying sweet-stuff on trays. I observed one very dark-eyed Hebrew boy chewing the hard-bake he vended—if it were not a substitute—with an expression of great enjoyment. Heaped-up trays of fresh-looking sponge-cakes are carried in tempting pyramids. Youths have stocks of large hard-looking biscuits, and walk about crying, " Ha'penny biscuits, ha'penny; three a penny, biscuits; " these, with a morsel of cheese, often supply a dinner or a luncheon. Dates and figs, as dry as they are cheap, constitute the stock in trade of other street-sellers. " Coker-nuts " are sold in pieces and entire; the Jew boy, when he invites to the purchase of an entire nut, shaking it at the ear of the customer. I was told by a costermonger that these juveniles had a way of drumming with their fingers on the shell so as to satisfy a " green " customer that the nut offered was a sound one.

Such are the summer eatables and drinkables which I have lately seen vended in the Petticoat-lane district. In winter there are, as long as daylight lasts—and in no other locality perhaps does it last so short a time—other street provisions, and, if possible, greater zeal in selling them, the hours of business being circumscribed. There is then the potato-can and the hot elder-wine apparatus, and smoking pies and puddings, and roasted apples and chestnuts, and walnuts, and the several fruits which ripen in the autumn—apples, pears, &c.

Hitherto I have spoken only of such eatables and drinkables as are ready for consumption, but to these the trade in the Petticoat-lane district is by no means confined. There is fresh fish, generally of the cheaper kinds, and smoked or dried fish (smoked salmon, moreover, is sold ready cooked), and costermongers' barrows, with their loads of green vegetables, looking almost out of place amidst the surrounding dinginess. The cries of "Fine cauliflowers," "Large penny cabbages," "Eight a shilling, mackarel," "Eels, live eels," mix strangely with the hubbub of the busier street.

Other street-sellers also abound. You meet one man who says mysteriously, and rather bluntly, "Buy a good knife, governor." His tone is remarkable, and if it attract attention, he may hint that he has smuggled goods which he *must* sell anyhow. Such men, I am told, look out mostly for seamen, who often resort to Petticoat-lane; for idle men like sailors on shore, and idle uncultivated men often love to lounge where there is bustle. Pocket and pen knives and scissors, "Penny a piece, penny a pair," rubbed over with oil, both to hide and prevent rust, are carried on trays, and spread on stalls, some stalls consisting of merely a tea-chest lid on a stool. Another man, carrying perhaps a sponge in his hand, and well-dressed, asks you, in a subdued voice, if you want a good razor, as if he almost suspected that you meditated suicide, and were looking out for the means! This is another ruse to introduce smuggled (or "duffer's") goods. Account-books are hawked. "Penny-a-quire," shouts the itinerant street stationer (who, if questioned, always declares he said "Penny half quire"). "Stockings, stockings, two pence a pair." "Here's your chewl-ry; penny, a penny; pick 'em and choose 'em." [I may remark that outside the window of one shop, or rather parlour, if there be any such distinction here, I saw the handsomest, as far as I am able to judge, and the best cheap jewellery I ever saw in the streets.] "Pencils, sir, pencils; steel-pens, steel-pens; ha'penny, penny; pencils, steel-pens; sealing-wax, wax, wax, wax!" shouts one, "Green peas, ha'penny a pint!" cries another.

These things, however, are but the accompaniments of the main traffic. But as such things accompany all traffic, not on a small scale, and may be found in almost every metropolitan thoroughfare, where the police are not required, by the householders, to interfere, I will point out, to show the distinctive character of the street-trade in this part, what is *not* sold and not encouraged. I saw no old books. There were no flowers; no music, which indeed could not be heard except at the outskirts of the din; and no beggars plying their vocation among the trading class.

Another peculiarity pertaining alike to this shop and street locality is, that everything is at the veriest minimum of price; though it may not be asked, it will assuredly be taken. The bottle of lemonade which is elsewhere a penny is here a halfpenny. The tarts, which among the street-sellers about the Royal Exchange are a halfpenny each, are here a farthing. When lemons are two a-penny in St. George's-market, Oxford-street, as the long line of street stalls towards the western extremity is called—they are three and four a-penny in Petticoat and Rosemary lanes. Certainly there is a difference in size between the dearer and the cheaper tarts and lemons, and perhaps there is a difference in quality also, but the rule of a minimized cheapness has no exceptions in this cheap-trading quarter.

But Petticoat-lane is essentially the old clothes district. Embracing the streets and alleys adjacent to Petticoat-lane, and including the rows of old boots and shoes on the ground, there is perhaps between two and three miles of old clothes. Petticoat-lane proper is long and narrow, and to look down it is to look down a vista of many coloured garments, alike on the sides and on the ground. The effect sometimes is very striking, from the variety of hues, and the constant flitting, or gathering, of the crowd into little groups of bargainers. Gowns of every shade and every pattern are hanging up, but none, perhaps, look either bright or white; it is a vista of dinginess, but many coloured dinginess, as regards female attire. Dress coats, frock coats, great coats, livery and game-keepers' coats, paletots, tunics, trowsers, knee-breeches, waistcoats, capes, pilot coats, working jackets, plaids, hats, dressing gowns, shirts, Guernsey frocks, are all displayed. The predominant colours are black and blue, but there is every colour; the light drab of some aristocratic livery; the dull brown-green of velveteen; the deep blue of a pilot jacket; the variegated figures of the shawl dressing-gown; the glossy black of the restored garments; the shine of newly turpentined black satin waistcoats; the scarlet and green of some flaming tartan; these things—mixed with the hues of the women's garments, spotted and striped—certainly present a scene which cannot be beheld in any other part of the greatest city of the world, nor in any other portion of the world itself.

The ground has also its array of colours. It is covered with lines of boots and shoes, their shining black relieved here and there by the admixture of females' boots, with drab, green, plum or lavender-coloured "legs," as the upper part of the boot is always called in the trade. There is, too, an admixture of men's "button-boots" with drab cloth legs; and of a few red, yellow, and russet coloured slippers; and of children's coloured morocco boots and shoes. Handkerchiefs, sometimes of a gaudy orange pattern, are heaped on a chair. Lace and muslins occupy small stands or are spread on the ground. Black and drab and straw hats are hung up, or piled one upon another and kept from falling by means of strings; while, incessantly threading their way through all this intricacy, is a mass of people, some of whose dresses speak of a recent purchase in the lane.

I have said little of the shopkeepers of Petticoat-lane, nor is it requisite for the full elucidation of my present subject (which relates more especially to *street-sale*), that I should treat of them otherwise than as being in a great degree connected with street-trade. They stand in the street (in front of their premises), they trade in the street, they smoke and read the papers in the street; and indeed the greater part of their lives seems passed in the street, for, as I have elsewhere remarked, the Saturday's or Sabbath's recreation to some of them, after synagogue hours, seems to be to stand by their doors looking about them.

In the earlier periods of the day—the Jewish Sabbath excepted, when there is no market at all in Petticoat-lane, not even among the Irish and other old clothes people, or a mere nothing of a market—the goods of these shops seem consigned to the care of the wives and female members of the families of the proprietors. The Old Clothes Exchange, like other places known by the name—the Royal Exchange, for example—has its daily season of "high change." This is, in summer, from about half-past two to five, in winter, from two to four o'clock. At those hours the crockman, and the bartering costermonger, and the Jew collector, have sought the Exchange with their respective bargains; and business there, and in the whole district, is at its fullest tide. Before this hour the master of the shop or *store* (the latter may be the more appropriate word) is absent buying, collecting, or transacting any business which requires him to leave home. It is curious to observe how, during this absence, the women, but with most wary eyes to the business, sit in the street carrying on their domestic occupations. Some, with their young children about them, are shelling peas; some are trimming vegetables; some plying their needles; some of the smaller traders' wives, as well as the street-sellers with a "pitch," are eating dinners out of basins (laid aside when a customer approaches), and occasionally some may be engaged in what Mrs. Trollope has called (in noticing a similar procedure in the boxes of an American theatre) "the most maternal of all offices." The females I saw thus occupied were principally Jewesses, for though those resorting to the Old Clothes Exchange and its concomitant branches may be but one-fourth Jews, more than half of the remainder being Irish people, the householders or shopkeepers of the locality, when capital is needed, are generally Israelites.

It must be borne in mind that, in describing Petticoat-lane, I have described it as seen on a fine summer's day, when the business is at its height. Until an hour or two after midday the district is quiet, and on very rainy days its aspect is sufficiently lamentable, for then it appears actually deserted. Perhaps on a winter's Saturday night—as the Jewish Sabbath terminates at sunset—the scene may be the most striking of all. The flaring lights from uncovered gas, from fat-fed lamps, from the paper-shaded candles, and the many ways in which the poorer street-folk throw some illumination over their goods, produce a multiplicity of lights and shadows, which, thrown and blended over the old clothes hanging up along the line of street, cause them to assume mysterious forms, and if the wind be high make them, as they are blown to and fro, look more mysterious still.

On one of my visits to Petticoat-lane I saw two foreign Jews—from Smyrna I was informed. An old street-seller told me he believed it was their first visit to the district. But, new as the scene might be to them, they looked on impassively at all they saw. They wore the handsome and peculiar dresses of their country. A glance was cast after them by the Petticoat-lane people, but that was all. In the Strand they would have attracted considerable attention; not a few heads would have been turned back to gaze after them; but it seems that only to those who may possibly be customers is any notice paid in Petticoat-lane.

ROSEMARY-LANE.

ROSEMARY-LANE, which has in vain been rechristened Royal Mint-street, is from half to three-quarters of a mile long—that is, if we include only the portion which runs from the junction of Leman and Dock streets (near the London Docks) to Sparrow-corner, where it abuts on the Minories. Beyond the Leman-street termination of Rosemary-lane, and stretching on into Shadwell, are many streets of a similar character as regards the street and shop supply of articles to the poor; but as the old clothes trade is only occasionally carried on there, I shall here deal with Rosemary-lane proper.

This lane partakes of some of the characteristics of Petticoat-lane, but without its so strongly marked peculiarities. Rosemary-lane is wider and airier, the houses on each side are loftier (in several parts), and there is an approach to a gin palace, a thing unknown in Petticoat-lane: there is no room for such a structure there.

Rosemary-lane, like the quarter I have last described, has its off-streets, into which the traffic stretches. Some of these off-streets are narrower, dirtier, poorer in all respects than Rosemary-lane itself, which indeed can hardly be stigmatized as very dirty. These are Glasshouse-street, Russell-court, Hairbrine-court, Parson's-court, Blue Anchor-yard (one of the poorest places and with a half-built look), Darby-street, Cartwright-street, Peter's-court, Princes-street, Queen-street, and beyond these and in the direction of the Minories, Rosemary-lane becomes Sharp's-buildings and Sparrow-corner. There are other small non-thoroughfare courts, sometimes called blind alleys, to which no name is attached, but which are very well known to the neighbourhood as Union-court, &c.; but as these are not scenes of street-traffic, although they may be the abodes of street-traffickers, they require no especial notice.

The dwellers in the neighbourhood or the off-streets of Rosemary-lane, differ from those of Petticoat-lane by the proximity of the former place to the Thames. The lodgings here are occupied by dredgers, ballast-heavers, coal-whippers, watermen, lumpers, and others whose trade is connected with the river, as well as the slop-workers and sweaters working for the Minories. The poverty of these workers compels them to lodge wherever the rent of the rooms is the lowest. As a few of the wives of the ballast-heavers, &c., are street-sellers in or about Rosemary-lane, the locality is often sought by them. About Petticoat-lane the off-streets are mostly occupied by the old clothes merchants.

In Rosemary-lane is a greater *street*-trade, as regards things placed on the ground for retail sale, &c., than in Petticoat-lane; for though the traffic in the last-mentioned lane is by far the greatest, it is more connected with the shops, and fewer traders whose dealings are strictly those of the street alone resort to it. Rosemary-lane, too, is more Irish. There are some cheap lodging-houses in the courts, &c., to which the poor Irish flock; and as they are very frequently street-sellers, on busy days the quarter abounds with them. At every step you hear the Erse tongue, and meet with the Irish physiognomy; Jews and Jewesses are also seen in the street, and they abound in the shops. The street-traffic does not begin until about one o'clock, except as regards the vegetable, fish, and oyster-stalls, &c.; but the chief business of this lane, which is as inappropriately as that of Petticoat is suitably named, is in the vending of the articles which have often been thrown aside as refuse, but from which numbers in London wring an existence.

One side of the lane is covered with old boots and shoes; old clothes, both men's, women's, and children's; new lace for edgings, and a variety of cheap prints and muslins (also new); hats and bonnets; pots, and often of the commonest kinds; tins; old knives and forks, old scissors, and old metal articles generally; here and there is a stall of cheap bread or American cheese, or what is announced as American; old glass; different descriptions of second-hand furniture of the smaller size, such as children's chairs, bellows, &c. Mixed with these, but only very scantily, are a few bright-looking swag-barrows, with china ornaments, toys, &c. Some of the wares are spread on the ground on wrappers, or pieces of matting or carpet; and some, as the pots, are occasionally placed on straw. The cotton prints are often heaped on the ground; where are also ranges or heaps of boots and shoes, and piles of old clothes, or hats, or umbrellas. Other traders place their goods on stalls or barrows, or over an old chair or clothes-horse. And amidst all this motley display the buyers and sellers smoke, and shout, and doze, and bargain, and wrangle, and eat and drink tea and coffee, and sometimes beer. Altogether Rosemary-lane is more of a *street* market than is Petticoat-lane.

This district, like the one I have first described, is infested with young thieves and vagrants from the neighbouring lodging-houses, who may be seen running about, often bare-footed, bare-necked, and shirtless, but "larking" one with another, and what may be best understood as "full of fun." In what way these lads dispose of their plunder, and how their plunder is in any way connected with the trade of these parts, I shall show in my account of the Thieves. One pickpocket told me that there was no person whom he delighted so much to steal from as any Petticoat-laner with whom he had professional dealings!

In Rosemary-lane there is a busy Sunday morning trade; there is a street-trade, also, on the Saturday afternoons, but the greater part of the shops are then closed, and the Jews do not participate in the commerce until after sunset.

The two marts I have thus fully described differ from all other street-markets, for in these two second-hand garments, and second-hand merchandize generally (although but in a small proportion), are the grand staple of the traffic. At the other street-markets, the second-hand commerce is the exception.

OF THE STREET-SELLERS OF MEN'S SECOND-HAND CLOTHES.

IN the following accounts of street-selling, I shall not mix up any account of the retailers' modes of buying, collecting, repairing, or "restoring" the second-hand garments, otherwise than incidentally. I have already sketched the systems pursued, and more will have to be said concerning them under the head of STREET-BUYERS. Neither have I thought it necessary, in the further accounts I have collected, to confine myself to the trade carried on in the Petticoat and Rosemary-lane districts. The greater portion relates to those places, but my aim, of course, is to give an account which will show the character of the second-hand trade of the metropolis generally.

"People should remember," said an intelligent shoemaker (not a street-seller) with whom I had some conversation about cobbling for the streets, "that such places as Rosemary-lane have their uses this way. But for them a very poor industrious widow, say, with only 2*d*. or 3*d*. to spare, couldn't get a pair of shoes for her child; whereas now, for 2*d*. or 3*d*., she can get them there, of some sort or other. There's a sort of decency, too, in wearing shoes. And what's more, sir—for I've bought old coats and other clothes in Rosemary-lane, both for my own wear and my family's, and know something about it—how is a poor creature to get such a decency as a petticoat for a poor little girl, if she'd only a penny, unless there were such places?"

In the present state of the very poor, it may be that such places as those described have, on the principle that half a loaf is better than no bread, their benefits. But whether the state of things in which an industrious widow, or a host of industrious persons, *can* spare but 1*d*. for a child's clothing (and nothing, perhaps, for their own), is one to be lauded in a Christian country, is another question, fraught with grave political and social considerations.

The man from whom I received the following account of the sale of men's wearing apparel was apparently between 30 and 40 years of age. His face presented something of the Jewish physiognomy, but he was a Christian, he said, though he never had time to go to church or chapel, and Sunday was often a busy day; besides, a man must live as others in his way lived. He had been connected with the sale of old clothes all his life, as were his parents, so that his existence had been monotonous enough, for he had never been more than five miles, he thought, from Whitechapel, the neighbourhood where he was born. In winter he liked a concert, and was fond of a hand at cribbage, but he didn't care for the play. His goods he sometimes spread on the ground—at other times he had a stall or a "horse" (clothes-horse).

"My customers," he said, "are nearly all working people, some of them very poor, and with large families. For anything I know, some of them works with their heads, though, as well, and not their hands, for I've noticed that their hands is smallish and seems smoothish, and suits a tight sleeve very well. I don't know what they are. How should I? I asks no questions, and they'll tell me no fibs. To such as them I sell coats mostly; indeed, very little else. They're often very perticler about the fit, and often asks, 'Does it look as if it was made for me?' Sometimes they is seedy, very seedy, and comes to such as me, most likely, 'cause we're cheaper than the shops. They don't like to try things on in the street, and I can always take a decent customer, or one as looks sich, in there, to try on (pointing to a coffee-shop). Bob-tailed coats (dress-coats) is far the cheapest. I've sold them as low as 1s., but not often; at 2s. and 3s. often enough; and sometimes as high as 5s. Perhaps a 3s. or 3s. 6d. coat goes off as well as any, but bob-tailed coats is little asked for. Now, I've never had a frock (surtout or frock coat), as well as I can remember, under 2s. 6d., except one that stuck by me a long time, and I sold it at last for 20d., which was 2d. less than what it cost. It was only a poor thing, in course, but it had such a rum-coloured velvet collar, that was faded, and had had a bit let in, and was all sorts of shades, and that hindered its selling, I fancy. Velvet collars isn't worn now, and I'm glad of it. Old coats goes better with their own collars (collars of the same cloth as the body of the coat). For frocks, I've got as much as 7s. 6d., and cheap at it too, sir. Well, perhaps (laughing) at an odd time they wasn't so very cheap, but that's all in the way of trade. About 4s. 6d. or 5s. is perhaps the ticket that a frock goes off best at. It's working people that buys frocks most, and often working people's wives or mothers—that is as far as I knows. They're capital judges as to what'll fit their men; and if they satisfy me it's all right, I'm always ready to undertake to change it for another if it don't fit. O, no, I never agree to give back the money if it don't fit; in course not; that wouldn't be business.

"No, sir, we're very little troubled with people larking. I have had young fellows come, half drunk, even though it might be Sunday morning, and say, 'Guv'ner, what'll you give me to wear that coat for you, and show off your cut?' We don't stand much of their nonsense. I don't know what such coves are. Perhaps 'torneys' journeymen, or pot-boys out for a Sunday morning's spree." [This was said with a bitterness that surprised me in so quiet-speaking a man.] "In greatcoats and cloaks I don't do much, but it's a very good sale when you can offer them well worth the money. I've got 10s. often for a greatcoat, and higher and lower, oftener lower in course; but 10s. is about the card for a good thing. It's the like with cloaks. Paletots don't sell well. They're mostly thinner and poorer cloth to begin with at the tailors—them new-fashioned named things often is so—and so they show when hard worn. Why no, sir, they can be done up, certainly; anything can be touched up; but they get thin, you see, and there's nothing to work upon as there is in a good cloth greatcoat. You'll excuse me, sir, but I saw you a little bit since take one of them there square books that a man gives away to people coming this way, as if to knock up the second-hand business, but he won't, though; I'll tell you how them slops, if they come more into wear, is sure to injure us. If people gets to wear them low-figured things, more and more, as they possibly may, why where's the second-hand things to come from? I'm not a tailor, but I understands about clothes, and I believe that no person ever saw anything green in my eye. And if you find a slop thing marked a guinea, I don't care what it is, but I'll undertake that you shall get one that'll wear longer, and look better to the very last, second-hand, at less than half the money, plenty less. It was good stuff and good make at first, and hasn't been abused, and that's the reason why it always bangs a slop, because it was good to begin with.

"Trousers sells pretty well. I sell them, cloth ones, from 6d. up to 4s. They're cheaper if they're not cloth, but very seldom less or so low as 6d. Yes, the cloth ones at that is poor worn things, and little things too. They're not men's, they're youth's or boy's size. Good strong cords goes off very well at 1s. and 1s. 6d., or higher. Irish bricklayers buys them, and paviours, and such like. It's easy to fit a man with a pair of second-hand trousers. I can tell by his build what'll fit him directly. Tweeds and summer trousers is middling, but washing things sells worse and worse. It's an expense, and expenses don't suit my customers—not a bit of it.

"Waistcoats isn't in no great call. They're often worn very hard under any sort of a tidy coat, for a tidy coat can be buttoned over anything that's 'dicky,' and so, you see, many of 'em's half-way to the rag-shop before they comes to us. Well, I'm sure I can hardly say what sort of people goes most for weskets" [so he pronounced it]. "If they're light, or there's anything 'fancy' about them, I thinks it's mothers as makes them up for their sons. What with the strings at the back and such like, it aint hard to make a wesket fit. They're poor people as buys certainly, but genteel people buys such things as fancy weskets, or how do you suppose they'd all be got through? O, there's ladies comes here for a bargain, I can tell you, and gentlemen, too; and many on 'em would go through fire for one. Second-hand satins (waistcoats) is good still, but they don't fetch the tin they did. I've sold weskets from 1½d. to 4s. Well, it's hard to say what the three-ha'pennies is made of; all sorts of things; we calls them 'serge.' Three-pence is a common price for a little wesket. There's no under-weskets wanted now, and there's no rolling collars. It was better for us when there was, as there was more stuff to work on. The double-breasted gets scarcer, too. Fashions grows to be cheap things now-a-days.

"I can't tell you anything about knee-breeches; they don't come into my trade, and they're never asked for. Gaiters is no go either. Liveries isn't a street-trade. I fancy all those sort of things is sent abroad. I don't know where. Perhaps where people doesn't know they was liveries. I wouldn't wear an old livery coat, if it was the Queen's, for five bob. I don't think wearing one would hinder trade. You may have seen a black man in a fine livery giving away bills of a slop in Holborn. If we was to have such a thing we'd be pulled up (apprehended) for obstructing.

"I sells a few children's (children's clothes), but only a few, and I can't say so much about them. They sells pretty freely though, and to very decent people. If they're good, then they're ready for use. If they ain't anything very prime, they can be mended—that is, if they was good to begin with. But children's woollen togs is mostly hardworn and fit only for the 'devil' (the machine which tears them up for shoddy). I've sold suits, which was tunics and trousers, but no weskets, for 3s. 6d. when they was tidy. That's a common price.

"Well, really, I hardly know how much I make every week; far too little, I know that. I could no more tell you how many coats I sell in a year, or how many weskets, than I could tell you how many days was fine, and how many wasn't. I can carry all in my head, and so I keeps no accounts. I know exactly what every single thing I sell has cost me. In course I must know *that*. I dare say I may clear about 12s. bad weeks, and 18s. good weeks, more and less both ways, and there's more bad weeks than good. I have cleared 50s. in a good week; and when it's been nothing but fog and wet, I haven't cleared 3s. 6d. But mine's a better business than common, perhaps. I can't say what others clears; more and less than I does."

The profit in this trade, from the best information I could obtain, runs about 50 per cent.

Of the Street-Sellers of Second-hand Boots and Shoes.

THE man who gave me the following account of this trade had been familiar with it a good many years, fifteen he believed, but was by no means certain. I saw at his lodgings a man who was finishing his day's work there, in cobbling and "translating." He was not in the employ of my informant, who had two rooms, or rather a floor; he slept in one and let the other to the "translator" who was a relation, he told me, and they went on very well together, as he (the street-seller) liked to sit and smoke his pipe of a night in the translator's room, which was much larger than his own; and sometimes, when times were "pretty bobbish," they clubbed together for a good supper of tripe, or had a "prime hot Jemmy a-piece," with a drop of good beer. A "Jemmy" is a baked sheep's head. The room was tidy enough, but had the strong odour of shoemaker's wax proper to the craft.

"I've been in a good many street-trades, and others too," said my informant, "since you want to know, and for a good purpose as well as I can understand it. I was a 'prentice to a shoemaker in Northampton, with a lot more; why, it was more like a factory than anything else, was my master's, and the place we worked in was so confined and hot, and we couldn't open the window, that it was worse than the East Ingees. O, I know what they is. I've been there. I was so badly treated I ran away from my master, for I had only a father, and he cared nothing about me, and so I broke my indentures. After a good bit of knocking about and living as I could, and starving when I couldn't, but I never thought of going back to Northampton, I 'listed and was a good bit in the Ingees. Well, never mind, sir, how long, or what happened me when I was soldier. I did nothing wrong, and that ain't what you was asking about, and I'd rather say no more about it."

I have met with other street-folk, who had been soldiers, and who were fond of talking of their "service," often enough to grumble about it, so that I am almost tempted to think my informant had deserted, but I questioned him no further on the subject.

"I had my ups and downs again, sir," he continued, "when I got back to England. God bless us all; I'm very fond of children, but I never married, and when I've been at the worst, I've been really glad that I hadn't no one depending on me. It's bad enough for oneself, but when there's others as you must love, what must it be then? I've smoked a pipe when I was troubled in mind, and couldn't get a meal, but could only get a pipe, and baccy's shamefully dear here; but if I'd had a young daughter now, what good would it have been my smoking a pipe to comfort her? I've seen that in people that's akin to me, and has been badly off, and with families. I had a friend or two in London, and I applied to them when I couldn't hold out no longer, and they gave me a bit of a rise, so I began as a costermonger. I was living among them as was in that line. Well, now, it's a pleasant life in fine weather. Why it was only this morning Joe (the translator) was reading the paper at breakfast time;—he gets it from the public-house, and if it's two, three, or four day's old, it's just as good for us;—and there was 10,000 pines had been received from the West Ingees. There's a chance for the costermongers, says I, if they don't go off too dear. Then cherries is in; and I was beginning to wish I was a costermonger myself still, but my present trade is *surer*. My boots and shoes'll keep. They don't spoil in hot weather. Cherries and strawberries does, and if it comes thunder and wet, you can't sell. I worked a barrow, and sometimes had only a bit of a pitch, for a matter of two year, perhaps, and then I got into this trade, as I understood it. I sells all sorts, but not so much women's or children's.

"Why, as to prices, there's two sorts of prices. You may sell as you buy, or you may sell new soled and heeled. They're never new welted for the streets. It wouldn't pay a bit. Not long since I had a pair of very good Oxonians that had been new welted, and the very first day I had them on sale—it was a dull drizzly day—a lad tried to prig them. I just caught him in time.

Did I give him in charge? I hope I've more sense. I've been robbed before, and I've caught young rips in the act. If it's boots or shoes they've tried to prig, I gives them a stirruping with whichever it is, and a kick, and lets them go."

"Men's shoes, the regular sort, isn't a very good sale. I get from 10d. to 4s. 6d. a pair; but the high priced 'uns is either soled and heeled, and mudded well, or they've been real well-made things, and not much worn. I've had gentlemen's shooting-shoes sometimes, that's flung aside for the least thing. The plain shoes don't go off at all. I think people likes something to cover their stocking-feet more. For cloth button-boots I get from 1s.—that's the lowest I ever sold at— to 2s. 6d. The price is according to what condition the things is in, and what's been done to them, but there's no regular price. They're not such good sale as they would be, because they soon show worn. The black 'legs' gets to look very seamy, and it's a sort of boot that won't stand much knocking about, if it ain't right well made at first. I've been selling Oxonian buttonovers ('Oxonian' shoes, which cover the instep, and are closed by being buttoned instead of being stringed through four or five holes) at 3s. 6d. and 4s. but they was really good, and soled and heeled; others I sell at 1s. 6d. to 2s. 3d. or 2s. 6d. Bluchers is from 1s. to 3s. 6d. Wellingtons from 1s.—yes, indeed, I've had them as low as 1s., and perhaps they weren't very cheap at that, them very low-priced things never is, neither new nor old—from 1s. to 5s.; but Wellingtons is more for the shops than the street. I do a little in children's boots and shoes. I sell them from 3d. to 15d. Yes, you can buy lower than 3d., but I'm not in that way. They sell quite as quick, or quicker, than anything. I've sold children's boots to poor women that wanted shoeing far worse than the child; aye, many a time, sir. Top boots (they're called 'Jockeys' in the trade) isn't sold in the streets. I've never had any, and I don't see them with others in my line. O no, there's no such thing as Hessians or backstraps (a top-boot without the light-coloured top) in my trade now. Yes, I always have a seat handy where anybody can try on anything in the street; no, sir, no boot-hooks nor shoe-horn; shoehorns is rather going out, I think. If what we sell in the streets won't go on without them they won't be sold at all. A good many will buy if the thing's only big enough—they can't bear pinching, and don't much care for a fine fit.

"Well, I suppose I take from 30s. to 40s. a week, 14s. is about my profit—that's as to the year through.

"I sell little for women's wear, though I do sell their boots and shoes sometimes."

Of the Street-Sellers of Old Hats.

The two street-sellers of old coats, waistcoats, and trousers, and of boots and shoes, whose statements precede this account, confined their trade, generally, to the second-hand merchandize I have mentioned as more especially constituting their stock. But this arrangement does not wholly prevail. There are many street-traders "in second-hand," perhaps two-thirds of the whole number, who sell indiscriminately anything which they can buy, or what they hope to turn out an advantage; but even they prefer to deal more in one particular kind of merchandize than another, and this is most of all the case as concerns the street-sale of old boots and shoes. Hats, however, are among the second-hand wares which the street-seller rarely vends unconnected with other stock. I was told that this might be owing to the hats sold in the streets being usually suitable only for one class, grown men; while clothes and boots and shoes are for boys as well as men. Caps may supersede the use of hats, but nothing can supersede the use of boots or shoes, which form the *steadiest* second-hand street-trade of any.

There are, however, occasions, when a street-seller exerts himself to become possessed of a cheap stock of hats, by the well-known process of "taking a quantity," and sells them without, or with but a small admixture of other goods. One man who had been lately so occupied, gave me the following account: He was of Irish parentage, but there was little distinctive in his accent:—

"Hats," he said, "are about the awkwardest things of any for the streets. Do as you will, they require a deal of room, so that what you'll mostly see isn't hats quite ready to put on your head and walk away in, but to be made ready. I've sold hats that way though, I mean ready to wear, and my father before me has sold hundreds —yes, I've been in the trade all my life—and it's the best way for a profit. You get, perhaps, the old hat in, or you buy it at 1d. or 2d. as may be, and so you kill two birds. But there's very little of that trade except on Saturday nights or Sunday mornings. People wants a decent tile for Sundays and don't care for work-days. I never hawks hats, but I sells to those as do. My customers for hats are mechanics, with an odd clerk or two. Yes, indeed, I sell hats now and then to my own countrymen to go decent to mass in. I go to mass myself as often as I can; sometimes I go to vespers. No, the Irish in this trade ain't so good in going to chapel as they ought, but it takes such a time; not just while you're there, but in shaving, and washing, and getting ready. My wife helps me in selling second-hand things; she's a better hand than I am. I have two boys; they're young yet, and I don't know what we shall bring them up to; perhaps to our own business; and children seems to fall naturally into it, I think, when their fathers and mothers is in it. They're at school now.

"I have sold hats from 6d. to 3s. 6d., but very seldom 3s. 6d. The 3s. 6d. ones would wear out two new gossamers, I know. It's seldom you see beaver hats in the street-trade now, they're nearly all silk. They say the beavers have got scarce in foreign parts where they're caught. I haven't an idea how many hats I sell in a year, for I don't stick to hats, you see, sir, but I like doing in them as well or better than in anything else. Sometimes I've sold nothing but hats for weeks together, wholesale and retail that is. It's only the regular-shaped hats I can sell. If you offer swells' hats, people 'll say: 'I may as well buy a new "wide-awake" at once.' I have made 20s. in a week on hats alone. But if I confined my trade to them now, I don't suppose I could clear 5s. one week with another the year through. It's only the hawkers that can sell them in wet weather. I wish we could sell under cover in all the places where there's what you call 'street-markets.' It would save poor people that lives by the street many a twopence by their things not being spoiled, and by people not heeding the rain to go and examine them."

Of the Street-Sellers of Women's Second-hand Apparel.

This trade, as regards the sale to retail customers in the streets, is almost entirely in the hands of women, seven-eighths of whom are the wives, relatives, or connections of the men who deal in second-hand male apparel. But gowns, cloaks, bonnets, &c., are collected more largely by men than by women, and the wholesale old clothes' merchants of course deal in every sort of habiliment. Petticoat and Rosemary-lanes are the grand marts for this street-sale, but in Whitecross-street, Leather-lane, Old-street (St. Luke's), and some similar Saturday-night markets in poor neighbourhoods, women's second-hand apparel is sometimes offered. "It is often of little use offering it in the latter places," I was told by a lace-seller who had sometimes tried to do business in second-hand shawls and cloaks, "because you are sure to hear, 'Oh, we can get them far cheaper in Petticoat-lane, when we like to go as far.'"

The different portions of female dress are shown and sold in the street, as I have described in my account of Rosemary-lane, and of the trading of the men selling second-hand male apparel. There is not so much attention paid to "set off" gowns that there is to set off coats. "If the gown be a washing gown," I was informed, "it is sure to have to be washed before it can be worn, and so it is no use bothering with it, and paying for soap and labour beforehand. If it be woollen, or some stuff that wont wash, it has almost always to be altered before it is worn, and so it is no use doing it up perhaps to be altered again." Silk goods, however, are carefully enough re-glossed and repaired. Most of the others "just take their chance."

A good-looking Irishwoman gave me the following account. She had come to London and had been a few years in service, where she saved a little money, when she married a cousin, but in what degree of cousinship she did not know. She then took part in his avocation as a crockman, and subsequently as a street-seller of second-hand clothes.

"Why, yis, thin and indeed, sir," she said, "I did feel rather quare in my new trade, going about from house to house, the Commercial-road and Stepney way, but I soon got not to mind, and indeed thin it don't matter much what way one gets one's living, so long as it's honest. O, yis, I know there's goings on in old clothes that isn't always honest, but my husband's a fair dealing man. I felt quarer, too, whin I had to sell in the strate, but I soon got used to that, too; and it's not such slavish work as the 'crocks.' But we sometimes 'crocks' in the mornings a little still, and sells in the evenings. No, not what we've collected—for that goes to Mr. Isaac's market almost always—but stock that's ready for wear.

"For *Cotton Gowns* I've got from 9d. to 2s. 3d. O, yis, and indeed thin, there's gowns chaper, 4d. and 6d., but there's nothing to be got out of them, and we don't sell them. From 9d. to 18d. is the commonest price. It's poor people as buys: O, yis, and indeed thin it is, thim as has families, and must look about thim. Many's the poor woman that's said to me, 'Well, and indeed, marm, it isn't my inclination to chapen anybody as I thinks is fair, and I was brought up quite different to buying old gowns, I assure you'—yis, that's often said; no, sir, it isn't my countrywomen that says it (laughing), it's yours. 'I wouldn't think,' says she, 'of offering you 1d. less than 1s., marm, for that frock for my daughter, marm, but it's such a hard fight to live.' Och, thin, and it is indeed; but to hear some of them talk you'd think they was born ladies. *Stuff-gowns* is from 2d. to 8d. higher than cotton, but they don't sell near so well. I hardly know why. Cotton washes, and if a dacent woman gets a chape second-hand cotton, she washes and does it up, and it seems to come to her fresh and new. That can't be done with stuff. *Silk* is very little in my way, but silk gowns sell from 3s. 6d. to 4s. Of satin and velvet gowns I can tell you nothing; they're never in the streets.

"*Second-hand Bonnets* is a very poor sale—very. The milliners, poor craitchers, as makes them up and sells them in the strate, has the greatest sale, but they makes very little by it. Their bonnets looks new, you see, sir, and close and nice for poor women. I've sold bonnets from 6d. to 3s. 6d., and some of them cost 3l. But whin they git faded and out of fashion, they're of no vally at all at all. *Shawls* is a very little sale; very little. I've got from 6d. to 2s. 6d. for them. Plaid shawls is as good as any, at about 1s. 6d.; but they're a winter trade. *Cloaks* (they are what in the dress-making trade are called mantles) isn't much of a call. I've had them from 1s. 6d. as high as 7s.—but only once 7s., and it was good silk. They're not a sort of wear that suits poor people. Will and indeed thin, I hardly know who buys them second-hand. Perhaps bad women buys a few, or they get men to buy them for them. I think your misses don't buy much second-hand thin in gineral; the less the better, the likes of them; yis, indeed, sir. *Stays* I don't sell, but you can buy them from 3d. to 15d.; it's a small trade. And I don't sell *Under Clothing*, or only now and thin, except *Children's*. Dear me, I can hardly tell the prices I get for the poor little things' dress—I've a little girl myself—the prices vary so, just as the frocks and other things is made for big children or little, and what they're made of. I've sold frocks—they sell best on Saturday and

Monday nights—from 2d. to 1s. 6d. Little petticoats is 1d. to 3d.; shifts is 1d. and 2d., and so is little shirts. If they wasn't so low there would be more rags than there is, and sure there's plinty.

"Will, thin and indeed, I don't know what we make in a week, and if I did, why should I tell? O, yes, sir, I know from the gentleman that sent you to me that you're asking for a good purpose: yis, indeed, thin; but I ralely can't say. We do pritty well, God's name be praised! Perhaps a good second-hand gown trade and such like is worth from 10s. to 15s. a week, and nearer 15s. than 10s. ivery week; but that's a *good* second-hand trade you understand, sir. A poor trade's about half that, perhaps. But thin my husband sells men's wear as well. Yis, indeed, and I find time to go to mass, and I soon got my husband to go after we was married, for he'd got to neglect it, God be praised; and what's all you can get here compared to making your sowl" [saving your soul —*making* your soul is not an uncommon phrase among some of the Irish people]. "Och, and indeed thin, sir, if you've met Father ——, you've met a good gintleman."

Of the street-selling of *women and children's second-hand boots and shoes*, I need say but little, as they form part of the stock of the men's ware, and are sold by the same men, not unfrequently assisted by their wives. The best sale is for black cloth boots, whether laced or buttoned, but the prices run only from 5d. to 1s. 9d. If the "legs" of a second-hand pair be good, they are worth 5d., no matter what the leather portion, including the soles, may be. Coloured boots sell very indifferently. Children's boots and shoes are sold from 2d. to 15d.

Of the Street-Sellers of Second-hand Furs.

Of furs the street-sale is prompt enough, or used to be prompt; but not so much so, I am told, last season, as formerly. A fur tippet is readily bought for the sake of warmth by women who thrive pretty well in the keeping of coffee-stalls, or any calling which requires attendance during the night, or in the chilliness of early morning, even in summer, by those who go out at early hours to their work. By such persons a big tippet is readily bought when the money is not an impediment, and to many it is a strong recommendation, that when new, the tippet, most likely, was worn by a real lady. So I was assured by a person familiar with the trade.

One female street-seller had three stalls or stands in the New Cut (when it was a great street market), about two years back, and all for the sale of second-hand furs. She has now a small shop in second-hand wearing apparel (women's) generally, furs being of course included. The business carried on in the street (almost always "the Cut") by the fur-seller in question, who was both industrious and respectable, was very considerable. On a Monday she has not unfrequently taken 3l., one-half of which, indeed more than half, was profit, for the street-seller bought in the summer, when furs "were no money at all," and sold in the winter, when they "were really tin, and no mistake." Before the season began, she sometimes had a small room nearly full of furs.

This trade is less confined to Petticoat-lane and the old clothes district, as regards the supply to retail customers, than is anything else connected with dress. But the fur trade is now small. The money, prudence, and forethought necessary to enable a fur-seller to buy in the summer, for ample profit in the winter, as regards street-trade, is not in accordance with the habits of the general run of street-sellers, who think but of the present, or hardly think even of that.

The old furs, like all the other old articles of wearing apparel, whether garbs of what may be accounted primary necessaries, as shoes, or mere comforts or adornments, as boas or muffs, are bought in the first instance at the Old Clothes Exchange, and so find their way to the street-sellers. The exceptions as to this first transaction in the trade I now speak of, are very trifling, and, perhaps, more trifling than in other articles, for one great supply of furs, I am informed, is from their being swopped in the spring and summer for flowers with the "root-sellers," who carry them to the Exchange.

Last winter there were sometimes as many as ten persons—three-fourths of the number of second-hand fur sellers, which fluctuates, being women—with fur-stands. They frequent the street-markets on the Saturday and Monday nights, not confining themselves to any one market in particular. The best sale is for *Fur Tippets*, and chiefly of the darker colours. These are bought, one of the dealers informed me, frequently by maid-servants, who could run of errands in them in the dark, or wear them in wet weather. They are sold from 1s. 6d. to 4s. 6d., about 2s. or 2s. 6d. being a common charge. Children's tippets "go off well," from 6d. to 1s. 3d. *Boas* are not vended to half the extent of tippets, although they are lower-priced, one of tolerably good gray squirrel being 1s. 6d. The reason of the difference in the demand is that boas are as much an ornament as a garment, while the tippet answers the purpose of a shawl. *Muffs* are not at all vendible in the streets, the few that are disposed of being principally for children. As muffs are not generally used by maid-servants, or by the families of the working classes, the absence of demand in the second-hand traffic is easily accounted for. They are bought sometimes to cut up for other purposes. *Victorines* are disposed of readily enough at from 1s. to 2s. 6d., as are *Cuffs*, from 4d. to 8d.

One man, who told me that a few years since he and his wife used to sell second-hand furs in the street, was of opinion that his best customers were women of the town, who were tolerably well-dressed, and who required some further protection from the night air. He could readily sell any "tidy" article, tippet, boa, or muff, to those females, if they had from 2s. 6d. to 5s. at command. He had so sold them in Clare-market, in Tottenham-court-road, and the Brill.

Of the Second-Hand Sellers of Smithfield-Market.

No small part of the second-hand trade of London is carried on in the market-place of Smithfield, on the Friday afternoons. Here is a mart for almost everything which is required for the harnessing of beasts of draught, or is required for any means of propulsion or locomotion, either as a whole vehicle, or in its several parts, needed by street-traders: also of the machines, vessels, scales, weights, measures, baskets, stands, and all other appliances of street-trade.

The scene is animated and peculiar. Apart from the horse, ass, and goat trade (of which I shall give an account hereafter), it is a grand Second-hand Costermongers' Exchange. The trade is not confined to that large body, though they are the principal merchants, but includes greengrocers (often the costermonger in a shop), carmen, and others. It is, moreover, a favourite resort of the purveyors of street-provisions and beverages, of street dainties and luxuries. Of this class some of the most prosperous are those who are "well known in Smithfield."

The space devoted to this second-hand commerce and its accompaniments, runs from St. Bartholomew's Hospital towards Long-lane, but isolated peripatetic traders are found in all parts of the space not devoted to the exhibition of cattle or of horses. The crowd on the day of my visit was considerable, but from several I heard the not-always-very-veracious remarks of "Nothing doing" and "There's nobody at all here to-day." The weather was sultry, and at every few yards arose the cry from men and boys, "Ginger-beer, ha'penny a glass! Ha'penny a glass," or "Iced lemonade here! Iced raspberriade, as cold as ice, ha'penny a glass, only a ha'penny!" A boy was elevated on a board at the end of a splendid affair of this kind. It was a square built vehicle, the top being about 7 feet by 4, and flat and surmounted by the lemonade fountain; long, narrow, champagne glasses, holding a raspberry coloured liquid, frothed up exceedingly, were ranged round, and the beverage dispensed by a woman, the mother or employer of the boy who was bawling. The sides of the machine, which stood on wheels, were a bright, shiny blue, and on them sprawled the lion and unicorn in gorgeous heraldry, yellow and gold, the artist being, according to a prominent announcement, a "herald painter." The apparatus was handsome, but with that exaggeration of handsomeness which attracts the high and low vulgar, who cannot distinguish between gaudiness and beauty. The sale was brisk. The ginger-beer sold in the market was generally dispensed from carts, and here I noticed, what occurs yearly in street-commerce, an innovation on the established system of the trade. Several sellers disposed of their ginger-beer in clear glass bottles, somewhat larger and fuller-necked than those introduced by M. Soyer for the sale of his "nectar," and the liquid was drank out of the bottle the moment the cork was undrawn, and so the necessity of a glass was obviated.

Near the herald-painter's work, of which I have just spoken, stood a very humble stall on which were loaves of bread, and round the loaves were pieces of fried fish and slices of bread on plates, all remarkably clean. "Oysters! Penny-a lot! Penny-a-lot, oysters!" was the cry, the most frequently heard after that of ginger-beer, &c. "Cherries! Twopence a-pound! Penny-a pound, cherries!" "Fruit-pies! Try my fruit-pies!" The most famous dealer in all kinds of penny pies is, however, not a pedestrian, but an equestrian hawker. He drives a very smart, handsome pie-cart, sitting behind after the manner of the Hansom cabmen, the lifting up of a lid below his knees displaying his large stock of pies. His "drag" is whisked along rapidly by a brisk chestnut poney, well-harnessed. The "whole set out," I was informed, poney included, cost 50*l*. when new. The proprietor is a keen Chartist and teetotaller, and loses no opportunity to inculcate to his customers the excellence of teetotalism, as well as of his pies. "Milk! ha'penny a pint! ha'penny a pint, good milk!" is another cry. "Raspberry cream! Iced raspberry-cream, ha'penny a glass!" This street-seller had a capital trade. Street-ices, or rather ice-creams, were somewhat of a failure last year, more especially in Greenwich-park, but this year they seem likely to succeed. The Smithfield man sold them in very small glasses, which he merely dipped into a vessel at his feet, and so filled them with the cream. The consumers had to use their fingers instead of a spoon, and no few seemed puzzled how to eat their ice, and were grievously troubled by its getting among their teeth. I heard one drover mutter that he felt "as if it had snowed in his belly!" Perhaps at Smithfield-market on the Friday afternoons every street-trade in eatables and drinkables has its representative, with the exception of such things as sweet-stuff, curds and whey, &c., which are bought chiefly by women and children. There were plum-dough, plum-cake, pastry, pea-soup, whelks, periwinkles, ham-sandwiches, hot-eels, oranges, &c., &c., &c.

These things are the usual accompaniment of street-markets, and I now come to the subject matter of the work, the sale of second-hand articles.

In this trade, since the introduction of a new arrangement two months ago, there has been a great change. The vendors are not allowed to vend barrows in the market, unless indeed with a poney or donkey harnessed to them, or unless they are wheeled about by the owner, and they are not allowed to spread their wares on the ground. When it is considered of what those wares are composed, the awkwardness of the arrangement, to the sales-people, may be understood. They consist of second-hand collars, pads, saddles, bridles, bits, traces, every description of worn harness, whole or in parts; the wheels, springs, axles, &c., of barrows and carts; the beams, chains, and bodies of scales;—these, perhaps, are the chief things which are sold separately, as parts of a whole. The traders have now no other option but to carry them as they best can, and offer them for sale. You saw men who really appear clad in harness. Portions were fastened round their bodies, collars slung on their arms, pads or small cart-saddles, with their shaft-gear, were planted on their shoulders. Some carried merely a collar, or a harness bridle, or even a bit or a pair of spurs. It was the same with the springs, &c., of the barrows and small carts. They were carried under men's arms, or poised on their shoulders. The wheels and other things which are too heavy for such modes of transport had to be placed in some sort of vehicle, and in the vehicles might be seen trestles, &c.

The complaints on the part of the second-hand sellers were neither few nor mild: "If it had been a fat ox that had to be accommodated," said one, "before he was roasted for an alderman, they'd have found some way to do it. But it don't matter for poor men; though why we shouldn't be suited with a market as well as richer people is not the ticket, that's the fact."

These arrangements are already beginning to be infringed, and will be more and more infringed, for such is always the case. The reason why they were adopted was that the ground was so littered, that there was not room for the donkey traffic and other requirements of the market. The donkeys, when "shown," under the old arrangement, often trod on boards of old metal, &c., spread on the ground, and tripped, sometimes to their injury, in consequence. Prior to the change, about twenty persons used to come from Petticoat-lane, &c., and spread their old metal or other stores on the ground.

Of these there are now none. These Petticoat-laners, I was told by a Smithfield frequenter, were men "who knew the price of old rags,"—a new phrase expressive of their knowingness and keenness in trade.

The statistics of this trade will be found under that head; the prices are often much higher and much lower. I speak of the regular trades. I have not included the sale of the superior butchers' carts, &c., as that is a traffic not in the hands of the regular second-hand street-sellers. I have not thought it requisite to speak of the hawking of whips, sticks, wash-leathers, brushes, curry-combs, &c., &c., of which I have already treated distinctively.

The accounts of the Capital and Income of the Street-Sellers of Second-Hand Articles I am obliged to defer till a future occasion.

OF THE STREET-SELLERS OF LIVE ANIMALS.

THE live animals sold in the streets include beasts, birds, fish, and reptiles, all sold in the streets of London.

The class of men carrying on this business—for they are nearly all men—is mixed; but the majority are of a half-sporting and half-vagrant kind. One informant told me that the bird-catchers, for instance, when young, as more than three-fourths of them are, were those who "liked to be after a loose end," first catching their birds, as a sort of sporting business, and then sometimes selling them in the streets, but far more frequently disposing of them in the bird-shops. "Some of these boys," a bird-seller in a large way of business said to me, "used to become rat-catchers or dog-sellers, but there's not such great openings in the rat and dog line now. As far as I know, they're the same lads, or just the same sort of lads, anyhow, as you may see 'helping,' holding horses, or things like that, at concerns like them small races at Peckham or Chalk Farm, or helping any way at the foot-races at Camberwell." There is in this bird-catching a strong manifestation of the vagrant spirit. To rise long before daybreak; to walk some miles before daybreak; from the earliest dawn to wait in some field, or common, or wood, watching the capture of the birds; then a long trudge to town to dispose of the fluttering captives; all this is done cheerfully, because there are about it the irresistible charms, to this class, of excitement, variety, and free and open-air life. Nor do these charms appear one whit weakened when, as happens often enough, all this early morn business is carried on fasting.

The old men in the bird-catching business are not to be ranked as to their enjoyment of it with the juveniles, for these old men are sometimes infirm, and can but, as one of them said to me some time ago, "hobble about it." But they have the same spirit, or the sparks of it. And in this part of the trade is one of the curious characteristics of a street-life, or rather of an open-air pursuit for the requirements of a street-trade. A man, worn out for other purposes, incapable of anything but a passive, or sort of lazy labour—such as lying in a field and watching the action of his trap-cages—will yet in a summer's morning, decrepid as he may be, possess himself of a dozen or even a score of the very freest and most aspiring of all our English small birds, a creature of the air beyond other birds of his "order"—to use an ornithological term—of sky-larks.

The dog-sellers are of a sporting, trading, idling class. Their sport is now the rat-hunt, or the ferret-match, or the dog-fight; as it was with the predecessors of their stamp, the cock-fight; the bull, bear, and badger bait; the shrove-tide cock-shy, or the duck hunt. Their trading spirit is akin to that of the higher-class sporting fraternity, the trading members of the turf. They love to sell and to bargain, always with a quiet exultation at the time—a matter of loud tavern boast afterwards, perhaps, as respects the street-folk—how they "do" a customer, or "do" one another. "It's not cheating," was the remark and apology of a very famous jockey of the old times, touching such measures; "it's not cheating, it's outwitting." Perhaps this expresses the code of honesty of such traders; not to cheat, but to outwit or over-reach. Mixed with such traders, however, are found a few quiet, plodding, fair-dealing men, whom it is difficult to classify, otherwise than that they are "in the line, just because they likes it." The idling of these street-sellers is a part of their business. To walk by the hour up and down a street, and with no manual labour except to clean their dogs' kennels, and to carry them in their arms, is but an idleness, although, as some of these men will tell you, "they work hard at it."

Under the respective heads of dog and bird-sellers, I shall give more detailed characteristics of the class, as well as of the varying qualities and inducements of the buyers.

The street-sellers of foreign birds, such as parrots, parroquets, and cockatoos; of gold and silver fish; of goats, tortoises, rabbits, leverets, hedgehogs; and the collectors of snails, worms, frogs, and toads, are also a mixed body. Foreigners, Jews, seamen, countrymen, costermongers, and boys form a part, and of them I shall give a description under the several heads. The prominently-characterized street-sellers are the traders in dogs and birds.

OF THE FORMER STREET-SELLERS, "FINDERS," STEALERS, AND RESTORERS OF DOGS.

BEFORE I describe the present condition of the street-trade in dogs, which is principally in spaniels, or in the description well known as lap-dogs, I will give an account of the former condition of the trade, if trade it can properly be called, for the "finders" and "stealers" of dogs were the more especial subjects of a parliamentary inquiry, from which I derive the official information on the matter. The Report of the Committee was ordered by the House of Commons to be printed, July 26, 1844.

In their Report the Committee observe, concerning the value of pet dogs:—"From the evidence of various witnesses it appears, that in one case a spaniel was sold for 105*l*., and in another, under a sheriff's execution, for 95*l*. at the hammer; and 50*l*. or 60*l*. are not unfrequently given for fancy dogs of first-rate breed and beauty." The hundred guineas' dog above alluded to was a "black and tan King Charles's spaniel;"—indeed, Mr. Dowling, the editor of *Bell's Life in London*, said, in his evidence before the Committee, "I have known as much as 150*l*. given for a dog." He said afterwards: "There are certain marks about the eyes and otherwise, which are considered 'properties;' and it depends entirely upon the property which a dog possesses as to its value."

I need not dwell on the general fondness of the English for dogs, otherwise than as regards what were the grand objects of the dog-finders' search —ladies' small spaniels and lap-dogs, or, as they are sometimes called, "carriage-dogs," by their being the companions of ladies inside their carriages. These animals first became fashionable by the fondness of Charles II. for them. That monarch allowed them undisturbed possession of the gilded chairs in his palace of Whitehall, and seldom took his accustomed walk in the park without a tribe of them at his heels. So "fashionable" were spaniels at that time and afterwards, that in 1712 Pope made the chief of all his sylphs and sylphides the guard of a lady's lapdog. The fashion has long continued, and still continues; and it was on this fashionable fondness for a toy, and on the regard of many others for the noble and affectionate qualities of the dog, that a traffic was established in London, which became so extensive and so lucrative, that the legislature interfered, in 1844, for the purpose of checking it.

I cannot better show the extent and lucrativeness of this trade, than by citing a list which one of the witnesses before Parliament, Mr. W. Bishop, a gunmaker, delivered in to the Committee, of "cases in which money had recently been extorted from the owners of dogs by dog-stealers and their confederates." There is no explanation of the space of time included under the vague term "recently;" but the return shows that 151 ladies and gentlemen had been the victims of the dog-stealers or dog-finders, for in this business the words were, and still are to a degree, synonymes, and of these 62 had been so victimized in 1843 and in the six months of 1844, from January to July. The total amount shown by Mr. Bishop to have been paid for the restoration of stolen dogs was 977*l*. 4*s*. 6*d*., or an average of 6*l*. 10*s*. per individual practised upon. This large sum, it is stated on the authority of the Committee, was only that which came within Mr. Bishop's knowledge, and formed, perhaps, "but a *tenth* part in amount" of the whole extortion. Mr. Bishop was himself in the habit of doing business "in obtaining the restitution of dogs," and had once known 18*l*.—the dog-stealers asked 25*l*.—given for the restitution of a spaniel. The full amount realized by this dog-stealing was, according to the above proportion, 9772*l*. 5*s*. In 1843, 227*l*. 3*s*. 6*d*. was so realized, and 97*l*. 14*s*. 6*d*. in the six months of 1844, within Mr. Bishop's personal knowledge; and if this be likewise a *tenth* of the whole of the commerce in this line, a year's business, it appears, averaged 2166*l*. to the stealers or finders of dogs. I select a few names from the list of those robbed of dogs, either from the amount paid, or because the names are well known. The first payment cited is from a public board, who owned a dog in their corporate capacity:

	£	s.	d.
Board of Green Cloth . .	8	0	0
Hon. W. Ashley (v. t.*) .	15	0	0
Sir F. Burdett . .	6	6	0
Colonel Udney (v. t.) .	12	0	0
Duke of Cambridge .	30	0	0
Count Kielmansegge .	9	0	0
Mr. Orby Hunter (v. t.) .	15	0	0
Mrs. Holmes (v. t.) . .	50	0	0
Sir Richard Phillips (v. t.) .	20	0	0
The French Amdassador .	1	11	6
Sir R. Peel . . .	2	0	0
Edw. Morris, Esq. . .	17	0	0

* "v. t." signifies "various times," of theft and of "restoration."

	£	s.	d.
Mrs. Ram (v. t.)	15	0	0
Duchess of Sutherland	5	0	0
Wyndham Bruce, Esq. (v. t.)	25	0	0
Capt. Alexander (v. t.)	22	0	0
Sir De Lacy Evans	3	0	0
Judge Littledale	2	0	0
Leonino Ippolito, Esq. (v. t.)	10	0	0
Mr. Commissioner Rae	5	0	0
Lord Cholmondeley (v. t.)	12	0	0
Earl Stanhope	8	0	0
Countess of Charlemont (v. t. in 1843)	12	0	0
Lord Alfred Paget	10	0	0
Count Leodoffe (v. t.)	7	0	0
Mr. Thorne (whipmaker)	12	12	0
Mr. White (v. t.)	15	0	0
Col. Barnard (v. t.)	14	14	0
Mr. T. Holmes	15	0	0
Earl of Winchelsea	6	0	0
Lord Wharncliffe (v. t.)	12	0	0
Hon. Mrs. Dyce Sombre	2	2	0
M. Ude (v. t.)	10	10	0
Count Batthyany	14	0	0
Bishop of Ely	4	10	0
Count D'Orsay	10	0	0

Thus these 36 ladies and gentlemen paid 438*l.* 5*s.* 6*d.* to rescue their dogs from professional dog-stealers, or an average, per individual, of upwards of 12*l.*

These dog appropriators, as they found that they could levy contributions not only on royalty, foreign ambassadors, peers, courtiers, and ladies of rank, but on public bodies, and on the dignitaries of the state, the law, the army, and the church, became bolder and more expert in their avocations—a boldness which was encouraged by the existing law. Prior to the parliamentary inquiry, dog-stealing was not an indictable offence. To show this, Mr. Commissioner Mayne quoted Blackstone to the Committee: "As to those animals which do not serve for food, and which therefore the law holds to have no intrinsic value, as dogs of all sorts, and other creatures kept for whim and pleasure—though a man may have a base property therein, and maintain a civil action for the loss of them, yet they are not of such estimation as that the crime of stealing them amounts to larceny." The only mode of punishment for dog-stealing was by summary conviction, the penalty being fine or imprisonment; but Mr. Commissioner Mayne did not know of any instance of a dog-stealer being sent to prison in default of payment. Although the law recognised no property in a dog, the animal was taxed; and it was complained at the time that an unhappy lady might have to pay tax for the full term upon her dog, perhaps a year and a half after he had been stolen from her. One old offender, who stole the Duke of Beaufort's dog, was transported, not for stealing the dog, but his collar. The difficulty of proving the positive theft of a dog was extreme. In most cases, where the man was not seen actually to seize a dog which could be identified, he escaped when carried before a magistrate. "The dog-stealers," said Inspector Shackell, "generally go two together; they have a piece of liver; they say it is merely bullock's liver, which will entice or tame the wildest or savagest dog which there can be in any yard; they give it him, and take him from his chain. At other times," continues Mr. Shackell, "they will go in the street with a little dog, rubbed over with some sort of stuff, and will entice valuable dogs away. . . . . If there is a dog lost or stolen, it is generally known within five or six hours where that dog is, and they know almost exactly what they can get for it, so that it is a regular system of plunder." Mr. G. White, "dealer in live stock, dogs, and other animals," and at one time a "dealer in lions, and tigers, and all sorts of things," said of the dog-stealers: "In turning the corners of streets there are two or three of them together; one will snatch up a dog and put into his apron, and the others will stop the lady and say, 'What is the matter?' and direct the party who has lost the dog in a contrary direction to that taken."

In this business were engaged from 50 to 60 men, half of them actual stealers of the animals. The others were the receivers, and the go-betweens or "restorers." The thief kept the dog perhaps for a day or two at some public-house, and he then took it to a dog-dealer with whom he was connected in the way of business. These dealers carried on a trade in "honest dogs," as one of the witnesses styled them (meaning dogs honestly acquired), but some of them dealt principally with the dog-stealers. Their depots could not be entered by the police, being private premises, without a search-warrant—and direct evidence was necessary to obtain a search-warrant—and of course a stranger in quest of a stolen dog would not be admitted. Some of the dog-dealers would not purchase or receive dogs known to have been stolen, but others bought and speculated in them. If an advertisement appeared offering a reward for the dog, a negotiation was entered into. If no reward was offered, the owner of the dog, who was always either known or made out, was waited upon by a restorer, who undertook "to restore the dog if terms could be come to." A dog belonging to Colonel Fox was once kept six weeks before the thieves would consent to the Colonel's terms. One of the most successful restorers was a shoemaker, and mixed little with the actual stealers; the dog-dealers, however, acted as restorers frequently enough. If the person robbed paid a good round sum for the restoration of a dog, and paid it speedily, the animal was almost certain to be stolen a second time, and a higher sum was then demanded. Sometimes the thieves threatened that if they were any longer trifled with they would inflict torture on the dog, or cut its throat. One lady, Miss Brown of Bolton-street, was so worried by these threats, and by having twice to redeem her dog, "that she has left England," said Mr. Bishop, "and I really do believe for the sake of keeping the dog." It does not appear, as far as the evidence shows, that these threats of torture or death were ever carried into execution;

some of the witnesses had merely heard of such things.

The shoemaker alluded to was named Taylor, and Inspector Shackell thus describes this person's way of transacting business in the dog "restoring" line: "There is a man named Taylor, who is one of the greatest restorers in London of stolen dogs, through Mr. Bishop." [Mr. Bishop was a gun-maker in Bond-street.] "It is a disgrace to London that any person should encourage a man like that to go to extort money from ladies and gentlemen, especially a respectable man. A gentleman applied to me to get a valuable dog that was stolen, with a chain on his neck, and the name on the collar; and I heard Mr. Bishop himself say that it cost 6*l*.; that it could not be got for less. Capt. Vansittart (the owner of the dog) came out; I asked him particularly, 'Will you give me a description of the dog on a piece of paper,' and that is his writing (producing a paper). I went and made inquiry; and the captain himself, who lives in Belgrave-square, said he had no objection to give 4*l*. for the recovery of the dog, but would not give the 6*l*. I went and took a good deal of trouble about it. I found out that Taylor went first to ascertain what the owner of the dog would give for it, and then went and offered 1*l*. for the dog, then 2*l*., and at last purchased it for 3*l*.; and went and told Capt. Vansittart that he had given 4*l*. for the dog; and the dog went back through the hands of Mr. Bishop."

The "restorers" had, it appears, the lion's share in the profits of this business. One witness had known of as much as ten guineas being given for the recovery of a favourite spaniel, or, as the witness styled it, for "working a dog back," and only two of these guineas being received by "the party." The wronged individual, thus delicately intimated as the "party," was the thief. The same witness, Mr. Hobdell, knew 14*l*. given for the restoration of a little red Scotch terrier, which he, as a dog-dealer, valued at four shillings!

One of the coolest instances of the organization and boldness of the dog-stealers was in the case of Mr. Fitzroy Kelly's "favourite Scotch terrier." The "parties," possessing it through theft, asked 12*l*. for it, and urged that it was a reasonable offer, considering the trouble they were obliged to take. "The dog-stealers were obliged to watch every night," they contended, through Mr. Bishop, "and very diligently; Mr. Kelly kept them out very late from their homes, before they could get the dog; he used to go out to dinner or down to the Temple, and take the dog with him; they had a deal of trouble before they could get it." So Mr. Kelly was expected not only to pay more than the value of his dog, but an extra amount on account of the care he had taken of his terrier, and for the trouble his vigilance had given to the thieves! The matter was settled at 6*l*. Mr. Kelly's case was but one instance.

Among the most successful of the practitioners in this street-finding business were Messrs. "Ginger" and "Carrots," but a parliamentary witness was inclined to believe that Ginger and Carrots were nicknames for the same individual, one Barrett; although he had been in custody several times, he was considered "a very superior dog-stealer."

If the stolen dog were of little value, it was safest for the stealers to turn him loose; if he were of value, and unowned and unsought for, there was a ready market abroad. The stewards, stokers, or seamen of the Ostend, Antwerp, Rotterdam, Hamburgh, and all the French steamers, readily bought stolen fancy dogs; sometimes twenty to thirty were taken at a voyage. A steward, indeed, has given 12*l*. for a stolen spaniel as a private speculation. Dealers, too, came occasionally from Paris, and bought numbers of these animals, and at what the dog foragers considered fair prices. One of the witnesses (Mr. Baker, a game dealer in Leadenhall-market) said:—"I have seen perhaps twenty or thirty dogs tied up in a little room, and I should suppose every one of them was stolen; a reward not sufficiently high being offered for their restoration, the parties get more money by taking them on board the different steam-ships and selling them to persons on board, or to people coming to this country to buy dogs and take them abroad."

The following statement, derived from Mr. Mayne's evidence, shows the extent of the dog-stealing business, but only as far as came under the cognizance of the police. It shows the number of dogs "lost" or "stolen," and of persons "charged" with the offence, and "convicted" or "discharged." Nearly all the dogs returned as lost, I may observe, were stolen, but there was no evidence to show the positive theft:—

	Dogs Stolen.	Dogs Lost.	Persons Charged.	Convicted.	Discharged.
1841	43	521	51	19	32
1842	54	561	45	17	28
1843	60	606	38	18	20

In what proportion the police-known thefts stood to the whole number, there was no evidence given; nor, I suppose, could it be given.

The dog-stealers were not considered to be connected with housebreakers, though they might frequent the same public-houses. Mr. Mayne pronounced these dog-stealers a genus, a peculiar class, "what they call dog-fanciers and dog-stealers; a sort of half-sporting, betting characters."

The law on the subject of dog-stealing (8 and 9 Vict., c. 47) now is, that "If any person shall steal any dog, every such offender shall be deemed guilty of a misdemeanor, and, being convicted thereof before any two or more justices of the peace, shall, for the first offence, at the discretion of the said justices, either be committed to the common gaol or house of correction, there to be imprisoned only, or be imprisoned and kept to hard labour, for any term not exceeding six calendar months, or shall forfeit and pay over and above the value of the said dog such sum of money, not exceeding 20*l*., as to the said justices shall seem meet. And if any person so convicted shall afterwards be guilty of the same offence, every such offender shall be guilty of an indictable misdemeanor, and, being convicted thereof, shall be liable to suffer such punishment, by fine or imprisonment, with or without hard labour, or by both, as the court in its discretion shall award, provided such imprisonment do not exceed eighteen months."

Of a Dog-"Finder."—A "Lurker's" Career.

Concerning a dog-finder, I received the following account from one who had received the education of a gentleman, but whom circumstances had driven to an association with the vagrant class, and who has written the dog-finder's biography from personal knowledge—a biography which shows the *variety* that often characterizes the career of the "lurker," or street-adventurer.

"If your readers," writes my informant, "have passed the Rubicon of 'forty years in the wilderness,' memory must bring back the time when the feet of their childish pilgrimage have trodden a beautiful grass-plot—now converted into Belgrave-square; when Pimlico was a 'village out of town,' and the 'five fields' of Chelsea were fields indeed. To write the biography of a living character is always delicate, as to embrace all its particulars is difficult; but of the truthfulness of my account there is no question.

"Probably about the year of the great frost (1814), a French Protestant refugee, named La Roche, sought asylum in this country, not from persecution, but from difficulties of a commercial character. He built for himself, in Chelsea, a cottage of wood, nondescript in shape, but pleasant in locality, and with ample accommodations for himself and his son. Wife he had none. This little bazaar of mud and sticks was surrounded with a bench of rude construction, on which the Sunday visitors to Ranelagh used to sit and sip their curds and whey, while from the entrance—far removed in those days from competition—

'There stood uprear'd, as ensign of the place,
 Of blue and red and white, a checquer'd mace,
 On which the paper lantern hung to tell
 How cheap its owner shaved you, and how well.'

Things went on smoothly for a dozen years, when the old Frenchman departed this life.

"His boy carried on the business for a few months, when frequent complaints of 'Sunday gambling' on the premises, and loud whispers of suspicion relative to the concealment of stolen goods, induced 'Chelsea George'—the name the youth had acquired—to sell the good-will of the house, fixtures, and all, and at the eastern extremity of London to embark in business as a 'mush or mushroom-faker.' Independently of his appropriation of umbrellas, proper to the mushfaker's calling, Chelsea George was by no means scrupulous concerning other little matters within his reach, and if the proprietors of the 'swell cribs' within his 'beat' had no 'umbrellas to mend,' or 'old 'uns to sell,' he would ease the pegs in the passage of the incumbrance of a greatcoat, and telegraph the same out of sight (by a colleague), while the servant went in to make the desired inquiries. At last he was 'bowl'd out' in the very act of 'nailing a yack' (stealing a watch). He 'expiated,' as it is called, this offence by three months' exercise on the 'cockchafer' (tread-mill). Unaccustomed as yet to the novelty of the exercise, he fell through the wheel and broke one of his legs. He was, of course, permitted to finish his time in the infirmary of the prison, and on his liberation was presented with five pounds out of 'the Sheriffs' Fund.'

"Although, as I have before stated, he had never been out of England since his childhood, he had some little hereditary knowledge of the French language, and by the kind and voluntary recommendation of one of the police-magistrates of the metropolis, he was engaged by an Irish gentleman proceeding to the Continent as a sort of supernumerary servant, to 'make himself generally useful.' As the gentleman was unmarried, and mostly stayed at hotels, George was to have permanent wages and 'find himself,' a condition he invariably fulfilled, if anything was left in his way. Frequent intemperance, neglect of duty, and unaccountable departures of property from the portmanteau of his master, led to his dismissal, and Chelsea George was left, without friends or character, to those resources which have supported him for some thirty years.

"During his 'umbrella' enterprise he had lived in lodging-houses of the lowest kind, and of course mingled with the most depraved society, especially with the vast army of trading sturdy mendicants, male and female, young and old, who assume every guise of poverty, misfortune, and disease, which craft and ingenuity can devise or well-tutored hypocrisy can imitate. Thus initiated, Chelsea George could 'go upon any lurk,' could be in the last stage of consumption—actually in his dying hour—but now and then convalescent for years and years together. He could take fits and counterfeit blindness, be a respectable broken-down tradesman, or a soldier maimed in the service, and dismissed without a pension.

"Thus qualified, no vicissitudes could be either very new or very perplexing, and he commenced operations without delay, and pursued them long without desertion. The 'first move' in his mendicant career was *taking them on the fly;* which means meeting the gentry on their walks, and beseeching or at times menacing them till something is given; something in general *was* given to get rid of the annoyance, and, till the 'game got stale,' an hour's work, morning and evening, produced a harvest of success, and ministered to an occasion of debauchery.

"His less popular, but more upright father, had once been a dog-fancier, and George, after many years vicissitude, at length took a 'fancy' to the same profession, but not on any principles recognised by commercial laws. With what success he has practised, the ladies and gentlemen about the West-end have known, to their loss and disappointment, for more than fifteen years past.

"Although the police have been and still are on the alert, George has, in every instance, hitherto escaped punishment, while numerous detections connected with escape have enabled the offender to hold these officials at defiance. The 'modus operandi' upon which George proceeds is to varnish his hands with a sort of gelatine, composed of the coarsest pieces of liver, fried, pulverised, and mixed up with tincture of myrrh." [This is the composition of which Inspector Shackell spoke before the Select Committee, but he did not seem to know of what the lure was concocted. My correspondent continues]: "Chelsea George caresses every animal who seems 'a likely spec,' and when his fingers have been rubbed over the dogs' noses they become easy and perhaps willing captives. A bag carried for the purpose, receives the victim, and away goes George, bag and all, to his printer's in Seven Dials. Two bills and no less—two and no more, for such is George's style of work—are issued to describe the animal that has thus been *found*, and which will be 'restored to its owner on payment of expenses.' One of these George puts in his pocket, the other he pastes up at a public-house whose landlord is 'fly' to its meaning, and poor 'bow-wow' is sold to a 'dealer in dogs,' not very far from Sharp's alley. In course of time the dog is discovered; the possessor refers to the 'establishment' where he bought it; the 'dealer makes himself *square*,' by giving the address of 'the chap he bought 'un of,' and Chelsea George shows a copy of the advertisement, calls in the publican as a witness, and leaves the place 'without the slightest imputation on his character.' Of this man's earnings I cannot speak with precision: it is probable that in a 'good year' his clear income is 200*l.*; in a bad year but 100*l.*, but, as he is very adroit, I am inclined to believe that the 'good' years somewhat predominate, and that the average income may therefore exceed 150*l.* yearly."

OF THE PRESENT STREET-SELLERS OF DOGS.

IT will have been noticed that in the accounts I have given of the former street-transactions in dogs, there is no mention of the *sellers*. The information I have adduced is a condensation of the evidence given before the Select Committee of the House of Commons, and the inquiry related only to the stealing, finding, and restoring of dogs, the selling being but an incidental part of the evidence. Then, however, as now, the street-sellers were not implicated in the thefts or restitution of dogs, "just except," one man told me, "as there was a black sheep or two in every flock." The black sheep, however, of this street-calling more frequently meddled with restoring, than with "finding."

Another street dog-seller, an intelligent man,— who, however did not know so much as my first informant of the state of the trade in the olden time,—expressed a positive opinion, that no dog-stealer was now a street-hawker ("hawker" was the word I found these men use). His reasons for this opinion, in addition to his own judgment from personal knowledge, are cogent enough: "It isn't possible, sir," he said, "and this is the reason why. We are not a large body of men. We stick pretty closely, when we are out, to the same places. We are as well-known to the police, as any men whom they most know, by sight at any rate, from meeting them every day. Now, if a lady or gentleman has lost a dog, or it's been stolen or strayed—and the most petted will sometimes stray unaccountably and follow some stranger or other—why where does she, and he, and all the family, and all the servants, first look for the lost animal? Why, where, but at the dogs we are hawking? No, sir, it can't be done now, and it isn't done in my knowledge, and it oughtn't to be done. I'd rather make 5*s.* on an honest dog than 5*l.* on one that wasn't, if there was no risk about it either." Other information convinces me that this statement is correct.

Of these street-sellers or hawkers there are now about twenty-five. There may be, however, but twenty, if so many, on any given day in the streets, as there are always some detained at home by other avocations connected with their line of life. The places they chiefly frequent are the Quadrant and Regent-street generally, but the Quadrant far the most. Indeed before the removal of the colonnade, one-half at least of all the dog-sellers of London would resort there on a very wet day, as they had the advantage of shelter, and generally of finding a crowd assembled, either lounging to pass the time, or waiting "for a fair fit," and so with leisure to look at dogs. The other places are the West-end squares, the banks of the Serpentine, Charing-cross, the Royal Exchange, and the Bank of England, and the Parks generally. They visit, too, any public place to which there may be a temporary attraction of the classes likely to be purchasers — a mere crowd of people, I was told, was no good to the dog-hawkers, it must be a crowd of people that had money—such as the assemblage of ladies and gentlemen who crowd the windows of Whitehall and Parliament-street, when the Queen opens or prorogues the houses. These spectators fill the street and the Horseguards' portion of the park as soon as the street mass has dispersed, and they often afford the means of a good day's work to the dog people.

Two dogs, carefully cleaned and combed, or brushed, are carried in a man's arms for street-vending. A fine chain is generally attached to a neat collar, so that the dog can be relieved from the cramped feel he will experience if kept off his feet too long. In carrying these little animals for sale—for it is the smaller dogs which are carried —the men certainly display them to the best advantage. Their longer silken ears, their prominent dark eyes and black noses, and the delicacy of their fore-paws, are made as prominent as possible, and present what the masses very well call "quite a pictur." I have alluded to the display of the *Spaniels*, as they constitute considerably more than half of the street trade in dogs, the "King Charleses" and the "Blenheims" being disposed of in nearly equal quantities. They are sold for lap-dogs, pets, carriage companions or companions in a walk, and are often intelligent and affectionate. Their colours are black, black and tan, white and liver-colour, chestnut, black and white, and entirely white, with many shades of these hues, and interblendings of them, one with another, and with gray.

The small *Terriers* are, however, coming more into fashion, or, as the hawkers call it, into "vogue." They are usually black, with tanned muzzles and feet, and with a keen look, their hair being short and smooth. Some, however, are preferred with long and somewhat wiry hair, and the colour is often strongly mixed with gray. A small Isle of Skye terrier—but few, I was informed know a "real Skye"—is sometimes carried in the streets, as well as the little rough dogs known as Scotch terriers. When a street-seller has a litter of terrier pups, he invariably selects the handsomest for the streets, for it happens—my informant did not know why, but he and others were positive that so it was—that the handsomest is the worst; "the worst," it must be understood as regards the possession of choice sporting qualities, more especially of pluck. The terrier's education, as regards his prowess in a rat-pit, is accordingly neglected; and if a gentleman ask, "Will he kill rats?" the answer is in the negative; but this is no disparagement to the sale, because the dog is sold, perhaps, for a lady's pet, and is not wanted to kill rats, or to "fight any dog of his weight."

The *Pugs*, for which, 40 to 50 years ago, and, in a diminished degree, 30 years back, there was, in the phrase of the day, "quite a rage," provided only the pug was hideous, are now never offered in the streets, or so rarely, that a well-known dealer assured me he had only sold one in the streets for two years. A Leadenhall tradesman, fond of dogs, but in no way connected with the trade, told me that it came to be looked upon, that a pug was a fit companion for only snappish old maids, and "so the women wouldn't have them any longer, least of all the old maids."

French Poodles are also of rare street-sale. One man had a white poodle two or three years ago, so fat and so round, that a lady, who priced it, was told by a gentleman with her, that if the head and the short legs were removed, and the inside scooped out, the animal would make a capital muff; yet even *that* poodle was difficult of sale at 50s.

Occasionally also an *Italian Greyhound*, seeming cold and shivery on the warmest days, is borne in a hawker's arms, or if following on foot, trembling and looking sad, as if mentally murmuring at the climate.

In such places as the banks of the Serpentine, or in the Regent's-park, the hawker does not carry his dogs in his arms, so much as let them trot along with him in a body, and they are sure to attract attention; or he sits down, and they play or sleep about him. One dealer told me that children often took such a fancy for a pretty spaniel, that it was difficult for either mother, governess, or nurse, to drag them away until the man was requested to call in the evening, bringing with him the dog, which was very often bought, or the hawker recompensed for his loss of time. But sometimes the dog-dealers, I heard from several, meet with great shabbiness among rich people, who recklessly give them no small trouble, and sometimes put them to expense without the slightest return, or even an acknowledgment or a word of apology. "There's one advantage in my trade," said a dealer in live animals, "we always has to do with principals. There's never a lady would let her most favouritest maid choose her dog for her. So no parkisits."

The species which I have enumerated are all that are now sold in the streets, with the exception of an odd "plum-pudding," or coach-dog (the white dog with dark spots which runs after carriages), or an odd bull-dog, or bull-terrier, or indeed with the exception of "odd dogs" of every kind. The hawkers are, however, connected with the trade in sporting dogs, and often through the medium of their street traffic, as I shall show under the next head of my subject.

There is one peculiarity in the hawking of fancy dogs, which distinguishes it from all other branches of street-commerce. The purchasers are all of the wealthier class. This has had its influence on the manners of the dog-sellers. They will be found, in the majority of cases, quiet and deferential men, but without servility, and with little of the quality of speech; and I speak only of speech which among English people is known as "gammon," and among Irish people as "blarney." This manner is common to many; to the established trainer of race-horses for instance, who is in constant communication with persons in a very superior position in life to his own, and to whom he is exceedingly deferential. But the trainer feels that in all points connected with his not very easy business, as well, perhaps, as in general turf knowingness, his royal highness (as was the case once), or his grace, or my lord, or Sir John, was inferior to himself; and so with all his deference there mingles a strain of quiet contempt, or rather, perhaps, of conscious superiority, which is one ingredient in the formation of the manners I have hastily sketched.

The customers of the street-hawkers of dogs are ladies and gentlemen, who buy what may have attracted their admiration. The kept mistresses of the wealthier classes are often excellent customers. "Many of 'em, I know," was said to me, "dotes on a nice spaniel. Yes, and I've known gentlemen buy dogs for their misses; I couldn't be mistaken when I might be sent on with them, which was part of the bargain. If it was a two-guinea dog or so, I was told never to give a hint of the price to the servant, or to anybody. *I* know why. It's easy for a gentleman that wants to please a lady, and not to lay out any great matter of tin, to say that what had really cost him two guineas, cost him twenty." If one of the working classes, or a small tradesman, buy a dog in the streets, it is generally because he is "of a fancy turn," and breeds a few dogs, and traffics in them in hopes of profit.

The homes of the dog-hawkers, as far as I had means of ascertaining—and all I saw were of the same character—are comfortable and very cleanly. The small spaniels, terriers, &c.,—I do not now allude to sporting dogs—are generally kept in kennels, or in small wooden houses erected for the purpose in a back garden or yard. These abodes are generally in some open court, or little square or "grove," where there is a free access of air. An old man who was sitting at his door in the summer evening, when I called upon a dog-seller, and had to wait a short time, told me that so quiet were his next-door neighbour's (the street-hawker's) dogs, that for some weeks, he did not know his newly-come neighbour was a dog-man; although he was an old nervous man himself, and couldn't bear any unpleasant noise or smell. The scrupulous observance of cleanliness is necessary in the rearing or keeping of small fancy dogs, for without such observance the dog would have a disagreeable odour about it, enough to repel any lady-buyer. It is a not uncommon declaration among dog-sellers that the animals are "as sweet as nuts." Let it be remembered that I have been describing the class of regular dog-sellers, making, by an open and established trade, a tolerable livelihood.

The spaniels, terriers, &c., the stock of these hawkers, are either bred by them—and they all breed a few or a good many dogs—or they are purchased of dog-dealers (not street-sellers), or of people who having a good fancy breed of "King Charleses," or "Blenheims," rear dogs, and sell them by the litter to the hawkers. The hawkers also buy dogs brought to them, "in the way of business," but they are wary how they buy any animal suspected to be stolen, or they may get into "trouble." One man, a carver and gilder, I was informed, some ten years back, made a good deal of money by his "black-patched" spaniels. These dogs had a remarkable black patch over their eyes, and so fond was the dog-fancier, or breeder of them, that when he disposed of them to street-sellers or others, he usually gave a portrait of the animals, of his own rude painting, into the bargain. These paintings he also sold, slightly framed, and I have seen them—but not so much lately—offered in the streets, and hung up in poor persons' rooms. This man lived in York-square, behind the Colosseum, then a not very reputable quarter. It is now Munster-square, and of a reformed character, but the seller of dogs and the donor of their portraits has for some time been lost sight of.

The prices at which fancy-dogs are sold in the streets are about the same for all kinds. They run from 10s. to 5l. 5s., but are very rarely so low as 10s., as "it's only a very scrubby thing for that." Two and three guineas are frequent street prices for a spaniel or small terrier. Of the dogs sold, as I have before stated, more than one-half are spaniels. Of the remainder, more than one-half are terriers; and the surplusage, after this reckoning, is composed in about equal numbers of the other dogs I have mentioned. The exportation of dogs is not above a twentieth of what it was before the appointment of the Select Committee, but a French or Belgium dealer sometimes comes to London to buy dogs.

It is not easy to fix upon any per-centage as to the profit of the street dog-sellers. There is the keep and the rearing of the animal to consider; and there is the same uncertainty in the traffic as in all traffics which depend, not upon a demand for use, but on the caprices of fashion, or—to use the more appropriate word, when writing on such a subject—of "fancy." A hawker may sell three dogs in one day, without any extraordinary effort, or, in the same manner of trading, and frequenting the very same places, may sell only one in three days. In the winter, the dogs are sometimes offered in public houses, but seldom as regards the higher-priced animals.

From the best data I can command, it appears that each hawker sells "three dogs and a half, if you take it that way, splitting a dog like, every week the year through; that is, sir, four or five one week in the summer, when trade's brisk and days are long, and only two or three the next week, when trade may be flat, and in winter when there isn't the same chance." Calculating, then, that seven dogs are sold by each hawker in a fortnight, at an average price of 50s. each, which is not a high average, and supposing that but twenty men are trading in this line the year through, we find that no less a sum than 9100l. is yearly expended in this street-trade. The weekly profit of the hawker is from 25s. to 40s. More than seven-eighths of these dogs are bred in this country, Italian greyhounds included.

A hawker of dogs gave me a statement of his life, but it presented so little of incident or of change, that I need not report it. He had assisted and then succeeded his father in the business; was a pains-taking, temperate, and industrious man, seldom taking even a glass of ale, so that the tenour of his way had been even, and he was prosperous enough.

I will next give an account of the connection of the hawkers of dogs with the "sporting" or "fancy" part of the business; and of the present state of dog "finding," to show the change since the parliamentary investigation.

I may observe that in this traffic the word "fancy" has two significations. A dog recommended by its beauty, or any peculiarity, so that it be suitable for a pet-dog, is a "fancy" animal; so is he if he be a fighter, or a killer of rats, however ugly or common-looking; but the term "sporting dog" seems to become more and more used in this case: nor is the first-mentioned use of the word "fancy," at all strained or very original, for it is lexicographically defined as "an opinion bred rather by the imagination than the reason, inclination, liking, caprice, humour, whim, frolick, idle scheme, vagary."

OF THE STREET-SELLERS OF SPORTING DOGS.

THE use, if use it may be styled, of sporting, or fighting dogs, is now a mere nothing to what it once was. There are many sports—an appellation of many a brute cruelty—which have become extinct, some of them long extinct. Herds of bears, for instance, were once maintained in this country, merely to be baited by dogs. It was even a part of royal merry-making. It was a sport altogether

THE STREET DOG-SELLER.

THE CRIPPLED STREET BIRD-SELLER.
[*From a Daguerreotype by* BEARD.]

congenial to the spirit of Henry VIII.; and when his daughter, then Queen Mary, visited her sister Elizabeth at Hatfield House, now the residence of the Marquess of Salisbury, there was a bear-baiting for their delectation—*after mass*. Queen Elizabeth, on her accession to the throne, seems to have been very partial to the baiting of bears and of bulls; for she not unfrequently welcomed a foreign ambassador with such exhibitions. The historians of the day intimate—they dared do no more—that Elizabeth affected these rough sports the most in the decline of life, when she wished to seem still sprightly, active, and healthful, in the eyes of her courtiers and her subjects. Laneham, whose veracity has not been impeached—though Sir Walter Scott has pronounced him to be as thorough a coxcomb as ever blotted paper—thus describes a bear-bait in presence of the Queen, and after quoting his description I gladly leave the subject. I make the citation in order to show and contrast the former with the present use of sporting dogs.

"It was a sport very pleasant to see the bear, with his pink eyes leering after his enemies, approach; the nimbleness and wait of the dog to take his advantage; and the force and experience of the bear again to avoid his assaults: if he were bitten in one place, how he would pinch in another to get free; that if he were taken once, then by what shift with biting, with clawing, with roaring, with tossing and tumbling, he would work and wind himself from them; and, when he was loose, to shake his ears twice or thrice, with the blood and the slaver hanging about his physiognomy."

The suffering which constituted the great delight of the *sport* was even worse than this, in bull-baiting, for the bull gored or tossed the dogs to death more frequently than the bear worried or crushed them.

The principal place for the carrying on of these barbarities was at Paris Garden, not far from St. Saviour's Church, Southwark. The clamour, and wrangling, and reviling, with and without blows, at these places, gave a proverbial expression to the language. "The place was like a bear-garden," for "gardens" they were called. These pastimes beguiled the *Sunday* afternoons more than any other time, and were among the chief delights of the people, "until," writes Dr. Henry, collating the opinions of the historians of the day, "until the refined amusements of the drama, possessing themselves by degrees of the public taste, if they did not mend the morals of the age, at least forced brutal barbarity to quit the stage."

Of this sport in Queen Anne's days, Strutt's industry has collected advertisements telling of bear and bull-baiting at Hockley-in-the-Hole, and "Tuttle"-fields, Westminster, and of dog-fights at the same places. Marylebone was another locality famous for these pastimes, and for its breed of mastiffs, which dogs were most used for baiting the bears, whilst bull-dogs were the antagonists of the bull. Gay, who was a sufficiently close observer, and a close observer of street-life too, as is well shown in his "Trivia," specifies these localities in one of his fables:—

"Both Hockley-hole and Mary-bone
The combats of my dog have known."

Hockley-hole was not far from Smithfield-market.

In the same localities the practice of these sports lingered, becoming less and less every year, until about the middle of the last century. In the country, bull-baiting was practised twenty times more commonly than bear-baiting; for bulls were plentiful, and bears were not. There are, perhaps, none of our older country towns without the relic of its bull-ring—a strong iron ring inserted into a large stone in the pavement, to which the baited bull was tied; or a knowledge of the site where the bull-ring was. The deeds of the baiting-dogs were long talked of by the vulgar. These sports, and the dog-fights, maintained the great demand for sporting dogs in former times.

The only sporting dogs now in request—apart, of course, from hunting and shooting (remnants of the old barbarous delight in torture or slaughter), for I am treating only of the street-trade, to which fox-hounds, harriers, pointers, setters, cockers, &c., &c., are unknown—are terriers and bull-terriers. Bull-dogs cannot now be classed as sporting, but only as fancy dogs, for they are not good fighters, I was informed, one with another, their mouths being too small.

The way in which the sale of sporting dogs is connected with street-traffic is in this wise: Occasionally a sporting-dog is offered for sale in the streets, and then, of course, the trade is direct. At other times, gentlemen buying or pricing the smaller dogs, ask the cost of a bull-dog, or a bull-terrier or rat-terrier, and the street-seller at once offers to supply them, and either conducts them to a dog-dealer's, with whom he may be commercially connected, and where they can purchase those dogs, or he waits upon them at their residences with some "likely animals." A dog-dealer told me that he hardly knew what made many gentlemen so fond of bull-dogs, and they were "the fonder on 'em the more blackguarder and varmint-looking the creatures was," although now they were useless for sport, and the great praise of a bull-dog, "never flew but at head in his life," was no longer to be given to him, as there were no bulls at whose heads he could now fly.

Another dog-dealer informed me—with what truth as to the judgment concerning horses I do not know, but no doubt with accuracy as to the purchase of the dogs—that Ibrahim Pacha, when in London, thought little of the horses which he saw, but was delighted with the bull-dogs, "and he weren't so werry unlike one in the face hisself," was said at the time by some of the fancy. Ibrahim, it seems, bought two of the finest and largest bull-dogs in London, of Bill George, giving no less than 70*l*. for the twain. The bull-dogs now sold by the street-folk, or through their agency in the way I have described, are from 5*l*. to 25*l*. each. The bull-terriers, of the best blood, are about the same price, or perhaps 10 to 15 per cent. lower, and rarely attaining the tip-top price.

The bull-terriers, as I have stated, are now the chief fighting-dogs, but the patrons of those combats—of those small imitations of the savage tastes of the Roman Colosseum, may deplore the decay of the amusement. From the beginning, until well on to the termination of the last century, it was not uncommon to see announcements of "twenty dogs to fight for a collar," though such advertisements were far more common at the commencement than towards the close of the century. Until within these twelve years, indeed, dog-matches were not unfrequent in London, and the favourite time for the regalement was on Sunday mornings. There were dog-pits in Westminster, and elsewhere, to which the admission was not very easy, for only known persons were allowed to enter. The expense was considerable, the risk of punishment was not a trifle, and it is evident that this Sunday game was *not supported by the poor or working classes.* Now dog-fights are rare. "There's not any public dog-fights," I was told, "and very seldom any in a pit at a public-house, but there's a good deal of it, I know, *at the private houses of the nobs.*" I may observe that "the nobs" is a common designation for the rich among these sporting people.

There are, however, occasionally dog-fights in a sporting-house, and the order of the combat is thus described to me: "We'll say now that it's a scratch fight; two dogs have each their corner of a pit, and they're set to fight. They'll fight on till they go down together, and then if one leave hold, he's sponged. Then they fight again. If a dog has the worst of it he mustn't be picked up, but if he gets into his corner, then he can stay for as long as may be agreed upon, minute or half-minute time, or more than a minute. If a dog won't go to the scratch out of his corner, he loses the fight. If they fight on, why to settle it, one must be killed—though that very seldom happens, for if a dog's very much punished, he creeps to his corner and don't come out to time, and so the fight's settled. Sometimes it's agreed beforehand, that the master of a dog may give in for him; sometimes that isn't to be allowed; but there's next to nothing of this now, unless it's in private among the nobs."

It has been said that a sportsman—perhaps in the relations of life a benevolent man—when he has failed to kill a grouse or pheasant outright, and proceeds to grasp the fluttering and agonised bird and smash its skull against the barrel of his gun, reconciles himself to the sufferings he inflicts by the *pride of art*, the consciousness of skill—he has brought down his bird at a long shot; that, too, when he cares nothing for the possession of the bird. The same feeling hardens him against the most piteous, woman-like cry of the hare, so shot that it cannot run. Be this as it may, it cannot be urged that in matching a favourite dog there can be any such feeling to destroy the sympathy. The men who thus amuse themselves are then utterly insensible to any pang at the infliction of pain upon animals, witnessing the infliction of it merely for a passing excitement: and in this insensibility the whole race who cater to such recreations of the wealthy, as well as the wealthy themselves, participate. There is another feeling too at work, and one proper to the sporting character—every man of this class considers the glories of his horse or his dog his own, a feeling very dear to selfishness.

The main sport now, however, in which dogs are the agents is rat-hunting. It is called hunting, but as the rats are all confined in a pit it is more like mere killing. Of this sport I have given some account under the head of rat-catching. The dogs used are all terriers, and are often the property of the street-sellers. The most accomplished of this terrier race was the famous dog Billy, the eclipse of the rat pit. He is now enshrined—for a stuffed carcase is all that remains of Billy—in a case in the possession of Charley Heslop of the Seven Bells behind St. Giles's Church, with whom Billy lived and died. His great feat was that he killed 100 rats in five minutes. I understand, however, that it is still a moot point in the sporting world, whether Billy did or did not exceed the five minutes by a very few seconds. A merely average terrier will easily kill fifty rats in a pit in eight minutes, but many far exceed such a number. One dealer told me that he would back a terrier bitch which did not weigh 12 lbs. to kill 100 rats in six minutes. The price of these dogs ranges with that of the bull-terriers.

The passion for rat-hunting is evidently on the increase, and seems to have attained the popularity once vouchsafed to cock-fighting. There are now about seventy regular pits in London, besides a few that are run up for temporary purposes. The landlord of a house in the Borough, familiar with these sports, told me that they would soon have to breed rats for a sufficient supply!

But it is not for the encounter with dogs alone, the issue being that so many rats shall be killed in a given time, that these vermin are becoming a trade commodity. Another use for them is announced in the following card:—

A FERRET MATCH.

A Rare Evening's Sport for the Fancy will take place at the

"——————,"

—— STREET, NEW ROAD,

On Tuesday Evening next, May 27.

Mr. ——————

has backed his Ferret against Mr. W. B——'s Ferret to kill 6 Rats each, for 10s. a-side.

He is still open to match his Ferret for £1 to £5 to kill against any other Ferret in London.

Two other Matches with Terriers will come off the same Evening.

Matches take place every —— Evening. Rats always on hand for the accommodation of Gentlemen to try their dogs.

Under the Management of ——————

As a rat-killer, a ferret is not to be compared to a dog; but his use is to kill rats in holes, inaccessible to dogs, or to drive the vermin out of their holes into some open space, where they can be destroyed. Ferrets are worth from 1*l*. to 4*l*. They are not animals of street-sale.

The management of these sports is principally in the hands of the street dog-sellers, as indeed is the dog-trade generally. They are the breeders, dealers, and sellers. They are compelled, as it were, to exhibit their dogs in the streets, that they may attract the attention of the rich, who would not seek them in their homes in the suburbs. The evening business in rat-hunting, &c., for such it is principally, perhaps doubles the incomes I have specified as earned merely by street-*sale*. The amount "turned over" in the trade in sporting-dogs yearly in London, was computed for me by one of the traders at from 12,000*l*. to 15,000*l*. He could not, however, lay down any very precise statistics, as some bull-dogs, bull-terriers, &c., were bred by butchers, tanners, publicans, horse-dealers, and others, and disposed of privately.

In my account of the former condition of the dog-trade, I had to dwell principally on the stealing and restoring of dogs. This is now the least part of the subject. The alteration in the law, consequent upon the parliamentary inquiry, soon wrought a great change, especially the enactment of the 6th Sect. in the Act 8 and 9 Vict. c. 47. "Any person who shall corruptly take any money or reward, directly or indirectly, under pretence or upon account of aiding any person to recover any dog which shall have been stolen, or which shall be in the possession of any person not being the owner thereof, shall be guilty of a misdemeanour, and punishable accordingly."

There may now, I am informed, be half a dozen fellows who make a precarious living by dog-stealing. These men generally keep out of the way of the street dog-sellers, who would not scruple, they assure me, to denounce their practices, as the more security a purchaser feels in the property and possession of a dog, the better it is for the regular business. One of these dog-stealers, dressed like a lime-burner—they generally appear as mechanics—was lately seen to attempt the enticing away of a dog. Any idle good-for-nothing fellow, slinking about the streets, would also, I was informed, seize any stray dog within his reach, and sell it for any trifle he could obtain. One dealer told me that there might still be a little doing in the "restoring" way, and with that way of life were still mixed up names which figured in the parliamentary inquiry, but it was a mere nothing to what it was formerly.

From a man acquainted with the dog business I had the following account. My informant was not at present connected with the dog and rat business, but he seemed to have what is called a "hankering after it." He had been a pot-boy in his youth, and had assisted at the bar of public-houses, and so had acquired a taste for sporting, as some "fancy coves" were among the frequenters of the tap-room and skittle-ground. He had speculated a little in dogs, which a friend reared, and he sold to the public-house customers. "At last I went slap into the dog-trade," he said, "but I did no good at all. There's a way to do it, I dare say, or perhaps you must wait to get known, but then you may starve as you wait. I tried Smithfield first—it's a good bit since, but I can't say how long—and I had a couple of tidy little terriers that we'd bred; I thought I'd begin cheap to turn over money quick, so I asked 12*s*. a-piece for them. O, in course they weren't a werry pure sort. But I couldn't sell at all. If a grazier, or a butcher, or anybody looked at them, and asked their figure, they'd say, 'Twelve shillings! a dog what ain't worth more nor 12*s*. ain't worth a d——n!' I asked one gent a sovereign, but there was a lad near that sung out, 'Why, you only axed 12*s*. a bit since; ain't you a-coming it?' After that, I was glad to get away. I had five dogs when I started, and about 1*l*. 8*s*. 6*d*. in money, and some middling clothes; but my money soon went, for I could do no business, and there was the rent, and then the dogs must be properly fed, or they'd soon show it. At last, when things grew uncommon taper, I almost grudged the poor things their meat and their sop, for they were filling their bellies, and I was an 'ung'ring. I got so seedy, too, that it was no use trying the streets, for any one would think I'd stole the dogs. So I sold them one by one. I think I got about 5*s*. apiece for them, for people took their advantage on me. After that I fasted oft enough. I helped about the pits, and looked out for jobs of any kind, cleaning knives and spittoons at a public-house, and such-like, for a bite and sup. And I sometimes got leave to sit up all night in a stable or any out-house with a live rat trap that I could always borrow, and catch rats to sell to the dealers. If I could get three lively rats in a night, it was good work, for it was as good as 1*s*. to me. I sometimes won a pint, or a tanner, when I could cover it, by betting on a rat-hunt with helpers like myself—but it was only a few places we were let into, just where I was known —'cause I'm a good judge of a dog, you see, and if I had it to try over again, I think I could knock a tidy living out of dog-selling. Yes, I'd like to try well enough, but it's no use trying if you haven't a fairish bit of money. I'd only myself to keep all this time, but that was one too many. I got leave to sleep in hay-lofts, or stables, or anywhere, and I have slept in the park. I don't know how many months I was living this way. I got not to mind it much at last. Then I got to carry out the day and night beers for a potman what had hurt his foot and couldn't walk quick and long enough for supplying his beer, as there was five rounds every day. He lent me an apron and a jacket to be decent. After that I got a potman's situation. No, I'm not much in the dog and rat line now, and don't see much of it, for I've very little opportunity. But I've a very nice Scotch terrier to sell if you should be wanting such a thing, or hear of any of your friends wanting one. It's dirt cheap at 30*s*., just about a year old. Yes, I generally has a dog, and swops and sells. Most masters allows that in a quiet respectable way."

Of the Street-Sellers of Live Birds.

The bird-*sellers* in the streets are also the bird-*catchers* in the fields, plains, heaths, and woods, which still surround the metropolis; and in compliance with established precedent it may be proper that I should give an account of the catching, before I proceed to any further statement of the procedures subsequent thereunto. The bird-catchers are precisely what I have described them in my introductory remarks. An intelligent man, versed in every part of the bird business, and well acquainted with the character of all engaged in it, said they might be represented as of "the fancy," in a small way, and always glad to run after, and full of admiration of, fighting men. The bird-catcher's life is one essentially vagrant; a few gipsies pursue it, and they mix little in street-trades, except as regards tinkering; and the mass, not gipsies, who become bird-catchers, rarely leave it for any other avocation. They "catch" unto old age. During last winter two men died in the parish of Clerkenwell, both turned seventy, and both bird-catchers—a profession they had followed from the age of six.

The mode of catching I will briefly describe. It is principally effected by means of nets. A bird-net is about twelve yards square; it is spread flat upon the ground, to which it is secured by four "stars." These are iron pins, which are inserted in the field, and hold the net, but so that the two "wings," or "flaps," which are indeed the sides of the nets, are not confined by the stars. In the middle of the net is a cage with a fine wire roof, widely worked, containing the "call-bird." This bird is trained to sing loudly and cheerily, great care being bestowed upon its tuition, and its song attracts the wild birds. Sometimes a few stuffed birds are spread about the cage as if a flock were already assembling there. The bird-catcher lies flat and motionless on the ground, 20 or 30 yards distant from the edge of the net. As soon as he considers that a sufficiency of birds have congregated around his decoy, he rapidly draws towards him a line, called the "pull-line," of which he has kept hold. This is so looped and run within the edges of the net, that on being smartly pulled, the two wings of the net collapse and fly together, the stars still keeping their hold, and the net encircles the cage of the call-bird, and incloses in its folds all the wild birds allured round it. In fact it then resembles a great cage of net-work. The captives are secured in cages—the call-bird continuing to sing as if in mockery of their struggles—or in hampers proper for the purpose, which are carried on the man's back to London.

The use of the call-bird as a means of decoy is very ancient. Sometimes—and more especially in the dark, as in the taking of nightingales—the bird-catcher imitates the notes of the birds to be captured. A small instrument has also been used for the purpose, and to this Chaucer, although figuratively, alludes: "So, the birde is begyled with the merry voice of the foulers' whistle, when it is closed in your nette."

Sometimes, in the pride of the season, a bird-catcher engages a costermonger's poney or donkey cart, and perhaps his boy, the better to convey the birds to town. The net and its apparatus cost 1*l*. The call-bird, if he have a good wild note—goldfinches and linnets being principally so used—is worth 10*s*. at the least.

The bird-cather's life has many, and to the constitution of some minds, irresistible charms. There is the excitement of "sport"—not the headlong excitement of the chase, where the blood is stirred by motion and exercise—but still sport surpassing that of the angler, who plies his finest art to capture one fish at a time, while the bird-catcher despises an individual capture, but seeks to ensnare a flock at one twitch of a line. There is, moreover, the attraction of idleness, at least for intervals, and sometimes long intervals—perhaps the great charm of fishing—and basking in the lazy sunshine, to watch the progress of the snares. Birds, however, and more especially linnets, are caught in the winter, when it is not quite such holiday work. A bird-dealer (not a street-seller) told me that the greatest number of birds he had ever heard of as having been caught at one pull was nearly 200. My informant happened to be present on the occasion. "Pulls" of 50, 100, and 150 are not very unfrequent when the young broods are all on the wing.

Of the bird-catchers, including all who reside in Woolwich, Greenwich, Hounslow, Isleworth, Barnet, Uxbridge, and places of similar distance, all working for the London market, there are about 200. The localities where these men "catch," are the neighbourhoods of the places I have mentioned as their residences, and at Holloway, Hampstead, Highgate, Finchley, Battersea, Blackheath, Putney, Mortlake, Chiswick, Richmond, Hampton, Kingston, Eltham, Carshalton, Streatham, the Tootings, Woodford, Epping, Snaresbrook, Walthamstow, Tottenham, Edmonton—wherever, in fine, are open fields, plains, or commons around the metropolis.

I will first enumerate the several birds sold in the streets, as well as the supply to the shops by the bird-catchers. I have had recourse to the best sources of information. Of the number of birds which I shall specify as "supplied," or "caught," it must be remembered that a not-very-small proportion die before they can be trained to song, or inured to a cage life. I shall also give the street prices. All the birds are caught by the nets with call-birds, excepting such as I shall notice. I take the singing birds first.

The *Linnet* is the cheapest and among the most numerous of what may be called the London-caught birds, for it is caught in the nearer suburbs, such as Holloway. The linnet, however,—the brown linnet being the species—is not easily reared, and for some time ill brooks confinement. About one-half of those birds die after having been caged a few days. The other evening a bird-catcher supplied 26 fine linnets to a shopkeeper in Pentonville, and next morning ten were dead. But in some of those bird shops, and bird chambers connected with the shops, the heat at the time the new broods are caught and caged, is excessive; and the atmosphere, from the crowded and compulsory fellowship of pigeons, and all descriptions of small birds, with white rats, hedgehogs, guinea-pigs, and other creatures, is often very foul; so that the wonder is, not that so many die, but that so many survive.

Some bird-connoisseurs prefer the note of the linnet to that of the canary, but this is far from a general preference. The young birds are sold in the streets at 3*d*. and 4*d*. each; the older birds, which are accustomed to sing in their cages, from 1*s*. to 2*s*. 6*d*. The "catch" of linnets—none being imported—may be estimated, for London alone, at 70,000 yearly. The mortality I have mentioned is confined chiefly to that year's brood. One-tenth of the catch is sold in the streets. Of the quality of the street-sold birds I shall speak hereafter.

The *Bullfinch*, which is bold, familiar, docile, and easily attached, is a favourite cage-bird among the Londoners; I speak of course as regards the body of the people. It is as readily sold in the streets as any other singing bird. Piping bullfinches are also a part of street-trade, but only to a small extent, and with bird-sellers who can carry them from their street pitches, or call on their rounds, at places where they are known, to exhibit the powers of the bird. The piping is taught to these finches when very young, and they must be brought up by their tutor, and be familiar with him. When little more than two months old, they begin to whistle, and then their training as pipers must commence. This tuition, among professional bullfinch-trainers, is systematic. They have schools of birds, and teach in bird-classes of from four to seven members in each, six being a frequent number. These classes, when their education commences, are kept unfed for a longer time than they have been accustomed to, and they are placed in a darkened room. The bird is wakeful and attentive from the want of his food, and the tune he is to learn is played several times on an instrument made for the purpose, and known as a bird-organ, its notes resembling those of the bullfinch. For an hour or two the young pupils mope silently, but they gradually begin to imitate the notes of the music played to them. When one commences—and he is looked upon as the most likely to make a good piper—the others soon follow his example. The light is then admitted and a portion of food, but not a full meal, is given to the birds. Thus, by degrees, by the playing on the bird-organ (a flute is sometimes used), by the admission of light, which is always agreeable to the finch, and by the reward of more and more, and sometimes more relishable food, the pupil "practises" the notes he hears continuously. The birds are then given into the care of boys, who attend to them without intermission in a similar way, their original teacher still overlooking, praising, or rating his scholars, till they acquire a tune which they pipe as long as they live. It is said, however, that only five per cent. of the number taught pipe in *perfect* harmony. The bullfinch is often pettish in his piping, and will in many instances not pipe at all, unless in the presence of some one who feeds it, or to whom it has become attached.

The system of training I have described is that practised by the Germans, who have for many years supplied this country with the best piping bullfinches. Some of the dealers will undertake to procure English-taught bullfinches which will pipe as well as the foreigners, but I am told that this is a prejudice, if not a trick, of trade. The mode of teaching in this country, by barbers, weavers, and bird-fanciers generally, who seek for a profit from their pains-taking, is somewhat similar to that which I have detailed, but with far less elaborateness. The price of a piping bullfinch is about three guineas. These pipers are also reared and taught in Leicestershire and Norfolk, and sent to London, as are the singing bullfinches which do not "pipe."

The bullfinches netted near London are caught more numerously about Hounslow than elsewhere. In hard winters they are abundant in the outskirts of the metropolis. The yearly supply, including those sent from Norfolk, &c., is about 30,000. The bullfinch is "hearty compared to the linnet," I was told, but of the amount which are the objects of trade, not more than two-thirds live many weeks. The price of a good young bullfinch is 2*s*. 6*d*. and 3*s*. They are often sold in the streets for 1*s*. The hawking or street trade comprises about a tenth of the whole.

The sale of piping bullfinches is, of course, small, as only the rich can afford to buy them. A dealer estimated it at about 400 yearly.

The *Goldfinch* is also in demand by street customers, and is a favourite from its liveliness, beauty, and sometimes sagacity. It is, moreover, the longest lived of our caged small birds, and will frequently live to the age of fifteen or sixteen years. A goldfinch has been known to exist twenty-three years in a cage. Small birds, generally, rarely live more than nine years. This finch is also in demand because it most readily of any bird pairs with the canary, the produce being known as a "mule," which, from its prettiness and powers of song, is often highly valued.

Goldfinches are sold in the streets at from 6*d*. to 1*s*. each, and when there is an extra catch, and they are nearly all caught about London, and the shops are fully stocked, at 3*d*. and 4*d*. each. The yearly catch is about the same as that of the linnet, or 70,000, the mortality being perhaps 30 per cent. If any one casts his eye over the stock of hopping, chirping little creatures in the window of a bird-shop, or in the close array of small cages hung outside, or at the stock of a street-seller, he will be struck by the preponderating number of goldfinches. No doubt the dealer, like any other shopkeeper, dresses his window to the best advantage, putting forward his smartest and prettiest birds. The demand for the goldfinch, especially among women, is steady and regular. The street-sale is a tenth of the whole.

The *Chaffinch* is in less request than either of its congeners, the bullfinch or the goldfinch, but the catch is about half that of the bullfinch, and with the same rate of mortality. The prices are also the same.

Greenfinches (called *green birds*, or sometimes *green linnets*, in the streets) are in still smaller request than are chaffinches, and that to about one-half. Even this smaller stock is little saleable, as the bird is regarded as "only a middling singer." They are sold in the open air, at 2*d*. and 3*d*. each, but a good "green bird" is worth 2*s*. 6*d*.

Larks are of good sale and regular supply, being perhaps more readily caught than other birds, as in winter they congregate in large quantities. It may be thought, to witness the restless throwing up of the head of the caged sky-lark, as if he were longing for a soar in the air, that he was very impatient of restraint. This does not appear to be so much the fact, as the lark adapts himself to the poor confines of his prison—poor indeed for a bird who soars higher and longer than any of his class—more rapidly than other wild birds, like the linnet, &c. The mortality of larks, however, approaches one-third.

The yearly "take" of larks is 60,000. This includes sky-larks, wood-larks, tit-larks, and mud-larks. The sky-lark is in far better demand than any of the others for his "stoutness of song," but some prefer the tit-lark, from the very absence of such stoutness. "Fresh-catched" larks are vended in the streets at 6*d*. and 8*d*., but a seasoned bird is worth 2*s*. 6*d*. One-tenth is the street-sale.

The larks for the supply of fashionable tables are never provided by the London bird-catchers, who catch only "singing larks," for the shop and street-traffic. The edible larks used to be highly esteemed in pies, but they are now generally roasted for consumption. They are principally the produce of Cambridgeshire, with some from Bedfordshire, and are sent direct (killed) to Leadenhall-market, where about 215,000 are sold yearly, being nearly two-thirds of the gross London consumption.

It is only within these twelve or fifteen years that the London dealers have cared to trade to any extent in *Nightingales*, but they are now a part of the stock of every bird-shop of the more flourishing class. Before that they were merely exceptional as cage-birds. As it is, the "domestication," if the word be allowable with reference to the nightingale, is but partial. Like all migratory birds, when the season for migration approaches, the caged nightingale shows symptoms of great uneasiness, dashing himself against the wires of his cage or his aviary, and sometimes dying in a few days. Many of the nightingales, however, let the season pass away without showing any consciousness that it was, with the race of birds to which they belonged, one for a change of place. To induce the nightingale to sing in the daylight, a paper cover is often placed over the cage, which may be gradually and gradually withdrawn until it can be dispensed with. This is to induce the appearance of twilight or night. On the subject of this night-singing, however, I will cite a short passage.

" The Nightingale is usually supposed to withhold his notes till the sun has set, and then to be the only songster left. This is, however, not quite true, for he sings in the day, often as sweetly and as powerfully as at night; but amidst the general chorus of other singing birds, his efforts are little noticed. Neither is he by any means the only feathered musician of the night. The Wood-lark will, to a very late hour, pour forth its rich notes, flying in circles round the female, when sitting on her nest. The Sky-lark, too, may frequently be heard till near midnight high in the air, soaring as if in the brightness of a summer's morning. Again we have listened with pleasure long after dark to the warblings of a Thrush, and been awakened at two in the morning by its sweet serenade." It appears, however, that this night-singing, as regards England, is on fine summer nights when the darkness is never very dense. In far northern climates larks sing all night.

I am inclined to believe that the mortality among nightingales, before they are reconciled to their new life, is higher than that of any other bird, and much exceeding one-half. The dealers may be unwilling to admit this; but such mortality is, I have been assured on good authority, the case; besides that, the habits of the nightingale unfit him for a cage existence.

The capture of the nightingale is among the most difficult achievements of the profession. None are caught nearer than Epping, and the catchers travel considerable distances before they have a chance of success. These birds are caught at night, and more often by their captor's imitation of the nightingale's note, than with the aid of the call-bird. Perhaps 1000 nightingales are reared yearly in London, of which three-fourths may be, more or less, songsters. The inferior birds are sold at about 2*s*. each, the street-sale not reaching 100, but the birds, "caged and singing," are worth 1*l*. each, when of the best; and 10*s*. 12*s*. and 15*s*. each when approaching the best. The mortality I have estimated.

Redbreasts are a portion of the street-sold birds, but the catch is not large, not exceeding 3000, with a mortality of about a third. Even this number, small as it is, when compared with the numbers of other singing birds sold, is got rid of with difficulty. There is a popular feeling repugnant to the imprisonment, or coercion in any way, of "a robin," and this, no doubt has its influence in moderating the demand. The redbreast is sold, when young, both in the shops and streets for 1*s*., when caged and singing, sometimes for 1*l*. These birds are considered to sing best by candlelight. The street-sale is a fifth, or sometimes a quarter, all young birds, or with the rarest exceptions.

The *Thrush, Throstle*, or (in Scottish poetry) *Mavis*, is of good sale. It is reared by hand, for the London market, in many of the villages and small towns at no great distance, the nests being robbed of the young, wherever they can be found. The nestling food of the infant thrush is grubs, worms, and snails, with an occasional moth or butterfly. On this kind of diet the young thrushes are reared until they are old enough for sale to the shopkeeper, or to any private patron. Thrushes are also netted, but those reared by hand are much the best, as such a rearing disposes the bird the more to enjoy his cage life, as he has never experienced the delights of the free hedges and thickets. This process the catchers call "rising" from the nest. A throstle thus "rose" soon becomes familiar with his owner—always supposing that he be properly fed and his cage duly cleaned, for all birds detest dirt—and among the working-men of England no bird is a greater favourite than the thrush; indeed few other birds are held in such liking by the artisan class. About a fourth of the thrushes supplied to the metropolitan traders have been thus "rose," and as they must be sufficiently grown before they will be received by the dealers, the mortality among them, when once able to feed themselves, in their wicker-work cages, is but small. Perhaps somewhere about a fourth perish in this hand-rearing, and some men, the aristocrats of the trade, let a number go when they have ascertained that they are hens, as these men exert themselves to bring up thrushes to sing well, and then they command good prices. Often enough, however, the hens are sold cheap in the streets. Among the catch supplied by netting, there is a mortality of perhaps more than a third. The whole take is about 35,000. Of the sale the streets have a tenth proportion. The prices run from 2s. 6d. and 3s. for the "fresh-caught," and 10s., 1l., and as much as 2l. for a seasoned throstle in high song. Indeed I may observe that for any singing bird, which is considered greatly to excel its mates, a high price is obtainable.

Blackbirds appear to be less prized in London than thrushes, for, though with a mellower note, the blackbird is not so free a singer in captivity. They are "rose" and netted in the same manner as the thrush, but the supply is less by one-fifth. The prices, mortality, street-sale, &c., are in the same ratio.

The street-sale of *Canaries* is not large; not so large, I am assured by men in the trade, as it was six or seven years ago, more especially as regarded the higher-priced birds of this open-air traffic. Canaries are now never brought from the group of islands, thirteen in number, situate in the North Atlantic and near the African coast, and from which they derive their name. To these islands and to these alone (as far as is known to ornithologists) are they indigenous. The canary is a slow flyer and soon wearied; this is one reason no doubt for its not migrating. This delightful songster was first brought into England in the reign of Elizabeth, at the era when so many foreign luxuries (as they were then considered, and stigmatised accordingly) were introduced; of these were potatoes, tobacco, turkeys, nectarines, and canaries. I have seen no account of what was the cost of a canary-bird when first imported, but there is no doubt that they were very dear, as they were found only in the abodes of the wealthy. This bird-trade seems, moreover, to have been so profitable to the Spaniards, then and now the possessors of the isles, that a government order for the killing or setting at liberty of all hen canaries, caught with the males, was issued in order that the breed might be confined to its native country; a decree not attended with successful results as regards the intention of the then ruling powers.

The foreign supply to this country is now principally from Holland and Germany, where canaries are reared in great numbers, with that care which the Dutch in especial bestow upon everything on which money-making depends, and whence they are sent or brought over in the spring of every year, when from nine to twelve months old. Thirty years ago, the Tyrolese were the principal breeders and purveyors of canaries for the London market. From about the era of the peace of 1814, on the first abdication of Napoleon, for ten or twelve years they brought over about 2000 birds yearly. They travelled the whole way on foot, carrying the birds in cages on their backs, until they reached whatever port in France or the Netherlands (as Belgium then was) they might be bound for. The price of a canary of an average quality was then from 5s. to 8s. 6d., and a fair proportion were street-sold. At that period, I was told, the principal open-air sale for canaries (and it is only of that I now write) was in Whitechapel and Bethnal-green. All who are familiar with those localities may smile to think that the birds chirping and singing in these especially urban places, were bred for such street-traffic in the valleys of the Rhætian Alps! I presume that it was the greater rapidity of communication, and the consequent diminished cost of carriage, between England, Holland, and Germany, that caused the Tyrolese to abandon the trade as one unremunerative—even to men who will live on bread, onions, and water.

I have, perhaps, dwelt somewhat at length on this portion of the subject, but it is the most curious portion of all, for the canary is the only one of all our singing-birds which is *solely* a household thing. Linnets, finches, larks, nightingales, thrushes, and blackbirds, are all free denizens of the open air, as well as prisoners in our rooms, but the canary with us is unknown in a wild state. "Though not very handy," wrote, in 1848, a very observant naturalist, the late Dr. Stanley, Bishop of Norwich, "canaries might possibly be naturalized in our country, by putting their eggs in the nests of sparrows, chaffinches, or other similar birds. The experiment has been partially tried in Berkshire, where a person for years kept them in an exposed aviary out of doors, and where they seemed to suffer no inconvenience from the severest weather."

The breeding of canaries in this country for the London supply has greatly increased. They are bred in Leicester and Norwich, weavers being generally fond of birds. In London itself, also, they are bred to a greater extent than used to be the case, barbers being among the most assiduous rearers of the canary. A dealer who trades in both foreign and home-bred birds thought that the supply from the country, and from the Continent, was about the same, 8000 to 9000 each, not including what were sold by the barbers, who are regarded as "fanciers," not to say interlopers, by the dealers. No species of birds are ever bred by the shop-dealers. The price of a brisk canary is 5s. or 6s.; but they are sold in the streets as low as 1s. each, a small cage worth 6d. being sometimes included. These, however, are hens. As in the life of a canary there is no transition from freedom to enthralment, for they are in a cage in the egg, and all their lives afterwards, they are subject to a far lower rate of mortality than other street-sold birds. A sixteenth of the number above stated as forming the gross supply are sold in the streets.

The foregoing enumeration includes all the singing-birds of street-traffic and street-folk's supply. The trade I have thus sketched is certainly one highly curious. We find that there is round London a perfect belt of men, employed from the first blush of a summer's dawn, through the heats of noon, in many instances during the night, and in the chills of winter; and all labouring to give to city-pent men of humble means one of the peculiar pleasures of the country—the song of the birds. It must not be supposed that I would intimate that the bird-catcher's life, as regards his field and wood pursuits, is one of hardship. On the contrary, it seems to me to be the very one which, perhaps unsuspected by himself, is best suited to his tastes and inclinations. Nor can we think similar pursuits partake much of hardship when we find independent men follow them for mere sport, to be rid of lassitude.

But the detail of the birds captured for the Londoners by no means ends here. I have yet to describe those which are not songsters, and which are a staple of street-traffic to a greater degree than birds of song. Of these my notice may be brief.

The trade in *Sparrows* is almost exclusively a street-trade and, numerically considered, not an inconsiderable one. They are netted in quantities in every open place near London, and in many places in London. It is common enough for a bird-catcher to obtain leave to catch sparrows in a wood-yard, a brick-field, or places where is an open space certain to be frequented by these bold and familiar birds. The sparrows are sold in the streets generally at 1d. each, sometimes halfpenny, and sometimes 1½d., and for no purpose of enjoyment (as in the case of the cheap song birds), but merely as playthings for children; in other words, for creatures wilfully or ignorantly to be tortured. Strings are tied to their legs and so they have a certain degree of freedom, but when they offer to fly away they are checked, and kept fluttering in the air as a child will flutter a kite. One man told me that he had sometimes sold as many as 200 sparrows in the back streets about Smithfield on a fine Sunday. These birds are not kept in cages, and so they can only be bought for a plaything. They oft enough escape from their persecutors.

But it is not merely for the sport of children that sparrows are purveyed, but for that of grown men, or—as Charles Lamb, if I remember rightly, qualifies it, when he draws a Pentonville sportsman with a little shrubbery for his preserve—for grown cockneys. The birds for adult recreation are shot in sparrow-matches; the gentleman slaughtering the most being, of course, the hero of a sparrow " *battue.*" One dealer told me that he had frequently supplied dozens of sparrows for these matches, at 2s. the dozen, but they were required to be fine bold birds! One dealer thought that during the summer months there were as many sparrows caught close to and within London as there were goldfinches in the less urban districts. These birds are sold direct from the hands of the catcher, so that it is less easy to arrive at statistics than when there is the intervention of dealers who know the extent of the trade carried on. I was told by several, who had no desire to exaggerate, that to estimate this sparrow-sale at 10,000 yearly, sold to children and idlers in the streets, was too low, but at that estimate, the outlay, at 1d. a sparrow, would be 850l. The adult sportsmen may slaughter half that number yearly in addition. The sporting sparrows are derived from the shopkeepers, who, when they receive the order, instruct the catchers to go to work.

Starlings used to be sold in very great quantities in the streets, but the trade is now but the shadow of its former state. The starling, too, is far less numerous than it was, and has lost much of its popularity. It is now seldom seen in flocks of more than 40, and it is rare to see a flock at all, although these birds at one period mustered in congregations of hundreds and even thousands. Ruins, and the roofs of ancient houses and barns—for they love the old and decaying buildings—were once covered with them. The starling was moreover the poor man's and the peasant's parrot. He was taught to speak, and sometimes to swear. But now the starling, save as regards his own note, is mute. He is seldom tamed or domesticated and taught tricks. It is true starlings may be seen carried on sticks in the street as if the tamest of the tame, but they are " braced." Tapes are passed round their bodies, and so managed that the bird cannot escape from the stick, while his fetters are concealed by his feathers, the street-seller of course objecting to allow his birds to be handled.

Starlings are caught chiefly Ilford way, I was told, and about Turnham-green. Some are " rose" from the nest. The price is from 9d. to 2s. each. About 3000 are sold annually, half in the streets. After having been braced, or ill-used, the starling, if kept as a solitary bird, will often mope and die.

Jackdaws and *Magpies* are in less demand than might be expected from their vivacity. Many of the other birds are supplied the year round, but daws and pies for only about two months, from the middle of June to the middle of August. The price is from 6d. to 1s. and about 1000 are thus disposed of, in equal quantities, one-half in the streets. These birds are for the most part reared from the nest, but little pains appear to be taken with them.

The *Redpole* is rather a favourite bird among street-buyers, especially where children are allowed to choose birds from a stock. I am told that they most frequently select a goldfinch or a redpole. These birds are supplied for about two months. About 800 or 1000 is the extent of the take. The mortality and prices are the same as with the goldfinch, but a goldfinch in high song is worth twice as much as the best redpole. About a third of the sale of the redpole is in the streets.

There are also 150 or 200 *Black-caps* sold annually in the open air, at from 3*d*. to 5*d*. each.

These are the chief birds, then, that constitute the trade of the streets, with the addition of an occasional yellow-hammer, wren, jay, or even cuckoo. They also, with the addition of pigeons, form the stock of the bird-shops.

I have shown the number of birds caught, the number which survive for sale, and the cost; and, as usual, under the head of "Statistics," will be shown the whole annual expenditure. This, however, is but a portion of the London outlay on birds. There is, in addition, the cost of their cages and of their daily food. The commonest and smallest cage costs 6*d*., a frequent price being 1*s*. A thrush's basket-cage cannot be bought, unless rubbish, under 2*s*. 6*d*. I have previously shown the amount paid for the green food of birds, and for their turfs, &c., for these are all branches of street-commerce. Of their other food, such as rape and canary-seed, German paste, chopped eggs, biscuit, &c., I need but intimate the extent by showing what birds will consume, as it is not a portion of street-trade.

A goldfinch, it has been proved by experimentalising ornithologists, will consume 90 grains, in weight, of canary-seed in 24 hours. A greenfinch, for whose use 80 grains of wheat were weighed out, ate 79 of them in 24 hours; and, on another occasion ate, in the same space of time, 100 grains of a paste of eggs and flour. Sixteen canaries consumed 100 grains' weight of food, each bird, in 24 hours. The amount of provision thus eaten was about one-sixth of the full weight of the bird's body, or an equivalent, were a man to swallow victuals in the same proportion, of 25 lbs. in 24 hours. I may remark, moreover, that the destruction of caterpillars, insects, worms, &c., by the small birds, is enormous, especially during the infancy of their nestlings. A pair of sparrows fed their brood 36 times an hour for 14 hours of a long spring day, and, it was calculated, administered to them in one week 3400 caterpillars. A pair of chaffinches, also, carried nearly as great a number of caterpillars for the maintenance of their young.

The singing-birds sold in the street are offered either singly in small cages, when the cage is sold with the bird, or they are displayed in a little flock in a long cage, the buyer selecting any he prefers. They always appear lively in the streets, or indeed a sale would be hopeless, for no one would buy a dull or sick bird. The captives are seen to hop and heard to chirp, but they are not often heard to sing when thus offered to the public, and it requires some little attention to judge what is but an impatient flutter, and what is the fruit of mere hilarity.

The places where the street-sellers more especially offer their birds are:—Smithfield, Clerkenwell-green, Lisson-grove, the City and New roads, Shepherdess-walk, Old Street-road, Shoreditch, Spitalfields, Whitechapel, Tower-hill, Ratcliffe-highway, Commercial-road East, Poplar, Billingsgate, Westminster Broadway, Covent-garden, Blackfriars-road, Bermondsey (mostly about Dockhead), and in the neighbourhood of the Borough Market. The street-sellers are also itinerant, carrying the birds in cages, holding them up to tempt the notice of people whom they see at the windows, or calling at the houses. The sale used to be very considerable in the "Cut" and Lambeth-walk. Sometimes the cages with their inmates are fastened to any contiguous rail; sometimes they are placed on a bench or stall; and occasionally in cages on the ground.

To say nothing, in this place, of the rogueries of the bird-trade, I will proceed to show how the street-sold birds are frequently inferior to those in the shops. The catcher, as I have stated, is also the street-seller. He may reach the Dials, or whatever quarter the dealer he supplies may reside in, with perhaps 30 linnets and as many goldfinches. The dealer selects 24 of each, refusing the remaining dozen, on account of their being hens, or hurt, or weakly birds. The man then resorts to the street to effect a sale of that dozen, and thus the streets have the refuse of the shops. On the other hand, however, when the season is at its height, and the take of birds is the largest, as at this time of year, the shops are "stocked." The cages and recesses are full, and the dealer's anxiety is to sell before he purchases more birds. The catchers proceed in their avocation; they must dispose of their stock; the shopkeeper will not buy "at any figure," and so the streets are again resorted to, and in this way fine birds are often sold very cheap. Both these liabilities prevail the year through, but most in the summer, and keep up a sort of poise; but I apprehend that the majority, perhaps the great majority, of the street-sold birds, are of an inferior sort, but then the price is much lower. On occasions when the bird-trade is overdone, the catchers will sell a few squirrels, or gather snails for the shops.

The buyers of singing-birds are eminently the working people, along with the class of tradesmen whose means and disposition are of the same character as those of the artisan. Grooms and coachmen are frequently fond of birds; many are kept in the several mews, and often the larger singing-birds, such as blackbirds and thrushes. The fondness of a whole body of artificers for any particular bird, animal, or flower, is remarkable. No better instance need be cited than that of the Spitalfields weavers. In the days of their prosperity they were the cultivators of choice tulips, afterwards, though not in so full a degree, of dahlias, and their pigeons were the best "fliers" in England. These things were accomplished with little cost, comparatively, for the weavers were engaged in tasks, grateful and natural to their tastes and habitudes; and what was expense in the garden or aviary of the rich, was an exercise of skill and industry on the part of the silk-weaver. The humanising and even refining influence of such pursuits is very great, and as regards these pure pleasures it is not seldom that the refinement which can appreciate them has proceeded not to but *from* the artisans. The operatives have often been in the van of those who have led the public taste from delighting in the cruelty and barbarity of bear and bull-baiting and of cock-fighting—among the worst of all possible schools, and very influential those schools were—to the delight in some of the most beautiful works of nature. It is easy to picture the difference of mood between a man going home from a dog-fight at night, or going home from a visit to his flowers, or from an examination to satisfy himself that his birds were "all right." The families of the two men felt the difference. Many of the rich appear to remain mere savages in their tastes and sports. Battues, lion and hippopotamus hunting, &c.,—all are mere civilized barbarisms. When shall we learn, as Wordsworth says,

"Never to blend our pleasure or our pride
With sorrow of the meanest thing that feels."

But the change in Spitalfields is great. Since the prevalence of low wages the weaver's garden has disappeared, and his pigeon-cote, even if its timbers have not rotted away, is no longer stocked with carriers, dragoons, horsemen, jacobins, monks, poulters, turtles, tumblers, fantails, and the many varieties of what is in itself a variety—the fancy-pigeon. A thrush, or a linnet, may still sing to the clatter of the loom, but that is all. The culture of the tulip, the dahlia, and (sometimes) of the fuchsia, was attended, as I have said, with small cost, still it *was* cost, and the weaver, as wages grew lower, could not afford either the outlay or the loss of time. To cultivate flowers, or rear doves, so as to make them a means of subsistence, requires a man's whole time, and to such things the Spitalfields man did not devote his time, but his leisure.

The readers who have perused this work from its first appearance will have noticed how frequently I have had to comment on the always realized indication of good conduct, and of a superior taste and generally a superior intelligence, when I have found the rooms of working people contain flowers and birds. I could adduce many instances. I have seen and heard birds in the rooms of tailors, shoemakers, coopers, cabinet-makers, hatters, dressmakers, curriers, and street-sellers,—all people of the best class. One of the most striking, indeed, was the room of a street-confectioner. His family attended to the sale of the sweets, and he was greatly occupied at home in their manufacture, and worked away at his peppermint-rock, in the very heart of one of the thickliest populated parts of London, surrounded by the song of thrushes, linnets, and gold-finches, all kept, not for profit, but because he "loved" to have them about him. I have seldom met a man who impressed me more favourably.

The flowers in the room are more attributable to the superintending taste of a wife or daughter, and are found in the apartments of the same class of people.

There is a marked difference between the buyers or keepers of birds and of dogs in the working classes, especially when the dog is of a sporting or "varmint" sort. Such a dog-keeper is often abroad and so his home becomes neglected; he is interested about rat-hunts, knows the odds on or against the dog's chance to dispatch his rats in the time allotted, loses much time and customers, his employers grumbling that the work is so slowly executed, and so custom or work falls off. The bird-lover, on the other hand, is generally a more domestic, and, perhaps consequently, a more prosperous and contented man. It is curious to mark the refining qualities of particular trades. I do not remember seeing a bull-dog in the possession of any of the Spitalfields silk-weavers: with them all was flowers and birds. The same I observed with the tailors and other kindred occupations. With slaughterers, however, and drovers, and Billingsgatemen, and coachmen, and cabmen, whose callings naturally tend to blunt the sympathy with suffering, the gentler tastes are comparatively unknown. The dogs are almost all of the "varmint" kind, kept either for rat-killing, fighting, or else for their ugliness. For "pet" or "fancy" dogs they have no feeling, and in singing birds they find little or no delight.

Of the Bird-Catchers who are Street-Sellers.

The street-sellers of birds are called by themselves "hawkers," and sometimes "bird hawkers."

Among the bird-catchers I did not hear of any very prominent characters at present, three of the best known and most prominent having died within these ten months. I found among all I saw the vagrant characteristics I have mentioned, and often united with a quietness of speech and manner which might surprise those who do not know that any pursuit which entails frequent silence, watchfulness, and solitude, forms such manners. Perhaps the man most talked of by his fellow-labourers, was Old Gilham, who died lately. Gilham was his real name, for among the bird-catchers there is not that prevalence of nicknames which I found among the costermongers and patterers. One reason no doubt is, that these bird-folk do not meet regularly in the markets. It is rarely, however, that they know each other's surnames, Old Gilham being an exception. It is Old Tom, or Young Mick, or Jack, or Dick, among them. I heard of no John or Richard.

For 60 years, almost without intermission, Old Gilham caught birds. I am assured that to state that his "catch" during this long period averaged 100 a week, hens included, is within the mark, for he was a most indefatigable man; even at that computation, however, he would have been the captor, in his lifetime, of three hundred and twelve thousand birds! A bird-catcher who used sometimes to start in the morning with Old Gilham, and walk with him until their roads diverged, told me that of late years the old man's talk was a good deal of where he had captured his birds in the old times: 'Why, Ned,' he would say to me, proceeded his companion, 'I've caught goldfinches in lots at Chalk Farm, and all where there's that railway smoke and noise just by the hill (Primrose Hill). I can't think where they'll drive all the birds to by and bye. I dare say the first time the birds saw a railway with its smoke, and noise to frighten them, and all the fire too, they just thought it was the devil was come.' He wasn't a fool, wasn't old Gilham, sir. 'Why,' he'd go on for to say, 'I've laid many a day at Ball's Pond there, where it's nothing but a lot of houses now, and catched hundreds of birds. And I've catched them where there's all them grand squares Pimlico way, and in Britannia Fields, and at White Condic. What with all these buildings, and them barbers, I don't know what the bird-trade'll come to. It's hard for a poor man to have to go to Finchley for birds that he could have catched at Holloway once, but people never thinks of that. When I were young I could make three times as much as I do now. I've got a pound for a good sound chaffinch as I brought up myself.' Ah, poor old Gilham, sir; I wish you could have seen him, he'd have told you of some queer changes in his time."

A shopkeeper informed me that a bird-catcher had talked to him of even "queerer" changes. This man died eight or ten years ago at an advanced age, but beyond the fact of his offering birds occasionally at my informant's shop, where he was known merely as "the old man," he could tell me nothing of the ancient bird-catcher, except that he was very fond of a talk, and used to tell how he had catched birds between fifty and sixty years, and had often, when a lad, catched them where many a dock in London now stands. "Where there's many a big ship now in deep water, I've catched flocks of birds. I never catched birds to be sure at them docks," he would add, "as was dug out of the houses. Why, master, you'll remember their pulling down St. Katherine's Church, and all them rummy streets the t'other side of the Tower, for a dock." As I find that the first dock constructed on the north side of the Thames, the West India dock, was not commenced until the year 1800, there seems no reason to discredit the bird-catcher's statement. Among other classes of street-sellers I have had to remark the little observation they extended to the changes all around, such as the extension of street-traffic to miles and miles of suburbs, unknown till recently. Two thousand miles of houses have been built in London within the last 20 years. But with the bird-catchers this want of observance is not so marked. Of necessity they must notice the changes which have added to the fatigues and difficulties of their calling, by compelling them, literally, to "go further a-field."

A young man, rather tall, and evidently active, but very thin, gave me the following account. His manners were quiet and his voice low. His dress could not so well be called mean as hard worn, with the unmistakable look of much of the attire of his class, that it was not made for the wearer; his surtout, for instance, which was fastened in front by two buttons, reached down to his ancles, and could have inclosed a bigger man. He resided in St. Luke's, in which parish there are more bird-catchers living than in any other. The furniture of his room was very simple. A heavy old sofa, in the well of which was a bed, a table, two chairs, a fender, a small closet containing a few pots and tins, and some twenty empty bird-cages of different sizes hung against the walls. In a sort of wooden loft, which had originally been constructed, he believed, for the breeding of fancy-pigeons, and which was erected on the roof, were about a dozen or two of cages, some old and broken, and in them a few live goldfinches, which hopped about very merrily. They were all this year's birds, and my informant, who had "a little connection of his own," was rearing them in hopes they would turn out good specs, quite "birds beyond the run of the streets." The place and the cages, each bird having its own little cage, were very clean, but at the time of my visit the loft was exceedingly hot, as the day was one of the sultriest. Lest this heat should prove too great for the finches, the timbers on all sides were well wetted and re-wetted at intervals, for about an hour at noon, at which time only was the sun full on the loft.

"I shall soon have more birds, sir," he said, "but you see I only put aside here such as are the very best of the take; all cocks, of course. O, I've been in the trade all my life; I've had a turn at other things, certainly, but this life suits me best, I think, because I have my health best in it. My father—he's been dead a goodish bit —was a bird-catcher as well, and he used to take me out with him as soon as I was strong enough; when I was about ten, I suppose. I don't remember my mother. Father was brought up to brick-making. I believe that most of the bird-catchers that have been trades, and that's not half a quarter perhaps, were brick-makers, or something that way. Well, I don't know the reason. The brick-making was, in my father's young days, carried on more in the country, and the bird-catchers used to fall in with the brick-makers, and so perhaps that led to it. I've heard my father tell of an old soldier that had been discharged with a pension being the luckiest bird-catcher he knowed. The soldier was a catcher before he first listed, and he listed drunk. I once —yes, sir, I dare say that's fifteen year back, for I was quite a lad—walked with my father and captain" (the pensioner's sobriquet) "till they parted for work, and I remember very well I heard him tell how, when on march in Portingal—I think that's what he called it, but it's in foreign parts—he saw flocks of birds; he wished he could be after catching them, for he was well tired of sogering. I was sent to school twice or thrice, and can read a little and write a little; and I should like reading better if I could manage it better. I read a penny number, or the 'police' in a newspaper, now and then, but very seldom. But on a fine day I hated being at school. I wanted to be at work, to make something at bird-catching. If a boy can make money, why shouldn't he? And if I'd had a net, or cage, and a mule of my own, then, I thought, I could make money." [I may observe that the mule longed for by my informant was a "cross" between two birds, and was wanted for the decoy. Some bird-catchers contend that a mule makes the best call-bird of any; others that the natural note of a linnet, for instance, was more alluring than the song of a mule between a linnet and a goldfinch. One birdman told me that the excellence of a mule was, that it had been bred and taught by its master, had never been at large, and was "better to manage;" it was bolder, too, in a cage, and its notes were often loud and ringing, and might be heard to a considerable distance.]

"I couldn't stick to school, sir," my informant continued, "and I don't know why, lest it be that one man's best suited for one business, and another for another. That may be seen every day. I was sent on trial to a shoemaker, and after that to a ropemaker, for father didn't seem to like my growing up and being a bird-catcher, like he was. But I never felt well, and knew I should never be any great hand at them trades, and so when my poor father went off rather sudden, I took to the catching at once and had all his traps. Perhaps, but I can't say to a niceness, that was eleven year back. Do I like the business, do you say, sir? Well, I'm forced to like it, for I've no other to live by." [The reader will have remarked how this man attributed the course he pursued, evidently from natural inclination, to its being the best and most healthful means of subsistence in his power.] "Last Monday, for my dealers like birds on a Monday or Tuesday best, and then they've the week before them,—I went to catch in the fields this side of Barnet, and started before two in the morning, when it was neither light nor dark. You must get to your place before daylight to be ready for the first flight, and have time to lay your net properly. When I'd done that, I lay down and smoked. No, smoke don't scare the birds; I think they're rather drawn to notice anything new, if all 's quite quiet. Well, the first pull I had about 90 birds, nearly all linnets. There was, as well as I can remember, three hedge-sparrows among them, and two larks, and one or two other birds. Yes, there's always a terrible flutter and row when you make a catch, and often regular fights in the net. I then sorted my birds, and let the hens go, for I didn't want to be bothered with them. I might let such a thing as 35 hens go out of rather more than an 80 take, for I've always found, in catching young broods, that I've drawn more cocks than hens. How do I know the difference when the birds are so young? As easy as light from dark. You must lift up the wing, quite tender, and you'll find that a cock linnet has black, or nearly black, feathers on his shoulder, where the hens are a deal lighter. Then the cock has a broader and whiter stripe on the wing than the hen has. It's quite easy to distinguish, quite. A cock goldfinch is straighter and more larger in general than a hen, and has a broader white on his wing, as the cock linnet has; he's black round the beak and the eye too, and a hen's greenish thereabouts. There's some gray-pates (young birds) would deceive any one until he opens their wings. Well, I went on, sir, until about one o'clock, or a little after, as well as I could tell from the sun, and then came away with about 100 singing birds. I sold them in the lump to three shopkeepers at 2s. 2d. and 2s. 6d. the doxen. That was a good day, sir; a very lucky day. I got about 17s., the best I ever did but once, when I made 19s. in a day.

"Yes, it's hard work is mine, because there's such a long walking home when you've done catching. O, when you're at work it's not work but almost a pleasure. I've laid for hours though, without a catch. I smoke to pass the time when I'm watching; sometimes I read a bit if I've had anything to take with me to read; then at other times I thinks. If you don't get a catch for hours, it's only like an angler without a nibble. O, I don't know what I think about; about nothing, perhaps. Yes, I've had a friend or two go out catching with me just for the amusement. They must lie about and wait as I do. We have a little talk of course: well, perhaps about sporting; no, not horse-racing, I care nothing for that, but it's hardly business taking any one with you. I supply the dealers and hawk as well. Perhaps I make 12s. a week the year through. Some weeks I've made between 3l. and 4l., and in winter, when there's rain every day, perhaps I haven't cleared a penny in a fortnight. That's the worst of it. But I make more than others because I have a connection and raise good birds.

"Sometimes I'm stopped by the farmers when I'm at work, but not often, though there is some of 'em very obstinate. It's no use, for if a catcher's net has to be taken from one part of a farm, after he's had the trouble of laying it, why it must be laid in another part. Some country people likes to have their birds caught."

My informant supplied shopkeepers and hawked his birds in the streets and to the houses. He had a connection, he said, and could generally get through them, but he had sometimes put a bird or two in a fancy house. These are the public-houses resorted to by "the fancy," in some of which may be seen two or three dozen singing-birds for sale on commission, through the agency of the landlord or the waiter. They are the property of hawkers or dealers, and must be good birds, or they will not be admitted.

The number of birds caught, and the proportion sold in the streets, I have already stated. The number of bird-catchers, I may repeat, is about the same as that of street bird-sellers, 200.

OF THE CRIPPLED STREET BIRD-SELLER.

FROM the bird-seller whose portrait will be given in the next number of this work I have received the following account. The statement previously given was that of a catcher and street-seller, as are the great majority in the trade; the following narrative is that of one who, from his infirmities, is merely a street-*seller*.

The poor man's deformity may be best understood by describing it in his own words: " I have no ancle." His right leg is emaciated, the bone is smaller than that of his other leg (which is not deformed), and there is no ancle joint. The joints of the wrists and shoulders are also defective, though not utterly wanting, as in the ancle. In walking this poor cripple seems to advance by means of a series of jerks. He uses his deformed leg, but must tread, or rather support his body, on the ball of the misformed foot, while he advances his sound leg; then, with a twist of his body, after he has advanced and stands upon his undeformed leg and foot, he throws forward the crippled part of his frame by the jerk I have spoken of. His arms are usually pressed against his ribs as he walks, and convey to a spectator the notion that he is unable to raise them from that position. This, however, is not the case; he can raise them, not as a sound man does, but with an effort and a contortion of his body to humour the effort. His speech is also defective, his words being brought out, as it were, by jerks; he has to prepare himself, and to throw up his chin, in order to converse, and then he speaks with difficulty. His face is sun-burnt and healthy-looking. His dress was a fustian coat with full skirts, cloth trowsers somewhat patched, and a clean coarse shirt. His right shoe was suited to his deformity, and was strapped with a sort of leather belt round the lower part of the leg.

A considerable number of book-stall keepers, as well as costermongers, swag-barrowmen, ginger-beer and lemonade sellers, orange-women, sweet-stuff vendors, root-sellers, and others, have established their pitches—some of them having stalls with a cover, like a roof—from Whitechapel workhouse to the Mile End turnpike-gate; near the gate they are congregated most thickly, and there they are mixed with persons seated on the forms belonging to adjacent innkeepers, which are placed there to allow any one to have his beer and tobacco in the open air. Among these street-sellers and beer-drinkers is seated the crippled bird-seller, generally motionless.

His home is near the Jews' burial-ground, and in one of the many "places" which by a misnomer, occasioned by the change in the character and appearance of what *were* the outskirts, are still called "Pleasant." On seeking him here, I had some little difficulty in finding the house, and asking a string of men, who were chopping fire-wood in an adjoining court, for the man I wanted, mentioning his name, no one knew anything about him; though when I spoke of his calling, " O," they said, " you want Old Billy." I then found Billy at his accustomed pitch, with a very small stock of birds in two large cages on the ground beside him, and he accompanied me to his residence. The room in which we sat had a pile of fire-wood opposite the door; the iron of the upper part of the door-latch being wanting was replaced by a piece of wood—and on the pile sat a tame jackdaw, with the inquisitive and askant look peculiar to the bird. Above the pile was a large cage, containing a jay—a bird seldom sold in the streets now—and a thrush, in different compartments. A table, three chairs, and a hamper or two used in the wood-cutting, completed the furniture. Outside the house were cages containing larks, goldfinches, and a very fine starling, of whose promising abilities the bird-seller's sister had so favourable an opinion that she intended to try and teach it to talk, although that was very seldom done now.

The following is the statement I obtained from the poor fellow. The man's sister was present at his desire, as he was afraid I could not understand him, owing to the indistinctness of his speech; but that was easy enough, after awhile, with a little patience and attention.

" I was born a cripple, sir," he said, " and I shall die one. I was born at Lewisham, but I don't remember living in any place but London. I remember being at Stroud though, where my father had taken me, and bathed me often in the sea himself, thinking it might do me good. I've heard him say, too, that when I was very young he took me to almost every hospital in London, but it was of no use. My father and mother were as kind to me and as good parents as could be. He's been dead nineteen years, and my mother died before him. Father was very poor, almost as poor as I am. He worked in a brick-field, but work weren't regular. I couldn't walk at all until I was six years old, and I was between nine and ten before I could get up and down stairs by myself. I used to slide down before, as well as I could, and had to be carried up. When I could get about and went among other boys, I was in great distress, I was teased so. Life was a burthen to me, as I've read something about. They used to taunt me by offering to jump me" (invite him to a jumping match), "and to say, I'll run you a race on one leg. They were bad to me then, and they are now. I've sometimes sat down and cried, but not often. No, sir, I can't say that I ever wished I was dead. I hardly know why I cried. I suppose because I was miserable. I learned to read at a Sunday school, where I went a long time. I like reading. I read the Bible and tracts, nothing else; never a newspaper. It don't come in my way, and if it did I shouldn't look at it, for I can't read over well and it's nothing to me who's king or who's queen. It can never have anything to do with me. It don't take my attention. There'll be no change for me in this world. When I was thirteen my father put me into the bird trade. He knew a good many catchers. I've been bird-selling in the streets for six-and-twenty years and more, for I was 39 the 24th of last January. Father didn't know what better he could put me to, as I hadn't the right use of my hands or feet, and at first I did very well. I liked the birds and do still. I used to think at first that they was like me; they was prisoners, and I was a cripple. At first I sold birds in Poplar, and

Limehouse, and Blackwall, and was a help to my parents, for I cleared 9s. or 10s. every week. But now, oh dear, I don't know where all the money's gone to. I think there's very little left in the country. I've sold larks, linnets, and goldfinches, to captains of ships to take to the West Indies. I've sold them, too, to go to Port Philip. O, and almost all those foreign parts. They bring foreign birds here, and take back London birds. I don't know anything about foreign birds. I know there's men dressed as sailors going about selling them; they're duffers—I mean the men. There's a neighbour of mine, that's very likely never been 20 miles out of London, and when he hawks birds he always dresses like a countryman, and duffs that way.

"When my father died," continued the man, "I was completely upset; everything in the world was upset. I was forced to go into the workhouse, and I was there between four and five months. O, I hated it. I'd rather live on a penny loaf a day than be in it again. I've never been near the parish since, though I've often had nothing to eat many a day. I'd rather be lamer than I am, and be oftener called silly Billy—and that sometimes makes me dreadful wild—than be in the workhouse. It was starvation, but then I know I'm a hearty eater, very hearty. Just now I know I could eat a shilling plate of meat, but for all that I very seldom taste meat. I live on bread and butter and tea, sometimes bread without butter. When I have it I eat a quartern loaf at three meals. It depends upon how I'm off. My health's good. I never feel in any pain now; I did when I first got to walk, in great pain. Beer I often don't taste once in two or three months, and this very hot weather one can't help longing for a drop, when you see people drinking it all sides of you, but they have the use of their limbs." [Here two little girls and a boy rushed into the room, for they had but to open the door from the outside, and, evidently to tease the poor fellow, loudly demanded "a ha'penny bird." When the sister had driven them away, my informant continued.] "I'm still greatly teased, sir, with children; yes, and with men too, both when they're drunk and sober. I think grown persons are the worst. They swear and use bad language to me. I'm sure I don't know why. I know no name they call me by in particular when I'm teased, if it isn't 'Old Hypocrite.' I can't say why they call me 'hypocrite.' I suppose because they know no better. Yes, I think I'm religious, rather. I would be more so, if I had clothes. I get to chapel sometimes." [A resident near the bird-seller's pitch, with whom I had some conversation, told me of "Billy" being sometimes teased in the way described. Some years ago, he believed it was at Limehouse, my informant heard a gentlemanly-looking man, tipsy, d—n the street bird-seller for Mr. *Hobbler*, and bid him go to the Mansion House, or to h—l. I asked the cripple about this, but he had no recollection of it; and, as he evidently did not understand the allusion to Mr. Hobbler, I was not surprised at his forgetfulness.]

"I like to sit out in the sunshine selling my birds," he said. "If it's rainy, and I can't go out, because it would be of no use, I'm moped to death. I stay at home and read a little; or I chop a little fire-wood, but you may be very sure, sir, its little I can do that way. I never associate with the neighbours. I never had any pleasure, such as going to a fair, or like that. I don't remember having ever spent a penny in a place of amusement in my life. Yes, I've often sat all day in the sun, and of course a deal of thoughts goes through my head. I think, shall I be able to afford myself plenty of bread when I get home? And I think of the next world sometimes, and feel quite sure, quite, that I shan't be a cripple there. Yes, that's a comfort, for this world will never be any good to me. I feel that I shall be a poor starving cripple, till I end, perhaps, in the workhouse. Other poor men can get married, but not such as me. But I never was in love in my life, never." [Among the vagrants and beggars, I may observe, there are men more terribly deformed than the bird-seller, who are married, or living in concubinage.] "Yes, sir," he proceeded, "I'm quite reconciled to my lameness, quite; and have been for years. O, no, I never fret about that now; but about starving, perhaps, and the workhouse.

"Before father died, the parish allowed us 1s. 6d. and a quartern loaf a week; but after he was buried, they'd allow me nothing; they'd only admit me into the house. I hadn't a penny allowed to me when I discharged myself and came out. I hardly know how ever I *did* manage to get a start again with the birds. I knew a good many catchers, and they trusted me. Yes, they was all poor men. I did pretty tidy by bits, but only when it was fine weather, until these five years or so, when things got terrible bad. Particularly just the two last years with me. Do you think times are likely to mend, sir, with poor people? If working-men had only money, they'd buy innocent things like birds to amuse them at home; but if they can't get the money, as I've heard them say when they've been pricing my stock, why in course they can't spend it."

"Yes, indeed," said the sister, "trade's very bad. Where my husband and I once earned 18s. at the fire-wood, and then 15s., we can't now earn 12s. the two of us, slave as hard as we will. I always dread the winter a-coming. Though there may be more fire-wood wanted, there's greater expenses, and it's a terrible time for such as us."

"I dream sometimes, sir," the cripple resumed in answer to my question, "but not often. I often have more than once dreamed I was starving and dying of hunger. I remember that, for I woke in a tremble. But most dreams is soon forgot. I've never seemed to myself to be a cripple in my dreams. Well, I can't explain how, but I feel as if my limbs was all free like—so beautiful. I dream most about starving I think, than about anything else. Perhaps that's when I have to go to sleep hungry. I sleep very well, though, take it altogether. If I had only plenty to live upon there would be nobody happier. I'm happy enough when times is middling with me, only one feels it won't last. I like a joke as well as anybody when times is good; but that's been very seldom lately.

"It's all small birds I sell in the street now, except at a very odd time. That jackdaw there, sir, he's a very fine bird. I've tamed him myself, and he's as tame as a dog. My sister's a very good hand among birds, and helps me. She once taught a linnet to say 'Joey' as plain as you can speak it yourself, sir. I buy birds of different catchers, but haven't money to buy the better kinds, as I have to sell at 3*d*., and 4*d*., and 6*d*. mostly. If I had a pound to lay out in a few nice cages and good birds, I think I could do middling, this fine weather particler, for I'm a very good judge of birds, and know how to manage them as well as anybody. Then birds is rather dearer to buy than they was when I was first in the trade. The catchers have to go further, and I'm afeared the birds is getting scarcer, and so there's more time taken up. I buy of several catchers. The last whole day that I was at my pitch I sold nine birds, and took about 3*s*. If I could buy birds ever so cheap, there's always such losses by their dying. I've had three parts of my young linnets die, do what I might, but not often so many. Then if they die all the food they've had is lost. There goes all for nothing the rape and flax-seed for your linnets, canary and flax for your goldfinches, chopped eggs for your nightingales, and German paste for your sky-larks. I've made my own German paste when I've wanted a sufficient quantity. It's made of peameal, treacle, hog's-lard, and moss-seed. I sell more goldfinches than anything else. I used to sell a good many sparrows for shooting, but I haven't done anything that way these eight or nine years. It's a fash'nable sport still, I hear. I've reared nightingales that sung beautiful, and have sold them at 4*s*. a piece, which was very cheap. They often die when the time for their departure comes. A shopkeeper as supplied such as I've sold would have charged 1*l*. a piece for them. One of my favouritest birds is redpoles, but they're only sold in the season. I think it's one of the most knowingest little birds that is; more knowing than the goldfinch, in my opinion.

"My customers are all working people, all of them. I sell to nobody else; I make 4*s*. or 5*s*.; I call 5*s*. a good week at this time of year, when the weather suits. I lodge with a married sister; her husband's a wood-chopper, and I pay 1*s*. 6*d*. a week, which is cheap, for I've no sticks of my own. If I earn 4*s*. there's only 2*s*. 6*d*. left to live on the week through. In winter, when I can make next to nothing, and must keep my birds, it is terrible—oh yes, sir, if you believe me, terrible!"

OF THE TRICKS OF THE BIRD-DUFFERS.

THE tricks practised by the bird-sellers are frequent and systematic. The other day a man connected with the bird-trade had to visit Holloway, the City, and Bermondsey. In Holloway he saw six men, some of whom he recognised as regular bird-catchers and street-sellers, offering sham birds; in the City he found twelve; and in Bermondsey six, as well as he could depend upon his memory. These, he thought, did not constitute more than a half of the number now at work as bird-"duffers," not including the sellers of foreign birds. In the summer, indeed, the duffers are most numerous, for birds are cheapest then, and these tricksters, to economise time, I presume, buy of other catchers any cheap hens suited to their purpose. Some of them, I am told, never catch their birds at all, but purchase them.

The greenfinch is the bird on which these men's art is most commonly practised, its light-coloured plumage suiting it to their purposes. I have heard these people styled "bird-swindlers," but by street-traders I heard them called "bird-duffers," yet there appears to be no very distinctive name for them. They are nearly all men, as is the case in the bird trade generally, although the wives may occasionally assist in the street-sale. The means of deception, as regards the greenfinch especially, are from paint. One aim of these artists is to make their finch resemble some curious foreign bird, "not often to be sold so cheap, or to be sold at all in this country." They study the birds in the window of the naturalists' shops for this purpose. Sometimes they declare these painted birds are young Java sparrows (at one time "a fashionable bird"), or St. Helena birds, or French or Italian finches. They sometimes get 5*s*. for such a "duffing bird;" one man has been known to boast that he once got a sovereign. I am told, however, by a bird-catcher who had himself supplied birds to these men for duffing, that they complained of the trade growing worse and worse.

It is usually a hen which is painted, for the hen is by far the cheapest purchase, and while the poor thing is being offered for sale by the duffers, she has an unlimited supply of hemp-seed, without other food, and hemp-seed beyond a proper quantity, is a very strong stimulus. This makes the hen look brisk and bold, but if newly caught, as is usually the case, she will perhaps be found dead next morning. The duffer will object to his bird being handled on account of its timidity; "but it is timid only with strangers!" When you've had him a week, ma'am," such a bird-seller will say, "you'll find him as lovesome and tame as can be." One jealous lady, when asked 5*s*. for a "very fine Italian finch, an excellent singer," refused to buy, but offered a deposit of 2*s*. 6*d*., if the man would leave his bird and cage, for the trial of the bird's song, for two or three days. The duffer agreed; and was bold enough to call on the third day to hear the result. The bird was dead, and after murmuring a little at the lady's mismanagement, and at the loss he had been subjected to, the man brought away his cage. He boasted of this to a dealer's assistant who mentioned it to me, and expressed his conviction that it was true enough. The paints used for the transformation of native birds into foreign are bought at the colour-shops, and applied with camel-hair brushes in the usual way.

When canaries are "a bad colour," or have

grown a paler yellow from age, they are re-dyed, by the application of a colour sold at the colour-shops, and known as "the Queen's yellow." Blackbirds are dyed a deeper black, the "grit" off a frying-pan being used for the purpose. The same thing is done to heighten the gloss and blackness of a jackdaw, I was told, by a man who acknowledged he had duffed a little; "people liked a gay bright colour." In the same way the tints of the goldfinch are heightened by the application of paint. It is common enough, moreover, for a man to paint the beaks and legs of the birds. It is chiefly the smaller birds which are thus made the means of cheating.

Almost all the "duffing birds" are hawked. If a young hen be passed off for a good singing bird, without being painted, as a cock in his second singing year, she is "brisked up" with hemp-seed, is half tipsy in fact, and so passed off deceitfully. As it is very rarely that even the male birds will sing in the streets, this is often a successful ruse, the bird appearing so lively.

A dealer calculated for me, from his own knowledge, that 2000 small birds were "duffed" yearly, at an average of from 2s. 6d. to 3s. each.

As yet I have only spoken of the "duffing" of English birds, but similar tricks are practised with the foreign birds.

In parrot-selling there is a good deal of "duffing." The birds are "painted up," as I have described in the case of the greenfinches, &c. Varnish is also used to render the colours brighter; the legs and beak are frequently varnished. Sometimes a spot of red is introduced, for as one of these duffers observed to a dealer in English birds, "the more outlandish you make them look, the better's the chance to sell." Sometimes there is little injury done by this paint and varnish, which disappear gradually when the parrot is in the cage of a purchaser; but in some instances when the bird picks himself where he has been painted, he dies from the deleterious compound. Of this mortality, however, there is nothing approaching that among the duffed small birds.

Occasionally the duffers carry really fine cockatoos, &c., and if they can obtain admittance into a lady's house, to display the beauty of the bird, they will pretend to be in possession of smuggled silk, &c., made of course for duffing purposes. The bird-duffers are usually dressed as seamen, and sometimes pretend they must sell the bird before the ship sails, for a parting spree, or to get the poor thing a good home. This trade, however, has from all that I can learn, and in the words of an informant, "seen its best days." There are now sometimes six men thus engaged; sometimes none: and when one of these men is "hard up," he finds it difficult to start again in a business for which a capital of about 1l. is necessary, as a cage is wanted generally. The duffers buy the very lowest priced birds, and have been known to get 2l. 10s. for what cost but 8s., but that is a very rare occurrence, and the men are very poor, and perhaps more dissipated than the generality of street-sellers. Parrot duffing, moreover, is seldom carried on regularly by any one, for he will often duff cigars and other things in preference, or perhaps vend really smuggled and good cigars or tobccco. Perhaps 150 parrots, paroquets, or cockatoos, are sold in this way annually, at from 15s. to 1l. 10s. each, but hardly averaging 1l., as the duffer will sell, or raffle, the bird for a small sum if he cannot dispose of it otherwise.

OF THE STREET-SELLERS OF FOREIGN BIRDS.

THIS trade is curious, but far from extensive as regards street-sale. There is, moreover, contrary to what might be expected, a good deal of "duffing" about it. The "duffer" in English birds disguises them so that they shall look like foreigners; the duffer in what are unquestionably foreign birds disguises them that they may look *more* foreign—more Indian than in the Indies.

The word "Duffer," I may mention, appears to be connected with the German *Durffen*, to want, to be needy, and so to mean literally a needy or indigent man, even as the word *Pedlar* has the same origin—being derived from the German *Bettler*, and the Dutch *Bedelaar*—a beggar. The verb *Durffen* means also to dare, to be so bold as to do; hence, to *Durff*, or *Duff*, would signify to resort to any impudent trick.

The supply of parrots, paroquets, cockatoos, Java sparrows, or St. Helena birds, is not in the regular way of consignment from a merchant abroad to one in London. The commanders and mates of merchant vessels bring over large quantities; and often enough the seamen are allowed to bring parrots or cockatoos in the homeward-bound ship from the Indies or the African coast, or from other tropical countries, either to beguile the tedium of the voyage, for presents to their friends, or, as in some cases, for sale on their reaching an English port. More, I am assured, although statistics are hardly possible on such a subject, are brought to London, and perhaps by one-third, than to all the other ports of Great Britain collectively. Even on board the vessels of the royal navy, the importation of parrots used to be allowed as a sort of boon to the seamen. I was told by an old naval officer that once, after a long detention on the west coast of Africa, his ship was ordered home, and, as an acknowledgment of the good behaviour of his men, he permitted them to bring parrots, cockatoos, or any foreign birds, home with them, not limiting the number, but of course under the inspection of the petty officers, that there might be no violation of the cleanliness which always distinguishes a vessel of war. Along the African coast, to the southward of Sierra Leone, the men were not allowed to land, both on account of the unhealthiness of the shores, and of the surf, which rendered landing highly dangerous, a danger, however, which the seamen would not have scrupled to brave, and recklessly enough, for any impulse of the minute. As if by instinct, however, the natives seemed to know what was wanted, for they came off from the shores in their light canoes, which danced like feathers on the surf, and brought boat-loads of birds; these the seamen bought of them, or possessed themselves of in the way of barter.

Before the ship took her final departure, however, she was reported as utterly uninhabitable below, from the incessant din and clamour: "We might as well have a pack of women aboard, sir," was the ungallant remark of one of the petty officers to his commander. Orders were then given that the parrots, &c., should be "thinned," so that there might not be such an unceasing noise. This was accordingly done. How many were set at liberty and made for the shore—for the seamen in this instance did not kill them for their skins, as is not unfrequently the case—the commander did not know. He could but conjecture; and he conjectured that something like a thousand were released; and even after that, and after the mortality which takes place among these birds in the course of a long voyage, a very great number were brought to Plymouth. Of these, again, a great number were sent or conveyed under the care of the sailors to London, when the ship was paid off. The same officer endeavoured on this voyage to bring home some very large pine-apples, which flavoured, and most deliciously, parts of the ship when she had been a long time at sea; but every one of them rotted, and had to be thrown overboard. He fell into the error, Captain —— said, of having the finest fruit selected for the experiment; an error which the Bahama merchants had avoided, and consequently they succeeded where he failed. How the sailors fed the parrots, my informant could hardly guess, but they brought a number of very fine birds to England, some of them with well-cultivated powers of speech.

This, as I shall show, is one of the ways by which the London supply of parrots, &c., is obtained; but the permission, as to the importation of these brightly-feathered birds, is, I understand, rarely allowed at present to the seamen in the royal navy. The far greater supply, indeed more than 90 per cent. of the whole of the birds imported, is from the merchant-service. I have already stated, on the very best authority, the motives which induce merchant-seamen to bring over parrots and cockatoos. That to bring them over is an inducement to some to engage in an African voyage is shown by the following statement, which was made to me, in the course of a long inquiry, published in my letters in the *Morning Chronicle*, concerning the condition of the merchant-seamen.

"I would never go to that African coast again, only I make a pound or two in birds. We buy parrots, gray parrots chiefly, of the natives, who come aboard in their canoes. We sometimes pay 6s. or 7s., in Africa, for a fine bird. I have known 200 parrots on board; they make a precious noise; but half the birds die before they get to England. Some captains won't allow parrots."

When the seamen have settled themselves after landing in England, they perhaps find that there is no room in their boarding-houses for their parrots; these birds are not admitted into the Sailors' Home; the seamen's friends are stocked with the birds, and look upon another parrot as but another intruder, an unwelcome pensioner. There remains but one course—to sell the birds, and they are generally sold to a highly respectable man, Mr. M. Samuel, of Upper East Smithfield; and it is from him, though not always directly, that the shopkeepers and street-sellers derive their stock-in-trade. There is also a further motive for the disposal of parrots, paroquets, and cockatoos to a merchant. The seafaring owner of those really magnificent birds, perhaps, squanders his money, perhaps he gets "skinned" (stripped of his clothes and money from being hocussed, or tempted to helpless drunkenness), or he chooses to sell them, and he or his boarding-house keeper takes the birds to Mr. Samuel, and sells them for what he can get; but I heard from three very intelligent seamen whom I met with in the course of my inquiry, and by mere chance, that Mr. Samuel's price was fair and his money sure, considering everything, for there is usually a qualification to every praise. It is certainly surprising, under these circumstances, that such numbers of these birds should thus be disposed of.

Parrots are as gladly, or more gladly, got rid of, in any manner, in different regions in the continents of Asia and America, than with us are even rats from a granary. Dr. Stanley, after speaking of the beauty of a flight of parrots, says:—" The husbandman who sees them hastening through the air, with loud and impatient screams, looks upon them with dismay and detestation, knowing that the produce of his labour and industry is in jeopardy, when visited by such a voracious multitude of pilferers, who, like the locusts of Egypt, desolate whole tracts of country by their unsparing ravages." A contrast with their harmlessness, in a gilded cage in the houses of the wealthy, with us! The destructiveness of these birds, is then, one reason why seamen can obtain them so readily and cheaply, for the natives take pleasure in catching them; while as to plentifulness, the tropical regions teem with bird, as with insect and reptile, life.

Of parrots, paroquets, and cockatoos, there are 3000 imported to London in the way I have described, and in about equal proportions. They are sold, wholesale, from 5s. to 30s. each.

There are now only three men selling these brilliant birds regularly in the streets, and in the fair way of trade; but there are sometimes as many as 18 so engaged. The price given by a hawker for a cockatoo, &c., is 8s. or 10s., and they are retailed at from 15s. to 30s., or more, " if it can be got." The purchasers are the wealthier classes who can afford to indulge their tastes. Of late years, however, I am told, a parrot or a cockatoo seems to be considered indispensable to an inn (not a gin-palace), and the innkeepers have been among the best customers of the street parrot-sellers. In the neighbourhood of the docks, and indeed along the whole river side below London-bridge, it is almost impossible for a street-seller to dispose of a parrot to an innkeeper, or indeed to any one, as they are supplied by the seamen. A parrot which has been taught to talk is worth from 4l. to 10l., according to its proficiency in speech. About 500 of these birds are sold yearly by the street-hawkers, at an outlay to the public of from 500*l.* to 600*l.*

Java sparrows, from the East Indies, and from the Islands of the Archipelago, are brought to London, but considerable quantities die during the voyage and in this country; for, though hardy enough, not more than one in three survives being "taken off the paddy seed." About 10,000, however, are sold annually, in London, at 1*s.* 6*d.* each, but a very small proportion by street-hawking, as the Java sparrows are chiefly in demand for the aviaries of the rich in town and country. In some years not above 100 may be sold in the streets; in others, as many as 500.

In St. Helena birds, known also as wax-bills and red-backs, there is a trade to the same extent, both as regards number and price; but the street-sale is perhaps 10 per cent. lower.

Of the Street-Sellers of Birds'-Nests.

The young gypsy-looking lad, who gave me the following account of the sale of birds'-nests in the streets, was peculiarly picturesque in his appearance. He wore a dirty-looking smock-frock with large pockets at the side; he had no shirt; and his long black hair hung in curls about him, contrasting strongly with his bare white neck and chest. The broad-brimmed brown Italian-looking hat, broken in and ragged at the top, threw a dark half-mask-like shadow over the upper part of his face. His feet were bare and black with mud: he carried in one hand his basket of nests, dotted with their many-coloured eggs; in the other he held a live snake, that writhed and twisted as its metallic-looking skin glistened in the sun; now over, and now round, the thick knotty bough of a tree that he used for a stick. The portrait of the youth is here given. I have never seen so picturesque a specimen of the English nomade. He said, in answer to my inquiries:—

"I am a seller of birds'-nesties, snakes, slow-worms, adders, 'effets'—lizards is their common name—hedgehogs (for killing black beetles); frogs (for the French—they eats 'em); snails (for birds); that's all I sell in the summer-time. In the winter I get all kinds of wild flowers and roots, primroses, 'butter-cups' and daisies, and snow-drops, and 'backing' off of trees; ('backing' it's called, because it's used to put at the back of nosegays, it's got off the yew trees, and is the green yew fern. I gather bulrushes in the summer-time, besides what I told you; some buys bulrushes for stuffing; they're the fairy rushes the small ones, and the big ones is bulrushes. The small ones is used for 'stuffing,' that is, for showing off the birds as is stuffed, and make 'em seem as if they was alive in their cases, and among the rushes; I sell them to the bird-stuffers at 1*d.* a dozen. The big rushes the boys buys to play with and beat one another—on a Sunday evening mostly. The birds'-nesties I get from 1*d.* to 3*d.* a-piece for. I never have young birds, I can never sell 'em; you see the young things generally dies of the cramp before you can get rid of them. I sell the birds'-nesties in the streets; the three-penny ones has six eggs, a half-penny a egg. The linnets has mostly four eggs, they're 4*d.* the nest; they're for putting under canaries, and being hatched by them. The thrushes has from four to five—five is the most; they're 2*d.*; they're merely for cur'osity—glass cases or anything like that. Moor-hens, wot build on the moors, has from eight to nine eggs, and is 1*d.* a-piece; they're for hatching underneath a bantam-fowl, the same as partridges. Chaffinches has five eggs; they're 3*d.*, and is for cur'osity. Hedge-sparrows, five eggs; they're the same price as the other, and is for cur'osity. The Bottletit—the nest and the bough are always put in glass cases; it's a long hanging nest, like a bottle, with a hole about as big as a sixpence, and there's mostly as many as eighteen eggs; they've been known to lay thirty-three. To the house-sparrow there is five eggs; they're 1*d.* The yellow-hammers, with five eggs, is 2*d.* The water-wagtails, with four eggs, 2*d.* Blackbirds, with five eggs, 2*d.* The golden-crest wren, with ten eggs—it has a very handsome nest—is 6*d.* Bulfinches, four eggs, 1*s.*; they're for hatching, and the bulfinch is a very dear bird. Crows, four eggs, 4*d.* Magpies, four eggs, 4*d.* Starlings, five eggs, 3*d.* The egg-chats, five eggs, 2*d.* Goldfinches, five eggs, 6*d.*, for hatching. Martins, five eggs, 3*d.* The swallow, four eggs, 6*d*; it's so dear because the nest is such a cur'osity, they build up again the house. The butcher-birds—hedge-murderers some calls them, for the number of birds they kills—five eggs, 3*d.* The cuckoo—they never has a nest, but lays in the hedge-sparrow's; there's only one egg (it's very rare you see the two, they has been got, but that's seldom) that is 4*d.*, the egg is such a cur'osity. The greenfinches has four or five eggs, and is 3*d.* The sparrer-hawk has four eggs, and they're 6*d.* The reed-sparrow—they builds in the reeds close where the bulrushes grow; they has four eggs, and is 2*d.* The wood-pigeon has two eggs, and they're 4*d.* The horned owl, four eggs; they're 6*d.* The woodpecker—I never see no more nor two—they're 6*d.* the two; they're a great cur'osity, very seldom found. The kingfishers has four eggs, and is 6*d.* That's all I know of.

"I gets the eggs mostly from Witham and Chelmsford, in Essex; Chelmsford is 20 mile from Whitechapel Church, and Witham, 8 mile further. I know more about them parts than anywhere else, being used to go after moss for Mr. Butler, of the herb-shop in Covent Garden. Sometimes I go to Shirley Common and Shirley Wood, that's three miles from Croydon, and Croydon is ten from Westminster-bridge. When I'm out bird-nesting I take all the cross country roads across fields and into the woods. I begin bird-nesting in May and leave off about August, and then comes the bulrushing, and they last till Christmas; and after that comes the roots and wild flowers, which serves me up to May again. I go out bird-nesting three times a week. I go away at night, and come up on the morning of the day after. I'm away a day and two nights. I start between one and two in the morning and walk all night—for the coolness—you see the weather's so hot you can't

STREET-SELLER OF BIRDS' NESTS.

THE JEW OLD-CLOTHES MAN.
Clo', Clo', Clo'.

[*From a Daguerreotype by* Beard.]

do it in the daytime. When I get down I go to sleep for a couple of hours. I 'skipper it'—turn in under a hedge or anywhere. I get down about nine in the morning, at Chelmsford, and about one if I go to Witham. After I've had my sleep I start off to get my nests and things. I climb the trees, often I go up a dozen in the day, and many a time there's nothing in the nest when I get up. I only fell once; I got on the end of the bough and slipped off. I p'isoned my foot once with the stagnant water going after the bulrushes,—there was horseleeches, and effets, and all kinds of things in the water, and they stung me, I think. I couldn't use my foot hardly for six weeks afterwards, and was obliged to have a stick to walk with. I couldn't get about at all for four days, and should have starved if it hadn't been that a young man kept me. He was a printer by trade, and almost a stranger to me, only he seed me and took pity on me. When I fell off the bough I wasn't much hurt, nothing to speak of. The house-sparrow is the worst nest of all to take; it's no value either when it *is* got, and is the most difficult of all to get at. You has to get up a sparapet (a parapet) of a house, and either to get permission, or run the risk of going after it without. Partridges' eggs (they has no nest) they gives you six months for, if they see you selling them, because it's game, and I haven't no licence; but while you're hawking, that is showing 'em, they can't touch you. The owl is a very difficult nest to get, they builds so high in the trees. The bottle-tit is a hard nest to find; you may go all the year round, and, perhaps, only get one. The nest I like best to get is the chaffinch, because they're in the hedge, and is no bother. Oh, you hasn't got the skylark down, sir; they builds on the ground, and has five eggs; I sell them for 4*d*. The robin-redbreast has five eggs, too, and is 3*d*. The ringdove has two eggs, and is 6*d*. The titlark—that's five blue eggs, and very rare—I get 4*d*. for them. The jay has five eggs, and a flat nest, very wiry, indeed; it's a ground bird; that's 1*s*.—the egg is just like a partridge egg. When I first took a kingfisher's nest, I didn't know the name of it, and I kept wondering what it was. I daresay I asked three dozen people, and none of them could tell me. At last a bird-fancier, the lame man at the Mile-end gate, told me what it was. I likes to get the nesties to sell, but I havn't no fancy for birds. Sometimes I get squirrels' nesties with the young in 'em—about four of 'em there mostly is, and they're the only young things I take—the young birds I leaves; they're no good to me. The four squirrels brings me from 6*s*. to 8*s*. After I takes a bird's nest, the old bird comes dancing over it, chirupping, and crying, and flying all about. When they lose their nest they wander about, and don't know where to go. Oftentimes I wouldn't take them if it wasn't for the want of the victuals, it seems such a pity to disturb 'em after they've made their little bits of places. Bats I never take myself—I can't get over 'em. If I has an order for 'em, I buys 'em of boys.

"I mostly start off into the country on Monday and come up on Wednesday. The most nesties as ever I took is twenty-two, and I generally get about twelve or thirteen. These, if I've an order, I sell directly, or else I may be two days, and sometimes longer, hawking them in the street. Directly I've sold them I go off again that night, if it's fine; though I often go in the wet, and then I borrow a tarpaulin of a man in the street where I live. If I've a quick sale I get down and back three times in a week, but then I don't go so far as Witham, sometimes only to Rumford; that is 12 miles from Whitechapel Church. I never got an order from a bird-fancier; they gets all the eggs they want of the countrymen who comes up to market.

"It's gentlemen I gets my orders of, and then mostly they tells me to bring 'em one nest of every kind I can get hold of, and that will often last me three months in the summer. There's one gentleman as I sells to is a wholesale dealer in window-glass—and he has a hobby for them. He puts 'em into glass cases, and makes presents of 'em to his friends. He has been one of my best customers. I've sold him a hundred nesties, I'm sure. There's a doctor at Dalston I sell a great number to—he's taking one of every kind of me now. The most of my customers is stray ones in the streets. They're generally boys. I sells a nest now and then to a lady with a child; but the boys of twelve to fifteen years of age is my best friends. They buy 'em only for cur'osity. I sold three partridges' eggs yesterday to a gentlemen, and he said he would put them under a bantam he'd got, and hatch 'em.

"The snakes, and adders, and slow-worms I get from where there's moss or a deal of grass. Sunny weather's the best for them, they won't come out when it's cold; then I go to a dung-heap, and turn it over. Sometimes, I find five or six there, but never so large as the one I had to-day, that's a yard and five inches long, and three-quarters of a pound weight. Snakes is 5*s*. a pound. I sell all I can get to Mr. Butler, of Covent-garden. He keeps 'em alive, for they're no good dead. I think it's for the skin they're kept. Some buys 'em to dissect: a gentleman in Theobalds-road does so, and so he does hedge-hogs. Some buys 'em for stuffing, and others for cur'osities. Adders is the same price as snakes, 5*s*. a pound after they first comes in, when they're 10*s*. Adders is wanted dead: it's only the fat and skin that's of any value; the fat is used for curing p'isoned wounds, and the skin is used for any one as has cut their heads. Farmers buys the fat, and rubs it into the wound when they gets bitten or stung by anything p'isonous. I kill the adders with a stick, or, when I has shoes, I jumps on 'em. Some fine days I get four or five snakes at a time; but then they're mostly small, and won't weigh above half a pound. I don't get many adders—they don't weigh many ounces, adders don't—and I mostly has 9*d*. a-piece for each I gets. I sells *them* to Mr. Butler as well.

"The hedgehogs is 1*s*. each; I gets them mostly in Essex. I've took one hedgehog with three young ones, and sold the lot for 2s. 6d. People in the streets bought them of me—they're wanted to kill the black-beetles; they're fed on bread and milk, and they'll suck a cow quite dry in their wild state. They eat adders, and can't be p'isoned, at least it says so in a book I've got about 'em at home.

"The effets I gets orders for in the streets. Gentlemen gives me their cards, and tells me to bring them one; they're 2d. apiece. I get them at Hampstead and Highgate, from the ponds. They're wanted for cur'osity.

"The snails and frogs I sell to Frenchmen. I don't know what part they eat of the frog, but I know they buy them, and the dandelion root. The frogs is 6d. and 1s. a dozen. They like the yellow-bellied ones, the others they're afraid is toads. They always pick out the yellow-bellied first; I don't know how to feed 'em, or else I might fatten them. Many people swallows young frogs, they're reckoned very good things to clear the inside. The frogs I catch in ponds and ditches up at Hampstead and Highgate, but I only get them when I've a order. I've had a order for as many as six dozen, but that was for the French hotel in Leicester-square; but I *have* sold three dozen a week to one man, a Frenchman, as keeps a cigar shop in R——r's-court.

"The snails I sell by the pailful—at 2s. 6d. the pail. There is some hundreds in a pail. The wet weather is the best times for catching 'em; the French people eats 'em. They boils 'em first to get 'em out of the shell and get rid of the green froth; then they boils them again, and after that in vinegar. They eats 'em hot, but some of the foreigners likes 'em cold. They say they're better, if possible, than whelks. I used to sell a great many to a lady and gentleman in Soho-square, and to many of the French I sell 1s.'s worth, that's about three or four quarts. Some persons buys snails for birds, and some to strengthen a sickly child's back; they rub the back all over with the snails, and a very good thing they tell me it is. I used to take 2s.'s worth a week to one woman; it's the green froth that does the greatest good. There are two more birds'-nest sellers besides myself, they don't do as many as me the two of 'em. They're very naked, their things is all to ribbins; they only go into the country once in a fortnight. They was never nothing, no trade—they never was in place—from what I've heard—either of them. I reckon I sell about 20 nesties a week take one week with another, and that I do for four months in the year. (This altogether makes 320 nests.) Yes, I should say, I do sell about 300 birds'-nests every year, and the other two, I'm sure, don't sell half that. Indeed they don't want to sell; they does better by what they gets give to them. I can't say what they takes, they're Irish, and I never was in conversation with them. I get about 4s. to 5s. for the 20 nests, that's between 2d. and 3d. apiece. I sell about a couple of snakes every week, and for some of them I get 1s., and for the big ones 2s. 6d.; but them I seldom find. I've only had three hedgehogs this season, and I've done a little in snails and frogs, perhaps about 1s. The many foreigners in London this season hasn't done me no good. I haven't been to Leicester-square lately, or perhaps I might have got a large order or two for frogs."

LIFE OF A BIRD'S-NEST SELLER.

"I am 22 years of age. My father was a dyer, and I was brought up to the same trade. My father lived at Arundel, in Sussex, and kept a shop there. He had a good business as dyer, scourer, calico glazer, and furniture cleaner. I have heard mother say his business in Arundel brought him in 300l. a year at least. He had eight men in his employ, and none under 30s. a week. I had two brothers and one sister, but one of my brothers is since dead. Mother died five years ago in the Consumption Hospital, at Chelsea, just after it was built. I was very young indeed when father died; I can hardly remember him. He died in Middlesex Hospital: he had abscesses all over him; there were six-and-thirty at the time of his death. I've heard mother say many times that she thinked it was through exerting himself too much at his business that he fell ill. The ruin of father was owing to his house being burnt down; the fire broke out at two in the morning; he wasn't insured: I don't remember the fire; I've only heerd mother talk about it. It was the ruin of us all she used to tell me; father had so much work belonging to other people; a deal of moreen curtains, five or six hundred yards. It was of no use his trying to start again: he lost all his glazing machines and tubs, and his drugs and 'punches.' From what I've heerd from mother they was worth some hundreds. The Duke of Norfolk, after the fire, gave a good lot of money to the poor people whose things father had to clean, and father himself came up to London. I wasn't two year old when that happened. We all come up with father, and he opened a shop in London and bought all new things. He had got a bit of money left, and mother's uncle lent him 60l. We lived two doors from the stage door of the Queen's Theatre, in Pitt-street, Charlotte-street, Fitzroy-square; but father didn't do much in London; he had a new connection to make, and when he died his things was sold for the rent of the house. There was only money enough to bury him. I don't know how long ago that was, but I think it was about three years after our coming to London, for I've heerd mother say I was six years old when father died. After father's death mother borrowed some more money of her uncle, who was well to do. He was perfumer to her Majesty: he's dead now, and left the business to his foreman. The business was worth 2000l. His wife, my mother's aunt, is alive still, and though she's a woman of large property, she won't so much as look at me. She keeps her carriage and two footmen; her address is, Mrs. Lewis, No. 10, Porchester-terrace, Bayswater. I have been in her drawing-room two or three times. I used to take letters to her from mother: she was very kind to me then, and give me several half-crowns. She knows the state I am in now. A young man wrote a letter to her, saying I had no clothes to look after work in, and that I was near starving, but she sent no answer to it. The last time I called at her house she sent me down nothing, and bid the servant tell me not to come any more. Ever since I've wanted it I've never had nothing from her, but before that she used to give me something whenever I took a letter from mother to her. The last half-crown I got at her house was from the cook, who gave it me out of her own money because she'd known my mother.

"I've got a grandmother living in Woburn-place; she's in service there, and been in the family for twenty years. The gentleman died lately and left her half his property. He was a foreigner and had no relations here. My grandmother used to be very good to me, and when I first got out of work she always gave me something when I called, and had me down in her room. She was housekeeper then. She never offered to get me a situation, but only gave me a meal of victuals and a shilling or eighteen-pence whenever I called. I was tidy in my dress then. At last a new footman came, and he told me as I wasn't to call again; he said, the family didn't allow no followers. I've never seen my grandmother since that time but once, and then I was passing with my basket of birds' nests in my hand just as she was coming out of the door. I was dressed about the same then as you seed me yesterday. I was without a shirt to my back. I don't think she saw me, and I was ashamed to let her see me as I was. She was kind enough to me, that is, she wouldn't mind about giving me a shilling or so at a time, but she never would do nothing else for me, and yet she had got plenty of money in the bank, and a gold watch, and all, at her side.

After father died, as I was saying, mother got some money from her uncle and set up on her own account; she took in glazing for the trade. Father had a few shops that he worked for, and they employed mother after his death. She kept on at this for eighteen months and then she got married again. Before this an uncle of mine, my father's brother, who kept some lime-kilns down in Bury St. Edmunds, consented to take my brother and sister and provide for them, and four or five year ago he got them both into the Duke of Norfolk's service, and there they are now. They've never seen me since I was a child but once, and that was a few year ago. I've never sent to them to say how badly I was off. They're younger than I am, and can only just take care of theirselves. When mother married again, her husband came to live at the house; he was a dyer. He behaved very well to me. Mother wouldn't send me down to uncle's, she was too fond of me. I was sent to school for about eighteen months, and after that I used to assist in the glazing at home, and so I went on very comfortable for some time. Nine year ago I went to work at a French dyer's, in Rathbone-place. My step-father got me there, and there I stopped six year. I lived in the house after the first eighteen months of my service. Five year ago mother fell ill; she had been ailing many years, and she got admitted into the Consumption Hospital, at Brompton. She was there just upon three months and was coming out the next day (her term was up), when she died on the over night. After that my step-father altered very much towards me. He didn't want me at home at all. He told me so a fortnight after mother was in her grave. He took to drinking very hearty directly she was gone. He would do anything for me before that. He used to take me with him to every place of amusement what he went to, but when he took to drinking he quite changed; then he got to beat me, and at last he told me I needn't come there any more.

"After that, I still kept working in Rathbone-place, and got a lodging of my own; I used to have 9s. a week where I was, and I paid 2s. a week for my bed, and washing, and mending. I had half a room with a man and his wife; I went on so for about two years, and then I was took bad with the scarlet fever and went to Gray's-inn-lane hospital. After I was cured of the scarlet fever, I had the brain fever, and was near my death; I was altogether eight weeks in the hospital, and when I come out I could get no work where I had been before. The master's nephew had come from Paris, and they had all French hands in the house. He wouldn't employ an English hand at all. He give me a trifle of money, and told me he would pay my lodgings for a week or two while I looked for work. I sought all about and couldn't find any; this was about three year ago. People wouldn't have me because I didn't know nothing about the English mode of business. I couldn't even tell the names of the English drugs, having been brought up in a French house. At last, my master got tired of paying for my lodging, and I used to try and pick up a few pence in the streets by carrying boxes and holding horses, it was all as I could get to do; I tried all I could to find employment, and they was the only jobs I could get. But I couldn't make enough for my lodging this way, and over and over again I've had to sleep out. Then I used to walk the streets most of the night, or lie about in the markets till morning came in the hopes of getting a job. I'm a very little eater, and perhaps that's the luckiest thing for such as me; half a pound of bread and a few potatoes will do me for the day. If I could afford it, I used to get a ha'porth of coffee and a ha'porth of sugar, and make it do twice. Sometimes I used to have victuals give to me, sometimes I went without altogether; and sometimes I couldn't eat. I can't always.

"Six weeks after I had been knocking about in the streets in the manner I've told you, a man I met in Covent-Garden market told me he was going into the country to get some roots (it was in the winter time and cold indeed; I was dressed about the same as I am now, only I had a pair of boots); and he said if I chose to go with him, he'd give me half of whatever he earned. I went to Croydon and got some primroses; my share came to 9d., and that was quite a God-send to me, after getting nothing. Sometimes before that I'd been two days without tasting anything; and when I got some victuals after that, I couldn't touch them. All I felt was giddy; I wasn't to say hungry, only weak and sicklified. I went with this man after the roots two or three times; he took me to oblige me, and show me the way how to get a bit of food for myself; after that, when I got to know all about it, I went to get roots on my own account. I never felt a wish to take nothing when I was very hard up. Sometimes when I got cold and was tired, walking about and weak from not having had nothing to eat, I used to think I'd break a window and take something out to get locked up; but I could never make my mind up to it; they never hurt me, I'd say to myself. I do fancy though, if anybody had refused me a bit of bread, I should have done something again them, but I couldn't, do you see, in cold blood like.

"When the summer came round a gentleman whom I seed in the market asked me if I'd get him half a dozen nesties—he didn't mind what they was, so long as they was small, and of different kinds—and as I'd come across a many in my trips after the flowers, I told him I would do so—and that first put it into my head; and I've been doing that every summer since then. It's poor work, though, at the best. Often and often I have to walk 30 miles out without any victuals to take with me, or money to get any, and 30 miles again back, and bring with me about a dozen nesties; and, perhaps, if I'd no order for them, and was forced to sell them to the boys, I shouldn't get more than a shilling for the lot after all. When the time comes round for it, I go Christmasing and getting holly, but that's more dangerous work than bird-nesting; the farmers don't mind your taking the nesties, as it prevents the young birds from growing up and eating their corn. The greater part of the holly used in London for trimming up the churches and sticking in the puddings, is stolen by such as me, at the risk of getting six months for it. The farmers brings a good lot to market, but we is obligated to steal it. Take one week with another, I'm sure I don't make above 5s. You can tell that to look at me. I don't drink, and I don't gamble; so you can judge how much I get when I've had to pawn my shirt for a meal. All last week I only sold two nesties—they was a partridge's and a yellow-hammer's; for one I got 6d., and the other 3d., and I had been thirteen miles to get them. I got beside that a fourpenny piece for some chickweed which I'd been up to Highgate to gather for a man with a bad leg (it's the best thing there is for a poultice to a wound), and then I earned another 4d. by some mash (marsh) mallow leaves (that there was to purify the blood of a poor woman): that, with 4d. that a gentleman give to me, was all I got last week; 1s. 9d. I think it is altogether. I had some victuals give to me in the street, or else I daresay I should have had to go without; but, as it was, I gave the money to the man and his wife I live with. You see they had nothing, and as they're good to me when I want, why, I did what I could for them. I've tried to get out of my present life, but there seems to be an ill luck again me. Sometimes I gets a good turn. A gentleman gives me an order, and then I saves a shilling or eighteenpence, so as to buy something with that I can sell again in the streets; but a wet day is sure to come, and then I'm cracked up, obligated to eat it all away. Once I got to sell fish. A gentleman give me a crown-piece in the street, and I borrowed a barrow at 2d. a day, and did pretty well for a time. In three weeks I had saved 18s.; then I got an order for a sack of moss from one of the flower-sellers, and I went down to Chelmsford, and stopped for the night in Lower Nelson-street, at the sign of "The Three Queens." I had my money safe in my fob the night before, and a good pair of boots to my feet then; when I woke in the morning my boots was gone, and on feeling in my fob my money was gone too. There was four beds in the rooms, feather and flock; the feather ones was 4d., and the flock 3d. for a single one, and 2½d. each person for a double one. There was six people in the room that night, and one of 'em was gone before I awoke—he was a cadger—and had took my money with him. I complained to the landlord—they call him George—but it was no good; all I could get was some victuals. So I've been obliged to keep to birds'-nesting ever since.

"I've never been in prison but once. I was took up for begging. I was merely leaning again the railings of Tavistock-square with my birds'-nesties in my hand, and the policemen took me off to Clerkenwell, but the magistrates, instead of sending me to prison, gave me 2s. out of the poors'-box. I feel it very much going about without shoes or without shirt, and exposed to all weathers, and often out all night. The doctor at the hospital in Gray's-inn-lane gave me two flannels, and told me that whatever I did I was to keep myself wrapped up; but what's the use of saying that to such as me who is obligated to pawn the shirt off our back for food the first wet day as comes? If you haven't got money to pay for your bed at a lodging-house, you must take the shirt off your back and leave it with them, or else they'll turn you out. I know many such. Sometimes I go to an artist. I had 5s. when I was drawed before the Queen. I wasn't 'xactly drawed before her, but my portrait was shown to her, and I was told that if I'd be there I might receive a trifle. I was drawed as a gipsy fiddler. Mr. Oakley in Regent-street was the gentleman as did it. I was dressed in some things he got for me. I had an Italian's hat, one with a broad brim and a peaked crown, a red plush waistcoat, and a yellow hankercher tied in a good many knots round my neck. I'd a black velveteen Newmarket-cut coat, with very large pearl buttons, and a pair of black knee-breeches tied with fine red strings. Then I'd blue stripe stockings and high-ancle boots with very thin soles. I'd a fiddle in one hand and a bow in the other. The gentleman said he drawed me for my head of hair. I've never been a gipsy, but he told me he didn't mind that, for I should make as good a gipsy fiddler as the real thing. The artists mostly give me 2s. I've only been three times. I only wish I could get away from my present life. Indeed I would do any work if I could get it. I'm sure I could have a good character from my masters in Rathbone-place, for I never done nothing wrong. But if I couldn't get work I might very well, if I'd money enough, get a few flowers to sell. As it is it's more than any one can do to save at bird-nesting, and I'm sure I'm as prudent as e'er a one in the streets. I never took the pledge, but still I never take no beer nor spirits—I never did. Mother told me never to touch 'em, and I haven't tasted a drop. I've often been in a public-house selling my things, and people has offered me something to drink, but I never touch any. I can't tell why I dislike doing so —but something seems to tell me not to taste such stuff. I don't know whether it's what my mother said to me. I know I was very fond of her, but I don't say it's that altogether as makes me do it. I don't feel to want it. I smoke a good bit, and would sooner have a bit of baccy than a meal at any time. I could get a goodish rig-out in the lane for a few shillings. A pair of boots would cost me 2s., and a coat I could get for 2s. 6d. I go to a ragged school three times a week if I can, for I'm but a poor scholar still, and I should like to know how to read; it's always handy you know, sir."

This lad has been supplied with a suit of clothes and sufficient money to start him in some of the better kind of street-trades. It was thought advisable not to put him to any more *settled* occupation on account of the vagrant habits he has necessarily acquired during his bird-nesting career. Before doing this he was employed as errand-boy for a week, with the object of testing his trustworthiness, and was found both honest and attentive. He appears a prudent lad, but of course it is difficult, as yet, to speak positively as to his character. He has, however, been assured that if he shows a disposition to follow some more reputable calling he shall at least be put in the way of so doing.

Of the Street-Sellers of Squirrels.

The street squirrel-sellers are generally the same men as are engaged in the open-air traffic in cage-birds. There are, however, about six men who devote themselves more particularly to squirrel-selling, while as many more sometimes "take a turn at it." The squirrel is usually carried in the vendor's arms, or is held against the front of his coat, so that the animal's long bushy tail is seen to advantage. There is usually a red leather collar round its neck, to which is attached some slender string, but so contrived that the squirrel shall not appear to be a prisoner, nor in general—although perhaps the hawker became possessed of his squirrel only that morning—does the animal show any symptoms of fear.

The chief places in which squirrels are offered for sale, are Regent-street and the Royal Exchange, but they are offered also in all the principal thoroughfares—especially at the West End. The purchasers are gentlefolk, tradespeople, and a few of the working classes who are fond of animals. The wealthier persons usually buy the squirrels for their children, and, even after the free life of the woods, the animal seems happy enough in the revolving cage, in which it "thinks it climbs."

The prices charged are from 2s. to 5s., "or more if it can be got," from a third to a half being profit. The sellers will oft enough state, if questioned, that they caught the squirrels in Epping Forest, or Caen Wood, or any place sufficiently near London, but such is hardly ever the case, for the squirrels are bought by them of the dealers in live animals. Countrymen will sometimes catch a few squirrels and bring them to London, and nine times out of ten they sell them to the shopkeepers. To sell three squirrels a day in the street is accounted good work.

I am assured by the best-informed parties that for five months of the year there are 20 men selling squirrels in the streets, at from 20 to 50 per cent. profit, and that they average a weekly sale of six each. The average price is from 2s. to 2s. 6d., although not very long ago one man sold a "wonderfully fine squirrel" in the street for three half-crowns, but they are sometimes parted with for 1s. 6d. or less, rather than be kept overnight. Thus 2400 squirrels are vended yearly in the streets, at a cost to the public of 240l.

Of the Street-Sellers of Leverets, Wild Rabbits, etc.

There are a few leverets, or young hares, sold in the streets, and they are vended for the most part in the suburbs, where the houses are somewhat detached, and where there are plenty of gardens. The softness and gentleness of the leveret's look pleases children, more especially girls, I am informed, and it is usually through their importunity that the young hares are bought, in order that they may be fed from the garden, and run tame about an out-house. The leverets thus sold, however, as regards nine out of ten, soon die. They are rarely supplied with their natural food, and all their natural habits are interrupted. They are in constant fear and danger, moreover, from both dogs and cats. One shopkeeper who sold fancy rabbits in a street off the Westminster-road told me that he had once tried to tame and rear leverets in hutches, as he did rabbits, but to no purpose. He had no doubt it might be done, he said, but not in a shop or a small house. Three or four leverets are hawked by the street-people in one basket and are seen lying on hay, the basket having either a wide-worked lid, or a net thrown over it. The hawkers of live poultry sell the most leverets, but they are vended also by the singing-bird sellers. The animals are nearly all bought, for this traffic, at Leadenhall, and are retailed at 1s. to 2s. each, one-third to one-half being profit. Perhaps 300 are sold this way yearly, producing 22l. 10s.

About 400 young wild rabbits are sold in the street in a similar way, but at lower sums, from 3d. to 6d. each, 4d. being the most frequent rate.

The yearly outlay is thus 6*l.* 13*s.* They thrive, in confinement, no better than the leverets.

OF THE STREET-SELLERS OF GOLD AND SILVER FISH.

OF these dealers, residents in London, there are about 70; but during my inquiry (at the beginning of July) there were not 20 in town. One of their body knew of ten who were at work live-fish selling, and there might be as many more, he thought, "working" the remoter suburbs of Blackheath, Croydon, Richmond, Twickenham, Isleworth, or wherever there are villa residences of the wealthy. This is the season when the gold and silver fish-sellers, who are altogether a distinct class from the bird-sellers of the streets, resort to the country, to vend their glass globes, with the glittering fish swimming ceaselessly round and round. The gold fish-hawkers are, for the most part, of the very best class of the street-sellers. One of the principal fish-sellers is in winter a street-vendor of cough drops, horehound candy, coltsfoot-sticks, and other medicinal confectionaries, which he himself manufactures. Another leading gold-fish seller is a costermonger now "on pine-apples." A third, "with a good connection among the innkeepers," is in the autumn and winter a hawker of game and poultry.

There are in London three wholesale dealers in gold and silver fish; two of whom—one in the Kingsland-road and the other close by Billingsgate—supply more especially the street-sellers, and the street-traffic is considerable. Gold fish is one of the things which people buy when brought to their doors, but which they seldom care to "order." The importunity of children when a man unexpectedly tempts them with a display of such brilliant creatures as gold fish, is another great promotive of the street-trade; and the street-traders are the best customers of the wholesale purveyors, buying somewhere about three-fourths of their whole stock. The dealers keep their fish in tanks suited to the purpose, but goldfish are never bred in London. The English-reared gold fish are "raised" for the most part, as respects the London market, in several places in Essex. In some parts they are bred in warm ponds, the water being heated by the steam from adjacent machinery, and in some places they are found to thrive well. Some are imported from France, Holland, and Belgium; some are brought from the Indies, and are usually sold to the dealers to improve their breed, which every now and then, I was told, "required a foreign mixture, or they didn't keep up their colour." The Indian and foreign fish, however, are also sold in the streets; the dealers, or rather the Essex breeders, who are often in London, have "just the pick of them," usually through the agency of their town customers. The English-reared gold fish are not much short of three-fourths of the whole supply, as the importation of these fishes is troublesome; and unless they are sent under the care of a competent person, or unless the master or steward of a vessel is made to incur a share in the venture, by being paid so much freight-money for as many gold and silver fishes as are landed in good health, and nothing for the dead or dying, it is very hazardous sending them on shipboard at all, as in case of neglect they may all die during the voyage.

The gold and silver fish are of the carp species, and are natives of China, but they were first introduced into this country from Portugal about 1690. Some are still brought from Portugal. They have been common in England for about 120 years.

These fish are known in the street-trade as "globe" and "pond" fish. The distinction is not one of species, nor even of the "variety" of a species, but merely a distinction of size. The larger fish are "pond;" the smaller, "globe." But the difference on which the street-sellers principally dwell is that the pond fish are far more troublesome to keep by them in a "slack time," as they must be fed and tended most sedulously. Their food is stale bread or biscuit. The "globe" fish are not fed at all by the street-dealer, as the animalcules and the minute insects in the water suffice for their food. Soft, rain, or sometimes Thames water, is used for the filling of the globe containing a street-seller's gold fish, the water being changed twice a day, at a public-house or elsewhere, when the hawker is on a round. Spring-water is usually rejected, as the soft water contains "more feed." One man, however, told me he had recourse to the street-pumps for a renewal of water, twice, or occasionally thrice a day, when the weather was sultry; but spring or well water "wouldn't do at all." He was quite unconscious that he was using it from the pump.

The wholesale price of these fish ranges from 5*s.* to 18*s.* per dozen, with a higher charge for "picked fish," when high prices must be paid. The cost of "large silvers," for instance, which are scarcer than "large golds," so I heard them called, is sometimes 5*s.* apiece, even to a retailer, and rarely less than 3*s.* 6*d.* The most frequent price, retail from the hawker—for almost all the fish are hawked, but only there, I presume, for a temporary purpose—is 2*s.* the pair. The gold fish are now always hawked in glass globes, containing about a dozen occupants, within a diameter of twelve inches. These globes are sold by the hawker, or, if ordered, supplied by him on his next round that way, the price being about 2*s.* Glass globes, for the display of gold fish, are indeed manufactured at from 6*d.* to 1*l.* 10*s.* each, but 2*s.* or 2*s.* 6*d.* is the usual limit to the price of those vended in the street. The fish are lifted out of the water in the globe to consign to a purchaser, by being caught in a neat net, of fine and different-coloured cordage, always carried by the hawker, and manufactured for the trade at 2*s.* the dozen. Neat handles for these nets, of stained or plain wood, are 1*s.* the dozen. The dealers avoid touching the fish with their hands. Both gold fish and glass globes are much cheaper than they were ten years ago; the globes are cheaper, of course, since the alteration in the tax on glass, and the street-sellers are, numerically, nearly double what they were.

From a well-looking and well-spoken youth of 21 or 22, I had the following account. He was the son, and grandson, of costermongers, but was —perhaps, in consequence of his gold-fish selling lying among a class not usually the costermongers' customers— of more refined manners than the generality of the costers' children.

"I've been in the streets, sir," he said, "helping my father, until I was old enough to sell on my own account, since I was six years old. *Yes, I like a street life, I'll tell you the plain truth, for I was put by my father to a paperstainer, and found I couldn't bear to stay in doors. It would have killed me.* Gold fish are as good a thing to sell as anything else, perhaps, but I've been a costermonger as well, and have sold both fruit and good fish—salmon and fine soles. Gold fish are not good for eating. I tried one once, just out of curiosity, and it tasted very bitter indeed; I tasted it boiled. I've worked both town and country on gold fish. I've served both Brighton and Hastings. The fish were sent to me by rail, in vessels with air-holes, when I wanted more. I never stopped at lodging-houses, but at respectable public-houses, where I could be well suited in the care of my fish. It's an expense, but there's no help for it." [A costermonger, when I questioned him on the subject, told me that he had sometimes sold gold fish in the country, and though he had often enough slept in common lodging-houses, he never could carry his fish there, for he felt satisfied, although he had never tested the fact, that in nine out of ten such places, the fish, in the summer season, would half of them die during the night from the foul air.] "Gold fish sell better in the country than town," the street-dealer continued; "much better. They're more thought of in the country. My father's sold them all over the world, as the saying is. I've sold both foreign and English fish. I prefer English. They're the hardiest; Essex fish. The foreign—I don't just know what part—are bred in milk ponds; kept fresh and sweet, of course; and when they're brought here, and come to be put in cold water, they soon die. In Essex they're bred in cold water. They live about three years; that's their lifetime if they're properly seen to. I don't know what kind of fish gold fish are. I've heard that they first came from China. No, I can't read, and I'm very sorry for it. If I have time next winter I'll get taught. Gentlemen sometimes ask me to sit down, and talk to me about fish, and their history (natural history), and I'm often at a loss, which I mightn't be if I could read. If I have fish left after my day's work, I never let them stay in the globe I've hawked them in, but put them into a large pan, a tub sometimes, three-parts full of water, where they have room. My customers are ladies and gentlemen, but I have sold to shopkeepers, such as buttermen, that often show gold fish and flowers in their shops. The fish don't live long in the very small globes, but they're put in them sometimes just to satisfy children. I've sold as many as two dozen at a time to stock a pond in a gentleman's garden. It's the best sale a little way out of town, in any direction. I sell six dozen a week, I think, one week with another; they'll run as to price at 1s. apiece. That six dozen includes what I sell both in town and country. Perhaps I sell them nearly three-parts of the year. Some hawk all the year, but it's a poor winter trade. Yes, I make a very fair living; 2s. 6d. or 3s. or so, a day, perhaps, on gold fish, when the weather suits."

A man, to whom I was referred as an experienced gold fish-seller, had just returned, when I saw him, from the sale of a stock of new potatoes, peas, &c., which he "worked" in a donkey cart. He had not this season, he said, started in the gold-fish line, and did very little last year in it, as his costermongering trade kept steady, but his wife thought gold fish-selling was a better trade, and she always accompanied him in his street rounds; so he might take to it again. In his youth he was in the service of an old lady who had several pets, and among them were gold fish, of which she was very proud, always endeavouring to procure the finest, a street-seller being sure of her as a customer if he had fish larger or deeper or brighter-coloured than usual. She kept them both in stone cisterns, or small ponds, in her garden, and in glass globes in the house. Of these fish my informant had the care, and was often commended for his good management of them. After his mistress's death he was very unlucky, he said, in his places. His last master having been implicated, he believed, in some gambling and bill-discounting transactions, left the kingdom suddenly, and my informant was without a character, for the master he served previously to the one who went off so abruptly was dead, and a character two years back was of no use, for people said, "But where have you been living since? Let me know all about that." The man did not know what to do, for his money was soon exhausted: "I had nothing left," he said, "which I could turn into money except a very good great coat, which had belonged to my last master, and which was given to me because he went off without paying me my wages. I thought of 'listing, for I was tired of a footman's life, *almost always in the house in such places as I had*, but I was too old, I feared, and if I could have got over that I knew I should be rejected because I was getting bald. I was sitting thinking whatever could be done—I wasn't married then—and had nobody to consult with; when I heard the very man as used to serve my old lady crying gold fish in the street. It struck me all of a heap, and I wonder I hadn't thought of it before, when I recollected how well I'd managed the fish, that I'd sell gold fish too, and hawk it as he did, as it didn't seem such a bad trade. So I asked the man all about it, and he told me, and I raised a sovereign on my great coat, and that was my start in the streets. I was nervous, and a little 'shamed at first, but I soon got over that, and in time turned my hand to fruit and other things. Gold fish saved my life, sir; I do believe that, for I might have pined into a consumption if I'd been without something to do, and something to eat much longer."

If we calculate, in order to allow for the cessation of the trade during the winter, and often in the summer when costermongering is at its best, that but half the above-mentioned number of gold-fish sellers hawk in the streets and that for but half a year, each selling six dozen weekly at 12s. the dozen, we find 65,520 fish sold, at an outlay of 3276l. As the country is also "worked" by the London street-sellers, and the supply is derived from London, the number and amount may be doubled to include this traffic, or 131,040 fish sold, and 6552l. expended.

Of the Street-Sellers of Tortoises.

The number of tortoises sold in the streets of London is far greater than might be imagined, for it is a creature of no utility, and one which is inanimate in this country for half its life.

Of live tortoises, there are 20,000 annually imported from the port of Mogadore in Morocco. They are not brought over, as are the parrots, &c., of which I have spoken, for amusement or as private ventures of the seamen, but are regularly consigned from Jewish houses in Mogadore, to Jewish merchants in London. They are a freight of which little care is taken, as they are brought over principally as ballast in the ship's hold, where they remain torpid.

The street-sellers of tortoises are costermongers of the smarter class. Sometimes the vendors of shells and foreign birds "work" also a few tortoises, and occasionally a wholesale dealer (the consignee of the Jewish house in Africa) will send out his own servants to sell barrow-loads of tortoises in the street on his own account. They are regularly ranged on the barrows, and certainly present a curious appearance—half-alive creatures as they are (when the weather is not of the warmest), brought from another continent for sale by thousands in the streets of London, and retention in the gardens and grounds of our civic villas. Of the number imported, one-half, or 10,000, are yearly sold in the streets by the several open-air dealers I have mentioned. The wholesale price is from 4s. to 6s. the dozen; they are retailed from 6d. to 1s., a very fine well-grown tortoise being sometimes worth 2s. 6d. The mass, however, are sold at 6d. to 9d. each, but many fetch 1s. They are bought for children, and to keep in gardens as I have said, and when properly fed on lettuce leaves, spinach, and similar vegetables, or on white bread sopped in water, will live a long time. If the tortoise be neglected in a garden, and have no access to his favourite food, he will eat almost any green thing which comes in his way, and so may commit ravages. During the winter, and the later autumn and earlier spring, the tortoise is torpid, and may be kept in a drawer or any recess, until the approach of summer "thaws" him, as I heard it called.

Calculating the average price of tortoises in street-sale at 8d. each, we find upwards of 333l. thus expended yearly.

Of the Street-Sellers of Snails, Frogs, Worms, Snakes, Hedgehogs, etc.

I class together these several kinds of live creatures, as they are all "gathered" and sold by the same persons—principally by the men who supply bird-food, of whom I have given accounts in my statements concerning groundsel, chickweed, plaintain, and turf-selling.

The principal *snail-sellers*, however, are the turf-cutters, who are young and active men, while the groundsel-sellers are often old and infirm and incapable of working all night, as the necessities of the snail-trade often require. Of turf-cutters there were, at the time of my inquiry last winter, 42 in London, and of these full one-third are regular purveyors of snails, such being the daintier diet of the caged blackbirds and thrushes. These men obtain their supply of snails in the market-gardens, the proprietors willingly granting leave to any known or duly recommended person who will rid them of these depredators. Seven-eighths of the quantity gathered are sold to the bird-dealers, to whom the price is 2d. a quart. The other eighth is sold on a street round at from 3d. to 6d. the quart. A quart contains at least 80 snails, not heaped up, their shells being measured along with them. One man told me there were "100 snails to a fair quart."

When it is moonlight at this season of the year, the snail gatherers sometimes work all night; at other times from an hour before sunset to the decline of daylight, the work being resumed at the dawn. To gather 12 quarts in a night, or a long evening and morning, is accounted a prosperous harvest. Half that quantity is "pretty tidy." An experienced man said to me :—

" The best snail grounds, sir, you may take my word for it, is in Putney and Barnes. It's the 'greys' we go for, the fellows with the shells on 'em; the black snails or slugs is no good to us. I think snails is the slowest got money of any. I don't suppose they get's scarcer, but there's good seasons for snails and there's bad. Warm and wet is best. We don't take the little 'uns. They come next year. I may make 1l. a year, or a little more, in snails. In winter there's hardly anything done in them, and the snails is on the ground; in summer they're on the walls or leaves. They'll keep six months without injury; they'll keep the winter round indeed in a proper place."

I am informed that the 14 snail gatherers on the average gather six dozen quarts each in a year, which supplies a total of 12,096 quarts, or individually, 1,189,440 snails. The labourers in the gardens, I am informed, may gather somewhat more than an equal quantity,—all being sold to the bird-shops; so that altogether the supply of snails for the caged thrushes and blackbirds of London is about two millions and a half. Computing them at 24,000 quarts, and only at 2d. a quart, the outlay is 200l. per annum.

The *Frogs* sold by street-people are, at the rate of about 36 dozen a year, disposed of in equal proportion to University and King's Colleges. Only two men collect the frogs, one for each hospital. They are charged 1*d*. each :—" I've sometimes," said one of the frog-purveyors, "come on a place where I could have got six or seven dozen in a day, but that's mostly been when I didn't want them. At other times I've gone days without collaring a single frog. I only want them four times a year, and four or five dozen at a time. The low part of Hampstead's the best ground for them, I think. The doctors like big fellows. They keep them in water 'til they're wanted to dissect." One man thought that there might be 50 more frogs or upwards ordered yearly, through the bird-shops, for experiments under air-pumps, &c. This gives about 500 frogs sold yearly by the street-people. One year, however, I was told, the supply was larger, for a Camberwell gentleman ordered 40 frogs to stock a watery place at the foot of his garden, as he liked to hear and see them.

The *Toad* trade is almost a nonentity. One man, who was confident he had as good a trade in that line as any of his fellows, told me that last year he only supplied one toad; in one year, he forgot the precise time, he collected ten. He was confident that from 12 to 24 a year was now the extent of the toad trade, perhaps 20. There was no regular price, and the men only "work to order." "It's just what the shopkeeper, mostly a herbalist, likes to give." I was told, from 1*d*. to 6*d*. according to size. "I don't know what they're wanted for, something about the doctors, I believe. But if you want any toads, sir, for anything, I know a place between Hampstead and Willesden, where there's real stunners."

Worms are collected in small quantities by the street-sellers, and very grudgingly, for they are to be supplied gratuitously to the shopkeepers who are the customers of the turf-cutters, and snail and worm collectors. "They expects it as a parquisite, like." One man told me that they only gathered ground worms for the bird-fanciers.

Of the *Snakes* and *Hedgehogs* I have already spoken, when treating of the collection of birds'-nests. I am told that some few *glow-worms* are collected.

OF THE STREET-SELLERS OF MINERAL PRODUCTIONS AND NATURAL CURIOSITIES.

THE class of which I have now to treat, including as it does the street-sellers of coal, coke, tan-turf, salt, and sand, seem to have been called into existence principally by the necessities of the poorer classes. As the earnings of thousands of men, in all the slop, "slaughter-house," or "scamping" branches of tailoring, shoe-making, cabinet-making, joining, &c. have become lower and lower, they are compelled to purchase the indispensable articles of daily consumption in the smallest quantities, and at irregular times, just as the money is in their possession. This is more especially the case as regards chamber-masters and garret-masters (among the shoemakers) and cabinet-makers, who, as they are small masters, and working on their own account, have not even such a regularity of payment as the journeyman of the slop-tailor. Among these poor artizans, moreover, the wife must slave with the husband, and it is often an object with them to save the time lost in going out to the chandler's-shop or the coal-shed, to have such things as coal, and coke brought to their very doors, and vended in the smallest quantities. It is the same with the women who work for the slop-shirt merchants, &c., or make cap-fronts, &c., on their own account, for the supply of the shopkeepers, or the wholesale swag-men, who sell low-priced millinery. The street-sellers of the class I have now to notice are, then, the principal purveyors of the very poor.

The men engaged in the street-sale of coal and coke—the chief articles of this branch of the street-sale—are of the costermonger class, as, indeed, is usually the case where an exercise of bodily strength is requisite. Costermongers, too, are better versed than any other street-folk in the management of barrows, carts, asses, ponies, or horses, so that when these vehicles and these animals are a necessary part of any open-air business, it will generally be found in the hands of the coster class.

Nor is this branch of the street-traffic confined solely to articles of necessity. Under my present enumeration will be found the street-sale of *shells*, an ornament of the mantel-piece above the fire-grate to which coal is a necessity.

The present division will complete the subject of Street *Sale* in the metropolis.

OF THE STREET-SELLERS OF COALS.

ACCORDING to the returns of the coal market for the last few years, there has been imported into London, on an average, 3,500,000 tons of sea-borne coal annually. Besides this immense supply, the various railways have lately poured in a continuous stream of the same commodity from the inland districts, which has found a ready sale without sensibly affecting the accustomed vend of the north country coals, long established on the Coal Exchange.

To the very poor the importance of coal can be scarcely estimated. Physiological and medical writers tell us that carbonaceous food is that which produces heat in the body, and is therefore the fuel of the system. Experience tells us that this is true; for who that has had an opportunity of visiting the habitations of the poor—the dwellers in ill-furnished rooms and garrets—has not remarked the more than half-starved slop needle-woman, the wretched half-naked children of the casually employed labourer, as the dock-man, or those whose earnings are extorted from them by their employers, such as the ballast-man, sitting crouched around the smouldering embers in the place where the fire ought to be? The reason of this is, because the system of the sufferer by long want of food has been deprived of the necessary internal heat, and so seeks instinctively to supply the deficiency by imbibing it from some outward source. It is on this account chiefly, I believe, that I have found the ill-paid and ill-fed workpeople prize warmth almost more than food. Among the poorest Irish, I have invariably found them crowding round the wretched fire when they had nothing to eat.

The census returns of the present year (according to the accounts published in the newspapers) estimate the number of the inhabitants of London at 2,363,141, and the number of inhabited houses as 307,722. Now if we take into consideration that in the immense suburbs of the metropolis, there are branching off from almost every street, labyrinths of courts and alleys, teeming with human beings, and that almost every room has its separate family—for it takes a multitude of poor to make one rich man—we may be able to arrive at the conclusion that by far the greater proportion of coals brought into London are consumed by the poorer classes. It is on this account of the highest importance, that honesty should be the characteristic of those engaged in the vend and distribution of an article so necessary not only to the comfort but to the very existence of the great masses of the population.

The modes in which the coals imported into London are distributed to the various classes of consumers are worthy of observation, as they unmistakably exhibit not only the wealth of the few, but the poverty of the many. The inhabitants of Belgravia, the wealthy shopkeepers, and many others periodically see at their doors the well-loaded waggon of the coal merchant, with two or three swarthy "coal-porters" bending beneath the black heavy sacks, in the act of laying in the 10 or 20 tons for yearly or half-yearly consumption. But this class is supplied from a very different quarter from that of the artizans, labourers, and many others, who, being unable to spare money sufficient to lay in at once a ton or two of coals, must have recourse to other means. To meet their limited resources, there may be found in every part, always in back streets, persons known as coal-shed men, who get the coals from the merchant in 7, 14, or 20 tons at a time, and retail them from $\frac{1}{4}$ cwt. upwards. The coal-shed men are a very numerous class, for there is not a low neighbourhood in any part of the city which contains not two or three of them in every street.

There is yet another class of purchasers of coals, however, which I have called the 'very poor,'—the inhabitants of two pairs back—the dwellers in garrets, &c. It seems to have been for the purpose of meeting the wants of this class that the street-sellers of coals have sprung into existence. Those who know nothing of the decent pride which often lingers among the famishing poor, can scarcely be expected to comprehend the great boon that the street-sellers of coals, if they could only be made honest and conscientious dealers, are calculated to confer on these people. "I have seen," says a correspondent, "the starveling child of misery, in the gloom of the evening, steal timidly into the shop of the coal-shed man, and in a tremulous voice ask, as if begging a great favour, for *seven pound of coals*. The coal-shed man has set down his pint of beer, taken the pipe from his mouth, blowing after it a cloud of smoke, and in a gruff voice, at which the little wretch has shrunk up (if it were possible) into a less space than famine had already reduced her to, and demanded —'Who told you as how I sarves seven pound o' coal?—Go to Bill C—— he may sarve you if he likes—I won't, and that's an end on 't—I wonders what people wants with seven pound o' coal.' The coal-shed man, after delivering himself of this enlightened observation, has placidly resumed his pipe, while the poor child, gliding out into the drizzling sleet, disappeared in the darkness."

The street-sellers vend any quantity at the very door of the purchaser, without rendering it necessary for them to expose their poverty to the prying eyes of the neighbourhood; and, as I have said were the street dealers only honest, they would be conferring a great boon upon the poorer portion of the people, but unhappily it is scarcely possible for them to be so, and realize a profit for themselves. The police reports of the last year show that many of the coal merchants, standing high in the estimation of the world, have been heavily fined for using false weights; and, did the present inquiry admit of it, there might be mentioned many other infamous practices by which the public are shamefully plundered in this commodity, and which go far to prove that the coal trade, *in toto*, is a gigantic fraud. May I ask how it is possible for the street-sellers, with such examples of barefaced dishonesty before their eyes, even to dream of acting honestly? If not actually certain, yet strongly suspecting, that they themselves are defrauded by the merchant, how can it be otherwise than that they should resort to every possible mode of defrauding their customers, and so add to the already almost unendurable burdens of the poorest of the poor, who by one means or other are made to bear all the burdens of the country?

The usual quantity of coals consumed in the poorest rooms, in which a family resides, is $\frac{1}{2}$ cwt. per week in summer, and 1 cwt. do. in winter, or about 2 tons per annum.

The street sale of coals was carried on to a considerable extent during the earlier part of the last century, "small coalmen" being among the regular street-traders. The best known of these was Tom Britton, who died through fright occasioned by a practical joke. He was a great fosterer of a taste for music among the people; for, after hawking his coals during the day, he had a musical gathering in his humble abode in the evening, to which many distinguished persons resorted. This is alluded to in the lines, by Hughes, under Tom Britton's portrait, and the allusion, according to the poetic fashion of the time being made by means of a strained classicality :—

"Cyllenius so, as fables tell, and Jove,
 Came willing guests to poor Philemon's grove."

The trade seems to have disappeared gradually, but has recently been revived in another form.

Some few years ago an ingenious and enterprising costermonger, during a "slack" in his own business, conceived the idea of purchasing some of the refuse of the coals at the wharfs, conveying them round the poorer localities of his beat, in his ass- or pony-cart, and vending them to "room-keepers" and others, in small quantities and at a reduced rate, so as to undersell the coal-shed men, while making for himself a considerable profit. The example was not lost upon his fraternity, and no long time had elapsed before many others had started in the same line; this eventually took so much custom from the regular coal-shed men, that, as a matter of self-defence, those among them who had a horse and cart, found it necessary to compete with the originators of the system in their own way, and, being possessed of more ample means, they succeeded, in a great measure, in driving the costers out of the field. The success of the coal-shed men was for a time so well followed up, that they began by degrees to edge away from the lanes and alleys, extending their excursions into quarters somewhat more aristocratic, and even there establishing a trade amongst those who had previously taken their ton or half ton of coals from the "brass-plate merchant," as he is called in the trade, being a person who merely procures orders for coals, gets some merchant who buys in the coal market to execute them in his name, and manages to make a living by the profits of these transactions. Some of this latter class consequently found themselves compelled to adopt a mode of doing their business somewhat similar, and for that purpose hired vans from the proprietors of those vehicles, loaded them with sacks of coals, drove round among their customers, prepared to furnish them with sacks or half sacks, as they felt disposed. Finally, many of the van proprietors themselves, finding that business might be done in this way, started in the line, and, being in general men of some means, established it as a regular trade. The van proprietors at the present time do the greater part of the business, but there may occasionally be seen, employed in this traffic, all sorts of conveyances, from the donkey-cart of the costermonger, or dock labourer, the latter of whom endeavours to make up for the miserable pittance he can earn at the rate of fourpence per hour, by the profits of this calling, to the aristocratic van, drawn along by two plump, well-fed horses, the property of a man worth 800*l*. or 900*l*.

The van of the street-seller of coals is easily distinguished from the waggon of the regular merchant. The merchant's waggon is always loaded with sacks standing perpendicularly; it is drawn by four immense horses, and is driven along by a gaunt figure, begrimed with coal-dust, and "sporting" ancle boots, or shoes and gaiters, white, or what ought to be white, stockings, velvet knee-breeches, short tarry smock-frock, and a huge fan-tail hat slouching half-way down his back. The street-seller's vehicle, on the contrary, has the coals shot into it without sacks; while, on a tailboard, extending behind, lie weights and scales. It is most frequently drawn by one horse, but sometimes by two, with bells above their collars jingling as they go, or else the driver at intervals rings a bell like a dustman's, to announce his approach to the neighbourhood.

The street-sellers formerly purchased their coals from any of the merchants along the river-side; generally the refuse, or what remained after the best had been picked out by "skreening" or otherwise; but always taking a third or fourth quality as most suitable for their purpose. But since the erection of machinery for getting coals out of the ships in the Regent's Canal basin, they have resorted to that place, as the coals are at once shot from the box in which they are raised from the hold of the ship, into the cart or van, saving all the trouble of being filled in sacks by coal porters, and carried on their backs from the ship, barge, or heap, preparatory to their being emptied into the van; thus getting them at a cheaper rate, and consequently being enabled to realize a greater profit.

Since the introduction of inland coals, also, by the railways, many of the street-sellers have either wholly, or in part, taken to sell them on account of the lower rate at which they can be purchased; sometimes they vend them unmixed, but more frequently they mix them up with "the small" of north country coals of better quality, and palm off the compound as "genuine Wallsend direct from the ship:" this (together with short weights) being, in fact, the principal source of their profit.

It occasionally happens that a merchant purchases in the market a cargo of coals which turns out to be damaged, very small, or of inferior quality. In such cases he usually refuses to take them, and it is difficult to dispose of them in any regular way of trade. Such cargoes, or parts of cargoes, are consequently at times bought up by some of the more wealthy van proprietors engaged in the coal line, who realize on them a great profit.

To commence business as a street-seller of coals requires little capital beyond the possession of a horse and cart. The merchants in all cases let street-sellers have any quantity of coals they may require till they are able to dispose of them; and the street-trade being a ready-money business, they can go on from day to day, or from week to week, according to their pre-arrangements, so that, as far as the commodity in which they deal is concerned, there is no outlay of capital whatever.

There are about 30 two-horse vans continually engaged in this trade, the price of each van being 70*l*. This gives . . . £2100
100 horses at 20*l*. each . . . 1200
160 carts at 10*l*. each . . . 1600
160 horses at 10*l*. each . . 1600
20 donkey or pony carts, value 1*l*. each 20
20 donkeys or ponies at 1*l*. 10*s*. each 30

Making a total of 210 vehicles continually employed, which, with the horses, &c., may be valued at . . 6550

This sum, with the price of 210 sets of weights and scales, at 1*l*. 10*s*. per set 315

Makes a total of £6865

This may be fairly set down as the gross amount of capital at present employed in the street-sale of coals.

It is somewhat difficult to ascertain correctly the amount of coals distributed in this way among the poorer classes. But I have found that they generally take two turns per day; that is they go to the wharfs in the morning, get their vans or carts loaded, and proceed on their various rounds. This first turn usually occupies them till dinner-time, after which they get another load, which is sufficient to keep them employed till night. Now if we allow each van to carry two and a half tons, it will make for all 150 tons per day, or 900 tons per week. In the same manner allowing the 160 carts to carry a ton each, it will give 320 tons per day, or 1920 tons per week, and the twenty pony carts half a ton each, 40 tons per day, or 240 tons per week, making a total of 3060 tons per week, or 159,120 tons per annum. This quantity purchased from the merchants at 14s. 6d. per ton amounts to 115,362l. annually, and sold at the rate of 1s. per cwt., or 1l. per ton, leaves 5s. 6d. per ton profit, or a total profit of 43,758l., and this profit divided according to the foregoing account gives the subjoined amounts, viz. :—

To each two-horse van regularly employed throughout the year, a profit of . . £429 0
To each one-horse cart, ditto, ditto, 171 12
To each pony cart, ditto, ditto, 121 12

From which must, of course, be made the necessary deductions for the keep of the animals and the repair of vehicles, harness, &c.

The keep of a good horse is 10s. per week; a pony 6s. Three horses can be kept for the price of two, and so on; the more there are, the less cost for each.

The localities where the street-sellers of coals may most frequently be met with, are Blackwall, Poplar, Limehouse, Stepney, St. George's East, Twig Folly, Bethnal Green, Spitalfields, Shoreditch, Kingsland, Haggerstone, and Islington. It is somewhat remarkable that they are almost unknown on the south side of the Thames, and are seldom or never to be encountered in the low streets and lanes in Westminster lying contiguous to the river, nor in the vicinity of Marylebone, nor in any place farther west than Shoreditch; this is on account of the distance from the Regent's Canal basin precluding the possibility of their making more than one turn in the day, which would greatly diminish their profits, even though they might get a higher price for their commodity.

It may be observed that the foregoing statement in figures is rather under the mark than otherwise, as it is founded on the amount of coals purchased at a certain rate, and sold at a certain profit, without taking into account any of the "dodges" which almost all classes of coal dealers, from the highest to the lowest, are known to practise, so that the rate of profit arising from this business may be fairly supposed to amount to much more than the above account can show in figures.

I received the following statement from a person engaged in the street traffic :—

"I kept a coal-shed and greengrocer's shop, and as I had a son grown up, I wanted to get something for him to do; so about six years ago, having a pony and cart, and seeing others selling coals through the street, I thought I'd make him try his hand at it. I went to Mr. B——'s, at Whiting's wharf, and got the cart loaded, and sent my son round our own neighbourhood. I found that he soon disposed of them, and so he went on by degrees. People think we get a great deal of profit, but we don't get near as much as they think. I paid 16s. a ton all the winter for coals and sold them for a shilling a hundred, and when I came to feed the horse I found that he 'll nearly eat it all up. A horse's belly is not so easy to fill. I don't think my son earns much more now, in summer, than feeds the horse. It's different in winter; he does not sell more nor half a ton a day now the weather's so warm. In winter he can always sell a ton at the least, and sometimes two, and on the Saturday he might sell three or four. My cart holds a ton; the vans hold from two to three tons. I can't exactly tell how many people are engaged in selling coals in the street, but there are a great many, that's certain. About eight o'clock what a number of carts and vans you'll see about the Regent's Canal! They like to get away before breakfast, because then they may have another turn after dinner. There's a great many go to other places for coals. The people who have vans do much better than those with the carts, because they carry so much that they save time. There are no great secrets in our business; we haven't the same chance of 'doing the thing' as the merchants have. They can mix the coals up as they like for their customers, and sell them for best; all we can do is to buy a low quality; then we may lose our customers if we play any tricks. To be sure, after that we can go to parts where we're not known. I don't use light weights, but I know it's done by a good many, and they mix up small coals a good deal, and that of course helps their profits. My son generally goes four or five miles before he sells a ton of coals, and in summer weather a great deal farther. It's hard-earned money that's got at it, I can tell you. My cart is worth 12l.; I have a van worth 20l. I wouldn't take 20l. for my horse. My van holds two tons of coals, and the horse draws it easily. I send the van out in the winter when there's a good call, but in the summer I only send it out on the Saturday. I never calculated how much profit I made. I haven't the least idea how much is got by it, but I'm sure there's not near as much as you say. Why, if there was, I ought to have made a fortune by this time." [It is right I should state that I received the foregoing account of the profits of the street trade in coals from one practically and eminently acquainted with it.] "Some in the trade have done very well, but they were well enough off before. I know very well I'll never make a fortune at anything; I'll be satisfied if I keep moving along, so as to keep out of the Union."

As to the habits of the street-sellers of coals,

they are as various as their different circumstances will admit; but they closely resemble each other in one general characteristic—their provident and careful habits. Many of them have risen from struggling costermongers, to be men of substance, with carts, vans, and horses of their own. Some of the more wealthy of the class may be met with now and then in the parlours of respectable public houses, where they smoke their pipes, sip their brandy and water, and are remarkable for the shrewdness of their remarks. They mingle freely with the respectable tradesmen of their own localities, and may be seen, especially on the Sunday afternoons, with their wives and showily-dressed daughters in the gardens of the New Globe, or Green Dragon—the Cremorne and Vauxhall of the east. I visited the house of one of those who I was told had originally been a costermonger. The front portion of the shop was almost filled with coals, he having added to his occupation of street-seller the business of a coal-shed man; this his wife and a little boy managed in his absence; while, true to his early training, the window-ledge and a bench before it were heaped up with cabbages, onions, and other vegetables. In an open space opposite his door, I observed a one-horse cart and two or three trucks with his name painted thereon. At his invitation, I passed through what may be termed the shop, and entered the parlour, a neat room nicely carpeted, with a round table in the centre, chairs ranged primly round the walls, and a long looking-glass reflecting the china shepherds and shepherdesses on the mantel-piece, while, framed and glazed, all around were highly-coloured prints, among which, Dick Turpin, in flash red coat, gallantly clearing the toll-gate in his celebrated ride to York, and Jack Sheppard lowering himself down from the window of the lock-up house, were most conspicuous. In the window lay a few books, and one or two old copies of *Bell's Life*. Among the well-thumbed books, I picked out the *Newgate Calendar*, and the "*Calendar of Orrers*," as he called it, of which he expressed a very high opinion. "Lor bless you," he exclaimed, "them there stories is the vonderfullest in the vorld! I 'd never ha believed it, if I adn't seed it vith my own two hies, but there can't be no mistake ven I read it hout o' the book, can there, now? I jist asks yer that ere plain question."

Of his career he gave me the following account:—"I vos at von time a coster, riglarly brought up to the business, the times vas good then; but lor, ve used to lush at sich a rate! About ten year ago, I ses to meself, I say Bill, I'm blowed if this here game 'ill do any longer. I had a good moke (donkey), and a tidyish box ov a cart; so vot does I do, but goes and sees von o' my old pals that gits into the coal-line somehow. He and I goes to the Bell and Siven Mackerels in the Mile End Road, and then he tells me all he knowed, and takes me along vith hisself, and from that time I sticks to the coals.

"I niver cared much about the lush myself, and ven I got avay from the old uns, I didn't mind it no how; but Jack my pal vos a awful lushy cove, he couldn't do no good at nothink, votsomever; he died they say of *lirium trumans*" [not understanding what he meant, I inquired of what it was he died]; "why, of *lirium trumans*, vich I takes to be too much of Trueman and Hanbury's heavy; so I takes varnin by poor Jack, and cuts the lush; but if you thinks as ve don't enjoy ourselves sometimes, I tells you, you don't know nothink about it. I'm gittin on like a riglar house a fire."

OF THE STREET-SELLERS OF COKE.

AMONG the occupations that have sprung up of late years is that of the purchase and distribution of the refuse cinders or coke obtained from the different gas-works, which are supplied at a much cheaper rate than coal. Several of the larger gas companies burn as many as 100,000 tons of coals per annum, and some even more, and every ton thus burnt is stated to leave behind two chaldrons of coke, returning to such companies 50 per cent. of their outlay upon the coal. The distribution of coke is of the utmost importance to those whose poverty forces them to use it instead of coal.

It is supposed that the ten gas companies in and about the metropolis produce at least 1,400,000 chaldrons of coke, which are distributed to the poorer classes by vans, one-horse carts, donkey carts, trucks, and itinerant vendors who carry one, and in some cases two sacks lashed together on their backs, from house to house.

The van proprietors are those who, having capital, contract with the companies at a fixed rate per chaldron the year through, and supply the numerous retail shops at the current price, adding 3*d*. per chaldron for carriage; thus speculating upon the rise or fall of the article, and in most cases carrying on a very lucrative business. This class numbers about 100 persons, and are to be distinguished by the words "coke contractor," painted on a showy ground on the exterior of their handsome well-made vehicles; they add to their ordinary business the occupation of conveying to their destination the coke that the companies sell from time to time. These men have generally a capital, or a reputation for capital, to the extent of 400*l*. or 500*l*., and in some cases more, and they usually enter into their contracts with the companies in the summer, when but small quantities of fuel are required, and the gas-works are incommoded for want of space to contain the quantity made. They are consequently able, by their command of means, to make advantageous bargains, and several instances are known of men starting with a wheelbarrow in this calling and who are now the owners of the dwellings in which they reside, and have goods, vans, and carts besides.

Another class, to whom may be applied much that has been said of the van proprietors, are the possessors of one-horse carts, who in many instances keep small shops for the sale of greens, coals, &c. These men are scattered over the whole metropolis, but as they do not exclusively obtain their living by vending this article, they do not properly belong to this portion of the inquiry.

A very numerous portion of the distributors of coke are the donkey-cart men, who are to be seen in all the poorer localities with a quantity shot in the bottom of their cart, and two or three sacks on the top or fastened underneath—for it is of a light nature—ready to meet the demand, crying "Coke! coke! coke!" morning, noon, and night. This they sell as low as 2*d*. per bushel, coke having, in consequence of the cheapness of coals, been sold at the gas-works by the single sack as low as 7*d*., and although there is here a seeming contradiction—that of a man selling and living by the loss—such is not in reality the case. It should be remembered that a bushel of good coke will weigh 40 lbs., and that the bushels of these men rarely exceed 25 lbs.; so that it will be seen that by this unprincipled mode of dealing they can seemingly sell for less than they give, and yet realize a good profit. The two last classes are those who own a truck or wheelbarrow or are the fortunate possessors of an athletic frame and broad shoulders, who roam about near the vicinity of the gas-works, soliciting custom, obtaining ready cash if possible, but in most cases leaving one sack on credit, and obtaining a profit of from 2*d*., 3*d*., 4*d*., or more. These men are to be seen going from house to house cleverly regulating their arrival to such times as when the head of the family returns home with his weekly wage, and in possession of ready cash enough to make a bargain with the coke contractor. Another fact in connection with this class, many of whom are women, who employ boys to drag or carry their wares to their customers, is this: when they fail through any cause, they put their walk up for sale, and find no difficulty to obtain purchasers from 2*l*. to as high as 8*l*., 10*l*., and 12*l*. The street-sellers of coke number in all not less than 1500 persons, who may be thus divided: van proprietors, 100; single horse carts, 300; donkey-cart men, 500; trucks, wheelbarrows, and "physical force men," 550; and women about 50, who penetrate to all the densely-crowded districts about town distributing this useful article; the major portion of those who are of anything like sober habits, live in comfort; and in spite of the opinion held by many, that the consumption of coke is injurious to health and sight, they carry on a large and increasing business.

At the present time coke may be purchased at the gas factories at 6*s*. per chaldron; but in winter it generally rises to 10*s*., so that, taking the average, 8*s*., it will be found, that the gas factories of the metropolis realize no less a sum than 560,000*l*. per annum, by the *coke* produced in the course of their operations. And 4*s*. per chaldron being considered a fair profit, it will be found, that the total profit arising from its sale by the various vendors is 280,000*l*.

It is impossible to arrive with any degree of certainty at the actual amount of business done by each of the above-named classes, and the profits consequent on that business: by dividing the above amount equally among all the coke sellers, it will be found to give 186*l*. per annum to each person. But it will be at once seen, that the same rule holds good in the coke trade that has already been explained in connection with coals: those possessing vans reaping the largest amount of profit; the one-horse cart men next; then the donkey carts, trucks, and wheelbarrows; and, least of all, the "backers," as they are sometimes called.

Concerning the amount of capital invested in the street-sale of coals it may be estimated as follows:—

If we allow 70*l*. for each of the 100 vans, it will give	£7,000
20*l*. for each of the horses	2,000
300 carts at 10*l*. each	3,000
300 horses at 10*l*. each	3,000
500 donkey-carts at 1*l*. each	500
500 donkeys at 1*l*. each	500
200 trucks and barrows at 10*s*. each	100
making a total of	£16,000

		£	*s*.	*d*.
To this must be added				
4800 sacks for the 100 vans at 3*s*. 6*d*. each		840	0	0
3600 sacks for the 300 carts		630	0	0
3000 „ „ 500 donkey carts		525	0	0
1652 „ „ 550 trucks and backers		288	15	0
300 „ „ 50 women		52	10	0
		£18,336	5	0

Which being added to the value of vans, carts, and horses employed in the street-sale of coals, viz.	6,865
gives a capital of	£252,015

employed in the street-sale of coal and coke.

The profits of both these trades added together, namely, that on coals	43,758
and the profit on coke	280,000
shows a total profit of	£323,758

to be divided among 1710 persons, who compose the class of itinerant coal and coke vendors of the metropolis.

The following statement as to the street-sale of coke was given by a man in good circumstances, who had been engaged in the business for many years:—

"I am a native of the south of Ireland. More nor twenty years ago I came to London. I had friends here working in a gas factory, and afther a time they managed to get me into the work too. My business was to keep the coals to the stokers, and when they emptied the retorts to wheel the coke in barrows and empty it on the coke heap. I worked for four or five years, off and on, at this place. I was sometimes put out of work in the summer-time, because they don't want as many hands then. There's not near so much gas burned in summer, and then, of course, it takes less hands to make it. Well, at last I got to be a stoker; I had betther wages thin, and a couple of pots of beer in the day. It was dhreadful hard work, and as hot, aye, as if you were in the inside of an oven. I don't know how I ever stood it. Be me soul, I don't know how anybody stands it; it's the divil's place of all you ever saw in your life, standing there before them retorts with a long heavy rake, pullin out the red-hot coke for the bare life, and then there's the rake red-hot in your hands, and the hissin and the bubblin of the wather, and the smoke and the smell—it's fit to melt a man like a rowl of fresh butther. I wasn't a bit too fond of it, at any rate, for it 'ud kill a horse; so I ses to the wife, 'I can't stand this much longer, Peggy.' Well, behold you, Peggy begins to cry and wring her hands, thinkin we'd starve; but I knew a grate dale betther nor that, for I was two or three times dhrinkin with some of thim that carry the coke out of the yard in sacks to sell to the poor people, and they had twice as much money to spind as me, that was working like a horse from mornin to night. I had a pound or two by me, for I was always savin, and by this time I knew a grate many people round about; so off I goes, and asks one and another to take a sack of coke from me, and bein knoun in the yard, and standin a dhrop o' dhrink now and thin for the fillers, I alway got good measure, and so I used to make four sacks out of three, and often three out of two. Well, at last I got tired carryin sacks on me back all day, and now I know I was a fool for doin it at all, for it's asier to dhrag a thruck with five or six sacks than to carry one; so I got a second-hand thruck for little or nothin, and thin I was able to do five times as much work in half the time. At last, I took a notion of puttin so much every Sathurday night in the savin bank, and faith, sir, that was the lucky notion for me, although Peggy wouldn't hear of it at all at all. She swore the bank 'ud be broke, and said she could keep the goold safer in her own stockin; that thim gintlemin in banks were all a set of blickards, and only desaved the poor people into givin them their money to keep it thimselves. But in spite of Peggy I put the money in, and it was well for me that I did so, for in a short time I could count up 30 or 40 guineas in bank, and whin Peggy saw that the bank wasn't broke she was quite satisfied; so one day I ses to myself, What the divil's the use of me breakin my heart mornin, noon, and night, dhraggin a thruck behind me, whin ever so little a bit of a horse would dhrag ten time as much as I can? so off I set to Smithfield, and bought a stout stump of a horse for 12*l*. 10*s*., and thin wint to a sale and bought an ould cart for little or nothin, and in less nor a month I had every farthin back again in the bank. Well, afther this, I made more and more every day, and findin that I paid more for the coke in winther than in summer, I thought as I had money if I could only get a place to put a good lot in summer to sell in winther it would be a good thing; so I begun to look about, and found this house for sale, so I bought it out and out. It was an ould house to be sure; but it's sthrong enough, and dune up well enough for a poor man—besides there's the yard, and see in that yard there's a hape o' coke for the winther. I'm buyin it up now, an it 'ill turn a nice pinny whin the could weather comes again. To make a long story short, I needn't call the king my cousin. I'm sure any one can do well, if he likes; but I don't mane that they can do well brakin their heart workin; divil a one that sticks to work 'ill ever be a hapenny above a beggar; and I know if I'd stuck to it myself I'd be a grate dale worse off now than the first day, for I'm not so young nor near so sthrong as I was thin, and if I hadn't lift it off in time I'd have nothin at all to look to in a few years more but to ind my days in the workhouse—bad luck to it."

Of the Street-Sellers of Tan-Turf.

Tan-turf is oak bark made into turf after its virtues have been exhausted in the tan-pits. To make it into turf the manufacturers have a mill which is turned by horse-power, in which they grind the bark to a considerable degree of fineness, after which it is shaped by a mould into thin cakes about six inches square, put out to dry and harden, and when thoroughly hardened it is fit for sale and for all the uses for which it is intended.

There is only one place in London or its neighbourhood where there are tan-pits—in Bermondsey—and there only is the turf made. There are not more than a dozen persons in London engaged in the sale of this commodity in the streets, and they are all of the tribe of the costermongers. The usual capital necessary for starting in the line being a donkey and cart, with 9*s*. or 10*s*. to purchase a few hundreds of the turf.

There is a tradition extant, even at the present day, that during the prevalence of the plague in London the houses where the tan-turf was used in a great measure escaped that awful visitation; and to this moment many people purchase and burn it in their houses on account of the peculiar smell, and under the belief that it is efficacious in repelling infectious diseases from the localities in which it is used.

The other purposes for which it is used are for forming a sort of compost or manure for plants of the heath kind, which delight in a soil of this description, growing naturally among mosses and bogs where the peat fuel is obtained. It is used also by small bakers for heating their ovens, as preferable for their purposes, and more economical than any other description of fuel. Sometimes it is used for burning under coppers; and very often for keeping alight during the night, on account of the slowness of its decomposition by fire, for a single cake will continue burning for a whole night, will be found in the morning completely enveloped in a white ash, which, on being removed, discovers the live embers in the centre.

The rate at which the tan-turf is sold to the dealers, at the tan-pits, is from 6*d*. to 9*d*. per hundred cakes. Those at 9*d*. per hundred are perfect and unbroken, while those at 6*d*. have been injured in some way or other. The quality of the article, however, remains the same, and by purchasing some of each sort the vendors are able to make somewhat more profit, which may be, on an average, about 4½*d*. per hundred, as they sell it at 1*s*.

While seeking information on this subject I obtained the address of a person in T—— mews, T—— square, engaged in the business. Running out of the square is a narrow street, which, about mid-way through, leads on the right-hand side to a narrow alley, at the bottom of which is the mews, consisting of merely an oblong court, surrounded by stables of the very smallest dimensions, not one of them being more than twelve feet square. Three or four men, in the long waistcoats and full breeches peculiar to persons engaged among horses, were lounging about, and, with the exception of the horses, appeared to be the only inhabitants of the place. On inquiring of one of the loungers, I was shown a stable in one corner of the court, the wide door of which stood open. On entering I found it occupied by a donkey-cart, containing a couple of hundred cakes of tan-turf; another old donkey-cart was turned up opposite, the tailboard resting on the ground, the shafts pointing to the ceiling, while a cock and two or three draggle-tailed hens were composing themselves to roost on the front portion of the cart between the shafts. Within the space thus inclosed by the two carts lay a donkey and two dogs, that seemed keeping him company, and were busily engaged in mumbling and crunching some old bones. On the wall hung "Jack's harness." In one corner of the ceiling was an opening giving access to the place above, which was reached by means of a long ladder. On ascending this I found myself in a very small attic, with a sloping ceiling on both sides. In the highest part, the middle of the room, it was not more than six feet high, but at the sides it was not more than three feet. In this confined apartment stood a stump bedstead, taking up the greater portion of the floor. In a corner alongside the fire-place I noticed what appeared to be a small turn-up bedstead. A little ricketty deal table, an old smoke-dried Dutch clock, and a poor old woman, withered and worn, were the only other things to be seen in the place. The old woman had been better off, and, as is not uncommon under such circumstances, she endeavoured to make her circumstances appear better than they really were. She made the following statement:—

"My husband was 23 years selling the tan turf. There used to be a great deal more of it sold than there is now; people don't seem to think so much of it now, as they once did, but there are some who still use it. There's an old lady in Kentish-town, who must have it regularly; she burns it on account of the smell, and has burned it for many years: my husband used to serve her. There's an old doctor at Hampstead —or rather he was there, for he died a few days ago—he always bought a deal of it, but I don't know whether he burned it or not; he used to buy 500 or 600 at a time, he was a very good customer, and we miss him now. The gardeners buy some of it, for their plants, they say it makes good manure, though you wouldn't think so to look at it, it's so hard and dry. My husband is dead three years; we were better off when he was alive; he was a very sober and careful man, and never put anything to waste. My youngest son goes with the cart now; he don't do as well as his father, poor little fellow! he's only fourteen years of age, but he does very well for a boy of his age. He sometimes travels 30 miles of a day, and can't sell a load—sometimes not half a load; and then he comes home of a night so foot-sore that you'd pity him. Sometimes he's not able to stir out, for a day or two, but he must do something for a living; there's nothing to be got by idleness. The cart will hold 1000 or 1200, and if he could sell that every day we'd do very well; it would leave us about 3*s*. 6*d*. profit, after keeping the donkey. It costs 9*d*. a day to keep our donkey; he's young yet, but he promises to be a good strong animal, and I like to keep him well, even if I go short myself, for what could we do without him? I believe there are one or two persons selling tan-turf who use trucks, but they're strong; besides they can't do much with a truck, they can't travel as far with a truck as a donkey can, and they can't take as much out with them. My son goes of a morning to Bermondsey for a load, and is back by breakfast time; from this to Bermondsey is a long way—then he goes out and travels all round Kentish-town and Hampstead, and what with going up one street and down another, by the time he comes home at night, he don't travel less than from 25 to 30 miles a day. I have another son, the eldest. He used to go with his father when he was alive; he was reared to the business, but after he died he thought it was useless for both to go out with the cart, so he left it to the little fellow, and now the eldest works among horses. He don't do much, only gets an odd job now and then among the ostlers, and earns a shilling now and then. They're both good lads, and would do well if they could; they do as well as they can, and I have a right to be thankful for it."

The poor woman, notwithstanding the extraordinary place in which she lived, and the confined dimensions of her single apartment (I ascertained that the two sons slept in the stump bedstead, while she used the turn-up), was nevertheless cleanly in her person and apparel, and superior in many respects to persons of the same class, and I give her statement verbatim, as it corroborates, in almost every particular, the statement of the unfortunate seller of salt, who is afflicted with a drunken disorderly wife, and who is also a man superior to the people with whom he is compelled to associate, but who in evident bitterness of spirit made this assertion: "Bad as I'm off now, if I had only a careful partner, I wouldn't want for anything."

Concerning the dogs that I have spoken of as being with the donkey, there is a curious story. During his rounds the donkey frequently met the bitch, and an extraordinary friendship grew up between the two animals, so that the dog at last forsook its owner, and followed the donkey in all his travels. For some time back she has accompanied him home, together with her puppy, and they all sleep cozily together during the night, Jack taking especial care not to hurt the young one. In the morning, when about to go out for the day's work, it is of no use to expect Jack to go without his friends, as he will not budge an inch, so he is humoured in his whim. The puppy, when tired, is put into the cart, and the mother forages for her living along the way; the poor woman not being able to feed them. The owner of the dogs came to see them on the day previous to my visit.

OF THE STREET-SELLERS OF SALT.

UNTIL a few years after the repeal of the duty on the salt, there were no street-sellers of it. It was first taxed in the time of William III., and during the war with Napoleon the impost was 15s. the bushel, or nearly thirty times the cost of the article taxed. The duty was finally repealed in 1823. When the tax was at the highest, salt was smuggled most extensively, and retailed at 4d. and 4½d. the pound. A licence to sell it was also necessary. Street salt-selling is therefore a trade of some twenty years standing. Considering the vast consumption of salt, and the trifling amount of capital necessary to start in the business, it might be expected that the street-sellers would be a numerous class, but they do not number above 150 at the outside. The reason assigned by a well-informed man was, that in every part of London there are such vast numbers of shopkeepers who deal in salt.

About one-half of those employed in street salt-selling have donkeys and carts, and the rest use the two-wheeled barrow of the costermonger, to which class the street salt-sellers, generally, belong. The value of the donkey and cart may be about 2l. 5s. on an average, so that 75 of the number possessing donkeys and carts will have a capital among them equal to the sum of . . . £168 15 0
The barrows of the remainder are worth about 10s. each, which will amount to . . . 37 10 0
To sell 3 cwt. of salt in a day is considered good work; and this, if purchased at 2s. per cwt., gives for stock-money the sum total of . . . 45 0 0

Thus the amount of capital which may be reasonably assumed to be embarked in this business is . £251 5 0

The street-sellers pay at the rate of 2s. per cwt. for the salt, and retail it at 3 lbs. for 1d., which leaves 1s. 1d. profit on every cwt. One day with another, taking wet and dry, for from the nature of the article it cannot be hawked in wet weather, the street-sellers dispose of about 2½ cwt. per day, or 18 tons 15 cwt. per day for all hands, which, deducting Sundays, makes 5825 tons in the course of the year. The profit of 1s. 1d. per cwt. amounts to a yearly aggregate profit of 6310l. 8s. 4d., or about 42l. per annum for each person in the trade.

The salt dealers, generally, endeavour to increase their profits by the sale of mustard, and sometimes by the sale of rock-salt, which is used for horses; but in these things they do little, the most profit they can realize in a day averaging about 4d.

The salt men who merely use the barrow are much better off than the donkey-cart men; the former are young men, active and strong, well able to drive their truck or barrow about from one place to another, and they can thereby save the original price and subsequent keep of the donkey. The latter are in general old men, broken down and weak, or lads. The daily cost of keeping a donkey is from 6d. to 9d.; if we reckon 7½d. as the average, it will annually amount to 11l. 8s. 1d. the year, which will reduce the profit of 42l. to about 30l., and so leave a balance of 11l. 8s. 1d. in favour of the truck or barrow man.

There are nine or ten places where the street-sellers purchase the salt:—Moore's, at Paddington, who get their salt by the canal, from Staffordshire; Welling's, at Battle-bridge; Baillie, of Thames-street, &c. Great quantities are brought to London by the different railways. The street-sellers have all regular beats, and seldom intrude on each other, though it sometimes happens, especially when any quarrel occurs among them, that they oppose and undersell one another in order to secure the customers.

During my inquiries on this subject, I visited Church-lane, Bloomsbury, to see a street-seller, about seven in the evening. Since the alterations in St. Giles's, Church-lane has become one of the most crowded places in London. The houses, none of which are high, are all old, time-blackened, and dilapidated, with shattered window-frames and broken panes. Stretching across the narrow street, from all the upper windows, might be seen lines crossing and recrossing each other, on which hung yellow-looking shirts, stockings, women's caps, and handkerchiefs looking like soiled and torn paper, and throwing the whole lane into shade. Beneath this ragged canopy, the street literally swarmed with human beings—young and old, men and women, boys and girls, wandering about amidst all kinds of discordant sounds. The footpaths on both sides of the narrow street were occupied here and there by groups of men and boys, some sitting on the flags and others leaning against the wall, while their feet, in most instances bare, dabbled in the black channel alongside the kerb, which being disturbed sent up a sickening stench. Some of these groups were playing cards for money, which lay on the ground near them. Men and women at intervals lay stretched out in sleep on the pathway; over these the passengers were obliged to jump; in some instances they stood on their backs as they stepped over them, and then the sleeper languidly raised his head, growled out a drowsy oath, and slept again. Three or four women, with bloated countenances, blood-shot eyes, and the veins of their necks swollen and distended till they resembled strong cords, staggered about violently quarrelling at the top of their drunken voices.

The street salt-seller—whom I had great difficulty in finding in such a place—was a man of about 50, rather sickly in his look. He wore an old cloth cap without a peak, a sort of dun-coloured waistcoat, patched and cobbled, a strong check shirt, not remarkable for its cleanliness, and what seemed to me to be an old pair of buckskin breeches, with fragments hanging loose about them like fringes. To the covering of his feet—I can hardly say shoes—there seemed to be neither soles nor uppers. How they kept on was a mystery.

In answer to my questions, he made the following statement, in language not to be anticipated from his dress, or the place in which he resided: "For many years I lived by the sale of toys, such as little chairs, tables, and a variety of other little things which I made myself and sold in the streets; and I used to make a good deal of money by them; I might have done well, but when a man hasn't got a careful partner, it's of no use what he does, he'll never get on, he may as well give it up at once, for the money'll go out ten times as fast as he can bring it in. I hadn't the good fortune to have a careful woman, but one who, when I wouldn't give her money to waste and destroy, took out my property and made money of it to drink; where a bad example like that is set, it's sure to be followed; the good example is seldom taken, but there's no fear of the bad one. You may want to find out where the evil lies, I tell you it lies in that pint pot, and in that quart pot, and if it wasn't for so many pots and so many pints, there wouldn't be half so much misery as there is. I know that from my own case. I used to sell toys, but since the foreign things were let come over, I couldn't make anything of them, and was obliged to give them up. I was forced to do something for a living, for a half loaf is better than no bread at all, so seeing two or three selling salt, I took to it myself. I buy my salt at Moore's wharf, Paddington; I consider it the purest; I could get salt 3d. or 2d. the cwt., or even cheaper, but I'd rather have the best. A man's not ashamed when he knows his articles are good. Some buy the cheap salt, of course they make more profit. We never sell by measure, always by weight; some of the street weights, a good many of them, are slangs, but I believe they are as honest as many of the shopkeepers after all; every one does the best he can to cheat everybody else. I go two or three evenings in the week, or as often as I want it, to the wharf for a load. I'm going there to-night, three miles out and three miles in. I sell, considering everything, about 2 cwt. a day; I sold 1½ to-day, but to-morrow (Saturday) I'll sell 3 or 4 cwt., and perhaps more. I pay 2s. the cwt. for it, and make about 1s. a cwt. profit on that. I sold sixpennyworth of mustard to-day; it might bring me in 2d. profit, every little makes something. If I wasn't so weak and broke down, I wouldn't trouble myself with a donkey, it's so expensive; I'd easily manage to drive about all I'd sell, and then I'd save the expense. It costs me 7d. or 8d. a day to keep him, besides other things. I got him a set of shoes yesterday, I said I'd shoe him first and myself afterwards; so you see there's other expenses. There's my son, too, paid off the other day from the *Prince of Wales*, after a four years' voyage, and he came home without a sixpence in his pocket. He might have done something for me, but I couldn't expect anything else from him after the example that was set to him. Even now, bad as I am, I wouldn't want for anything if I had a careful woman; but she's a shocking drunkard, and I can do nothing with her." This poor fellow's mind was so full of his domestic troubles that he recurred to them again and again, and was more inclined to talk about what so nearly concerned himself than on any matter of business.

OF THE STREET-SELLERS OF SAND.

Two kinds of sand only are sold in the streets, scouring or floor sand, and bird sand for birds. In scouring sand the trade is inconsiderable to what it was, saw-dust having greatly superseded it in the gin-palace, the tap-room, and the butcher's shop. Of the supply of sand, a man, who was working at the time on Hampstead-heath, gave the following account:—"I've been employed here for five-and-thirty years, under Sir Thomas Wilson. Times are greatly changed, sir; we used to have from 25 to 30 carts a day hawking sand, and taking six or seven men to fill them every morning; besides large quantities which went to brass-founders, and for cleaning dentists' cutlery, for stone-sawing, lead and silver casting, and such like. This heath, sir, contains about every kind of sand, but Sir Thomas won't allow us to dig it. The greatest number of carts filled now is eight or ten a day, which I fill myself. Sir Thomas has raised the price from 3s. 6d. to 4s. a load, of about 2½ tons. Bless you, sir, some years ago, one might go into St. Luke's, and sell five or six cart-loads of house-sand a week; now, a man may roar himself hoarse, and not sell a load in a fortnight. Saw-dust is used in all the public-houses and gin-palaces. People's sprung up who don't use sand at all; and many of the old people are too poor to buy it. The men who get sand here now are old customers, who carry it all over the town, and round Holloway, Islington, and such parts. Twelve year ago I would have taken here 6l. or 7l. in a morning, to-day I have only taken 9s. Fine weather is greatly against the sale of house-sand; in wet, dirty weather, the sale is greater."

One street sand-seller gave the following account of his calling:—

"I have been in the sand business, man and

boy, for 40 years. I was at it when I was 12 years old, and am now 52. I used to have two carts hawking sand, but it wouldn't pay, so I have just that one you see there. Hawking sand is a poor job now. I send two men with that 'ere cart, and pay one of 'em 3*s.* 4*d.* and the other 3*s.* a day. Now, with beer-money, 2*s.* a week, to the man at the heath, and turnpike gates, I reckon every load of sand to cost me 5*s.* Add to that 6*s.* 4*d.* for the two men, the wear and tear, and horse's keep (and, to do a horse justice, you cannot in these cheap times keep him at less than 10*s.* a week, in dear seasons, it will cost 15*s.*), and you will find each load of sand stands me in a good sum. So suppose we get a guinea a load, you see we have no great pull. Then there's the licence, 8*l.* a year. Many years ago we resisted this, and got Mr. Humphreys to defend us before the magistrates at Clerkenwell; but we were 'cast,' several hawkers were fined 10*l.*, and I was brought up before old Sir Richard Birnie, at Bow-street, and had to find bail that I would not sell another bushel of sand till I took out a licence. Soon after that Sir Thomas Wilson shut up the heath from us; he said he would not have it cut about any more, for that a poor animal could not pick up a crumb without being in danger of breaking its leg. This was just after we took out our licences, and, as we'd paid dearly for being allowed to sell the sand, some of us, and I was one, we waited upon Sir Thomas, and asked to be allowed to work out our licences, which was granted, and we have gone on ever since. My men work very hard for their money, sir; they are up at 3 o'clock of the morning, and are knocking about the streets, perhaps till 5 or 6 o'clock in the evening."

The yellow house-sand is also found at Kingsland, and at the Kensington Gravel-pits; but at the latter place street-sellers are not supplied. The sand here is very fine, and mostly disposed of to plasterers. There is also some of this kind of sand at Wandsworth. In the street-selling of house-sand, there are now not above 30 men employed, and few of these trade on their own account. Reckoning the horses and carts employed in the trade at the same price as our Camden-town informant sets on his stock, we have 20 horses, at 10*l.* each, and 20 carts, at 3*l.* each, with 3 baskets to each, at 2*s.* apiece, making a total of 236*l.* of capital employed in the carrying machinery of the street-selling of sand. Allowing 3*s.* a day for each man, the wages would amount for 30 men to 27*l.* weekly; and the expenses for horses' keep, at 10*s.* a head, would give, for 20 horses, 10*l.* weekly, making a total of 38*l.* weekly, or an annual expenditure for man and horse of 2496*l.* Calculating the sale at a load per day, for each horse and cart, at 21*s.* a load, we have 6573*l.* annually expended in the purchase of house or floor-sand.

Bird-sand, or the fine and dry sand required for the use of cage-birds, is now obtained altogether of a market gardener in Hackney. It is sold at 8*d.* the barrow-load; as much being shovelled on to a coster's barrow "as it will carry." A good-sized barrow holds 3½ bushels; a smaller size, 3 bushels, and the buyer is also the shoveller. Three-fourths of the quantity conveyed by the street-sellers from Hackney is sold to the bird-shop keepers at 6*d.* for 3 pecks. The remainder is disposed of to such customers as purchase it in the street, or is delivered at private houses, which receive a regular supply. The usual charge to the general public is a halfpenny or a penny for sand to fill any vessel brought to contain it. A penny a gallon is perhaps an average price in this retail trade.

A man, " in a good way of business," disposes of a barrow-load once a week; the others once a fortnight. In wet or windy weather great care is necessary, and much trouble incurred in supplying this sand to the street-sellers, and again in their vending it in the streets. The street-vendors are the same men as supply the turf, &c., for cage-birds, of whom I have treated, p. 156, vol. i. They are 40 in number, and although they do not all supply sand, a matter beyond the strength of the old and infirm, a few costermongers convey a barrow-load of sand now and then to the bird-sellers, and this addition ensures the weekly supply of 40 barrow-loads. Calculating these at the wholesale, or bird-dealer's price—2*s.* 3*d.* a barrow being an average—we find 234*l.* yearly expended in this sand. What is vended at 2*s.* 3*d.* costs but 8*d.* at the wholesale price; but the profit is hardly earned considering the labour of wheeling a heavy barrow of sand for miles, and the trouble of keeping over night what is unsold during the day.

OF THE STREET-SELLERS OF SHELLS.

THE street-trade in shells presents the characteristics I have before had to notice as regards the trade in what are not necessaries, or an approach to necessaries, in contradistinction of what men must have to eat or wear. Shells, such as the green snail, ear shell, and others of that class, though extensively used for inlaying in a variety of ornamental works, are comparatively of little value; for no matter how useful, if shells are only well known, they are considered of but little importance; while those which are rarely seen, no matter how insignificant in appearance, command extraordinary prices. As an instance I may mention that on the 23rd of June there was purchased by Mr. Sowerby, shell-dealer, at a public sale in King-street, Covent-garden, a small shell not two inches long, broken and damaged, and withal what is called a "dead shell," for the sum of 30 guineas. It was described as the *Conus Glory Mary,* and had it only been perfect would have fetched 100 guineas.

Shells, such as conches, cowries, green snails, and ear shells (the latter being so called from their resemblance to the human ear), are imported in large quantities, as parts of cargoes, and are sold to the large dealers by weight. Conch shells are sold at 8*s.* per cwt; cowries and clams from 10*s.* to 12*s.* per cwt; the green snail, used for inlaying, fetches from 1*l.* to 1*l.* 10*s.* per cwt.; and the ear shell, on account of its superior quality and richer variety of colours, as much as 3*l.* and 5*l.* per cwt.

The conches are found only among the West India Islands, and are used principally for garden ornaments and grotto-work. The others come principally from the Indian Ocean and the China seas, and are used as well for chimney ornaments, as for inlaying, for the tops of work-tables and other ornamental furniture.

The shells which are considered of the most value are almost invariably small, and of an endless variety of shape. They are called "cabinet" shells, and are brought from all parts of the world —land as well as sea—lakes, rivers, and oceans furnishing specimens to the collection. The Australian forests are continually ransacked to bring to light new varieties. I have been informed that there is not a river in England but contains valuable shells; that even in the Thames there are shells worth from 10s. to 1l. each. I have been shown a shell of the snail kind, found in the woods of New Holland, and purchased by a dealer for 2l., and on which he confidently reckoned to make a considerable profit.

Although "cabinet" shells are collected from all parts, yet by far the greater number come from the Indian Ocean. They are generally collected by the natives, who sell them to captains and mates of vessels trading to those parts, and very often to sailors, all of whom frequently speculate to a considerable extent in these things, and have no difficulty in disposing of them as soon as they arrive in this country, for there is not a shell dealer in London who has not a regular staff of persons stationed at Gravesend to board the homeward-bound ships at the Nore, and sometimes as far off as the Downs, for the purpose of purchasing shells. It usually happens that when three or four of these persons meet on board the same ship, an animated competition takes place, so that the shells on board are generally bought up long before the ship arrives at London. Many persons from this country go out to various parts of the world for the sole purpose of procuring shells, and they may be found from the western coast of Africa to the shores of New South Wales, along the Persian Gulf, in Ceylon, the Mallaccas, China, and the Islands of the Pacific, where they employ the natives in dredging the bed of the ocean, and are by this means continually adding to the almost innumerable varieties which are already known.

To show the extraordinary request in which shells are held in almost every place, while I was in the shop of Mr. J. C. Jamrach, naturalist, and agent to the Zoological Society at Amsterdam—one of the largest dealers in London, and to whom I am indebted for much valuable information on this subject—a person, a native of High Germany, was present. He had arrived in London the day before, and had purchased on that day a collection of shells of a low quality for which he paid Mr. Jamrach 36l.; to this he added a few birds. Placing his purchase in a box furnished with a leather strap, he slung it over his shoulder, shook hands with Mr. Jamrach, and departed. Mr. Jamrach informed me that the next morning he was to start by steam for Rotterdam, then continue his journey up the Rhine to a certain point, from whence he was to travel on foot from one place to another, till he could dispose of his commodities; after which he would return to London, as the great mart for a fresh supply. He was only a very poor man, but there are a great many others far better off, continually coming backwards and forwards, who are able to purchase a larger stock of shells and birds, and who, in the course of their peregrinations, wander through the greater part of Germany, extending their excursions sometimes through Austria, the Tyrol, and the north of Italy. A visit to the premises of Mr. Jamrach, Ratcliff-highway, or Mr. Samuel, Upper East Smithfield, would well repay the curious observer. The front portion of Mr. Jamrach's house is taken up with a wonderful variety of strange birds that keep up an everlasting screaming; in another portion of the house are collected confusedly together heaps of nondescript articles, which might appear to the uninitiated worth little or nothing, but on which the possessor places great value. In a yard behind the house, immured in iron cages, are some of the larger species of birds, and some beautiful varieties of foreign animals—while in large presses ranged round the other rooms, and furnished with numerous drawers, are placed his real valuables, the cabinet shells. The establishment of Mr. Samuel is equally curious.

In London, the dealers in shells, keeping shops for the sale of them, amount to no more than ten; they are all doing a large business, and are men of good capital, which may be proved by the following quotation from the day-books of one of the class for the present year, viz.:—

	£	s.	d.
Shells sold in February	275	0	0
Ditto, ditto, March	471	0	0
Ditto, ditto, April	1389	0	0
Ditto, ditto, May	475	0	0
Total	£2610	0	0
Profit on same, February	£75	12	0
Ditto, ditto, March	140	0	0
Ditto, ditto, April	323	0	0
Ditto, ditto, May	127	0	0
Total	£665	12	0

Besides these there are about 20 private dealers who do not keep shops, but who nevertheless do a considerable business in this line among persons at the West End of London. All shell dealers add to that occupation the sale of foreign birds and curiosities.

There is yet another class of persons who seem to be engaged in the sale of shells, but it is only seeming. They are dressed as sailors, and appear at all times to have just come ashore after a long voyage, as a man usually follows them with that sort of canvas bag in use among sailors, in which they stow away their clothes; the men themselves go on before carrying a parrot or some rare bird in one hand, and in the other a large shell. These men are the "duffers" of whom I have spoken in my account of the sale of foreign birds. They make shells a more frequent medium for the introduction of their real avocation, as a shell is a far less troublesome thing either to hawk or keep by them than a parrot.

I now give a description of these men, as general duffers, and from good authority.

"They are known by the name of '*duffers*,' and have an exceedingly cunning mode of transacting their business. They are all united in some secret bond; they have persons also bound to them, who are skilled in making shawls in imitation of those imported from China, and who, according to the terms of their agreement, must not work for any other persons. The duffers, from time to time, furnish these persons with designs for shawls, such as cannot be got in this country, which, when completed, they (the duffers) conceal about their persons, and start forward on their travels. They contrive to gain admission to respectable houses by means of shells and sometimes of birds, which they purchase from the regular dealers, but always those of a low quality; after which they contrive to introduce the shawls, their real business, for which they sometimes have realized prices varying from 5l. to 20l. In many instances, the cheat is soon discovered, when the duffers immediately decamp, to make place for a fresh batch, who have been long enough out of London to make their faces unknown to their former victims. These remain till they also find danger threaten them, when they again start away, and others immediately take their place. While away from London, they travel through all parts of the country, driving a good trade among the country gentlemen's houses; and sometimes visiting the seaports, such as Liverpool, Portsmouth, and Plymouth."

An instance of the skill with which the duffers sometimes do business, is the following. One of these persons some time ago came into the shop of a shell dealer, having with him a beautiful specimen of a three-coloured cockatoo, for which he asked 10l. The shell dealer declined the purchase at that price, saying, that he sold these birds at 4l. a piece, but offered to give 3l. 10s. for it, which was at once accepted; while pocketing the money, the man remarked that he had paid ten guineas for that bird. The shell dealer, surprised that so good a judge should be induced to give so much more than the value of the bird, was desirous of hearing further, when the duffer made this statement:—"I went the other day to a gentleman's house, he was an old officer, where I saw this bird, and, in order to get introduced, I offered to purchase it. The gentleman said he knew it was a valuable bird, and couldn't think of taking less than ten guineas. I then offered to barter for it, and produced a shawl, for which I asked twenty-five guineas, but offered to take fifteen guineas and the bird. This was at length agreed to, and now, having sold it for 3l. 10s., it makes 19l. 5s. I got for the shawl, and not a bad day's work either."

Of shells there are about a million of the commoner sorts bought by the London street-sellers at 3s. the gross. They are retailed at 1d. apiece, or 12s. the gross, when sold separately; a large proportion, as is the case with many articles of taste or curiosity rather than of usefulness, being sold by the London street-folk on country rounds; some of these rounds stretch half-way to Bristol or to Liverpool.

OF THE RIVER BEER-SELLERS, OR PURL-MEN.

THERE is yet another class of itinerant dealers who, if not traders in the streets, are traders in what was once termed the silent highway—the river beer-sellers, or purl-men, as they are more commonly called. These should strictly have been included among the sellers of eatables and drinkables; they have, however, been kept distinct, being a peculiar class, and having little in common with the other out-door sellers.

I will begin my account of the river-sellers by enumerating the numerous classes of labourers, amounting to many thousands, who get their living by plying their respective avocations on the river, and who constitute the customers of these men. There are first the sailors on board the corn, coal, and timber ships; then the "lumpers," or those engaged in discharging the timber ships; the "stevedores," or those engaged in stowing craft; and the "riggers," or those engaged in rigging them; ballast-heavers, ballast-getters, corn-porters, coal-whippers, watermen and lightermen, and coal-porters, who, although engaged in carrying sacks of coal from the barges or ships at the river's side to the shore, where there are public-houses, nevertheless, when hard worked and pressed for time, frequently avail themselves of the presence of the purl-man to quench their thirst, and to naval stimulate them to further exertion.

It would be a remarkable circumstance if the fact of so many persons continually employed in severe labour, and who, of course, are at times in want of refreshment, had not called into existence a class to supply that which was evidently required; under one form or the other, therefore, river-dealers boast of an antiquity as old as the navel commerce of the country.

The prototype of the river beer-seller of the present day is the bumboat-man. Bumboats (or rather *Baum*-boats, that is to say, the boats of the harbour, from the German *Baum*, a haven or bar) are known in every port where ships are obliged to anchor at a distance from the shore. They are stored with a large assortment of articles, such as are likely to be required by people after a long voyage. Previously to the formation of the various docks on the Thames, they were very numerous on the river, and drove a good trade with the homeward-bound shipping. But since the docks came into requisition, and steam-tugs brought the ships from the mouth of the river to the dock entrance, their business died away, and they gradually disappeared; so that a bumboat on the Thames at the present day would be a sort of curiosity, a relic of times past.

In former times it was *not* in the power of any person who chose to follow the calling of a bumboat man on the Thames. The Trinity Company had the power of granting licences for this purpose. Whether they were restrained by some special clause in their charter, or not, from giving licences indiscriminately, it is difficult to say. But it is certain that none got a licence but a sailor—one who had "served his country;" and it was quite common in those days to see an old fellow with a pair of wooden legs, perhaps blind of an eye, or wanting an arm, and with a face rugged as a rock, plying about among the shipping, accompanied by a boy whose duty it was to carry the articles to the purchasers on shipboard, and help in the management of the boat. In the first or second year of the reign of her present Majesty, however, when the original bumboat-men had long degenerated into the mere beer-sellers, and any one who wished traded in this line on the river (the Trinity Company having for many years paid no attention to the matter), an inquiry took place, which resulted in a regulation that all the beer-sellers or purl-men should thenceforward be regularly licensed for the river-sale of beer and spirits from the Waterman's Hall, which regulation is in force to the present time.

It appears to have been the practice at some time or other in this country to infuse wormwood into beer or ale previous to drinking it, either to make it sufficiently bitter, or for some medicinal purpose. This mixture was called *purl*—why I know not, but Bailey, the philologist of the seventeenth century, so designates it. The drink originally sold on the river was purl, or this mixture, whence the title, purl-man. Now, however, the wormwood is unknown; and what is sold under the name of purl is beer warmed nearly to boiling heat, and flavoured with gin, sugar, and ginger. The river-sellers, however, still retain the name, of *purl*-men, though there is not one of them with whom I have conversed that has the remotest idea of the meaning of it.

To set up as a purl-man, some acquaintance with the river, and a certain degree of skill in the management of a boat, are absolutely necessary; as, from the frequently-crowded state of the pool, and the rapidity with which the steamers pass and repass, twisting and wriggling their way through craft of every description, the unskilful adventurer would run in continual danger of having his boat crushed like a nutshell. The purl-men, however, through long practice, are scarcely inferior to the watermen themselves in the management of their boats; and they may be seen at all times easily working their way through every obstruction, now shooting athwart the bows of a Dutch galliot or sailing-barge, then dropping astern to allow a steam-boat to pass till they at length reach the less troubled waters between the tiers of shipping.

The first thing required to become a purl-man is to procure a licence from the Waterman's Hall, which costs 3s. 6d. per annum. The next requisite is the possession of a boat. The boats used are all in the form of skiffs, rather short, but of a good breadth, and therefore less liable to capsize through the swell of the steamers, or through any other cause. Thus equipped he then goes to some of the small breweries, where he gets two "pins," or small casks of beer, each containing eighteen pots; after this he furnishes himself with a quart or two of gin from some publican, which he carries in a tin vessel with a long neck, like a bottle—an iron or tin vessel to hold the fire, with holes drilled all round to admit the air and keep the fuel burning, and a huge bell, by no means the least important portion of his fit out. Placing his two pins of beer on a frame in the stern of the boat, the spiles loosened and the brass cocks fitted in, and with his tin gin bottle close to his hand beneath the seat, two or three measures of various sizes, a black tin pot for heating the beer, and his fire pan secured on the bottom of the boat, and sending up a black smoke, he takes his seat early in the morning and pulls away from the shore, resting now and then on his oars, to ring the heavy bell that announces his approach. Those on board the vessels requiring refreshment, when they hear the bell, hail "Purl ahoy;" in an instant the oars are resumed, and the purl-man is quickly alongside the ship.

The bell of the purl-man not unfrequently performs another very important office. During the winter, when dense fogs settle down on the river, even the regular watermen sometimes lose themselves, and flounder about bewildered perhaps for hours. The direction once lost, their shouting is unheeded or unheard. The purl-man's bell, however, reaches the ear through the surrounding gloom, and indicates his position; when near enough to hear the hail of his customers, he makes his way unerringly to the spot by now and then sounding his bell; this is immediately answered by another shout, so that in a short time the glare of his fire may be distinguished as he emerges from the darkness, and glides noiselessly alongside the ship where he is wanted.

The amount of capital necessary to start in the purl line may be as follows:—I have said that the boats are all of the skiff kind—generally old ones, which they patch up and repair at but little cost. They purchase these boats at from 3*l*. to 6*l*. each. If we take the average of these two sums, the items will be—

	£	s.	d.
Boat	4	10	0
Pewter measures	0	5	0
Warming-pot	0	1	6
Fire stove	0	5	0
Gallon can	0	2	6
Two pins of beer	0	8	0
Quart of gin	0	2	6
Sugar and ginger	0	1	0
Licence	0	3	6
Total	£5	19	0

Thus it requires, at the very least, a capital of 6*l*. to set up as a purl-man.

Since the Waterman's Hall has had the granting of licences, there have been upwards of 140 issued; but out of the possessors of these many are dead, some have left for other business, and others are too old and feeble to follow the occupation any longer, so that out of the whole number there remain only 35 purl-men on the river, and these are thus divided:—23 ply their trade in what is called "the pool," that is, from Execution Dock to Ratcliff Cross, among the coal-laden ships, and do a tolerable business amongst the sailors and the hard-working and thirsty coal-whippers; 8 purl-men follow their calling from Execution Dock to London Bridge, and sell their commodity among the ships loaded with corn, potatoes, &c.; and 4 are known to frequent the various reaches below Limehouse Hole, where the colliers are obliged to lie at times in sections, waiting till they are sold on the Coal Exchange, and some even go down the river as far as the ballast-lighters of the Trinity Company, for the purpose of supplying the ballast-getters. The purl-men cannot sell much to the unfortunate ballast-heavers, for they are suffering under all the horrors of an abominable truck system, and are compelled to take from the publicans about Wapping and Shadwell, who are their employers, large quantities of filthy stuff compounded especially for their use, for which they are charged exorbitant prices, being thus and in a variety of other ways mercilessly robbed of their earnings, so that they and their families are left in a state of almost utter destitution. One of the purl-men, whose boat is No. 44, has hoops like those used by gipsies for pitching their tents; these he fastens to each side of the boat, over which he draws a tarred canvas covering, water-proof, and beneath this he sleeps the greater part of the year, seldom going ashore except for the purpose of getting a fresh supply of liquors for trade, or food for himself. He generally casts anchor in some unfrequented nook down the river, where he enjoys all the quiet of a Thames hermit, after the labour of the day. To obtain the necessary heat during the winter, he fits a funnel to his fire-stove to carry away the smoke, and thus warmed he sleeps away in defiance of the severest weather.

It appears from the facts above given that 210*l*. is the gross amount of capital employed in this business. On an average all the year round each purl-man sells two "pins" of beer weekly, independent of gin; but little gin is thus sold in the summer, but in the winter a considerable quantity of it is used in making the purl. The men purchase the beer at 4*s*. per pin, and sell it at 4*d*. per pot, which leaves them a profit of 4*s*. on the two pins, and, allowing them 6*d*. per day profit on the gin, it gives 1*l*. 7*s*. per week profit to each, or a total to all hands of 47*l*. 5*s*. per week, and a gross total of 2457*l*. profit made on the sale of 98,280 gallons of beer, beside gin sold on the Thames in the course of the year. From this amount must be deducted 318*l*. 10*s*., which is paid to boys, at the rate of 3*s*. 6*d*. per week; it being necessary for each purl-man to employ a lad to take care of the boat while he is on board the ships serving his customers, or traversing the tiers. This deduction being made leaves 61*l*. 2*s*. per annum to each purl-man as the profit on his year's trading.

The present race of purl-men, unlike the weather-beaten tars who in former times alone were licensed, are generally young men, who have been in the habit of following some river employment, and who, either from some accident having befallen them in the course of their work, or from their preferring the easier task of sitting in their boat and rowing leisurely about to continuous labour, have started in the line, and ultimately superseded the old river dealers. This is easily explained. No man labouring on the river would purchase from a stranger when he knew that his own fellow-workman was afloat, and was prepared to serve him with as good an article; besides he might not have money, and a stranger could not be expected to give trust, but his old acquaintance would make little scruple in doing so. In this way the customers of the purl-men are secured; and many of these people do so much more than the average amount of business above stated, that it is no unusual thing to see some of them, after four or five years on the river, take a public-house, spring up into the rank of licensed victuallers, and finally become men of substance.

I conversed with one who had been a coal-whipper. He stated that he had met with an accident while at work which prevented him from following coal-whipping any longer. He had fallen from the ship's side into a barge, and was for a long time in the hospital. When he came out he found he could not work, and had no other prospect before him but the union. "I thought I'd be by this time toes up in Stepney churchyard," he said, "and grinning at the lid of an old coffin." In this extremity a neighbour, a waterman, who had long known him, advised him to take to the purl business, and gave him not only the advice, but sufficient money to enable him to put it in practice. The man accordingly got a boat, and was soon afloat among his old workmates. In this line he now makes out a living for himself and his family, and reckons himself able to clear, one week with the other, from 18*s*. to 20*s*. "I should do much better," he said, "if people would only pay what they owe; but there are some who never think of paying anything." He has between 10*l*. and 20*l*. due to him, and never expects to get a farthing of it.

The following is the form of licence issued by the Watermen's Company:—

INCORPORATED 1827.

BUMBOAT.

Height 5 feet 8 inches, 30 years of age, dark hair, sallow complexion. 2nd & 3rd Vic. cap. 47, sec. 25.

I hereby certify that   of   , in the parish of   in the county of Middlesex, is this day registered in a book of the Company of the Master, Wardens, and Commonalty of Watermen and Lightermen of the river Thames, kept for that purpose, to use, work, or navigate a boat called a skiff, named   , number   , for the purpose of selling, disposing of, or exposing for sale to and amongst the seamen, or other persons employed in and about any of the ships or vessels upon the said river, any liquors, slops, or other articles whatsoever, between London Bridge and Limehouse Hole; but the said boat is not to be used on the said river for any other purpose than the aforesaid.

Waterman's Hall,
JAS. BANYON, *Clerk*.

Beside the regular purl-men, or, as they may be called, bumboat-men, there are two or three others who, perhaps unable to purchase a boat, and take out the licence, have nevertheless for a number of years contrived to carry on a traffic in spirits among the ships in the Thames. Their practice is to carry a flat tin bottle concealed about their person, with which they go on board the first ship in a tier, where they are well known by those who may be there employed. If the seamen wish for any spirit the river-vendor immediately supplies it, entering the name of the customers served, as none of the vendors ever receive, at the time of sale, any money for what they dispose of; they keep an account till their customers receive their wages, when they always contrive to be present, and in general succeed in getting what is owing to them. What their profits are it is impossible to tell, perhaps they may equal those of the regular purl-man, for they go on board of almost every ship in the course of the day. When their tin bottle is empty they go on shore to replenish it, doing so time after time if necessary.

It is remarkable that although these people are perfectly well known to every purl-man on the river, who have seen them day by day, for many years going on board the various ships, and are thoroughly cognizant of the purpose of their visits, there has never been any information laid against them, nor have they been in any way interrupted in their business.

There is one of these river spirit-sellers who has pursued the avocation for the greater part of his life; he is a native of the south of Ireland, now very old, and a little shrivelled-up man. He may still be seen every day, going from ship to ship by scrambling over the quarters where they are lashed together in tiers—a feat sometimes attended with danger to the young and strong; yet he works his way with the agility of a man of 20, gets on board the ship he wants, and when there, were he not so well known, he might be thought to be some official sent to take an inventory of the contents of the ship, for he has at all times an ink-bottle hanging from one of his coat buttons, a pen stuck over his ear, spectacles on his nose, a book in his hand, and really has all the appearance of a man determined on doing business of some sort or other. He possesses a sort of ubiquity, for go where you will through any part of the pool you are sure to meet him. He seems to be expected everywhere; no one appears to be surprised at his presence. Captains and mates pass him by unnoticed and unquestioned. As suddenly as he comes does he disappear, to start up in some other place. His visits are so regular, that it would scarcely look like being on board ship if "old D——, the whiskey man," as he is called, did not make his appearance some time during the day, for he seems to be in some strange way identified with the river, and with every ship that frequents it.

OF THE NUMBERS, CAPITAL, AND INCOME OF THE STREET-SELLERS OF SECOND-HAND ARTICLES, LIVE ANIMALS, MINERAL PRODUCTIONS, ETC.

THE hawkers of second-hand articles, live animals, mineral productions, and natural curiosities, form, as we have seen, large important classes of the street-sellers. According to the facts already given, there appear to be at present in the streets, 90 sellers of metal wares, including the sellers of second-hand trays and Italian-irons; 30 sellers of old linen, as wrappers and towelling; 80 vendors of second-hand (burnt) linen and calico; 30 sellers of curtains; 30 sellers of carpeting, &c.; 30 sellers of bed-ticking, &c.; 6 sellers of old crockery and glass; 25 sellers of old musical instruments; 6 vendors of second-hand weapons; 6 sellers of old curiosities; 6 vendors of telescopes and pocket glasses; 30 to 40 sellers of other miscellaneous second-hand articles; 100 sellers of men's second-hand clothes; 30 sellers of old boots and shoes; 15 vendors of old hats; 50 sellers of women's second-hand apparel; 30 vendors of second-hand bonnets, and 10 sellers of old furs; 116 sellers of second-hand articles at Smithfield-market;—making altogether 725 street-sellers of second-hand commodities.

But some of the above trades are of a temporary character only, as in the case of the vendors of old linen towelling or wrappers, carpets, bed-ticking, &c.—the same persons who sell the one often selling the others; the towels and wrappers, moreover, are offered for sale only on the Monday and Saturday nights. Assuming, then, that upwards of 100 or one-sixth of the above number sell two different second-hand articles, or are not continually employed at that department of street-traffic, we find the total number of street-sellers belonging to this class to be about 500.

Concerning the number selling live animals in the streets, there are 50 men vending fancy and sporting dogs; 200 sellers and "duffers" of English birds; 10 sellers of parrots and other foreign birds; 3 sellers of birds'-nests, &c.; 20 vendors of squirrels; 6 sellers of leverets and wild rabbits; 35 vendors of gold and silver fish; 20 vendors of tortoises; and 14 sellers of snails, frogs, worms, &c.; or, allowing for the temporary and mixed character of many of these trades, we may say that there are 200 constantly engaged in this branch of street-commerce.

Then of the street-sellers of mineral productions and natural curiosities, there are 216 vendors of coals; 1500 sellers of coke; 14 sellers of tan-turf; 150 vendors of salt; 70 sellers of sand; 26 sellers of shells; or 1969 in all. From this number the sellers of shells must be deducted, as the shell-trade is not a special branch of street-traffic. We may, therefore, assert that the number of people engaged in this latter class of street-business amounts to about 1900.

Now, adding all these sums together, we have the following table as to the numbers of individuals comprised in the *first* division of the London street-folk, viz. the street-sellers :—

1. Costermongers (including men, women, and children engaged in the sale of fish, fruit, vegetables, game, poultry, flowers, &c.)	30,000
2. Street-sellers of "green stuff," including water-cresses, chickweed and gru'n'sel, turf, &c.	2,000
3. Street-sellers of eatables and drinkables	4,000
4. Street-sellers of stationery, literature, and fine arts	1,000
5. Street-sellers of manufactured articles of metal, crockery, glass, textile, chemical, and miscellaneous substances	4,000
6. Street-sellers of second-hand articles, including the sellers of old metal articles, old glass, old linen, old clothes, old shoes, &c.	500
7. Street-sellers of live animals, as dogs, birds, gold and silver fish, squirrels, leverets, tortoises, snails, &c.	200
8. Street-sellers of mineral productions and natural curiosities, as coals, coke, tan-turf, salt, sand, shells, &c.	1,900

TOTAL NUMBER OF STREET-SELLERS 43,640

These numbers, it should be remembered, are given rather as an approximation to the truth than as the absolute fact. It would therefore be safer to say, making all due allowance for the temporary and mixed character of many branches of street-commerce, that there are about 40,000 people engaged in selling articles in the streets of London. I am induced to believe that this is very near the real number of street-sellers, from the *wholesale* returns of the places where the street-sellers purchase their goods, and which I have always made a point of collecting from the best authorities connected with the various branches of street-traffic. The statistics of the fish and green markets, the swag-shops, the old clothes exchange, the bird-dealers, which I have caused to be collected for the first time in this country, all tend to corroborate this estimate.

The next fact to be evolved is the amount of capital invested in the street-sale of Second-hand Articles, of Live Animals, and of Mineral Productions. And, first, as to the money employed in the Second-hand Street-Trade.

The following tables will show the amount of capital invested in this branch of street-business.

Street-Sellers of Second-hand Metal Wares.

	£	s.	d.
30 stalls, 5s. each; 20 barrows, 1l. each; stock-money for 50 vendors, at 10s. per head	52	10	0

Street-Sellers of Second-hand Metal Trays.

Stock-money for 20 sellers, at 5s. each	5	0	0

Street-Sellers of other Second-hand Metal Articles, as Italian and Flat Irons.

Stock-money for 20 vendors, at 5s. each; 20 stalls, at 3s. each	8	0	0

Street-Sellers of Second-hand Linen, &c.

Stock-money for 30 vendors, at 5s. per head	7	10	0

Street-Sellers of Second-hand (burnt) Linen and Calico.

Stock-money for 80 vendors, at 10s. each	40	0	0

Street-Sellers of Second-hand Curtains.

Stock-money for 30 sellers, at 5s. each	7	10	0

Street-Sellers of Second-hand Carpeting, Flannels, Stocking-legs, &c.

Stock-money for 30 sellers, at 6s. each	9	0	0

Street-Sellers of Second-hand Bed-ticking, Sacking, Fringe, &c.

Stock-money for 30 sellers, at 4s. each	6	0	0

Street-Sellers of Second-hand Glass and Crockery.

6 barrows, 15s. each; 6 baskets, 1s. 6d. each; stock-money for 6 vendors, at 5s. each	6	9	0

Street-Sellers of Second-hand Miscellaneous Articles.

Stock-money for 5 vendors, at 15s. each	3	15	0

Street-Sellers and Duffers of Second-hand Music.

Stock-money for 25 sellers, at 1l. each	25	0	0

Street-Sellers of Second-hand Weapons.

Stock-money for 6 vendors, at 1l. each	6	0	0

Street-Sellers of Second-hand Curiosities.

6 barrows, 15s. each; stock-money for 6 vendors, at 15s. per head	9	0	0

Street-Sellers of Second-hand Telescopes and Pocket-Glasses.

Stock-money for 6 vendors, at 4l. each	24	0	0

Street-Sellers of other Miscellaneous Articles.

30 stalls, 5s. each; stock-money for 30 sellers, at 15s. each	30	0	0

Street-Sellers of Men's Second-hand Clothes.

	£	s.	d.
100 linen bags, at 2s. each; stock-money for 100 sellers, at 15s. each	85	0	0

Street-Sellers of Second-hand Boots and Shoes.

	£	s.	d.
10 stalls, at 3s. each; 30 baskets, at 2s. 6d. each; stock-money for 30 sellers, at 10s. each	20	5	0

Street-Sellers of Second-hand Hats.

	£	s.	d.
30 irons, two to each man, at 2s. each; 60 blocks, at 1s. 6d. per block; stock-money for 15 vendors, at 10s. each	15	0	0

Street-Sellers of Women's Second-hand Apparel.

	£	s.	d.
Stock-money for 50 sellers, at 10s. each; 50 baskets, at 2s. 6d. each	31	5	0

Street-Sellers of Second-hand Bonnets.

	£	s.	d.
10 umbrellas, at 3s. each; 30 baskets, at 2s. 6d. each; stock-money for 30 sellers, at 5s. each	12	15	0

Street-Sellers of Second-hand Furs.

	£	s.	d.
Stock-money for 10 vendors, at 7s. 6d. each	3	15	0

Street-Sellers of Second-hand Articles in Smithfield-market.

	£	s.	d.
30 sellers of harness sets and collars, at an average capital of 15s. each; 6 sellers of saddles and pads, at 15s. each; 10 sellers of bits, at 3s. each; 6 sellers of wheel-springs and trays, at 15s. each; 6 sellers of boards and trestles for stalls, at 10s. each; 20 sellers of barrows, small carts, and trucks, at 5l. each; 6 sellers of goat carriages, at 3l. each; 6 sellers of shooting galleries and guns for ditto, and drums for costers, at 15s. each; 10 sellers of measures, weights, and scales, at 25s. each; 5 sellers of potato cans and roasted-chestnut apparatus, at 5l. each; 3 sellers of ginger-beer trucks, at 5l. each; 6 sellers of pea-soup cans and pickled-eel kettles, 15s. each; 2 sellers of elder-wine vessels, at 15s. each. Thus we find that the average number of street-sellers frequenting Smithfield-market once a week is 116, and the average capital	217	0	0
TOTAL AMOUNT OF CAPITAL BELONGING TO STREET-SELLERS OF SECOND-HAND ARTICLES	621	14	0

STREET-SELLERS OF LIVE ANIMALS.

Street-Sellers of Dogs.

	£	s.	d.
Stock-money for 20 sellers (including kennels and keep), at 5l. 15s. each seller	115	0	0

Street-Sellers and Duffers of Birds (English).

	£	s.	d.
2400 small cages (reckoning 12 to each seller), at 6d. each; 1200 long cages (allowing 6 cages to each seller), at 2s. each; 1800 large cages (averaging 9 cages to each seller), at 2s. 6d. each. Stock-money for 200 sellers, at 20s. each	605	0	0

Street-Sellers of Parrots, &c.

	£	s.	d.
20 cages, at 10s. each; stock-money for 10 sellers, at 30s. each	25	0	0

Street-Sellers of Birds'-Nests.

	£	s.	d.
3 hamper baskets, at 6d. each		1	6

Street-Sellers of Squirrels.

	£	s.	d.
Stock-money for 20 vendors, at 10s. each	10	0	0

Street-Sellers of Leverets, Wild Rabbits, &c.

	£	s.	d.
6 baskets, at 2s. each; stock-money for 6 vendors, at 5s. each	2	2	0

Street-Sellers of Gold and Silver Fish.

	£	s.	d.
35 glass globes, at 2s. each; 35 small nets, at 6d. each; stock-money for 35 vendors, at 15s. each	30	12	6

Street-Sellers of Tortoises.

	£	s.	d.
Stock-money for 20 vendors, at 10s. each	25	0	0

Street-Sellers of Snails, Frogs, Worms, Snakes, Hedgehogs, &c.

	£	s.	d.
14 baskets, at 1s. each		14	0
TOTAL AMOUNT OF CAPITAL BELONGING TO STREET-SELLERS OF LIVE ANIMALS	798	10	0

STREET-SELLERS OF MINERAL PRODUCTIONS AND NATURAL CURIOSITIES.

Street-Sellers of Coals.

	£	s.	d.
30 two-horse vans, at 70l. each; 100 horses, at 20l. each; 100 carts, at 10l. each; 160 horses, at 10l. each; 20 donkey or pony carts, at 1l. each; 20 donkeys or ponies, at 1l. 10s. each; 210 sets of weights and scales, at 1l. 10s. each; stock-money for 210 vendors, at 2l. each	7,485	0	0

Street-Sellers of Coke.

	£	s.	d.
100 vans, at 70l. each; 100 horses, at 20l. each; 300 carts, at 10l. each; 300 horses, at 10l. each; 500 donkey-carts, at 1l. each; 500 donkeys, at 1l. each; 200 trucks and barrows, at 10s. each; 4800 sacks for the 100 vans, at 3s. 6d. each; 3600 sacks for the 300 carts; 3000 sacks for the 500 donkey carts; 1652 sacks for the 550 trucks and barrows; 300 sacks for the 50 women; stock-money for 1500 vendors, at 1l. per head	19,936	12	0

Street-Sellers of Tan-Turf.

12 donkeys and carts, at 2l. each;

2 trucks, at 15s. each; stock-money for 14 vendors, at 10s. each . . . £ s. d.
32 10 0

Street-Sellers of Salt.

75 donkeys and carts, at 2l. 5s. each; 75 barrows, at 10s. each; stock-money for 150 vendors, at 6s. each 251 5 0

Street-Sellers of Sand.

20 horses, at 10l. each; 20 carts, at 3l. each; 60 baskets, at 2s. each; wages of 30 men, at 3s. per day for each; expenses for keep of 20 horses, at 10s. per head; estimated stock-money for 30 sellers, at 5s. each; 40 barrows, at 15s. each; stock-money for the barrow-men, at 1s. 6d. each . 320 5 0

Street-Sellers of Shells.

Stock-money for 70 vendors, at 5s. each 17 10 0

TOTAL CAPITAL BELONGING TO STREET-SELLERS OF MINERAL PRODUCTIONS, ETC. 28,043 2 0

River-Sellers of Purl.

35 boats, at 4l. 10s. each; 35 sets of measures, at 5s. the set; 35 warming pots, at 1s. 6d. each; 35 fire-stoves, at 5s. each; 35 gallon cans, at 2s. 6d. each; 70 "pins" of beer, at 4s. per "pin;" 35 quarts of gin, at 2s. 6d. the quart; 35 licences, at 3s. 6d.; stock-money for spice, &c., at 1s. each 208 5 0

Hence it would appear that the gross amount of property belonging to the street-sellers may be reckoned as follows:—

Value of stock-in-trade belonging to costermongers 25,000 0 0
Ditto street-sellers of green-stuff . 149 0 0
Ditto street-sellers of eatables and drinkables 9,000 0 0
Ditto street-sellers of stationery, literature, and the fine arts . . . 400 0 0
Ditto street-sellers of manufactured articles 2,800 0 0
Ditto street-sellers of second-hand articles 621 14 0
Ditto street-sellers of live animals 798 10 0
Ditto street-sellers of mineral productions, &c. 28,043 2 0
Ditto river-sellers of purl . . . 208 5 0

TOTAL AMOUNT OF CAPITAL BELONGING TO THE LONDON STREET-SELLERS 67,023 11 0

The gross value of the stock in trade of the London street-sellers may then be estimated at about 60,000l.

INCOME, OR "TAKINGS," OF THE STREET-SELLERS OF SECOND-HAND ARTICLES.

We have now to estimate the receipts of each of the above-mentioned classes.

Street-Sellers of Second-hand Metal Wares.

I was told by several in this trade that there were 200 old metal sellers in the streets, but, from the best information at my command, not more than 50 appear to be strictly street-sellers, unconnected with shopkeeping. Estimating a weekly receipt, per individual, of 15s. (half being profit), the yearly street outlay among this body amounts to . . 1,950 0 0
£ s. d.

Street-Sellers of Second-hand Metal-Trays, &c.

Calculating that 20 persons take in the one or two nights' sale 4s. a week each, on second-hand trays (33 per cent. being the rate of profit), the street expenditure amounts yearly to 208 0 0

Street-Sellers of other Second-hand Metal Articles, as Italian and Flat Irons, &c.

There are, I am informed, 20 persons selling Italian and flat irons regularly throughout the year in the streets of London; each takes upon an average 6s. weekly, which gives an annual expenditure of upwards of 312 0 0

Street-Sellers of Second-hand Linen, &c.

There are at present 30 men and women who sell towelling and canvas wrappers in the streets on Saturday and Monday nights, each taking in the sale of those articles 9s. per week, thus giving an annual outlay of 702 0 0

Street-Sellers of Second-hand (burnt) Linen and Calico.

The most intelligent man whom I met with in this trade calculated that there were 80 of these second-hand street-folk plying their trade two nights in the week; and that they took 8s. each weekly, about half of it being profit; thus the annual street expenditure would be 1,664 0 0

Street-Sellers of Second-hand Curtains.

From the best data at my command there are 30 individuals who are engaged in the street-sale of second-hand curtains, and reckoning the weekly takings of each to be 5s., we find the yearly sum spent in the streets upon second-hand curtains amounts to 390 0 0

Street-Sellers of Second-hand Carpeting, Flannels, Stocking-legs, &c.

I am informed that the same persons selling curtains sell also second-hand carpeting, &c.; their weekly average takings appear to be about 6s. each in the sale of the above articles, thus we have a yearly outlay of . . . 468 0 0

Street-Sellers of Second-hand Bed-ticking, Sacking, Fringe, &c.

The street-sellers of curtains, carpeting, &c., of whom there are 30, are also the street-sellers of bed-ticking, sacking, fringe, &c. Their weekly takings for the sale of these articles amount to 4s. each. Hence we find that the sum spent yearly in the streets upon the purchase of bed-ticking, &c., amounts to 312 0 0

Street-Sellers of Second-hand Glass and Crockery.

Calculating that each of the six dealers takes 12s. weekly, with a profit of 6s. or 7s., we find there is annually expended in this department of street-commerce 187 4 0

Street-Sellers of Second-hand Miscellaneous Articles.

From the best data I have been able to obtain, it appears that there are five street-sellers engaged in the sale of these second-hand articles of amusement, and the receipts of the whole are 10l. weekly, about half being profit, thus giving a yearly expenditure of 520 0 0

Street-Sellers and Duffers of Second-hand Music.

A broker who was engaged in this traffic estimated—and an intelligent street-seller agreed in the computation—that, take the year through, at least 25 individuals are regularly, but few of them fully, occupied with this traffic, and that their weekly takings average 30s. each, or an aggregate yearly amount of 1950l. The weekly profits run from 10s. to 15s., and sometimes the well-known dealers clear 40s. or 50s. a week, while others do not take 5s. 1,950 0 0

Street-Sellers of Second-hand Weapons.

In this traffic it may be estimated, I am assured, that there are 20 men engaged, each taking, as an average, 1l. a week. In some weeks a man may take 5l.; in the next month he may sell no weapons at all. From 30 to 50 per cent. is the usual rate of profit, and the yearly street outlay on these second-hand offensive or defensive weapons is 1,040 0 0

Street-Sellers of Second-hand Curiosities.

There are not now more than six men who carry on this trade apart from other commerce. Their average takings are 15s. weekly each man, about two-thirds being profit, or early 234 0 0

Street-Sellers of Second-hand Telescopes and Pocket-Glasses.

There are only six men at present engaged in the sale of telescopes and pocket-glasses, and their weekly average takings are 30s. each, giving a yearly expenditure in the streets of 468 0 0

Street-Sellers of other Second-hand Miscellaneous Articles.

If we reckon that there are 30 street-sellers carrying on a traffic in second-hand miscellaneous articles, and that each takes 10s. weekly, we find the annual outlay in the streets upon these articles amounts to . . 780 0 0

Street-Sellers of Men's Second-hand Clothes.

The street-sale of men's second-hand wearing apparel is carried on principally by the Irish and others. From the best information I can gather, there appear to be upwards of 1200 old clothes men buying left-off apparel in the metropolis, one-third of whom are Irish. There are, however, not more than 100 of these who sell in the streets the articles they collect; the average-takings of each of the sellers are about 20s. weekly, their trading being chiefly on the Saturday nights and Sunday mornings. Their profits are from 50 to 60 per cent. Estimating the number of sellers at 100, and their weekly takings at 20s. each, we have an annual expenditure of 5,200 0 0

Street-Sellers of Second-hand Boots and Shoes.

There are at present about 30 individuals engaged in the street-sale of second-hand boots and shoes of all kinds; some take as much as 30s. weekly, while others do not take more than half that amount; their profits being about 50 per cent. Reckoning that the weekly average takings are 20s. each, we have a yearly expenditure on second-hand boots and shoes of 1,560 0 0

Street-Sellers of Second-hand Hats.

Throughout the year there are not more than 15 men constantly "working" this branch of street-traffic. The average weekly gains of each are about 10s., and in order to clear that sum they must take 20s. Hence the gross gains of the class will be 390l. per annum, while the sum yearly expended in the streets upon second-hand hats will amount altogether to 780 0 0

Street-Sellers of Women's Second-hand Apparel.

The number of persons engaged in the street-sale of women's second-hand apparel is about 50, each of whom take, upon an average, 15s. per week; one-half of this is clear gain. Thus we find the annual outlay in the streets upon women's second-hand apparel is no less than . . . . £1,950 0s. 0d.

Street-Sellers of Second-hand Bonnets.

There are at present 30 persons (nearly one-half of whom are milliners, and the others street-sellers) who sell second-hand straw and other bonnets; some of these are placed in an umbrella turned upside down, while others are spread upon a wrapper on the stones. The average takings of this class of street-sellers are about 12s. each per week, and their clear gains not more than one-half, thus giving a yearly expenditure of 936 0 0

Street-Sellers of Second-hand Furs.

During five months of the year there are as many as 8 or 12 persons who sell furs in the street-markets on Saturday nights, Sunday mornings, and Monday nights. The weekly average takings of each is about 12s., nearly three-fourths of which is clear profit. Reckoning that 10 individuals are engaged 20 weeks during the year, and that each of these takes weekly 12s., we find the sum annually expended in the streets on furs amounts to 120 0 0

Street-Sellers of Second-hand Articles in Smithfield-market.

I am informed, by those who are in a position to know, that there are sold on an average every year in Smithfield-market about 624 sets of harness, at 14s. per set; 1560 collars, at 2s. each; 686 pads, at 1s. each; 1560 saddles, at 5s. each; 936 bits, at 6d. each; 520 pair of wheels, at 10s. per pair; 624 pair of springs, at 8s. 4d. per pair; 832 pair of trestles, at 2s. 6d. per pair; 520 boards, at 4s. each; 1820 barrows, at 25s. each; 312 trucks, at 50s. each; 208 trays, at 1s. 3d. each; 1040 small carts, at 63s. each; 156 goat-carriages, at 20s. each; 520 shooting-galleries, at 14s. each; 312 guns for shooting-galleries, at 10s. each; 1040 drums for costers, at 3s. each; 2080 measures, at 3d. each; 2080 pair of large scales, at 5s. per pair; 2080 pair of hand-scales, at 5d. per pair; 30 roasted chestnut-apparatus, at 20s. each; 100 ginger-beer trucks, at 30s. each; 20 eel-kettles, at 5s. each; 100 potato-cans, at 17s. each; 10 pea-soup cans, at 5s. each; 40 elderwine vessels, at 8s. each; giving a yearly expenditure of 10,242 3 8

Total Sum of Money Annually taken by the Street-Sellers of Second-hand Articles . . . 33,461 1 4

Street-Sellers of Live Animals.

Street-Sellers of Dogs (Fancy Pets).

From the best data it appears that each hawker sells "four or five occasionally in one week in the summer, when trade's brisk and days are long, and only two or three the next week, when trade may be flat, and during each week in winter, when there isn't the same chance." Calculating, then, that seven dogs are sold by each hawker in a fortnight, at an average price of 50s. each (many fetch 3l., 4l., and 5l.), and supposing that but 20 men are trading in this line the year through, we find that no less a sum is yearly expended in this street-trade than . . 9,100 0 0

Street-Sellers of Sporting Dogs.

The amount "turned over" in the trade in sporting dogs yearly, in London, is computed by the best informed at about 12,000 0 0

Street-Sellers and Duffers of Live Birds. (English).

There are in the metropolis 200 street-sellers of English birds, who may be said to sell among them 7000 linnets, at 3d. each; 3000 bullfinches, at 2s. 6d. each; 400 piping bullfinches, at 63s. each; 7000 goldfinches, at 9d. each; 1500 chaffinches, at 2s. 6d. each; 700 greenfinches, at 3d. each; 6000 larks, at 1s. each; 200 nightingales, at 1s. each; 600 redbreasts, at 1s. each; 3500 thrushes and thrustles, at 2s. 6d. each; 1400 blackbirds, at 2s. 6d. each; 1000 canaries, at 1s. each; 10,000 sparrows, at 1d. each; 1500 starlings, at 1s. 6d. each; 500 magpies and jackdaws, at 9d. each; 300 redpoles, at 9d. each; 150 blackcaps, at 4d. each; 2000 "duffed," birds, at 2s. 6d. each. Thus making the sum annually expended in the purchase of birds in the streets, amount to 3,624 12 2

Street-Sellers of Parrots, &c.

The number of individuals at present hawking parrots and other foreign birds in the streets is 10, who sell among them during the year about 500 birds. Reckoning each bird to sell at 1l., we find the annual outlay upon parrots bought in the streets to be 500l.; adding to this the sale of 110 Java sparrows and St. Helena birds, as Wax-bills and Red-beaks at 1s. 6d. each, we have for the sum yearly expended in the streets on the sale of foreign birds 508 5 0

Street-Sellers of Birds'-Nests.

	£	s.	d.

There are at present only three persons hawking birds'-nests, &c., in the streets during the season, which lasts from May to August; these street-sellers sell among them 400 nests, at 2½d. each; 144 snakes, at 1s. 6d. each; 4 hedgehogs, at 1s. each; and about 2s.'s worth of snails. This makes the weekly income of each amount to about 8s. 6d. during a period of 12 weeks in the summer, and the sum annually expended on these articles to come to 15 6 0

Street-Sellers of Squirrels.

For five months of the year there are 20 men selling squirrels in the streets, at from 20 to 50 per cent. profit, and averaging a weekly sale of six each. The average price is from 2s. to 2s. 6d. Thus 2400 squirrels are vended yearly in the streets, at a cost to the public of 240 0 0

Street-Sellers of Leverets, Wild Rabbits, &c.

During the year there are about six individuals exposing for sale in the streets young hares and wild rabbits. These persons sell among them 300 leverets, at 1s. 6d. each; and 400 young wild-rabbits, at 4d. each, giving a yearly outlay of 29 3 4

Street-Sellers of Gold and Silver Fish.

If we calculate, in order to allow for the cessation of the trade during the winter, and often in the summer when costermongering is at its best, that but 35 gold-fish sellers hawk in the streets and that for but half a year, each selling six dozen weekly, at 12s. the dozen, we find 65,520 fish sold, at an outlay of 3,276 0 0

Street-Sellers of Tortoises.

Estimating the number of individuals selling tortoises to be 20, and the number of tortoises sold to be 10,000, at an average price of 8d. each, we find there is expended yearly upon these creatures upwards of . . 333 6 8

Street-Sellers of Snails, Frogs, &c.

There are 14 snail gatherers, and they, on an average, gather six dozen quarts each in a year, which supplies a total of 12,096 quarts of snails. The labourers in the gardens, I am informed, gather somewhat more than an equal quantity, the greater part being sold to the bird-shops; so that altogether the supply of snails for the caged thrushes and blackbirds of London is about two millions and a half. Computing them at 24,000 quarts, and at 2d. a quart, the annual outlay is 200l. Besides snails, there are collected annually 500 frogs and 18 toads, at 1d. each, giving a yearly expenditure of 202 3 2

TOTAL, OR GROSS "TAKINGS," OF THE STREET-SELLERS OF LIVE ANIMALS 23,868 16 4

INCOME, OR "TAKINGS," OF THE STREET-SELLERS OF MINERAL PRODUCTIONS AND NATURAL CURIOSITIES.

Street-Sellers of Coals.

The number of individuals engaged in the street-sale of coals is 210; these distribute 2940 tons of coals weekly, giving an annual trade of 152,880 tons, at 1l. per ton, and consequently a yearly expenditure by the poor of 152,880 0 0

Street-Sellers of Coke.

The number of individuals engaged in the street-sale of coke is 1500; and the total quantity of coke sold annually in the streets is computed at about 1,400,000 chaldrons. These are purchased at the gas factories at an average price of 8s. per chaldron. Reckoning that this is sold at 4s. per chaldron for profit, we find that the total gains of the whole class amount to 280,000l. per annum, and their gross annual takings to . . . 840,000 0 0

Street-Sellers of Tan-Turf.

The number of tan-turf sellers in the metropolis is estimated at 14; each of these dispose of, upon an average, 20,000 per week, during the year; selling them at 1s. per hundred, and realizing a profit of 4½d. for each hundred. This makes the annual outlay in the street-sale of the above article amount to . . 7,280 0 0

Street-Sellers of Salt.

There are at present 150 individuals hawking salt in the several streets of London; each of these pay at the rate of 2s. per cwt. for the salt, and retail it at 3 lbs. for 1d., which leaves 1s. 1d. profit on every cwt. One day with another, wet and dry, each of the street-sellers disposes of about 2½ cwt., or 18 tons 15 cwt. per day for all hands, and this, deducting Sundays, makes 5868 tons 15 cwt. in the course of the year. The profit of 1s. 1d. per cwt. amounts to a yearly aggregate profit of 6357l. 16s. 3d., or about 42l. per annum for each person in the trade; while the sum annually expended upon this article in the streets amounts to 18,095 6 3

Street-Sellers of Sand.

Calculating the sale at a load of sand per day, for each horse and cart, at 21s. per load, we find the sum annually expended in house-sand to be 6573l.; adding to this the sum of 234l. spent yearly in bird-sand, the total street-expenditure is . . £6,807 0 0

Street-Sellers of Shells.

There are about 50 individuals disposing of shells at different periods of the year. These sell among them 1,000,000 at 1d. each, giving an annual expenditure of £4,166 13 4

TOTAL, OR GROSS TAKINGS, OF THE STREET-SELLERS OF MINERAL PRODUCTIONS AND NATURAL CURIOSITIES £1,029,228 19 7

River-Sellers of Purl.

There are at present 35 men following the trade of purl-selling on the river Thames to colliers. The weekly profits of this class amount to 117l. 5s. per week, and yearly to 6097l., while their annual takings is £8,190 0 0

Now, adding together the above and the other foregone results, we arrive at the following estimate as to the amount of money annually expended on the several articles purchased in the streets of the metropolis.

	£	£
"Wet" fish	1,177,200	
Dry fish	127,000	
Shell fish	156,600	
Fish of all kinds . .		1,460,800
Vegetables	292,400	
Green fruit	332,200	
Dry fruit	1,000	
Fruit and Vegetables		625,600
Game, poultry, rabbits, &c. . . .		80,000
Flowers, roots, &c.		14,800
Water-cresses		13,900
Chickweed, gru'nsel, and turf for birds		14,570
Eatables and drinkables.		203,100
Stationery, literature, and fine arts .		33,400
Manufactured articles		188,200
Second-hand articles		29,900
Live animals (*including dogs, birds, and gold fish*)		29,300
Mineral productions (*as coals, coke, salt, sand, &c.*)		1,022,700

TOTAL SUM EXPENDED UPON THE VARIOUS ARTICLES VENDED BY THE STREET-SELLERS £3,716,270

Hence it appears that the street-sellers, of all ages, in the metropolis are about forty thousand in number—their stock-in-trade is worth about sixty thousand pounds—and their gross annual takings or receipts amount to no less than three millions and a half sterling.

OF THE STREET-BUYERS.

THE persons who traverse the streets, or call periodically at certain places to purchase articles which are usually sold at the door or within the house, are—according to the division I laid down in the first number of this work—STREET-BUYERS. The largest, and, in every respect, the most remarkable body of these traders, are the buyers of old clothes, and of them I shall speak separately, devoting at the same time some space to the STREET-JEWS. It will also be necessary to give a brief account of the Jews generally, for they are still a peculiar race, and street and shop-trading among them are in many respects closely blended.

The principal things bought by the itinerant purchasers consist of waste-paper, hare and rabbit skins, old umbrellas and parasols, bottles and glass, broken metal, rags, dripping, grease, bones, tea-leaves, and old clothes.

With the exception of the buyers of waste-paper, among whom are many active, energetic, and intelligent men, the street-buyers are of the lower sort, both as to means and intelligence. The only further exception, perhaps, which I need notice here is, that among some umbrella-buyers, there is considerable smartness, and sometimes, in the repair or renewal of the ribs, &c., a slight degree of skill. The other street-purchasers—such as the hare-skin and old metal and rag buyers, are often old and infirm people of both sexes, of whom—perhaps by reason of their infirmities—not a few have been in the trade from their childhood, and are as well known by sight in their respective rounds, as was the "long-remembered beggar" in former times.

It is usually the lot of a poor person who has been driven to the streets, or has adopted such a life when an adult, to *sell* trifling things—such as are light to carry and require a small outlay—in advanced age. Old men and women totter about offering lucifer-matches, boot and stay-laces, penny memorandum books, and such like. But the elder portion of the street-folk I have now to speak of do not sell, but *buy*. The street-seller commends his wares, their cheapness, and excellence. The same sort of man, when a buyer, depreciates everything offered to him, in order to ensure a cheaper bargain, while many of the things thus obtained find their way into street-sale, and are then as much commended for cheapness and goodness, as if they were the stock-in-trade of an acute slop advertisement-monger, and this is done sometimes by the very man who, when a buyer, condemned them as utterly valueless. But this is common to all trades.

Of the Street-Buyers of Rags, Broken Metal, Bottles, Glass, and Bones.

I class all these articles under one head, for, on inquiry, I find no individual supporting himself by the trading in any one of them. I shall, therefore, describe the buyers of rags, broken metal, bottles, glass, and bones, as a body of street-traders, but take the articles in which they traffic seriatim, pointing out in what degree they are, or have been, wholly or partially, the staple of several distinct callings.

The traders in these things are not unprosperous men. The poor creatures who may be seen picking up rags in the street are "street-finders," and not buyers. It is the same with the poor old men who may be seen bending under an unsavoury sack of bones. The bones have been found, or have been given for charity, and are not purchased. One feeble old man whom I met with, his eyes fixed on the middle of the carriage-way in the Old St. Pancras-road, and with whom I had some conversation, told me that the best friend he had in the world was a gentleman who lived in a large house near the Regent's-park, and gave him the bones which his dogs had done with! "If I can only see hisself, sir," said the old man, "he's sure to give me any coppers he has in his coat-pocket, and that's a very great thing to a poor man like me. O, yes, I'll buy bones, if I have any ha'pence, rather than go without them; but I pick them up, or have them given to me mostly."

The street-buyers, who are only buyers, have barrows, sometimes even carts with donkeys, and, as they themselves describe it, they "buy everything." These men are little seen in London, for they "work" the more secluded courts, streets, and alleys, when in town; but their most frequented rounds are the poorer parts of the populous suburbs. There are many in Croydon, Woolwich, Greenwich, and Deptford. "It's no use," a man who had been in the trade said to me, "such as us calling at fine houses to know if they've any old keys to sell! No, we trades with the poor." Often, however, they deal with the servants of the wealthy; and their usual mode of business in such cases is to leave a bill at the house a few hours previous to their visit. This document has frequently the royal arms at the head of it, and asserts that the "firm" has been established since the year ——, which is seldom less than half a century. The hand-bill usually consists of a short preface as to the increased demand for rags on the part of the paper-makers, and this is followed by a liberal offer to give the very best prices for any old linen, or old metal, bottles, rope, stair-rods, locks, keys, dripping, carpeting, &c., "in fact, no rubbish or lumber, however worthless, will be refused;" and generally concludes with a request that this "bill" may be shown to the mistress of the house and preserved, as it will be called for in a couple of hours.

The papers are delivered by one of the "firm," who marks on the door a sign indicative of the houses at which the bill has been taken in, and the probable reception there of the gentleman who is to follow him. The road taken is also pointed by marks before explained, see vol. i. pp. 218 and 247. These men are residents in all quarters within 20 miles of London, being most numerous in the places at no great distance from the Thames. They work their way from their suburban residences to London, which, of course, is the mart, or "exchange," for their wares. The reason why the suburbs are preferred is that in those parts the possessors of such things as broken metal, &c., cannot so readily resort to a marine-store dealer's as they can in town. I am informed, however, that the shops of the marine-store men are on the increase in the more densely-peopled suburbs; still the dwellings of the poor are often widely scattered in those parts, and few will go a mile to sell any old thing. They wait in preference, unless very needy, for the *visit* of the street-buyer.

A good many years ago—perhaps until 30 years back—*rags*, and especially white and good linen rags, were among the things most zealously inquired for by street-buyers, and then 3*d.* a pound was a price readily paid. Subsequently the paper-manufacturers brought to great and economical perfection the process of boiling rags in lye and bleaching them with chlorine, so that colour became less a desideratum. A few years after the peace of 1815, moreover, the foreign trade in rags increased rapidly. At the present time, about 1200 tons of woollen rags, and upwards of 10,000 tons of linen rags, are imported yearly. These 10,000 tons give us but a vague notion of the real amount. I may therefore mention that, when reduced to a more definite quantity, they show a total of no less than twenty-two millions four hundred thousand pounds. The woollen rags are imported the most largely from Hamburg and Bremen, the price being from 5*l.* to 17*l.* the ton. Linen rags, which average nearly 20*l.* the ton, are imported from the same places, and from several Italian ports, more especially those in Sicily. Among these ports are Palermo, Messina, Ancona, Leghorn, and Trieste (the Trieste rags being gathered in Hungary). The value of the rags annually brought to this country is no less than 200,000*l.* What the native rags may be worth, there are no facts on which to ground an estimate; but supposing each person of the 20,000,000 in Great Britain to produce one pound of rags annually, then the rags of this country may be valued at very nearly the same price as the foreign ones, so that the gross value of the rags of Great Britain imported and produced at home, would, in such a case, amount to 400,000*l.* From France, Belgium, Holland, Spain, and other continental kingdoms, the exportation of rags is prohibited, nor can so bulky and low-priced a commodity be smuggled to advantage.

Of this large sum of rags, which is independent of what is collected in the United Kingdom, the Americans are purchasers on an extensive scale. The wear of cotton is almost unknown in many parts of Italy, Germany, and Hungary; and al-

although the linen in use is coarse and, compared to the Irish, Scotch, or English, rudely manufactured, the foreign rags *are* generally linen, and therefore are preferred at the paper mills. The street-buyers in this country, however, make less distinction than ever, as regards price, between linen and cotton rags.

The linen rag-buying is still prosecuted extensively by itinerant " gatherers " in the country, and in the further neighbourhoods of London, but the collection is not to the extent it was formerly. The price is lower, and, owing to the foreign trade, the demand is less urgent; so common, too, is now the wear of cotton, and so much smaller that of linen, that many people will not sell linen rags, but reserve them for use in case of cuts and wounds, or for giving to their poor neighbours on any such emergency. This was done doubtlessly to as great, or to a greater extent, in the old times, but linen rags were more plentiful then, for cotton shirting was not woven to the perfection seen at present, and many good country housewives spun their own linen sheetings and shirtings.

A street-buyer of the class I have described, upon presenting himself at any house, offers to buy rags, broken metal, or glass, and for rags especially there is often a serious bargaining, and sometimes, I was told by an itinerant street-seller, who had been an ear-witness, a little joking not of the most delicate kind. For coloured rags these men give $\frac{1}{2}d.$ a pound, or $1d.$ for three pounds; for inferior white rags $\frac{1}{2}d.$ a pound, and up to $1\frac{1}{2}d.$; for the best, $2d.$ the pound. It is common, however, and even more common, I am assured, among masters of the old rag and bottle shops, than among street-buyers, to announce $2d.$ or $3d.$, or even as much as $6d.$, for the *best* rags, but, somehow or other, the rags taken for sale to those buyers never are of the best. To offer $6d.$ a pound for rags is ridiculous, but such an offer may be seen at some rag-shops, the figure **6**, perhaps, crowning a painting of a large plum-pudding, as a representation of what may be a Christmas result, merely from the thrifty preservation of rags, grease, and dripping. Some of the street-buyers, when working the suburbs or the country, attach a similar " illustration " to their barrows or carts. I saw the winter placard of one of these men, which he was reserving for a country excursion as far as Rochester, "when the plum-pudding time was a-coming." In this pictorial advertisement a man and woman, very florid and full-faced, were on the point of enjoying a huge plum-pudding, the man flourishing a large knife, and looking very hospitable. On a scroll which issued from his mouth were the words: " From our rags! The best prices given by —— ——, of London." The woman in like manner exclaimed: " From dripping and house fat! The best prices given by —— ——, of London."

This man told me that at some times, both in town and country, he did not buy a pound of rags in a week. He had heard the old hands in the trade say, that 20 or 30 years back they could "gather" (the word generally used for buying) twice and three times as many rags as at present. My formant attributed this change to two causes, depending more upon what he had heard from experienced street-buyers than upon his own knowledge. At one time it was common for a mistress to allow her maid-servant to "keep a rag-bag," in which all refuse linen, &c., was collected for sale for the servant's behoof; a privilege now rarely accorded. The other cause was that working-people's wives had less money at their command now than they had formerly, so that instead of gathering a good heap for the man who called on them periodically, they ran to a marine store-shop and sold them by one, two, and three pennyworths at a time. This related to all the things in the street-buyer's trade, as well as to rags.

" I 've known this trade ten years or so," said my informant, " I was a costermonger before that, and I work coster-work now in the summer, and buy things in the winter. Before Christmas is the best time for second-hand trade. When I set out on a country round—and I 've gone as far as Guildford and Maidstone, and St. Alban's—I lays in as great a stock of glass and crocks as I can raise money for, or as my donkey or pony—I 've had both, but I 'm working a ass now—can drag without distressing him. I swops my crocks for anythink in the second-hand way, and when I 've got through them I buys outright, and so works my way back to London. I bring back what I 've bought in the crates and hampers I 've had to pack the crocks in. The first year as I started I got hold of a few very tidy rags, coloured things mostly. The Jew I sold 'em to when I got home again gave me more than I expected. O, lord no, not more than I asked! He told me, too, that he 'd buy any more I might have, as they was wanted at some town not very far off, where there was a call for them for patching quilts. I haven't heard of a call for any that way since. I get less and less rags every year, I think. Well, I can't say what I got last year; perhaps about two stone. No, none of them was woollen. They 're things as people 's seldom satisfied with the price for, is rags. I 've bought muslin window curtains or frocks as was worn, and good for nothink but rags, but there always seems such a lot, and they weighs so light and comes to so little, that there 's sure to be grumbling. I 've sometimes bought a lot of old clothes, by the lump, or I 've swopped crocks for them, and among them there 's frequently been things as the Jew in Petticoat-lane, what I sells them to, has put o' one side as rags. If I 'd offered to give rag prices, them as I got 'em of would have been offended, and have thought I wanted to cheat. When you get a lot at one go, and 'specially if it 's for crocks, you must make the best of them. This for that, and t'other for t'other. I stay at the beer-shops and little inns in the country. Some of the landlords looks very shy at one, if you 're a stranger, acause, if the police detectives is after anythink, they go as hawkers, or barrowmen, or somethink that way." [This statement as to the police is correct; but the man did not know how it came to his knowledge; he had " heard of it," he believed.] " I 've very seldom slept in a common lodging-house. I 'd rather sleep on my barrow." [I have before had occasion to remark the aversion of the costermonger class to sleep in low lodging-houses. These men, almost always, and from the necessities of their calling, have rooms of their own in London; so that, I presume, they hate to sleep *in public*, as the accommodation for repose in many a lodging-house may very well be called. At any rate the costermongers, of all classes of street-sellers, when on their country excursions, resort the least to the lodging-houses.] "The last round I had in the country, as far as Reading and Pangbourne, I was away about five weeks, I think, and came back a better man by a pound; that was all. I mean I had 30 shillings' worth of things to start with, and when I'd got back, and turned my rags, and old metal, and things into money, I had 50s. To be sure Jenny (the ass) and me lived well all the time, and I bought a pair of half-boots and a pair of stockings at Reading, so it weren't so bad. Yes, sir, there's nothing I likes better than a turn into the country. It does one's health good, if it don't turn out so well for profits as it might."

My informant, the rag-dealer, belonged to the best order of costermongers; one proof of this was in the evident care which he had bestowed on Jenny, his donkey. There were no loose hairs on her hide, and her harness was clean and whole, and I observed after a pause to transact business on his round, that the animal held her head towards her master to be scratched, and was petted with a mouthful of green grass and clover, which the costermonger had in a corner of his vehicle.

Tailor's cuttings, which consist of cloth, satin, lining materials, fustian, waistcoatings, silk, &c., are among the things which the street-buyers are the most anxious to become possessed of on a country round; for, as will be easily understood by those who have read the accounts before given of the Old Clothes Exchange, and of Petticoat and Rosemary lanes, they are available for many purposes in London.

Dressmaker's cuttings are also a portion of the street-buyer's country traffic, but to no great extent, and hardly ever, I am told, unless the street-buyer, which is not often the case, be accompanied on his round by his wife. In town, tailor's cuttings are usually sold to the piece-brokers, who call or send men round to the shops or workshops for the purpose of buying them, and it is the same with the dressmaker's cuttings.

Old metal, or *broken metal*, for I heard one appellation used as frequently as the other, is bought by the same description of traders. This trade, however, is prosecuted in town by the street-buyers more largely than in the country, and so differs from the rag business. The carriage of old iron bolts and bars is exceedingly cumbersome; nor can metal be packed or stowed away like old clothes or rags. This makes the street-buyer indifferent as to the collecting of what I heard one of them call "country iron." By "metal" the street-folk often mean copper (most especially), brass, or pewter, in contradistinction to the cheaper substances of iron or lead. In the country they are most anxious to buy "metal;" whereas, in town, they as readily purchase "iron." When the street-buyers give merely the worth of any metal by weight to be disposed of, in order to be remelted, or re-wrought in some manner, by the manufacturers, the following are the average prices:—Copper, 6d. per lb.; pewter, 5d.; brass, 5d.; iron, 6 lbs. for 1d., and 8 lbs. for 2d. (a smaller quantity than 6 lbs. is seldom bought); and 1d. and 1$\frac{1}{4}d$. per lb. for lead. Old zinc is not a metal which "comes in the way" of the street-buyer, nor—as one of them told me with a laugh —old silver. Tin is never bought by weight in the streets.

It must be understood that the prices I have mentioned are those given for old or broken metal, valueless unless for re-working. When an old metal article is still available, or may be easily made available, for the use for which it was designed, the street-purchase is by "the piece," rather than the weight.

The broken pans, scuttles, kettles, &c., concerning one of the uses of which I have quoted Mr. Babbage, in page 6 of the present volume, as to the conversion of these worn-out vessels into the light and japanned edgings, or clasps, called "clamps," or "clips," by the trunk-makers, and used to protect or strengthen the corners of boxes and packing-cases, are purchased sometimes by the street-buyers, but fall more properly under the head of what constitutes a portion of the stock-in-trade of the street-finder. They are not bought by weight, but so much for the pan, perhaps so much along with other things; a halfpenny, a penny, or occasionally two-pence, and often only a farthing, or three pans for a penny. The uses for these things which the street-buyers have more especially in view, are not those mentioned by Mr. Babbage (the trunk clamps), but the conversion of them into the "iron shovels," or strong dust-pans sold in the streets. One street artisan supports himself and his family by the making of dust-pans from such grimy old vessels.

As in the result of my inquiry among the street-*sellers* of old metal, I am of opinion that the street-*buyers* also are not generally mixed up with the receipt of stolen goods. That they may be so to some extent is probable enough; in the same proportion, perhaps, as highly respectable tradesmen have been known to buy the goods of fraudulent bankrupts, and others. The street-buyers are low itinerants, seen regularly by the police and easy to be traced, and therefore, for one reason, cautious. In one of my inquiries among the young thieves and pickpockets in the low lodging-houses, I heard frequent accounts of their selling the metal goods they stole, to "fences," and in one particular instance, to the mistress of a lodging-house, who had conveniences for the melting of pewter pots (called "cats and kittens" by the young thieves, according to the size of the vessels), but I never heard them speak of any connection, or indeed any transactions, with street-folk.

Among the things purchased in great quantities by the street-buyers of old metal are keys. The keys so bought are of every size, are generally very rusty, and present every form of manufacture, from the simplest to the most complex wards. On my inquiring how such a number of keys without locks came to be offered for street-sale, I was informed that there were often duplicate or triplicate keys to one lock, and that in sales of household furniture, for instance, there were often numbers of odd keys found about the premises and sold "in a lump;" that locks were often spoiled and unsaleable, wearing out long before the keys. Twopence a dozen is an usual price for a dozen "mixed keys," to a street-buyer. Bolts are also freely bought by the street-people, as are holdfasts, bed-keys, and screws, "and everything," I was told, "which some one or other among the poor is always a-wanting."

A little old man, who had been many years a street-buyer, gave me an account of his purchases of *bottles* and *glass*. This man had been a soldier in his youth; had known, as he said, "many ups and downs;" and occasionally wheels a barrow, somewhat larger and shallower than those used by masons, from which he vends iron and tin wares, such as cheap gridirons, stands for hand-irons, dust-pans, dripping trays, &c. As he sold these wares, he offered to buy, or swop for, any second-hand commodities. "As to the bottle and glass buying, sir," he said, "it's dead and buried in the streets, and in the country too. I've known the day when I've cleared 2*l*. in a week by buying old things in a country round. How long was that ago, do you say, sir? Why perhaps twenty years; yes, more than twenty. Now, I'd hardly pick up odd glass in the street." [He called imperfect glass wares "odd glass."] "O, I don't know what's brought about such a change, but everything changes. I can't say anything about the duty on glass. No, I never paid any duty on my glass; it ain't likely. I buy glass still, certainly I do, but I think if I depended on it I should be wishing myself in the East Injes again, rather than such a poor consarn of a business—d——n me if I shouldn't. The last glass bargain I made about two months back, down Limehouse-way, and about the Commercial-road, I cleared 7*d*. by; and then I had to wheel what I bought—it was chiefly bottles—about five mile. It's a trade would starve a cat, the buying of old glass. I never bought glass by weight, but I've heard of some giving a halfpenny and a penny a pound. I always bought by the piece: from a halfpenny to a shilling (but that's long since) for a bottle; and farthings and halfpennies, and higher and sometimes lower, for wine and other glasses as was chipped or cracked, or damaged, for they could be sold in them days. People's got proud now, I fancy that's one thing, and must have everything slap. O, I do middling: I live by one thing or other, and when I die there'll just be enough to bury the old man." [This is the first street-trader I have met with who made such a statement as to having provided for his interment, though I have heard these men occasionally express repugnance at the thoughts of being buried by the parish.] "I have a daughter, that's all my family now; she does well as a laundress, and is a real good sort; I have my dinner with her every Sunday. She's a widow without any young ones. I often go to church, both with my daughter and by myself, on Sunday evenings. It does one good. I'm fond of the music and singing too. The sermon I can very seldom make anything of, as I can't hear well if any one's a good way off me when he's saying anythink. I buy a little old metal sometimes, but it's coming to be all up with street glass-people; everybody seems to run with their things to the rag-and-bottle-shops."

The same body of traders buy also *old sacking, carpeting, and moreen bed-curtains and window-hangings;* but the trade in them is sufficiently described in my account of the buying of rags, for it is carried on in the same way, so much per pound (1*d*. or 1½*d*. or 2*d*.), or so much for the lot.

Of *Bones* I have already spoken. They are bought by any street-collector with a cart, on his round in town, at a halfpenny a pound, or three pounds for a penny; but it is a trade, on account of the awkwardness of carriage, little cared for by the regular street-buyers. Men, connected with some bone-grinding-mill, go round with a horse and cart to the knackers and butchers to collect bones; but this is a portion, not of street, but of the mill-owner's, business. These bones are ground for manure, which is extensively used by the agriculturists, having been first introduced in Yorkshire and Lincolnshire about 30 years ago. The importation of bones is now very great; more than three times as much as it was 20 years back. The value of the foreign bones imported is estimated at upwards of 300,000*l*. yearly. They are brought from South America (along with hides), from Germany, Holland, and Belgium.

The men who most care to collect bones in the streets of London are old and infirm, and they barter toys for them with poor children; for those children sometimes gather bones in the streets and put them on one side, or get them from dustholes, for the sake of exchanging them for a plaything; or, indeed, for selling them to any shopkeeper, and many of the rag-and-bottle-tradesmen buy bones. The toys most used for this barter are paper "wind-mills." These toy-barterers, when they have a few pence, will buy bones of children or any others, if they cannot become possessed of them otherwise; but the carriage of the bones is a great obstacle to much being done in this business.

In the regular way of street-buying, such as I have described it, there are about 100 men in London and the suburbs. Some buy only during a portion of the year, and none perhaps (except in the way of barter) the year round. They are chiefly of the costermonger class, some of the street-buyers however, have been carmen's servants, or connected with trades in which they had the care of a horse and cart, and so became habituated to a street-life.

There are still many other ways in which the commerce in refuse and the second-hand street-trade is supplied. As the windmill-seller for bones, so will the puppet-show man for old bottles or broken table-spoons, or almost any old trifle, allow children to regale their eyes on the beauties of his exhibition.

The trade expenditure of the street-buyers it is not easy to estimate. Their calling is so mixed with selling and bartering, that very probably not one among them can tell what he expends in *buying*, as a separate branch of his business. If 100 men expend 15s. each weekly, in the purchase of rags, old metal, &c., and if this trade be prosecuted for 30 weeks of the year, we find 2250*l*. so expended. The profits of the buyers range from 20 to 100 per cent.

OF THE " RAG-AND-BOTTLE," AND THE " MARINE-STORE," SHOPS.

The principal purchasers of any refuse or worn-out articles are the proprietors of the rag-and-bottle-shops. Some of these men make a good deal of money, and not unfrequently unite with the business the letting out of vans for the conveyance of furniture, or for pleasure excursions, to such places as Hampton Court. The stench in these shops is positively sickening. Here in a small apartment may be a pile of rags, a sack-full of bones, the many varieties of grease and " kitchen-stuff," corrupting an atmosphere which, even without such accompaniments, would be too close. The windows are often crowded with bottles, which exclude the light; while the floor and shelves are thick with grease and dirt. The inmates seem unconscious of this foulness,—and one comparatively wealthy man, who showed me his horses, the stable being like a drawing-room compared to his shop, in speaking of the many deaths among his children, could not conjecture to what cause it could be owing. This indifference to dirt and stench is the more remarkable, as many of the shopkeepers have been gentlemen's servants, and were therefore once accustomed to cleanliness and order. The door-posts and windows of the rag-and-bottle-shops are often closely placarded, and the front of the house is sometimes one glaring colour, blue or red; so that the place may be at once recognised, even by the illiterate, as the "red house," or the "blue house." If these men are not exactly street-buyers, they are street-billers, continually distributing hand-bills, but more especially before Christmas. The more aristocratic, however, now send round cards, and to the following purport:—

No. —   No. —

THE —— HOUSE IS ——'S
RAG, BOTTLE, AND KITCHEN STUFF
WAREHOUSE,
—— STREET, —— TOWN,

Where you can obtain Gold and Silver to any amount.
ESTABLISHED ——.
THE HIGHEST PRICE GIVEN
For all the undermentioned articles, viz:—

Wax and Sperm Pieces	Old Copper, Brass, Pewter, &c.
Kitchen Stuff, &c.	
Wine & Beer Bottles	Lead, Iron, Zinc, Steel, &c., &c.
Eau de Cologne, Soda Water	
Doctors' Bottles, &c.	Old Horse Hair, Mattresses, &c.
White Linen Rags	Old Books, Waste Paper, &c.
Bones, Phials, & Broken Flint Glass	
	All kinds of Coloured Rags

The utmost value given for all kinds of Wearing Apparel.
Furniture and Lumber of every description bought, and full value given at his Miscellaneous Warehouse.
Articles sent for.

Some content themselves with sending hand-bills to the houses in their neighbourhood, which many of the cheap printers keep in type, so that an alteration in the name and address is all which is necessary for any customer.

I heard that suspicions were entertained that it was to some of these traders that the facilities with which servants could dispose of their pilferings might be attributed, and that a stray silver spoon might enhance the weight and price of kitchen-stuff. It is not pertaining to my present subject to enter into the consideration of such a matter; and I might not have alluded to it, had not I found the regular street-buyers fond of expressing an opinion of the indifferent honesty of this body of traders; but my readers may have remarked how readily the street-people have, on several occasions, justified (as they seem to think) their own delinquencies by quoting what they declared were as great and as frequent delinquencies on the part of shopkeepers: "I know very well," said an intelligent street-seller on one occasion, "that two wrongs can never make a right; but tricks that shopkeepers practise to grow rich upon we must practise, just as they do, to live at all. As long as they give short weight and short measure, the streets can't help doing the same."

The *rag-and-bottle* and the *marine-store shops* are in many instances but different names for the same description of business. The chief distinction appears to be this: the marine-store shopkeepers (proper) do not meddle with what is a very principal object of traffic with the rag-and-bottle man, the purchase of dripping, as well as of every kind of refuse in the way of fat or grease. The marine-store man, too, is more miscellaneous in his wares than his contemporary of the rag-and-bottle-store, as the former will purchase any of the smaller articles of household furniture, old tea-caddies, knife-boxes, fire-irons, books, pictures, draughts and backgammon boards, bird-cages, Dutch clocks, cups and saucers, tools and brushes. The rag-and-bottle tradesman will readily purchase any of these things to be disposed of as old metal or waste-paper, but his brother tradesman buys them to be re-sold and re-used for the purposes for which they were originally manufactured. When furniture, however, is the staple of one of these second-hand storehouses, the proprietor is a furniture-broker, and not a marine-store dealer. If, again, the dealer in these stores confine his business to the purchase of old metals, for instance, he is classed as an old metal dealer, collecting it or buying it of collectors, for sale to iron-founders, coppersmiths, brass-founders, and plumbers. In perhaps the majority of instances there is little or no distinction between the establishments I have spoken of. The *dolly* business is common to both, but most common to the marine-store dealer, and of it I shall speak afterwards.

These shops are exceedingly numerous. Perhaps in the poorer and smaller streets they are more numerous even than the chandlers' or the beer-sellers' places. At the corner of a small street, both in town and the nearer suburbs, will frequently be found the chandler's shop, for the sale of small quantities of cheese, bacon, groceries, &c., to the poor. Lower down may be seen the beer-seller's; and in the same street there is certain to be one rag-and-bottle or marine-store shop, very often two, and not unfrequently another in some adjacent court.

I was referred to the owner of a marine-store shop, as to a respectable man, keeping a store of the best class. Here the counter, or table, or whatever it is to be called, for it was somewhat nondescript, by an ingenious contrivance could be pushed out into the street, so that in bad weather the goods which were at other times exposed in the street could be drawn inside without trouble. The glass frames of the window were removable, and were placed on one side in the shop, for in the summer an open casement seemed to be preferred. This is one of the remaining old trade customs still seen in London; for previously to the great fire in 1666, and the subsequent rebuilding of the city, shops with open casements, and protected from the weather by overhanging eaves, or by a sloping wooden roof, were general.

The house I visited was an old one, and abounded in closets and recesses. The fire-place, which apparently had been large, was removed, and the space was occupied with a mass of old iron of every kind; all this was destined for the furnace of the iron-founder, wrought iron being preferred for several of the requirements of that trade. A chest or range of very old drawers, with defaced or worn-out labels—once a grocer's or a chemist's—was stuffed, in every drawer, with old horse-shoe nails (valuable for steel manufacturers), and horse and donkey shoes; brass knobs; glass stoppers; small bottles (among them a number of the cheap cast "hartshorn bottles"); broken pieces of brass and copper; small tools (such as shoemakers' and harness-makers' awls), punches, gimlets, plane-irons, hammer heads, &c.; odd dominoes, dice, and backgammon-men; lock escutcheons, keys, and the smaller sort of locks, especially padlocks; in fine, any small thing which could be stowed away in such a place.

In one corner of the shop had been thrown, the evening before, a mass of old iron, then just bought. It consisted of a number of screws of different lengths and substance; of broken bars and rails; of the odds and ends of the cogged wheels of machinery, broken up or worn out; of odd-looking spikes, and rings, and links; all heaped together and scarcely distinguishable. These things had all to be assorted; some to be sold for re-use in their then form; the others to be sold that they might be melted and cast into other forms. The floor was intricate with hampers of bottles; heaps of old boots and shoes; old desks and work-boxes; pictures (all modern) with and without frames; waste-paper, the most of it of quarto, and some larger sized, soiled or torn, and strung closely together in weights of from 2 to 7 lbs.; and a fire-proof safe, stuffed with old fringes, tassels, and other upholstery goods, worn and discoloured. The miscellaneous wares were carried out into the street, and ranged by the door-posts as well as in front of the house. In some small out-houses in the yard were piles of old iron and tin pans, and of the broken or separate parts of harness.

From the proprietor of this establishment I had the following account:—

"I've been in the business more than a dozen years. Before that, I was an auctioneer's, and then a furniture broker's, porter. I wasn't brought up to any regular trade, but just to jobbing about, and a bad trade it is, as all trades is that ain't regular employ for a man. I had some money when my father died—he kept a chandler's shop—and I bought a marine." [An elliptical form of speech among these traders.] "I gave 10*l*. for the stock, and 5*l*. for entrance and good-will, and agreed to pay what rents and rates was due. It was a smallish stock then, for the business had been neglected, but I have no reason to be sorry for my bargain, though it might have been better. There's lots taken in about good-wills, but perhaps not so many in my way of business, because we're rather 'fly to a dodge.' It's a confined sort of life, but there's no help for that. Why, as to my way of trade, you'd be surprised, what different sorts of people come to my shop. I don't mean the regular hands; but the chance comers. I've had men dressed like gentlemen—and no doubt they was respectable when they was sober—bring two or three books, or a nice cigar case, or anythink that don't show in their pockets, and say, when as drunk as blazes, 'Give me what you can for this; I want it sold for a particular purpose.' That particular purpose was more drink, I should say; and I've known the same men come back in less than a week, and buy what they'd sold me at a little extra, and be glad if I had it by me still. O, we sees a deal of things in this way of life. Yes, poor people run to such as me. I've known them come with such things as teapots, and old hair mattresses, and flock beds, and *then* I'm sure they're hard up—reduced for a meal. I don't like buying big things like mattresses, though I do purchase 'em sometimes. Some of these sellers are as keen as Jews at a bargain; others seem only anxious to get rid of the things and have hold of some bit of money anyhow. Yes, sir, I've known their hands tremble to receive the money, and mostly the women's. They haven't been used to it, I know, when that's the case. Perhaps they comes to sell to me what the pawns won't take in, and what they wouldn't like to be seen selling to any of the men that goes about buying things in the street.

"Why, I've bought everythink; at sales by auction there's often 'lots' made up of different things, and they goes for very little. I buy of people, too, that come to me, and of the regular hands that supply such shops as mine. I sell retail, and I sell to hawkers. I sell to anybody, for gentlemen 'll come into my shop to buy anythink that's took their fancy in passing. Yes, I've bought old oil paintings. I've heard of some being bought by people in my way as have turned out stunners, and was sold for a hundred pounds or more, and cost, perhaps, half-a-crown or only a shilling. I never experienced such a thing myself. There's a good deal of gammon about it. Well, it's hardly possible to say anything about a scale of prices. I give 2d. for an old tin or metal teapot, or an old saucepan, and sometimes, two days after I've bought such a thing, I've sold it for 3d. to the man or woman I've bought it of. I'll sell cheaper to them than to anybody else, because they come to me in two ways—both as sellers and buyers. For pictures I've given from 3d. to 1s. I fancy they're among the last things some sorts of poor people, which is a bit fanciful, parts with. I've bought them of hawkers, but often I refuse them, as they've given more than I could get. Pictures requires a judge. Some brought to me was published by newspapers and them sort of people. Waste-paper I buy as it comes. I can't read very much, and don't understand about books. I take the backs off and weighs them, and gives 1d., and 1½d., and 2d. a pound, and there's an end. I sell them at about ¼d. a pound profit, or sometimes less, to men as we calls 'waste' men. It's a poor part of our business, but the books and paper takes up little room, and then it's clean and can be stowed anywhere, and is a sure sale. Well, the people as sells 'waste' to me is not such as can read, I think; I don't know what they is; perhaps they're such as obtains possession of the books and whatnot after the death of old folks, and gets them out of the way as quick as they can. I know nothink about what they are. Last week, a man in black—he didn't seem rich—came into my shop and looked at some old books, and said 'Have you any black lead?' He didn't speak plain, and I could hardly catch him. I said, 'No, sir, I don't sell black lead, but you'll get it at No. 27,' but he answered, 'Not black lead, but black letter,' speaking very pointed. I said, 'No,' and I haven't a notion what he meant.

"Metal (copper) that I give 5d. or 5½d. for, I can sell to the merchants from 6½d. to 8d. the pound. It's no great trade, for they'll often throw things out of the lot and say they're not metal. Sometimes, it would hardly be a farthing in a shilling, if it war'n't for the draught in the scales. When we buys metal, we don't notice the quarters of the pounds; all under a quarter goes for nothink. When we buys iron, all under half pounds counts nothink. So when we buys by the pound, and sells by the hundredweight, there's a little help from this, which we calls the draught.

"Glass bottles of all qualities I buys at three for a halfpenny, and sometimes four, up to 2d. a-piece for 'good stouts' (bottled-porter vessels), but very seldom indeed 2d., unless it's something very prime and big like the old quarts (quart bottles). I seldom meddles with decanters. It's very few decanters as is offered to me, either little or big, and I'm shy of them when they are. There's such a change in glass. Them as buys in the streets brings me next to nothing now to buy; they both brought and bought a lot ten year back and later. I never was in the street-trade in second-hand, but it's not what it was. I sell in the streets, when I put things outside, and know all about the trade.

"It ain't a fortnight back since a smart female servant, in slap-up black, sold me a basket-full of doctor's bottles. I knew her master, and he hadn't been buried a week before she come to me, and she said, 'missus is glad to get rid of them, for they makes her cry.' They often say their missusses sends things, and that they're not on no account to take less than so much. That's true at times, and at times it ain't. I gives from 1½d. to 3d. a dozen for good new bottles. I'm sure I can't say what I give for other odds and ends; just as they're good, bad, or indifferent. It's a queer trade. Well, I pay my way, but I don't know what I clear a week—about 2l. I dare say, but then there's rent, rates, and taxes to pay, and other expenses."

The *Dolly* system is peculiar to the rag-and-bottle man, as well as to the marine-store dealer. The name is derived from the black wooden doll, in white apparel, which generally hangs dangling over the door of the marine-store shops, or of the "rag-and-bottles," but more frequently the last-mentioned. This type of the business is sometimes swung above their doors by those who are not dolly-shop keepers. The dolly-shops are essentially pawn-shops, and pawn-shops for the very poorest. There are many articles which the regular pawnbrokers decline to accept as pledges. Among these things are blankets, rugs, clocks, flock-beds, common pictures, "translated" boots, mended trowsers, kettles, saucepans, trays, &c. Such things are usually styled "lumber." A poor person driven to the necessity of raising a few pence, and unwilling to part finally with his lumber, goes to the dolly-man, and for the merest trifle advanced, deposits one or other of the articles I have mentioned, or something similar. For an advance of 2d. or 3d., a halfpenny a week is charged, but the charge is the same if the pledge be redeemed next day. If the interest be paid at the week's end, another 1d. is occasionally advanced, and no extra charge exacted for interest. If the interest be not paid at the week or fortnight's end, the article is forfeited, and is sold at a large profit by the dolly-shop man. For 4d. or 6d. advanced, the weekly interest is 1d.; for 9d. it is 1½d.; for 1s. it is 2d., and 2d. on each 1s. up to 5s., beyond which sum the "dolly" will rarely go; in fact, he will rarely advance as much. Two poor Irish flower girls, whom I saw in the course of my inquiry into that part of street-traffic, had in the winter very often to pledge the rug under which they slept at a dolly-shop in the morning for 6d., in order to provide themselves with stock-money to buy forced violets, and had to redeem it on their return in the evening, when they could, for 7d. Thus 6d. a week was sometimes paid for a daily advance of that sum. Some of these "*illicit*" pawnbrokers even give tickets.

This incidental mention of what is really an immense trade, as regards the number of pledges, is all that is necessary under the present head of inquiry, but I purpose entering into this branch of the subject fully and minutely when I come to treat of the class of "distributors."

The *iniquities* to which the poor are subject are positively monstrous. A halfpenny a day interest on a loan of 2*d*. is at the rate of 7280 *per cent. per annum!*

OF THE BUYERS OF KITCHEN-STUFF, GREASE, AND DRIPPING.

THIS body of traders cannot be classed as street-buyers, so that only a brief account is here necessary. The buyers are not now chance people, itinerant on any round, as at one period they were to a great extent, but they are the proprietors of the rag and bottle and marine-store shops, or those they employ.

In this business there has been a considerable change. Until of late years women, often wearing suspiciously large cloaks and carrying baskets, ventured into perhaps every area in London, and asked for the cook at every house where they thought a cook might be kept, and this often at early morning. If the well-cloaked woman was known, business could be transacted without delay: if she were a stranger, she recommended herself by offering very liberal terms for "kitchen-stuff." The cook's, or kitchen-maid's, or servant-of-all-work's "perquisites," were then generally disposed of to these collectors, some of whom were charwomen in the houses they resorted to for the purchase of the kitchen-stuff. They were often satisfied to purchase the dripping, &c., by the lump, estimating the weight and the value by the eye. In this traffic was frequently mixed up a good deal of pilfering, directly or indirectly. Silver spoons were thus disposed of. Candles, purposely broken and crushed, were often part of the grease; in the dripping, butter occasionally added to the weight; in the "stock" (the remains of meat boiled down for the making of soup) were sometimes portions of excellent meat fresh from the joints which had been carved at table; and among the broken bread, might be frequently seen small loaves, unbroken.

There is no doubt that this mode of traffic by itinerant charwomen, &c., is still carried on, but to a much smaller extent than formerly. The cook's perquisites are in many cases sold under the inspection of the mistress, according to agreement; or taken to the shop by the cook or some fellow-servant; or else sent for by the shopkeeper. This is done to check the confidential, direct, and immediate trade-intercourse between merely two individuals, the buyer and seller, by making the transaction more open and regular. I did not hear of any persons who merely purchase the kitchen-stuff, as street-buyers, and sell it at once to the tallow-melter or the soap-boiler; it appears all to find its way to the shops I have described, even when bought by charwomen; while the shopkeepers send for it or receive it in the way I have stated, so that there is but little of street traffic in the matter.

One of these shopkeepers told me that in this trading, as far as his own opinion went, there was as much trickery as ever, and that many gentlefolk quietly made up their minds to submit to it, while others, he said, "kept the house in hot water" by resisting it. I found, however, the general opinion to be, that when servants could only dispose of these things to known people, the responsibility of the buyer as well as the seller was increased, and acted as a preventive check.

The price for kitchen-stuff is 1*d*. and 1½*d*. the pound; for dripping—used by the poor as a substitute for butter—3½*d*. to 5*d*.

OF THE STREET-BUYERS OF HARE AND RABBIT SKINS.

THESE buyers are for the most part poor, old, or infirm people, and I am informed that the majority have been in some street business, and often as buyers, all their lives. Besides having derived this information from well-informed persons, I may point out that this is but a reasonable view of the case. If a mechanic, a labourer, or a gentleman's servant, resorts to the streets for his bread, or because he is of a vagrant "turn," he does not become a *buyer*, but a *seller*. Street-selling is the easier process. It is easy for a man to ascertain that oysters, for example, are sold wholesale at Billingsgate, and if he buy a bushel (as in the present summer) for 5*s*., it is not difficult to find out how many he can afford for "a penny a lot." But the street-buyer must not only know what to *give*, for hare-skins for instance, but what he can depend upon *getting* from the hat-manufacturers, or hat-furriers, and upon having a regular market. Thus a double street-trade knowledge is necessary, and a novice will not care to meddle with any form of open-air traffic but the simplest. Neither is street-buying (old clothes excepted) generally cared for by adults who have health and strength.

In the course of a former inquiry I received an account of hareskin-buying from a woman, upwards of fifty, who had been in the trade, she told me, from childhood, "as was her mother before her." The husband, who was lame, and older than his wife, had been all *his* life a field-catcher of birds, and a street-seller of hearth-stones. They had been married 31 years, and resided in a garret of a house, in a street off Drury-lane—a small room, with a close smell about it. The room was not unfurnished—it was, in fact, crowded. There were bird-cages, with and without birds, over what *was* once a bed; for the bed, just prior to my visit, had been sold to pay the rent, and a month's rent was again in arrear; and there were bird-cages on the wall by the door, and bird-cages over the mantelshelf. There was furniture, too, and crockery; and a vile oil painting of "still life;" but an eye used to the furniture in the rooms of the poor could at once perceive that there was not *one* article which could be sold to a broker or marine-store dealer, or pledged at a pawn-shop. I was told the man and woman both drank hard. The woman said:—

"I've sold hareskins all my life, sir, and was born in London; but when hareskins isn't in, I sells flowers. I goes about now (in November) for my skins every day, wet or dry, and all day long—that is, till it's dark. To-day I've not laid out a penny, but then it's been such a day for rain. I reckon that if I gets hold of eighteen hare and rabbit skins in a day, that is my greatest day's work. I gives 2d. for good hares, what's not riddled much, and sells them all for 2½d. I sells what I pick up, by the twelve or the twenty, if I can afford to keep them by me till that number's gathered, to a Jew. I don't know what is done with them. I can't tell you just what use they 're for—something about hats." [The Jew was no doubt a hat-furrier, or supplying a hat-furrier.] "Jews gives us better prices than Christians, and buys readier; so I find. Last week I sold all I bought for 3s. 6d. I take some weeks as much as 8s. for what I pick up, and if I could get that every week I should think myself a lady. The profit left me a clear half-crown. There's no difference in any perticler year—only that things gets worse. The game laws, as far as I knows, hasn't made no difference in my trade. Indeed, I can't say I knows anything about game laws at all, or hears anything consarning 'em. I goes along the squares and streets. I buys most at gentlemen's houses. We never calls at hotels. The servants, and the women that chars, and washes, and jobs, manages it there. Hareskins is in—leastways I c'lects them—from September to the end of March, when hares, they says, goes mad. I can't say what I makes one week with another—perhaps 2s. 6d. may be cleared every week."

These buyers go regular rounds, carrying the skins in their hands, and crying, "Any hareskins, cook? Hareskins." It is for the most part a winter trade; but some collect the skins all the year round, as the hares are now vended the year through; but by far the most are gathered in the winter. Grouse may not be killed excepting from the 12th, and black-game from the 20th of August to the 10th of December; partridges from the 1st of September to the 1st of February; while the pheasant suffers a shorter season of slaughter, from the 1st of October to the 1st of February; but there is no time restriction as to the killing of hares or of rabbits, though custom causes a cessation for a few months.

A lame man, apparently between 50 and 60, with a knowing look, gave me the following account. When I saw him he was carrying a few tins, chiefly small dripping-pans, under his arm, which he offered for sale as he went his round collecting hare and rabbit-skins, of which he carried but one. He had been in the streets all his life, as his mother—he never knew any father—was a rag-gatherer, and at the same time a street-seller of the old brimstone matches and papers of pins. My informant assisted his mother to make and then to sell the matches. On her last illness she was received into St. Giles's workhouse, her son supporting himself out of it; she had been dead many years. He could not read, and had never been in a church or chapel in his life. "He had been married," he said, "for about a dozen years, and had a very good wife, who was also a street-trader until her death; but "we didn't go to church or anywhere to be married," he told me, in reply to my question, "for we really couldn't afford to pay the parson, and so we took one another's words. If it's so good to go to church for being married, it oughtn't to cost a poor man nothing; he shouldn't be charged for being good. I doesn't do any business in town, but has my regular rounds. This is my Kentish and Camden-town day. I buys most from the servants at the bettermost houses, and I'd rather buy of them than the missusses, for some missusses sells their own skins, and they often want a deal for 'em. Why, just arter last Christmas, a young lady in that there house (pointing to it), after ordering me round to the back-door, came to me with two hareskins. They certainly was fine skins—werry fine. I said I'd give 4½d. 'Come now, my good man,' says she," and the man mimicked her voice, "'let me have no nonsense. I can't be deceived any longer, either by you or my servants; so give me 8d., and go about your business.' Well, I went about my business; and a woman called to buy them, and offered 4d. for the two, and the lady was so wild, the servant told me arter; howsomever she only got 4d. at last. She's a regular screw, but a fine-dressed one. I don't know that there's been any change in my business since hares was sold in the shops. If there's more skins to sell, there's more poor people to buy. I never tasted hares' flesh in my life, though I've gathered so many of their skins. I've smelt it when they've been roasting them where I've called, but don't think I could eat any. I live on bread and butter and tea, or milk sometimes in hot weather, and get a bite of fried fish or anything when I'm out, and a drop of beer and a smoke when I get home, if I can afford it. I don't smoke in my own place, I uses a beer-shop. I pay 1s. 6d. a week for a small room; I want little but a bed in it, and have my own. I owe three weeks' rent now; but I do best both with tins and hareskins in the cold weather. Monday's my best day. O, as to rabbit-skins, I do werry little in them. Them as sells them gets the skins. Still there *is* a few to be picked up; such as them as has been sent as presents from the country. Good rabbit-skins is about the same price as hares, or perhaps a halfpenny lower, take them all through. I generally clears 6d. a dozen on my hare and rabbit-skins, and sometimes 8d. Yes, I should say that for about eight months I gathers four dozen every week, often five dozen. I suppose I make 5s. or 6s. a week all the year, with one thing or other, and a lame man can't do wonders. I never begged in my life, but I've twice had help from the parish, and that only when I was very bad (ill). O, I suppose I shall end in the great house."

There are, as closely as I can ascertain, at least 50 persons buying skins in the street; and calculating that each collects 50 skins weekly for 32 weeks of the year, we find 80,000 to be the total. This is a reasonable computation, for there are upwards of 102,000 hares consigned yearly to Newgate and Leadenhall markets; while the rabbits sold yearly in London amount to about

1,000,000; but, as I have shown, very few of their skins are disposed of to street-buyers.

OF THE STREET-BUYERS OF WASTE (PAPER).
BEYOND all others the street-purchase of waste paper is the most curious of any in the hands of the class I now treat of. Some may have formed the notion that waste paper is merely that which is soiled or torn, or old numbers of newspapers, or other periodical publications; but this is merely a portion of the trade, as the subsequent account will show.

The men engaged in this business have not unfrequently an apartment, or a large closet, or recess, for the reception of their purchases of paper. They collect their paper street by street, calling upon every publisher, coffee-shop keeper, printer, or publican (but rarely on a publican), who may be a seller of "waste." I heard the refuse paper called nothing but "waste" after the general elliptical fashion. Attorneys' offices are often visited by these buyers, as are the offices of public men, such as tax or rate collectors, generally.

One man told me that until about ten years ago, and while he was a youth, he was employed by a relation in the trade to carry out waste paper sold to, or ordered by cheesemongers, &c., but that he never "collected," or bought paper himself. At last he thought he would start on his own account, and the first person he called upon, he said, was a rich landlady, not far from Hungerford-market, whom he saw sometimes at her bar, and who was always very civil. He took an opportunity to ask her if she "happened to have any waste in the house, or would have any in a week or so?" Seeing the landlady look surprised and not very well pleased at what certainly appeared an impertinent inquiry, he hastened to explain that he meant old newspapers, or anything that way, which he would be glad to buy at so much a pound. The landlady however took in but one daily and one weekly paper (both sent into the country when a day or so old), and having had no dealings with men of my informant's avocation, could not understand his object in putting such questions.

Every kind of paper is purchased by the "waste-men." One of these dealers said to me: "I've often in my time 'cleared out' a lawyer's office. I've bought old briefs, and other law papers, and 'forms' that weren't the regular forms then, and any d——d thing they had in my line. You'll excuse me, sir, but I couldn't help thinking what a lot of misery was caused, perhaps, by the cwts. of waste I've bought at such places. If my father hadn't got mixed up with law he wouldn't have been ruined, and his children wouldn't have had such a hard fight of it; so I hate law. All that happened when I was a child, and I never understood the rights or the wrongs of it, and don't like to think of people that's so foolish. I gave 1½d. a pound for all I bought at the lawyers, and done pretty well with it, but very likely that's the only good turn such paper ever did any one—unless it were the lawyers themselves."

The waste-dealers do not confine their purchases to the tradesmen I have mentioned. They buy of any one, and sometimes act as middlemen or brokers. For instance, many small stationers and newsvendors, sometimes tobacconists in no extensive way of trade, sometimes chandlers, announce by a bill in their windows, "Waste Paper Bought and Sold in any Quantity," while more frequently perhaps the trade is carried on, as an understood part of these small shopmen's business, without any announcement. Thus the shop-buyers have much miscellaneous waste brought to them, and perhaps for only some particular kind have they a demand by their retail customers. The regular itinerant waste dealer then calls and "clears out everything" the "everything" being not an unmeaning word. One man, who "did largely in waste," at my request endeavoured to enumerate all the kinds of paper he had purchased as waste, and the packages of paper he showed me, ready for delivery to his customers on the following day, confirmed all he said as he opened them and showed me of what they were composed. He had dealt, he said—and he took great pains and great interest in the inquiry, as one very curious, and was a respectable and intelligent man—in "books on *every* subject" [I give his own words] "on which a book can be written." After a little consideration he added: "Well, perhaps *every* subject is a wide range; but if there are any exceptions, it's on subjects not known to a busy man like me, who is occupied from morning till night every week day. The only worldly labour I do on a Sunday is to take my family's dinner to the bakehouse, bring it home after chapel, and read *Lloyd's Weekly*. I've had Bibles—the backs are taken off in the waste trade, or it wouldn't be fair weight—Testaments, Prayer-books, Companions to the Altar, and Sermons and religious works. Yes, I've had the Roman Catholic books, as is used in their public worship—at least so I suppose, for I never was in a Roman Catholic chapel. Well, it's hard to say about proportions, but in my opinion, as far as it's good for anything, I've not had *them* in anything like the proportion that I've had Prayer-books, and Watts' and Wesley's hymns. More shame; but you see, sir, perhaps a godly old man dies, and those that follow him care nothing for hymn-books, and so they come to such as me, for they're so cheap now they're not to be sold second-hand at all, I fancy. I've dealt in tragedies and comedies, old and new, cut and uncut—they're best uncut, for you can make them into sheets then—and farces, and books of the opera. I've had scientific and medical works of every possible kind, and histories, and travels, and lives, and memoirs. I needn't go through them—everything, from a needle to an anchor, as the saying is. Poetry, ay, many a hundred weight; Latin and Greek (sometimes), and French, and other foreign languages. Well now, sir, as you mention it, I think I never *did* have a Hebrew work; I think not, and I know the Hebrew letters when I see them. Black letter, not once in a couple of years; no, nor in three or four years, when I think of it. I have met with it, but I always take anything I've got that way to Mr. ——, the bookseller, who uses a poor man well. Don't you think, sir, I'm complaining of poverty; though I have been very poor, when I was recovering from cholera at the first break-out of it, and I'm anything but rich now. Pamphlets I've had by the ton, in my time; I think we should both be tired if I could go through all they were about. Very many were religious, more 's the pity. I've heard of a page round a quarter of cheese, though, touching a man's heart."

In corroboration of my informant's statement, I may mention that in the course of my inquiry into the condition of the fancy cabinet-makers of the metropolis, one elderly and very intelligent man, a first-rate artisan in skill, told me he had been so reduced in the world by the underselling of slop-masters (called "butchers" or "slaughterers," by the workmen in the trade), that though in his youth he could take in the *News* and *Examiner* papers (each he believed 9*d*. at that time, but was not certain), he could afford, and enjoyed, no reading when I saw him last autumn, beyond the book-leaves in which he received his quarter of cheese, his small piece of bacon or fresh meat, or his saveloys; and his wife schemed to go to the shops who "wrapped up their things from books," in order that he might have something to read after his day's work.

My informant went on with his specification: " Missionary papers of all kinds. Parliamentary papers, but not so often new ones, very largely. Railway prospectuses, with plans to some of them, nice engravings; and the same with other joint-stock companies. Children's copy-books, and cyphering-books. Old account-books of every kind. A good many years ago, I had some that must have belonged to a West End perfumer, there was such French items for Lady this, or the Honourable Captain that. I remember there was an Hon. Capt. G., and almost at every second page was '100 tooth-picks, 3*s*. 6*d*.' I think it was 3*s*. 6*d*.; in arranging this sort of waste one now and then gives a glance to it. Dictionaries of every sort, I've had, but not so commonly. Music books, lots of them. Manuscripts, but only if they're rather old; well, 20 or 30 years or so: I call that old. Letters on every possible subject, but not, in my experience, any very modern ones. An old man dies, you see, and his papers are sold off, letters and all; that's the way; get rid of all the old rubbish, as soon as the old boy's pointing his toes to the sky. What's old letters worth, when the writers are dead and buried? why, perhaps 1½*d*. a pound, and it's a rattling big letter that will weigh half-an-ounce. O, it's a queer trade, but there's many worse."

The letters which I saw in another waste-dealer's possession were 45 in number, a small collection, I was told; for the most part they were very dull and common-place. Among them, however, was the following, in an elegant, and I presume a female hand, but not in the modern fashionable style of handwriting. The letter is evidently old, the address is of West-end gentility, but I leave out name and other particularities:—

" Mrs. —— [it is not easy to judge whether the flourished letters are ' Mrs.' or ' Miss,' but certainly more like ' Mrs.'] Mrs. —— (Zoological Artist) presents her compliments to Mr. ——, and being commissioned to communicate with a gentleman of the name, recently arrived at Charing-cross, and presumed by description to be himself, in a matter of delicacy and confidence, indispensably verbal; begs to say, that if interested in the ecclaircissement and necessary to the same, she may be found in attendance, any afternoon of the current week, from 3 to 6 o'clock, and no other hours.

" —— street, —— square.

" Monday Morn. for the aftn., at home."

Among the books destined to a butcher, I found three perfect numbers of a sixpenny periodical, published a few years back. Three, or rather two and a half, numbers of a shilling periodical, with "coloured engravings of the fashions." Two (imperfect) volumes of French Plays, an excellent edition; among the plays were Athalie, Iphigénie, Phèdre, Les Frères Ennemis, Alexandre, Andromaque, Les Plaideurs, and Esther. A music sheet, headed " A lonely thing I would not be." A few pages of what seems to have been a book of tales: " Album d'un Sourd-Muet " (36 pages in the pamphlet form, quite new). All these constituted about twopennyworth to the butcher. Notwithstanding the variety of sources from which the supply is derived, I heard from several quarters that "waste never was so scarce" as at present; it was hardly to be had at all.

The purchasers of the waste-paper from the collectors are cheesemongers, buttermen, butchers, fishmongers, poulterers, pork and sausage-sellers, sweet-stuff-sellers, tobacconists, chandlers—and indeed all who sell provisions or such luxuries as I have mentioned in retail. Some of the wholesale provision houses buy very largely and sell the waste again to their customers, who pay more for it by such a medium of purchase, but they have it thus on credit. Any retail trader in provisions at all "in a large way," will readily buy six or seven cwt. at a time. The price given by them varies from 1¼*d*. to 3½*d*. the pound, but it is very rarely either so low or so high. The average price may be taken at 18*s*. the cwt., which is not quite 2*d*. a pound, and at this rate I learn from the best-informed parties there are twelve tons sold weekly, or 1624 tons yearly (1,397,760 lbs.), at the cost of 11,232*l*. One man in the trade was confident the value of the waste paper sold could not be less than 12,000*l*. in a year.

There are about 60 men in this trade, nearly 50 of whom live entirely, as it was described to me, " by their waste," and bring up their families upon it. The others unite some other avocation with it. The earnings of the regular collectors vary from 15*s*. weekly to 35*s*. accordingly as they meet with a supply on favourable terms, or, as they call it, " a good pull in a lot of waste." They usually reside in a private room with a recess, or a second room, in which they sort, pack, and keep their paper.

One of these traders told me that he was satisfied that stolen paper seldom found its way, directly, into the collectors' hands, "particularly publisher's paper," he added. "Why, not long since there was a lot of sheets stolen from Alderman Kelly's warehouse, and the thief didn't take them to a waste dealer; he knew better. He took them, sir, to a tradesman in a large respectable way over the water—a man that uses great lots of waste—and sold them at just what was handed to him: I suppose no questions asked. The thief was tried and convicted, but nothing was done to the buyer."

It must not be supposed that the waste-paper used by the London tradesmen costs no more than 12,000*l.* in a year. A large quantity is bought direct by butchers and others from poor persons going to them with a small quantity of their own accumulating, or with such things as copybooks.

Of the Street-Buyers of Umbrellas and Parasols.

The street-traders in old umbrellas and parasols are numerous, but the buying is but one part, and the least skilled part, of the business. Men, some tolerably well-dressed, some swarthy-looking, like gipsies, and some with a vagabond aspect, may be seen in all quarters of the town and suburbs, carrying a few ragged-looking umbrellas, or the sticks or ribs of umbrellas, under their arms, and crying "Umbrellas to mend," or "Any old umbrellas to sell?" The traffickers in umbrellas are also the crockmen, who are always glad to obtain them in barter, and who merely dispose of them at the Old Clothes Exchange, or in Petticoat-lane.

The umbrella-menders are known by an appellation of an appropriateness not uncommon in street language. They are *mushroom-fakers.* The form of the expanded umbrella resembles that of a mushroom, and it has the further characteristic of being rapidly or suddenly raised, the mushroom itself springing up and attaining its full size in a very brief space of time. The term, however, like all street or popular terms or phrases, has become very generally condensed among those who carry on the trade—they are now *mushfakers,* a word which, to any one who has not heard the term in full, is as meaningless as any in the vocabulary of slang.

The mushroom-fakers will repair any umbrella on the owner's premises, and their work is often done adroitly, I am informed, and as often bunglingly, or, in the trade term, "botched." So far there is no traffic in the business, the mushroom-faker simply performing a piece of handicraft, and being paid for the job. But there is another class of street-folk who buy the old umbrellas in Petticoat-lane, or of the street buyer or collector, and "sometimes," as one of these men said to me, "we are our own buyers on a round." They mend the umbrellas—some of their wives, I am assured, being adepts as well as themselves—and offer them for sale on the approaches to the bridges, and at the corners of streets.

The street umbrella trade is really curious. Not so very many years back the use of an umbrella by a man was regarded as partaking of effeminacy, but now they are sold in thousands in the streets, and in the second-hand shops of Monmouth-street and such places. One of these street-traders told me that he had lately sold, but not to an extent which might encourage him to proceed, old silk umbrellas in the street for gentlemen to protect themselves from the rays of the sun.

The purchase of umbrellas is in a great degree mixed up with that of old clothes, of which I have soon to treat; but from what I have stated it is evident that the umbrella trade is most connected with street-artisanship, and under that head I shall describe it.

OF THE STREET-JEWS.

Although my present inquiry relates to London life in London streets, it is necessary that I should briefly treat of the Jews generally, as an integral, but distinct and peculiar part of street-life.

That this ancient people were engaged in what may be called street-traffic in the earlier ages of our history, as well as in the importation of spices, furs, fine leather, armour, drugs, and general merchandise, there can be no doubt; nevertheless concerning this part of the subject there are but the most meagre accounts.

Jews were settled in England as early as 730, and during the sway of the Saxon kings. They increased in number after the era of the Conquest; but it was not until the rapacity to which they were exposed in the reign of Stephen had in a great measure exhausted itself, and until the measures of Henry II. had given encouragement to commerce, and some degree of security to property in cities or congregated communities, that the Jews in England became numerous and wealthy. They then became active and enterprising attendants at fairs, where the greater portion of the internal trade of the kingdom was carried on, and especially the traffic in the more valuable commodities, such as plate, jewels, armour, cloths, wines, spices, horses, cattle, &c. The agents of the great prelates and barons, and even of the ruling princes, purchased what they required at these fairs. St. Giles's fair, held at St. Giles's hill, not far from Winchester, continued sixteen days. The fair was, as it were, a temporary city. There were streets of tents in every direction, in which the traders offered and displayed their wares. During the continuance of the fair, business was strictly prohibited in Winchester, Southampton, and in every place within seven miles of St. Giles's hill. Among the tent-owners at such fairs were the Jews.

At this period the Jews may be considered as one of the bodies of "merchant-strangers," as they were called, settled in England for purposes of commerce. Among the other bodies of these "strangers" were the German "merchants of the steel-yard," the Lombards, the Caursini of Rome, the "merchants of the staple," and others. These were all corporations, and thriving corporations (when unmolested), and the Jews had also their Jewerie, or Judaisme, not for a "corporation" merely, but also for the requirements of their faith and worship, and for their living together. The London Jewerie was established in a place of which no vestige of its establishment now remains beyond the name—the Old Jewry. Here was erected the first synagogue of the Jews in England, which was defaced or demolished, Maitland states, by the citizens, after they had slain 700 Jews (other accounts represent that number as greatly exaggerated). This took place in 1263, during one of the many disturbances in the uneasy reign of Henry III.

All this time the Jews amassed wealth by trade and usury, in spite of their being plundered and maltreated by the princes and other potentates— every one has heard of King John's having a Jew's teeth drawn—and in spite of their being reviled by the priests and hated by the people. The sovereigns generally encouraged " merchant-strangers." When the city of London, in 1289, petitioned Edward I. for " the expulsion of all merchant-strangers," that monarch answered, with all a monarch's peculiar regard for " great " men and " great " men only, " No ! the merchant-strangers are useful and beneficial to the great men of the kingdom, and I will not expel them." But though the King encouraged, the people detested, *all* foreign traders, though not with the same intensity as they detested and contemned the Jews, for in *that* detestation a strong religious feeling was an element. Of this dislike to the merchant-strangers, very many instances might be cited, but I need give only one. In 1379, nearly a century after the banishment of the Jews, a Genoese merchant, a man of great wealth, petitioned Richard II. for permission to deposit goods for safe keeping in Southampton Castle, promising to introduce so large a share of the commerce of the East into England, that pepper should be 4*d.* a pound. " Yet the Londoners," writes Walsingham, but in the quaint monkish Latin of the day, " enemies to the prosperity of their country, hired assassins, who murdered the merchant in the street. After this, what stranger will trust his person among a people so faithless and so cruel ? who will not dread our treachery, and abhor our name ?"

In 1290, by a decree of Edward I., the Jews were banished out of England. The causes assigned for this summary act, were "their extortions, their debasing and diminishing the coin, and for other crimes." I need not enter into the merits or demerits of the Jews of that age, but it is certain that any ridiculous charge, any which it was impossible could be true, was an excuse for the plundering of them at the hands of the rich, and the persecution of them at the hands of the people. At the period of this banishment, their number is represented by the contemporaneous historians to have been about 16,000, a number most probably exaggerated, as perhaps all statements of the numbers of a people are when no statistical knowledge has been acquired. During this period of their abode in England, the Jews were protected as the villeins or bondsmen of the king, a protection disregarded by the commonalty, and only giving to the executive government greater facilities of extortion and oppression.

In 1655 an Amsterdam Jew, Rabbi Manasseh Ben-Israel, whose name is still highly esteemed among his countrymen, addressed Cromwell on the behalf of the Jews that they should be re-admitted into England with the sanction, and under the protection, of the law. Despite the absence of such sanction, they had resided and of course traded in this country, but in small numbers, and trading often in indirect and sometimes in contraband ways. Chaucer, writing in the days of Richard II., three reigns after their expulsion, speaks of Jews as living in England. It is reputed that, in the reigns of Elizabeth and the first James, they supplied, at great profit, the materials required by the alchymists for their experiments in the transmutation of metals. In Elizabeth's reign, too, Jewish physicians were highly esteemed in England. The Queen at one time confided the care of her health to Rodrigo Lopez, a Hebrew, who, however, was convicted of an attempt to poison his royal mistress. Francis I., of France, carried his opinion of Jewish medical skill to a great height; he refused on one occasion, during an illness, to be attended by the most eminent of the Israelitish physicians, because the learned man had just before been converted to Christianity. The most Christian king, therefore, applied to his ally, the Turkish sultan, Solyman II., who sent him "a true hardened Jew," by whose directions Francis drank asses' milk and recovered.

Cromwell's response to the application of Manasseh Ben Israel was favourable; but the opposition of the Puritans, and more especially of Prynne, prevented any public declaration on the subject. In 1656, however, the Jews began to arrive and establish themselves in England, but not until after the restoration of Charles II., in 1660, could it be said that, as a body, they were settled in England. They arrived from time to time, and without any formal sanction being either granted or refused. One reason alleged at the time was, that the Jews were well known to be money-lenders, and Charles and his courtiers were as well known money-borrowers!

I now come to the character and establishment of the Jews in the capacity in which I have more especially to describe them—as street-traders. There appears no reason to doubt that they commenced their principal street traffic, the collecting of old clothes, soon after their settlement in London. At any rate the cry and calling of the Jew old clothesman were so established, 30 or 40 years after their return, or early in the last century, that one of them is delineated in Tempest's "Cries of London," published about that period. In this work the street Jew is represented as very different in his appearance to that which he presents in our day. Instead of merely a dingy bag, hung empty over his arm, or carried, when partially or wholly filled, on his shoulder, he is depicted as wearing, or rather carrying, three cocked hats, one over the other, upon his head; a muff, with a scarf or large handkerchief over it, is attached to his right hand and arm, and two dress swords occupy his left hand. The apparel which he himself wears is of the full-skirted style of the day, and his long hair, or periwig, descends to his shoulders. This difference in appearance, however, between the street Jew of 1700 and of a century and a half later, is simply the effect of circumstances, and indicates no change in the character of the man. Were it now the fashion for gentlemen to wear muffs, swords, and cocked hats, the Jew would again have them in his possession.

During the eighteenth century the popular feeling ran very high against the Jews, although to the masses they were almost strangers, except as men employed in the not-very-formidable occupation of collecting and vending second-hand clothes. The old feeling against them seems to have lingered among the English people, and their own greed in many instances engendered other and lawful causes of dislike, by their resorting to unlawful and debasing pursuits. They were considered—and with that exaggeration of belief dear to any ignorant community—as an entire people of misers, usurers, extortioners, receivers of stolen goods, cheats, brothel-keepers, sheriff's-officers, clippers and sweaters of the coin of the realm, gaming-house keepers; in fine, the charges, or rather the accusations, of carrying on every disreputable trade, and none else, were " bundled at their doors." That there was too much foundation for many of these accusations, and still *is*, no reasonable Jew can now deny; that the wholesale prejudice against them was absurd, is equally indisputable.

So strong was this popular feeling against the Israelites, that it not only influenced, and not only controlled the legislature, but it coerced the Houses of Parliament to repeal, in 1754, an act which they had passed the previous session, and that act was merely to enable foreign Jews to be naturalized without being required to take the sacrament! It was at that time, and while the popular ferment was at its height, unsafe for a Hebrew old clothesman, however harmless a man, and however long and well known on his beat, to ply his street-calling openly; for he was often beaten and maltreated. Mobs, riots, pillagings, and attacks upon the houses of the Jews were frequent, and one of the favourite cries of the mob was certainly among the most preposterously stupid of any which ever tickled the ear and satisfied the mind of the ignorant:—

"No Jews!
No wooden shoes!!"

Some mob-leader, with a taste for rhyme, had in this distich cleverly blended the prejudice against the Jews with the easily excited but vague fears of a French invasion, which was in some strange way typified to the apprehensions of the vulgar as connected with slavery, popery, the compulsory wearing of wooden shoes (*sabots*), and the eating of frogs! And this sort of feeling was often revenged on the street-Jew, as a man mixed up with wooden shoes! Cumberland, in the comedy of "The Jew," and some time afterwards Miss Edgeworth, in the tale of "Harrington and Ormond," and both at the request of Jews, wrote to moderate this rabid prejudice.

In what estimation the street, and, incidentally, all classes of Jews are held at the present time, will be seen in the course of my remarks; and in the narratives to be given. I may here observe, however, that among some the dominant feeling against the Jews on account of their faith still flourishes, as is shown by the following statement:—A gentleman of my acquaintance was one evening, about twilight, walking down Brydges-street, Covent-garden, when an elderly Jew was preceding him, apparently on his return from a day's work, as an old clothesman. His bag accidentally touched the bonnet of a dashing woman of the town, who was passing, and she turned round, abused the Jew, and spat at him, saying with an oath: "You old rags humbug! *You* can't do that!"—an allusion to a vulgar notion that Jews have been unable to do more than *slobber*, since spitting on the Saviour.

The number of Jews now in England is computed at 35,000. This is the result at which the Chief Rabbi arrived a few years ago, after collecting all the statistical information at his command. Of these 35,000, more than one-half, or about 18,000, reside in London. I am informed that there may now be a small increase to this population, but only small, for many Jews have emigrated—some to California. A few years ago—a circumstance mentioned in my account of the Street-Sellers of Jewellery—there were a number of Jews known as "hawkers," or "travellers," who traverse every part of England selling watches, gold and silver pencil-cases, eye-glasses, and all the more portable descriptions of jewellery, as well as thermometers, barometers, telescopes, and microscopes. This trade is now little pursued, except by the stationary dealers; and the Jews who carried it on, and who were chiefly foreign Jews, have emigrated to America. The foreign Jews who, though a fluctuating body, are always numerous in London, are included in the computation of 18,000; of this population two-thirds reside in the city, or the streets adjacent to the eastern boundaries of the city.

OF THE TRADES AND LOCALITIES OF THE STREET-JEWS.

THE trades which the Jews most affect, I was told by one of themselves, are those in which, as they describe it, "there's a chance;" that is, they prefer a trade in such commodity as is not subjected to a fixed price, so that there may be abundant scope for speculation, and something like a gambler's chance for profit or loss. In this way, Sir Walter Scott has said, trade has "all the fascination of gambling, without the moral guilt;" but the absence of moral guilt in connection with such trading is certainly dubious.

The wholesale trades in foreign commodities which are now principally or solely in the hands of the Jews, often as importers and exporters, are, watches and jewels, sponges—fruits, especially green fruits, such as oranges, lemons, grapes, walnuts, cocoa-nuts, &c., and dates among dried fruits—shells, tortoises, parrots and foreign birds, curiosities, ostrich feathers, snuffs, cigars, and pipes; but cigars far more extensively at one time.

The localities in which these wholesale and retail traders reside are mostly at the East-end—indeed the Jews of London, as a congregated body, have been, from the times when their numbers were sufficient to institute a "settlement" or "colony," peculiar to themselves, always resident in the eastern quarter of the metropolis.

Of course a wealthy Jew millionaire—merchant, stock-jobber, or stock-broker—resides where he pleases—in a villa near the Marquis of Hertford's in the Regent's-park, a mansion near the Duke of Wellington's in Piccadilly, a house and grounds at Clapham or Stamford-hill; but these are exceptions. The quarters of the Jews are not difficult to describe. The trading-class in the capacity of shopkeepers, warehousemen, or manufacturers, are the thickest in Houndsditch, Aldgate, and the Minories, more especially as regards the "swag-shops" and the manufacture and sale of wearing apparel. The wholesale dealers in fruit are in Duke's-place and Pudding-lane (Thames-street), but the superior retail Jew fruiterers—some of whose shops are remarkable for the beauty of their fruit—are in Cheapside, Oxford-street, Piccadilly, and most of all in Covent-garden market. The inferior jewellers (some of whom deal with the first shops) are also at the East-end, about Whitechapel, Bevis-marks, and Houndsditch; the wealthier goldsmiths and watchmakers having, like other tradesmen of the class, their shops in the superior thoroughfares. The great congregation of working watchmakers is in Clerkenwell, but in that locality there are only a few Jews. The Hebrew dealers in second-hand garments, and second-hand wares generally, are located about Petticoat-lane, the peculiarities of which place I have lately described. The manufacturers of such things as cigars, pencils, and sealing-wax; the wholesale importers of sponge, bristles and toys, the dealers in quills and in "looking-glasses," reside in large private-looking houses, when display is not needed for purposes of business, in such parts as Maunsell-street, Great Prescott-street, Great Ailie-street, Leman-street, and other parts of the eastern quarter known as Goodman's-fields. The wholesale dealers in foreign birds and shells, and in the many foreign things known as "curiosities," reside in East Smithfield, Ratcliffe-highway, High-street (Shadwell), or in some of the parts adjacent to the Thames. In the long range of river-side streets, stretching from the Tower to Poplar and Blackwall, are Jews, who fulfil the many capacities of slop-sellers, &c., called into exercise by the requirements of seafaring people on their return from or commencement of a voyage. A few Jews keep boarding-houses for sailors in Shadwell and Wapping. Of the localities and abodes of the poorest of the Jews I shall speak hereafter.

Concerning the street-trades pursued by the Jews, I believe there is not at present a single one of which they can be said to have a monopoly; nor in any one branch of the street-traffic are there so many of the Jew traders as there were a few years back.

This remarkable change is thus to be accounted for. Strange as the fact may appear, the Jew has been undersold in the streets, and he has been beaten on what might be called his own ground—the buying of old clothes. The Jew boys, and the feebler and elder Jews, had, until some twelve or fifteen years back, almost the monopoly of orange and lemon street-selling, or street-hawking. The costermonger class had possession of the theatre doors and the approaches to the theatres; they had, too, occasionally their barrows full of oranges; but the Jews were the daily, assiduous, and itinerant street-sellers of this most popular of foreign, and perhaps of all, fruits. In their hopes of sale they followed any one a mile if encouraged, even by a few approving glances. The great theatre of this traffic was in the stage-coach yards in such inns as the Bull and Mouth, (St. Martin's-le-Grand), the Belle Sauvage (Ludgate-hill), the Saracen's Head (Snow-hill), the Bull (Aldgate), the Swan-with-two-Necks (Lad-lane, City), the George and Blue Boar (Holborn), the White Horse (Fetter-lane), and other such places. They were seen too, "with all their eyes about them," as one informant expressed it, outside the inns where the coaches stopped to take up passengers—at the White Horse Cellar in Piccadilly, for instance, and the Angel and the (now defunct) Peacock in Islington. A commercial traveller told me that he could never leave town by any "mail" or "stage," without being besieged by a small army of Jew boys, who most pertinaciously offered him oranges, lemons, sponges, combs, pocket-books, pencils, sealing-wax, paper, many-bladed pen-knives, razors, pocket-mirrors, and shaving-boxes—as if a man could not possibly quit the metropolis without requiring a stock of such commodities. In the whole of these trades, unless in some degree in sponges and blacklead-pencils, the Jew is now out-numbered or displaced.

I have before alluded to the underselling of the Jew boy by the Irish boy in the street-orange trade; but the characteristics of the change are so peculiar, that a further notice is necessary. It is curious to observe that the most assiduous, and hitherto the most successful of street-traders, were supplanted, not by a more persevering or more skilful body of street-sellers, but simply by a more *starving* body.

Some few years since poor Irish people, and chiefly those connected with the culture of the land, "came over" to this country in great numbers, actuated either by vague hopes of "bettering themselves" by emigration, or working on the railways, or else influenced by the restlessness common to an impoverished people. These men, when unable to obtain employment, without scruple became street-sellers. Not only did the adults resort to street-traffic, generally in its simplest forms, such as hawking fruit, but the children, by whom they were accompanied from Ireland, in great numbers, were put into the trade; and if two or three children earned 2*d*. a day each, and their parents 5*d*. or 6*d*. each, or even 4*d*., the subsistence of the family was better than they could obtain in the midst of the miseries of the southern and western part of the Sister Isle. An Irish boy of fourteen, having to support himself by street-trade, as was often the case, owing to the death of parents and to divers casualties, would undersell the Jew boys similarly circumstanced.

The Irish boy could live *harder* than the Jew—often in his own country he subsisted on a stolen turnip a day; he could lodge harder—lodge for 1*d*. a night in any noisome den, or sleep in the open air, which is seldom done by the Jew boy; he could dispense with the use of shoes and stockings—a dispensation at which his rival in trade revolted; he drank only water, or if he took tea or coffee, it was as a meal, and not merely as a beverage; to crown the whole, the city-bred Jew boy required some evening recreation, the penny or twopenny concert, or a game at draughts or dominoes; but this the Irish boy, country bred, never thought of, for *his* sole luxury was a deep sleep, and, being regardless or ignorant of all such recreations, he worked longer hours, and so sold more oranges, than his Hebrew competitor. Thus, as the Munster or Connaught lad could live on less than the young denizen of Petticoat-lane, he could sell at smaller profit, and did so sell, until gradually the Hebrew youths were displaced by the Irish in the street orange trade.

It is the same, or the same in a degree, with other street-trades, which were at one time all but monopolised by the Jew adults. Among these were the street-sale of spectacles and sponges. The prevalence of slop-work and slop-wages, and the frequent difficulty of obtaining properly-remunerated employment—the pinch of want, in short—have driven many mechanics to street-traffic; so that the numbers of street-traffickers have been augmented, while no small portion of the new comers have adopted the more knowing street avocations, formerly pursued only by the Jews.

Of the other class of street-traders who have interfered largely with the old-clothes trade, which, at one time, people seemed to consider a sort of birthright among the Jews, I have already spoken, when treating of the dealings of the crockmen in bartering glass and crockery-ware for second-hand apparel. These traders now obtain as many old clothes as the Jew clothes men themselves; for, with a great number of "ladies," the offer of an ornament of glass or spar, or of a beautiful and fragrant plant, is more attractive than the offer of a small sum of money, for the purchase of the left-off garments of the family.

The crockmen are usually strong and in the prime of youth or manhood, and are capable of carrying heavy burdens of glass or china-wares, for which the Jews are either incompetent or disinclined.

Some of the Jews which have been thus displaced from the street-traffic have emigrated to America, with the assistance of their brethren.

The principal street-trades of the Jews are now in sponges, spectacles, combs, pencils, accordions, cakes, sweetmeats, drugs, and fruits of all kinds; but, in all these trades, unless perhaps in drugs, they are in a minority compared with the "Christian" street-sellers.

There is not among the Jew street-sellers generally anything of the concubinage or cohabitation common among the costermongers. Marriage is the rule.

OF THE JEW OLD-CLOTHES MEN.

FIFTY years ago the appearance of the street-Jews, engaged in the purchase of second-hand clothes, was different to what it is at the present time. The Jew then had far more of the distinctive garb and aspect of a foreigner. He not unfrequently wore the gabardine, which is never seen now in the streets, but some of the long loose frock coats worn by the Jew clothes' buyers resemble it. At that period, too, the Jew's long beard was far more distinctive than it is in this hirsute generation.

In other respects the street-Jew is unchanged. Now, as during the last century, he traverses every street, square, and road, with the monotonous cry, sometimes like a bleat, of "Clo'! Clo'!" On this head, however, I have previously remarked, when describing the street Jew of a hundred years ago.

In an inquiry into the condition of the old-clothes dealers a year and a half ago, a Jew gave me the following account. He told me, at the commencement of his statement, that he was of opinion that his people were far more speculative than the Gentiles, and therefore the English liked better to deal with them. "Our people," he said, "will be out all day in the wet, and begrudge themselves a bit of anything to eat till they go home, and then, may be, they'll gamble away their crown, just for the love of speculation." My informant, who could write or speak several languages, and had been 50 years in the business, then said, "I am no bigot; indeed I do not care where I buy my meat, so long as I can get it. I often go into the Minories and buy some, without looking to how it has been killed, or whether it has a seal on it or not."

He then gave me some account of the Jewish children, and the number of men in the trade, which I have embodied under the proper heads. The itinerant Jew clothes man, he told me, was generally the son of a former old-clothes man, but some were cigar-makers, or pencil-makers, taking to the clothes business when those trades were slack; but that nineteen out of twenty had been born to it. If the parents of the Jew boy are poor, and the boy a sharp lad, he generally commences business at ten years of age, by selling lemons, or some trifle in the streets, and so, as he expressed it, the boy "gets a round," or street-connection, by becoming known to the neighbourhoods he visits. If he sees a servant, he will, when selling his lemons, ask if she have any old shoes or old clothes, and offer to be a purchaser. If the clothes should come to more than the Jew boy has in his pocket, he leaves what silver he has as " an earnest upon them," and then seeks some regular Jew clothes man, who will advance the purchase money. This the old Jew agrees to do upon the understanding that he is to have " half Rybeck," that is, a moiety of the profit, and then he will accompany the boy to the house, to pass his judgment on the goods, and satisfy himself that the stripling has not made a blind bargain, an error into which he very rarely falls. After this he goes with the lad to Petticoat-lane, and there they share whatever money the clothes may bring over and above what has been paid for them. By such means the Jew boy gets his knowledge of the old-clothes business; and so quick are these lads generally, that in the course of two months they will acquire sufficient experience in connection with the trade to begin dealing on their own account. There are some, he told me, as sharp at 15 as men of 50.

"It is very seldom," my informant stated, " very seldom indeed, that a Jew clothes man takes away any of the property of the house he may be called into. I expect there's a good many of 'em," he continued, for he sometimes spoke of his co-traders, as if they were not of his own class, " is fond of cheating—that is, they won't mind giving only 2s. for a thing that's worth 5s. They are fond of money, and will do almost anything to get it. Jews are perhaps the most money-loving people in all England. There are certainly some old-clothes men who will buy articles at such a price that they must know them to have been stolen. Their rule, however, is to ask no questions, and to get as cheap an article as possible. A Jew clothes man is seldom or never seen in liquor. They gamble for money, either at their own homes or at public-houses. The favourite games are tossing, dominoes, and cards. I was informed, by one of the people, that he had seen as much as 30l. in silver and gold lying upon the ground when two parties had been playing at throwing three halfpence in the air. On a Saturday, some gamble away the morning and the greater part of the afternoon." [Saturday, I need hardly say, is the Hebrew Sabbath.] " They meet in some secret back place, about ten, and begin playing for 'one a time'—that is, tossing up three halfpence, and staking 1s. on the result. Other Jews, and a few Christians, will gather round and bet. Sometimes the bets laid by the Jew bystanders are as high as 2l. each; and on more than one occasion the old-clothes men have wagered as much as 50l., but only after great gains at gambling. Some, if they *can*, will cheat, by means of a halfpenny with a head or a tail on both sides, called a 'gray.' The play lasts till the Sabbath is nearly over, and then they go to business or the theatre. They seldom or never say a word while they are losing, but merely stamp on the ground; it is dangerous, though, to interfere when luck runs against them. The rule is, when a man is losing to let him alone. I have known them play for three hours together, and nothing be said all that time but 'head' or 'tail.' They seldom go to synagogue, and on a Sunday evening have card parties at their own houses. They seldom eat anything on their rounds. The reason is, not because they object to eat meat killed by a Christian, but because they are afraid of losing a 'deal,' or the chance of buying a lot of old clothes by delay. They are generally too lazy to light their own fires before they start of a morning, and nineteen out of twenty obtain their breakfasts at the coffee-shops about Houndsditch.

"When they return from their day's work they have mostly some stew ready, prepared by their parents or wife. If they are not family men they go to an eating-house. This is sometimes a Jewish house, but if no one is looking they creep into a Christian ' cook-shop,' not being particular about eating ' tryfer'—that is, meat which has been killed by a Christian. Those that are single generally go to a neighbour and agree with him to be boarded on the Sabbath; and for this the charge is generally about 2s. 6d. On a Saturday there's cold fish for breakfast and supper; indeed, a Jew would pawn the shirt off his back sooner than go without fish then; and in holiday-time he *will* have it, if he has to get it out of the stones. It is not reckoned a holiday unless there's fish."

" Forty years ago I have made as much as 5l. in a week by the purchase of old clothes in the streets," said a Jew informant. " Upon an average then, I could earn weekly about 2l. But now things are different. People are more wide awake. Every one knows the value of an old coat now-a-days. The women know more than the men. The general average, I think, take the good weeks with the bad throughout the year, is about 1l. a week; some weeks we get 2l., and some scarcely nothing."

I was told by a Jewish professional gentleman that the account of the *spirit* of gambling prevalent among his people was correct, but the amounts said to be staked, he thought, rare or exaggerated.

The Jew old-clothes men are generally far more cleanly in their habits than the poorer classes of English people. Their hands they always wash before their meals, and this is done whether the party be a strict Jew or " Meshumet," a convert, or apostate from Judaism. Neither will the Israelite ever use the same knife to cut his meat that he previously used to spread his butter, and he will not even put his meat on a plate that has had butter on it; nor will he use for his soup the spoon that has had melted butter in it. This objection to mix butter with meat is carried so far, that, after partaking of the one, Jews will not eat of the other for the space of two hours. The Jews are generally, when married, most exemplary family men. There are few fonder fathers than they are, and they will starve themselves sooner than their wives and children should want. Whatever their faults may be, they are good fathers, husbands, and sons. Their principal characteristic is their extreme love of money; and, though the strict Jew does not trade himself on the Sabbath, he may not object to employ either one of his tribe, or a Gentile, to do so for him.

The capital required for commencing in the old-clothes line is generally about 1*l.* This the Jew frequently borrows, especially after holiday-time, for then he has generally spent all his earnings, unless he be a provident man. When his stock-money is exhausted, he goes either to a neighbour or to a publican in the vicinity, and borrows 1*l.* on the Monday morning, "to strike a light with," as he calls it, and agrees to return it on the Friday evening, with 1*s.* interest for the loan. This he always pays back. If he was to sell the coat off his back he would do this, I am told, because to fail in so doing would be to prevent his obtaining any stock-money for the future. With this capital he starts on his rounds about eight in the morning, and I am assured he will frequently begin his work without tasting food, rather than break into the borrowed stock-money. Each man has his particular walk, and never interferes with that of his neighbour; indeed, while upon another's beat he will seldom cry for clothes. Sometimes they go half "Rybeck" together— that is, they will share the profits of the day's business, and when they agree to do this the one will take one street, and the other another. The lower the neighbourhood the more old clothes are there for sale. At the east end of the town they like the neighbourhoods frequented by sailors, and there they purchase of the girls and the women the sailors' jackets and trowsers. But they buy most of the Petticoat-lane, the Old-Clothes Exchange, and the marine-store dealers; for as the Jew clothes man never travels the streets by night-time, the parties who then have old clothes to dispose of usually sell them to the marine-store or second-hand dealers over-night, and the Jew buy's them in the morning. The first thing that he does on his rounds is to seek out these shops, and see what he can pick up there. A very great amount of business is done by the Jew clothes man at the marine-store shops at the west as well as at the east end of London.

At the West-end the itinerant clothes men prefer the mews at the back of gentlemen's houses to all other places, or else the streets where the little tradesmen and small genteel families reside. My informant assured me that he had once bought a Bishop's hat of his lordship's servant for 1*s.* 6*d.* on a Sunday morning.

These traders, as I have elsewhere stated, live at the East-end of the town. The greater number of them reside in Portsoken Ward, Houndsditch; and their favourite localities in this district are either Cobb's-yard, Roper's-building, or Wentworth-street. They mostly occupy small houses, about 4*s.* 6*d.* a week rent, and live with their families. They are generally sober men. It is seldom that a Jew leaves his house and owes his landlord money; and if his goods should be seized the rest of his tribe will go round and collect what is owing.

The rooms occupied by the old-clothes men are far from being so comfortable as those of the English artizans whose earnings are not superior to the gains of these clothes men. Those which I saw had all a littered look; the furniture was old and scant, and the apartment seemed neither shop, parlour, nor bed-room. For domestic and family men, as some of the Jew old-clothes men are, they seem very indifferent to the comforts of a home.

I have spoken of "Tryfer," or meat killed in the Christian fashion. Now, the meat killed according to the Jewish law is known as "Coshar," and a strict Jew will eat none other. In one of my letters in the *Morning Chronicle* on the meat markets of London, there appeared the following statement, respecting the Jew butchers in Whitechapel-market.

"To a portion of the meat here exposed for sale, may be seen attached the peculiar seal which shows that the animal was killed conformably to the Jewish rites. According to the injunctions of this religion the beast must die from its throat being cut, instead of being knocked on the head. The slaughterer of the cattle for Jewish consumption, moreover, must be a Jew. Two slaughterers are appointed by the Jewish authorities of the synagogue, and they can employ others, who must be likewise Jews, as assistants. The slaughterers I saw were quiet-looking and quiet-mannered men. When the animal is slaughtered and skinned, an examiner (also appointed by the synagogue) carefully inspects the 'inside.' 'If the lights be grown to the ribs,' said my informant, who had had many years' experience in this branch of the meat trade, 'or if the lungs have any disease, or if there be any disease anywhere, the meat is pronounced unfit for the food of the Jews, and is sent entire to a carcase butcher to be sold to the Christians. This, however, does not happen once in 20 times.' To the parts exposed for sale, when the slaughtering has been according to the Jewish law, there is attached a leaden seal, stamped in Hebrew characters with the name of the examining party sealing. In this way, as I ascertained from the slaughterers, are killed weekly from 120 to 140 bullocks, from 400 to 500 sheep and lambs, and about 30 calves. All the parts of the animal thus slaughtered may be and are eaten by the Jews, but three-fourths of the purchase of this meat is confined, as regards the Jews, to the fore-quarters of the respective animals; the hind-quarters, being the choicer parts, are sent to Newgate or Leadenhall-markets for sale on commission." The Hebrew butchers consider that the Christian mode of slaughter is a far less painful death to the ox than was the Jewish.

I am informed that of the Jew Old-Clothes Men there are now only from 500 to 600 in London; at one time there might have been 1000. Their average earnings may be something short of 20*s.* a week in second-hand clothes alone; but the gains are difficult to estimate.

Of a Jew Street-Seller.

An elderly man, who, at the time I saw him, was vending spectacles, or bartering them for old clothes, old books, or any second-hand articles, gave me an account of his street-life, but it presented little remarkable beyond the not unusual vicissitudes of the lives of those of his class.

He had been in every street-trade, and had on four occasions travelled all over England, selling quills, sealing-wax, pencils, sponges, braces, cheap or superior jewellery, thermometers, and pictures. He had sold barometers in the mountainous parts of Cumberland, sometimes walking for hours without seeing man or woman. "*I liked it then,*" he said, "*for I was young and strong, and didn't care to sleep twice in the same town.* I was afterwards in the old-clothes line. I buy a few odd hats and light things still, but I'm not able to carry heavy weights, as my breath is getting rather short." [I find that the Jews generally object to the more laborious kinds of street-traffic.] "Yes, I've been twice to Ireland, and sold a good many quills in Dublin, for I crossed over from Liverpool. Quills and wax were a great trade with us once; now it's quite different. I've had as much as 60*l.* of my own, and that more than half-a-dozen times, but all of it went in speculations. Yes, some went in gambling. I had a share in a gaming-booth at the races, for three years. O, I dare say that's more than 20 years back; but we did very little good. There was such fees to pay for the tent on a race-ground, and often such delays between the races in the different towns, and bribes to be given to the town-officers—such as town-sergeants and chief constables, and I hardly know who—and so many expenses altogether, that the profits were mostly swamped. Once at Newcastle races there was a fight among the pitmen, and our tent was in their way, and was demolished almost to bits. A deal of the money was lost or stolen. I don't know how much, but not near so much as my partners wanted to make out. I wasn't on the spot just at the time. I got married after that, and took a shop in the second-hand clothes line in Bristol, but my wife died in child-bed in less than a year, and the shop didn't answer; so I got sick of it, and at last got rid of it. O, I work both the country and London still. I shall take a turn into Kent in a day or two. I suppose I clear between 10*s.* and 20*s.* a week in anything, and as I've only myself, I do middling, and am ready for another chance if any likely speculation offers. I lodge with a relation, and sometimes live with his family. No, I never touch any meat but 'Coshar.' I suppose my meat now costs me 6*d.* or 7*d.* a day, but it has cost me ten times that—and 2*d.* for beer in addition."

I am informed that there are about 50 adult Jews (besides old-clothes men) in the streets selling fruit, cakes, pencils, spectacles, sponge, accordions, drugs, &c.

Of the Jew-Boy Street-Sellers.

I have ascertained, and from sources where no ignorance on the subject could prevail, that there are now in the streets of London, rather more than 100 Jew-boys engaged principally in fruit and cake-selling in the streets. Very few Jewesses are itinerant street-sellers. Most of the older Jews thus engaged have been street-sellers from their boyhood. The young Jews who ply in street-callings, however, are all men in matters of traffic, almost before they cease, in years, to be children. In addition to the Jew-boy street-sellers above enumerated, there are from 50 to 100, but usually about 50, who are occasional, or "casual" street-traders, vending for the most part cocoa-nuts and grapes, and confining their sales chiefly to the Sundays.

On the subject of the street-Jew boys, a Hebrew gentleman said to me: "When we speak of street-Jew boys, it should be understood, that the great majority of them are but little more conversant with or interested in the religion of their fathers, than are the costermonger boys of whom you have written. They are Jews by the accident of their birth, as others in the same way, with equal ignorance of the assumed faith, are Christians."

I received from a Jew boy the following account of his trading pursuits and individual aspirations. There was somewhat of a thickness in his utterance, otherwise his speech was but little distinguishable from that of an English street-boy. His physiognomy was decidedly Jewish, but not of the handsomer type. His hair was light-coloured, but clean, and apparently well brushed, without being oiled, or, as I heard a street-boy style it, "greased"; it was long, and he said his aunt told him it "wanted cutting sadly;" but he "liked it that way;" indeed, he kept dashing his curls from his eyes, and back from his temples, as he was conversing, as if he were somewhat vain of doing so. He was dressed in a corduroy suit, old but not ragged, and wore a tolerably clean, very coarse, and altogether buttonless shirt, which he said "was made for one bigger than me, sir." He had bought it for 9½*d.* in Petticoat-lane, and accounted it a bargain, as its wear would be durable. He was selling sponges when I saw him, and of the commonest kind, offering a large piece for 3*d.*, which (he admitted) would be rubbed to bits in no time. This sponge, I should mention, is frequently "dressed" with sulphuric acid, and an eminent surgeon informed me that on his servant attempting to clean his black dress coat with a sponge that he had newly bought in the streets, the colour of the garment, to his horror, changed to a bright purple. The Jew boy said—

"I believe I'm twelve. I've been to school, but it's long since, and my mother was very ill then, and I was forced to go out in the streets to have a chance. I never was kept to school. I can't read; I've forgot all about it. I'd rather now that I could read, but very likely I could soon learn if I could only spare time, but if I stay long in the house I feel sick; it's not healthy. O, no, sir, inside or out it would be all the same to me, just to make a living and keep my health. I can't say how long it is since I began to sell, it's a good long time; one must do something. I could keep myself now, and do sometimes, but my father — I live with him (my mother's dead) is often laid up. Would you like to see him, sir? He knows a deal. No, he can't write, but he can read a little. Can I speak Hebrew? Well, I know what you mean. O, no, I can't. I don't go to synagogue; I haven't time. My father goes, but only sometimes; so he says, and he tells me to look out, for we must both go by-and-by." [I began to ask him what he knew of Joseph, and others recorded in the Old Testament, but he bristled up, and asked if I wanted to make a Meshumet (a convert) of him?] " I have sold all sorts of things," he continued, " oranges, and lemons, and sponges, and nuts, and sweets. I should like to have a real good ginger-beer fountain of my own; but I must wait, and there's many in the trade. I only go with boys of my own sort. I sell to all sorts of boys, but that's nothing. Very likely they're Christians, but that's nothing to me. I don't know what's the difference between a Jew and Christian, and I don't want to talk about it. The Meshumets are never any good. Anybody will tell you that. Yes, I like music and can sing a bit. I get to a penny and sometimes a two-penny concert. No, I haven't been to Sussex Hall—I know where it is—I shouldn't understand it. You get in for nothing, that's one thing. I've heard of Baron Rothschild. He has more money than I could count in shillings in a year. I don't know about his wanting to get into parliament, or what it means; but he's sure to do it or anything else, with his money. He's very charitable, I've heard. I don't know whether he's a German Jew, or a Portegee, or what. He's a cut above me, a precious sight. I only wish he was my uncle. I can't say what I should do if I had his money. Perhaps I should go a travelling, and see everything everywhere. I don't know how long the Jews have been in England; always perhaps. Yes, I know there's Jews in other countries. This sponge is Greek sponge, but I don't know where it's grown, only it's in foreign parts. Jerusalem! Yes, I've heard of it. I'm of no tribe that I know of. I buy what I eat about Petticoat-lane. No, I don't like fish, but the stews, and the onions with them is beautiful for two-pence; you may get a pennor'th. The pickles—cowcumbers is best—are stunning. But they're plummiest with a bit of cheese or anything cold—that's my opinion, but you may think different. Pork! Ah! No, I never touched it; I'd as soon eat a cat; so would my father. No, sir, I don't think pork smells nice in a cook-shop, but some Jew boys, as I knows, thinks it does. I don't know why it shouldn't be eaten, only that it's wrong to eat it. No, I never touched a ham-sandwich, but other Jew boys have, and laughed at it, I know.

"I don't know what I make in a week. I think I make as much on one thing as on another. I've sold strawberries, and cherries, and gooseberries, and nuts and walnuts in the season. O, as to what I make, that's nothing to nobody. Sometimes 6*d.* a day, sometimes 1*s.*; sometimes a little more, and sometimes nothing. No, I never sells inferior things if I can help it, but if one hasn't stock-money one must do as one can, but it isn't so easy to try it on. There was a boy beaten by a woman not long since for selling a big pottle of strawberries that was rubbish all under the toppers. It was all strawberry leaves, and crushed strawberries, and such like. She wanted to take back from him the two-pence she'd paid for it, and got hold of his pockets and there was a regular fight, but she didn't get a farthing back though she tried her very hardest, 'cause he slipped from her and hooked it. So you see it's dangerous to try it on." [This last remark was made gravely enough, but the lad told of the feat with such manifest glee, that I'm inclined to believe that he himself was the culprit in question.] " Yes, it was a Jew boy it happened to, but other boys in the streets is just the same. Do I like the streets? I can't say I do, there's too little to be made in them. *No, I wouldn't like to go to school, nor to be in a shop, nor be anybody's servant but my own.* O, I don't know what I shall be when I'm grown up. I shall take my chance like others."

OF THE PURSUITS, DWELLINGS, TRAFFIC, ETC., OF THE JEW-BOY STREET-SELLERS.

To speak of the street Jew-boys as regards their traffic, manners, haunts, and associations, is to speak of the same class of boys who may not be employed regularly in street-sale, but are the comrades of those who are; a class, who, on any cessation of their employment in cigar manufactories, or indeed any capacity, will apply themselves temporarily to street-selling, for it seems to these poor and uneducated lads a sort of natural vocation.

These youths, *uncontrolled* or *incontrollable* by their parents (who are of the lowest class of the Jews, and who often, I am told, care little about the matter, so long as the child can earn his own maintenance), frequently in the evenings, after their day's work, resort to coffee-shops, in preference even to a cheap concert-room. In these places they amuse themselves as men might do in a tavern where the landlord leaves his guests to their own caprices. Sometimes one of them reads aloud from some exciting or degrading book, the lads who are unable to read listening with all the intentness with which many of the uneducated attend to any one reading. The reading is, however, not unfrequently interrupted by rude comments from the listeners. If a newspaper be read, the "police," or "crimes," are mostly the parts preferred. But the most approved way of passing the evening, among the Jew boys, is to play at draughts, dominoes, or cribbage, and to bet on the play. Draughts and dominoes are unpractised among the costermonger boys, but some of the young Jews are adepts in those games.

A gentleman who took an interest in the Jew lads told me that he had often heard the sort of reading and comments I have described, when he had called to talk to and perhaps expostulate with these youths in a coffee-shop, but he informed me that they seldom regarded any expostulation, and seemed to be little restrained by the presence of a stranger, the lads all muttering and laughing in a box among themselves. I saw seven of them, a little after eight in the evening, in a coffee-shop in the London-road,—although it is not much of a Jewish locality,—and two of them were playing at draughts for coffee, while the others looked on, betting halfpennies or pennies with all the eagerness of gamblers, unrestrained in their expressions of delight or disappointment as they thought they were winning or losing, and commenting on the moves with all the assurance of connoisseurship; sometimes they squabbled angrily and then suddenly dropped their voices, as the master of the coffee-shop had once or twice cautioned them to be quiet.

The dwellings of boys such as these are among the worst in London, as regards ventilation, comfort, or cleanliness. They reside in the courts and recesses about Whitechapel and Petticoat-lane, and generally in a garret. If not orphans they usually dwell with their father. I am told that the care of a mother is almost indispensable to a poor Jew boy, and having that care he seldom becomes an outcast. The Jewesses and Jew girls are rarely itinerant street-sellers—not in the proportion of one to twelve, compared with the men and boys; in this respect therefore the street Jews differ widely from the English costermongers and the street Irish, nor are the Hebrew females even stall-keepers in the same proportion.

One Jew boy's lodging which I visited was in a back garret, low and small. The boy lived with his father (a street-seller of fruit), and the room was very bare. A few sacks were thrown over an old palliass, a blanket seemed to be used for a quilt; there were no fire-irons nor fender; no cooking utensils. Beside the bed was an old chest, serving for a chair, while a board resting on a trestle did duty for a table (this was once, I presume, a small street-stall). The one not very large window was thick with dirt and patched all over. Altogether I have seldom seen a more wretched apartment. The man, I was told, was addicted to drinking.

The callings of which the Jew boys have the monopoly are not connected with the sale of any especial article, but rather with such things as present a variety from those ordinarily offered in the streets, such as cakes, sweetmeats, fried fish, and (in the winter) elder wine. The cakes known as "boolers"—a mixture of egg, flour, and candied orange or lemon peel, cut very thin, and with a slight colouring from saffron or something similar—are now sold principally, and used to be sold exclusively, by the Jew boys. Almond cakes (little round cakes of crushed almonds) are at present vended by the Jew boys, and their sponge biscuits are in demand. All these dainties are bought by the street-lads of the Jew pastry-cooks. The difference in these cakes, in their sweetmeats, and their elder wine, is that there is a dash of spice about them not ordinarily met with. It is the same with the fried fish, a little spice or pepper being blended with the oil. In the street-sale of pickles the Jews have also the monopoly; these, however, are seldom hawked, but generally sold from windows and door-steads. The pickles are cucumbers or gherkins, and onions—a large cucumber being 2*d.*, and the smaller 1*d.* and ½*d.*

The faults of the Jew lad are an eagerness to make money by any means, so that he often grows up a cheat, a trickster, a receiver of stolen goods, though seldom a thief, for he leaves that to others. He is content to profit by the thief's work, but seldom *steals* himself, however he may cheat. Some of these lads become rich men; others are vagabonds all their lives. None of the Jew lads confine themselves to the sale of any one article, nor do they seem to prefer one branch of street-traffic to another. Even those who cannot read are exceedingly quick.

I may here observe in connection with the receipt of stolen goods, that I shall deal with this subject in my account of the LONDON THIEVES. I shall also show the connection of Jewesses and Jews with the *prostitution of the metropolis*, in my forthcoming exposition of the LONDON PROSTITUTES.

OF THE STREET JEWESSES AND STREET JEW-GIRLS.

I HAVE mentioned that the Jewesses and the young Jew girls, compared with the adult Jews and Jew boys, are not street-traders in anything like the proportion which the females were found to bear to the males among the Irish street-folk and the English costermongers. There are, however, a few Jewish females who are itinerant street-sellers as well as stall keepers, in the proportion, perhaps, of one female to seven or eight males. The majority of the street Jew-girls whom I saw on a round were accompanied by boys who were represented to be their brothers, and I have little doubt such was the facts, for these young Jewesses, although often pert and ignorant, are not unchaste. Of this I was assured by a medical gentleman who could speak with sufficient positiveness on the subject.

Fruit is generally sold by these boys and girls together, the lad driving the barrow, and the girl inviting custom and handing the purchases to the buyers. In tending a little stall or a basket at a regular pitch, with such things as cherries or strawberries, the little Jewess differs only from her street-selling sisters in being a brisker trader. The stalls, with a few old knives or scissors, or odds and ends of laces, that are tended by the Jew girls in the streets in the Jewish quarters (I am told there are not above a dozen of them) are generally near the shops and within sight of their parents or friends. One little Jewess, with whom I had some conversation, had not even heard the name of the Chief Rabbi, the Rev. Dr. Adler, and knew nothing of any distinction between German and Portuguese Jews; she had, I am inclined to believe, never heard of either. I am told that the whole, or nearly the whole, of these young female traders reside with parents or friends, and that there is among them far less than the average number of runaways. One Jew told me he thought that the young female members of his tribe did not tramp with the juveniles of the other sex—no, not in the proportion of one to a hundred in comparison, he said with a laugh, with "young women of the Christian persuasion." My informant had means of knowing this fact, as although still a young man, he had traversed the greater part of England hawking perfumery, which he had abandoned as a bad trade. A wire-worker, long familiar with tramping and going into the country—a man upon whose word I have every reason to rely—told me that he could not remember a single instance of his having seen a young Jewess "travelling" with a boy.

There are a few adult Jewesses who are itinerant traders, but very few. I met with one who carried on her arm a not very large basket, filled with glass wares; chiefly salt-cellars, cigar-ash plates, blue glass dessert plates, vinegar-cruets, and such like. The greater part of her wares appeared to be blue, and she carried nothing but glass. She was a good-looking and neatly-dressed woman. She peeped in at each shop-door, and up at the windows of every private house, in the street in which I met her, crying, "Clo', old clo' !" She bartered her glass for old clothes, or bought the garments, dealing principally in female attire, and almost entirely with women. She declined to say anything about her family or her circumstances, except that she had nothing that way to complain about, but—when I had used some names I had authority to make mention of—she said she would, with pleasure, tell me all about her trade, which she carried on rather than do nothing. "When I hawk," she said with an English accent, her face being unmistakeably Jewish, "I hawk only good glass, and it can hardly be called hawking, as I swop it for more than I sell it. I always ask for the mistress, and if she wants any of my glass we come to a bargain if we can. O, it's ridiculous to see what things some ladies—I suppose they must be called ladies—offer for my glass. Children's green or blue gauze veils, torn or faded, and not worth picking up, because no use whatever; old ribbons, not worth dyeing, and old frocks, not worth washing. People say, 'as keen as a Jew,' but ladies can't think we're very keen when they offer us such rubbish. I do most at the middle kind of houses, both shops and private. I sometimes give a little money for such a thing as a shawl, or a fur tippet, as well as my glass—but only when I can't help it—to secure a bargain. Sometimes, but not often, I get the old thing and a trifle for my glass. Occasionally I buy outright. I don't do much, there's so many in the line, and I don't go out regularly. I can't say how many women are in my way—very few ; O, I do middling. I told you I had no complaints to make. I don't calculate my profits or what I sell. My family do that and I don't trouble myself."

Of the Synagogues and the Religion of the Street and other Jews.

The Jews in this country are classed as "Portuguese" and "German." Among them are no distinctions of tribes, but there is of rites and ceremonies, as is set forth in the following extract (which shows also the mode of government) from a Jewish writer : " The Spanish and Portuguese Congregation of Jews, who are also called Sephardin (from the word Sepharad, which signifies Spain in Hebrew), are distinct from the German and Polish Jews in their ritual service. The prayers both daily and for the Sabbath materially differ from each other, and the festival prayers differ still more. Hence the Portuguese Jews have a distinct prayer-book, and the German Jews likewise.

"The fundamental laws are equally observed by both sects, but in the ceremonial worship there exists numerous differences. The Portuguese Jews eat some food during the Passover, which the German Jews are prohibited doing by *some* Rabbis, but their authority is not acknowledged by the Portuguese Rabbis. Nor are the present ecclesiastical authorities in London of the two sects the same. The Portuguese Jews have their own Rabbis, and the German have their own. The German Jews are much more numerous than the Portuguese ; the chief Rabbi of the German Jews is the Rev. Dr. Nathan Marcus Adler, late Chief Rabbi of Hanover, who wears no beard, and dresses in the German costume. The presiding Rabbi of the Portuguese Jews is the Rev. David Meldola, a native of Leghorn ; his father filled the same office in London. Each chief Rabbi is supported by three other Rabbis, called Dayamin, which signifies in Hebrew 'Judges.' Every Monday and Thursday the Chief Rabbi of the German Jews, Dr. Adler, supported by his three colleagues, sits for two hours in the Rabbinical College (Beth Hamedrash), Smith's-buildings, Leadenhall-street, to attend to all applications from the German Jews, which may be brought before him, and which are decided according to the Jewish law. Many disputes between Jews in religious matters are settled in this manner ; and if the Lord Mayor or any other magistrate is told that the matter has already been settled by the Jewish Rabbi he seldom interferes. This applies only to civil and not to criminal cases. The Portuguese Jews have their own hospital and their own schools. Both congregations have their representatives in the Board of Deputies of British Jews, which board is acknowledged by government, and is triennial. Sir Moses Montefiore, a Jew of great wealth, who distinguished himself by his mission to Damascus, during the persecution of the Jews in that place, and also by his mission to Russia, some years ago, is the President of the Board. All political matters, calling for communications with government, are within the province of that useful board."

The Jews have eight synagogues in London, besides some smaller places which may perhaps, adopting the language of another church, be called synagogues of ease. The great synagogue in Duke's-place (a locality of which I have often had to speak) is the largest, but the new synagogue, St. Helen's, Bishopgate, is the one which most betokens the wealth of the worshippers. It is rich with ornaments, marble, and painted glass; the pavement is of painted marble, and presents a perfect round, while the ceiling is a half dome. There are besides these the Hamburg Synagogue, in Fenchurch-street; the Portuguese Synagogue, in Bevis-marks; two smaller places, in Cutler-street and Gun-yard, Houndsditch, known as Polish Synagogues; the Maiden-lane (Covent-garden), Synagogue; the Western Synagogue, St. Alban's-place, Pall-mall; and the West London Synagogue of British Jews, Margaret-street, Cavendish-square. The last-mentioned is the most aristocratic of the synagogues. The service there is curtailed, the ritual abbreviated, and the days of observance of the Jewish festival reduced from two to one. This alteration is strongly protested against by the other Jews, and the practices of this synagogue seem to show a yielding to the exactions or requirements of the wealthy. In the old days, and in almost every country in Europe, it was held to be sinful even for a king—reverenced and privileged as such a potentate then was—to prosecute any undertaking before he heard mass. In some states it was said in reproach of a noble or a sovereign, " he breakfasts before he hears mass," and, to meet the impatience of the Great, " hunting masses," as they were styled, or epitomes of the full service, were introduced. The Jews, some eight or nine years back in this country, seem to have followed this example; such was the case, at least, as regards London and the wealthier of the professors of this ancient faith.

The synagogues are not well attended, the congregations being smaller in proportion to the population than those of the Church of England. Neither, during the observance of the Jewish worship, is there any especial manifestation of the service being regarded as of a sacred and divinely-ordained character. There is a buzzing talk among the attendants during the ceremony, and an absence of seriousness and attention. Some of the Jews, however, show the greatest devotion, and the same may be said of the Jewesses, who sit apart in the synagogues, and are not required to attend so regularly as the men.

I should not have alluded to this absence of the solemnities of devotion, as regards the congregations of the Hebrews, had I not heard it regretted by Hebrews themselves. "It is shocking," one said. Another remarked, "To attend the synagogue is looked upon too much as a matter of *business*; but perhaps there is the same spirit in some of the Christian churches."

As to the street-Jews, religion is little known among them, or little cared for. They are indifferent to it—not to such a degree, indeed, as the costermongers, for they are not so ignorant a class—but yet contrasting strongly in their neglect with the religious intensity of the majority of the Roman Catholic Irish of the streets. In common justice I must give the remark of a Hebrew merchant with whom I had some conversation on the subject:—" I can't say much about street-Jews, for my engagements lead me away from them, and I don't know much about street-Christians. But if out of a hundred Jews you find that only ten of them care for their religion, how many out of a hundred Christians of any sort will care about theirs? Will ten of them care? If you answer, but they are only nominal Christians, my reply is, the Jews are only nominal Jews—Jews by birth, and not by faith."

Among the Jews I conversed with—and of course only the more intelligent understood, or were at all interested in, the question—I heard the most contemptuous denunciation of all converts from Judaism. One learned informant, who was by no means blind to the short-comings of his own people, expressed his conviction that no Jew had ever been really *converted*. He had abandoned his faith from interested motives. On this subject I am not called upon to express any opinion, and merely mention it to show a prevalent feeling among the class I am describing.

The street-Jews, including the majority of the more prosperous and most numerous class among them, the old-clothes men, are far from being religious in feeling, or well versed in their faith, and are, perhaps, in that respect on a level with the mass of the members of the Church of England; I say of the Church of England, because of that church the many who do not profess religion are usually accounted members.

In the Rabbinical College, I may add, is the finest Jewish library in the world. It has been collected for several generations under the care of the Chief Rabbis. The public are admitted, having first obtained tickets, given gratuitously, at the Chief Rabbi's residence in Crosby-square.

Of the Politics, Literature, and Amusements of the Jews.

Perhaps there is no people in the world, possessing the average amount of intelligence in busy communities, who care so little for politics as the general body of the Jews. The wealthy classes may take an interest in the matter, but I am assured, and by those who know their countrymen well, that even with them such a quality as patriotism is a mere word. This may be accounted for in a great measure, perhaps, from an hereditary feeling. The Jew could hardly be expected to love a land, or to strive for the promotion of its general welfare, where he felt he was but a sojourner, and where he was at the best but tolerated and often proscribed. But this feeling becomes highly reprehensible when it extends—as I am assured it does among many of the rich Jews—to their own people, for whom, apart from conventionalities, say my informants, *they care nothing whatever;* for so long as they are undisturbed in money-getting at home, their brethren may be persecuted all over the world, while the rich Jew merely shrugs his shoulders. An honourable exception, however, exists in Sir Moses Montefiore, who has honourably distinguished himself in the relief of his persecuted brethren on more than one occasion. The great of the earth no longer spit upon the gabardine of the Jewish millionaire, nor do they draw his teeth to get his money, but the great Jew capitalists, with powerful influence in many a government, do not seek to direct that influence for the bettering of the lot of their poorer brethren, who, at the same time, brook the restrictions and indignities which they have to suffer with a perfect philosophy. In fact, the Jews have often been the props of the courts who have persecuted them; that is to say, two or three Jewish firms occasionally have not hesitated to lend millions to the governments by whom they and their people have been systematically degraded and oppressed.

I was told by a Hebrew gentleman (a professional man) that so little did the Jews themselves care for "Jewish emancipation," that he questioned if one man in ten, actuated solely by his own feelings, would trouble himself to walk the length of the street in which he lived to secure Baron Rothschild's admission into the House of Commons. This apathy, my informant urged with perfect truth, in nowise affected the merits of the question, though he was convinced it formed a great obstacle to Baron Rothschild's success; "for governments," he said, "won't give boons to people who don't care for them; and, though this is called a boon, I look upon it as only a *right*."

When such is the feeling of the comparatively wealthier Jews, no one can wonder that I found among the Jewish street-sellers and old-clothes men with whom I talked on the subject—and their more influential brethren gave me every facility to prosecute my inquiry among them—a perfect indifference to, and nearly as perfect an ignorance of, politics. Perhaps no men buy so few newspapers, and read them so little, as the Jews generally. The street-traders, when I alluded to the subject, said they read little but the "Police Reports."

Among the body of the Jews there is little love of Literature. They read far less (let it be remembered I have acquired all this information from Jews themselves, and from men who could not be mistaken in the matter), and are far less familiar with English authorship, either historical or literary, than are the poorer English artizans. Neither do the wealthiest classes of the Jews care to foster literature among their own people. One author, a short time ago, failing to interest the English Jews, to promote the publication of his work, went to the United States, and his book was issued in Philadelphia, the city of Quakers!

The Amusements of the Jews—and here I speak more especially of the street or open-air traders—are the theatres and concert-rooms. The City of London Theatre, the Standard Theatre, and other playhouses at the East-end of London, are greatly resorted to by the Jews, and more especially by the younger members of the body, who sometimes constitute a rather obstreperous gallery. The cheap concerts which they patronize are generally of a superior order, for the Jews are fond of music, and among them have been many eminent composers and performers, so that the trash and jingle which delights the costermonger class would not please the street Jew boys;

hence their concerts are superior to the general run of cheap concerts, and are almost always "got up" by their own people.

Sussex-hall, in Leadenhall-street, is chiefly supported by Israelites; there the "Jews' and General Literary and Scientific Institution" is established, with reading-rooms and a library; and there lectures, concerts, &c., are given as at similar institutions. Of late, on every Friday evening, Sussex-hall has been thrown open to the general public, without any charge for admission, and lectures have been delivered gratuitously, on literature, science, art, and general subjects, which have attracted crowded audiences. The lecturers are chiefly Jews, but the lectures are neither theological nor sectarian. The lecturers are Mr. M. H. Bresslau, the Rev. B. H. Ascher, Mr. J. L. Levison (of Brighton), and Mr. Clarke, a merchant in the City, a Christian, whose lectures are very popular among the Jews. The behaviour of the Jew attendants, and the others, the Jews being the majority, is decorous. They seem "to like to receive information," I was told; and a gentleman connected with the hall argued that this attention showed a readiness for proper instruction, when given in an attractive form, which favoured the opinion that the young Jews, when not thrown in childhood into the vortex of money-making, were very easily teachable, while their natural quickness made them both ready and willing to be taught.

My old-clothes buying informant mentioned a Jewish eating-house. I visited one in the Jew quarter, but saw nothing to distinguish it from Christian resorts of the same character and cheapness (the "plate" of good hot meat costing 4*d*., and vegetables 1*d*.), except that it was fuller of Jews than of Christians, by three to two, perhaps, and that there was no "pork" in the waiter's specification of the fare.

Of the Charities, Schools, and Education of the Jews.

The Jewish charities are highly honourable to the body, for they allow none of their people to live or die in a parish workhouse. It is true that among the Jews in London there are many individuals of immense wealth; but there are also many rich Christians who care not one jot for the need of their brethren. It must be borne in mind also, that not only do the Jews voluntarily support their own poor and institutions, but they contribute—compulsorily it is true—their quota to the support of the English poor and church; and, indeed, pay their due proportion of all the parliamentary or local imposts. This is the more honourable and the more remarkable among the Jews, when we recollect their indisputable greed of money.

If a Jew be worn out in his old age, and unable to maintain himself, he is either supported by the contributions of his friends, or out of some local or general fund, or provided for in some asylum, and all this seems to be done with a less than ordinary fuss and display, so that the recipient of the charity feels himself more a pensioner than a pauper.

The Jews' Hospital, in the Mile-end Road, is an extensive building, into which feeble old men and destitute children of both sexes are admitted. Here the boys are taught trades, and the girls qualified for respectable domestic service. The Widows' Home, in Duke-street, Aldgate, is for poor Hebrew widows. The Orphan Asylum, built at the cost of Mr. A. L. Moses, and supported by subscription, now contains 14 girls and 8 boys; a school is attached to the asylum, which is in the Tenter Ground, Goodman's-fields. The Hand-in-Hand Asylum, for decayed old people, men and women, is in Duke's-place, Aldgate. There are likewise alms-houses for the Jews, erected also by Mr. A. L. Moses, at Mile-end, and other alms-houses, erected by Mr. Joel Emanuel, in Wellclose-square, near the Tower. There are, further, three institutions for granting marriage dowers to fatherless children; an institution in Bevis-marks, for the burial of the poor of the congregation; "Beth Holim;" a house for the reception of the sick poor, and of poor lying-in women belonging to the congregation of the Spanish and Portuguese Jews; "Magasim Zobim," for lending money to aid apprenticeships among boys, to fit girls for good domestic service, and for helping poor children to proceed to foreign parts, when it is believed that the change will be advantageous to them; and "Noten Lebem Larcebim;" to distribute bread to the poor of the congregation on the day preceding the Sabbath.

I am assured that these institutions are well-managed, and that, if the charities are abused by being dispensed to undeserving objects, it is usually with the knowledge of the managers, who often let the abuse pass, as a smaller evil than driving a man to theft or subjecting him to the chance of starvation. One gentleman, familiar with most of these establishments, said to me with a laugh, "I believe, if you have had any conversation with the gentlemen who manage these matters, you will have concluded that they are not the people to be imposed upon very easily."

There are seven Jewish schools in London, four in the city, and three at the West-end, all supported by voluntary contributions. The Jews' Free School, in Bell-lane, Spitalfields, is the largest, and is adapted for the education of no fewer than 1200 boys and girls. The late Baroness de Rothschild provided clothing, yearly, for all the pupils in the school. In the Infant School, Houndsditch, are about 400 little scholars. There are also the Orphan Asylum School, previously mentioned; the Western Jewish schools, for girls, in Dean-street, and, for boys, in Greek-street, Soho, but considered as one establishment; and the West Metropolitan School, for girls, in Little Queen-street, and, for boys, in High Holborn, also considered as one establishment.

Notwithstanding these means of education, the body of the poorer, or what in other callings might be termed the working-classes, are not even tolerably well educated; they are indifferent to the matter. With many, the multiplication table seems to constitute what they think the acme of all knowledge needful to a man. The great majority of the Jew boys, in the street, cannot read. A smaller portion can read, but so imperfectly that their ability to read detracts nothing from their ignorance. So neglectful or so necessitous (but I heard the ignorance attributed to neglect far more frequently than necessity) are the poorer Jews, and so soon do they take their children away from school, "to learn and do something for themselves," and so irregular is their attendance, on the plea that the time cannot be spared, and the boy must do something for himself, that many children leave the free-schools not only about as ignorant as when they entered them, but almost with an incentive to continued ignorance; for they knew nothing of reading, except that to acquire its rudiments is a pain, a labour, and a restraint. On some of the Jew boys the vagrant spirit is strong; they *will* be itinerants, if not wanderers,—though this is a spirit in no way confined to the Jew boys.

Although the wealthier Jews may be induced to give money towards the support of their poor, I heard strong strictures passed upon them concerning their indifference towards their brethren in all other respects. Even if they subscribed to a school, they never cared whether or not it was attended, and that, much as was done, far more was in the power of so wealthy and distinct a people. "This is all the more inexcusable," was said to me by a Jew, "because there are so many rich Jews in London, and if they exerted and exercised a broader liberality, as they might in instituting Jewish colleges, for instance, to promote knowledge among the middle-classes, and if they cared more about employing their own people, their liberality would be far more fully felt than similar conduct in a Christian, because they have a smaller sphere to influence. As to employing their own people, there are numbers of the rich Jews who will employ any stranger in preference, if he work a penny a week cheaper. This sort of *clan* employment," continued my Jew informant, "should never be exclusive, but there might, I think, be a judicious preference."

I shall now proceed to set forth an account of the sums yearly subscribed for purposes of education and charity by the Jews.

The Jews' Free School in Spitalfields is supported by voluntary contributions to the amount of about 1200*l.* yearly. To this sum a few Christians contribute, as to some other Hebrew institutions (which I shall specify), while Jews often are liberal supporters of Christian public charities—indeed, some of the wealthier Jews are looked upon by the members of their own faith as inclined to act more generously where Christian charities, with the prestige of high aristocratic and fashionable patronage, are in question, than towards their own institutions. To the Jews' Free School the Court of Common Council of the Corporation of London lately granted 100*l.*, through the exertions of Mr. Benjamin S. Phillips, of Newgate-street, a member of the court. The Baroness Lionel de Rothschild (as I have formerly stated of the late Baroness) supplies clothing for the scholars. The school is adapted for the reception of 1200 boys and girls in equal proportion; about 900 is the average attendance.

The Jews' Infant School in Houndsditch, with an average attendance approaching 400, is similarly supported at a cost of from 800*l.* to 1000*l.* yearly.

The Orphan Asylum School, in Goodman's-fields, receives a somewhat larger support, but in the expenditure is the cost of an asylum (before mentioned, and containing 22 inmates). The funds are about 1500*l.* yearly. Christians subscribe to this institution also—Mr. Frederick Peel, M.P., taking great interest in it. The attendance of pupils is from 300 to 400.

It might be tedious to enumerate the other schools, after having described the principal; I will merely add, therefore, that the yearly contributions to each are from 700*l.* to 1000*l.*, and the pupils taught in each from 200 to 400. Of these further schools there are four already specified.

The Jews' Hospital, at Mile End, is maintained at a yearly cost of about 3000*l.*, to which Christians contribute, but not to a twentieth of the amount collected. The persons benefited are worn-out old men, and destitute children, while the number of almspeople is from 150 to 200 yearly.

The other two asylums, &c., which I have specified, are maintained at a cost of about 800*l.* each, as a yearly average, and the Almshouses, three in number, at about half that sum. The persons relieved by these last-mentioned institutions number about 250, two-thirds, or thereabouts, being in the asylums.

The Loan Societies are three: the Jewish Ladies Visiting and Benevolent Loan Society; the Linusarian Loan Society (why called Linusarian a learned Hebrew scholar could not inform me, although he had asked the question of others); and the Magasim Zobim (the Good Deeds), a Portuguese Jews' Loan Society.

The business of these three societies is conducted on the same principle. Money is lent on personal or any security approved by the managers, and no interest is charged to the borrower. The amount lent yearly is from 600*l.* to 700*l.* by each society, the whole being repaid and with sufficient punctuality; a few weeks' "grace" is occasionally allowed in the event of illness or any unforeseen event. The Loan Societies have not yet found it necessary to proceed against any of their debtors; my informant thought this forbearance extended over six years.

There is not among the Jewish street-traders, as among the costermongers and others, a class forming part, or having once formed part of themselves, and living by usury and loan mongering, where they have amassed a few pounds. Whatever may be thought of the Jews' usurious dealings as regards the general public, the poorer classes of their people are not subjected to the exactions of usury, with all its clogs to a struggling man's well-doing. Sometimes the amount required by an old-clothes man, or other street-trader, is obtained by or for him at one of these loan societies. Sometimes it is advanced by the usual buyer of the second-hand garments collected by the street-Jew. No security in such cases is given beyond —strange as it may sound—the personal honour of an old-clothes man! An experienced man told me, that taking all the class of Jew street-sellers, who are a very fluctuating body, with the exception of the old-clothes men, the sum thus advanced as stock-money to them might be seldom less in any one year than 300*l.*, and seldom more than 500*l.* There is a prevalent notion that the poorer Jews, when seeking charity, are supplied with goods for street-sale by their wealthy brethren, and never with money—this appears to be unfounded.

Now to sum up the above items we find that the yearly cost of the Jewish schools is about 7000*l.*, supplying the means of instruction to 3000 children (out of a population of 18,000 of all ages, one-half of whom, perhaps, are under 20 years). The yearly outlay in the asylums, &c., is, it appears, 5800*l.* annually, benefiting or maintaining about 420 individuals (at a cost of nearly 14*l.* per head). If we add no more than 200*l.* yearly for the minor charities or institutions I have previously alluded to, we find 14,000*l.* expended annually in the public schools and charities of the Jews of London, independently of about 2000*l.*, which is the amount of the loans to those requiring temporary aid.

We have before seen that the number of Jews in London is estimated by the best informed at about 18,000; hence it would appear that the charitable donations of the Jews of London amount on an average to a little less than 1*l.* per head. Let us compare this with the benevolence of the Christians. At the same ratio the sum devoted to the charities of England and Wales should be very nearly 16,000,000*l.*, but, according to the most liberal estimates, it does not reach half that amount; the rent of the land and other fixed property, together with the interest of the money left for charitable purposes in England and Wales, is 1,200,000*l.* If, however, we add to the voluntary contributions the sum raised compulsorily by assessment in aid of the poor (about 7,000,000*l.* per annum), the ratio of the English Christian's contributions to his needy brethren throughout the country will be very nearly the same as that of the Jew's. Moreover, if we turn our attention to the benevolent bequests and donations of the Christians of London, we shall find that their munificence does not fall far short of that of the metropolitan Jews. The gross amounts of the charitable contributions of London are given below, together with the numbers of institutions; and it will thus be seen that the sum devoted to such purposes amounts to no less than 1,764,733*l.*, or upwards of a million and three-quarters sterling for a population of about two millions!

	Income derived from voluntary contributions.	Income derived from property.
12 General medical hospitals	£31,265	£111,641
50 Medical charities for special purposes	27,974	68,690
35 General dispensaries	11,470	2,954
12 Preservation of life and public morals	8,730	2,773
18 Reclaiming the fallen and staying the progress of crime	16,299	13,737
14 Relief of general destitution and distress	20,646	3,234
12 Relief of specified distress	19,473	10,408
14 Aiding the resources of the industrious	4,677	2,569
11 For the blind, deaf, and dumb	11,965	22,797
103 Colleges, hospitals, and other asylums for the aged	5,857	77,190
16 Charitable pension societies	15,790	3,199
74 Charitable and provident, chiefly for specified classes	19,905	83,322
31 Asylums for orphans and other necessitous children	55,466	25,549
10 Educational foundations	15,000	78,112
4 Charitable modern ditto	4,000	9,300
40 School societies, religious books, church aiding, and Christian visitings, &c.	159,853	158,336
35 Bible and missionary	494,494	63,058
491 Total	1,022,864	741,869

In connection with the statistical part of this subject I may mention that the Chief Rabbis each receive 1200*l.* a year; the Readers of the Synagogues, of whom there are twelve in London, from 300*l.* to 400*l.* a year each; the Secretaries of the Synagogues, of whom there are also twelve, from 200*l.* to 300*l.* each; the twelve under Secretaries from 100*l.* to 150*l.*; and six Dayanim 100*l.* a year each. These last-mentioned officers are looked upon by many of the Jews, as the "poor curates" may be by the members of the Church of England — as being exceedingly under-paid. The functions of the Dayanim have been already mentioned, and, I may add, that they must have received expensive scholarly educations, as for about four hours daily they have to read the Talmud in the places of worship.

The yearly payment of these sacerdotal officials, then, independent of other outlay, amounts to about 11,700*l.*; this is raised from the profits of the seats in the synagogues and voluntary contributions, donations, subscriptions, bequests, &c., among the Jews.

I have before spoken of a Board of Deputies, in connection with the Jews, and now proceed to describe its constitution. It is not a parliament among the Jews, I am told, nor a governing power, but what may be called a directing or regulating body. It is authorized by the body of Jews, and recognised by her Majesty's Government, as an established corporation, with powers to treat and determine on matters of civil and political policy affecting the condition of the Hebrews in this country, and interferes in no way with religious matters. It is neither a metropolitan nor a local nor a detached board, but, as far as the Jews in England may be so described, a national board. This board is elected triennially. The electors are the "seat-holders" in the Jewish synagogues; that is to say, they belong to the class of Jews who promote the support of the synagogues by renting seats, and so paying towards the cost of those establishments.

There are in England, Ireland, and Scotland, about 1000 of these seat-holders exercising the franchise, or rather entitled to exercise it, but many of them are indifferent to the privilege, as is often testified by the apathy shown on the days of election. Perhaps three-fourths of the privileged number may vote. The services of the representatives are gratuitous, and no qualification is required, but the elected are usually the leading metropolitan Jews. The proportion of the electors voting is in the ratio of the deputies elected. London returns 12 deputies; Liverpool, 2; Manchester, 2; Birmingham, 2; Edinburgh, Dublin, (the only places in either Scotland or Ireland returning deputies), Dover, Portsmouth, Southampton, Plymouth, Canterbury, Norwich, Swansea, Newcastle-on-Tyne, and two other places (according to the number of seat-holders), each one deputy, thus making up the number to 30. On election days the attendance, as I have said, is often small, but fluctuating according to any cause of excitement, which, however, is but seldom.

The question which has of late been discussed by this Board, and which is now under consideration, and negotiation with the Education Commissioners of her Majesty's Privy Council, is the obtaining a grant of money in the same proportion as it has been granted to other educational establishments. Nothing has as yet been given to the Jewish schools, and the matter is still undetermined.

With religious or sacerdotal questions the Board of Deputies does not, or is not required to meddle; it leaves all such matters to the bodies or tribunals I have mentioned. Indeed the deputies concern themselves only with what may be called the *public* interests of the Jews, both as a part of the community and as a distinct people. The Jewish institutions, however, are not an exception to the absence of unanimity among the professors of the same creeds, for the members of the Reform Synagogue in Margaret-street, Cavendish-square, are not recognised as entitled to vote, and do not vote, accordingly, in the election of the Jewish deputies. Indeed, the Reform members, whose synagogue was established eight years ago, were formally excommunicated by a declaration of the late Chief Rabbi, but this seems now to be regarded as a mere matter of form, for the members have lately partaken of all the rites to which orthodox Jews are entitled.

Of the Funeral Ceremonies, Fasts, and Customs of the Jews.

The funeral ceremonies of the Jews are among the things which tend to preserve the distinctness and peculiarity of this people. Sometimes, though now rarely, the nearest relatives of the deceased wear sackcloth (a coarse crape), and throw ashes and dust on their hair, for the term during which the corpse remains unburied, this term being the same as among Christians. When the corpse is carried to the Jews' burial-ground for interment the coffin is frequently opened, and the corpse addressed, in a Hebrew formula, by any relative, friend, or acquaintance who may be present. The words are to the following purport: "If I have done anything that might be offensive—pardon, pardon, pardon." After that the coffin is carried round the burial-ground in a circuit, children chanting the 90th Psalm in its original Hebrew, "a prayer of Moses, the man of God." The passages which the air causes to be most emphatic are these verses:—

"3. Thou turnest man to destruction; and sayest, Return, ye children of men.

"4. For a thousand years in thy sight are but as yesterday when it is past, and as a watch in the night.

"5. Thou carriest them away as with a flood; they are as a sleep: in the morning they are like grass which groweth up.

"6. In the morning it flourisheth, and groweth up; in the evening it is cut down, and withereth.

"10. The days of our years are threescore years and ten; and if by reason of strength they be fourscore years, yet is their strength labour and sorrow; for it is soon cut off, and we fly away."

The coffin is then carried into a tent, and the funeral prayers, in Hebrew, are read. When it has been lowered into the grave, the relatives, and indeed all the attendants at the interment, fill up the grave, shovelling in the earth. In the Jews' burial-ground are no distinctions, no vaults or provisions for aristocratic sepulture. The very rich and the very poor, the outcast woman and the virtuous and prosperous gentlewoman, "grossly familiar, side by side consume." A Jewish funeral is a matter of high solemnity.

The burial fees are 12s. for children, and from 2l. to 3l. for adults. These fees are not the property of the parties officating, but form a portion of the synagogue funds for general purposes, payment of officers, &c. No fees are charged to the relatives of poor Jews.

Two fasts are rigidly observed by the Jews, and even by those Jews who are usually indifferent to the observances of their religion. These are the Black Fast, in commemoration of the destruction of Jerusalem, and the White Fast, in commemoration of the atonement. On each of those occasions the Jews abstain altogether from food for 24 hours, or from sunset to sunset.

Of the Jew Street-Sellers of Accordions, and of their Street Musical Pursuits.

I conclude my account of the Street-Jews with an account of the accordion sellers.

Although the Jews, as a people, are musical, they are little concerned at present either in the sale of musical instruments in the streets, or in street-music or singing. Until within a few years, however, the street-sale of accordions was carried on by itinerant Jews, and had previously been carried on most extensively in the country, even in the far north of England. Some years back well-dressed Jews "travelled" with stocks of accordions. In many country towns and in gentlemen's country mansions, in taverns, and schools also, these accordions were then a novelty. The Jew could play on the instrument, and carried a book of instructions, which usually formed part of the bargain, and by the aid of which, he made out, any one, even without previous knowledge of the practical art of music, could easily teach himself —nothing but a little practice in fingering being wanted to make a good accordion-player. At first the accordions sold by the Jew hawkers were good, two guineas being no unusual price to be paid for one, even to a street-seller, while ten and twenty shillings were the lower charges. But the accordions were in a few years "made slop," cheap instruments being sent to this country from Germany, and sold at less than half their former price, until the charge fell as low as 3s. 6d. or even 2s. 6d.—but only for "rubbish," I was told. When the fragility and inferior musical qualities of these instruments came to be known, it was found almost impossible to sell in the streets even superior instruments, however reasonable in price, and thus the trade sunk to a nonentity. So little demand is there now for these instruments that no pawnbroker, I am assured, will advance money on one, however well made.

The itinerant accordion trade was always much greater in the country than in London, for in town, I was told, few would be troubled to try, or even listen, to the tones of an accordion played by a street-seller, at their own doors, or in their houses. While there were 100 or 120 Jews hawking accordions in the country, there would not be 20 in London, including even the suburbs, where the sale was the best.

Calculating that, when the trade was at its best, 130 Jews hawked accordions in town and country, and that each sold three a week, at an average price of 20s. each, or six in a week at an average price of 10s. each, the profit being from 50 to 100 per cent., we find upwards of 20,000l. expended in the course of the year in accordions of which, however, little more than a sixth part, or about 3000l., was expended in London. This was only when the trade had all the recommendations of novelty, and in the following year perhaps not half the amount was realized. One informant thought that the year 1828–9 was the best for the sale of these instruments, but he spoke only from memory. At the present time I could not find or hear of one street-Jew selling accordions; I remember, however, having seen one within the present year. Most of the Jews who travelled with them have emigrated.

It is very rarely indeed that, fond as the Jews are of music, any of them are to be found in the bands of street-musicians, or of such street-performers as the Ethiopian serenaders. If there be any, I was told, they were probably not pure Jews, but of Christian parentage on one side or the other, and not associating with their own people. At the cheap concert-rooms, however, Jews are frequently singers, but rarely the Jewesses, while some of the twopenny concerts at the East-end are got up and mainly patronized by the poorer class of Jews. Jews are also to be found occasionally among the supernumeraries of the theatres; but, when not professionally engaged, these still live among their own people. I asked one young Jew who occasionally sang at a cheap concert-room, what description of songs they usually sung, and he answered " all kinds." He, it seems, sang comic songs, but his friend Barney, who had just left him, sang sentimental songs. He earned 1s. and sometimes 2s., but more frequently 1s., three or four nights in the week, as he had no regular engagement. In the daytime he worked at cigar-making, but did not like it, it was "*so confining*." He had likewise sung, but gratuitously, at concerts got up for the benefit of any person " bad off." He knew nothing of the science and art of music. Of the superior class of Jew vocalists and composers, it is not of course necessary here to speak, as they do not come within the scope of my present subject. Of Hebrew youths thus employed in cheap and desultory concert-singing, there are in the winter season, I am told, from 100 to 150, few, if any, depending entirely upon their professional exertions, but being in circumstances similar to those of my young informant.

Of the Street-Buyers of Hogs'-Wash.

The trade in hogs'-wash, or in the refuse of the table, is by no means insignificant. The street-buyers are of the costermonger class, and some of them have been costermongers, and "when not kept going regular on wash," I was told, are " costers still," but with the advantage of having donkeys, ponies, or horses and carts, and frequently shops, as the majority of the wash-buyers have; for they are often greengrocers as well as costermongers.

The hogs' food obtained by these street-folk, or, as I most frequently heard it called, the " wash," is procured from the eating-houses, the coffee-houses which are also eating-houses (with " hot joints from 12 to 4 "), the hotels, the club-houses, the larger mansions, and the public institutions. It is composed of the scum and lees of all broths and soups; of the washings of cooking utensils, and of the dishes and plates used at dinners and suppers; of small pieces of meat left on the plates of the diners in taverns, clubs, or cook-shops; of pieces of potato, or any remains of vegetables; of any viands, such as puddings, left in the plates in the same manner; of gristle; of pieces of stale bread, or bread left at table; occasionally of meat kept, whether cooked or uncooked, until " blown," and unfit for consumption (one man told me that he had found whole legs of mutton in the wash he bought from a great eating-house, but very rarely): of potato-peelings; of old and bad potatoes; of " stock," or the remains of meat stewed for soup, which was not good enough for sale to be re-used by the poor; of parings of every kind of cheese or meat; and of the many things which are considered " only fit for pigs."

It is not always, however, that the unconsumed food of great houses or of public bodies (where the dinners are a part of the institution) goes to the wash-tub. At Buckingham-palace, I am told, it is given to poor people who have tickets for the receipt of it. At Lincoln's-inn the refuse or leavings of the bar dinners are sold to men who retail them, usually small chandlers, and the poor people, who have the means, buy this broken meat very readily at 4d., 6d., and 8d. the pound, which is cheap for good cooked meat. Pie-crust, obtained by its purveyors in the same way, is sold, perhaps with a small portion of the contents of the pie, in penny and twopenny-worths. A man familiar with this trade told me that among the best customers for this kind of second-hand food were women of the town of the poorer class, who were always ready, whenever they had a few pence at command, to buy what was tasty, cheap, and ready-cooked, because " they hadn't no trouble with it, but only just to eat it."

One of the principal sources of the " wash" supply is the cook-shops, or eating-houses, where the "leavings" on the plates are either the perquisites of the waiters or waitresses, or looked sharply after by master or mistress. There are also in these places the remains of soups, and the potato-peelings, &c., of which I have spoken, together with the keen appropriation to a profitable use of every crumb and scrap—when it is a portion of the gains of a servant, or when it adds to the receipts of the proprietor. In calculating the purchase-value of the good-will of an eating-house, the " wash" is as carefully considered as is the number of daily guests.

One of the principal street-buyers from the eating-houses, and in several parts of town, is Jemmy Divine, of Lambeth. He is a pig-dealer, but also sells his wash to others who keep pigs. He sends round a cart and horse under the care of a boy, or of a man, whom he may have employed, or drives it himself, and he often has more carts than one. In his cart are two or three tubs, well secured, so that they may not be jostled out, into which the wash is deposited. He contracts by the week, month, or quarter, with hotel-keepers and others, for their wash, paying from 10l. to as high as 50l. a year, about 20l. being an average for well-frequented taverns and " dining-rooms." The wash-tubs on the premises of these buyers are often offensive, sometimes sending forth very sour smells.

In Sharp's-alley, Smithfield, is another man buying quantities of wash, and buying fat and grease extensively. There is one also in Prince's-street, Lambeth, who makes it his sole business to collect hogs'-wash; he was formerly a coal-heaver and wretchedly poor, but is now able to make a decent livelihood in this trade, keeping a pony and cart. He generally keeps about 30 pigs, but also sells hogs' food retail to any pig-keeper, the price being 4*d.* to 6*d.* a pail-full, according to the quality, as the collectors are always anxious to have the wash "rich," and will not buy it if cabbage-leaves or the parings of green vegetables form a part of it. This man and the others often employ lads to go round for wash, paying them 2*s.* a week, and finding them in board. They are the same class of boys as those I have described as coster-boys, and are often strong young fellows. These lads—or men hired for the purpose—are sometimes sent round to the smaller cook-shops and to private houses, where the wash is given to them for the trouble of carrying it away, in preference to its being thrown down the drain. Sometimes only 1*d.* a pail is paid by the street-buyer, provided the stuff be taken away punctually and regularly. These youths or men carry pails after the fashion of a milkman.

The supply from the workhouses is very large. It is often that the paupers do not eat all the rice-pudding allowed, or all the bread, while soup is frequently left, and potatoes; and these leavings are worthless, except for pig-meat, as they would soon turn sour. It is the same, though not to the same extent, in the prisons.

What I have said of some of the larger eating-houses relates also to the club-houses.

There are a number of wash-buyers in the suburbs, who purchase, or obtain their stock gratuitously, at gentlemen's houses, and retail it either to those who feed pigs as a business, or else to the many, I was told, who live a little way out of town, and "like to grow their own bacon." Many of these men perform the work themselves, without a horse and cart, and are on their feet every day and all day long, except on Sundays, carrying hogs'-wash from the seller, or to the buyer. One man, who had been in this trade at Woolwich, told me that he kept pigs at one time, but ceased to do so, as his customers often murmured at the thin quality of the wash, declaring that he gave all the best to his own animals.

If it be estimated that there are 200 men daily buying hogs'-wash in London and the suburbs, within 15 miles, and that each collects only 20 pails per day, paying 2*d.* per pail (thus allowing for what is collected without purchase), we find 10,400*l.* expended annually in buying hogs'-wash.

Of the Street-Buyers of Tea-Leaves.

An extensive trade, but less extensive, I am informed, than it was a few years ago, is carried on in tea-leaves, or in the leaves of the herb after their having been subjected, in the usual way, to decoction. These leaves are, so to speak, re-manufactured, in spite of great risk and frequent exposure, and in defiance of the law. The 17th Geo. III., c. 29, is positive and stringent on the subject:—

"Every person, whether a dealer in or seller of tea, or not, who shall dye or fabricate any sloe-leaves, liquorice-leaves *or the leaves of tea that have been used,* or the leaves of the ash, elder or other tree, shrub or plant, in imitation of tea, or who shall mix or colour such leaves with terra Japonica, copperas, sugar, molasses, clay, logwood or other ingredient, or who shall sell or expose to sale, or have in custody, any such adulterations in imitation of tea, shall for every pound forfeit, on conviction, by the oath of one witness, before one justice, 5*l.*; or, on non-payment, be committed to the House of Correction for not more than twelve or less than six months."

The same act also authorizes a magistrate, on the oath of an excise officer, or any one, by whom he suspects this illicit trade to be carried on, to seize the herbs, or spurious teas, and the whole apparatus that may be found on the premises, the herbs to be burnt and the other articles sold, the proceeds of such a sale, after the payment of expenses, going half to the informer and half to the poor of the parish.

It appears evident, from the words of this act which I have *italicised*, that the use of tea-leaves for the robbery of the public and the defrauding of the revenue has been long in practice. The extract also shows what other cheats were formerly resorted to—the substitutes most popular with the tea-manufacturers at one time being sloe-leaves. If, however, one-tenth of the statements touching the applications of the leaves of the sloe-tree, and of the juice of its sour, astringent fruit, during the war-time, had any foundation in truth, the sloe must have been regarded commercially as one of the most valuable of our native productions, supplying our ladies with their tea, and our gentlemen with their port-wine.

Women and men, three-fourths of the number being women, go about buying tea-leaves of the female servants in the larger, and of the shopkeepers' wives in the smaller, houses. But the great purveyors of these things are the char-women. In the houses where they char the tea-leaves are often reserved for them to be thrown on the carpets when swept, as a means of allaying the dust, or else they form a part of their perquisites, and are often asked for if not offered. The mistress of a coffee-shop told me that her charwoman, employed in cleaning every other morning, had the tea-leaves as a part of her remuneration, or as a matter of course. What the charwoman did with them her employer never inquired, although she was always anxious to obtain them, and she referred me to the poor woman in question. I found her in a very clean apartment on the second floor of a decent house in Somers-town; a strong hale woman, with what may be called an industrious look. She was middle-aged, and a widow, with one daughter, then a nursemaid in the neighbourhood, and had regular employment.

"Yes," she said, "I get the tea-leaves whenever I can, and the most at two coffee-shops that I work at, but neither of them have so many as they used to have. I think it's because cocoa's come so much to be asked for in them, and so they sell less tea. I buy tea-leaves only at one place. It's a very large family, and I give the servant 4*d*. and sometimes 3*d*. or 2*d*. a fortnight for them, but I'm nothing in pocket, for the young girl is a bit of a relation of mine, and it's like a trifle of pocket-money for her. She gives a penny every time she goes to her chapel, and so do I; there's a box for it fixed near the door. O yes, her mistress knows I buy them, for her mistress knew me before she was married, and that's about 15 or 16 years since. When I've got this basin (producing it) full I sell it, generally for 4*d*. I don't know what the leaves in it will weigh, and I have never sold them by weight, but I believe some have. Perhaps they might weigh, as damp as some of them are, about a pound. I sell them to a chandler now. I have sold them to a rag-and-bottle-shop. I've had men and women call upon me and offer to buy them, but not lately, and I never liked the looks of them, and never sold them any. I don't know what they're wanted for, but I've heard that they're mixed with new tea. I have nothing to do with that. I get them honestly and sell them honestly, and that's all I can say about it. Every little helps, and if rich people won't pay poor people properly, then poor people can't be expected to be very nice. But I don't complain, and that's all I know about it."

The chandler in question knew nothing of the trade in tea-leaves, he said; he bought none, and he did not know that any of the shopkeepers did, and he could not form a notion what they could be wanted for, if it wasn't to sweep carpets!

This mode of buying or collecting is, I am told the commonest mode of any, and it certainly presents some peculiarities. The leaves which are to form the spurious tea are collected, in great measure, by a class who are perhaps more likely than any other to have themselves to buy and drink the stuff which they have helped to produce! By charwomen and washer-women a "nice cup of tea" in the afternoon during their work is generally classed among the comforts of existence, yet they are the very persons who sell the tea-leaves which are to make their "much prized beverage." It is curious to reflect also, that as tea-leaves are used indiscriminately for being re-made into what is considered new tea, what must be the strength of our tea in a few years. Now all housewives complain that twice the quantity of tea is required to make the infusion of the same strength as formerly, and if the collection of old tea-leaves continues, and the refuse leaves are to be dried and re-dried perpetually, surely we must get to use pounds where we now do ounces.

A man formerly in the tea-leaf business, and very anxious not to be known—but upon whose information, I am assured from a respectable source, full reliance may be placed—gave me the following account:—

"My father kept a little shop in the general line, and I helped him; so I was partly brought up to the small way. But I was adrift by myself when I was quite young—18 or so perhaps. I can read and write well enough, but I was rather of too gay a turn to be steady. Besides, father was very poor at times, and could seldom pay me anything, if I worked ever so. He was very fond of his belly too, and I've known him, when he's had a bit of luck, or a run of business, go and stuff hisself with fat roast pork at a cook-shop till he could hardly waddle, and then come home and lock hisself upstairs in his bedroom and sleep three parts of the afternoon. (My mother was dead.) But father was a kind-hearted man for all that, and for all his roast pork, was as thin as a whipping-post. I kept myself when I left him, just off and on like, by collecting grease, and all that; it can't be done so easy now, I fancy; so I got into the tea-leaf business, but father had nothing to do with it. An elderly sort of a woman who I met with in my collecting, and who seemed to take a sort of fancy to me, put me up to the leaves. She was an out-and-out hand at anything that way herself. Then I bought tea-leaves with other things, for I suppose for four or five years. How long ago is it? O, never mind, sir, a few years. I bought them at many sorts of houses, and carried a box of needles, and odds and ends, as a sort of introduction. There wasn't much of that wanted though, for I called, when I could, soon in the mornings before the family was up, and some ladies don't get up till 10 or 11 you know. The masters wasn't much; it was the mistresses I cared about, because they are often such Tartars to the maids and always a-poking in the way.

"I've tried to do business in the great lords' houses in the squares and about the parks, but there was mostly somebody about there to hinder you. Besides, the servants in such places are often on board wages, and often, when they're not on board wages, find their own tea and sugar, and little of the tea-leaves is saved when every one has a separate pot of tea; so there's no good to be done there. Large houses in trade where a number of young men is boarded, drapers or grocers, is among the best places, as there is often a housekeeper there to deal with, and no mistress to bother. I always bought by the lot. If you offered to weigh you would not be able to clear anything, as they'd be sure to give the leaves a extra wetting. I put handfuls of the leaves to my nose, and could tell from the smell whether they were hard drawn or not. When they isn't hard drawn they answer best, and them I put to one side. I had a bag like a lawyer's blue bag, with three divisions in it, to put my leaves into, and so keep them 'sunder. Yes, I've bought of charwomen, but somehow I think they did'nt much admire selling to me. I hardly know how I made them out, but one told me of another. They like the shops better for their leaves, I think; because they can get a bit of cheese, or snuff, or candles for them there; though I don't know much about the shop-work in this line. I've often been tried to be took in by the servants. I've found leaves in the lot offered to me to buy what was all dusty, and had been used for sweeping; and if I'd sold them with my stock they'd have been stopped out of the next money. I've had tea-leaves given me by servants oft enough, for I used to sweetheart them a bit, just to get over them; and they've laughed, and asked me whatever I could want with them. As for price, why, I judged what a lot was worth, and gave accordingly—from 1$d.$ to 1$s.$ I never gave more than 1$s.$ for any one lot at a time, and that had been put to one side for me in a large concern, for about a fortnight I suppose. I can't say how many people had been tea'd on them. If it was a housekeeper, or anybody that way, that I bought of, there was never anything said about what they was wanted for. What *did* I want them for? Why, to sell again; and though him as I sold them to never said so, I knew they was to dry over again. I know nothing about who he was, or where he lived. The woman I told you of sent him to me. I suppose I cleared about 10$s.$ a week on them, and did a little in other things beside; perhaps I cleared rather more than 10$s.$ on leaves some weeks, and 5$s.$ at others. The party as called upon me once a week to buy my leaves was a very polite man, and seemed quite the gentleman. There was no weighing. He examined the lot, and said 'so much.' He wouldn't stand 'bating, or be kept haggling; and his money was down, and no nonsense. What cost me 5$s.$ I very likely got three half-crowns for. It was no great trade, if you consider the trouble. I've sometimes carried the leaves that he'd packed in papers, and put into a carpet-bag, where there was others, to a coffee-shop; they always had 'till called for' marked on a card then. I asked no questions, but just left them. There was two, and sometimes four boys, as used to bring me leaves on Saturday nights. I think they was charwomen's sons, but I don't know for a positive, and I don't know how they made me out. I think I was one of the tip-tops of the trade at one time; some weeks I've laid out a sov. (sovereign) in leaves. I haven't a notion how many's in the line, or what's doing now; but much the same I've no doubt. I'm glad *I've* done with it."

I am told by those who are as well-informed on the subject as is perhaps possible, when a surreptitious and dishonest traffic is the subject of inquiry, that although less spurious tea is sold, there are more makers of it. Two of the principal manufacturers have of late, however, been prevented carrying on the business by the intervention of the excise officers. The spurious tea-men are also the buyers of " wrecked tea," that is, of tea which has been part of the salvage of a wrecked vessel, and is damaged or spoiled entirely by the salt water. This is re-dried and dyed, so as to appear fresh and new. It is dyed with Prussian blue, which gives it what an extensive tea-dealer described to me as an " intensely fine green." It is then mixed with the commonest Gunpowder teas and with the strongest Young Hysons, and has always a kind of " metallic" smell, somewhat like that of a copper vessel after friction in its cleaning. These teas are usually sold at 4$s.$ the pound.

Sloe-leaves for spurious tea, as I have before stated, were in extensive use, but this manufacture ceased to exist about 20 years ago. Now the spurious material consists only of the old tea-leaves, at least so far as experienced tradesmen know. The adulteration is, however, I am assured, more skilfully conducted than it used to be, and its staple is of far easier procuration. The law, though it makes the use of old tea-leaves, as components of what is called tea, punishable, is nevertheless silent as to their sale or purchase; they can be collected, therefore, with a comparative impunity.

The tea-leaves are dried, dyed (or re-dyed), and shrivelled on plates of hot metal, carefully tended. The dyes used are those I have mentioned. These teas, when mixed, are hawked in the country, but not in town, and are sold to the hawkers at 7 lbs. for 21$s.$ The quarters of pounds are retailed at 1$s.$ A tea-dealer told me that he could recognise this adulterated commodity, but it was only a person skilled in teas who could do so, by its *coarse* look. For green tea—the mixture to which the prepared leaves are mostly devoted—the old tea is blended with the commonest Gunpowders and Hysons. No dye, I am told, is required when black tea is thus re-made; but I know that plumbago is often used to simulate the bloom. The inferior shopkeepers sell this adulterated tea, especially in neighbourhoods where the poor Irish congregate, or any of the lowest class of the poor English.

To obtain the statistics of a trade which exists in spite not only of the vigilance of the excise and police officers but of public reprobation, and which is essentially a secret trade, is not possible. I heard some, who were likely to be well-informed, conjecture—for it cannot honestly be called more than a conjecture—that between 500 and 1000 lbs., perhaps 700 lbs., of old tea-leaves were made up weekly in London; but of this he thought that about an eighth was spoilt by burning in the process of drying.

Another gentleman, however, thought that, at the very least, double the above quantity of old tea-leaves was weekly manufactured into new tea. According to his estimate, and he was no mean authority, no less than 1500 lbs. weekly, or 78,000 lbs. per annum of this trash are yearly poured into the London market. The average consumption of tea is about 1$\frac{1}{4}$ lb. per annum for each man, woman, or child in the kingdom; coffee being the *principal* unfermented beverage of the poor. Those, however, of the poorest who drink tea consume about two ounces per week (half an ounce serving them twice), or one pound in the course of every two months. This makes the annual consumption of the adult tea-drinking poor amount to 6 lbs., and it is upon this class the spurious tea is chiefly foisted.

OF THE STREET-FINDERS OR COLLECTORS.

These men, for by far the great majority are men, may be divided, according to the nature of their occupations, into three classes:—

1. The bone-grubbers and rag-gatherers, who are, indeed, the same individuals, the pure-finders, and the cigar-end and old wood collectors.
2. The dredgermen, the mud-larks, and the sewer-hunters.
3. The dustmen and nightmen, the sweeps and the scavengers.

The first class go abroad daily to *find* in the streets, and carry away with them such things as bones, rags, "pure" (or dogs'-dung), which no one appropriates. These they sell, and on that sale support a wretched life. The second class of people are also as strictly *finders*; but their industry, or rather their labour, is confined to the river, or to that subterranean city of sewerage unto which the Thames supplies the great outlets. These persons may not be immediately connected with the *streets* of London, but their pursuits are carried on in the open air (if the sewer-air may be so included), and are all, at any rate, out-of-door avocations. The third class is distinct from either of these, as the labourers comprised in it are not finders, but *collectors* or *removers* of the dirt and filth of our streets and houses, and of the soot of our chimneys.

The two first classes also differ from the third in the fact that the sweeps, dustmen, scavengers, &c., are paid (and often large sums) for the removal of the refuse they collect; whereas the bone-grubbers, and mud-larks, and pure-finders, and dredgermen, and sewer-hunters, get for their pains only the value of the articles they gather.

Herein, too, lies a broad distinction between the street-finder, or collector, and the street-buyer: though both deal principally with refuse, the buyer *pays* for what he is permitted to take away; whereas the finder or collector is either paid (like the sweep), or else he neither pays nor is paid (like the bone-grubber), for the refuse that he removes.

The third class of street-collectors also presents another and a markedly distinctive characteristic. They act in the capacity of servants, and do not depend upon chance for the result of their day's labour, but are put to stated tasks, being employed and paid a fixed sum for their work. To this description, however, some of the sweeps present an exception; as when the sweep works on his own account, or, as it is worded, "is his own master."

The public health requires the periodical cleaning of the streets, and the removal of the refuse matter from our dwellings; and the man who contracts to carry on this work is decidedly a street-collector; for on what he collects or removes depends the amount of his remuneration. Thus a wealthy contractor for the public scavengery, is as entirely one of the street-folk as the unskilled and ignorant labourer he employs. The master lives, and, in many instances, has become rich, on the results of his street employment; for, of course, the actual workmen are but as the agents or sources of his profit. Even the collection of "pure" (dogs'-dung) in the streets, if conducted by the servants of any tanner or leather dresser, either for the purposes of his own trade or for sale to others, might be the occupation of a wealthy man, deriving a small profit from the labour of each particular collector. The same may also be said of bone-grubbing, or any similar occupation, however insignificant, and now abandoned to the outcast.

Were the collection of mud and dust carried on by a number of distinct individuals—that is to say, were each individual dustman and scavenger to collect on his own account, there is no doubt that no *one man* could amass a fortune by such means—while if the collection of bones and rags and even dogs'-dung were carried on "in the large way," that is to say, by a number of individual collectors working for one "head man," even the picking up of the most abject refuse of the metropolis might become the source of great riches.

The bone-grubber and the mud-lark (the searcher for refuse on the banks of the river) differ little in their pursuits or in their characteristics, excepting that the mud-larks are generally boys, which is more an accidental than a definite distinction. The grubbers are with a few exceptions stupid, unconscious of their degradation, and with little anxiety to be relieved from it. They are usually taciturn, but this taciturn habit is common to men whose callings, if they cannot be called solitary, are pursued with little communication with others. I was informed by a man who once kept a little beer-shop near Friar-street, Southwark Bridge-road (where then and still, he thought, was a bone-grinding establishment), that the bone-grubbers who carried their sacks of bones thither sometimes had a pint of beer at his house when they had received their money. They usually sat, he told me, silently looking at the corners of the floor—for they rarely lifted their eyes up—as if they were expecting to see some bones or refuse there available for their bags. Of this inertion, perhaps fatigue and despair may be a part. I asked some questions of a man of this class whom I saw pick up in a road in the suburbs something that appeared to have been a coarse canvas apron, although it was wet after a night's rain and half covered with mud. I inquired of him what he thought about when he trudged along looking on the ground on every side. His answer was, "Of nothing, sir." I believe that no better description could be given of that vacuity of mind or mental inactivity which seems to form a part of the most degraded callings. The minds of such men, even without an approach to idiotcy, appear to be a blank. One characteristic of these poor fellows, bone-grubbers and mud-larks, is that they are very poor, although I am told some of them, the older men, have among the poor the reputation of being misers. It is not unusual for the youths belonging to these callings to live with their parents and give them the amount of their earnings.

The sewer-hunters are again distinct, and a far more intelligent and adventurous class; but they work in gangs. They must be familiar with the course of the tides, or they might be drowned at high water. They must have quick eyes too, not merely to descry the objects of their search, but to mark the points and bearings of the subterraneous roads they traverse; in a word, "to know their way underground." There is, moreover, some spirit of daring in venturing into a dark, solitary sewer, the chart being only in the memory, and in braving the possibility of noxious vapours, and the by no means insignificant dangers of the rats infesting these places.

The dredgermen, the finders of the water, are again distinct, as being watermen, and working in boats. In some foreign parts, in Naples, for instance, men carrying on similar pursuits are also divers for anything lost in the bay or its confluent waters. One of these men, known some years ago as "the Fish," could remain (at least, so say those whom there is no reason to doubt) three hours under the water without rising to the surface to take breath. He was, it is said, web-footed, naturally, and partially web-fingered. The King of the Two Sicilies once threw a silver cup into the sea for "the Fish" to bring up and retain as a reward, but the poor diver was never seen again. It was believed that he got entangled among the weeds on the rocks, and so perished. The dredgermen are necessarily well acquainted with the sets of the tide and the course of the currents in the Thames. Every one of these men works on his own account, being as it were a "small master," which, indeed, is one of the great attractions of open-air pursuits. The dredgermen also depend for their maintenance upon the sale of what they find, or the rewards they receive.

It is otherwise, however, as was before observed, with the third class of the street-finders, or rather collectors. In all the capacities of dustmen, nightmen, scavengers, and sweeps, the employers of the men are *paid* to do the work, the proceeds of the street-collection forming only a portion of the employer's remuneration. The sweep has the soot in addition to his 6*d*. or 1*s*.; the master scavenger has a payment from the parish funds to sweep the streets, though the clearance of the cesspools, &c., in private houses, may be an individual bargain. The whole refuse of the streets belongs to the contractor to make the best of, but it must be cleared away, and so must the contents of a dust-bin; for if a mass of dirt become offensive, the householder may be indicted for a nuisance, and municipal by-laws require its removal. It is thus made a matter of compulsion that the dust be removed from a private house; but it is otherwise with the soot. Why a man should be permitted to let soot accumulate in his chimney—perhaps exposing himself, his family, his lodgers, and his neighbours to the dangers of fire, it may not be easy to account for, especially when we bear in mind that the same man may not accumulate cabbage-leaves and fish-tails in his yard.

The dustmen are of the plodding class of labourers, mere labourers, who require only bodily power, and possess little or no mental development. Many of the agricultural labourers are of this order, and the dustman often seems to be the stolid ploughman, modified by a residence in a city, and engaged in a peculiar calling. They are generally uninformed, and no few of them are dustmen because their fathers were. The same may be said of nightmen and scavengers. At one time it was a popular, or rather a vulgar notion that many dustmen had become possessed of large sums, from the plate, coins, and valuables they found in clearing the dust-bins — a manifest absurdity; but I was told by a marine-store dealer that he had known a young woman, a dustman's daughter, sell silver spoons to a neighbouring marine-store man, who was "not very particular."

The circumstances and character of the chimney-sweeps have, since Parliament "put down" the climbing boys, undergone considerable change. The sufferings of many of the climbing boys were very great. They were often ill-lodged, ill-fed, barely-clad, forced to ascend hot and narrow flues, and subject to diseases—such as the chimney-sweep's cancer—peculiar to their calling. The child hated his trade, and was easily tempted to be a thief, for prison was an asylum; or he grew up a morose tyrannical fellow as journeyman or master. Some of the young sweeps became very bold thieves and house-breakers, and the most remarkable, as far as personal daring is concerned: the boldest feat of escape from Newgate was performed by a youth who had been brought up a chimney-sweep. He climbed up the two bare rugged walls of a corner of the interior of the prison, in the open air, to the height of some 60 feet. He had only the use of his hands, knees, and feet, and a single slip, from fear or pain, would have been death; he surmounted a parapet after this climbing, and gained the roof, but was recaptured before he could get clear away. He was, moreover, a sickly, and reputed a cowardly, young man, and ended his career in this country by being transported.

A master sweep, now in middle age, and a man "well to do," told me that when a mere child he had been apprenticed out of the workhouse to a sweep, such being at that time a common occurrence. He had undergone, he said, great hardships while learning his business, and was long, from the indifferent character of his class, ashamed of being a sweep, both as journeyman and master; but the sweeps were so much improved in character now, that he no longer felt himself disgraced in his calling.

The sweeps are more intelligent than the mere ordinary labourers I have written of under this head, but they are, of course, far from being an educated body.

The further and more minute characteristics of the curious class of street-finders or collectors will be found in the particular details and statements.

Among the finders there is perhaps the greatest poverty existing, they being the very lowest class of all the street-people. Many of the very old live on the hard dirty crusts they pick up out of the roads in the course of their rounds, washing them and steeping them in water before they eat them. Probably that vacuity of mind which is a distinguishing feature of the class is the mere atony or emaciation of the mental faculties proceeding from—though often producing in the want of energy that it necessarily begets—the extreme wretchedness of the class. But even their liberty and a crust—as it frequently literally is—appears preferable to these people to the restrictions of the workhouse. Those who are unable to comprehend the inertia of both body and mind begotten by the despair of long-continued misfortune are referred to page 357 of the first volume of this work, where it will be found that a tinman, in speaking of the misery connected with the early part of his street-career, describes the effect of extreme want as producing not only an absence of all hope, but even of a desire to better the condition. Those, however, who have studied the mysterious connection between body and mind, and observed what different creatures they themselves are before and after dinner, can well understand that a long-continued deficiency of food must have the same weakening effect on the muscles of the mind and energy of the thoughts and will, as it has on the limbs themselves.

Occasionally it will be found that the utter abjectness of the bone-grubbers has arisen from the want of energy begotten by intemperate habits. The workman has nothing but this same energy to live upon, and the permanent effect of stimulating liquors is to produce an amount of depression corresponding to the excitement momentarily caused by them in the frame. The operative, therefore, who spends his earnings on "drink," not only squanders them on a brutalising luxury, but deprives himself of the power, and consequently of the disposition, to work for more, and hence that idleness, carelessness, and neglect which are the distinctive qualities of the drunkard, and sooner or later compass his ruin.

For the poor wretched children who are reared to this the lowest trade of all, surely even the most insensible and unimaginative must feel the acutest pity. There is, however, this consolation: I have heard of none, with the exception of the more prosperous sewer-hunters and dredgermen, who have remained all their lives at street-finding. Still there remains much to be done by all those who are impressed with a sense of the trust that has been confided to them, in the possession of those endowments which render their lot in this world so much more easy than that of the less lucky street-finders.

Bone-Grubbers and Rag-Gatherers.

The habits of the bone-grubbers and rag-gatherers, the "pure," or dogs'-dung collectors, and the cigar-end finders, are necessarily similar. All lead a wandering, unsettled sort of life, being compelled to be continually on foot, and to travel many miles every day in search of the articles in which they deal. They seldom have any fixed place of abode, and are mostly to be found at night in one or other of the low lodging-houses throughout London. The majority are, moreover, persons who have been brought up to other employments, but who from some failing or mishap have been reduced to such a state of distress that they were obliged to take to their present occupation, and have never after been able to get away from it.

Of the whole class it is considered that there are from 800 to 1000 resident in London, one-half of whom, at the least, sleep in the cheap lodging-houses. The Government returns estimate the number of mendicants' lodging-houses in London to be upwards of 200. Allowing two bone-grubbers and pure-finders to frequent each of these lodging-houses, there will be upwards of 400 availing themselves of such nightly shelters. As many more, I am told, live in garrets and ill-furnished rooms in the lowest neighbourhoods. There is no instance on record of any of the class renting even the smallest house for himself.

Moreover there are in London during the winter a number of persons called "trampers," who employ themselves at that season in street-finding. These people are in the summer country labourers of some sort, but as soon as the harvest and potato-getting and hop-picking are over, and they can find nothing else to do in the country, they come back to London to avail themselves of the shelter of the night asylums or refuges for the destitute (usually called "straw-yards" by the poor), for if they remained in the provinces at that period of the year they would be forced to have recourse to the unions, and as they can only stay one night in each place they would be obliged to travel from ten to fifteen miles per day, to which in the winter they have a strong objection. They come up to London in the winter, not to look for any regular work or employment, but because they know that they can have a nightly shelter, and bread night and morning for nothing, during that season, and can during the day collect bones, rags, &c. As soon as the "straw-yards" close, which is generally about the beginning of April, the "trampers" again start off to the country in small bands of two or three, and without any fixed residence keep wandering about all the summer, sometimes begging their way through the villages and sleeping in the casual wards of the unions, and sometimes, when hard driven, working at hay-making or any other light labour.

Those among the bone-grubbers who do not belong to the regular "trampers" have been either navvies, or men who have not been able to obtain employment at their own business, and have been driven to it by necessity as a means of obtaining a little bread for the time being, and without any intention of pursuing the calling regularly; but, as I have said, when once in the

THE BONE-GRUBBER.

[*From a Daguerreotype by* BEARD.]

THE MUD-LARK.

[*From a Daguerreotype by* BEARD.]

business they cannot leave it, for at least they make certain of getting a few halfpence by it, and their present necessity does not allow them time to look after other employment. There are many of the street-finders who are old men and women, and many very young children who have no other means of living. Since the famine in Ireland vast numbers of that unfortunate people, particularly boys and girls, have been engaged in gathering bones and rags in the streets.

The bone-picker and rag-gatherer may be known at once by the greasy bag which he carries on his back. Usually he has a stick in his hand, and this is armed with a spike or hook, for the purpose of more easily turning over the heaps of ashes or dirt that are thrown out of the houses, and discovering whether they contain anything that is saleable at the rag-and-bottle or marine-store shop. The bone-grubber generally seeks out the narrow back streets, where dust and refuse are cast, or where any dust-bins are accessible. The articles for which he chiefly searches are rags and bones—rags he prefers—but waste metal, such as bits of lead, pewter, copper, brass, or old iron, he prizes above all. Whatever he meets with that he knows to be in any way saleable he puts into the bag at his back. He often finds large lumps of bread which have been thrown out as waste by the servants, and occasionally the housekeepers will give him some bones on which there is a little meat remaining; these constitute the morning meal of most of the class. One of my informants had a large rump of beef bone given to him a few days previous to my seeing him, on which "there was not less than a pound of meat."

The bone-pickers and rag-gatherers are all early risers. They have all their separate beats or districts, and it is most important to them that they should reach their district before any one else of the same class can go over the ground. Some of the beats lie as far as Peckham, Clapham, Hammersmith, Hampstead, Bow, Stratford, and indeed all parts within about five miles of London. In summer time they rise at two in the morning, and sometimes earlier. It is not quite light at this hour—but bones and rags can be discovered before daybreak. The "grubbers" scour all quarters of London, but abound more particularly in the suburbs. In the neighbourhood of Petticoat-lane and Ragfair, however, they are the most numerous on account of the greater quantity of rags which the Jews have to throw out. It usually takes the bone-picker from seven to nine hours to go over his rounds, during which time he travels from 20 to 30 miles with a quarter to a half hundredweight on his back. In the summer he usually reaches home about eleven of the day, and in the winter about one or two. On his return home he proceeds to sort the contents of his bag. He separates the rags from the bones, and these again from the old metal (if he be lucky enough to have found any). He divides the rags into various lots, according as they are white or coloured ; and if he have picked up any pieces of canvas or sacking, he makes these also into a separate parcel. When he has finished the sorting he takes his several lots to the rag-shop or the marine-store dealer, and realizes upon them whatever they may be worth. For the white rags he gets from 2d. to 3d. per pound, according as they are clean or soiled. The white rags are very difficult to be found; they are mostly very dirty, and are therefore sold with the coloured ones at the rate of about 5 lbs. for 2d. The bones are usually sold with the coloured rags at one and the same price. For fragments of canvas or sacking the grubber gets about three-farthings a pound; and old brass, copper, and pewter about 4d. (the marine-store keepers say 5d.), and old iron one farthing per pound, or six pounds for 1d. The bone-grubber thinks he has done an excellent day's work if he can earn 8d.; and some of them, especially the very old and the very young, do not earn more than from 2d. to 3d. a day. To make 10d. a day, at the present price of rags and bones, a man must be remarkably active and strong,—"ay ! and lucky, too," adds my informant. The average amount of earnings, I am told, varies from about 6d. to 8d. per day, or from 3s. to 4s. a week ; and the highest amount that a man, the most brisk and persevering at the business, can by any possibility earn in one week is about 5s., but this can only be accomplished by great good fortune and industry—the usual weekly gains are about half that sum. In bad weather the bone-grubber cannot do so well, because the rags are wet, and then they cannot sell them. The majority pick up bones only in wet weather; those who *do* gather rags during or after rain are obliged to wash and dry them before they can sell them. The state of the shoes of the rag and bone-picker is a very important matter to him; for if he be well shod he can get quickly over the ground; but he is frequently lamed, and unable to make any progress from the blisters and gashes on his feet, occasioned by the want of proper shoes.

Sometimes the bone-grubbers will pick up a stray sixpence or a shilling that has been dropped in the street. "The handkerchief I have round my neck," said one whom I saw, "I picked up with 1s. in the corner. The greatest prize I ever found was the brass cap of the nave of a coach-wheel; and I *did* once find a quarter of a pound of tobacco in Sun-street, Bishopsgate. The best bit of luck of all that I ever had was finding a cheque for 12l. 15s. lying in the gateway of the mourning-coach yard in Titchborne-street, Haymarket. I was going to light my pipe with it, indeed I picked it up for that purpose, and then saw it was a cheque. It was on the London and County Bank, 21, Lombard-street. I took it there, and got 10s. for finding it. I went there in my rags, as I am now, and the cashier stared a bit at me. The cheque was drawn by a Mr. Knibb, and payable to a Mr. Cox. I *did* think I should have got the odd 15s. though."

It has been stated that the average amount of the earnings of the bone-pickers is 6d. per day, or 3s. per week, being 7l. 16s. per annum for each person. It has also been shown that the number of persons engaged in the business may be estimated at about 800; hence the earnings of the entire number will amount to the sum of 20*l*. per day, or 120*l*. per week, which gives 6240*l*. as the annual earnings of the bone-pickers and rag-gatherers of London. It may also be computed that each of the grubbers gathers on an average 20 lbs. weight of bone and rags; and reckoning the bones to constitute three-fourths of the entire weight, we thus find that the gross quantity of these articles gathered by the street-finders in the course of the year, amounts to 3,744,000 lbs. of bones, and 1,240,000 lbs. of rags.

Between the London and St. Katherine's Docks and Rosemary Lane, there is a large district interlaced with narrow lanes, courts, and alleys ramifying into each other in the most intricate and disorderly manner, insomuch that it would be no easy matter for a stranger to work his way through the interminable confusion without the aid of a guide, resident in and well conversant with the locality. The houses are of the poorest description, and seem as if they tumbled into their places at random. Foul channels, huge dust-heaps, and a variety of other unsightly objects, occupy every open space, and dabbling among these are crowds of ragged dirty children who grub and wallow, as if in their native element. None reside in these places but the poorest and most wretched of the population, and, as might almost be expected, this, the cheapest and filthiest locality of London, is the head-quarters of the bone-grubbers and other street-finders. I have ascertained on the best authority, that from the centre of this place, within a circle of a mile in diameter, there dwell not less than 200 persons of this class. In this quarter I found a bone-grubber who gave me the following account of himself:—

"I was born in Liverpool, and when about 14 years of age, my father died. He used to work about the Docks, and I used to run on errands for any person who wanted me. I managed to live by this after my father's death for three or four years. I had a brother older than myself, who went to France to work on the railroads, and when I was about 18 he sent for me, and got me to work with himself on the Paris and Rouen Railway, under McKenzie and Brassy, who had the contract. I worked on the railroads in France for four years, till the disturbance broke out, and then we all got notice to leave the country. I lodged at that time with a countryman, and had 12*l*., which I had saved out of my earnings. This sum I gave to my countryman to keep for me till we got to London, as I did not like to have it about me, for fear I'd lose it. The French people paid our fare from Rouen to Havre by the railway, and there put us on board a steamer to Southampton. There was about 50 of us altogether. When we got to Southampton, we all went before the mayor; we told him about how we had been driven out of France, and he gave us a shilling a piece; he sent some one with us, too, to get us a lodging, and told us to come again the next day. In the morning the mayor gave every one who was able to walk half-a-crown, and for those who were not able he paid their fare to London on the railroad. I had a sore leg at the time, and I came up by the train, and when I gave up my ticket at the station, the gentleman gave me a shilling more. I couldn't find the man I had given my money to, because he had walked up; and I went before the Lord Mayor to ask his advice; he gave me 2*s*. 6*d*. I looked for work everywhere, but could get nothing to do; and when the 2*s*. 6*d*. was all spent, I heard that the man who had my money was on the London and York Railway in the country; however, I couldn't get that far for want of money then; so I went again before the Lord Mayor, and he gave me two more, but told me not to trouble him any further. I told the Lord Mayor about the money, and then he sent an officer with me, who put me into a carriage on the railway. When I got down to where the man was at work, he wouldn't give me a farthing; I had given him the money without any witness bring present, and he said I could do nothing, because it was done in another country. I staid down there more than a week trying to get work on the railroad, but could not. I had no money and was nearly starved, when two or three took pity on me, and made up four or five shillings for me, to take me back again to London. I tried all I could to get something to do, till the money was nearly gone; and then I took to selling lucifers, and the fly-papers that they use in the shops, and little things like that; but I could do no good at this work, there was too many at it before me, and they knew more about it than I did. At last, I got so bad off I didn't know what to do; but seeing a great many about here gathering bones and rags, I thought I'd do so too—a poor fellow must do something. I was advised to do so, and I have been at it ever since. I forgot to tell you that my brother died in France. We had good wages there, four francs a day, or 3*s*. 4*d*. English; I don't make more than 3*d*. or 4*d*. and sometimes 6*d*. a day at bone-picking. I don't go out before daylight to gather anything, because the police takes my bag and throws all I've gathered about the street to see if I have anything stolen in it. I never stole anything in all my life, indeed I'd do anything before I'd steal. Many a night I've slept under an arch of the railway when I hadn't a penny to pay for my bed; but whenever the police find me that way, they make me and the rest get up, and drive us on, and tell us to keep moving. I don't go out on wet days, there's no use in it, as the things won't be bought. I can't wash and dry them, because I'm in a lodging-house. There's a great deal more than a 100 bone-pickers about here, men, women, and children. The Jews in this lane and up in Petticoat-lane give a good deal of victuals away on the Saturday. They sometimes call one of us in from the street to light the fire for them, or take off the kettle, as they must not do anything themselves on the Sabbath; and then they put some food on the footpath, and throw rags and bones into the street for us, because they must not hand anything to us. There are some about here who get a couple of shillings' worth of goods, and go on board the ships in the Docks, and exchange them for bones and bits of old canvas among the sailors; I'd buy and do so too if I only had the money, but can't get it. The summer is the worst time for us, the winter is much better, for there is more meat used in winter, and then there are more bones." (Others say differently.) "I intend to go to the country this season, and try to get something to do at the hay-making and harvest. I make about 2s. 6d. a week, and the way I manage is this: sometimes I get a piece of bread about 12 o'clock, and I make my breakfast of that and cold water; very seldom I have any dinner,—unless I earn 6d. I can't get any,—and then I have a basin of nice soup, or a penn'orth of plum-pudding and a couple of baked 'tatoes. At night I get $\frac{1}{4}d.$ worth of coffee, $\frac{1}{2}d.$ worth of sugar, and $1\frac{1}{4}d.$ worth of bread, and then I have 2d. a night left for my lodging; I always try to manage that, for I'd do anything sooner than stop out all night. I'm always happy the day when I make 4d., for then I know I won't have to sleep in the street. The winter before last, there was a straw-yard down in Black Jack's-alley, where we used to go after six o'clock in the evening, and get $\frac{1}{2}$ lb. of bread, and another $\frac{1}{2}$ lb. in the morning, and then we'd gather what we could in the daytime and buy victuals with what we got for it. We were well off then, but the straw-yard wasn't open at all last winter. There used to be 300 of us in there of a night, a great many of the dock-labourers and their families were there, for no work was to be got in the docks; so they weren't able to pay rent, and were obliged to go in. I've lost my health since I took to bone-picking, through the wet and cold in the winter, for I've scarcely any clothes, and the wet gets to my feet through the old shoes; this caused me last winter to be nine weeks in the hospital of the Whitechapel workhouse."

The narrator of this tale seemed so dejected and broken in spirit, that it was with difficulty his story was elicited from him. He was evidently labouring under incipient consumption. I have every reason to believe that he made a truthful statement,—indeed, he did not appear to me to have sufficient intellect to invent a falsehood. It is a curious fact, indeed, with reference to the London street-finders generally, that they seem to possess less rational power than any other class. They appear utterly incapable of trading even in the most trifling commodities, probably from the fact that buying articles for the purpose of selling them at a profit, requires an exercise of the mind to which they feel themselves incapable. Begging, too, requires some ingenuity or tact, in order to move the sympathies of the well-to-do, and the street-finders being incompetent for this, they work on day after day as long as they are able to crawl about in pursuit of their unprofitable calling. This cannot be fairly said of the younger members of this class, who are sent into the streets by their parents, and many of whom are afterwards able to find some more reputable and more lucrative employment. As a body of people, however, young and old, they mostly exhibit the same stupid, half-witted appearance.

To show how bone-grubbers occasionally manage to obtain shelter during the night, the following incident may not be out of place. A few mornings past I accidentally encountered one of this class in a narrow back lane; his ragged coat—the colour of the rubbish among which he toiled—was greased over, probably with the fat of the bones he gathered, and being mixed with the dust it seemed as if the man were covered with bird-lime. His shoes—torn and tied on his feet with pieces of cord —had doubtlessly been picked out of some dust-bin, while his greasy bag and stick unmistakably announced his calling. Desirous of obtaining all the information possible on this subject, I asked him a few questions, took his address, which he gave without hesitation, and bade him call on me in the evening. At the time appointed, however, he did not appear; on the following day therefore I made way to the address he had given, and on reaching the spot I was astonished to find the house in which he had said he lived was uninhabited. A padlock was on the door, the boards of which were parting with age. There was not a whole pane of glass in any of the windows, and the frames of many of them were shattered or demolished. Some persons in the neighbourhood, noticing me eyeing the place, asked whom I wanted. On my telling the man's name, which it appeared he had not dreamt of disguising, I was informed that he had left the day before, saying he had met the landlord in the morning (for such it turned out he had fancied me to be), and that the gentleman had wanted him to come to his house, but he was afraid to go lest he should be sent to prison for breaking into the place. I found, on inspection, that the premises, though locked up, could be entered by the rear, one of the window-frames having been removed, so that admission could be obtained through the aperture. Availing myself of the same mode of ingress, I proceeded to examine the premises. Nothing could well be more dismal or dreary than the interior. The floors were rotting with damp and mildew, especially near the windows, where the wet found easy entrance. The walls were even slimy and discoloured, and everything bore the appearance of desolation. In one corner was strewn a bundle of dirty straw, which doubtlessly had served the bone-grubber for a bed, while scattered about the floor were pieces of bones, and small fragments of dirty rags, sufficient to indicate the calling of the late inmate. He had had but little difficulty in removing his property, seeing that it consisted solely of his bag and his stick.

The following paragraph concerning the chiffoniers or rag-gatherers of Paris appeared in the London journals a few weeks since:—

"The fraternal association of rag-gatherers (chiffoniers) gave a grand banquet on Saturday last (21st of June). It took place at a public-house called the *Pot Tricolore*, near the *Barrière de Fontainbleau*, which is frequented by the rag-gathering fraternity. In this house there are three rooms, each of which is specially devoted to the use of different classes of rag-gatherers: one, the least dirty, is called the 'Chamber of Peers,' and is occupied by the first class—that is, those who possess a basket in a good state, and a crook ornamented with copper; the second, called the 'Chamber of Deputies,' belonging to the second class, is much less comfortable, and those who attend it have baskets and crooks not of first-rate quality; the third room is in a dilapidated condition, and is frequented by the lowest class of rag-gatherers who have no basket or crook, and who place what they find in the streets in a piece of sackcloth. They call themselves the '*Réunion des Vrais Prolétaires.*' The name of each room is written in chalk above the door; and generally such strict etiquette is observed among the rag-gatherers that no one goes into the apartment not occupied by his own class. At Saturday's banquet, however, all distinctions of rank were laid aside, and delegates of each class united fraternally. The president was the oldest rag-gatherer in Paris; his age is 88, and he is called 'the Emperor.' The banquet consisted of a sort of *olla podrida*, which the master of the establishment pompously called *gibelotte*, though of what animal it was composed it was impossible to say. It was served up in huge earthen dishes, and before it was allowed to be touched payment was demanded and obtained; the other articles were also paid for as soon as they were brought in; and a deposit was exacted as a security for the plates, knives, and forks. The wine, or what did duty as such, was contained in an earthen pot called the *Petit Père Noir*, and was filled from a gigantic vessel named *Le Moricaud*. The dinner was concluded by each guest taking a small glass of brandy. Business was then proceeded to. It consisted in the reading and adoption of the statutes of the association, followed by the drinking of numerous toasts to the president, to the prosperity of rag-gathering, to the union of rag-gatherers, &c. A collection amounting to 6f. 75c. was raised for sick members of the fraternity. The guests then dispersed; but several of them remained at the counter until they had consumed in brandy the amount deposited as security for the crockery, knives, and forks."

OF THE "PURE"-FINDERS.

Dogs'-dung is called "Pure," from its cleansing and purifying properties.

The name of "Pure-finders," however, has been applied to the men engaged in collecting dogs'-dung from the public streets only, within the last 20 or 30 years. Previous to this period there appears to have been no men engaged in the business, old women alone gathered the substance, and they were known by the name of "bunters," which signifies properly gatherers of rags; and thus plainly intimates that the rag-gatherers originally added the collecting of "Pure" to their original and proper vocation. Hence it appears that the bone-grubbers, rag-gatherers, and pure-finders, constituted formerly but one class of people, and even now they have, as I have stated, kindred characteristics.

The pure-finders meet with a ready market for all the dogs'-dung they are able to collect, at the numerous tanyards in Bermondsey, where they sell it by the stable-bucket full, and get from 8d. to 10d. per bucket, and sometimes 1s. and 1s. 2d. for it, according to its quality. The "dry limy-looking sort" fetches the highest price at some yards, as it is found to possess more of the alkaline, or purifying properties; but others are found to prefer the dark moist quality. Strange as it may appear, the preference for a particular kind has suggested to the finders of Pure the idea of adulterating it to a very considerable extent; this is effected by means of mortar broken away from old walls, and mixed up with the whole mass, which it closely resembles; in some cases, however, the mortar is rolled into small balls similar to those found. Hence it would appear, that there is no business or trade, however insignificant or contemptible, without its own peculiar and appropriate tricks.

The pure-finders are in their habits and mode of proceeding nearly similar to the bone-grubbers. Many of the pure-finders are, however, better in circumstances, the men especially, as they earn more money. They are also, to a certain extent, a better educated class. Some of the regular collectors of this substance have been mechanics, and others small tradesmen, who have been reduced. Those pure-finders who have "a good connection," and have been granted permission to cleanse some kennels, obtain a very fair living at the business, earning from 10s. to 15s. a week. These, however, are very few; the majority have to seek the article in the streets, and by such means they can obtain only from 6s. to 10s. a week. The average weekly earnings of this class are thought to be about 7s. 6d.

From all the inquiries I have made on this subject, I have found that there cannot be less than from 200 to 300 persons constantly engaged solely in this business. There are about 30 tanyards large and small in Bermondsey, and these all have their regular Pure collectors from whom they obtain the article. Leomont and Roberts's, Bavingtons', Beech's, Murrell's, Cheeseman's, Powell's, Jones's, Jourdans', Kent's, Moorcroft's, and Davis's, are among the largest establishments, and some idea of the amount of business done in some of these yards may be formed from the fact, that the proprietors severally employ from 300 to 500 tanners. At Leomont and Roberts's there are 23 regular street-finders, who supply them with pure, but this is a large establishment, and the number supplying them is considered far beyond the average quantity; moreover, Messrs. Leomont and Roberts do more business in the particular branch of tanning in which the article is principally used, viz., in dressing the leather for book-covers, kid-gloves, and a variety of other articles. Some of the other tanyards, especially the smaller ones, take the substance only as they happen to want it, and others again employ but a limited number of hands. If, therefore, we strike an average, and reduce the number supplying each of the several yards to eight, we shall have 240 persons regularly engaged in the business: besides these, it may be said that numbers of the starving and destitute Irish have taken to picking up the material, but not knowing where to sell it, or how to dispose of it, they part with it for 2*d*. or 3*d*. the pail-full to the regular purveyors of it to the tanyards, who of course make a considerable profit by the transaction. The children of the poor Irish are usually employed in this manner, but they also pick up rags and bones, and anything else which may fall in their way.

I have stated that some of the pure-finders, especially the men, earn a considerable sum of money per week; their gains are sometimes as much as 15*s*.; indeed I am assured that seven years ago, when they got from 3*s*. to 4*s*. per pail for the pure, that many of them would not exchange their position with that of the best paid mechanic in London. Now, however, the case is altered, for there are twenty now at the business for every one who followed it then; hence each collects so much the less in quantity, and, moreover, from the competition gets so much less for the article. Some of the collectors at present do not earn 3*s*. per week, but these are mostly old women who are feeble and unable to get over the ground quickly; others make 5*s*. and 6*s*. in the course of the week, while the most active and those who clean out the kennels of the dog fanciers may occasionally make 9*s*. and 10*s*. and even 15*s*. a week still, but this is of very rare occurrence. Allowing the finders, one with the other, to earn on an average 5*s*. per week, it would give the annual earnings of each to be 13*l*., while the income of the whole 200 would amount to 50*l*. a week, or 2600*l*. per annum. The kennel "pure" is not much valued, indeed many of the tanners will not even buy it, the reason is that the dogs of the "fanciers" are fed on almost anything, to save expense; the kennel cleaners consequently take the precaution of mixing it with what is found in the street, previous to offering it for sale.

The pure-finder may at once be distinguished from the bone-grubber and rag-gatherer; the latter, as I have before mentioned, carries a bag, and usually a stick armed with a spike, while he is most frequently to be met with in back streets, narrow lanes, yards and other places, where dust and rubbish are likely to be thrown out from the adjacent houses. The pure-finder, on the contrary, is often found in the open streets, as dogs wander where they like. The pure-finders always carry a handle basket, generally with a cover, to hide the contents, and have their right hand covered with a black leather glove; many of them, however, dispense with the glove, as they say it is much easier to wash their hands than to keep the glove fit for use. The women generally have a large pocket for the reception of such rags as they may chance to fall in with, but they pick up those only of the very best quality, and will not go out of their way to search even for them. Thus equipped they may be seen pursuing their avocation in almost every street in and about London, excepting such streets as are now cleansed by the "street orderlies," of whom the pure-finders grievously complain, as being an unwarrantable interference with the privileges of their class.

The pure collected is used by leather-dressers and tanners, and more especially by those engaged in the manufacture of morocco and kid leather from the skins of old and young goats, of which skins great numbers are imported, and of the roans and lambskins which are the sham morocco and kids of the "slop" leather trade, and are used by the better class of shoemakers, bookbinders, and glovers, for the inferior requirements of their business. Pure is also used by tanners, as is pigeon's dung, for the tanning of the thinner kinds of leather, such as calf-skins, for which purpose it is placed in pits with an admixture of lime and bark.

In the manufacture of moroccos and roans the pure is rubbed by the hands of the workman into the skin he is dressing. This is done to "purify" the leather, I was told by an intelligent leather-dresser, and from that term the word "pure" has originated. The dung has astringent as well as highly alkaline, or, to use the expression of my informant, "scouring," qualities. When the pure has been rubbed into the flesh and grain of the skin (the "flesh" being originally the interior, and the "grain" the exterior part of the cuticle), and the skin, thus purified, has been hung up to be dried, the dung removes, as it were, all such moisture as, if allowed to remain, would tend to make the leather unsound or imperfectly dressed. This imperfect dressing, moreover, gives a disagreeable smell to the leather—and leather-buyers often use both nose and tongue in making their purchases—and would consequently prevent that agreeable odour being imparted to the skin which is found in some kinds of morocco and kid. The peculiar odour of the Russia leather, so agreeable in the libraries of the rich, is derived from the bark of young birch trees. It is now manufactured in Bermondsey.

Among the morocco manufacturers, especially among the old operatives, there is often a scarcity of employment, and they then dress a few roans, which they hawk to the cheap warehouses, or sell to the wholesale shoemakers on their own account. These men usually reside in small garrets in the poorer parts of Bermondsey, and carry on their trade in their own rooms, using and keeping the pure there; hence the "homes" of these poor men are peculiarly uncomfortable, if not unhealthy. Some of these poor fellows or their wives collect the pure themselves, often starting at daylight for the purpose; they more frequently, however, buy it of a regular finder.

The number of pure-finders I heard estimated, by a man well acquainted with the tanning and other departments of the leather trade, at from 200 to 250. The finders, I was informed by the same person, collected about a pail-full a day, clearing 6*s*. a week in the summer—1*s*. and 1*s*. 2*d*. being the charge for a pail-full; in the short days of winter, however, and in bad weather, they could not collect five pail-fulls in a week.

In the wretched locality already referred to as lying between the Docks and Rosemary-lane, redolent of filth and pregnant with pestilential diseases, and whither all the outcasts of the metropolitan population seem to be drawn, either in the hope of finding fitting associates and companions in their wretchedness (for there is doubtlessly something attractive and agreeable to them in such companionship), or else for the purpose of hiding themselves and their shifts and struggles for existence from the world,—in this dismal quarter, and branching from one of the many narrow lanes which interlace it, there is a little court with about half-a-dozen houses of the very smallest dimensions, consisting of merely two rooms, one over the other. Here in one of the upper rooms (the lower one of the same house being occupied by another family and apparently *filled* with little ragged children), I discerned, after considerable difficulty, an old woman, a Pure-finder. When I opened the door the little light that struggled through the small window, the many broken panes of which were stuffed with old rags, was not sufficient to enable me to perceive who or what was in the room. After a short time, however, I began to make out an old chair standing near the fire-place, and then to discover a poor old woman resembling a bundle of rags and filth stretched on some dirty straw in the corner of the apartment. The place was bare and almost naked. There was nothing in it except a couple of old tin kettles and a basket, and some broken crockeryware in the recess of the window. To my astonishment I found this wretched creature to be, to a certain extent, a "superior" woman; she could read and write well, spoke correctly, and appeared to have been a person of natural good sense, though broken up with age, want, and infirmity, so that she was characterized by all that dull and hardened stupidity of manner which I have noticed in the class. She made the following statement:—

"I am about 60 years of age. My father was a milkman, and very well off; he had a barn and a great many cows. I was kept at school till I was thirteen or fourteen years of age; about that time my father died, and then I was taken home to help my mother in the business. After a while things went wrong; the cows began to die, and mother, alleging she could not manage the business herself, married again. I soon found out the difference. Glad to get away, anywhere out of the house, I married a sailor, and was very comfortable with him for some years; as he made short voyages, and was often at home, and always left me half his pay. At last he was pressed, when at home with me, and sent away; I forget now where he was sent to, but I never saw him from that day to this. The only thing I know is that some sailors came to me four or five years after, and told me that he deserted from the ship in which he had gone out, and got on board the *Neptune*, East Indiaman, bound for Bombay, where he acted as boatswain's mate; some little time afterwards, he had got intoxicated while the ship was lying in harbour, and, going down the side to get into a bumboat, and buy more drink, he had fallen overboard and was drowned. I got some money that was due to him from the India House, and, after that was all gone, I went into service, in the Mile-end Road. There I stayed for several years, till I met my second husband, who was bred to the water, too, but as a waterman on the river. We did very well together for a long time, till he lost his health. He became paralyzed like, and was deprived of the use of all one side, and nearly lost the sight of one of his eyes; this was not very conspicuous at first, but when we came to get pinched, and to be badly off, then any one might have seen that there was something the matter with his eye. Then we parted with everything we had in the world; and, at last, when we had no other means of living left, we were advised to take to gathering 'Pure.' At first I couldn't endure the business; I couldn't bear to eat a morsel, and I was obliged to discontinue it for a long time. My husband kept at it though, for he could do *that* well enough, only he couldn't walk as fast as he ought. He couldn't lift his hands as high as his head, but he managed to work under him, and so put the Pure in the basket. When I saw that he, poor fellow, couldn't make enough to keep us both, I took heart and went out again, and used to gather more than he did; that's fifteen years ago now; the times were good then, and we used to do very well. If we only gathered a pail-full in the day, we could live very well; but we could do much more than that, for there wasn't near so many at the business then, and the Pure was easier to be had. For my part I can't tell where all the poor creatures have come from of late years; the world seems growing worse and worse every day. They have pulled down the price of Pure, that's certain; but the poor things must do something, they can't starve while there's anything to be got. Why, no later than six or seven years ago, it was as high as 3s. 6d. and 4s. a pail-full, and a ready sale for as much of it as you could get; but now you can only get 1s. and in some places 1s. 2d. a pail-full; and, as I said before, there are so many at it, that there is not much left for a poor old creature like me to find. The men that are strong and smart get the most, of course, and some of them do very well, at least they manage to live. Six years ago, my husband complained that he was ill, in the evening, and lay down in the bed—we lived in Whitechapel then—he took a fit of coughing, and was smothered in his own blood. O dear" (the poor old soul here ejaculated), "what troubles I have gone through! I had eight children at one time, and there is not one of them alive now. My daughter lived to 30 years of age, and then she died in childbirth, and, since then, I have had nobody in the wide world to care for me—none but myself, all alone as I am. After my husband's death I couldn't do much, and all my things went away, one by one, until I've nothing but bare walls, and that's the reason why I was vexed at first at your coming in, sir. I was yesterday out all day, and went round Aldgate, Whitechapel, St. George's East, Stepney, Bow, and Bromley, and then came home; after that, I went over to Bermondsey, and there I got only 6d. for my pains. To-day I wasn't out at all; I wasn't well; I had a bad headache, and I'm so much afraid of the fevers that are all about here—though I don't know why I should be afraid of them—I was lying down, when you came, to get rid of my pains. There's such a dizziness in my head now, I feel as if it didn't belong to me. No, I have earned no money to-day. I have had a piece of dried bread that I steeped in water to eat. I haven't eat anything else to-day; but, pray, sir, don't tell anybody of it. I could never bear the thought of going into the 'great house' [workhouse]; I'm so used to the air, that I'd sooner die in the street, as many I know have done. I've known several of our people, who have sat down in the street with their basket alongside them, and died. I knew one not long ago, who took ill just as she was stooping down to gather up the Pure, and fell on her face; she was taken to the London Hospital, and died at three o'clock in the morning. I'd sooner die like them than be deprived of my liberty, and be prevented from going about where I liked. No, I'll never go into the workhouse; my master is kind to me" [the tanner whom she supplies]. "When I'm ill, he sometimes gives me a sixpence; but there's one gentleman has done us great harm, by forcing so many into the business. He's a poor-law guardian, and when any poor person applies for relief, he tells them to go and gather Pure, and that he'll buy it of them (for he's in the line), and so the parish, you see, don't have to give anything, and that's one way that so many have come into the trade of late, that the likes of me can do little or no good at it. Almost every one I've ever known engaged at Pure-finding were people who were better off once. I knew a man who went by the name of Brown, who picked up Pure for years before I went to it; he was a very quiet man; he used to lodge in Blue Anchor-yard, and seldom used to speak to anybody. We two used to talk together sometimes, but never much. One morning he was found dead in his bed; it was of a Tuesday morning, and he was buried about 12 o'clock on the Friday following. About 6 o'clock on that afternoon, three or four gentlemen came searching all through this place, looking for a man named Brown, and offering a reward to any who would find him out; there was a whole crowd about them when I came up. One of the gentlemen said that the man they wanted had lost the first finger of his right hand, and then I knew that it was the man that had been buried only that morning. Would you believe it, Mr. Brown was a real gentleman all the time, and had a large estate, of I don't know how many thousand pounds, just left him, and the lawyers had advertised and searched everywhere for him, but never found him, you may say, till he was dead. We discovered that his name was not Brown; he had only taken that name to hide his real one, which, of course, he did not want any one to know. I've often thought of him, poor man, and all the misery he might have been spared, if the good news had only come a year or two sooner."

Another informant, a Pure-collector, was originally in the Manchester cotton trade, and held a lucrative situation in a large country establishment. His salary one year exceeded 250*l*., and his regular income was 150*l*. "This," he says, "I lost through drink and neglect. My master was exceedingly kind to me, and has even assisted me since I left his employ. He bore with me patiently for many years, but the love of drink was so strong upon me that it was impossible for him to keep me any longer." He has often been drunk, he tells me, for three months together; and he is now so reduced that he is ashamed to be seen. When at his master's it was his duty to carve and help the other assistants belonging to the establishment, and his hand used to shake so violently that he has been ashamed to lift the gravy spoon.

At breakfast he has frequently waited till all the young men had left the table before he ventured to taste his tea; and immediately, when he was alone, he has bent his head down to his cup to drink, being utterly incapable of raising it to his lips. He says he is a living example of the degrading influence of drink. All his friends have deserted him. He has suffered enough, he tells me, to make him give it up. He earned the week before I saw him 5*s*. 2*d*.; and the week before that, 6*s*.

Before leaving me I prevailed upon the man to "take the pledge." This is now eighteen months ago, and I have not seen him since.

OF THE CIGAR-END FINDERS.

THERE are, strictly speaking, none who make a living by picking up the ends of cigars thrown away as useless by the smokers in the streets, but there are very many who employ themselves from time to time in collecting them. Almost all the street-finders, when they meet with such things, pick them up, and keep them in a pocket set apart for that purpose. The men allow the ends to accumulate till they amount to two or three pounds weight, and then some dispose of them to a person residing in the neighbourhood of Rosemary-lane, who buys them all up at from 6*d*. to 10*d*. per pound, according to their length and quality. The long ends are considered the best, as I am told there is more sound tobacco in them, uninjured by the moisture of the mouth. The children of the poor Irish, in particular, scour Ratcliff-highway, the Commercial-road, Mile-end-road, and all the leading thoroughfares of the East, and every place where cigar smokers are likely to take an evening's promenade. The quantity that each of them collects is very trifling indeed—perhaps not more than a handful during a morning's search. I am informed, by an intelligent man living in the midst of them, that these children go out in the morning not only to gather cigar-ends, but to pick up out of dust bins, and from amongst rubbish in the streets, the smallest scraps and crusts of bread, no matter how hard or filthy they may be. These they put into a little bag which they carry for the purpose, and, after they have gone their rounds and collected whatever they can, they take the cigar-ends to the man who buys them—sometimes getting not more than a halfpenny or a penny for their morning's collection. With this they buy a halfpenny or a pennyworth of oatmeal, which they mix up with a large quantity of water, and after washing and steeping the hard and dirty crusts, they put them into the pot or kettle and boil all together. Of this mass the whole family partake, and it often constitutes all the food they taste in the course of the day. I have often seen the bone-grubbers eat the black and soddened crusts they have picked up out of the gutter.

It would, indeed, be a hopeless task to make any attempt to get at the number of persons who occasionally or otherwise pick up cigar-ends with the view of selling them again. For this purpose almost all who ransack the streets of London for a living may be computed as belonging to the class; and to these should be added the children of the thousands of destitute Irish who have inundated the metropolis within the last few years, and who are to be found huddled together in all the low neighbourhoods in every suburb of the City. What quantity is collected, or the amount of money obtained for the ends, there are no means of ascertaining.

Let us, however, make a conjecture. There are in round numbers 300,000 inhabited houses in the metropolis; and allowing the married people living in apartments to be equal in number to the unmarried "housekeepers," we may compute that the number of families in London is about the same as the inhabited houses. Assuming one young or old gentleman in every ten of these families to smoke one cigar per diem in the public thoroughfares, we have 30,000 cigar-ends daily, or 210,000 weekly cast away in the London streets. Now, reckoning 150 cigars to go to a pound, we may assume that each end so cast away weighs about the thousandth part of a pound; consequently the gross weight of the ends flung into the gutter will, in the course of the week, amount to about 2 cwt.; and calculating that only a sixth part of these are picked up by the finders, it follows that there is very nearly a ton of refuse tobacco collected annually in the metropolitan thoroughfares.

The aristocratic quarters of the City and the vicinity of theatres and casinos are the best for the cigar-end finders. In the Strand, Regent-street, and the more fashionable thoroughfares, I am told, there are many ends picked up; but even in these places they do not exclusively furnish a means of living to any of the finders. All the collectors sell them to some other person, who acts as middle-man in the business. How he disposes of the ends is unknown, but it is supposed that they are resold to some of the large manufacturers of cigars, and go to form the component part of a new stock of the "best Havannahs;" or, in other words, they are worked up again to be again cast away, and again collected by the finders, and so on perhaps, till the millennium comes. Some suppose them to be cut up and mixed with the common smoking tobacco, and others that they are used in making snuff. There are, I am assured, five persons residing in different parts of London, who are known to purchase the cigar-ends.

In Naples the sale of cigar-ends is a regular street-traffic, the street-seller carrying them in a small box suspended round the neck. In Paris, also, *le Remasseur de Cigares* is a well-known occupation: the "ends" thus collected are sold as cheap tobacco to the poor. In the low lodging-houses of London the ends, when dried, are cut up, and frequently vended by the finders to such of their fellow-lodgers as are anxious to enjoy their pipe at the cheapest possible rate.

OF THE OLD WOOD GATHERERS.

ALL that has been said of the cigar-end finders may, in a great measure, apply to the wood-gatherers. No one can make a living exclusively by the gathering of wood, and those who *do* gather it, gather as well rags, bones, and bits of metal. They gather it, indeed, as an adjunct to their other findings, on the principle that "every little helps." Those, however, who most frequently look for wood are the very old and feeble, and the very young, who are both unable to travel far, or to carry a heavy burden, and they may occasionally be seen crawling about in the neighbourhood of any new buildings in the course of construction, or old ones in the course of demolition, and picking up small odds and ends of wood and chips swept out amongst dirt and shavings; these they deposit in a bag or basket which they carry for that purpose. Should there happen to be what they call "pulling-down work," that is, taking down old houses, or palings, the place is immediately beset by a number of wood-gatherers, young and old, and in general all the poor people of the locality join with them, to obtain their share of the spoil. What the poor get they take home and burn, but the wood-gatherers sell all they procure for some small trifle.

Some short time ago a portion of the wood-pavement in the city was being removed; a large number of the old blocks, which were much worn and of no further use, were thrown aside, and became the perquisite of the wood-gatherers. During the repair of the street, the spot was constantly besieged by a motley mob of men, women, and children, who, in many instances, struggled and fought for the wood rejected as worthless. This wood they either sold for a trifle as they got it, or took home and split, and made into bundles for sale as firewood.

All the mudlarks (of whom I shall treat specially) pick up wood and chips on the bank of the river; these they sell to poor people in their own neighbourhood. They sometimes "find" large pieces of a greater weight than they can carry; in such cases they get some other mudlark to help them with the load, and the two "go halves" in the produce. The only parties among the street-finders who do not pick up wood are the Pure-collectors and the sewer-hunters, or, as they call themselves, shore-workers, both of whom pass it by as of no value.

It is impossible to estimate the quantity of wood which is thus gathered, or what the amount may be which the collector realizes in the course of the year.

Of the Dredgers, or River Finders.

The dredgermen of the Thames, or river finders, naturally occupy the same place with reference to the street-finders, as the purlmen or river beer-sellers do to those who get their living by selling in the streets. It would be in itself a curious inquiry to trace the origin of the manifold occupations in which men are found to be engaged in the present day, and to note how promptly every circumstance and occurrence was laid hold of, as it happened to arise, which appeared to have any tendency to open up a new occupation, and to mark the gradual progress, till it became a regularly-established employment, followed by a separate class of people, fenced round by rules and customs of their own, and who at length grew to be both in their habits and peculiarities plainly distinct from the other classes among whom they chanced to be located.

There has been no historian among the dredgers of the Thames to record the commencement of the business; and the utmost that any of the river-finders can tell is that his father had been a dredger, and so had his father before him, and that *that's* the reason why they are dredgers also. But no such people as dredgers were known on the Thames in remote days; and before London had become an important trading port, where nothing was likely to be got for the searching, it is not probable that people would have been induced to search. In those days, the only things searched for in the river were the bodies of persons drowned, accidentally or otherwise. For this purpose, the Thames fishermen of all others, appeared to be the best adapted. They were on the spot at all times, and had various sorts of tackle, such as nets, lines, hooks, &c. The fishermen well understood everything connected with the river, such as the various sets of the tide, and the nature of the bottom, and they were therefore on such occasions invariably applied to for these purposes.

It is known to all who remember anything of Old London Bridge, that at certain times of the tide, in consequence of the velocity with which the water rushed through the narrow apertures which the arches then afforded for its passage, to bring a boat in safety through the bridge was a feat to be attempted only by the skilful and experienced. This feat was known as "shooting" London Bridge; and it was no unusual thing for accidents to happen even to the most expert. In fact, numerous accidents occurred at this bridge, and at such times valuable articles were sometimes lost, for which high rewards were offered to the finder. Here again the fishermen came into requisition, the small drag-net, which they used while rowing, offering itself for the purpose; for, by fixing an iron frame round the mouth of the drag-net, this part of it, from its specific gravity, sunk first to the bottom, and consequently scraped along as they pulled forward, collecting into the net everything that came in its way; when it was nearly filled, which the rower always knew by the weight, it was hauled up to the surface, its contents examined, and the object lost generally recovered.

It is thus apparent that the fishermen of the Thames were the men originally employed as dredgermen; though casually, indeed, at first, and according as circumstances occurred requiring their services. By degrees, however, as the commerce of the river increased, and a greater number of articles fell overboard from the shipping, they came to be more frequently called into requisition, and so they were naturally led to adopt the dredging as part and parcel of their business. Thus it remains to the present day.

The fishermen all serve a regular apprenticeship, as they say themselves, "duly and truly" for seven years. During the time of their apprenticeship they are (or rather, in former times they *were*) obliged to sleep in their master's boat at night to take care of his property, and were subject to many other curious regulations, which are foreign to this subject.

I have said that the fishermen of the Thames to the present day unite the dredging to their proper calling. By this I mean that they employ themselves in fishing during the summer and autumn, either from Barking Creek downwards, or from Chelsea Reach upwards, catching dabs, flounders, eels, and other sorts of fish for the London markets. But in winter when the days are short and cold, and the weather stormy, they prefer stopping at home, and dredging the bed of the river for anything they may chance to find. There are others, however, who have started wholly in the dredging line, there being no hindrance or impediment to any one doing so, nor any licence required for the purpose : these dredge the river winter and summer alike, and are, in fact, the only real dredgermen of the present day living solely by that occupation.

There are in all about 100 dredgermen at work on the river, and these are located as follows :—

	Dredgermen.
From Putney to Vauxhall there are	20
From Vauxhall to London-bridge	40
From London-bridge to Deptford	20
And from Deptford to Gravesend	20
	100

All these reside, in general, on the south side of the Thames, the two places most frequented by them being Lambeth and Rotherhithe. They do not, however, confine themselves to the neighbourhoods wherein they reside, but extend their operations to all parts of the river, where it is likely that they may pick up anything; and it is perfectly marvellous with what rapidity the intelligence of any accident calculated to afford them employment is spread among them; for should a loaded coal barge be sunk over night, by daylight the next morning every dredgerman would be sure to be upon the spot, prepared to collect what he could from the wreck at the bottom of the river.

The boats of the dredgermen are of a peculiar shape. They have no stern, but are the same fore and aft. They are called Peter boats, but not one of the men with whom I spoke had the least idea as to the origin of the name. These boats are to be had at almost all prices, according to their condition and age—from 30s. to 20l. The boats used by the fishermen dredgermen are decidedly the most valuable. One with the other, perhaps the whole may average 10l. each ; and this sum will give 1000l. as the value of the entire number. A complete set of tackle, including drags, will cost 2l., which comes to 200l. for all hands; and thus we have the sum of 1200l. as the amount of capital invested in the dredging of the Thames.

It is by no means an easy matter to form any estimate of the earnings of the dredgermen, as they are a matter of mere chance. In former years, when Indiamen and all the foreign shipping lay in the river, the river finders were in the habit of doing a good business, not only in their own line, through the greater quantities of rope, bones, and other things which then were thrown or fell overboard, but they also contrived to smuggle ashore great quantities of tobacco, tea, spirits, and other contraband articles, and thought it a bad day's work when they did not earn a pound independent of their dredging. An old dredger told me he had often in those days made 5l. before breakfast time. After the excavation of the various docks, and after the larger shipping had departed from the river, the finders were obliged to content themselves with the chances of mere dredging; and even then, I am informed, they were in the habit of earning one week with another throughout the year, about 25s. per week, each, or 6500l. per annum among all. Latterly, however, the earnings of these men have greatly fallen off, especially in the summer, for then they cannot get so good a price for the coal they find as in the winter—6d. per bushel being the summer price; and, as they consider three bushels a good day's work, their earnings at this period of the year amount only to 1s. 6d. per day, excepting when they happen to pick up some bones or pieces of metal, or to find a dead body for which there is a reward. In the winter, however, the dredgermen can readily get 1s. per bushel for all the coals they find; and far more coals are to be found then than in summer, for there are more colliers in the river, and far more accidents at that season. Coal barges are often sunk in the winter, and on such occasions they make a good harvest. Moreover there is the finding of bodies, for which they not only get the reward, but 5s., which they call inquest money; together with many other chances, such as the finding of money and valuables among the rubbish they bring up from the bottom; but as the last-mentioned are accidents happening throughout the year, I am inclined to think that they have understated the amount which they are in the habit of realizing even in the summer.

The dredgers, as a class, may be said to be altogether uneducated, not half a dozen out of the whole number being able to read their own name, and only one or two to write it; this select few are considered by the rest as perfect prodigies. " Lor' bless you!" said one, " I on'y wish you'd 'ear Bill S—— read; I on'y jist wish you'd 'ear him. Why that ere Bill can read faster nor a dog can trot. And, what's more, I seed him write an ole letter hisself, ev'ry word on it! What do you think o' that now ?" The ignorance of the dredgermen may be accounted for by the men taking so early to the water; the bustle and excitement of the river being far more attractive to them than the routine of a school. Almost as soon as they are able to do anything, the dredgermen's boys are taken by their fathers afloat to assist in picking out the coals, bones, and other things of any use, from the midst of the rubbish brought up in their drag-nets; or else the lads are sent on board as assistants to one or other of the fishermen during their fishing voyages. When once engaged in this way it has been found impossible afterwards to keep the youths from the water; and if they have learned anything previously they very soon forget it.

It might be expected that the dredgers, in a manner depending on chance for their livelihood, and leading a restless sort of life on the water, would closely resemble the costermongers in their habits; but it is far otherwise. There can be no two classes more dissimilar, except in their hatred of restraint. The dredgers are sober and steady; gambling is unknown amongst them; and they are, to an extraordinary degree, laborious, persevering, and patient. They are in general men of short stature, but square built, strong, and capable of enduring great fatigue, and have a silent and thoughtful look. Being almost always alone, and studying how they may best succeed in finding what they seek, marking the various sets of the tide, and the direction in which things falling into the water at a particular place must necessarily be carried, they become the very opposite to the other river people, especially to the watermen, who are brawling and clamorous, and delight in continually " chaffing" each other. In consequence of the sober and industrious habits of the dredgermen their homes are, as they say, " pretty fair" for working men, though there is nothing very luxurious to be found in them, nor indeed anything beyond what is absolutely necessary. After their day's work, especially if they have "done well," these men smoke a pipe over a pint or two of beer at the nearest publichouse, get home early to bed, and if the tide answers may be found on the river patiently dredging away at two or three o'clock in the morning.

Whenever a loaded coal barge happens to sink, as I have already intimated, it is surprising how short a time elapses before that part of the river is alive with the dredgers. They flock thither from all parts. The river on such occasions presents a very animated appearance. At first they are all in a group, and apparently in confusion, crossing and re-crossing each other's course; some with their oars pulled in while they examine the contents of their nets, and empty the coals into the bottom of their boats; others rowing and tugging against the stream, to obtain an advantageous position for the next cast; and when they consider they have found this, down go the dredging-nets to the bottom, and away they row again with the stream, as if pulling for a wager, till they find by the weight of their net that it is full; then they at once stop, haul it to the surface, and commence another course. Others who have been successful in getting their boats loaded may be seen pushing away from the main body, and making towards the shore. Here they busily employ themselves, with what help they can get, in emptying the boat of her cargo—carrying it ashore in old coal baskets, bushel measures, or anything else which will suit their purpose; and when this is completed they pull out again to join their comrades, and commence afresh. They continue working thus till the returning tide puts an end to their labours, but these are resumed after the tide has fallen to a certain depth; and so they go on, working night and day while there is anything to be got.

The dredgerman and his boat may be immediately distinguished from all others; there is nothing similar to them on the river. The sharp cutwater fore and aft, and short rounded appearance of the vessel, marks it out at once from the skiff or wherry of the waterman. There is, too, always the appearance of labour about the boat, like a ship returning after a long voyage, daubed and filthy, and looking sadly in need of a thorough cleansing. The grappling irons are over the bow, resting on a coil of rope; while the other end of the boat is filled with coals, bones, and old rope, mixed with the mud of the river. The ropes of the dredging-net hang over the side. A short stout figure, with a face soiled and blackened with perspiration, and surmounted by a tarred sou'-wester, the body habited in a soiled check shirt, with the sleeves turned up above the elbows, and exhibiting a pair of sunburnt brawny arms, is pulling at the sculls, not with the ease and lightness of the waterman, but toiling and tugging away like a galley slave, as he scours the bed of the river with his dredging-net in search of some hoped-for prize.

The dredgers, as was before stated, are the men who find almost all the bodies of persons drowned. If there be a reward offered for the recovery of a body, numbers of the dredgers will at once endeavour to obtain it, while if there be no reward, there is at least the inquest money to be had—beside other chances. What these chances are may be inferred from the well-known fact, that no body recovered by a dredgerman ever happens to have any money about it, when brought to shore. There may, indeed, be a watch in the fob or waistcoat pocket, for that article would be likely to be traced. There may, too, be a purse or pocket-book forthcoming, but somehow it is invariably empty. The dredgers cannot by any reasoning or argument be made to comprehend that there is anything like dishonesty in emptying the pockets of a dead man. They consider them as their just perquisites. They say that any one who finds a body does precisely the same, and that if they did not do so the police would. After having had all the trouble and labour, they allege that they have a much better right to whatever is to be got, than the police who have had nothing whatever to do with it. There are also people who shrewdly suspect that some of the coals from the barges lying in the river, very often find their way into the dredgers' boats, especially when the dredgers are engaged in night-work; and there are even some who do not hold them guiltless of, now and then, when opportunity offers, smuggling things ashore from many of the steamers coming from foreign parts. But such things, I repeat, the dredgers consider in the fair way of their business.

One of the most industrious, and I believe one of the most skilful and successful of this peculiar class, gave me the following epitome of his history.

"Father was a dredger, and grandfather afore him; grandfather was a dredger and a fisherman too. A'most as soon as I was able to crawl, father took me with him in the boat to help him to pick the coals, and bones, and other things out of the net, and to use me to the water. When I got bigger and stronger, I was sent to the parish school, but I didn't like it half as well as the boat, and couldn't be got to stay two days together. At last I went above bridge, and went along with a fisherman, and used to sleep in the boat every night. I liked to sleep in the boat; I used to be as comfortable as could be. Lor bless you! there's a tilt to them boats, and no rain can't git at you. I used to lie awake of a night in them times, and listen to the water slapping ag'in the boat, and think it fine fun. I might a got bound 'prentice, but I got aboard a smack, where I stayed three or four year, and if I'd a stayed there, I'd a liked it much better. But I heerd as how father was ill, so I com'd home, and took to the dredging, and am at it off and on ever since. I got no larnin', how could I? There's on'y one or two of us dredgers as knows anything of larnin', and they're no better off than the rest. Larnin's no use to a dredger, he hasn't got no time to read; and if he had, why it wouldn't tell him where the holes and furrows is at the bottom of the river, and where things is to be found. To be sure there's holes and furrows at the bottom. I know a good many. I know a furrow off Lime'us Point, no wider nor the dredge, and I can go there, and when others can't git anything but stones and mud, I can git four or five bushel o' coal. You see they lay there; they get in with the set of the tide, and can't git out so easy like. Dredgers don't do so well now as they used to do. You know Pelican Stairs? well, before the Docks was built, when the ships lay there, I could go under Pelican Pier and pick up four or five shilling of a morning. What was that tho' to father? I hear him say he often made 5*l*. afore breakfast, and nobody ever the wiser. Them were fine times! there was a good livin' to be picked up on the water them days. About ten year ago, the fishermen at Lambeth, them as sarves their time 'duly and truly' thought to put us off the water, and went afore the Lord Mayor, but they couldn't do nothink after all. They do better nor us, as they go fishin' all the summer, when the dredgin' is bad, and come back in winter. Some on us down here" [Rotherhithe] "go a deal-portering in the summer, or unloading 'tatoes, or anything else we can get; when we have nothin' else to do, we go on the river. Father don't dredge now, he's too old for that; it takes a man to be strong to dredge, so father goes to ship scrapin'. He on'y sits on a plank outside the ship, and scrapes off the old tar with a scraper. We does very well for all that—why he can make his half a bull a day [2s. 6d.] when he gits work, but that's not always; howsomever I helps the old man at times, when I'm able. I've found a good many bodies. I got a many rewards, and a tidy bit of inquest money. There's 5s. 6d. inquest money at Rotherhithe, and on'y a shillin' at Deptford; I can't make out how that is, but that's all they give, I know. I never finds anythink on the bodies. Lor bless you! people don't have anythink in their pockets when they gits drowned, they are not such fools as all that. Do you see them two marks there on the back of my hand? Well, one day—I was on'y young then—I was grabblin' for old rope in Church Hole, when I brings up a body, and just as I was fixing the rope on his leg to tow him ashore, two swells comes down in a skiff, and lays hold of the painter of my boat, and tows me ashore. The hook of the drag went right thro' the trowsers of the drowned man and my hand, and I couldn't let go no how, and tho' I roared out like mad, the swells didn't care, but dragged me into the stairs. When I got there, my arm, and the corpse's shoe and trowsers, was all kivered with my blood. What do you think the gents said?—why, they told me as how they had done me good, in towin' the body in, and ran away up the stairs. Tho' times ain't near so good as they was, I manages purty tidy, and hasn't got no occasion to hollor much; but there's some of the dredgers as would hollor, if they was ever so well off."

OF THE SEWER-HUNTERS.

SOME few years ago, the main sewers, having their outlets on the river side, were completely open, so that any person desirous of exploring their dark and uninviting recesses might enter at the river side, and wander away, provided he could withstand the combination of villanous stenches which met him at every step, for many miles, in any direction. At that time it was a thing of very frequent occurrence, especially at the spring tides, for the water to rush into the sewers, pouring through them like a torrent, and then to burst up through the gratings into the streets, flooding all the low-lying districts in the vicinity of the river, till the streets of Shadwell and Wapping resembled a Dutch town, intersected by a series of muddy canals. Of late, however, to remedy this defect, the Commissioners have had a strong brick wall built within the entrance to the several sewers. In each of these brick walls there is an opening covered by a strong iron door, which hangs from the top and is so arranged that when the tide is low the rush of the water and other filth on the inner side, forces it back and allows the contents of the sewer to pass into the river, whilst when the tide rises the door is forced so close against the wall by the pressure of the water outside that none can by any possibility enter, and thus the river neighbourhoods are secured from the deluges which were heretofore of such frequent occurrence.

Were it not a notorious fact, it might perhaps be thought impossible, that men could be found who, for the chance of obtaining a living of some sort or other, would, day after day, and year after year, continue to travel through these underground channels for the offscouring of the city; but such is the case even at the present moment. In former times, however, this custom prevailed much more than now, for in those days the sewers were entirely open and presented no obstacle to any one desirous of entering them. Many wondrous tales are still told among the people of men having lost their way in the sewers, and of having wandered among the filthy passages—their lights extinguished by the noisome vapours—till, faint and overpowered, they dropped down and died on the spot. Other stories are told of sewer-hunters beset by myriads of enormous rats, and slaying thousands of them in their struggle for life, till at length the swarms of the savage things overpowered them, and in a few days afterwards their skeletons were discovered picked to the very bones. Since the iron doors, however, have been placed on the main sewers a prohibition has been issued against entering them, and a reward of 5l. offered to any person giving information so as to lead to the conviction of any offender. Nevertheless many still travel through these foul labyrinths, in search of such valuables as may have found their way down the drains.

The persons who are in the habit of searching the sewers, call themselves "shore-men" or "shore-workers." They belong, in a certain degree, to the same class as the "mud-larks," that is to say, they travel through the mud along shore in the neighbourhood of ship-building and ship-breaking yards, for the purpose of picking up copper nails, bolts, iron, and old rope. The shore-men, however, do not collect the lumps of coal and wood they meet with on their way, but leave them as the proper perquisites of the mud-larks. The sewer-hunters were formerly, and indeed are still, called by the name of "Toshers," the articles which they pick up in the course of their wanderings along shore being known among themselves by the general term "tosh," a word more particularly applied by them to anything made of copper. These "Toshers" may be seen, especially on the Surrey side of the Thames, habited in long greasy velveteen coats, furnished with pockets of vast capacity, and their nether limbs encased in dirty canvas trowsers, and any old slops of shoes, that may be fit only for wading through the mud. They carry a bag on their back, and in their hand a pole seven or eight feet long, on one end of which there is a large iron hoe. The uses of this instrument are various; with it they try the ground wherever it appears unsafe, before venturing on it, and, when assured of its safety, walk forward steadying their footsteps with the staff. Should they, as often happens, even to the most experienced, sink in some quagmire, they immediately throw out the long pole armed with the hoe, which is always held uppermost for this purpose, and with it seizing hold of any object within their reach, are thereby enabled to draw themselves out; without the pole, however, their danger would be greater, for the more they struggled to extricate themselves from such places, the deeper they would sink; and even with it, they might perish, I am told, in some part, if there were nobody at hand to render them assistance. Finally, they make use of this pole to rake about the mud when searching for iron, copper, rope, and bones. They mostly exhibit great skill in discovering these things in unlikely places, and have a knowledge of the various sets of the tide, calculated to carry articles to particular points, almost equal to the dredgermen themselves. Although they cannot "pick up" as much now as they formerly did, they are still able to make what they call a fair living, and can afford to look down with a species of aristocratic contempt on the puny efforts of their less fortunate brethren the "mudlarks."

To enter the sewers and explore them to any considerable distance is considered, even by those acquainted with what is termed "working the shores," an adventure of no small risk. There are a variety of perils to be encountered in such places. The brick-work in many parts—especially in the old sewers—has become rotten through the continual action of the putrefying matter and moisture, and parts have fallen down and choked up the passage with heaps of rubbish; over these obstructions, nevertheless, the sewer-hunters have to scramble "in the best way they can." In such parts they are careful not to touch the brick-work over head, for the slightest tap might bring down an avalanche of old bricks and earth, and severely injure them, if not bury them in the rubbish. Since the construction of the new sewers, the old ones are in general abandoned by the "hunters;" but in many places the former channels cross and re-cross those recently constructed, and in the old sewers a person is very likely to lose his way. It is dangerous to venture far into any of the smaller sewers branching off from the main, for in this the "hunters" have to stoop low down in order to proceed; and, from the confined space, there are often accumulated in such places, large quantities of foul air, which, as one of them stated, will "cause instantious death." Moreover, far from there being any romance in the tales told of the rats, these vermin are really numerous and formidable in the sewers, and have been known, I am assured, to attack men when alone, and even sometimes when accompanied by others, with such fury that the people have escaped from them with difficulty. They are particularly ferocious and dangerous, if they be driven into some corner whence they cannot escape, when they will immediately fly at any one that opposes their progress. I received a similar account to this from one of the London flushermen. There are moreover, in some quarters, ditches or trenches which are filled as the water rushes up the sewers with the tide; in these ditches the water is retained by a sluice, which is shut down at high tide, and lifted again at low tide, when it rushes down the sewers with all the violence of a mountain torrent, sweeping everything before it. If the sewer-hunter be not close to some branch sewer, so that he can run into it, whenever the opening of these sluices takes place, he must inevitably perish. The trenches or water reservoirs for the cleansing of the sewers are chiefly on the south side of the river, and, as a proof of the great danger to which the sewer-hunters are exposed in such cases, it may be stated, that not very long ago, a sewer on the south side of the Thames was opened to be repaired; a long ladder reached to the bottom of the sewer, down which the bricklayer's labourer was going with a hod of bricks, when the rush of water from the sluice, struck the bottom of the ladder, and instantly swept away ladder, labourer, and all. The bricklayer fortunately was enjoying his "pint and pipe" at a neighbouring public-house. The labourer was found by my informant, a "shore-worker," near the mouth of the sewer quite dead, battered, and disfigured in a frightful manner. There was likewise great danger in former times from the rising of the tide in the sewers, so that it was necessary for the shore-men to have quitted them before the water had got any height within the entrance. At present, however, this is obviated in those sewers where the main is furnished with an iron door towards the river.

The shore-workers, when about to enter the sewers, provide themselves, in addition to the long hoe already described, with a canvas apron, which they tie round them, and a dark lantern similar to a policeman's; this they strap before them on their right breast, in such a manner that on removing the shade, the bull's-eye throws the light straight forward when they are in an erect position, and enables them to see everything in advance of them for some distance; but when they stoop, it throws the light directly under them, so that they can then distinctly see any object at their feet. The sewer-hunters usually go in gangs of three or four for the sake of company, and in order that they may be the better able to defend themselves from the rats. The old hands who have been often up (and every gang endeavours to include at least one experienced person), travel a long distance, not only through the main sewers, but also through many of the branches. Whenever the shore-men come near a street grating, they close their lanterns and watch their opportunity of gliding silently past unobserved, for otherwise a crowd might collect over head and intimate to the policeman on duty, that there were persons wandering in the sewers below. The shore-workers never take dogs with them, lest their barking when hunting the rats might excite attention. As the men go along they search the bottom of the sewer, raking away the mud with their hoe, and pick, from between the crevices of the brick-work, money, or anything else that may have lodged there. There are in many parts of the sewers holes where the brick-work has been worn away, and in these holes clusters of articles are found, which have been washed into them from time to time, and perhaps been collecting there for years; such as pieces of iron, nails, various scraps of metal, coins of every description, all rusted into a mass like a rock, and weighing from a half hundred to two hundred weight altogether. These "conglomerates" of metal are too heavy for the men to take out of the sewers, so that if unable to break them up, they are compelled to leave them behind; and there are very many such masses, I am informed, lying in the sewers at this moment, of immense weight, and growing larger every day by continual additions. The shore-men find great quantities of money— of copper money especially; sometimes they dive their arm down to the elbow in the mud and filth and bring up shillings, sixpences, half-crowns, and occasionally half-sovereigns and sovereigns. They always find the coins standing edge uppermost between the bricks in the bottom, where the mortar has been worn away. The sewer-hunters occasionally find plate, such as spoons, ladles, silver-handled knives and forks, mugs and drinking cups, and now and then articles of jewellery; but even while thus "in luck" as they call it, they do not omit to fill the bags on their backs with the more cumbrous articles they meet with—such as metals of every description, rope and bones. There is always a great quantity of these things to be met with in the sewers, they being continually washed down from the cesspools and drains of the houses. When the sewer-hunters consider they have searched long enough, or when they have found as much as they can conveniently take away, the gang leave the sewers and, adjourning to the nearest of their homes, count out the money they have picked up, and proceed to dispose of the old metal, bones, rope, &c.; this done, they then, as they term it, "whack" the whole lot; that is, they divide it equally among all hands. At these divisions, I am assured, it frequently occurs that each member of the gang will realise from 30s. to 2l.—this at least *was* a frequent occurrence some few years ago. Of late, however, the shore-men are obliged to use far more caution, as the police, and especially those connected with the river, who are more on the alert, as well as many of the coal-merchants in the neighbourhood of the sewers, would give information if they saw any suspicious persons approaching them.

The principal localities in which the shore-hunters reside are in Mint-square, Mint-street, and Kent-street, in the Borough—Snow's-fields, Bermondsey—and that never-failing locality between the London Docks and Rosemary-lane which appears to be a concentration of all the misery of the kingdom. There were known to be a few years ago nearly 200 sewer-hunters, or "toshers," and, incredible as it may appear, I have satisfied myself that, taking one week with another, they could not be said to make much short of 2l. per week. Their probable gains, I was told, were about 6s. per day all the year round. At this rate the property recovered from the sewers of London would have amounted to no less than 20,000l. per annum, which would make the amount of property lost down the drains of each house amount to 1s. 4d. a year. The shore-hunters of the present day greatly complain of the recent restrictions, and inveigh in no measured terms against the constituted authorities. "They won't let us in to work the shores," say they, "'cause there's a little danger. They fears as how we'll get suffocated, at least they tells us so; but they don't care if we get starved! no, they doesn't mind nothink about that."

It is, however, more than suspected that these men find plenty of means to evade the vigilance of the sewer officials, and continue quietly to reap a considerable harvest, gathered whence it might otherwise have rotted in obscurity.

The sewer-hunters, strange as it may appear, are certainly smart fellows, and take decided precedence of all the other "finders" of London, whether by land or water, both on account of the greater amount of their earnings, and the skill and courage they manifest in the pursuit of their dangerous employment. But like all who make a living as it were by a game of chance, plodding, carefulness, and saving habits cannot be reckoned among their virtues; they are improvident, even to a proverb. With their gains, superior even to those of the better-paid artizans, and far beyond the amount received by many clerks, who have to maintain a "respectable appearance," the shore-men might, with but ordinary prudence, live well, have comfortable homes, and even be able to save sufficient to provide for themselves in their old age. Their practice, however, is directly the reverse. They no sooner make a "haul," as they say, than they adjourn to some low public-house in the neighbourhood, and seldom leave till empty pockets and hungry stomachs drive them forth to procure the means for a fresh debauch. It is principally on this account that, despite their large gains, they are to be found located in the most wretched quarter of the metropolis.

It might be supposed that the sewer-hunters (passing much of their time in the midst of the noisome vapours generated by the sewers, the odour of which, escaping upwards from the gratings in the streets, is dreaded and shunned by all as something pestilential) would exhibit in their pallid faces the unmistakable evidence of their unhealthy employment. But this is far from the fact. Strange to say, the sewer-hunters are strong, robust, and healthy men, generally florid in their complexion, while many of them know illness only by name. Some of the elder men, who head the gangs when exploring the sewers, are between 60 and 80 years of age, and have followed the employment during their whole lives. The men appear to have a fixed belief that the odour of the sewers contributes in a variety of ways to their general health; nevertheless, they admit that accidents occasionally occur from the air in some places being fully impregnated with mephitic gas.

I found one of these men, from whom I derived

much information, and who is really an active intelligent man, in a court off Rosemary-lane. Access is gained to this court through a dark narrow entrance, scarcely wider than a doorway, running beneath the first floor of one of the houses in the adjoining street. The court itself is about 50 yards long, and not more than three yards wide, surrounded by lofty wooden houses, with jutting abutments in many of the upper stories that almost exclude the light, and give them the appearance of being about to tumble down upon the heads of the intruders. This court is densely inhabited; every room has its own family, more or less in number; and in many of them, I am assured, there are two families residing, the better to enable the one to whom the room is let to pay the rent. At the time of my visit, which was in the evening, after the inmates had returned from their various employments, some quarrel had arisen among them. The court was so thronged with the friends of the contending individuals and spectators of the fight that I was obliged to stand at the entrance, unable to force my way through the dense multitude, while labourers and streetfolk with shaggy heads, and women with dirty caps and fuzzy hair, thronged every window above, and peered down anxiously at the affray. There must have been some hundreds of people collected there, and yet all were inhabitants of this very court, for the noise of the quarrel had not yet reached the street. On wondering at the number, my informant, when the noise had ceased, explained the matter as follows: "You see, sir, there's more than 30 houses in this here court, and there's not less than eight rooms in every house; now there's nine or ten people in some of the rooms, I knows, but just say four in every room, and calculate what that there comes to." I did, and found it, to my surprise, to be 960. "Well," continued my informant, chuckling and rubbing his hands in evident delight at the result, "you may as well just tack a couple a hundred on to the tail o' them for make-weight, as we're not werry pertikler about a hundred or two one way or the other in these here places."

In this court, up three flights of narrow stairs that creaked and trembled at every footstep, and in an ill-furnished garret, dwelt the shore-worker —a man who, had he been careful, according to his own account at least, might have money in the bank and be the proprietor of the house in which he lived. The sewer-hunters, like the street-people, are all known by some peculiar nickname, derived chiefly from some personal characteristic. It would be a waste of time to inquire for them by their right names, even if you were acquainted with them, for none else would know them, and no intelligence concerning them could be obtained; while under the title of Lanky Bill, Long Tom, One-eyed George, Short-armed Jack, they are known to every one.

My informant, who is also dignified with a title, or as he calls it a "handle to his name," gave me the following account of himself: "I was born in Birmingham, but afore I recollects anythink, we came to London. The first thing I remembers is being down on the shore at Cuckold's P'int, when the tide was out and up to my knees in mud, and a gitting down deeper and deeper every minute till I was picked up by one of the shore-workers. I used to git down there every day, to look at the ships and boats a sailing up and down; I'd niver be tired a looking at them at that time. At last father 'prenticed me to a blacksmith in Bermondsey, *and then I couldn't git down to the river when I liked, so I got to hate the forge and the fire, and blowing the bellows, and couldn't stand the confinement no how,—at last I cuts and runs.* After some time they gits me back ag'in, but I cuts ag'in. I was determined not to stand it. I wouldn't go home for fear I'd be sent back, so I goes down to Cuckold's P'int and there I sits near half the day, when who should I see but the old un as had picked me up out of the mud when I was a sinking. I tells him all about it, and he takes me home along with hisself, and gits me a bag and an o, and takes me out next day, and shows me what to do, and shows me the dangerous places, and the places what are safe, and how to rake in the mud for rope, and bones, and iron, and that's the way I comed to be a shore-worker. Lor' bless you, I've worked Cuckold's P'int for more nor twenty year. I know places where you'd go over head and ears in the mud, and jist alongside on 'em you may walk as safe as you can on this floor. But it don't do for a stranger to try it, he'd wery soon git in, and it's not so easy to git out agin, I can tell you. I stay'd with the old un a long time, and we used to git lots o' tin, specially when we'd go to work the sewers. I liked that well enough. I could git into small places where the old un couldn't, and when I'd got near the grating in the street, I'd search about in the bottom of the sewer; I'd put down my arm to my shoulder in the mud and bring up shillings and half-crowns, and lots of coppers, and plenty other things. I once found a silver jug as big as a quart pot, and often found spoons and knives and forks and every thing you can think of. Bless your heart the smells nothink; it's a roughish smell at first, but nothink near so bad as you thinks, 'cause, you see, there's sich lots o' water always a coming down the sewer, and the air gits in from the gratings, and that helps to sweeten it a bit. There's some places, 'specially in the old sewers, where they say there's foul air, and they tells me the foul air 'ill cause instantious death, but I niver met with anythink of the kind, and I think if there was sich a thing I should know somethink about it, for I've worked the sewers, off and on, for twenty year. When we comes to a narrow-place as we don't know, we takes the candle out of the lantern and fastens it on the hend of the o, and then runs it up the sewer, and if the light stays in, we knows as there a'n't no danger. We used to go up the city sewer at Blackfriars-bridge, but that's stopped up now; it's boarded across inside. The city wouldn't let us up if they knew it, 'cause of the danger, they say, but they don't care if we hav'n't got nothink to eat nor a place to put our heads in, while there's plenty of money lying there and good for nobody. If you was caught up it and brought afore the Lord Mayor, he'd give you fourteen days on it, as safe as the bellows, so a good many on us now is afraid to wenture in. We don't wenture as we used to, but still it's done at times. There's a many places as I knows on where the bricks has fallen down, and that there's dangerous; it's so delaberated that if you touches it with your head or with the hend of the o, it 'ill all come down atop o' you. I've often seed as many as a hundred rats at once, and they're woppers in the sewers, I can tell you; them there water rats, too, is far more ferociouser than any other rats, and they'd think nothink of tackling a man, if they found they couldn't get away no how, but if they can why they runs by and gits out o' the road. I knows a chap as the rats tackled in the sewers; they bit him hawfully: you must ha' heard on it; it was him as the watermen went in arter when they heard him a shouting as they was a rowin' by. Only for the watermen the rats would ha' done for him, safe enough. Do you recollect hearing on the man as was found in the sewers about twelve year ago?—oh you must—the rats eat every bit of him, and left nothink but his bones. I knowed him well, he was a rig'lar shore-worker.

"The rats is wery dangerous, that's sartain, but we always goes three or four on us together, and the varmint's too wide awake to tackle us then, for they know they'd git off second best. You can go a long way in the sewers if you like; I don't know how far. I niver was at the end on them myself, for a cove can't stop in longer than six or seven hour, 'cause of the tide; you must be out before that's up. There's a many branches on ivery side, but we don't go into all; we go where we know, and where we're always sure to find somethink. I know a place now where there's more than two or three hundred weight of metal all rusted together, and plenty of money among it too; but it's too heavy to carry it out, so it 'ill stop there I s'pose till the world comes to an end. I often brought out a piece of metal half a hundred in weight, and took it under the harch of the bridge, and broke it up with a large stone to pick out the money. I've found sovereigns and half sovereigns over and over ag'in, and three on us has often cleared a couple of pound apiece in one day out of the sewers. But we no sooner got the money than the publican had it. I only wish I'd back all the money I've guv to the publican, and I wouldn't care how the wind blew for the rest of my life. I never thought about taking a hammer along with me into the sewer, no; I never thought I'd want it. You can't go in every day, the tides don't answer, and they're so pertikler now, far more pertikler than formerly; if you was known to touch the traps, you'd git hauled up afore the beak. It's done for all that, and though there *is* so many eyes about. The "Johnnys" on the water are always on the look out, and if they sees any on us about, we has to cut our lucky. We shore-workers sometimes does very well other ways. When we hears of a fire anywheres, we goes and watches where they shoots the rubbish, and then we goes and sifts it over, and washes it afterwards, then all the metal sinks to the bottom. The way we does it is this here: we takes a barrel cut in half, and fills it with water, and then we shovels in the siftings, and stirs 'em round and round and round with a stick; then we throws out that water and puts in some fresh, and stirs that there round ag'in; arter some time the water gets clear, and every thing heavy's fell to the bottom, and then we sees what it is and picks it out. I've made from a pound to thirty shilling a day, at that there work on lead alone. The time the Parliament Houses was burnt, the rubbish was shot in Hyde Park, and Long J— and I goes to work it, and while we were at it, we didn't make less nor three pounds apiece a day; we found sovereigns and half sovereigns, and lots of silver half melted away, and jewellery, such as rings, and stones, and brooches; but we never got half paid for them. I found two sets of bracelets for a lady's arms, and took 'em to a jeweller, and he tried them jist where the "great" heat had melted the catch away, and found they was only metal double plated, or else he said as how he'd give us thirty pounds for them; howsomever, we takes them down to a Jew in Petticoat-lane, who used to buy things of us, and he gives us 7*l.* 10*s.* for 'em. We found so many things, that at last Long J— and I got to quarrel about the "whacking;" there was cheatin' a goin' on; it wasn't all fair and above board as it ought to be, so we gits to fightin', and kicks up sich a jolly row, that they wouldn't let us work no more, and takes and buries the whole on the rubbish. There's plenty o' things under the ground along with it now, if anybody could git at them. There was jist two loads o' rubbish shot at one time in Bishop Bonner's-fields, which I worked by myself, and what do you think I made out of that there?—why I made 3*l.* 5*s.* The rubbish was got out of a cellar, what hadn't been stirred for fifty year or more, so I thinks there ought to be somethink in it, and I keeps my eye on it, and watches where it's shot; then I turns to work, and the first thing I gits hold on is a chain, which I takes to be copper; it was so dirty, but it turned out to be all solid goold, and I gets 1*l.* 5*s.* for it from the Jew; arter that I finds lots o' coppers, and silver money, and many things besides. *The reason I likes this sort of life is, 'cause I can sit down when I likes, and nobody can't order me about. When I'm hard up, I knows as how I must work, and then I goes at it like sticks a breaking;* and tho' the times isn't as they was, I can go now and pick up my four or five bob a day, where another wouldn't know how to get a brass farden."

There is a strange tale in existence among the shore-workers, of a race of wild hogs inhabiting the sewers in the neighbourhood of Hampstead. The story runs, that a sow in young, by some accident got down the sewer through an opening, and, wandering away from the spot, littered and reared her offspring in the drain, feeding on the offal and garbage washed into it continually. Here, it is alleged, the breed multiplied exceedingly, and have become almost as ferocious as they are numerous. This story, apocryphal as it seems, has nevertheless its believers, and it is ingeniously argued, that the reason why none of the subterranean animals have been able to make their way to the light of day is, that they could only do so by reaching the mouth of the sewer at the river-side, while, in order to arrive at that point, they must necessarily encounter the Fleet ditch, which runs towards the river with great rapidity, and as it is the obstinate nature of a pig to swim *against* the stream, the wild hogs of the sewers invariably work their way back to their original quarters, and are thus never to be seen. What seems strange in the matter is, that the inhabitants of Hampstead never have been known to see any of these animals pass beneath the gratings, nor to have been disturbed by their gruntings. The reader of course can believe as much of the story as he pleases, and it is right to inform him that the sewer-hunters themselves have never yet encountered any of the fabulous monsters of the Hampstead sewers.

OF THE MUD-LARKS.

THERE is another class who may be termed river-finders, although their occupation is connected only with the shore; they are commonly known by the name of "mud-larks," from being compelled, in order to obtain the articles they seek, to wade sometimes up to their middle through the mud left on the shore by the retiring tide. These poor creatures are certainly about the most deplorable in their appearance of any I have met with in the course of my inquiries. They may be seen of all ages, from mere childhood to positive decrepitude, crawling among the barges at the various wharfs along the river; it cannot be said that they are clad in rags, for they are scarcely half covered by the tattered indescribable things that serve them for clothing; their bodies are grimed with the foul soil of the river, and their torn garments stiffened up like boards with dirt of every possible description.

Among the mud-larks may be seen many old women, and it is indeed pitiable to behold them, especially during the winter, bent nearly double with age and infirmity, paddling and groping among the wet mud for small pieces of coal, chips of wood, or any sort of refuse washed up by the tide. These women always have with them an old basket or an old tin kettle, in which they put whatever they chance to find. It usually takes them a whole tide to fill this receptacle, but when filled, it is as much as the feeble old creatures are able to carry home.

The mud-larks generally live in some court or alley in the neighbourhood of the river, and, as the tide recedes, crowds of boys and little girls, some old men, and many old women, may be observed loitering about the various stairs, watching eagerly for the opportunity to commence their labours. When the tide is sufficiently low they scatter themselves along the shore, separating from each other, and soon disappear among the craft lying about in every direction. This is the case on both sides of the river, as high up as there is anything to be found, extending as far as Vauxhall-bridge, and as low down as Woolwich. The mud-larks themselves, however, know only those who reside near them, and whom they are accustomed to meet in their daily pursuits; indeed, with but few exceptions, these people are dull, and apparently stupid; this is observable particularly among the boys and girls, who, when engaged in searching the mud, hold but little converse one with another. The men and women may be passed and repassed, but they notice no one; they never speak, but with a stolid look of wretchedness they plash their way through the mire, their bodies bent down while they peer anxiously about, and occasionally stoop to pick up some paltry treasure that falls in their way.

The mud-larks collect whatever they happen to find, such as coals, bits of old-iron, rope, bones, and copper nails that drop from ships while lying or repairing along shore. Copper nails are the most valuable of all the articles they find, but these they seldom obtain, as they are always driven from the neighbourhood of a ship while being new-sheathed. Sometimes the younger and bolder mud-larks venture on sweeping some empty coal-barge, and one little fellow with whom I spoke, having been lately caught in the act of so doing, had to undergo for the offence seven days' imprisonment in the House of Correction: this, he says, he liked much better than mud-larking, for while he staid there he wore a coat and shoes and stockings, and though he had not over much to eat, he certainly was never afraid of going to bed without anything at all—as he often had to do when at liberty. He thought he would try it on again in the winter, he told me, saying, it would be so comfortable to have clothes and shoes and stockings then, and not be obliged to go into the cold wet mud of a morning.

The coals that the mud-larks find, they sell to the poor people of the neighbourhood at 1d. per pot, holding about 14 lbs. The iron and bones and rope and copper nails which they collect, they sell at the rag-shops. They dispose of the iron at 5 lbs. for 1d., the bones at 3 lbs. a 1d., rope a ½d. per lb. wet, and ¾d. per lb. dry, and copper nails at the rate of 4d. per lb. They occasionally pick up tools, such as saws and hammers; these they dispose of to the seamen for biscuit and meat, and sometimes sell them at the rag-shops for a few halfpence. In this manner they earn from 2½d. to 8d. per day, but rarely the latter sum; their average gains may be estimated at about 3d. per day. The boys, after leaving the river, sometimes scrape their trousers, and frequent the cab-stands, and try to earn a trifle by opening the cab-doors for those who enter them, or by holding gentlemen's horses. Some of them go, in the evening, to a ragged school, in the neighbourhood of which they live; more, as they say, because other boys go there, than from any desire to learn.

At one of the stairs in the neighbourhood of the pool, I collected about a dozen of these unfortunate children; there was not one of them over twelve years of age, and many of them were but six. It would be almost impossible to describe the wretched group, so motley was their appearance, so extraordinary their dress, and so stolid and inexpressive their countenances. Some carried baskets, filled with the produce of their morning's work, and others old tin kettles with iron handles. Some, for want of these articles, had old hats filled with the bones and coals they had picked up; and others, more needy still, had actually taken the caps from their own heads, and filled them with what they had happened to find. The muddy slush was dripping from their clothes and utensils, and forming a puddle in which they stood. There did not appear to be among the whole group as many filthy cotton rags to their backs as, when stitched together, would have been sufficient to form the material of one shirt. There were the remnants of one or two jackets among them, but so begrimed and tattered that it would have been difficult to have determined either the original material or make of the garment. On questioning one, he said his father was a coal-backer; he had been dead eight years; the boy was nine years old. His mother was alive; she went out charing and washing when she could get any such work to do. She had 1s. a day when she could get employment, but that was not often; he remembered once to have had a pair of shoes, but it was a long time since. "It is very cold in winter," he said, "to stand in the mud without shoes," but he did not mind it in summer. He had been three years mud-larking, and supposed he should remain a mud-lark all his life. What else could he be? for there was nothing else that he knew *how* to do. Some days he earned 1d., and some days 4d.; he never earned 8d. in one day, that would have been a "jolly lot of money." He never found a saw or a hammer, he "only wished" he could, they would be glad to get hold of them at the dolly's. He had been one month at school before he went mud-larking. Some time ago he had gone to the ragged-school; but he no longer went there, for he forgot it. He could neither read nor write, and did not think he could learn if he tried "ever so much." He didn't know what religion his father and mother were, nor did know what religion meant. God was God, he said. He had heard he was good, but didn't know what good he was to him. He thought he was a Christian, but he didn't know what a Christian was. He had heard of Jesus Christ once, when he went to a Catholic chapel, but he never heard tell of who or what he was, and didn't "particular care" about knowing. His father and mother were born in Aberdeen, but he didn't know where Aberdeen was. London was England, and England, he said, was in London, but he couldn't tell in what part. He could not tell where he would go to when he died, and didn't believe any one could tell *that*. Prayers, he told me, were what people said to themselves at night. *He* never said any, and didn't know any; his mother sometimes used to speak to him about them, but he could never learn any. His mother didn't go to church or to chapel, because she had no clothes. All the money he got he gave to his mother, and she bought bread with it, and when they had no money they lived the best way they could.

Such was the amount of intelligence manifested by this unfortunate child.

Another was only seven years old. He stated that his father was a sailor who had been hurt on board ship, and been unable to go to sea for the last two years. He had two brothers and a sister, one of them older than himself; and his elder brother was a mud-lark like himself. The two had been mud-larking more than a year; they went because they saw other boys go, and knew that they got money for the things they found. They were often hungry, and glad to do anything to get something to eat. Their father was not able to earn anything, and their mother could get but little to do. They gave all the money they earned to their mother. They didn't gamble, and play at pitch and toss when they had got some money, but some of the big boys did on the Sunday, when they didn't go a mud-larking. He couldn't tell why they did nothing on a Sunday, "only they didn't;" though sometimes they looked about to see where the best place would be on the next day. He didn't go to the ragged school; he should like to know how to read a book, though he couldn't tell what good it would do him. He didn't like mud larking, would be glad of something else, but didn't know anything else that he could do.

Another of the boys was the son of a dock labourer,—casually employed. He was between seven and eight years of age, and his sister, who was also a mud-lark, formed one of the group. The mother of these two was dead, and there were three children younger than themselves.

The rest of the histories may easily be imagined, for there was a painful uniformity in the stories of all the children: they were either the children of the very poor, who, by their own improvidence or some overwhelming calamity, had been reduced to the extremity of distress, or else they were orphans, and compelled from utter destitution to seek for the means of appeasing their hunger in the mud of the river. That the majority of this class are ignorant, and without even the rudiments of education, and that many of them from time to time are committed to prison for petty thefts, cannot be wondered at. Nor can it even excite our astonishment that, once within the walls of a prison, and finding how much more comfortable it is than their previous condition, they should return to it repeatedly. As for the females growing up under such circumstances, the worst may be anticipated of them; and in proof of this I have found, upon inquiry, that very many of the unfortunate creatures who swell the tide of prostitution in Ratcliff-highway, and other low neighbourhoods in the East of London, have originally been mud-larks; and only remained at that occupation till such time as they were capable of adopting the more easy and more lucrative life of the prostitute.

As to the numbers and earnings of the mud-larks, the following calculations fall short of, rather than exceed, the truth. From Execution Dock to the lower part of Limehouse Hole, there are 14 stairs or landing-places, by which the mud-larks descend to the shore in order to pursue their employment. There are about as many on the opposite side of the water similarly frequented.

At King James' Stairs, in Wapping Wall, which is nearly a central position, from 40 to 50 mud-larks go down daily to the river; the mud-larks "using" the other stairs are not so numerous. If, therefore, we reckon the number of stairs on both sides of the river at 28, and the average number of mud-larks frequenting them at 10 each, we shall have a total of 280. Each mud-lark, it has been shown, earns on an average 3*d*. a day, or 1*s*. 6*d*. per week; so that the annual earnings of each will be 3*l*. 18*s*., or say 4*l*., a year, and hence the gross earnings of the 280 will amount to rather more than 1000*l*. per annum.

But there are, in addition to the mud-larks employed in the neighbourhood of what may be called the pool, many others who work down the river at various places as far as Blackwall, on the one side, and at Deptford, Greenwich, and Woolwich, on the other. These frequent the neighbourhoods of the various "yards" along shore, where vessels are being built; and whence, at certain times, chips, small pieces of wood, bits of iron, and copper nails, are washed out into the river. There is but little doubt that this portion of the class earn much more than the mud-larks of the pool, seeing that they are especially convenient to the places where the iron vessels are constructed; so that the presumption is, that the number of mud-larks "at work" on the banks of the Thames (especially if we include those above bridge), and the value of the property extracted by them from the mud of the river, may be fairly estimated at double that which is stated above, or say 550 gaining 2000*l*. per annum.

As an illustration of the doctrines I have endeavoured to enforce throughout this publication, I cite the following history of one of the above class. It may serve to teach those who are still sceptical as to the degrading influence of circumstances upon the poor, that many of the humbler classes, if placed in the same easy position as ourselves, would become, perhaps, quite as "respectable" members of society.

The lad of whom I speak was discovered by me now nearly two years ago "mud-larking" on the banks of the river near the docks. He was a quick, intelligent little fellow, and had been at the business, he told me, about three years. He had taken to mud-larking, he said, because his clothes were too bad for him to look for anything better. He worked every day, with 20 or 30 boys, who might all be seen at daybreak with their trowsers tucked up, groping about, and picking out the pieces of coal from the mud on the banks of the Thames. He went into the river up to his knees, and in searching the mud he often ran pieces of glass and long nails into his feet. When this was the case, he went home and dressed the wounds, but returned to the river-side directly, "for should the tide come up," he added, "without my having found something, why I must starve till next low tide." In the very cold weather he and his other shoeless companions used to stand in the hot water that ran down the river side from some of the steam-factories, to warm their frozen feet.

At first he found it difficult to keep his footing in the mud, and he had known many beginners fall in. He came to my house, at my request, the morning after my first meeting with him. It was the depth of winter, and the poor little fellow was nearly destitute of clothing. His trousers were worn away up to his knees, he had no shirt, and his legs and feet (which were bare) were covered with chilblains. On being questioned by me he gave the following account of his life:—

He was fourteen years old. He had two sisters, one fifteen and the other twelve years of age. His father had been dead nine years. The man had been a coal-whipper, and, from getting his work from one of the publican employers in those days, had become a confirmed drunkard. When he married he held a situation in a warehouse, where his wife managed the first year to save 4*l*. 10*s*. out of her husband's earnings; but from the day he took to coal-whipping she had never saved one halfpenny, indeed she and her children were often left to starve. The man (whilst in a state of intoxication) had fallen between two barges, and the injuries he received had been so severe that he had lingered in a helpless state for three years before his death. After her husband's decease the poor woman's neighbours subscribed 1*l*. 5*s*. for her; with this sum she opened a greengrocer's shop, and got on very well for five years.

When the boy was nine years old his mother sent him to the Red Lion school at Green-bank, near Old Gravel-lane, Ratcliffe-highway; she paid 1*d*. a week for his learning. He remained there for a year; then the potato-rot came, and his mother lost upon all she bought. About the same time two of her customers died 30*s*. in her debt; this loss, together with the potato-disease, completely ruined her, and the whole family had been in the greatest poverty from that period. Then she was obliged to take all her children from their school, that they might help to keep themselves as best they could. Her eldest girl sold fish in the streets, and the boy went to the river-side to "pick up" his living. The change, however, was so great that shortly afterwards the little fellow lay ill eighteen weeks with the ague. As soon as the boy recovered his mother and his two sisters were "taken bad" with a fever. The poor woman went into the "Great House," and the children were taken to the Fever Hospital. When the mother returned home she was too weak to work, and all she had to depend on was what her boy brought from the river. They had nothing to eat and no money until the little fellow had been down to the shore and picked up some coals, selling them for a trifle. "And hard enough he had to work for what he got, poor boy," said his mother to me on a future occasion, sobbing; "still he never complained, but was quite proud when he brought home enough for us to get a bit of meat with; and when he has sometimes seen me down-hearted, he has clung round my neck, and assured me that one day God would see us cared for if I would put my trust in Him." As soon as his mother was well enough she sold fruit in the streets, or went out washing when she could get a day's work.

The lad suffered much from the pieces of broken glass in the mud. Some little time before I met with him he had run a copper nail into his foot. This lamed him for three months, and his mother was obliged to carry him on her back every morning to the doctor. As soon, however, as he could "hobble" (to use his mother's own words) he went back to the river, and often returned (after many hours' hard work in the mud) with only a few pieces of coal, not enough to sell even to get them a bit of bread. One evening, as he was warming his feet in the water that ran from a steam factory, he heard some boys talking about the Ragged School in High-street, Wapping.

"They was saying what they used to learn there," added the boy. "They asked me to come along with them for it was great fun. They told me that all the boys used to be laughing and making game of the master. They said they used to put out the gas and chuck the slates all about. They told me, too, that there was a good fire there, so I went to have a warm and see what it was like. When I got there the master was very kind to me. They used to give us tea-parties, and to keep us quiet they used to show us the magic lantern. I soon got to like going there, and went every night for six months. There was about 40 or 50 boys in the school. The most of them was thieves, and they used to go thieving the coals out of barges along shore, and cutting the ropes off ships, and going and selling it at the rag-shops. They used to get $\frac{3}{4}d.$ a lb. for the rope when dry, and $\frac{1}{2}d.$ when wet. Some used to steal pudding out of shops and hand it to those outside, and the last boy it was handed to would go off with it. They used to steal bacon and bread sometimes as well. About half of the boys at the school was thieves. Some had work to do at ironmongers, lead-factories, engineers, soap-boilers, and so on, and some had no work to do and was good boys still. After we came out of school at nine o'clock at night, some of the bad boys would go a thieving, perhaps half-a-dozen and from that to eight would go out in a gang together. There was one big boy of the name of C——; he was 18 years old, and is in prison now for stealing bacon; I think he is in the House of Correction. This C—— used to go out of school before any of us, and wait outside the door as the other boys came out. Then he would call the boys he wanted for his gangs on one side, and tell them where to go and steal. He used to look out in the daytime for shops where things could be 'prigged,' and at night he would tell the boys to go to them. He was called the captain of the gangs. He had about three gangs altogether with him, and there were from six to eight boys in each gang. The boys used to bring what they stole to C——, and he used to share it with them. I belonged to one of the gangs. There were six boys altogether in my gang; the biggest lad, that knowed all about the thieving, was the captain of the gang I was in, and C—— was captain over him and over all of us.

"There was two brothers of them; you seed them, sir, the night you first met me. The other boys, as was in my gang, was B—— B——, and B—— L——, and W—— B——, and a boy we used to call 'Tim;' these, with myself, used to make up one of the gangs, and we all of us used to go a thieving every night after school-hours. When the tide would be right up, and we had nothing to do along shore, we used to go thieving in the daytime as well. It was B—— B——, and B—— L——, as first put me up to go thieving; they took me with them, one night, up the lane [New Gravel-lane], and I see them take some bread out of a baker's, and they wasn't found out; and, after that, I used to go with them regular. Then I joined C——'s gang; and, after that, C—— came and told us that his gang could do better than ourn, and he asked us to join our gang to his'n, and we did so. Sometimes we used to make $3s.$ or $4s.$ a day; or about $6d.$ apiece. While waiting outside the school-doors, before they opened, we used to plan up where we would go thieving after school was over. I was taken up once for thieving coals myself, but I was let go again."

I was so much struck with the boy's truthfulness of manner, that I asked him, *would*, he really lead a different life, if he saw a means of so doing? He assured me he would, and begged me earnestly to try him. Upon his leaving me, $2s.$ were given him for his trouble. This small sum (I afterwards learned) kept the family for more than a fortnight. The girl laid it out in sprats (it being then winter-time); these she sold in the streets.

I mentioned the fact to a literary friend, who interested himself in the boy's welfare; and eventually succeeded in procuring him a situation at an eminent printer's. The subjoined letter will show how the lad conducted himself while there.

"Whitefriars, April 22, 1850.
"Messrs. Bradbury and Evans beg to say that the boy J. C. has conducted himself in a very satisfactory manner since he has been in their employment."

The same literary friend took the girl into his service. She is in a situation still, though not in the same family.

The boy now holds a good situation at one of the daily newspaper offices. So well has he behaved himself, that, a few weeks since, his wages were increased from $6s.$ to $9s.$ per week. His mother (owing to the boy's exertions) has now a little shop, and is doing well.

This simple story requires no comments, and is narrated here in the hope that it may teach many to know how often the poor boys reared in the gutter are thieves, merely because society forbids them being honest lads.

OF THE LONDON DUSTMEN, NIGHTMEN, SWEEPS, AND SCAVENGERS.

THESE men constitute a large body, and are a class who, all things considered, do their work silently and efficiently. Almost without the cognisance of the mass of the people, the refuse is removed from our streets and houses; and London, as if in the care of a tidy housewife, is *always* being cleaned. Great as are the faults and absurdities of many parts of our system of public cleansing, nevertheless, when compared with the state of things in any continental capital, the superiority of the metropolis of Great Britain is indisputable.

In all this matter there is little merit to be attributed to the workmen, except that they may be well drilled; for the majority of them are as much machines, apart from their animation, as are the cane and whalebone made to cleanse the chimney, or the clumsy-looking machine which, in its progress, is a vehicular scavenger, sweeping as it goes.

These public cleansers are to be thus classified:—

1. Dustmen, or those who empty and remove the collection of ashes, bones, vegetables, &c., deposited in the dust-bins, or other refuse receptacles throughout the metropolis.
2. Nightmen, or those who remove the contents of the cesspools.
3. Sweeps, or those who remove the soot from the chimneys.
4. Scavengers, or those who remove the dirt from the streets, roads, and markets.

Let me, however, before proceeding further with the subject, lay before the reader the following important return as to the extent and contents of this prodigious city: for this document I am indebted to the Commissioners of Police, gentlemen from whom I have derived the most valuable information since the commencement of my inquiries, and to whose courtesy and consideration I am anxious to acknowledge my many obligations.

RETURN SHOWING THE EXTENT, POPULATION, AND POLICE FORCE IN THE METROPOLITAN POLICE DISTRICT AND THE CITY OF LONDON IN SEPTEMBER, 1850.

	Metropolitan Police District*.			City of London ‡.	Grand Total.
	Inner District †.	Outer District.	Total.		
Area . . . . . (in square miles)	91	609½	700½	1¾	702¼
Parishes	82	136	218	97	315
Streets, Roads, &c. (length of, in miles)	1,700	1,936	3,636	50	3,686
Number of Houses inhabited . .	289,912	59,995	349,907	15,613	365,520
,, ,, uninhabited .	11,868	1,437	13,305	387	13,692
,, ,, being built .	4,634	1,097	5,731	23	5,754
Population	1,986,629	350,331	2,336,960	125,000	2,461,960
Police Force	4,844	660	5,504	568	6,072

18*th September*, 1850.

* The Metropolitan Police District comprises a circle, the radius of which is 15 miles from Charing Cross; the extreme boundary on the N. includes the parish of Cheshunt and South Mimms; on the S., Epsom; on the E., Dagenham and Crayford; and on the W., Uxbridge and Staines.
† The inner district includes the parish of St. John, Hampstead, on the N.; Tooting and Streatham on the S.; Ealing and Brentford on the W.; and Greenwich on the E.
The Registrar General's District is equal, or nearly so, to the inner Metropolitan Police District.
‡ The City of London is bounded on the S. by the River, on the E. by Whitechapel, on the W. by Chancery Lane, and N. by Finsbury.

The total here given can hardly be considered as the dimensions of the metropolis; though, where the capital begins and ends, it is difficult to say. If, however, London be regarded as concentring within the Inner Police District, then, adding the extent and contents of that district to those of the City, as above detailed, we have the subjoined statement as to the dimensions and inhabitants of the

Metropolis Proper.

Area	92¾ square miles.
Parishes . . .	179
Length of street, roads, &c.	1750 miles.
Number of inhabited houses . .	305,525
Ditto uninhabited .	12,255
Ditto being built .	4657
Population . .	2,111.629
Police force . .	5412

But if the extent of even this "inner district" be so vast as almost to overpower the mind with its magnitude—if its population be greater than that of the entire kingdom of Hanover, and almost equal to that of the republic of Switzerland—if its houses be so numerous that placed side by side they would form one continuous line of dwellings from its centre to Moscow—if its streets and roads be nearly equal in length to one quarter of the diameter of the earth itself,—what a task must the cleansing of such a bricken wilderness be, and yet, assuredly, though it be by far the greatest, it is at the same time by far the cleanest city in the world.

The removal of the refuse of a large town is, perhaps, one of the most important of social operations. Not only is it necessary for the well-being of a vast aggregation of people that the ordure should be removed from both within and around their dwellings as soon as it is generated, but nature, ever working in a circle and reproducing in the same ratio as she destroys, has made this same ordure not only the cause of present disease when allowed to remain within the city, but the means of future health and sustenance when removed to the fields.

In a leading article in the *Morning Chronicle*, written about two years since, I said—

"That man gets his bones from the rocks and his muscles from the atmosphere, is beyond all doubt. The iron in his blood and the lime in his teeth were originally in the soil. But these could not be in his body unless they had previously formed part of his food. And yet we can neither live on air nor on stones. We cannot grow fat upon lime, and iron is positively indigestible in our stomachs. It is by means of the vegetable creation alone that we are enabled to convert the mineral into flesh and blood. The only apparent use of herbs and plants is to change the inorganic earth, air, and water, into organic substances fitted for the nutrition of animals. The little lichen, which, by means of the oxalic acid that it secretes, decomposes the rocks to which it clings, and fits their lime for 'assimilation' with higher organisms, is, as it were, but the primitive bone-maker of the world. By what subtle transmutation inorganic nature is changed into organic, and dead inert matter quickened with life, is far beyond us even to conjecture. Suffice it that an express apparatus is required for the process—a special mechanism to convert the 'crust of the earth,' as it is called, into food for man and beast.

"Now, in Nature everything moves in a circle—perpetually changing, and yet ever returning to the point whence it started. Our bodies are continually decomposing and recomposing—indeed, the very process of breathing is but one of decomposition. As animals live on vegetables, even so is the refuse of the animal the vegetable's food. The carbonic acid which comes from our lungs, and which is poison for us to inhale, is not only the vital air of plants, but positively their nutriment. With the same wondrous economy that marks all creation, it has been ordained that what is unfitted for the support of the superior organisms, is of all substances the best adapted to give strength and vigour to the inferior. That which we excrete as pollution to our system, they secrete as nourishment to theirs. Plants are not only Nature's scavengers but Nature's purifiers. They remove the filth from the earth, as well as disinfect the atmosphere, and fit it to be breathed by a higher order of beings. Without the vegetable creation the animal could neither have been nor be. Plants not only fitted the earth originally for the residence of man and the brute, but to this day they continue to render it habitable to us. For this end their nature has been made the very antithesis to ours. The process by which we live is the process by which they are destroyed. That which supports respiration in us produces putrefaction in them. What our lungs throw off, their lungs absorb—what our bodies reject, their roots imbibe.

"Hence, in order that the balance of waste and supply should be maintained—that the principle of universal compensation should be kept up, and that what is rejected by us should go to the sustenance of plants, Nature has given us several instinctive motives to remove our refuse from us. She has not only constituted that which we egest the most loathsome of all things to our senses and imagination, but she has rendered its effluvium highly pernicious to our health—sulphuretted hydrogen being at once the most deleterious and offensive of all gases. Consequently, as in all other cases where the great law of Nature has to be enforced by special sanctions, a double motive has been given us to do that which it is necessary for us to do, and thus it has been made not only advantageous to us to remove our refuse to the fields, but positively detrimental to our health, and disgusting to our senses, to keep it in the neighbourhood of our houses.

"In every well-regulated State, therefore, an effective and rapid means for carrying off the ordure of the people to a locality where it may be fruitful instead of destructive, becomes a most important consideration. Both the health and the wealth of the nation depend upon it. If to make two blades of wheat grow where one grew before is to confer a benefit on the world, surely to remove that which will enable us at once to do this, and to purify the very air which we breathe, as well as the water which we drink, must be a still greater boon to society. It is, in fact, to give the community not only a double amount of food, but a double amount of health to enjoy it. We are now beginning to understand this. Up to the present time we have only thought of removing our refuse—the idea of using it never entered our minds. It was not until science taught us the dependence of one order of creation upon another, that we began to see that what appeared worse than worthless to us was Nature's capital—*wealth set aside for future production.*"

In connection with this part of the subject, viz., the use of human refuse, I would here draw attention to those erroneous notions, as to the multiplication of the people, which teach us to look upon the increases of the population beyond certain limits as the greatest possible evil that can befall a community. Population, it is said, multiplies itself in a geometrical ratio, whereas the produce of the land is increased only in arithmetical proportion; that is to say, while the people are augmented after the rate of—

2   4   8   16   32   64

the quantity of food for them can be extended only in the following degrees:—

2   4   6   8   10   12

The cause of this is said to be that, after a certain stage in the cultivation of the soil, the increase of the produce from land is not in proportion to the increase of labour devoted to it; that is to say, doubling the labour does not double the crop; and hence it is asserted that the human race increasing at a quicker rate than the food, insufficient sustenance must be the necessary lot of a portion of the people in every densely-populated community.

That men of intelligence and education should have been persuaded by so plausible a doctrine at the time of its first promulgation may be readily conceived, for then the notions concerning organic chemistry were vague in the extreme, and the great universal law of Waste and Supply remained to be fully developed; but that men pretending to the least scientific knowledge should in these days be found advocating the Population Theory is only another of the many proofs of the indisposition of even the strongest minds to abandon their pet prejudices. Assuredly Malthus and Liebig are incompatible. If the new notions as to the chemistry of vegetation be true, then must the old notions as to population be utterly unfounded. If what we excrete plants secrete—if what we exhale they inspire—if our refuse is their food—then it follows that to increase the population is to increase the quantity of manure, while to increase the manure is to augment the food of plants, and consequently the plants themselves. If the plants nourish us, we at least nourish them. It seems never to have occurred to the economists that plants themselves required sustenance, and consequently they never troubled themselves to inquire whence they derived the elements of their growth. Had they done this they would never have even expected that a double quantity of mere labour upon the soil should have doubled the produce; but they would rather have seen that it was utterly impossible for the produce to be doubled without the food in the soil being doubled likewise; that is to say, they would have perceived that plants could not, whatever the labour exerted upon their cultivation, extract the elements of their organization from the earth and air, unless those elements previously existed in the land and atmosphere in which they grew, and that such elements, moreover, could not exist there without some organic being to egest them.

This doctrine of the universal Compensation extending throughout the material world, and more especially through the animal and vegetable kingdom, is, perhaps, one of the grandest and most consoling that science has yet revealed to us, making each mutually dependent on the other, and so contributing each to the other's support. Moreover it is the more comforting, as enabling us almost to demonstrate the falsity of a creed which is opposed to every generous impulse of our nature, and which is utterly irreconcilable with the attributes of the Creator.

"Thanks to organic chemistry," I said two years ago in the *Morning Chronicle*, "we are beginning to wake up. Science has taught us that the removal of the ordure of towns to the fields is a question that concerns not only our health, but, what is a far more important consideration with us, our breeches pockets. What we, in our ignorance, had mistaken for refuse of the vilest kind, we have now learned to regard as being, with reference to its fertilizing virtues, 'a precious ore, running in rich veins beneath the surface of our streets.' Whereas, if allowed to reek and seethe in cesspools within scent of our very hearths, or to pollute the water that we use to quench our thirst and cook our food, it becomes, like all wealth badly applied, converted into 'poison:' as Romeo says of gold to the apothecary—

'Doing more murders in this loathsome world
Than those poor compounds which thou mayst not sell.'

"Formerly, in our eagerness to get rid of the pollution, we had literally not looked beyond our noses: hence our only care was to carry off the nuisance from the immediate vicinity of our own residences. It was no matter to us what became of it, so long as it did not taint the atmosphere around us. This the very instincts of our nature had made objectionable to us; so we laid down just as many drains and sewers as would carry our night-soil to the nearest stream; and thus, instead of poisoning the air that we breathed, we poisoned the water that we drank. Then, as the town extended—for cities, like mosaic work, are put together piecemeal—street being dovetailed to street, like county to county in our children's geographical puzzles—each new row of houses tailed on its drains to those of its neighbours, without any inquiry being made as to whether they were on the same level or not. The consequence of this is, that the sewers in many parts of our metropolis are subject to an ebb and flood like their central stream, so that the pollution which they remove at low-water, they regularly bring back at high-water to the very doors of the houses whence they carried it.

"According to the average of the returns, from 1841 to 1846, we are paying two millions every year for guano, bone-dust, and other foreign fertilizers of our soil. In 1845, we employed no fewer than 683 ships to bring home 220,000 tons of animal manure from Ichaboe alone; and yet we are every day emptying into the Thames 115,000 tons of a substance which has been proved to be possessed of even greater fertilizing powers. With 200 tons of the sewage that we are wont to regard as refuse, applied to the irrigation of one acre of meadow land, seven crops, we are told, have been produced in the year, each of them worth from 6*l*. to 7*l*.; so that, considering the produce to have been doubled by these means, we have an increase of upwards of 20*l*. per acre per annum effected by the application of that refuse to the surface of our fields. This return is at the rate of 10*l*. for every 100 tons of sewage; and, since the total amount of refuse discharged into the Thames from the sewers of the metropolis is, in round numbers, 40,000,000 tons per annum, it follows that, according to such estimate, we are positively wasting 4,000,000*l*. of money every year; or, rather, *it costs us that amount to poison the waters about us*. Or, granting that the fertilizing power of the metropolitan refuse is—as it is said to be—as great for arable as for pasture-lands, then for every 200 tons of manure that we now cast away, we might have an increase of at least 20 bushels of corn per acre. Consequently the entire 40,000,000 tons of sewage, if applied to fatten the land instead of to poison the water, would, at such a rate of increase, swell our produce to the extent of 4,000,000 bushels of wheat per annum. Calculating then that each of these bushels would yield 16 quartern loaves, it would follow that we fling into the Thames no less than 246,000,000 lbs. of bread every year; or, still worse, by pouring into the river that which, if spread upon our fields, would enable thousands to live, we convert the elements of life and health into the germs of disease and death, changing into slow but certain poisons that which, in the subtle transmutation of organic nature, would become acres of life-sustaining grain." I shall have more to say subsequently on this waste and its consequences.

These considerations show how vastly important it is that in the best of all possible ways we should *collect, remove,* and *use* the scavengery and excrementitious matter of our streets and houses.

Now the removal of the refuse of London is no slight task, consisting, as it does, of the cleansing of 1750 miles of streets and roads; of collecting the dust from 300,000 dust-bins; of emptying (according to the returns of the Board of Health) the same number of cesspools, and sweeping near upon 3,000,000 chimneys.

A task so vast it might naturally be imagined would give employment to a number of hands, and yet, if we trusted the returns of the Occupation Abstract of 1841, the whole of these stupendous operations are performed by a limited number of individuals.

RETURN OF THE NUMBER OF SWEEPS, DUSTMEN, AND NIGHTMEN IN THE METROPOLIS, ACCORDING TO THE CENSUS OF 1841.

	Total.	Males.		Females.	
		20 years and upwards.	Under 20.	20 years and upwards.	Under 20.
Chimney Sweepers	1033	619	370	44	
Scavengers and Nightmen . . .	254	227	10	17	

I am informed by persons in the trade that the "females" here mentioned as chimney-sweepers, and scavengers, and nightmen, must be such widows or daughters of sweeps and nightmen as have succeeded to their businesses, for that no women *work* at such trades; excepting, perhaps, in the management and care of the soot, in assisting to empty and fill the bags. Many females, however, are employed in sifting dust, but the calling of the dustman and dustwoman is not so much as noticed in the population returns.

According to the occupation abstract of the previous decennial period, the number of males of 20 years and upwards (for none others were mentioned) pursuing the same callings in the metropolis in 1831, were as follows:—

Soot and chimney-sweepers . . . 421
Nightmen and scavengers . . . 130

Hence the increase in the adult male operatives belonging to these trades, between 1831 and 1841, was, for Chimney-sweeps, 198; and Scavengers and Nightmen, 97.

But these returns are preposterously incorrect. In the first place it was not until 1842 that the parliamentary enactment prohibiting the further employment of climbing-boys for the purpose of sweeping chimneys came into operation. At that time the number of inhabited houses in the metropolis was in round numbers 250,000, and calculating these to have contained only eight rooms each, there would have been at the least 2,000,000 chimneys to sweep. Now, according to the government returns above cited—the London climbing-boys (for the masters did not and could not climb) in 1841 numbered only 370; at which rate there would have been but one boy to no less than 5400 chimneys! Pursuing the same mode of testing the validity of the "official" statements, we find, as the nightmen generally work in gangs of four, that each of the 63, or say 64, gangs comprised in the census returns, would have had 4000 cesspools to empty of their contents; while, working both as scavengers and nightmen (for, according to the census, they were the *only* individuals following those occupations in London), they would after their nocturnal labours have had about 27 miles of streets and roads to cleanse—a feat which would certainly have thrown the scavengering prowess of Hercules into the shade.

Under the respective heads of the dustmen, nightmen, sweeps, and scavengers, I shall give an account of the numbers, &c., employed, and a resumé of the whole. It will be sufficient here to mention that my investigations lead to the conclusion that, of men working as dustmen (a portion of whom are employed as nightmen and scavengers) there are at present about 1800 in the metropolis. The census of 1841, as I have pointed out, mentions no dustman whatever!

But I have so often had instances of the defects of this national numbering of the people that I have long since ceased to place much faith in its returns connected with the humbler grades of labour. The costermongers, for example, I estimate at about 10,000, whereas the government reports, as has been before mentioned, ignore the very existence of such a class of people, and make the entire hawkers, hucksters, and pedlars of the metropolis to amount to no more than 2045. Again, the London "coal labourers, heavers, and porters" are said, in the census of 1841, to be only 1700 in number; I find, however, that there are no less than 1800 "registered" coal-whippers, and as many coal porters; so that I am in no way inclined to give great credence to the "official enumerations." The difficulties which beset the perfection of such a document are almost insuperable, and I have already heard of returns for the forthcoming document, made by ignorant people as to their occupations, which already go far to nullify the facts in connection with the employment of the ignorant and profligate classes of the metropolis.

Before quitting this part of the subject, viz., the extent of surface, the length of streets, and the number of houses throughout the metropolis requiring to be continually cleansed of their refuse, as well as the number of people as continually engaged in so cleansing them, let me here append the last returns of the Registrar General, copied from the census of 1851, as to the dimensions and contents of the metropolis according to that functionary, so that they may be compared with those of the metropolitan police before given.

In Weale's "*London Exhibited,*" which is by far the most comprehensive description of the metropolis that I have seen, it is stated that it is "only possible to adopt a general idea of the giant city," as its precise boundaries and extent cannot be defined. On the north of the Thames, we are told, London extends to Edmonton and Finchley; on the west it stretches to Acton and Hammersmith; on the east it reaches Leyton and Ham; while on the south of the Thames the metropolis is said to embrace Wandsworth, Streatham, Lewisham, Woolwich, and Plumstead. "To each of these points," says Mr. Weale, but upon what authority he does not inform us, "continuous streets of houses reach; but the solid mass of houses lies within narrow bounds—with these several long arms extending from it. The greatest length of street, from east to west," he adds, "is about fourteen miles, and from north to south about thirteen miles. The solid mass is about seven miles by four miles, so that the ground covered with houses is not less than 20 square miles."

Mr. McCulloch, in his "*London in* 1850-51," has a passage to the same effect. He says, "The continued and rapid increase of buildings renders it difficult to ascertain the extent of the metropolis at any particular period. If we include in it those parts only that present a solid mass of houses, its length from east to west may be taken at six miles, and its breadth from north to south at about three miles and a half. There is, however, a nearly continuous line of houses from Blackwall to Chelsea, a distance of about seven miles, and from Walworth to Holloway, of four and a half miles. The extent of surface covered by buildings is estimated at about sixteen square miles, or above 10,000 acres, so that M. Say, the celebrated French economist, did not really indulge in hyperbole when he said, '*Londres n'est plus une ville : c'est une province couverte de maisons!*' (London is no longer a town: it is a province covered with houses)."

The Government authorities, however, appear to have very different notions from either of the above gentlemen as to the extent of the metropolis.

The limits of London, as at present laid down by the Registrar General, include 176 parishes, besides several precincts, liberties, and extra-parochial places, comprising altogether about 115 square miles. According to the old bills of mortality, London formerly included only 148 parishes, which were located as follows:—

Parishes within the walls of the city	97
Parishes without the walls	17
Parishes in the city and liberties of Westminster	10
Out parishes in Middlesex and Surrey	24
	148

The parishes which have been annexed to the above at different periods since the commencement of the present century are:—

Parishes added by the late Mr. Rickman (see Pop. Abstracts, 1801–31) (including Chelsea, Kensington, Paddington, St. Marylebone, and St. Pancras)	5
Parishes added by the Registrar General, 1838 (including Hammersmith, Fulham, Stoke Newington, Stratford-le-Bow, Bromley, Camberwell, Deptford, Greenwich, and Woolwich)	10
Parishes added by the Registrar General in 1844 (including Clapham, Battersea, Wandsworth, Putney, Lower Tooting, and Streatham)	6
Parishes added by the Registrar General in 1846 (comprising Hampstead, Charlton, Plumstead, Eltham, Lee, Kidbroke, and Lewisham)	7
Total number of parishes in the metropolis, as defined by the Registrar General	176

The extent of London, according to the limits assigned to it at the several periods above mentioned, was—

	Stat. Acres.	Sq. miles.
London within the old bills of mortality, from 1726	21,080	32
London, within the limits adopted by the late Mr. Rickman, 1801–31	29,850	46
London, within the limits adopted by the Registrar General, 1838-43	44,850	70
London, within the limits adopted by the Registrar General, 1844-46	55,650	87
London, within the limits adopted by the Registrar General in 1847-51	74,070	115

"London," observes Mr. Weale, "has now swallowed up many cities, towns, villages, and separate jurisdictions. The four commonwealths, or kingdoms, of the Middle Saxons, East Saxons, the South Rick, and the Kentwaras, once ruled over its surface. It now embraces the episcopal cities of London and Westminster, the towns of Woolwich, Deptford, and Wandsworth, the watering places of Hampstead, Highgate, Islington, Acton, and Kilburn, the fishing town of Barking, the once secluded and ancient villages of Ham, Hornsey, Sydenham, Lee, Kensington, Fulham, Lambeth, Clapham, Paddington, Hackney, Chelsea, Stoke Newington, Newington Butts, Plumstead, and many others.

The 176 parishes now included by the Registrar General within the boundaries of the metropolis, are arranged by him into five districts, of which the areas, population, and number of inhabited houses were on the 31st of March, 1851, as undermentioned:—

TABLE SHOWING THE AREA, NUMBER OF INHABITED HOUSES, AND POPULATION OF THE DIFFERENT PARTS OF THE METROPOLIS, 1841-51.

Divisions of Metropolis.	Statute Acres.	Population.		Inhabited Houses.	
		1841.	1851.	1841.	1851.
West Districts.					
Kensington	7,860	74,898	119,990	10,962	17,292
Chelsea	780	40,243	56,543	5,648	7,629
St. George's, Hanover-square	1,090	66,657	73,207	7,630	8,795
Westminster	840	56,802	65,609	6,439	6,647
St. Martin's-in-the-Fields	260	25,132	24,557	2,439	2,323
St. James's, Westminster	165	37,457	36,426	3,590	3,460
North Districts.					
Marylebone	1,490	138,383	157,679	14,169	15,955
Hampstead (added 1846)	2,070	10,109	11,986	1,411	1,719
Pancras	2,600	129,969	167,198	14,766	18,731
Islington	3,050	55,779	95,154	8,508	13,558
Hackney	3,950	42,328	58,424	7,192	9,861
Central Districts.					
St. Giles's	250	54,378	54,062	4,959	4,778
Strand	163	43,667	44,446	4,327	3,938
Holborn	188	44,532	46,571	4,603	4,517
Clerkenwell	320	56,799	64,705	6,946	7,259
St. Luke's	240	49,908	54,058	6,385	6,421
East London	} †230	39,718	44,407	4,796	4,785
West London		29,188	28,829	3,010	2,745
London, City of	‡370	56,009	55,908	7,921	7,329
East Districts.					
Shoreditch	620	83,564	109,209	12,642	15,433
Bethnal Green	760	74,206	90,170	11,782	13,370
Whitechapel	316	71,879	79,756	8,834	8,832
St. George's in the East	230	41,416	48,375	5,985	6,151
Stepney	2,518	90,831	110,669	14,364	16,346
Poplar	1,250	31,171	47,157	5,066	6,882
South Districts.					
St. Saviour's, Southwark	*	33,027	35,729	4,659	4,613
St. Olave's, Southwark	*	19,869	19,367	2,523	2,365
Bermondsey	620	35,002	48,128	5,674	7,095
St. George's, Southwark	*590	46,718	51,825	6,663	7,005
Newington	630	54,693	64,805	9,370	10,468
Lambeth	3,640	116,072	139,240	17,791	20,520
Wandsworth (added 1843)	10,800	39,918	50,770	6,459	8,290
Camberwell	4,570	39,931	54,668	6,843	9,417
Rotherhithe	690	13,940	17,778	2,420	2,834
Greenwich	4,570	81,125	99,404	11,995	14,423
Lewisham (added 1846)	16,350	23,051	34,831	3,966	5,936
Total London Division	74,070	1,948,369	2,361,640	262,737	307,722

* The area of the districts of St. Saviour and St. Olave is included in that returned for St. George, Southwark.
† The area here stated is that of the city without the walls, and includes White Friars precinct and Holy Trinity, Minories, both belonging to other districts.
‡ This area is that of the city within the walls, and does not include White Friars, which belongs to the district¹

In order to be able to compare the average density of the population in the various parts of London, I have made a calculation as to the number of persons and houses to the acre, as well as the number of inhabitants to each house. I have also computed the annual rate of increase of the population from 1841–51, in the several localities here mentioned, and append the result. It will be seen that, while what are popularly known as the suburbs have increased, both in houses and population, at a considerable rate, some of the more central parts of London, on the contrary, have decreased not only in the number of people, but in the number of dwellings as well. This has been the case in St. Martin's-in-the-Fields, St. James's, Westminster, St. Giles's, and the City of London.

TABLE SHOWING THE INCREASE OF THE POPULATION AND INHABITED HOUSES, AS WELL AS THE NUMBER OF PEOPLE AND HOUSES TO EACH ACRE, AND THE NUMBER OF PERSONS TO EACH HOUSE IN THE DIFFERENT PARTS OF THE METROPOLIS IN 1841-51.

	Yearly Increase of Population per annum, from 1841–51.	Yearly Increase of Inhabited Houses, from 1841–51.	Number of People to the Acre, 1851.	Number of Inhabited Houses to the Acre, 1851.	Number of Persons to each House, 1851.
WEST DISTRICTS.					
Kensington	4,509·2	633·0	15·2	2·2	6·9
Chelsea	1,630·0	198·1	72·4	9·7	7·4
St. George's, Hanover-square	655·0	11·6	67·1	8·0	8·3
Westminster	880·7	20·8	80·4	8·2	9·8
St. Martin's-in-the-Fields	decr. 57·5*	decr. 11·6*	94·3	8·9	10·5
St. James's, Westminster	103·1*	13·0*	220·7	20·9	10·5
NORTH DISTRICTS.					
Marylebone	1,926·6	178·6	105·8	10·3	9·8
Hampstead	187·7	30·8	5·7	·8	6·9
St. Pancras	3,722·9	396·5	64·3	7·2	8·9
Islington	3,937·5	505·0	31·5	4·4	7·0
Hackney	1,609·6	719·2	14·7	2·3	5·9
CENTRAL DISTRICTS.					
St. Giles's	decr. 31·6*	decr. 18·1*	216·2	19·1	11·3
Strand	77·9	decr. 38·9*	272·2	24·1	11·2
Holborn	203·9	decr. 8·6*	247·7	24·0	10·3
Clerkenwell	790·6	31·3	202·2	22·6	8·9
St. Luke's	415·0	3·6	225·2	26·7	8·4
East and West London	433·0	decr. 27·6*	318·4	32·7	9·7
London City	decr. 10·1*	decr. 59·2*	151·0	19·8	7·6
EAST DISTRICTS.					
Shoreditch	2,564·5	279·1	176·1	24·8	7·0
Bethnal-green	1,596·4	158·8	118·6	17·5	6·7
Whitechapel	787·7	decr. ·2*	252·3	27·9	9·0
St. George's-in-the-East	695·9	16·6	210·3	26·7	7·8
Stepney	1,983·8	198·2	43·9	6·4	6·7
Poplar	1,598·6	181·6	37·7	5·5	6·8
SOUTH DISTRICTS.					
St. Saviour's, St. Olave's, and St. George's, Southwark	730·7	13·8	181·2	23·7	7·6
Bermondsey	1,312·6	142·1	77·6	11·2	6·7
Newington	1,011·2	109·8	102·8	16·6	6·1
Lambeth	2,316·8	272·9	38·2	5·6	6·7
Wandsworth	1,085·2	183·1	4·7	·7	6·1
Camberwell	1,473·7	257·4	12·4	2·0	5·8
Rotherhithe	383·8	41·4	25·7	4·1	6·2
Greenwich	1,827·9	242·8	21·7	3·1	6·8
Lewisham	1,178·0	197·0	2·1	·3	5·6
Total for all London	41,327·1	4,498·5	31·8	4·1	7·6

* The population and number of inhabited houses in these districts has decreased annually to this extent since 1841.

By the above table we perceive that St. Martin's-in-the-Fields, St. James's, Westminster, St. Giles's, the Strand, and the City have all decreased both in population and houses since 1841. The population has diminished most of all in St. James's, and the houses the most in the City. The suburban districts, however, such as Chelsea, Marylebone, St. Pancras, Islington, Hackney, Shoreditch, Bethnal-green, Stepney, Poplar, Bermondsey, Newington, Lambeth, Wandsworth, Camberwell, Greenwich, and Lewisham, have all increased greatly within the last ten years, both in dwellings and people. The greatest increase of the population, as well as houses, has been in Kensington, where the yearly addition has been 4500 people, and 630 houses.

The more densely-populated districts are, St. James's, Westminster, St. Giles's, the Strand, Holborn, Clerkenwell, St. Luke, Whitechapel, and St. George's-in-the-East, in all of which places there are upwards of 200 people to the acre, while in East and West London, in which the population is the most dense of all, the number of people exceeds 300 to the acre. The least densely populated districts are Hampstead, Wandsworth, and Lewisham, where the people are not more than six, and as few as two to the acre.

The districts in which there are the greatest number of houses to a given space, are St. James's, Westminster, the Strand, Holborn, Clerkenwell, St. Luke's, Shoreditch, and St. George's-in-the-East, in all of which localities there are upwards of 20 dwellings to each acre of ground, while in East and West London, which is the most closely built over of all, the number of houses to each acre are as many as 32. Hampstead and Lewisham appear to be the most open districts; for there the houses are not more than eight and three to every ten acres of ground.

The localities in which the houses are the most crowded with inmates are the Strand and St. Giles's, where there are more than eleven people to each house, and St. Martin's-in-the-Fields, and St. James's, Westminster, and Holborn, where each house has on an average ten inmates, while in Lewisham and Wandsworth the houses are the least crowded, for there we find only five people to every house.

Now, comparing this return with that of the metropolitan police, we have the following results as to the extent and contents of the Metropolis Proper:—

	According to Registrar General.	According to Metropolitan Police.
Area (in statute acres)	74,070	58,880
Parishes	176	179
Number of inhabited houses	307,722	305,525
Population	2,361,640	2,111,629

Hence it will be seen that both the extent and contents of these two returns differ most materially.

1st. The superficies of the Registrar General's metropolis is very nearly 13 square miles, or 15,190 statute acres, greater than the metropolis of the police commissioners.

2nd. The number of inhabited houses is 2197 more in the one than in the other.

3rd. The population of London, according to the Registrar General's limits, is 250,011, or a quarter of a million, more than it is according to the limits of the metropolitan police.

It were much to be desired that some more definite and scientific mode, not only of limiting, but of dividing the metropolis, were to be adopted. At present there are, perhaps, as many different metropolises, so to speak, and as many different modes of apportioning the several parts of the whole into districts, as there are public bodies whose operations are specially confined to the capital. The Registrar General has, as we have seen, one metropolis divided into western, northern, central, eastern, and southern districts. The metropolitan police commissioners have another metropolis apportioned into its A divisions, B divisions, and so forth; and the Post Office has a third metropolis parcelled out in a totally different manner; while the London City Mission, the Scripture Readers, the Ragged Schools, and the many other similar metropolitan institutions, all seem to delight in creating a distinct metropolis for themselves, thus tending to make the statistical "confusion worse confounded."

OF THE DUSTMEN OF LONDON.

DUST and rubbish accumulate in houses from a variety of causes, but principally from the residuum of fires, the white ash and cinders, or small fragments of unconsumed coke, giving rise to by far the greater quantity. Some notion of the vast amount of this refuse annually produced in London may be formed from the fact that the consumption of coal in the metropolis is, according to the official returns, 3,500,000 tons per annum, which is at the rate of a little more than 11 tons per house; the poorer families, it is true, do not burn more than 2 tons in the course of the year, but then many such families reside in the same house, and hence the average will appear in no way excessive. Now the ashes and cinders arising from this enormous consumption of coal would, it is evident, if allowed to lie scattered about in such a place as London, render, ere long, not only the back streets, but even the important thoroughfares, filthy and impassable. Upon the Officers of the various parishes, therefore, has devolved the duty of seeing that the refuse of the fuel consumed throughout London is removed almost as fast as produced; this they do by entering into an agreement for the clearance of the "dustbins" of the parishioners as often as required, with some person who possesses all necessary appliances for the purpose—such as horses, carts, baskets, and shovels, together with a plot of waste ground whereon to deposit the refuse. The persons with whom this agreement is made are called "dust-contractors," and are generally men of considerable wealth.

The collection of "dust," is now, more properly speaking, the removal of it. The collection of an article implies the voluntary seeking after it, and this the dustmen can hardly be said to do; for though they parade the streets shouting for the dust as they go, they do so rather to fulfil a certain duty they have undertaken to perform than in any expectation of profit to be derived from the sale of the article.

Formerly the custom was otherwise; but then, as will be seen hereafter, the residuum of the London fuel was far more valuable. Not many years ago it was the practice for the various master dustmen to send in their tenders to the vestry, on a certain day appointed for the purpose, offering to pay a considerable sum yearly to the parish authorities for liberty to collect the dust from the several houses. The sum formerly paid to the parish of Shadwell, for instance, though not a very extensive one, amounted to between 400*l.* or 500*l.* per annum; but then there was an immense demand for the article, and the contractors were unable to furnish a sufficient supply from London; ships were frequently freighted with it from other parts, especially from Newcastle and the northern ports, and at that time it formed an article of considerable international commerce—the price being from 15*s.* to 1*l.* per chaldron. Of late years, however, the demand has fallen off greatly, while the supply has been progressively increasing, owing to the extension of the metropolis, so that the Contractors have not only declined paying anything for liberty to collect it, but now stipulate to receive a certain sum for the removal of it. It need hardly be stated that the parishes always employ the man who requires the least money for the performance of what has now become a matter of duty rather than an object of desire. Some idea may be formed of the change which has taken place in this business, from the fact, that the aforesaid parish of Shadwell, which formerly received the sum of 450*l.* per annum for liberty to collect the dust, now pays the Contractor the sum of 240*l.* per annum for its removal.

The Court of Sewers of the City of London, in 1846, through the advice of Mr. Cochrane, the president of the National Philanthropic Association, were able to obtain from the contractors the sum of 5000*l.* for liberty to clear away the dirt from the streets and the dust from the bins and houses in that district. The year following, however, the contractors entered into a combination, and came to a resolution not to bid so high for the privilege; the result was, that they obtained their contracts at an expense of 2200*l.* By acting on the same principle in the year after, they not only offered no premium whatever for the contract, but the City Commissioners of Sewers were obliged to pay them the sum of 300*l.* for removing the refuse, and at present the amount paid by the City is as much as 4900*l.*! This is divided among four great contractors, and would, if equally apportioned, give them 1250*l.* each.

I subjoin a list of the names of the principal contractors and the parishes for which they are engaged :—

DISTRICTS CONTRACTED FOR.	NAMES OF CONTRACTORS.
Four divisions of the City.	Redding. Rook. J. Sinnott. J. Gould.
Finsbury-square	J. Gould.
St. Luke's	H. Dodd.
Shoreditch	Ditto
Norton Folgate	J. Gould.
Bethnal-green	E. Newman.
Holborn	Pratt and Sewell.
Hatton-garden	Ditto.
Islington	Stroud, Brickmaker.
St. Martin's	Wm. Sinnott, Junior.
St. Mary-le-Strand	J. Gore.
St. Sepulchre	Ditto.
Savoy	Ditto.
St. Clement Danes	Rook.
St. James's, Clerkenwell	H. Dodd.
St. John's, ditto	J. Gould.
St. Margaret's, Westminster	W. Hearne.
St. John's, ditto	Stapleton and Holdsworth.
Lambeth	W. Hearne.
Chelsea	C. Humphries.
St. Marylebone	J. Gore.
Blackfriars-bridge	Jenkins.
St. Paul's, Covent-garden	W. Sinnott.
Piccadilly	H. Tame.
Regent-street and Pall-mall	W. Ridding.
St. George's, Hanover-sq.	H. Tame.
Paddington	C. Humphries.
Camden-town	Milton.
St. Pancras, S.W. Division	W. Stapleton.
Southampton estate	C. Starkey.
Skinner's ditto	H. North.
Brewer's ditto	C. Starkey.
Cromer ditto	Ditto.
Calthorpe ditto	Ditto.
Bedford ditto	Gore.
Doughty ditto	Martin.
Union ditto	J. Gore.
Foundling ditto	Pratt and Sewell.
Harrison ditto	Martin.
St. Ann's, Soho	J. Gore.
Whitechapel	Parsons.
Goswell-street	Redding.
Commercial-road, East	J. Sinnott.
Mile-end	Newman.
Borough	Hearne.
Bermondsey	The parish.
Kensington	H. Tame.
St. Giles's-in-the-Fields and St. George's, Bloomsbury	Redding.
Shadwell	Westley.
St. George's-in-the-East	Ditto.
Battle-bridge	Starkey.
Berkeley-square	Clutterbuck.
St. George's, Pimlico	Redding.
Woods and Forests	Ditto.
St. Botolph	Westley.
St. John's, Wapping	Ditto.
Somers-town	H. North.
Kentish-town	J. Gore.
Rolls (Liberty of the)	Pratt and Sewell.
Edward-square, Kensington	C. Humphries.

All the metropolitan parishes now pay the contractors various amounts for the removal of the dust, and I am credibly informed that there is a system of underletting and jobbing in the dust contracts extensively carried on. The contractor for a certain parish is often a different person from the master doing the work, who is unknown in the contract. Occasionally the work would appear to be subdivided and underlet a second time.

The parish of St. Pancras is split into no less than 21 districts, each district having a separate and independent "Board," who are generally at war with each other, and make separate contracts for their several divisions. This is also the case in other large parishes, and these and other considerations confirm me in the conclusion that of large and small dust-contractors, job-masters, and middle-men, of one kind or the other, throughout the metropolis, there cannot be less than the number I have stated—90. With the exception of Bermondsey, there are no parishes who remove their own dust.

It is difficult to arrive at any absolute statement as to the gross amount paid by the different parishes for the removal of the entire dust of the metropolis. From Shadwell the contractor, as we have seen, receives 250*l.*; from the city the four contractors receive as much as 5000*l.*; but there are many small parishes in London which do not pay above a tithe of the last-mentioned sum. Let us, therefore, assume, that one with another, the several metropolitan parishes pay 200*l.* a year each to the dust contractor. According to the returns before given, there are 176 parishes in London. Hence, the gross amount paid for the removal of the entire dust of the metropolis will be between 30,000*l.* and 40,000*l.* per annum.

The removal of the dust throughout the metropolis, is, therefore, carried on by a number of persons called Contractors, who undertake, as has been stated, for a certain sum, to cart away the refuse from the houses as frequently as the inhabitants desire it. To ascertain the precise numbers of these contractors is a task of much greater difficulty than might at first be conceived.

The London Post Office Directory gives the following number of tradesmen connected with the removal of refuse from the houses and streets of the metropolis.

Dustmen	9
Scavengers	10
Nightmen	14
Sweeps	32

But these numbers are obviously incomplete, for even a cursory passenger through London must have noticed a greater number of names upon the various dust carts to be met with in the streets than are here set down.

A dust-contractor, who has been in the business upwards of 20 years, stated that, from his knowledge of the trade, he should suppose that at present there might be about 80 or 90 contractors in the metropolis. Now, according to the returns before given, there are within the limits of the Metropolitan Police District 176 parishes, and comparing this with my informant's statement, that many persons contract for more than one parish (of which, indeed, he himself is an instance), there remains but little reason to doubt the correctness of his supposition—that there are, in all, between 80 or 90 dust-contractors, large and small, connected with the metropolis. Assuming the aggregate number to be 88, there would be one contractor to every two parishes.

These dust-contractors are likewise the contractors for the cleansing of the streets, except where that duty is performed by the Street-Orderlies; they are also the persons who undertake the emptying of the cesspools in their neighbourhood; the latter operation, however, is effected by an arrangement between themselves and the landlords of the premises, and forms no part of their parochial contracts. At the office of the Street Orderlies in Leicester Square, they have knowledge of only 30 contractors connected with the metropolis; but this is evidently defective, and refers to the "large masters" alone; leaving out of all consideration, as it does, the host of small contractors scattered up and down the metropolis, who are able to employ only two or three carts and six or seven men each; many of such small contractors being merely master sweeps who have managed to "get on a little in the world," and who are now able to contract, "in a small way," for the removal of dust, street-sweepings, and night-soil. Moreover, many of even the "great contractors" being unwilling to venture upon an outlay of capital for carts, horses, &c., when their contract is only for a year, and may pass at the end of that time into the hands of any one who may underbid them—many such, I repeat, are in the habit of underletting a portion of their contract to others possessing the necessary appliances, or of entering into partnership with them. The latter is the case in the parish of Shadwell, where a person having carts and horses shares the profits with the original contractor. The agreement made on such occasions is, of course, a secret, though the practice is by no means uncommon; indeed, there is so much secrecy maintained concerning all matters connected with this business, that the inquiry is beset with every possible difficulty. The gentleman who communicated to me the amount paid by the parish of Shadwell, and who informed me, moreover, that parishes in his neighbourhood paid twice and three times more than Shadwell did, hinted to me the difficulties I should experience at the commencement of my inquiry, and I have certainly found his opinion correct to the letter. I have ascertained that in one yard intimidation was resorted to, and the men were threatened with instant dismissal if they gave me any information but such as was calculated to mislead.

I soon discovered, indeed, that it was impossible to place any reliance on what some of the contractors said; and here I may repeat that the indisputable result of my inquiries has been to meet with far more deception and equivocation from employers generally than from the employed; working men have little or no motive for mis-stating their wages; they know well that the ordinary rates of remuneration for their labour are easily ascertainable from other members of the trade, and seldom or never object to produce accounts of their earnings, whenever they have been in the habit of keeping such things. With employers, however, the case is far different; to seek to ascertain from them the profits of their trade is to meet with evasion and prevarication at every turn; they seem to feel that their gains are dishonestly large, and hence resort to every means to prevent them being made public. That I have met with many honourable exceptions to this rule, I most cheerfully acknowledge; but that the *majority* of tradesmen are neither so frank, communicative, nor truthful, as the men in their employ, the whole of my investigations go to prove. I have already, in the *Morning Chronicle*, recorded the character of my interviews with an eminent Jew slop-tailor, an army clothier, and an enterprising free-trade stay-maker (a gentleman who subscribed his 100 guineas to the League), and I must in candour confess that now, after two years' experience, I have found the industrious poor a thousand-fold more veracious than the trading rich.

With respect to the amount of business done by these contractors, or gross quantity of dust collected by them in the course of the year, it would appear that each employs, on an average, about 20 men, which makes the number of men employed as dust-men through the streets of London amount to 1800. This, as has been previously stated, is grossly at variance with the number given in the Census of 1841, which computes the dustmen in the metropolis at only 254. But, as I said before, I have long ceased to place confidence in the government returns on such subjects. According to the above estimate of 254, and deducting from this number the 88 master-dustmen, there would be only 166 labouring men to empty the 300,000 dust-bins of London, and as these men always work in couples, it follows that every two dustmen would have to remove the refuse from about 3600 houses; so that assuming each bin to require emptying once every six weeks they would have to cart away the dust from 2400 houses every month, or 600 every week, which is at the rate of 100 a day ! and as each dust-bin contains about half a load, it would follow that at this rate each cart would have to collect 50 loads of dust daily, whereas 5 loads is the average day's work.

Computing the London dust-contractors at 90, and the inhabited houses at 300,000, it follows that each contractor would have 3333 houses to remove the refuse from. Now it has been calculated that the ashes and cinders alone from each house average about three loads per annum, so that each contractor would have, in round numbers, 10,000 loads of dust to remove in the course of the year. I find, from inquiries, that every two dustmen carry to the yard about five loads a day, or about 1500 loads in the course of the year, so that at this rate, there must be between six and seven carts, and twelve and fourteen collectors employed by each master. But this is exclusive of the men employed in the yards. In one yard that I visited there were fourteen people busily employed. Six of these were women, who were occupied in sifting, and they were attended by three men who shovelled the dust into their sieves, and the foreman, who was hard at work loosening and dragging down the dust from the heap, ready for the "fillers-in." Besides these there were two carts and four men engaged in conveying the sifted dust to the barges alongside the wharf. At a larger dust-yard, that formerly stood on the banks of the Regent's-canal, I am informed that there were sometimes as many as 127 people at work. It is but a small yard, which has not 30 to 40 labourers connected with it; and the lesser dust-yards have generally from four to eight sifters, and six or seven carts. There are, therefore, employed in a medium-sized yard twelve collectors or cartmen, six sifters, and three fillers-in besides the foreman or forewoman, making altogether 22 persons; so that, computing the contractors at 90, and allowing 20 men to be employed by each, there would be 1800 men thus occupied in the metropolis, which appears to be very near the truth.

One who has been all his life connected with the business estimated that there must be about ten dustmen to each metropolitan parish, large and small. In Marylebone he believed there were eighteen dust-carts, with two men to each, out every day; in some small parishes, however, two men are sufficient. There would be more men employed, he said, but some masters contracted for two or three parishes, and so "kept the same men going," working them hard, and enlarging their regular rounds. Calculating, then, that ten men are employed to each of the 176 metropolitan parishes, we have 1760 dustmen in London. The suburban parishes, my informant told me, were as well "dustmaned" as any he knew; for the residents in such parts were more particular about their dust than in busier places.

It is curious to observe how closely the number of men engaged in the collection of the " dust " from the coals burnt in London agrees, according to the above estimate, with the number of men engaged in delivering the coals to be burnt. The coal-whippers, who "discharge the colliers," are about 1800, and the coal-porters, who carry the coals from the barges to the merchants' wagons, are about the same in number. The amount of residuum from coal after burning cannot, of course, be equal either in bulk or weight to the original substance; but considering that the collection of the dust is a much slower operation than the delivery of the coals, the difference is easily accounted for.

We may arrive, approximately, at the quantity of dust annually produced in London, in the following manner:—

The consumption of coal in London, per annum, is about 3,500,000 tons, exclusive of what is brought to the metropolis per rail. Coals are made up of the following component parts, viz. (1) the inorganic and fixed elements; that is to say, the ashes, or the bones, as it were, of the fossil trees, which cannot be burnt; (2) coke, or the residuary carbon, after being deprived of the volatile matter; (3) the volatile matter itself given off during combustion in the form of flame and smoke.

The relative proportions of these materials in the various kinds of coals are as follows.—

	Carbon, per cent.	Volatile, per cent.	Ashes, per cent.
Cannel or gas coals.	40 to 60	60 to 40	10
Newcastle or "house" coals.	57	37	5
Lancashire and Yorkshire coals.	50 to 60	35 to 40	4
South Welsh or "steam" coals.	81 to 85	11 to 15	3
Anthracite or "stone" coals.	80 to 95	None	a little.

In the metropolis the Newcastle coal is chiefly

used, and this, we perceive, yields five per cent. ashes and about 57 per cent. carbon. But a considerable part of the carbon is converted into carbonic acid during combustion; if, therefore, we assume that two-thirds of the carbon are thus consumed, and that the remaining third remains behind in the form of cinder, we shall have about 25 per cent. of "dust" from every ton of coal. On inquiry of those who have had long experience in this matter, I find that a ton of coal may be fairly said on an average to yield about one-fourth its weight in dust; hence the gross amount of "dust" annually produced in London would be 900,000 tons, or about three tons per house per annum.

It is impossible to obtain any definite statistics on this part of the subject. Not one in every ten of the contractors keeps any account of the amount that comes into the "yard." An intelligent and communicative gentleman whom I consulted on this matter, could give me no information on this subject that was in any way satisfactory. I have, however, endeavoured to check the preceding estimate in the following manner. There are in London upwards of 300,000 inhabited houses, and each house furnishes a certain quota of dust to the general stock. I have ascertained that an average-sized house will produce, in the course of a year, about three cart-loads of dust, while each cart holds about 40 bushels (baskets)—what the dustmen call a chaldron. There are, of course, many houses in the metropolis which furnish three and four times this amount of dust, but against these may be placed the vast preponderance of small and poor houses in London and the suburbs, where there is not one quarter of the quantity produced, owing to the small amount of fuel consumed. Estimating, then, the average annual quantity of dust from each house at three loads, or chaldrons, and the houses at 300,000, it follows that the gross quantity collected throughout the metropolis will be about 900,000 chaldrons per annum.

The next part of the subject is—what becomes of this vast quantity of dust—to what use it is applied.

The dust thus collected is used for two purposes, (1) as a manure for land of a peculiar quality; and (2) for making bricks. The fine portion of the house-dust called "soil," and separated from the "brieze," or coarser portion, by sifting, is found to be peculiarly fitted for what is called breaking up a marshy heathy soil at its first cultivation, owing not only to the dry nature of the dust, but to its possessing in an eminent degree a highly separating quality, almost, if not quite, equal to sand. In former years the demand for this finer dust was very great, and barges were continually in the river waiting their turn to be loaded with it for some distant part of the country. At that time the contractors were unable to supply the demand, and easily got 1*l*. per chaldron for as much as they could furnish, and then, as I have stated, many ships were in the habit of bringing cargoes of it from the North, and of realizing a good profit on the transaction. Of late years, however—and particularly, I am told, since the repeal of the corn-laws—this branch of the business has dwindled to nothing. The contractors say that the farmers do not cultivate their land now as they used; it will not pay them, and instead, therefore, of bringing fresh land into tillage, and especially such as requires this sort of manure, they are laying down that which they previously had in cultivation, and turning it into pasture grounds. It is principally on this account, say the contractors, that we cannot sell the dust we collect so well or so readily as formerly. There are, however, some cargoes of the dust still taken, particularly to the lowlands in the neighbourhood of Barking, and such other places in the vicinity of the metropolis as are enabled to realize a greater profit, by growing for the London markets. Nevertheless, the contractors are obliged now to dispose of the dust at 2*s*. 6*d*. per chaldron, and sometimes less.

The finer dust is also used to mix with the clay for making bricks, and barge-loads are continually shipped off for this purpose. The fine ashes are added to the clay in the proportion of one-fifth ashes to four-fifths clay, or 60 chaldrons to 240 cubic yards, which is sufficient to make 100,000 bricks (where much sand is mixed with the clay a smaller proportion of ashes may be used). This quantity requires also the addition of about 15 chaldrons, or, if mild, of about 12 chaldrons of "brieze," to aid the burning. The ashes are made to mix with the clay by collecting it into a sort of reservoir fitted up for the purpose; water in great quantities is let in upon it, and it is then stirred till it resembles a fine thin paste, in which state the dust easily mingles with every part of it. In this condition it is left till the water either soaks into the earth, or goes off by evaporation, when the bricks are moulded in the usual manner, the dust forming a component part of them.

The ashes, or cindered matter, which are thus dispersed throughout the substance of the clay, become, in the process of burning, gradually ignited and consumed. But the "brieze" (from the French *briser*, to break or crush), that is to say, the coarser portion of the coal-ash, is likewise used in the burning of the bricks. The small spaces left among the lowest courses of the bricks in the kiln, or "clamp," are filled with "brieze," and a thick layer of the same material is spread on the top of the kilns, when full. Frequently the "brieze" is mixed with small coals, and after having been burnt the ashes are collected, and then mixed with the clay to form new bricks. The highest price at present given for "brieze" is 3*s*. per ton.

The price of the dust used by the brickmakers has likewise been reduced; this the contractors account for by saying that there are fewer brick-fields than formerly near London, as they have been nearly all built over. They assert, that while the amount of dust and cinders has increased proportionately to the increase of the houses, the demand for the article has decreased in a like ratio; and that, moreover, the greater portion of the bricks now used in London for the new buildings come from other quarters. Such dust, however, as the contractors sell to the brick-makers, they in general undertake, for a certain sum, to cart to the brick-fields, though it often happens that the brick-makers' carts coming into town with their loads of bricks to new buildings, call on their return at the dust-yards, and carry thence a load of dust or cinders back, and so save the price of cartage.

But during the operation of sifting the dust, many things are found which are useless for either manure or brick-making, such as oyster shells, old bricks, old boots and shoes, old tin kettles, old rags and bones, &c. These are used for various purposes.

The bricks, &c., are sold for sinking beneath foundations, where a thick layer of concrete is spread over them. Many old bricks, too, are used in making new roads, especially where the land is low and marshy. The old tin goes to form the japanned fastenings for the corners of trunks, as well as to other persons, who re-manufacture it into a variety of articles. The old shoes are sold to the London shoemakers, who use them as stuffing between the in-sole and the outer one; but by far the greater quantity is sold to the manufacturers of Prussian blue, that substance being formed out of refuse animal matter. The rags and bones are of course disposed of at the usual places—the marine-store shops.

A dust-heap, therefore, may be briefly said to be composed of the following things, which are severally applied to the following uses:—

1. "Soil," or fine dust, sold to brickmakers for making bricks, and to farmers for manure, especially for clover.
2. "Brieze," or cinders, sold to brickmakers, for burning bricks.
3. Rags, bones, and old metal, sold to marine-store dealers.
4. Old tin and iron vessels, sold for "clamps" to trunks, &c., and for making copperas.
5. Old bricks and oyster shells, sold to builders, for sinking foundations, and forming roads.
6. Old boots and shoes, sold to Prussian-blue manufacturers.
7. Money and jewellery, kept, or sold to Jews.

The dust-yards, or places where the dust is collected and sifted, are generally situated in the suburbs, and they may be found all round London, sometimes occupying open spaces adjoining back streets and lanes, and surrounded by the low mean houses of the poor; frequently, however, they cover a large extent of ground in the fields, and there the dust is piled up to a great height in a conical heap, and having much the appearance of a volcanic mountain. The reason why the dust-heaps are confined principally to the suburbs is, that more space is to be found in the outskirts than in a thickly-peopled and central locality. Moreover, the fear of indictments for nuisance has had considerable influence in the matter, for it was not unusual for the yards in former times, to be located within the boundaries of the city.

They are now, however, scattered round London, and always placed as near as possible to the river, or to some canal communicating therewith. In St. George's, Shadwell, Ratcliffe, Limehouse, Poplar, and Blackwall, on the north side of the Thames, and in Redriffe, Bermondsey, and Rotherhithe, on the south, they are to be found near the Thames. The object of this is, that by far the greater quantity of the soil or ashes is conveyed in sailing-barges, holding from 70 to 100 tons each, to Feversham, Sittingbourne, and other places in Kent, which are the great brick-making manufactories for London. These barges come up invariably loaded with bricks, and take home in return a cargo of soil. Other dust-yards are situated contiguous to the Regent's and the Surrey canal; and for the same reason as above stated—for the convenience of water carriage. Moreover, adjoining the Limehouse cut, which is a branch of the Lea River, other dust-yards may be found; and again travelling to the opposite end of the metropolis, we discover them not only at Paddington on the banks of the canal, but at Maiden-lane in a similar position. Some time since there was an immense dust-heap in the neighbourhood of Gray's-inn-lane, which sold for 20,000l.; but that was in the days when 15s. and 1l. per chaldron could easily be procured for the dust. According to the present rate, not a tithe of that amount could have been realized upon it.

A visit to any of the large metropolitan dust-yards is far from uninteresting. Near the centre of the yard rises the highest heap, composed of what is called the "soil," or finer portion of the dust used for manure. Around this heap are numerous lesser heaps, consisting of the mixed dust and rubbish carted in and shot down previous to sifting. Among these heaps are many women and old men with sieves made of iron, all busily engaged in separating the "brieze" from the "soil." There is likewise another large heap in some other part of the yard, composed of the cinders or "brieze" waiting to be shipped off to the brickfields. The whole yard seems alive, some sifting and others shovelling the sifted soil on to the heap, while every now and then the dust-carts return to discharge their loads, and proceed again on their rounds for a fresh supply. Cocks and hens keep up a continual scratching and cackling among the heaps, and numerous pigs seem to find great delight in rooting incessantly about after the garbage and offal collected from the houses and markets.

In a dust-yard lately visited the sifters formed a curious sight; they were almost up to their middle in dust, ranged in a semi-circle in front of that part of the heap which was being "worked;" each had before her a small mound of soil which had fallen through her sieve and formed a sort of embankment, behind which she stood. The appearance of the entire group at their work was most peculiar. Their coarse dirty cotton gowns were tucked up behind them, their arms were bared above their elbows, their black bonnets crushed and battered like those of fish-women; over their gowns they wore a strong leathern apron, extending from their necks to the extremities of their petticoats, while over this, again, was another leathern apron, shorter, thickly padded, and fastened by a stout string or strap round the waist. In the process of their work they pushed the sieve from them and drew it back again with apparent violence, striking it against the outer leathern apron with such force that it produced each time a hollow sound, like a blow on the tenor drum. All the women present were middle aged, with the exception of one who was very old—68 years of age she told me—and had been at the business from a girl. She was the daughter of a dustman, the wife, or woman of a dustman, and the mother of several young dustmen—sons and grandsons—all at work at the dust-yards at the east end of the metropolis.

We now come to speak of the labourers engaged in collecting, sifting, or shipping off the dust of the metropolis.

The dustmen, scavengers, and nightmen are, to a certain extent, the same people. The contractors generally agree with the various parishes to remove both the dust from the houses and the mud from the streets; the men in their employ are indiscriminately engaged in these two diverse occupations, collecting the dust to-day, and often cleansing the streets on the morrow, and are designated either dustmen or scavengers, according to their particular avocation at the moment. The case is somewhat different, however, with respect to the nightmen. There is no such thing as a contract with the parish for removing the nightsoil. This is done by private agreement with the landlord of the premises whence the soil has to be removed. When a cesspool requires emptying, the occupying tenant communicates with the landlord, who makes an arrangement with a dust-contractor or sweep-nightman for this purpose. This operation is totally distinct from the regular or daily labour of the dust-contractor's men, who receive extra pay for it; sometimes one set go out at night and sometimes another, according either to the selection of the master or the inclination of the men. There are, however, some dustmen who have never been at work as nightmen, and could not be induced to do so, from an invincible antipathy to the employment; still, such instances are few, for the men generally go whenever they can, and occasionally engage in nightwork for employers unconnected with their masters. It is calculated that there are some hundreds of men employed nightly in the removal of the nightsoil of the metropolis during the summer and autumn, and as these men have often to work at dust-collecting or cleansing the streets on the following day, it is evident that the same persons cannot be thus employed every night; accordingly the ordinary practice is for the dustmen to "take it in turns," thus allowing each set to be employed every third night, and to have two nights' rest in the interim.

The men, therefore, who collect the dust on one day may be cleaning the streets on the next, especially during wet weather, and engaged at night, perhaps, twice during the week, in removing nightsoil; so that it is difficult to arrive at any precise notion as to the number of persons engaged in any one of these branches *per se*.

But these labourers not only work indiscriminately at the collection of dust, the cleansing of the streets, or the removal of nightsoil, but they are employed almost as indiscriminately at the various branches of the dust business; with this qualification, however, that few men apply themselves continuously to any one branch of the business. The labourers employed in a dust-yard may be divided into two classes: those paid by the contractor; and those paid by the foreman or forewoman of the dust-heap, commonly called hill-man or hill-woman.

They are as follows:—

I. LABOURERS PAID BY THE CONTRACTORS, OR,
1. *Yard foreman*, or superintendent. This duty is often performed by the master, especially in small contracts.
2. *Gangers* or *dust-collectors*. These are called "fillers" and "carriers," from the practice of one of the men who go out with the cart filling the basket, and the other carrying it on his shoulder to the vehicle.
3. *Loaders* of carts in the dust-yard for shipment.
4. *Carriers* of cinders to the cinder-heap, or bricks to the brick-heap.
5. *Foreman* or *forewoman* of the heap.

II. LABOURERS PAID BY THE HILL-MAN OR HILL-WOMAN.
1. *Sifters*, who are generally women, and mostly the wives or concubines of the dustmen, but sometimes the wives of badly-paid labourers.
2. *Fillers-in*, or shovellers of dust into the sieves of the sifters (one man being allowed to every two or three women).
3. *Carriers off* of bones, rags, metal, and other perquisites to the various heaps; these are mostly children of the dustmen.

A medium-sized dust-yard will employ about twelve collectors, three fillers-in, six sifters, and one foreman or forewoman; while a large yard will afford work to about 150 people.

There are four different modes of payment prevalent among the several labourers employed at the metropolitan dust-yards:—(1) by the day; (2) by the piece or load; (3) by the lump; (4) by perquisites.

1st. The foreman of the yard, where the master does not perform this duty himself, is generally one of the regular dustmen picked out by the master, for this purpose. He is paid, the sum of 2*s.* 6*d.* per day, or 15*s.* per week. In large yards there are sometimes two and even three yard-foremen at the same rate of wages. Their duty is merely to superintend the work. They do not labour themselves, and their exemption in this respect is considered, and indeed looked on by themselves, as a sort of premium for good services.

2nd. The gangers or collectors are generally

THE LONDON DUSTMAN.

Dust Hoi! Dust Hoi!

[*From a Daguerreotype by* Beard.]

VIEW OF A DUST YARD.
(From a Sketch taken on the spot.)

paid 8d. per load for every load they bring into the yard. This is, of course, piece work, for the more hours the men work the more loads will they be enabled to bring, and the more pay will they receive. There are some yards where the carters get only 6d. per load, as, for instance, at Paddington. The Paddington men, however, are not considered inferior workmen to the rest of their fellows, but merely to be worse paid. In 1826, or 25 years ago, the carters had 1s. 6d. per load; but at that time the contractors were able to get 1l. per chaldron for the soil and "brieze" or cinders; then it began to fall in value, and according to the decrease in the price of these commodities, so have the wages of the dust-collectors been reduced. It will be at once seen that the reduction in the wages of the dustmen bears no proportion to the reduction in the price of soil and cinders, but it must be borne in mind that whereas the contractors formerly paid large sums for liberty to collect the dust, they now are paid large sums to remove it. This in some measure helps to account for the apparent disproportion, and tends, perhaps, to equalize the matter. The gangers, therefore, have 4d. each, per load when best paid. They consider from four to six loads a good day's work, for where the contract is large, extending over several parishes, they often have to travel a long way for a load. It thus happens that while the men employed by the Whitechapel contractor can, when doing their utmost, manage to bring only four loads a day to the yard, which is situated in a place called the "ruins" in Lower Shadwell, the men employed by the Shadwell contractor can easily get eight or nine loads in a day. Five loads are about an average day's work, and this gives them 1s. 8$\frac{1}{2}d$. per day each, or 10s. per week. In addition to this, the men have their perquisites "in aid of wages." The collectors are in the habit of getting beer or money in lieu thereof, at nearly all the houses from which they remove the dust, the public being thus in a manner compelled to make up the rate of wages, which should be paid by the employer, so that what is given to benefit the men really goes to the master, who invariably reduces the wages to the precise amount of the perquisites obtained. This is the main evil of the "perquisite system of payment" (a system of which the mode of paying waiters may be taken as the special type). As an instance of the injurious effects of this mode of payment in connection with the London dustmen, the collectors are forced, as it were, to extort from the public that portion of their fair earnings of which their master deprives them; hence, how can we wonder that they make it a rule when they receive neither beer nor money from a house to make as great a mess as possible the next time they come, scattering the dust and cinders about in such a manner, that, sooner than have any trouble with them, people mostly give them what they look for? One of the most intelligent men with whom I have spoken, gave me the following account of his perquisites for the last week, viz.: Monday, 5$\frac{1}{2}d$.; Tuesday, 6d.; Wednesday, 4$\frac{1}{2}d$.; Thursday, 7d.; Friday, 5$\frac{1}{2}d$.; and Saturday, 5d. This he received in money, and was independent of beer. He had on the same week drawn rather more than five loads each day, to the yard, which made his gross earnings for the week, wages and perquisites together, to be 14s. 0$\frac{1}{2}d$. which he considers to be a fair average of his weekly earnings as connected with dust.

3rd. The loaders of the carts for shipment are the same persons as those who collect the dust, but thus employed for the time being. The pay for this work is by the "piece" also, 2d. per chaldron between four persons being the usual rate, or $\frac{1}{2}d$. per man. The men so engaged have no perquisites. The barges into which they shoot the soil or "brieze," as the case may be, hold from 50 to 70 chaldrons, and they consider the loading of one of these barges a good day's work. The average cargo is about 60 chaldrons, which gives them 2s. 6d. per day, or somewhat more than their average earnings when collecting.

4th. The carriers of cinders to the cinder heap. I have mentioned that, ranged round the sifters in the dust-yard, are a number of baskets, into which are put the various things found among the dust, some of these being the property of the master, and others the perquisites of the hill man or woman, as the case may be. The cinders and old bricks are the property of the master, and to remove them to their proper heaps boys are employed by him at 1s. per day. These boys are almost universally the children of dustmen and sifters at work in the yard, and thus not only help to increase the earnings of the family, but qualify themselves to become the dustmen of a future day.

5th. The hill-man or hill-woman. The hill-man enters into an agreement with the contractor to sift *all* the dust in the yard throughout the year at so much per load and perquisites. The usual sum per load is 6d., nor have I been able to ascertain that any of these people undertake to do it at a less price. Such is the amount paid by the contractor for Whitechapel. The perquisites of the hill-man or hill-woman, are rags, bones, pieces of old metal, old tin or iron vessels, old boots and shoes, and one-half of the money, jewellery, or other valuables that may be found by the sifters.

The hill-man or hill-woman employs the following persons, and pays them at the following rates.

1st. The sifters are paid 1s. per day when employed, but the employment is not constant. The work cannot be pursued in wet weather, and the services of the sifters are required only when a large heap has accumulated, as they can sift much faster than the dust can be collected. The employment is therefore precarious; the payment has not, for the last 30 years at least, been more than 1s. per day, but the perquisites were greater. They formerly were allowed one-half of whatever was found; of late years, however, the hill-man has gradually reduced the perquisites "first one thing and then another," until the only one they have now remaining is half of whatever money or other valuable article may be found in the process of sifting. These valuables the sifters often pocket, if able to do so unperceived, but if discovered in the attempt, they are immediately discharged.

2nd. "The fillers-in," or shovellers of dust into the sieves of sifters, are in general any poor fellows who may be straggling about in search of employment. They are sometimes, however, the grown-up boys of dustmen, not yet permanently engaged by the contractor. These are paid 2s. per day for their labour, but they are considered more as casualty men, though it often happens, if "hands" are wanted, that they are regularly engaged by the contractors, and become regular dustmen for the remainder of their lives.

3rd. The little fellows, the children of the dustmen, who follow their mothers to the yard, and help them to pick rags, bones, &c., out of the sieve and put them into the baskets, as soon as they are able to carry a basket between two of them to the separate heaps, are paid 3d. or 4d. per day for this work by the hill-man.

The wages of the dustmen have been increased within the last seven years from 6d. per load to 8d. among the large contractors—the "small masters," however, still continue to pay 6d. per load. This increase in the rate of remuneration was owing to the men complaining to the commissioners that they were not able to live upon what they earned at 6d.; an enquiry was made into the truth of the men's assertion, and the result was that the commisioners decided upon letting the contracts to such parties only as would undertake to pay a fair price to their workmen. The contractors, accordingly, increased the remuneration of the labourers; since then the principal masters have paid 8d. per load to the collectors. It is right I should add, that I could not hear—though I made special enquiries on the subject—that the wages had been in any one instance reduced since Free-trade has come into operation.

The usual hours of labour vary according to the mode of payment. The "collectors," or men out with the cart, being paid by the load, work as long as the light lasts; the "fillers-in" and sifters, on the other hand, being paid by the day, work the ordinary hours, viz., from six to six, with the regular intervals for meals.

The summer is the worst time for all hands, for then the dust decreases in quantity; the collectors, however, make up for the "slackness" at this period by nightwork, and, being paid by the "piece" or load at the dust business, are not discharged when their employment is less brisk.

It has been shown that the dustmen who perambulate the streets usually collect five loads in a day; this, at 8d. per load, leaves them about 1s. 8d. each, and so makes their weekly earnings amount to about 10s. per week. Moreover, there are the "perquisites" from the houses whence they remove the dust; and further, the dust-collectors are frequently employed at the night-work, which is always a distinct matter from the dust-collecting, &c., and paid for independent of their regular weekly wages, so that, from all I can gather, the average wages of the men appear to be rather more than 15s. Some admitted to me, that in busy times they often earned 25s. a week.

Then, again, dustwork, as with the weaving of silk, is a kind of family work. The husband, wife, and children (unfortunately) all work at it. The consequence is, that the earnings of the whole have to be added together in order to arrive at a notion of the aggregate gains.

The following may therefore be taken as a fair average of the earnings of a dustman and his family *when in full employment*. The elder boys when able to earn 1s. a day set up for themselves, and do not allow their wages to go into the common purse.

	£. s. d.	£. s. d.
Man, 5 loads per day, or 30 loads per week, at 4d. per load	0 10 0	
Perquisites, or beer money	0 2 9½	
Night-work for 2 nights a week	0 5 0	
		0 17 9½
Woman, or sifter, per week, at 1s. per day	0 6 0	
Perquisites, say 3d. a day	0 1 6	
		0 7 6
Child, 3d. per day, carrying rags, bones, &c.		0 1 6
Total		1 6 9½

These are the earnings, it should be borne in mind, of a family in full employment. Perhaps it may be fairly said that the earnings of the single men are, on an average, 15s. a week, and 1l. for the family men all the year round.

Now, when we remember that the wages of many agricultural labourers are but 8s. a week, and the earnings of many needlewomen not 6d. a day, it must be confessed that the remuneration of the dustmen, and even of the dustwomen, is *comparatively* high. This certainly is not due to what Adam Smith, in his chapter on the Difference of Wages, terms the "disagreeableness of the employment." "The wages of labour," he says, "vary with the ease or hardship, the cleanliness or dirtiness, the honourableness or dishonourableness, of the employment." It will be seen — when we come to treat of the nightmen — that the most offensive, and perhaps the least honourable, of all trades, is far from ranking among the best paid, as it should, if the above principle held good. That the disagreeableness of the occupation may in a measure tend to decrease the competition among the labourers, there cannot be the least doubt, but that it will consequently induce, as political economy would have us believe, a larger amount of wages to accrue to each of the labourers, is certainly another of the many assertions of that science which must be pronounced "not proven." For the dustmen are paid, if anything, less, and certainly not more, than the usual rate of payment to the London labourers; and if the earnings rank high, as times go, it is because all the members of the family, from the very earliest age, are able to work at the business, and so add to the general gains.

The dustmen are, generally speaking, an hereditary race; when children they are reared in the dust-yard, and are habituated to the work gradually as they grow up, after which, almost as a natural consequence, they follow the business for the remainder of their lives. These may be said to be born-and-bred dustmen. The numbers of the regular men are, however, from time to time recruited from the ranks of the many ill-paid labourers with which London abounds. When hands are wanted for any special occasion an employer has only to go to any of the dock-gates, to find at all times hundreds of starving wretches anxiously watching for the chance of getting something to do, even at the rate of 4d. per hour. As the operation of emptying a dust-bin requires only the ability to handle a shovel, which every labouring man can manage, all workmen, however unskilled, can at once engage in the occupation; and it often happens that the men thus casually employed remain at the calling for the remainder of their lives. There are no houses of call whence the men are taken on when wanting work. There are certainly public-houses, which are denominated houses of call, in the neighbourhood of every dust-yard, but these are merely the drinking shops of the men, whither they resort of an evening after the labour of the day is accomplished, and whence they are furnished in the course of the afternoon with beer; but such houses cannot be said to constitute the dustman's "labour-market," as in the tailoring and other trades, they being never resorted to as hiring-places, but rather used by the men only when hired. If a master have not enough "hands" he usually inquires among his men, who mostly know some who—owing, perhaps, to the failure of their previous master in getting his usual contract—are only casually employed at other places. Such men are immediately engaged in preference to others; but if these cannot be found, the contractors at once have recourse to the system already stated.

The manner in which the dust is collected is very simple. The "filler" and the "carrier" perambulate the streets with a heavily-built high box cart, which is mostly coated with a thick crust of filth, and drawn by a clumsy-looking horse. These men used, before the passing of the late Street Act, to ring a dull-sounding bell so as to give notice to housekeepers of their approach, but now they merely cry, in a hoarse unmusical voice, "Dust oy-eh!" Two men accompany the cart, which is furnished with a short ladder and two shovels and baskets. These baskets one of the men fills from the dust-bin, and then helps them alternately, as fast as they are filled, upon the shoulder of the other man, who carries them one by one to the cart, which is placed immediately alongside the pavement in front of the house where they are at work. The carrier mounts up the side of the cart by means of the ladder, discharges into it the contents of the basket on his shoulder, and then returns below for the other basket which his mate has filled for him in the interim. This process is pursued till all is cleared away, and repeated at different houses till the cart is fully loaded; then the men make the best of their way to the dust-yard, where they shoot the contents of the cart on to the heap, and again proceed on their regular rounds.

The dustmen, in their appearance, very much resemble the waggoners of the coal-merchants. They generally wear knee-breeches, with ancle boots or gaiters, short dirty smockfrocks or coarse gray jackets, and fantail hats. In one particular, however, they are at first sight distinguishable from the coal-merchants' men, for the latter are invariably black from coal dust, while the dustmen, on the contrary, are gray with ashes.

In their personal appearance the dustmen are mostly tall stalwart fellows; there is nothing sickly-looking about them, and yet a considerable part of their time is passed in the yards and in the midst of effluvia most offensive, and, if we believe "zymotic theorists," as unhealthy to those unaccustomed to them; nevertheless, the children, who may be said to be reared in the yard and to have inhaled the stench of the dust-heap with their first breath, are healthy and strong. It is said, moreover, that during the plague in London the dustmen were the persons who carted away the dead, and it remains a tradition among the class to the present day, that not one of them died of the plague, even during its greatest ravages. In Paris, too, it is well known, that, during the cholera of 1849, the quarter of Belleville, where the night-soil and refuse of the city is deposited, escaped the freest from the pestilence; and in London the dustmen boast that, during both the recent visitations of the cholera, they were altogether exempt from the disease. "Look at that fellow, sir!" said one of the dust-contractors to me, pointing to his son, who was a stout red-cheeked young man of about twenty. "Do you see anything ailing about him? Well, he has been in the yard since he was born. There stands my house just at the gate, so you see he hadn't far to travel, and when quite a child he used to play and root away here among the dust all his time. I don't think he ever had a day's illness in his life. The people about the yard are all used to the smell and don't complain about it. It's all stuff and nonsense, all this talk about dust-yards being unhealthy. I've never done anything else all my days and I don't think I look very ill. I shouldn't wonder now but what I'd be set down as being fresh from the sea-side by those very fellows that write all this trash about a matter that they don't know just *that* about;" and he snapped his fingers contemptuously in the air, and, thrusting both hands into his breeches pockets, strutted about, apparently satisfied that he had the best of the argument. He was, in fact, a stout, jolly, red-faced man. Indeed, the dustmen, as a class, appear to be healthy, strong men, and extraordinary instances of longevity are common among them. I heard of one dustman who lived to be 115 years; another, named Wood, died at 100; and the well-known Richard Tyrrell died only a short time back at the advanced age of 97. The misfortune is, that we have no large series of facts on this subject, so that the longevity and health of the dustmen might be compared with those of other classes.

In almost all their habits the Dustmen are similar to the Costermongers, with the exception that they seem to want their cunning and natural quickness, and that they have little or no predilection for gaming. Costermongers, however, are essentially traders, and all trade is a species of gambling—the risking of a certain sum of money to obtain more; hence spring, perhaps, the gambling propensities of low traders, such as costers, and Jew clothes-men; and hence, too, that natural sharpness which characterizes the same classes. The dustmen, on the contrary, have regular employment and something like regular wages, and therefore rest content with what they can earn in their usual way of business.

Very few of them understand cards, and I could not learn that they ever play at "pitch and toss." I remarked, however, a number of parallel lines such as are used for playing "shove halfpenny," on a deal table in the tap-room frequented by them. The great amusement of their evenings seems to be, to smoke as many pipes of tobacco and drink as many pots of beer as possible.

I believe it will be found that all persons in the habit of driving horses, such as cabmen, 'busmen, stage-coach drivers, &c., are peculiarly partial to intoxicating drinks. The cause of this I leave others to determine, merely observing that there would seem to be two reasons for it: the first is, their frequent stopping at public-houses to water or change their horses, so that the idea of drinking is repeatedly suggested to their minds even if the practice be not *expected* of them; while the second reason is, that being out continually in the wet, they resort to stimulating liquors as a preventive to "colds" until at length a habit of drinking is formed. Moreover, from the mere fact of passing continually through the air, they are enabled to drink a greater quantity with comparative impunity. Be the cause, however, what it may, the dustmen spend a large proportion of their earnings in drink. There is always some public-house in the neighbourhood of the dust-yard, where they obtain credit from one week to another, and here they may be found every night from the moment their work is done, drinking, and smoking their long pipes—their principal amusement consisting in "chaffing" each other. This "chaffing" consists of a species of scurrilous jokes supposed to be given and taken in good part, and the noise and uproar occasioned thereby increases as the night advances, and as the men get heated with liquor. Sometimes the joking ends in a general quarrel; the next morning, however, they are all as good friends as ever, and mutually agree in laying the blame on the "cussed drink."

One-half, at least, of the dustmen's earnings, is, I am assured, expended in drink, both man and woman assisting in squandering their money in this way. They usually live in rooms for which they pay from 1s. 6d. to 2s. per week rent, three or four dust-men and their wives frequently lodging in the same house. These rooms are cheerless-looking, and almost unfurnished—and are always situate in some low street or lane not far from the dust-yard. The men have rarely any clothes but those in which they work. For their breakfast the dustmen on their rounds mostly go to some cheap coffee-house, where they get a pint or half-pint of coffee, taking their bread with them as a matter of economy. Their midday meal is taken in the public-house, and is almost always bread and cheese and beer, or else a saveloy or a piece of fat pork or bacon, and at night they mostly "wind up" by deep potations at their favourite house of call.

There are many dustmen now advanced in years born and reared at the East-end of London, who have never in the whole course of their lives been as far west as Temple-bar, who know nothing whatever of the affairs of the country, and who have never attended a place of worship. As an instance of the extreme ignorance of these people, I may mention that I was furnished by one of the contractors with the address of a dustman whom his master considered to be one of the most intelligent men in his employ. Being desirous of hearing his statement from his own lips I sent for the man, and after some conversation with him was proceeding to note down what he said, when the moment I opened my note-book and took the pencil in my hand, he started up, exclaiming,—" No, no! I'll have none of that there work— I'm not such a b—— fool as you takes me to be —I doesn't understand it, I tells you, and I'll not have it, now that's plain;" —and so saying he ran out of the room, and descended the entire flight of stairs in two jumps. I followed him to explain, but unfortunately the pencil was still in one hand and the book in the other, and immediately I made my appearance at the door he took to his heels, again with three others who seemed to be waiting for him there. One of the most difficult points in my labours is to make such men as these comprehend the object or use of my investigations.

Among 20 men whom I met in one yard, there were only five who could read, and only two out of that five could write, even imperfectly. These two are looked up to by their companions as prodigies of learning and are listened to as oracles, on all occasions, being believed to understand every subject thoroughly. It need hardly be added, however, that their acquirements are of the most meagre character.

The dustmen are very partial to a song, and always prefer one of the doggrel street ballads, with what they call a "jolly chorus" in which, during their festivities, they all join with stentorian voices. At the conclusion there is usually a loud stamping of feet and rattling of quart pots on the table, expressive of their approbation.

The dustmen never frequent the twopenny hops, but sometimes make up a party for the "theaytre." They generally go in a body with their wives, if married, and their "gals," if single. They are always to be found in the gallery, and greatly enjoy the melodramas performed at the second-class minor theatres, especially if there be plenty of murdering scenes in them. The Garrick, previous to its being burnt, was a favourite resort of the East-end dustmen. Since that period they have patronized the Pavilion and the City of London.

The politics of the dustmen are on a par with their literary attainments—they cannot be said to have any. I cannot say that they are Chartists, for they have no very clear knowledge of what "the charter" requires. They certainly have a confused notion that it is something against the Government, and that the enactment of it would make them all right; but as to the nature of the benefits which it would confer upon them, or in what manner it would be likely to operate upon their interest, they have not, as a body, the slightest idea. They have a deep-rooted antipathy to the police, the magistrates, and all connected with the administration of justice, looking upon them as their natural enemies. They associate with none but themselves; and in the public-houses where they resort there is a room set apart for the special use of the "dusties," as they are called, where no others are allowed to intrude, except introduced by one of themselves, or at the special desire of the majority of the party, and on such occasions the stranger is treated with great respect and consideration.

As to the morals of these people, it may easily be supposed that they are not of an over-strict character. One of the contractors said to me, "I'd just trust one of them as far as I could fling a bull by the tail; *but then*," he added, with a callousness that proved the laxity of discipline among the men was due more to his neglect of his duty to them than from any special perversity on their parts, "*that's none of my business; they do my work, and that's all I want with them, and all I care about.* You see they're not like other people, they're reared to it. Their fathers before them were dustmen, and when lads they go into the yard as sifters, and when they grow up they take to the shovel, and go out with the carts. They learn all they know in the dust-yards, and you may judge from that what their learning is likely to be. If they find anything among the dust you may be sure that neither you nor I will ever hear anything about it; ignorant as they are, they know a little too much for that. They know, as well as here and there one, where the dolly-shop is; *but, as I said before, that's none of my business. Let every one look out for themselves, as I do, and then they need not care for any one.*" [With such masters professing such principles—though it should be stated that the sentiments expressed on this occasion are but similar to what I hear from the lower class of traders every day—how can it be expected that these poor fellows can be above the level of the mere beasts of burden that they use.] "As to their women," continued the master, "I don't trouble my head about such things. I believe the dustmen are as good to them as other men; and I'm sure their wives would be as good as other women, if they only had the chance of the best. But you see they're all such fellows for drink that they spend most of their money that way, and then starve the poor women, and knock them about at a shocking rate, so that they have the life of dogs, or worse. I don't wonder at anything they do. Yes, they're all married, as far as I know; that is, they live together as man and wife, though they're not very particular, certainly, about the ceremony. The fact is, a regular dustman don't understand much about such matters, and, I believe, don't care much, either."

From all I could learn on this subject, it would appear that, for one dustman that is married, 20 live with women, but remain constant to them; indeed, both men and women abide faithfully by each other, and for this reason—the woman earns nearly half as much as the man. If the men and women were careful and prudent, they might, I am assured, live well and comfortable; but by far the greater portion of the earnings of both go to the publican, for I am informed, on competent authority, that a dustman will not think of sitting down for a spree without his woman. The children, as soon as they are able to go into the yard, help their mothers in picking out the rags, bones, &c., from the sieve, and in putting them in the basket. They are never sent to school, and as soon as they are sufficiently strong are mostly employed in some capacity or other by the contractor, and in due time become dustmen themselves. Some of the children, in the neighbourhood of the river, are mud-larks, and others are bone-grubbers and rag-gatherers, on a small scale; neglected and thrown on their own resources at an early age, without any but the most depraved to guide them, it is no wonder to find that many of them turn thieves. To this state of the case there are, however, some few exceptions.

Some of the dustmen are prudent well-behaved men and have decent homes; many of this class have been agricultural labourers, who by distress, or from some other cause, have found their way to London. This was the case with one whom I talked with: he had been a labourer in Essex, employed by a farmer named Izzod, whom he spoke of as being a kind good man. Mr. Izzod had a large farm on the Earl of Mornington's estate, and after he had sunk his capital in the improvement of the land, and was about to reap the fruits of his labour and his money, the farmer was ejected at a moment's notice, beggared and broken-hearted. This occurred near Roydon, in Essex. The labourer, finding it difficult to obtain work in the country, came to London, and, discovering a cousin of his engaged in a dust-yard, got employed through him at the same place, where he remains to the present day. This man was well clothed, he had good strong lace boots, gray worsted stockings, a stout pair of corduroy breeches, a short smockfrock and fantail. He has kept himself aloof, I am told, from the drunkenness and dissipation of the dustmen. He says that many of the new hands that get to dustwork are mechanics or people who have been "better off," and that these get thinking about what they have been, till to drown their care they take to drinking, and often become, in the course of a year or so, worse than the "old hands" who have been reared to the business and have "nothing at all to think about."

Among the dustmen there is no "Society" nor "Benefit Club," specially devoted to the class—no provident institution whence they can obtain "relief" in the event of sickness or accident. The consequence is that, when ill or injured, they are obliged to obtain letters of admission to some of the hospitals, and there remain till cured. In cases of total incapacity for labour, their invariable refuge is the workhouse; indeed they look forward (whenever they foresee at all) to this asylum as their resting-place in old age, with the greatest equanimity, and talk of it as "the house" par excellence, or as "the big house," "the great house," or "the old house." There are, however, scattered about in every part of London numerous benefit clubs made up of working-men of every description, such as Old Friends, Odd Fellows, Foresters, and Birmingham societies, and with some one or other of these the better class of dustmen are connected. The general rule, however, is, that the men engaged in this trade belong to no benefit club whatever, and that in the season of their adversity they are utterly unprovided for, and consequently become burdens to the parishes wherein they happen to reside.

I visited a large dust-yard at the east end of London, for the purpose of getting a statement from one of the men. My informant was, at the time of my visit, shovelling the sifted soil from one of the lesser heaps, and, by a great effort of strength and activity, pitching each shovel-full to the top of a lofty mound, somewhat resembling a pyramid. Opposite to him stood a little woman, stoutly made, and with her arms bare above the elbow; she was his partner in the work, and was pitching shovel-full for shovel-full with him to the summit of the heap. She wore an old soiled cotton gown, open in front, and tucked up behind in the fashion of the last century. She had clouts of old rags tied round her ancles to prevent the dust from getting into her shoes, a sort of coarse towel fastened in front for an apron, and a red handkerchief bound tightly round her head. In this trim she worked away, and not only kept pace with the man, but often threw two shovels for his one, although he was a tall, powerful fellow. She smiled when she saw me noticing her, and seemed to continue her work with greater assiduity. I learned that she was deaf, and spoke so indistinctly that no stranger could understand her. She had also a defect in her sight, which latter circumstance had compelled her to abandon the sifting, as she could not well distinguish the various articles found in the dust-heap. The poor creature had therefore taken to the shovel, and now works with it every day, doing the labour of the strongest men.

From the man above referred to I obtained the following statement:—"Father vos a dustie;—vos at it all his life, and grandfather afore him for I can't tell how long. Father vos allus a rum 'un;—sich a beggar for lush. Vhy I'm blowed if he vouldn't lush as much as half-a-dozen on 'em can lush now; somehow the dusties hasn't got the stuff in 'em as they used to have. A few year ago the fellers 'u'd think nothink o' lushin avay for five or six days without niver going anigh their home. I niver vos at a school in all my life; I don't know what it's good for. It may be wery well for the likes o' you, but I doesn't know it 'u'd do a dustie any good. You see, ven I'm not out with the cart, I digs here all day; and p'raps I'm up all night, and digs avay agen the next day. Vot does I care for reading, or anythink of that there kind, ven I gets home arter my vork? I tell you vot I likes, though! vhy, I jist likes two or three pipes o' baccer, and a pot or two of good heavy and a song, and then I tumbles in with my Sall, and I'm as happy as here and there von. That there Sall of mine's a stunner—a riglar stunner. There ain't never a voman can sift a heap quickerer nor my Sall. Sometimes she yarns as much as I does; the only thing is, she's sitch a beggar for lush, that there Sall of mine, and then she kicks up sitch jolly rows, you niver see the like in your life. That there's the only fault, as I know on, in Sall; but, barring that, she's a hout-and-houter, and worth a half-a-dozen of t'other sifters—pick 'em out vare you likes. No, we ain't married 'zactly, though it's all one for all that. I sticks to Sall, and Sall sticks to I, and there's an end on't:—vot is it to any von? I rec'lects a-picking the rags and things out of mother's sieve, when I were a young'un, and a putting 'em all in the heap jist as it might be there. I vos allus in a dust-yard. I don't think I could do no how in no other place. You see I vouldn't be 'appy like; I only knows how to vork at the dust 'cause I'm used to it, and so vos father afore me, and I'll stick to it as long as I can. I yarns about half-a-bull [2s. 6d.] a day, take one day with another. Sall sometimes yarns as much, and ven I goes out at night I yarns a bob or two more, and so I gits along pretty tidy; sometimes yarnin more and sometimes yarnin less. I niver vos sick as I knows on; I've been queerish of a morning a good many times, but I doesn't call that sickness; it's only the lush and nothink more. The smells nothink at all, ven you gits used to it. Lor' bless you! you'd think nothink on it in a veek's time,—no, no more nor I do. There's twenty on us vorks here—riglar. I don't think there's von on 'em 'cept Scratchey Jack can read, but he can do it stunning; he's out vith the cart now, but he's the chap as can patter to you as long as he likes."

Concerning the capital and income of the London dust business, the following estimate may be given as to the amount of property invested in and accruing to the trade.

It has been computed that there are 90 contractors, large and small; of these upwards of two-thirds, or about 35, may be said to be in a considerable way of business, possessing many carts and horses, as well as employing a large body of people; some yards have as many as 150 hands connected with them. The remaining 55 masters are composed of "small men," some of whom are known as "running dustmen," that is to say, persons who collect the dust without any sanction from the parish; but the number belonging to this class has considerably diminished since the great deterioration in the price of "brieze." Assuming, then, that the great and little master dustmen employ on an average between six and seven carts each, we have the following statement as to the

CAPITAL OF THE LONDON DUST TRADE.

600 Carts, at 20*l.* each	£12,000
600 Horses, at 25*l.* each	15,000
600 Sets of harness, at 2*l.* per set.	1,200
600 Ladders, at 5*s.* each	150
1200 Baskets, at 2*s.* each	120
1200 Shovels, at 2*s.* each	120
Being a total capital of	£28,590

If, therefore, we assert that the capital of this trade is between 25,000*l.* and 30,000*l.* in value, we shall not be far wrong either way.

Of the annual income of the same trade, it is almost impossible to arrive at any positive results; but, in the absence of all authentic information on the subject, we may make the subjoined conjecture.

INCOME OF THE LONDON DUST TRADE.

Sum paid to contractors for the removal of dust from the 176 metropolitan parishes, at 200*l.* each parish	£35,200
Sum obtained for 900,000 loads of dust, at 2*s.* 6*d.* per load	112,500
	£147,700

Thus it would appear that the total income of the dust trade may be taken at between 145,000*l.* and 150,000*l.* per annum.

Against this we have to set the yearly outgoings of the business, which may be roughly estimated as follows:—

EXPENDITURE OF THE LONDON DUST TRADE.

Wages of 1800 labourers, at 10*s.* a week each (including sifters and carriers)	£46,800
Keep of 600 horses, at 10*s.* a week each	15,600
Wear and tear of stock in trade	4000
Rent for 90 yards, at 100*l.* a year each (large and small)	9000
	£75,400

The above estimates give us the following aggregate results:—

Total yearly incomings of the London dust trade	£147,700
Total yearly out-goings	75,400
Total yearly profit	£72,300

Hence it would appear that the profits of the dust-contractors are very nearly at the rate of 100*l.* per cent. on their expenditure. I do not think I have over estimated the incomings, or under estimated the out-goings; at least I have striven to avoid doing so, in order that no injustice might be done to the members of the trade.

This aggregate profit, when divided among the 90 contractors, will make the clear gains of each master dustman amount to about 800*l.* per annum: of course some derive considerably more than this amount, and some considerably less.

OF THE LONDON SEWERAGE AND SCAVENGERY.

THE subject I have now to treat—principally as regards street-labour, but generally in its sanitary, social, and economical bearings—may really be termed vast. It is of the cleansing of a capital city, with its thousands of miles of streets and roads *on* the surface, and its thousands of miles of sewers and drains *under* the surface of the earth. And first let me deal with the subject in a historical point of view.

Public scavengery or street-cleansing, from the earliest periods of our history, since municipal authority regulated the internal economy of our cities, has been an object of some attention. In the records of all our civic corporations may be found bye-laws, or some equivalent measure, to enforce the cleansing of the streets. But these regulations were little enforced. It was ordered that the streets should be swept, but often enough men were not employed by the authorities to sweep them; until after the great fire of London, and in many parts for years after that, the tradesman's apprentice swept the dirt from the front of his master's house, and left it in the street, to be removed at the leisure of the scavenger. This was in the streets most famous for the wealth and commercial energy of the inhabitants. The streets inhabited by the poor, until about the beginning of the present century, were rarely swept at all. The unevenness of the pavement, the accumulation of wet and mud in rainy weather, the want of foot-paths, and sometimes even of grates and kennels, made Cowper, in one of his letters, describe a perambulation of some of these streets as "going by water."

Even this state of things was, however, an improvement. In the accounts of the London street-broils and fights, from the reign of Henry III., more especially during the war of the Roses, down to the civil war which terminated in the beheading of Charles I., mention is more or less made of the combatants having availed themselves of the shelter of the rubbish in the streets. These mounds of rubbish were then kinds of street-barricades, opposing the progress of passengers, like the piles of overturned omnibuses and other vehicles of the modern French street-combatants. There is no doubt that in the older times these mounds were composed, first, of the earth dug out for the foundation of some building, or the sinking of some well, or (later on) the formation of some drain; for these works were often long in hand, not only from the interruptions of civil strife and from want of funds, but from indifference, owing to the long delay in their completion, and were often altogether abandoned. After dusk the streets of the capital of England could not be traversed without lanterns or torches. This was the case until the last 40 or 50 years in nearly all the smaller towns of England, but there the darkness was the principal obstacle; in the inferior parts of "Old London," however, there were the additional inconveniences of broken limbs and robbery.

It would be easy to adduce instances from the olden writers in proof of all the above statements, but it seems idle to cite proofs of what is known to all.

The care of the streets, however, as regards the removal of the dirt, or, as the weather might be, the dust and mud, seems never to have been much of a national consideration. It was left to the corporations and the parishes. Each of these had its own especial arrangements for the collection and removal of dirt in its own streets; and as each parochial or municipal system generally differed in some respect or other, taken as a whole, there was no one general mode or system adopted. To all this the street-management of our own days, in the respect of scavengery, and, as I shall show, of sewerage, presents a decided improvement. This improvement in street-management is not attributable to any public agitation—to any public, and, far less, national manifestation of feeling. It was debated sometimes in courts of Common Council, in ward and parochial meetings, but the public generally seem to have taken no express interest in the matter. The improvement seems to have established itself gradually from the improved tastes and habits of the people.

Although *generally* left to the local powers, the subject of street-cleansing and management, however, has not been *entirely* overlooked by Parliament. Among parliamentary enactments is the measure best known as "Michael Angelo Taylor's Act," passed early in the present century, which requires all householders every morning to remove from the front of their premises any snow which may have fallen during the night, &c., &c.; the late Police Acts also embrace subordinately the subject of street-management.

On the other hand the sewers have long been the object of national care. "The daily great damages and losses which have happened in many and divers parts of this realm" (I give the spirit of the preamble of several Acts of Parliament), " as well by the reason of the outrageous flowings, surges, and course of the river in and upon the marsh grounds and other low places, heretofore through public wisdom won and made profitable for the great commonwealth of this realm, as also by occasion of land waters and other outrageous springs in and upon meadows, pastures, and other low grounds adjoining to rivers, floods, and other water-courses," caused parliamentary attention to be given to the subject.

Until towards the latter part of the last century, however, the streets even of the better order were often flooded during heavy and continuous rains, owing to the sewers and drains having been choked, so that the sewage forced its way through the gratings into the streets and yards, flooding all the underground apartments and often the ground floors of the houses, as well as the public thoroughfares with filth.

It is not many months since the neighbourhood of so modern a locality as Waterloo-bridge was flooded in this manner, and boats were used in the Belvidere and York-roads. On the 1st of August, 1846, after a tremendous storm of thunder, hail, and rain, miles of the capital were literally under water; hundreds of publicans' beer-cellars contained far more water than beer, and the damage done was enormous. These facts show that though much has been accomplished towards the efficient sewerage of the metropolis, much remains to be accomplished still.

The first statute on the subject of the public sewerage was as early as the 9th year of the reign of Henry III. There were enactments, also, in most of the succeeding reigns, but they were all partial and conflicting, and related more to local desiderata than to any system of sewerage for the public benefit, until the reign of Henry VIII., when the "Bill of Sewers" was passed (in 1531). This act provided for a more general system of sewerage in the cities and towns of the kingdom, requiring the main channels to be of certain depths and dimensions, according to the localities, situation, &c. In many parts of the country the sewerage is still carried on according to the provisions in the act of Henry VIII., but those provisions were modified, altered, or "explained," by many subsequent statutes.

Any uniformity which might have arisen from the observance of the same principles of sewerage was effectually checked by the measures adopted in London, more especially during the last 100 years. As the metropolis increased new sewerage became necessary, and new local bodies were formed for its management. These were known as the Commissions of Sewers, and the members of those bodies acted independently one of another, under the authority of their own Acts of Parliament, each having its own board, engineers, clerks, officers, and workmen. Each commission was confined to its own district, and did what was accounted best for its own district with little regard to any general plan of sewerage, so that London was, and in a great measure is, sewered upon different principles, as to the size of the sewers and drains, the rates of inclination, &c. &c. In 1847 there were eight of these districts and bodies: the City of London, the Tower Hamlets, Saint Katherine's, Poplar and Blackwall, Holborn and Finsbury, Westminster and part of Middlesex, Surrey and Kent, and Greenwich. In 1848 these several bodies were concentrated by act of parliament, and entitled the "Metropolitan Commission of Sewers;" but the City of London, as appears to be the case with every parliamentary measure affecting the metropolis, presents an exception, as it retains a separate jurisdiction, and is not under the control of the general commissioners, to whom parliament has given authority over such matters.

The management of the metropolitan scavengery and sewerage, therefore, differs in this respect. The scavengery is committed to the care of the several parishes, each making its own contract; the sewerage is consigned by Parliament to a body of commissioners. In both instances, however, the expenses are paid out of local rates.

I shall now proceed to treat of each of these subjects separately, beginning with the cleansing of the streets.

OF THE STREETS OF LONDON.

THERE are now three modes of pavement in the streets of the metropolis.
1. *The stone pavement* (commonly composed of Aberdeen granite).
2. *The macadamized pavement,* or rather *road.*
3. *The wood pavement.*

The stone pavement has generally, in the several towns of England, been composed of whatever material the quarries or rocks of the neighbourhood supplied, limestone being often thus used. In some places, where there were no quarries available, the stones of a river or rivuletside were used, but these were rounded and slippery, and often formed but a rugged pathway. For London pavement, the neighbourhood not being rich in stone quarries, granite has usually been brought by water from Scotland, and a small quantity from Guernsey for the pavement of the streets. The stone pavement is made by the placing of the granite stones, hewn and shaped ready for the purpose, side by side, with a foundation of concrete. The concrete now used for the London street-pavement is Thames ballast, composed of shingles, or small stones, and mixed with lime, &c.

Macadamization was not introduced into the *streets* of London until about 25 years ago. Before that, it had been carried to what was accounted a great degree of perfection on many of the principal mail and coach roads. Some 50 miles on the Great North Road, or that between London and Carlisle, were often pointed out as an admirable specimen of road-making on Mac Adam's principles. This road was well known in the old coaching days as Leming-lane, running from Boroughbridge to Greta Bridge, in Yorkshire.

The first thoroughfare in London which was macadamized, a word adapted from the name of Sir W. Mac Adam, the originator or great improver of the system, was St. James's-square; after that, some of the smaller streets in the aristocratic parishes of St. James and St. George were thus paved, and then, but not without great opposition, Piccadilly. The opposition to the macadamizing of the latter thoroughfare assumed many forms. Independently of the conflicting statements as to extravagance and economy, it was urged by the opponents, that the dust and dirt of the new style of paving would cause the street to be deserted by the aristocracy—that the noiselessness of the traffic would cause the deaths of the deaf and infirm—that the aristocracy promoted this new-fangled street-making, that they might the better " sleep o' nights," regardless of all else. One writer especially regretted that the Duke of Queensberry, popularly known as " Old Q.," who resided at the western end of Piccadilly, had not lived to enjoy, undisturbed by vulgar noises, his bed of down, until it was his hour to rise and take his bath of perfumed milk! In short, there was all the fuss and absurdity which so often characterise local contests.

The macadamized street is made by a layer of stones, broken small and regular in size, and spread evenly over the road, so that the pressure and friction of the traffic will knead, grind, crush, and knit them into one compact surface. Until road-making became better understood, or until the early part of the present century, the roads even in the suburbs immediately connected with London, such as Islington, Kingsland, Stoke Newington, and Hackney, were " repaired when they wanted it." If there were a " rut," or a hole, it was filled up or covered over with stones, and as the drivers usually avoided such parts, for the sake of their horses' feet, another rut was speedily formed alongside of the original one. Under the old system, road-mending was patch-work; defects were sought to be remedied, but there was little or no knowledge of constructing or of reconstructing the surface as a whole.

The wood pavement came last, and was not established, even partially, until eleven or twelve years ago. One of the earliest places so paved was the Old Bailey, in order that the noise of the street-traffic might be deadened in the Criminal Courts. The same plan was adopted alongside some of the churches, and other public buildings, where external quietude, or, at any rate, diminished noise, was desired. At the first, there were great complaints made, and frequent expostulations addressed to the editors of the newspapers, as to the slipperiness of the wooden ways. The wood pavement is formed of blocks of wood, generally deal, fitted to one another by grooves, by joints, or by shape, for close adjustment. They are placed on the road over a body of concrete, in the same way as granite.

" In constructing roads, or rather streets, through towns or cities, where the amount of traffic is considerable, it will be found desirable," says Mr. Law, in his 'Treatise on the Constructing and Repairing of Roads,' " to pave their surface. The advantages belonging to pavements in such situations over macadamized roads are considerable; where the latter are exposed to an incessant and heavy traffic, their surface becomes rapidly worn, rendering constant repairs requisite, which are not only attended with very heavy expense, but also render the road very unpleasant for being travelled upon while being done; they also require much more attention in the way of scraping or sweeping, and in raking in ruts. And some difficulty would be experienced in towns to find places in which the materials, which would be constantly wanted for repairing the road, could be deposited. In dry weather the macadamized road would always be dusty, and in wet weather it would be covered with mud. The only advantage which such a road really possesses over a pavement is the less noise produced by carriages in passing over it; but this advantage is very small when the pavement is properly laid."

Concerning wood pavements the same gentleman says, "Of late years wood has been introduced as a material for paving streets, and has been rather extensively employed both in Russia and America. It has been tried in various parts of London, and generally with small success, the cause of its failure being identical with the cause of the enormous sums being spent annually in the repairs of the streets generally, namely, the want of a proper foundation; a want which was sooner felt with wood than with granite, in consequence of the less weight and inertia of the wood. The comfort resulting from the use of wooden pavement, both to those who travelled, and those who lived in the streets, from the diminished jolting and noise, was so great, that it is just matter of surprise that so little care was taken in forming that which a very little consideration would have shown to be indispensable to its success, namely, a good foundation. Slipperiness of its surface, in particular states of the weather, was also found to be a disadvantage belonging to wooden pavement; but means might be devised which would render its surface at all times safe, and afford a secure footing for horses. As regards durability, it has scarcely been used for a sufficient period to allow a comparison being made with other materials, but from the result of some observations communicated by Mr. Hope to the Scottish Society of Arts, it appears that wooden blocks when placed with the end of the grain exposed, wear *less than granite*. At first sight, this result might appear questionable, but it is a well-ascertained fact that, where wood and iron move in contact in machinery, the iron generally wears more rapidly than the wood, the reason appearing to be, that the surface of the wood soon becomes covered with particles of dust and grit, which become partially embedded in it, and, while they serve to protect the wood, convert its surface into a species of file, which rapidly wears away whatever it rubs against."

Such then are the different modes of constructing the London roads or streets. I shall now endeavour to show the relative length, and relative cost of the streets thus severally prepared for the commercial, professional, and pleasurable transit of the metropolis.

The comparative extent of the macadamized, of the stone, and of the wood pavement of the streets of the metropolis has not as yet been ascertained, for no general account has appeared condensing the reports, returns, accounts, &c., of the several specific bodies of management into one grand total.

It is, however, possible to arrive at an approximation as to the comparative extent I have spoken of; and in this attempt at approximation, in the absence of all means of a definite statistical computation, I have had the assistance of an experienced and practical surveyor, familiar with the subject.

Macadamization prevails beyond the following boundaries:—

North of the New-road and of its extension, as the City-road, and westward of the New-road's junction with Lisson-grove.

Westward of Park-lane and of the West-end parks.

Eastward of Brick-lane (Spitalfields) and of the Whitechapel High-street.

Southward (on the Surrey side) from the New-cut and Long-lane, Bermondsey, and both in the eastern and western direction of Southwark, Lambeth, and the other southern parishes.

Stone pavement, on the other hand, prevails in the district which may be said to be within this boundary, bearing down upon the Thames in all directions.

It is, doubtlessly, the fact that in both the districts thus indicated exceptions to the general rule may prevail—that in one, for instance, there may be some miles of macadamized way, and in the other some miles of granite pavements; but such exceptions, I am told by a Commissioner of Paving, may fairly be dismissed as balancing each other.

The wooden pavement, I am informed on the same authority, does not now comprise five miles of the London thoroughfares; little notice, therefore, need be taken of it.

The miles of streets in the City in which stone only affords the street medium of locomotion are 50. The stone pavement in the localities outside of this area are six times, or approaching to seven times, the extent of that in the City. I have no actual admeasurement to demonstrate this point, for none exists, and no private individual can offer to measure hundreds of miles of streets in order to ascertain the composition of their surface. But the calculation has been made for me by a gentleman thoroughly conversant with the subject, and well acquainted with the general relative proportion of the defined districts, parishes, and boroughs of the metropolis.

We have thus the following result, as regards the inner police district, or Metropolis Proper:—

	Miles.
Granite paved streets	400
Macadamized ditto (or roads)	1350
Wood ditto	5
Total	1755

This may appear a disproportionate estimate, but when it is remembered that the inner police district of the metropolis extends as far as Hampstead, Tooting, Brentford, and Greenwich, it will be readily perceived that the relative proportions of the macadamized and paved roads are much about the same as is here stated.

As to the cost of these several roads, I will, before entering upon that part of the subject, state the prices of the different materials used in their manufacture.

Aberdeen granite is now 1*l.* 5*s.* per ton, delivered, and prepared for paving, or, as it is often called, "pitching." A ton of "seven inch" granite, that is, granite sunk seven inches in the ground, will cover from two and three-quarters to three square yards, superficial measure, or nine feet per yard. The cost, labour included, is, therefore, from 9s. to 12s. the square yard. This appears very costly; but in some of the more quiet streets, such as those in the immediate neighbourhood of Golden and Fitzroy-squares, a good granite pavement will endure for 20 years, requiring little repair. In other streets, such as Cheapside, for instance, it lasts from three to four years, without repavement being necessary, supposing the best construction has been originally adopted.

For macadamized streets, where there is a traffic like that of Tottenham Court-road, three layers of small broken granite a year are necessary; the cost of this repavement being about 2s. 6d. a yard superficial measure. The repairs and relayings on macadamized roads of regular traffic range from 4s. to 6s. 6d. yearly, the square yard.

The wood pavement, which endures, with a trifling outlay for repairs, for about three years, costs, on an average, 11s. the square yard.

The concrete used as a foundation in this street-construction costs 4s. 6d. a cube yard, or 27 feet, by which admeasurement it is always calculated. A cube yard of Thames ballast weighs about 1¼ ton.

The average cost of street-building, new, taking an average breadth, or about ten yards, from footpath to footpath, is then—

	Per Mile.		
	£.	s.	d.
Granite built	96	0	0
Macadamized	44	0	0
Wood	88	0	0

Or, as a total,

	£	s.	d.
400 miles of granite paved streets at £96 per mile	38,400	0	0
1350 macadamized ditto, at £44 per mile	59,400	0	0
5 wood ditto, at £88 per mile	440	0	0
	98,240	0	0

This, then (about £100,000), is the *original cost* of the roads of the metropolis.

The cost of repairs, &c., annually, is shown by the amount of the paving rate, which may be taken as an average.

	£	s.	d.
400 miles of granite, at 20s. per mile	400	0	0
1350 macadamized ditto, at £13 4s. per mile	17,820	0	0
5 wood* ditto, at 20s. per mile	5	0	0
Total	18,225	0	0

According to a "General Survey of the Metropolitan Highways," by Mr. Thomas Hughes, the principal roads leading out of London are:—

1. *The Cambridge Road*, from Shoreditch through Kingsland.

2. *The Epping and Chelmsford Roads*, from Whitechapel, through Bow and Stratford.

3. *The Barking Road*, along the Commercial Road past Limehouse.

4. *The Dover Road*, from the Elephant and Castle, across Blackheath.

5. *The Brighton Roads*, (a) through Croydon, (b) through Sutton.

6. *The Guildford Road*, along the Westminster Road through Battersea and Wandsworth.

7. *The Staines*, or *Great Western Road*, from Knightsbridge through Brentford.

8. *The Amersham and Aylesbury Road*, along the Harrow Road, and through Harrow-on-the-Hill.

9. *The St. Alban's Road*, along the Edgeware Road through Elstree.

10. *The Oxford Road*, from Bayswater through Ealing.

11. *The Great Holyhead Road.*
12. *The Great North Road.* } From Islington, by and through Barnet.

As to the amount of resistance to traction offered by different kinds of pavement, or the same pavement under different circumstances, the following are the general results of the experiments made by M. Morin, at the expense of the French Government:—

1st. The traction is directly proportional to the load, and inversely proportional to the diameter of the wheel.

2nd. Upon a paved, or hard macadamized road, the resistance is independent of the width of the tire, when it exceeds from three to four inches.

3rd. At a walking pace the traction is the same, under the same circumstances, for carriages with springs and without them.

4th. Upon hard macadamized, and upon paved roads, the traction increases with the velocity: the increments of traction being directly proportional to the increments of velocity above the velocity 3·28 feet per second, or about 2¼ miles per hour. The equal increment of traction thus due to each equal increment of velocity is less as the road is more smooth, and the carriage less rigid or better hung.

5th. Upon soft roads of earth, or sand, or turf, or roads fresh and thickly gravelled, the traction is independent of the velocity.

6th. Upon a well-made and compact pavement of hewn stones, the traction at a walking pace is not more than three-fourths of that upon the best macadamized roads under similar circumstances; at a trotting pace it is equal to it.

7th. The destruction of the road is in all cases greater, as the diameters of the wheels are less, and it is greater in carriages without than with springs.

In Sir H. Parnell's book on roads, p. 73, we are told that Sir John Macneill, by means of an instrument invented by himself for measuring the tractive force required on different kinds of road, obtained the following general results as to the power requisite to move a ton weight under ordinary circumstances, at a very low velocity.

* This relates merely to the repairs to the wooden pavement, but if a renewal of the blocks be necessary, then the cost approaches that of a new road; and a renewal is considered necessary about once in three years.

Description of Road.	Force, in pounds, required to move a ton.
On a well-made pavement	33
On a road made with six inches of broken stone of great hardness, laid either on a foundation of large stones, set in the form of a pavement, or upon a bottoming of concrete	46
On an old flint road, or a road made with a thick coating of broken stone, laid on earth	65
On a road made with a thick coating of gravel, laid on earth	147

In the same work the relative degrees of resistance to traction on the several kinds of roads are thus expressed:—

On a timber surface	2
On a paved road	2
On a well-made broken stone road, in a dry clean state	5
On a well-made broken stone road, covered with dust	8
On a well-made broken stone road, wet and muddy	10
On a gravel or flint road, in a dry clean state	13
On a gravel or flint road, in a wet muddy state	32

Of the Traffic of London.

I HAVE shown (at p. 159, vol. ii.) that the number of miles of streets included in the Inner District of the Metropolitan Police is 1750.

Mr. Peter Cunningham, in his excellent "Handbook of Modern London," tells us that "the streets of the Metropolis, if put together, would measure 3000 miles in length;" but he does not inform us what limits he assigns to the said metropolis; it would seem, however, that he refers to the Outer Police District: and in another place he cites the following as the extent of some of the principal thoroughfares:—

New-road	5115 yds. long, or nearly 3 miles.			
Oxford-street	2304	,,	,,	1½ ,,
Regent-street	1730	,,	,,	1 ,,
Piccadilly	1690	,,		
City-road	1690	,,		
Strand	1396	,,		

Of the two great lines of streets parallel to the river, the one extending along Oxford-street, Holborn, Cheapside, Cornhill, and Whitechapel to the Regent's-canal, Mile-end, is, says Mr. McCulloch, "above six miles in length;" while that which stretches from Knightsbridge along Piccadilly, the Haymarket, Pall-mall East, the Strand, Fleet-street, Watling-street, Eastcheap, Tower-street, and so on by Ratcliffe-highway to the West India Docks, is, according to the same authority, about equal in length to the other. Mr. Weale asserts, as we have already seen, that the greatest length of street from east to west is about fourteen miles, and from north to south about thirteen miles. The number of streets in London is said to be 10,000, though upon what authority the statement is made, and within what compass it is meant to be applied, I have not been able to ascertain. It is calculated, however, that there are 1900 miles of gas "mains" laid down in London and the suburbs; so that adopting the estimate of the Commissioners of Police, or 1760 miles of streets, within an area of about 90 square miles, we cannot go far wrong.

Now, as to the amount of *traffic* that takes place daily over this vast extent of paved road, it is almost impossible to predicate anything definitely. As yet there are only a few crude facts existing in connection with the subject. All we know is, that the London streets are daily traversed by 1500 omnibuses—such was the number of drivers licensed by the Metropolitan Commissioners in 1850—and about 3000 cabs—the number of drivers licensed in 1850 was 5000, but many "cabs" have a day and night driver as well, and the Return from the Stamp and Tax Office cited below, represents the number of licensed cabriolets, in 1849, at 2846: besides these public conveyances, there are the private carriages and carts, so that the metropolitan vehicles may be said to employ altogether upwards of 20,000 horses.

In the *Morning Chronicle* I said, when treating of the London omnibus-drivers and conductors:—"The average journey, as regards the distance travelled by each omnibus, is six miles, and that distance is, in some cases, travelled twelve times a day, or as it is called, 'six there and six back.' Some omnibuses perform the journey only ten times a day, and some, but a minority, a less number of times. Now, taking the average distance travelled by each omnibus at between 45 and 50 miles a day—and this, I am assured, on the best authority, is within the mark, while 60 miles a day might exceed it—and computing the omnibuses running daily at 1500, we find 'a travel,' as it was worded to me, of upwards of 70,000 miles daily, or a yearly 'travel' of more than 25,000,000 miles; an extent which is upwards of a thousand times more than the circumference of the earth; and that this estimate in no way exceeds the truth is proved by the sum annually paid to the Excise for 'mileage,' which amounts on an average to 9*l*. each 'bus' per month, or collectively to 162,000*l*. per annum, and this, at 1½*d*. per mile (the rate of duty charged), gives 25,920,000 miles as the aggregate distance travelled by the entire number of omnibuses every year through the London streets."

The distance travelled by the London cabs may be estimated as follows:—Each driver may be said to receive on an average 10*s*. a day all the year through. Now, the number of licences prove that there are 5000 cab-drivers in London, and as each of these must travel at the least ten miles in order to obtain the daily 10*s*., we may safely assert that the whole 5000 go over 50,000 miles of ground a day, or, in round numbers, 18,250,000 miles in the course of the year.

According to a return obtained by Mr. Charles Cochrane from the Stamp and Tax Office, Somerset House, there were in the metropolis, in 1849–50, the following number of horses:—

Private carriage, job, and cart horses (in London)	3,683
Ditto . . . (in Westminster)	6,339
Cabriolets licensed 2846 (having two horses each)	5,692
Omnibuses licensed 1350 (four horses each)	5,500
Total number of horses in the metropolis	21,214

I am assured, by persons well acquainted with the omnibus trade, that the number of omnibus horses here cited is far too low—as many proprietors employ ten horses to each "bus," and none less than six. Hence we may fairly assume that there are at the least 25,000 horses at work every day in the streets of London. Besides the horses above mentioned, it is estimated that the number daily coming to the metropolis from the surrounding parts is 3000 ; and calculating that each of the 25,000, which may be said to be at work out of the entire number, travels eight miles a day, the aggregate length of ground gone over by the whole would amount to 200,000 miles per diem, or about 70,000,000 miles throughout the year. There are, as we have seen, upwards of 1750 miles of streets in London. It follows, therefore, that each piece of pavement would be traversed no less than 40,000 times per annum, or upwards of a hundred times a day, by some horse or vehicle.

As I said before, the facts that have been collected concerning the absolute traffic of the several parts of London are of the most meagre description. The only observations of any character that have been made upon the subject are—as far as my knowledge goes—those of M. D'Arcey, which are contained in a French report upon the roads of London, as compared with those of Paris.

This gentleman, speaking of the relative number of vehicles passing and repassing over certain parts of the two capitals, says :—"The Boulevards of Paris are the parts where the greatest traffic takes place. On the *Boulevard des Capucins* there pass, every 24 hours, 9070 horses drawing carriages ; on the *Boulevard des Italiens,* 10,750 ; *Boulevard Poissonière,* 7720 ; *Boulevard St. Denis,* 9609 ; *Boulevard des Filles du Calvaire,* 5856 : general average of the above, 8600. *Rue du Faubourg St. Antoine,* 4300 ; *Avenue des Champs Elysées,* 8959. At London, in Pall Mall, opposite Her Majesty's Theatre, there pass at least 800 carriages every hour. On London-bridge the number of vehicles passing and repassing is not less than 13,000 every hour. On Westminster-bridge the annual traffic amounts to 8,000,000 horses at the least. By this it will be seen that the traffic in Paris does not amount to one-half of what it is in the streets of London."

OF THE DUST AND DIRT OF THE STREETS OF LONDON.

WE have merely to reflect upon the vast amount of traffic just shown to be daily going on throughout London—to think of the 70,000,000 miles of journey through the metropolis annually performed by the entire vehicles (which is more than two-thirds the distance from the earth to the sun)—to bear in mind that each part of London is on the average gone over and over again 40,000 times in the course of the year, and some parts as many as 13,000 times in a day—and that every horse and vehicle by which the streets are traversed are furnished, the one with four iron-bound hoofs, and the other with iron-bound wheels—to have an imperfect idea of the enormous weights and friction continually operating upon the surface of the streets—as well as the amount of grinding and pulverising, and wear and tear, that must be perpetually taking place in the paving-stones and macadamized roads of London ; and thus we may be able to form some mental estimate as to the quantity of dust and dirt annually produced by these means alone.

But the table in pp. 186-7, which has been collected at great trouble, will give us still more accurate notions on the subject. It is not given as perfect, but as being the best information, in the absence of positive returns, that was procurable even from the best informed.

Here, then, we have an aggregate total of dust collected from the *principal* parts of the metropolis amounting to no less than 141,466 loads. The value of this refuse is said to be as much as 21,221*l.* 8*s.,* but of this and more I shall speak hereafter. At present I merely seek to give the reader a general notion upon the matter. I wish to show him, before treating of the labourers engaged in the scavenging of the London streets, the amount of work they have to do.

OF THE STREET-DUST OF LONDON, AND THE LOSS AND INJURY OCCASIONED BY IT.

THE daily and nightly grinding of thousands of wheels, the iron friction of so many horses' hoofs, the evacuations of horses and cattle, and the ceaseless motion of pedestrians, all decomposing the substance of our streets and roads, give rise to many distinct kinds of street-dirt. These are severally known as

(1) *Dust.*
(2) *Horse-dung* and *cattle-manure.*
(3) *Mud,* when mixed with water and with general refuse, such as the remains of fruit and other things thrown into the street and swept together.
(4) *Surface-water* when mixed with street-sewage.

These productions I shall treat severally, and first of the street-dust.

The "*detritus*" of the streets of London assumes many forms, and is known by many names, according as it is combined with more or less water.

A TABLE SHOWING THE SEVERAL DIVISIONS OF THE METROPOLIS CLEANSED BY THE SCAVENGERS AND PARISH MEN, THE NAMES OF THE CONTRACTORS, THE NUMBER OF MEN AND CARTS EMPLOYED IN COLLECTING, THE QUANTITY OF DUST AND MUD COLLECTED DAILY IN THE STREETS IN DRY AND WET WEATHER, WITH THE ANNUAL VALUE OF THE WHOLE.

Divisions and Districts.	Names of Contractors.	Number of Men employed at scavenging.		Number of Carts used daily in scavenging.		Number of loads collected daily.		Number of Cart-Loads annually collected by the Scavengers.	Annual value of Dirt collected by Scavengers.
		In dry weather.	In wet weather.	In dry weather.	In wet weather.	In dry weather.	In wet weather.		£ s. d.
Kensington	Parish	3	5	1	2	3	5	1252	187 16 0
Chelsea	Ditto	3	5	1	2	4	6	1565	234 15 0
Ditto (Hans' Town)	Mr. C. Humphries	3	4	1	1	3	5	1252	187 16 0
St. George's, Pimlico	Mr. Redding	2	4	1	2	5	7	1878	281 14 0
Ditto, Hanover Square	Parish	2	5	1	1	1½	2½	626	93 18 0
St. Margaret's, Westminster	Ditto	5	7	2	3	8	10	2817	422 11 0
St. John's, ditto	Mr. Hearne	5	7	1	2	8	10	2817	422 11 0
St. Martin's	Machine	6	9	4	4	4	6	1565	234 15 0
Hungerford-market	Mr. J. Gore	2	2	1	2	1	3	626	93 18 0
St. James's, Westminster	Parish and Machine	2	4	2	2	5	7	1873	281 14 0
Piccadilly	Parish and Machine	20	28	2	2	8	12	3130	469 10 0
Regent-street and Pall-mall	Ditto, ditto	8	12	2	2	4	6	1565	234 15 0
St. Ann's, Soho	Ditto	3	4	1	2	4	6	1565	234 15 0
Woods and Forests	Machine	3	4	1	2	5	7	1878	281 14 0
Paddington	Parish	4	6	1	2	6	8	2191	328 13 0
Marylebone (Five Districts)	Ditto	20	35	3	4	15	25	6260	939 0 0
Portland-market	Mr. Tame	3	5	1	1	2	4	939	140 17 0
Hampstead	Parish	2	4	1	1	2	4	939	140 17 0
Highgate	Ditto	2	4	1	1	2	4	939	140 17 0
St. Pancras, South-west Division	Mr. Stapleton	2	4	1	2	4	6	1565	234 15 0
Somers-town	Mr. Starkey	3	5	1	2	7	9	2504	375 12 0
Southampton Estate	Mr. C. Starkey	4	5	1	1	3	5	1252	187 16 0
Bedford ditto	Mr. J. Gore	2	2	1	1	1	3	626	93 18 0
Brewers' ditto	Mr. C. Starkey	2	2	1	1	1	3	626	93 18 0
Calthorpe ditto	Ditto	2	2	1	1	1	3	626	93 18 0
Cromer ditto	Ditto	2	2	1	1	1	3	626	93 18 0
Doughty ditto	Mr. Martin	2	2	1	1	1	3	626	93 18 0
Foundling ditto	Ditto	2	2	1	1	1	3	626	93 18 0
Harrison ditto	Ditto	2	2	1	1	1	3	626	93 18 0
Skinners' ditto	Mr. H. North	2	2	1	1	1	3	626	93 18 0
Union ditto	Mr. J. Gore	2	2	1	1	1	3	626	93 18 0
Islington District	Parish	6	8	1	2	3	5	1252	187 16 0
Battle-bridge	Mr. Starkey	4	6	1	2	5	7	1878	281 14 0
Hackney	Parish	5	7	1	1	2	4	939	140 17 0

Parish	Contractor						Loads yearly		£	s	d
St. Giles-in-the-Fields and St. George, Bloomsbury	Mr. Redding	7	9	2	3	6	10	2504	375	12	0	0
St. Mary-le-Strand	Mr. J. Gore	2	5	1	2	4	6	1565	234	15	0
Savoy	Ditto	2	3	1	1	1	3	626	93	18	0
St. Clement Danes	Parish	5	7	3	3 waggons.	2	6	1252	187	16	0
St. Paul's, Covent Garden	Ditto	3	5	3	2 carts.	3	5	1252	187	16	0
Covent Garden-market	Mr. Stapleton	5	7	5	6	9	12	3130	469	10	0
Holborn	Parish	6	9	2	3	4	6	1565	234	15	0
St. Sepulchre's	Mr. J. Gore	6	4	1	3	2	4	939	140	17	0
Hatton-garden	Messrs. Pratt and Sewell	3	2	1	1	1	3	626	93	18	0
St. James's, Clerkenwell	Mr. Dodd	2	5	1	3	8	10	2817	422	11	0
St. John's, ditto	Mr. J. Gould	5	7	1	3	6	8	2191	328	13	0
St. Luke's	Mr. Dodd	7	10	1	6	8	8	2817	422	11	0
Goswell-street	Mr. Redding	3	4	1	2	4	6	1565	234	15	0
Liberty of the Rolls	Messrs. Pratt and Sewell	2	2	1	1	1	3	626	93	18	0
Blackfriars Bridge	Mr. Jenkins	3	5	1	1	4	6	1565	234	15	0
City Division, Eastern, A	Mr. G. Sinnott	10	16	4	6	12	16	4382	657	6	0
Ditto, North Middle, B	Mr. T. Rooke	9	13	4	6	8	12	3130	469	10	0
Ditto, Western, C	Mr. C. Redding	12	14	4	6	14	18	5008	751	4	0
Ditto, South Middle, D	Mr. J. Gould	10	12	3	4	9	11	3130	469	10	0
Shoreditch	Mr. Dodd	6	9	2	2	8	12	3130	469	10	0
Norton Folgate	Mr. J. Gould	3	5	1	1	4	6	1565	234	15	0
Finsbury Square District	Ditto	3	4	1	1	6	8	2191	328	13	0
St. Botolph	Mr. Westley	3	4	2	2	4	6	1565	234	15	0
Spitalfields District	Mr. Newman	2	6	1	2	3	5	1252	187	16	0
Spitalfields-market	Mr. Parsons	3	7	3	4	5	6	1565	234	15	0
Bethnal-green	Mr. E. Newman	5	6	3	4	8	10	2817	422	11	0
Whitechapel	Mr. Parsons	4	5	2	3	4	8	2191	328	13	0
Commercial-road	Parish	3	6	2	3	4	6	1565	234	15	0
Mile-end	Mr. Newman	3	5	1	2	3	5	1252	187	16	0
Ditto, New-town	Mr. Parsons	2	6	1	2	2	4	939	140	17	0
St. John's, Wapping	Mr. Westley	2	4	1	2	2	4	939	140	17	0
Shadwell	Ditto	4	6	2	3	3	5	1252	187	16	0
St. George's-in-the-East	Mr. E. Newman	4	6	2	3	6	8	2191	328	13	0
Stepney	Parish	4	4	1	2	4	6	1565	234	15	0
Poplar	Mr. Redding	2	6	1	1	3	4	939	140	17	0
East Borough	Ditto	4	6	2	3	2	5	1252	187	16	0
West ditto	Mr. W. Sinnott	3	4	1	2	2	4	939	140	17	0
Borough Clink	Parish	3	5	2	3	2	4	939	140	17	0
Bermondsey	Ditto	4	6	2	3	9	15	3376	563	18	0
Newington	Ditto	4	6	2	3	3	5	1252	187	16	0
Lambeth	Ditto	12	16	2	3	8	10	2817	422	11	0
Ditto (Christchurch)	Ditto	14	20	2	3	6	9	2191	328	13	0
Wandsworth	Ditto	2	4	1	1	1	3	626	93	18	0
Camberwell and Walworth	Ditto	4	6	2	2	5	7	1878	281	14	0
Rotherhithe	Ditto	3	5	1	2	3	5	1252	187	16	0
Greenwich	Ditto	3	5	1	2	4	6	1565	234	15	0
Deptford	Ditto	3	4	1	2	6	8	2191	328	13	0
Woolwich	Ditto	3	5	1	2	2	5	1252	187	16	0
Lewisham	Ditto	2	4	1	1	1	3	626	93	18	0
Scavengers' Total		358	531	130	183	355½	548½	140,983	21,147	9	0

Average total .... 444½ men. 156½ carts. 452 loads daily. 140,983 loads yearly. £21,147 9 0
Orderlies .... 546 ditto. 9 ditto. 2,817 ditto. 352 2 6

Gross total .... 990½ men. 156½ 461 loads daily. 143,800 loads yearly. £21,499 11 6

1st. In a perfectly dry state, so that the particles no longer exist either in a state of cohesion or aggregation, but are minutely divided and distinct, it is known by the name of "dust."

2nd. When in combination with a small quantity of water, so that it assumes the consistency of a pap, the particles being neither free to move nor yet able to resist pressure, the detritus is known by the name of "mac mud," or simply "mud," according as it proceeds from a macadamized or stone paved road.

3rd. When in combination with a greater quantity of water, so that it is rendered almost liquid, it is known as "slop-dirt."

4th. When in combination with a still greater quantity of water, so that it is capable of running off into the sewers, it is known by the name of "street surface-water."

The mud of the streets of London is then merely the dust or detritus of the granite of which they are composed, agglutinated either with rain or the water from the watering-carts. Granite consists of silex, felspar, and mica. Silex is sand, while felspar and mica are also silex in combination with alumina (clay), and either potash or magnesia. Hence it would appear to be owing to the affinity of the alumina or clay for moisture, as well as the property of silex to "gelatinize" with water under certain conditions, that the particles of dry dust derive their property of *agglutinating*, when wetted, and so forming what is termed "mud"—either "mac," or simple mud, according, as I said before, to the nature of the paving on which it is formed.

By *dust* the street-cleansers mean the collection of every kind of refuse in the dust-bins; but I here speak, of course, of the fine particles of earthy matter produced by the attrition of our roads when in a dry state. Street-dust is, more properly speaking, mud deprived of its moisture by evaporation. Miss Landon (L. E. L.) used to describe the London dust as "mud in high spirits," and perhaps no figure of speech could convey a better notion of its character.

In some parts of the suburbs on windy days London is a perfect dust-mill, and although the dust may be allayed by the agency of the water-carts (by which means it is again converted into "mac," or mud), it is not often thoroughly allayed, and is a source of considerable loss, labour, and annoyance. Street-dust is not collected for any useful purpose, so that as there is no return to be balanced against its prejudicial effects it remains only to calculate the quantity of it annually produced, and thus to arrive at the extent of the mischief.

Street-dust is disintegrated granite, that is, pulverized quartz and felspar, felspar being principally composed of alumina or clay, and quartz silex or sand; it is the result of the attrition, or in a word it is the *detritus*, of the stones used in pavements and in macadamization; it is further composed of the pulverization of all horse and cattle-dung, and of the almost imperceptible, but still, I am assured, existent powder which arises from the friction of the wooden pavement even when kept moist. In the roads of the nearest suburbs, even around such places as the Regent's-park, at many seasons this dust is produced largely, so that very often an open window for the enjoyment of fresh air is one for the intrusion of fresh dust. This may be less the case in the busier and more frequently-watered thoroughfares, but even there the annoyance is great.

I find in the "Reports" in which this subject is mentioned but little said concerning the influence of dust upon the public health. Dr. Arnott, however, is very explicit on the subject. "It is," says he, "scarcely conceivable that the immense quantities of granite dust, pounded by one or two hundred thousand pairs of wheels (!) working on macadamized streets, should not greatly injure the public health. In houses bordering such streets or roads it is found that, notwithstanding the practice of watering, the furniture is often covered with dust, even more than once in the day, so that writing on it with the finger becomes legible, and the lungs and air tubes of the inhabitants, with a moist lining to detain the dust, are constantly pumping in the same atmosphere. The passengers by a stage-coach in dry weather, when the wind is moving with them so as to keep them enveloped in the cloud of dust raised by the horses' feet and the wheels of the coach, have their clothes soon saturated to whiteness, and their lungs are charged in a corresponding degree. A gentleman who rode only 20 miles in this way had afterwards to cough and expectorate for ten days to clear his chest again."

In order that the deleteriousness to health incident to the inhalation of these fine and offensive particles may be the better estimated, I may add, that in every 24 hours an adult breathes 36 hogsheads of air; and Mr. Erasmus Wilson, in his admirable work on the Skin, has the following passage concerning the extent of surface presented by the lungs:—

"The lungs receive the atmospheric air through the windpipe. At the root of the neck the windpipe, or trachea, divides into two branches, called bronchi, and each bronchus, upon entering its respective lung, divides into an infinity of small tubes; the latter terminate in small pouches, called air-cells, and a number of these little air-cells communicate together at the extremity of each small tube. The number of air-cells in the two lungs has been estimated at 1,744,000,000, and the extent of the skin which lines the cells and tubes together at 1500 square feet. This calculation of the number of air-cells, and the extent of the lining membrane, rests, I believe, on the authority of Dr. Addison of Malvern."

What is the amount of atmospherical granite, dung, and refuse-dust received in a given period into the human lungs, has never, I am informed, been ascertained even by approximation; but according to the above facts it must be something fearful to contemplate.

After this brief recital of what is known concerning the sanitary part of the question, I proceed to consider the damage and loss occasioned by street-dust. In no one respect, perhaps, can this be ascertained with perfect precision, but still even a rough approximation to the extent of the evil is of value, as giving us more definite ideas on the subject.

It will be seen, on reference to the preceding table, that the quantity of street-refuse collected in dry weather throughout the metropolis is between 300 and 400 cart-loads daily, or upwards of 100,000 cart-loads, the greater proportion of which may be termed street-dust.

The damage occasioned by the street-dust arises from its penetrating, before removal, the atmosphere both without and within our houses, and consists in the soiling of wearing apparel, the injury of the stock-in-trade of shopkeepers, and of household furniture.

Washing is, of course, dependent upon the duration of time in which it is proper, in the estimation of the several classes of society, to retain wearing apparel upon the person, on the bed or the table, without what is termed a "change;" and this duration of time with thousands of both men and women is often determined by the presence or absence of dirt on the garment; and not arbitrarily, as among wealthier people, with whom a clean shirt every morning, and a clean table-cloth every one, two, three, or more days, as may happen, are regarded as things of course, no matter what may be the state of the displaced linen.

The Board of Health, in one of their Reports, speak very decisively and definitely on this subject. "Common observation of the rate at which the skin, linen, and clothes (not to speak of paper, books, prints, and furniture) become dirty in the metropolis," say they, "as compared with the time that elapses before a proportionate amount of deterioration and uncleanliness is communicated in the rural districts, will warrant the estimate, that *full one-half the expense of washing to maintain a passable degree of cleanliness*, is rendered necessary by the excess of smoke generated in open fires, and the *excess of dust arising from the imperfect scavenging of the roads and streets*. Persons engaged in washing linen on a large scale, state that it is dirtied in the crowded parts of the metropolis in *one-third* the time in which the like degree of uncleanliness would be produced in a rural district; but all attest the fact, that linen is more rapidly destroyed by washing than by the wear on the person. The expense of the more rapid destruction of linen must be added to the extra expense of washing. These expenses and inconveniences, the greater portion of which are due to *local maladministration, occasion an extra expenditure of upwards of two to three millions per annum*—exclusive of the injury done to the general health and the medical and other expenses consequent thereon."

Here, then, we find the evil effects of the imperfect scavenging of the metropolis estimated at between two and three millions sterling per annum, and this in the mere matter of extra washing and its necessary concomitant extra wear and tear of clothes.

As this estimate, however, appears to me to exaggerate the evil beyond all due bounds, I will proceed to adduce a few facts, bearing upon the point: and first as to the expense of washing.

In order to ascertain as accurately as possible, the actual washing expenses of labouring men and their families whose washing was done at home, Mr. John Bullar, the Honorary Secretary to the Association for the Promotion of Baths and Washhouses, tells us in a Report presented to Parliament, "that inquiries were made of several hundred families of labouring men, and it was found that, *taking the wife's labour as worth 5s. a week!* the total cost of washing at home, for a man and wife and four children, averaged very closely on 2s. 6d. a week, = 5d. a head. The cost of coals, soda, soap, starch, blue, and sometimes water, was rather less than one-third of the amount. The time occupied was rarely less than two days, and more often extended into a third day, so that the value of the labour was rather more than two-thirds of the amount.

"The cost of washing to single men among the labouring classes, whose washing expenditure might be expected to be on a very low scale, such as hod-men and street-sweepers, was found to be 4½d. a head.

"The cost of washing to very small tradesmen could not be safely estimated at much more than 6d. a head a week.

"It may, perhaps," continues the Report, "be safe to reckon the weekly washing expenses of the poorer half of the inhabitants of the metropolis at not exceeding 6d. a head; but the expenditure for washing rapidly increases as the inquiry ascends into what are called the 'middle classes.'

"The washing expenses of families in which servants are employed may be considered as double that of the servants', and, therefore, as ranging from 1s. 6d. to 5s. a week a head.

"There is considerable difficulty in ascertaining with any exactness the washing expenditure of private families, but the conclusion is that, taking the whole population, the washing bills of London are nearly 1s. a week a head, or 5,000,000*l*. a year.

"Of course," adds Mr. Bullar, "I give this as but a rough estimate, and many exceptions may easily be taken to it; but I feel pretty confident that *it is not very far* from the truth."

As I before stated, I am in no way disposed to go to the extent of the calculation here made. It appears to me that in parliamentary investigations by the agency of select committees, or by gentlemen appointed to report on any subject, there is an aptitude to deal with the whole body of the people as if they were earning the wages of well and regularly-employed labourers, or even mechanics. To suppose that the starving ballast-heaver, the victim of a vicious truck system, which condemns him to poverty and drunkenness, or the sweep, or the dustman, or the street-seller—all very numerous classes—expends 1s. a week in his washing, is far beyond the fact. Still less is expended in the washing of these people's children. Even the well-conducted artizan, with two clean shirts a week (costing him 6*d*.), with the washing of stockings, &c. (costing 1*d*. or 2*d*.), does not expend 1*s*. a week; so that, though the washing bills of many ladies and of some gentlemen may average 10*s*. weekly, if we consider how few are rich and how many poor, the extra payment seems insufficient to make up the average of the weekly shilling for the washing of all classes.

A prosperous and respectable master greengrocer, who was what may be called "particular" in his dress, as he had been a gentleman's servant, and was now in the habit of waiting upon the wealthy persons in his neighbourhood, told me that the following was the average of his washing bill. He was a bachelor; all his washing was put out, and he considered his expenditure far *above* the average of his class, as many used no night-shirt, but slept in the shirts they wore during the day, and paid only 3*d*., and even less, per shirt to their washer-woman, and perhaps, and more especially in winter, made one shirt last the week.

Two shirts (per week)	7*d*.
Stockings	1
Night-shirt (worn two weeks generally, average per week)	0¾
Sheets, blankets, and other household linens or woollens	2
Handkerchiefs	0¼
	11*d*.

My informant was satisfied that he had put his expenditure at the highest. I also ascertained that an industrious wife, who was able to attend to her household matters, could wash the clothes of a small tradesman's family,—for a man, his wife, and four small children,—" well," at the following rate:—

1 lb. soap	4½*d*. or 5*d*.
Soda and starch	0½
¼ cwt. coals (extra)	3½
	8½*d*.

or less than 1½*d*. per head.

In this calculation it will be seen the cheapest soap is reckoned, and that *there is no allowance for the wife's labour.* When I pointed out the latter circumstance, my informant said: "I look on it that the washing labour is part of the wife's keep, or what she gives in return for it; and that as she'd have to be kept if she didn't do it, why there shouldn't be no mention of it. If she was working for others it would be quite different, but washing is a family matter; that's my way of looking at it. Coke, too, is often used instead of coals; besides, a bit of bacon, or potatoes, or the tea-kettle, will have to be boiled, and that's managed along with the hot water for the suds, and would have to be done anyhow, especially in winter."

One decent woman, who had five children, "all under eight," told me she often sat up half, and sometimes the whole night to wash, when busy other ways. She was not in poverty, for she earned "a good bit" in going out to cook, and her husband was employed by a pork-butcher.

I may further add, that a great many single men wash their own clothes. Many of the street-sellers in particular do this; so do such of the poor as live in their own rooms, and occasionally the dwellers in the low lodging-houses. One street-seller of ham sandwiches, whose aprons, sleeves, and tray-cloth, were remarkably white, told me that he washed them himself, as well as his shirt, &c., and that it was the common practice with his class. This washing—his aprons, tray-cloths, shirts, and stockings included—cost him, every three weeks, 4¼*d*. or 5*d*. for 1 lb. of soap, which is less than 1½*d*. a week. Among such people it is considered that the washing of a shirt is, as they say, "a penn'orth of soap, and the stockings in," meaning that a penny outlay is sufficient to wash for both.

But not only does Mr. Bullar's estimate exceed the truth as regards the cost of washing among the poorer classes, but it also errs in the proportion they are said to bear to the other ranks of society. That gentleman speaks of "the poorer *half* of the inhabitants of the metropolis," as if the rich and poor were equal in numbers! but with all deference, it will be found that the ratio between the well-to-do and the needy is as 1 to 2, that is to say, the property and income-tax returns teach us there are at least two persons with an income *below* 150*l*. per annum, to every one having an income *above* it. Hence, the population of London being, within a fraction, 2,400,000; the numbers of the metropolitan well-to-do and needy would be respectively 800,000 and 1,600,000, and, allowing the cost of the washing of the former to average 1*s*. per head (adults and children), and, the washing of the labouring classes to come to 2*d*. a head, young and old (the expense of the materials, when the work is done at home, average, it has been shown, about 1½*d*. for each member of the family), we shall then have the following statement:—

Annual cost of washing for 800,000 people, at 1*s*. per head per week	£2,080,000
Annual cost of washing for 1,600,000 people, at 2*d*. per head per week	693,333
Total cost of washing of metropolis	£2,773,333

I am convinced, low as the estimate of 2*d*. a week may appear for all whose incomes are under 150*l*. a year, from many considerations, that the above computation is rather over than under the truth. As, for instance, Mr. Hawes has said concerning the consumption of soap in the metropolis, — " Careful inquiry has proved that the quantity used is much greater than that indicated by the Excise returns; but reducing the results obtained by inquiry in one uniform proportion, the quantity used by the labouring classes earning from 10*s*. to 30*s*. per week is 10 lbs. each per annum, including every member of the family. Dividing the population of the metropolis into three classes: (1) the wealthy; (2) the shopkeepers and tradesmen; (3) labourers and the poor, and allowing 15 lbs., 10 lbs., and 4 lbs. to each respectively, the consumption of the metropolis will be nearly 200 tons per week." The cost of each ton of soap Mr. Hawes estimates at 45*l*.

Professor Clarke, however, computes the metropolitan consumption of soap at 250 ton. per week, and the cost per ton at 50*l*.

According to the above estimates, the total quantity of soap used every year in the metropolis is 12,000 tons, and this, at 50*l*. per ton, comes to . . £600,000

Professor Clarke reckons the gross consumption of soda in the metropolis, at 250 tons per month, costing 10*l*. a ton; hence for the year the consumption will be 3000 tons, costing 30,000

The cost of water, according to the same authority, is 3*s*. 4*d*. per head per annum, and this, for the whole metropolis, amounts to 400,000

Estimating the cost of the coals used in heating the water to be equal to that of the soap, we have for the gross expense of fuel annually consumed in washing 600,000

There are 21,000 laundresses in London, and, calculating that the wages of these average 10*s*. a week each all the year round, the gross sum paid to them, would be in round numbers 550,000
Profit of employers, say 550,000
Add for sundries, as starch, &c. . 50,000

Total cost of washing of metropolis £2,780,000

Hence it would appear, that viewed either by the individual expense of the great bulk of society, or else by the aggregate cost of the materials and labour used in cleansing the clothes of the people of London, the total sum annually expended in the washing of the metropolis may be estimated at the outside at two millions and three quarters sterling per annum, or about 1*l*. 3*s*. 4*d*. per head.

And yet, though the data for the calculation here given, as to the cost and quantity of the principal materials used in cleansing the clothes of London, are derived from the same Report as that in which the expense of the metropolitan washing is estimated at 5,000,000*l*. per annum, the Board of Health do not hesitate in that document to say that,—" Of the fairness of the estimate of the expense of washing to the higher and middle classes, and to the great bulk of the householders, and the better class of artizans, we entertain no doubt whatever. Whatsoever deductions, if any, may be made from the above estimate, it is, nevertheless, an *under-estimate* for maintaining, at the present expense of washing, a proper amount of cleanliness in linen."

Proceeding, however, with the calculation as to the loss from the imperfect scavenging of the metropolis, we have the following results:—

LOSS FROM DUST AND DIRT IN THE STREETS OF THE METROPOLIS, OWING TO THE EXTRA WASHING ENTAILED THEREBY.

According to the Board of Health, taking the yearly amount of the washing of the metropolis at 5,000,000*l*., and assuming the washing to be doubled by street-dirt, the loss will be £2,500,000

Calculating the washing, however, for reasons above adduced, to be only 2,750,000*l*., and to be as much again as it might be under an improved system of scavenging, the loss will be 1,375,000

Or calculating, *as a minimum*, that the remediable loss is less than one-half, the cost is £1,000,000

Hence it would appear that the loss from dust and dirt is *really enormous*.

In a work entitled " Sanatory Progress," being the Fifth Report of the National Philanthropic Association, I find a calculation as to the losses sustained from dust and dirt upon our clothes. Owing to the increased wear from daily brushing to remove the dust, and occasional scraping to remove the mud, the loss is estimated at from 3*l*. to 7*l*. per annum for each well-dressed man and woman, and 1*l*. for inferiorly-dressed persons, including their Sunday and holiday clothing.

I inquired of a West-end tailor, who previously to his establishment in business had himself been an operative, and had had experience both in town and country as to the wear of clothes, and I learned from him the following particulars.

With regard to the clothes of the wealthy classes, of those who could always command a carriage in bad weather, there are no means of judging as to the loss caused by bad scavengery.

My informant, however, obliged me with the following calculations, the results of his experience. His trade is what I may describe as a medium business, between the low slop and the high fashionable trades. The garments of which he spoke were those worn by clerks, shopmen, students, tradesmen, town-travellers, and others not engaged in menial or handicraft labour.

Altogether, and after consulting his books relative to town and country customers, my informant thought it might be easy to substantiate the following estimate as regards the duration and cost of clothes in town and country among the classes I have specified.

TABLE SHOWING THE COMPARATIVE COST OF CLOTHES WORN IN TOWN AND COUNTRY.

Garments.	Original cost.	Town.		Country.		Difference of cost.
		Duration.	Annual cost.	Duration.	Annual cost.	
	£ s. d.	Years.	£ s. d.	Years.	£ s. d.	£ s. d.
Coat	2 10 0	2	1 5 0	3	0 16 8	0 8 4
Waistcoat	0 15 0	2½	0 6 0	3	0 5 0	0 1 0
Trowsers	1 5 0	1¼	1 0 0	2	0 12 6	0 7 6
Total Suit	4 10 0		2 11 0		1 14 2	0 16 10

Here, then, it appears that the annual outlay for clothes in town, by the classes I have specified, is about 2*l*. 11*s*.; while the annual outlay in the country for the same garments is 1*l*. 14*s*. 2*d*.; the difference of expense being 16*s*. 10*d*. per annum. I consulted another tailor on the subject, and his estimate was a trifle above that of my informant.

I should remark that the proportion thus adduced holds, *whatever be the number of garments* worn in the year, or in a series of years, for the calculation was made not as to individual garments, but as to the general wear, evinced by the average outlay, as shown in the tradesman's books, of the same class of persons in town and country.

In the calculation given in the publication of the National Philanthropic Association, the loss on a well-dressed Londoner's clothing, arising from excessive dust and dirt, is estimated at from 3*l*. to 7*l*. per annum. By the above table it will be seen that the clothes which cost 1*l*. 14*s*. 2*d*. per annum in the cleanliness of a country abode, cost 2*l*. 11*s*., or, within a fraction, half as much again, in the uncleanliness of a London atmosphere and roads. If, therefore, any London inhabitant, of the classes I have specified, expend four times 2*l*. 11*s*. in his clothes yearly, as many do, or 10*l*. 4*s*., he loses 3*l*. 5*s*. 4*d*., or 5*s*. 4*d*. more than the minimum mentioned in the Report alluded to.

Now estimating 2*l*. 10*s*. as the yearly tailor's bill among the well-to-do (boys and men), and calculating that one-sixth of the metropolitan population (that is, half of the one-third who may be said to belong to the class having incomes above 150*l*. a year) spend this sum yearly in clothes, we have the following statement:—

AGGREGATE LOSS UPON CLOTHES WORN IN LONDON.

	£ s. d.
400,000 persons living in London expend in clothing (at 2*l*. 10*s*. per annum)	1,000,000 0 0
400,000 persons living in better atmospheres in rural parts, and with the same stock of clothes, expend one-third less, or	666,666 13 4
Difference	333,333 6 8

It would be pushing the inquiry to exceeding minuteness were I to enter into calculations as to the comparative expense of boots, hats, and ladies' dresses worn in town and country; suffice it, that competent persons in each of the vestiary trades have been seen, and averages drawn for the accounts of their town and country customers.

All things, then, being duly considered, the following conclusion would seem to be warranted by the facts:—

Annual cost of clothes to 800,000 of the metropolitan population (those belonging to the class who have incomes *above* 150*l*. per annum) at 4*l*. per year each	£3,200,000
Annual cost of clothes to 1,600,000 of the metropolitan population (those belonging to the class who have incomes *below* 150*l*. per annum), at 1*l*. per year each	1,600,000
	£4,800,000
Annual cost of the same clothes if worn in the country	3,600,000
Extra expense annually entailed by dust and dirt of metropolis	£1,200,000

In the above estimate I have included the cost of wear and tear of linen from extra washing when worn in London, and this has been stated on the authority of the Board of Health to be double that of linen worn in the country.

In connection with this subject I may cite the following curious calculation, taken from a Parliamentary Report, as to the cost of a working man's new shirt, comprising four yards of strong calico.

Material.—Cotton at 6*d*. per lb. 1¼ lb., with loss thereupon		*d.* 8·25
Manufacture,—	*d.*	
Spinning	2·25	
Weaving	3·00	
Profit	·25	
		5·50
		13·75
Bleaching about		1·25
		15·00

Grey (calico) 13·75*d*. +9*d*. (making) = 1*s*. 10¾*d*.
Bleached 15*d*. +9*d*. „ = 2*s*.

As regards the loss and damage occasioned by the injury to household furniture and decorations, and to stocks-in-trade, which is another important consideration connected with this subject, I find the following statement in the Report of the Philanthropic Institution :—" The loss by goods and furniture is incalculable : shopkeepers lose from 10*l*. to 150*l*. a-year by the spoiling of their goods for sale; dealers in provisions especially, who cannot expose them without being deteriorated in value, from the dust that is incessantly settling upon them. Nor is it much better with clothiers of all kinds :—Mr. Holmes, shawl merchant, in Regent-street, has stated that his losses from road-dust alone exceed 150*l*. per annum." . . . . "In a communication with Mr. Mivart, respecting the expenses of mud and road-dust to him, that gentleman stated that the rent of the four houses of which his hotel is composed, was 896*l*.; and that he could not (considering the cost of cleaning and servants) estimate the expense of repairing the damage done by the dirt and dust, carried and blown into these houses, at a less annual sum than that of his rent!"

An upholsterer obliged me with the following calculations, but so many were the materials, and so different the rates of wear or the liability to injury in different materials in his trade, that he could only calculate generally.

The same quality, colour, and pattern of curtains, silk damasks, which he had furnished to a house in town, and to a country house belonging to the same gentleman, looked far fresher and better after five years' wear in the country than after three in town. Both windows had a southern aspect, but the occupant would have his windows partially open unless the weather was cold, foggy, or rainy. It was the same, or nearly the same, he thought, with the carpets on the two places, for London dust was highly injurious to all the better qualities of carpets. He was satisfied, also, it was the same generally in upholstery work subjected to town dust.

I inquired at several West-end and city shops, and of different descriptions of tradesmen, of the injury done to their shop and shop-window goods by the dust, but I found none who had made any calculations on the subject. All, however, agreed that the dust was an excessive annoyance, and entailed great expense; a ladies' shoemaker and a bookseller expressed this particularly—on the necessity of making the window a sort of small glass-house to exclude the dust, which, after all, was not sufficiently excluded. All thought, or with but one hesitating exception, that the estimation as to the loss sustained by the Messrs. Holmes, considering the extent of their premises, and the richness of the goods displayed in the windows, &c., was not in excess.

I can, then, but indicate the injury to household furniture and stock-in-trade as a corroboration of all that has been advanced touching the damaging effects of road dirt.

Of the Horse-Dung of the Streets of London.

" Familiarity with streets of crowded traffic deadens the senses to the perception of their actual condition. Strangers coming from the country frequently describe the streets of London as smelling of dung like a stable-yard."

Such is one of the statements in a Report submitted to Parliament, and there is no reason to doubt the fact. Every English visitor to a French city, for instance, must have detected street-odours of which the inhabitants were utterly unconscious. In a work which between 20 and 30 years ago was deservedly popular, Mathews's "Diary of an Invalid," it is mentioned that an English lady complaining of the villanous rankness of the air in the first French town she entered—Calais, if I remember rightly—received the comfortable assurance, "It is the smell of the Continent, ma'am." Even in Cologne itself, the "most stinking city of Europe," as it has been termed, the citizens are insensible to the foul airs of their streets, and yet possess great skill in manufacturing perfumed and distilled waters for the toilet, pluming themselves on the delicacy and discrimination of their nasal organs. What we perceive in other cities, as strangers, those who visit London detect in our streets—that they smell of dung like stable-yards. It is idle for London denizens, because they are unconscious of the fact, to deny the existence of any such effluvia. I have met with nightmen who have told me that there was " nothing particular" in the smell of the cesspools they were emptying; they "hardly perceived it." One man said, "Why, it's like the sort of stuff I've smelt in them ladies' smelling-bottles." An eminent tallow-melter said, in the course of his evidence before Parliament during a sanitary inquiry, that the smell from the tallow-melting on his premises was not only healthful and reviving —for invalids came to inhale it—but agreeable. I mention these facts to meet the scepticism which the official assertion as to the stable-like odour of the streets may, perhaps, provoke. When, however, I state the *quantity* of horse-dung and "cattle-droppings" voided in the streets, all incredulity, I doubt not, will be removed.

"It has been ascertained," says the Report of the National Philanthropic Association, "that four-fifths of the street-dirt consist of horse and cattle-droppings."

Let us, therefore, endeavour to arrive at definite notions as to the absolute quantity of this element of street-dirt.

And, first, as to the number of cattle and horses traversing the streets of London.

In the course of an inquiry in November, 1850, into Smithfield-market, I adduced the following results as to the number of cattle entering the metropolis, deriving the information from the experience of Mr. Deputy Hicks, confirmed by returns to Parliament, by the amount of tolls, and further ratified by the opinion of some of the most experienced "live salesmen" and "dead salesmen" (sellers on commission of live and dead cattle), whose assistance I had the pleasure of obtaining.

The return is of the stock *annually* sold in Smithfield-market, and includes not only English but foreign beasts, sheep, and calves; the latter averaging weekly in 1848 (the latest return then published), beasts, 590; sheep, 2478; and calves, 248.

224,000 horned cattle.
1,550,000 sheep.
27,300 calves.
40,000 pigs.

Total . . 1,841,300.

I may remark that this is not a criterion of the consumption of animal food in the metropolis, for there are, besides the above, the daily supplies from the country to the "dead salesmen." The preceding return, however, is sufficient for my present purpose, which is to show the quantity of cattle manure "dropped" in London.

The number of cattle entering the metropolis, then, are 1,841,300 per annum.

The number of horses daily traversing the metropolis has been already set forth. By a return obtained by Mr. Charles Cochrane from the Stamp and Tax Office, we have seen that there are altogether

In London and Westminster, of private carriage, job, and cart horses . . . 10,022
Cab horses 5,692
Omnibus horses 5,500
Horses daily coming to metropolis . . 3,000

Total number of horses daily in London 24,214

The total here given includes the returns of horses which were either taxed or the property of those who employ them in hackney-carriages in the metropolis. But the whole of these 24,214 horses are not at work in the streets every day. Perhaps it might be an approximation to the truth, if we reckoned five-sixths of the horses as being worked regularly in the public thoroughfares; so that we arrive at the conclusion that 20,000 horses are daily worked in the metropolis; and hence we have an aggregate of 7,300,000 horses traversing the streets of London in the twelvemonth. The beasts, sheep, calves, and pigs driven and conveyed to and from Smithfield are, we have seen, 1,841,300 in number. These, added together, make up a total of 9,141,300 animals appearing annually in the London thoroughfares. The circumstance of Smithfield cattle-market being held but twice a week in no way detracts from the amount here given; for as the gross number of individual cattle coming to that market in the course of the year is given, each animal is estimated as appearing only once in the metropolis.

The next point for consideration is—what is the quantity of dung dropped by each of the above animals while in the public thoroughfares?

Concerning the quantity of excretions passed by a horse in the course of 24 hours there have been some valuable experiments made by philosophers whose names alone are a sufficient guarantee for the accuracy of their researches.

The following Table from Boussingault's experiments is copied from the "Annales de Chimie et de Physique," t. lxxi.

FOOD CONSUMED BY AND EXCRETIONS OF A HORSE IN TWENTY-FOUR HOURS.

Food.			Excretions.		
	Weight in a fresh state in grammes.	Weight in a fresh state in pounds.		Weight in a fresh state in grammes.	Weight in a fresh state in pounds.
		lbs. oz.			lbs. oz.
Hay . . .	7,500	20 0	Excrements .	14,250	38 2
Oats . . .	2,270	6 1	Urine . . .	1,330	3 7
	9,770	26 1			
Water . . .	16,000	42 10			
Total . .	25,770	68 11	Total . . .	15,580	41 9

Here it will be seen that the quantity of solid food given to the horse in the course of the 24 hours amounted only to 26 lbs.; whereas it is stated in the Report of the National Philanthropic Association, on the authority of the veterinary surgeon to the Life Guards, that the regulation horse rations in all cavalry regiments is 30 lbs. of solid food; viz., 10 lbs. of oats, 12 lbs. of hay, together with 8 lbs. of straw, for the horse to lie upon and munch at his leisure. "This quantity of solid food, with five gallons of water, is considered sufficient," we are told, "for all regimental horses, who have but little work to perform, in comparison with the draught horses of the metropolis, many of which consume daily 35 lbs. and upwards of solid food, with at least six gallons of water.

"At a conference held with the secretary and professors of the Veterinary College in College-street, Camden-town," continues the Report, "those gentlemen kindly undertook to institute a series of experiments in this department of equine physiology; the subject being one which interested themselves, professionally, as well as the council of the National Philanthropic Association. The experiments were carefully conducted under the superintendence of Professor Varnell. The food, drink, and voidances of several horses, kept in stable all day long, were separately weighed and measured; and the following were the results with an animal of medium size and sound health:—

"'Royal Veterinary College,
Sept. 29, 1849.

"'Brown horse of middle size ate in 24 hours, of hay, 16 lbs.; oats, 10 lbs.; chaff, 4 lbs.; in all . . . . . . 30 lbs.
Drank of water, in 24 hours, 6 gallons, or . . . . 48 lbs.

Total . . . 78 lbs.
Voided in the form of fæces . . . 49 lbs.

Allowance for nutrition, supply of waste in system, perspiration, and urine 29 lbs.
(Signed)
"'GEORGE VARNELL,
"'Demonstrator of Anatomy.'"

Here we find the excretions to be 11 lbs. more than those of the French horse experimented upon by M. Boussingault; but then the solid food given to the English horse was 4 lbs. more, and the liquid upwards of 7 lbs. extra.

We may then, perhaps, assume, without fear of erring, that the excrements voided by horses in the course of 24 hours, weigh, at the least, 45 lbs.

Hence the gross quantity of dung produced by the 7,300,000 horses which traverse the London streets in the course of the twelvemonth will be 7,300,000 × 45, or 328,500,000 lbs., which is upwards of 146,651 tons. But these horses cannot be said to be at work above six hours each day; we must, therefore, divide the above quantity by four, and thus we find that there are 36,662 tons of horse-dung annually dropped in the streets of London.

I am informed, on good authority, that the evacuations of an ox, in 24 hours, will, on the average, exceed those of a horse in weight by about a fifteenth, while, if the ox be disturbed by being driven, the excretions will exceed the horse's by about a twelfth. As the oxen are not driven in the streets, or detained in the market for so long a period as horses are out at work, it may be fair to compute that their droppings are about the same, individually, as those of the horses.

Hence, as there are 224,000 horned cattle yearly brought to London, we have 224,000 × 45 lbs. = 10,080,000 lbs., or 4500 tons, for the gross quantity of ordure dropped by this number of animals in the course of 24 hours, so that, dividing by 4, as before, we find that there are 1125 tons of ordure annually dropped by the "horned cattle" in the streets of London.

Concerning the sheep, I am told that it may be computed that the ordure of five sheep is about equal in weight to that of two oxen. As regards the other animals it may be said that their "droppings" are insignificant, the pigs and calves being very generally carted to and from the market, as, indeed, are some of the fatter and more valuable sheep and lambs. All these facts being taken into consideration, I am told, by a regular frequenter of Smithfield market, that it will be best to calculate the droppings of each of the 1,617,300 sheep, calves, and pigs yearly coming to the metropolis at about one-fourth of those of the horned cattle; so that multiplying 1,617,300 by 10, instead of 45, we have 16,173,000 lbs., or 7220 tons, for the weight of ordure deposited by the entire number of sheep, calves, and pigs annually brought to the metropolis, and then dividing this by 4, as usual, we find that the droppings of the calves, sheep, and pigs in the streets of London amount to 1805 tons per annum.

Now putting together all the preceding items we obtain the following results:—

GROSS WEIGHT OF THE HORSE-DUNG AND CATTLE-DROPPINGS ANNUALLY DEPOSITED IN THE STREETS OF LONDON:—

	Tons.
Horse-dung	36,662
Droppings of horned cattle . . .	1,125
Droppings of sheep, calves, and pigs	1,805
	39,592

Hence we perceive that the gross weight of animal excretions dropped in the public thoroughfares of the metropolis is about 40,000 tons per annum, or, in round numbers, 770 tons every week-day—say 100 tons a day.

This, I am well aware, is a low estimate, but it appears to me that the facts will not warrant any other conclusion. And yet the Board of Health, who seem to delight in "large" estimates, represent the amount of animal manure deposited in the streets of London at no less than 200,000 tons per annum.

"Between the Quadrant in Regent-street and Oxford-street," says the first Report on the Supply of Water to the Metropolis, "a distance of a third of a mile, three loads, on the average, of dirt, almost all horse-dung, are removed daily. On an estimate made from the working of the street-sweeping machine, in one quarter of the City of London, which includes lines of considerable traffic, the quantity of dung dropped must be upwards of 60 tons, or about 20,000 tons per annum, and this, on a City district, which comprises about one-twentieth only of the covered area of the metropolis, though within that area there is the greatest proportionate amount of traffic. Though the data are extremely imperfect, it is considered that the horse-dung which falls in the streets of the whole metropolis *cannot be less than* 200,000 *tons a year.*"

Hence, although the data are imperfect, the Board of Health do not hesitate to conclude that the gross quantity of horse-dung dropped throughout every part of London—back streets and all—is equal to one-half of that let fall in the greatest London thoroughfares. According to this estimate, all and every of the 24,000 London horses must void, in the course of the six hours that they are at work in the streets, not less than 51 lbs. of excrement, which is at the rate of very nearly 2 cwt. in the course of the day, or voiding only 49 lbs. in the twenty-four hours, they must remain out altogether, and never return to the stable for rest !!!

Mr. Cochrane is far less hazardous than the Board of Health, and appears to me to arrive at his result in a more scientific and conclusive manner. He goes first to the Stamp Office to ascertain the number of horses in the metropolis, and then requests the professors of the Veterinary College to estimate the average quantity of excretions produced by a horse in the course of 24 hours. All this accords with the soundest principles of inquiry, and stands out in startling contrast with the unphilosophical plan pursued by the Board of Health, who obtain the result of the most crowded thoroughfare, and then halving this, frame an exaggerated estimate for the whole of the metropolis.

But Mr. Cochrane himself appears to me to exceed that just caution which is so necessary in all statistical calculations. Having ascertained that a horse voids 49 lbs. of dung in the course of 24 hours, he makes the whole of the 24,214 horses in the metropolis drop 30 lbs. daily in the streets, so that, according to his estimate, not only must every horse in London be out every day, but he must be at work in the public thoroughfares for very nearly 15 hours out of the 24 !

The following is the estimate made by Mr. Cochrane :—

Daily weight of manure deposited in the streets by 24,214 horses × 30 lbs. = 726,420 lbs., or 324 tons, 5 cwt., 100 lbs.
Weekly weight, 2270 tons, 1 cwt., 28 lbs.
Annual weight, 118,043 tons, 5 cwt.
Tons or cart-loads deposited annually, valued at 6s. × 118,043 = 35,412l. 19s. 6d.

It has, then, been here shown that, assuming the number of horses worked daily in the streets of London to be 20,000, and each to be out six hours *per diem*, which, it appears to me, is all that can be fairly reckoned, the quantity of horse-dung dropped weekly is about 700 tons, so that, including the horses of the cavalry regiments in London, which of course are not comprised in the Stamp-Office returns, as well as the animals taken to Smithfield, we may, perhaps, assert that the annual ordure let fall in the London streets amounts, at the outside, to somewhere about 1000 tons weekly, or 52,000 tons per annum.

The next question becomes—what is done with this vast amount of filth?

The Board of Health is a much better guide upon this point than upon the matter of quantity: "Much of the horse-dung dropped in the London streets, under ordinary circumstances," we are told, "dries and is pulverized, and with the common soil is carried into houses as dust, and dirties clothes and furniture. The odour arising from the surface evaporation of the streets when they are wet is chiefly from horse-dung. Susceptible persons often feel this evaporation, after partial wetting, to be highly oppressive. The surface-water discharged into sewers from the streets and roofs of houses is found to contain as much filth as the soil-water from the house-drains."

Here, then, we perceive that the whole of the animal manure let fall in the streets is worse than wasted, and yet we are assured that it is an article, which, if properly collected, is of considerable value. "It is," says the Report of the National Philanthropic Association, "an article of Agricultural and Horticultural commerce which has ever maintained a high value with the farmers and market-gardeners, wherever conveniently obtainable. When these cattle-droppings can be collected *unmixed*, in dry weather, they bear an acknowledged value by the grazier and root-grower;—there being no other kind of manure which fertilizes the land so bounteously. Mr. Marnock, Curator of the Royal Botanical Society, has valued them at from 5s. to 10s. per load; according to the season of the year. The United Paving Board of St. Giles and St. George, since the introduction of the Street Orderly System into their parishes, has wisely had it collected in a state separate from all admixture, and sold it at highly remunerative prices, rendering it the means of considerably lessening the expense of cleansing the streets."

Now, assuming the value of the street-dropped manure to be 6s. per ton when collected free from dirt, we have the following statement as to the value of the horse and cattle-voidances let fall in the streets of London:—

52,000 tons of cattle-droppings, at 6s. per ton £15,600 0 0

Mr. Cochrane, who considers the quantity of animal-droppings to be much greater, attaches of course a greater value to the aggregate quantity. His computation is as follows :—

118,043 tons of cattle-droppings, at 6s. per ton £35,412 19 6

It seems to me that the calculations of the quantity of horse and cattle-dung in the streets, are based on such well-authenticated and scientific foundations, that their accuracy can hardly be disputed, unless it be that a higher average might fairly be shown.

Whatever estimate be adopted, the worth of street-dropped animal manure, if properly secured and made properly disposable, is great and indisputable; most assuredly between 10,000l. and 20,000l. in value.

OF STREET "MAC" AND OTHER MUD.

FIRST of that kind of mud known by the name of "mac."

The scavengers call mud all that is *swept* from the granite or wood pavements, in contradistinction to "mac," which is both *scraped* and swept on the macadamized roads. The mud is usually carted apart from the "mac," but some contractors cause their men to shovel every kind of dirt they meet with into the same cart.

The introduction of Mac Adam's system of road-making into the streets of London called into existence a new element in what is accounted street refuse. Until of late years little attention was paid to "Mac," for it was considered in no way distinct from other kinds of street-dirt, nor as being likely to possess properties which might adapt it for any other use than that of a component part of agricultural manure.

"Mac" is found principally on the roads from which it derives its name, and is, indeed, the grinding and pounding of the imbedded pieces of granite, which are the staple of those roads. It is, perhaps, the most adhesive street-dirt known, as respects the London specimen of it; for the exceeding traffic works and kneads it into a paste which it is difficult to remove from the texture of any garment splashed or soiled with it.

"Mac" is carted away by the scavengers in great quantities, being shovelled, in a state of more or less fluidity or solidity, according to the weather, from the road-side into their carts. Quantities are also swept with the rain into the drains of the streets, and not unfrequently quantities are found deposited in the sewers.

The following passage from "Sanatory Progress," a work before alluded to, cites the opinion of Lord Congleton as to the necessity of continually removing the mud from roads. I may add that Lord Congleton's work on road-making is of high authority, and has frequently been appealed to in parliamentary discussions, inquiries, and reports on the subject.

"The late Lord Congleton (Sir Henry Parnell) stated before a Committee of the House of Commons, in June, 1838, 'a road should be cleansed from time to time, so as *never* to have half an inch of mud upon it; and this is particularly necessary to be attended to where the materials are *weak;* for, if the surface be not kept clean, so as to admit of its becoming dry in the intervals between showers of rain, it will be rapidly worn away.' How truly," adds the Report, "is his Lordship's opinion verified every day on the macadamized roads in and around London ! * * * * * * The horse-manure and other filth are there allowed to accumulate, and to be carried about by the horses and carriage-wheels; the road is formed into cavities and mud-hollows, which, being wetted by the rain and the constantly plying *watering-carts,* retain the same. Thus, not only are vast quantities of offensive mud formed, but puddles and *pools of water* also ; which water, not being allowed to run off to the side gutter, by declivity, owing to the *mud embankments* which surround it, naturally *percolates through the surface of the road, dissolving and loosening the soft earthy matrix* by which the broken granite is surrounded and fixed."

The quantity of "mac" produced is the next consideration, and in endeavouring to ascertain this there are no specific data, though there are what, under other circumstances, might be called circumstantial or inferential evidence.

I have shown both the length of the streets and roads and the proportion which might be pronounced macadamized ways in the Metropolis Proper. But as in the macadamized proportion many thoroughfares cannot be strictly considered as yielding "mac," I will assume that the roads and streets producing this kind of dirt, more or less fully, are 1200 miles in length.

On the busier macadamized roads in the vicinity of what may be called the interior of London, it is common, I was told by experienced men, in average weather, to collect daily two cart-loads of what is called mac, from every mile of road. The mass of such road-produce, however, is mixed, though the "mac" unquestionably predominates. It was described to me as mac, general dirt, and droppings, more than the half being "mac." In wet weather there is at least twenty times more "mac" than dung scavenged; but in dry weather the dung and other street-refuse constitute, perhaps, somewhat less than three-fourths of each cart-load. The "mac" in dry weather is derived chiefly from the fluid from the watering carts mixing with the dust, and so forming a paste capable of being removed by the scraper of the scavenger.

It may be fair to assume that every mile of the roads in question, some of them being of considerable width, yields at least one cart-load of "mac," as a daily average, Sunday of course excepted. An intelligent man, who had the management of the "mac" and other street collections in a contractor's wharf, told me that in a load of "mac" carted from the road to any place of deposit, there was (I now use his own words) "a good deal of water; for there's great difference," he added, "in the *stiffness* of the "mac" on different roads, that seem very much the same to look at. But that don't signify a halfpenny-piece," he said, "for if the 'mac' is wanted for any purpose, and let be for a little time, you see, sir, the water will dry up, and leave the proper stuff. I haven't any doubt whatever that two loads a mile are collected in the way you've been told, and that a load and a quarter of the two is 'mac,' though after the water is dried up out of it there mightn't be much more than a load. So if you want to calculate what the quantity of 'mac' is by itself, I think you had best say one load a mile."

But it is only in the more frequented approaches to the City or the West-end, such as the Knightsbridge-road, the New-road, the Old Kent-road, and thoroughfares of similar character as regards the extent of traffic, that two loads of refuse are daily collected. On the more distant roads, beyond the bounds traversed by the omnibuses for instance, or beyond the roads resorted to by the market gardeners on their way to the metropolitan "green" markets, the supply of street-refuse is hardly a quarter as great; one man thought it was a third, and another only a sixth of a load a day in quiet places.

Calculating then, in order to be within the mark,

that the macadamized roads afford daily two loads of dirt per mile, and reckoning the great macadamized streets at 100 miles in length, we have the following results:—

QUANTITY OF STREET-REFUSE COLLECTED FROM THE MORE FREQUENTED MACADAMIZED THOROUGHFARES.

	Loads.
100 miles, 2 loads per day	200
,, Weekly amount	1,200
,, Yearly amount	62,400

PROPORTION OF "MAC" IN THE ABOVE.

100 miles, 1 load per day	100
,, Weekly	600
,, Yearly	31,200

To this amount must be added the quantity supplied by the more distant and less frequented roads situate within the precincts of the Metropolis Proper. These I will estimate at one-eighth less than that of the roads of greater traffic. Some of the more quiet thoroughfares, I should add, are not scavenged more than once a week, and some less frequently; but on some there is considerable traffic.

QUANTITY OF STREET-REFUSE COLLECTED FROM THE LESS FREQUENTED MACADAMIZED THOROUGHFARES.

	Loads.
1100 miles, ¼ load per day	275
,, Weekly	1,650
,, Yearly	85,800

The proportion of mac to the gross dirt collected is greater in the more distant roads than what I have already described, but to be safe I will adopt the same ratio.

PROPORTION OF "MAC."

	Loads.
1100 miles of road, ⅛ load per day	137
,, Weekly	825
,, Yearly	42,900

YEARLY TOTAL OF THE GROSS QUANTITY OF STREET-REFUSE, WITH THE PROPORTIONATE QUANTITY OF "MAC" COLLECTED FROM THE MACADAMIZED THOROUGHFARES OF THE METROPOLIS.

	Street Refuse.	"Mac."
	Cart-loads.	Loads.
100 miles of macadamized roads	62,400	31,200
1100 miles ditto ditto	85,800	42,900
	148,200	74,100

Thus upwards of 74,000 cart-loads of "mac" are, at a low computation, annually scraped and swept from the metropolitan thoroughfares.

So far as to the *quantity* of "mac" collected, and now as to its *uses*.

"'Mac.' or *Macadam*," says one of Mr. Cochrane's Reports, "is a grand prize to the scavenging contractor, who finds ready vend and a high price for it among the builders and brickmakers. Those who *paid* for the road—and their surveyors, *possibly*—know nothing of its value, or of their own loss by its removal from the road; they consider it in the light of *dirt*—*offensive* dirt—and are glad to *pay* the scavenger for carrying it away! When the *broom* comes, the scavenger's men take care to go *deep* enough; and many of them are, moreover, instructed to keep the 'mac' as free from admixture with foreign substances as possible; for, though cattle-dung be valuable enough in itself, the '*mac*' loses *its* value to the builder and brickmaker by being *mixed with it*. Indeed, both are valuable for their respective uses if kept separate, not otherwise."

On my first making inquiries as to the uses and value of "mac," I was frequently told that it was utterly valueless, and that great trouble and expense were incurred in merely getting rid of it. That this is the case with many contractors is, doubtlessly, the fact; for now, unless the "mac," or, rather, the general road-dirt, be ordered, or a market for it be assured, it must be got rid of without a remuneration. Even when the contractor can shoot the "mac" in his own yard, and keep it there for a customer, there is the cost of re-loading and re-carting; a cost which a customer requiring to use it at any distance may not choose to incur. Great quantities of "mac," therefore, are wasted; and more would be wasted, were there places to waste it in.

Let me, therefore, before speaking of the uses and sale of it, point out some of the reasons for this wasting of the "mac" with other street-dirt. In the first place, the weight of a cart-load of street-refuse of any kind is usually estimated at a ton; but I am assured that the weight of a cart-load of "stiff mac" is a ton and a quarter at the least; and this weight becomes so trying to a scavenger's horse, as the day's work advances, that the contractor, to spare the animal, is often glad to get rid of the "mac" in any manner and without any remuneration. Thousands of loads of "mac," or rather of mixed street-dirt, have for this, and other reasons, been thrown away; and no small quantity has been thrown down the gulley-holes, to find its way into that main metropolitan sewer, the Thames. Of this matter, however, I shall have to speak hereafter.

There is no doubt that it is common for contractors to represent the "mac" they collect as being utterly valueless, and indeed an incumbrance. The "mixed mac," as I have said, may be so. Some contractors urge, especially in their bargains with the parish board, that all kinds of street dirt are not only worthless, but expensive to be got rid of. Five or six years ago, this was urged very strenuously, for then there was what was accounted a combination among the contractors. The south-west district of St. Pancras, until within the last six years, *received* from the contractor for the public scavengery, 100*l.* for the year's aggregation of street and house dirt. Since then, however, they have had to pay him 500*l.* for removing it.

Notwithstanding the reluctance of some of the

contractors to give information on this, or indeed any subject connected with their trade, I have ascertained from indubitable authority, that "mac" is disposed of in the following manner. Some, but this is mostly the mixed kind, is got rid of in *any* manner; it has even been diluted with water so as to be driven down the drains. Some is mixed with the general street ordure—about a quarter of "mac," I was told, to three-quarters of dung and street mud—and shipped off in barges as manure. Some is given to builders, when they require it for the foundations of any edifices that are "handy," or rather it is carted thither for a nominal price, such as a trifle as beer-money for the men. Some, however, is *sold* for the same purpose, the contractors alleging that the charge is merely for cartage. Some, again, is given away or sold (with the like allegation) for purposes of levelling, of filling up cavities, or repairing unevennesses in any ground where improvements are being carried on; and, finally, some is sold to masons, plasterers, and brickmakers, for the purposes of their trade.

Even for such purposes as "filling up," there must be in the "mixed mac" supplied, at least a considerable preponderance of the pure material, or there would not be, as I heard it expressed, a sufficient "setting" for what was required.

As a set-off to what is sold, however, I may here state that 30*s.* has been paid for the privilege of depositing a barge-load of mixed street dirt in Battersea-fields, merely to get rid of it.

The principal use of the unmixed "mac" is as a component part of the mortar, or lime, of the mason in the exterior, and of the plasterer in the interior, construction of buildings, and as an ingredient of the mill in brick-grounds.

The accounts I received of the properties of "mac" from the vendors of it, were very contradictory. One man, until lately connected with its sale, informed me that as far as his own experience extended, "mac" was most in demand among scamping builders, and slop brickmakers, who looked only to what was cheap. To a notorious "scamper," he one morning sent three cart-loads of "mac" at 1*s.* a load, all to be used in the erection of the skeleton of one not very large house; and he believed that when it was used instead of sand with lime, it was for inferior work only, and was mixed, either for masons' or plasterers' work, with bad, low-priced mortar. Another man, with equal knowledge of the trade, however, represented "mac" as a most valuable article for the builder's purposes, it was "so *binding*," and this he repeated emphatically. A working builder told me that "mac" was as good as the best sand; it made the mortar "hang," and without either that or sand, the lime would "brittle" away.

"Mac" may be said to be composed of pulverised granite and rain water. Granite is composed of quartz, felspar, and mica, each in granular crystals. Hence, alumina being clay, and silex a substance which has a strong tendency to enter into combination with the lime of the mortar, the pulverizing of granite tends to produce a substance which has necessarily great binding and indurating properties.

From this reduction of "mac" to its elements, it is manifest that it possesses qualities highly valuable in promoting the cohesive property of mortar, so that, were greater attention paid to its collection by the scavenger, there would, in all probability, be an improved demand for the article, for I find that it is already used in the prosecution of some of the best masons' work. On this head I can cite the authority of a gentleman, at once a scientific and practical architect, who said to me—

"'Mac' is used by many respectable builders for making mortar. The objection to it is, that it usually contains much extraneous decaying matter."

Increased care in the collection of the material would, perhaps, remove this cause of complaint.

I heard of one West-end builder, employing many hands, however, who had totally or partially discontinued the use of "mac," as he had met with some which he considered showed itself *brittle* in the plastering of walls.

"Mac," is pounded, and sometimes sifted, when required for use, and is then mixed and "worked up" with the lime for mortar, in the same way as sand. By the brickmakers it is mixed with the clay, ground, and formed into bricks in a similar manner.

Of the proportion sold to builders, plasterers, and brickmakers, severally, I could learn no precise particulars. The general opinion appears to be, that "mac" is sold most to brickmakers, and that it would find even a greater sale with them, were not brick-fields becoming more and more remote. I moreover found it universally admitted, that "mac" was in less demand—some said by onehalf—than it was five or six years back.

Such are the *uses* of "mac," and we now come to the question of its *value*.

The price of the purer "mac" seems, from the best information I can procure, to have varied considerably. It is now generally cheap. I did not hear any very sufficing reason advanced to account for the depreciation, but one of the contractors expressed an opinion that this was owing to the "disturbed" state of the trade. Since the passing of the Sanitary Bill, the contractors for the public scavengery have been prevented "shooting" any valueless street-dirt, or dirt "not worth carriage" in convenient waste-places, as they were once in the habit of doing. Their yards and wharfs are generally full, so that, to avoid committing a nuisance, the contractor will not unfrequently sell his "mac" at reduced rates, and be glad thus to get rid of it. To this cause especially Mr. ——— attributed the deterioration in the price of "mac," but if he had convenience, he told me, and any change was made in the present arrangements, he would not scruple to store 1000 loads for the demands of next summer, as a speculation. I am of opinion, moreover, notwithstanding what seemed something very like unanimity of opinion on the part of the sellers of "mac," that what is given or thrown away is usually, if not always, *mixed* or inferior "mac," and that what is sold at the lowest rate is only a degree or two better; unless, indeed, it be under the immediate pressure of some of the circumstances I have pointed out, as want of room, &c.

On inquiring the price of "mac," I believe the answer of a vendor will almost invariably be found to be "a shilling a load;" a little further inquiry, however, shows that an extra sum may have to be paid. A builder, who gave me the information, asked a parish contractor the price of "mac." The contractor at once offered to supply him with 500 loads at 1s. a load, if the "mac" were ordered beforehand, and could be shot at once; but it would be 6d. a mile extra if delivered a mile out of the mac-seller's parish circuit, or more than a mile from his yard; while, if extra care were to be taken in the collection of the "mac," it would be 2d., 3d., 4d., or 6d. a load higher. This, it must be understood, was the price of "*wet* mac."

Good "*dry* mac," that is to say, "mac" ready for use, is sold to the builder or the brickmaker at from 2s. to 3s. the load; 2s. 6d., or something very near it, being now about an average price. It is dried in the contractor's yard by being exposed to the sun, or it is sometimes protected from the weather by a shed, while being dried. More wet "mac" would be shot for the trade, and kept until dry, but for want of room in the contractors' yards and wharfs; for "mac" must give way to the more valuable dung, and the dust and ashes from the bins. The best "mac" is sometimes described as "country mac," that is to say, it is collected from those suburban roads where it is likely to be little mixed with dung, &c.

A contractor told me that during the last twelve months he had sold 300 loads of "mac;" he had no account of what he had given away, to be rid of it, or of what he had sold at nominal prices. Another contractor, I was told by his managing man, sold last year about 400 loads. But both these parties are "in a large way," and do not supply the data upon which to found a calculation as to an average yearly sale; for though in the metropolis there are, according to the list I have given in p. 167 of the present volume, 63 contracts, for cleansing the metropolis, without including the more remote suburbs, such as Greenwich, Lewisham, Tooting, Streatham, Ealing, Brentford, and others—still some of the districts contracted for yield no "mac" at all.

From what I consider good authority, I may venture upon the following moderate computation as to the quantity of "mac" sold last year.

Estimating the number of contracts for cleansing the more central parishes at 35, and adding 20 for all the outlying parishes of the metropolis— in some of which the supply of road "mac" is very fine, and by no means scarce—it may be accurate enough to state that, out of the 55 individual contracts, 300 loads of "mac" were sold by each in the course of last year. This gives 16,500 loads of "mac" disposed of per annum. It may, moreover, be a reasonable estimate to consider this "mac," wet and dry together, as fetching 1s. 6d. a load, so that we have for the sum realized the following result :—

16,500 loads of "mac," at 1s. 6d. per load £1237 10

It may probably be considered by the contractors that 1s. 6d. is too high an average of price per load: if the price be minimized the result will be—

16,500 loads of "mac," at 1s. per load £825

Then if we divide the first estimate among the 55 contractors, we find that they receive upwards of 22*l.* each; the second estimate gives nearly 15*l.* each.

I repeat, that in this inquiry I can but approximate. One gentleman told me he thought the quantity of "mac" thus sold in the year was twice 1600 loads; another asserted that it was not 1000. I am assured, however, that my calculation does not exceed the truth.

I have given the full quantity of "mac," as nearly, I believe, as it can be computed, to be yielded by the metropolitan thoroughfares; the surplusage, after deducting the 1600 loads sold, must be regarded as consisting of mixed, and therefore useless, "mac;" that is to say, "mac" rendered so *thin* by continuous wet weather, that it is little worth; "mac" wasted because it is not storeable in the contractor's yard; and "mac" used as a component part of a barge-load of manure.

In the course of my inquiries I heard it very generally stated that until five or six years ago 2s. 6d. might be considered a regular price for a load of "mac," while 4s., 5s., or even 6s. have been paid to one contractor, according to his own account, for the better kind of this commodity.

OF THE MUD OF THE STREETS.

THE dirt yielded by a macadamized road, no matter what the composition, is always termed by the scavengers "*mac;*" what is yielded by a granite-paved way is always "*mud.*" Mixed mud and "mac" are generally looked upon as useless.

I inquired of one man, connected with a contractor's wharf, if he could readily distinguish the difference between "mac" and other street or mixed dirts, and he told me that he could do so, more especially when the stuff was sufficiently dried or set, at a glance. "If mac was darker," he said, "it always looked brighter than other street-dirts, as if all the colour was not ground out of the stone." He pointed out the different kinds, and his definition seemed to me not a bad one, although it may require a practised eye to make the distinction readily.

Street-mud is only partially mud, for mud is earthy particles saturated with water, and in the composition of the scavenger's street-mud are dung, general refuse (such as straw and vegetable remains), and the many things which in poor neighbourhoods are still thrown upon the pavement.

In the busier thoroughfares of the metropolis— apart from the City, where there is no macadamization requiring notice—it is almost impossible to keep street "mac" and mud distinct, even if the scavengers cared more to do so than is the case at present; for a waggon, or any other vehicle, entering a street paved with blocks of wrought granite from a macadamized road must convey "mac" amongst mud; both "mac" and mud, however, as I have stated, are the most valuable separately.

In a Report on the Supply of Water, Appendix No. III., Mr. Holland, Upper Stamford-street, Waterloo-road, is stated to have said, in reply to a question on the subject:—"Suppose the inhabitants of one parish are desirous of having their streets in good order and clean: unless the adjoining districts concur, a great and unjust expense is imposed upon the cleaner parish; because every vehicle which passes from a dirty on to a clean street carries dirt from the former to the latter, and renders cleanliness more difficult and expensive. The inhabitants of London have an interest in the condition of other streets besides those of their own parish. Besides the inhabitants of Regent-street, for instance, all the riders in the 5000 vehicles that daily pass through that great thoroughfare are affected by its condition; and the inhabitants of Regent-street, who have to bear the cost of keeping that street in good repair and well cleansed, *for others' benefit as well as for their own*, may fairly feel aggrieved if they do not experience the benefits of good and clean streets when they go into other districts."

In the admixture of street-dirt there is this material difference—the dung, which spoils good " mac," makes good mud more valuable.

After having treated so fully of the road-produce of "mac," there seems no necessity to say more about mud than to consider its quantity, its value, and its uses.

In the Haymarket, which is about an eighth of a mile in length, and 18 yards in width, a load and a half of street-mud is collected daily (Sundays excepted), take the year through. As a farmer or market-gardener will give 3s. a load for common street-mud, and cart it away at his own cost, we find that were all this mud sold separately, at the ordinary rate, the yearly receipt for one street alone would be 70l. 4s. This public way, however, furnishes no criterion of the general mud-produce of the metropolis. We must, therefore, adopt some other basis for a calculation; and I have mentioned the Haymarket merely to show the great extent of street-dirt accruing in a largely-frequented locality.

But to obtain other data is a matter of no small difficulty when returns are not published nor even kept. I have, however, been fortunate enough to obtain the assistance of gentlemen whose public employment has given them the best means of forming an accurate opinion.

The street mud from the Haymarket, it has been positively ascertained, is 1¼ load each wet day the year through. Fleet-street, Ludgate-hill, Cheapside, Newgate-street, the "off" parts of St. Paul's Church-yard, Cornhill, Leadenhall-street, Bishopsgate-street, the free bridges, with many other places where locomotion never ceases, are, in proportion to their width, as productive of street mud as the Haymarket.

Were the Haymarket a mile in length, it would supply, at its present rate of traffic, to the scavenger 6 loads of street mud daily, or 36 loads for the scavenger's working week. In this yield, however, I am assured by practical men, the Haymarket is six times in excess of the average streets; and when compared with even "great business" thoroughfares, of a narrow character, such as Watling-street, Bow-lane, Old-change, and other thoroughfares off Cheapside and Cornhill, the produce of the Haymarket is from 10 to 40 per cent. in excess.

I am assured, however, and especially by a gentleman who had looked closely into the matter —as he at one time had been engaged in preparing estimates for a projected company purposing to deal with street-manures—that the 50 miles of the City may be safely calculated as yielding daily 1½ load of street mud per mile. Narrow streets—Thames-street for instance, which is about three-quarters of a mile long—yield from 2½ to 3½ loads daily, according to the season; but a number of off-streets and open places, such as Long-alley, Alderman's-walk, America-square, Monument-yard, Bridgewater-square, Austin-friars, and the like, are either streets without horse-thoroughfares, or are seldom traversed by vehicles. If, then, we calculate that there are 100 miles of paved streets adjoining the City, and yielding the same quantity of street mud daily as the above estimate, and 200 more miles in the less central parts of the metropolis, yielding only half that quantity, we find the following daily sum during the wet season:—

	Loads.
150 miles of paved streets, yielding 1½ load of street mud per mile	225
200 miles of paved streets, yielding ¾ load of street mud per mile	150
	375
Weekly amount of street mud during the wet season	2,250
Total ditto for six months in the year	58,500

63,000 loads of street mud, at 3s. per load £8775

The great sale for this mud, perhaps nineteen-twentieths, is from the barges. A barge of street-manure, about one-fourth (more or less) " mac," or rather " mac" mixed with its street proportion of dung, &c., and three-fourths mud, dung, &c., contains from 30 to 40 tons, or as many loads. These manure barges are often to be seen on the Thames, but nearly three-fourths of them are found on the canals, especially the Paddington, the Regent's, and the Surrey, these being the most immediately connected with the interior part of the metropolis. A barge-load of this manure is usually sold at from 5l. to 6l. Calculating its average weight at 35 tons, and its average sale at 5l. 10s., the price is rather more than 3s. a load. "Common street mud," I have been informed on good authority, "fetches 3s. per load from the farmer, when he himself carts it away."

The price of the barge-load of manure is tolerably uniform, for the quality is generally the same.

Some of the best, because the cleanest, street mud —as it is mixed only with horse-dung—is obtained from the wood streets, but this mode of pavement is so circumscribed that the contractors pay no regard to its manure produce, as a general rule, and mix it carelessly with the rest. Such, at least, is the account they themselves give, and they generally represent that the street manure is, owing to the outlay for cartage and boatage, little remunerative to them at the prices they obtain; notwithstanding, they are paid to remove it from the streets. Indeed, I heard of one contractor who was said to be so dissatisfied with the demand for, and the prices fetched by, his street-manure, that he has rented a few acres not far from the Regent's Canal, to test the efficacy of street dirt as a fertilizer, and to ascertain if to cultivate might not be more profitable than to sell.

OF THE SURFACE-WATER OF THE STREETS OF LONDON.

THE consideration of what Professor Way has called the "street waters" of the metropolis, is one of as great moment as any of those I have previously treated in my details concerning street refuse, whether "mac," mud, or dung. Indeed, water enters largely into the composition of the two former substances, while even the street dung is greatly affected by the rain.

The *feeders* of the street, as regards the street surface-water, are principally the rains. I will first consider the amount of surface-water supplied by the rain descending upon the area of the metropolis: upon the roofs of the houses, and the pavement of the streets and roads.

The depth of rain falling in London in the different months, according to the observations and calculations of the most eminent meteorologists, is as follows:—

Months.	Depth of Rain in inches.			Quantity of rain falling in the different seasons.	Number of days on which rain falls.
	Royal Society, according to observation.	Howard, according to observation.	Daniell according to calculation.		
January	1·56	1·907	1·483		14·4
February ..	1·45	1·643	0·746	Winter.	15·8
March	1·36	1·542	1·440	5·868	12·7
April	1·55	1·719	1·786		14·0
May	1·67	2·036	1·853		15·8
June	1·98	1·964	1·830	Spring.	11·8
July	2·44	2·592	2·516	4·813	16·1
August	2·37	2·134	1·453		16·3
September .	2·97	1·644	2·193	Summer.	12·3
October....	2·46	2·872	2·073	6·682	16·2
November .	2·58	2·637	2·400	Autumn.	15·0
December .	1·65	2·489	2·426	7·441	17·7
Totals	24·04	25·179	22·199	24·804	173·1

The rainfall in London, according to a ten years' average of the Royal Society's observations, amounts to 23 inches; in 1848 it was as high as 28 inches, and in 1847 as low as 15 inches. The depth of rain annually falling near London is stated by Mr. Luke Howard to be, on an average of 23 years (1797–1819), as much as 25·179 inches. Mr. Daniel says that the average annual fall is $23\frac{1}{10}$ inches. The mean of the observations made at Greenwich between the years 1838 and 1849 was 24·84 inches.

The following extract from an account of the "Soft Water Springs of the Surrey Sands," by the Hon. Wm. Napier, is interesting.

"The amount of rainfall," says the Author, "is taken from a register kept at the Royal Military College, Sandhurst, from the year 1818 to 1846.

"The average fall of the last 15 years, during which time the register appears to have been correctly kept, is 22·64 inches. I consider this to be a very low estimate, however, of the average rainfall over the whole district. The fall on the ranges of the Hindhead must considerably exceed this amount, for I find in White's 'Selborne,' a register for ten years at that place; the greatest fall being in 1782, 50·26 inches, the lowest, in 1788, 22·50 inches, and the average of all 37·58 inches. The elevation of the Hindhead is about 800 feet above mean tide.

"With reference to the measurement of rainfall, it is difficult indeed to obtain more than a very approximate idea for a given district of not very great extent; the method of measurement is so uncertain, as liable to be affected by currents of air and evaporation. It is well known that elevated regions attract by condensation more rain than low lands, and yet a rain-gauge placed on the ground will register a greater fall than one placed immediately, and even at a small height, above it.

"M. Arago has shown from 12 years' observations at Paris, that the average depth of rain on the terrace of the Observatory was 19·88 inches, while 30 yards lower it was 22·21 inches. Dr. Heberden has shown the rainfall on the top of Westminster Cathedral, during a certain period to be only 12·09 inches, and at a lower level on the top of a house in the neighbourhood to be 22·608 inches. This fact has been observed all over the world, and I can only account for it as arising partly from the greater amount of condensation the nearer the earth's surface, but probably also from currents of air depriving a rain-gauge at a high elevation of its fair share."

The results of the above observations, as to the yearly quantity of rain falling in the metropolis, may be summed up as follows:—

	Inches of Rain falling Annually.
Royal Society (average of 20 years)	24·04
Mr. Howard (average of 23 years)	25·179
Professor Daniell	22·199
Dr. Heberden	22·608
Mean	23·506

The "mean mean," or average of all the averages here given is within a fraction the average of the Royal Society's Observations for 10 years, and this is the quantity that I shall adopt in my calculations as to the gross volume of rain falling over the entire area of London.

I have shown, by a detail of the respective districts in the Registrar General's department, that the metropolis contains 74,070 statute acres. Every square inch of this extent, as garden, arable, or pasture ground, or as road or street, or waste place, or house, or inclosed yard or lawn, of course receives its modicum of rain. Each acre comprises 6,272,640 square inches, and we thus find the whole metropolitan area to contain a number of square inches, almost beyond the terms of popular arithmetic, and best expressible in figures.

Area of metropolis in square inches, 464,614,444,800. Now, multiplying these four hundred and sixty four thousand, six hundred and fourteen millions, four hundred and forty-four thousand, eight hundred square inches, by 23, the number of inches of rain falling every year in London, we have the following result:—

Total quantity of rain falling yearly in the metropolis, 10,686,132,230,400 cubic inches.

Then, as a fraction more than $277\frac{1}{4}$ cubic inches of water represent a weight of 10 lbs., and an admeasurement of a gallon, we have the following further results:—

	Weight in pounds and tons.	Admeasurement in gallons.
Yearly Rainfall in the Metropolis	385,399,721,220 lbs., or 172,053,447 tons.	38,539,972,122 gals.

The total quantity of water mechanically supplied every day to the metropolis is said to be in round numbers 55,000,000 gallons, the amount being made up in the following manner:—

DAILY MECHANICAL SUPPLY OF WATER TO METROPOLIS.

Sources of Supply.	Average No. of Gallons per day.
New River	14,149,315
East London	8,829,462
Chelsea	3,940,730
West Middlesex	3,334,054
Grand Junction	3,532,013
Lambeth	3,077,260
Southwark and Vauxhall	6,313,716
Kent	1,079,311
Hampstead	427,468
Total from Companies	44,383,329
Artesian Wells	8,000,000
Land Spring Pumps	3,000,000
Total daily	55,383,329

YEARLY MECHANICAL SUPPLY OF WATER.

From Companies	16,200,000,000 gals.
„ Artesian Wells	1,920,000,000 „
„ Land Spring Pumps	1,095,000,000 „
Total yearly	19,215,000,000 „

Hence it would appear that the rain falling in London in the course of the year is *rather more* than double that of the entire quantity of water annually supplied to the metropolis by mechanical means, the rain-water being to the other as 2·005 to 1·000.

Now, in order to ascertain what proportion of the entire volume of rain comes under the denomination of street surface-water, we must first deduct from the gross quantity falling the amount said to be caught, and which, in contradistinction to that mechanically *supplied* to the houses of the metropolis is termed, "catch." This is estimated at 1,000,000 gallons per diem, or 365,000,000 gallons yearly.

But we must also subtract from the gross quantity of rain-water that which falls on the roofs as well as on the "back premises" and yards of houses, and is carried off directly to the drains without appearing in the streets. This must be a considerable proportion of the whole, since the streets themselves, allowing them to be ten yards wide on an average, would seem to occupy only about one-tenth part of the entire metropolitan area, so that the rain falling *directly* upon the public thoroughfares will be but a tithe of the aggregate quantity. But the surface-water of the streets is increased largely by tributary shoots from courts and drainless houses, and hence we may fairly assume the *natural* supply to be doubled by such means. At this rate the volume of rain-water annually poured into and upon the metropolitan thoroughfares by natural means, will be between five and six thousand millions of gallons, or one hundred times the quantity that is daily supplied to the houses of the metropolis by mechanical agency.

Still only a part of this quantity appears in the form of surface-water, for a considerable portion of it is absorbed by the ground on which it falls—especially in dry weather—serving either to "lay the dust," or to convert it into mud. Due regard, therefore, being had to all these considerations, we cannot, consistently with that caution which is necessary in all statistical inquiries, estimate the surface-water of the London streets at more than one thousand millions of gallons per annum, or twenty times the daily mechanical supply to the houses of the entire metropolis, and which it has been asserted is sufficient to exhaust a lake covering the area of St. James's-park, 30 inches in depth.

The quantity of water annually poured upon the streets in the process of what is termed "watering" amounts, according to the returns of the Board of Health, to 275,000,000 gallons per annum! But as this seldom or never assumes the form of street surface-water, it need form no part of the present estimate.

What proportion of the thousand million gallons of "slop dirt" produced annually in the London streets is carried off down the drains, and what proportion is ladled up by the scavengers, I have no means of ascertaining, but that vast quantities run away into the sewers and there form large deposits of mud, everything tends to prove.

Mr. Lovick, on being asked, "How many loads of deposit have been removed in any one week in the Surrey and Kent district? What is the total quantity of deposit removed in any one week in the whole of the metropolitan district?" replied:

"It is difficult, if not impossible, to ascertain correctly the quantity removed, owing to the variety of forms of sewers and the ever-varying forms assumed by the deposit from the action of varying volumes of water; but I have had observations made on the rate of accumulation, from which I have been enabled roughly to approximate it. In one week, in the Surrey and Kent district, about 1000 yards were removed. In one week, in the whole of the metropolitan districts, including the Surrey and Kent district, between 4000 and 5000 yards were removed; but in portions of the districts these operations were not in progress."

It is not here stated of what the deposit consisted, but there is no doubt that "mac" from the streets formed a great portion of it. Neither is it stated what period of time had sufficed for the accumulation; but it is evident enough that such deposits in the course of a year must be very great.

The street surface-water has been analyzed by Professor Way, and found to yield different constituents according to the different pavements from which it has been discharged. The results are as follows:—

"*Examination of Samples of Water from Street Drainage, taken from the Gullies in the Sewers during the rain of 6th May, 1850.*

"The waters were all more or less turbid, and some of them gave off very noxious odours, due principally to the escape of sulphuretted hydrogen gas.

"Some of them were alkaline to test-paper, but the majority were neutral.

"The following table exhibits the quantity of matter (both in solution and in solid state) contained in an imperial gallon of each specimen.

"STREET WATERS.

Number of Bottle.	Name of Street.	Quality of Paving.	Quality of Traffic.	Residue in an Imperial Gallon.		
				Soluble.	Insoluble.	Both.
				Grains.	Grains.	Grains.
1	Duke-street, Manchester-square	Macadam	Middling	92·80	105·95	198·75
7	Foley-street (upper part)	,,	Little	95·13	116·30	211·43
5	Gower-street	Granite	Middling	126·00	168·30	294·30
12	Norton-street	,,	Little	123·87	3·00	126·87
3	Hampstead-road (above the canal)	Ballasted	Great	96·00	84·00	180·00
4	Ferdinand-street	,,	Middling	44·00	48·30	92·30
2	Ferdinand-place	,,	Little	50·80	34·30	85·10
10	Oxford-street	Granite	Great	276·23	537·10	813·33
6	,,	Macadam	,,	194·62	390·30	584·92
11	,,	Wood	,,	34·00	5·00	39·00

"The influence of the quality of the paving on the composition of the drainage water," says Professor Way, "is well seen in the specimens Nos. 10, 6, and 11, all of them from Oxford-street, the traffic being described as 'Great.'

"The quantity of soluble salts is here found to be greatest from the granite matter from the macadamized road, and very inconsiderable from the wood pavement.

"The same relation between the granite and macadam pavement seems to hold good in the other instances; the granite for any quality of traffic affording more soluble salts to the water than the macadam.

"The ballasted pavement holds a position intermediate between the macadam and the wood, giving more soluble salts than the wood, but less than the macadam.

"The quantity of solid (insoluble) matter in the different samples of water, *which is a measure of the mechanical waste of the different kinds of pavement*, appears also to follow the same relation as that of the soluble salts; that is to say, granite greatest, next macadam, then ballasted, and, lastly, wood pavement, which affords a quantity of solid deposit almost too small to deserve notice.

"The influence of the quality of traffic on the composition of the different specimens of drainage is well marked in nearly all cases; the greatest amount of matter both insoluble and soluble being found in the water obtained from the streets of great traffic.

"The following table shows the composition of the soluble salts of four specimens, two of them being from the granite, and two from the macadam pavement.

"It appears from the table that the granite furnishes little or no magnesia to the water, whilst the quantity from the macadam is considerable.

"On the other hand, the quantity of potash is far greatest in the water derived from the granite.

"The traffic, as was before seen, has a very great influence on the quantity of the soluble salts. It seems also to influence their composition, for we find no carbonates either in the water from the granite, or that from the macadam, where the traffic is little; whereas, when it is great, carbonates of lime and potash are found in the water in large quantity, a circumstance which is no doubt attributable to the action of decaying organic matter on the mineral substances of the pavement.

"ANALYSIS OF THE SOLUBLE MATTER IN DIFFERENT SPECIMENS OF STREET DRAINAGE WATER.

	Grains in an Imperial Gallon.			
	Great Traffic.		Little Traffic.	
	Granite. No. 10.	Macadam. No. 6.	Granite. No. 12.	Macadam. No. 7.
Water of combination and some soluble organic matter	77·56	29·07	22·72	13·73
Silica	·51	2·81	...	...
Carbonic Acid	15·84	12·23	None	None
Sulphuric Acid	36·49	38·23	46·48	34·08
Lime	6·65	13·38	25·90	16·10
Magnesia	None	23·51	Trace	3·50
Oxide of Iron and Alumina, with a little Phosphate of Lime	2·58	1·25	...	...
Chloride of Potassium	None	10·99	None	2·79
" Sodium	53·84	44·88	18·44	19·70
Potash	82·76	18·27	8·75	5·23
Soda	...	...	1·58	...
	276·23	194·62	123·87	95·13

"The insoluble matter in the waters consists of the comminuted material of the road itself, with small fragments of straw and broken dung.

"The quantity of soluble salts (especially of salts of potash) in many of these samples of water is quite as great, and in some cases greater, than that found in the samples of sewer-water that have been examined; and it is open to question and further inquiry, whether the water obtained from the street-drainage of a crowded city might not often be of nearly equal value as liquid manure with the sewer-water with which it is at present allowed to mix."

With regard to the "ballasted pavement" mentioned by Professor Way, I may observe that it cannot be considered a *street*-pavement, unless exceptionally. It is formed principally of Thames ballast mixed with gravel, and is used in the construction of what are usually private or pleasure walks, such as the "gravel walks" in the inclosures of some of the parks, and upon Primrose-hill, &c.

OF THE MASTER SCAVENGERS IN FORMER TIMES.

DEGRADED as the occupation of the scavenger may be in public estimation; though "I'd rather sweep the streets" may be a common remark expressive of the lowest deep of humiliation among those who never handled a besom in their lives; yet the very existence of a large body who are public cleansers betokens civilization. Their occupation, indeed, was defined, or rather was established or confirmed, in the early periods of our history, when municipal regulations were a sort of charter of civic protection, of civic liberties, and of general progress.

The noun *Scavenger* is said by lexicographers to be derived from the German *schaben*, to shave or scrape, "applied to those who scrape and clear away the filth from public streets or other places." The more direct derivation, however, is from the Danish verb *skaver*, the Saxon equivalent of which is *sceafan*, whence the English *shave*. Formerly the word was written *Scavager*, and meant simply one who was engaged in removing the *Scrapeage* or *Rakeage* (the working men, it will be seen, were termed also "rakers") from the surface of the streets. Hence it would appear that there is no authority for the verb to scavenge, which has lately come into use. The term from which the personal substantive is directly made, is *scavage*, a word formed from the verb in the same manner as *sewage* and *rubbage* (now fashionably corrupted into rubbish), and meaning the refuse which is or should be scraped away from the roads. The Latin equivalent from the Danish verb *skave*, is *scabere*.

I believe that the first mention of a scavenger in our earlier classical literature, is by Bishop Hall, one of the lights of the Reformation, in one of his "Satires."

"To see the Pope's blacke knight, a cloaked frere,
Sweating in the channel *like a scavengere*."

Many similar passages from the old poets and dramatists might be adduced, but I will content myself with one from the "Martial Maid" of Beaumont and Fletcher, as bearing immediately on the topic I have to discuss:—

"Do I not know thee for the alguazier,
Whose dunghil *all the parish scavengers*
Could never rid."

Johnson defines a scavenger to be "a petty

magistrate, whose province is to keep the streets clean;" and in the earlier times, certainly the scavenger was an officer to whom a certain authority was deputed, as to beadles and others.

One or two of these officials were appointed, according to the municipal or by-laws of the City of London, not to each parish, but to each ward. Of course, in the good old days, nothing could be done unless under "the sanction of an oath," and the scavengers were sworn accordingly on the Gospel, the following being the form as given in the black letter of the laws relating to the city in the time of Henry VIII.

"*The Oath of Scavagers, or Scavengers, of the Ward.*

"Ye shal swear, That ye shal wel and diligently oversee that the pavements in every Ward be wel and rightfully repaired, and not haunsed to the noyaunce of the neighbours; and that the Ways, Streets, and Lanes, be kept clean from Donge and other Filth, for the Honesty of the City. And that all the Chimneys, Redosses, and Furnaces, be made of Stone for Defence of Fire. And if ye know any such ye shall shew it to the Alderman, that he may make due Redress therefore. And this ye shall not lene. So help you God."*

To aid the scavengers in their execution of the duties of the office, the following among others were the injunctions of the civic law. They indicate the former state of the streets of London better than any description. A "Goung (or dung) fermour" appears to be a nightman, a dung-carrier or bearer, the servant of the master or ward scavenger.

"No Goungfermour shall spill any ordure in the Street, under pain of Thirteen Shillings and Four Pence.

"No Goungfermour shall carry any ordure till after nine of the clock in the Night, under pain of Thirteen Shillings and Four Pence. No man shall cast any urine boles, or ordure boles, into the Streets by Day or Night, *afore the Hour of nine in the Night*. And also he shall not cast it out, but bring it down and lay it in the Canel, under Pain of Three Shillings and Four Pence. And if he do so cast it upon any Person's Head, the Person to have a lawful Recompense, *if he have hurt thereby*.

"No man shall bury any Dung, or Goung, within the Liberties of this City, under Pain of Forty Shillings."

I will not dwell on the state of things which caused such enactments to be necessary, or on the barbarism of the law which ordered a lawful recompense to any person assailed in the manner intimated, only when he had "hurt thereby."

These laws were for the government of the city, where a body of scavengers was sometimes called

* "Haunsed" is explained by Strype to signify "made too high," and the "Redosses" to be "Reredoughs." A mason informed me that he believed these Redosses were what were known in some old country-houses as "Back-Flues," or flues connecting any fire-grate in the out-offices with the main chimney. The term "lene" is the Teutonic *Lehn*, and signifies "let, lease," or literally *loan*.

a "street-ward." Until about the reign of Charles II., however, to legislate concerning such matters for the city was to legislate for the metropolis, as Southwark was then more or less under the city jurisdiction, and the houses of the nobility on the north bank of the Thames (the Strand), would hardly require the services of a public scavenger.

As new parishes or districts became populous, and established outside the city boundaries, the authorities seem to have regulated the public scavengery after the fashion of the city; but the whole, in every respect of cleanliness, propriety, regularity, or celerity, was most grievously defective.

Some time about the middle of the last century, the scavengers were considered and pronounced by the administrators or explainers of municipal law, to be "two officers chosen yearly in each parish in London and the suburbs, by the constables, churchwardens, and other inhabitants," and their business was declared to be, that they should "hire persons called 'rakers,' with carts to clean the streets, and carry away the dirt and filth thereof, under a penalty of 40s."

The scavengers thus appointed we should now term surveyors. There is little reason to doubt that in the old times the duly-appointed scavagers or scavengers, laboured in their vocation themselves, and employed such a number of additional hands as they accounted necessary; but how or when the master scavenger ceased to be a labourer, and how or when the office became merely nominal, I can find no information. So little attention appears to have been paid to this really important matter, that there are hardly any records concerning it. The law was satisfied to lay down provisions for street-cleansing, but to enforce these provisions was left to chance, or to some idle, corrupt, or inefficient officer or body.

Neither can I find any precise account of what was formerly done with the dirt swept and scraped from the streets, which seems always to have been left to the discretion of the scavenger to deal with as he pleased, and such is still the case in a great measure. Some of this dirt I find, however, promoted "the goodly nutriment of the land" about London, and some was "delivered in waste places apart from habitations." These waste places seem to have been the nuclei of the present dust-yards, and were sometimes "presented," that is, they were reported by a jury of nuisances (or under other titles), as "places of obscene resort," for lewd and disorderly persons, the lewd and disorderly persons consisting chiefly of the very poor, who came to search among the rubbish for anything that might be valuable or saleable; for there were frequent rumours of treasure or plate being temporarily hidden in such places by thieves. Some outcast wretches, moreover, slept within the shelter of these scavengers' places, and occasionally a vigilant officer—even down to our own times, or within these few years—apprehended such wretches, charged them with destitution, and had them punished accordingly. Much of the street refuse thus "delivered," especially the "dry rubbish," was thrown into the streets from houses under repair, &c., (I now speak of the past century,) and no use seems to have been made of any part of it unless any one requiring a load or two of rubbish chose to cart it away.

I have given this sketch to show what master scavengers were in the olden times, and I now proceed to point out what is the present condition of the trade.

OF THE SEVERAL MODES AND CHARACTERISTICS OF STREET-CLEANSING.

WE here come to the practical part of this complex subject. We have ascertained the length of the streets of London—we have estimated the amount of daily, weekly, and yearly traffic—calculated the quantity of mud, dung, "mac," dust, and surface-water formed and collected annually throughout the metropolis—we have endeavoured to arrive at some notion as to the injury done by all this vast amount of filth owing to what the Board of Health has termed "imperfect scavenging,"—and we now come to treat of the means by which the loads of street refuse—the loads of dust—loads of "mac" and mud, and the tons of dung, are severally and collectively removed throughout the year.

There are two distinct, and, in a measure, diametrically opposed, methods of street-cleansing at present in operation.

1. That which consists in cleaning the streets when dirtied.

2. That which consists in cleaning them and *keeping* them clean.

These modes of scavenging may not appear, to those who have paid but little attention to the matter, to be *very* widely different means of effecting the same object. The one, however, removes the refuse from the streets (sooner or later) *after it has been formed,* whereas the other removes it *as fast as it is formed.* By the latter method the streets are never allowed to get dirty —by the former they must be dirty before they are cleansed.

The plan of street-cleansing *before* dirtied, or the pre-scavenging system, is of recent introduction, being the mode adopted by the " street-orderlies ;" that of cleansing after having dirtied, or the post-scavenging system, is (so far as the more *general* or common method is concerned) the same as that pursued two centuries ago. I shall speak of each of these modes in due course, beginning with that last mentioned.

By the ordinary method of scavenging, the dirt is still swept or scraped to one side of the public way, then shovelled into a cart and conveyed to the place of deposit. In wet weather the dirt swept or scraped to one side is so liquified that it is known as "slop," and is "lifted" into the cart in shovels hollowed like sugar-spoons. The only change of which I have heard in this mode of scavenging was in one of the tools. Until about nine years ago birch, or occasionally heather, brooms or besoms were used by the street-sweepers, but they soon became clogged in dirty weather, and then, as one working scavenger explained it to me, " they scattered and drove the dirt to the sides 'stead of making it go right ahead as you wants it." The material now used for the street-sweeper's broom is known as " bass," and consists of the stems or branches of a New Zealand plant, a substance which has considerable strength and elasticity of fibre, and both " sweeps " and " scrapes " in the process of scavenging. The broom itself, too, is differently constructed, having divisions between the several insertions of bass in the wooden block of the head, so that clogging is less frequent, and cleaning easier, whereas the birch broom consisted of a close mass of twigs, and thus scattered while it swept the dirt. There was, of course, some outcry on the part of the " established-order-of-things " gentry among scavengers, against the innovation, but it is now general. As all the scavengers, no matter how they vary in other respects, work with the brooms described, this one mention of the change will suffice. No doubt the cleansing of the streets is accomplished with greater efficiency and with greater celerity than it was, but the mere process of manual toil is little altered.

In a work like the present, however, we have more particularly to deal with the labourers engaged ; and, viewing the subject in this light, we may arrange the several modes of street-cleansing into the four following divisions :—

1. By paid manual-labourers, or men employed by the contractors, and paid in the ordinary ways of wages.

2. By paid " Machine "-labourers, differing from the first only or mainly in the means by which they attain their end.

3. By pauper labourers, or men employed by the parishes in which they are set to work, and either paid in money or in food, or maintained in the workhouses.

4. By street-orderlies, or men employed by philanthropists—a body of workmen with particular regulations and more organized than other scavengers.

By one or other of these modes of scavengery all the public ways of the metropolis are cleansed ; and the subject is most peculiar, as including within itself all the several varieties of labour, if we except that of women and children—viz., manual labour, mechanical labour, pauper labour, and philanthropic labour.

By these several varieties of labour the highways and by-ways of the entire metropolis are cleansed, with one exception—the Mews, concerning which a few words here may not be out of place. *All* these localities, whether they be what are styled Private or Gentlemen's Mews, or Public Mews, where stables, coach-houses, and dwelling-rooms above them, may be taken by any one (a good many of such places being, moreover, public or partial thoroughfares) ; or whether they be job-masters' or cab-proprietors' mews ; are scavenged by the occupants, for the manure is valuable. The mews of London, indeed, constitute a world of their own. They are tenanted by one class— coachmen and grooms, with their wives and families—men who are devoted to one pursuit, the care of horses and carriages ; who live and associate one among another; whose talk is of horses (with something about masters and mistresses) as if to ride or to drive were the great ends of human existence, and who thus live as much together as the Jews in their compulsory quarters in Rome. The mews are also the "chambers" of unemployed coachmen and grooms, and I am told that the very sicknesses known in such places have their own peculiarities. These, however, form matter for *future* inquiry.

Concerning the private scavenging of the metropolitan mews, the *Medical Times*, of July 26, 1851, contains a letter from Mr. C. Cochrane, in which that gentleman says:—

"It will be found, that in all the mews throughout the metropolis, the manure produced from each stable is packed up in a separate stack, until there is sufficient for a load for some market-gardener or farmer to remove. The groom or stable-man makes an arrangement, or agreement as it is called, with the market-gardener, to remove it at his convenience, and a gratuity of 1s. or 1s. 6d. per load is usually presented to the stable-man. In some places there are dung-pits containing the collectings of a fortnight's dung, which, when disturbed for removal, casts out an offensive effluvium, as sickening as it is disgusting to the whole neighbourhood. In consequence of the arrangement in question, if a third party wished to buy some of this manure, he could not get it; and if he wished to get rid of any by giving it away, the stable-man would not receive it, as it would not be removed sufficiently quick by the farmer. The result is, that whilst the air is rendered offensive and insalubrious, manure becomes difficult to be removed or disposed of, and frequently is washed away into the sewer.

"Of this manure there are always (at a moderate computation) remaining daily, in the mews and stable-yards of the metropolis, at least 2000 cart-loads.

"To remedy these evils, I would suggest that a brief Act of Parliament should be passed, giving municipal and parochial authorities the same complete control over the manure as they have over the 'ashes,' with the provision, that owners should have the right of removing it themselves for their own use; but if they did not do so daily, then the control to return to the above authorities, who should have the right of selling it, and placing the proceeds in the parish funds. By this simple means immense quantities of valuable manure would be saved for the purposes of agriculture—food would be rendered cheaper and more abundant—more people would be employed—whilst the metropolis would be rendered clean, sweet, and healthy."

I may dismiss this part of the subject with the remark, that I was informed that the mews' manure was in regular demand and of ready sale, being removed by the market-gardeners with greater facility than can street-dirt, which the contractors with the parishes prefer to vend by the barge-load.

Having enumerated the four several modes of street-cleansing, I will now proceed to point out briefly the characteristics of each class of cleansing. This will also denote the quality of the employers and the nature of the employment.

1. *The Paid Manual Labourers* constitute the bulk of those engaged in scavenging, and the chief pay-masters are the contractors. Many of these labourers consider themselves the only "regular hands," having been "brought up to the business;" but unemployed or destitute labourers or mechanics, or reduced tradesmen, will often endeavour to obtain employment in street-sweeping; this is the necessary evil of all *unskilled* labour, for since every one can do it (without previous apprenticeship), it follows that the beaten-out artisans or discarded trade assistants, beggared tradesmen, or reduced gentlemen, must necessarily resort to it as their only means of independent support; and hence the reason why dock labour and street labour, and indeed all the several forms of unskilled work, have a tendency to be overstocked with hands—the *unskilled* occupations being, as it were, the sink for all the refuse *skilled* labour and beggared industry of the country.

The "contractors," like other employers, are separated by their men into two classes—such as, in more refined callings, are often designated the "honourable" and "dishonourable" traders—according as they pay or do not pay what is reputed "fair wages."

I cannot say that I heard any especial appellation given by the working scavengers to the better-paying class of employers, unless it were the expressive style of "good-'uns." The inferior paying class, however, are very generally known among their work-people as "scurfs."

2. *The Street-sweeping Machine Labourers.*— Of the men employed as "attendant" scavengers, for so they may be termed, in connection with these mechanical and vehicular street-sweepers, little need here be said, for they are generally of the class of ordinary scavengers. It may, however, be necessary to explain that each of those machines must have the street refuse, for the "lick-in" of the machine, swept into a straight line wherever there is the slightest slope at the sides of a street towards the foot-path; the same, too, must sometimes be done, if the pavement be at all broken, even when the progress of the machine is, what I heard, not very appropriately, termed "plain sailing." Sometimes, also, men follow the course of the street-sweeping machine, to "sweep up" any dirt missed or scattered, as the vehicle proceeds on a straightforward course, for at all to diverge would be to make the labour, where the machine alone is used, almost double.

3. *The Pauper, or Parish-employed Scavengers* present characteristics peculiarly their own, as regards open-air labour in London. They are employed less to cleanse the streets, than to prevent their being chargeable to the poor's rate as outdoor recipients, or as inmates of the workhouses. When paid, they receive a lower amount of wages than any other scavengers, and they are sometimes paid in food as well as in money, while a difference may be made between the wages of the

married and of the unmarried men, and even between the married men who have and have not children; some, again, are employed in scavengery without any money receipt, their maintenance in the workhouse being considered a sufficient return for the fruits of their toil.

Some of these men are feeble, some are unskilful (even in tasks in which skill is but little of an element), and most of them are dissatisfied workmen. Their ranks comprise, or may comprise, men who have filled very different situations in life. It is mentioned in the second edition of one of the publications of the National Philanthropic Association, "Sanatory Progress" (1850), "that the once high-salaried cashier of a West-end bank died lately in St. Pancras-workhouse;—that the architect of several of the most fashionable West-end club-houses is now an inmate of St. James's-workhouse;—and that the architect of St. Pancras' New Church lately died in a back garret in Somers-town. "These recent instances (a few out of many)" says the writer, "prove that 'wealth has wings,' and that Genius and Industry have but leaden feet, when overtaken by Adversity. A late number of the *Globe* newspaper states that, 'among the police constables on the Great Western Railway, there are at present eight members of the Royal College of Surgeons, and three solicitors;'—and the *Limerick Examiner*, a few weeks ago, announced the fact, that 'a gentlewoman is now an inmate of the workhouse of that city, whose husband, a few years ago, filled the office of High Sheriff of the county.'"

I do not know that either the cashier or the architect in the two workhouses in question was employed as a street-sweeper.

This second class, then, are situated differently to the paid street-sweepers (or No. 1 of the present division), who may be considered, more or less, independent or self-supporting labourers, while the paupers are, of course, dependent.

4. *The "Street Orderlies."*—These men present another distinct body. They are not merely in the employment, but many of them are under the care, of the National Philanthropic Association, which was founded by, and is now under the presidency of, Mr. Cochrane. The objects of this society, as far as regards the street orderlies' existence as a class of scavengers, are sufficiently indicated in its title, which declares it to be "For the Promotion of Street Cleanliness and the Employment of the Poor; so that able-bodied men may be prevented from burthening the parish rates, and preserved independent of workhouse alms and degradation. Supported by the contributions of the benevolent."

The street orderlies, men and boys, are paid a fixed weekly wage, a certain sum being stopped from those single men who reside in houses rented for them by the association, where their meals, washing, &c., are provided. Among them are men of many callings, and some educated and accomplished persons.

The system of street orderlyism is, moreover, distinguished by one attribute unknown to any other mode; it is an effort, persevered in, despite of many hindrances and difficulties, to amend our street scavengery, indeed to reform it altogether; so that dust and dirt may be checked in their very origination.

The corporation, if I may so describe it, of the street orderlies, presents characteristics, again, varying from the other orders of what can only be looked upon either as the self-supporting or pauper workers.

These, then, are the several modes or methods of street-scavengery, and they show the following:—

CLASSES OF STREET-SWEEPING EMPLOYERS.

(1.) *Traders,* who undertake contracts for scavengery as a speculation. Under this denomination may be classed the contractors with parishes, districts, boards, liberties, divisions and subdivisions of parishes, markets, &c.

(2.) *Parishes,* who employ the men as a matter of parochial policy, with a view to the reduction of the rates, and with little regard to the men.

(3.) *Philanthropists,* who seek, more particularly, to benefit the men whom they employ, while they strive to promote the public good by increasing public cleanliness and order.

Under the head of "Traders" are the contractors with the parishes, &c., and the proprietors of the sweeping-machines, who are in the same capacity as the "regular contractors" respecting their dealings with labourers, but who substitute mechanical for manual operations.

Of these several classes of masters engaged in the scavengery of the metropolis I have much to say, and, for the clearer saying of it, I shall treat each of the several varieties of labour separately.

OF THE CONTRACTORS FOR SCAVENGERY.

THE scavenging of the streets of the metropolis is performed *directly* or *indirectly* by the authorities of the several parishes "without the City," who have the power to levy rates for the cleansing of the various districts; within the City, however, the office is executed under the direction of the Court of Sewers.

When the cleansing of the streets is performed indirectly by either the parochial or civic authorities, it is effected by contractors, that is to say, by traders who undertake for a certain sum to remove the street-refuse at stated intervals and under express conditions, and who employ paid servants to execute the work for them. When it is performed *directly,* the authorities employ labourers, generally from the workhouse, and usually enter into an agreement with some contractor for the use of his carts and appliances, together with the right to deposit in his wharf or yard the refuse removed from the streets.

I shall treat first of the *indirect* mode of scavenging—that is to say, of cleansing the streets by contract—beginning with the contractors, setting forth, as near as possible, the receipts and expenditure in connection with the trade, and then proceeding in due order to treat of the labourers employed by them in the performance of the task.

Some of the contractors agree with the parochial

or district authorities to remove the dust from the house-bins as well as the dirt from the streets under one and the same contract; some undertake to execute these two offices under separate contracts; and some to perform only one of them. It is most customary, however, for the same contractor to serve the parish, especially the larger parishes, in both capacities.

There is no established or legally required *form* of agreement between a contractor and his principals; it is a bargain in which each side strives to get the best of it, but in which the parish representatives have often to contend against something looking like a monopoly; a very common occurrence in our day when capitalists choose to combine, which *is* legal, or unnoticed, but very heinous on the part of the working men, whose capital is only in their strength or skill. One contractor, on being questioned by a gentleman officially connected with a large district, as to the existence of combination, laughed at such a notion, but said there might be "a sort of understanding one among another," as among people who "must look to their own interests, and see which way the cat jumped;" concluding with the undeniable assertion that "no man ought reasonably to be expected to ruin himself for a parish."

There does not appear, however, to have been any countervailing qualities on the part of the parishes to this understanding among the contractors; for some of the authorities have found themselves, when a new or a renewed contract was in question, suddenly "on the other side of the hedge." Thus, in the south-west district of St. Pancras, the contractor, five or six years ago, paid 100*l*. per annum for the removal and possession of the street-dirt, &c.; but the following year the district authorities had to pay him 500*l*. for the same labour and with the same privileges! Other changes took place, and in 1848-9 a contractor again paid the district 95*l*. I have shown, too, that in Shadwell the dust-contractor now *receives* 450*l*. per annum, whereas he formerly *paid* 240*l*. To prove, however, that a spirit of combination does *occasionally* exist among these contractors, I may cite the following minute from one of the parish books.

Extract from Minute-book, Nov. 7, 1839.
Letter C, Folio 437.

"Commissioner's Office,
"30, Howland-street,
"Nov. 7, 1839.

"REPORT of the Paving Committee to the General Board, relating to the watering the district for the past year.

"Your Committee beg leave to report that for the past three years the sums paid by contract for watering were respectively:—

"For 1836 . . . . . £230
„ 1837 220
„ 1838 200

"That in the month of February in the present year the Board advertised in the usual manner for tenders to water the district, when the following were received, viz.:—

"Mr. Darke £315
„ Gore 318
„ Nicholls 312
„ Starkey 285
which was the lowest.

"Your Committee, anxious to prevent any increase in the watering-rate from being levied, and considering the amount required by the contractors for this service as excessive and exorbitant, and even evincing a spirit of combination, resolved to make an inroad upon this system, and after much trouble and attention adopted other measures for watering the district, the results of which they have great pleasure in presenting to the Board, by which it will be seen that a saving over the very lowest of the above tenders of 102*l*. 3*s*. has been effected; the sum of 18*l*. 18*s*. has been paid for pauper labour at the same time. Your Committee regret that, notwithstanding the efforts of themselves and their officers, the state of insubordination and insult of most of the paupers (in spite of all encouragement to industry) was such, that the Committee, on the 12th of July last, were reluctantly compelled to discontinue their services. The Committee cannot but congratulate the Board upon the result of their experiment, which will have the effect of breaking up a spirit of combination highly dangerous to the community at large, at the same time that their labours have caused a very considerable saving to the ratepayers; and they trust the work, considering all the numerous disadvantages under which they have laboured, has been performed in a satisfactory manner.

"P. CUNNINGHAM,
"Surveyor,
"30, Howland-street, Fitzroy-square."

The following regulations sufficiently show the nature of the agreements made between the contractors and the authorities as to the cleansing of the more important thoroughfares especially. It will be seen that in the regulations I quote every street, court, or alley, must now be swept *daily*, a practice which has only been adopted within these few years in the City.

"SEWERS' OFFICE, GUILDHALL, LONDON, RAKERS' DUTIES,[*] MIDSUMMER, 1851, TO MIDSUMMER, 1852.

"*CLEANSING.*

"*The whole surface* of every Carriage-way, Court, and Alley shall be swept *every day* (Sundays excepted), and all mud, dust, filth, and rubbish, all frozen or partially frozen matter, and snow, animal and vegetable matter, and everything offensive or injurious, shall be properly pecked, scraped, swept up, and carted away therefrom; and the iron gutters laid across or along the footways, the air-grates over the sewers, the gulley-

[*] The reader will remember that in the historical sketch given of the progress of public scavengery, the word "Rakers" occurred in connection with the sworn master scavengers, &c., &c.; the word is now unknown to the trade, except that it appears on city documents.

grates in the carriage-way of the streets respectively; and all public urinals are to be daily raked out, swept, and made clean and clear from all obstructions; and the Contractor or Contractors shall, in time of frost, continually keep the channels in the Streets and Places clear for water to run off: and cleanse and cart away refuse hogan or gravel (when called upon by the Inspector to do so) from all streets newly paved.

"The Mud and Dirt, &c., is to be carted away immediately that it is swept up.

"N.B. The Inspector of the District may, at any time he may think it necessary, order any Street or Place to be cleansed and swept a second time in any one day, and the Contractor or Contractors are thereupon bound to do the same.

"The Markets and their approaches are also to be thus cleansed DAILY, and the approaches thereto respectively are also to be thus cleansed at such an hour in the night of Saturday in each week as the Inspector of the District may direct.

"Every Street, Lane, Square, Yard, Court, Alley, Passage, and Place (except certain main Streets hereinafter enumerated), are to be thus cleansed within the following hours Daily: namely—

"In the months of April, May, June, July, August, and September. To be begun not earlier than 4 o'Clock in the morning, and finished not later than 1 o'Clock in the afternoon.

"In the months of October, November, December, January, February, and March. To be begun not earlier than 5 o'Clock in the morning, and finished not later than 2 o'Clock in the afternoon.

"The following main Streets are to be cleansed DAILY throughout the year (except Sundays), to be begun not earlier than 4 o'Clock in the morning, and finished not later than 9 o'Clock in the morning.

Fleet Street	Old Bailey
Ludgate Hill and Street	Lombard Street
St. Paul's Church Yard	New Bridge Street
Cheapside	Farringdon Street
Newgate Street	Aldersgate Street
Poultry	St. Martin-le-grand
Watling Street, Budge Row, and Cannon St.	Prince's Street
	Moorgate Street
Mansion House Street	The Street called 'The Pavement'
Cornhill	
Leadenhall Street	Finsbury Place, South
Aldgate Street and Aldgate	Gracechurch Street
	Bishopsgate St., within and without
King William Street and London Bridge	The Minories
Fenchurch Street	Wood Street
Holborn	Gresham Street
Holborn Bridge	Coleman Street.
Skinner Street	

"N.B. In times of frost and snow these hours of executing the work may be extended at the discretion of the Local Commissioners."

The other conditions relate to the removal of the dust from the houses (a subject I have already treated), and specify the fines, varying from 1l. to 5l., to be paid by the contractors, for the violation or neglect of any of the provisions of the contract. It is further required that "Each Foreman, Sweeper, and Dustman, in the employ of either of the Contractors," (of whom there are four, Messrs. Sinnott, Rooke, Reddin, and Gould), "will be required to wear a Badge on the arm with these words thereon,—

"'London Sewers,
N°. —
Guildhall,'

by which means any one having cause of complaint against any of the men in the performance of their several duties, may, by taking down the number of the man and applying at the Sewers' Office, Guildhall, have reference to his name and employer.

"Any man working without his Badge, for each day he offends, the Contractor is liable to the penalty of Five Shillings.

"All the sweepings of the Streets, and all the dust and ashes from the Houses, are to be entirely carted away from the City of London, on a Penalty of *Ten Pounds* for each cart-load."

These terms sufficiently show the general nature of the contracts in question; the principal difference being that in some parts, the contractor is not required to sweep the streets more than once, twice, or thrice a week in ordinary weather.

The number of individuals in London styling themselves Master Scavengers is 34. Of these, 10 are at present without a contract either for dust or scavenging, and 5 have a contract for removing the dust only; so that, deducting these two numbers, the gross number 34 is reduced to 19 scavenging contractors. Of the latter number 16 are in a large way of business, having large yards, possessing several carts and some waggons, and employing a vast number of men daily in sweeping the streets, carting rubbish, &c. The other 3 masters, however, are only in a small way of business, being persons of more limited means. A *large* master scavenger employs from 3 to 18 carts, and from 18 to upwards of 40 men at scavengery alone, while a small master employs only from 1 to 3 carts and from 3 to 6 men. By the table I have given, p. 186, vol. ii., it is shown that there are 52 *contracts* between the several district authorities and master scavengers, and nineteen *contractors*, without counting members of the same family, as distinct individuals; this gives an average of nearly three distinct contracts per individual. The contracts are usually for a twelvemonth.

Although the table above referred to shows but 19 contractors for public scavenging, there are, as I have said, more, or about 24, in London, most of them in a "large way," and next year some of those who have no contracts at present may enter into agreements with the parishes. The smallness of this number, when we consider the vast extent of the metropolis, confirms the notion of the sort of monopoly and combination to which I have alluded. In the Post-Office Directory for 1851 there are no names under the heads of

Scavengers or Dustmen, but under the head of "Rubbish Carters," 28 are given, 9 names being marked as "Dust Contractors" and 10 as "Nightmen."

Of large contractors, however, there are, as I have said, about 24, but they may not all obtain contracts every year, and in this number are included different members of the same family or firm, who may undertake specific contracts, although in the trade it is looked upon as "one concern." The smaller contractors were represented to me as rather more numerous than the others, and perhaps numbered 40, but it is not easy to define what is to be accounted a contractor. In the table given in pp. 213, 214, I cite only 7 as being the better known. The others may be considered as small rubbish-carters and flying-dustmen.

There are yet other transactions in which the contractors are engaged with the parishes, independently of their undertaking the whole labour of street and house cleansing. In the parishes where pauper, or "poor" labour is resorted to— for it is not always that the men employed by the parishes are positive "paupers," but rather the unemployed poor of the parish—in such parishes, I say, an agreement is entered into with a contractor for the deposit of the collected street dirt at his yard or wharf. For such deposit the contractor must of course be paid, as it is really an occupation and renting of a portion of his premises for a specific purpose. The street dirt, however, is usually left to the disposal of the contractor, for his own profit, and where he once paid 50*l.* for the possession of the street-collected dirt of a parish, collected by labour which was no cost to him, he may now *receive* half of such 50*l.*, or whatever the terms of the agreement may be. I heard of one contractor who lately received 25*l.* where he once paid 50*l.*

In another way, too, contractors are employed by parishes. Where pauper or poor labour in street cleansing is the practice, a contractor's horses, carts, and cart-drivers are hired for the conveyance of the dirt from the streets. This of course is for a specific payment, and is in reality the work of the tradesmen who in the Post Office Directory are described as "Rubbish Carters," and of whom I shall have to speak afterwards. Some parishes or paving boards have, however, their own horses and vehicles, but in the other respects they have dealings with the contractors.

To come to as correct a conclusion as possible in this complicated and involved matter, I have obtained the aid of some gentlemen long familiar with such procedures. One of them said that to procure the accounts of such transactions for a series of years, with all their chops and changes, or to obtain a perfectly precise return, for any three years, affecting the whole metropolis, would be the work of a parliamentary commission with full powers "to send for papers," &c., &c., and that even *then* the result might not be satisfactory as a clear exposition. However, with the aid of the gentlemen alluded to, I venture upon the following approximation.

As my present inquiry relates only to the Scavenging Contractors in the metropolis, I will take the number of districts, markets, &c., which are specified in the table, p. 186, vol. ii. These are 83 in number, of which 29 are shown to be scavenged by the "parish." I will not involve in this computation any of the more rural places which may happen to be in the outskirts of the metropolitan area, but I will take the contracts as 54, where the contractors do the entire work, and as 29 where they are but the rubbish-carters and dirt receivers of the parishes.

I am assured that it is a fair calculation that the scavengery of the streets, apart from the removal of the dust from the houses, costs in payments to the contractors, 150*l.* as an average, to each of the several 54 districts; and that in the 29 localities in which the streets are cleansed by parish labour, the sum paid is at the rate of 50*l.* per locality, some of them, as the five districts of Marylebone for instance, being very large. This is calculated regardless of the cases where parishes may have their own horses and vehicles, for the cost to the rate-payers may not be very materially different, between paying for the hire of carts and horses, and investing capital in their purchase and incurring the expense of wear and tear. The account then stands thus:—

Parish payment on 54 contracts, 150*l.* each	£8100
Parish payment on 29 contracts, 50*l.* each	1450
Yearly total sum paid for Scavenging of the Metropolis	£9550

or, apportioned among 19 *contractors*, upwards of 500*l.* each; and among 83 *contracts*, about 115*l.* per *contract*. Even if other contractors are employed where parish labour is pursued, the cost to the rate-payers is the same. This calculation is made, as far as possible, as regards scavengery alone; and is independent of the value of the refuse collected. It is about the scavengery that the grand fight takes place between the parishes and contractors; the house dust, being uninjured by rain or street surface-water, is more available for trade purposes.

From this it would appear that the cost of cleansing the streets of London may be estimated in round numbers at 10,000*l.* per annum.

The next point in the inquiry is, What is the value of the street dirt annually collected?

The price I have adduced for the dirt gained from the streets is 3*s.* per load, which is a very reasonable average. If the load be dung, or even chiefly dung, it is worth 5*s.* or 6*s.* With the proportion of dung and street refuse to be found in such a thoroughfare as the Haymarket, in dry, or comparatively dry weather, a load, weighing about a ton, is worth about 3*s.* in the purchaser's own cart. On the other hand, as I have shown that quantities of mixed or slop "mac" have to be wasted, that some is sold at a nominal price, and a good deal at 1*s.* the load, 3*s.* is certainly a fair average.

Thus the annual sum of the street-dirt, as re-

A TABLE SHOWING THE NUMBER OF MEN AND CARTS EMPLOYED IN COLLECTING DUST, IN SCAVENGERY, AND AT RUBBISH CARTING, AS WELL AS THE NUMBER OF MEN, WOMEN, AND BOYS WORKING IN THE DUST-YARDS OF THE SEVERAL METROPOLITAN CONTRACTORS.

Contractors (Large).	Dust.		Scavengery.		Rubbish Carting.		Working in the Yard.		
	Number of Men employed.	Number of Carts used.	Number of Men employed.	Number of Carts, Waggons, or Machines used.	Number of Men employed.	Number of Carts used.	Number of Men employed.	Number of Women employed.	Number of Boys working.
Mr. Dodd	20	10	26	13	20	20	9	12	4
,, Gould	20	10	28	11	11	11	5	15	4
,, Redding	32	16	41	18	22	22	5	12	4
,, Gore	32	16	18	7	none.	none.	4	20	6
,, Rooke	16	8	16	6	16	16	2	6	3
,, Stapleton & Holdsworth	10	5	11	8	10	10	4	8	2
,, Tame	20	10	5	1	12	12	4	8	2
,, Starkey	10	5	22	8	none.	none.	4	12	3
,, Newman	8	4	23	10	8	8	4	8	2
,, Pratt and Sewell	10	5	4	2	20	20	2	6	2
,, W. Sinnott, Sen.	28	14	5	2	none.	none.	5	15	5
,, J. Sinnott	8	4	16	6	ditto.	ditto.	none.	none.	none.
,, Westley	10	5	18	9	ditto.	ditto.	3	9	2
,, Parsons	10	5	18	3	ditto.	ditto.	2	6	1
,, Hearne	18	9	7	2	20	20	3	9	3
,, Humphries	20	10	4	1	6	6	3	9	3
,, Calvert	6	3	none.	none.	7	7	2	6	2
	278	139	262	107	152	152	61	161	48
Contractors (Small).									
Mr. North	4	2	2	1	4	4	1	2	1
,, Milton	6	3	none.	none.	none.	none.	3	6	2
,, Jenkins	2	1	5	1	ditto.	ditto.	1	2	1
,, Stroud	10	5	none.	none.	ditto.	ditto.	4	9	3
,, Martin	2	1	6	3	ditto.	ditto.	1	2	1
,, Clutterbuck	4	2	none.	none.	5	5	1	3	1
,, W. Sinnott, Jun.	4	2	ditto.	ditto.	6	6	1	2	1
	32	16	13	5	15	15	12	26	10
Contractors, but not having any contract at present, only carting rubbish, &c.									
Mr. Darke	...	...	...	...	36	36			
,, Tomkins	...	...	...	...	6	6			
,, J. Cooper	...	...	...	...	8	8			
,, T. Cooper, Sen.	...	...	...	...	12	12			
,, Athill	...	...	...	...	6	6			
,, Barnett (lately sold off)									
,, Brown	...	...	...	...	4	4			
,, Ellis	...	...	...	...	6	6			
,, Limpus	...	...	...	...	10	10			
,, Emmerson	...	...	...	...	6	6			
					94	94			

Machines.	Dust.		Scavengers.		Rubbish.		Employed in Yard.		
	Men.	Carts.	Men.	Carts.	Men.	Carts.	Men.	Women.	Children
Woods and Forests	none.	none.	4	2 machines.	none.	none.	none.	none.	none.
Regent-street and Pall-mall.	ditto.	ditto.	12	2 ,,	ditto.	ditto.	ditto.	ditto.	ditto.
St. Martin's	ditto.	ditto.	9	4 ,,	ditto.	ditto.	ditto.	ditto.	ditto.
			25	8 ,,					
Parishes.									
Kensington *	...	...	5	2					
Chelsea *	...	...	5	2					
St. George's, Hanover-sq.*.	...	...	5	1					
St. Margaret's, Westminster*	...	...	7	3					
Piccadilly *	...	...	28	2					
St. Ann's, Soho *	...	...	4	2					
Paddington *	...	...	6	2					
St. Marylebone *(5 Districts)	...	...	35	4					
St. James's, Westminster...	...	...	2	1					
Hampstead	No parochial removal of dust.		4	1					
Highgate	ditto.		4	1					
Islington *	...	...	8	1					
Hackney	8	4	7	1	...	...	2	6	2
St. Clement Danes *	...	...	7	3 waggons.					
Commercial-road, East * ...	...	...	6	3 carts.					
Poplar	4	2	4	1	...	...	2	4	1
Bermondsey	6	3	6	3	...	...	3	6	2
Newington	8	4	6	2	...	...	2	6	2
Lambeth *	...	...	16	3					
Ditto (Christchurch).........	4	2	20	3	...	...	1	4	1
Wandsworth	4	2	4	1	...	...	1	4	1
Camberwell and Walworth	8	4	6	2	...	...	2	5	3
Rotherhithe	6	3	5	2	...	...	1	5	2
Greenwich	4	2	5	2	...	...	1	3	1
Deptford	4	2	4	2	...	...	1	3	1
Woolwich	none.	none.	5	2					
Lewisham......................	ditto.	ditto	4	1					
Total for Parishes	56	28	218	50 carts. 3 waggons.			16	46	16
Total for large contractors.	278	139	262	107	152	152	61	161	48
Total for small contractors.	32	16	13	5	15	15	12	26	10
Total for machines	...	...	25	8 machines.					
Total for street orderlies ...	...	...	60	9					
Gross total	366	183	578	179 carts. 3 waggons.	167	167	89	233	74

	Men.	Carts.
Total employed at dust	366	183
,, ,, scavenging	578	179
,, ,, rubbish carting..........................	167	167
,, (men, women, and children), in yard	396	
Total employed in the removal of house and street refuse	1507	529

* The parishes marked thus * have their dustmen and dust-carts, as well as the rubbish carting and the individuals in the dust-yard, reckoned in the numbers employed by the contractors.

gards the quantity collected by the contracting scavengers (as shown in the table given at page 186), is, in round numbers, 89,000 cart-loads; that collected by parish labour, with or without the aid of the street-sweeping machines, at 52,000 cart-loads, or a total (I do not include what is collected by the orderlies) of 141,000 loads.

This result shows, then, that the contractors yearly collect by scavenging the streets with their own paid labourers, and receive as the produce of pauper labour, as follows:—

	Loads of Street Dirt.	Per Load.	Total.
By Contractors	89,000	3s.	£13,350
By Parishes	52,000	3s.	7,800
Total	141,000		£21,150

or a value of rather more than 1113*l*. as the return to each individual contractor in the table, or about 255*l*. as the average on each contract. As, however, the whole of the parish-collected manure does not come into the hands of the contractors, it will be fair, I am assured, to compute the total at 19,000*l*., a sum of 1000*l*. to each contractor, or nearly 229*l*. on each contract.

It would appear, then, that the total receipts of the contractors for the scavenging of London amount to very nearly 30,000*l*.; that is to say, 10,000*l*. as remuneration for the office, and 20,000*l*. as the value of the dirt collected. But against this sum as received, we have to set the gross expense of wages paid to men, wear and tear of carts and appliances, rent of wharfs, interest for money, &c.

Concerning the amount paid in wages, it appears by the table at pp. 186, 187, that the men employed by the scavenging contractors in wet weather, are 260 daily (being nearly half of the whole force of 531 men, the orderlies excepted). In dry weather, however, there are only 194 men employed. I will therefore calculate upon 194 men employed daily, and 66 employed half the year, making the total of 260. By the table here given, it will be seen that the total number of scavengers employed by the large and small contractors, is 275.

Number of Men.	Weekly Wage.	Yearly.
194 (for 12 months)	16s. *	£8070 8s.
66 (for 6 months)	16s.	1372 16s.
Total		£9443 4s.

There remains now to show the amount of capital which a large contractor must embark in his business: I include the amount of rent, and the expenditure on what must be provided for business purposes, and which is subject to wear and tear, to decay, and loss.

* I have computed all the weekly wages at 16s., though some of the men are paid only 14s. My object in this is to give the contractors the benefit of the difference.

There are not now, I am told, more than twelve scavengers' wharfs and 20 yards (the wharf being also a yard) in the possession of the contractors in regular work. These are the larger contractors, and their capital, I am assured, may be thus estimated:—

CAPITAL OF THE MASTER SCAVENGERS.

	£	s.	d.
179 Carts, 21*l*. each	3,759	0	0
3 Waggons, 32*l*. each	96	0	0
230 Horses, 25*l*. each	5,750	0	0
230 Sets of harness, 2*l*. each	460	0	0
600 Brooms, 9*d*. each	22	10	0
300 Shovels, 1s. each	15	0	0
100 Barges, 50*l*. each	5,000	0	0
Total	15,102	10	0

I have estimated according to what may be the *present* value, not the original cost, of the implements, vehicles, &c. A broom, when new, costs 1s. 2d., and is worn out in two or three weeks. A shovel, when new, costs 2s.

The following appears to be the

YEARLY EXPENDITURE OF THE MASTER SCAVENGERS.

	£	s.	d.
Wages to working scavengers (as before shown)	9,443	0	0
Wages to 48 bargemen, engaged in unloading the vessels with street-dirt, 4 men to each of 12 wharfs, at 16s. weekly wage	1,996	0	0
Keep of 300 horses (26*l*. each)	7,800	0	0
Wear and tear (say 15 per cent. on capital)	2,250	0	0
Rent of 20 wharfs and yards (average 100*l*. each)	2,000	0	0
Interest on 15,000*l*. capital, at 10 per cent.	1,500	0	0
	£24,989	0	0

I have endeavoured in this estimate to confine myself, as much as possible, to the separate subject of scavengery, but it must be borne in mind that as the large contractors are dustmen as well as scavengers, the great charges for rent and barges cannot be considered as incurred solely on account of the street-dirt trade. Including, then, the payments from parishes, the account will stand thus:—

YEARLY RECEIPTS OF MASTER SCAVENGERS.

From Parishes	£9,450
From Manure, &c.	19,000
Total Income	£28,450
Deduct yearly Expenditure	25,000
Profit	£3,450

This gives a profit of nearly 182*l*. to each contractor, if equally apportioned, or a little more than 41*l*. on each contract for street-scavenging alone, and a profit no doubt affected by circumstances which cannot very well be reduced to figures. The profit may appear small, but it should be remembered that it is *independent* of the profits on the dust.

OF THE CONTRACTORS' (OR EMPLOYERS') PREMISES, &c.

AT page 171 of the present volume I have described one of the yards devoted to the trade in house-dust, and I have little to say in addition regarding the premises of the contracting or employing scavengers. They are the same places, and the industrious pursuits carried on there, and the division and subdivision of labour, relate far more to the dustmen's department than to the scavengers'. When the produce of the sweeping of the streets has been thrown into the cart, it is so far ready for use that it has not to be sifted or prepared, as has the house-dust, for the formation of brieze, &c., the " mac " being sifted by the purchaser.

These yards or wharfs are far less numerous and better conducted now than they were ten years ago. They are at present fast disappearing from the banks of the Thames (there is, however, one still at Whitefriars and one at Milbank). They are chiefly to be found on the banks of the canals. Some of the principal wharfs near Maiden-lane, St. Pancras, are to be found among unpaven, or ill-paved, or imperfectly macadamized roads, along which run rows of what were once evidently pleasant suburban cottages, with their green porches and their trained woodbine, clematis, jasmine, or monthly roses; these tenements, however, are now occupied chiefly by the labourers at the adjacent stone, coal, lime, timber, dust, and general wharfs. Some of the cottages still presented, on my visits, a blooming display of dahlias and other autumnal flowers; and in one corner of a very large and very black-looking dust-yard, in which rose a huge mound of dirt, was the cottage residence of the man who remained in charge of the wharf all night, and whose comfortable-looking abode was embedded in flowers, blooming luxuriantly. The gay-tinted holly-hocks and dahlias are in striking contrast with the dinginess of the dust-yards, while the canal flows along, dark, sluggish, and muddy, as if to be in keeping with the wharf it washes.

The dust-yards must not be confounded with the "night-yards," or the places where the contents of the cess-pools are deposited, places which, since the passing of the Sanatory Act, are rapidly disappearing.

Upon entering a dust-yard there is generally found a heavy oppressive sort of atmosphere, more especially in wet or damp weather. This is owing to the tendency of charcoal to absorb gases, and to part with them on being saturated with moisture. The cinder-heaps of the several dust-yards, with their million pores, are so many huge gasometers retaining all the offensive gases arising from the putrefying organic matters which usually accompany them, and parting with such gases immediately on a fall of rain. It would be a curious calculation to estimate the quantity of deleterious gas thus poured into the atmosphere after a slight shower.

The question has been raised as to the propriety of devoting some special locality to the purposes of dust-yards, and it is certainly a question deserving public attention.

The chief disposal of the street manure is from barges, sent by the Thames or along the canals, and sold to farmers and gardeners. In the larger wharfs, and in those considered removed from the imputation of "scurfdom," six men, and often but four, are employed to load a barge which contains from 30 to 40 tons. In such cases the dust-yard and the wharf are one and the same place. The contents of these barges are mixed, about one-fourth being "mac," the rest street-mud and dung. This admixture, on board the vessel, is called by the bargemen and the contractors' servants at the wharfs Leicester (properly Læsta, a load). We have the same term at the end of our word bal-*last*.

I am assured by a wharfinger, who has every means of forming a correct judgment, it may be estimated that there are dispatched from the contractors' wharfs twelve barges daily, freighted with street-manure. This is independent of the house-dust barged to the country brick-fields. The weight of the cargo of a barge of manure is about 40 tons; 36 tons being a low average. This gives 3744 barge-loads, or 132,784 tons, or loads, yearly ; for it must be recollected that the dirt gathered by pauper labour is dispatched from the contractors' yards or wharfs, as well as that collected by the immediate servants of the contractors. The price per barge-load at the canal, basin, or wharf, in the country parts where agriculture flourishes, is from 5*l.* to 6*l.*, making a total of 20,594*l.* The difference of that sum, and the total given in the table (21,147*l.*) may be accounted for on the supposition that the remainder is sold in the yards and carted away thence. The slop and valueless dirt is not included in this calculation.

OF THE WORKING SCAVENGERS UNDER THE CONTRACTORS.

I HAVE now to deal with what throughout the whole course of my inquiry into the state of London Labour and the London Poor I have considered the great object of investigation—the condition and characteristics of the working men; and what is more immediately the "labour question," the relation of the labourer to his employer, as to rates of payment, modes of payment, hiring of labourers, constancy or inconstancy of work, supply of hands, the many points concerning wages, perquisites, family work, and parochial or club relief.

First, I shall give an account of the class employment, together with the labour season and earnings of the labourers, or "economical" part of the subject. I shall then pass to the social points, concerning their homes, general expenditure, &c., and then to the more moral and intellectual questions of education, literature, politics, religion, marriage, and concubinage of the men and of their families. All this will refer, it should be remembered, only to the working scavagers in the honourable or better-paid trade; the cheaper labourers I shall treat separately as a distinct class; the details in both cases I shall illustrate with the statement of men of the class described.

The first part of this multifarious subject appertains to the division of labour. This in the scavaging trade consists rather of that kind of "gang-work" which Mr. Wakefield styles "simple co-operation," or the working together of a number of people at the same thing, as opposed to "complex co-operation," or the working together of a number at *different branches* of the same thing. Simple co-operation is of course the ruder kind; but even this, rude as it appears, is far from being barbaric. "The savages of New Holland," we are told, "never help each other even in the most simple operations; and their condition is hardly superior—in some respects it is inferior—to that of the wild animals which they now and then catch."

As an instance of the advantages of "simple co-operation," Mr. Wakefield tells us that "in a vast number of simple operations performed by human exertion, it is quite obvious that two men working together will do more than four, or four times four men, each of whom should work alone. In the lifting of heavy weights, for example, in the felling of trees, in the gathering of much hay and corn during a short period of fine weather, in draining a large extent of land during the short season when such a work may be properly conducted, in the pulling of ropes on board ship, in the rowing of large boats, in some mining operations, in the erection of a scaffolding for a building, and in the breaking of stones for the repair of a road, so that the whole road shall always be kept in good repair—in all these simple operations, and thousands more, it is absolutely necessary that many persons should work together at the same time, in the same place, and in the same way."

To the above instances of simple co-operation, or gang-working, as it may be briefly styled in Saxon English, Mr. Wakefield might have added dock labour and scavaging.

The principle of complex co-operation, however, is not entirely unknown in the public cleansing trade. This business consists of as many branches as there are distinct kinds of refuse, and these appear to be four. There are (1) the wet and (2) the dry *house*-refuse (or dust and night-soil), and (3) the wet and (4) the dry *street*-refuse (or mud and rubbish); and in these four different branches of the one general trade the principle of complex co-operation is found commonly, though not invariably, to prevail.

The difference as to the class employments of the general body of public cleansers—the dustmen, street-sweepers, nightmen, and rubbish carters—seems to be this:—any nightman will work as a dustman or scavager; but it is not all the dustmen and scavagers who will work as nightmen. The reason is almost obvious. The avocations of the dustman and the nightman are in some degree hereditary. A rude man provides for the future maintenance of his sons in the way which is most patent to his notice; he makes the boy share in his own labour, and grow up unfit for anything else.

The regular working scavagers are then generally a distinct class from the working dustmen, and are all paid by the week, while the dustmen are paid by the load. In very wet weather, when there is a great quantity of "slop" in the streets, a dustman is often called upon to lend a helping hand, and sometimes when a working scavager is out of employ, in order to keep himself from want, he goes to a "job of dust work," but seldom from any other cause.

In a parish where there is a crowded population, the dustman's labours consume, on an average, from six to eight hours a day. In scavagery, the average hours of daily work are twelve (Sundays of course excepted), but they sometimes extended to fifteen, and even sixteen hours, in places of great business traffic; while in very fine dry weather, the twelve hours may be abridged by two, three, four, or even more. Thus it is manifest that the consumption of time alone prevents the same working men being simultaneously dustmen and scavagers. In the more remote and quiet parishes, however, and under the management of the smaller contractors, the opposite arrangement frequently exists; the operative is a scavager one day, and a dustman the next. This is not the case in the busier districts, and with the large contractors, unless exceptionally, or on an emergency.

If the scavagers or dustmen have completed their street and house labours in a shorter time than usual, there is generally some sort of employment for them in the yards or wharfs of the contractors, or they may sometimes avail themselves of their leisure to enjoy themselves in their own way. In many parts, indeed, as I have shown, the street-sweeping must be finished by noon, or earlier.

Concerning the *division of labour*, it may be said, that the principle of complex co-operation in the scavaging trade exists only in its rudest form, for the characteristics distinguishing the labour of the working scavagers are far from being of that complicated nature common to many other callings.

As regards the act of sweeping or scraping the streets, the labour is performed by the *gangsman* and his *gang*. The gangsman usually loads the cart, and occasionally, when a number are employed in a district, acts as a foreman by superintending them, and giving directions; he is a working scavager, but has the office of overlooker confided to him, and receives a higher amount of wage than the others.

For the completion of the street-work there are the *one-horse carmen* and the *two-horse carmen*, who are also working scavagers, and so called from their having to load the carts drawn by one or two horses. These are the men who shovel into the cart the dirt swept or scraped to one side of the public way by the gang (some of it mere slop), and then drive the cart to its destination, which is generally their master's yard. Thus far only does the street-labour extend. The carmen have the care of the vehicles in cleaning them, greasing the wheels, and such like, but the horses are usually groomed by stablemen, who are not employed in the streets.

The division of labour, then, among the working scavagers, may be said to be as follows:—

1st. The *ganger*, whose office it is to superintend the gang, and shovel the dirt into the cart.

2nd. The gang, which consists of from three to ten or twelve men, who sweep in a row and collect the dirt in heaps ready for the ganger to shovel into the cart.

3rd. The carman (one-horse or two-horse, as the case may be), who attends to the horse and cart, brushes the dirt into the ganger's shovel, and assists the ganger in wet sloppy weather in carting the dirt, and then takes the mud to the place where it is deposited.

There is only one *mode of payment* for the above labours pursued among the master scavagers, and that is by the week.

1st. The ganger receives a weekly salary of 18s. when working for an "honourable" master; with a "scurf," however, the ganger's pay is but 16s. a week.

2nd. The gang receive in a large establishment each 16s. per week, but in a small one they usually get from 14s. to 15s. a week. When working for a small master they have often, by working over hours, to "make eight days to the week instead of six."

3rd. The one-horse carman receives 16s. a week in a large, and 15s. in a small establishment.

4th. The two-horse carman receives 18s. weekly, but is employed only by the larger masters.

On the opposite page I give a table on this point.

Some of these men are paid by the day, some by the week, and some on Wednesdays and Saturdays, perhaps in about equal proportions, the "casuals" being mostly paid by the day, and the regular hands (with some exceptions among the scurfs) once or twice a week. The chance hands are sometimes engaged for a half day, and, as I was told, "jump at a bob and a joey (1s. 4d.), or at a bob." I heard of one contractor who not unfrequently said to any foreman or gangsman who mentioned to him the applications for work, "O, give the poor devils a turn, if it's only for a day now and then."

Piece-work, or, as the scavagers call it, " by the load," *did* at one time prevail, but not to any great extent. The prices varied, according to the nature and the state of the road, from 2s. to 2s. 6d. the load. The system of piece-work was never liked by the men; it seems to have been resorted to less as a system, or mode of labour, than to insure assiduity on the part of the working scavagers, when a rapid street-cleansing was desirable. It was rather in the favour of the working man's *individual* emoluments than otherwise, as may be shown in the following way. In Battle-bridge, four men collect five loads in dry, and six men seven loads in wet weather. If the average piece hire be 2s. 3d. a load, it is 2s. 9¾d. for each of the five men's day's work; if 2s. 2d. a load, it is 2s. 8½d. (the regular wage, and an extra halfpenny); if 2s., it is 2s. 6d.; and if less (which has been paid), the day's wage is not lower than 2s. At the lowest rates, however, the men, I was informed, could not be induced to take the necessary pains, as they *would* struggle to "make up half-a-crown;" while, if the streets were scavaged in a slovenly manner, the contractor was sure to hear from his friends of the parish that he was not acting up to his contract. I could not hear of any men now set to piece-work within the precincts of the places specified in the table. This extra work and scamping work are the two great evils of the piece system.

In their payments to their men the contractors show a superiority to the practices of some traders, and even of some dock-companies—the men are never paid at public-houses; the payment, moreover, is always in money. One contractor told me that he would like all his men to be teetotallers, if he could get them, though he was not one himself.

But these remarks refer only to the *nominal* wages of the scavagers; and I find the nominal wages of operatives in many cases are widely different (either from some additions by way of perquisites, &c., or deductions by way of fines, &c., but oftener the latter) from the *actual* wages received by them. Again, the average wages, or gross yearly income of the casually-employed men, are very different from those of the constant hands; so are the gains of a particular individual often no criterion of the general or average earnings of the trade. Indeed I find that the several varieties of wages may be classified as follows:—

1. *Nominal Wages.*—Those said to be paid in a trade.

2. *Actual Wages.*—Those *really* received, and which are equal to the nominal wages, *plus* the additions to, or *minus* the deductions from, them.

3. *Casual Wages.*—The earnings of the men who are only occasionally employed.

4. *Average Casual or Constant Wages.*—Those obtained throughout the year by such as are either occasionally or regularly employed.

5. *Individual Wages.*— Those of particular hands, whether belonging to the scurf or honourable trade, whether working long or short hours, whether partially or fully employed, and the like.

6. *General Wages.*—Or the *average* wages of the whole trade, constant or casual, fully or partially employed, honourable or scurf, long and short hour men, &c., &c., all lumped together and the mean taken of the whole.

Now in the preceding account of the working scavagers' mode and rate of payment I have spoken only of the nominal wages; and in order to arrive at their actual wages we must, as we have seen, ascertain what additions and what deductions are generally made to and from this

TABLE SHOWING THE DIVISION OF LABOUR, MODE AND RATES OF PAYMENT, NATURE OF WORK PERFORMED, TIME UNEMPLOYED, AND AVERAGE EARNINGS OF THE OPERATIVE SCAVAGERS OF LONDON.

OPERATIVE SCAVAGERS.	Mode of Payment.	Rates of Payment.	Nature of Work performed.	Time unemployed during the Year.	Average casual (or constant) gains throughout the Year.
I. *Manual Labourers.*					
A. *Better Paid.*					
Ganger	By the day.	18s. weekly, and 2s. allowance.	To load the cart and superintend the men.	Not two days during the year.	20s. per week.
Carman (2 horse)	,,	18s. weekly, and 2s. allowance.	To take care of the horses, help to load the cart, and take the dirt and slop to the dust-yard.	Seldom or never out of employment.	20s. ,,
Ditto (1 horse)	,,	16s. weekly, and 2s. allowance.	Ditto. ditto. ditto.	ditto.	18s. ,,
Sweepers	,,	16s. weekly, and 2s. allowance.	To sweep the district to which they are sent, and collect the dirt or slop ready for carting away.	About three months during the year.	13s. 6d. ,,
B. *Worse Paid.*					
Ganger	,,	16s. weekly, and 1s. allowance.	To load the cart and superintend the men.	Three months during the year.	12s. 9d. ,,
Carman	,,	15s. weekly, and 1s. allowance.	To take charge of the horse and cart, help to load the cart, and take the dirt or slop to the dust-yard.	Ditto.	12s. ,,
Sweepers	,,	15s. weekly, and 1s. allowance.	To sweep the district, collect the dirt or slop ready for carting off, work in the yard, and load the barge.	Ditto.	12s. ,,
II. *Machine Men.*					
Carman	,,	16s. weekly.	To take charge of the horse and machine, collect the dirt and take it to the yard.	Ditto.	12s. ,,
Sweepers	,,	16s. weekly.	To sweep where the machine cannot touch, work in the yard, and load the barges.	Ditto.	12s. ,,
III. *Parish Men.*					
A. Out-door Paupers.					
1. Paid in Money.					
Married men	,,	9s. weekly.	Sweep the streets and courts belonging to the parish, and collect the dirt or slop ready for carting away.	Six months during the year.	4s. 6d. ,,
Single men	,,	6s. weekly.	Ditto. ditto. ditto.	Ditto.	3s. ,,
2. Paid part in kind.					
Married men	,,	6s. 9d. weekly, and 3 quartern loaves.	Ditto. ditto. ditto.	Ditto.	3s. 4½d. and 3 quartern loaves weekly.
Single men	,,	5s. and 3 half-quartern loaves.	Ditto. ditto. ditto.	Ditto.	2s. 6d. and 3 half-quartern loaves weekly.
B. In-door Paupers	All in kind.	Food, lodging, and clothes.	Ditto. ditto. ditto.	....	Food, lodging, and clothes.
IV. *Street-Orderlies.*					
Foreman or Ganger	By the day.	15s. weekly.	Superintend the men and see that their work is done well.		
Sweepers	,,	12s. weekly.	Collect the dirt or slop ready for carting away.		
Barrow men	,,	....	Collect the short dung as it gathers in the district to which they are appointed.		
Barrow boys	,,	....	Ditto. ditto.		

amount. The deductions in the honourable trade are, as usual, inconsiderable.

All the *tools* used by operative scavagers are supplied to them by their employers—the tools being only brooms and shovels; and for this supply there are *no stoppages* to cover the expense.

Neither by *fines* nor by way of *security* are the men's wages reduced.

The *truck system*, moreover, is unknown, and has never prevailed in the trade. I heard of only one instance of an approach to it. A yard foreman, some years ago, who had a great deal of influence with his employer, had a chandler's-shop, managed by his wife, and it was broadly intimated to the men that they must make their purchases there. Complaints, however, were made to the contractor, and the foreman dismissed. One man of whom I inquired did not even know what the "truck system" meant; and when informed, thought they were "pretty safe" from it, as the contractor had nothing which he *could* truck with the men, and if "he polls us hisself," the man said, "he's not likely to let anybody else do it."

There are, moreover, no trade-payments to which the men are subjected; there are no trade-societies among the working men, no benefit nor sick clubs; neither do parochial relief and family labour characterize the regular hands in the honourable trade, although in sickness they may have no other resource.

Indeed, the working scavagers employed by the more honourable portion of the trade, instead of having any deductions made from their nominal wages, have rather additions to them in the form of perquisites coming from the public. These perquisites consist of allowances of beer-money, obtained in the same manner as the dustmen—not through the medium of their employers (though, to say the least, through their sufferance), but from the householders of the parish in which their labours are prosecuted.

The scavagers, it seems, are not required to sweep any places considered "private," nor even to sweep the public foot-paths; and when they *do* sweep or carry away the refuse of a butcher's premises, for instance—for, by law, the butcher is required to do so himself—they receive a gratuity. In the contract entered into by the city scavagers, it is expressly covenanted that no men employed shall accept gratuities from the householders; a condition little or not at all regarded, though I am told that these gratuities become less every year. I am informed also by an experienced butcher, who had at one time a private slaughter-house in the Borough, that, until within these six or seven years, he thought the scavagers, and even the dustmen, would carry away entrails, &c., in the carts, from the butcher's and the knacker's premises, for an allowance.

I cannot learn that the contractors, whether of the honourable or scurf trade, take any advantage of these "allowances." A working scavager receives the same wage, when he enjoys what I heard called in another trade "the height of perquisites," or is employed in a locality where there are no such additions to his wages. I believe, however, that the contracting scavagers let their best and steadiest hands have the best perquisited work.

These perquisites, I am assured, average from 1s. to 2s. a week, but one butcher told me he thought 1s. 6d. might be rather too high an average, for a pint of beer (2d.) was the customary sum given, and that was, or ought to be, divided among the gang. "In my opinion," he said, "there 'll be no allowances in a year or two." By the amount of these perquisites, then, the scavagers' gains are so far enhanced.

The wages, therefore, of an operative scavager in full employ, and working for the "honourable" portion of the trade, may be thus expressed:—

Nominal weekly wages . . . . 16s.
Perquisites in the form of allowances
for beer from the public . . . . 2s.

Actual weekly wages . . . . 18s.

OF THE "CASUAL HANDS" AMONG THE SCAVAGERS.

OF the scavagers proper there are, as in all classes of unskilled labour, that is to say, of labour which requires no previous apprenticeship, and to which any one can "turn his hand" on an emergency, two distinct orders of workmen, "the *regulars* and *casuals*" to adopt the trade terms; that is to say, the labourers consist of those who have been many years at the trade, constantly employed at it, and those who have but recently taken to it as a means of obtaining a subsistence after their ordinary resources have failed. This mixture of *constant* and *casual* hands is, moreover, a necessary consequence of all trades which depend upon the seasons, and in which an additional number of labourers are required at different periods. Such is necessarily the case with dock labour, where an easterly wind prevailing for several days deprives *thousands of work*, and where the change from a foul to a fair wind causes an equally inordinate demand for workmen. The same temporary increase of employment takes place in the agricultural districts at harvesting time, and the same among the hop growers in the picking season; and it will be hereafter seen that there are the same labour fluctuations in the scavaging trade, a greater or lesser number of hands being required, of course, according as the season is wet or dry.

This occasional increase of employment, though a benefit in some few cases (as enabling a man suddenly deprived of his ordinary means of living to obtain "a job of work" until he can "turn himself round"), is generally a most alarming evil in a State. What are the casual hands to do when the extra employment ceases? Those who have paid attention to the subject of dock labour and the subject of casual labour in general, may form some notion of the vast mass of misery that must be generally existing in London. The subject of hop-picking again belongs to the same question. Here are thousands of the very poorest employed only for a few days in the year. What, the mind naturally asks, do they after their short term of honest independence has ceased? With dock labour the poor man's bread depends upon the very winds; in scavaging and in street life generally it depends upon the rain; and in market-gardening, harvesting, hop-picking, and the like, it depends upon the sunshine. How many thousands in this huge metropolis have to look immediately to the very elements for their bread, it is overwhelming to contemplate; and yet, with all this fitfulness of employment we wonder that an extended knowledge of reading and writing does not produce a decrease of crime! We should, however, ask ourselves whether men can stay their hunger with alphabets or grow fat on spelling books; and wanting employment, and consequently food, and objecting to the *incarceration* of the workhouse, can we be astonished— indeed is it not a natural law—that they should help themselves to the property of others?

Concerning the "regular hands" of the contracting scavagers, it may, perhaps, be reasonable to compute that little short of one-half of them have been "to the manner born." The others are, as I have said, what these regular hands call "casuals," or "casualties." As an instance of the peculiar mixture of the regular and casual hands in the scavaging trade, I may state that one of my informants told me he had, at one period, under his immediate direction, fourteen men, of whom the former occupations had been as follows:—

7 Always Scavagers (or dustmen, and six of them nightmen when required).
1 Pot-boy at a public-house (but only as a boy).
1 Stable-man (also nightman).
1 Formerly a pugilist, then a showman's assistant.
1 Navvy.
1 Ploughman (nightman occasionally).
2 Unknown, one of them saying, but gaining no belief, that he had once been a gentleman.

14

In my account of the street orderlies will be given an interesting and elaborate statement of the former avocations, the habits, expenditure, &c., of a body of street-sweepers, 67 in number. This table will be found very curious, as showing what classes of men have been *driven* to street-sweeping, but it will not furnish a criterion of the character of the "regular hands" employed by the contractors.

The "casuals" or the "casualties" (always called among the men "cazzelties"), may be more properly described as men whose employment is accidental, chanceful, or uncertain. The regular hands of the scavagers are apt to designate any new comer, even for a permanence, any sweeper not reared to or versed in the business, a casual ("cazzel"). I shall, however, here deal with the "casual hands," not only as hands newly introduced into the trade, but as men of chanceful and irregular employment.

These persons are now, I understand, numerous in all branches of unskilled labour, willing to undertake or attempt any kind of work, but perhaps there is a greater tendency on the part of the surplus unskilled to turn to scavaging, from the fact that any broken-down man seems to account himself competent to sweep the streets.

To ascertain the number of these casual or outside labourers in the scavaging trade is difficult, for, as I have said, they are willing in their need to attempt any kind of work, and so may be "casuals" in divers departments of unskilled labour.

I do not think that I can better approximate the number of casuals than by quoting the opinion of a contracting scavager familiar with his workmen and their ways. He considered that there were always nearly as many hands on the look-out for a job in the streets, as there were regularly employed at the business by the large contractors; this I have shown to be 262, let us estimate therefore the number of casuals at 200.

According to the table I have given at pp. 213, 214, the number of men regularly or constantly employed at the metropolitan trade is as follows:—

Scavagers employed by large contractors	262
Ditto small contractors	13
Ditto machines	25
Ditto parishes	218
Ditto street-orderlies	60
Total working scavagers in London	578

But the prior table given at pp. 186, 187, shows the number of scavagers employed throughout the metropolis in wet and dry weather (*exclusive of the street-orderlies*) to be as follows:—

Scavagers employed in wet weather	531
Ditto in dry weather	358
Difference	173

Hence it would appear that about one-third less hands are required in the dry than in the wet season of the year. The 170 hands, then, discharged in the dry season are the casually employed men, but the whole of these 170 are not turned adrift immediately they are no longer wanted, some being kept on "odd jobs" in the yard, &c.; nor can that number be said to represent the entire amount of the surplus labour in the trade; but only that portion of it which *does* obtain even casual employment. After much trouble, and taking the average of various statements, it would appear that the number of casualty or quantity of occasional surplus labour in the scavaging trade may be represented at between 200 and 250 hands.

The scavaging trade, however, is not, I am informed, so overstocked with labourers now as it was formerly. Seven years ago, and from that to ten, there were usually between 200 and 300 hands out of work; this was owing to there being a less extent of paved streets, and comparatively few contractors; the scavaging work, moreover, was "scamped," the men, to use their own phrase, "licking the work over any how," so that fewer hands were required. Now, however, the inhabitants are more particular, I am told, "about the crooks and corners," and require the streets to be swept oftener. Formerly a gang of operative scavagers would only collect six loads of dirt a day, but now a gang will collect nine loads daily. The causes to which the surplus of labourers at present may be attributed are, I find, as follows:—Each operative has to do nearly double the work to what he formerly did, the extra cleansing of the streets having tended not only to employ more hands, but to make each of those employed do more work. The result has, however been followed by an increase in the wages of the operatives; seven years ago the labourers received but 2s. a day, and the ganger 2s. 6d., but now the labourers receive 2s. 8d. a day, and the ganger 3s.

In the city the men have to work very long hours, sometimes as many as 18 hours a day without any extra pay. This practice of overworking is, I find, carried on to a great extent, even with those master scavagers who pay the regular wages. One man told me that when he worked for a certain large master, whom he named, he has many times been out at work 28 hours in the wet (saturated to the skin) without having any rest. This plan of overworking, again, is generally adopted by the small masters, whose men, after they have done a regular day's labour, are set to work in the yard, sometimes toiling 18 hours a day, and usually not less than 16 hours daily. Often so tired and weary are the men, that when they rise in the morning to pursue their daily labour, they feel as fatigued as when they went to bed. "Frequently," said one of my informants, "have I gone to bed so worn out, that I haven't been able to sleep. However" (he added), "there is the work to be done, and we must do it or be off."

This system of overwork, especially in those trades where the quantity of work to be done is in a measure fixed, I find to be a far more influential cause of surplus labour than "over-population." The mere number of labourers in a trade is, *per se*, no criterion as to the quantity of labour employed in it; to arrive at this three things are required:—

(1) The number of hands;
(2) The hours of labour;
(3) The rate of labouring;

for it is a mere point of arithmetic, that if the hands in the scavaging trade work 18 hours a day, there must be one-third less men employed than there otherwise would, or in other words one-third of the men who are in work must be thus deprived of it. This is one of the crying evils of the day, and which the economists, filled as they are with their over-population theories, have entirely overlooked.

There are 262 men employed in the Metropolitan Scavaging Trade; one-half of these at the least may be said to work 16 hours per diem instead of 12, or one-third longer than they should; so that if the hours of labour in this trade were restricted to the usual day's work, there would be employment for one-sixth more hands, or nearly 50 individuals extra.

The other causes of the present amount of surplus labour are—

The many hands thrown out of employment by the discontinuance of railway works.

A less demand for unskilled labour in agricultural districts, or a smaller remuneration for it.

A less demand for some branches of labour (as ostlers, &c.), by the introduction of machinery (applied to roads), or through the caprices of fashion.

It should, however, be remembered, that men often found their opinions of such causes on prejudices, or express them according to their class interests, and it is only a few employers of unskilled labourers who care to inquire into the antecedent circumstances of men who ask for work.

As regards the population part of the question, it cannot be said that the surplus labour of the scavaging trade is referable to any inordinate increase in the families of the men. Those who are married appear to have, on the average, four children, and about one-half of the men have no family at all. Early marriages are by no means usual. Of the casual hands, however, full three-fourths are married, and one-half have families.

There are not more than ten or a dozen Irish labourers who have taken to the scavaging, though several have "tried it on;" the regular hands say that the Irish are too lazy to continue at the trade; but surely the labour of the hodman, in which the Irish seem to delight, is sufficient to disprove this assertion, be the cause what it may. About one-fourth of the scavagers entering the scavaging trade as casual hands have been agricultural labourers, and have come up to London from the several agricultural districts in quest of work; about the same proportion appear to have been connected with horses, such as ostlers, carmen, &c.

The *brisk and slack seasons* in the scavaging trade depend upon the state of the weather. In the depth of winter, owing to the shortness of the days, more hands are usually required for street cleansing; but a "clear frost" renders the scavager's labour in little demand. In the winter, too, his work is generally the hardest, and the hardest of all when there is snow, which soon becomes mud in London streets; and though a continued frost is a sort of lull to the scavagers' labour, after "a great thaw" his strength is taxed to the uttermost; and then, indeed, new hands have had to be put on. At the West End, in the height of the summer, which is usually the height of the fashionable season, there is again a more than usual requirement of scavaging industry in wet weather; but perhaps the greatest exercise of such industry is after a series of the fogs peculiar to the London atmosphere, when the men cannot *see* to sweep. The table I have given shows the influence of the weather, as on wet days 531 men are employed, and on dry days only 358; this, however, does not influence the Street-Orderly system, as under it the men are employed every day, unless the weather make it an actual impossibility.

According to the rain table given at p. 202, there would appear to be, on an average of 23 years, 178 wet days in London out of the 365, that is to say, about 100 in every 205 days are "rainy ones." The months having the greatest and least number of wet days are as follows:—

	No. of days in the month in which rain falls.
December	17
July, August, October	16
February, May, November	15
January, April	14
March, September	12
June	11

Hence it would appear that June is the least and December the most showery month in the course of the year; the greatest *quantity* of rain falling in any month is, however, in October, and the least quantity in March. The number of wet days, and the quantity of rain falling in each half of the year, may be expressed as follows:—

	Total in No. of wet days.	Total depth of rain falling in inches.
The first six months in the year ending June there are	84	10
The second six months in the year ending December there are	93	14

Hence we perceive that the quantity of work for the scavagers would fluctuate in the first and last half of the year in the proportion of 10 to 14, which is very nearly in the ratio of 358 to 531, which are the numbers of hands given in table pp. 186, 187, as those employed in wet and dry weather throughout the metropolis.

If, then, the labour in the scavaging trade varies in the proportion of 5 to 7, that is to say, that 5 hands are required at one period and 7 at another to execute the work, the question consequently becomes, how do the 2 casuals who are discharged out of every 7 obtain their living when the wet season is over?

When a scavager is out of employ, he seldom or never applies to the parish; this he does, I am informed, only when he is fairly "beaten out" through sickness or old age, for the men "hate the thought of going to the big house" (the union workhouse). An unemployed operative scavager will go from yard to yard and offer his services to do anything in the dust trade or any other kind of employment in connection with dust or scavaging.

Generally speaking, an operative scavager who is casually employed obtains work at that trade for six or eight months during the year, and the remaining portion of his time is occupied either at rubbish-carting or brick-carting, or else he gets a job for a month or two in a dust-yard.

Many of these men seem to form a body of street-jobbers or operative labourers, ready to work at the docks, to be navvies (when strong enough), bricklayers' labourers, street-sweepers, carriers of trunks or parcels, window-cleaners, errand-goers, porters, and (occasionally) nightmen. Few of the class seem to apply themselves to trading, as in the costermonger line. They are the loungers about the boundaries of trading, but seldom take any onward steps. The street-sweeper of this week, a "casual" hand, may be a rubbish-carter or a labourer about buildings the next, or he may be a starving man for days together, and the more he is starving with the less energy will he exert himself to obtain work: "it's not in" a starving or ill-fed man to exert himself otherwise than what may be called *passively*; this is well known to all who have paid attention to the subject. The want of energy and carelessness begotten by want of food was well described by the tinman, at p. 355 in vol. i.

One casual hand told me that last year he was out of work altogether three months, and the year before not more than six weeks, and during the six weeks he got a day's work sometimes at rubbish carting and sometimes at loading bricks. Their wives are often employed in the yards as sifters, and their boys, when big enough, work also at the heap, either in carrying off, or else as fillers-in; if there are any girls, one is generally left at home to look after the rest and get the meals ready for the other members of the family. If any of the children go to school, they are usually sent to a ragged school in the neighbourhood, though they seldom attend the school more than two or three times during the week.

The additional hands employed in wet weather are either men who at other times work in the yards, or such as have their "turns" in street-sweeping, if not regularly employed. There appears, however, to be little of system in the arrangement. If more hands are wanted, the gangsman, who receives his orders from the contractor or the contractor's managing man, is told to put on so many new hands, and over-night he has but to tell any of the men at work that Jack, and Bob, and Bill will be wanted in the morning, and they, if not employed in other work, appear accordingly.

There is nothing, however, which can be designated a *labour market* appertaining to the trade. No "house of call," no trade society. If men seek such employment, they must apply at the contractor's premises, and I am assured that poor men not unfrequently ask the scavagers whom they see at work in the streets where to apply "for a job," and sometimes receive gruff or abusive replies. But though there is nothing like a labour market in the scavager's trade, the employers have not to "look out" for men, for I was told by one of their foremen, that he would undertake, if necessary, which it never was, by a mere "round of the docks," to select 200 new hale men, of all classes, and strong ones, too, if properly fed, who in a few days would be tolerable street-sweepers. It is a calling to which agricultural labourers are glad to resort, and a calling to which *any* labourer or any mechanic may resort, more especially as regards sweeping or scraping, apart from shovelling, which is regarded as something like the high art of the business.

We now come to estimate the earnings of the casual hands, whose yearly incomes must, of course, be very different from those of the regulars. The *constant* weekly wages of any workman are of course the average of his casual—and hence we shall find the wages of those who are *regularly* employed far exceed those of the *occasionally* employed men:—

	£	s.	d.
Nominal yearly wages at scavaging for 25 weeks in the year, at 16s. per week	20	16	0
Perquisites for 26 weeks, at 2s.	2	12	0
Actual yearly wages at scavaging	23	8	0
Nominal and actual weekly wages at rubbish carting for 20 weeks in the year, at 12s.	12	0	0
Unemployed six weeks in the year	0	0	0
Gross yearly earnings	35	8	0
Average casual or constant weekly wages throughout the year		15	4½

Hence the difference between the earnings of the casual and the regular hand would appear to be one-sixth. But the great evil of all casual labour is the uncertainty of the income—for where there is the greatest chance connected with an employment, there is not only the greatest necessity for providence, but unfortunately the greatest tendency to improvidence. It is only when a man's income becomes regular and fixed that he grows thrifty, and lays by for the future; but where all is chance-work there is but little ground for reasoning, and the accident which assisted the man out of his difficulties at one period is continually expected to do the same good turn for him at another. Hence the casual hand, who passes the half of the year on 18s., and twenty weeks on 12s., and *six weeks on nothing*, lives a life of excess both ways—of excess of "guzzling" when in work, and excess of privation when out of it—oscillating, as it were, between surfeit and starvation.

A man who had worked in an iron-foundry, but who had "lost his work" (I believe through some misconduct) and was glad to get employment as a street-sweeper, as he had a good recommendation to a contractor, told me that " the misery of the thing" was the want of regular work. "I've worked," he said, "for a good master for four months an end at 2s. 8d. a day, and they were prime times. Then I hadn't a stroke of work for a fortnight, and very little for two months, and if my wife hadn't had middling work with a laundress we might have starved, or I might have made a hole in the Thames, for it's no good living to be miserable and feel you can't help yourself any how. We was sometimes half-starved, as it was. I'd rather at this minute have regular work at 10s. a week all the year round, than have chance-work that I could earn 20s. a week at. I once had 15s. in relief from the parish, and a doctor to attend us, when my wife and I was both laid up sick. O, there's no difference in the way of doing the work, whatever wages you're on for; the streets must be swept clean, of course. The plan's the same, and there's the same sort of management, any how."

STATEMENT OF A "REGULAR SCAVAGER."

THE following statement of his business, his sentiments, and, indeed, of the subjects which concerned him, or about which he was questioned, was given to me by a street-sweeper, so he called himself, for I have found some of these men not to relish the appellation of "scavager." He was a short, sturdy, somewhat red-faced man, without anything particular in his appearance to distinguish him from the mass of mere labourers, but with the sodden and sometimes dogged look of a man contented in his ignorance, and—for it is not a very uncommon case—rather proud of it.

"I don't know how old I am," he said—I have observed, by the by, that there is not any excessive vulgarity in these men's tones or accent so much as grossness in some of their expressions— "and I can't see what that consarns any one, as I's old enough to have a jolly rough beard, and so can take care of myself. I should think so. My father was a sweeper, and I wanted to be a waterman, but father—he hasn't been dead long— didn't like the thoughts on it, as he said they was all drownded one time or 'nother; so I ran away and tried my hand as a Jack-in-the-water, but I was starved back in a week, and got a h—— of a clouting. After that I sifted a bit in a dust-yard, and helped in any way; and I was sent to help at and larn honey-pot and other pot making, at Deptford; but honey-pots was a great thing in the business. Master's foreman married a relation of mine, some way or other. I never tasted honey, but I've heered it's like sugar and butter mixed. The pots was often wanted to look like foreign pots; I don't know nothing what was meant by it; some b—— dodge or other. No, the trade didn't suit me at all, master, so I left. I don't know why it didn't suit me; cause it didn't. Just then, father had hurt his hand and arm, in a jam again' a cart, and so, as I was a big lad, I got to take his place, and gave every satisfaction to Mr. ——. Yes, he was a contractor and a great man. I can't say as I knows how contracting's done; but it's a bargain atween man and man. So I got on. I'm now looked on as a stunning good workman, I can tell you.

"Well, I can't say as I thinks sweeping the streets is hard work. I'd rather sweep two hours than shovel one. It tires one's arms and back so, to go on shovelling. You can't change, you see, sir, and the same parts keeps getting gripped more and more. Then you must mind your eye, if you're shovelling slop into a cart, perticler so; or some feller may run off with a complaint that he's been splashed o' purpose. *Is* a man ever splashed o' purpose? No, sir, not as I knows on, in coorse not. [Laughing.] Why should he?

"The streets *must* be done as they're done now. It always was so, and will always be so. Did I ever hear what London streets were like a thousand years ago? It's nothing to me, but they must have been like what they is now. Yes, there was always streets, or how was people that has tin to get their coals taken to them, and how was the public-houses to get their beer? It's talking nonsense, talking that way, a-asking sich questions." [As the scavager seemed likely to lose his temper, I changed the subject of conversation.]

"Yes," he continued, "I have good health. I never had a doctor but twice; once was for a hurt, and the t'other I won't tell on. Well, I think nightwork's healthful enough, but I'll not say so much for it as you may hear some on 'em say. I don't like it, but I do it when I's obligated under a necessity. It pays one as overwork; and werry like more one's in it, more one may be suited. I reckon no men works harder nor sich as me. O, as to poor journeymen tailors and sich like, I knows they're stunning badly off, and many of their masters is the hardest of beggars. I have a nephew as works for a Jew slop, but I don't reckon that *work ;* anybody might do it. You think not, sir? Werry well, it's all the same. No, I won't say as I could make a veskit, but I've sowed my own buttons on to one afore now.

"Yes, I've heered on the Board of Health. They've put down some night-yards, and if they goes on putting down more, what's to become of the night-soil? I can't think what they're up to; but if they don't touch wages, it may be all right in the end on it. I don't know that them there consarns does touch wages, but one's naterally afeard on 'em. I could read a little when I was a child, but I can't now for want of practice, or I might know more about it. I yarns my money gallows hard, and requires support to do hard work, and if wages goes down, one's strength goes down. I'm a man as understands what things belongs. I was once out of work, through a mistake, for a good many weeks, perhaps five or six or more; I larned then what short grub meant. I got a drop of beer and a crust sometimes with men as I knowed, or I might have dropped in the street. What did I do to pass my time when I was out of work? Sartinly the days seemed wery long; but I went about and called at dust-yards, till I didn't like to go too often; and I met men I know'd at tap-rooms, and spent time that way, and axed if there was any openings for work. I've been out of collar odd weeks now and then, but when this happened, I'd been on slack work a goodish bit, and was bad for rent three weeks and more. My rent was 2s. a week then; its 1s. 9d. now, and my own traps.

"No, I can't say I was sorry when I was forced to be idle that way, that I hadn't kept up my reading, nor tried to keep it up, because I couldn't then have settled down my mind to read; I know I couldn't. I likes to hear the paper read well enough, if I's resting; but old Bill, as often wolunteers to read, has to spell the hard words so, that one can't tell what the devil he's reading about. I never heers anything about books; I never heered of Robinson Crusoe, if it wasn't once at the Wic. [Victoria Theatre]; I think there was some sich a name there. He lived on a deserted island, did he, sir, all by hisself? Well, I think, now you mentions it, I have heered on him. But one needn't believe all one hears, whether out of books or not. I don't know much good that ever anybody as I knows ever got out of books; they're fittest for idle people. Sartinly I've seen working people reading in coffee-shops; but they might as well be resting theirselves to keep up their strength. Do I think so? I'm sure on it, master. I sometimes spends a few browns a-going to the play; mostly about Christmas. It's werry fine and grand at the Wic., that's the place I goes to most; both the pantomimers and t' other things is werry stunning. I can't say how much I spends a year in plays; I keeps no account; perhaps 5s. or so in a year, including expenses, sich as beer, when one goes out after a stopper on the stage. I don't keep no accounts of what I gets, or what I spends, it would be no use; money comes and it goes, and it often goes a d——d sight faster than it comes; so it seems to me, though I ain't in debt just at this time.

"I never goes to any church or chapel. Sometimes I hasn't clothes as is fit, and I s'pose I couldn't be admitted into sich fine places in my working dress. I was once in a church, but felt queer, as one does in them strange places, and never went again. They're fittest for rich people. Yes, I've heered about religion and about God Almighty. *What* religion have I heered on? Why, the regular religion. I'm satisfied with what I knows and feels about it, and that's enough about it. I came to tell you about trade and work, because Mr. —— told me it might do good; but religion hasn't nothing to do with it. Yes, Mr. ——'s a good master, and a religious man; but I've known masters as didn't care a d—n for religion, as good as him; and so you see it comes to much the same thing. I cares nothing about politics neither; but I'm a chartist.

"I'm not a married man. I was a-going to be married to a young woman as lived with me a goodish bit as my housekeeper" [this he said very demurely]; "but she went to the hopping to yarn a few shillings for herself, and never came back. I heered that she'd taken up with an Irish hawker, but I can't say as to the rights on it. Did I fret about her? Perhaps not; but I was wexed.

"I'm sure I can't say what I spends my wages in. I sometimes makes 12s. 6d. a week, and sometimes better than 21s. with night-work. I suppose grub costs 1s. a day, and beer 6d.; but I keeps no accounts. I buy ready-cooked meat; often cold b'iled beef, and eats it at any tap-room. I have meat every day; mostly more than once a day. Wegetables I don't care about, only ingans and cabbage, if you can get it smoking hot, with plenty of pepper. The rest of my tin goes for rent and baccy and togs, and a little drop of gin now and then."

The statement I have given is sufficiently explicit of the general opinions of the "regular scavagers" concerning literature, politics, and religion. On these subjects the great majority of the regular scavagers have no opinions at all, or opinions distorted, even when the facts seem clear and obvious, by ignorance, often united with its nearest of kin, prejudice and suspiciousness. I am inclined to think, however, that the man whose narrative I noted down was more dogged in his ignorance than the body of his fellows. All the intelligent men with whom I conversed, and whose avocations had made them familiar for years with this class, concurred in representing them as grossly ignorant.

This description of the scavagers' ignorance, &c., it must be remembered, applies only to the "regular hands." Those who have joined the ranks of the street-sweepers from other callings are more intelligent, and sometimes more temperate.

The system of concubinage, with a great degree of fidelity in the couple living together without the sanction of the law—such as I have described as prevalent among the costermongers and dustmen—is also prevalent among the regular scavagers.

I did not hear of habitual unkindness from the parents to the children born out of wedlock, but there is habitual neglect of all or much which a child should be taught—a neglect growing out of ignorance. I heard of two scavagers with large families, of whom the treatment was sometimes very harsh, and at others mere petting.

Education, or rather the ability to read and write, is not common among the adults in this calling, so that it cannot be expected to be found among their children. Some labouring men, ignorant themselves, but not perhaps constituting a class or a clique like the regular scavagers, try hard to procure for their children the knowledge, the want of which they usually think has barred their own progress in life. Other ignorant men, mixing only with "their own sort," as is generally the case with the regular scavagers, and in the several branches of the business, often think and say that what *they* did without their children could do without also. I even heard it said by one scavager that it wasn't right a child should ever think himself wiser than his father. A man who knew, in the way of his business as a private contractor for night-work, &c., a great many regular scavagers, "ran them over," and came to the conclusion that about four or five out of twenty could read, ill or tolerably well, and about three out of forty could write. He told me, moreover, that one of the most intelligent fellows generally whom he knew among them, a man whom he had heard read well enough, and always understood to be a tolerable writer, the other day brought a letter from his son, a soldier abroad with his regiment in Lower Canada, and requested my informant to read it to him, as "that kind of writing," although plain enough, was "beyond him." The son, in writing, had availed himself of the superior skill of a corporal in his company, so that the letter, on family matters and feelings, was written by deputy and read by deputy. The costermongers, I have shown, when themselves unable to read, have evinced a fondness for listening to exciting stories of courts and aristocracies, and have even bought penny periodicals to have their contents read to them. The scavagers appear to have no taste for this mode of enjoying themselves; but then their leisure is far more circumscribed than that of the costermongers.

It must be borne in mind that I have all along spoken of the regular (many of them hereditary) scavagers employed by the more liberal contractors.

There are yet accounts of habitations, statements of wages, &c., &c., to be given, in connection with men working for the honourable masters, before proceeding to the scurf-traders.

The working scavagers usually reside in the neighbourhood of the dust-yards, occupying "second-floor backs," kitchens (where the entire house is sublet, a system often fraught with great extortion), or garrets; they usually, and perhaps always, when married, or what they consider "as good," have their own furniture. The rent runs from 1s. 6d. to 2s. 3d. weekly, an average being 1s. 9d. or 1s. 10d. One room which I was in was but barely furnished,—a sort of dresser, serving also for a table; a chest; three chairs (one almost bottomless); an old turn-up bedstead, a Dutch clock, with the minute-hand broken, or as the scavager very well called it when he saw me looking at it, "a stump;" an old "corner cupboard," and some pots and domestic utensils in a closet without a door, but retaining a portion of the hinges on which a door had swung. The rent was 1s. 10d., with a frequent intimation that it ought to be 2s. The place was clean enough, and the scavager seemed proud of it, assuring me that his old woman (wife or concubine) was "a good sort," and kept things as nice as ever she could, washing everything herself, where "other old women lushed." The only ornaments in the room were three profiles of children, cut in black paper and pasted upon white card, tacked to the wall over the fire-place, for mantel-shelf there was none, while one of the three profiles, that of the eldest child (then dead), was "framed," with a glass, and a sort of bronze or "cast" frame, costing, I was told, 15d. This was the apartment of a man in regular employ (with but a few exceptions).

Another scavager with whom I had some conversation about his labours as a nightman, for he was both, gave me a full account of his own diet, which I find to be sufficiently specific as to that of his class generally, but only of the regular hands.

The diet of the regular working scavager (or nightman) seems generally to differ from that of mechanics, and perhaps of other working men, in the respect of his being fonder of salt and *strong-flavoured* food. I have before made the same

THE LONDON SCAVENGER.

[*From a Daguerreotype by* BEARD.]

STREET ORDERLIES.

remark concerning the diet of the poor generally. I do not mean, however, that the scavagers are fond of such animal food as is called "high," for I did not hear that nightmen or scavagers were more tolerant of what approached putridity than other labouring men, and, despite their calling, might sicken at the rankness of some haunches of venison; but they have a great relish for highly-salted cold boiled beef, bacon, or pork, with a saucer-full of red pickled cabbage, or dingy-looking pickled onions, or one or two big, strong, raw onions, of which most of them seem as fond as Spaniards of garlic. This sort of meat, sometimes profusely mustarded, is often eaten in the beer-shops with thick "shives" of bread, cut into big mouthfuls with a clasp pocket-knife, while vegetables, unless indeed the beer-shop can supply a plate of smoking hot potatoes, are uncared for. The drink is usually beer. The same style of eating and the same kind of food characterize the scavager and nightman, when taking his meal at home with his wife or family; but so irregular, and often of necessity, are these men's hours, that they may be said to have no homes, merely places to sleep or dose in.

A working scavager and nightman calculated for me his expenses in eating and drinking, and other necessaries, for the previous week. He had earned 15s., but 1s. of this went to pay off an advance of 5s. made to him by the keeper of a beer-shop, or, as he called it, a "jerry."

	Daily. d.	Weekly. s. d.
Rent of an unfurnished room		1 9
Washing (average)		3
[The man himself washed the dress in which he worked, and generally washed his own stockings.]		
Shaving (when twice a week)		1
Tobacco	1	7
[Short pipes are given to these men at the beer-shops, or public-houses which they "use."]		
Beer	4	2 4
[He usually spent more than 4d. a day in beer, he said, "it was only a pot;" but this week more beer than usual had been given to him in nightwork.]		
Gin	2	1 2
[The same with gin.]		
Cocoa (pint at a coffee-shop)	1½	10½
Bread (quartern loaf) (sometimes 5½d.)	6	3 6
Boiled salt beef (¾ lb. or ½ lb. daily, "as happened," for two meals, 6d. per pound, average	4	2 4
Pickles or Onions	0¼	1¾
Butter		1
Soap		1
		13 2¼

Perhaps this informant was excessive in his drink. I believe he was so; the others not drinking so much regularly. The odd 9d., he told me, he paid to "a snob," because he said he was going to send his half-boots to be mended.

This man informed me he was a "widdur," having lost his old 'oman, and he got all his meals at a beer or coffee-shop. Sometimes, when he was a street-sweeper by day and a nightman by night, he had earned 20s. to 22s.; and then he could have his pound of salt meat a day, for *three* meals, with a "baked tatur or so, when they was in." I inquired as to the apparently low charge of 6d. per pound for cooked meat, but I found that the man had stated what was correct. In many parts good boiled "brisket," fresh cut, is 7d. and 8d. per lb., with mustard into the bargain; and the cook-shop keepers (not the eating-house people) who sell boiled hams, beef, &c., in retail, but not to be eaten on the premises, vend the hard remains of a brisket, and sometimes of a round, for 6d., or even less (also with mustard), and the scavagers like this better than any other food. In the brisk times my informant sometimes had "a hot cut" from a shop on a Sunday, and a more liberal allowance of beer and gin. If he had any piece of clothing to buy he always bought it at once, before his money went for other things. These were his proceedings when business was brisk.

In slacker times his diet was on another footing. He then made his supper, or second meal, for tea he seldom touched, on "fagots." This preparation of baked meats costs 1d. hot— but it is seldom sold hot except in the evening— and ¾d., or more frequently two for 1½d., cold. It is a sort of cake, roll, or ball, a number being baked at a time, and is made of chopped liver and lights, mixed with gravy, and wrapped in pieces of pig's caul. It weighs six ounces, so that it is unquestionably a cheap, and, to the scavager, a savoury meal; but to other nostrils its odour is not seductive. My informant regretted the capital fagots he used to get at a shop when he worked in Lambeth; superior to anything he had been able to meet with on the Middlesex side of the water. Or he dined off a saveloy, costing 1d., and bread; or bought a pennyworth of strong cheese, and a farthing's worth of onions. He would further reduce his daily expenditure on cocoa (or coffee sometimes) to 1d., and his bread to three-quarters of a loaf. He ate, however, in average times, a quarter of a quartern loaf to his breakfast (sometimes buying a halfpennyworth of butter), a quarter or more to his dinner, the same to his supper, and the other, with an onion for a relish, to his beer. He was a great bread eater, he said; but sometimes, if he slept in the day-time, half a loaf would "stand over to next day." He was always hungriest when at work among the street-mud or night-soil, or when he had finished work.

On my asking him if he meant that he partook of the meals he had described daily, "he answered "no," but that was *mostly* what he had; and if he bought a bit of cold boiled, or even roast pork, "what offered cheap," the expense was about the same. When he was drinking, and he did "make a break sometimes," he ate nothing, and "wasn't inclined to," and he seemed rather to plume himself on this, as a point of economy. He had tasted fruit pies, but cared nothing for them; but liked four penn'orth of a hot meat or giblet pie on a Sunday. Batter-pudding he only liked if smoking hot; and it was "uncommon improved," he said, "with an ingan!" Rum he preferred to gin, only it was dearer, but most of the scavagers, he thought, liked Old Tom (gin) best; but "they was both good."

Of the drinking of these men I heard a good deal, and there is no doubt that some of them tope hard, and by their conduct evince a sort of belief that the great end of labour is beer. But it must be borne in mind that if inquiries are made as to the man best adapted to give information concerning any rude calling (especially), some talkative member of the body of these working men, some pot-house hero who has persuaded himself and his ignorant mates that he is an oracle, is put forward. As these men are sometimes, from being trained to, and long known in their callings, more prosperous than their fellows, their opinions seem ratified by their circumstances. But in such cases, or in the appearance of such cases, it has been my custom to make subsequent inquiries, or there might be frequent misleadings, were the statements of these men taken as typical of the feelings and habits of the *whole* body. The statement of the working scavager given under this head is unquestionably typical of the character of a portion of his co-workers, and more especially of what was, and in the sort of hereditary scavagers I have spoken of *is*, the character of the regular hands. There are now, however, many checks to prolonged indulgence in "lush," as every man of the ruder street-sweeping class *will* call it. The contractors must be served regularly; the most indulgent will not tolerate any unreasonable absence from work, so that the working scavagers, at the jeopardy of their means of living, must leave their carouse at an hour which will permit them to rise soon enough in the morning.

The beer which these men imbibe, it should be also remembered, they regard as a proper part of their diet, in the same light, indeed, as they regard so much bread, and that among them the opinion is almost universal, that beer is necessary to "keep up their strength;" there are a few teetotallers belonging to the class; one man thought he *knew* five, and had *heard* of five others.

I inquired of the landlord of a beer-shop, frequented by these men, as to their potations, but he wanted to make it appear that they took a half-pint, *now and then*, when thirsty! He was evidently tender of the character of his customers. The landlord of a public-house also frequented by them informed me that he really could not say what they expended in beer, for labourers of all kinds "used his tap," and as all tap-room liquor was paid for on delivery in his and all similar establishments, he did not know the quantity supplied to any particular class. He was satisfied these men, as a whole, drank less than they did at one time; though he had no doubt some (he seemed to know no distinctions between scavagers, dustmen, and nightmen) spent 1s. a day in drink. He knew one scavager who was dozing about not long since for nearly a week, "sleepy drunk," and the belief was that he had "found something." The absence of all accounts prevents my coming to anything definite on this head, but it seems positive that these men drink less than they did. The landlord in question thought the statement I have given as to diet and drink perfectly correct for a regular hand in good earnings. I am assured, however, and it is my own opinion, after long inquiry, that one-third of their earnings is spent in drink.

OF THE INFLUENCE OF FREE TRADE ON THE EARNINGS OF THE SCAVAGERS.

As regards the influence of Free Trade upon the scavaging business, I could gain little or no information from the body of street-sweepers, because they have never noticed its operation, and the men, with the exception of such as have sunk into street-sweeping from better-informed conditions of life, know nothing about it. Among *all*, however, I have heard statements of the blessing of cheap bread; always cheap *bread*. "There's nothing like bread," say the men, "it's not all poor people can get meat; but they *must* get bread." Cheap food all labouring men pronounce a blessing, as it unquestionably is, but "somehow," as a scavager's carman said to me, "the thing ain't working as it should."

In the course of the present and former inquiries among unskilled labourers, street-sellers, and costermongers, I have found the great majority of the more intelligent declare that Free Trade had not worked well for them, because there were more labourers and more street-sellers than were required, for each man to live by his toil and traffic, and because the numbers increased yearly, and the demand for their commodities did not increase in proportion. Among the ignorant, I heard the continual answers of, "I can't say, sir, what it's owing to, that I'm so bad off;" or, "Well, I can't tell anything about that."

It is difficult to state, however, without positive inquiry, whether this extra number of hands be due to diminished employment in the agricultural districts, since the repeal of the Corn Laws, or whether it be due to the insufficiency of occupation generally for the increasing population. One thing at least is evident, that the increase of the trades alluded to cannot be said to arise directly from diminished agricultural employment, for but few farm labourers have entered these businesses since the change from Protection to Free Trade. If, therefore, Free-Trade principles *have* operated injuriously in reducing the work of the unskilled labourers, street-sellers, and the poorer classes generally, it can have done so only *indirectly*; that is to say, by throwing a mass of displaced country labour into the towns, and so displacing other labourers from their ordinary occupations, as well as by decreasing the wages of working-men generally. Hence it becomes almost impossible, I repeat, to tell whether the increasing difficulty that the poor experience in living by their labour, is a consequence or merely a concomitant of the repeal of the Corn Laws; if it be a consequence, of course the poor are no better for the alteration; if, however, it be a coincidence rather than a necessary result of the measure, the circumstances of the poor are, of course, as much improved as they would have been impoverished provided that measure had never become law. I candidly confess I am as yet without the means of coming to any conclusion on this part of the subject.

Nor can it be said that in the scavagers' trade wages have in any way declined since the repeal of the Corn Laws; so that were it not for the difficulty of obtaining employment among the *casual* hands, this class must be allowed to have been considerable gainers by the reduction in the price of food, and even as it is, the *constant* hands must be acknowledged to be so.

I will now endeavour to reduce to a tabular form such information as I could obtain as to the expenditure of the labourer in scavaging before and after the establishment of Free Trade. I inquired, the better to be assured of the accuracy of the representations and accounts I received from labourers, the price of meat then and now. A butcher who for many years has conducted a business in a populous part of Westminster and in a populous suburb, supplying both private families with the best joints, and the poor with their "little bits" their "block ornaments" (meat in small pieces exposed on the chopping-block), their purchases of liver, and of beasts' heads. In 1845, the year I take as sufficiently prior to the Free-Trade era, my informant from his recollection of the state of his business and from consulting his books, which of course were a correct guide, found that for a portion of the year in question, mutton was as much as $7\frac{1}{2}d.$ per lb. (Smithfield prices), now the same quality of meat is but $5d.$ This, however, was but a temporary matter, and from causes which sometimes are not very ostensible or explicable. Taking the butcher's trade that year as a whole, it was found sufficiently conclusive, that meat was generally $1d.$ per lb. higher then than at present. My informant, however, was perfectly satisfied that, although situated in the same way, and with the same class of customers, he did *not* sell so much meat to the poor and labouring classes as he did five or six years ago, *he believed not by one-eighth*, although perhaps "pricers of his meat" among the poor were more numerous. For this my informant accounted by expressing his conviction that the labouring men spent their money in drink more than ever, and were a longer time in recovering from the effects of tippling. This supposition, from what I have observed in the course of the present inquiry, is negatived by facts.

Another butcher, also supplying the poor, said they bought less of him; but he could not say exactly to what extent, perhaps an eighth, and he attributed it to less work, there being no railways about London, fewer buildings, and less general employment. About the wages of the labourers he could not speak as influencing the matter. From this tradesmen also I received an account that meat generally was $1d.$ per lb. higher at the time specified. Pickled Australian beef was four or five years ago very low—$3d.$ per lb.—salted and prepared, and "swelling" in hot water, but the poor "couldn't eat the stringy stuff, for it was like pickled ropes." "It's better now," he added, "but it don't sell, and there's no nourishment in such beef."

But these tradesmen agreed in the information that poor labourers bought less meat, while one pronounced Free Trade a blessing, the other declared it a curse. I suggested to each that cheaper fish might have something to do with a smaller consumption of butcher's meat, but both said that cheap fish was the great thing for the Irish and the poor needle-women and the like, who were never at any time meat eaters.

From respectable bakers I ascertained that bread might be considered $1d.$ a quartern loaf dearer in 1845 than at present. Perhaps the following table may throw a fuller light on the matter. I give it from what I learned from several men, who were without accounts to refer to, but speaking positively from memory; I give the statement per week, as for a single man, without charge for the support of a wife and family, and without any help from other resources.

	Before Free Trade.	After Free Trade.	Saving since Free Trade.
Rent	1s. 6d.	1s. 6d.	...
Bread (5 loaves)	2s. 11d.	2s. 6d.	5d
Butter ($\frac{1}{2}$ lb.)	5d.	5d.	...
Tea (2 oz.)	8d.	8d.	...
Sugar ($\frac{1}{4}$ lb.)	3d.	2d.	1d.
Meat (3 lb.)	1s. 6d.	1s. 3d.	3d.
Bacon (1 lb.)	5d.	5d.	...
Fish (a dinner a day, 6 days)	3d., or 1s. 6d. weekly.	2d., or 1s. weekly.	6d.
Potatoes or Vegetables ($\frac{1}{2}d.$ a day)	$3\frac{1}{2}d.$	$3\frac{1}{2}d.$	...
Beer (pot)	$3\frac{1}{2}d.$	$3\frac{1}{2}d.$	...

Total saving, per week, since Free Trade 1s. 3d.

In butter, bacon, potatoes, &c., and beer, I could hear of no changes, except that bacon might be a trifle cheaper, but instead of a good quality selling better, although cheaper, there was a demand for an inferior sort.

In the foregoing table the weekly consumption of several necessaries is given, but it is not to be understood that one man consumes them all in a week; they are what may generally be consumed when such things are in demand by the poor, one week after another, or one day after another, forming an aggregate of weeks.

Thus, Free Trade and cheap provisions are an unquestionable benefit, if unaffected by drawbacks, to the labouring poor.

The above statement refers only to a fully employed hand.

The following table gives the change since Free Trade in the earnings of casual hands, and relates to the past and the present expenditure of a scavager. The man, who was formerly a house painter, said he could bring me 50 men similarly circumstanced to himself.

In 1845, per Week.			In 1851, per Week.		
	s.	d.		s.	d.
Rent	1	4	Rent	1	8
5 loaves	2	11	4 loaves	2	0
Butter	0	5	Butter	0	5
Tea	0	6	Tea	0	5
Meat (3 lbs.)	1	6	Meat (3 lbs.)	1	0
Potatoes	0	3	Potatoes	0	2
Beer (a pot)	0	4	Beer (a pint)	0	2
	7	3		5	10

Here, then, we find a positive saving in the expenditure of 1s. 5d. per week in this man's wages, since the cheapening of food.

His earnings, however, tell a different story.

	1845.		1851.	
	s.	d.	s.	d.
Earnings of 6 days	15	0		
Ditto 3 days			7	6
Weekly Income	15	0	7	6
Expenditure	7	3	5	10
Difference	7	9	1	8

Thus we perceive that the beneficial effects of cheapness are defeated by the dearth of employment among labourers.

It is impossible to come to *precise* statistics in this matter, but all concurrent evidence, as regards the unskilled work of which I now treat, shows that attainable is attainable at almost any rate.

Another drawback to the benefits of cheap food I heard of first in my inquiries (for the Letters on Labour and the Poor, in the *Morning Chronicle*) among the boot and shoemakers—their rents had been raised in consequence of their landlords' property having been subjected to the income tax. Numbers of large houses are now let out in single rooms, in the streets off Tottenham-court-road, and near Golden-square, as well as in many other quarters—to men, who, working for West-end tradesmen, must live, for economy of time, near the shops from which they derive their work. Near and in Cunningham-street and other streets, two men, father and son, rent upwards of 30 houses, the whole of which they let out in one or two rooms, it is believed at a very great profit; in fact they live by it.

The rent of these houses, among many others, was raised when the income tax was imposed, the sub-lettors declaring, with what truth no one knew, that the rents were raised to them. It is common enough for capitalists to fling such imposts on the shoulders of the poor, and I heard scavagers complain, that every time they had to change their rooms, they had either to pay more rent by 2d. or 3d. a week, or put up with a worse place. One man who lived at the time of the passing of the Income Tax Bill in Shoe-lane, found his rent raised suddenly 3d. a week, a non-resident landlord or agent calling for it weekly. He was told that the advance was to meet the income tax. "I know nothing about what income tax means," he said, "but it's some —— roguery as is put on the poor." I heard complaints to the same purport from several working scavagers, and the lettors of rooms are the most exacting in places crowded with the poor, and where the poor think or feel they must reside "to be handy for work." What connection there may be between the questions of Free Trade and the necessity of the income tax, it is not my business now to dilate upon, but it is evident that the circumstances of the country are not sufficiently prosperous to enable parliament to repeal this "temporary" impost.

From a better informed class than the scavagers, I might have derived data on which to form a calculation from account books, &c., but I could hear of none being kept. I remember that a lady's shoemaker told me that the weekly rents of the ten rooms in the house in which he lived were 4s. 3d. higher than before the income tax, which "came to the same thing as an extra penny on over 50 loaves a week." It is certain that the great tax-payers of London are the labouring classes.

I have endeavoured to ascertain the facts in connection with this complex subject in as calm and just a manner as possible, leaning neither to the Protectionist nor the Free-Trade side of the question, and I must again in honesty acknowledge, that to the *constant* hands among the scavagers and dustmen of the metropolis, the repeal of the Corn Laws appears to have been an unquestionable benefit.

I shall conclude this exposition of the condition and earnings of the working scavagers employed by the more honourable masters, with an account of the average income and expenditure of the better-paid hands (regular and casual, as well as single and married), and first, of the unmarried regular hand.

The following is an estimate of the income and expenditure of an *unmarried* operative scavager *regularly* employed, working for a large contractor:—

LONDON LABOUR AND THE LONDON POOR.

WEEKLY INCOME.				WEEKLY EXPENDITURE.			
	£	s.	d.		£	s.	d.
Constant Wages.				Rent	0	2	0
Nominal weekly wages	0	16	0	Washing and mending......	0	0	10
Perquisites	0	2	0	Clothes, and repairing ditto..	0	0	10
Actual weekly wages	0	18	0	Butcher's meat..	0	3	6
				Bacon	0	0	8
				Vegetables......	0	0	4
				Cheese	0	0	4
				Beer.............	0	3	0
				Spirits.........	0	1	0
				Tobacco.........	0	0	10½
				Butter..........	0	0	7½
				Sugar	0	0	4
				Tea	0	0	3
				Coffee	0	0	3
				Fish............	0	0	4
				Soap	0	0	2
				Shaving	0	0	1
				Fruit	0	0	4
				Keep of 2 dogs..	0	0	6
				Amusements, as skittles, &c. ..	0	1	9
					0	18	0

The subjoined represents the income of an *unmarried* operative scavager *casually* employed by a small master scavager six months during the year, at 15s. a week, and 20 weeks at sand and rubbish carting, at 12s. a week.

Casual Wages.	£	s.	d.
Nominal weekly wages at scavaging, 16s. for 26 weeks during the year	20	16	0
Perquisites, 2s. for 26 weeks during the year ..	2	12	0
Actual weekly wages for 26 weeks during the year	0	16	0
Nominal and actual weekly wages at rubbish carting, 12s. for 20 weeks more during the year	12	0	0
Average casual or constant weekly wages throughout the year	0	15	4½

The expenditure of this man when in work was nearly the same as that of the regular hand; the main exceptions being that his rent was 1s. instead of 2s., and no dogs were kept. When in work he saved nothing, and when out of work lived as he could.

The *married* scavagers are differently circumstanced from the *unmarried;* their earnings are generally increased by those of their family.

The labour of the wives and children of the scavagers is not unfrequently in the capacity of sifters in the dust-yards, where the wives of the men employed by the contractors have the preference, and in other but somewhat rude capacities. One of their wives I heard of as a dresser of sheep's trotters; two as being among the most skilful dressers of tripe for a large shop; one as "a cat's-meat seller" (her father's calling); but I still speak of the regular scavagers—I could not meet with one woman "working a slop-needle." One, indeed, I saw who was described to me as a "feather dresser to an out-and-out negur," but the woman assured me she was neither badly paid nor badly off. Perhaps by such labour, as an average on the part of the wives, 9d. a day is cleared, and 1s. "on tripe and such like." Among the "casual's" wives there are frequent instances of the working for slop shirt-makers, &c., upon the coarser sorts of work, and at "starvation wages," but on such matters I have often dwelt. I heard from some of these men that it was looked upon as a great thing if the wife's labour could clear the week's rent of 1s. 6d. to 2s.

The following may be taken as an estimate of the income and outlay of a *better paid and fully* employed operative scavager, with his wife and two children:—

WEEKLY INCOME OF THE FAMILY.				WEEKLY EXPENDITURE OF THE FAMILY.			
	£	s.	d.		£	s.	d.
Nominal weekly wages of man, 16s.				Rent	0	3	0
				Candle	0	0	3½
				Bread	0	2	1
Perquisites, 2s.				Butter.........	0	0	10
Actual weekly wages of man.	0	18	0	Sugar	0	0	8
				Tea	0	0	10
Nominal weekly wages of wife, 6s.				Coffee	0	0	4
				Butcher's meat..	0	3	6
Perquisites in coal and wood, 1s. 4d.				Bacon	0	1	2
				Potatoes.......	0	0	10
				Raw fish.......	0	0	4
Actual weekly wages of wife.	0	7	4	Herrings	0	0	4
				Beer (at home)..	0	2	0
Nominal weekly wages of boy..	0	3	0	,, (at work)..	0	1	6
	1	8	4	Spirits.........	0	1	0
				Cheese	0	0	6
				Flour	0	0	3
				Suet............	0	0	3
				Fruit	0	0	3
				Rice...........	0	0	0½
				Soap	0	0	6
				Starch.........	0	0	0½
				Soda and blue ..	0	0	1
				Dubbing	0	0	0½
				Clothes for the whole family, and repairing ditto	0	2	0
				Boots and shoes for ditto, ditto	0	1	6
				Milk	0	0	7
				Salt, pepper, and mustard	0	0	1
				Tobacco........	0	0	9
				Wear and tear of bedding, crocks, &c.	0	0	3
				Schooling for girl	0	0	3
				Baking Sunday's dinner........	0	0	2
				Mangling	0	0	3
				Amusements and sundries......	0	1	0
					1	7	6

The subjoined, on the other hand, gives the income and outlay of a *casually employed* operative scavager (*better paid*) with his wife and two boys in constant work :—

WEEKLY INCOME OF THE FAMILY.				WEEKLY EXPENDITURE OF THE FAMILY.			
	£	s.	d.		£	s.	d.
Nominal wages of man at scavaging for six months, at 16s. weekly.				Rent	0	3	6
				Candle	0	0	6
				Soap	0	0	4
Ditto at rubbish carting three months, 12s. weekly.				Soda, starch, and blue............	0	0	2½
				Bread	0	2	6
				Butter.........	0	0	9
Average casual wages throughout the year ..	0	15	0	Dripping	0	0	5
				Sugar	0	0	8
				Tea	0	0	8
Nominal weekly wages of wife, 6s. (constant).				Coffee	0	0	6
				Butcher's meat..	0	3	6
				Bacon	0	1	0
Perquisites in wood and coal, 1s 4d.				Potatoes........	0	1	0
				Cheese	0	0	6
				Raw fish........	0	0	4
				Herrings.......	0	0	3
Actual weekly wages of wife.	0	7	4	Fried fish	0	0	3
				Flour	0	0	3
				Suet............	0	0	2

	£	s.	d.		£	s.	d.
Nominal weekly wages of two boys, 7s. the two				Fruit	0	0	6
				Rice	0	0	1½
				Beer (at home)	0	2	0
Perquisites for running on messages, 1s. the two (constant).				,, (at work)	0	1	9
				Spirits	0	1	0
				Tobacco	0	0	9
				Pepper, salt, and mustard	0	0	1
				Milk	0	0	7
Actual weekly wages of the two boys	0	8	0	Clothes for man, wife, and family	0	2	0
				Repairing ditto for ditto	0	0	6
	1	10	4	Boots and shoes for ditto	0	1	6
				Repairing ditto for ditto	0	0	8
				Wear and tear of bedding, crocks, &c.	0	0	3
				Baking Sunday's dinner	0	0	2
				Mangling	0	0	2
				Amusements, sundries, &c.	0	1	0
					1	10	4

OF THE WORSE PAID SCAVAGERS, OR THOSE WORKING FOR SCURF* EMPLOYERS.

THERE are in the scavagers' trade the same distinct classes of employers as appertain to all other trades; these consist of:—

1. The large capitalists.
2. The small capitalists.

As a rule (with some few honourable and dishonourable exceptions, it is true) I find that the large capitalists in the several trades are generally the employers who pay the higher wages, and the small men those who pay the lower. The reasons for this conduct are almost obvious. The power of the capital of the "large master" must be contended against by the small one; and the usual mode of contention in all trades is by reducing the wages of the working men. The wealthy master has, of course, many advantages over the poor one. (1) He can pay ready money, and obtain discounts for immediate payment. (2) He can buy in large quantities, and so get his stock cheaper. (3) He can purchase what he wants in the best markets, and that *directly* of the producer, without the intervention and profit of the middleman. (4) He can buy at the best times and seasons; and "lay in" what he requires for the purposes of his trade long before it is needed, provided he can obtain it "a bargain." (5) He can avail himself of the best tools and mechanical contrivances for increasing the productiveness or "economizing the labour" of his workmen. (6) He can build and arrange his places of work upon the most approved plan and in the best situations for the manufacture and distribution of the commodities. (7) He can employ the highest talent for the management or design of the work on which he is engaged. (8) He can institute a more effective system for the surveillance and checking of his workmen. (9) He can employ a large number of hands, and so reduce the secondary expenses (of firing, lighting, &c.) attendant upon the work, as well as the number of superintendents and others engaged to "look after" the operatives. (10) He can resort to extensive means of making his trade known. (11) He can sell cheaper (even if his cost of production be the same), from employing a larger capital, and being able to "do with" a less rate of profit. (12) He can afford to give credit, and so obtain customers that he might otherwise lose.

The small capitalist, therefore, enters the field of competition by no means equally matched against his more wealthy rival. What the little master wants in "substance," however, he generally endeavours to make up in cunning. If he cannot buy his materials as cheap as a trader of larger means, he uses an inferior or cheaper article, and seeks by some trick or other to palm it off as equal to the superior and dearer kind. If the tools and appliances of the trade are expensive, he either transfers the cost of providing them to the workmen, or else he charges them a rent for their use; and so with the places of work, he mulcts their wages of a certain sum per week for the gas by which they labour, or he makes them do their work at home, and thus saves the expense of a workshop; and, lastly, he pays his men either a less sum than usual for the same quantity of labour, or exacts a greater quantity from them for the same sum of money. By one or other of these means does the man of limited capital seek to counterbalance the advantages which his more wealthy rival obtains by the possession of extensive "resources." The large employer is enabled to work cheaper by the sheer force of his larger capital. He reduces the cost of production, not by employing a cheaper labour, but by "economizing the labour" that he does employ. The small employer, on the other hand, seeks to keep pace with his larger rival, and strives to work cheap, not by "the economy of labour" (for this is hardly possible in the small way of production), but by reducing the wages of his labourers. Hence the *rule* in almost every trade is that the smaller capitalists pay a lower rate of wages. To this, however, there are many honourable exceptions among the small masters, and many as dishonourable among the larger ones in different trades. Messrs. Moses, Nicoll, and Hyams, for instance, are men who certainly cannot plead deficiency of means as an excuse for reducing the ordinary rate of wages among the tailors.

Those employers who seek to reduce the prices of a trade are known technologically as "*cutting employers*," in contradistinction to the standard employers, or those who pay their workpeople and sell their goods at the ordinary rates.

Of "cutting employers" there are several kinds, differently designated, according to the different means by which they gain their ends. These are:—

---

* The Saxon *Sceorfa*, which is the original of the English Scurf, means a scab, and scab is the term given to the "cheap men" in the shoemaking trade. Scab is the root of our word *Shabby*; hence Scurf and Scab, deprived of their offensive associations, both mean shabby fellows.

1. "*Drivers*," or those who compel the men in their employ to do more work for the same wages; of this kind there are two distinct varieties:—
   a. *The long-hour masters*, or those who make the men work longer than the usual hours of labour.
   b. *The strapping masters*, or those who make the men (by extra supervision) "strap" to their work, so as to do a greater quantity of labour in the usual time.
2. *Grinders*, or those who compel the workmen (through their necessities) to do the same amount of work for less than the ordinary wages.

The reduction of wages thus brought about may or may not be attended with a corresponding reduction in the price of the goods to the public; if the price of the goods be reduced in proportion to the reduction of wages, the consumer, of course, is benefited at the expense of the producer. When it is not followed by a like diminution in the selling price of the article, and the wages of which the men are mulct go to increase the profits of the capitalist, the employer alone is benefited, and is then known as a "*grasper*."

Some cutting tradesmen, however, endeavour to undersell their more wealthy rivals, by reducing the ordinary rate of profit, and extending their business on the principle of small profits and quick returns, the "nimble ninepence" being considered "better than the slow shilling." Such traders, of course, cannot be said to reduce wages directly—indirectly, however, they have the same effect, for in reducing prices, other traders, ever ready to compete with them, but, unwilling, or perhaps unable, to accept less than the ordinary rate of profit, seek to attain the same cheapness by diminishing the cost of production, and for this end the labourers' wages are almost invariably reduced.

Such are the characteristics of the cheap employers in all trades. Let me now proceed to point out the peculiarities of what are called the scurf employers in the scavaging trade.

The insidious practices of capitalists in other callings, in reducing the hire of labour, are not unknown to the scavagers. The evils of which these workmen have to complain under scurf or slop masters are:—
1. *Driving*, or being compelled to do more work for the *same pay*.
2. *Grinding*, or being compelled to do the same or a greater amount of work for *less pay*.

1. Under the first head, if the employment be at all regular, I heard few complaints, for the men seemed to have learned to look upon it as an inevitable thing, that one way or other they *must* submit, by the receipt of a reduced wage, or the exercise of a greater toil, to a deterioration in their means.

The system of driving, or, in other words, the means by which extra work is got out of the men for the same remuneration, in the scavagers' trade is as follows:—some employers cause their scavagers after their day's work in the streets, to load the barges with the street and house-collected manure, without any additional payment; whereas, among the more liberal employers, there are bargemen who are employed to attend to this department of the trade, and if their street scavagers *are* so employed, which is not very often, it is computed as extra work or "over hours," and paid for accordingly. This same indirect mode of reducing wages (by getting more work done for the same pay) is seen in many piece-work callings. The slop boot and shoe makers pay the same price as they did six or seven years ago, but they have "knocked off the extras," as the additional allowance for greater than the ordinary height of heel, and the like. So the slop Mayor of Manchester, Sir Elkanah Armitage, within the last year or two, sought to obtain from his men a greater length of "cut" to each piece of woven for the same wages.

Some master scavagers or contractors, moreover, reduce wages by making their men do what is considered the work of "a man and a half" in a week, without the recompense due for the labour of the "half" man's work; in other words, they require the men to condense eight or nine days' labour into six, and to be paid for the six days only; this again is usual in the strapping shops of the carpenters' trade.

Thus the class of street-sweepers do not differ materially in the circumstances of their position from other bodies of workers skilled and unskilled.

Let me, however, give a practical illustration of the loss accruing to the working scavagers by the *driving* method of reducing wages.

A is a large contractor and a driver. He employs 16 men, and pays them the "regular wages" of the honourable trade; but, instead of limiting the hours of labour to 12, as is usual among the better class of employers, he compels each of his men to work at the least 16 hours per diem, which is one-third more, and for which the men should receive one-third more wages. Let us see, therefore, how much the men in his employ lose annually by these means.

	Sum received per Annum.	Sum they should receive.	Difference.
	£ s.	£ s.	£ s.
4 Gangers, at 18s. a week, for 9 months in the year........	140 8	210 12	70 4
12 Sweepers, at 16s. a week, for 9 months in the year........	374 8	499 4	124 16
Total wages per Ann.	514 16	709 16	195 0

Here, then, we find the annual loss to these men through the system of "driving" to be 195*l*. per annum.

But A is not the only driver in the scavagers' trade; out of the 19 masters having contracts for scavaging, as cited in the table given at pp. 213, 214, there are 4 who are regular drivers; and, making the same calculation as above, we have the following results:—

	Sum received per Annum.	Sum they should receive.	Difference.
	£ s.	£ s.	£ s.
26 Gangers, at 18s. a week, for 9 months in the year........	912 12	1216 16	304 4
80 Sweepers, at 16s. a week, for 9 months in the year........	2496 0	3328 0	832 0
	3308 12	4544 16	1136 4

Thus we find that the gross sum of which the men employed by these drivers are deprived, is no less than 1136*l*. per annum.

2. The second or indirect mode of reducing the wages of the men in the scavaging trade is by *Grinding;* that is to say, by making the men do the same amount of work for less pay. It requires nothing but a practical illustration to render the injury of this particular mode of reduction apparent to the public.

B is a master scavager (a small contractor, though the instances are not confined to this class), and a "*Grinder.*" He pays 1s. a week less than the "regular wages" of the honourable trade. He employs six men; hence the amount that the workmen in his pay are mulct of every year is as follows:—

	Sum received per Annum.	Sum they should receive.	Difference.
	£ s.	£ s.	£ s.
6 men, at 15s. a week, for 9 months in the year	175 10	187 4	11 14

Here the loss to the men is 11*l*. 14*s*. per annum, and there is but one such grinder among the 19 master scavagers who have contracts at present.

3. The third and last method of reducing the earnings of the men as above enumerated, is by a combination of both the systems before explained, viz., by *grinding* and *driving* united, that is to say, by not only paying the men a smaller wage than the more honourable masters, but by compelling them to work longer hours as well. Let me cite another illustration from the trade.

C is a large contractor, and both a grinder and driver. He employs 28 men, and not only pays them less wages, but makes them work longer hours than the better class of employers. The men in his pay, therefore, are annually mulct of the following sums.

SUMS THE MEN RECEIVE.	SUMS THEY SHOULD RECEIVE.
£ s. d.	£ s. d.
7 Gangers, at 16s. a week, for 9 months in the year.......... 218 8 0	7 Gangers, at 18s. a week, for 9 months in the year.......... 245 14 0
21 Sweepers, at 15s. a week.... 614 5 0	Over work, 4 hours per day. 61 8 6
832 13 0	21 Sweepers, at 16s. a week, 12 hours a day .. 655 4 0
	Over work, 4 hours a day .. 163 6 0
	1125 12 6

Here the annual loss to the men employed by this one master is 292*l*. 19*s*. 6*d*.

Among the 19 master scavagers there are altogether 7 employers who are both grinders and drivers. These employ among them no less than 111 hands; hence, the gross amount of which their workmen are yearly defrau—no, let me adhere to the principles of political economy, and say deprived—is as under:—

SUM THE MEN ANNUALLY RECEIVE.	SUM THEY SHOULD ANNUALLY RECEIVE.
£ s. d.	£ s. d.
28 Gangers, at 16s. a week, employed for 9 months in the year.......... 873 12 0	28 Gangers, at 18s. a week (12 hours a day), for 9 months in the year 982 16 0
83 Sweepers, at 15s. a week, employed for 9 months in the year 2427 15 0	Over work, 4 hours per day 245 14 0
	83 Sweepers, at 16s. a week, 12 hours a day 2589 12 0
3301 7 0	Over work, 4 hours per day 647 8 0
	4465 10 0

Here we perceive the gross loss to the operatives from the system of combined grinding and driving to be no less than 1164*l*. 3*s*. per annum.

Now let us see what is the aggregate loss to the working men from the several modes of reducing their wages as above detailed.

	£. s. d.
Loss to the working scavagers by the "driving" of employers.	1136 4 0
Ditto by the "grinding" .	11 14 0
Ditto by the "grinding *and* driving" of employers . .	1164 3 0
Total loss to the working scavagers per annum . . .	2312 1 0

Now this is a large sum of money to be wrested annually out of the workmen—that it is so wrested is demonstrated by the fact cited at p. 174 in connection with the dust trade.

The wages of the dustmen employed by the large contractors, it is there stated, have been increased within the last seven years from 6*d*. to 8*d*. per load. This increase in the rate of remuneration was owing to complaints made by the men to the Commissioners of Sewers, that they were not able to live on their earnings; an inquiry took place, and the result was that the Commissioners decided upon letting the contracts only to such parties as would undertake to pay a fair price to their workmen. The contractors accordingly increased the remuneration of the labourers as mentioned.

Now political economy would tell us that the Commissioners *interfered* with wages in a most reprehensible manner—preventing the natural operation of the law of Supply and Demand; but both justice and benevolence assure us that the Commissioners did perfectly right. The masters in the dust trade were forced to make good to the men what they had previously taken from them, and the same should be done in the scavaging trade—the contracts should be let only to those masters who will undertake to pay the regular rate of wages, and employ their men only the regular hours; for by such means, and by such means alone, can *justice* be done to the operatives.

This brings me to the *cause of the reduction of wages in the scavaging trade*. The scurf trade, I am informed, has been carried on among the master scavagers upwards of 20 years, and arose partly from the contractors having *to pay* the parishes for the house-dust and street-sweepings, brieze and street manure at that period often selling for 30*s*. the chaldron or load. The demand for this kind of manure 20 years ago was so great, that there was a competition carried on among the contractors themselves, each out-bidding the other, so as to obtain the right of collecting it; and in order not to lose anything by the large sums which they were induced to bid for the contracts, the employers began gradually to "grind down" their men from 17*s*. 6*d*. (the sum paid 20 years back) to 17*s*. a week, and eventually to 15*s*., and even 12*s*. weekly. This is a curious and instructive fact, as showing that even an increase of prices will, *under the contract system*, induce a reduction of wages. The greed of traders becomes, it appears, from the very height of the prices, proportionally intensified, and from the desire of each to reap the benefit, they are led to outbid one another to such an extent, and to offer such large premiums for the right of appropriation, as to necessitate a reduction of every possible expense in order to make any profit at all upon the transaction. Owing, moreover, to the surplus labour in the trade, the contractors were enabled to offer any premiums and reduce wages as they pleased; for the casually-employed men, when the wet season was over, and their services no longer required, were continually calling upon the contractors, and offering their services at 2*s*. and 3*s*. less per week than the regular hands were receiving. The consequence was, that five or six of the master scavagers began to reduce the wages of their labourers, and since that time the number has been gradually increasing, until now there are no less than 21 scurf masters (8 of whom have no contracts) out of the 34 contractors; so that nearly three-fifths of the entire trade belong to the *grinding* class. Within the last seven or eight years, however, there has been an increase of wages in connection with the city operative scavagers. This was owing mainly to the operatives complaining to the Commissioners that they could not live upon the wages they were then receiving—12*s*. and 14*s*. a week. The circumstances inducing the change, I am informed, were as follows:—one of the gangers asked a tradesman in the city to give the street-sweepers "something for beer," whereupon the tradesman inquired if the men could not find beer out of their wages, and on being assured that they were receiving only 12*s*. a week, he had the matter brought before the Board. The result was, that the wages of the operatives were increased from 12*s*. to 15*s*. and 16*s*. weekly, since which time there has been neither an increase nor a decrease in their pay. The cheapness of provisions seems to have caused no reduction with them.

Now there are but two "efficient causes" to account for the reduction of wages among the scurf employers in the scavagers' trade:—(1) The employers may diminish the pay of their men from a disposition to "*grind*" out of them an inordinate rate of profit. (2) The price paid for the work may be so reduced that, consistent with the ordinary rate of profit on capital, and remuneration for superintendence, greater wages cannot be paid. If the first be the fact, then the employers are to blame, and the parishes should follow the example of the Commissioners of Sewers, and let the work to those contractors only who will undertake to pay the "regular wages" of the honourable trade; but if the latter be the case, as I strongly suspect it is, though some of the masters seem to be more "grasping" than the rest—but in the paucity of returns on this matter, it is difficult to state positively whether the price paid for the labour of the working scavager is in all the parishes proportional to the price paid to the employers for the work (a most important fact to be solved)—if, however, I repeat, the decrease of the wages be mainly due to the decrease in the sums given for the performance of the contract, then the parishes are to blame for seeking to get their work done *at the expense of the working men*.

The contract system of work, I find, necessarily tends to this diminution of the men's earnings in a trade. Offer a certain quantity of work to the lowest bidder, and the competition will assuredly be maintained at *the operative's expense*. It is idle to expect that, as a general rule, traders will take less than the ordinary rate of profit. Hence, he who underbids will usually be found to underpay. This, indeed, is almost a necessity of the system, and one which the parochial functionaries more than all others should be guarded against—seeing that a decrease of the operative's wages can but be attended with an increase of the very paupers, and consequently of the parochial expenses, which they are striving to reduce.

A labourer, in order to be self-supporting and avoid becoming a "burden" on the parish, requires something more than bare subsistence-money in remuneration for his labour, and yet this is generally the mode by which we test the *sufficiency of wages*. "A man can live very comfortably upon that!" is the exclamation of those who have seldom thought upon what constitutes the *minimum* of self-support in this country. A man's wages, to prevent pauperism, should include, besides present subsistence, what Dr. Chalmers has called "his secondaries;" viz., a sufficiency to pay for his maintenance : 1st, during the slack season ; 2nd, when out of employment ; 3rd, when ill; 4th, when old*. If insufficient to do

* These items wages *must* include to prevent pauperism, *even with providence*. But this is only on the supposition that the labourer is unmarried; if married, however, and having a family, then his wages should include, moreover, the keep of at least three extra persons, as well as the education of the children. If not, one of two results is self-evident—either the wife must toil, to the neglect of her young ones, and they be allowed to run about and pick their morals and education, as I have before said, out of the gutter, or else the whole family must be transferred to the care of the parish.

this, it is evident that the man at such times must seek parochial relief; and it is by the reduction of wages down to bare subsistence, that the cheap employers of the present day shift the burden of supporting their labourers when unemployed on to the parish; thus virtually perpetuating the allowance system or relief in aid of wages under the old Poor Law. Formerly the mode of hiring labourers was by the year, so that the employer was bound to maintain the men when unemployed. But now journey-work, or hiring by the day, prevails, and the labourers being paid—and that mere subsistence-money—only when wanted, are necessitated to become either paupers or thieves when their services are no longer required. It is, moreover, this change from yearly to daily hirings, and the consequent discarding of men when no longer required, that has partly caused the immense mass of surplus labourers, who are continually vagabondizing through the country begging or stealing as they go—men for whom there is but some two or three weeks' work (harvesting, hop-picking, and the like) throughout the year.

That there is, however, a large system of *jobbing pursued by the contractors* for the house-dust and cleansing of the streets, there cannot be the least doubt. The minute I have cited at page 210 gives us a slight insight into the system of combination existing among the employers, and the extraordinary fluctuations in the prices obtained by the contractors would lead to the notion that the business was more a system of gambling than trade. The following returns have been procured by Mr. Cochrane within the last few days:—

"Average yearly cost of cleansing the whole of the public ways within the City of London, including the removal of dust, ashes, &c., from the houses of the inhabitants, for eight years, terminating at Michaelmas in the year 1850 . . . . £4,643

Square yards of carriage-way, estimated at 430,000

Square yards of footway, estimated at 300,000

A more specific and later return is as follows:—

	Received for Dust.			Paid for cleansing, &c.			
	£	s.	d.	£	s.	d.	
1845	0	0	0	2833	2	0	Streets not cleansed daily.
1846	1354	5	0	6034	6	0	
1847	4455	5	0	8014	2	0	Streets cleansed daily.
1848	1328	15	0	7226	1	6	
1849	0	0	0	7486	11	6	
1850	0	0	0	6779	16	0	

"From the above return," says Mr. Cochrane, "it may be *inferred* that the annual sums paid for cleansing in each year of 1844 and 1843 did not exceed 2281*l*., as this would make up the eight years' average calculation of 4643*l*."

Since the streets have been cleansed daily, it will be seen that the average has been 7188*l*. The smallest amount, in 1846, was 6034*l*.; and the largest, in 1847, 8014*l*.; which was a sudden increase of 1980*l*.

Here, then, we perceive an immediate increase in the price paid for scavaging between 1846 and 1847 of nearly 33 per cent., and since the wages of the workmen were not proportionately increased in the latter year by the employers, it follows that the profits of the contractors must have been augmented to that enormous extent. The only effectual mode of preventing this system of jobbing being persevered in, *at the expense of the workmen*, is by the insertion of a clause in each parish contract similar to that introduced by the Commissioners of Sewers—that at least a fair living rate of wages shall be paid by each contractor to the men employed by him. This may be an interference with the freedom of labour, according to the economists' "cant" language, but at least it is a restriction of the tyranny of capital, for free labour means, when literally translated, *the unrestricted use of capital*, which is (especially when the moral standard of trade is not of the highest character) perhaps the greatest evil with which a State can be afflicted.

Let me now speak of the *Scurf labourers*. The moral and social characteristics of the working scavagers who labour for a lower rate of hire do not materially differ from those of the better paid and more regularly employed body, unless, perhaps, in this respect, that there are among them a greater proportion of the "casuals," or of men reared to the pursuit of other callings, and driven by want, misfortune, or misconduct, to "sweep the streets;" and not only that, but to regard the "leave to toil" in such a capacity a boon. These constitute, as it were, the cheap labourers of this trade.

Among the parties concerned in the lower-priced scavaging, are the usual criminations. The parish authorities will not put up any longer with the extortions of the contractors. The contractors cannot put up any longer with the stinginess of the parishes. The *working* scavagers, upon whose shoulders the burthen falls the heaviest—as it does in all depreciated tradings—grumble at both. I cannot aver, however, that I found among the men that bitter hatred of their masters which I found actuating the mass of operative tailors, shoemakers, dressmakers, &c., toward the slop capitalists who employed them.

I have pointed out in what the "scurf" treatment of the labourers was chiefly manifested—in extra work for inferior pay; in doing eight or nine days' work in six; and in being paid for only six days' labour, and not always at the ordinary rate even for the lighter toil—not 2*s*. 8*d*., but 2*s*. 6*d*. or even 2*s*. 4*d*. a day. To the wealthy, this 2*d*. or 4*d*. a day may seem but a trifling matter, but I heard a working scavager (formerly a house-painter) put it in a strong light: "that 3*d*. or 4*d*. a day, sir, is a poor family's rent." The rent, I may observe, as a result of my inquiries among the more decent classes of labourers, is often the primary consideration: "You see, sir, we must have a roof over our heads."

A scavager, working for a scurf master, gave

me the following account. He was a middle-aged man, decently dressed, for when I saw him, he was in his "Sunday clothes," and was quiet in his tones, even when he spoke bitterly.

"My father," he said, "was once in business as a butcher, but he failed, and was afterwards a journeyman butcher, but very much respected, I know, and I used to job and help him. O dear, yes! I can read and write, but I have very seldom to write, only I think one never forgets it, it's like learning to swim, that way; and I read sometimes at coffee-shops. My father died rather sudden, and me and a brother had to look out. My brother was older than me, he was 20 or 21 then, and he went for a soldier, I believe to some of the Ingees, but I've never heard of him since. I got a place in a knacker's yard, but I didn't like it at all, *it was so confining*, and should have hooked it, only I left it honourable. I can't call to mind how long that's back, perhaps 16 or 18 years, but I know there was some stir at the time about having the streets and yards cleaner. A man called and had some talk with the governor, and says he, says the governor, says he, 'if you want a handy lad with his besom, and he's good for nothing else'—but that was his gammon—'here's your man;' so I was engaged as a young sweeper at 10s. a week. I worked in Hackney, but I heard so much about railways, that I saved my money up to 10s., and popped [pledged] a suit of mourning I'd got after my father's death for 22s., and got to York, both on foot and with lifts. I soon got work on a rail; there was great call for rails then, but I don't know how long it's since, and I was a navvy for six or seven years, or better. Then I came back to London. I don't know just what made me come back, *but I was restless*, and I thought I could get work as easy in London as in the country, but I couldn't. I brought 21 gold sovereigns with me to London, twisted in my fob for safeness, in a wash-leather bag. They didn't last so long as they ought to. I didn't care for drinking, only when I was in company, but I was a little too gay. One night I spent over 12s. in the St. Helena Gardens at Rotherhithe, and that sort of thing soon makes money show taper. I got some work with a rubbish carter, a regular scurf. I made only about 8s. a week under him, for he didn't want me this half day or that whole day, and if I said anything, he told me I might go and be d—d, he could get plenty such, and I knew he could. I got on then with a gangsman I knew, at street-sweeping. I had 15s. a week, but not regular work, but when the work wer'n't regular, I had 2s. 8d. a day. I then worked under another master for 14s. a week, and was often abused that I wasn't better dressed, for though that there master paid low wages, he was vexed if his men didn't look decent in the streets. I've heard that he said he paid the best of wages when asked about it. I had another job after that, at 15s., and then 16s. a week, with a contractor as had a wharf; but a black nigger slave was never slaved as I was. I've worked all night, when it's been very moonlight, in loading a barge, and I've worked until three and four in the morning that way, and then me and another man slept an hour or two in a shed as joined his stables, and then must go at it again. Some of these masters is ignorant, and treats men like dirt, but this one was always civil, and made his people be civil. But, Lord, I hadn't a rag left to my back. Everything was worn to bits in such hard work, and then I got the sack. I was on for Mr. —— next. He's a jolly good 'un. I was only on for him temp'ry, but I was told it was for temp'ry when I went, so I can't complain. I'm out of work this week, but I've had some jobs from a butcher, and I'm going to work again on Monday. I don't know at what wages. The gangsmen said they'd see what I could do. It'll be 15s., I expect, and over-work if it's 16s.

"Yes, I like a pint of beer now and then, and one requires it, but I don't get drunk. I dusted for a fortnight once while a man was ill, and got more beer and twopences give me than I do in a year now; aye, twice as much. My mate and me was always very civil, and people has said, ' there's a good fellow, just sweep together this bit of rubbish in the yard here, and off with it.' That was beyond our duty, but we did it. I have very little night-work, only for one master; he's a sweep as well. I get 2s. 6d. a job for it. Yes, there's mostly something to drink, but you can't demand nothing. Night-work's nothing, sir; no more ain't a knacker's yard.

"I pay 2s. a week rent, but I'm washed for and found soap as well. My landlady takes in washing, and when her husband, for they're an old couple, has the rheumatics, I make a trifle by carrying out the clothes on a barrow, and Mrs. Smith goes with them and sees to the delivery. I've my own furniture.

"Well, I don't know what I spend in my living in a week. I have a bit of meat, or a saveloy or two, or a slice of bacon every day, mostly when I'm at work. I sometimes make my own meals ready in my room. No, I keep no accounts. There'd be very little use or pleasure in doing it when one has so little to count. When I'm past work, I suppose I must go to the workhouse. I sometimes wish I'd gone for a soldier when I was young enough. I shouldn't have minded going abroad. I'd have liked it better than not, for *I like to be about; yes, I like a change.*

"I go to chapel every Sunday night, and have regularly since Mr. —— (the butcher) gave me this cast-off suit. I promised him I would when I got the togs.

"Things would be well enough with me if I'd constant work and fair pay. I don't know what makes wages so low. I suppose it's rich people trying to get all the money they can, and caring nothing for poor men's rights, and poor men's sometimes forced to undersell one another, 'cause half a loaf you know, sir, is better than no bread at all " (a proverb, by the way, which has wrought no little mischief).

In conclusion, I may remark, that although I was told, in the first instance, there was sub-letting in street sweeping, I could not hear of any facts to prove it. I was told, indeed, by a gentleman who took great interest in parochial matters, with a view to "reforms" in them, that such a thing was most improbable, for if a contractor sub-let any of his work it would soon become known, and as it would be evident that the work could be accomplished at a lower rate, the contractor would be in a worse position for his next contract.

Of the Street-Sweeping Machine, and the Street-Sweepers employed with it.

Until the introduction of the machines now seen in London, I believe that no mechanical contrivances for sweeping the streets had been attempted, all such work being executed by manual labour, and employing throughout the United Kingdom a great number of the poor. The street-sweeping machine, therefore, assumes an importance as another instance of the displacement, or attempted displacement, of the labour of man by the mechanism of an engine.

The street-sweeping machines were introduced into London about five years ago, after having been previously used, under the management of a company, in Manchester, the inventor and maker being Mr. Whitworth, of that place. The novelty and ingenuity of the apparatus soon attracted public attention, and for the first week or two the vehicular street-sweeper was accompanied in its progress by a crowd of admiring and inquisitive pedestrians, so easily attracted together in the metropolis. In the first instance the machines were driven through the streets merely to display their mode and power of work, and the drivers and attendants not unfrequently came into contact with the regular scavagers, when a brisk interchange of street wit took place, the populace often enough encouraging both sides. At present the street-sweeping machine proceeds on its line of operation as little noticed, except by visitors, and foreigners especially, as any other vehicle. The body of the sweeping machine, although the sizes may not all be uniform, is about 5 feet in length, and 2 feet 8 inches or 3 feet in width; the height is about 5 feet 6 inches or 6 feet, and the form that of a covered cart, with a rounded top. The sides of the exterior are of cast iron, the top being of wood. At the hinder part of the cart is fixed the sweeping-machine itself, covered by sloping boards which descend from the top of the cart, projecting slightly behind the vehicle to the ground; under the sloping boards is an endless chain of brushes as wide as the cart, 16 in number, placed at equal distances, and so arranged, that when made to revolve, each brush in turn passes over the ground, sweeping the mud along with it to the bottom sloping board, and so carrying it up to the interior of the cart. The chain of brushes is set in motion, over the surface of the pavement, by the agency of three cog wheels of cast iron; these are worked by the rotation of the wheels of the cart, the cogs acting upon the spindles to which the brooms are attached. The spindles, brushes, and the sloped boards can be raised or lowered by the winding of an instrument called the broom winder; or the whole can be locked. The brooms are raised when any acclivity is to be swept, and lowered at a declivity. The vehicle must be water-tight, in order to contain the slop.

When full the machine holds about half a cart load or half a ton of dirt; this is emptied by letting down the back in the manner of a trap door. If the contents be solid, they have to be forked out; if more sloppy, they are "shot" out, as from a cart, the interior generally being roughly scraped to complete the emptying.

The districts which have as yet been cleansed by the machines are what may be considered a government domain, being the public thoroughfares under the control of the Commissioners of the Woods and Forests, running from Westminster Abbey to the Regent-circus in Piccadilly, and including Spring-gardens, Carlton-gardens, and a portion of the West Strand, where they were first employed in London; they have been used also in parts of the City; and are at present employed by the parish of St. Martin-in-the-Fields. The company by whom the mechanical street-sweeping business is carried on employ 12 machines, 4 water carts, 19 horses, and 24 men. They have also the use, but not the sole use, of two wharfs and barges at Whitefriars and Millbank. The machines altogether collect about 30 cart-loads of street-dirt a day, which is equivalent to four or five barge-loads in a week, if all were boated. Two barges per week are usually sent to Rochester, the others up the river to Fulham, &c. The average price is 5*l.* 10*s.* to 6*l.* per barge load, but when the freight has been chiefly dung, as much as 8*l.* has been paid for it by a farmer.

The street-sweeping machine seems to have commanded the approbation of the General Board of Health, although the Board's expression of approval is not without qualification. "Even that efficient and economical implement," says one of the Reports, "the street-sweeping machine, leaves much filth between the interstices of the stones and some on the surface." One might have imagined, however, that an efficient and economical implement would not have left this "much filth" in its course; but the Board, I presume, spoke comparatively.

The reason of the circumscribed adoption of the machine—I say it with some reluctance, but from concurrent testimony—appears to be that it does *not* sweep sufficiently clean. It sweeps the surface, but only the surface; not cleansing what the scavagers call the "nicks" and "holes," and the Board of Health the "interstices," in the pavement.

One man is obliged to go along with each machine, to sweep the ridge of dirt invariably left at the edge of the track of the vehicle into the line of the next machine, so that it may be "licked up." In fine weather this work is often light enough. It is also the occupation of the accompanying scavager to sweep the dirt from the sloping edges of the public ways into the direct course of the machine, for the brushes are of no service along such slopes; he must also sweep out the contents of any hole or hollow there may be in the streets, as is frequently the case when the pavement has been disturbed in the relaying or repairing of the gas or water pipes. But for this arrangement, I was told, the brushes would pass "clean over" such places, or only disturb without clearing away the dirt. Indeed irregularities of any kind in the pavement are great obstructions to the efficiency of the street-sweeping machine.

There are some places, moreover, wholly unsweepable by the machine; in many parts of St. Martin's parish, for instance, there are localities where the machine cannot be introduced; such are—St. Martin's-court; the flagged ways about the National Gallery; and the approach, alongside the church, to the Lowther Arcade; the pavement surrounding the fountains which adorn the "noblest site in Europe;" and a variety of alleys, passages, yards, and minor streets, which must be cleansed by manual labour.

In fair weather, again, water carts are indispensable before machine sweeping, for if the ground be merely dry and dusty, the set of brooms will not "bite."

We now come to estimate the *relative values of the mechanical and manual labour applied to the scavaging of the streets*. The average progress of the street-sweeping machine, in the execution of the scavagers' work, is about two miles an hour. It must not be supposed, however, that two streets each a mile in length, could be swept in one hour; for to do this the vehicle would have to travel up and down those streets as many times as the streets are wider than the machine. The machines, sometimes two, sometimes three or four, follow alongside each other's tracks in sweeping a street, so as to leave no part unswept. Thus, supposing a street half a mile long and nine yards wide, and that each machine swept a breadth of a yard, then three such machines, driven once up, and once again down, and once more up such a street, would cleanse it in three quarters of an hour. To do this by manual labour in the same or nearly the same time, would require the exertions of five men. Each machine has been computed to have mechanical power equal to the industry of five street-sweepers; and such, from the above computation, would appear to be the fact. I do not include the drivers in this enumeration, as of course the horse in the scavagers' cart, and in the machine require alike the care of a man, and there is to each vehicle (whether mechanical or not) one hand (besides the carman) to sweep after the ordinary work. Hence every two men with the machine do the work of seven men by hand.

Having, then, ascertained the relative values of the two forces employed in cleansing the streets, let me now proceed to set forth what is "the economy of labour" resulting from the use of the sweeping machine. In the following table are given the number of men at present engaged by the machine company in the cleansing of those districts where the machine is in operation, as well as the annual amount of wages paid to the machine labourers; these facts are then collocated with the number of manual labourers that would be required to do the same work under the ordinary contract system (assuming every two labourers with the machine to do the work of seven labourers by hand), as well as the amount of wages that would be paid to such manual labourers; and finally, the number of men and amount of wages under the one system of street-cleansing is subtracted from the other, in order to arrive at the number of street-sweepers at present displaced by manual labour, and the annual loss in wages to the men so displaced; or, to speak economically, the last column represents the amount by which the Wage Fund of the street-sweepers is diminished by the employment of the machine.

TABLE SHOWING THE DIFFERENCE BETWEEN THE NUMBER OF MEN AT PRESENT ENGAGED IN STREET-SWEEPING BY MACHINES, AND THE NUMBER THAT WOULD BE REQUIRED TO SWEEP THE SAME DISTRICTS BY HAND, TOGETHER WITH THE ANNUAL AMOUNT OF WAGES ACCRUING TO EACH.

Districts.	Machine Labour.		Manual Labour.		Difference.	
	Number of Men employed to attend Machines.	Annual Wages received by Machine Men, at 16s. a Week.	Number of men that would be required to sweep the Streets by Manual labour.	Annual Wages that would be received by Manual Labourers, at 15s. a Week.	Number of Men displaced by Machine-work.	Annual Loss in Wages to Manual Labourers by Machine-work.
		£ s.		£ s.		£ s.
St. Martin's-in-the Fields . . .	8	332 16	28	1092 0	20	759 4
Regent-street and Pall-mall (see table, p. 214) .	12	499 4	42	1638 0	30	1138 16
Other places, connected with Woods and Forests . .	4	166 8	14	546 0	10	379 12
Total. . .	24	998 8	84	3276 0	60	2277 12

Hence, we perceive that no less than 60 street-sweepers are deprived of work by the street-sweeping machine, and that the gross Wage Fund of the men is diminished by the employment of mechanical labour no less than 2277*l.* per annum.

But let us suppose the street-sweeping machine to come into general use, and all the men who are at present employed by the contractors, both large and small, to sweep the street by hand to be superseded by it, what would be the result? how much money would the manual labourers be deprived of per annum, and how many self-supporting labourers would be pauperized thereby? The following table will show us: in the first compartment given below we have the number of manual labourers employed throughout London by the large and small contractors, and the amount of wages annually received by them*; in the second compartment is given the number of men that would be required to sweep the same districts by the machine, and the amount of wages that would be received by them at the present rate; and the third and last compartment shows the gross number of hands that would be displaced, and the annual loss that would accrue to the operatives by the substitution of mechanical for manual labour in the sweeping of the streets.

TABLE SHOWING THE DIFFERENCE BETWEEN THE NUMBER OF CONTRACTORS' MEN AT PRESENT EMPLOYED TO SWEEP THE STREETS BY HAND, AND THE NUMBER THAT WOULD BE REQUIRED TO SWEEP THE SAME DISTRICTS BY MACHINE WORK, TOGETHER WITH THE AMOUNT OF WAGES ACCRUING TO EACH.

	Manual Labour.		Machine Labour.		Difference.	
	Number of Men at present employed by Contractors to sweep the streets.	Annual Wages received by Contractors' Men for sweeping the Streets, at 15*s.* a Week.	Number of Machine Men that would be required to attend the Street-sweeping Machines.	Annual Wages that would be received by Machine Men, at 16*s.* a Week.	Number of Men that would be displaced by Machine-work.	Annual Loss that would accrue to Manual Labourers by Machine-work.
		£ *s.*		£ *s.*		£ *s.*
Districts at present swept by large contractors (see table, p. 214)	262	10,218 0	75	3120 0	187	7098 0
Districts swept by small contractors.	13	507 0	4	166 8	9	340 12
Total. . .	275	10,725 0	79	3286 8	196	7438 12

Here we find that nearly 200 men would be pauperized, losing upwards of 7000*l.* per annum, if the street-sweeping machine came into general use throughout London. But, before the introduction of machines, the thoroughfares of St. Martin's parish were swept only once a week in dry weather, and three times a week in sloppy weather, and since the introduction of the machines they have been swept daily; allowing, therefore, the extra cleansing to have arisen from the extra cheapness of the machine work—though it seems to have been the result of improved sanatory regulations, for in parts where the machine has not been used the same alteration has taken place—making such allowance, however, it may, perhaps, be fair to say, that the same increase of cleansing would take place throughout London; that is to say, that the streets would be swept by the machines, were they generally used, twice as often as they are at present by hand. At this rate 158 machine men, instead of 79 as above calculated, would be required for the work; so that, reckoning for the increased employment which might arise from the increased cheapness of the work, we see that, were the street-sweeping machines used throughout the metropolis, nearly 120 of the 275 manual labourers now employed at scavaging by the large and small contractors, would be thrown out of work, and deprived of no less a sum than 4680*l.* per annum.

This amount, of course, the parishes would pocket, minus the sum that it would cost them to keep the displaced scavagers as paupers, so that in this instance, at least, we perceive that, however great a benefit cheapness may be to the wealthy classes, to the poorer classes it is far from being of the same advantageous character; for, just as much as the rate-payers are the gainers in the matter of street-cleansing must the labourers be the losers—the economy of labour in a trade where there are too many labourers already, and where the quantity of work does not admit of indefinite increase, meaning simply the increase of pauperism†.

* I have estimated the whole at 15*s.* a week the year through, gangers, "honourable men," regular hands and all, so as to allow for the diminished receipts of the casual hands.
† The usual argument in favour of machinery, viz., that "by reducing prices it extends the market, and so, causing a greater demand for the commodities, induces a greater quantity of employment," would also be an argument in favour of over population, since this, by

The "*labour question*" as connected with the sweeping-machine work, requires but a brief detail, as it presents no new features. The majority of the machine men may be described as having been "general (unskilled) labourers" before they embarked in their present pursuits: labourers for builders, brick-makers, rubbish-carters, the docks, &c.

Among them there is but one who was brought up as a mechanic; the others have all been labourers, brick-makers, and what I heard called "barrow-workers" on railways, the latter being the most numerous.

Employment is obtained by application at the wharfs. There is nothing of the character of a trade society among the machine-men; nothing in the way of benefit or sick clubs, unless the men choose to enrol themselves in a general benefit society, of which I did not hear one instance.

The payment is by the week, and without drawback in the guise or disguise of fines, or similar inflictions for the use of tools, &c.; the payment, moreover, is always in money.

The only perquisite is in the case of anything being found in the streets; but the rule as to perquisites seems to be altogether an understanding among the men. The disposal of what may be picked up in the streets appears, moreover, to be very much in the discretion of the picker up. If anything be found in the contents of the vehicle, when emptied, it is the perquisite of the driver, who is also the unloader; he, however, is expected to treat the men "on the same beat" out of any such "treasure trove," when the said treasure is considerable enough to justify such bounty. Odd sixpences, shillings, or copper coin, I was informed, were found almost every week, but I could ascertain no general average. One man, some time ago, found a purse inside the vehicle containing 20s., and "spent it out and out all on hisself," in a carouse of three days. He lost his situation in consequence.

The number of men employed by the company in this trade is 24, and these perform all the work required in the driving and attendance upon the machines in the street, in loading the barges, grooming the horses, &c. There is, indeed, a twenty-fifth man, but he is a blacksmith, and his wages of 35s. weekly are included in the estimate as to wear and tear given below, for he shoes the horses and repairs the machines.

The rate of wages paid by the machine company is 16s. a week, so that the full amount of wages is paid to the men.

But though the company cannot be ranked among the grinders of the scavaging trade, they *must* be placed among "the drivers."

cheapening, labour must have the same effect as machinery on prices, and, consequently (according to the above logic), induce a greater quantity of employment! But granting that machinery really does benefit the labourer in cases *where the market, and therefore the quantity of work, is largely extensible,* surely it cannot but be an injury in those callings where *the quantity of work is fixed.* Such is the fact with the sawing of wood, the reaping of corn, the threshing of corn, the sweeping of the streets, &c., and hence the evil of mechanical labour applied to such trades.

I am assured, by those who are familiar with such labour, that the 24 men employed by the machine masters do the work of upwards of 30 in the honourable trade, with a corresponding saving to their employers, from an adherence to the main point of the scurf system, the overworking of the men without extra payment.

It has been before stated that, in dry weather, the roads require to be watered before being swept, so that the brushes may *bite*. In summer the machine-men sometimes commence this part of their business at three in the morning; and at the other periods of the year, sometimes at early morning, when moonlight. In summer the hours of labour in the streets are from three, four, five, or six in the morning, to half-past four in the afternoon; in winter, from light to light, and after street there may be yard and barge work.

The saving by this scurf system, then, is:—

30 men (honourable trade), 16s. weekly . . . . . . £1248 yearly.
24 men (scurf-trade) doing same work), 16s. weekly . . 998 „

Saving to capitalist and loss to labourer . . . . . £250 „

It now but remains to sum up the capital, income, and expenditure of the machine-scavaging trade.

The cost of a street-sweeping machine is 50l. to 60l., with an additional 5l. 5s. for the set of brooms. The wear and tear of these machines are very considerable. A man who had the care of one told me that when there was a heavy stress on it he had known the iron cogs of the inner wheels "go rattle, rattle, snap, snap," until it became difficult to proceed with the work. The brooms, too, in hard work and "cloggy" weather, are apt to snap short, and in the regular course of wear have to be renewed every four or five weeks. The sets of brooms are of bass, worked strongly with copper wire. The whole apparatus can be unscrewed and taken to pieces, to be cleaned or repaired. The repairs, independently of the renewal of the brooms, have been calculated at 7l. yearly each machine. The capital invested, then, in twelve street-sweeping machines, in the horses, and what may be considered the appurtenances of the trade, together with the yearly expenditure, may be thus calculated:—

CAPITAL OF STREET-SWEEPING MACHINE TRADE.

12 machines, 60l. each	£720
12 sets of brooms, 5l. 5s. each set .	63
19 horses, 25l. each	475
4 water-carts, 20l. each	80
19 sets of harness (new), 7l. each set	133
4 barges, 50l. each	200
	£1671

YEARLY EXPENDITURE.

24 men, 16s. weekly	£998
120 sets of brooms for 12 machines, 4l. per set	480
Wear and tear, &c. (15 per cent.)	255
Keep of 19 horses, 10s. each weekly	494
Rent (say)	150
Clerk (say)	100
Interest on capital, at 10 per cent.	179
	£2674

In this calculation I have included wear and tear of the whole of the implements of the stock-in-trade, &c., taking that of the brooms on the most moderate estimate. According to the scale of payment by the parish of St. Martin (which is now 1000l. per annum) the probable receipts of a single year will be:—

YEARLY RECEIPTS.

	£	s.	d.
For hire of 12 machines	2500	0	0
200 barge-loads of manure, 5l. 15s. per barge	1150	10	0
	3650	10	0
Yearly expenditure	2674	0	0
Profit	976	10	0

OF THE CLEANSING OF THE STREETS BY PAUPER LABOUR.

UNDER the head of the several modes and characteristics of street-cleansing, I stated at p. 207 of the present volume that there were no less than four distinct kinds of labourers employed in the scavaging of the public thoroughfares of the metropolis. These were:—
1. The self-supporting manual labourers.
2. The self-supporting machine labourers.
3. The pauper labourers.
4. The "philanthropic" labourers.

I have already set forth the distinguishing features of the first two of these different orders of workmen in connection with the scavaging trade, and now proceed in due order to treat of the characteristics of the third.

The subject of pauper labour generally is one of the most difficult topics that the social philosopher can deal with. It is not possible, however, to do more here than draw attention to the salient points of the question. The more comprehensive consideration of the matter must be reserved till such time as I come to treat of the poor specially under the head of those that cannot work.

By the 43 Eliz., which is generally regarded as the basis of the existing poor laws in this country, it was ordained that in every parish a fund should be raised by local taxation, not merely for the relief of the aged and infirm, but *for setting to work all persons having no means to maintain themselves, and using no ordinary or daily trade of life to get their living by.*

It was, however, soon discovered that it was one thing to pass an act for setting able-bodied paupers to work, and another thing to do so. "In every place," as Mr. Thornton truly says in his excellent treatise on "Over Population," "there is only a certain amount of work to be done," (limited by the extent of the market) "and only a certain amount of capital to pay for it; and, if the number of workmen be more than proportionate to the work, employment can only be given to those who want it by taking from those who have."

Let me illustrate this by the circumstances of the scavaging trade. There are 1760 miles of streets throughout London, and these would seem to require about 600 scavagers to cleanse them. It is self-evident, therefore, that if 400 paupers be "set" to sweep particular districts, the same number of self-supporting labourers must be deprived of employment, and if these cannot obtain work elsewhere, they of course must become paupers too, and, seeking relief, be put upon the same kind of work as they were originally deprived of, and that only to displace and pauperize in their turn a similar number of independent operatives.

The work of a country then being limited (by the capital and market for the produce), there can be but two modes of setting paupers to labour: (1) by throwing the self-supporting operatives out of employment altogether, and substituting pauper labourers in their stead; (2) by giving a portion of the work to the paupers, and so decreasing the employment, and consequently the wages, of the regular operatives. In either case, however, the independent labourers must be reduced to a state of comparative or positive dependence, for *it is impossible to make labourers of the paupers of an over-populated country without making paupers of the labourers.*

Some economists argue that, as paupers are consumers, they should, whenever they are able to work, be made producers also, or otherwise they exhaust the national wealth, to which they do not contribute. This might be a sound axiom were there work sufficient for all. But in an over-populated country there is not work enough, as is proven by the mere fact of the over-population; and the able-bodied paupers *are* paupers simply *because they cannot obtain work*, so that to employ those who are out of work is to throw out those who are in work, and thus to pauperize the self-supporting.

The whole matter seems to hinge upon this one question—

Who are to maintain the paupers? The rate-paying traders or the non-ratepaying workmen?

If the paupers be set to work in a country like Great Britain, they must necessarily be brought into competition with the self-supporting workmen, and so be made to share the wage fund with them, decreasing the price of labour in proportion to the extra number of such pauper labourers among whom the capital of the trade has to be shared. Hence the burden of maintaining the paupers will be virtually shifted from the capitalist to the labourer, the poor-rate being thus really paid out of the wages of the operatives, instead of the profits of the traders, as it should be.

And here lies the great wrong of pauper labour. It saddles the poor with the maintenance of their poorer brethren, while the rich not only contribute nothing to their support, but are made still richer by the increased cheapness resulting from the depreciation of labour and their consequent ability to obtain a greater quantity of commodities for the same amount of money.

In illustration of this argument let us say the wages of 600 independent scavagers amount, at 15s. a week each the year through, to 23,400l. per annum; and let us say, moreover, that the keep of 400 paupers amounts, at 5s. a week each, to, altogether, 5200l.; hence the total annual expense to the several metropolitan parishes for cleansing the streets and maintaining 400 paupers would be 23,400l. + 5200l. = 28,600l.

If, however, the 400 paupers be set to scavaging work, and made to do something for their keep, one of two things *must* follow: (1) either the 400 extra hands will receive their share of the 23,400l. devoted to the payment of the operative scavagers, in which case the wages of each of the regular hands will be reduced from 15s. to 9s. a week; hence the maintenance of the paupers will be saddled upon the 600 independent operatives, who will lose no less than 9360l. per annum, while the ratepayers will be saved the maintenance of the 400 paupers and so gain 5200l. per annum by the change; (2) or else 400 of the self-supporting operatives must be thrown out of work, in which case the displaced labourers will lose no less than 15,600l., while the ratepayers will gain upwards of 5000l.

The reader is now, I believe, in a position to comprehend the wrong done to the self-supporting scavagers by the employment of pauper labour in the cleansing of the streets.

The preparation of the material of the roads of a parish seems, as far as the metropolis is concerned, at one time to have supplied the chief "test," to which parishes have resorted, as regards the willingness to labour on the part of the able-bodied applicants for relief. When the casual wards of the workhouses were open for the reception of all vagrants who sought a night's shelter, each tramper was required to break so many stones in the morning before receiving a certain allowance of bread, soup, or what not for his breakfast; and he then might be received again into the shelter of this casual asylum. In some parishes the wards were open without the test of stone-breaking, and there was a crowded resort to them, especially during the prevalence of the famine in Ireland and the immigration of the Irish peasants to England. The favourite resort of the vagrants was Marylebone workhouse, and Irish immigrants very frequently presented slips of paper on which some tramper whom they had met with on their way had written "*Marylebone workhouse,*" as the best place at which they could apply, and these the simple Irish offered as passports for admission!

Gradually, the asylum of these wards, with or without labour tests, was discontinued, and in one where the labour test used to be strongly insisted upon—in St. Pancras—a school for pauper children has been erected on the site of the stone-yard.

This labour test was unequal when applied to all comers; for what was easy work to an agricultural labourer, a railway excavator, a quarryman, or to any one used to wield a hammer, was painful and blistering to a starving tailor. Nor was the test enforced by the overseers or regarded by the paupers as a proof of willingness to work, but simply as a punishment for poverty, and as a means of deterring the needy from applying for relief. To make labour a punishment, however, is *not* to destroy, but really to confirm, idle habits; it is to give a deeper root to the vagrant's settled aversion to work. "Well, I always thought it was unpleasant," the vagabond will say to himself "*that* working for one's bread, and now I'm *convinced* of it!" Again, in many of the workhouses the labour to which the paupers were set was of a manifestly unremunerative character, being work for mere work's sake; and to apply people to unproductive labour is to destroy all the ordinary motives to toil—to take away the only stimulus to industry, and remove the very will to work which the labour test was supposed to discover *.

The labour test, then, or setting the poor to work as a proof of their willingness to labour, appears to be as foolish as it is vicious; the objections to it being—(1) the inequality of the test applied to different kinds of work-people; (2) the tendency of it to confirm rather than weaken idle habits by making labour inordinately repulsive; (3) the removal of the ordinary stimulus to industry by the unproductiveness of the work to which the poor are generally applied.

And now, having dealt with the subject of parish labour as a test of the willingnes to work on the part of the applicants for relief, I will proceed to deal with that portion of the work itself which is connected with the cleansing of the streets.

And first as to the employment of paupers at all in the streets. If pauperism be a disgrace, then it is unjust to turn a man into the public thoroughfares, wearing the badge of beggary, to be pointed at and scorned for his poverty, especially when we are growing so particularly studious of our criminals that we make them wear masks to prevent even their faces being seen †. Nor is it consistent with the principles of an enlightened national morality that we should force a body of honest men to labour upon the highways, branded with a degrading garb, like convicts. Neither is it *wise* to do so, for the shame of poverty soon becomes deadened by the repeated exposure to public scorn; and thus the occasional recipient of parish relief is ultimately

* Mr. Sidney Herbert informed me, that when he was connected with the Ordnance Department the severest punishment they could discover for idleness was the piling and unpiling of cannon shot; but surely this was the consummation of official folly! for idleness being simply an aversion to work, it is almost self-evident that it is *impossible* to remove this aversion by making labour inordinately irksome and repulsive. Until we understand the means by which work is made pleasant, and can discover other modes of employing our paupers and criminals, all our workhouse and prison discipline is idle tyranny.

† This is done at the Model Prison, Pentonville.

converted into the hardened and habitual pauper. "Once a pauper always a pauper," I was assured was the parish rule; and here lies the *rationale* of the fact. Not long ago this system of employing *badged* paupers to labour in the public thoroughfares was carried to a much more offensive extent than it is even at present. At one time the pauper labourers of a certain parish had the attention of every passer-by attracted to them while at their work, for on the back of each man's garb—a sort of smock-frock—was marked, with sufficient prominence, "CLERKENWELL. STOP IT!" This public intimation that the labourers were not only paupers, but regarded as thieves, and expected to purloin the parish dress they wore, attracted public attention, and was severely commented upon at a meeting. The "STOP IT!" therefore was cancelled, and the frocks are now *merely* lettered "CLERKENWELL." Before the alteration the men very generally wore the garment inside out.

The present dress of the parish scavagers is usually a loose smock-frock, costing 1s. 6d. to 2s, and a glazed hat of about the same price. In some cases, however, the men may wear these things or not, at their option.

The pauper scavagers employed by the several metropolitan parishes may be divided into three classes:—

1. The in-door paupers, who receive no wages whatever (their lodging, food, and clothing being considered to be sufficient remuneration for their labour).

2. The out-door paupers, who are paid partly in money and partly in kind, and employed in some cases three days and in others six days in the week.

These may be subdivided into—(*a*) the single men, who receive, or rather used to receive, 9*d*. and a quartern loaf for each of the three or more days they were so employed; (*b*) the married men with families, who receive 7*s*. and 3 quartern loaves a week to 1*s*. 1½*d*. and 1 quartern loaf for each day's labour.

3. The unemployed labourers of the district, who are set to scavaging work by the parish, and paid a regular money wage—the employment being constant, and the rate of remuneration ranging from 1s. 3d. to 2s. 6d. a day for each of the six days, or from 7s. 6d. to 15s. a week.

In pp. 246, 247, I give a table of the wages paid by each of the metropolitan parishes. This has been collected at great trouble in order to arrive at the truth on this most important matter, and for which purpose the several parishes have been personally visited. It will be seen on reference to this document, that there is only one parish at present that employs its in-door paupers in the scavaging of the public streets; and 3 parishes employing 48 out-door paupers, who are paid partly in money and partly in bread; the money remuneration ranging from 1*s*. 1½*d*. a day (paid by Clerkenwell) to 7*s*. a week (paid by Chelsea), and moreover 31 parishes employing 408 applicants for relief (paupers they cannot be called), and paying them wholly in money, the remuneration ranging from 15*s*. per week to 7*s*. 6*d*. (paid by the Liberty of the Rolls), and the employment from 6 to 3 days weekly. As a general rule it was found that the greatest complaints were made by the authorities as to the idleness of the poor, and by the poor as to the tyranny of the authorities, in those parishes where the remuneration was the least. In St. Luke's, Chelsea, for instance, where the remuneration is but 7*s*. a week and three loaves, the criminations and recriminations by the parish functionaries and the paupers were almost equally harsh and bitter. I should, however, observe that the men employed in this parish spoke in terms of great commendation of Mr. Pattison the surveyor, saying he always gave them to understand that they were free labourers, and invariably treated them as such. The men at work for Bermondsey parish also spoke very highly of their superintendent, who, it seems, has interested himself to obtain for them a foul-weather coat. Some of the highway boards or trusts take all the pauper labourers sent them by the parish, while others give employment only to such as please them. These boards generally pay good wages, and are in favour with the men.

The mode of working, as regards the use of the implements and the manual labour, is generally the same among the pauper scavagers as I have described in connection with the scavagers generally.

The consideration of what is the rate of parish pay to the poor who are employed as scavagers, is complicated by the different modes in which the employment is carried out, for, as we see, there is—1st, the scavaging labour, by workhouse inmates, without any payment beyond the cost of maintenance and clothing; 2nd, the "short" or three-days-a-week labour, with or without "relief" in the bestowal of bread; and 3rd, the six days' work weekly, with a money wage and no bread, nor anything in the form of payment in kind or of "relief."

Let me begin with the first system of labour above mentioned, viz. the employment of the in-door paupers without wages of any kind, their food, lodging, and clothing being considered as equivalents for their work. The principal evil in connection with this form of parish work is its compulsory character, the men regarding it not as so much work given in exchange for such and such comforts, but as something *exacted* from them; and, to tell the truth, it is precisely the counterpart of slavery, being equally deficient in all inducement to toil, and consequently requiring almost the same system of compulsion and supervision in order to keep the men at their labour. All interest in the work is destroyed, there being no reward connected with it; and consequently the same organized system of setting to work is required as with cattle. There are but two inducements to voluntary action—pain to be avoided or pleasure to be derived—or, in other words, the attractiveness and repulsiveness of objects. Take away the pecuniary attraction of labour, and men become mere beasts of burden, capable of being set to work only by the dread of some punishment; hence the system of parish labour, which has no reward directly connected with it, must necessarily be tyrannical, and so tend to induce idleness and a hatred of work altogether.

Of the different forms of pauper work, street-sweeping is, I am inclined to believe, the most unpopular of all among the poor. The scavaging is generally done in the workhouse dress, and that to all, except the hardened paupers, and sometimes even to them, is highly distasteful. Neither have such labourers, as I have said, the incentive of that hope of the reward which, however diminutive, still tends to sweeten the most repulsive labour. I am informed by an experienced gangsman under a contractor, that it is notorious that the workhouse hands are the least industrious scavagers in the streets. "They don't sweep as well," he said, "and don't go about it like regular men; they take it quite easy." It is often asserted that this labour of the workhouse men is applied as a *test;* but this opinion seems rather to bear on the past than the present.

One man thus employed gave me the following account. He was garrulous but not communicative, as is frequently the case with men who love to hear themselves talk, and are not very often able to command listeners. He was healthy looking enough, but he told me he was, or had been "delicate." He querulously objected to be questioned about his youth, or the reason of his being a pauper, but seemed to be abounding in workhouse stories and workhouse grievances.

"Street-sweeping," he said, "degrades a man, and if a man's poor he hasn't no call to be degraded. Why can't they set the thieves and pickpockets to sweep? they could be watched easy enough; there's always idle fellers as reckons theirselves real gents, as can be got for watching and sitch easy jobs, for they gets as much for them, as three men's paid for hard work in a week. I never was in a prison, but I've heerd that people there is better fed and better cared for than in workusses. What's the meaning of that, sir, I'd like for to know? You can't tell me, but I can tell you. The workus is made as ugly as it can be, that poor people may be got to leave it, and chance dying in the street rather." [Here the man indulged in a gabbled detail of a series of pauper grievances which I had a difficulty in diverting or interrupting. On my asking if the other paupers had the same opinion as to street-sweeping as he had, he replied:—] "To be sure they has; all them that has sense to have a 'pinion at all has; there's not two sides to it any how. No, I don't want to be kept and do nothink. I want *proper* work. And by the rights of it I might as well be kept with nothink to do as —— or ——" [parish officials]. "Have they nothing to do," I asked? "Nothink, but to make mischief and get what ought to go to the poor. It's salaries and such like as swallers the rates, and that's what every poor family knows as knows anythink. Did I ever like my work better? Certainly not. Do I take any pains with it? Well, where would be the good? I can sweep well enough, when I please, but if I could do more than the best man as ever Mr. Darke paid a pound a week to, it wouldn't be a bit better for me—not a bit, sir, I assure you. We all takes it easy whenever we can, but the work *must* be done. The only good about it is that you get outside the house. It's a change that way certainly. But we work like horses and is treated like asses." [On my reminding him that he had just told me that they all took it easy when they could, and *that* rather often, he replied:] "Well, don't horses? But it ain't much use talking, sir. It's only them as has been in workusses and in parish work as can understand all the ins and outs of it."

In giving the above and the following statements I have endeavoured to elicit the *feelings* of the several paupers whom I conversed with. Poor, ignorant, or prejudiced men may easily be mistaken in their opinions, or in what they may consider their "facts," but if a clear exposition of their sentiments be obtained, it is a guide to the truth. I have, therefore, given the statement of the in-door pauper's opinions, querulously as they were delivered, as I believe them to be the sentiments of those of his class who, as he said, had any opinion at all.

It seems indeed, from all I could learn on the subject, that pauper street-work, even at the best, is unwilling and slovenly work, pauper workmen being the worst of all workmen. If the streets be swept clean, it is because a dozen paupers are put to the labour of eight, nine, or ten regular scavagers who are independent labourers, and who may have some "pride of art," or some desire to show their employers that they are to be depended upon. This feeling does not actuate the pauper workman, who thinks or knows that if he did evince a desire and a perseverance to please, it would avail him little beyond the sneers and ill-will of his mates; so that, even with a disposition to acquire the good opinion of the authorities, there is this obstacle in his way, and to most men who move in a circumscribed sphere it is a serious obstacle.

Of the second mode of pauper scavaging, viz., that performed by out-door paupers, and paid for partly in money and partly in kind, I heard from officials connected with pauper management very strong condemnations, as being full of mischievous and degrading tendencies. The payment to the out-door pauper scavager averages, as I have stated, 9*d.* a day to a single man, with, perhaps, a quartern loaf; and this, in some cases, is for only three days in the week; while to a married man with a family, it varies between 1*s.* 1½*d.* and 1*s.* 2*d.* a day, with a quartern, and sometimes two quartern loaves; and this, likewise, is occasionally from three to six days in the week. On this the single or family men must subsist, if they have no other means of earning an addition. The men thus employed are certainly not independent labourers, nor are they, in the full sense of the word as popularly understood, paupers; for their means of subsistence are partly the fruits of their toil; and although they are wretchedly dependent, they seem to feel that they have a sort of right to be set to work, as the law ordains such modicum of relief, in or out of the workhouse, as will only ward off death through hunger. This "three-

*TABLE SHOWING THE NUMBER OF MEN EMPLOYED BY SCAVAGING, AS WELL AS THE NUMBER OF HOURS PER DAY AMOUNT OF WAGES ACCRUING TO EACH, AND THE TOTAL

PARISHES.	No. of married men employed by parishes daily in scavaging the streets.	Number of single men employed by parishes daily in scavaging the streets.	Number of Superintendents employed by parishes.	Number of Foremen or Gangers employed by parishes.	Daily or weekly wages of the married parish-men.
Paid in Money (by Parishes).					s.
Greenwich	7	1	1	1	15
Walworth	12	8		3	15
Newington					
Lambeth	30		1	5	15
Poplar	20			4	15
St. Ann's, Soho	4	1			15
Rotherhithe	4			1	14
Wandsworth	6			1	12
Hackney	12	4		4	12
St. Mary's, Paddington	8	5	1	2	12
St. Giles's, and St. George's, Bloomsbury	20	4		4	12
St. Pancras (South-west Division)	10		2		12
St. Clement Danes	6	2		1	11
St. Paul's, Covent-garden	2	5		1	11
St. James's, Westminster	6			1	10
Ditto	6			1	10
Ditto	6			1	9
St. Andrew's, Holborn	10		1	1	9
Marylebone	80	15	1	10	9
St. George's, Hanover-square	30	6	1	4	9s. a week.
Liberty of the Rolls	1				7s. 6d.
Bermondsey	13	1	1		1s. 4d. per day.
Paid in Money (by Highway Boards).					
St. James's, Clerkenwell (1st Division)	5				15
Islington	7	1		1	15
Commercial Road East	4	1	1		15
Hampstead	4			1	15
Highgate	3	2		1	14
Kensington	6	1		1	12
Lewisham	4			1	12
Camberwell	10			1	12
Christchurch, Lambeth	6			1	12
Woolwich	5			1	12
Deptford	4			1	9
Paid partly in kind.					
St. Luke's, Chelsea	27	9		3	7s., and on an average 3 loaves each at 4d. a loaf.
Hans-town „	6			1	7s., and average loaves per head.
St. James's, Clerkenwell	6				1s. 1½d. a day, and 1 quartern loaf.
Paid wholly in kind.					
St. Pancras (Highways)	10		1		estimated expense of food, 2s. 4d. weekly.
Total	400	66	8	62	

* The number of men here given as employed by the parishes in the scavaging of the streets will be found to differ from that of the table at page 213; but the present table includes *all* the parish-men employed throughout London whereas the other referred to only a portion of the localities there mentioned.

THE METROPOLITAN PARISHES AND HIGHWAY BOARDS IN AND NUMBER OF DAYS PER WEEK, TOGETHER WITH THE ANNUAL WAGES OF THE WHOLE.

Daily or weekly wages of the single parish-men.	Weekly wages of the Superintendents employed by parishes.	Weekly wages of Foremen or Gangers employed by parishes.	Number of hours per day each parish-man is employed to sweep the streets.	Number of days in the week each parish-man is employed in sweeping the streets.	Total annual wages of the whole, including the estimated value of food and clothes.
s.	s.	s.			£. s. d.
15	30s. and a house to live in.	18	10	6	456 16 0
14		18	12	6	899 12 0
	20	18	10	6	1456 0 0
		18	10	6	967 4 0
15			12	6	195 0 0
		16	10	6	187 4 0
		18	10	6	234 0 0
10		18	10	6	665 12 0
10	20	15	12	6	509 12 0
12		18	12	6	936 0 0
		18	12	6	93 12 0
11		15	10	6	267 16 0
11		13	12	6	234 0 0
		12	10	6	187 4 0
		12	10	6	187 4 0
		12	10	6	166 12 0
	15	12	10	6	304 4 0
9	18	16	10	6	2685 16 0
9s. a week.	20	16	10	6	1060 16 0
			10	6	19 10 0
1s. 4d. per day.	28s. and clothing.		10	5	321 3 4
			10	6	195 0 0
15		18	10	6	405 0 0
15	100l. a year.		12	6	295 0 0
		18	10	6	202 10 0
14		18	10	6	228 16 0
12		18	12	6	265 4 0
		18	10	6	171 12 0
		18	12	6	358 16 0
		15	10	6	226 4 0
		18	10	6	202 16 0
		18	10	3	140 8 0
7		14	10	6	834 12 0
		14	10	6	161 4 0
			10	3	70 4 0
	21s. and food.		8	4	128 5 4
					15,919 8 8

days-a-week work" is by the poor or pauper labourers looked upon as being, after the in-door pauper work, the worst sort of employment.

From a married man employed by the parish under this mode, I had the following account.

He was an intelligent-looking man, of about 35, but with nothing very particular in his appearance unless it were a head of very curly hair. He gave me the statement in his own room, which was larger than I have usually found such abodes, and would have been very bare, but that it was somewhat littered with the vessels of his trade as a street-seller of Nectar, Persian Sherbet, Raspberryade, and other decoctions of coloured ginger-beer, with high-sounding names and indifferent flavour: in the summer he said he could live better thereby, with a little costering, than by street-sweeping, but being often a sickly man he could not do so during the uncertainties of a winter street trade. His wife, a decent looking woman, was present occasionally, suckling one child, about two years old—for the poor often protract the weaning of their children, as the mother's nutriment is the *cheapest* of all food for the infant, and as the means of postponing the further increase of their family—whilst another of five or six years of age sat on a bench by her side. There was nothing on the walls in the way of an ornament, as I have seen in some of the rooms of the poor, for the couple had once been in the workhouse, and might be driven there again, and with such apprehensions did not care, perhaps, to make a home otherwise than they found it, even if the consumption of only a little spare time were involved.

The husband said:—

"I was brought up as a type-founder; my father, who was one, learnt me his trade; but he died when I was quite a young man, or I might have been better perfected in it. I was comfortably off enough then, and got married. Very soon after that I was taken ill with an abscess in my neck, you can see the mark of it still." [He showed me the mark.] "For six months I wasn't able to do a thing, and I was a part of the time, I don't recollect how long, in St. Bartholomew's Hospital. I was weak and ill when I came out, and hardly fit for work; I couldn't hear of any work I could get, for there was a great bother in the trade between master and men. Before I went into the hospital, there was money to pay to doctors; and when I came out I could earn nothing, so everything went, yes, sir, everything. My wife made a little matter with charing for families she'd lived in, but things are in a bad way if a poor woman has to keep her husband. She was taken ill at last, and then there was nothing but the parish for us. I suffered a great deal before it come to that. It was awful. No one can know what it is but them that suffers it. But I didn't know what in the world to do. We lived then in St. Luke's, and were passed to our own parish, and were three months in the workhouse. The living was good enough, better then than it is now, I've heard, but I was miserable." ["And I was *very* miserable," interposed the wife, "for I had been brought up comfortable; my father was a respectable tradesman in St. George's-in-the-East, and I had been in good situations."]

"We made ourselves," said the husband, "as useful as we could, but we were parted of course. At the three months' end, I had 10s. given to me to come out with, and was told I might start costermongering on it. But to a man not up to the trade, 10s. won't go very far to keep up costering. I didn't feel master enough of my own trade by this time to try for work at it, and work wasn't at all regular. There were good hands earning only 12s. a week. The 10s. soon went, and I had again to apply for relief, and got an order for the stone-yard to go and break stones. Ten bushels was to be broken for 15d. It was dreadful hard work at first. My hands got all blistered and bloody, and I've gone home and cried with pain and wretchedness. At first it was on to three days before I could break the ten bushels. I felt shivered to bits all over my arms and shoulders, and my head was splitting. I then got to do it in two days, and then in one, and it grew easier. But all this time I had only what was reckoned three days' work in a week. That is, you see, sir, I had only three times ten bushels of stones given to break in the week, and earned only 3s. 9d. Yes, I lived on it, and paid 1s. 6d. a week rent, for the neighbours took care of a few sticks for us, and the parish or a broker wouldn't have found them worth carriage. My wife was then in the country with a sister. I lived upon bread and dripping, went without fire or candle (or had one only very seldom) though it wasn't warm weather. I can safely say that for eight weeks I never tasted one bite of meat, and hardly a bite of butter. When I couldn't sleep of a night, but that wasn't often, it was terrible, very. I washed what bits of things I had then myself, and had sometimes to get a ha'porth of soap as a favour, as the chandler said she 'didn't make less than a penn'orth.' If I eat too much dripping, it made me feel sick. I hardly know how much bread and dripping I eat in a week. I spent what money I had in it and bread, and sometimes went without. I was very weak, you may be sure, sir; and if I'd had the influenza or anything that way, I should have gone off like a shot, for I seemed to have no constitution left. But my wife came back again and got work at charing, and made about 4s. a week at it; but we were still very badly off. Then I got to work on the roads every day, and had 1s. and a quartern loaf a day, which was a rise. I had only one child then, but men with larger families got two quartern loaves a day. Single men got 9d. a day. It was far easier work than stone-breaking too. The hours were from eight to five in winter, and from seven to six in summer. But there's always changes going on, and we were put on 1s. 1½d. a day and a quartern loaf, and only three days a week. All the same as to time of course. The bread wasn't good; it was only cheap. I suppose there was 20 of us working most of the times as I was. The gangsman, as you call him, but that's more for the regular hands, was a servant of the parish, and a great tyrant.

Yes, indeed, when we had a talk among ourselves, there was nothing but grumbling heard of. Some of the tales I've heard were shocking; worse than what I've gone through. Everybody was grumbling, except perhaps two men that had been 20 years in the streets, and were like born paupers. They didn't feel it, for there's a great difference in men. They knew no better. But anybody might have been frightened to hear some of the men talk and curse. We've stopped work to abuse the parish officers as might be passing. We've mobbed the overseers, and a number of us, I was one, were taken before the magistrate for it; but we told him how badly we were off, and he discharged us, and gave us orders into the workhouse, and told 'em to see if nothing could be done for us. We were there till next morning, and then sent away without anything being said.

"It's a sad life, sir, is a parish worker's. I wish to God I could get out of it. But when a man has children he can't stop and say 'I can't do this,' and 'I won't do that.' Last week, now, I lost 6s.'" [he meant that his expenses, of every kind, exceeded his receipts by 6s.], and though I can distil nectar, or anything that way" [this was said somewhat laughingly], "it's only when the weather's hot and fine that any good at all can be done with it. I think, too, that there's not the money among working men that there once was. Anything regular in the way of pay must always be looked at by a man with a family.

"Of course the streets must be properly swept, and if I can sweep them as well as Mr. Dodd's men, for I know one of them very well, why should I have only 3s. 4½d. a week and three loaves, and he have 16s, I think it is? I don't drink, my wife knows I don't" [the wife assented], "and it seems as if in a parish a man must be kept down when he is down, and then blamed for it. I may not understand all about it, but it looks queer."

From an *unmarried* man, looking like a mere boy in the face, although he assured me he was nearly 24, as far as he knew, I heard an account of his labour and its fruits as a parish scavager; also of his former career, which partakes greatly in its characteristics of the narratives I gave, toward the close of the first volume, of deserted, neglected, and runaway children.

He lived from his earliest recollection with an old woman whom he first called "grandmother," and was then bid to call "aunt," and she, some of the neighbours told him, had "kept him out of his rights," for she had 4s. a week with him, so that there ought to have been money coming to him when he grew up. I have sometimes heard similar statements from the ignorant poor, for it is agreeable enough to them to fancy that they have been wronged out of fortunes to which they were justly entitled, and deprived of the position and consequence in life which they ought to have possessed "by rights." In the course of my inquiries among the poor women who supply the slop milliners' shops with widows' caps, cap fronts, women's collars, &c., &c., I was told by one middle-aged cap-maker, a very silly person, that she would be worth 100,000*l*, "if she had her rights." What those "rights" were she could not explain, only that there was and had been a great deal of money in the family, and of course she had a right to her share, only she was kept out of it.

The youth in question never heard of a father, and had been informed that his mother had died when he was a baby. From what he told me, I think it most probable that he was an illegitimate child, for whose maintenance his father possibly paid the 4s. a week, perhaps to some near relative of the deceased mother. The old woman, as well as I could make the matter out from his narrative, died suddenly, and, as little was known about her, she was buried by the parish, and the lad, on the evening of the funeral, was to have been taken by the landlord of the house where they lodged into the workhouse; but the boy ran away before this could be accomplished; the parish of course not objecting to be relieved of an incumbrance. He thought he was then about twelve or thirteen years of age, and he had before run away from two schools, one a Ragged-school, to which he had been sent, "*for it was so confining*," he said, "and one master, not he as had the raggeds, leathered him," to use his own words, "tightly." He knew his letters now, he thought, but that was all, and very few," he said, gravely, "would have put up with it so long as I did." He subsisted as well as he could by selling matches, penny memorandum books, onions, &c., after he had run away, sleeping under hedges in the country, or in lodging-houses in town, and living on a few pence a day, or "starving on nothink." He was taken ill, and believed it was of a fever, at or somewhere about Portsmouth, and when he was sufficiently recovered, and had given the best account he could of himself, was passed to his parish in London. The relieving officer, he said, would have given him a pair of shoes and half-a-crown, and let him "take his chance, but the doctor wouldn't sartify any ways." He meant, I think, that the medical officer found him too ill to be at large on his own account. He discharged himself, however, in a few weeks from this parish workhouse, as he was convalescent. "The grub there, you see, sir," he said, "was stunning good when I first went, but it fell off." As the probability is that there was no change in the diet, it may not be unfair to conclude that the regular meals of the establishment were very relishable at first, and that afterwards their very regularity and their little variation made the recipient critical.

"When I left, sir," he stated, "they guv me 2s. 6d., and a tidy shirt, and a pair of blucherers, and mended up my togs for me decent. I tried all sorts of goes then. I went to Chalk-farm and some other fairs with sticks for throwing, and used to jump among them as throwing was going on, and to sing out, 'break my legs and miss my pegs.' I got many a knock, and when I did, oh! there *was* such larfing at the fun on it. I sold garden sticks too, and garden ropes, and posts sometimes; but it was all wery poor pay. Sometimes I made 10d., but not never I think but twice 1*s.* a day at it, and oftener 6*d.*, and in bad weather there was nothink to be done. If I made 6*d.* clear, it was 1*d.* for cawfee—for I often went out fasting in a morning —and 1*d.* for bread and butter, and 1*d.* for pudden for dinner, and another 1*d.* perhaps for beer—half-pint and a farden out at the public bar—and 2*d.* for a night's lodging. I've had sometimes to leave half my stock in flue with a deputy for a night's rest. O, I didn't much mind the bugs, so I could rest; and next day had to take my things out if I could, and pay a hexter ha'penny or penny, for hintrest, like. Yes, I've made 18*d.* a hevening at a fair; but there's so many a going it there that one ruins another, and wet weather ruins the whole biling, the pawillion, theaytres and all. I never was a hactor, never; but I've thought sometimes I'd like to try my hand at it. I may some day, 'cause I'm tall. I was forced to go to the parish again, for I got ill and dreadful weak, and then they guv me work on the roads. I can't just say how long it's since, two or three year perhaps, but I had 9*d.* a day at first, and reglar work, and then three days and three loaves a week, and then three days and no loaves. I haven't been at it werry lately. I've rayther taken the summer out of myself, but I must go back soon, for cold weather's a coming. Vy, I lived a good deal on carrying trunks from the busses to Euston Railway; a good many busses stops in the New-road, in the middle of the square. Some was foreigners, and they was werry scaly. No, I never said nothink but once, ven I got two French ha'pennies for carrying a heavy old leather thing, like a coach box, as seemed to belong to a family; and then the railway bobbies made me hold my tongue. I jobbed about in other places too, but the time's gone by now. O, I had a deal to put up with last winter. What is 9*d.* a day for three days? and if poor men had their rights, times 'ud be different. I'd like to know where all the money goes. I never counted how many parish sweepers there was; too many by arf. I've a rights to work, and it's as little as a parish can do to find it. I pay 1*s.* a week for half a bed, and not half enough bed-clothes; but me and Jack Smith sometimes sleeps in our clothes, and sometimes spreads 'em o' top. No, poor Jack, he hasn't no hold on a parish; he's a mud-lark and a gatherer [bone-grubber]. Do I like the overseers and the parish officers? In course not, nobody does. Why don't they? Well, how can they? that's just where it is. Ven I haven't been at sweeping, I've staid in bed as long as I was let; but Mother B.—I don't know no other name she has—wouldn't stand it after ten. O no, it wern't a common lodging-house, a sort of private lodging-house perhaps, where you took by the week. If I made nothink but my ninepences, I lived on bread and cawfee, or bread and coker, and sometimes a red herring, and I've bought 'em in the Brill at five and six a penny. Mother B. charged ½*d.* for leave to toast 'em on her gridiron. She *is* a scaly old ——. *I've oft spent all my money in a tripe supper at night, and fasted all next day.* I used to walk about and look in at the cook-shop windows, and try for a job next day. *I'd have gone five miles for anybody for a penn'orth of pudden.* No, I never thought of making away with myself; never. Nor I never thought of going for a soldier; *it wouldn't suit me to be tied so.* What I want is this here—regular work and no jaw. O, I'm sometimes as miserable as hunger'll make a parson, if ever he felt it. Yes, I go to church sometimes when I'm at work for the parish, if I'm at all togged. No doubt I shall die in the workus. You see there's nobody in the world cares for me. I can't tell just how I spend my money; just as it comes into my head. No, I don't care about drinking; it don't agree with me; but there's some can live on it. I don't think as I shall ever marry, though who knows?"

The third and last system of parish work is where the labourer is employed regularly, and paid a fixed wage, out of the parochial fund certainly, but not in the same manner as the paupers are paid, nor with any payment in kind (as in loaves), but all in money. The payment in this wise is usually 1*s.* 6*d.* a day, and, but for such employment, the poor so employed, would, in most instances, apply for relief.

In one parish, where the poor are regularly employed in street sweeping, and paid a regular wage in money, the whole scavaging work is done by the paupers, as they are usually termed, though they are not "on the rate." By them the streets are swept and the houses dusted, the granite broken for macadamization, and the streets and roads repaved or repaired. This is done by about 50 men, the labour in the different departments I have specified being about equally apportioned as to the number employed in each. The work is executed without any direct intervention of the parish officers employed in administering *relief* to the poor, but through the agency of a board. All the men, however, are the poor of the parish, and but for this employment would or might claim relief, or demand admittance with their families into the workhouse. The system, therefore, is one of indirect pauper labour. Nearly all the men have been unskilled labourers, the exception being now and then a few operatives in such handicrafts as were suffering from the dearth of employment. Some of the artizans, I was informed, would be earning their 9*s.* in the stone-yard one week, and the next getting 30*s.* at their business. The men thus labouring for the parish are about three-fifths Irishmen, a fifth Welchmen, or rather more than a fifth, and the remainder Englishmen. There is not a single Scotchman among them.

There is no difference, in the parish I allude to, between the wages of married and single men, but men with families are usually preferred among the applicants for such work. They all reside in their own rooms, or sometimes in lodging-houses, but this rests with themselves.

I had the following account from a heavy and healthy-looking middle-aged man, dressed in a jacket and trousers of coarse corduroy. There is so little distinctive about it, however, that I will not consume space in presenting it in the narrative form in which I noted it down. It may suffice that the man seemed to have little recollection as to the past, and less care as to the future. His life, from all I could learn from him, had been spent in what may be called menial labour, as the servant, not of an individual, but of a parish; but there was nothing, he knew of, that he had to thank anybody for—parish or any one. They wanted *him* and he wanted *them*. On my asking him if he had never tried to "better himself," he said that he *had* once as a navvy, but a blow on the head and eye, from a portion of rock shivered by his pick-axe, disabled him for awhile, and he left railway work. He went to church, as was expected of him, and he and his wife liked it. He had forgotten how to read, but never was "a dab at it," and so "didn't know nothing about the litany or the psalms." He couldn't say as he knew any difference between the Church of England and the Roman Catholic church-goers, "cause the one was a English and the t' other a Irish religion," and he "wasn't to be expected to understand Irish religion." He saw no necessity to put by money (this he said hesitatingly), supposing he could; what was his parish for? and he would take care he didn't lose his settlement. If he'd ever had such a chance as some had he might have saved money, but he never had. He had no family, and his wife earned about 4s. a week, but not every week, in a wool warehouse, and they did middling.

The above, then, are the modes in which paupers, or imminent paupers, so to speak, are employed, and in one way or other are *paid* for their labour, or what is called paid, and who, although parish menials, still reside in their own abodes, with the opportunity, such as it is, of "looking out" for better employment.

As to the *moral qualities of the street-sweeping paupers* I do not know that they differ from those of paupers generally. All men who feel themselves sunk into compulsory labour and a degraded condition are dissatisfied, and eager to throw the blame of their degradation from their own shoulders. But it is evident that these men are unwilling workers, because their work is deprived of its just reward; and although I did not hear of any difficulty being experienced in getting them to work, I was assured by many who knew them well, that they do not go about it with any alertness. Did any one ever hear a pauper whistle or sing at his street-work? I believe that every experienced vestryman will agree to the truth of the statement that it is very rarely a confirmed pauper rises from his degradation. His thoughts and aspirations seem bounded by the workhouse and the parish. The reason appears to be because the workhouse authorities seek rather to degrade than to elevate the man, resorting to every means of shaming the pauper, until at last he becomes so utterly callous to the disgrace of pauperism that he does not care to alter his position. The system, too, adopted by the parish authorities of not paying for work, or paying less than the ordinary prices of the trade, causes the pauper labourers to be unwilling workers; and finding that industry brings no reward, or less than its fair reward, to them, they get to hate all work, and to grow up habitual burdens on the State. Crabbe, the poet, who in all questions of borough and parish life is an authority, makes his workhouse boy, Dick Monday, who when a boy got more kicks than halfpence, die Sir Richard Monday, of Monday-place; but this is a flight on the wings of poetical licence; certainly not impossible, and that is all which can be said for its likelihood.

The following remarks on the payment of the parish street-sweepers are from one of Mr. Cochrane's publications:—

"The council considers it a duty to the poor to touch upon the niggardly manner in which parish scavengers are generally paid, and the deplorable and emaciated condition which they usually present, with regard to their clothing and personal appearance. One contractor pays 16s. 6d. per week; 2 pay 16s.; 12 (including a Highway Board) pay 15s. each; 1 pays 14s. 6d.; 2 pay 14s.; and 1 pays so low as 12s. On the other hand, five parish boards of 'guardians of the poor,' pay only 9s. each, to their miserable mudlarks; one pays 8s.; another 7s. 5d.; a third 7s.; a fourth compensates its labourers—in the British metropolis, where rent and living are necessarily higher than elsewhere—with 5s. 8d. per week! whilst a fifth pays 3 men 15s. each, 12 men 10s. each, and 6 men 7s. 6d. each, for exactly the same kind of work!!! But what renders this mean torture of men (because they happen to be poor) absurd as well as cruel, are the anomalous facts, that whilst the guardians of one parish pay 5 men 7s. each, the contractor for another part of the same parish, pays his 4 men 14s. each;—and whilst the guardians of a second parish pay only 5s. 8d., the Highway Board pays 15s. to each of its labourers, for performing exactly the same work in the same district!—Mr. Darke, scavenging contractor of Paddington, lately stated that he never had, and never would, employ any man at less than 16s. or 18s. per week;—and Mr. Sinnott, of Belvidere-road, Lambeth, about three months since, offered to certain West-End guardians, to take 40 paupers out of their own workhouse to cleanse their own parish, on the street-orderly system;—and to pay them 15s. per week each man*; but the economical guardians preferred filth and a full workhouse, to cleanliness, Christian charity, and common sense;—and so the proposal of this considerate contractor was rejected! It is certainly far from being creditable to boards of gentlemen and wealthy tradesmen who manage parish affairs, to pay little more than one-half the wages that an individual does, to poor labourers who cannot choose their employment or their masters. . . . .

"The broken-down tradesman, the journeyman deprived of his usual work by panic or by poverty of the times, the ingenious mechanic, or the unsuccessful artist, applies at the parish labour-market for leave to live by other labour than that

* To the honourable conduct of the above-named contractors to their men, I am glad to be able to bear witness. All the men speak in the highest terms of them.

which hitherto maintained him in comfort. . . . . . The usual language of such persons, even when applying for private alms or parochial relief, is, not that they want money, but 'that they have long been out of work;' 'that their particular trade has been overstocked with apprentices, or superseded by machinery;' or, 'that their late employer has become bankrupt, or has discharged the majority of his hands from the badness of the times.' To a man of this class, the guardian of the poor replies, 'We will test your willingness to labour, by employing you in the stone-yard, or to sweep the streets; but the parish being heavily burthened with rates, we cannot afford more than 7s. or 8s. a week.' The poor creature, conscious of his own helplessness, accepts the miserable pittance, in order to preserve himself and family from immediate starvation. . . . . .

"The council has taken much pains to ascertain the wages, and mode of expenditure of them, by this uncared-for, and almost pariah, class of labourers throughout the metropolitan parishes; and it possesses undeniable proofs, that few possess any further garment than the rags upon their backs; some being even without a change of linen; that they never enter a place of worship, on account of their want of decent clothing; that their wives and children are starved and in rags, and the latter without the least education; that they never by any chance taste fresh animal food; that one-third of their hard earnings is paid for rent; and that their only sustenance (unless their wives happen to go out washing or charing), consists of bread, potatoes, coarse tea without milk or sugar, a salt herring two or three times a week, and a slice of rusty bacon on Sunday morning! The meal called dinner they never know; their only refection being breakfast and 'tea:' beer they do not taste from year's end to year's end; and any other luxury, or even necessary, is out of the question.

"Of the 21 scavengers employed by St. James's parish in 1850, no less than 16," says Mr. Cochrane's report, "were married, with from one to four children each. How the poor creatures who receive but 7s. 6d. a week support their families, is best known to themselves."

Let me now, in conclusion, endeavour to arrive at a rough estimate as to the sum of which the pauper labours annually are mulct by the beforementioned rates of remuneration, estimating their labour at the market value or amount paid by the honourable contractors, viz. 16s. a week; for if private individuals can afford to pay that wage, and yet reap a profit out of the transaction, the guardians of the poor surely could and should pay the same prices, and not avail themselves of starving men's necessities to reduce the wages of a trade to the very quick of subsistence. If it be a sound principle that the condition of the pauper should be rendered *less* desirable than that of the labourer, assuredly the principle is equally sound that the condition of the labourer should be made *more* desirable than that of the pauper; for if to pamper the pauper be to make indolence more agreeable than industry, certainly to grind down the wages of the labourer is to render industry as unprofitable as indolence. In either case the same premium is proffered to pauperism. As yet the Poor-Law Commissioners have seen but one way of reducing the poor-rates, viz., by rendering the state of the pauper as *unenviable* as possible, and they have wholly lost sight of the other mode of attaining the same end, viz., by making the state of the labourer as *desirable* as possible. To institute a terrible poor law without maintaining an attractive form of industry, is to hold out a boon to crime. If the wages of the working man are to be reduced to bare subsistence, and the condition of the pauper is to be rendered worse than that of the working man, what atrocities will not be committed upon the poor. Elevate the condition of the labourer, and there will be no necessity to depress the pauper. Make work more attractive by increasing the reward for it, and laziness will necessarily become more repulsive. As it is, however, the pauper is not only kept at the very lowest point of subsistence, but his half-starved labour is brought into competition with that of men living in a comparative state of comfort; and the result, of course, is, that instead of decreasing the number of paupers or poor-rates, we make paupers of our labourers, and fill our workhouses by such means. If a scavager's labour be worth from 12s. to 15s. per week in the market, what moral right have the *guardians of the poor* to pay 5s. 8d. for the same commodity? If the paupers are set to do work which is fairly worth 15s., then to pay them little more than one-third of the regular value is not only to make unwilling workers of the paupers, but to drag down all the better workmen to the level of the worst.

It may be estimated that the outlay on pauper labour, as a whole, after deducting the sum paid to superintendents and gangers, does not exceed 10s. weekly per individual; consequently the lowering of the price of labour is in this ratio: There are now, in round numbers, 450 pauper scavagers in the metropolis, and the account stands thus:—

	Yearly.
450 scavagers, at the regular weekly wages of 16s. each . .	£18,710
450 pauper labourers, 10s. each weekly	11,700
Lower price of pauper work . .	£7,020

Hence we see, that the great scurf employers of the scavagers, after all, are the guardians of the poor compared with whom the most grasping contractor is a model of liberality.

That the minimum of remuneration paid by the parishes has tended, and is tending more and more, to the general depreciation of wages in the scavaging trade, there is no doubt. It has done so directly and indirectly. One man, who had been a last-maker, told me that he left his employment as a London scavager, for he had "come down to the parish," and set off at the close of the summer into Kent for the harvest and hopping, for, when in the country, he had been more used to agricultural labour than to last, clog, or patten making. He considered that he had not been successful; still he returned to London a richer man by 26s. 6d. Nearly 20s. of this soon went for shoes and necessary clothing, and to pay some arrears of rent, and a chandler's bill he owed, after which he could be trusted again where he was known. He applied to the foreman of a contractor, whom he knew, for work. "What wage?" said the foreman. "Fifteen shillings a week," was the reply. "Why, what did you get from the parish for sweeping?" "Nine shillings." "Well," said the foreman, "I know you're a decent man, and you were recommended before, and so I *can* give you four or five days a week at 2s. 4d. a day, and no nonsense about hours; *for you know yourself I can get 50 men as have been parish workers at 1s. 9d. a day, and jump at it, and so you mustn't be cheeky.*" The man closed with the offer, knowing that the foreman spoke the truth.

A contractor told me that he could obtain "plenty of hands," used to parish scavaging work, at 10s. 6d. to 12s. a week, whereas he paid 16s.

It is evident, then, that the system of pauper work in scavaging has created an increasing market for cheap and deteriorated labour, a market including hundreds of the unemployed at other unskilled labours; and it is hardly to be doubted that the many who have faith in the doctrine that it is the best policy to buy in the cheapest and sell in the dearest market, will avail themselves of the low-priced labour of this pauper-constituted mart.

It is but right to add, that those parishes which pay 15s. a week are as worthy of commendation as those which pay 9s., 7s. 6d. and 7s. per week, and 1s. 4d. and 1s. 1½d. a day are reprehensible; and, unfortunately, the latter have a tendency to regulate all the others.

OF THE STREET-ORDERLIES.

THIS constitutes the last of the four varieties of labour employed in the cleansing of the public thoroughfares of London. I have already treated of the self-supporting manual labour, the self-supporting machine labour, and the pauper labour, and now proceed to the consideration of the philanthropic labour of the streets.

In the first place, let us understand clearly what is meant by philanthropic labour, and how it is distinguished from pauper labour on the one hand, and self-supporting labour on the other. Self-supporting labour I take to be that form of work which returns not less, and generally something more, than is expended upon it. Pauper labour, on the other hand, is work to which the applicants for parish relief are "set," not with a view to the profit to be derived from it, but partly as a test of their willingness to work, and partly as a means of employing the unemployed; while philanthropic labour is employment provided for the unemployed with the same disregard of profit as distinguishes pauper labour, but with a greater regard for the poor, and as a means of affording them relief in a less degrading manner than is done under the present Poor Law. Pauper and philanthropic labour, then, differ essentially from self-supporting labour in being *non-profitable* modes of employment; that is to say, they yield so bare an equivalent for the sum expended upon the labourers, that none, in the ordinary way of trade, can be found to provide the means necessary for putting them into operation: while pauper labour differs from philanthropic labour, in the fact that the funds requisite for "setting the poor on work" are provided by law as a matter of social policy, whereas, in the case of philanthropic labour, the funds, or a part of them, are supplied by voluntary contributions, out of a desire to improve the labourers' condition. There are, then, two distinguishing features in all philanthropic labour—the one is, that it yields no profit (if it did it would become a matter of trade), and the other, that it is instituted and maintained from a wish to benefit the labourer.

The Street-Orderly system forms part of the operations on behalf of the poor adopted by a society, of which Mr. Charles Cochrane is the president, entitled the "National Philanthropic Association," which is said to have for its object "the promotion of social and salutiferous improvements, street cleanliness, and the employment of the poor, so that able-bodied men may be prevented from burthening the parish-rate, and preserved independent of workhouse, alms, and degradation." Here a twofold object is expressed: the Philanthropic Association seeks not only to benefit the poor by giving them employment, and "preserving them independent of workhouse, alms, and degradation," but to benefit the public likewise, by "promoting social and salutiferous improvements and street cleanliness." I shall deal with each of these objects separately; but first let me declare, so as to remove all suspicion of private feelings tending in any way to bias my judgment in this most important matter, that I am an utter stranger to the President and Council of the Philanthropic Association; and that, whatever I may have to say on the subject of the street-orderlies, I do simply in conformity with my duty to the public—to state truthfully all that concerns the labourers and the poor of the metropolis.

Viewed economically, philanthropic and pauper work may be said to be the regulators of the minimum rate of wages—establishing the lowest point to which competition can possibly drive down the remuneration for labour; for it is evident, that if the self-supporting labourer cannot obtain greater comforts by the independent exercise of his industry than the parish rates or private charity will afford him, he will at once give over working for the trading employer, and declare on the funds raised by assessment or voluntary subscription for his support. Hence, those who wish well to the labourer, and who believe that cheapness of commodities is desirable "only," as Mr. Stewart Mill says (p. 502, vol. ii.), "when the cause of it is, that their production costs little labour, and not when occasioned by that labour's being ill-remunerated;" and who believe, moreover, that the labourer is to be benefited solely by the cultivation of a high standard of comfort among the people — to such, I say, it is evident, that a poor law which reduces the relief to able-bodied labourers to the smallest modicum of food consistent with the continuation of life must be about the greatest curse that can possibly come upon an over-populated country, admitting, as it does, of the reduction of wages to so low a point of mere brutal existence as to induce that recklessness and improvidence among the poor which is known to give so strong an impetus to the increase of the people. A minimized rate of parish relief is necessarily a minimized rate of wages, and admits of the labourers' pay being reduced, by pauper competition, to little short of starvation; and such, doubtlessly, would have been the case long ago in the scavaging trade by the employment of parish labour, had not the Philanthropic Association instituted the system of street-orderlies, and by the payment of a higher rate of wages than the more grinding parishes afforded—by giving the men 12s. instead of 9s. or even 7s. a week—prevented the remuneration of the regular hands being dragged down to an approximation to the parish level. Hence, rightly viewed, philanthropic labour—and, indeed, pauper labour too—comes under the head of a remedy for low wages, as preventing, if properly regulated, the undue depreciation of industry from excessive competition, and it is in this light that I shall now proceed to consider it.

The several plans that have been propounded from time to time, as remedies for an insufficient rate of remuneration for work, are as multifarious as the circumstances influencing the three requisites for production—labour, capital, and land. I will here run over as briefly as possible—abstaining from the expression of all opinion on the subject—the various schemes which have been proposed with this object, so that the reader may come as prepared as possible to the consideration of the matter.

The remedies for low wages may be arranged into two distinct groups, viz., those which seek to increase the labourer's rate of pay *directly*, and those which seek to do so *indirectly*.

The *direct* remedies for low wages that have been propounded are :—

A. *The establishment of a standard rate of remuneration for labour.* This has been proposed to be brought about by three different means, viz. :—
1. By law or government authority; either (*a*) fixing the minimum rate of wages, and leaving the variations above that point to be adjusted by competition (this, as we have seen, is the effect of the poor-law); or, (*b*) settling the rate of wages generally by means of local boards of trade for *conseils de prud'hommes*, consisting of delegates from the workmen and employers, to determine, by the principles of natural equity, a *reasonable* scale of remuneration in the several trades, their decision being binding in law on both the employers and the employed.
2. By public opinion; this has been generally proposed by those who are what Mr. Mill terms "shy of admitting the interference of authority in contracts for labour," fearing that if the law intervened it would do so rashly and ignorantly, and desiring to compass by *moral* sanction what they consider useless or dangerous to attempt to bring about by *legal* means. "Every employer," says Mr. Mill, "they think, *ought* to give *sufficient wages*," and if he does not give such wages willingly, he should be compelled to do so by public opinion.
3. By trade societies or combination among the workmen; that is to say, by the payment of a small sum per week out of the wages of the workmen, towards the formation of a fund for the support of such of their fellow operatives as may be out of employment, or refuse to work for those employers who seek to give less than the standard rate of wages established by the trade.

B. *The prohibition of stoppages or deductions of all kinds from the nominal wages of workmen.* This is principally the object of the Anti-Truck Society, which seeks to obtain an Act of Parliament, enjoining the payment in full of all wages. The stoppages or extortions from workmen's wages generally consist of :—
1. Fines for real or pretended misconduct.
2. Rents for tools, frames, gas, and sometimes lodgings.
3. Sale of trade appliances (as trimmings, thread, &c.) at undue prices.
4. Sale of food, drink, &c., at an exorbitant rate of profit.
5. Payment in public-houses; as the means of inducing the men to spend a portion of their earnings in drink.
6. Deposit of money as security before taking out work; so that the capital of the employer is increased without payment of interest to the workpeople.

C. *The institution of certain aids or additions to wages;* as—
1. Perquisites or gratuities obtained from the public; as with waiters, boxkeepers, coachmen, dustmen, vergers, and others.
2. Beer money, and other "allowances" to workmen.
3. Family work; or the co-operation of the wife and children as a means of increasing the workman's income.
4. Allotments of land, to be cultivated after the regular day's labour.
5. The parish "allowance system," or relief in aid of wages, as practised under the old Poor Law.

D. *The increase of the money value of wages;* by—

1. Cheap food.
2. Cheap lodgings; through building improved dwellings for the poor, and doing away with the profit of sub-letting.
3. Co-operative stores; or the "club system" of obtaining provisions at wholesale prices.
4. The abolition of the payment of wages on Sunday morning, or at so late an hour on the Saturday night as to prevent the labourer availing himself of the Saturday's market.
5. Teetotalism; as causing the men to spend nothing in fermented drinks, and so leaving them more to spend on food.

Such are the *direct* modes of remedying low wages, viz., either by preventing the price of labour itself falling below a certain standard; prohibiting all stoppages from the pay of the labourer; instituting certain aids or additions to such pay; or increasing the money value of the ordinary wages by reducing the price of provisions.

The *indirect* modes of remedying low wages are of a far more complex character. They consist of, first, the remedies propounded by political economists, which are—

A. *The decrease of the number of labourers;* for gaining this end several plans have been proposed, as—
1. Checks against the increase of the population, for which the following are the chief Malthusian proposals:—
    a. Preventive checks for the hindrance of impregnation.
    b. Prohibition of early marriages among the poor.
    c. Increase of the standard of comfort, or requirements, among the people; as a means of inducing prudence and restraint of the passions.
    d. Infanticide; as among the Chinese.
2. Emigration; as a means of draining off the surplus labourers.
3. Limitation of apprentices in skilled trades; as a means of preventing the undue increase of particular occupations. This, however, is advocated not by economists, but generally by operatives.
4. Prevention of family work; or the discouragement of the labour of the wives and children of operatives. This, again, cannot be said to be an "economist" remedy.

B. *Increase of the circulating capital, or sum set aside for the payment of the labourers.*
1. By government imposts. "Governments," says Mr. Mill, "can create additional industry by creating capital. They may lay on taxes, and employ the amount productively." This was the object of the original Poor Law (43 Eliz.), which empowered the overseers of the poor to "raise weekly, or otherwise, by taxation of every inhabitant, &c., such sums of money as they shall require for providing a sufficient stock of flax, hemp, wool, and other ware or stuff, to set the poor on work."
2. By the issue of paper money. The proposition of Mr. Jonathan Duncan is, that the government should issue notes equivalent to the taxation of the country, with the view of affording increased employment to the poor; the people being set to work as it were upon credit, in the same manner as the labourers were employed to build the market-house at Guernsey.

C. *The extension of the markets of the country;* by the abolition of all restrictions on commerce, and the encouragement of the free interchange of commodities, so that, by increasing the demand for our products, we may be able to afford employment to an extra number of producers.

The above constitute what, with a few exceptions, may be termed, more particularly, the "economist" remedies for low wages.

D. *The regulation of the quantity of work done by each workman, or the prevention of the undue economizing of labour.* For this end, several means have been put forward.
1. The shortening the hours of labour, and abolition of Sunday-work.
2. Alteration of the mode of work; as the substitution of day-work for piece-work, as a means of decreasing the stimulus to overwork.
3. Extension of the term of hiring; by the substitution of annual engagements for daily or weekly hirings, with a view to the prevention of "casual labour."
4. Limitation of the number of hands employed by one capitalist; so as to prevent the undue extension of "the large system of production."
5. Taxation of machinery; with the object, not only of making it contribute its quota to the revenue of the country, but of impeding its undue increase.
6. The discountenance of every form of work that tends to the making up of a greater quantity of materials with a less quantity of labour; and consequently to the expenditure of a greater proportion of the capital of the country on machinery or materials, and a correspondingly less proportion on the labourers.

E. *"Protective imposts,"* or high import duties on such foreign commodities as can be produced in this country; with the view of preventing the labour of the comparatively untaxed and uncivilized foreigner being brought into competition with that of the taxed and civilized producer at home.

F. *"Financial reform,"* or reduction of the taxation of the country; as enabling the home labourer the better to compete with the foreigner.

The two latter proposals, and that of the extension of the markets, may be said to seek to remedy low wages by expanding or circumscribing the foreign trade of the country.

G. *A different division of the proceeds of labour.* For this object several schemes have been propounded:—

1. The "tribute system" of wages; or payment of labour according to the additional value which it confers on the materials on which it operates.
2. The abolition of the middleman; whether "sweater," "piece-master," "lumper," or what not, coming between the employer and employed.
3. Co-operation; or joint-stock associations of labourers, with the view of abolishing the profit of the capitalist employer.

H. *A different mode of distributing the products of labour;* with the view of abolishing the profit of the dealer, between the producer and consumer—as co-operative stores, where the consumers club together for the purchase of their goods directly of the producers.

I. *A more general and equal division of the wealth of the country:* for attaining this end there are but two known means:—
1. Communism; or the abolition of all rights to individual property.
2. Agapism; or the voluntary sharing of individual possessions with the less fortunate or successful members of the community.

These remedies may, with a few exceptions (such as the tribute system of wages, and the abolition of middlemen), be said to constitute the socialist and communist schemes for the prevention of distress.

J. *Creating additional employment for the poor;* and so removing the surplus labour from the market. Two modes of effecting this have been proposed:—
1. Home colonization, or the cultivation of waste lands by the poor.
2. Orderlyism, or the employment of the poor in the promotion of public cleanliness, and the increased sanitary condition of the country.

K. *The prevention of the enclosure of commons;* as the means of enabling the poor to obtain gratuitous pasturage for their cattle.

L. *The abolition of primogeniture;* with the view of dividing the land among a greater number of individuals.

M. *The holding of the land by the State,* and equal apportionment of it among the poor.

N. *Extension of the suffrage among the people;* and so allowing the workman, as well as the capitalist and the landlord, to take part in the formation of the laws of the country. For this purpose there are two plans:—
1. "The freehold-land movement," which seeks to enable the people to become proprietors of as much land as will, under the present law, give them "a voice" in the country.
2. Chartism, or that which seeks to alter the law concerning the election of members of Parliament, and to confer the right of voting on every male of mature age, sound mind, and non-criminal character.

O. *Cultivation of a higher moral and Christian character among the people.* This form of remedy, which is advocated by many, is based on the argument, that, without some mitigation of the "selfishness of the times," all other schemes for improving the condition of the people will be either evaded by the cunning of the rich, or defeated by the servility of the poor.

The above I believe to be a full and fair statement of the several plans that have been proposed, from time to time, for alleviating the distress of the people. This enumeration is as comprehensive as my knowledge will enable me to make it; and I have abstained from all comment on the several schemes, so that the reader may have an opportunity of impartially weighing the merits of each, and adopting that, which in his own mind, seems best calculated to effect what, after all, we every one desire—whether protectionist, economist, freetrader, philanthropist, socialist, communist, or chartist—the good of the country in which we live, and the people by whom we are surrounded.

Now we have to deal here with that particular remedy for low wages or distress which consists in creating additional employment for the poor, and of which the street-orderly system is an example.

The increase of employment for the poor was the main object of the 43 Eliz., for which purpose, as we have seen, the overseers of the several parishes were empowered to raise a fund by assessments upon the property of the rich, for providing " a sufficient stock of flax, hemp, wool, and other ware or stuff, to set the poor on work." But though economists, to this day, tell us that " while, on the one hand, industry is limited by capital, so, on the other, every increase of capital gives, or is capable of giving, additional employment to industry, and this without assignable limit,"* nevertheless the great difficulty of carrying out the provisions of the original poor-law has consisted in finding a market for the products of pauper labour, for the frequent gluts in our manufactures are sufficient to teach us that it is one thing to produce and another to dispose of the products; so that to create additional employment for the poor something besides capital is requisite: it is necessary either that they shall be engaged in producing that which they themselves immediately consume, or that for which the market admits of being extended.

The two plans proposed for the employment of the poor, it will be seen, consist (1) in the cultivation of waste lands; (2) in promoting public cleanliness, and so increasing the sanitary condition of the country. The first, it is evident, removes the objection of a market being needed for the products of the labour of the poor, since it pro-

* This is Mr. Mills's second *fundamental* proposition respecting capital (see " Principles of Pol. Econ." p. 82, vol. i.). " What I intend to assert is," says that gentleman, " that the portion (of capital) which is destined to the maintenance of the labourers may—supposing no increase in anything else—be indefinitely increased, without creating an impossibility of finding them employment—in other words, if there are human beings capable of work, and food to feed them, they may always be employed in producing something."

poses that their energies should be devoted to the production of the food which they themselves consume; while the second seeks to create additional employment in effecting that increased cleanliness which more enlightened physiological views have not only made more desirable, but taught us to be absolutely necessary to the health and enjoyment of the community.

The great impediment, however, to the profitable employment of the poor, has generally been the unproductive or unavailing character of pauper labour. This has been mainly owing to the fact that the able-bodied who are deprived of employment are necessarily the lowest grade of operatives; for, in the displacement of workmen, those are the first discarded whose labour is found to be the least efficient, either from a deficiency of skill, industry, or sobriety, so that pauper labour is necessarily of the least productive character.

Another great difficulty with the employment of the poor is, that the idle, or those to whom work is more than usually irksome, require a stronger inducement than ordinary to make them labour, and the remuneration for parish work being necessarily less than for any other, those who are pauperized through idleness (the most benevolent among us must allow there are such) are naturally less than ever disposed to labour when they become paupers. All pauper work, therefore, is generally unproductive or unavailing, because it is either inexpert or unwilling work. The labour of the in-door paupers, who receive only their food for their pains, is necessarily of the same compulsory character as slavery; while that of the out-door paupers, with the remuneration often cut down to the lowest subsisting point, is scarcely of a more willing or more availing kind.

Owing to this general unproductiveness, (as well as the difficulty of finding a field for the profitable employment of the unemployed poor,) the labour of paupers has been for a long time past directed mainly to the cleansing of the public thoroughfares. Still, from the degrading nature of the occupation, and the small remuneration for the toil, pauper labourers have been found to be such unwilling workers that many parishes have long since given over employing their poor even in this capacity, preferring to entrust the work to a contractor, with his paid self-supporting operatives, instead.

The founder of the Philanthropic Association appears to have been fully aware of the two great difficulties besetting the profitable employment of the poor, viz., (1) finding a field for the exercise of their labours where they might be "set on work" with benefit to the community, and without injury to the independent operatives already engaged in the same occupation; and (2) overcoming the unwillingness, and consequently the unavailingness, of pauper labour.

The first difficulty Mr. Cochrane has endeavoured to obviate by taking advantage of that growing desire for greater public cleanliness which has arisen from the increased knowledge of the principles governing the health of towns; and the second, by giving the men 12s. instead of 9s. or 7s. a week, or worse than all, 1s. 1½d. and a quartern loaf a day for three days in the week, and so not only augmenting the stimulus to work (for it should be remembered that wages are to the human machine what the fire is to the steam-engine), but preventing the undue depreciation of the labour of the independent workman. He who discovers the means of increasing the rewards of labour, is as great a friend to his race as he who strives to depreciate them is the public enemy; and I do not hesitate to confess, that I look upon Mr. Charles Cochrane as one of the illustrious few who, in these days of unremunerated toil, and their necessary concomitants—beggars and thieves, has come forward to help the labourers of this country from their daily-increasing degradation. His benevolence is of that enlightened order which seeks to extend rather than destroy the self-trust of the poor, not only by creating additional employment for them, but by rendering that employment less repulsive.

The means by which Mr. Cochrane has endeavoured to gain these ends constitutes the system called Street-Orderlyism, which therefore admits of being viewed in two distinct aspects—first, as a new mode of improving "the health of towns," and, secondly, as an improved method of employing the poor.

Concerning the first, I must confess that the system of scavaging or cleansing the public thoroughfares pursued by the street-orderlies assumes, when contemplated in a sanitary point of view, all the importance and simplicity of a great discovery. It has been before pointed out that this system consists not only in cleansing the streets, but in *keeping* them clean. By the street-orderly method of scavaging, the thoroughfares are continually being cleansed, and so never allowed to become dirty; whereas, by the ordinary method, they are not cleansed *until* they are dirty. Hence the two modes of scavaging are diametrically opposed; under the one the streets are cleansed as fast as dirtied, while under the other they are dirtied as fast as cleansed; so that by the new system of scavaging the public thoroughfares are maintained in a perpetual state of cleanliness, whereas by the old they may be said to be kept in a continual state of dirt.

The street-orderly system of scavaging, however, is not only worthy of high commendation as a more efficient means of gaining a particular end—a simplification of a certain process—but it calls for our highest praise as well for the end gained as for the means of gaining it. If it be really a sound physiological principle, that the Creator has made dirt offensive to every rightly-constituted mind, because it is injurious to us, and so established in us an instinct, before we could discover a reason, for removing all refuse from our presence, it becomes, now that we have detected the cause of the feeling in us, at once disgusting and irrational to allow the filth to accumulate in our streets in front of our houses. If typhus, cholera, and other pestilences are but divine punishments inflicted on us for the infraction of that most kindly law by which the health of a people has been made to depend on that which is naturally agreeable—cleanliness, then our instinct for self-preservation should force us, even if our sense of enjoyment would not lead us, to remove as fast as it is formed what is at once as dangerous as it should be repulsive to our natures. Sanitarily regarded, the cleansing of a town is one of the most important objects that can engage the attention of its governors; the removal of its refuse being quite as necessary for the continuance of the existence of a people as the supply of their food. In the economy of Nature there is no loss: this the great doctrine of waste and supply has taught us; the detritus of one rock is the conglomerate of another; the evaporation of the ocean is the source of the river; the poisonous exhalations of animals the vital air of plants; and the refuse of man and beasts the food of their food. The dust and cinders from our fires, the "slops" from the washing of our houses, the excretions of our bodies, the detritus and "surface-water" of our streets, have all their offices to perform in the great scheme of creation; and if left to rot and fust about us not only injure our health, but diminish the supplies of our food. The filth of the thoroughfares of the metropolis forms, it would appear, the staple manure of the market-gardens in the suburbs; out of the London mud come the London cabbages : so that an improvement in the scavaging of the metropolis tends not only to give the people improved health, but improved vegetables; for that which is nothing but a pestiferous muck-heap in the town becomes a vivifying garden translated to the country.

Dirt, however, is not only as prejudicial to our health and offensive to our senses, when allowed to accumulate in our streets, as it is beneficial to us when removed to our gardens,—but it is a most expensive commodity to keep in front of our houses. It has been shown, that the cost to the people of London, in the matter of extra washing induced by defective scavaging, is at the least 1,000,000*l.* sterling per annum (the Board of Health estimate it at 2,500,000*l.*); and the loss from extra wear and tear of clothes from brushing and scrubbing, arising from the like cause, is about the same prodigious sum; while the injury done to the furniture of private houses, and the goods exposed for sale in shops, though impossible to be estimated—appears to be something enormous : so that the loss from the defective scavaging of the metropolis seems, at the lowest calculation, to amount to several millions per annum; and hence it becomes of the highest possible importance, economically as well as physiologically, that the streets should be cleansed in the most effective manner.

Now, that the street-orderly system is the only rational and efficacious mode of street cleansing both theory and practice assure us. To allow the filth to accumulate in the streets before any steps are taken to remove it, is the same as if we were never to wash our bodies until they were dirty—it is to be perpetually striving to cure the disease, when with scarcely any more trouble we might prevent it entirely. There is, indeed, the same difference between the new and the old system of scavaging, as there is between a bad and a good housewife : the one never cleaning her house until it is dirty, and the other continually cleaning it, so as to prevent it being ever dirty.

Hence it would appear, that the street-orderly system of scavaging would be a great public benefit, even were there no other object connected with it than the increased cleanliness of our streets; but in a country like Great Britain, afflicted as it is with a surplus population (no matter from what cause), that each day finds the difficulty of obtaining work growing greater, the opening up of new fields of employment for the poor is perhaps the greatest benefit that can be conferred upon the nation. Without the discovery of such new fields, " the setting the poor on work" is merely, as I have said, to throw out of employment those who are already employed; it is not to decrease, but really to increase, the evil of the times—to add to, rather than diminish, the number of our paupers or our thieves. The increase of employment in a nation, however, requires, not only a corresponding increase of capital, but a like increase in the demand or desire, as well as in the pecuniary means, of the people to avail themselves of the work on which the poor are set (that is to say, in the extension of the home market); it requires, also, some mode of stimulating the energies of the workers, so as to make them labour more willingly, and consequently more availingly, than usual. These conditions appear to have been fulfilled by Mr. Cochrane, in the establishment of the street-orderlies. He has introduced, in connection with this body, a system of scavaging which, while it employs a greater number of hands, produces such additional benefits as cannot but be considered an equivalent for the increased expenditure; though it is even doubtful whether, by the collection of the street manure unmixed with the mud, the extra value of that article alone will not go far to compensate for the additional expense; if, however, there be added to this the saving to the metropolitan parishes in the cost of watering the streets—for under the street-orderly system this is not required, the dust never being allowed to accumulate, and consequently never requiring to be "laid" —as well as the greater saving of converting the paupers into self-supporting labourers; together with the diminished expense of washing and doctors' bills, consequent on the increased cleanliness of the streets—there cannot be the least doubt that the employment of the poor as street-orderlies is no longer a matter of philanthropy, but of mere commercial prudence.

Such appear to me to be the principal objects of Mr. Cochrane's street-orderly system of scavaging; and it is a subject upon which I have spoken the more freely, because, being unacquainted with that gentleman, none can suspect me of being prejudiced in his favour, and because I have felt that the good which he has done and is likely to do to the poor, has been comparatively unacknowledged by the public, and that society and the people owe him a heavy debt of gratitude*.

I shall now proceed to set forth the character of the labour, and the condition and remuneration of the labourers in connection with the street-orderly system of scavaging the metropolitan thoroughfares.

The first appearance of the street-orderlies in the metropolis was in 1843. Mr. Charles Cochrane, who had previously formed the National Philanthropic Association, with its eleemosynary soup-kitchens, &c., then introduced the system of street-orderlies, as one enabling many destitute men to support themselves by their labour; as well as, in his estimation, a better, and eventually a more economical, mode of street-cleansing, and partaking also somewhat of the character of a street police.

The first "demonstration," or display of the street-orderly system, took place in Regent-street, between the Quadrant and the Regent-circus, and in Oxford-street, between Vere-street and Charles-street. The streets were thoroughly swept in the morning, and then each man or boy, provided with a hand-broom and dust-pan, removed any dirt as soon as it was deposited. The demonstration was pronounced highly successful and the system effective, in the opinion of eighteen influential inhabitants of the locality who acted as a committee, and who publicly, and with the authority of their names, testified their conviction that "the most efficient means of keeping streets clean, and more especially great thoroughfares, was to prevent the accumulation of dirt, by removing the manure within a few minutes after it has been deposited by the passing cattle; the same having, hitherto, remained during several days."

The cost of this demonstration amounted to about 400*l.*, of which, the Report states, "200*l.* still remains due from the shop-keepers to the Association; which," it is delicately added, "from late commercial difficulties they have not yet repaid" (in 1850).

Whilst the street-orderlies were engaged in cleansing Regent-street, &c., the City Commissioners of the sewers of London were invited to depute some person to observe and report to them concerning the method pursued; but with that instinctive sort of repugnance which seems to animate the great bulk of city officials against improvement of any kind, the reply was, that they "did not consider the same worthy their attention." The matter, however, was not allowed to drop, and by the persevering efforts of Mr. Cochrane, the president, and of the body of gentlemen who form the council of the Association, Cheapside, Cornhill, and the most important parts of the very heart of the city were at length cleansed according to the new method. The ratepayers then showed that *they*, at least, *did* consider "the same worthy of attention," for 8000 out of 12,000 within a few days signed memorials recommending the adoption of what they pronounced an improvement, and a public meeting was held in Guildhall (May 4, 1846), at which resolutions in favour of the street-orderly method were passed. The authorities did not adopt these recommendations, but they ventured so far to depart from their venerable routine as to order the streets to be "swept every day!" This employed upwards of 300 men, whereas at the period when the sages of the city sewers did not consider any proposed improvement in scavagery worthy their attention, the number of men employed by them in cleansing the streets did not exceed 30.

The street-orderly system was afterwards tried in the parishes of St. Paul, Covent-garden, St. James (Westminster), St. Martin-in-the-Fields, St. Anne, Soho, and others—sometimes calling forth opposition, of course from the authorities connected with the established modes of paving, scavaging, &c.

It is not my intention to write a complete history of the street-orderlies, but merely to sketch their progress, as well as describe their peculiar characteristics.

Within these few months public meetings have been held in almost every one of the 26 wards of the City, at which approving resolutions were either passed unanimously or carried by large majorities; and the street-orderly system is now about to be introduced into St. Martin's parish instead of the street-sweeping machine.

As far as the street-orderly system has been tried, and judging only by the testimony of public examination and public record of opinion, the trial has certainly been a success. A memorial to the Court of Sewers, from the ward of Broad-street, supported by the leading merchants of that locality, in recommendation of the employment of street-orderlies, seems to bear more closely on the subject than any I have yet seen.

"Your memorialists," they state, "have observed that those public thoroughfares within the city of London which are now cleansed by street-orderlies, *are so remarkably clean* as to be *almost free from mud in wet, and dust in dry weather*—that *such extreme cleanliness is of great comfort to the public*, and tends to improve the sanitary condition of the ward."

But it is not only in the metropolis that the street-orderlies seem likely to become the established scavagers. The streets of Windsor, I am informed, are now in the course of being cleansed upon the orderly plan. In Amsterdam, there are at present 16 orderlies regularly employed upon scavaging a portion of the city, and in Paris and Belgium, I am assured, arrangements are being made for the introduction of the system into both those cities. Were the street-orderly mode of scavaging to become general throughout this country, it is estimated that employment would be given to 100,000 labourers, so that, with the families of these men, not less than half a million of people would be supported in a state of independence by it. The total number of adult able-bodied paupers relieved—in-door and out-door—throughout England and Wales, on January 1, 1850, was 154,525.

The following table shows the route of the street-orderly operations in the metropolis. A further

---

* Mr. Cochrane is said, in the Reports of the National Philanthropic Association, to have expended no less than 6000*l.* of his fortune in the institution of the Street-Orderly system of scavaging.

column, in the Report from which the table has been extracted, contained the names of thirteen clergymen who have "weekly read prayers and delivered discourses to the street-orderlies at their respective stations, and recorded flattering testimonials of their conduct and demeanour."

EMPLOYMENT OF STREET-ORDERLIES.

LOCALITIES CLEANSED.	No. of Street-Orderlies.	Wives and Children dependent.	Money expended. £ s. d.
1843-4. Oxford and Regent Streets	50	256	560 0 0
1845. Strand	8	—	38 0 0
1845-6. Cheapside, Cornhill, &c., City of London	100	363	1540 2 0
1846-7. St. Margaret's and St. John's, Westminster	15	65	306 0 0
1847. Piccadilly, St. James's, &c.	8	32	115 0 0
1848. Strand	8	31	35 0 0
1848. St. Martin's Lane, &c.	38	138	153 0 0
1848. Piccadilly, St. James's, &c.	48	108	341 3 0
1848-9. St. Paul's, Covent Garden	13	38	38 10 0
1849. Regent Street, Whitehall, &c.	18	68	98 0 0
1849. St. Giles's and St. George's, Bloomsbury	14	71	58 1 0
1849. St. Pancras, New Road, &c.	16	46	177 6 0
1849. St. Andrew's and St. George's, Holborn.	23	83	63 4 9
1849. Lambeth Parish	16	41	84 16 0
1851. St. Martin's-in-the-Fields	68	179	119 3 4
1851. City of London, Central Districts (per week, during 6 weeks last past)	103	378	55 0 0
Total	546	1897	3782 6 1

The period of nine years comprised in the above statement (1843 and 1851 being both included) gives a yearly average, as to the number of the poor employed, exceeding 60, with a similar average of 210 wives and children, and a yearly average outlay of 420*l*. The number of orderlies now employed by the Association is from 80 to 90.

Such, then, is a brief account of the rise and progress of this new mode of street-sweeping, and we now come to a description of the work itself.

"The orderlies," says the Report of the Association, "keep the streets free from mud in winter, and dust in summer; and that with the least possible personal drudgery:—adhering to the principle of operation laid down, viz., that of '*Cleansing and keeping Clean,*' they have merely, after each morning's sweeping and removal of dirt, to keep a vigilant look-out over the surface of street allotted to them; and to remove with the handbrush and dust-pan, from any particular spot, whatever dirt or rubbish may fall upon it, *at the moment of its deposit.* Thus are the streets under their care kept constantly clean.

"But sweeping and removing dirt," continues the Report, "is not the only occupation of the street-orderly, whilst keeping up a careful inspection of the ground allotted to him. He is also the watchman of house-property and shop-goods; the guardian of reticules, pocketbooks, purses, and watch-pockets;—the experienced observer and detector of pickpockets; the ever ready, though unpaid, auxiliary to the police constable. Nay, more;—he is always at hand, to render assistance to both equestrian and pedestrian: if a horse slip, stumble, or fall,—if a carriage break down, or vehicles come into collision,—the street-orderly darts forward to raise and rectify them: if foot-passengers be run over, or knocked down, or incautiously loiter on a crossing, the street-orderly rescues them from peril or death; or warns them of the approaching danger of carriages driving in opposite directions: if other accidents befall pedestrians,—if they fall on the pavement, from sudden illness, faintness, or apoplexy, the street-orderly is at hand to render assistance, or convey them to the nearest surgery or hospital. If strangers are at fault as to the localities of London, or the place of their destination, the orderly, in a civil and respectful manner, directs them on their way. If habitual or professional mendicants are importunate or troublesome, the street-orderly warns them off; or hands them to the care of the policeman. And if a *really* poor or starving fellow-creature wanders in search of food or alms, he leads him to a workhouse or soup-kitchen*.

"Should the system become general (*of which there is now every good prospect*), it will be the

---

* A street-orderly in St. Martin's-lane recovered a piece of broad-cloth from a man who had just stolen it from a warehouse; others in Drury-lane detected several thefts from provision-shops. Two orderlies in Holborn saved the lives of the guard and driver of one of Her Majesty's mail-carts, the horse having become unmanageable in consequence of the shafts being broken. In St. Mary's Church, Lambeth, a gentleman having fallen down in apoplexy, the orderlies who were attending Divine service, carried him out into the air, and promptly procured him medical aid, but unhappily life was extinct. Many instances have occurred, however, in which they have rendered essential service to the public and to individuals.

means of rescuing no less than TEN THOUSAND PERSONS *and their families from destitution and distress* (in London alone)*;*—from the forlorn and wretched condition which tempts to criminality and outrage, to that of comfort, independence, and happiness—produced by their own industry, aided by the kind consideration of those who are more the favourites of fortune than themselves.

"In conclusion it may be stated, that the street-orderly system will keep the streets and pavements of London and Westminster as clean as the court-yard and hall of any gentleman's private dwelling: it will not only secure the general comfort and health of upwards of two millions of people, but save a vast annual amount to shopkeepers, housekeepers, and others, with regard to the spoiling of their goods by dust and dirt; in the wear and tear of clothes and furniture, by an eternal round of brushing, dusting, scouring, and scrubbing."

The foregoing extract fully indicates the system pursued and results of street-orderlyism. I will now deal with what may be considered *the labour or trade part of the question.*

By the street-orderly plan a district is duly apportioned. To one man is assigned the care of a series of courts, a street, or 500, 1000, 1200, 1500, or 2000 yards of a public way, according to its traffic, after the whole surface has been swept "the first thing in the morning." In Oxford-street, for instance, it has been estimated that 500 yards can be kept clear of the dirt continually being deposited by one man; in the squares, where there is no great traffic, 2000 yards; while in so busy a part as Cheapside, some nine men will be required to be hourly on the look-out. These street-orderlies are confined to their beats as strictly as are policeman, and as they soon become known to the inhabitants, it is a means of checking any disposition to loiter, or to shirk the work; to say nothing of the corps of inspectors and superintendents.

The *division of labour* among the street-orderlies is as follows:—

1. The *foreman,* whose duty is to "look over the men" (one such over-looker being employed to about every 20 men), and who receives 15s. per week.

2. The *barrow-men,* or sweepers, consisting of men and boys; the former receiving 12s. and the latter generally 7s. per week.

The *tools and implements* used, and their cost, are as follows:—wooden scoops, to throw up the slop, 1s. 2d. each (they used to be made of iron, weighing 8 lbs. each, but the men then complained that the weight "broke their arms"); shovel, 2s. 3d.; hoe and scraper, 1s. 3d.; hand-broom, 8d.; scavager's broom, 1s. 2d.; barrow, 12s.; covered barrow, 24s.

In the amount of his receipts, the street-orderly appears to a disadvantage, as many of the "regular hands" of the contractors receive 16s. weekly, and he but 12s. The reason for this circumscribed payment I have already alluded to—the deficiency of funds to carry out the full purposes of the Association. Contrasted with the remuneration of the great majority of the pauper scavagers, the street-orderly is in a state of comparative comfort, for he receives nearly double as much as the Guardians of the Poor of Chelsea and the Liberty of the Rolls pay their labourers, and full 25 per cent. more than is paid by Bermondsey, Deptford, Marylebone, St. James's, Westminster, St. George's, Hanover-square, and St. Andrew's, Holborn; and, I am assured, it is the intention of the Council to pay the full rate of wages given by the more respectable scavagers, viz., 16s. a week each man. *If traders can do this, philanthropists, who require no profit, at least should be equally liberal.* The labourer never can be benefited by depreciating the ordinary wages of his trade; and I must in justice confess, that there are scattered throughout the Report repeated regrets that the funds of the Association will not admit of a higher rate of wages being paid.

The street-orderly is not subjected to any fines or drawbacks, and is paid always in money, every Saturday evening at the office of the Association. In this respect, however, he does not differ from other bodies of scavagers.

The usual mode of obtaining employment among the street-orderlies is by personal application at the office of the Association in Leicester-square; but sometimes letters, well-penned and well-worded, are addressed to the president.

The daily number of applicants for employment is far from demonstrative of that unbroken prosperity of the country, of which we hear so much. On my inquiring into the number, I ascertained towards the end of August, that, for the previous fortnight, during fine summer weather, London being still full of the visitors to the Exhibition, on an average 30 men, of nearly all conditions of life, applied personally each day for work at street-sweeping, at 12s. a week. Certainly this labour is not connected with the feeling of pauper degradation, but it does not look well for the country that in twelve days 360 men should apply for such work. On the year's average, I am assured, there are 30 applications daily, but only ten new applicants, as men call to solicit an engagement again and again. Thus in the year there are *nine thousand, three hundred, and ninety* applications, and 3130 individual applicants. In the course of one month last winter, there were applications from 300 boys in Spitalfields alone, to be set to work; and I am told, that had they been successful, 3000 lads would have applied the next month.

When an application is made by any one recommended by subscribers, &c., to the Association, or where the case seems worthy of attention, the names and addresses are entered in a book, with a slight sketch of the circumstances of the person wishing to become a street-orderly, so that inquiries may be made. I give a few of the more recent of these entries and descriptions, which are really "histories in little":—

"Thomas M'G——, aged 50, W— L— street, Chelsea Hospital, single man. Taught a French and English school in Lyons, France. Driven out of France at the Revolution of 1848. Penniless.

"Rich. M——, 13, C—— street, H—— garden, 42 years. Married. Can read and write. Has been a seaman in the royal service ten years. Chairmaker by trade. Has jobbed as a porter in Rochester, Kent.

"Phil. S——, 1, R— L— street, High Holborn. From Killarney, co. Kerry. Bred a gardener. Fifteen years in constabulary force, for which he has a character from Col: Macgregor, and received the compensation of 50*l*., which he bestowed on his father and mother to keep them at home. Nine months in England, viz., in Bristol, Bath, and London. Aged 35. Can read and write.

"Edw. C——, 79, M—— street, Hackney. Aged 27. Married. Army-pensioner, 6*d*. a day. Can read and write. Recommended by Rev. T. Gibson, rector of Hackney.

"Chas. J——, 11, D—— street, Chelsea. Aged 38. Gentleman's servant."

In my account of the "regular hands" employed by the contracting scavagers, I have stated that the street-orderlies were a more miscellaneous body, as they had not been reared in the same proportion to street work. They are also, I may add, a better-conducted and better-informed class than the general run of unskilled labourers, as they know, before applying for street-orderly work, that inquiries are made concerning them, and that men of reprobate character will not be employed.

Many of those employed as orderlies have since returned to their original employments; others have procured, and been recommended to, superior situations in life to that of street-orderlies, by the Council of the Association, but *no instance has occurred of any street-orderly having returned back to his parish workhouse or stoneyard.*" This certainly looks well.

One street-orderly, I may add, is now a reputable school-master, and has been so for some time; another is a clerk under similar circumstances. Another is a good theoretical and practical musician, having officiated as organist in churches and at concerts; he is also a neat music copyist. Another tells of his correspondence with a bishop on theological topics. Another, with a long and well-cultured beard, has been a model for artists. One had 150*l*. left to him not long ago, which was soon spent; his wife spent it, he said, and then he quietly applied to be permitted to be again a street-orderly. Several have got engagements as seamen, their original calling—indeed, I am assured, that a few months of street-orderly labour is looked upon as an excellent ordeal of character, after which the Association affirms good behaviour on the part of the employed.

The subscribers to the funds not unfrequently recommend destitute persons to the good offices of the Association, apart from their employment as street-orderlies. Thus, it is only a few weeks ago, that twelve Spanish refugees, none of them speaking English, were recommended to the Association; one of them it was ultimately enabled to establish as a waiter in an hotel resorted to by foreigners, another as an interpreter, another as a gentleman's servant, and another (with a little boy, his son) in shoe-blacking in Leicester-square.

Thus among street-orderlies are to be found a great diversity of career in life, and what may be called adventures.

One great advantage, however, which the orderly possesses over his better paid brethren is in the greater probability of his "rising out of the street." This is very rarely the case with an ordinary scavager.

I now give the following account from one of the street-orderlies, a tall, soldierly-looking man:—

"I'm 42 now," he said, "and when I was a boy and a young man I was employed in the *Times* machine office, but got into a bit of a row—a bit of a street quarrel and frolic, and was called on to pay 3*l*., something about a street-lamp: that was out of the question; and as I was taking a walk in the park, not just knowing what I'd best do, I met a recruiting sergeant, and enlisted on a sudden—all on a sudden—in the 16th Lancers. When I came to the standard, though, I was found a little bit too short. Well, I was rather frolicsome in those days, I confess, and perhaps *had rather a turn for a roving life*, so when the sergeant said he'd take me to the East India Company's recruiting sergeant, I consented, and was accepted at once. I was taken to Calcutta, and served under General Nott all through the Affghan war. I was in the East India Company's artillery, 4th company and 2nd battalion. Why, yes, sir, I saw a little of what you may call 'service.' I was at the fighting at Candahar, Bowlinglen, Bowling-pass, Clatigillsy, Ghuznee, and Caboul. The first real warm work I was in was at Candahar. I've heard young soldiers say that they've gone into action the first time as merry as they would go to a play. Don't believe them, sir. Old soldiers will tell you quite different. You *must* feel queer and serious the first time you're in action: it's not fear—it's nervousness. The crack of the muskets at the first fire you hear in real hard earnest is uncommon startling; you see the flash of the fire from the enemy's line, but very little else. Indeed, oft enough you see nothing but smoke, and hear nothing but balls whistling every side of you. And then you get excited, just as if you were at a hunt; but after a little service—I can speak for myself, at any rate—you go into action as you go to your dinner.

"I served during the time when there was the Affghanistan retreat; when the 44th was completely cut up, before any help could get up to them. We suffered a good deal from want of sufficient food; but it was nothing like so bad, at the very worst, as if you're suffering in London. In India, in that war time, if you suffered, you were along with a number in just the same boat as yourself; and there's always something to hope for when you're an army. It's different if you're walking the streets of London by yourself—I felt it, sir, for a little bit after my return—and if you haven't a penny, you feel as if there wasn't a hope. If you have friends it may be different, but I had none. It's no comfort if

THE ABLE-BODIED PAUPER STREET-SWEEPER.

[*From a Daguerreotype by* BEARD.]

THE RUBBISH-CARTER.
[*From a Daguerreotype by* BEARD.]

you know hundreds are suffering as you are, for you can't help and cheer one another as soldiers can.

"Well, sir, as I've told you, I saw a good deal of service all through that war. Indeed I served thirteen years and four months, and was then discharged on account of ill health. If I'd served eight months longer that would have been fourteen years, and I should have been entitled to a pension. I believe my illness was caused by the hardships I went through in the campaigns, fighting and killing men that I never saw before, and until I was in India had never heard of, and that I had no ill-will to; certainly not, why should I? they never did me any wrong. But when it comes to war, if you can't kill them they'll kill you. When I got back to London I applied at the East India House for a pension, but was refused. I hadn't served my time, though that wasn't my fault.

"I then applied for work in the *Times* machine office, and they were kind enough to put me on. But I wasn't master of the work, for there was new machinery, wonderful machinery, and a many changes. So I couldn't be kept on, and was some time out of work, and very badly off, as I've said before, and then I got work as a scavenger. O, I knew nothing about sweeping before that. I'd never swept anything except the snow in the north of India, which is quite a different sort of thing to London dirt. But I very soon got into the way of it. I found no difficulty about it, though some may pretend there is an art in it. I had 15s. a week, and when I was no longer wanted I got employment as a street-orderly. I never was married, and have only myself to provide for. I'm satisfied that the street-orderly is far the best plan for street-cleaning. Nothing else can touch it, in my opinion, and I thought so before I was one of them, and I believe most working scavengers think so now, though they mayn't like to say so, for fear it might go again their interest.

"Oh, yes, I'm sometimes questioned by gentlemen that may be passing in the streets while I'm at work, all about our system. They generally say, 'and a very good system, too.' One said once, 'It shows that scavengers can be decent men; they weren't when I was first in London, above 40 years ago.' Well, I sometimes get the price of a pint of beer given to me by gentlemen making inquiries, but very seldom."

Until about eighteen months ago none but unmarried men were employed by the Association, and these all resided in one locality, and under one general superintendence or system. The boarding and lodging of the men has, however, been discontinued about fifteen months; for I am told it was found difficult to encourage industrial and self-reliant pursuits in connection with public eleemosynary aid. Married men are now employed, and all the street-orderlies reside at their own homes; the adults, married or single, receiving 12s. a week each; the boys, 6s.; while to each man is gratuitously supplied a blouse of blue serge, costing 2s. 6d., and a glazed hat, costing the same amount.

The system formerly adopted was as follows:—

The men were formed into a distinct body, and established in houses taken for them in Ham-yard, Great Windmill-street, Haymarket.

"The wages of the men," states the Report, "were fixed at 12s. each per week; that is, 9s. were charged for board and lodging, and 3s. were paid in money to each man on Saturday afternoon, out of which he was expected to pay for his clothing and washing. The men had provided for them clean wholesome beds and bedding, a common sitting-room, with every means of ablution and personal cleanliness, including a warm bath once a week. Their food was abundant and of the best quality, viz., coffee and bread and butter for breakfast, at eight o'clock; round of beef, bread, and vegetables, four times a week for dinner, at one o'clock; nutritious soup and bread, or bread and cheese, forming the afternoon repast of the other three days. At six in the evening, when they returned from their labours, they were refreshed with tea or coffee, and bread and butter; or for supper, at nine, each had a large basin of soup, with bread. Thus, three-fourths of their wages being laid out for them to advantage, the men were well lodged and fed; and they have always declared themselves satisfied, comfortable, and happy, under the arrangements that were made for them. Under the charge of their intelligent and active superintendent, the street-orderlies soon fell into a state of the most exact discipline and order; and when old orderlies were drafted off, either to enter the service of parish boards who adopted the system, or were recommended into service, or some other superior position in life, and when new recruits came to supply their places, the latter found no difficulty in conforming to the rules laid down for the performance of their duties, as well as for their general conduct. 'Military time' regulated their hours of labour, refreshment, and rest; due attention was required from all; and each man (though a scavenger) was expected to be cleanly in his person, and respectful in his demeanour; indeed, nothing could be more gratifying than the conduct of these men, both at home and abroad."

"In their domicile in Ham Yard," continues the Report, "the street-orderlies have invariably been encouraged to follow pursuits which were useful and improving, after their daily labours were at an end; for this, a small library of history, voyages, travels, and instructive and entertaining periodical works, was placed at their disposal; and it is truly gratifying to the Council to be able to state, that the men evinced great satisfaction, and even avidity, in availing themselves of this source of intellectual pleasure and improvement. Writing materials also were provided for them, for the purpose of practice and improvement, as well as for mutual instruction in this most necessary and useful art; and it must be gratifying to the members of the Association to be informed, that, in April last, 34 out of 40 men appended their signatures, distinctly and well written, to a document which was submitted to them. Such a fact will at least prove, that when poor persons are employed, well fed, and lodged, and cared for in the way of instruction, they do not always mis-spend their time, nor, from mere preference, run riot in pot-houses and scenes of low debauchery. It is to be borne in mind, however, that one-half of these men were persons of almost every trade and occupation, from the artizan to the shopman and clerk, and therefore previously educated; the other half consisted of labourers and persons forsaken and indigent from their birth, and formerly dependent on workhouse charity or chance employment for their scanty subsistence; consequently in a state of utter ignorance as to reading and writing.

"Every night, after supper, prayers were read by the superintendent; and it has frequently been a most edifying as well as gratifying sight to members of your council, as well as to other persons of rank and station in society, who have visited the Hospice in Ham Yard at that interesting hour, to observe the decorum with which these poor men demeaned themselves; and the heartfelt solemnity with which they joined in the invocations and thanks to their Creator and Preserver!

"Each Sunday morning, at 8 o'clock, a portion of the church service was read, followed by an extemporaneous discourse or exhortation by the secretary to the Hospice. They were marshalled to church twice on the Sabbath, headed by the superintendent and foremen; and generally divided into two or three bodies, each taking a direction to St. James's, St. Anne's, or St. Paul's, Covent Garden; in all of which places of worship they had sitting accommodation provided by the kindness of the clergy and churchwardens. On Tuesday evenings they had the benefit of receiving pastoral visits and instruction from several of the worthy clergymen of the surrounding parishes."

This is all very benevolent, but still very wrong. There is but one way of benefiting the poor, viz., by developing their powers of self-reliance, and certainly not in treating them like children. Philanthropists always seek to do too much, and in this is to be found the main cause of their repeated failures. The poor are expected to become angels in an instant, and the consequence is, they are merely made *hypocrites*. Moreover, no men of any independence of character will submit to be washed, and dressed, and fed like schoolboys; hence none but the worst classes come to be experimented upon. It would seem, too, that this overweening disposition to play the part of *ped-agogues* (I use the word in its literal sense) to the poor, proceeds rather from a love of power than from a sincere regard for the people. Let the rich become the advisers and assistants of the poor, giving them the benefit of their superior education and means—but *leaving the people to act for themselves*—and they will do a great good, developing in them a higher standard of comfort and moral excellence, and so, by improving their tastes, inducing a necessary change in their habits. But such as seek merely to *lord it* over those whom distress has placed in their power, and strive to bring about the *villeinage* of benevolence, making the people the philanthropic, instead of the feudal, serfs of our nobles, should be denounced as the arch-enemies of the country. Such persons may mean well, but assuredly they achieve the worst towards the poor. The curfew-bell, whether instituted by benevolence or tyranny, has the same degrading effect on the people —destroying their principle of self-action, without which we are all but as the beasts of the field.

Moreover, the laying out of the earnings of the poor is sure, after a time, to sink into "a job;" and I quote the above passage to show that, despite the kindest management, eleemosynary help is *not* a fitting adjunct to the industrial toil of independent labourers.

The residences of the street-orderlies are now in all quarters where unfurnished rooms are about 1s. 9d. or 2s. a week. The addresses I have cited show them residing in the outskirts and the heart of the metropolis. The following returns, however, will indicate the ages, the previous occupations, the education, church-going, the personal habits, diet, rent, &c., of the class constituting the street-orderlies, better than anything I can say on the matter.

Before any man is employed as a street-orderly, he is called upon to answer certain questions, and the replies from 67 men to these questions supply a fund of curious and important information—important to all but those who account the lot of the poor of *no* importance. In presenting these details, I beg to express my obligations to Mr. Colin Mackenzie, the enlightened and kindly secretary of the Association.

I shall first show what is the order of the questioning, then what were the answers, and I shall afterwards recapitulate, with a few comments, the salient characteristics of the whole.

The questions are after this fashion; the one I adduce having been asked of a scavager to whom a preference was given:—

The Parish of St. Mary, Paddington.—Questions asked of Parish Scavagers, applying for employment as Street-Orderlies, with the answers appended.

Name ?—W—— C——.
Age ?—35 years.
How long a scavenger ?—Three months.
What occupation previously ? — Gentleman's footman.
Married or single ?—Married.
Reading, writing, or other education ?—Yes.
Any children ?—One.
Their ages ?—Three years.
Wages ?—Nine shillings per week.
Any parish relief ?—No.

What and how much food the applicants have usually purchased in a week.

Meat ?—2s. 6d.
Bacon ?—None.
Fish ?—None.
Bread ?—2s.
Potatoes ?—4d.
Butter ?—6d.

Tea and sugar?—1s.
Cocoa?—None.
What rent they pay?—2s.
Furnished or unfurnished lodgings?—Unfurnished.
Any change of dress?—No.
Sunday clothing?—No.
How many shirts?—Two shirts.
Boots and shoes?—One pair.
How much do they lay out for clothes in a year?—I have nothing but what I stand upright in.
Do they go to church or chapel?—Sometimes.
If not, why not?—It is from want of clothes.
Do they ever bathe?—No.
Does the wife go out to, or take in work?—Yes.
What are her earnings?—Uncertain.
Do they have anything from charitable institutions or families?—No.
When ill; where do they resort to?—Hospitals, dispensaries, and the parish doctor.
Do their children go to any school; and what?—Paddington.
Do they ever save any money; how much, and where?—
How much do they spend per week in drink?
Do not passers by, as charitable ladies, &c., give them money; and how much per week?—No.

Such are the questions asked, and I now give the answers of 67 individuals.

Their ages were:—
10 were from 20 to 30   15 from 50 to 60
13   „   30 „ 40   4   „   60 „ 70.
24   „   40 „ 50   1   „   70

The greatest number of any age was 7 persons of 45 years respectively.

Their previous occupations had been:—

22 labourers.	1 sweep.
3 at the business "all their lives."	1 haybinder.
	1 gaslighter.
3 dustmen.	1 dairyman.
3 ostlers.	1 ploughman.
2 stablemen.	1 gardener.
2 carmen.	1 errand boy.
2 porters.	1 fur dresser.
2 gentlemen's servants.	1 fur dyer.
2 greengrocers.	1 skinner.
1 following dust-cart.	1 leather dresser.
1 excavator.	1 letter-press printer.
1 gravel digging.	1 paper stainer.
1 stone breaking in yards.	1 glass blower.
	1 farrier.
1 at work in the brick-fields.	1 plasterer.
	1 clerk.
1 at work in the lime-works.	1 vendor of goods.
	1 licensed victualler.
1 coal porter.	

Therefore, of 67 scavagers
12 had been artizans.
55   „   unskilled workmen.

Hence about five-sixths belong to the unskilled class of operatives.

Time of having been at scavagering.
3 "all their lives" at the business.
1 about 27 years.
6 from 15 to 20 years.
6   „   10 „ 15   „
4 from 5 to 10 years.
34   „   1   „   5   „
13 twelve months and less.

Hence it would appear, that few have been at the business a long time. The greater number have not been acting as scavagers more than five years.

State of education.—Could they read and write?
45 answered yes.
4 replied that they could read and write.
5 could read only.
12 could do neither.
1 was deaf and dumb.

Hence it would appear, that rather more than two-thirds of the scavagers have received *some little* education.

Did they go to church or chapel?
22 answered yes.
9 went to church.
4   „   chapel.
4   „   the Catholic chapel.
1   „   both church and chapel.
5 went sometimes.
1 not often.
17 never went at all.
1 was ashamed to go.
1 went out of town to enjoy himself.
2 made no return (1 being deaf and dumb).

Thus it would seem, that not quite two-thirds regularly attend some place of worship; that about one-eleventh go occasionally; and that about one-fourth never go at all.

Why did they not go to church?
12 had no clothes.
55 returned no answer (1 being deaf and dumb).

Hence of those who never go (19 out of 67), very nearly two-thirds (say 12 in 19) have no clothes to appear in.

Did they bathe?
59 answered no.
3 replied yes.
2 said they did in the Thames.
2 returned "sometimes."
1 was deaf and dumb.

Hence it appeared, that about seven-eighths never bathe, although following the filthiest occupation.

Were they married or single?
56 were married.   6 were single.
5   „   widowers.

Thus it would seem, that about ten-elevenths are or have been married men.

How many children had they?
1 had 15.
1   „   6.
2   „   5 each.
11   „   4   „
19   „   3   „
9   „   2   „
6 had 1 each.
16   „   none (6 of these being single men).
2 returned their family as grown up without stating the number.

Consequently 51 out of 61, or five-sixths, are married, and have families numbering altogether 165 children; the majority had only 3 children, and this was about the average family.

What were the ages of their children?

11	were grown up.	8	were 1 year and under.
2	between 30 and 40.		
9	„ 20 and 30.	5	were returned at home.
49	„ 10 and 20.		
80	„ 1 and 10.	1	returned as dead.

One-half of the scavagers' children, therefore, are between 1 and 10 years of age; the majority would appear to be 8 years old.

Some were said to be grown up, but no number was given.

Did their children go to school?

13 answered yes.
13 to the National School
5 to the Ragged School.
2 to Catholic.
2 to Parish.
6 to local schools.
1 replied that he went sometimes.
2 returned no.
1 replied that his children were "not with him."
22 (of whom 16 had no children, and 1 was deaf and dumb) made no reply.

From this it would seem, that a large majority—41 out of 51, or four-fifths—of the parents who have children send them to school.

Did their wives work?

15 returned no.
6 said their wives were "unable."
1 had lost the use of her limbs.
2 did, but "not often."
4 did "when they could."
10 worked "sometimes."
12 answered yes.
1 sold cresses.
15 made no return (11 having no wives and 1 being deaf and dumb).

Hence two-fifths of the wives (22 out of 56) do no work, 16 do so occasionally, and 13, or one-fourth, are in the habit of working.

What were wives' earnings?

10 returned them as "uncertain."
1 "didn't know."
1 estimated them at 1s. 6d. per week.
1 at 1s. to 2s. „
2 at 2s. „
3 at 2s. or 3s. „
2 at about 3s. „
1 at 2s. to 4s. per week.
1 at 3s. or 4s. „
1 at 3d. or 4d. per day.
43 gave no returns (having either no wives, or their wives not working).
1 was deaf and dumb.

So that, out of 29 wives who were said to work, 16 occasionally and 13 regularly, there were returns for 23. Nearly half of their earnings were given as uncertain from their seldom doing work, while the remainder were stated to gain from 1s. to 4s. per week; about 2s. 6d. perhaps would be a fair average.

What wages were they themselves in the habit of receiving?

3 had 16s. 6d. per week.
2 „ 16s. „
28 „ 15s. „
3 „ 14s. 6d. „
1 „ 14s. „
2 „ 12s. „
15 had 9s. per week.
4 „ 8s. „
5 „ 7s. „
4 „ 1s. 1½d. a day and 2 loaves.

Hence it is evident, that one-half receive 15s. or more a week, and about a fourth 9s.

It was not the parishes, however, but the contractors with the parishes, who paid the higher rates of wages: Mr. Dodd, for St. Luke's; Mr. Westley, for St. Botolph's, Bishopsgate; Mr. Parsons, for Whitechapel; Mr. Newman, for Bethnal-green, &c.

These wages the scavagers laid out in the following manner:—

For rent, per week.

1 paid 4s.
1 „ 3s. 6d.
8 „ 3s.
14 „ 2s. 6d.
33 „ 2s.
4 „ 1s. 6d.
1 paid 1s. 3d.
2 „ 1s.
1 lived rent free.
1 paid for board and lodging.
1 lived with mother.

Hence it would appear, that near upon half the number paid 2s. rent. The usual rent paid seems to be between 2s. and 3s., five-sixths of the entire number paying one or other of those amounts. Only three lived in furnished lodgings, and the rents of these were, respectively, two at 2s. 6d. and the other at 2s.

For bread, per week.

1 expended 5s. 3d.
1 „ 5s.
1 „ 4s. 7d.
1 „ 4s. 6d.
1 „ 4s. 3d.
7 „ 4s.
13 „ 3s. 6d.
8 „ 3s.
3 „ 2s. 6d.
4 „ 2s. 3d.
13 „ 2s.
4 expended 1s. 6d.
1 „ 1s. 9d.
4 two loaves a day from parish.
3 gave a certain sum per week to their wives or mothers to lay out for them, and 1 boarded and lodged.
1 was deaf and dumb.

Thus it would seem, that the general sum expended weekly on bread varies between 2s. and 4s. The average saving from free-trade, therefore, would be between 4d. and 8d., or say 6d., per week.

For meat, per week.

4 expended 4s.
5 „ 3s. 6d.
11 „ 3s.
12 „ 2s. 6d.
1 „ 2s. 4d.
5 „ 2s.
4 „ 1s. 6d.
1 „ 1s. 2d.
9 „ 1s.
2 „ 10d.
2 „ 6d.
1 expended 8d.
1 once a week.
4 had none.
5 no returns (3 of this number gave a weekly allowance to wives or mothers, 1 was deaf and dumb, and 1 paid for board and lodging).

By the above we see, that the sum usually expended on meat is between 2s. 6d. and 3s. per week, about one-third of the entire number expending that sum. All those who expended 1s. and less per week had 9s. and less for their week's labour. The average saving from the cheapening of provisions would here appear to be between 5d. and 6d. per week at the outside.

For tea and sugar, per week.

2 paid 2s. 6d.
1 „ 2s. 4d.
1 „ 2s. 3d.
19 „ 2s.
2 „ 1s. 9d.
4 „ 1s. 8d.
12 „ 1s. 6d.
5 „ 1s. 4d.
5 paid 1s. 3d.
5 „ 1s. 2d.
13 „ 1s.
2 „ 8d.
5 no returns: 1 deaf and dumb, 1 board and lodging, and 3 making allowances.

The sum usually expended on tea and sugar seems to be between 1s. 6d. and 2s. per week.

For fish, per week.

3 expended	1s.	4 allowed so much per week to wives, or mother, or landlady.	
5 „	8d.		
23 „	6d.		
8 „	4d.	1 deaf and dumb.	
23 „	nothing.		

Hence one-third spent 6d. weekly in fish, and one-third nothing.

For bacon, per week.

1 expended	1s.	1 expended	4d.
2 „	10d.	43 „	nothing.
1 „	9d.	4 allowances to wives, &c.	
5 „	8d.		
9 „	6d.	1 deaf and dumb.	

The majority (two-thirds), therefore, do not have bacon. Of those that do eat bacon, the usual sum spent weekly is 6d. or 8d.

For butter, per week.

1 expended	1s. 8d.	1 expended	3d.
24 „	1s.	2 „	nothing.
11 „	10d.	4 made allowances.	
12 „	8d.	1 deaf and dumb.	
11 „	6d.		

Thus one-third expended 1s., and about one-sixth spent 10d.; another sixth, 8d.; and another sixth, 6d. a week, for butter.

For potatoes, per week.

1 spent	1s.	6 spent	4d.
2 „	10d.	28 spent nothing.	
6 „	8d.	4 made allowances.	
1 „	7d.	1 deaf and dumb.	
18 „	6d.		

About one-fourth spent 6d.; the greater proportion, however (nearly one-half), expended nothing upon potatoes weekly.

For clothes, yearly.

2 expended	2l.	1 had 2 pairs of boots a year, but no clothes.	
2 „	1l. 10s.		
2 „	1l. 5s.	2 expended "not much."	
3 „	1l.		
1 „	18s.	2 got them as they could.	
1 „	17s.	1 expended a few shillings.	
1 „	15s.		
4 „	12s.	1 said it "all depends."	
1 „	10s.	2 returned "nothing."	
34 couldn't say.		1 was deaf and dumb.	
		6 made no return.	

Hence 43 out of 67, or nearly two-thirds, spent little or nothing upon their clothes.

Had they a change of dress?

28 had a change of dress.   1 was deaf and dumb.
38 had not.

Above one-half, therefore, had no other clothes but those they worked in.

Had they any Sunday clothing?

20 had some.   21 made no return.
45 had none.   1 deaf and dumb.

More than two-thirds, then, had no Sunday clothes.

How many shirts had they?

10 had 3 shirts.   2 had 1 shirt.
54 „ 2 „   1 was deaf and dumb.

The greater number, therefore, had two shirts.

How many shoes had they?

27 had 2 pairs.   1 was deaf and dumb.
39 „ 1 „

Thus the majority had only one pair of shoes.

How much did they spend in drink?

1 expended	2s. a week.	1 said he "wouldn't say."	
1 „	1s. or 2s. „		
2 „	1s. 6d. „	1 said "that all depends."	
4 „	1s. „		
1 „	6d. „	2 said they "had none to spend."	
1 „	3d. or 5d. „		
7 said they "couldn't say."		2 expended nothing.	
		44 gave no return (1 deaf and dumb).	

Hence answers were given by one-third, of whom the greatest number "couldn't say." (?) Of the ten who acknowledged spending anything upon drink, the greater number, or 4, said they spent 1s. a week only. But?

Did they save any money?

36 answered no.
31 gave no reply (1 being deaf and dumb).

What did they in case of illness coming upon themselves or families?

28 went to the dispensary	1 went to the workhouse.
8 went to the hospital.	2 said "nothing."
6 „ parish doctor.	1 "never troubled any."
	8 made no reply (1 being deaf and dumb).
3 wives went to the lying-in hospital.	

The greater number, then, go, when ill, to the dispensary.

Were they in receipt of alms?

56 answered no.		6 made no returns (1 being deaf and dumb).
2 „ sometimes.		
3 „ yes.		

Did the passers-by give them anything?

49 answered no.	1 answered very seldom.
2 „ sometimes beer.	12 no returns (1 being deaf and dumb).
1 answered never.	
2 „ seldom.	

Did they receive any relief from their parishes?

56 replied no.	1 had 15 lbs. of bread.
4 had 2 loaves and 1s. a day as wages.	2 answered "not at present."
1 had 4 loaves a week.	2 made no returns.
1 „ a 4-lbs. loaf.	

Thus the greater proportion (five-sixths), it will be seen, had no relief; two of those who had relief received 9s. wages a week, and two others only 7s., while four received part of their wages from the parish in bread.

These analyses are not merely the characteristics of the applicant or existent street-orderlies; they are really the annals of the poor in all that relates to their domestic management in regard to meat and clothes, the care of their children, their church-going, education, previous callings, and parish relief. The inquiry is not discouraging as to the character of the poor, and I must call attention to the circumstance of how rarely it is that so large a collection of facts is placed at the command of a public writer. In many of the public offices the simplest information is as jealously withheld as if statistical knowledge were the first and last steps to high treason. I trust that Mr. Cochrane's example in the skilful arrangement of the returns connected with the Association over which he presides, and his courteous readiness to supply the information, gained at no small care and cost, will be more freely followed, as such a course unquestionably tends to the public benefit.

It will be seen from these statements, how hard the struggle often is to obtain work in unskilled labour, and, when obtained, how bare the living. Every farthing earned by such workpeople is necessarily expended in the support of a family; and in the foregoing details we have another proof as to the diminution of the purchasing fund of the country, being in direct proportion to the diminution of the wages. If 100 men receive but 7s. a week each for their work, their yearly outlay, to "keep the bare life in them," is 1820l. If they are paid 16s. a week, their outlay is 4160l.; an expenditure of 2340l. more in the productions of our manufactures, in all textile, metal, or wooden fabrics; in bread, meat, fruit, or vegetables; and in the now necessaries, the grand staple of our foreign and colonial trade—tea, coffee, cocoa, sugar, rice, and tobacco. *Increase your wages, therefore, and you increase your markets.* For manufacturers to underpay their workmen is to cripple the demand for manufactures. To talk of the over-production of our cotton, linen, and woollen goods is idle, when thousands of men engaged in such productions are in rags. It is not that there are too many makers, but too few who, owing to the decrease of wages, are able to be buyers. Let it be remembered that, out of 67 labouring men, three-fourths could not afford to buy proper clothing, expending thereupon "little" or "nothing," and, I may add, *because* earning little or nothing, and so having scarcely anything to expend.

I now come to *the cost of cleansing the streets upon the street-orderly system,* as compared with that of the ordinary modes of payment to contractors, &c. It will have been observed, from what has been previously stated, that the Council of the Association contend that far higher amounts may be realized for street manure when collected clean, according to the street-orderly plan. If, by a better mode of collecting the street dirt, it be kept unmixed, its increase in value and in price may be most positively affirmed.

Before presenting estimates and calculations of cost, I may remind the reader; that under the street-orderly system no watering carts are required, and none are used where the system is carried out in its integrity. To be able to dispense with the watering of the streets is not merely to get rid of a great nuisance, but to effect a considerable saving in the rates.

I now give two estimates, both relating to the same district:—

"COMPARATIVE EXPENSE OF CLEANING AND WATERING THE STREETS, &C., OF ST. JAMES'S PARISH; under the system now in operation by the Paving Board, and under the sanitary system of employing street-orderlies, as recommended by 779 ratepayers. It is assumed, from reasonable data, that the superficial contents of all the streets, lanes, courts, and alleys in the parish, do not amount to more than 80,000 square yards.

"*Present Annual Expense of Cleansing St. James's Parish:—*

Paid to contractor for carrying away slop, including expense of brooms	£800	0 0
Paid to 23 men, average wages, 10s. per week, 52 weeks	598	0 0
	£1398	0 0

"*Annual Expense of Street-Orderly System:—*

30 men (including those with hand-barrows), at 10s. per week, 52 weeks	£780	0 0	
Expense of brooms	30	0 0	
Cartage of slop	100	0 0	
		£910	0 0
		£488	0 0
Saving by diminished expense of street-watering throughout the parish		450	0 0
Annual prospective saving		£938	0 0

"Obs.—The sum of 800l. per annum was paid to the contractor on account of expenses incurred for the removal of slop. During the three years previous to 1849, the contractor paid money to the parish for permission to remove the house-ashes, the value of which was then 2s. per load; it is now 2s. 6d. In St. Giles's and St. George's parishes, whose surface is more than twice the extent of St. James's, the expense of slop-cartage, in 1850, was 304l. 14s. 0d., whilst the sum received for cattle-manure collected by street-orderlies, was 73l. 14s. 0d.; and the slop-expenses for the four months ending November 29, were 59l. 18s. 6d., whilst the manure sold for 21l. 6s. 0d. Thus has the slop-expense in these extensive united parishes been reduced to less than 120l. per annum. Since the preceding estimate was submitted to the Commissioners of Paving, the street-orderly system has been introduced into St. James's parish; and it is confidently expected that the 'Annual Prospective saving' of 938l., will be fully realised."

A similar estimate has just been sent into the authorities of the great parish of St. Marylebone, but its results do not differ from the one I have just cited.

I next present an estimate contrasting the expense of the street-orderly method with the cost of employing sweeping-machines:—

"COMPARATIVE EXPENSE OF CLEANSING AND WATERING THE STREETS, &C., OF ST. MARTIN'S PARISH, under the system now in operation by the Paving Board, and under the sanatory system of employing street-orderlies, as recommended by 703 ratepayers. It is assumed, from reasonable data, that the superficial contents of all the streets, lanes, courts, and alleys in the parish, amount to about 70,000 square yards.

"Expenses by Machinery in St. Martin's Parish.

	£	s.	d
Annual payment to street-machine proprietor	980	0	0
Watering rate (1847)	644	16	8½
Salaries to clerks	391	0	0
Support of 28 able-bodied men in workhouse, thrown out of work, at 4s. 6d. per man	327	12	0
	£2343	8	8½

I now give an estimate concerning a smaller district, *one of the divisions of St. Pancras parish*. It was embodied in a Report read at a meeting in Camden-town, on the desirableness of introducing the street-orderly system:—

The Report set forth that the Committee had "made a minute investigation into the present systems of street-cleansing, as adopted under the superintendence of Mr. Bird, the parish surveyor, and under that of the National Philanthropic Association.

"From the 26th of March, 1848, to the 26th of March, 1849, the Directors of the Poor expended in paving and cleansing, &c., the three and a quarter miles under their charge, 3545*l*. 19*s*. 7*d*.; of this the following items were for cleansing, viz.—

	£	s.	d.
Labour	249	13	0
Tools	10	12	0
Slop carting	496	0	0
Proportion of foreman's salary	39	0	0
	795	5	0

"Expenditure by the Employment of Street-Orderlies.

	£	s.	d.
Maintenance of 28 street-orderlies to keep clean 70,000 yards (presumed contents), at 2500 yards each man, at 12s. per week	768	0	0
Two inspectors of orderlies, at 15s. per week	78	0	0
One superintendent of ditto, at 1*l*. per week	52	0	0
Wear and tear of brooms	36	8	0
Interest on outlay for barrows, brooms, and shovels	26	19	0
Watering rate (not required)			
Value of manure pays for cartage			
	961	7	0
Annual saving by street-orderlies	1382	1	8½
	2343	8	8½

"*The street-orderly system of cleansing* the said roads in the most efficient manner would give the following expenditure per annum:—

	£	s.	d.
Thirty-four men to cleanse 3¼ miles, at the rate of 2000 superficial yards each man, 12s. per week each	1060	16	0
Two inspectors of orderlies, at 15s. per week each	78	0	0
Superintendent	104	0	0
Cost of brooms, shovels, &c.	83	0	0
No allowance for slop-carting, the National Philanthropic Association holding that the manure, properly collected, will more than pay for its removal			
	1325	16	0
Deduct cost of cleansing by the old mode	795	5	0
	530	11	0

"The apparent extra cost, therefore, would be 530*l*. 11*s*. The vestry, however, would see that the charge for supporting 34 able-bodied men in the workhouse is at least 5s. per week each, or 442*l*. per annum. This, therefore, must be deducted from the 530*l*. 11*s*., leaving the extra cost 88*l*. 11*s*. per annum. This sum, the committee were assured, will be not only repaid by the reduced outlay for repairs, which the new system will effect; but a very great saving will be the result of the thorough cleansed state in which the roads will be constantly maintained. Under the late system, to find the roads in a cleansed state was the exception, not the rule; and when all the advantages likely to result from the new system were taken into consideration, the committee did not hesitate to recommend it for adoption in its most efficient form."

Concerning the *expense of cleansing the City by the street-orderly system*, Mr. Cochrane says:—

"The number required for the whole surface (including the footways, courts, &c.) would be about 250 men and boys.

"Upon the present system this number would be formed in three divisions:—

"First division.—170 to begin work at 6 a.m., and end 6 p.m. Second division, called relief and aids.—30 boys boys from 12 at noon to 10. Third division.—50 men from 6 p.m. to 6 a.m. Total, 250.

"The men and boys are now working at from 6s. to 12s. per week.

These 250 men and boys would cost for wages during the year about £5100

Twelve foremen, at 40*l*. per annum		480
Two superintendents at 50*l*. each		100
Brooms, &c.		325
Barrows		100
Two clerks, at 100*l*. each		200
Manager		100
		£6405

"No items are given for slopping or cartage, as, if the streets are properly attended to, there ought to be no slop, whilst the value of the manure may be more than equivalent for the expense of its removal.

"Some slop-carts will, however, be occasionally required for Smithfield-market and similar localities; making, therefore, ample allowance for contingencies, it is confidently considered that the expense for cleansing the whole of the city of London by street-orderlies would not exceed 8000*l*. per annum."

"Expenses of Cleansing and Watering the Streets, &c., *of the City of London, on the old system of Scavaging, from June*, 1845, *to June*, 1846.

	Annual Expense.
To scavaging contractors	£6040
Value of ashes and dust of the city of London, given gratis to the above contractors in the year ending 1846, and now purchased by them for the year ending 1847	5500
Estimated contributions levied for watering streets	4000
Salaries to surveyors, inspectors, beadles, clerks, &c., of Sewers' Office, according to printed account, March 3, 1846	2485
Expense for cleaning out sewers and gully-holes (not known)	

Annual expense under the imperfect system of street-cleansing . £18,025

"Number of men employed, 58.

"State of the Streets:—Inhabitants always complaining of their being muddy in winter and dusty in summer."

Two estimates, then, show an expectation of a yearly saving of no less than 2320*l*. to the ratepayers of two parishes alone; 938*l*. to St. James's, and 1382*l*. to St. Martin's. And this, too, if all that be augured of this system be realized, with a freedom from street dust and dirt unknown under other methods of scavagery. I think it right, however, to express my opinion that even in the reasonable prospect of these great savings being effected, it is a paltry, or rather a false, because miscalled, economy to speculate on the payment of 10s. and 12s. a week to street-labourers in the parishes of St. James and St. Martin respectively, when so many of the contractors pay their men 16s. weekly. If this low hire be justifiable in the way of an experiment, it can never be justifiable as a continuance of the *reward* of labour.

If the street-orderly system is to be the means of *permanently* reducing the wages of the regular scavagers from 16s. to 12s. a week, then we had better remain afflicted with the physical dirt of our streets, than the moral filth which is sure to proceed from the poverty of our people—but if it is to be a means of elevating the pauper to the dignity of the independent labour, rather than dragging the independent labourer down to the debasement of the pauper, then let all who wish well to their fellows encourage it as heartily and strenuously as they can—otherwise the sooner it is denounced as an insidious mode of defrauding the poor of one-fourth of their earnings the better; and it is merely in the belief that Mr. Cochrane and the Council of the Association *mean* to keep faith with the public and increase the men's wages to those of the regular trade, that the street-orderly system is advocated here. If our philanthropists are to reduce wages 25 per cent., then, indeed, the poor man may cry, "*save me from my friends.*"

As to the positive and definite working of the street-orderly system as an *economical* system, no information can be given beyond the estimates I have cited, as it has never been duly tested on a sufficiently large scale. Its working has been, of necessity, desultory. It has, however, been introduced into St. George's, Bloomsbury; St. James's, Westminster; and is about to be established in St. Martin's-in-the-Fields; and in the course of a year or two it seems that it will be sufficiently tested. That its working has hitherto been desultory is a necessity in London, where "vested interests" look grimly on any change or even any inquiry. That it deserves a full and liberal testing seems undeniable, from the concurrent assent of all parishioners who have turned their attention to it.

It remains to show the expenses of the Philanthropic Association, for I am unable to present an account of street-orderlyism separately. The two following tables fully indicate to what an extent the association is indebted to the private purse of Mr. Cochrane, who by this time has advanced between 6000*l.* and 7000*l.*

"Balance Sheet.

Receipts and Expenditure of the National Philanthropic Association, for the Promotion of Social and Sanatory Improvements and the Employment of the Poor, from 29*th September,* 1846, *to* 29*th September,* 1849.

Dr.	£	s.	d.	Cr.	£	s.	d.
To subscriptions and donations from the 29th September, 1846, to 29th September, 1849	1393	16	7	By balance due to president, as per Balance Sheet, Sept. 29, 1846	2935	17	9
Balance due to president, 29th September, 1849	5739	19	9	Secretary's salary	300	0	0
	7133	16	4	Rent of offices, &c.	248	10	0
				Salaries to clerks, messengers, &c.	371	19	4
				Do. to collectors	312	18	1
				Commission to do.	130	5	6
				Printing and stationery	556	17	0
				Hire of rooms for public meetings	60	10	0
				Advertisements and newspapers	244	5	3
				Bill posting	8	12	6
				Salaries to persons in charge of free lavatories in Ham-yard, Great Windmill-st., St. James's	10	18	2
				Brooms, barrows, and shovels, for the use of street-orderlies	86	8	0
				Charges of contractors and others for removal of street slop, &c.	58	9	6
				Food, lodging, and wages to street-orderlies, domiciled in Ham-yard, Great Windmill-street, St. James's	980	11	4
				Clothing for the street-orderlies	13	3	2
				Baths provided for do.	5	15	10
				Sundry expenses for offices, including postage-stamps, &c.	92	7	11
				Law expenses	8	10	10
				Builder's charges for free lavatories in Ham-yard	95	13	10
				Amount advanced to the late secretary for improving the dwellings of the poor	20	0	0
				Farther advances made by president on various occasions for the general purposes of the Association	592	2	4
					7133	16	4

Audited by us, Oct. 19th, 1849, Charles Shepherd Lenton, 33, Leicester-square; and Joseph Child, 43, Leicester-square."

Street-Orderlies.—City Surveyor's Report.

I have been favoured with a Report "upon street-cleansing and in reference to the Street-Orderly System," by the author, Mr. W. Haywood, the Surveyor to the City Commission of Sewers, who has invited my attention to the matter, in consequence of the statements which have appeared on the subject in "London Labour and the London Poor."

Mr. Haywood, whose tone of argument is courteous and moderate, and who does not scruple to do justice to what he accounts the good points of the street-orderly system, although he condemns it as a whole, gives an account of the earlier scavaging of the city, not differing in any material respect from that which I have already printed. He represents the public ways of the City, which I have stated to be about 50 miles, as "about 51 miles lineal, about 770,157 superficial yards in area." This area, it appears, comprehends 1000 different places.

In 1845 the area of the carriage-way of the City was estimated at 418,000 square yards, and the footway at 316,000, making a total of 734,000; but since that period new streets have been made and others extensively widened. The precincts of Bridewell, St. Bartholomew, St. James's, Duke's-place, Aldgate, and others, have been added to the jurisdiction of the Sewers Commission by Act of Parliament, so that the Surveyor now estimates the area of the carriage-way of the City of London at 441,250 square yards, and the footway at 328,907, making a total of 770,157 square yards.

"I am fully impressed," observes Mr. Haywood, "with the great importance to a densely-populated city of an efficient cleansing of the public ways. Probably after a perfect system of sewage and drainage (which implies an adequate water supply), and a well-paved surface (which I have always considered to be little inferior in its importance to the former, and which is indispensable to obtaining clean sweeping), good surface cleansing ranks next in its beneficial sanitary influence; and most certainly the comfort gained by all through having public thoroughfares in a high degree of cleanliness is exceedingly great."

Mr. Haywood expresses his opinion that streets "ordure soddened"—smelling like "stable yards,"—dangerous to the health of the inhabitants—impassable from mud in winter and from dust in summer—and inflicting constant pecuniary loss, "can only exist in an appreciable degree in thoroughfares swept much less frequently" than the streets within the jurisdiction of the City Commissioners of Sewers. In this opinion, however, Mr. Haywood comes into direct collision with the statements put forth by the Board of Health, who have insisted upon the insanitary state of the metropolitan streets, more strongly, perhaps, in their several Reports, than has Mr. Cochrane.

But Mr. Haywood believes that not only are the assertions of the Board of Health as to the unwholesome state of the metropolitan thoroughfares unfounded as regards the city of London, but he asserts that from the daily street-sweeping, "the surface there is maintained in as high an average condition of cleanliness, as the means hitherto adopted will enable to be attained."

"Nor does this apply," says Mr. Haywood, "to the main thoroughfares only. In the poorer courts and alleys within the city, where a high degree of cleanliness is, at least, as needful, in a sanitary point of view, as in the larger and wider thoroughfares, the facilities for efficient sweeping are as great, if not greater, than in other portions of your jurisdiction. For many years past the whole of the courts and alleys which carts do not enter, have been paved with flagstone, laid at a good inclination, and presenting an uniform smooth *non-absorbent* surface: in many of these courts where the habits of the people are cleanly, the scavenger's broom is almost unneeded for weeks together; in others, where the habit prevails of throwing the refuse of the houses upon the pavements, the daily sweeping is highly essential; but in all these courts the surface presents a condition which renders good clean sweeping a comparatively easy operation, that which is swept away being mostly dry, or nearly so."

After alluding to the street-orderly principle of scavaging, "to clean and keep clean," Mr. Haywood observes, "between the '*street-orderly system*' and the periodical or intermittent sweeping there is this difference, that upon the former system there should be (if it fulfils what it professes) no deposit of any description allowed to remain much longer than a few minutes upon the surface, and that there should be neither mud in the wet weather, nor dust in the dry weather, upon the public ways; whilst, upon the latter system, the deposit necessarily accumulates between the periods of sweeping, commencing as soon as one sweeping has terminated, gradually increasing, and being at its point of extreme accumulation at the period when the next sweeping takes place: the former, then, is, or should be, a system of prevention; the latter, confessedly, but a system of palliation or cure.

"The more frequent the periodical sweeping, therefore, the nearer it approximates in its results to the '*street-orderly system*,' inasmuch as the accumulations, being frequently removed, must be smaller, and the evils of mud, dust, effluvia, &c., less in proportion.

"Now to fulfil its promise: upon the 'street-orderly system,' there should be men both day and night within the streets, who should constantly remove the manure and refuse, and, failing this, if there be only cessation for six hours out of the twenty-four of the 'continuous cleansing,' it becomes at once a periodical cleansing but a degree in advance of the daily sweeping, which has been now for years in operation within the city of London."

This appears to me to be an extreme conclusion:—because the labours of the street orderly system cease when the great traffic ceases, and when, of course, there is comparatively little or no dirt deposited in the thoroughfares, therefore, says Mr. Haywood, "the City system of cleansing once per day is *only a degree* behind that system of which the principle is incessant cleansing at such time as the dirtying is incessant." The two principles are surely as different as light and darkness:—in the one the cleansing is intermittent and the dirt constant; in the other the dirt is intermittent and the cleanliness constant—constant, at least, so long as the causes of impurity are so.

Mr. Haywood, however, states that the Commissioners were so pleased with the appearance of the streets, when cleansed on the street-orderly system, which "was *certainly much to be admired*," that they introduced a somewhat similar system, calling their scavagers "daymen," as they had the care of *keeping* the streets clean, *after* a daily morning sweeping by the contractor's men. They commenced their work at 9 A.M. and ceased at 6 P.M. in the summer months, and at half-past 4 P.M. in the winter. In the summer months 36 daymen were employed on the average; in the winter months, 46. The highest number of scavaging daymen employed on any one day was 63; the lowest was 34. The area cleansed was about 47,000 yards (superficial measure), and with the following results, and the following cost, from June 24, 1846, to the same date, 1847:—

	Yards Superficial.
The average area cleansed during the summer months, per man per diem, was	1298
Ditto during winter, per man per diem, was	1016
The average of both summer and winter months was, per man per diem	1139

	£	s.
The cost of the experiment was for daymen (including brooms, barrows, shovels, cartage, &c. *	1450	18
One Foreman at	78	0
And the total cost of the experiment	£1528	18

"The daily sweeping," Mr. Haywood says, "which for the previous two years had been established throughout the City, gave at that time *very great satisfaction*. It was quite true that the streets which the daymen attended to, *looked superior* to those cleansed only *periodically*, but the practical value of the difference was considered by many not to be worth the sum of money paid for it. It was also felt that, if it was continued, it should upon principle be extended at least to all streets of similar traffic to those upon which it had been tried; and as, after due consideration, the Commission thought that one daily sweeping was sufficient, both for health and comfort, the day or continuous sweeping was abandoned, and the whole City only received, from that time to the present, the usual daily sweeping."

The "present" time is shown by the date of Mr. Haywood's Report, October 13, 1851. The

* The wages paid are not stated.

reason assigned for the abandonment of the system of the daymen is peculiar and characteristic. The system of continuous cleansing gave very great satisfaction, although it was but a degree in advance of the once-a-day cleansing. The streets which the daymen attended to "looked," and of course were, "superior" in cleanliness to those scavaged periodically. It was also felt that the principle should "be extended at least to all streets of similar traffic;" and why was it not so extended? Because, in a word, "it was not worth the money;" though by what standard the value of public cleanliness was calculated, is not mentioned.

The main question, therefore, is, what is the difference in the cost of the two systems, and *is* the admitted "superior cleanliness" produced by the continuous mode of scavaging, in comparison with that obtained by the intermittent mode, of sufficient public value to warrant the increased expense (if any)—in a word, as the City people say—is it *worth the money?*

First, as to the comparative cost of the two systems: after a statement of the contracts for the dusting and cleansing of the City (matters I have before treated of) Mr. Haywood, for the purpose of making a comparison of the present City system of scavaging with the street-orderly system, gives the table in the opposite page to show the cost of street cleansing and dusting within the jurisdiction of the City Court of Sewers.

Mr. Haywood then invites attention to the subjoined statement of the National Philanthropic Association, on the occurrence of a demonstration as to the efficiency and economy of the street-orderly system.

"Association for the Promotion of Street Paving, Cleansing, Draining, &c., 20, Vere Street, Oxford Street, January 26th, 1846.

"Approximation to the total Expenses connected with cleansing, as an experiment, certain parts of the City of London, commencing December, 1845, for the period of two months.

	£.	s.	d.
"350 brooms, being an average of 5 brooms for each man	25	18	10
For carting	99	1	9
For advertising	65	0	0
For rent of store-room, 3l. 14s.; Clerks' salaries, 12l.; Messengers, 5l. 5s.; wooden clogs for men, 2l. 5s. 10d.; expenses of washing wood pavement, 5l.	28	4	10
Expenses of barrows	24	14	0
Christmas dinner to men, foremen, and superintendents (97)	15	12	6
83 men (averaging at 2s. 6d. per day) for 9 weeks	573	15	0
4 superintendents at 25s. 4d., foreman at 18s., cart foreman 20s., storekeeper 18s., chief superintendents 2l., for 9 weeks	112	10	0
For various small articles, brushes, rakes, &c.	36	7	8
Petty expenses of the office, postages, &c., and stationery	6	0	0
Approximation to the total cost of the expense	£987	4	7

Signed, M. DAVIES, Secretary."

"I will now," says Mr. Haywood, "without further present reference to the Report of the Association, proceed to form an estimate of the expenses of the system as they would have been if it had been extended to the whole City, and which estimate will be based upon the informa-

TABLE SHOWING THE COST OF STREET CLEANSING AND DUSTING WITHIN THE JURISDICTION OF THE CITY COURT OF SEWERS.

Date.	Mode of Contracting, whether Contracts for Dusting and Scavenging were let separately or together.	Leading or Principal feature in the Regulations for the Dusting and Cleansing.	Sum paid for Scavenging and Dusting, or for Scavenging only during the year.			Sum received by Commission for Sale of Dust when the Contracts were let separately.			Total Disbursements by the Commission for Scavenging and Dusting.		
			£	s.	d.	£	s.	d.	£	s.	d.
Year ending Michaelmas, 1841	separately	Main streets of largest traffic running east and west cleansed *daily*, other principal streets *every other day*, the whole of the remainder of the public ways *twice* a week; dust to be removed at least *twice* a week.	4590	6	0				4590	6	0
,, 1842	separately		3633	17	0	Amounts paid and received are balanced			3633	17	0
,, 1843	together		2084	4	6				2084	4	6
		Average per Annum for 3 Years.							3436	2	6
,, 1844	separately	Main line of streets cleansed *daily*, other principal streets *every other day*, and all other place *twice* in every week; dust to be removed at least *twice* a week.	3826	12	6	Amounts paid and received are balanced			3826	12	6
,, 1845	separately		2033	2	0				2833	2	0
		Average per Annum of the 2 Years							3329	17	3
,, 1846	separately		6034	6	0	1354	5	0	4680	1	0
,, 1847	separately		8014	2	0	4455	5	0	3558	17	0
,, 1848	separately	*Daily cleansing* throughout every public way of every description; dust to be removed twice a week.	7226	1	6	1328	15	0	5897	6	6
,, 1849	together		7486	11	6				7486	11	6
,, 1850	together		6779	16	0				6779	16	0
,, 1851	together		6328	17	0				6328	17	0
		Average per Annum of the last 6 Years							5788	11	6

NOTE.—From 24th June, 1846, to 24th June, 1847, the Commission made their own experiment upon the Street-Orderly System—the expenses of such experiment are included in the above amounts. In 1849 the area of the jurisdiction of the Commission was increased by the addition of various precincts under the City of London Sewers' Act.

tion as to the expenses of the system, furnished by the experiment or demonstration made by the Association within your jurisdiction.

"The total cost of the experiment was £987 4s. 7d., and, deducting the charges under the head of advertising, Christmas dinner, and petty cash expenses, and also that for office-rent, clerks, messengers, &c., and assigning £50 as the value of the implements at that time for future use, there is left a balance of £822 7s. 3d. as the clear cost of the experiment.

"The experiment was tried for a period of eight weeks exactly, according to the return made to the Commission by the Superintendent of the Association, but as in the statement of expenses the wages appear to be included for a period of nine weeks, I have assumed nine weeks as the correct figure, and the experiment must therefore have cost a sum of £822 7s. 3d. for that period, or at the rate of about £91 per week.

	Squ. Yards
"Now the total area of the carriage-way of the City of London was at that time	418,000
"And the area of the foot-way	316,000
"Making a total of	734,000
"And the area of the carriage-way cleaned by the street-orderlies was	30,670
"And the area of the foot-way	18,590
"Making a total of	49,260

"The total area of foot-way and carriage-way cleansed was therefore 1-15th of the whole of the carriage-way and foot-way of the City; or, taken separately, the carriage-way cleansed was somewhat more than 1-14th of the whole of the City carriage-way.

"It has been seen also that the total cost of cleansing this 1-14th portion of the carriage-way, after deducting all extraneous expenses, was at the rate per week of £91
Or at the rate, per annum, of £4732

"To assign an expenditure in the same proportion for the remaining 13-14ths of the whole carriage-way area of the City would not be just, for, in the first place, allowance must be made, owing to the dirt brought off from the adjacent streets, which, it is assumed, would not have been the case had they also been cleansed upon the street-orderly system; and moreover, as the majority of the streets cleansed were those of large traffic, a larger proportion of labour was needed to them than would have been the case had the experiment been upon any equal area of carriage-way, taken from a district comprehending streets of all sizes and degrees of traffic; but if I assume that the 1-14th portion of the City cleansed represents 1-11th of the whole in the labour needed for cleansing the whole of the City upon the same system, I believe I shall have made a very fair deduction, and shall, if anything, err in favour of the experiment.

"Estimating, therefore, the expense of cleansing the whole of the City carriage-way upon the street-orderly system according to the expenses of the experiment made in 1845-6, and from the data then furnished, it appears that cleansing upon such system would have come to an annual sum of 52,052l.

"It will be seen that there is a remarkable difference between this estimate of 52,052l. per annum and that of 18,000l. per annum estimated by the Association, and given in their Report of the 26th January, 1846; and what is more remarkable is, that my estimate is framed not upon any assumption of my own, but is a dry calculation based upon the very figures of expense furnished by the Association itself, and hereinbefore recited."

A second demonstration, carried on in the City by the street-orderlies, is detailed by Mr. Haywood, but as he draws the same conclusions from it, there is no necessity to do other than allude to it here.

According to the above estimate, it certainly must be admitted that the difference between the two accounts is, as Mr. Haywood says, "remarkable"—the one being nearly three times more than the other. But let us, for fairness' sake, test the cost of cleansing the City thoroughfares upon the continuous plan of scavaging by the figures given in Mr. Haywood's own report, and see whether the above conclusion is warranted by the facts there stated. From June, 1846, to June, 1847, we have seen that several of the main streets in the City were cleansed continuously throughout the day by what were called "day-men"—that is to say, 47,000 superficial yards of the principal thoroughfares were *kept* clean (*after* the daily cleansing of them by the contractor's men) by a body of men similar in their mode of operation to the street-orderlies, and who removed all the dirt as soon as deposited between the hours of the principal traffic. The cost of this experiment (for such it seems to have been) was, for the twelve months, as we have seen, 1528l. 18s. Now if the expense of cleansing 47,000 superficial yards upon the continuous method was 1529l., then, according to Cocker, 770,157 yards (the total area of the public ways of the City) would cost 25,054l.; and, adding to this 6328l. for the sum paid to the contractors for the daily scavaging, we have only 31,382l. for the gross expense of cleansing the whole of the City thoroughfares once a day by the "regular scavagers," and *keeping* them clean *afterwards* by a body similar to the street-orderlies—a difference of upwards of 20,000l. between the facts and figures of the City Surveyor.

It would appear to me, therefore, that Mr. Haywood has erred, in estimating the probable expense of the street-orderly system of scavaging applied to the City at 52,000l. per annum, for, by his own showing, it actually cost the authorities for the one year when it was tried there, only 1529l. for 47,000 superficial yards, at which rate 770,000 yards could not cost more than 31,500l., and this, even allowing that the same amount of labour would be required for the continuous cleansing of the minor thoroughfares as needed for the principal ones. That the error is an oversight on the part of the City Surveyor, the whole tone of his Report is sufficient to assure us, for it is at once moderate and candid.

It must, on the other hand, be admitted, that Mr. Haywood is perfectly correct as to the difference between the cost of the "demonstration" of the street-orderly system of cleansing in the City, and the estimated cost of that mode of scavaging when brought into regular operation there; this, however, the year's experience of the City "day-men" shows, could not possibly exceed 32,000l., and might and probably would be much less, when we take into account the smaller quantity of labour required for the minor thoroughfares—the extra value of the street manure when collected free from mud—the saving in the expense of watering the streets (this not being required under the orderly system)—and the abolition of the daily scavaging, which is included in the sum above cited, but which would be no longer needed were the orderlies employed, such work being performed by them at the commencement of their day's labours; so that I am disposed to believe, all things considered, that somewhere about 20,000*l.* per annum might be the gross expense of continuously cleansing the City. Mr. Cochrane estimates it at 18,000*l.* But whether the admitted superior cleanliness of the streets, and the employment of an extra number of people, will be held by the citizens to be worth the extra money, it is not for me to say. If, however, the increased cleanliness effected by the street-orderlies is to be brought about by a decrease of the wages of the regular scavagers from 16*s.* to 12*s.* a week, which is the amount upon which Mr. Cochrane forms his estimate, then I do not hesitate to say the City authorities will be gainers, in the matter of poor-rates at least, by an adherence to the present method of scavaging, paying as they do the best wages, and indeed affording an illustrious example to all the metropolitan parishes, in refusing to grant contracts to any master scavagers but such as consent to deal fairly with the men in their employ. And I do hope and trust, for the sake of the working-men, the City Commissioners of Sewers will, should they decide upon having the City cleansed *continuously*, make the same requirement of Mr. Cochrane, before they allow his street-orderlies to displace the regular scavagers at present employed there.

Benefits to the community, gained at the expense of "the people," are really great evils. The street-orderly system is a good one when applied to parishes employing paupers and paying them 1*s.* 1½*d.* and a loaf per day, or even nothing, except their food, for their labour. Here it elevates paupers into independent labourers; but, applied to those localities where the highest wages are paid, and there is the greatest regard shown for the welfare of the workmen, it is merely a scurf-system of degrading the independent labourers to the level of paupers, by reducing the wages of the regular scavagers from 16*s.* to 12*s.* per week. The avowed object of the street-orderly system is to provide employment for able-bodied men, and so to *prevent* them becoming a *burthen to the parish.* But is not a reduction of the scavager's wages to the extent of 25 per cent. a week, more likely to *encourage* than to *prevent* such a result? This is the weak point of the orderly system, and one which gentlemen calling themselves *philanthropists* should really blush to be parties to.

After all, the opinion to which I am led is this— the street-orderly system is incomparably the best mode of scavaging, and the payment of the men by "*honourable*" masters the best mode of employing the scavagers. The evils of the scavaging trade appear to me to spring chiefly from the parsimony of the parish authorities—either employing their own paupers without adequate remuneration, or else paying such prices to the contractors as almost necessitates the under-payment of the men in their employ. Were I to fill a volume, this is all that could be said on the matter.

OF THE "JET AND HOSE" SYSTEM OF SCAVAGING.

THERE appears at the present time a bent in the public mind for an improved system of scavagery. Until the ravages of the cholera in 1832, and again in 1848, roused the attention of Government and of the country, men seemed satisfied to dwell in dirty streets, and to congratulate themselves that the public ways were dirtier in the days of their fathers; a feeling or a spirit which has no doubt existed in all cities, from the days of those original scavagers, the vultures and hyenas of Africa and the East, the adjutants of Calcutta, and the hawks—the common glades or kites of this country—and which, we are told, in the days of Henry VIII. used to fly down among the passengers to remove the offal of the butchers and poulterers' stalls in the metropolitan markets, and in consideration of which services it was forbidden to kill them—down to the mechanical sweeping of the streets of London, and even to Mr. Cochrane's excellent street-orderlies.

Besides the plan suggested by Mr. Cochrane, whose orderlies cleanse the streets without wetting, and consequently without dirtying, the surface by the use of the watering-cart, there is the opposite method proposed by Mr. Lee, of Sheffield, and other gentlemen, who recommend street-cleansing by the hose and jet, that is to say, by flushing the streets with water at a high pressure, as the sewers are now flushed; and so, by *washing* rather than *sweeping* the dirt of the streets into the sewers, through the momentum of the stream of water, dispensing altogether with the scavager's broom, shovel, and cart.

In order to complete this account of the scavaging of the streets of London, I must, in conclusion, say a few words on this method, advocated as it is by the Board of Health, and sanctioned by scientific men. By the application of a hose, with a jet or water pipe attached to a fire-plug, the water being at high pressure, a stream of fluid is projected along the street's surface with force enough to *wash* away all before it into the sewers, while by the same apparatus it can be thrown over the fronts of the houses. This mode of street-cleansing prevails in some American cities, especially in Philadelphia, where the principal thoroughfares are said to be kept admirably clean by it; while the fronts of the houses are as bright as those in the towns of Holland, where they are washed, not by mechanical appliances, but by water thrown over them out of scoops by hand labour—one of the instances of the minute and indefatigable industry of the Dutch.

It is stated in one of the Reports of the Board of Health, that "unless cleansing be general and simultaneous, much of the dirt of one district is carried by traffic into another. By the subdivision of the metropolis into small districts, the duty of cleansing the *public* carriage-way is thrown upon a number of obscure and irresponsible authorities; while the duty of cleansing the *public* footways, which are no less important, *are* charged upon multitudes of private individuals." [The grammar is the Board of Health's grammar.] "It is a false pecuniary economy, in the case of the poorest inhabitants of court or alley, who obtain their livelihood by any regular occupation, to charge upon each family the duty of cleansing the footway before their doors. The performance of this service daily, at a rate of 1*d. per week* per house or per family, would be an economy in soap and clothes to persons the average value of whose time is never less than 2*d.* per hour." [This is at the rate of 2*s.* a day; did this most innocent Board *never* hear of work yielding 1*s.* 6*d.* a week? But the sanitary authorities seem to be as fond as teetotallers of "going to extremes."]

In another part of the same Report the process and results are described. It is also stated that for the success of this method of street purification the pavement must be good; for "a powerful jet, applied by the hose, would scoop out hollows in unpaved places, and also loosen and remove the stones in those that are badly paved." As every public place ought to be well-paved, this necessity of new and good pavement is no reasonable objection to the plan, though it certainly admits of a question as to the durability of the roads—the macadamized especially—under this continual soaking. Sir Henry Parnell, the great road authority, speaks of wet as the main destroyer of the highways.

It is stated in the Report, after the mention of experiments having been made by Mr. Lovick, Mr. Hale, and Mr. Lee (Mr. Lee being one of the engineering inspectors of the Board), that

"Mr. Lovick, at the instance of the Metropolitan Commissioners of Sewers, conducted his experiments with such jets as could be obtained from the water companies' mains in eligible places; but the pressure was low and insufficient. Nevertheless, it appeared that, taking the extra quantity of water required at the actual expense of pumping, the paved surfaces might be washed clean at one-half the price of the scavagers' manual labour in sweeping. Mr. Lee's trials were made at Sheffield, with the aid of a more powerful and suitable pressure, and he found that with such pressure as he obtained the cleansing might be effected in one-third the time, and at one-third the usual expense, of the scavagers' labour of sweeping the surface with the broom." [This expense varies, and the Board nowhere states at what rate it is computed; the scavagers' wages varying 100 per cent.]

"The effect of this mode of cleansing in close courts and streets," it is further stated, "was found to be peculiarly grateful in hot weather. The water was first thrown up and diffused in a thin sheet, it was then applied rapidly to cleansing the surface and the side walls, as well as the pavements." Mr. Lovick states that the immediate effect of this operation was to lower the temperature, and to produce a sense of freshness, similar to that experienced after a heavy thunder-shower in hot weather. But there is nothing said as to the probable effect of this state of things in winter—a hard frost for instance. The same expedient was resorted to for cooling the yards and outer courts of hospitals, and the shower thrown on the windows of the wards afforded great relief. Mr. Lovick, in his Report on the trial works for cleansing courts, states:—

"The importance of water as an agent in the improvement and preservation of health being in proportion to the unhealthiness or depressed condition of districts, its application to close courts and densely-populated localities, in which a low sanitary condition must obtain, is of primary importance. Having shown the practicability of applying this system (cleansing by jets of water) to the general cleansing of the streets, my further labours have been, and are now, directed to this end.

"For the purpose of ascertaining the effect produced by operations of this nature upon the atmosphere, two courts were selected: Church-passage, New Compton-street, open at both ends, with a carriage-way in the centre, and footway on each side; and Lloyd's-court, Crown-street, St. Giles's, a close court, with, at one entrance, a covered passage about 40 feet in length: both courts were in a very filthy condition; in Church-passage there were dead decaying cats and fish, with offal, straw, and refuse scattered over the surface; at one end an entrance to a private yard was used as a urinal; in every part there were most offensive smells.

"Lloyd's-court was in a somewhat similar condition, the covered entrance being used as a general urinal, presenting a disgusting appearance; the whole atmosphere of the court was loaded with highly-offensive effluvia; in the covered entrance this was more particularly discernible.

"The property of water, as an absorbent, was rendered strikingly apparent in the immediate and marked effects of its application, a purity and freshness remarkably contrasted to the former close and foul condition prevailing throughout. A test of this, striking and unexpected, was the change at different periods in the relative condition of atmosphere of the courts and of the contiguous streets. In their ordinary condition, as might have been expected, the atmosphere was purer in the streets than in the courts; it was to be inferred that the cleansing would have more nearly assimilated these conditions. This was not only the case, but it was found to have effected a complete change; the atmosphere of the courts at the close of the operations being far fresher and purer than the atmosphere of the streets. The effect produced was in every respect satisfactory and complete; and was the theme of conversation with the lookers-on, and with the men who conducted the operations.

"The expense of these operations, including water, would be, for—

"Church-passage (time, five minutes), $1\frac{1}{2}d.$

"Lloyd's-court (time, ten minutes), $3\frac{1}{4}d.$

"Mr. Hale, another officer, gave a similar statement."

Other experiments are thus detailed:—

"Lascelles-court, Broad-street, St. Giles's. This court was pointed out to me as one of the worst in London. Before cleansing it smelt *intolerable*," [*sic*] "and looked disgusting. Besides an abundance of ordinary filth arising from the exposure of refuse, the surface of the court contained heaps of human excrement, there being only one privy to the whole court, and that not in a state to be publicly used. . . . . . The cleansing operations were commenced by sprinkling the court with deodorising fluid, mixed with 20 times its volume of water; a great change, from a very pungent odour to an imperceptible smell, was immediately effected; after which the refuse of the court was washed away, and the pavement thoroughly cleansed by the hose and jet; and now this place, which before was in a state almost indescribable, presented an appearance of comparative comfort and respectability."

It is stated as the result of another experiment in "an ordinary wide street with plenty of traffic," that "water-carts and ordinary rains only create the mud which the jet entirely removes, giving to the pavement the appearance of having been as thoroughly cleansed as the private stone steps in front of the houses."

With respect to Mr. Lee's experiments in Sheffield, I find that Messrs. Guest, of Rotherham, are patentees of a tap for the discharge of water at high pressures, and that they had adapted their invention to the purpose of a fire-plug and stand pipe suitable for street-cleansing by the hose and jet. Church-street, one of the principal thoroughfares, was experimentally cleansed by this process: "The carriage-way is from 20 to 24 feet wide, and about 150 yards long. It was washed almost as clean as a house-floor in five minutes." Mr. Lee expresses his conviction that, by the agency of the hose and jet, every street in that populous borough might be cleansed at about 1s. per annum for each house. "The principal thoroughfares," he states, "could be thus made perfectly clean, three times every week, before business hours, and the minor streets and lanes twice, or once per week, at later hours in the day, by the agency of an abundant supply of water, at *less than half the sum necessary for the cartage alone* of an equal quantity of refuse in a solid or semi-fluid condition."

The highways most frequented in Sheffield constitute about one-half of the whole extent of the streets and roads in the borough, measuring 47 miles. This length, Mr. Lee computes, might be effectually cleansed with the hose and jet, ten miles of it three times a week, 21 miles twice a week, and 16 miles once a week, a total of 88 miles weekly, or 4576 miles yearly. The quantity of Water required would be 3000 gallons a mile, or a yearly total of 13,728,000 gallons. This water might be supplied, Mr. Lee opines, at 1d. per 1000 gallons (57l. 4s. per annum), although the price obtained by the Water-works Company was 6½d. per 1000 gallons (371l. 16s. per annum). "I now proceed," he says, "to the cost of labour: 4576 miles per annum is equal to 14⅔ miles for each working day, or to six sets of two men cleansing 2½ miles per day each set. To these must be added three horses and carts, and three carters, for the removal of such *débris* as cannot be washed away and for such parts of the town as cannot be cleansed by this system, making a total of fifteen men. Their wages I would fix at 50l. per annum each. The estimate is as follows:—

"Annual interest upon the first cost of hose and pipes, three horses and carts £30
Fifteen men's wages 750
Three horses' provender . . . 150
Wear, tear, and depreciation of hose, &c. 250
Management and incidentals, say . . 120

£1300."

The estimate, it will be seen, is based on the supposition that *the water supply should be at the public cost*, and not a specific charge for the purposes of street-cleansing.

The 47 miles of highway of Sheffield is but three miles less than those of the city of London, the cost of cleansing which is, according to the estimate before given, no less than 18,000l.

The Sheffield account is divested of all calculations as to house-dust and ashes, and the charge for watering-carts; but, taking merely the sum paid to scavaging contractors, and assigning 1000l. (out of the 2485l.), as the proportion of salaries, &c., under the department of scavagery in the management of the City Commissioners, we find that while the expense of street-cleansing by the Sheffield hose and jet was little more than 34l., in London, by the ordinary mode, it was upwards of 140l. per mile, or more than four times as much. The hose and jet system is said to have washed the streets of Sheffield as clean as a house-floor, which could not be said of it in London. The streets of the City, it should also be borne in mind, are now swept daily; Mr. Lee proposes only a periodical cleaning for Sheffield, or once, twice, and thrice a week. Of the cost of the experiments made in London with the hose and jet, in Lascelles-court, &c., nothing is said.

Street-cleansing by the hose and jet is, then, as yet but an experiment. It has not, like the street-orderly mode, been tested continuously or systematically; but the experiments are so curious and sometimes so startling in their results that it was necessary to give a brief account of them here, in order to render this account of the cleansing of the streets of the metropolis as comprehensive as possible. For my own part, I must confess the street-orderly system appears to excel all other modes of scavagery, producing at once the greatest cleanliness with the greatest employment to the poor. Nor am I so convinced as the theoretic and crotchety Board of Health as to the healthfulness of dampness, or the daily evaporation of a sheet of even clean water equal in extent to the entire surface of the London streets. It is certainly *doubtful*, to say the least, whether so much additional moisture might *improve* the public health, which the Board are instituted to protect; rain certainly contributes to cleanliness, and yet no one would advocate continued wet weather as a source of general convalescence.

I shall conclude this account of the scavaging

of London, with the following brief statement as to the mode in which these matters are conducted abroad.

In Paris, where our system of parochial legislation and management is unknown, the scavaging of the streets—so frequently matters of private speculation with us—is under the immediate direction of the municipality, and the Government publish the returns, as they do of the revenue of their capital from the abattoirs, the interments, and other sources.

In the *Moniteur* for December 10, 1848, it is stated that the refuse of the streets of Paris sells for 500,500 francs (20,020*l*.), when sold by auction in the mass; and 3,800,000 francs (equal to 152,000*l*.) when, after having lain in the proper receptacles, until fit for manure, it is sold by the cubic foot. In 1823, the streets of Paris were leased for 75,000 francs (3000*l*.) per annum in 1831 the value was 166,000 francs (6640*l*.); and since 1845 the price has risen to the sum first named, viz., 500,500 francs (20,020*l*.); from which, however, is to be deducted the expense of cleansing, &c. I may add, that the receptacles alluded to are large places provided by Government, where the manure is deposited and left to ferment for twelve or eighteen months.

OF THE COST AND TRAFFIC OF THE STREETS OF LONDON.

I HAVE, at page 183 of the present volume, given a brief statement of the annual cost attending the keeping of the streets of the metropolis in working order.

The formation of the streets of a capital like London, the busiest in the world—streets traversed daily by what Cowper, even in his day, described as "the ten thousand wheels" of commerce—is an elaborate and costly work.

In my former account I gave an estimate which referred to the amount dispensed weekly in wages for the labour of the workmen engaged in laying down the paved roads of the metropolis. This was at the rate of 100,000*l*. per week; that is to say, calculating the operation of relaying the streets to occupy one year in every five, there is no less than 5,200,000*l*. expended in that time among the workpeople so engaged. The sum expended in labour for the continued repairs of the roads, after being so relaid, appears to be about 20,000*l*. per week *, or, in round numbers, about 1,000,000*l*. a year; so that the gross sum annually disbursed to the labourers engaged in the construction of the roads of London would seem to be about 2,250,000*l*., that is to say, 1,000,000*l*. for repairing the old roads, and 1,250,000*l*. per annum for laying down new ones in their place.

It now remains for me to set forth the gross cost of the metropolitan highways, that is to say, the sum annually expended in both labour and materials, as well for relaying as for repairing the roads.

The granite-built streets cost, when relaid,

* At p. 183 the sum of 18,225*l*. is said to be expended in repairs *annually*; it should have been *weekly*.

about 11,000*l*. the mile, of ten yards' width, which is at the rate of 12*s*. 6*d*. the square yard, materials and labour included, the granite (Aberdeen) being 1*l*. 5*s*. per ton, and one ton of "seven-inch" being sufficient to cover about three square yards.

The average cost of a macadamized road, materials and labour included, if constructed from the foundation, is about 4400*l*. per street mile (ten yards wide)—5*s*. the superficial yard being a fair price for materials and labour.

Wood pavement, on the other hand, costs about 9680*l*. a mile of ten yards' width for materials and labour, which is at the rate of 11*s*. the superficial yard.

The cost of *repairs*, materials and labour included, is, for granite pavement about 1½*d*. per square yard, or 100*l*. the street mile of ten yards wide; for "Macadam" it is from 6*d*. to 3*s*. 6*d*., or an average of 1*s*. 6*d*. per superficial yard, which is at the rate of 1320*l*. the street mile; while the wood pavement costs about the same for repairs as the granite.

The total cost of repairing the streets of London, then, may be taken as follows:—

	£
Repairing granite-built streets, per mile of ten yards wide . .	100
Repairing macadamized roads, per street mile	1320
Repairing wood pavement, per street mile	100

Or, as a total for all London,—

Repairing 400 miles of granite-built streets, at 100*l*. per mile . .	40,000
Repairing 1350 miles of macadamized streets, at 1320*l*. per mile .	1,782,000
Repairing five miles of wood, at 100*l*. per mile	500
	£1,822,500

The following, on the other hand, may be taken as the total cost of *reconstructing* the London streets:—

	£
Granite-built streets, per mile ten yards wide	11,000
Macadamized streets, per street mile	4,400
Wood „ „ .	9,680

Or, as a total for the entire streets and roads of London,—

	£
Relaying 400 miles of granite-built streets, at 11,000*l*. per mile . .	4,400,000
Relaying 1350 miles of macadamized streets, at 4400*l*. per mile .	5,940,000
Relaying five miles of wood-built streets, at 9680*l*. . . .	48,400
	£10,388,400

But the above refers only to the road, and besides this, there is, as a gentleman to whom I am much indebted for valuable information on the subject, reminds me, the foot paving, granite curb, and granite channel not included. The usual price for *paving* is 8*d*. per foot superficial, when laid—granite curb 1s. 7d. per foot run, and granite channel 12s. per square yard.

"Now, presuming that three-fourths of the roads," says my informant, "have paved footpaths on each side at an average width of six feet exclusive of curb, and that one-half of the macadamized roads have granite channels on each side, and that one-third of all the roads have granite curb on each side; these items for 400 miles of granite road, 1350 macadamized, and 5 miles of wood—together 1755 miles—will therefore amount to

	£	s.	d.
Three-fourths of 1755 miles of streets paved on each side, six feet wide, at 8d. per foot superficial	2,779,392	0	0
One-half of 1350 miles of macadamized roads with one foot of granite channel on each side, at 12s. per yard square .	458,537	4	5
One-third of 1755 miles of road with granite curb on each side, at 1s. 7d. per foot run .	489,060	0	0
	3,726,989	4	5
Cost of constructing 1755 miles of roadway . . .	10,388,400	0	0
Total cost of constructing the streets of London . .	£14,115,389	4	5

"Accordingly the original cost of the metropolitan pavements exceeds fourteen millions sterling, and, calculating that this requires renewal every five years, the gross annual expenditure will be at the rate of 2,500,000l. per annum, which, added to 1,822,500l., gives 4,322,500l., or upwards of four millions and a quarter sterling for the entire annual cost of the London roadways.

"From rather extensive experience," adds my informant, "in building operations, and consequently in making and paying for roads, I am of opinion that the amount I have shown is under rather than above the actual cost.

"In a great many parts of the metropolis the roads are made by the servants of a body of Commissioners appointed for the purpose; and from dear-bought experience I can say they are a public nuisance, and would earnestly caution speculating builders against taking building ground or erecting houses in any place where the roads are under their control. The Commissioners are generally old retired tradesmen, and have very little to occupy their attention, and are often quite ignorant of their duties; I have reason to believe, too, that some of them even use their little authority to gratify their dislike to some poor builder in their district, by meddling and quibbling, and while that is going on the houses which have been erected can neither be let nor sold; so that as the bills given for the materials keep running, the builder, when they fall due, is ruined, for his creditors will not take his unlet houses for their debts, and no one else will purchase them until let, for none will rent them without proper accesses. I feel certain that in those parts where the roads are made by Commissioners three times more builders, in proportion to their number, get into difficulties than in the districts where they are permitted to make the roads themselves."

The paved ways and roads of London, then, it appears, cost in round numbers 10,000,000l. sterling, and require nearly 2,000,000l. to be expended upon them annually for repairs.

But this is not the sole expense attendant upon the construction of the streets of the metropolis. Frequently, in the formation of new lines of thoroughfare, large masses of property have to be bought up, removed, and new buildings erected at considerable cost. In a return made pursuant to an order of the Court of Common Council, dated 23rd October, 1851, for "An account of all moneys which have been raised for public works executed, buildings erected, or street improvements effected, out of the Coal Duties receivable by the Corporation of London in the character of trustees for administration or otherwise, since the same were made chargeable by Parliament for such purposes in the year 1766," the following items are given relating to the cost of the formation of new streets and improvements of old ones :—

Street Improvements forming New Thoroughfares.

	Amount raised for Public Works, &c.		
	£.	s.	d.
Building the bridge across the river Thames, from Blackfriars, in the city of London, to Upper Ground-street, in the county of Surrey, now called Blackfriars Bridge, and forming the avenues thereto, and embanking the north abutment of the said bridge—(Entrusted to the Corporation of the city of London)	210,000	0	0
Making a new line of streets from Moorfields, opposite Chiswell-street, towards the east into Bishopsgate-street (now Crown-street and Sun-street), also from the east end of Chiswell-street westward into Barbican—(Corporation of the city of London) . .	16,500	0	0
Making a new street from Crispin-street, near Spitalfields Church, into Bishopsgate-street (now called Union-street), in the city of London and in the county of Middlesex—(Commissioners named in Act 18, George III., c. 78) .	9,000	0	0
Opening communications between Wapping-street and Ratcliffe-highway, and between Old Gravel-lane and Virginia-street, all in the county of Middlesex—(Commissioners appointed under Act 17, Geo. III., c. 22) . . .	1,000	0	0
Formation of Farringdon-street, removal of Fleet-market, and erection of Farringdon-market, in the city of London—(Corporation of the city of London).	250,000	0	0

Formation of a new street from the end of Coventry-street to the junction of Newport-street and Long-acre (Cranbourn-street), continuing the line of street from Waterloo Bridge, already completed to Bow-street (Upper Wellington-street), and thence northward into Broad-street, Holborn, and thence to Charlotte-street, Bloomsbury, extending Oxford-street in a direct line through St. Giles's, so as to communicate with Holborn at or near Southampton-street (New Oxford-street); also widening the northern and

	£	s.	d.
Brought forward . .	436,500	0	0

southern extremities of Leman-street, Goodman's-fields, and forming a new street from the northern side of Whitechapel to the front of Spitalfields Church (Commercial-street), and forming a new street from Rosemary-lane to East Smithfield, near to the entrance of the London-docks; also formation of a street from the neighbourhood of the Houses of Parliament towards Buckingham Palace, in the city of Westminster (Victoria-street), all in the county of Middlesex; also formation of a line of new street between Southwark and Westminster Bridges, in the county of Surrey—(Her Majesty's Commissioners of Woods, Forests, and Land Revenues) £65,000 0 0

NOTE.—The Commissioners of Her Majesty's Woods have been authorised to raise further moneys on the credit of the duty of 1d. per ton for further improvements in the neighbourhood of Spitalfields, but the Chamberlain is not officially cognizant of the amount.

Forming a new street from the northern end of Victoria-street, Holborn (formed by the Corporation to Clerkenwell-green, all in the county of Middlesex)—(Clerkenwell Improvement Commissioners) 25,000 0 0

Formation of a new line of streets from King William-street, London Bridge, to the south side of St. Paul's Cathedral, by widening and improving Cannon-street, making a new street from Cannon-street, near Bridge-row, to Queen-street, and another street from the west side of Queen-street, in a direct line to St. Paul's-churchyard, and widening Queen-street, from the junction of the said new street to Southwark Bridge; also improving Holborn Bridge and Field-lane, and effecting an improvement in Grace-church-streeet and Ship Tavern-passage, all in the city of London—(Corporation of the city of London) . 500,000 0 0

Finishing the new street left incomplete by the Clerkenwell Improvement Commissioners, from the end of Victoria-street, Farringdon-street, to Coppice-row, Clerkenwell, all in the county of Middlesex—(Corporation of the City of London) 88,000 0 0

Total cost of forming the above-mentioned new thoroughfares . . . 1,734,500 0 0

Improving existing Thoroughfares.

Improving existing approaches, and forming new approaches to new London Bridge, viz., in High-street, Tooley-street, Montague-close, Pepper-alley, Whitehorse-court, Chequer-court, Chaingate, Churchyard-passage, St. Saviour's churchyard, Carter-lane, Boar's-head-place, Fryingpan-alley, Green Dragon-court, Joyner-street, Red Lion-street, Counter-street, Three Crown-court, and the east front of the Town Hall, all in the Borough of Southwark; also ground and premises at the north-west foot of London Bridge, Upper Thames-street, Red-cross-wharf, Mault's-wharf, High Timber-street and Broken-wharf, Swan-passage, Churchyard-alley, site of Fishmonger's Hall, Great East-cheap, Little Eastcheap, Star-court, Fish-street-hill, Little Tower-street, Idol-lane, St. Mary-at-hill, Crooked-lane, Miles-lane, Three Tun-alley, Warren-court, Cannon-street, Grace-church-street, Bell-yard, Martin's-lane, Nicholas-lane, Clement's-lane, Abchurch-lane, Sherborne-lane, Swithin's-lane, Cornhill, Lombard-street, Dove-court, Fox Ordinary-court, Old Post Office Chambers, Mansion-house-street, Princes-street, Coleman-street, Coleman-street-buildings, Moorgate-street, London Wall, Lothbury, Tokenhouse-yard, King's Arms-yard, Great Bell-alley, Packer's-court, White's-alley, Great Swan-alley, Crown-court, George-yard, Red Lion-court, Cateaton-street, Gresham-street, Milk-street, Wood-street, King-street, Basinghall-street, Houndsditch, Lad-lane, Threadneedle-street, Aldgate High-street, and Maiden-lane, all in the City of London—(Corporation of the City of London) 1,016,421 18 1

Widening and improving the entrance into London near Temple-bar, improving the Strand and Fleet-street, and formation of Pickett-street, and for making a new street from the east end of Snow-hill to the bottom of Holborn-hill, now called Skinner-street—(Corporation of the City of London) 246,300 0 0

Widening and improving Dirty-lane and part of Brick-lane, leading from Whitechapel to Spitalfields, and for paving Dirty-lane, Petticoat-lane, Wentworth-street, Old Montague-street, Chapel-street, Princes-row, &c., all in the county of Middlesex—(Commissioners appointed by the Act 18, Geo. III., c. 80) 1,500 0 0

Widening the avenues from the Minories, through Goodman's-yard into Prescott-street, and through Swan-street and Swan-alley into Mansell-street, and from Whitechapel through Somerset-street into Great Mansell-street, all in the county of Middlesex—(Commissioners named in Act 18, George III., c. 50) . . . 1,500 0 0

Total cost of improving the above-mentioned thoroughfares . . 1,265,721 18 1

Paving.

Paving the road from Aldersgate Bars to turnpike in Goswell-street, in the county of Middlesex—(Commissioners Sewers, &c., of the City of London) . 5,500 0 0

Completing the paving of the town borough of Southwark and certain parts adjacent—(Commissioners for executing Act 6, George III., for paving town and borough of Southwark) 4,000 0 0

Total cost of paving the above-mentioned thoroughfares 9,500 0 0

Hence the aggregate expense of the preceding improvements has been upwards of 3,000,000l. sterling.

I have now, in order to complete this account of the cost of paving and cleansing the thoroughfares of the metropolis, only to add the following statement as to the traffic of the principal thoroughfares in the city of London, for which I am indebted to Mr. Haywood, the City Surveyor.

By the subjoined Return it will be seen that there are two tides as it were in the daily current of locomotion in the City—the one being at its flood at 11 o'clock A.M., after which it falls gradually till 2 o'clock, when it is at its lowest ebb, and then begins to rise, gradually till 5 o'clock, when it reaches its second flood, and then begins to decline once more. The point of greatest traffic in the City is London-bridge, where the conveyances passing and repassing amount to 13,099 in the course of twelve hours*.

* At p. 185 the traffic of London Bridge is stated to be 13,000 conveyances per hour, instead of per 12 hours.

Of these it would appear, that 9351 consist of one-horse vehicles and equestrians, 3389 of two-horse conveyances, and only 359 of vehicles drawn by more than two horses. The one horse vehicles would seem to be between two and three times as many as the two-horse, which form about one-fourth of the whole, while those drawn by more than two horses constitute about one-sixtieth of the entire number.

The Return does not mention the state of the weather on the several days and hours at which the observations were made, nor does it tell us whether there was any public event occurring on those days which was likely to swell or diminish the traffic beyond its usual proportions. The table, moreover, it should be remembered, is confined to the observations of only one day in each locality, so that we must be guarded in receiving that which records a mere accidental set of circumstances as an example of the general course of events. It would have been curious to have extended the observations throughout the night, and so have ascertained the difference in the traffic; and also to have noted the decrease in the number of vehicles passing during a continuously wet as well as a showery day. The observations should be further carried out to different seasons, in order to be rendered of the highest value. Mr. Haywood and the City authorities would really be conferring a great boon on the public by so doing.

Of the Rubbish Carters.

The public cleansing trade, I have before said, consists of as many divisions as there are distinct species of refuse to be removed, and these appear to be four. There is the *house*-refuse, consisting of two different kinds, as (1) the wet house-refuse or "slops," and "night-soil," and (2) the dry house-refuse, or dust and soot; and there is the *street*-refuse, also consisting of two distinct kinds, as (3) the wet street-refuse, or mud and dirt; and (4) the dry street-refuse or "rubbish."

I now purpose dealing with the labourers engaged in the collection and removal of the last-mentioned kind of refuse.

Technologically there are several varieties of "rubbish," or rather "*dirt*," for such appears to be the generic term, of which "rubbish" is *strictly* a species. Dirt, according to the understanding among the rubbish-carters, would seem to consist of any solid earthy matter, which is of an useless or refuse character. This dirt the trade divides into two distinct kinds, viz. :—

1. "Soft dirt," or refuse clay (of which "dry dirt," or refuse soil or mould, is a variety).

2. "Hard-dirt," or "hard-core," consisting of the refuse bricks, chimney-pots, slates, &c., when a house is pulled down, as well as the broken bottles, pans, pots, or crocks, and oyster-shells, &c., which form part of the contents of the dust-man's cart.

The phrase "hard-core"* seems strictly to

* The *core* in this term may be a corruption of the Saxon *Carr*, a rock, rather than that which would at first suggest itself as its origin, viz., the Latin *cor*, the heart. *Hard-core* would therefore mean hard rock-like rubbish, instead of lumps of rubbish having a hard nucleus or heart.

mean all such refuse matter as will admit of being used as the foundation of roads, buildings, &c. "Rubbish," on the other hand, appears to be limited, by the trade, to "dry dirt;" out of the trade, however, and etymologically speaking, it signifies all such *dry* and *hard* refuse matter as is rendered useless by wear and tear*. The term *dirt*, on the other hand, is generally applied to *soft* refuse matter, and *dust* to *dry* refuse matter in a state of minute division, while *slops* is the generic term for all *wet* or *liquid* refuse matter. I shall here restrict the term rubbish to all that dry and hard refuse matter which is the residuum of certain worn-out or "used-up" earthen commodities, as well as the surplus earth which is removed whenever excavations are made, either for the building of houses, the cutting of railways, the levelling of roads, the laying down of pipes or drains, and the sinking of wells.

The commodities whose residuum goes to swell the annual supply of *rubbish*, are generally of an earthy nature. Such commodities as are made of *fibrous* or *textile* materials, go, when "used up," chiefly to form manure if of an animal nature, and to be converted into paper if of a vegetable origin. The refuse materials of our woollen clothes, our old coats and trousers, are either torn to pieces and re-manufactured into shoddy, or become the invigorators of our hop and other plants ; whereas those of our linen or cotton garments, our old shirts and petticoats, form the materials of our books and letters ; while our old ropes, &c., are converted into either brown paper or oakum. Those commodities, on the other hand, which are made of *leathern* materials, become, when worn out, the ingredients of the prussiate of potash and other nitrogenised products manufactured by our chemists. Our old *wooden* commodities, again, are used principally to kindle our fires; while the refuse of our fires themselves, whether the soot which is deposited in the chimney above, or the ashes which fall below, are employed mainly to increase the fertility of our land. Our worn-out *metal* commodities, on the other hand, are newly melted, and go to form fresh commodities when the metals are of the scarcer kind, as gold, silver, copper, brass, lead, and even iron; and when of the more common kind, as is the case with old tin, and occasionally iron vessels, they either become the ingredients in some of our chemical manufactures, or else when formed of tin are cut up into smaller and inferior commodities. Even the detritus of our *streets* is used as the soil of our market gardens. All this we have already seen, and we have now to deal more particularly with

* The term *rubbish* is a polite corruption of the original word *rubbage*, which is still used by uneducated people; *ish* is an *adjectival* termination, as whitish, slavish, brutish, &c., and is used only in connection with such substantives as are derived from adjectives, as English, Scottish, &c. Whereas the affix *age* is strictly substantival, as sewage, garbage, wharfage, &c., and is found applied only to adjectives derived from substantives, as *savage*. A like polite corruption is found in the word *pudding*, which should be strictly *pudden*: the addition of the g is as gross a mistake as saying *garding* for *garden*. There is no such verb as to *pud* whence could come the substantival participle *pudding*: and the French word from which we derive our term is *poudin* without the g, like *jardin*, the root of our *garden*.

STREET TRAFFIC.

TABLE SHOWING THE NUMBER OF VEHICLES AND HORSES PASSING THROUGH [certain streets between the] HOURS OF 8 A.M. AND 8 P.M., UPON CERTAIN [days].

Date.	Situation.	Hour ending 9 A.M. Vehicles drawn by			Hour ending 10 A.M. Vehicles drawn by			Hour ending 11 A.M. Vehicles drawn by			Hour ending 12 A.M. Vehicles drawn by			
		1 Horse and Equestrians.	2 Horses.	3 Horses or more.	1 Horse and Equestrians.	2 Horses.	3 Horses or more.	1 Horse and Equestrians.	2 Horses.	3 Horses or more.	1 Horse and Equestrians.	2 Horses.	3 Horses or more.	
8th July, 1850.	Temple Bar Gate	230	61	20	292	192	42	448	235	21	505	222	30	A
9th ,, ,,	Holborn Hill, by St. Andrew's Church	250	65	12	380	166	6	480	181	9	530	154	14	B
10th ,, ,,	Ludgate Hill, by Pilgrim-street	268	76	17	290	170	16	454	261	13	420	210	6	C
11th ,, ,,	Newgate-street, by Old Bailey	250	59	11	360	155	13	433	184	11	367	137	5	D
12th ,, ,,	Aldersgate-street, by Fann-street	140	20	8	198	52	11	150	44	14	147	36	13	E
13th ,, ,,	Cheapside, by Foster-lane	345	110	18	483	301	21	703	385	36	768	390	11	F
15th ,, ,,	Poultry, by Mansion House	287	103	24	437	315	10	654	398	19	690	373	17	G
16th ,, ,,	Finsbury Pavement, by South-place	185	63	14	252	123	10	330	138	7	250	129	8	H
17th ,, ,,	Cornhill, by Royal Exchange	98	56	7	172	177	15	252	210	17	270	184	7	I
18th ,, ,,	Threadneedle-street	47	47	4	67	77	1	162	97	3	160	50	4	J
19th ,, ,,	Gracechurch-street, by St. Peter's-alley	202	50	6	200	99	23	308	113	18	320	175	12	K
20th ,, ,,	Lombard-street, by Birchin-lane	121	15	1	87	28	2	140	12	4	174	14	..	L
22nd ,, ,,	Bishopsgate Within, by Great St. Helen's	194	58	7	253	144	11	323	164	13	277	143	10	M
23rd ,, ,,	London Bridge	519	139	22	744	339	45	955	334	43	820	274	30	N
24th ,, ,,	Bishopsgate-street Witht, by City boundr.	148	51	4	197	121	11	310	134	3	170	109	7	O
25th ,, ,,	Aldgate High-street, by ditto	335	68	22	291	111	20	292	115	10	287	145	10	P
26th ,, ,,	Leadenhall-st., rear of East India House	193	45	13	272	141	16	388	196	11	340	150	5	Q
27th ,, ,,	Eastcheap, by Philpot-lane	274	35	26	293	40	13	340	46	12	320	34	18	R
29th ,, ,,	Tower-street, by Mark-lane	132	22	15	180	37	5	220	32	10	220	39	12	S
30th ,, ,,	Lower Thames-street, by Botolph-lane	79	7	2	117	10	3	153	15	7	90	7	8	T
31st ,, ,,	Blackfriars Bridge	268	42	17	280	78	23	409	99	10	393	89	34	U
1st Aug. ,,	Upper Thames-street, rear of Queen-street	97	28	15	172	43	12	126	28	11	160	42	21	V
2nd ,, ,,	Smithfield Bars	180	16	7	206	18	6	180	16	6	254	14	9	W
3rd ,, ,,	Fenchurch-street	175	20	11	198	60	4	205	41	7	298	39	6	X
		5017	1256	303	6421	2997	339	8415	3478	315	8230	3159	297	

STREET TRAFFIC.

TABLE SHOWING TOTALS OF EVERY DESCRIPTION OF VEHICLE PASSING PER HOUR AND PER DAY OF 12 HOURS THROUGH CERTAIN STREETS WITHIN THE CITY OF LONDON.

Date.	Situation.	Hours Ending												Total of 12 Hours	Average per Hour.
		9 A.M.	10 A.M.	11 A.M.	12 Noon	1 P.M.	2 P.M.	3 P.M.	4 P.M.	5 P.M.	6 P.M.	7 P.M.	8 P.M.		
1850. July 8	Temple Bar Gate	311	526	704	757	691	664	791	737	738	671	537	614	7741	645
,, 9	Holborn-hill, by St. And. Ch.	327	552	670	698	623	606	535	377	915	445	841	317	6906	575
,, 10	Ludgate-hill, by Pilgrim-st.	361	476	728	636	789	514	628	531	619	584	543	420	6829	569
,, 11	Newgate-st., by Old Bailey	320	528	628	509	555	537	564	738	572	563	467	394	6375	531
,, 12	Aldersgate-st., by Fann-st.	168	261	208	196	214	235	194	219	235	233	229	198	2590	215
,, 13	Cheapside, by Foster-lane	473	805	1124	1169	1020	1009	1007	1076	1106	964	808	492	11053	921
,, 15	Poultry, by Mansion House	414	762	1071	1080	1043	941	875	910	956	825	802	595	10274	856
,, 16	Finsbury-pave., by South-pl	262	385	475	387	364	345	293	347	483	475	400	244	4460	371
,, 17	Cornhill, by Roy. Exchange	161	364	479	461	487	441	493	451	468	430	354	327	4916	409
,, 18	Threadneedle-street	98	145	262	214	211	154	212	195	198	205	148	108	2150	179
,, 19	Gracech-st., by St. Pet.-alley	258	322	439	507	392	423	464	516	461	436	338	331	4887	407
,, 20	Lombard-st., by Birchin-la	137	117	156	188	169	232	237	304	243	209	130	106	2228	185
,, 22	Bishopsg.-st., by Gt. St. Hel.	259	408	500	430	396	238	439	432	541	450	404	345	4842	403
,, 23	London Bridge	680	1128	1332	1124	1094	1048	1101	1180	1344	1308	962	798	13099	1091
,, 24	Bishp.-st. out, by Cy. Bound	203	329	447	286	307	342	390	335	430	439	323	279	4110	342
,, 25	Aldgate High-street, ditto	425	422	417	442	445	379	389	409	405	401	331	289	4754	396
,, 26	Leadenhall-st., E. I. House	251	429	495	495	594	563	525	569	466	588	437	418	5930	494
,, 27	Eastcheap, by Philpot-lane	335	346	398	372	378	343	368	393	398	349	294	128	4102	341
,, 29	Tower-street, by Mark-lane	169	222	262	271	292	324	290	262	282	238	164	114	2890	240
,, 30	L. Thames-st, by Botolph-la	88	130	175	105	105	108	118	147	168	121	69	46	1380	115
,, 31	Blackfriars Bridge	327	381	518	516	465	336	385	416	570	548	463	337	5262	438
Aug. 1	U. Thames-st., rear of Qn.-st	140	227	165	223	205	160	164	213	253	312	176	93	2331	194
,, 2	Smithfield Bars	203	230	202	277	276	255	334	267	328	289	288	159	3108	259
,, 3	Fenchurch-street	206	262	253	343	293	269	272	327	364	259	249	545	3642	303
		6576	9757	12208	11686	11408	10466	11068	11351	12543	11342	9757	7697	125859	10488

TRAFFIC.

CERTAIN THOROUGHFARES WITHIN THE CITY OF LONDON, BETWEEN THE DAYS DURING THE YEAR 1850.

	Hour ending 1 P.M.			Hour ending 2 P.M.			Hour ending 3 P.M.			Hour ending 4 P.M.			Hour ending 5 P.M.			Hour ending 6 P.M.			Hour ending 7 P.M.			Hour ending 8 P.M.		
	Vehicles drawn by			Vehicles drawn by			Vehicles drawn by			Vehicles drawn by			Vehicles drawn by			Vehicles drawn by			Vehicles drawn by			Vehicles drawn by		
	1 Horse and Equestrians.	2 Horses.	3 Horses or more.	1 Horse and Equestrians.	2 Horses.	3 Horses or more.	1 Horse and Equestrians.	2 Horses.	3 Horses or more.	1 Horse and Equestrians.	2 Horses.	3 Horses or more.	1 Horse and Equestrians.	2 Horses.	3 Horses or more.	1 Horse and Equestrians.	2 Horses.	3 Horses or more.	1 Horse and Equestrians.	2 Horses.	3 Horses or more.	1 Horse and Equestrians.	2 Horses.	3 Horses or more.
A	460	218	13	415	230	19	550	231	10	496	237	4	470	255	13	435	219	17	329	200	8	405	198	11
B	453	160	10	435	158	13	373	150	12	270	100	7	639	251	25	330	111	4	615	209	17	219	92	6
C	530	256	3	330	180	4	400	221	7	288	242	1	375	235	9	360	220	4	330	210	3	214	202	4
D	390	156	9	377	155	5	390	167	7	525	201	12	390	177	5	415	142	6	337	126	4	250	136	8
E	165	40	9	180	49	6	150	32	12	172	40	7	187	36	12	185	40	8	175	44	10	141	46	11
F	680	334	6	664	336	9	665	338	4	730	339	7	671	427	8	645	303	16	482	319	7	271	212	9
G	680	358	5	595	337	9	548	321	6	575	330	5	565	381	10	505	310	10	455	344	3	292	299	4
H	243	115	6	223	118	4	184	107	2	215	128	4	340	135	8	300	159	16	242	142	16	140	101	3
I	275	208	4	253	180	8	305	185	3	276	172	3	255	206	7	242	180	8	177	176	1	186	140	1
J	160	50	1	120	32	2	164	46	2	157	37	1	150	45	3	157	45	3	115	30	3	77	31	..
K	295	87	10	330	81	12	360	93	11	375	123	18	302	135	24	310	113	13	253	79	6	250	75	6
L	160	9	..	215	15	2	227	9	1	283	20	1	223	20	..	180	26	3	115	15	..	94	12	..
M	260	125	11	164	70	4	320	113	6	287	140	5	380	150	11	320	123	7	270	127	7	222	120	3
N	775	296	23	765	255	28	793	284	24	845	305	30	975	336	33	970	305	33	680	264	18	510	258	30
O	191	112	4	243	96	3	285	97	8	231	103	1	309	113	8	305	126	8	203	112	8	177	99	3
P	300	135	10	249	123	7	260	112	17	274	122	13	248	141	16	276	110	15	220	100	11	190	96	3
Q	415	168	11	385	171	7	353	158	14	387	172	10	295	166	5	390	183	15	292	139	6	260	152	6
R	340	27	11	300	28	15	310	38	20	345	40	8	340	43	15	280	58	11	230	59	5	109	16	3
S	260	26	6	270	39	15	252	34	4	226	26	10	230	39	13	195	34	9	137	25	2	94	16	4
T	83	21	1	100	8	..	100	15	3	130	13	4	143	23	2	100	15	6	52	14	3	40	4	2
U	365	78	22	253	65	18	302	73	10	340	66	10	450	103	17	446	87	15	361	89	13	265	66	6
V	160	35	10	120	31	9	125	33	6	160	44	9	185	52	16	241	54	17	139	25	12	71	13	9
W	252	18	6	232	19	4	305	20	9	250	11	6	305	17	6	265	20	4	269	10	9	145	14	..
X	240	45	8	223	39	7	220	46	6	267	54	6	300	57	7	215	36	8	193	53	3	516	28	1
	8132	3077	199	7441	2815	210	7941	2923	204	8104	3065	182	8727	3543	273	8067	3019	256	6671	2911	175	5138	2426	133

STREET TRAFFIC.

TABLE SHOWING THE TOTAL NUMBER OF EACH DESCRIPTION OF VEHICLE PASSING THROUGH CERTAIN STREETS WITHIN THE CITY OF LONDON, BETWEEN THE HOURS OF 8 A.M. AND 8 P.M. (12 HOURS.)

Date.	Situation.	Total Number of Vehicles drawn by			Total of the whole.	Average Number per Hour.			Average of the whole.
		1 Horse and Equestrians.	2 Horses.	3 Horses or more.		1 Horse and Equestrians.	2 Horses.	3 Horses or more.	
8th July, 1850.	Temple Bar Gate	5035	2498	208	7741	419	208	17	645
9th ,, ,,	Holborn Hill, by St. Andrew's Church	4974	1797	135	6906	414	149	11	575
10th ,, ,,	Ludgate Hill, by Pilgrim-street	4259	2483	87	6829	354	207	7	569
11th ,, ,,	Newgate-street, by Old Bailey	4484	1795	96	6375	373	149	8	531
12th ,, ,,	Aldersgate-street, by Fann-street	1990	479	121	2590	165	40	10	215
13th ,, ,,	Cheapside, by Foster-lane	7107	3794	152	11053	592	316	12	921
15th ,, ,,	Poultry, by Mansion House	6283	3869	122	10274	523	332	10	856
16th ,, ,,	Finsbury Pavement, by South-place	2904	1458	98	4460	242	121	8	371
17th ,, ,,	Cornhill, by Royal Exchange	2761	2074	81	4916	230	172	7	409
18th ,, ,,	Threadneedle-street	1536	587	27	2150	128	49	2	179
19th ,, ,,	Gracechurch-st., by St. Peter's-alley	3505	1223	159	4887	292	102	13	407
20th ,, ,,	Lombard-street, by Birchin-lane	2019	195	14	2228	168	16	1	185
22nd ,, ,,	Bishopsgate-st., by Great St. Helen's	3270	1477	95	4842	272	123	8	403
23rd ,, ,,	London Bridge	9351	3389	359	13099	779	282	30	1091
24th ,, ,,	Bishopsgate-st., out, by City Boundy.	2769	1273	68	4110	230	106	5	342
25th ,, ,,	Aldgate High-street, ditto	3222	1378	154	4754	268	114	12	396
26th ,, ,,	Leadenhall-street, East India House	3970	1841	119	5930	330	153	10	494
27th ,, ,,	Eastcheap, by Philpot-lane	3481	464	157	4102	290	38	13	341
29th ,, ,,	Tower-street, by Mark-lane	2416	369	105	2890	201	30	8	240
30th ,, ,,	Lower Thames-st., by Botolph-lane	1187	152	41	1380	98	12	3	115
31st ,, ,,	Blackfriars Bridge	4132	935	195	5262	344	78	16	438
1st Aug. ,,	Upper Thames-st., rear of Queen-st.	1756	428	147	2331	146	35	12	194
2nd ,, ,,	Smithfield Bars	2843	193	72	3108	237	16	6	259
3rd ,, ,,	Fenchurch-street	3050	518	74	3642	254	43	6	303
		88304	34669	2886	125859	7358	2889	240	10488

the refuse of the sole remaining materials, viz., those of an *earthy* kind, and out of which are made our bricks, our earthenware and porcelain, as well as our glass, plaster, and stone commodities. What becomes of all these materials when the articles made of them are no longer fit for use? The old glass is, like the old metal, remelted and made into new commodities; some broken bottles are used for the tops of walls as a protection against trespassers; and the old bricks, when sound, are employed again for inferior brickwork; but what becomes of the rest of the earthen materials—the unsound bricks or "bats," the old plaster and mortar, the refuse slates and tiles and chimney-pots, the broken pans, and dishes, and other crocks—in a word, the potsherds and pansherds*, as the rubbish-carters call them—what is done with these?

But rubbish, as we have seen, consists not only of refuse earthen commodities, but of refuse earth itself: such as the soil removed during excavations for the foundations of houses, for the cuttings of railways, the levelling of roads, the formation of parks, the laying down of pipes or drains, and the sinking of wells. For each and all of these operations there is necessarily a certain quantity of soil removed, and the question that naturally occurs to the mind is, what is done with it?

There is, moreover, a third kind of rubbish, which, though having an animal origin, consists chiefly of earthy matter, and that is the shells of oysters, and other shell-fish. Whence go they, since these shells are of a comparatively indestructible nature, and thousands of such fish are consumed annually in the metropolis? What, the inquirer asks, becomes of the refuse bony coverings of such fish?

Let us first, however, endeavour to estimate what quantity of each of these three kinds of rubbish is annually produced in London, beginning with the refuse earthen commodities.

There is no published account of the quantity of *crockeryware* annually manufactured in this country. Mr. McCulloch tells us, "It is estimated, that the *value* of the various sorts of earthenware produced at the potteries may amount to about 1,700,000*l*. or 1,800,000*l*. a year; and that the earthenware produced at Worcester, Derby, and other parts of the country, may amount to about 850,000*l*. or more, making the whole value of the manufacture 2,550,000*l*. or 2,650,000*l*. a year." What proportion of this quantity may fall to the share of the metropolis, and what proportion of the whole may be annually destroyed, I know of no means of judging. We must therefore go some other way to work in order to arrive at the required information. Now, it has been before shown, that the quantity of "dust," or dry refuse from houses, annually collected, amounts to 900,000 tons or chaldrons yearly; and I find, on inquiry at the principal "yards," that the average quantity of Potsherds

* This is the Saxon *sceard*, which means a sheard, remnant, or fragment, and is from the verb *sceran*, signifying both to shear and to share or divide. The low Dutch *schaard* is a piece of pot, a fragment.

and broken crockery is at the rate of about half a bushel to every load of dust, or say 1 per cent. out of the entire quantity collected. At other yards, I find the proportion of sherds to be about the same, so that we may fairly assume that the gross quantity of broken earthenware produced in London is in round numbers 9000 loads or tons per annum. The sherds run about 250 pieces to the bushel, and assuming every five of such pieces to be the remains of an entire article, there would be in each bushel the fragments of fifty earthenware vessels; and thus the total quantity of crockeryware destroyed yearly in the metropolis will amount to 18,000,000 vessels.

As to the quantity of *refuse bricks*, the number annually produced, which is between 1,500,000,000 and 2,000,000,000, will give us no knowledge of the quantity yearly converted into rubbish. In order to arrive at this, we must ascertain the number of houses pulled down in the course of the twelvemonth; and I find, by the Returns of the Registrar-General, that the buildings removed between 1841 and 1851 have been as follows:—

DECREASE IN THE NUMBER OF HOUSES THROUGHOUT LONDON BETWEEN 1841 AND 1851.

	Total Decrease in 10 Years.	Annual Average Decrease.
St. Martin's	116	11·6
St. James's, Westminster	130	13·0
St. Giles's	181	18·1
Strand	389	38·9
Holborn	86	8·6
East London	11	1·1
West London	265	26·5
London, City of	592	59·2
Whitechapel	2	·2
St. Saviour's, Southwark	46	4·6
St. Olave's	158	15·8
Total	1976	197·6

Thus, then, we perceive that there have been, upon an average, very nearly 200 houses annually pulled down in London within the last ten years, and I find, on inquiry among those who are likely to be the best-informed on such matters, that each house so pulled down will yield from 40 to 50 loads of rubbish; so that, altogether, the quantity of refuse bricks, slates, tiles, chimney-pots, &c., annually produced in London must be no less than 8000 loads.

But the above estimate refers only to those houses which have been pulled down and never rebuilt; so that, in order to arrive at the gross quantity of this kind of rubbish yearly produced in the metropolis, we must add to the preceding amount the quantity accruing from such houses as are pulled down and built up again, or newly fronted and repaired, which are by far the greater number. These, I find, may be estimated at between 5 and 10 per cent. of the gross number of houses in the metropolis. In some quarters (the older parts of London, for instance,) the proportion is much higher, while in the suburbs, or newer districts, it is scarcely half per cent. Each of the houses so new-fronted or repaired may be said to yield, on an average, 10 loads of rubbish, and, at this rate, the yearly quantity of refuse bricks, mortar, &c., proceeding from such a source, will be 150,000 loads per annum; so that the total amount of rubbish produced in London by the demolition and reparation of houses would appear to be about 160,000 loads yearly.

The quantity of refuse *oyster shells* may easily be found by the number of oysters annually sold in Billingsgate-market. These, from the returns which I obtained from the market salesmen, and printed at p. 63 of the first volume of this work, appear to be, in round numbers, 500,000,000; and, calculating that one-third of this quantity is sent into the country, the total number of shells remaining in the metropolis may be estimated at about 650,000,000. Reckoning, then, that 500 shells go to the bushel (the actual number was found experimentally to be between 525 and 550), and consequently that 20,000 are contained in every load, we may conclude that the gross quantity of refuse oyster shells annually produced in London average somewhere about 30,000 loads. That this is an approximation to the true quantity there can be little doubt, for, on inquiry at one of the largest dust-yards, I was informed by the hillman that the quantity of oyster-shells collected with the refuse dust from houses in the vicinity of Shoreditch, Whitechapel, and other localities at the east-end of the metropolis, averages 6 bushels to the load of dust; about the west-end, however, half a bushel or a bushel to each load is the average ratio; while from the City there is none, the house "dust" there being free from oyster-shells. In taking one district, however, with another, I am assured that the average may be safely computed at 2 bushels of oyster-shells to every 3 loads of dust; hence, as the gross amount of house-dust is equal to 900,000 tons or loads per annum, the quantity of refuse oyster-shells collected yearly by the dustmen may be taken at 15,000 loads. But, besides these, there is the quantity got rid of by the costermongers, which seldom or never appear in the dust-bins. The costers sell about 124,000,000 oysters per annum, and thus the extra quantity of shells resulting from these means would be about 12,400 loads; so that the gross quantity of refuse oyster-shells actually produced in London may be said to average between 25,000 and 30,000 loads per annum.

There still remains the quantity of *refuse earth* to be calculated; this may be estimated as follows:—

1. *Foundations of Houses.*—Each house that is built requires the ground to be excavated from two to three yards deep, the average area of each being about nine yards square. This gives between 160 and 200 cubic yards of earth removed from the foundation of each house. A cubic yard of earth is a load, so that there are between 160 and 200 loads of earth displaced in the building of every new house.

The following statement shows—

THE NUMBER OF HOUSES BUILT THROUGHOUT LONDON BETWEEN 1841 AND 1851.

	Total No. of Houses built in 10 Years.	Average No. of Houses built per Year.
West Districts	9,624	962·4
North Districts	13,778	1377·8
Central Districts	349	34·9
East Districts	8,343	834·3
South Districts	14,807	1480·7
Total	46,901	4690·1

Hence, estimating the number of new houses built yearly in the metropolis at 4500, the total quantity of earth removed for the foundations of the buildings throughout London would be 800,000 loads per annum.

2. *The Cuttings of Railways.*—The railways formed within the area of the metropolis during the last ten years have been—the Great Northern; the Camden Town, and Bow; the West India Docks and Bow; and the North Kent Lines. The extension of the Southampton Railway from Vauxhall to Waterloo-bridge, as well as the Richmond Line, has also been formed within the same period, but for these no cuttings have been made.

The Railway Cuttings made within the area of the Metropolis Proper during the last ten years have been to the following extent:—

RAILWAYS.	Length of Cutting.	Width of Cutting.		Depth of Cutting.	Quantity of earth Removed.
		At top.	At bottom.		
	Miles.	Yards.	Yards.	Yards.	Loads.
Great Northern	1½	12	10	10	290,400
Camden Town and Bow	1½	12	10	10	290,400
West India Docks and Bow	2	15	10	12	528,000
North Kent	2	15	10	12	528,000

Hence, the gross quantity of earth removed from railway cuttings within the last ten years has been 1,636,800 loads, or say, in round numbers, 160,000 loads per annum.

3. *The Cutting of Roads and Streets.*—According to a Return presented to Parliament, there were 200 miles of new streets formed within the metropolitan police district between the years 1839-49; but in the formation of these no earth has been taken away; on the contrary a considerable quantity has been required for their construction. In the case of the lowering of Holborn-hill, that which was removed from the top was used to fill up the hollow.

4. *The Formation of Parks.*—The only park that has been constructed during the last ten years in the metropolis is Victoria Park, at the east end of the town; but I am informed that, in the course of the works there, no earth was carted away, the soil which was removed from one part being used for the levelling of another.

5. *Pipe and Sewer Works.*—The earth displaced in the course of these operations is usually put back into the ground whence it was taken, excepting in the formation of some new sewer, and then a certain proportion has to be carted away. Upon inquiry among those who are likely to be best informed, I am assured that 1000 loads may be taken as the quantity carted away in the course of the last year.

6. *Well-sinking.*—In this there has been but little done. Those who are best informed assure me that within the last ten years no such works of any magnitude have been executed.

The account as to the quantity of rubbish removed in London, then, stands thus:—

Refuse Earthen Materials.	Loads per Annum.
Potsherds and Pansherds	9,000
Old bricks, tiles, slates, mortar, &c.	160,000
Oyster-shells	25,000
Refuse Earth.	
Foundations of houses	800,000
Railway cuttings	160,000
Pipe and sewer laying	1,000
	1,155,000

Thus, then, we perceive that the gross quantity of rubbish that has to be annually removed throughout the metropolis is upwards of 1,000,000 loads per annum.

Now what is done with the vast amount of refuse matter? Whither is it carried? How is it disposed of?

The rubbish from the house building or removing is of no value to the master carter, and is shot gratuitously wherever there is the privilege of shooting it; this privilege, however, is very often usurped. Great quantities used to be shot in what were, until these last eight years, Bishop Bonner's Fields, but now Victoria Park. At the present time this sort of rubbish is often slily deposited in localities generally known as "the ruins," being places from which houses, and indeed streets, have been removed, and the sites left bare and vacant.

But the main localities for the deposition of this kind of refuse are in the fields round about the metropolis. Each particular district appears to have its own special "shoot," as it is called, for rubbish, of which the following are the principal.

Rubbish shoots.

The rubbish of Kensington and Chelsea is shot in the Pottery Grounds and Kensington-fields.

The rubbish of St. George's Hanover-square, Marylebone, and Paddington, is shot in the fields about Notting-hill and Kilburn.

The rubbish of Westminster, Strand, Holborn, St. Martin's, St. Giles's, St. James's, Westminster, West London, and Southwark, is shot in Cubitt's fields at Millbank and Westminster improvements.

The rubbish of Hampstead is shot in the fields at back of Haverstock-hill.

The rubbish of Saint Pancras is shot in the Copenhagen-fields.

The rubbish of Islington, Clerkenwell, and St. Luke's, is shot in the Eagle Wharf-road and Shepherdess-fields.

The rubbish of East London and City is shot in the Haggerstone-fields.

The rubbish of Whitechapel, St. George's in the East, and Stepney, is shot in Stepney fields.

The rubbish of Hackney, Bethnal-green, and Shoreditch, is shot in the Bonkers-pond, Hackney-road.

The rubbish of Poplar is shot in the fields at back of New Town, Poplar.

The rubbish of Bermondsey is shot in the Bermondsey fields.

The rubbish of Newington, Camberwell, and Lambeth, is shot in Walworth-common and Kennington-fields.

The rubbish of Wandsworth is shot in Pottershole, Wandsworth-common.

The rubbish of Greenwich and Lewisham is shot in Russia-common, near Lewisham.

The rubbish of Rotherhithe is used for ballast.

The quantity of rubbish annually shot in each of the above-mentioned localities appears to range from 5000 up to as high as 30,000 and 40,000 loads.

Of the earth removed in forming the foundation of new houses, between one-fourth and one-sixth of the whole is used to make the gardens at the back, and the bed of the roads in front of them, while the entire quantity of the soil displaced in the execution of the "cuttings" of railways is carted away in the trucks of the company to form embankments in other places. Hence there would appear to be about from 160,000 to 200,000 loads of refuse bricks, potsherds, pansherds, and oyster-shells, and about 600,000 loads of refuse earth deposited every year in the fields or "shoots" in the vicinity of the metropolis.

The refuse earth displaced in forming the foundations of houses is generally carted away by the builders' men, so that it is principally the refuse bricks, &c., that the rubbish-carters are engaged in removing; these they usually carry to the shoots already indicated, or to such other localities where the hard core may be needed for forming the foundation of roads, or the rubbish be required for certain other purposes.

The principal *use to which the "rubbish" is put*

is for levelling, when the hollow part of any newly-made road has to be filled up, or garden or lawn ground has to be levelled for a new mansion. Rubbish, at one time, was in demand for the ballasting of small coasting vessels. For such ballasting 2*d*. a ton has to be paid to the corporation of the Trinity House. This rubbish has been used, but sometimes surreptitiously, for ballast, unmixed with other things. It is, however, light and inferior ballast, and occupies more space than the gravel ballast from the bed of the Thames.

Suppose that a collier requires ballast to the extent of 60 tons; if house rubbish be used it will occupy the hold to a greater height by about 10 inches than would the ballast derived from the bed of the Thames. The Thames ballast is supplied at 1*s*. a ton; the rubbish-ballast, however, was only 3*d*. to 6*d*. a ton, but now it is seldom used unless to mix with manure, which might be considered too wet and soft, and likely to ferment on the voyage to a degree unpleasant even to the mariners used to such freights. The rubbish, I am told, checks the fermentation, and gives consistency to the manure.

I am assured by a tradesman, who ships a considerable quantity of stable manure collected from the different mews of the metropolis, that comparatively little rubbish is now used for ballast (unless in the way I have stated); even for mixing, but a few tons a week are required up and down the river, and perhaps a small quantity from the wharfs on the several canals. Nothing was ever paid for the use of this rubbish as ballast, the carters being well satisfied to have the privilege of shooting it. Two of the principal shoots by the river side were at Bell-wharf, Shadwell, and off Wapping-street. The rubbish of Rotherhithe, it will be seen, is mainly "shot" as ballast.

The "*hard-core*" is readily got rid of; sometimes it is shot gratuitously (or merely with a small gratuity for beer to the men); but if it have to be carted three or four miles, it is from 2*s*. 6*d*. to 3*s*. a load. This is used for the foundations of houses, the groundwork of roads, and other purposes where a hard substratum is required. The hard-core on a new road is usually about nine inches deep. There are on an average 20 miles of streets, 15 yards wide, formed annually in London. Hence there would be upwards of 100,000 loads of hard-core required for this purpose alone. Where the soil is of a gravelly nature, but little hard rubbish is needed. Oyster-shells *did* form a much greater portion than they do now of the hard substratum of roads. Eight or nine years ago the costermongers could sell their oyster-shells for 6*d*. a bushel. Now they cannot, or do not, sell them at all; and the law not only forbids their deposit in any place whatever, but forbids their being scattered in the streets, under a penalty of 5*l*. But as the same law provides no place where these shells may be deposited, the costermongers are in what one of them described to me as "a quandary." One man, who with his wife kept two stalls in Tottenham Court-road, one for fish (fresh and dried) and for shell-fish, and the other for fruit and vegetables, told me that he gave "one of those poor long-legged fellows who were neither men nor boys, and who were always starving and hanging about for a two-penny job, two-pence to carry away a hamper-full of shells and get rid of them as he best could. O, where he put them, sir," said the man, "I don't know, I wouldn't know; and I shouldn't have mentioned it to you, only I saw you last winter and know you're inquiring for an honest purpose."

Another costermonger who has a large barrow of oysters and mussels, and sometimes of "wet fish" near King's-cross, and at the junction of Leather-lane with Back-hill, Hatton-garden, was more communicative: "If you'll walk on with me, sir," he said, "*I'll* show you where they're shot. You may mention my name if you like, sir; I don't care a d—— for the crushers; not a blessed d——." He accordingly conducted me to a place which seemed adapted for the special purpose. At the foot of Saffron-hill and the adjacent streets runs the Fleet-ditch, now a branch of the common sewers; not covered over as in other parts, but open, noisome, and, as the dark water flows on, throwing up a sickening stench. The ditch is indifferently fenced, so that any one with a little precaution may throw what he pleases into it. "There, sir," said my companion, "there's the place where more oyster-shells is thrown than anywhere in London. They're thrown in in the dark." Assuredly the great share of blame is not to those who avail themselves of such places for illegal purposes, but to those who leave such filthy receptacles available. The scattered oyster-shells along all the approaches, on both sides, to this part of the open Fleet-ditch, evince the use that is made of it in violation of the law. Many of the costers, however, keep the shells by them till they amount to several bushels, and then give the rubbish-carters a few pence to dispose of them for them.

Some of the costermongers, again, obtain leave to deposit their oyster-shells in the dustmen's yards, where quantities may be seen whitening the dingy dust-heaps, and a large quantity are collected with the house-dust and ashes, together with the broken crockery from the dust-bins of the several houses. The oyster-shells are carted away with the pan-sherds, &c., for the purposes I have mentioned.

I now come to deal with the rubbish-carters, that is to say, with the labourers engaged in the removal of the "hard" species of refuse; of which we have seen there are between 160,000 and 200,000 loads annually carted away; the refuse earth, or "soft dirt," being generally removed by the builders' men, and the refuse, crockeryware, &c., by the dustmen, when collecting the dust from the "bins" of the several houses.

The master *Rubbish-Carters* are those who keep carts and horses to be hired for carting away the old materials when houses or walls are pulled down. They are also occasionally engaged in carrying away the soil or rubbish thrown up from the foundations of buildings; the excavations of docks, canals, and sewers; the digging of artesian wells, &c. This seems to comprise what in this carrying or removing trade is accounted "rubbish."

Perhaps not one of these tradesmen is solely a rubbish-carter, for they are likewise the carters of new materials for the use of builders, such as lime, bricks, stone, gravel, slates, timber, ironwork, chimney-pieces, &c. Some of them are public carmen; licensed carmen if they work, or ply, in the City; but beyond the City boundaries no licence is necessary. This complication perplexes the inquiry, but I purpose to confine it, as much as possible, to the rubbish-carters proper, having defined what may be understood by "rubbish." These carters are also employed in digging, pick-axing, &c., at the buildings, the rubbish of which they are engaged to remove.

Among the conveyors of rubbish are no distinctions as to the kind. Any of them will one week cart old bricks from a house which has been pulled down, and the next week be busy in removing the soil excavated where the foundations and cellars of a new mansion have been dug.

From inquiries made in each of the different districts of the metropolis, there appear to be from 140 to 150 tradesmen who, with the carting of bricks, lime, and other building commodities, add also that of rubbish-carting. These "masters" among them find employment for 840 labouring men, some of whom I find to have been in the service of the same employer upwards of 20 years.

The Post-Office Directory, under the head of rubbish-carters, gives the names of only 35 of the principal masters, of whom several are marked as scavagers, dust-contractors, nightmen, and road-contractors. The occupation abstract of the census, on the other hand, totally ignores the existence of any such class of workmen, masters as well as operatives. I find, however, by actual visitation and inquiry in each of the metropolitan districts, and thus learning the names of the several masters as well as the number of men in their employment, that there may be said to be, in round numbers, 150 master rubbish-carters, employing among them 840 operatives throughout London.

A large proportion of this number of labouring men, however, are casual hands, who have been taken on when the trade was busy during the summer (which is the the "brisk season" of rubbish-cartage), and who are discharged in the slack time; during which period they obtain jobs at dust-carting or scavaging, or some such outdoor employment. Among the employers there are scarcely any who are purely rubbish-carters, the large majority consisting of dust and road-contractors, carmen, dairymen, and persons who have two or three horses and carts at their disposal. When a master builder or bricklayer obtains a contract, he hires horses and carts to take away any rubbish which may previously have been deposited. The contract of the King's Cross Terminus of the Great Northern Railway, for instance, has been undertaken by Mr. W. Jay, the builder; and, not having sufficient conveyances to cart the rubbish away, he has hired horses and carts of others to assist in the removal of it. The same mode is adopted in other parts of the metropolis, where any improvements are going on. The owners of horses and carts let them out to hire at from 7s. for one horse, to 14s. for two per day. If, however, the job be unusually large, the master rubbish-carters often take it by contract themselves.

Although the *operative rubbish-carters* may be classed among unskilled labourers, they are, perhaps, less miscellaneous, as a body, than other classes of open-air workers. Before they can obtain work of the best description it is necessary that they should have some knowledge of the management of a horse in the drawing of a loaded carriage, or of the way in which the animal should be groomed and tended in the stable. I was told by an experienced carman, that he, or any one with far less than his experience, could in a moment detect, merely by the mode in which a man would put the harness on a horse and yoke him to the cart, whether he was likely to prove a master of his craft in that line or not. My informant had noticed, more especially many years ago, when labour was not so abundantly obtainable as it was last year, that men out of work would offer him their services as carmen even if they had never handled a whip in their lives, as if little more were wanted than to walk by the horse's side. An experienced carter knows how to ease and direct the animal when heavily burdened, or when the road is rugged; and I am assured by the same informant, that he had known one of his horses more fatigued after traversing a dozen miles with a "yokel" (as he called him), or an incompetent man, than the animal had been after a fifteen miles' journey with the same load under the care of a careful and judicious driver. This knowledge of the management of a horse is most essential when men are employed to work "single-handed," or have confided to them singly a horse and cart; when they work in gangs it is not insisted upon, except as regards the "carman," or the man having charge of the horse or the team.

The master rubbish-carters generally are more particular than they used to be as to the men to whom they commit the care of their horses. It may be easy enough to learn to drive a horse and cart, but a casual labourer will now hardly get employment in rubbish-carting of a "good sort" unless he has attained that preliminary knowledge. The foreman of one of the principal contractors said to me, "It would never do to let a man learn his business by practising on our horses." I mention this to show, that although rubbish-carting is to be classed among unskilled labours, *some* training is necessary.

I am informed that one-third of the working rubbish-carters have been rubbish-carters from their youth, or cart, car, or waggon-drivers, for they all seem to have known changes; or they have been used to the care of horses in the capacity of ostlers, stable-men, helpers, coaching-inn porters, coachmen, grooms, and horse-breakers. Of the remainder, one-half, I am informed, have "had a turn" at such avocations as scavagery, bricklayers' labouring, dock work, railway excavating, night work, and the many toils to which such men resort in their struggles to obtain bread, whatever may have been their original occupation, which is rarely that of an artizan. The other, and what may be called the greater half of the remaining number, is composed of agricultural labourers who were rubbish-carters in the country, and of the many men who have had the care of horses and vehicles in the provinces, and who have sought the metropolis, depending upon their thews and sinews for a livelihood, as porters, or carmen, or labourers in almost any capacity. The most of these men at the plough, the harrow, the manure-cart, the hay and corn harvests, have been practised carters and horse drivers before they sought the expected gold in the streets of London. Full a third of the whole body of rubbish-carters are Irishmen, who in Ireland were small farmers, or cottiers, or agricultural labourers, or belonged to some of the classes I have described.

The mechanics among rubbish-carters I heard estimated, by men with equal means of information, as one in twenty and one in fifteen. Among these *quondam* mechanics were more farriers, cart and wheel wrights, than of other classes.

It seems to be regarded as an indispensable thing that working rubbish-carters should have one quality—bodily strength. I am told that one employer, who died a few weeks ago, used to say to any applicant for work, "It's no use asking for it, if you wish to keep it, unless you can lift a horse up when he's down."

As I have shown of the scavagers, &c., the employers in rubbish-carting may be classed as "honourable" and "scurfs." The men do not use the word "honourable," nor any equivalent term, but speak of their masters, though with no great distinctiveness, as being either "good," or "scurfs." As in other branches of unskilled labour where there are no trade societies or general trade regulations among the operatives, there are few distinctive appellations.

From the facts I have collected in connection with this trade, it would appear that there are 180 master rubbish-carters in the metropolis, about 140 of whom pay 18s. or more per week as wages, while the remaining 40 pay less than that amount. The latter constitute what the men term the scurf portion of the trade; so that the honourable masters among the rubbish-carters may be said to comprise seven-ninths of the whole.

I will first treat of the circumstances, characteristics, and wages of the men employed in the honourable trade.

And first, as regards *the division of labour* among the operative rubbish-carters, the work is as simple as possible.

There are—

1. *The Rubbish-Carters* proper, or "carmen," who are engaged principally in conveying the refuse brick or earth to the several shoots.

2. *The Rubbish-Shovellers,* or "gangers," who are engaged principally in filling the cart with the rubbish to be removed. Generally speaking, the two offices are performed by the same individual, who is both carter and shoveller, and it is only in large works that the gangers are employed.

Master builders and others who require the aid of rubbish-carters for the removal of earth or any other kind of rubbish from ground about to be built upon, or from old buildings about to be repaired or pulled down, either hire horses, carts, and carmen, by the day, of the master rubbish-carters, or pay a certain price per load for the removal of the rubbish. If the job be likely to last some length of time, the builders pay the masters so much per load for carting away the rubbish; but if the job be only for a short period, the horses, carts, and carmen are hired of the masters for the time. The price paid to the master rubbish-carter ranges from 2s. 6d. to 3s. 6d. per load for the removal of rubbish and bringing back such bricks, lime, or sand as may be required for the building. The master rubbish-carter, in all cases, pays the men engaged in the removal of the rubbish.

The operative rubbish-carters (except in a very few instances) never work in gangs, either in the construction of new buildings or in old buildings about to be pulled down or repaired. In digging the foundations of new houses, the master builders, or speculators, building upon their own ground employ their own excavators, and engage rubbish-carters to remove the refuse earth, the latter being merely occupied in carting it away.

The principle of simple co-operation or gang-work occasionally prevails; and, when this is the case, the gang is employed in shovelling and picking, while the carman, as the shovellers throw out the rubbish, fills or shovels the rubbish into the cart.

Each rubbish-carter will, on an average, convey away from two to five loads a day, according to the distance he has to take it. Calculating 850 men to remove four loads per diem for five months in a year, the gross quantity of rubbish annually removed would be very nearly 326,000 loads.

In the regular trade *the hours of daily labour* are twelve, or from six to six; but the men are allowed half an hour for breakfast, an hour for dinner, and half an hour for tea, and almost invariably leave at half-past five, so postponing the "tea" half-hour until after the termination of their work. In winter the hours are generally "between the lights," but on very short, dark, or foggy days, lanterns are used. The men employed by one firm "often made up," I was told by one of them, "for lost time, by shovelling by moonlight." The carman, however, has to get to his stable in the summer at four o'clock in the morning, and to tend his horse after he has done work at night; so that the usual hours of labour with him are fifteen and sixteen per day, as well as Sunday-work.

The rubbish-carters are *paid by the week,* 18s. to 20s. being the weekly amount; and by *the load,* which is indeed piece-work. The payment to the

TABLE SHOWING THE NUMBER OF OPERATIVE RUBBISH-CARTERS EMPLOYED THROUGHOUT LONDON, THE WAGES RECEIVED BY THEM, THE NUMBER OF WEEKS THEY ARE EMPLOYED, AS WELL AS THE QUANTITY OF RUBBISH REMOVED BY THEM IN THE COURSE OF THE YEAR.

District	Master Rubbish Carters	No. of Operative Rubbish-Carters	No. of Shovellers working in Gangs	Quantity of Rubbish carted Daily (lds.)	Quantity of Rubbish carted Annually (loads)	No. of days in the week each Operative is employed at Rubbish-Carting	No. of weeks during the year each Operative is engaged in Removing Rubbish	Weekly Wages of Rubbish-Carters (s.)	Weekly Wages of the Operatives working in Gangs at Rubbish-Carting (s.)
Kensington	Mr. J. Bird	5	…	15	2340	6	26	18	…
	Hough	3	…	9	1404	6	26	18	…
	Dubbins	3	…	9	1404	6	26	18	…
	Taylor	3	…	12	1872	6	26	18	…
	Gale	3	…	12	1872	6	26	18	…
	G. Bird	10	…	20	3120	6	26	18	…
	Nicholls	10	…	20	3120	6	26	18	…
Chelsea	Emmerson	5	…	15	2340	6	26	18	…
	Freeman	5	…	15	2340	6	26	18	…
	Pattison	2	…	6	936	6	26	18	…
	Porter	6	…	18	2808	6	26	18	…
St. George's, Hanover-sq.	Rawlins	4	…	16	1248	6	13	18	…
	Wells	2	…	8	624	6	13	18	…
	Watkins	5	…	15	1170	6	13	18	…
	Liddiard	5	…	15	1170	6	13	18	…
Westminster	Farmer	4	…	16	1920	6	20	18	…
	Bugbee	6	4	30	2340	6	13	18	18
	Reddin	6	4	20	2340	6	13	18	18
	Francis	5	…	15	2340	6	26	18	…
	Chadwick	3	…	20	3120	6	26	18	…
	Francis	5	…	15	2340	6	26	18	…
Westminster Improvements	Farmer	5	…	20	3120	6	26	18	…
	Duggan	8	…	40	6240	6	26	18	…
St. Martin's	T. Cooper	3	3	24	1872	6	13	18	20
	Wall	2	2	16	1248	6	13	18	20
	Duggan	4	…	16	1248	6	13	18	…
St. James's, Westminster	Nicolls	5	…	20	1560	6	13	18	…
	Wells	2	…	8	624	6	13	18	…
	Watkins	5	…	15	810	6	9	18	…
Marylebone	Freeman	3	…	12	2808	6	39	18	…
	Curmock	4	…	16	2496	6	26	18	…
	Nicolls	8	…	24	1872	3	26	18	…
	Watkins	10	…	40	4160	4	26	18	…
	Perkins	5	…	20	3120	6	26	18	…
	Culverwell	5	…	20	3120	6	26	18	…
West London	Mr. Rutty	3	…	12	360	5	6	18	…
	Kitchener	3	…	12	360	6	4	18	…
	Wickham	3	…	12	240	6	4	18	…
	Porter	4	…	16	864	6	9	18	…
	Crook	3	…	6	468	6	13	18	…
West London Improvements	M'Carthy	6	…	30	4680	6	26	20	…
	Reddin	5	…	25	3900	6	26	18	…
	Rooke	6	…	30	4680	6	26	18	…
	Bugbee	5	…	25	3900	6	26	18	…
	Chadwick	5	…	25	3900	6	4	18	…
London City	Bateman	3	…	12	288	6	3	18	…
	Tame	4	…	12	216	6	3	18	…
	Walker	3	…	9	144	6	4	18	…
	Harmadu	2	…	9	216	3	4	18	…
	Bindy	3	…	6	72	3	2	18	…
London City Improvements	Duggan	10	…	50	7800	6	26	16	…
	Bugbee	20	…	100	15600	6	26	18	18
	Gould	10	…	50	7800	6	26	18	18
	Booth	5	…	20	360	3	6	18	…
Shoreditch	Styles	2	…	8	96	3	4	18	…
	Wood	5	…	20	780	3	13	18	…
	Gould	5	…	20	1560	3	13	18	…
Bethnal Green	Calvert	2	…	8	240	3	10	18	…
	Newman	2	…	6	234	3	13	18	…
	Rooke	4	…	16	624	6	13	15	…
Whitechapel	Tilley	3	…	12	936	3	13	18	…
	Newman	3	…	9	216	3	8	18	…
	Tomkins	2	…	6	234	3	13	16	…
	Abbott	2	…	6	90	3	13	18	…
St. George's in the East	Clarke	6	…	18	360	4	5	18	…
	Calvert	4	…	16	192	3	4	18	…
	Newman	3	…	6	216	3	6	15	…
	Tomkins	3	…	6	108	3	6	18	…
	Abbott	6	…	18	432	3	8	16	…
Stepney	Newman	4	…	16	288	3	8	18	…
	Potter	3	…	12	180	3	5	16	…
	Church	3	…	12	216	3	6	15	…

LONDON LABOUR AND THE LONDON POOR.

Paddington.	Mr. Curmock	3	..	12	936	6	13	18		Poplar.	Mr. Pine	3	..	12	324	3	9	18
	„ Tame	6	..	18	432	3	8	18			„ Monk	3	..	12	780	5	13	18
	„ Humphries	6	..	18	702	3	13	16			„ Tingey	2	..	8	240	3	10	18
	„ Nicolls	3	..	12	268	3	8	20			„ Gabriel	4	..	16	624	3	13	18
	„ Seal & Jackson	3	..	6	936	6	26	20			„ Jones	3	..	12	192	4	4	18
Hampstead.	„ Kirtland	2	..	6	468	3	26	20		St. George's.	„ Reddin	10	..	40	3120	6	13	18
	„ Hingston	1	..	3	117	3	13	18			„ G. Whitten	2	..	10	780	6	13	18
	„ Batterbury	1	..	3	117	3	13	18			„ Webbon	3	..	10	936	6	13	18
	„ Smith	1	..	3	384	4	12	18		St. Olave's.	„ Reddin	10	..	40	3120	6	13	18
	„ Perkins	8	..	24	1872	6	13	18			„ Bugbee	2	..	6	72	3	4	18
St. Pancras.	„ Reddin	8	..	24	2304	6	16	18		St. Saviour's, Southwark.	„ Ryder	2	..	6	72	3	4	18
	„ Jay	6	..	24	2304	6	16	18			„ Wright	1	..	3	36	3	4	18
	„ M. Rose	3	..	12	468	3	13	18			„ Peake	5	..	12	3120	6	26	18
	„ Eldred	4	..	20	1920	6	26	16		Bermondsey.	„ Duckett	12	..	36	5616	6	26	18
	„ Croot	3	..	12	936	6	13	16			„ Elworthy	8	..	24	3744	6	26	18
Islington.	„ Speller	2	..	20	288	3	6	16			„ Slee	5	2	20	3120	6	26	18
	„ J. Rose	2	..	9	1560	6	13	18			„ Adams	4	..	20	4680	6	39	18
	„ Piper	5	..	18	702	3	13	16		Newington.	„ Gutteris	3	..	9	270	6	5	18
Hackney.	„ Rumball	3	..	15	2808	6	26	18			„ Crawley	2	..	8	256	4	8	18
	„ Booth	6	..	15	1170	3	13	16			„ Martainbody	6	..	24	960	4	10	17
	„ Duggan	5	..	12	936	6	13	18			„ Nicholson	5	..	15	1170	6	13	17
	„ Freeman	3	..	12	624	3	13	18		Wandsworth.	„ Mears	3	..	6	468	3	13	17
St. Giles's.	„ Bugbee	4	..	16	768	6	16	18			„ Parsons	4	..	16	864	3	9	19
	„ Wall	2	..	8	288	6	6	16			„ Easton	3	..	15	720	6	8	18
	„ Mildwater	2	..	6	180	3	5	18			„ J. Whitton	10	..	40	2080	4	13	18
St. Giles's Improvements.	„ Reddin	10	..	50	3900	6	13	18			„ G. Whitton	8	..	24	1248	4	13	18
	„ Bugbee	10	..	50	3900	6	13	18		Lambeth.	„ Kenning	2	..	10	390	3	10	18
	„ North	3	..	12	432	3	6	18			„ Hook	6	..	18	540	3	8	18
	„ Nicolls	5	..	20	1560	6	13	16			„ Michel	2	..	8	384	6	4	15
Strand.	„ Piper	4	..	16	384	3	4	18		Camberwell.	„ Marsland	2	..	8	128	4	6	18
	„ Reddin	5	..	12	480	4	4	18			„ Walton	2	..	6	144	4	5	15
	„ Ellis	3	..	12	180	4	5	18			„ Evans	1	..	6	90	4	6	18
	„ Cooper	3	..	8	108	3	5	18			„ Walker	10	..	30	3240	6	18	15
	„ Lovell	2	..	8	312	3	6	18			„ Brown	8	..	24	936	6	13	18
Holborn.	„ M'Carthy	6	..	24	1872	3	10	18		Rotherhithe.	„ Hobman	12	..	36	1404	3	13	18
	„ Wells	3	..	12	468	6	9	18			„ East	6	..	18	702	3	13	18
	„ Ellis	3	..	12	324	3	13	18			„ Stevens	5	..	20	1560	6	10	15
Holborn and New Oxford-street Improvements.	„ Reddin	20	..	80	6240	6	13	18		Greenwich.	„ Jeffry	5	..	10	600	6	6	14
	„ Bugbee	10	..	40	3120	6	13	18			„ Turtle	2	..	15	720	6	8	17
	„ Nicolls	5	..	20	480	3	8	18			„ Hiscock	2	..	6	432	6	12	16
	„ Ellis	6	..	24	936	3	13	17			„ Allen	5	..	10	780	6	13	18
	„ T. Brown	3	..	12	624	4	6	16			„ Connall	3	..	6	432	6	26	18
Clerkenwell.	„ Wood	4	..	16	576	3	4	18		Woolwich.	„ Waller	6	..	12	468	6	13	16
	„ Johnstone	3	..	15	360	6	3	16			„ Miller	8	..	36	936	6	13	18
	„ Clarkson	6	..	24	432	3	4	18			„ Fuller	8	..	16	960	6	10	18
	„ North	3	..	12	144	5	5	18			„ Barnes	4	..	12	648	6	9	16
	„ J. Brown	2	..	6	180	5	6	18			„ Sharpe	12	..	36	1404	3	13	18
St. Luke's.	„ Rhodes	5	..	20	500	5	10	18			„ Taylor	2	..	24	2016	6	14	18
	„ Wood	5	..	20	360	5	13	18			„ Ginno	8	..	20	780	3	13	16
	„ Dodd	10	..	30	1200	6	13	18			„ Millard	5	..	10	390	3	10	18
	„ Gould	3	..	20	2340	3	13	18		Lewisham.	„ Graham	4	..	9	270	3	9	18
East London.	„ Pratt & Sewell	2	..	9	351	3	13	18			„ Peakes	5	..	15	810	6	13	15
	„ Tomkins	2	..	6	234	3	13	18			„ Wellard	3	..	12	936	6	13	15
	„ Crook	2	..	6	234	3	13	18			„ Fleckell	6	..	18	1404	6	13	15
	„ Abbott	2	..	8	384	6	8	18			„ Hollis	4	..	12	288	3	8	15
											Total	840	15	3134	259831			

operatives by the load varies from 6*d*. to 1*s*. 6*d*., for it is necessarily regulated by the distance to be traversed. If the rubbish have to be carted a mile to its destination—or, as the men call it, to "the shoot"—of course it is to be so conveyed at a proportionally lower rate than if it had to be driven two or three miles. The employment of men by the load, however, becomes less every year, and the reason, I am assured, is this:— The great stress of the labour falls upon the horse. If the animal be strong and manageable, a man, for the sake of conveying an extra load a day, might overtax its powers, injure it gradually, and deteriorate its strength and its value. The operative carters, on their part, have complained that sometimes even "good" employers have set them to work by the load with "hard old horses," which no management could get out of their slow, long-accustomed pace. Thus a man might clear by the piece-work but 1*s*. 6*d*. a day, with a horse not worth 15*l*.; while another carter, with a superior animal worth twice as much, might clear 3*s*. or 3*s*. 6*d*. Some "hard" masters, I was informed, liked these old horses, because they were bought cheap, and though they brought in less than superior animals they were easier kept; while if less were earned by the piece-work with such horses, less was paid in wages; and if the horse broke its leg, or was killed, or injured, it was more easily replaced. This mode of employment is, as I have said, less and less carried into effect; but it is still one of the ways in which a working carter may be made a sufferer, because a principal accessary of his work—the horse—may not be capable of the requisite exertion.

The nominal wages of the rubbish-carters in the best employ are from 18*s*. to 20*s*. a week; in the worse-paid trade 15*s*. is the more general price; but even as little as 12*s*. is given by some masters.

The actual wages are the same as the nominal in the honourable trade, with the addition of perquisites in beer to the men of from 1*s*. to 2*s*. weekly, and of "findings," especially to the carmen, of an amount I could not ascertain, but perhaps realizing 6*d*. a week. One carman put all he found on one side to buy new year's clothes for his children, and on new year's eve last year he had 48*s*. 0½*d*., "money, and what brought money;" but this is far from an usual case.

The rate of wages paid to the operative rubbish-carters throughout the different districts of London, I find, by inquiries in each locality, to be by no means uniform. For instance, at Hampstead the wages are unexceptionally 20*s*. per week; while at Kensington, Chelsea, and indeed the whole of the west districts of London, they are 18*s*. weekly; in St. Martin's parish, however, 19*s*. a week is paid by two masters. In the north districts again, 18*s*. a week is generally paid; with the exception of Hampstead, where the weekly wages for the same labour are as high as 20*s*., and Islington where they are as low as 16*s*. In the central districts, too, the wages are generally 18*s*.; the lower rate of 17*s*. and 16*s*. per week being paid in certain places by "cutting" and "grasping" individuals, who form isolated exceptions to the rule. In a certain portion of the eastern districts, such as Bethnal Green, St. George's in the East, and Stepney, 16*s*. and 15*s*. a week appears to be the rule; while in Shoreditch and Poplar 18*s*. is paid by all the masters. The southern districts of the metropolis are equally irregular in their rates of wages. Lewisham pays as low as 15*s*., and Woolwich the same weekly sum, with one exception. Wandsworth, on the other hand, pays uniformly 17*s*.; while in Southwark, Bermondsey, Newington, and Camberwell, the wages paid by all are 18*s*. In Lambeth as much as 19*s*. is given by two masters out of three; whereas, in Greenwich one master pays 14*s*., and the other even as low as 12*s*. a week. When I come to treat of the lower-paid trade, I shall explain the causes of the above difference as regards wages.

The analysis of the facts I have collected on this subject is as follows:—Out of 180 masters, employing among them 840 men, there are—

						Wages per Week.
5 masters employing	11 men, and paying	20*s*.
5	,,	,,	30	,,	,,	19*s*.
127	,,	,,	605	,,	,,	18*s*.
6	,,	,,	20	,,	,,	17*s*.
16	,,	,,	70	,,	,,	16*s*.
19	,,	,,	97	,,	,,	15*s*.
1	,,	,,	5	,,	,,	14*s*.
1	,,	,,	2	,,	,,	12*s*.

Hence, three-fourths of the operatives may be said to receive 18*s*. weekly, and about one-sixth 16*s*.

The perquisites in this trade are more in beer than in money, nor are they derived from the employers, unless exceptionally. They are given to the rubbish-carters by the owners of the premises where they work, and may, in the best trade, amount, in beer or in money to buy beer, to from 1*s*. 6*d*. to 2*s*. weekly per man. The other perquisites are what is found in the digging of the rubbish for the carts, and in the shooting of it. As in other trades of a not dissimilar character, there appears to be no fixed rule as to "treasure trove." One man told me that in digging or shovelling each man kept what he found; another said the men drank it. Anything found, however, when the cart is emptied is the perquisite of the carman. "It's luck as is everything;" said one carman. "There was a mate of mine as hadn't not no better work nor me, once found an old silver coin, like a bad half-crown, as a gen'lman he knowed gave him five good shillings for, and he found a silver spoon as fetched 1*s*. 9*d*., in one week, and that same week on the same ground *I* got nothing but five bad ha'pennies. I once worked in the City where the Sun office now is, just by the Hall of Commerce in Threadneedle-street, and something was found in the Hall as now is; it was a French church once; and an old gent gave us on the sly 1*s*. a day for beer, to show him or tell him of anything we turned up queer. We did show him things as we thought queer, and they looked queer, but he all'us said 'Chi-ish,' or 'da-amn.' From what I've heard him say to another old cove as sometimes was with him, they looked for something Roman Catholic." My informant no doubt meant "Roman," as in digging the foundations of the Hall of Commerce a tesselated Roman pavement was found at a great depth.

Among these workmen are *no Trade Societies, no Benefit or Sick-Clubs*, and, indeed, no measures whatever for the upholding of accustomed wages, or providing "for a rainy day," unless individually. If a rubbish-carter be sick, the men in the same employ, whatever their number, 10 or 40, contribute on the Saturday evenings 6d. each, towards his support, until the patient's convalescence. There are no Houses of Call.

The *payment is in the master's yard* on the Saturday evening, and always in money. There are no drawbacks, unless for any period during the hours of regular labour, when a man may have been absent from his work. Fines there are none, except in large establishments among the carmen where many horses are kept, and then, if a man do not keep his regular stable-hours in the mornings, especially the Sunday mornings, he is fined 6d. These fines are spent by the carmen generally, and most frequently in beer.

The *usual way of applying for work* is to call at the yards or premises, or, more frequently, to take a round in the districts where it is known that buildings or excavations are being carried on, to inquire of the men if a hand be wanted. Sometimes a foreman may be there who has authority to "put on" new hands; if not, the applicant, with the prospect of an engagement in view, calls upon any party he may be directed to. Several men told me that when they were engaged nothing was said about character. The employers seem to be much influenced by the applicant's appearance.

I must now give a brief description of the rubbish-carter, and the scene of his labours.

Any one who observes, and does not merely see, the labour of the rubbish-carter, will have been struck with the stolid indifference with which these men go about their work, however much the scene of their labours, from its historical associations, may interest the better informed. So it was when the rubbish carters were employed in removing the ruins of the old Houses of Parliament, and of that portion of the Tower which suffered from the ravages of the fire; and so it would be if they were directed to-morrow to commence the demolition and rubbish-carting of Westminster Abbey, the Temple Church, or St. Paul's, even in their present integrity.

Sometimes the scene of the rubbish-carter's industry presents what may be called a "piteous aspect." This was not long ago the case in Cannon-street, City, and the adjacent courts and alleys; when the houses had been cleared of their furniture, the windows were removed (giving the house what may be styled a "blind" look); most of the doors had been taken away, as well as some of the floors. Large cyphers, scrawled in whitewash on the walls and woodwork, intimated the different "lots," and all spoke of desertion; the only moving thing to be seen, perhaps, was some flapping paper, torn from the sides of a room and which fluttered in the wind.

A scene of exceeding bustle follows the apparent desolateness of the premises. When the whole has been disposed of to the several purchasers, the further and final work of demolition begins. Baskets filled with the old bricks are rapidly lowered by ropes and pulleys into the carts below, it being the carter's business to empty them, and then up the empty baskets are drawn, as if by a single jerk. The sound of the hammer used in removing and separating the old bricks of the building, the less frequent sound of the pickaxe, the rumble of the stones and bricks into the cart, the noise of the pulleys, the shouts of the men aloft, crying "be-low there!" the half-articulate exclamations of the carters choked with dust, form a curious medley of noises. The atmosphere is usually a cloud of dust, which sticks to the men's hair like powder. The premises are boarded round, and if adjoining a thoroughfare the boards are closely fitted, to prevent the curious and the loiterers obstructing the current of passengers. The work within is confined to the labourers; "no persons admitted except on business" seems a rule rigidly enforced. The only men inside who appear idle are the over-lookers, or surveyors. They stand with their hands in their breeches' pockets; and a stranger to the business might account them uninterested spectators, but for the directions they occasionally give, now quietly, and now snappishly; while the Irishmen show an excessive degree of activity, the assumption of which never deceives an overlooker.

From twelve to one is the customary dinner-hour, and then all is quiet. On visiting some new buildings at Maida-hill, I found seven men, out of about 30, all fast asleep in the nooks and corners of the piles of bricks and rubbish, the day being fine. The others were eating their dinners at the public-houses or at their own homes.

In the progress of pulling down, the work of removal goes on very rapidly where a strong force is employed—the number varying from about twelve to 30 men. A four-storied house is often pulled down to its basement, and the contents of the walls, floors, &c., removed, in ten days or a fortnight.

As the work of demolition goes on, the rubbish-carter loads the cart with the old bricks, mortar, and refuse which the labourers have displaced. In some places, where a number of buildings is being removed at the same time, an inclined plane or road is formed by the rubbish-carters, up and down which the horses and vehicles can proceed. Until such means of carriage have been employed, the rubbish from the interior foundation is often shot in a mound within the premises, and carried off when the way has been formed, excepting such portion as may be retained for any purpose.

In hot weather, many of the rubbish-carters in the fair trade work in their shirts, a broad woollen belt being strapped round the waist, which, they say, supports "the small of the back" in their frequent bending and stooping. Some wear woollen night-caps at this work when there is much dust; and nearly all the men in the honourable trade wear the "strong men's" half-boots, laced up in the front, as the best protectors of the feet from the intrusion of rubbish.

In the cold weather, the rubbish-carter's working dress is usually a suit of strong drab-white fustian. The suit comprises a jacket with two large pockets. The cost of such a suit, new, at a slop-tailor's, is from 28s. to 35s.; from a good shop, and of better materials, 40s. to 55s. Some prefer stout corduroy to fustian trowsers; and some work in short smock-frocks.

Having thus shown the nature of the work, the class of men employed, and the amount of remuneration, I proceed to describe the characteristics of the rubbish-carters employed by the honourable masters; I will then describe the state of the labourers who are *casually* rather than *constantly* employed; and finally speak of the condition and habits of the lower-paid workers under the cheap masters.

The Ability to Read and Write.—I think I heard of fewer instances of defective education among the rubbish-carters than among other classes of unskilled labourers. The number of men who could read and not write, I found computed at about one-half. It appears that the children of these men are very generally sent to school, which is certainly a healthful sign as to the desire of the parents to do justice to their offspring. As among other classes, I met with uneducated men who had exaggerated notions of the advantages of the capability of reading and writing, and men who possessed such capability representing it as a worthless acquirement.

The *majority of the Rubbish-Carters* in the honourable trade *are*, I am informed, *really married men*, and have families "born in lawful wedlock." One decent and intelligent man, to whom I was referred, said (his wife being present and confirming his statement): "I don't know how it is, sir, but they say one scabbed sheep will affect a flock." "Oh! it's dreadful," said the wife; "but some way it seems to run in places. Now, we've lived among people much in our own way of life in Clerkenwell, and Pentonville, and Paddington. Well, we've reason to believe, that there wasn't much living together unmarried in Clerkenwell or Pentonville, but a goodish deal in Paddington. I don't know why, for they seemed to live one with another, just as men do with their wives. But if there's daughters, sir, as is growing up and gets to know it, as they're like enough to do, ain't it a bad example? Yes, indeed," said the wife, "and I'm told they call going together in that bad way—they ought all to be punished—without ever entering a church or chapel, getting 'ready married.'" I inquired if they were not perhaps married quietly at the Registrar's office? "O, that," said Mrs. B——, "ain't like being married at all. *I* would never have consented to such a way, but I'm pretty certain they don't as much as do that. No, sir," (in answer to another inquiry), "I hope, and think, it ain't so bad among young couples as it was, but its bad enough as it is, God he knows." The proportions of Wedlock and Concubinage I could not learn, for the woman, I was assured, always took the man's name; and both man and woman, unless in their cups or their quarrels, declared they were man and wife, only there was no good in wasting money to get their "marriage lines" all for no use.

The Politics of the rubbish-carters are, I am assured by some of the best informed among them, of no fixity, or principle, or inclination whatever, as regards one-half of the entire body; and that the other half, whether ignorant or not, are Chartists, the Irish generally excepted; and they, I understood, as I had learned on previous occasions, had no political opinions, unless such as were entertained by their priests. Strong, rude, and ignorant as many of these carters are, I am told that few of them took part in any public manifestation of opinion, or in any disturbance, unless they were out of work. "I think I know them well," one of their body said to me, "and as long as they have pretty middling of work, it'll take a very great thing indeed to move 'em. If they was longish out of work and felt a pinch, very likely they'd be found ready for anything."

With respect to Free Trade, I am told that these men sometimes discuss it, and formerly discussed it far more frequently among themselves, but that it was not above one in a dozen, and of the better sort only, who cared to talk about it either now or then. There seems no doubt that the majority, whether they understand its principles and working or not, are favourable to it; I may say, from all I could learn, that the *great* majority are. I heard of one rubbish-carter, formerly a small farmer, who left London for some other employment, in the spring, contending, and taking pains to enforce his conviction, that Free Trade would ruin the best interests of rubbish-carters, as year by year there would be more agricultural labourers resorting to the great towns to look for such work as rubbish-carting, for every farmer would employ more Irish labourers at his own terms, and even the 8s. a week, the extent of the earnings of the agricultural labourers in some parishes, would be undersold by the Irish. Last winter, he said, very many countrymen came to London, and would do so the next, and more and more every year, and so make labour cheaper.

As far as I could extend my inquiries and observations, this man's arguments—although I cannot say I heard any one offer to controvert them—were not considered sound, nor his facts fully established. There were certainly great numbers of good hands out of employment last winter, and many new applicants for work; "but buildings," I was told by a carman, "are of course always slacker carried on in the winter. Now, this year, so far (beginning of October), things seem to promise pretty well in our business, and so if it's good this winter and was bad the last, why, as there's the same Free Trade, it seems as if it had nothing to do with it. There's not so much building going on now as there was a few years ago, but trade's steadier, I think."

Other rubbish-carters, in the best trade, said that they had found little difference for six or eight years, only as bread was cheaper or dearer; and, if Free Trade made bread cheap, no man ought to say a word against it, "no matter about anything else." Of course I give these opinions as they came to me.

As to Food, these labourers, when in full work, generally live what they consider *well;* that is, they eat meat and have beer to their meals every day. Three of them told me that they could not say what their living cost separately, as they took all their meals at home with their families, their wives laying out the money. One couple had six children, and the husband said they cost him about 17s. a week in food, or about 2s. 6d. per head, reckoning a pint of beer a day for himself, and not including the youngest, which was an infant at the breast. The father earned 22s. weekly, and the eldest child, a boy, 3s. 6d. a week for carrying out and collecting the papers for a news'-agent. The wife could earn nothing, although an excellent washerwoman, the cares of her family occupying her whole time. She always had "the cold shivers," she said, "if ever she thought of John's being out of work, but he was a steady man, and had been pretty fortunate." If these men were engaged on a job at any distance, they sometimes breakfasted before starting, or carried bread and butter with them, and eat it to a pint of coffee if near enough to a coffee-shop, but in some places they were not near enough. Their dinners they carried with them, generally cold meat and bread, in a basin covered with a plate, a handkerchief being tied round it so as to keep the plate firm and afford a hold to the bearer. "It's not always, you see, sir," said a rubbish-carter, "that there's a butcher's shop near enough to run to and buy a bit of steak and get it dressed at a tap-room fire, just for buying a pint of beer, and have a knife and fork, and a plate, and salt found you into the bargain, and pepper and mustard too, if you'll give the girl or the man 1d. a week or so. But we're glad to get a good cold dinner. O, as to beer, it would be a queer out-of-the-way place indeed where a landlord didn't send out a man to a building with beer." One single man, who told me he was only a small eater, gave me the following as his *daily* bill of fare, as he rarely took any meals at his lodgings :

	s.	d.
Half-quartern loaf	0	2¾
Butter	0	1
Coffee (twice a day) . . .	0	3
Eleven o'clock beer, sometimes a pint and sometimes half-a-pint, but often obtained as a perquisite . . . (average)	0	1½
½ lb. of beef steak, or a chop, or four or five pennyworth of cold meat from a cook-shop . . . (average)	0	5
Potatoes	0	1
Dinner beer	0	2
Bread and cheese and beer for supper	0	4
	1	8¼

This was the average cost of his daily food, while on Sundays he generally paid 1s. 6d. for breakfast and tea, and a good dinner off a hot joint with baked potatoes from the oven, along with the family and other lodgers. He had a good walk every Sunday morning, he said, but liked to sleep away the afternoon. He found his own Sunday beer, costing 4d. dinner and supper, but he didn't eat anything at supper, as he wasn't inclined after resting all day, and so his weekly expenses in food were :—

	s.	d.
Six working days, at 1s. 8¼d. a day	10	1½
Sunday	1	10
Week's food	11	11½

To this, in the way of drink or luxuries, I might add, the carter said, 2d. a day for gin (although he wasn't a drinker and was very seldom tipsy), "for I treat a friend to a quartern one day and may-be he stands treat the next." Also 4d. for Sunday gin, as he and the other men took a glass just before dinner for an appetite, and he took one after dinner to send him asleep. Add, too, 3d. a week for tobacco. In all 1s. 7d., which swells the weekly cost of eating, drinking, and smoking to 13s. 6½d. His washing was 4d. a week (he washed his working jacket and trowsers himself), his rent 2s. 6d. for a bed to himself; so that, 16s. 4½d. being spent out of an earning of 18s., he had but 1s. 5½d. a week left for his clothes, shoes, &c. If he wanted a shilling or two for anything, he said, he knocked off his supper, and then nothing was allowed in his reckoning for perquisites, so he might be 2s. in hand, at least 2s., every week in a regular way of living. This man expressed his conviction that no man, who had to work hard, could live at smaller cost than he did. That numbers of men did so, he admitted, but he "couldn't make it out." The two ways of living which I have described may be taken as the modes prevalent among this class of labourers, who seek to live "comfortably." Others who "rough it" live at less cost, dining, for instance, off a pennyworth of pudding and half a pint of beer.

I ascertained that among the rubbish-carters, *those most frequently attendant on public worship are the Irish Roman Catholics*, and such Englishmen as had been agricultural labourers in rural parishes, and had been reared in the habit of church-going; a habit in which, but not without many exceptions, they still persevere. Among London-bred labourers such habits are rarely formed.

The abodes of the better description of rubbish-carters are not generally in those localities which are crowded with the poor. They reside in the streets off the Edgeware and Harrow-roads, as building has been carried on to a very great extent in Westbourne, Maida-hill, &c.; in Portland-town, Camden-town, Somers-town, about King's-cross; in Islington, Pentonville, and Clerkenwell; off the Commercial and Mile-end-roads; in Walworth, Camberwell, Kennington, and Newington; and, indeed, in all the quarters where building has been prosecuted on an extensive scale. I was in some of their apartments, and found them tidy and comfortable-looking: one was especially so. Some stone-fruit on the mantel-shelf shone as if newly painted, and the fender and fire-irons glittered from their brightness to the fire of the small grate. The husband, however, was in good earnings, and the wife cleared about 5s. weekly on superior needlework. There was one thing painful to observe—the contrast between the robust and sun-burnt look of the husband, and the delicate and pallid, not to say sickly, appearance of the wife. The rents for unfurnished apartments vary from 2s. to 5s., but rarely the latter, unless the wife take in a little washing. I heard of some at 2s., but very few; 2s. 6d. to 3s. 6d. are common prices.

I heard of no partiality for amusements among the rubbish-carters, beyond what my informant spoke of—a visit to the play. Some, I was told, but principally the younger men, never missed going to a fair, which was not too far off. I think not quite one-half of those I spoke to, with the best earnings, had been to the Exhibition. Of the worst paid, I am told, not one in 50 went; one man told me that he had no amusements but his pipe and his beer. Some of them, I was assured, drank half a gallon of beer in a day, but at intervals, so as not to be intoxicated. "A hand at cribbage" is a favourite public-house game among a few of these men; but not above one in half-a-dozen, I was assured, "knew the cards," and not one in two dozen played them.

These, then, are the characteristics of the labouring rubbish-carters employed in the honourable trade.

A fine-looking man, upwards of six feet in stature and of proportionate bulk, with so smart a set to his bushy whiskers, and a look of such general tidiness (after he had left off work in the evening), that he might have been taken for a life-guardsman had it not been for a slight slouch of the shoulders, and a very unmilitary gait, gave me the following account:—

"I'm a London man," he said, "and though I'm not yet 25, I've kept myself for the last five years. I've worked at rubbish-carting and general ground-work (digging for pipe-laying, &c.,) as we nearly all do, but mainly at rubbish-carting, and I'm at that now. My friends are in the same line, so I helped them: I was big enough, and was brought up that way. O, yes, I can read and write, but I haven't time, or very seldom, to read anything but a newspaper now and again. I'm a carman now, and have a very good master. I've served him, more or less, for three years. I have had 25s. a week, and I have had 29s., but that included over-work. Two hours extra work a day makes an extra day in the week, you see, sir. O, yes, I might have saved money, and I'm trying to save 25l. now to see if I can't raise a horse and cart, and begin for myself in a small way, general jobbing. I've been used to cart mould, and gravel, and turf for gentlemen's gardens, or when gardens have been laid out in new buildings, as well as rubbish, for the same master. Last year I set to work in hard earnest in the same way, and this is where it is that always stops me. Mr. —— [his employer] is very busy now, and things look pretty well about here [Camden-town], but I don't know how it is in other parts. It was the same last year, but trade fell off in the winter, and I was three months out of work. O, that's a common case, especial with young men, for of course the old hands has the preference. That's where it is, you see, sir; it's a *uncertain* trade. It's always that new shoes is wanted, but it ain't always new houses. My money all went, and then all my things went to the pawn, and when I got fairly to work again, I had a shirt and a shilling left, and owed some little matters. I'd saved well on to 50s., and could have gone on saving, but for being thrown out. Then, when you get into regular wages again, there's your uncle to meet, and there's always something wanted—a pair of half-boots, or a new shirt, or a new tool, or something; so one loses heart about it, and I can't abear not to appear respectable.

"I pay 2s. a week for my lodging, but it's only for half a bed. The house is let out that way to single men like me, so each bed brings in 4s. a week. There's two beds in the room where I sleep; I don't know how many in all. Why, yes, it's a respectable sort of a place, but I don't much like it. There's plenty such places; some's decent and some's not. Oh, certainly, a place of your own's best, if it's ever so humble, but it wouldn't suit a man like me. I may work one week at Paddington, and the next at Bow, and if I had a furnished room at Paddington, what good would it be if I went to work at Bow? Only the bother and expense of removing my sticks again and again. O, people that find lodgings for such as me, know that well enough, and makes a prey of us, of course.

"I take my meals at a public-house or a coffee-shop. O yes, I live well enough. I have meat every day to dinner; a man like me must keep up his strength, and you can't do that without good meat. It's all nonsense about vegetables and all that, as if men's stomachs were like cows'. I have bread and butter and tea or coffee for breakfast and tea, sometimes a few cresses with it just to sweeten the blood, which is the proper use of vegetables. A pint of beer or so for supper, but I don't care about supper, though now and then I take a bit of bread and cheese with a nice fresh onion to it. Well, I'm sure I can't say what I lay out in my living in a week; sometimes more and sometimes less. I keep no account; I pay my way as I go on. Some weeks when I get my Saturday night's wage, I have from 2s. 6d. to 6s. 6d. left from last Saturday night's money, but that's only when I've had nothing to lay out beyond common. Now, last week I was 4s. 9d. to the good, and this week I shall be about the ditto; but then I want a waistcoat and a silk handkerchief for my neck for Sunday wear; so I must draw on my Saturday night. There's a gentleman takes care of my money for me, and I carry him what I have over in a week, and he takes care of it for me. I did a good deal of work about his houses—he has a block of them—and his own place, and I've gardened for him; and from what I've heard, my money's safer with him than with a Savings' Bank. When I want to draw he likes to be satisfied what it's for, and he's lent me as much as 33s. in different sums, when I was hard up. He's what I call a real gentleman. He says if I ever go to him tipsy to draw, and says it quite solemn like, he'll take me by the scruff of the neck and kick me out; though [laughing] he can't be much above five foot, and has gray hairs, and seems a feeble sort of a man, I mean of a gentleman. He enters all I pay in a book. Here it is, sir, for this year, if you'd like to see it. I wasn't able to put anything by for a goodish bit. I lost my book once, but I knew how much, and so did Mr. ——, and he put it down in a lump.

		£	s.	d.
July 18	In hand	1	3	0
25	Received	0	3	6
Aug. 9	,,	0	3	6
23	,,	0	5	0
Sept. 13	,,	0	9	6
20	,,	0	4	0
27	,,	0	4	0
		£2	12	6

"If I can't save a little to start myself on when I'm a single man, I can't ever after, I fancy; so I'm a trying.

"No, my expenses, over and above my living and lodging and washing, and all that, ain't heavy. Yes, I'm very fond of a good play, very. Some galleries is 6d., and some 3d; but then there's refreshment and that, so it costs 1s. a time. Perhaps I go once a week, but only in autumn and winter, when nights get long, and we leave work at half-past five. The last time I was at the play was at the Marylebone, but there was some opera pieces that don't suit me; such stuff and nonsense. I like something very lively, or else a deep tragedy. Sadler's Wells is the place, sir. I mean to go there to-morrow night. Yes, I'm very fond of the pantomimes. Concerts I've been at, but don't care for them. They're as dear at 2d. as an egg a penny, and an egg's only a bite.

"Well, I've gone to church sometimes, but a carman hasn't time, for he has his horses to attend to on Sunday mornings, and that uses up his morning. No, I never go now. Work must be done. It ain't my fault. I'm sure, if I could have my wish, I'd never do anything on a Sunday.

"Yes, there's far too many as undersells us in work. I know that, but I don't like to think about them or to talk about them." [He seemed desirous to ignore the very existence of the scurf rubbish-carters.] "They're Irish many of them. They're often quarrelsome and blood-thirsty, but I know many decent men among the Irishmen in our gangs. There's good and bad among them, as there is among the English. There's very few of the Irish that are carmen; they haven't been much used to horses.

"I have done a little as a nightman when I worked for Mr. ——. He was a parish contractor, and undertook such jobs, and liked to put strong men on to them. I didn't like it. I can't think it's a healthy trade. I can't say, but I heard it represented, that in this particular calling there was a great deal of under-contracting going on when the railway undertakings generally received a severe check, and when a great number of hands were thrown out of employment, and sought employment in rubbish-carting generally, and apart from railway-work. These hands suffered greatly for a long time. The tommy-shops and the middle-man system were enough to swallow the largest amount of railway wages, so that very few had saved money, and they were willing to work for very low wages. A good many of these people went to endeavour to find work at the large new docks being erected at Great Grimsby, near Boston, in Lincolnshire. Some of the more prudent were able to raise the means of emigrating, and from one cause or other the pressure of this surplus labour among rubbish-carters and excavators, as regards the metropolis, became relieved."

OF CASUAL LABOUR IN GENERAL, AND THAT OF THE RUBBISH-CARTERS IN PARTICULAR.

THE subject of casual labour is one of such vast importance in connection with the welfare of a nation and its people, and one of which the causes as well as consequences seem to be so utterly ignored by economical writers and unheeded by the public, that I purpose here saying a few words upon the matter in general, with the view of enabling the reader the better to understand the difficulties that almost all unskilled and many skilled labourers have to contend with in this country.

By *casual* labour I mean such labour as can obtain only *occasional* as contradistinguished from *constant* employment. In this definition I include all classes of workers, literate and illiterate, skilled and unskilled, whose professions, trades, or callings expose them to be employed temporarily rather than continuously, and whose incomes are in a consequent degree fluctuating, casual, and uncertain.

In no country in the world is there such an extent, and at the same time such a diversity, of casual labour as in Great Britain. This is attributable to many causes—commercial and agricultural, natural and artificial, controllable and uncontrollable.

I will first show what are the causes of casual labour, and then point out its effects.

The causes of casual labour may be grouped under two heads:—

I. *The Brisk and Slack Seasons, and Fit Times*, or periodical increase and decrease of work in certain occupations.

II. *The Surplus Hands* appertaining to the different trades.

First, as to the briskness or slackness of employment in different occupations. This depends in different trades on different causes, among which may be enumerated—

A. The weather.

B. The seasons of the year.
C. The fashion of the day.
D. Commerce and accidents.

I shall deal with each of these causes *seriatim*.

A. The labour of thousands is influenced by the *weather;* it is suspended or prevented in many instances by stormy or rainy weather; and in some few instances it is promoted by such a state of things.

Among those whose labour cannot be executed on *wet days*, or executed but imperfectly, and who are consequently deprived of their ordinary means of living on such days, are—paviours, pipe-layers, bricklayers, painters of the exteriors of houses, slaters, fishermen, watermen (plying with their boats for hire), the crews of the river steamers, a large body of agricultural labourers (such as hedgers, ditchers, mowers, reapers, ploughmen, thatchers, and gardeners), costermongers and all classes of street-sellers (to a great degree), street-performers, and showmen.

With regard to the degree in which agricultural (or indeed in this instance woodland) labour may be influenced by the weather, I may state that a few years back there had been a fall of oaks on an estate belonging to Col. Cradock, near Greta-bridge, and the poor people, old men and women, in the neighbourhood, were selected to strip off the bark for the tanners, under the direction of a person appointed by the proprietor: for this work they were paid by the basket-load. The trees lay in an open and exposed situation, and the rain was so incessant that the "barkers" could scarcely do any work for the whole of the first week, but kept waiting under the nearest shelter in the hopes that it would "clear up." In the first week of this employment nearly one-third of the poor persons, who had commenced their work with eagerness, had to apply for some temporary parochial relief. A rather curious instance this, of a parish suffering from the casualty of a very humble labour, and actually from the attempt of the poor to earn money, and do work prepared for them.

On the other hand, some few classes may be said to be benefited by the rain which is impoverishing others: these are cabmen (who are the busiest on *showery* days), scavagers, umbrella-makers, clog and patten-makers. I was told by the omnibus people that their vehicles filled better in hot than in wet weather.

But the labour of thousands is influenced also by the *wind;* an easterly wind prevailing for a few days will throw out of employment 20,000 dock labourers and others who are dependent on the shipping for their employment; such as lumpers, corn-porters, timber-porters, ship-builders, sail-makers, lightermen, watermen, and, indeed, almost all those who are known as 'long-shoremen. The same state of things prevails at Hull, Bristol, Liverpool, and all our large ports.

Frost, again, is equally inimical to some labourers' interests; the frozen-out market-gardeners are familiar to almost every one, and indeed all those who are engaged upon the land may be said to be deprived of work by severely cold weather.

In the weather alone, then, we find a means of starving thousands of our people. Rain, wind, and frost are many a labourer's natural enemies, and to those who are fully aware of the influence of "the elements" upon the living and comforts of hundreds of their fellow-creatures, the changes of weather are frequently watched with a terrible interest. I am convinced that, altogether, a wet day deprives not less than 100,000, and probably nearer 200,000 people, including builders, bricklayers, and agricultural labourers, of their ordinary means of subsistence, and drives the same number to the public-houses and beer-shops (on this part of the subject I have collected some curious facts); thus not only decreasing their income, but positively increasing their expenditure, and that, perhaps, in the worst of ways.

Nor can there be fewer dependent on the winds for their bread. If we think of the vast number employed either directly or indirectly at the various ports of this country, and then remember that at each of these places the prevalence of a particular wind must prevent the ordinary arrival of shipping, and so require the employment of fewer hands; we shall have some idea of the enormous multitude of men in this country who can be starved by "a nipping and an eager air." If in London alone there are 20,000 people deprived of food by the prevalence of an easterly wind (and I had the calculation from one of the principal officers of the St. Katherine Dock Company), surely it will not be too much to say that throughout the country there are not less than 50,000 people whose living is thus precariously dependent.

Altogether I am inclined to believe, that we shall not be over the truth if we assert there are between 100,000 and 200,000 individuals and their families, or half a million of people, dependent on the elements for their support in this country.

But this calculation refers to those classes only who are deprived of a certain number of *days'* work by an alteration of the weather, a cause that is essentially *ephemeral* in its character. The other series of natural events influencing the demand for labour in this country are of a more *continuous* nature—the stimulus and the depression enduring for weeks rather than days. I allude to the *second* of the four circumstances above-mentioned as inducing briskness or slackness of employment in different occupations, viz.:—

B. The seasons.

These are the seasons of the year, and not the arbitrary seasons of fashion, of which I shall speak next.

The following classes are among those exposed to the uncertainty of employment, and consequently of income, from the above cause, since it is only in particular seasons that particular works, such as buildings, will be undertaken, or that open-air pleasure excursions will be attempted: carpenters, builders, brickmakers, painters, plasterers, paper-hangers, rubbish-carters, sweeps, and riggers and lumpers, the latter depending mainly on the arrival of the timber ships to the Thames (and this, owing to the ice in the Baltic Sea and in the river St. Lawrence, &c., takes place only at certain seasons of the year), coal-whippers and coal-porters (the coal trade being much brisker in winter), market-porters, and those employed in summer in steam-boat, railway, van, and barge excursions.

Then there are the casualties attending agricultural labour, for, although the operations of nature are regular "even as the seed time follows the harvest," there is, almost invariably, a smaller employment of labour after the completion of the haymaking, the sheep-shearing, and the grain-reaping labours.

For the hay and corn harvests it is well known that there is a periodical immigration of Irishmen and women, who clamour for the *casual* employment; others, again, leave the towns for the same purpose; the same result takes place also in the fruit and pea-picking season for the London green-markets; while in the winter such people return some to their own country, and some to form a large proportion of the casual class in the metropolis. A tall Irishman of about 34 or 35 (whom I had to see when treating of the religion of the street Irish) leaves his accustomed crossing-sweeping at all or most of the seasons I have mentioned, and returns to it for the winter at the end of October; while his wife and children are then so many units to add to the casualties of the street sale of apples, nuts, and onions, by over-stocking the open-air markets.

The autumnal season of hop-picking is the grand rendezvous for the vagrancy of England and Ireland, the stream of London vagrancy flowing freely into Kent at that period, and afterwards flowing back with increased volume. Men, women, and children are attracted to the hop harvest. The season is over in less than a month, and then the casual labourers engaged in it (and they are nearly all casual labourers) must divert their industry, or their endeavours for a living, into other channels, swelling the amount of casualty in unskilled work or street-trade.

Numerically to estimate the influence of the seasons on the labour-market of this country is almost an overwhelming task. Let us try, however: there are in round numbers one million agricultural labourers in this country; saying that in the summer four labourers are employed for every three in the winter, there would be 250,000 people and their families, or say 1,000,000 of individuals, deprived of their ordinary subsistence in the winter time; this, of course, does not include those who come from Ireland to assist at the harvest-getting—how many these may be I have no means of ascertaining. Added to these there are the natural vagabonds, whom I have before estimated at another hundred thousand (see p. 408, vol. i.), and who generally help at the harvest work or the fruit or hop-picking.

Then there are the carpenters, who are 163,000 in number; the builders, 9200; the brickmakers, 18,000; the painters, 48,200; the coal-whippers, 9200; the coal-miners, 110,000; making altogether 350,000 people, and estimating that for every four hands employed in the brisk season, there are only three required in the slack, we have 80,000 more families, or 300,000 people, deprived of their living by the casualty of labour; so that if we assert that there are, at the least, including agricultural labourers, 1,250,000 people thus deprived of their usual means of living, we shall not be very wide of the truth.

The next cause of the briskness or slackness of different employments is—

C. Fashion.

The London fashionable season is also the parliamentary season, and is the "briskest" from about the end of February to the middle of July.

The workmen most affected by the aristocratic, popular, or general fashions, are—

Tailors, ladies' habit-makers, boot and shoemakers, hatters, glovers, milliners, dress-makers, mantua-makers, drawn and straw bonnet-makers, artificial flower-makers, plumassiers, stay-makers, silk and velvet weavers, saddlers, harness-makers, coach-builders, cabmen, job-coachmen, farriers, livery stable keepers, poulterers, pastry-cooks, confectioners, &c., &c.

The above-mentioned classes may be taken, according to the Occupation Abstract of the last Census, at between 500,000 and 600,000; and, assuming the same ratio as to the difference of employment between the brisk and the slack seasons of the trades, or, in other words, that 25 per cent. less hands are required at the slack than at the brisk time of these trades, we have another 150,000 people, who, with their families, may be estimated altogether at say 500,000, who are thrown out of work at a certain season, and have to starve on as best they can for at least three months in the year.

The last-mentioned of the causes inducing briskness or slackness of employment are—

D. Commerce and Accidents.

Commerce has its periodical fits and starts. The publishers, for instance, have their season, generally from October to March, as people read more in winter than in summer; and this arrangement immediately effects the printers and bookbinders; there is no change, however, as regards the newspapers and periodicals. Again, the early importation to this country of the new foreign fruits gives activity to the dock and wharf labourers and porters and carmen. Thus the arrival here, generally in autumn, of the nut, chestnut, and grape (raisin) produce of Spain; of the almond crops in Portugal, Spain, and Barbary; the date harvest in Morocco, and different parts of Africa; the orange gathering in Madeira, and in St. Michael's, Terceira, and other islands of the Azores; the fig harvest from the Levant; the plum harvest of the south of France; the currant picking of Zante, Ithaca, and other Ionian Islands;—all these events give an activity, as new fruit is always most saleable, to the traders in these southern productions; and more shopmen, shop-porters, wharf labourers, and assistant lightermen are required—casually required—for the time.

I was told by a grocer, with a country connection, and in a large way of business, that for three weeks or a month before Christmas he required the aid of four fresh hands, a shopman, an errand-boy, and two porters (one skilled in packing), for whom he had nothing to do after Christmas. If in the wide sweep of London trade there be 1000 persons, including the market salesmen, the retail butchers, the carriers, &c., so circumstanced, then 4000 men are *casually* employed, and for a very brief time.

The brief increase of the carrying business generally about Christmas, by road, water, or railway, is sufficiently indicated by the foregoing account.

The employment, again, in the cotton and woollen manufacturing districts may be said to depend for its briskness on commerce rather than on the seasons.

Accidents, or extraordinary social events, promote casual labour and then depress it. Often they depress without having promoted it.

During the display of the Great Exhibition, there were some thousands employed in the different capacities of police, packing, cleaning, porterage, watching, interpreting, door-keeping and money-taking, cab-regulating, &c.; and after the close of the Exhibition how many were retained? Thus the Great Exhibition fostered casual, or uncertain labour. Foreign revolutions, moreover, affect the trade of England: speculators become timid and will not embark in trade or in any proposed undertaking; the foreign import and export trades are paralysed; and fewer clerks and fewer labourers are employed. Home political agitations, also, have the same effect; as was seen in London during the corn-law riots, about 35 years ago (when only eight members of the House of Commons supported a change in those laws); the Spafields riots in 1817; the affair in St. Peter's-field, Manchester, in 1819; the disturbances and excitement during the trial of Queen Caroline, in 1820-1, and the loss of life on the occasion of her funeral in 1821; the agitation previously to the passing of the Reform Bill had a like effect; the meeting on Kennington Common on the 10th of April;—in all these periods, indeed, employment decreased. Labour is affected also by the death of a member of the royal family, and the hurried demand for general mourning, but in a very small degree to what was once the case. A West-End tailor employing a great number of hands did not receive a single order for mourning on the death of Queen Adelaide; while on the demise of the Princess Charlotte (in 1817) thousands of operative tailors, throughout the three kingdoms, worked day and night, and for double wages, on the general mourning. Gluts in the markets, an increase of heavy bankruptcies and "panics," such as were experienced in the money market in 1825-6, and again in 1846, with the failure of banks and merchants, likewise have the effect of augmenting the mass of casual labour; for capitalists and employers, under such circumstances, expend as little as possible in wages or employment until the storm blows over. Bad harvests have a similar depressing effect.

There are also the consequences of changes of taste. The abandonment of the fashions of gentlemen's wearing swords, as well as embroidered garments, flowing periwigs, large shoe-buckles, all reduced able artizans to poverty by depriving them of work. So it was, when, to carry on the war with France, Mr. Pitt introduced a tax on hair powder. Hundreds of hair-dressers were thrown out of employment, many persons abandoning the fashion of wearing powder rather than pay the tax. There are now city gentlemen, who can remember that when clerks, they had sometimes to wait two or three hours for "their turn" at a barber's shop on a Sunday morning; for they could not go abroad until their hair was dressed and powdered, and their queues trimmed to the due standard of fashion. So it has been, moreover, in modern times in the substitution of silk for metal buttons, silk hats for stuff, and in the supersedence of one material of dress by another.

These several causes, then, which could only exist in a community of great wealth and great poverty have rendered, and are continually rendering, the labour market uncertain and over-stocked; to what extent they do and have done this, it is, of course, almost impossible to say *precisely;* but, even with the strongest disposition to avoid exaggeration, we may assert that there are in this country no less than 125,000 families, or 500,000 people, who depend on the weather for their food; 300,000 families, or 1,250,000 people, who can obtain employment only at particular seasons; 150,000 more families, or 500,000 people, whose trade depends upon the fashionable rather than the natural seasons, are thrown out of work at the cessation of the brisk time of their business; and, perhaps, another 150,000 of families, or 500,000 people, dependent on the periodical increase and decrease of commerce, and certain social and political accidents which tend to cause a greater or less demand for labour. Altogether we may assert, with safety, that there are at the least 725,000 families, or three millions of men, women, and children, whose means of living, far from being certain and constant, are of a precarious kind, depending either upon the rain, the wind, the sunshine, the caprice of fashion, or the ebbings and flowings of commerce.

But there is a still more potent cause at work to increase the amount of *casual* labour in this country. Thus far we have proceeded on the assumption that at the brisk season of each trade there is full employment for all; but this is far from being the case in the great majority, if not the whole, of the instances above cited. In almost all occupations there is in this country a *superfluity of labourers*, and this alone would tend to render the employment of a vast number of the hands of a casual rather than a regular character. In the generality of trades the calculation is that one-third of the hands are fully employed, one-third partially, and one-third unemployed throughout the year. This, of course, would be the case if there were twice too many workpeople; for suppose the number of work-people in a given trade to be 6000, and the work sufficient to employ (fully) only half the quantity, then, of course, 2000 might be occupied their whole time, 2000 more might have work sufficient to occupy them half their time, and the remaining 2000 have no work at all; or the whole 4000 might, on the average, obtain three months' employment out of the twelve; and this is frequently the case. Hence we see that a surplusage of hands in a trade tends to change the employment of the great majority from a state of constancy and regularity into one of casualty and precariousness. Consequently it becomes of the highest importance that we should endeavour to ascertain what are the circumstances inducing a surplusage of hands in the several trades of the present day. A *surplusage of hands* in a trade may proceed from three different causes, viz. :—

1. The alteration of the hours, rate, or mode of working, or else the term of hiring.
2. The increase of the hands themselves.
3. The decrease of the work.

Each of these causes is essentially distinct; in the first case there is neither an increase in the number of hands nor a decrease in the quantity of work, and yet a surplusage of labourers is the consequence, for it is self-evident that if there be work enough in a given trade to occupy 6000 men all the year round, labouring twelve hours per day for six days in the week, the same quantity of work will afford occupation to only 4000 men, or one-third less, labouring between fifteen and sixteen hours per diem for seven days in the week. The same result would, of course, take place, if the workman were made to labour one-third more *quickly*, and so to get through one-third more work in the same time (either by increasing their interest in their work, by the invention of a new tool, by extra supervision, or by the subdivision of labour, &c., &c.), the same result would, of course, ensue as if they laboured one-third longer hours, viz., one-third of the hands must be thrown out of employment. So, again, by altering the *mode or form of work*, as by producing on the large scale, instead of the small, a smaller number of labourers are required to execute the same amount of work; and thus (if the market for such work be necessarily limited) a surplusage of labourers is the result. Hence we see that the alteration of the hours, rate, or mode of working may tend as positively to overstock a country with labourers as if the labourers themselves had unduly increased.

But this, of course, is on the assumption that both the quantity of work and the number of hands remain the same. The next of the three causes, above mentioned as inducing a surplusage of hands, is that which arises from a positive *increase in the number of labourers*, while the quantity of work remains the same or increases at a less rate than the labourers; and the third cause is, where the surplusage of labourers arises not from any alteration in the number of hands, but from a positive *decrease in the quantity of work*.

These are distinctions necessary to be borne clearly in mind for the proper understanding of this branch of the subject.

In the first case both the number of hands and the quantity of work remain the same, but the term, rate, or mode of working is changed.

In the second, hours, rate, or mode of working remain the same, as well as the quantity of work, but the number of hands is increased.

And in the third case, neither the number of hands nor the hours, rate, or mode of working is supposed to have been altered, but the work only to have decreased.

The surplusage of hands will, of course, be the same in each of these cases.

I will begin with the first, viz., that which induces a surplusage of labourers in a trade by enabling fewer hands to get through the ordinary amount of work. This is what is called the "economy of labour."

There are, of course, only three modes of economizing labour, or causing the same quantity of work to be done by a smaller number of hands.

1st. By causing the men to work *longer*.

2nd. By causing the men to work *quicker*, and so get through more work in the same time.

3rd. By *altering the mode* of work, or hiring, as in the "large system of production," where fewer hands are required; or the custom of temporary hirings, where the men are retained only so long as their services are needed, and discharged immediately afterwards.

First, of that mode of economizing labour which depends on an *increase of either the ordinary hours or days for work*. This is what is usually termed over-work and Sunday-work, both of which are largely creative of surplus hands. The hours of labour in mechanical callings are usually twelve, two of them devoted to meals, or 72 hours (less by the permitted intervals) in a week. In the course of my inquiries for the *Chronicle*, I met with slop cabinet-makers, tailors, and milliners who worked sixteen hours and more daily, their toil being only interrupted by the necessity of going out, if small masters, to purchase materials, and offer the goods for sale; or, if journeymen in the slop trade, to obtain more work and carry what was completed to the master's shop. They worked on Sundays also; one tailor told me that the coat he worked at on the previous Sunday was for the Rev. Mr. ——, who "little thought it," and these slop-workers rarely give above a few minutes to a meal. Thus they toil 40 hours beyond the hours usual in an honourable trade (112 hours instead of 72), in the course of a week, or between three and four days of the regular hours of work of the six working days. In other words, two such men will in less than a week accomplish work which should occupy three men a full week; or 1000 men will execute labour fairly calculated to employ 1500 at the least. A paucity of employment is thus caused among the general body, by this system of over-labour decreasing the share of work accruing to the several operatives, and so adding to surplus hands.

Of over-work, as regards excessive labour, both in the general and fancy cabinet trade, I heard the following accounts, which different operatives concurred in giving; while some represented the labour as of longer duration by at least an hour, and some by two hours, a day, than I have stated.

The labour of the men who depend entirely on "the slaughter-houses" for the purchase of their articles is usually seven days a week the year through. That is, seven days—for Sunday work is all but universal—each of 13 hours, or 91 hours in all; while the established hours of labour in the "honourable trade" are six days of the week, each of 10 hours, or 60 hours in all. Thus 50 per cent. is added to the extent of the production of low-priced cabinet-work, merely from "over-hours;" but in some cases I heard of 15 hours for seven days in the week, or 105 hours in all.

Concerning the hours of labour in this trade, I had the following minute particulars from a garret-master who was a chair-maker:—

"I work from six every morning to nine at night; some work till ten. My breakfast at eight stops me for ten minutes. I can breakfast in less time, but it's a rest; my dinner takes me say twenty minutes at the outside; and my tea, eight minutes. All the rest of the time I'm slaving at my bench. How many minutes' rest is that, sir? Thirty-eight; well, say three-quarters of an hour, and that allows a few sucks at a pipe when I rest; but I can smoke and work too. I have only one room to work and eat in, or I should lose more time. Altogether I labour 14¼ hours every day, and I must work on Sundays—at least 40 Sundays in the year. One may as well work as sit fretting. But on Sundays I only work till it's dusk, or till five or six in summer. When it's dusk I take a walk. I'm not well-dressed enough for a Sunday walk when it's light, and I can't wear my apron on that day very well to hide patches. But there's eight hours that I reckon I take up every week one with another, in dancing about to the slaughterers. I'm satisfied that I work very nearly 100 hours a week the year through; deducting the time taken up by the slaughterers, and buying stuff—say eight hours a week—it gives more than 90 hours a week for my work, and there's hundreds labour as hard as I do, just for a crust.'

The East-end turners generally, I was informed, when inquiring into the state of that trade, labour at the lathe from six o'clock in the morning till eleven and twelve at night, being 18 hours' work per day, or 108 hours per week. They allow themselves two hours for their meals. It takes them, upon an average, two hours more every day fetching and carrying their work home. Some of the East-end men work on Sundays, and not a few either, said my informant. "Sometimes I have worked hard," said one man, "from six one morning till four the next, and scarcely had any time to take my meals in the bargain. I have been almost suffocated with the dust flying down my throat after working so many hours upon such heavy work too, and sweating so much. It makes a man drink where he would not."

This system of over-work exists in the "slop" part of almost every business—indeed, it is the principal means by which the cheap trade is maintained. Let me cite from my letters in the *Chronicle* some more of my experience on this subject. As regards the London mantua-makers, I said:—"The workwomen for good shops that give fair, or tolerably fair wages, and expect good work, can make six average-sized mantles in a week, *working from ten to twelve hours a day;* but the slop-workers, by toiling from thirteen to sixteen hours a day, will make *nine* such sized mantles in a week. In a season of twelve weeks 1000 workers for the slop-houses and warehouses would at this rate make 108,000 mantles, or 36,000 more than workers for the fair trade. Or, to put it in another light, these slop-women, by being compelled, in order to live, to work such over-hours as inflict lasting injury on the health, supplant, by their over-work and over-hours, the labour of 500 hands, working the regular hours."

The following are the words of a chamber-master, working for the cheap shoe trade:—

"From people being obliged to work twice the hours they once *did* work, or that in reason they *ought* to work, a glut of hands is the consequence, and the masters are led to make reductions in the wages. They take advantage of our poverty and lower the wages, so as to undersell each other, and command business. My daughters have to work fifteen hours a day that we may make a bare living. They seem to have no spirit and no animation in them; in fact, such very hard work takes the youth out of them. They have no time to enjoy their youth, and, with all their work, they can't present the respectable appearance they ought." "I" (interposed my informant's wife) "often feel a faintness and oppression from my hard work, as if my blood did not circulate."

The better class of artizans denounce the system of Sunday working as the most iniquitous of all the impositions. They object to it, not only on moral and religious grounds, but economically also. "Every 600 men employed on the Sabbath," say they, "deprive 100 individuals of a week's work. Every six men who labour seven days in the week must necessarily throw one other man out of employ for a whole week. The seventh man is thus deprived of his fair share of work by the overtoiling of the other six." This Sunday working is a necessary consequence of the cheap slop-trade. The workmen cannot keep their families by their six days' labour, and therefore they not only, under that system, get less wages and do more work, but by their extra labour throw so many more hands out of employment.

Here then, in the over-work of many of the trade, we find a vast cause of surplus hands, and, consequently, of casual labour; and that the work in these trades has not proportionately increased is proven by the fact of the existence of a superfluity of workmen.

Let us now turn our attention to the second of the causes above cited, viz., *the causing of men to* work quicker, and so to accomplish more in the same time. There are several means of attaining this end; it may be brought about either (a) by making the workman's gains depend directly on the quantity of work executed by him, as by the substitution of piece-work for day-work; (b) by the omission of certain details or parts necessary for the perfection of the work; (c) by decreasing the workman's pay, and so increasing the necessity for him to execute a greater quantity of work in order to obtain the same income; (d) increasing the supervision, and encouraging a spirit of emulation among the workpeople; (e) by dividing the labour into a number of simple and minute processes, and so increasing the expertness of the labourers; (f) by the invention of some new tool or machine for expediting the operations of the workman.

I shall give a brief illustration of each of these causes *seriatim*, showing how they tend to produce a surplusage of hands in the trades to which they are severally applied. And first, as to *making the workman's gains depend directly on the quantity of work executed by him*.

Of course there are but two direct modes of paying for labour—either by the day or by the piece. Over-work by day-work is effected by means of what is called the "strapping system" (as described in the *Morning Chronicle* in my letter upon the carpenters and joiners), where a whole shop are set to race over their work in silence one with another, each striving to outdo the rest, from the knowledge that anything short of extraordinary exertion will be sure to be punished with dismissal. Over-work by piece-work, on the other hand, is almost a necessary consequence of that mode of payment—for where men are paid by the quantity they do, of course it becomes the interest of a workman to do more than he otherwise would.

"Almost all who work by the day, or for a fixed salary, that is to say, those who labour for the gain of others, not for their own, have," it has been well remarked, "no interest in doing more than the smallest quantity of work that will pass as a fulfilment of the mere terms of their engagement. Owing to the insufficient interest which day labourers have in the result of their labour, there is a natural tendency in such labour to be extremely inefficient—a tendency only to be overcome by vigilant superintendence on the part of the persons who *are* interested in the result. The 'master's eye' is notoriously the only security to be relied on. But superintend them as you will, day labourers are so much inferior to those who work by the piece, that, as was before said, the latter system is practised in all industrial occupations where the work admits of being put out in definite portions, without involving the necessity of too troublesome a surveillance to guard against inferiority (or scamping) in the execution." But if the labourer at piece-work is made to produce a greater quantity than at day-work, and this solely by connecting his own interest with that of his employer, how much more largely must the productiveness of workmen be increased when labouring wholly on their own account! Accordingly it has been invariably found that whenever the operative unites in himself the double function of capitalist and labourer, as the "garret-master" in the cabinet trade, and the "chamber-master" in the shoe trade, making up his own materials or working on his own property, his productiveness, single-handed, is considerably greater than can be attained even under the large system of production, where all the arts and appliances of which extensive capital can avail itself are brought into operation.

As regards the increased production by *omitting certain details necessary for the due perfection of the work*, it may be said that "scamping" adds at least 200 per cent. to the productions of the cabinet-maker's trade. I ascertained, in the course of my previous inquiries, several cases of this over-work from scamping, and adduce two. A very quick hand, a little master, working, as he called it, "at a slaughtering pace," for a warehouse, made 60 plain writing-desks in a week of 90 hours; while a first-rate workman, also a quick hand, made 18 in a week of 70 hours. The scamping hand said he must work at the rate he did to make 14s. a week from a slaughter-house; and so used to such style of work had he become, that, though a few years back he did West-end work in the best style, he could not now make eighteen desks in a week, if compelled to finish them in the style of excellence displayed in the work of the journeyman employed for the honourable trade. Perhaps, he added, he couldn't make them in that style at all. The frequent use of rosewood veneers in the fancy cabinet, and their occasional use in the general cabinet trade gives, I was told, great facilities for scamping. If in his haste the scamping hand injure the veneer, or if it have been originally faulty, he takes a mixture of gum shellac and "colour" (colour being a composition of Venetian red and lamp black), which he has ready by him, rubs it over the damaged part, smooths it with a slightly-heated iron, and so blends it with the colour of the rosewood that the warehouseman does not detect the flaw. In the general, as contradistinguished from the fancy, cabinet trade I found the same ratio of "scamping." A good workman in the better-paid trade made a four-foot mahogany chest of drawers in five days, working the regular hours, and receiving, at piece-work price, 35s. A scamping hand made five of the same size in a week, and had time to carry them for sale to the warehouses, wait for their purchase or refusal, and buy material. But for the necessity of doing this the scamping hand could have made seven in the 91 hours of his week, though of course in a very inferior manner. "They would hold together for a time," I was assured, "and that was all; but the slaughterer cared only to have them viewly and cheap." These two cases exceed the average, and I have cited them to show what *can* be done under the scamping system.

We now come to the *increased rate of working induced by a reduction of the ordinary rate of remuneration of the workman*. Not only is it true that over-work makes under-pay, but the converse of the proposition is equally true, that under-pay makes over-work—that is to say, it is true of those trades where the system of piece-work or small mastership admits of the operative doing the utmost amount of work that he is able to accomplish; for the workman in such cases seldom or never thinks of reducing his expenditure to his income, but rather of increasing his labour, so as still to bring his income, by extra production, up to his expenditure. Hence we find that, as the wages of a trade descend, so do the labourers extend their hours of work to the utmost possible limits—they not only toil earlier and later than before, but the Sunday becomes a work-day like the rest (amongst the "sweaters" of the tailoring trade Sunday labour, as I have shown, is almost universal); and when the hours of work are carried to the extreme of human industry, then more is sought to be done in a given space of time, either by the employment of the members of their own family, or apprentices, upon the inferior portion of the work, or else by "scamping it." "My employer," I was told by a journeyman tailor working for the Messrs. Nicoll, "reduces my wages one-third, and the consequence is, I put in two stitches where I used to give three." "I must work from six to eight, and later," said a pembroke-table-maker to me, "to get 18s. now for my labour, where I used to get 54s. a week—that's just a third. I could in the old times give my children good schooling and good meals. Now children have to be put to work very young. I have four sons working for me at present. Not only, therefore, does any stimulus to extra production make over-work, and over-work make under-pay; but under-pay, by becoming an additional provocative to increased industry, again gives rise in its turn to over-work. Hence we arrive at a plain unerring law—*over-work makes under-pay and under-pay makes over-work.*

But the above means of increasing the rate of working refer solely to those cases where the extra labour is induced by making it the *interest* of the workman so to do. The other means of extra production is *by stricter supervision of journeymen, or those paid by the day.* The shops where this system is enforced are termed "strapping-shops," as indicative of establishments where an undue quantity of work is expected from a journeyman in the course of the day. Such shops, though not directly making use of cheap labour (for the wages paid in them are generally of the higher rate), still, by exacting more work, may of course be said, in strictness, to encourage the system now becoming general, of less pay and inferior skill. These strapping establishments sometimes go by the name of "scamping shops," on account of the time allowed for the manufacture of the different articles not being sufficient to admit of good workmanship.

Concerning this "*strapping*" system I received the following extraordinary account from a man after his heavy day's labour. Never in all my experience had I seen so sad an instance of over-work. The poor fellow was so fatigued that he could hardly rest in his seat. As he spoke he sighed deeply and heavily, and appeared almost spirit-broken with excessive labour:—

"I work at what is called a strapping shop," he said, "and have worked at nothing else for these many years past in London. I call 'strapping' doing as much work as a human being or a horse possibly can in a day, and that without any hanging upon the collar, but with the foreman's eyes constantly fixed upon you, from six o'clock in the morning to six o'clock at night. The shop in which I work is for all the world like a prison; the silent system is as strictly carried out there as in a model gaol. If a man was to ask any common question of his neighbour, except it was connected with his trade, he would be discharged there and then. If a journeyman makes the least mistake, he is packed off just the same. A man working at such places is almost always in fear; for the most trifling things he's thrown out of work in an instant. And then the quantity of work that one is forced to get through is positively awful; if he can't do a plenty of it, he don't stop long where I am. No one would think it was possible to get so much out of blood and bones. No slaves work like we do. At some of the strapping shops the foreman keeps continually walking about with his eyes on all the men at once. At others the foreman is perched high up, so that he can have the whole of the men under his eye together. I suppose since I knew the trade that a *man does four times the work that he did formerly.* I know a man that's done four pairs of sashes in a day, and one is considered to be a good day's labour. What's worse than all, the men are every one striving one against the other. Each is trying to get through the work quicker than his neighbours. Four or five men are set the same job, so that they may be all pitted against one another, and then away they go every one striving his hardest for fear that the others should get finished first. They are all tearing along from the first thing in the morning to the last at night, as hard as they can go, and when the time comes to knock off they are ready to drop. I was hours after I got home last night before I could get a wink of sleep; the soles of my feet were on fire, and my arms ached to that degree that I could hardly lift my hand to my head. Often, too, when we get up of a morning, we are more tired than when we went to bed, for we can't sleep many a night; but we mustn't let our employers know it, or else they'd be certain we couldn't do enough for them, and we'd get the sack. So, tired as we may be, we are obliged to look lively, somehow or other, at the shop of a morning. If we're not beside our bench the very moment the bell's done ringing, our time's docked—they wont give us a single minute out of the hour. If I was working for a fair master, I should do nearly one-third, and sometimes a half, less work than I am now forced to get through, and, even to manage that much, I shouldn't be idle a second of my time. It's quite a mystery to me how they *do* contrive to get so much work out of the men. But they are very clever people. They know how to have the most out of a man, better than any one in the world. They are all picked men in the shop—regular 'strappers,' and no mistake. The most of them are five foot ten, and fine broad-shouldered, strong-backed fellows too—if they weren't they wouldn't have them. Bless you, they make no words with the men, they sack them if they're not strong enough to do all they want; and they can pretty soon tell, the very first shaving a man strikes in the shop, what a chap is made of. Some men are done up at such work—quite old men and gray with spectacles on, by the time they are forty. I have seen fine strong men, of 36, come in there and be bent double in two or three years. They are most all countrymen at the strapping shops. If they see a great strapping fellow, who they think has got some stuff about him that will come out, they will give him a job directly. We are used for all the world like cab or omnibus horses. Directly they've had all the work out of us, we are turned off, and I am sure, after my day's work is over, my feelings must be very much the same as one of the London cab horses. As for Sunday, it is *literally* a day of rest with us, for the greater part of us lay a-bed all day, and even that will hardly take the aches and pains out of our bones and muscles. When I'm done and flung by, of course I must starve."

The next means of inducing a quicker rate of working, and so economizing the number of labourers, is by the *division* and *subdivision of labour*. In perhaps all the skilled work of London, of the better sort, this is more or less the case; it is the case in a much smaller degree in the country.

The nice subdivision makes the operatives perfect adepts in their respective branches, working at them with a greater and a more assured facility than if their care had to be given to the whole work, and in this manner the work is completed in less time, and consequently by fewer hands.

In illustration of the extraordinary increased productiveness induced by the division of labour, I need only cite the well-known cases:—

"It is found," says Mr. Mill, "that the productive power of labour is increased by carrying the separation further and further; by breaking down more and more every process of industry into parts, so that each labourer shall confine himself to an even smaller number of simple operations. And thus, in time, arise those remarkable cases of what is called the division of labour, with which all readers on subjects of this nature are familiar. Adam Smith's illustration from pin-making, though so well-known, is so much to the point, that I will venture once more to transcribe it. 'The business of making a pin is divided into eighteen distinct operations. One man draws out the wire, another straightens it, a third cuts it, a fourth points it, and a fifth grinds it at the top for receiving the head; to make the head requires two or three distinct operations; to put it on, is a peculiar business; to whiten the pins is another; it is even a trade by itself to put them into the paper. I have seen a small manufactory where ten men only were employed, and were some of them, consequently, performed two or three distinct operations. But though they were very poor, and therefore but indifferently accommodated with the necessary machinery, they could, when they exerted themselves, make among them about twelve pounds of pins in a day. There are in a pound upwards of 4000 pins of a middling size.

"'Those ten persons, therefore, could make among them upwards of 48,000 pins in a day. Each person, therefore, making a tenth part of 48,000 pins, might be considered as making 4800 pins in a day. But if they had all wrought separately and independently, and without any of them having been educated to this peculiar business, they certainly could not each of them have made 20, perhaps not one pin in a day.'"

M. Say furnishes a still stronger example of the effects of division of labour, from a not very important branch of industry certainly, the manufacture of playing cards. "It is said by those engaged in the business, that each card, that is, a piece of pasteboard of the size of the hand, before being ready for sale, does not undergo fewer than 70 operations, every one of which might be the occupation of a distinct class of workmen. And if there are not 70 classes of work-people in each card manufactory, it is because the division of labour is not carried so far as it might be; because the same workman is charged with two, three, or four distinct operations. The influence of this distribution of employment is immense. I have seen a card manufactory where thirty workmen produced daily 15,500 cards, being above 500 cards for each labourer; and it may be presumed that if each of these workmen were obliged to perform all the operations himself, even supposing him a practised hand, he would not, perhaps, complete two cards in a day; and the 30 workmen, instead of 15,500 cards, would make only 60."

One great promoter of the decrease of manual labour is to be found in the economy of labour from a very different cause to any I have pointed out as tending to the increase of surplus hands and casual labour, viz., to *the use of machinery*.

In this country the use of machinery has economised the labour both of man and horse to a greater extent than is known in any other land, and that in nearly all departments of commerce or traffic. The total estimated machine power in the kingdom is 600,000,000 of human beings, and this has been all produced within the last century. In agriculture, for example, the threshing of the corn was the peasant's work of the later autumn and of a great part of the winter, until towards the latter part of the last century. The harvest was hardly considered complete until the corn was threshed by the peasants. On the first introduction of the threshing machines, they were demolished in many places by the country labourers, whose rage was excited to find that their winter's work, instead of being regular, had become *casual*.

But the use of these machines is now almost

universal. It would, of course, be the height of absurdity to say that threshing machines could possibly increase the number of threshers, even as the reaping machines cannot possibly increase the number of reapers; their effect is rather to displace the greater number of labourers so engaged, and hence indeed the "economy" of them. It is not known what number of men were, at any time, employed in threshing corn. Their displacement was gradual, and in some of the more remote parts of the provinces, the flails of the threshers may be heard still, but if a threshing machine—for they are of different power—do the work, as has been stated, of six labourers, the economization or displacement of manual labour is at once shown to be the economization and displacement of the whole labour (for a season) of a country side; thus increasing surplus hands.

In other matters—in the unloading vessels by cranes, in *all* branches of manufactures, and even in such minor matters as the grinding of coffee berries, and the cutting and splitting of wood for lucifer matches, an immense amount of manual labour has been minimized, economized, or displaced by steam machinery. On my inquiry into the condition of the London sawyers, I found that the labour of 2000 men had been displaced by the steam saw-mills of the metropolis alone. At one of the largest builder's I saw machines for making mortises and tenons, for sticking mouldings, and, indeed, performing all the operations of the carpenter—one such machine doing the work, perhaps, of a hundred men. I asked the probable influence that such an instrument was likely to have on the men? "Ruin them all," was the laconic reply of the superintendent of the business! Within the last year casks have been made by machinery—a feat that the coopers declared impossible. Wheels, also, have been lately produced by steam. I need, however, as I have so recently touched upon the subject, do no more than call attention to the information I have given (p. 240, vol. ii.) concerning the use of machinery in lieu of human labour. It is there shown that if the public street-sweeping were effected, throughout the metropolis, by the machines, nearly 196 of the 275 manual labourers, now scavaging for the parish contractors, would be thrown out of work, and deprived of 7438*l*., out of their joint earnings, in the year.

It is the fashion of political economists to insist on the general proposition that machinery increases the demand for labour, rather than decreases it; when they write unguardedly, however, they invariably betray a consciousness that the benefits of machinery to manual labourers are not quite so invariable as they would otherwise make out. Here, for instance, is a confession from the pamphlet on "the Employer and Employed," published by the Messrs. Chambers, gentlemen who surely cannot be accused of being averse to economical doctrines. It is true the pamphlet is intended to show the evils of strikes to working men, but it likewise points out the evils of mechanical power to the same class when applied to certain operations.

"Strikes also lead to *the superseding of hand labour by machines*," says this little work. "In 1831, on the occasion of a strike at Manchester, several of the capitalists, afraid of their business being driven to other countries, had recourse to the celebrated machinists, Messrs. Sharp and Co. of Manchester, requesting them to direct the inventive talents of their partner, Mr. Roberts, to the construction of a self-acting mule, in order to emancipate the trade from galling slavery and impending ruin. Under assurances of the most liberal encouragement in the adoption of his invention, Mr. Roberts suspended his professional pursuits as an engineer, and set his fertile genius to construct a spinning automaton. In the course of a few months he produced a machine, called the 'Self-acting Mule,' which, in 1834, was in operation in upwards of 60 factories; *doing the work of the head spinners so much better than they could do it themselves, as to leave them no chance against it.*

"In his work on the 'Philosophy of Manufactures,' Dr. Ure observes on the same subject—'The elegant art of calico-printing, which embodies in its operations the most elegant problems of chemistry, as well as mechanics, had been for a long period the sport of foolish journeymen, who turned the liberal means of comfort it furnished them into weapons of warfare against their employers and the trade itself. They were, in fact, by their delirious combinations, plotting to kill the goose which laid the golden eggs of their industry, or to force it to fly off to a foreign land, where it might live without molestation. In the spirit of Egyptian task-masters, the operative printers dictated to the manufacturers the number and quality of the apprentices to be admitted into the trade, the hours of their own labour, and the wages to be paid them. At length capitalists sought deliverance from this intolerable bondage in the resources of science, and were speedily reinstated in their legitimate dominion of the head over the inferior members. The four-colour and five-colour machines, which now render calico-printing an unerring and expeditious process, are mounted in all great establishments. It was under the high-pressure of the same despotic confederacies, that self-acting apparatus for executing the dyeing and rinsing operations has been devised.'

"The croppers of the West Riding of Yorkshire, and the hecklers or flax-dressers, can unfold 'a tale of wo' on this subject. Their earnings exceeded those of most mechanics; but the frequency of strikes among them, and the irregularities in their hours and times of working, compelled masters to substitute machinery for their manual labour. *Their trades, in consequence, have been in a great measure superseded.*"

It must, then, be admitted that machinery, *in some cases at least*, does displace manual labour, and so tend to produce a surplusage of labourers, even as over-work, Sunday-work, scamping-work, strapping-work, piece-work, minutely-divided work, &c., have the same effect so long as the quantity of work to be done remains unaltered. *The extensibility of the market* is the one circumstance which determines whether the economy of labour produced by these means is a blessing or a curse to the nation. To apply mechanical power, the division of labour, the large system of production, or indeed any other means of enabling a less number of labourers to do the same amount of work *when the quantity of work to be done is limited in its nature*, as, for instance, the threshing of corn, the sawing of wood, &c., is necessarily to make either paupers or criminals of those who were previously honest independent men, living by the exercise of their industry in that particular direction. Economize your labour one-half, in connection with a particular article, and you must sell twice the quantity of that article or displace a certain number of the labourers; that is to say, suppose it requires 400 men to produce 4000 commodities in a given time, then, if you enable 200 men to produce the same quantity in the same time, you must get rid of 8000 commodities, or deprive a certain number of labourers of their ordinary means of living. Indeed, the proposition is almost self-evident, though generally ignored by social philosophers: economize your labour at a greater rate than you expand your markets, and you must necessarily increase your paupers and criminals in precisely the same ratio. "The division of labour," says Mr. Mill, following Adam Smith, "is limited by the extent of the market. If by the separation of pin-making into ten distinct employments 48,000 pins can be made in a day, this separation will only be advisable if the number of accessible consumers is such as to require every day something like 48,000 pins. If there is a demand for only 25,000, the division of labour can be advantageously carried but to the extent which will every day produce that smaller number." Again, as regards the large system of production, the same authority says, "the possibility of substituting the large system of production for the small depends, of course, on the extent of the market. The large system can only be advantageous when a large amount of business is to be done; it implies, therefore, either a populous and flourishing community, or a great opening for exportation." But these are mere glimmerings of the broad incontrovertible principle, that *the economization of labour at a greater rate than the expansion of the markets, is necessarily the cause of surplus labour in a community.*

The effect of machinery in depriving the families of agricultural labourers of their ordinary sources of income is well established. "Those countries," writes Mr. Thornton, "in which the class of agricultural labourers is most depressed, have all one thing in common. Each of them was formerly the seat of a flourishing manufacture carried on by the cottagers at their own homes, which has now decayed or been withdrawn to other situations. Thus, in Buckinghamshire and Bedfordshire, the wives and children of labouring men had formerly very profitable occupation in making lace; during the last war a tolerable lacemaker, working eight hours a day, could easily earn 10s. or 12s. a week; the profits of this employment have been since so much reduced by the use of machinery, that a pillow lacemaker must now work twelve hours daily to earn 2s. 6d. a week."

The last of the conditions above cited, as causing the same or a greater amount of work to be executed with a less quantity of labour, is *the large system of production* Mr. Babbage and Mr. Mill have so well and fully pointed out "the economy of labour" effected in this manner, that I cannot do better than quote from them upon this subject:—

"Even when no additional subdivision of the work," says Mr. Mill, "would follow an enlargement of the operations, there will be good economy in enlarging them to the point at which every person to whom it is convenient to assign a special occupation will have full employment in that occupation." This point is well illustrated by Mr. Babbage:—"If machines be kept working through the 24 hours" [which is evidently the only economical mode of employing them], "it is necessary that some person shall attend to admit the workmen at the time they relieve each other; and whether the porter or other servant so employed admit one person or twenty, his rest will be equally disturbed. It will also be necessary occasionally to adjust or repair the machine; and this can be done much better by a workman accustomed to machine-making than by the person who uses it. Now, since the good performance and the duration of machines depend, to a very great extent, upon correcting every shake or imperfection in their parts as soon as they appear, the prompt attention of a workman resident on the spot will considerably reduce the expenditure arising from the wear and tear of the machinery. But in the case of a single lace-frame, or a single loom, this would be too expensive a plan. Here, then, arises another circumstance, which tends to enlarge the extent of the factory. It ought to consist of such a number of machines as shall occupy the whole time of one workman in keeping them in order. If extended beyond that number the same principle of economy would point out the necessity of doubling or tripling the number of machines, in order to employ the whole time of two or three skilful workmen. Where one portion of the workman's labour consists in the exertion of mere physical force, as in weaving, and in many similar arts, it will soon occur to the manufacturer that, if that part were executed by a steam-engine, the same man might, in the case of weaving, attend to two or more looms at once; and, since we already suppose that one or more operative engineers have been employed, the number of looms may be so arranged that their time shall be fully occupied in keeping the steam-engine and the looms in order.

"Pursuing the same principles, the manufactory becomes gradually so enlarged that the expense of lighting during the night amounts to a considerable sum; and as there are already attached to the establishment persons who are up all night, and can therefore constantly attend to it, and also engineers to make and keep in repair any machinery, the addition of an apparatus for making gas to light the factory leads to a new extension, at the same time that it contributes, by diminishing the expense of lighting and the risk of accidents from fire, to reduce the cost of manufacturing.

"Long before a factory has reached this extent it will have been found necessary to establish an accountant's department, with clerks to pay the workmen, and to see that they arrive at their stated times; and this department must be in communication with the agents who purchase the raw produce, and with those who sell the manufactured article. It will cost these clerks and accountants little more time and trouble to pay a large number of workmen than a small number, to check the accounts of large transactions than of small. If the business doubled itself it would probably be necessary to increase, but certainly not to double, the number either of accountants or of buying and selling agents. *Every increase of business would enable the whole to be carried on with a proportionally smaller amount of labour.* As a general rule, the expenses of a business do not increase by any means proportionally to the quantity of business. Let us take as an example a set of operations which we are accustomed to see carried on by one great establishment—that of the Post Office.

"Suppose that the business, let us say only of the London letter-post, instead of being centralised in a single concern, were divided among five or six competing companies. Each of these would be obliged to maintain almost as large an establishment as is now sufficient for the whole. Since each must arrange for receiving and delivering letters in all parts of the town, each must send letter-carriers into every street, and almost every alley, and this, too, as many times in the day as is now done by the Post Office, if the service is to be as well performed. Each must have an office for receiving letters in every neighbourhood, with all subsidiary arrangements for collecting the letters from the different offices and re-distributing them. I say nothing of the much greater number of superior officers who would be required to check and control the subordinates, implying not only a greater cost in salaries for such responsible officers, but the necessity, perhaps, of being satisfied in many instances with an inferior standard of qualification, and so failing in the object."

But this refers solely to the "large system of business" as applied to purposes of manufacture and distribution. In connection with agriculture there is the same saving of labour effected. "The large farmer," says Mr. Mill, "has some advantage in the article of buildings. It does not cost so much to house a great number of cattle in one building, as to lodge them equally well in several buildings. There is also some advantage in implements. A small farmer is not so likely to possess expensive instruments. But the principal agricultural implements, even when of the best construction, are not expensive. It may not answer to a small farmer to own a threshing machine for the small quantity of corn he has to thresh; but there is no reason why such a machine should not in every neighbourhood be owned in common, or provided by some person to whom the others pay a consideration for its use. The large farmer can make some saving in cost of carriage. There is nearly as much trouble in carrying a small portion of produce to market, as a much greater produce; in bringing home a small, as a much larger quantity of manure, and articles of daily consumption. There is also the greater cheapness of buying things in large quantities."

A short time ago I went into Buckinghamshire to look into the allotment system. And, in one parish of 1800 acres, I found that some years ago there were seventeen farmers who occupied, upon the average, 100 acres each, and who, previous to the immigration of the Irish harvest-men, *constantly* employed six men a-piece, or, in the aggregate, upwards of 100 hands. Now, however, the farmers in the same parish occupy to the extent of 300 acres each, and respectively employ only six men *and a few extra hands at harvest time.* Thus the number of hands employed by this system has been decreased one-half. I learned, moreover, from a clergyman there, who had resided in Wiltshire, that the same thing was going on in that county also; that small farms were giving way to large farms, and that at least half the labourers had been displaced. The agricultural labourers, at the time of taking the last census, were 1,500,000 in number; so that, if this system be generally carried out, there must be 750,000 labourers and their families, or 3,000,000 people, deprived of their living by it.

Sir James Graham, in his evidence before the Committee on Criminal Commitments, has given us some curious particulars as to the decrease of the number of hands required for agricultural purposes, where the large system of production is pursued in place of the small: he has told us how many hands he was enabled to get rid of by these means, the proportion of labour displaced, it will be seen, amounted to about 10 per cent. of the labouring population. In answer to a question relative to the increase of population in his district, he replied:—

"I have myself taken *very strong means to prevent it,* for it so happens that my whole estate came out of lease in the year 1822, after the currency of a lease of fourteen years; and by *consolidation of farms, and the destruction of cottages, I have diminished, upon my own property, the population to the extent of from 300 to 400 souls.*"

"On how many acres?—On about 30,000 acres." [This is at the rate of one in every 100 acres].

"What was the whole extent of population?—It was under 4000 before I reduced it.

"What became of those 300 or 400?—The greater part of them, being small tenants were, enabled to find farms on the estates of other proprietors, who pursued the opposite course of subdividing their estates for the purpose of obtaining higher nominal rents; *others have become day labourers,* and as day labourers, I have reason to know, they are more thriving than they were on my estate as small farmers, subject to a high rent, which their want of capital seldom enabled them to pay; two or three of these families went to America.

"Have you any out of work?—None entirely out of work, some only partially employed; but since the *dispersion of this large mass of population,* the supply of labour has not much exceeded the demand, for *whenever I removed a family, I pulled down the house,* and the parochial jealousy respecting settlements is an ample check on the influx of strangers."

Similar to the influence of the large system of production in its displacement of labourers, as enabling a larger quantity of work to be executed by one establishment with a smaller number of hands than would be required were the amount of work to be divided into a number of smaller establishments,—similar to this mode of economizing labour, is that mode of work which, by altering the produce rather than the mode of production, and by substituting an article that requires less labour for one that required more, gets rid of a large quantity of labour, and, consequently, adds to the surplusage of labourers. An instance of this is in the substitution of pasturage for tillage. "*Plough less and graze more,*" says Sir J. Graham, the great economist of labour, simply because fewer people will be required to attend to the land. But this plan of grazing instead of ploughing was adopted in this country some centuries back, and with what effect to the labourers and the people at large, the following extract from the work of Mr. Thornton, on over-population, will show:—

"The extension of the woollen manufacture was raising the price of wool; and the little attendance which sheep require was an additional motive for causing sheep farming to be preferred to tillage. Arable land, therefore, began to be converted into pasture; and the seemingly-interminable corn fields, which, like those of Germany at this day, probably extended for miles without having their even surface broken by fences or any other visible boundaries, disappeared. After being sown with grass they were surrounded and divided by inclosures, to prevent the sheep from straying, and to do away with the necessity of having shepherds always on the watch. By these changes the quantity of work to be done upon a farm was exceedingly diminished, and most of the servants, whom it had been usual to board and lodge in the manor and farm-houses, were dismissed. This was not all. The married farm-servants were ousted from their cottages, which were pulled down, and their gardens and fields were annexed to the adjoining meadows. The small farmers were treated in the same way, as their leases fell in, *and were sent to join the daily increasing crowd of competitors for work that was daily increasing in quantity.*

"Even freeholders were in some instances ejected from their lands. This social revolution had probably commenced even before the prosperity of the peasantry had reached its climax; but in 1487 it attracted the notice of Parliament, and an Act was passed to restrain its progress; for already it was observed that inclosures were becoming 'more frequent, whereby arable land, *which could not be manured without people and families,* was turned into pasture, which was easily rid by a few herdsmen;' and that 'tenancies for years, lives, and at will, whereupon most of the yeomanry lived, were turned into demesnes'*. In 1533†, An act was passed strongly condemning the practice of 'accumulating' farms, which it was declared had reduced 'a marvellous multitude' of the people to poverty and misery, and left them no alternative but to steal, or to die 'pitifully' of cold and hunger. In this Act it was stated that single farms might be found with flocks of from 10,000 to 20,000 sheep upon them; and it was ordained that no man should keep more than 2000 sheep, except upon his own land, or rent more than two farms.

"Two years later it was enacted that the king should have a moiety of the profits of land converted (subsequently to a date specified) from tillage to pastures, until a suitable house was erected, and the land was restored to tillage. In 1552, a law ‡ was made which required that on all estates as large a quantity of land as had been kept in tillage for four years together at any time since the accession of Henry VIII., should be so continued in tillage. But these, and many subsequent enactments of the same kind, had not the smallest effect in checking the consolidation of farms. We find Roger Ascham, in Queen Elizabeth's reign, lamenting the dispersion of families, the ruin of houses, the breaking up and destruction of 'the noble yeomanry, the honour and strength of England.' Harrison also speaks of towns pulled down for sheep-walks; 'and of the tenements that had fallen either down or into the lord's hands;' or had been 'brought and united together by other men, so that in some one manor, seventeen, eighteen, or twenty houses were shrunk.'§

"'Where have been a great many householders and inhabitants,' says Bishop Latimer, ' there is now but a shepherd and his dog.'∥ And in a curious tract, published in 1581, by one William Stafford, a husbandman is made to exclaim, 'Marry, these inclosures do and undo us all, for they make us pay dearer for our land that we occupy, and causeth that we can have no land to put to tillage; all is taken up for pasture, either for sheep or for grazing of cattle, insomuch that I have known of late a dozen ploughs, within less compass than six miles about me, laid down within this seven years; and where threescore persons or upwards had their livings, now one man, with his cattle, hath all. Those sheep is

---

* Lord Bacon's Hist. of King Henry VII., Works, vol. v. p. 61.
† 25th Henry VIII. cap. 13.
‡ 5 & 6 Edw. VI., cap. 5.
§ Eden's Hist. of the Poor, vol. i. p. 118.
∥ Latimer's Sermons, p. 100.

the cause of all our mischief, for they have driven husbandry out of the country, by which was increased before all kinds of victuals, and now altogether sheep, sheep, sheep.'* While numbers of persons were thus continually driven from their homes, and deprived of their means of livelihood, we need not be at a loss to account for the increase of vagrancy, without ascribing it to the increase of population."

As an instance, within our time, of the same mode of causing a surplusage of labourers, and so adding to the quantity of casual labour in the kingdom, viz., by the extension of pasturage and consequent diminution of tillage, we may cite the "clearances," as they were called, which took place, some few years back, in the Highlands of Scotland. "It is only within the last few years," says the author above quoted, "that the strathes and glens of Sutherland have been *cleared of their inhabitants, and that the whole country has been converted into one immense sheepwalk*, over which the traveller may proceed for 40 miles together without seeing a tree or a stone wall, or anything, but a heath dotted with sheep and lambs † . . . . . . The example of Sutherland is imitated in the neighbouring counties. During the last four years *some hundreds of families* have been 'weeded' out of Ross-shire, and nearly 400 more have received notice to quit next year. Similar notice has been given to 34 families in Cromarty, and only the other day eighteen families, who were living in peace and comfort, in Glencalvie, in Ross-shire, were expelled from the farms occupied for ages by themselves and their forefathers, to make room for sheep." And still we are told to "*plough less and graze more!*"

We now come to the last-mentioned of the circumstances inducing a surplusage of labourers, and, consequently, augmenting the amount of casual labour throughout the kingdom, viz., by *altering the mode of hiring the labourers*. At page 236 of the present volume, I have said, in connection with this part of the subject,—

"Formerly the mode of hiring farm-labourers was by the year, so that the employer was bound to maintain the men when unemployed. But now weekly hirelings and even journey-work, or hiring by the day, prevail, and the labourers being paid mere subsistence-money only when wanted are necessitated to become either paupers or thieves when their services are no longer required. It is, moreover, this change from yearly to weekly and daily hirings, and the consequent discarding of men when no longer wanted, that has partly caused the immense mass of surplus labourers, who are continually vagabondizing through the country, begging or stealing as they go—men for whom there is but some two or three weeks' work (harvesting, hop-picking, and the like) throughout the year."

Blackstone, in treating of the laws relating to master and servant (the greater part of the farm labourers or farm servants, as they were then called, being included under the latter head), tells us at page 425 of his first volume—

"The first sort of servants, acknowledged by the laws of England, are MENIAL SERVANTS; so called from being *inter mœnia*, or domestic. The contract between them and their masters arises upon the hiring. If the hiring be generally, without any particular *time limited*, the law construes it to be a *hiring for a year* (Co. Lit. 42); upon a principle of natural equity, that the servant shall serve, and the master maintain him, throughout all the revolutions of the respective seasons, as well when *there is work to be* done, *as when there is not*."

Mr. Thornton says, "until recently it had been common for farm servants, even when married and living in their own cottages, to take their meals with their master; and, what was of more consequence, in every farm-house, many unmarried servants, of both sexes, were lodged, as well as boarded. The latter, therefore, even if ill paid, might be tolerably housed and fed, and many of them fared, no doubt, much better than they could have done if they had been left to provide for themselves, with treble their actual wages."

Formerly throughout the kingdom—and it is a custom *still* prevalent in some parts, more especially in the north—single men and women seeking engagements as farm-servants, congregated at what were called the "Hirings," held usually on the three successive market days, which were nearest to May-day and Martinmas-day. The hiring was thus at two periods of the year, but the engagement was usually for the twelvemonth. By the concurrent consent, however, of master and servant, when the hiring took place, either side might terminate it at the expiration of the six months, by giving due notice; or a further hiring for a second twelvemonth could be legally effected without the necessity of again going to the hirings. The servants, even before their term of service had expired, could attend a hiring (generally held under the authority of the town's charter) as a matter of right; the master and mistress having no authority to prevent them. The Market Cross was the central point for the holding of the hirings, and the men and women, the latter usually the most numerous, stood in rows around the cross. The terms being settled, the master or mistress gave the servant "a piece of money," known as a "god's penny" (the "handsel penny"), the offer and acceptance of this god's penny being a legal ratification of the agreement, without any other step. In the old times such engagements had almost always (as shown in the term "God's penny") a character of religious obligation. At the earliest period, the hirings were held in the church-yards; afterwards by the Market Cross.

I have spoken of this matter more in the past than the present tense, for the system is greatly changed as regards the male farm-servant, though little as regards the female. Now the male farm-labourers, instead of being hired for a specific term, are more generally hired by week, by job, or by day; indeed, even "half-a-day's" work is known. At one period it was merely the

---

* Pictorial History of England, vol. ii. p. 900.
† Reports of the "Commissioner" of the *Times* Newspaper, in June, 1845.

married country labourers, residing in their own cottages, who were temporarily engaged, but it is now the general body, married and unmarried, old and young, with a few exceptions. Formerly the farmer was bound to find work for six or twelve months (for both terms existed) for his hired labourers. If the land did not supply it, still the man must be maintained, and be paid his full wages when due. By such a provision, the labour and wage of the hired husbandman were regular and rarely *casual;* but this arrangement is now seldom entered into, and the hired husbandman's labour is consequently generally casual and rarely regular. This principle of hiring labourers only for so long as they are wanted, as contradistinguished from the "*principle of natural equity*," spoken of by Blackstone, which requires that "the servant shall serve and the master maintain him *throughout all the revolutions of the respective seasons, as well when there is work to be done as when there is not,*" has been the cause, perhaps, of more casual labour and more pauperism and crime, in this country, than, perhaps, any other of the antecedents before mentioned. The harvest is now collected solely by casual labourers, by a horde of squalid immigrants, or the tribe of natural and forced vagabonds who are continually begging or stealing their way throughout the country; our hops are picked, our fruit and vegetables gathered by the same precarious bands—wretches who, perhaps, obtain some three months' harvest labour in the course of the year. The ships at our several ports are discharged by the same "*casual hands,*" who may be seen at our docks scrambling like hounds for the occasional bit of bread that is vouchsafed to them; there numbers loiter throughout the day, even on the chance of *an hour's employment;* for the term of hiring has been cut down to the finest possible limits, so that the labourer may not be paid for even a second longer than he is wanted. And since he gets only bare subsistence money when employed, "What," we should ask ourselves, "*must* be his lot when unemployed?"

I now come to consider the circumstances causing an undue increase of the labourers in a country. Thus far we have proceeded on the assumption that both the quantity of work to be done and the number of hands to do it remained stationary, and we have seen that by the mere alteration of the time, rate, and mode of working, a vast amount of surplus, and, consequently, casual labour may be induced in a community. We have now to ascertain how, still assuming the quantity of work to remain unaltered, the same effect may be brought about by an undue *increase of the number of labourers.*

There are many means by which the number of labourers may be increased besides that of a positive increase of the people. These are—

1. By the undue increase of apprentices.
2. By drafting into the ranks of labour those who should be otherwise engaged, as women and children.
3. By the importation of labourers from abroad.
4. By the migration of country labourers to towns, and so overcrowding the market in the cities.
5. By the depression of other trades.
6. By the undue increase of the people themselves.

Each and every of the first-mentioned causes are as effective a circumstance for the promotion of surplus labour, as even the positive extension of the population of the country.

Let me begin with the undue increase of a trade by means of *apprentices.*

This is, perhaps, one of the chief aids to the cheap system. For it is principally by apprentice labour that the better masters, as well as workmen, are undersold, and the skilled labourer consequently depressed to the level of the unskilled. But the great evil is, that the cheapening of goods by this means causes an undue increase in the trade. The apprentices grow up and become labourers, and so the trade is glutted with workmen, and casual labour is the consequence.

This apprentice system is the great bane of the printer's trade. Country printers take an undue number of boys to help them cheap; these lads grow up, and then, finding wages in the provinces depressed through this ·system of apprentice labour, they flock to the towns, and so tend to glut the labour market, and consequently to increase the number of casual hands.

One cause of the increased surplus and casual labour in such trades as dressing-case, work-box, writing-desk-making and other things in the fancy cabinet trade (among the worst trades even in Spitalfields and Bethnal Green), shoemaking, and especially of women and children's shoes, is the taking of many apprentices by small masters (supplying the great warehouses). As journey-work is all but unknown in the slop fancy cabinet trade, an apprentice, when he has "served his time," must start on his own account in the same wretched way of business, or become a casual labourer in some unskilled avocation, and this is one way in which the hands surely, although gradually, increase beyond the demand. It is the same with the general slop cabinet-maker's trade in the same parts. The small masters supply the "slaughter-houses," the linen-drapers, &c., who sell cheap furniture; they work in the quickest and most scamping manner, and do more work (which is nearly all done on the chance of sale), as they must confine themselves to one branch. The slop chair-makers cannot make tables, nor the slop table-makers, chairs; nor the cheffonier and drawer-makers, bedsteads; for they have not been taught. Even if they knew the method, and *could* accomplish other work, the want of practice would compel them to do it slowly, and the slop mechanic can never afford to work slowly. Such classes of little masters, then, to meet the demand for low-priced furniture, rear their sons to the business, and frequently take apprentices, to whom they pay small amounts. The hands so trained (as in the former instances) are not skilled enough to work for the honourable trade, so that they can only adopt the course pursued by their parents, or masters, before them. Hence a rapid, although again gradual, increase of surplus hands; or hence a resort to some unskilled labour, to be wrought casually. This happens too, but in a smaller degree, in trades which are not slop, from the same cause. Concerning the *apprentice system* in the boot and shoe trade, when making my inquiries into the condition of the London workmen, I received the following statements:—

"My employer had seven apprentices when I was with him; of these, two were parish apprentices (I was one), and the other five from the Refuge for the Destitute, at Hoxton. With each Refuge boy he got 5*l*. and three suits of clothes, and a kit (tools). With the parish boys of Coventgarden and St. Andrew's, Holborn, he got 5*l*. and two suits of clothes, reckoning what the boy wore as one. My employer was a journeyman, and by having all us boys he was able to get up work very cheap, though he received good wages for it. We boys had no allowance in money, only board, lodging, and clothing. The board was middling, the lodging was too, and there was nothing to complain about in the clothing. He was severe in the way of flogging. I ran away six times myself, but was forced to go back again, as I had no money and no friend in the world. When I first ran away I complained to Mr. ——— the magistrate, and he was going to give me six weeks. He said it would do me good; but Mr. ——— interfered, and I was let go. I don't know what he was going to give me six weeks for, unless it was for having a black eye that my master had given me with the stirrup. Of the seven only one served his time out. He let me off two years before my time was up, as we couldn't agree. The mischief of taking so many apprentices is this:—The master gets money with them from the parish, and can feed them much as he likes as to quality and quantity; and if they run away soon, the master's none the worse, for he's got the money; and so boys are sent out to turn vagrants when they run away, as such boys have no friends. Of us seven boys (at the wages our employer got) one could earn 19*s*., another 15*s*., another 12*s*., another 10*s*., and the rest not less than 8*s*. each, for all worked sixteen hours a day—that's 4*l*. 8*s*. a week for the seven, or 225*l*. 10*s*. a year. You must recollect I reckon this on nearly the best wages in the women's trade. My employer you may call a sweater, and he made money fast, though he drank a good deal. We seldom saw him when he was drunk; but he *did* pitch into us when he was getting sober. Look how easily such a man with apprentices can undersell others when he wants to work as cheap as possible for the great slop warehouses. They serve haberdashers so cheap that oft enough it's starvation wages for the same shops."

Akin to the system of using a large number of apprentices is that of *employing boys and girls* to displace the work of men, at the less laborious parts of the trade.

"It is probable," said a working shoemaker to me, "that, independent of apprentices, 200 additional hands are added to our already overburdened trade yearly. Sewing boys soon learn the use of the knife. Plenty of poor men will offer to finish them for a pound and a month's work; and men, for a few shillings and a few weeks' work, will teach other boys to sew. There are many of the wives of chamber-masters teach girls entirely to make children's work for a pound and a few months' work, and there are many in Bethnal-green who have learnt the business in this way. These teach some other members of their families, and then actually set up in business in opposition to those who taught them, and in cutting offer their work for sale at a much lower rate of profit; and shopkeepers in town and country, having circulars sent to solicit custom, will have their goods from a warehouse that will serve them cheapest; then the warehouseman will have them cheap from the manufacturer; and he in his turn cuts down the wages of the workpeople, who fear to refuse offers at the warehouse price, knowing the low rate at which chambermasters will serve the warehouse."

As in all trades where lowness of wages is the rule, the boy system of labour prevails among the cheap cabinet-workers. It prevails, however, among the garret-masters, by very many of them having one, two, three or four youths to help them, and so the number of boys thus employed through the whole trade is considerable. This refers principally to the general cabinet trade. In the fancy trade the number is greater, as the boys' labour is more readily available; but in this trade the greatest number of apprentices is employed by such warehousemen as are manufacturers, as some at the East end are, or rather by the men that they constantly keep at work. Of these men, one has now eight and another fourteen boys in his service, some apprenticed, some merely " engaged " and dischargeable at pleasure. A sharp boy, in six or eight months, becomes "handy;" but four out of five of the workmen thus brought up can do nothing well but their own particular branch, and that only well as far as celerity in production is considered.

It is these boys who are put to make, or as a master of the better class distinguished to me, not to *make* but to put together, ladies' workboxes at 5*d*. a piece, the boy receiving 2½*d*. a box. 'Such boxes,' said another workman, 'are nailed together; there's no dove-tailing, nothing of what I call *work*, or workmanship, as you say, about them, but the deal's nailed together, and the veneer's dabbed on, and if the deal's covered, why the thing passes. The worst of it is, that people don't understand either good work or good wood. Polish them up and they look well. Besides—and that's another bad thing, for it encourages bad work—there's no stress on a lady's work-box, as on a chair or a sofa, and so bad work lasts far too long, though not half so long as good; in solids especially, if not in veneers."

To such a pitch is this demand for children's labour carried, that there is a market in Bethnal-green, where boys and girls stand twice a week to be hired as binders and sewers. Hence it will be easily understood that it is impossible for the skilled and grown artizan to compete with the labour of mere children, who are thus literally brought into the market to undersell him!

Concerning this market for boys and girls, in Bethnal-green, I received, during my inquiries into the boot and shoe trade, the following statements from shopkeepers on the spot:—

"Mr. H—— has lived there sixteen years. The market-days are Monday and Tuesday mornings, from seven to nine. The ages of persons who assemble there vary from ten to twenty, and they are often of the worst character, and a decideded nuisance to the inhabitants. A great many of both sexes congregate together, and most market days there are three females to one male. They consist of sewing boys, shoe-binders, winders for weavers, and girls for all kinds of slop needlework, girls for domestic work, nursing children, &c. No one can testify, for a fact, that they (the females) are prostitutes; but, by their general conduct, they are fit for anything. The market, some years since, was held at the top of Abbey-street; but, on account of the nuisance, it was removed to the other end of Abbey-street. When the schools were built, the nuisance became so intolerable that it was removed to a railway arch in White-street, Bethnal-green. There are two policemen on market mornings to keep order, but my informant says they require four to maintain anything like subjection."

But *family work, or the conjoint labour of a workman's wife and children*, is an equally extensive cause of surplus and casual labour.

A small master, working, perhaps, upon goods to be supplied at the lowest rates to wholesale warehousemen, will often contribute to this result by the way in which he brings up his children. It is less expensive to him to teach them his own business, and he may even reap a profit from their labour, than to have them brought up to some other calling. I met with an instance of this in an inquiry among the toy-makers. A maker of common toys brought up five children to his own trade, for boys and girls can be made useful in such labour at an early age. His business fell off rapidly, which he attributed to the great and numerous packages of cheap toys imported from Germany, Holland, and France, after the lowering of the duty by Sir Robert Peel's tariff. The chief profit to the toy-maker was derived from the labour, as the material was of trifling cost. He found, on the change in his trade, that he could not employ all his family. His fellow tradesmen, he said, were in the same predicament; and thus surplus hands were created, so leading to casualty in labour.

"The system which has, I believe, the worst effect on the women's trade in the boot and shoe business throughout England is," I said in the *Morning Chronicle*, "chamber-mastering. There are between 300 and 400 chamber-masters. Commonly the man has a wife, and three or four children, ten years old or upwards. The wife cuts out the work for the binders, the husband does the knife-work, the children sew with uncommon rapidity. The husband, when the work is finished at night, goes out with it, though wet and cold, and perhaps hungry—his wife and children waiting his return. He returns sometimes, having sold his work at cost price, or not cleared 1s. 6d. for the day's labour of himself and family. In the winter, by this means, the shopkeepers and warehouses can take the advantage of the chamber-master, buying the work at their own price. By this means haberdashers' shops are supplied with boots, shoes, and slippers; they can sell women's boots at 1s. 9d. per pair; shoes, 1s. 3d. per pair; children's, 6d., 8d., and 9d. per pair, getting a good profit, having bought them of the poor chamber-master for almost nothing, and he glad to sell them at any price, late at night, his children wanting bread, and he having walked about for hours, in vain trying to get a fair price for them; thus, women and children labour as well as husbands and fathers, and, with their combined labours, they only obtain a miserable living."

The labour of the wife, and indeed the whole family—family work, as it is called—is attended with the same evil to a trade, introducing a large supply of fresh hands to the labour market, and so tending to glut with workpeople each trade into which they are introduced, and thus to increase the casual labour, and decrease the earnings of the whole.

"The only means of escape from the inevitable poverty," I said in the same letters, "which sooner or later overwhelms those in connection with the cheap shoe trade, seems to the workmen to be by the employment of his whole family as soon as his children are able to be put to the trade—and yet this only increases the very depression that he seeks to avoid. I give the statement of such a man residing in the suburbs of London, and working with three girls to help him:—

"'I have known the business,' he said, 'many years, but was not brought up to it. I took it up because my wife's father was in the trade, and taught me. I was a weaver originally, but it is a bad business, and I have been in this trade seventeen years. Then I had only my wife and myself able to work. At that time my wife and I, by hard work, could earn 1l. a week; on the same work we could not now earn 12s. a week. As soon as the children grew old enough the falling off in the wages compelled us to put them to work one by one—as soon as a child could make threads. One began to do that between eight and nine. I have had a large family, and with very hard work too. We have had to lie on straw oft enough. Now, three daughters, my wife, and myself work together, in chamber-mastering; the whole of us may earn, one week with another, 28s. a week, and out of that I have eight to support. Out of that 28s. I have to pay for grindery and candles, which cost me 1s. a week the year through. I now make children's shoes for the wholesale houses and anybody. About two years ago I travelled from Thomas-street, Bethnal-green, to Oxford-street, "on the hawk." I then positively had nothing in my inside, and in Holborn I had to lean against a house, through weakness from hunger. I was compelled, as I could sell nothing at that end of the town, to walk down to Whitechapel at ten at night. I went into a shop near Mile-end turnpike, and the same articles (children's patent leather shoes) that I received 8s. a dozen for from the wholesale houses, I was compelled to sell to the shopkeeper for 6s. 6d. This is a very frequent case—very frequent—with persons circumstanced as I am, and so trade is injured and only some hard man gains by it.'"

Here is the statement of a worker at "fancy cabinet" work on the same subject:—

"The most on us has got large families. We put the children to work as soon as we can. My little girl began about six, but about eight or nine is the usual age." "*Oh, poor little things,*" *said the wife,* "*they are obliged to begin the very minute they can use their fingers at all.*" "The most of the cabinet-makers of the East end have from five to six in family, and they are generally all at work for them. The small masters mostly marry when they are turned of 20. You see our trade's coming to such a pass, that unless a man has children to help him he can't live at all. *I've worked more than a month together, and the longest night's rest I've had has been an hour and a quarter; aye, and I've been up three nights a week besides.* I've had my children lying ill, and been obliged to wait on them into the bargain. You see, we couldn't live if it wasn't for the labour of our children, though it makes 'em—poor little things!—old people long afore they are growed up."

"Why, I stood at this bench," said the wife, "with my child, only ten years of age, from four o'clock on Friday morning till ten minutes past seven in the evening, without a bit to eat or drink. I never sat down a minute from the time I began till I finished my work, and then I went out to sell what I had done. I walked all the way from here [Shoreditch] down to the Lowther Arcade, to get rid of the articles." *Here she burst out in a violent flood of tears, saying,* "*Oh, sir, it is hard to be obliged to labour from morning till night as we do, all of us, little ones and all, and yet not be able to live by it either.*"

"And you see the worst of it is, this here children's labour is of such value now in our trade, that there's more brought into the business every year, so that it's really for all the world *like breeding slaves.* Without my children I don't know how we should be able to get along." "There's that little thing," said the man, pointing to the girl ten years of age before alluded to, as she sat at the edge of the bed, "why she works regularly every day from six in the morning till ten at night. She never goes to school. We can't spare her. There's schools enough about here for a penny a week, but we could not afford to keep her without working. If I'd ten more children I should be obliged to employ them all the same way, and there's hundreds and thousands of children now slaving at this business. There's the M——'s; they have a family of eight, and the youngest to the oldest of all works at the bench; and the oldest ain't fourteen. I'm sure, of the 2500 small masters in the cabinet line, you may safely say that 2000 of them, at the very least, has from five to six in family, *and that's upwards of* 12,000 *children that's been put to the trade since prices has come down.* Twenty years ago I don't think there was a child at work in our business; and I am sure there is not a small master now whose whole family doesn't assist him. But what I want to know is, what's to become of the 12,000 children when they're growed up, and come regular into the trade? Here are all my young ones growing up without being taught anything but a business that I know they must starve at."

In answer to my inquiry as to what dependence he had in case of sickness, "Oh, bless you," he said, "there's nothing but the parish for us. I *did* belong to a Benefit Society about four years ago, but I couldn't keep up my payments any longer. I was in the society above five-and-twenty year, and then was obliged to leave it after all. I don't know of one as belongs to any Friendly Society, and I don't think there is a man as can afford it in our trade now. They must all go to the workhouse when they're sick or old."

The following is from a journeyman tailor, concerning the employment of women in his trade:—

"When I first began working at this branch, there were but very few females employed in it: a few white waistcoats were given out to them, under the idea that women would make them cleaner than men—and so indeed they can. But since the last five years the sweaters have employed females upon cloth, silk, and satin waistcoats as well, and before that time the idea of a woman making a cloth waistcoat would have been scouted. But since the increase of the puffing and the sweating system, masters and sweaters have sought everywhere for such hands as would do the work below the regular ones. Hence the wife has been made to compete with the husband, and the daughter with the wife: they all learn the waistcoat business, and must all get a living. If the man will not reduce the price of his labour to that of the female, why he must remain unemployed; and if the full-grown woman will not take the work at the same price as the young girl, why she must remain without any. The female hands, I can confidently state, have been sought out and introduced to the business by the sweaters, from a desire on their part continually to ferret out hands who will do the work cheaper than others. The effect that this continual reduction has had upon me is this: Before the year 1844 I could live comfortably, and keep my wife and children (I had five in family) by my own labour. My wife then attended to her domestic and family duties; but since that time, owing to the reduction in prices, she has been compelled to resort to her needle, as well as myself, for her living." [On the table was a bundle of crape and bombazine ready to be made up into a dress.] "I cannot afford now to let her remain idle—that is, if I wish to live, and keep my children out of the streets, and pay my way. My wife's earnings are, upon an average, 8s. per week. She makes dresses. I never would teach her to make waistcoats, because I knew the introduction of female hands had been the ruin of my trade. With the labour of myself and wife now I can only earn 32s. a week, and six years ago I could make my 36s. If I had a daughter I should be obliged to make her work as well, and then probably, with the labour of the three of us, we could make up at the week's end as much money, as, up to 1844, I could get by my own single hands. My wife, since she took to dressmaking, has become sickly from over-exertion. Her work, and her domestic and family duties altogether, are too much for her. Last night I was up all night with her, and was compelled to call in a female to attend her as well. The over-exertion now necessary for us to maintain a decent appearance, has so ruined her constitution that she is not the same woman as she was. In fact, ill as she is, she has been compelled to rise from her bed to finish a mourning-dress against time, and I myself have been obliged to give her a helping-hand, and turn to at women's work in the same manner as the women are turning to at men's work."

"The cause of the serious decrease in our trade," said another tailor to me, "is the employment given to workmen at their own homes; or, in other words, to the 'sweaters.' The sweater is the greatest evil to us; as the sweating system increases the number of hands to an almost incredible extent—wives, sons, daughters, and extra women, all working 'long days'—that is, labouring from sixteen to eighteen hours per day, and Sundays as well. I date the decrease in the wages of the workman from the introduction of piece-work and giving out garments to be made off the premises of the master; for the effect of this was, that the workman making the garment, knowing that the master could not tell whom he got to do his work for him, employed women and children to help him, and paid them little or nothing for their labour. This was the beginning of the sweating system. The workmen gradually became transformed from journeymen into 'middlemen,' living by the labour of others. Employers soon began to find that they could get garments made at a less sum than the regular price, and those tradesmen who were anxious to force their trade, by underselling their more honourable neighbours, readily availed themselves of this means of obtaining cheap labour. The consequence was, that the sweater sought out where he could get the work done the cheapest, and so introduced a fresh stock of hands into the trade. Female labour, of course, could be had cheaper than male, and the sweater readily availed himself of the services of women on that account. Hence the males who had formerly been employed upon the garments were thrown out of work by the females, and obliged to remain unemployed, unless they would reduce the price of their work to that of the women. It cannot, therefore, be said that the reduction of prices originally arose from there having been more workmen than there was work for them to do. There was no superabundance of hands until female labour was generally introduced—and even if the workmen had increased 25 per cent. more than what they were twenty years back, still that extra number of hands would be required now to make the same number of garments, owing to the work put into each article being at least one-fourth more than formerly. So far from the trade being over-stocked with male hands, if the work were confined to the men or the masters' premises, there would not be sufficient hands to do the whole."

According to the last Census (1841, G.B.), out of a population of 18,720,000 the proportions of the people occupied and unoccupied were as follows:—

Occupied	7,800,000
Unoccupied (including women and children) , . . .	10,920,000

Of those who were occupied the following were the proportions:—

Engaged in productive employments*	5,350,000
Engaged in non-productive employments	2,450,000

Of those who were engaged in productive employments, the proportion (in round numbers) ran as follows:—

Men	3,785,000
Women	660,000
Boys and girls . . .	905,000

Here, then, we find nearly one-fifth, or 20 per cent., of our producers to be boys and girls, and upwards of 10 per cent. to be women. Such was the state of things in 1841. In order to judge of the possible and probable condition of the labour market of the country, if this introduction of women and children into the ranks of the labourers be persisted in, let us see what were the proportions of the 10,920,000 men, women, and children who ten years ago still remained unoccupied among us. The ratio was as follows:—

Men . . .	275,000
Women . . .	3,570,000
Boys and girls . . .	7,075,000

Here the unoccupied men are about 5 per cent. of the whole, the children nearly two-thirds, and the wives about one-third. Now it appears that out of say 19,000,000 people, 8,000,000 were, in 1841, occupied, and by far the greater number, 11,000,000, unoccupied.

Who were the remaining eleven millions, and what were they doing? They, of course, consisted principally of the unemployed wives and children of the eight millions of people before specified, three millions and a half of the number

---

* I have here included those engaged in Trade and Commerce, and employers as well as the employed among the *producers*.

being females of twenty years of age and upwards, and seven millions being children of both sexes under twenty. Of these children, four millions, according to the "age abstract," were under ten years, so that we may fairly assume that, at the time of taking the last census, *there were very nearly seven millions of wives and children of a workable age still unoccupied.* Let us suppose, then, that these seven millions of people are brought in competition with the five million producers. What is to be the consequence? If the labour market be overstocked at present with only five millions of people working for the support of nineteen millions (I speak according to the Census of 1841), what would it be if another seven millions were to be dragged into it? And if wages are low now, and employment is precarious on account of this, what will not both work and pay sink to when the number is again increased, and the people clamouring for employment are at least treble what they are at present? When the wife has been taught to compete for work with the husband, and son and daughter to undersell their own father, what will be the state of our labour market then?

But the labour of wives, and children, and apprentices, is not the only means of glutting a particular trade with hands. There is another system becoming every day more popular with our enterprising tradesmen, and this is the *importation of foreign labourers.* In the cheap tailoring this is made a regular practice. Cheap labour is regularly imported, not only from Ireland (the wives of sweaters making visits to the Emerald Isle for the express purpose), but small armies of working tailors, ready to receive the lowest pittance, are continually being shipped into this country. That this is no exaggeration let the following statement prove:—

"I am a native of Pesth, having left Hungary about eight years ago. By the custom of the country I was compelled to travel three years in foreign parts, before I could settle in my native place. I went to Paris, after travelling about in the different countries of Germany. I stayed in Paris about two years. My father's wish was that I should visit England, and I came to London in June, 1847. I first worked for a West end show shop—not *directly* for them—but through the person who is their middleman getting work done at what rates he could for the firm, and obtaining the prices they allowed for making the garments. I once worked four days and a half for him, finding my own trimmings, &c., for 9s. For this my employer would receive 12s. 6d. He then employed 190 hands; he *has* employed 300. Many of those so employed set their wives, children, and others to work, some employing as many as five hands this way. The middleman keeps his carriage, and will give fifty guineas for a horse. I became unable to work from a pain in my back, from long sitting at my occupation. The doctor told me not to sit much, and so, as a countryman of mine was doing the same, I employed hands, making the best I could of their labour. I have now four young women (all Irish girls) so employed. Last week one of them received 4s., another 4s. 2d., the other two 5s. each. They find their board and lodging, but I find them a place to work in, a small room, the rent of which I share with another tailor, who works on his own account. There are not so many Jews come over from Hungary or Germany as from Poland. The law of travelling three years brings over many, but not more than it did. The revolutions have brought numbers this year and last. They are Jew tailors flying from Russian and Prussian Poland to avoid the conscription. I never knew any of these Jews go back again. *There is a constant communication among the Jews, and when their friends in Poland, and other places, learn they are safe in England, and in work and out of trouble, they come over too. I worked as a journeyman in Pesth, and got 2s. 6d. a week, my board and washing, and lodging, for my labour.* We lived well, everything being so cheap. The Jews come in the greatest number about Easter. They try to work their way here, most of them. Some save money here, but they never go back; if they leave England it is to go to America."

The labour market of a particular place, however, comes to be overstocked with hands, not only from the introduction of an inordinate number of apprentices and women and children into the trade, as well as the importation of workmen from abroad, but the same effect is produced by *the migration of country labourers to towns.* This, as I have before said, is specially the case in the printer's and carpenter's trades, where the cheap provincial work is executed chiefly by apprentices, who, when their time is up, flock to the principal towns, in the hopes of getting better wages than can be obtained in the country, owing to the prevalence of the apprentice system of work in those parts. The London carpenters suffer greatly from what are called "improvers," who come up to town to get perfected in their art, and work for little or no wages. The work of some of the large houses is executed mainly in this way; that of Mr. Myers was, for instance, against whom the men lately struck.

But the unskilled labour of towns suffers far more than the skilled from the above cause.

The employment of unskilled labourers in towns is being constantly rendered more casual by the migrations from the country parts. The peasants, owing to the insufficiency of their wages, and the wretchedness of their dwellings and diet, in Wilts, Somerset, Dorset, and elsewhere, leave their native places without regret, and swell the sum of unskilled labour in towns. This is shown by the increase of population far beyond the excess of births over deaths in those counties where there are large manufacturing or commercial towns; whilst in purely agricultural counties the increase of population does not keep pace with the excess of births. "Thus in Lancashire," writes Mr. Thornton, in his work on Over-Population, "the increase of the population in the ten years ending in 1841, was 330,210, and in Cheshire, 60,919; whilst the excess of births was only 150,150 in the former, and 28,000 in the latter. In particular towns the contrast is still more striking. In Liverpool and Bristol the annual deaths actually exceed the births, so that these towns are only saved from depopulation by their rural recruits, yet the first increased the number of its inhabitants in ten years by more than one-third, and the other by more than one-sixth. In Manchester, the annual excess of births could only have added 19,390 to the population between 1831 and 1841; the actual increase was 68,375. The number of emigrants (immigrants) into Birmingham, during the same period, may, in the same way, be estimated at 40,000; into Leeds, at 8000; into the metropolis, at 130,000. On the other hand, in Dorset, Somerset, and Devon, the actual addition to the population, in the same decennial period, was only 15,491, 31,802, and 39,253 respectively; although the excess of births over deaths in the same counties was about 20,000, 38,600, and 48,700."

The unskilled labour market suffers, again, from the depression of almost any branch of skilled labour; for whatever branch of labour be depressed, and men so be deprived of a sufficiency of employment, one especial result ensues—the unskilled labour market is glutted. The skilled labourer, a tailor, for instance, may be driven to work for the wretched pittance of an East end slop-tailor, but he cannot "turn his hand" to any other description of skilled labour. He cannot say, " I will make billiard-tables, or book-cases, or boots, or razors;" so that there is no resource for him but in unskilled labour. The Spitalfields weavers have often sought dock labour; the turners of the same locality, whose bobbins were once in great demand by the silk-winders, and for the fringes of upholsterers, have done the same; and in this way the increase of casual labour increases the poverty of the poor, and so tends directly to the increase of pauperism.

We have now seen what a vast number of surplus labourers may be produced by an extension of time, rate, or mode of working, as well as by the increase of the hands, by other means than by *the increase of the people themselves*. If, however, we are increasing our workers at a greater rate than we are increasing the means of work, the excess of workmen must, of course, remain unemployed. But are we doing this?

Let us test the matter on the surest data. In the first instance let us estimate the increase of population, both according to the calculations of the late Mr. Rickman and the returns of the several censuses. The first census, I may observe, was taken in 1801, and has been regularly continued at intervals of ten years. The table first given refers to the population of England and Wales:—

INCREASE IN THE POPULATION OF ENGLAND AND WALES.

Years.	Population, England and Wales.	Numerical Increase.	Increase per Cent.	Annual Increase per cent.	Increase per Cent. in 50 Years, from 1801 to 1851 = 101.	Annual average increase per Cent., 1·41.
*1570	4,038,879					
1600	4,811,718	772,839	19	0·6		
1630	5,601,517	789,799	16	0·5		
1670	5,773,646	172,129	3	0·08		
1700	6,045,008	271,362	5	0·2		
1750	6,517,035	472,027	8	0·2		
†1801	8,892,536	2,375,501	37	0·7		
1811	10,164,068	1,271,532	14	1·4		
1821	11,999,322	1,835,250	18	1·8		
1831	13,896,797	1,897,475	16	1·6		
1841	15,914,148	1,982,489	14	1·4		
1851	17,922,768	1,968,341	13	1·3		

* The amount of the population from 1570 to 1750, as here given, is copied from Rickman's tables, as published by the Registrar-General.

† The population at the decennial term, as here given, is the amended calculation of the Registrar-General, as given in the new census tables.

INCREASE IN THE POPULATION OF SCOTLAND.

Years.	Population, Scotland.	Numerical Increase.	Increase per Cent.	Annual Increase per Cent.	Increase per Cent. in 50 years, from 1801 to 1851 = 78.	Annual rate of Increase per Cent., 1·16.
*1755	1,265,380					
†1801	1,608,420	343,040	27	0·6		
1811	1,805,864	197,444	12	1·3		
1821	2,091,512	285,657	16	1·6		
1831	2,364,386	272,865	13	1·3		
1841	2,620,184	255,798	11	1·1		
1851	2,870,784	245,237	10	1·0		

* From returns furnished by the clergy.

† The returns here cited are copied from those given by the Registrar-General in the new census.

INCREASE IN THE POPULATION OF IRELAND.

Years.	Population, Ireland.	Numerical Increase and Decrease. † denotes Increase. * ,, Decrease.	Increase and Decrease per Cent.	Annual rate of Increase and Decrease per Cent.	Total Decrease in 30 Years, from 1821 to 1851 = 4 per Cent.	Annual rate of Decrease for 30 Years, from 1821 to 1851, ·1 per Cent.
1731[a]	2,010,221					
1754[b]	2,372,634	† 362,413	†19			
1767	2,544,276	† 171,642	† 7			
1777	2,690,556	† 146,280	† 6			
1785	2,845,932	† 155,376	† 6			
1788	4,040,000	†1,194,068	†42			
1805[c]	5,395,456	†1,355,456	†34			
1813[d]	5,937,858	† 542,402	†10			
1821[e]	6,801,827	† 863,969	†15	†1·4		
1831	7,767,401	† 965,574	†14	†1·3		
1841	8,175,124	† 407,723	† 5	†·5		
1851	6,515,794	*1,659,330	*20	*1·8		

[a] Returns obtained through an inquiry instituted by the Irish House of Lords.
[b] The population from 1754–1788 is estimated from the "hearth money" returns.
[c] Newenham's Inquiry into the Population of Ireland.
[d] Estimate from incomplete census.
[e] First complete census.

INCREASE IN THE POPULATION OF THE UNITED KINGDOM.

Years.	Population.	Numerical Increase.	Decennial Increase per Cent.	Annual Increase per Cent.	Increase in 30 years, from 1821 to 1851 = 31 per Cent.	Annual Rate of Increase ·9 per Cent.
1821	20,892,670					
1831	24,028,584	3,135,914	15	1·4		
1841	26,709,456	2,680,872	11	1·1		
1851	27,309,346	599,890	2	0·2		

Discarding, then, all conjectural results, and adhering solely to the returns of the censuses, we find that, according to the official numberings of the people *throughout the kingdom*, the increased rate of population is, in round numbers, 10 per cent. every ten years; that is to say, where 100 persons were living in the United Kingdom in 1821, there are 130 living in the present year of 1851. The average increase in England and Wales for the last 50 years may, however, be said to be 1·5 per cent. per annum, the population having doubled itself during that period.

How, then, does this rate of increase among the people, and consequently the labourers and artizans of the country, correspond with the rate of increase in the production of commodities, or, in plain English, the means of employment? *This is the main inquiry.*

The only means of determining the total amount of commodities produced, and consequently the quantity of work done in the country, is from official returns, submitted to the Parliament and the public as part of the "revenue" of the kingdom. These afford a broad and accurate basis for the necessary statistics; and to get rid of any speculating or calculating on the subject, I will confine my notice to such commodities; giving, however, further information bearing on the subject, but still derived from official sources, so that there may be no doubt on the matter. The facts in connection with this part of the subject are exhibited in the table given in the next page.

The majority of the articles there specified supply the elements of trade and manufacture in furnishing the materials of our clothing, in all its appliances of decency, comfort, and luxury. The table relates, moreover, to our commerce with other countries—to the ships which find profitable employment, and give such employment to our people, in the aggregate commerce of the nation. Under almost every head, it will be seen, the increase in the means of labour has been more extensive than has the increase in the number of labourers; in some instances the difference is wide indeed.

The annual rate of increase among the population has been ·9 per cent. From 1801 to 1841 the population of the kingdom at the outside cannot be said to have doubled itself. Yet the productions in cotton goods *were not less than ten times greater in 1851 than in 1801.* The increase in the use of wool from 1821 to 1851 was more than sixfold; that of the population, I may repeat, *not* twofold. In *twenty* years (1831 to 1851) the hides were more than doubled in amount as a means of production; in *fifty* years the population has not increased to the same amount. Can any one, then, contend that the labouring population has extended itself at a greater rate than the means of labour, or that the vast mass of surplus labour throughout the country is owing to the working classes having increased more rapidly than the means of employing them?

Thus, it is evident, that the means of labour

TABLE SHOWING THE INCREASE IN THE PRODUCTIONS AND COMMERCE OF THE UNITED KINGDOM, FROM 1801-1850.

† denotes increase.
* „ decrease.

	1801.	1811.	Increase and Decrease per Cent. from 1801 to 1811.	1821.	Increase per Cent. from 1811 to 1821.	1831.	Increase and Decrease per Cent. from 1821 to 1831.	1841.	Increase per Cent. from 1831 to 1841.	1850.	Increase per Cent. from 1841 to 1850.	Total Increase per Cent.	Average Annual Increase per Cent.
Soap ....in lbs.	55,500,000	80,000,000	†44	97,000,000	†21	127,500,000	†31	170,500,000	†34	205,000,000	20	269	5·3
Cotton .... „	56,000,000	92,000,000	†64	137,000,000	†49	273,000,000	†99	437,000,000	†60	664,700,000	52	1087	21·7
Wool .... „				10,000,000		30,000,000	†200	53,000,000	†77	72,675,000	37	627	20·9
Silk .... „	1,000,000	1,500,000	†50	2,250,000	†50	4,250,000	†89	7,159,000	†18	......	43	616	12·3
Flax .... „						104,000,000	†89	151,000,000	†45	204,000,000	35	271	9·0
Hemp .... „				55,000,000		56,500,000		73,000,000	†29	117,447,000	61	108	5·4
Hides .... „						26,000,000		51,000,000	†96	66,300,000	30	155	7·7
Official Value of Exports in £	24,500,000	21,750,000	*11	40,250,000	†85	60,000,000	†49	101,750,000	†70	197,309,000	94	705	14·1
Official Value of Imports „		25,500,000		29,750,000	†17	48,250,000	†62	62,750,000	†30	100,460,000	60	294	7·3
Tonnage of Vessels belonging to British Empire ...				2,550,203		2,581,964	†1	3,512,480	†36	4,232,962	21	65	2·2
Tonnage of Vessels entering Ports				1,895,000		3,241,927	†71	4,652,376	†44	7,110,476	53	274	9·1

*The *official* value was established long ago; it represents a price put upon merchandise or commodities; it is in reality a fixed value, and serves to indicate the relative extent of imports and exports in different years. The *declared* value is simply the market price.

have increased at a more rapid pace than the labouring population. But the increase in "property" of the country, in that which is sometimes called the "staple" property, being the assured possessions of the class of proprietors or capitalists, as well as in the profits, prove that, if the labourers of the country have been hungering for want of employment, at least the wealth of the nation has kept pace with the increase of the people, while the profits of trade have exceeded it.

AMOUNT OF THE PROPERTY AND INCOME OF GREAT BRITAIN.

Year.	Property assessed to Property-tax.	Annual Profits of Trade.
1815	£60,000,000	£37,000,000
1842	95,250,000	
1844	......	60,000,000
Increase	58 per cent.	
„	......	62 per cent.
Annual rate of increase	1·7 per cent.	1·7 per cent.

Here, then, we find, that the property assessed to the property tax has increased 35,250,000*l*. in 27 years, from 1815 to 1842, or upwards of 1,000,000*l*. sterling a year; this is at the rate of 1·7 per cent. every year, whereas the population of Great Britain has increased at the rate of only 1·4 per cent. per annum. But the amount of assessment under the property tax, it should be borne in mind, does not represent the full value of the possessions, so that among this class of proprietors there is far greater wealth than the returns show.

As regards the annual profits of trade, the increase between the years 1815 and 1844 has been 23,000,000*l*. in 29 years. This is at the rate of 1·7 per cent. per annum, and the annual increase in the population of Great Britain is only 1·4 per cent. But the amount of the profits of trade is unquestionably greater than appears in the financial tables of the revenue of the country; consequently there is a greater increase of wealth over population than the figures indicate.

The above returns show the following results:—

	Increase per Cent. per Ann.
Population of the United Kingdom	·9
Productions from	21 to 5
Exports	14
Imports	5
Shipping entering Ports	9
Property	1·7
Profits of trade	1·7

Far, very far indeed then, beyond the increase of the population, has been the increase of the wealth and work of the country.

And now, after this imposing array of wealth, let us contemplate the reverse of the picture: let us inquire if, while we have been increasing in riches and productions far more rapidly than we have been increasing in people and producers—let us inquire, I say, if we have been numerically increasing also in the sad long lists of paupers and criminals. Has our progress in poverty and crime been "*pari passu*," or been more than commensurate in the rapidity of its strides?

TABLE SHOWING THE NUMBER OF PAUPERS IN ENGLAND AND WALES.[a]

Years.	Number of Paupers relieved, Quarters ending Lady-day.	Numerical Increase and Decrease. † denotes Increase. * ,, Decrease.	Annual Increase and Decrease per Cent.	Increase per Cent. from 1840 to 1848 = 56. Annual Increase, 7 per Cent.
1840	1,199,529			
1841	1,299,048	† 99,519	† 8	
1842	1,427,187	†128,139	†10	
1843	1,539,490	†112,303	† 8	
1844	1,477,561	†938,071	†60	
1845	1,470,970	* 6,591	* 0·4	
1846	1,332,089	* 38,881	* 3	
1847	1,721,350	†389,261	†29	
1848	1,876,541	†155,191	† 9	

Here, then, we have an increase of 56 per cent. in less than ten years, though the increase of the population of England and Wales, in the same time, was but 13 per cent.; and let it be remembered that the increase of upwards of 650,000 paupers, in nine years, has accrued since the New Poor Law has been in what may be considered full working; a law which many were confident would result in a diminution of pauperism, and which certainly cannot be charged with offering the least encouragement to it. Still in *nine* years, our poverty increases while our wealth increases, and our paupers grow nearly four times as quick as our people, while the profits on trade nearly double themselves in little more than a quarter of a century.

We now come to the records of criminality:—

TABLE SHOWING THE INCREASE IN THE NUMBER OF CRIMINALS IN ENGLAND AND WALES FROM 1805-1850.

	Annual Average Number of Criminals Committed.	Numerical Increase.	Decennial Increase per Cent.	Annual Increase per Cent.	Increase per Cent. in the 43 years.	
1805	4,605					Annual Average Increase per Cent., 11·7.
1811	5,375	770	17	2·8		
1821	9,783	4408	82	8·2		
1831	15,318	5535	57	5·7	504	
1841	22,305	6987	46	4·6		
1850	27,814	5509	25	3·6		

From these results—and such figures are facts, and therefore stubborn things—the people cannot be said to have increased beyond the wealth or the means of employing them, for it is evident that *we increase in poverty and crime as we increase in wealth, and in both far beyond our increase in numbers.* The above are the bare facts of the country—it is for the reader to explain them as he pleases.

As yet we have dealt with those causes of casual labour only which may induce a surplusage of labourers without any *decrease taking place in the quantity of work.* We have seen, first, how the number of the unemployed may be increased either by altering the hours, rate, or mode of working, or else by changing the term of hiring, and this while the number of labourers remains the same; and, secondly, we have seen how the same results may ensue from increasing the number of labourers, while the conditions of working and hiring are unaltered. Under both these circumstances, however, the actual quantity of work to be done in the country has been supposed to undergo no change whatever; and at present we have to point out not only how the amount of surplus, and, consequently, of casual labour, in the kingdom, may be increased by *a decrease of the work,* but also how the work itself may be made to decrease. To know the causes of the one we must ascertain the antecedents of the other. What, then, are the circumstances inducing a decrease in the quantity of work? and,

---

[a] The official returns as to the number of paupers are most incomplete and unsatisfactory. In the 10th annual Report of the Poor Law Commissioners, p. 480 (1844), a table is printed which is said to give the returns from the earliest period for which authentic Parliamentary documents have been received, and this sets forth the number of paupers in England and Wales, for the *entire twelve months* in the years 1803, 1813, 1814, and 1815; then comes a long interval of "no returns," and after 1839 we have the numbers for only *three months* in each year, from 1840 up to 1843; in the first annual Report (1848) these returns for one quarter in each year are continued up to 1848; and then we get the returns for only two days in each year, the 1st of July and the 1st of January, so that to come to any conclusion amid so much inconsistency is utterly impossible. The numbers above given would have been continued to the present period, could any comparison have been instituted. The numbers for the periods (not above given) are—

1803	1,040,716	} Number of paupers for the entire twelve months.
1813	1,426,065	
1814	1,402,576	
1815	1,319,851	
1849 (1st Jan.)	940,851	} Number of paupers for two separate days in each year.
,, (1st July)	846,988	
1850 (1st Jan.)	889,830	
,, (1st July)	796,318	
1851 (1st Jan.)	829,440	

consequently, what the circumstances inducing an increase in the amount of surplus and casual labour?

In the first place we may induce a large amount of casual labour *in particular districts*, not by decreasing the gross quantity of work required by the country, but by merely shifting the work into new quarters, and so decreasing the quantity in the ordinary localities. "The west of England," says Mr. Dodd, in his account of the textile manufactures of Great Britain, "was formerly, and continued to be till a comparatively recent period, the most important clothing district in England. The changes which the woollen manufacture, as respects both localization and mode of management, has been and is now undergoing, are very remarkable. Some years ago the 'west of England cloths' were the test of excellence in this manufacture; while the productions of Yorkshire were deemed of a coarser and cheaper character. At present, although the western counties have not deteriorated in their product, the West Riding of Yorkshire has made giant strides, by which equal skill in every department has been attained; while the commercial advantages resulting from coal-mines, from water-power, from canals and railroads, and from vicinage to the eastern port of Hull and the western port of Liverpool, give to the West Riding a power which Gloucestershire and Somersetshire cannot equal. The steam-engine, too, and various machines for facilitating some of the manufacturing processes, have been more readily introduced into the former than into the latter; a circumstance which, even without reference to other points of comparison, is sufficient to account for much of the recent advance in the north."

Of late years the products of many of the west of England clothing districts have considerably declined. Shepton Mallet, Frome and Trowbridge, for instance, which were at one time the seats of a flourishing manufacture for cloth, have now but little employment for the workmen in those parts; and so with other towns. "At several places in Wiltshire, Somersetshire, and Gloucestershire, and others of the western counties," says Mr. Thornton, "most of the cottagers, fifty years ago, were weavers, whose chief dependence was their looms, though they worked in the field at harvest time and other busy seasons. By so doing they kept down the wages of agricultural labourers, who had no other employment; and now that they have themselves become dependent upon agriculture, in consequence of the removal of the woollen manufacture from the cottage to the factory" [as well as to the north of England], "these reduced wages have become their own portion also;" or, in other words, since the shifting of the woollen manufacture in these parts, the quantity of casual labour in the cultivation of the land has been augmented.

The same effect takes place, of course, if the work be shifted to the Continent, instead of merely to another part of our own country. This has been the main cause of the misery of the straw-plaiters of Buckinghamshire and Bedfordshire. "During the last war," says the author before quoted, "there were examples of women (the wives and children of labouring men) earning as much as 22s. a week. The profits of this employment have been so much reduced by the competition of Leghorn hats and bonnets, that a straw-plaiter cannot earn much more than 2s. 6d. in the week."

But the work of particular localities may not only decrease, and the casual labour, in those parts, increase in the same proportion, by shifting it to other localities (either at home or abroad), even while the gross quantity of work required by the nation remains the same, but the quantity of work may be less than ordinary at *a particular time*, even while the same gross quantity annually required undergoes no change. This is the case in those periodical gluts which arise from over-production, in the cotton and other trades. The manufacturers, in such cases, have been increasing the supplies at a too rapid rate in proportion to the demand of the markets, so that, though there be no decrease in the requirements of the country, there ultimately accrues such a surplus of commodities beyond the wants and means of the people, that the manufacturers are compelled to stop producing until such time as the regular demand carries off the extra supply. And during all this time either the labourers have to work half-time at half-pay, or else they are thrown out of employment altogether.

Thus far we have proceeded in the assumption that the actual quantity of work required by the nation *does not decrease in the aggregate, but only in particular places or at particular times*, owing to a greater quantity than usual being done in other places or at other times *. We have still to consider what are the circumstances which tend to *diminish the gross quantity of work required by the country*. To understand these we must know the conditions on which all work depends; these are simply the conditions of demand and supply, and hence to know what it is that regulates the demand for commodities, and what it is that regulates the supply of them, is also to know what it is that regulates the quantity of work required by the nation.

Let me begin with the decrease of work arising from a *decrease of the demand* for certain commodities. This decrease of demand may proceed from one of three causes:—

1. An increase of cost.
2. A change of taste or fashion.
3. A change of circumstances.

The *increase of cost* may be brought about either by an increase in the expense of production or by a tax laid upon the article, as in the case of hair-powder, before quoted. Of the *change of taste or fashion*, as a means of decreasing the

---

* It might at first appear that, when the work is shifted to the Continent, there would be a proportionate decrease of the aggregate quantity at home, but a little reflection will teach us that the foreigners must take something from us in *exchange* for their work, and so increase the quantity of our work in certain respects as much as they depress it in others.

demand for a certain article of manufacture, and, consequently, of a particular form of labour, many instances have already been given; to these the following may be added:—" In Dorsetshire," says Mr. Thornton, "the making of wire shirt-buttons (now in a great measure superseded by the use of mother-o'-pearl) once employed great numbers of women and children." So it has been with the manufacture of metal coat-buttons; the change to silk has impoverished hundreds.

The decrease of work arising from a *change of circumstances* may be seen in the fluctuations of the iron trade; in the railway excitement the demand for labour in the iron districts was at least tenfold as great as it is at present, and so again with the demand for arms during war time; at such periods the quantity of work in that particular line at Birmingham is necessarily increased, while the contrary effects, of course, ensue immediately the requirements cease, and a large mass of surplus and casual hands is the result. It is the same with the soldiers themselves, as with the gun and sword makers; on the disbanding of certain portions of the army at the conclusion of a war, a vast amount of surplus labourers are poured into the country to compete with those already in work, and either to drag down their weekly earnings, or else, by obtaining *casual* employment in their stead, to reduce the gross quantity of work accruing to each, and so to render their incomes not only less in amount but less constant and regular. Within the last few weeks no less than 1000 policemen employed during the Exhibition have been discharged, of course with a like result to the labour market.

The circumstances tending to *diminish the supply* of certain commodities, are—

1. Want of capital.
2. Want of materials.
3. Want of labourers.
4. Want of opportunity.

The *decrease of the quantity of capital* in a trade may be brought about by several means: it may be produced by a want of security felt among the moneyed classes, as at the time of revolutions, political agitations, commercial depressions, or panics; or it may be produced by a deficiency of enterprise after the bursting of certain commercial "bubbles," or the decline of particular manias for speculation, as on the cessation of the railway excitement; so, again, it may be brought about by a failure of the ordinary produce of the year, as with bad harvests.

The *decrease of the quantity of materials*, as tending to diminish the supply of certain commodities, may be seen in the failure of the cotton crops, which, of course, deprive the cotton manufacturers of their ordinary quantity of work. The same diminution in the ordinary supply of particular articles ensues when the men engaged in the production of them "strike" either for an advance of wages, or more generally to resist the attempt of some cutting employer to reduce their ordinary earnings; and lastly, a like decrease of work necessarily ensues when the *opportunity of working is changed*. Some kinds of work, as we have already seen, depend on the weather—on either the wind, rain, or temperature; while other kinds can only be pursued at certain seasons of the year, as brick-making, building, and the like; hence, on the cessation of the opportunities for working in these trades, there is necessarily a great decrease in the quantity of work, and consequently a large increase in the amount of surplus and therefore casual labour.

We have now, I believe, exhausted the several causes of that vast national evil—casual labour. We have seen that it depends,

First, upon certain times and seasons, fashions and accidents, which tend to cause a periodical briskness or slackness in different employments;

And secondly, upon the number of surplus labourers in the country.

The circumstances inducing surplus labour we have likewise ascertained to be three.

1. An alteration in the hours, rate, or mode of working, as well as in the mode of hiring.
2. An increase of the hands.
3. A decrease of the work, either in particular places, at particular times, or in the aggregate, owing to a decrease either in the demand or means of supply.

Any one of these causes, it has been demonstrated, must necessarily tend to induce an over supply of labourers and consequently a casualty of labour, for it has been pointed out that an over supply of labourers does not depend *solely* on an increase of the workers beyond the means of working, but that a decrease of the ordinary quantity of work, or a general increase of the hours or rate of working, or an extension of the system of production, or even a diminution of the term of hiring, will also be attended with the same result—facts which should be borne steadily in mind by all those who would understand the difficulties of the times, and which the "economists" invariably ignore.

On a careful revision of the whole of the circumstances before detailed, I am led to believe that there is considerable truth in the statement lately put forward by the working classes, that only one-third of the operatives of this country are fully employed, while another third are partially employed, and the remaining third wholly unemployed; that is to say, estimating the working classes as being between four and five millions in number, I think we may safely assert—considering how many depend for their employment on particular times, seasons, fashions, and accidents, and the vast quantity of over-work and scamp-work in nearly all the cheap trades of the present day, the number of women and children who are being continually drafted into the different handicrafts with the view of reducing the earnings of the men, the displacement of human labour in some cases by machinery, and the tendency to increase the division of labour, and to extend the large system of production beyond the requirements of the markets, as well as the temporary mode of hiring—all these things being considered, I say I believe we may safely conclude that, out of the four million five hundred thousand people who have to depend on their industry for the livelihood of themselves and families, there is (owing to the extraordinary means of economizing labour which have been developed of late years, and the discovery as to how to do the work of the nation with fewer people) barely sufficient work for the *regular* employment of half of our labourers, so that only 1,500,000 are fully and constantly employed, while 1,500,000 more are employed only half their time, and the remaining 1,500,000 wholly unemployed, obtaining a day's work *occasionally* by the displacement of some of the others.

Adopt what explanation we will of this appalling deficiency of employment, one thing at least is certain: we cannot *consistently with the facts of the country*, ascribe it to an increase of the population beyond the means of labour; for we have seen that, while the people have increased during the last fifty years at the rate of ·9 per cent. per annum, the wealth and productions of the kingdom have far exceeded that amount.

Of the Casual Labourers among the Rubbish-Carters.

The casual labour of so large a body of men as the rubbish-carters is a question of high importance, for it affects the whole unskilled labour market. And this is one of the circumstances distinguishing unskilled from skilled labour. Unemployed cabinet-makers, for instance, do not apply for work to a tailor; so that, with skilled labourers, only one trade is affected in the slack season by the scarcity of employment among its operatives. With unskilled labourers it is otherwise. If in the course of next week 100 rubbish-carters were from any cause to be thrown out of employment, and found an impossibility to obtain work at rubbish-carting, there would be 100 fresh applicants for employment among the bricklayer's-labourers, scavagers, nightmen, sewermen, dock-workers, lumpers, &c. Many of the 100 thus unemployed would, of course, be willing to work at reduced wages merely that they might subsist; and thus the hands employed by the regular and "honourable" part of those trades are exposed to the risk of being underworked, as regards wages, from the surplusage of labour in other unskilled occupations.

The employment of the rubbish-carters depends, in the first instance, upon the *season*. The services of the men are called into requisition when houses are being built or removed. In the one case, the rubbish-carters cart away the refuse earth; in the other they remove the old materials. The *brisk season* for the builders, and consequently for the rubbish-carters, is, as I heard several of them express it, "when days are long." From about the middle of April to the middle of October is the *brisk* season of the rubbish-carters, for during those six months more buildings are erected than in the winter half of the year. There is an advantage in fine weather in the masonry becoming *set;* and efforts are generally made to complete at least the carcase of a house before the end of October, at the latest.

I am informed that the difference in the employment of labourers about buildings is 30 per cent.—one builder estimated it at 50 per cent.—less in winter than in summer, from the circumstance of fewer buildings being then in the course of erection. It may be thought that, as rubbish-carters are employed frequently on the foundation of buildings, their business would not be greatly affected by the season or the weather. But the work is often more difficult in wet weather, the ground being heavier, so that a smaller extent of work only can be accomplished, compared to what can be done in fine weather; and an employer may decline to pay six days' wages for work in winter, which he might get done in five days in summer. If the men work by the piece or the load the result is the same; the rubbish-carter's employer has a smaller return, for there is less work to be charged to the customer, while the cost in keeping the horses is the same.

Thus it appears that under the most favourable circumstances about *one-fourth* of the rubbish-carters, even in the honourable trade, may be exposed to the evils of non-employment merely from the state of the weather influencing, more or less, the custom of the trade, and this even during *the* six months' employment out of the year; after which the men must find some other means of earning a livelihood.

There are, in round numbers, 850 operative rubbish-carters employed in the brisk season throughout the metropolis; hence 212 men, at this calculation, would be regularly deprived of work every year for six months out of the twelve. It will be seen, however, on reference to the table here given, that the average number of weeks each of the rubbish-carters is employed throughout the twelve months is far below 26; indeed many have but three and four weeks work out of the 52.

By an analysis of the returns I have collected on this subject I find the following to have been the actual term of employment for the several rubbish-carters in the course of last year:—

Men.	Employment in the Year.			
9 had	39 weeks,	or	9	months.
214 ,,	26 ,,		6	,,
4 ,,	20 ,,		5	,,
10 ,,	18 ,,			
28 ,,	16 ,,		4	,,
8 ,,	14 ,,			
353 ,,	13 ,,		3	,,
4 ,,	12 ,,			
34 ,,	10 ,,			
29 ,,	9 ,,			
38 ,,	8 ,,		2	,,
38 ,,	6 ,,			
27 ,,	5 ,,			
45 ,,	4 ,,		1	,,
15 ,,	3 ,,			
856				

Hence about one-fourth of the trade appear to have been employed for six months, while upwards of one-half had work for only three months or less throughout the year—many being at work only three days in the week during that time.

The rubbish-carter is exposed to another casualty over which he can no more exercise control than he can over the weather; I mean to what is generally called *speculation*, or a rage for building. This is evoked by the state of the money market, and other causes upon which I need not dilate; but the effect of it upon the labourers I am describing is this: capitalists may in one year embark sufficient means in building speculations to erect, say 500 new houses, in any particular district. In the following year they may not erect more than 200 (if any), and thus, as there is the same extent of unskilled labour in the market, the number of hands required is, if the trade be generally less speculative, less in one year than in its predecessor by the number of rubbish-carters required to work at the foundations of 300 houses. Such a cause may be exceptional; but during the last ten years the inhabited houses in the five districts of the Registrar-General have increased to the extent of 45,000, or from 262,737 in 1841, to 307,722 in 1851. It appears, then, that the annual increase of our metropolitan houses, concluding that they increase in a regular yearly ratio, is 4500. Last year, however, as I am informed by an experienced builder, there were rather fewer buildings erected (he spoke only from his own observations and personal knowledge of the business) than the yearly average of the decennial term.

The casual and constant wages of the rubbish-carters may be thus detailed. The whole system of the labour, I may again state, must be regarded as *casual*, or—as the word imports in its derivation from the Latin *casus*, a chance—the labour of men who are occasionally employed. Some of the most respectable and industrious rubbish-carters with whom I met, told me they generally might make up their minds, though they might have excellent masters, to be six months of the year unemployed at rubbish-carting; this, too, is less than the average of this chance employment.

Calculating, then, the rubbish-carter's receipt of *nominal wages* at 18s., and his *actual wages* at 20s. in the honourable trade, I find the following amount to be paid.

By nominal wages, I have before explained, I mean what a man is *said* to receive, or has been *promised* that he shall be paid weekly. Actual wages, on the other hand, are what a man positively *receives*, there being sometimes additions in the form of perquisites or allowances; sometimes deductions in the way of fines and stoppages; the additions in the rubbish-carting trade appear to average about 2s. a week. But these *actual wages* are received only so long as the men are employed, that is to say, they are the *casual* rather than the *constant* earnings of the men working at a trade, which is essentially of an occasional or temporary character; the average employment at rubbish-carting being only three months in the year.

Let us see, therefore, what would be the constant earnings or income of the men working at the better-paid portion of the trade.

	£	s.	d.
The gross actual wages of ten rubbish-carters, casually employed for 39 weeks, at 20s. per week, amount to	390	0	0
The gross actual wages of 250 rubbish-carters, casually employed for 26 weeks, at 20s. per week .	6500	0	0
The gross actual wages of 360 rubbish-carters, casually employed for 13 weeks, at 20s. per week .	4600	0	0
Total gross actual wages of 620 of the better-paid rubbish-carters .	11,490	0	0

But this, as I said before, represents only the *casual* wages of the better-paid operatives—that is to say, it shows the amount of money or money's worth that is positively received by the men while they are in employment. To understand what are the *constant* wages of these men, we must divide their gross casual earnings by 52, the number of weeks in the year: thus we find that the constant wages of the ten men who were employed for 39 weeks, were 15s. instead of 20s. per week—that is to say, their wages, equally divided throughout the year, would have yielded that constant weekly income. By the same reasoning, the 20s. per week casual wages of the 250 men employed for 26 weeks out of the 52, were equal to only 10s. constant weekly wages; and so the 360 men, who had 20s. per week casually for only three months in the year, had but 5s. a week *constantly* throughout the whole year. Hence we see the enormous difference there may be between a man's casual and his constant earnings at a given trade.

The next question that forces itself on the mind is, how do the rubbish-carters live when no longer employed at this kind of work?

When the slack season among rubbish-carters commences, nearly one-fifth of the operatives are discharged. These take to scavaging or dustman's work, as well as that of navigators, or, indeed, any form of unskilled labour, some obtaining full employ, but the greater part being able to "get a job only now and then." Those masters who keep their men on throughout the year are some of them large dust contractors, some carmen, some dairymen, and (in one or two instances in the suburbs, as at Hackney) small farmers. The dust-contractors and carmen, who are by far the more numerous, find employment for the men employed by them as rubbish-carters in the season, either at the dust-yard or carrying sand, or, indeed, carting any materials they may have to move—the wages to the men remaining the same; indeed such is the transient character of the rubbish-carting trade, that there are no masters or operatives who devote themselves solely to the business.

The Effects of Casual Labour in General.

Having now pointed out the causes of casual labour, I proceed to set forth its effects.

All casual labour, as I have said, is necessarily *uncertain* labour; and wherever uncertainty exists, there can be no foresight or pro-vidence. Had the succession of events in nature been irregular,—had it been ordained by the Creator that similar causes under similar circumstances should *not* be attended with similar effects,—it would have been impossible for us to have had any knowledge of the future, or to have made any preparations concerning it. Had the seasons followed each other fitfully,—had the sequences in the external world been variable instead of invariable, and what are now termed "constants" from the regularity of their succession been changed into inconstants,—what provision could even the most prudent of us have made? Where all was dark and unstable, we could only have guessed instead of reasoned as to what was to come; and who would have deprived himself of present enjoyments to avoid future privations, which could appear neither probable nor even possible to him? Pro-vidence, therefore, is simply the result of certainty, and whatever tends to increase our faith in the uniform sequences of outward events, as well as our reliance on the means we have of avoiding the evils connected with them, necessarily tends to make us more prudent. Where the means of sustenance and comfort are fixed, the human being becomes conscious of what he has to depend upon; and if he feel *assured* that such means may fail him in old age or in sickness, and be fully impressed with the *certainty* of suffering from either, he will immediately proceed to make some provision against the time of adversity or infirmity. If, however, his means be *uncertain*—abundant at one time, and deficient at another—a spirit of speculation or gambling with the future will be induced, and the individual get to believe in "luck" and "fate" as the arbiters of his happiness rather than to look upon himself as "the architect of his fortunes" —trusting to "chance" rather than his own powers and foresight to relieve him at the hour of necessity. The same result will necessarily ensue if, from defective reasoning powers, the ordinary course of nature be not sufficiently apparent to him, or if, being in good health, he grow too confident upon its continuance, and, either from this or other causes, is led to believe that death will overtake him before his powers of self-support decay.

The ordinary effects of uncertain labour, then, are to drive the labourers to improvidence, recklessness, and pauperism.

Even in the classes which we do not rank among labourers, as, for instance, authors, artists, musicians, actors, uncertainty or irregularity of employment and remuneration produces a spirit of wastefulness and carelessness. The steady and daily accruing gains of trade and of some of the professions form a certain and staple income; while in other professions, where a large sum may be realized at one time, and then no money be earned until after an interval, incomings are rapidly spent, and the interval is one of suffering. This is part of the very nature, the very essence, of the casualty of employment and the delay of remuneration. The past privation gives a zest to the present enjoyment; while the present enjoyment renders the past privation faint as a remembrance and unimpressive as a warning. "Want of providence," writes Mr. Porter, "on the part of those who live by the labour of their hands, and whose employments so often depend upon circumstances beyond their control, is a theme which is constantly brought forward by many whose lot in life has been cast beyond the reach of want. It is, indeed, greatly to be wished, for their own sakes, that the habit were general among the labouring classes of saving some part of their wages when fully employed, against less prosperous times; but it is difficult for those who are placed in circumstances of ease to *estimate the amount of virtue that is implied in this self-denial*. It must be a hard trial for one who has recently, perhaps, seen his family enduring want, to deny them the small amount of indulgences, which are, at the best of times, placed within their reach."

It is easy enough for men in smooth circumstances to say, "the privation is a man's own fault, since, to avoid it, he has but to apportion the sum he may receive in a lump over the interval of non-recompense which he knows will follow." Such a course as this, experience and human nature have shown not to be easy—perhaps, with a few exceptions, not to be possible. It is the starving and not the well-fed man that is in danger of surfeiting himself. When pestilence or revolution are rendering life and property *casualties* in a country, the same spirit of improvident recklessness breaks forth. In London, on the last visitation of the plague, in the reign of Charles II., a sort of Plague Club indulged in the wildest excesses in the very heart of the pestilence. To these orgies no one was admitted who had not been bereft of some relative by the pest. In Paris, during the reign of terror in the first revolution, the famous Guillotine Club was composed of none but those who had lost some near relative by the guillotine. When they met for their half-frantic revels every one wore some symbol of death: breast pins in the form of guillotines, rings with death's-heads, and such like. The duration of their own lives these Guillotine Clubbists knew to be uncertain, not merely in the ordinary uncertainty of nature, but from the character of the times; and this feeling of the jeopardy of existence, from the practice of violence and bloodshed, wrought the effects I have described. Life was more than naturally casual. When the famine was at the worst in Ireland, it was remarked in the *Cork Examiner*, that in that city there never had been seen more street "larking" or street gambling among the poor lads and young men who were really starving. This was a natural result of the casualty of labour and the consequent casualty of food. Persons, it should be remembered, do not insure houses or shops that are "doubly or trebly hazardous;" they gamble on the uncertainty.

Mr. Porter, in his "Progress of the Nation," cites a fact bearing immediately upon the present subject.

"The formation of a canal, which has been in progress during the last five years, in the north of Ireland (this was written in 1847), has afforded steady employment to a portion of the peasantry, who before that time were suffering all the evils, so common in that country, which result from the precariousness of employment. Such work as they could previously get came at uncertain intervals, and was sought by so many competitors, that the remuneration was of the scantiest amount. In this condition of things the men were improvident, to recklessness; their wages, insufficient for the comfortable sustenance of their families, were wasted in procuring for themselves a temporary forgetfulness of their misery at the whiskey-shop, and the men appeared to be sunk into a state of hopeless degradation. From the moment, however, that work was offered to them which was *constant in its nature and certain in its duration*, and on which their weekly earnings would be sufficient to provide for their comfortable support, *men who had been idle and dissolute were converted into sober hard-working labourers, and proved themselves kind and careful husbands and fathers;* and it is stated as a fact, that, notwithstanding the distribution of several hundred pounds weekly in wages, the whole of which must be considered as so much additional money placed in their hands, the consumption of whiskey was absolutely and *permanently* diminished in the district. During the comparatively short period in which the construction of this canal was in progress, some of the most careful labourers—men who most probably before then never knew what it was to possess five shillings at any one time—saved sufficient money to enable them to emigrate to Canada."

There can hardly be a stronger illustration of the blessing of constant and the curse of casual labour. We have competence and frugality as the results of one system; poverty and extravagance as the results of the other; and among the very same individuals.

In the evidence given by Mr. Galloway, the engineer, before a parliamentary committee, he remarks, that "when employers are competent to show their men that their business is *steady and certain*, and when men find that they are likely to have *permanent* employment, they have always *better habits and more settled notions*, which will make them *better men* and *better workmen*, and will produce great benefits to all who are interested in their employment."

Moreover, even if payment be assured to a working man regularly, *but deferred for long intervals*, so as to make the returns lose all appearance of regularity, he will rarely be found able to resist the temptation of a tavern, and, perhaps, a long-continued carouse, or of some other extravagance to his taste, when he receives a month's dues at once. I give an instance of this in the following statement:—

For some years after the peace of 1815 the staffs of the militias were kept up, but not in any active service. During the war the militias performed what are now the functions of the regular troops in the three kingdoms, their stations being changed more frequently than those of any of the regular regiments at the present day. Indeed, they only differed from the "regulars" in name. There was the same military discipline, and the sole difference was, that the militia-men—who were balloted for periodically—could not, by the laws regulating their embodiment, be sent out of the United Kingdom for purposes of warfare. The militias were embodied for twenty-eight days' training, once in four years (seldom less) after the peace, and the staff acted as the drill sergeants. They were usually steady, orderly men, working at their respective crafts when not on duty after the militia's disembodiment, and some who had not been brought up to any handicraft turned out —perhaps from their military habits of early rising and orderliness—very good gardeners, both on their own account and as assistants in gentlemen's grounds. No few of them saved money. Yet these men, with very few exceptions, when they received a month's pay, fooled away a part of it in tippling and idleness, to which they were not at all addicted when attending regularly to their work with its regular returns. If they got into any trouble in consequence of their carousing, it was looked upon as a sort of legitimate excuse, "Why you see, sir, it was the 24th" (the 24th of each month being the pension day).

The thoughtless extravagance of sailors when, on their return to port, they receive in one sum the wages they have earned by severe toil amidst storms and dangers during a long voyage, I need not speak of; it is a thing well known.

These soldiers and seamen cannot be said to have been *casually* employed, but the results were the same as if they had been so employed; the money came to them in a lump at so long an interval as to appear uncertain, and was consequently squandered.

I may cite the following example as to the effects of uncertain earnings upon the household outlay of labourers who suffer from the casualties of employment induced by the season of the year. "In the long fine days of summer, the little daughter of a working brickmaker," I was told, "used to order chops and other choice dainties of a butcher, saying, 'Please, sir, father don't care for the price just a-now; but he must have his chops good; line-chops, sir, and tender, please—'cause he's a brickmaker.' In the winter, it was, 'O please, sir, here's a fourpenny bit, and you must send father something cheap. He don't care what it is, so long as it's cheap. It's winter, and he hasn't no work, sir—'cause he's a brickmaker.'"

I have spoken of the tendency of casual labour to induce intemperate habits. In confirmation of this I am enabled to give the following account as to the increase of the sale of malt liquor in the metropolis *consequent upon wet weather*. The account is derived from the personal observations of a gentleman long familiar with the brewing trade, in connection with one of the largest houses. In short, I may state that the account is given on the very best authority.

There are *nine* large brewers in London; of these the two firms transacting the greatest extent of business supply, daily, 1000 barrels each firm to their customers; the seven others, among them, dispose, altogether, of 3000 barrels daily. All these 5000 barrels a day are solely for town consumption; and this may be said to be the *average* supply the year through, but the public-house sale is far from regular.

After a wet day the sale of malt liquor, principally beer (porter), to the metropolitan retailers is from 500 to 1000 barrels more than when a wet day has not occurred; that is to say, the supply increases from 5000 barrels to 5500 and 6000. Such of the publicans as keep small stocks go the next day to their brewers to order a further supply; those who have better-furnished cellars may not go for two or three days after, but the result is the same.

The reason for this increased consumption is obvious; when the weather prevents workmen from prosecuting their respective callings in the open air, they have recourse to drinking, to pass away the idle time. Any one who has made himself familiar with the habits of the working classes has often found them crowding a public-house during a hard rain, especially in the neighbourhood of new buildings, or any public open-air work. The street-sellers, themselves prevented from plying their trades outside, are busy in such times in the "publics," offering for sale braces, belts, hose, tobacco-boxes, nuts of different kinds, apples, &c. A bargain may then be struck for so much and a half-pint of beer, and so the consumption is augmented by the trade in other matters.

Now, taking 750 barrels as the average of the extra sale of beer in consequence of wet weather, we have a consumption beyond the demands of the ordinary trade in malt liquor of 27,000 gallons, or 216,000 pints. This, at 2*d.* a pint, is 3000*l.* for a day's needless, and often prejudicial, outlay caused by the casualty of the weather and the consequent casualty of labour. A censor of morals might say that these men should go home under such circumstances; but their homes may be at a distance, and may present no great attractions; the single men among them may have no homes, merely sleeping-places; and even the more prudent may think it advisable to wait awhile under shelter in hopes of the weather improving, so that they could resume their labour, and only an hour or so be deducted from their wages. Besides, there is the attraction to the labourer of the warmth, discussion, freedom, and excitement of the public-house.

That the great bulk of the consumers of this *additional* beer are of the classes I have mentioned is, I think, plain enough, from the increase being experienced only in that beverage, the consumption of gin being little affected by the same means. Indeed, the statistics showing the ratio of beer and gin-drinking are curious enough (were this the place to enter into them), the most gin, as a general rule, being consumed in the most depressed years.

"It is a fact worth notice," said a statistical journal, entitled "Facts and Figures," published in 1841, "as illustrative of the *tendency of the times of pressure to increase spirit drinking*, that whilst under the privations of last year (1840) the poorer classes paid 2,628,286*l.* tax for spirits; in 1836, a year of the greatest prosperity, the tax on British spirits amounted only to 2,390,188*l.* *So true is it that to impoverish is to demoralise.*"

The numbers who imbibe, in the course of a wet day, these 750 barrels, cannot, of course, be ascertained, but the following calculations may be presented. The class of men I have described rarely have spare money, but if known to a landlord, they probably may obtain credit until the Saturday night. Now, putting their *extra* beer-drinking on wet days—for on fine days there is generally a pint or more consumed daily per working man—putting, I say, the *extra* potations at a pot (quart) each man, we find *one hundred and eight thousand* consumers (out of 2,000,000 people, or, discarding the women and children, not 1,000,000)! A number doubling, and trebling, and quadrupling the male adult population of many a splendid continental city.

Of the data I have given, I may repeat, no doubt can be entertained; nor, as it seems to me, can any doubt be entertained that the increased consumption is directly attributable to the casualty of labour*.

OF THE SCURF TRADE AMONG THE RUBBISH-CARTERS.

Before proceeding to treat of the cheap or "scurf" labourers among the rubbish-carters, I shall do as I have done in connection with the casual labourers of the same trade, say a few words on that kind of labour in general, both as to the means by which it is usually obtained and as to the distinctive qualities of the scurf or low-priced labourers; for experience teaches me that the mode by which labour is cheapened is more or less similar in all trades, and it will therefore save much time and space if I here—as with the casual labourers—give the general facts in connection with this part of my subject.

In the first place, then, there are but two direct modes of cheapening labour, viz.:—

1. By making the workmen do *more* work for the *same* pay.

2. By making them do the *same* work for *less* pay.

The first of these modes is what is technically termed "*driving*," especially when effected by compulsory "overwork;" and it is called the "economy of labour" when brought about by more elaborate and refined processes, such as the division of labour, the large system of production, the invention

---

* The Great Exhibition, I am informed, produced a very small effect on the consumption of porter; and, according to the official returns, 160,000 gallons less spirits were consumed in the first nine months of the present year, than in the corresponding months of the last: thus showing that any occupation of mind or body is incompatible with intemperate habits, for drunkenness is essentially the vice of idleness, or want of something better to do.

of machinery, and the *temporary*, as contradistinguished from the *permanent*, mode of hiring.

Each of these modes of making workmen do *more* work for the *same* pay, can but have the same depressing effect on the labour market, for not only is the *rate* of remuneration (or ratio of the work to the pay) reduced when the operative is made to do a greater quantity of work for the same amount of money, but, unless the means of disposing of the extra products be proportionately increased, it is evident that just as many workmen must be displaced thereby as the increased term or rate of working exceeds the extension of the markets; that is to say, if 4000 workpeople be made to produce each twice as much as formerly (either by extending the hours of labour or increasing their rate of labouring), then if the markets or means of disposing of the extra products be increased only one-half, 1000 hands must, according to Cocker, be deprived of their ordinary employment; and these competing with those who are in work will immediately tend to reduce the wages of the trade generally, so that not only will the *rate* of wages be decreased, since each will have more work to do, but the actual earnings of the workmen will be diminished likewise.

Of the economy of labour itself, as a means of cheapening work, there is no necessity for me to speak here. It is, indeed, generally admitted, that to economize labour without proportionally extending the markets for the products of such labour, is to deprive a certain number of workmen of their ordinary means of living; and under the head of casual labour so many instances have been given of this principle that it would be wearisome to the reader were I to do other than allude to the matter at present. There are, however, several other means of causing a workman to do more than his ordinary quantity of work. These are:—

1. By extra supervision when the workmen are paid by the day. Of this mode of increased production an instance has already been cited in the account of the strapping-shops given at p. 304, vol. ii.
2. By increasing the workman's interest in his work; as in piece-work, where the payment of the operative is made proportional to the quantity of work done by him. Of this mode examples have already been given at p. 303, vol. ii.
3. By large quantities of work given out at one time; as in "lump-work" and "contract work."
4. By the domestic system of work, or giving out materials to be made up at the homes of the workpeople.
5. By the middleman system of labour.
6. By the prevalence of small masters.
7. By a reduced rate of pay, as forcing operatives to labour both longer and quicker, in order to make up the same amount of income.

Of several of these modes of work I have already spoken, citing facts as to their pernicious influence upon the greater portion of those trades where they are found to prevail. I have already shown how, by extra supervision—by increased interest in the work—as well as by decreased pay, operatives can be made to do more work than they otherwise would, and so be the cause, unless the market be proportionately extended, of depriving some of their fellow-labourers of their fair share of employment. It now only remains for me to set forth the effect of those modes of employment which have not yet been described, viz., the domestic system, the middleman system, and the contract and lump system, as well as the small-master system of work.

Let me begin with the first of the last-mentioned modes of cheapening labour, viz., *the domestic system of work.*

I find, by investigation, that in trades where the system of working on the master's premises has been departed from, and a man is allowed to take his work home, there is invariably a tendency to cheapen labour. These home workers, whenever opportunity offers, will use other men's ill-paid labour, or else employ the members of their family to enhance their own profits.

The domestic system, moreover, naturally induces *over-work and Sunday-work, as well as tends to change journeymen into trading operatives, living on the labour of their fellow-workmen.* When the work is executed off the master's premises, of course there are neither definite hours nor days for labour; and the consequence is, the generality of home workers labour early and late, Sundays as well as week-days, availing themselves at the same time of the co-operation of their wives and children; thus the trade becomes overstocked with workpeople by the introduction of a vast number of new hands into it, as well as by the overwork of the men themselves who thus obtain employment. When I was among the tailors, I received from a journeyman to whom I was referred by the Trades' Society as the one best able to explain the causes of the decline of that trade, the following lucid account of the evils of this system of labour:—

"The principal cause of the decline of our trade is the employment given to workmen at their own homes, or, in other words, to the 'sweaters.' The sweater is the greatest evil in the trade; as the sweating system increases the number of hands to an almost incredible extent—wives, sons, daughters, and extra women, all working 'long days'—that is, labouring from sixteen to eighteen hours per day, and Sundays as well. By this system two men obtain as much work as would give employment to three or four men working regular hours in the shop. Consequently, the sweater being enabled to get the work done by women and children at a lower price than the regular workman, obtains the greater part of the garments to be made, while men who depend upon the shop for their living are obliged to walk about idle. A greater quantity of work is done under the sweating system at a lower price. I consider that the decline of my trade dates from the change of day-work into piece-work. According to the old system, the journeyman was paid by the day, and consequently must have done his work under the eye of his employer. It is true that work was given out by the master before the change from day-work to piece-work was regularly acknowledged in the trade. But still it was morally impossible for work to be given out and not be paid by the piece. Hence *I date the decrease in the wages of the workman from the introduction of piece-work, and giving out garments to be made off the premises of the master.* The effect of this was, that the workman making the garment, knowing that the master could not tell whom he got to do his work for him, employed women and children to help him, and paid them little or nothing for their labour. This was the beginning of the sweating system. The workmen gradually became transformed from journeymen into 'middlemen,' living by the labour of others. Employers soon began to find that they could get garments made at a less sum than the regular price, and those tradesmen who were anxious to force their trade, by underselling their more honourable neighbours, readily availed themselves of this means of obtaining cheap labour."

The *middleman system of work* is so much akin to the domestic system, of which, indeed, it is but a necessary result, that it forms a natural addendum to the above. Of this indirect mode of employing workmen, I said, in the *Chronicle*, when treating of the timber-porters at the docks:—

"The middleman system is the one crying evil of the day. Whether he goes by the name of 'sweater,' 'chamber-master,' 'lumper,' or contractor, it is this *trading operative* who is the great means of reducing the wages of his fellow working-men. To make a profit out of the employment of his brother operatives he must, of course, obtain a lower class and, consequently, cheaper labour. Hence it becomes a *business* with him to hunt out the lowest grades of working men—that is to say, those who are either morally or intellectually inferior in the craft—the drunken, the dishonest, the idle, the vagabond, and the unskilful; these are the instruments that he seeks for, because, these being unable to obtain employment at the regular wages of the sober, honest, industrious, and skilful portion of the trade, he can obtain their labour at a lower rate than what is usually paid. Hence drunkards, tramps, men without character or station, apprentices, children—all suit him. Indeed, the more degraded the labourers, the better they answer his purpose, for the cheaper he can get their work, and consequently the more he can make out of it.

"'Boy labour or thief labour,' said a middleman, on a large scale, to me, 'what do I care, so long as I can get my work done cheap?' That this *seeking out* of cheap and inferior labour really takes place, and is a necessary consequence of the middleman system, we have merely to look into the condition of any trade where it is extensively pursued. I have shown, in my account of the tailors' trade printed in the *Chronicle*, that the wives of the sweaters not only parade the streets of London on the look-out for youths raw from the country, but that they make periodical trips to the poorest provinces of Ireland, in order to obtain workmen at the lowest possible rate. I have shown, moreover, that foreigners are annually imported from the Continent for the same purpose, and that among the chamber-masters in the shoe trade, the child-market at Bethnal-green, as well as the workhouses, are continually ransacked for the means of obtaining a cheaper kind of labour. All my investigations go to prove, that it is chiefly by means of this middleman system that the wages of the working men are reduced. It is this contractor—this trading operative—who is invariably the prime mover in the reduction of the wages of his fellow-workmen. He uses the most degraded of the class as a means of underselling the worthy and skilful labourers, and of ultimately dragging the better down to the abasement of the worst. He cares not whether the trade to which he belongs is already overstocked with hands, for, be those hands as many as they may, and the ordinary wages of his craft down to bare subsistence point, it matters not a jot to him; *he* can live solely by reducing them still lower, and so he immediately sets about drafting or importing a fresh and cheaper stock into the trade. If *men* cannot subsist on lower prices, then he takes apprentices, or hires children; if women of chastity cannot afford to labour at the price he gives, then he has recourse to prostitutes; or if workmen of character and worth refuse to work at less than the ordinary rate, then he seeks out the moral refuse of the trade—those whom none else will employ; or else he flies, to find labour meet for his purpose, to the workhouse and the gaol. Backed by this cheap and refuse labour, he offers his work at lower prices, and so keeps on reducing and reducing the wages of his brethren, until all sink in poverty, wretchedness, and vice. Go where we will, look into whatever poorly-paid craft we please, we shall find this *trading operative*, this *middleman* or contractor, at the bottom of the degradation."

The "contract system" or "lump work," as it is called, is but a corollary, as it were, of the foregoing; for it is an essential part of the middleman system, that the work should be obtained by the trading operative in large quantities, so that those upon whose labour he lives should be kept continually occupied, and the more, of course, that he can obtain work for, the greater his profit. When a quantity of work, usually paid for by the piece, is given out at one time, the natural tendency is for the piece-work to pass into lump-work; that is to say, if there be in a trade a number of distinct parts, each requiring, perhaps, from the division of labour, a distinct hand for the execution of it, or if each of these parts bear a different price, it is frequently the case that the master will contract with some one workman for the execution of the whole, agreeing to give a certain price for the job "in the lump," and allowing the workman to get whom he pleases to execute it. This is the case with the piece-working masters in the coach-building trade; but it is not essential to the contract or lump system of work, that other hands should be employed; the main distinction between it and piece-work being that the work is given out in large quantities, and a certain allowance or reduction of price effected from that cause alone.

It is this contract or lump work which constitutes the great evil of the carpenter's, as well as of many other trades; and as in those crafts, so in this, we find that the lower the wages are reduced the greater becomes the number of trading operatives or middlemen. For it is when workmen find the difficulty of living by their labour increased that they take to scheming and trading upon the labour of their fellows. In the slop trade, where the pay is the worst, these creatures abound the most; and so in the carpenter's trade, where the wages are the lowest—as among the speculative builders—there the system of contracting and sub-contracting is found in full force.

Of this contract or lump work, I received the following account from the foreman to a large speculating builder, when I was inquiring into the condition of the London carpenters:—

"The way in which the work is done is mostly by letting and subletting. The masters usually prefer to let work, because it takes all the trouble off their hands. They know what they are to get for the job, and of course they let it as much under that figure as they possibly can, all of which is clear gain without the least trouble. How the work is done, or by whom, it's no matter to them, so long as they can make what they want out of the job, and have no bother about it. Some of our largest builders are taking to this plan, and a party who used to have one of the largest shops in London has within the last three years discharged all the men in his employ (he had 200 at least), and has now merely an office, and none but clerks and accountants in his pay. He has taken to letting his work out instead of doing it at home. The parties to whom the work is let by the speculating builders are generally working men, and these men in their turn look out for other working men, who will take the job cheaper than they will; and so I leave you, sir, and the public to judge what the party who really executes the work gets for his labour, and what is the quality of work that he is likely to put into it. The speculating builder generally employs an overlooker to see that the work is done sufficiently well to pass the surveyor. That's all he cares about. Whether it's done by thieves, or drunkards, or boys, it's no matter to him. The overlooker, of course, sees after the first party to whom the work is let, and this party in his turn looks after the several hands that he has sublet it to. The first man who agrees to the job takes it in the lump, and he again lets it to others in the piece. I have known instances of its having been let again a third time, but this is not usual. The party who takes the job in the lump from the speculator usually employs a foreman, whose duty it is to give out the materials and to make working drawings. The men to whom it is sublet only find labour, while the 'lumper,' or first contractor, agrees for both labour and materials. It is usual in contract work, for the first party who takes the job to be bound in a large sum for the due and faithful performance of his contract. He then, in his turn, finds out a sub-contractor, who is mostly a small builder, who will also bind himself that the work shall be properly executed, and there the binding ceases—those parties to whom the job is afterwards let, or sublet, employing foremen or overlookers to see that their contract is carried out. The first contractor has scarcely any trouble whatsoever; he merely engages a gentleman, who rides about in a gig, to see that what is done is likely to pass muster. The sub-contractor has a little more trouble; and so it goes on as it gets down and down. Of course I need not tell you that the first contractor, who does the *least* of all, gets the *most* of all; while the poor wretch of a working man, who positively executes the job, is obliged to slave away every hour, night after night, to get a bare living out of it; and this is the contract system."

A tradesman, or a speculator, will contract, for a certain sum, to complete the skeleton of a house, and render it fit for habitation. He will sublet the flooring to some working joiner, who will, in very many cases, take it on such terms as to allow himself, by working early and late, the regular journeymen's wages of 30s. a week, or perhaps rather more. Now this sub-contractor cannot complete the work within the requisite time by his own unaided industry, and he employs men to assist him, often subletting again, and such assistant men will earn perhaps but 4s. a day. It is the same with the doors, the staircases, the balustrades, the window-frames, the room-skirtings, the closets; in short, all parts of the building.

The subletting is accomplished without difficulty. Old men are sometimes employed in such work, and will be glad of any remuneration to escape the workhouse; while stronger workmen are usually sanguine that by extra exertion, "though the figure is low, they may make a tidy thing out of it after all." In this way labour is cheapened. "Lump" work, "piece" work, work by "the job," are all portions of the contract system. The principle is the same. "Here is this work to be done, what will you undertake to do it for?"

In number after number of the *Builder* will be found statements headed "Blind Builders." One firm, responding to an advertisement for "estimates" of the building of a church, sends in an offer to execute the work in the best style for 5000*l*. Another firm may offer to do it for somewhere about 3000*l*. The first-mentioned firm would do the work well, paying the "honourable" rate of wages. The under-working firm *must* resort to the scamping and subletting system I have alluded to. It appears that the building of churches and chapels, of all denominations, is one of the greatest encouragement to slop, or scamp, or under-paid work. The same system prevails in many trades with equally pernicious effects.

"If you will allow me," says a correspondent, "I would state that there is one cause of hardship and suffering to the labouring or handicraftsman, which, to my mind, is far more productive of distress and poor-grinding than any other, or than all other causes put together: I allude to the *contract* system, and especially in reference to printing. Depend upon it, sir, the father of wickedness himself could not devise a more malevolent or dishonest course than that now very generally pursued by those who should be, of all others, the friends of the poor and working man. The Government and the great West-end clubs have reduced their transactions to such a low level in this respect that it seems to be the only question with them, Who will work lowest or supply goods at the lowest figure? And this, too, totally irrespective of the circumstance whether it may not reduce wages or bankrupt the contractor. No matter whether a party who has executed the work required for years be noted for paying a fair and remunerating price to his workmen or sub-tradesmen, and bears the character of a responsible and trustworthy man—all this is as nothing; for somebody, who may be, for aught that is cared, deficient in all these points, will do what is needful at *so much* less; and then, unless willing to reduce the wage of his workpeople, the long-employed tradesman has but the alternative of losing his business or cheating his creditors. And then, to give a smack to the whole affair, the 'Stationery Office' of the Government, or the committee of the club, will congratulate themselves and their auditors on the fact that a diminution in expenses has been effected; a result commemorated perhaps by an addition of salary to the officials in the former case, and of a 'cordial vote of thanks' in the latter. I do not write 'without book,' I can assure you, on these matters; for I have long and earnestly watched the subject, and could fill many a page with the details."

Of the ruinous effects of the contract system in connection with the army clothing, Mr. Pearse, the army clothier, gave the following evidence before the Select Committee on Army and Navy Appointments.

"When the contract for soldier's great coats was opened, Mr. Maberly took it at the same price (13s.) in December, 1808; this shows the effect of wild competition. In February following, Esdailes' house, who were accoutrement makers, and not clothiers, got knowledge of what was Mr. Maberly's price, and *they* tendered at 12s. 6½d. a month afterwards; it was evidently then a struggle for the price, and how the quality the least good (if we may use such a term) could pass. Mr. Maberly did not like to be outbidden by Esdailes; *Esdailes stopped subsequently*, and Mr. Maberly bid 12s. 6d. three months after, and Mr. Dixon bid again, and got the contract for 11s. 3d. in October, and in December of that year another public tender took place, and Messrs. A. and D. Cock took it at 11s. 5½d., *and they subsequently broke*. It went on in this sort of way,—changing hands every two or every three months, by bidding against each other. Presently, though it was calculated that the great coat was to wear four years, it was found that *those great coats were so inferior in quality, that they wore only two years*, and representations were accordingly made to the Commander-in-Chief, when it was found necessary that great care should be taken to go back to the original good quality that had been established by the Duke of York."

Mr. Shaw, another army clothier, and a gentleman with whose friendship, I am proud to say, I have been honoured since the commencement of my inquiries—a gentleman actuated by the most kindly and Christian impulses, and of whom the workpeople speak in terms of the highest admiration and regard; this gentleman, impressed with a deep sense of the evils of the contract system to the under-paid and over-worked operatives of his trade, addressed a letter to the Chairman of the Committee on Army, Navy, and Ordnance Estimates, from which the following are extracts:—

"My Lord, my object more particularly is, to request your lordship will submit to the committee, *as an evidence of the evils of contracts*, the great coat sent herewith, made similar to those supplied to the army, and I would respectfully appeal to them as men, gentlemen, *as Christians*, whether *fivepence*, the price now being given to poor females for making up those coats, is a fair and just price for six, seven, and eight hours' work. . . . My Lord, *the misery amongst the workpeople is most distressing*—of a mass of people, *willing to work*, who cannot obtain it, and of a mass, especially women, most iniquitously paid for their labour, who are in a state of oppression disgraceful to the Legislature, the Government, the Church, and the consuming public. . . . . I would, therefore, most humbly and earnestly call upon your lordship, and the other members of the committee, to recommend an *immediate stop to be put to the system of contracting* now pursued by the different government departments, as being one of false economy, as a system most *oppressive to the poor*, and *being most injurious*, in every way, to the best *interests of the country.*"

In another place the same excellent gentleman says:—

"I could refer to the screwing down of other things by the government authorities, but the above will be sufficient to show *how cruelly the workpeople employed in making up this clothing are oppressed; and some of the men will tell you they are tired of life. Last week I found one man making a country police coat, who said his wife and child were out begging.*"

The last mentioned of the several modes of cheapening labour is the "*small-master system*" of work, that is to say, the operatives taking to make up materials on their own account rather than for capitalist employers. In every trade where there are *small* masters, trades into which it requires but little capital to embark, there is certain to be a cheapening of labour. Such a man works himself, and to get work, to meet the exigences of the rent and the demands of the collectors of the parliamentary and parochial taxes, he will often underwork the very journeymen whom he occasionally employs, doing "the job" in such cases with the assistance of his family and apprentices, at a less rate of profit than the amount of journeymen's wages.

Concerning these garret masters I said, when treating of the Cabinet trade, in the *Chronicle*, " The cause of the extraordinary decline of wages in the Cabinet trade (even though the hands decreased and the work increased to an unprecedented extent) will be found to consist in the increase that has taken place within the last 20 years of what are called ' garret masters' in the cabinet trade. These garret masters are a class of small ' trade-working masters,' the same as the ' chamber masters' in the shoe trade, supplying both capital and labour. They are in manufacture what ' the peasant proprietors' are in agriculture—their own employers and their own workmen. There is, however, this one marked distinction between the two classes—the garret master cannot, like the peasant proprietor, *eat* what he produces; the consequence is, that he is obliged to convert each article into food immediately he manufactures it—no matter what the state of the market may be. The capital of the garret master being generally sufficient to find him in materials for the manufacture of only one article at a time, and his savings being but barely enough for his subsistence while he is engaged in putting those materials together, he is compelled, the moment the work is completed, to part with it for whatever he can get. He cannot afford to keep it even a day, for to do so is generally to remain a day unfed. Hence, if the market be at all slack, he has to force a sale by offering his goods at the lowest possible price. What wonder, then, that the necessities of such a class of individuals should have created a special race of employers, known by the significant name of ' slaughter-house men'—or that these, being aware of the inability of the 'garret masters' to hold out against any offer, no matter how slight a remuneration it affords for their labour, should continually lower and lower their prices, until the entire body of the competitive portion of the cabinet trade is sunk in utter destitution and misery? Moreover, it is well known how strong is the stimulus among peasant proprietors, or, indeed, any class working for themselves, to extra production. So it is, indeed, with the garret masters; their industry is almost incessant, and hence a greater quantity of work is turned out by them, and continually forced into the market, than there would otherwise be. What though there be a brisk and a slack season in the cabinet-maker's trade as in the majority of others?—slack or brisk, the garret masters must produce the same excessive quantity of goods. In the hope of extricating himself from his overwhelming poverty, he toils on, producing more and more—and yet the more he produces the more hopeless does his position become; for the greater the stock that he thrusts into the market, the lower does the price of his labour fall, until at last, he and his whole family work for less than half what he himself could earn a few years back by his own unaided labour."

The small-master system of work leads, like the domestic system, with which, indeed, it is intimately connected, to the employment of wives, children, and apprentices, as a means of assistance and extra production—for as the prices decline so do the small masters strive by further labour to compensate for their loss of income.

Such, then, are the several modes of work by which labour is cheapened. There are, as we have seen, but two ways of *directly* effecting this, viz., first by making men do more work for the same pay, and secondly, by making them do the same work for less pay. The way in which men are made to do more, it has been pointed out, is, by causing them either to work longer or quicker, or else by employing fewer hands in proportion to the work; or engaging them only for such time as their services are required, and discharging them immediately afterwards. These constitute the several modes of economizing labour, which lowers the rate of remuneration (the ratio of the pay to the work) rather than the pay itself. The several means by which this result is attained are termed "systems of work, production, or engagement," and such are those above detailed.

Now it is a necessity of these several systems, though the actual amount of remuneration is not directly reduced by them, that a cheaper labour should be obtained for carrying them out. Thus, in contract or lump work, perhaps, the price may not be immediately lowered; the saving to the employer consisting chiefly in supervision, he having in such a case only one man to look to instead of perhaps a hundred. The contractor, or lumper, however, is differently situated; he, in order to reap any benefit from the contract, must, since he cannot do the whole work himself, employ others to help him, and to reap any benefit from the contract, this of course must be done at a lower price than he himself receives; so it is with the middleman system, where a profit is derived from the labour of other operatives; so, again, with the domestic system of work, where the several members of the family, or cheaper labourers, are generally employed as assistants; and even so is it with the small-master system, where the labour of apprentices and wives and children is the principal means of help. Hence the operatives adopting these several systems of work are rather the instruments by which cheap labour is obtained than the cheap labourers themselves. It is true that a sweater, a chamber master, or garret master, a lumper or contractor, or a home worker, generally works cheaper than the ordinary operatives, but this he does chiefly by the cheap labourers he employs, and then, finding that he is able to underwork the rest of the trade, and that the more hands he employs the greater becomes his profit, he offers to do work at less than the usual rate. It is not a necessity of the system that the middleman operative, the domestic worker, the lumper, or garret master should be himself underpaid, but simply that he should employ others who are so, and it is thus that such systems of work tend to cheapen the labour of those trades in which they are found to prevail. Who, then, are the cheap labourers?—who the individuals, by means of whose services the sweater, the smaller master, the lumper, and others, is enabled to underwork the rest of his trade?—what the general characteristics of those who, in the majority of handicrafts, are found ready to do the same work for less pay, and how are these usually distinguished from such as obtain the higher rate of remuneration?

The cheap workmen in all trades, I find, are divisible into three classes:—
1. The unskilful.
2. The untrustworthy.
3. The inexpensive.

First, as regards the *unskilful*. Long ago it has been noticed how frequently boys were put to trades to which their tastes and temperaments were antagonistic. Gay, who in his quiet, unpretending style often elicited a truth, tells how a century and a half ago the generality of parents never considered for what business a boy was best adapted—

"But ev'n in infancy decree
What this or t'other son shall be."

A boy thus brought up to a craft for which he entertains a dislike can hardly become a proficient in it. At the present time thousands of parents are glad to have their sons reared to *any* business which their means or opportunities place within their reach, even though the lad be altogether unsuited to the craft. The consequence is, that these boys often grow up to be unskilful workmen. There are technical terms for them in different trades, but perhaps the generic appellation is "muffs." Such workmen, however well conducted, can rarely obtain employment in a good shop at good wages, and are compelled, therefore, to accept second, third, and fourth-rate wages, and are often driven to slop work.

Other causes may be cited as tending to form unskilful workmen: the neglect of masters or foremen, or their incapacity to teach apprentices; irregular habits in the learner; and insufficient practice during a master's paucity of employment. I am assured, moreover, that hundreds of mechanics yearly come to London *from the country parts,* whose skill is altogether inadequate to the demands of the "honourable trade." Of course, during the finishing of their education they can only work for inferior shops at inferior wages; hence another cause of cheap labour. Of this I will cite an instance: a bootmaker, who for years had worked for first-rate West-end shops, told me that when he came to London from a country town he was sanguine of success, because he knew that he was a *ready* man (a quick workman.) He very soon found out, however, he said, that as he aspired to do the best work, he "had his business to learn all over again;" and until he attained the requisite skill, he worked for "just what he could get:" he was a cheap, because then an unskilful, labourer.

There is, moreover, the cheaper labour of *apprentices,* the great prop of many a slop-trader; for as such traders disregard all the niceties of work, as they disregard also the solidity and perfect finish of any work (finishing it, as it was once described to me, "just to the eye"), a lad is soon made useful, and his labour remunerative to his master, as far as slop remuneration goes, which, though small in a small business, is wealth in a "monster business."

There are, again, the "*improvers.*" These are the most frequent in the dress-making and millinery business, as young women find it impossible to form a good connection among a wealthier class of ladies in any country town, unless the "patronesses" are satisfied that their skill and taste have been perfected in London. In my inquiry (in the course of two letters in the *Morning Chronicle*) into the condition of the workwomen in this calling, I was told by a retired dressmaker, who had for upwards of twenty years carried on business in the neighbourhood of Grosvenor-square, that she had sometimes met with "improvers" so tasteful and quick, from a good provincial tuition, that they had really little or nothing to learn in London. And yet their services were secured for one, and oftener for two years, merely for board and lodging, while others employed in the same establishment had not only board and lodging, but handsome salaries. The improver's, then, is generally a cheap labour, and often a very cheap labour too. The same form of cheap labour prevails in the carpenter's trade.

There is, moreover, the labour of *old men.* A tailor, for instance, who may have executed the most skilled work of his craft, in his old age, or before the period of old age, finds his eyesight fail him,—finds his tremulous fingers have not a full and rapid mastery of the needle, and he then labours, at greatly reduced rates of payment, on the making of soldiers' clothing—"sanc-work," * as it is called—or on any ill-paid and therefore ill-wrought labour.

The inferior, as regards the quality of the work, and under-paid class of *women,* in tailoring, for example, again, cheapen labour. It is cheapened, also, by the employment of *Irishmen* (in, perhaps, all branches of skilled or unskilled labour), and of *foreigners,* more especially of Poles, who are inferior workmen to the English, and who will work *very* cheap, thus supplying a low-price labour to those who seek it.

I may remark further, that if a first-rate workman be driven to slop work, he soon loses his skill; he can only work slop; this has been shown over and over again, and so *his* labour becomes cheap in the mart.

2. Of *Untrustworthy Labour* (as a cause of cheap labour) I need not say much. It is obvious that a drunken, idle, or dishonest workman or workwoman, when pressed by want, will and must labour, not for the recompense the labour merits, but for whatever pittance an employer will accord. There is no reliance to be placed in him. Such a man cannot "hold out" for terms, for he is perhaps starving, and it is known that "he cannot be depended upon." In the sweep's trade many of those who work at a lower rate than the rest of

---

* The term *sanc* in "sanc-work" is the Norman word for blood (Latin, *sanguis*; French, *sang*), so that "sanc-work" means, literally, bloody work, this called either from the sanguinary trade of the soldier, or from the blood-red colour of the cloth.

the trade are men who have lost their regular work by dishonesty.

3. The *Inexpensive class* of workpeople are very numerous. They consist of three sub-divisions:—
  (*a.*) Those who have been accustomed to a coarser kind of diet, and who, consequently, requiring less, can afford to work for less.
  (*b.*) Those who derive their subsistence from other sources, and who, consequently, do not live by their labour.
  (*c.*) Those who are in receipt of certain "aids to their wages," or who have other means of living beside their work.

Of course these causes can alone have influence where the wages are *minimized* or reduced to the lowest ebb of subsistence, in which case they become so many means of driving down the price of labour still lower.

a. Those who, being what is designated hard-reared that is to say, accustomed to a scantier or coarser diet, and who, therefore, "can do" with a less quantity or less expensive quality of food than the average run of labourers, can of course live at a lower cost, and so *afford* to work at a lower rate. Among such (unskilled) labourers are the peasants from many of the counties, who seek to amend their condition by obtaining employment in the towns. I will instance the agricultural labourers of Dorsetshire.

"Bread and potatoes," writes Mr. Thornton, in his work on Over-Population and its Remedy, p. 21, "do really form the staple of their food. As for meat, most of them would not know its taste, if, once or twice *in the course of their lives*,—on the squire's having a son and heir born to him, or on the young gentleman's coming of age,—they were not regaled with a dinner of what the newspapers call 'old English fare.' Some of them contrive to have a little bacon, in the proportion, it seems, of *half a pound a week to a dozen persons*, but they more commonly use fat to give the potatoes a relish ; and, as one of them said to Mr. Austin (a commissioner), they don't *always* go without cheese.'"

With many poor Irishmen the rearing has been still harder. I had some conversation with an Irish rubbish-carter, who had been thrown out of work (and was entitled to no allowance from any trade society) in consequence of a strike by Mr. Myers's men. On my asking him how he subsisted in Ireland, "Will, thin, sir," he said, "and it's God's truth, I once lived for days on green things I picked up by the road side, and the turnips, and that sort of mate I stole from the fields. It was called staling, but it was the hunger, 'deed was it. That was in the county Limerick, sir, in the famine and 'viction times; and, glory be to God, I 'scaped when others didn't."

I may observe that the chief local paper, the *Limerick and Clare Examiner*, published twice a week, gave, twice a week, at the period of "the famine and evictions," statements similar to that of my informant.

Now, would not a poor man, reared as the Limerick peasant I have spoken of, who was actually driven to eat the grass, which biblical history shows was once a signal punishment to a great offender—would not such a man work for the veriest dole, rather than again be subjected to the pangs of hunger? In my inquiries among the costermongers, one of them said of the Irish in his trade, and without any bitterness, " they'll work for nothing, and live on less." The meaning is obvious enough, although the assertion is, of course, a contradiction in itself.

"This department of labour," says Mr. Baines, in his History of the Hand-Loom Weavers, is "greatly overstocked, and the price necessarily falls. The evil is aggravated by the multitudes of Irish who have flocked into Lancashire, some of whom, having been linen weavers, naturally resort to the loom, and others learn to weave as the easiest employment they can adopt. Accustomed to a wretched mode of living in their own country, they are contented with wages that would starve an English labourer. They have, in fact, so lowered the *rate* of wages as to drive many of the English out of the employment, and to drag down those who remain in it to their own level."

b. Those who derive their subsistence from other sources can, of course, afford to work cheaper than those who have to live by their labour. To this class belongs the labour of wives and children, who, being supposed to be maintained by the toil of the husband, are never paid "living wages" for what they do ; and hence the misery of the great mass of needlewomen, widows, unmarried and friendless females, and the like, who, having none to assist them, are forced to starve upon the pittance they receive for their work. The labour of those who are in prisons, workhouses, and asylums, and who consequently have their subsistence found them in such places, as well as the work of prostitutes, who obtain their living by other means than work, all come under the category of those who can afford to labour at a lower rate than such as are condemned to toil for an honest living. It is the same with apprentices and "improvers," for whose labour the instruction received is generally considered to be either a sufficient or partial recompense, and who consequently look to other means for their support. Under the same head, too, may be cited the labour of amateurs, that is to say, of persons who either are not, or who are too proud to acknowledge themselves, regular members of the trade at which they work. Such is the case with very many of the daughters of tradesmen, and of many who are considered *genteel* people. These young women, residing with their parents, and often in comfortable homes, at no cost to themselves, will, and do, undersell the regular needlewomen ; the one works merely for pocket-money (often to possess herself of some article of finery), while the other works for what is called "the bare life."

c. The last-mentioned class, or those who are in possession of what may be called "aids to wages," are differently circumstanced. Such are the men who have other employment besides that for which they accept less than the ordinary pay, as is the case with those who attend at gentlemen's houses for one or two hours every morning, cleaning boots, brushing clothes, &c., and who, having the remainder of the day at their own disposal, can afford to work at any calling cheaper than others, because not solely dependent upon it for their living.

The army and navy pensioners (non-commissioned officers and privates) were, at one period, on the disbanding of the militia and other forces, a very numerous body, but it was chiefly the military pensioners whose position had an effect upon the labour of the country. The naval pensioners found employment as fishermen, or in some avocation connected with the sea. The military pensioners, however, were men who, after a career of soldiership, were not generally disposed to settle down into the drudgery of regular work, even if it were in their power to do so; and so, as they always had their pensions to depend upon, they were a sort of universal jobbers, and jobbed cheaply. At the present time, however, this means of cheap labour is greatly restricted, compared with what was the case, the number of the pensioners being considerably diminished. Many of the army pensioners turn the wheels for turners at present.

The allotment of gardens, which yield a partial support to the allottee, are another means of cheap labour. The allotment demands a certain portion of time, but is by no means a thorough employment, but merely an "aid," and consequently a *means*, to low wages. Such a man has the advantage of obtaining his potatoes and vegetables at the cheapest rate, and so can afford to work cheaper than other men of his class. It was the same formerly with those who received "relief" under the old Poor-Law.

And even under the present system it has been found that the same practice is attended with the same result. In the Sixth Annual Report of the Poor-Law Commissioners, 1840, at p. 31, there are the following remarks on the subject:—

"Whilst upon the subject of relief to widows in aid of wages, we must not omit to bring under your Lordship's notice an illustration of the *depressing effect* which is produced by the practice of giving relief in aid of wages to widows upon the earnings of females. Colonel A'Court states:—

"'As regards females, the instance to which I have alluded presents itself in the Portsea Island Union, where, from the insufficiency of workhouse accommodation, as well as from benevolent feelings, small allowances of 1s. 6d. or 2s. a week are given to widows with or without small children, or to married women deserted by their husbands. *Having this certain income, however small, they are enabled to work at lower wages than those who do not possess this advantage.* The consequence is, that competition has enabled the shirt and stay manufacturers, who abound in the Union, and who furnish in great measure the London as well as many foreign markets with these articles of their trade, to get their work done at the extraordinary low prices of—stays, complete, 9d.; shirts, from 1s. to 1s. 6d. per dozen.

"'The women all declare that they cannot possibly, after working from twelve to fifteen hours per day, earn more than 1s. 6d. per week. The manufacturers assert that, by steady work, 4s. to 6s. a week may be earned under ordinary circumstances.

"'In the meantime *the demand for workwomen increases*, and it is by no means unusual to see hand-bills posted over the town requiring from 500 to 1000 additional stitchers.'"

Such, then, is the character of the cheap workers in all trades; go where we will, we shall find the low-priced labour of the trade to consist of either one or other of the three classes above-mentioned; while the *means* by which this labour is brought into operation will be generally by one of the "systems of work" before specified.

The cheap labour of the rubbish-carters' trade appears to be a consequence of two distinct antecedents, viz., casual labour and the prevalence of the contract system among builder's work. The small-master system also appears to have some influence upon it.

First as regards the influence of casual labour in reducing the ordinary rate of wages.

The tables given at p. 290, vol. ii., showing the wages paid to the rubbish-carters, present what appears, and indeed is, a strange discrepancy of payment to the labourers in rubbish-carting. About three-fourths of the rubbish-carters throughout London receive 18s. weekly, when in work; in Hampstead, however, the rate of their wages is (uniformly) 20s. a week; in Lambeth (but less uniformly), it is 19s.; in Wandsworth, 17s.; in Islington, 16s.; and in Greenwich, 14s. and 12s. The character of the work, whether executed for 12s. or 20s. weekly, is the same; why, then, can a rubbish-carter, who works at Hampstead, earn 8s. a week more than one who works at Greenwich? An employer of rubbish-carters, and of similar labourers, on a large scale, a gentleman thoroughly conversant with the subject in all its industrial bearings, accounts for the discrepancy in this manner:—

After the corn and the hop-harvests have terminated, there is always an influx of unskilled labourers into Gravesend, Woolwich, and Greenwich. These are the men who, from the natural bent of their dispositions, or from the necessity of their circumstances, resort to the casual labour afforded by the revolution of the seasons, when to gather the crops before the weather may render the harvest precarious and its produce unsound, is a matter of paramount necessity, and the increase of hands employed during this season is, as a consequence, proportionately great. The chief scene of such labour in the neighbourhood of the metropolis, is in the county of Kent; and on the cessation of this work, of course there is a large amount of labour "turned adrift," to seek, the next few days, for any casual employment that may "turn up." In this way, I am assured, a large amount of cheap and unskilled labour is being constantly placed at the command of those masters who, so to speak, occupy the line of march to London, and are, therefore, first applied to for employment by casual labourers; who, when engaged, are employed as inferior, or unskilful, workmen, at an inferior rate of remuneration. Greenwich may be looked upon as the first stage or halt for casual labourers, on their way to London.

My informant assured me, as the result of his own observations, that an English labourer would, as a general rule, execute more work by one-sixth, in a week, than an Irish labourer (a large proportion of the casual hands are Irish); that is, the extent of work which would occupy the Irishman six, would occupy the Englishman but five days, were it so calculated. The Englishman was, however, usually more skilled and persevering, and far more to be depended upon. So different was the amount of work, even in rubbish-carting, between an able and experienced hand and one unused to the toil, or one inadequate from want of alertness or bodily strength, or any other cause, to its full and quick execution, that two "good" men in a week have done as much work as three indifferent hands. Thus two men at 18s. weekly each are as cheap (only employers cannot always see it), when they are thorough masters of their business, as three unready hands at 12s. a week each. The misfortune, however, is, that the 12s. a week men have a tendency to reduce the 16s. to their level.

With regard to the difference between the wages of Hampstead and Greenwich, I am informed that stationary working rubbish-carters are not too numerous in Hampstead, which is considered as rather "out of the way;" and as that metropolitan suburb is surrounded in every direction by pasture-land and wood-land, it is not in the line of resort of the class of men who seek the casual labour in harvesting, &c., of which I have spoken; it is rarely visited by them, and consequently, the regular hands are less interfered with than elsewhere, and wages have not been deteriorated.

The mode of work among the scurf labourers differs somewhat from that of the honourable part of the trade; the work executed by the scurf masters being for the most part on a more limited scale than that of the others. To meet the demands of builders or of employers generally, when "time" is an object, demands the use of relays of men, and of strong horses. This demand the smaller or scurf master cannot always meet. He may find men, but not always horses and carts, and he will often enough undertake work beyond his means and endeavour to aggrandise his profits by screwing his labourers. The *hours of scurf-employed labour* are nominally the same as the regular trade, but as an Irish carter said, "it's ralely the hours the masther plases, and they're often as long as it's light." The *scurf labourer is often paid by the day*, with "a day's hire, and no notice beyond." I am informed that scurf labourers generally work an hour a day, without extra remuneration, longer than those in the honourable trade.

The rubbish-carters employed by the scurf masters are not, as a body, I am assured, so badly paid as they were a few years back. It is rarely that labouring men can advance any feasible reason for the changes in their trade.

One of the main causes of the deteriorated wages of the rubbish-carters is the system of contracting and subletting. This, however, is but a branch of the ramified system of subletting in the construction of the " scamped" houses of the speculative builders. The building of such houses is sublet, literally from cellar to chimney. The rubbish-carting may be contracted for at a certain sum. The contractor may sublet it to men who will do it for one-fourth less perhaps, and who may sublet the labour in their turn. For instance, the calculation may be founded on the working men's receiving 15s. weekly. A contractor, a man possessing a horse, perhaps, and a couple of carts, and hiring another horse, will undertake it on the knowledge of his being able to engage men at 12s. or 13s. weekly, and so obtain a profit; indeed the reduction of price in such cases must all come out of the labour.

This subletting, I say, is but a small part of a gigantic system, and it is an unquestionable cause of the grinding down of the rubbish-carters' wages, and that by a class who have generally been working men themselves, and risen to be the owners of one or two carts and horses.

From one of these men, now a working carter, I had the following account, which further illustrates the mode of labour as well as of employment.

" I got a little a-head," he stated, " from railway jobbing and such like, and my father-in-law, as soon as I got married, made me a present of 20l. unexpected. I started for myself, thinking to get on by degrees, and get a fresh horse and cart every year. But it couldn't be done, sir. If I offered to take a contract to cart the rubbish and dig it, a builder would say,—'I can't wait; you haven't carts and horses enough from your own account, and I can't wait. If you have to hire them I can do that myself.' I was too honest, sir, in telling the plain truth, or I might have got more jobs. It's not a good trade in a small way, for if your horses aren't at work, they're eating their heads off, and you're fretting your heart out. Then I got to do sub-contracting, as you call it. No, it weren't that, it was under-working. I'd go to Mr. V—— as I knew, and say, ' You're on such a place, sir, have you room for me?' ' I think not,' he'd say, ' I've only the regular thing and no advantages—10s. 6d. for a day's work, horse and cart, or 4s. a load.' Those are the regular terms. Then I'd say, ' Well, sir, I'll do it for 8s. 6d., and be my own carman;' and so perhaps I'd get the job, and masters often say: ' I know I shall lose at 10s. 6d., but if I don't, you shall have something over.' Get anything over! Of course not, sir. I could have lived if I had constant work for two horses and carts, for I would have got a cheap man; such as me must get cheap men to drive the second cart, and under my own eye, whenever I could; but one of my poor horses broke his leg, and had to be sent to the knacker's, and I sold the other and my carts, and have worked ever since as a labouring man; mainly at pipe-work. O, yes, and rubbish-carting. I get 18s. a week now, but not regular.

"Well, sir, I'm sure I can't say, and I think no man could say, how much there's doing in sub-contracting. If I'm at work in Cannon-street, I don't know what's doing at Notting-hill, or beyond Bow and Stratford. No, I'm satisfied there's not so much of it as there was, but it's done so on the sly; who knows how much is done still, or how little? It's a system as may be carried on a long time, and is carried on, as far as men's labour goes, but it's different where there's horses, and stable rent. They can't be screwed, or under-fed, beyond a certain pitch, or they couldn't work at all, and so there's not as much under-work about horse-labour."

These small men are among the scurf and petty rubbish-carters, and are often the means of depressing the class to which they have belonged.

The employment in the honourable trade at rubbish-carting would be one of the best among unskilled labourers, were it continuous. But it is not continuous, and three-fourths of those engaged in it have only six months' work at it in the year. In the scurf-masters' employ, the work is really "casual," or, as I heard it quite as often described, "chance." In both departments of this trade, the men out of work look for a job in scavagery, and very generally in night-work, or, indeed, in any labour that offers. The Irish rubbish-carters will readily became hawkers of apples, oranges, walnuts, and even nuts, when out of employ, so working in concert with their wives. I heard of only four instances of a similar resource by the English rubbish-carters.

What I have said of the education, religion, politics, concubinage, &c., &c., of the better-paid rubbish-carters would have but to be repeated, if I described those of the under-paid. The latter may be more reckless when they have the means of enjoyment, but their diet, amusements, and expenditure would be the same, were their means commensurate. As it is, they sometimes live very barely and have hardly any amusements at their command. Their dinners, when single men, are often bread and a saveloy; when married, sometimes tea and bread and butter, and occasionally some "block ornaments;" the Irish being the principal consumers of cheap fish.

The labour of the wives of the rubbish-carters is far more frequently that of char-women than of needle-women, for the great majority of these women before their marriage were servant-maids. All the information I received was concurrent in that respect. The wife of a carman who keeps a chandler's shop near the Edgeware-road, greatly resorted to by the class to which her husband belonged, told me that out of somewhere about 25 wives of rubbish-carters or similar workmen, whom she knew, 20 had been domestic servants; what the others had been she did not know.

"I can tell you, sir," said the woman, "charing is far better than needle-work; far. If a young woman has conducted herself well in service, she can get charing, and then if she conducts herself well again, she makes good friends. That's, of course, if they're honest, sir. I know it from experience. My husband—before we were able to open this shop—was in the hospital a long time, and I went out charing, and did far better than a sister I have, who is a capital shirt-maker. There's broken victuals, sometimes, for your children. It's a hard world, sir, but there's a many good people in it."

One woman (before mentioned) earned not less than 5s. weekly in superior shirt-making, as it was described to me, which was evidently looked upon as a handsome remuneration for such toil. Another earned 3s. 6d.; another 2s. 6d.; and others, with uncertain employ, 2s., 1s. 6d., and in some weeks nothing. Needle-work, however, is, I am informed, not the work of one-tenth of the rubbish-carters' wives, whatever the earnings of the husband. From all I could learn, too, the wives of the under-paid rubbish-carters earned more, by from 10 to 20 per cent., than those of the better-paid. The earnings of a char-woman in average employ, as regards the wives of the rubbish-carters, is about 4s. weekly, without the exhausting toil of the needle-woman, and with the advantage of sometimes receiving broken meat, dripping, fat, &c., &c. The wives of the Irish labourers in this trade are often all the year street-sellers, some of wash-leathers, some of cabbage-nets, and some of fruit, clearing perhaps from 6d. to 9d. a day, if used to street-trading, as the majority of them are.

The under-paid labourers in this trade are chiefly poor Irishmen. The Irish workmen in this branch of the trade have generally been brought up "on the land," as they call it, in their own country, and after the sufferings of many of them during the famine, 12s. a week is regarded as "a rise in the world."

From one of this class I learned the following particulars. He seemed a man of 26 or 28 :—

"I was brought up on the land, sir," he said, "not far from Cullin, in the county Wexford. I lived with my father and mother, and shure we were badly off. Shure, thin, we were. Father and mother—the Heavens be their bed—died one soon after another, and some friends raised me the manes to come to this country. Well, thin, indeed, sir, and I can't say how they raised them, God reward them. I got to Liverpool, and walked to London, where I had some relations. I sold oranges in the strates the first day I was in London. God help me, I was glad to do anything to get a male's mate. I've lived on 6d. a-day sometimes. I have indeed. There was 2d. for the lodging, and 4d. for the mate, the tay and bread and butter. Did I live harder than that in Ireland, your honour? Well, thin, I have. I've lived on a dish of potatoes that might cost a penny there, where things is bhutiful and chape. Not like this country. No, no. I wouldn't care to go back. I have no friends there now. Thin I got ingaged by a man—yis, he was a rubbish-carter—to help him to fill his cart, and then we shot it on some new garden grounds, and had to shovel it about to make the grounds livil, afore the top soil was put on, for the bhutiful flowers and the gravel walks. Tim—yis, he was a counthryman of mine, but a Cor-rk man—said he'd made a bad bargain, for he was bad off, and he only clared 4*d*. a load, and he'd divide it wid me. We did six loads in a day, and I got 1*s*. every night for a wake. This was a rise. But one Sunday evening I was standing talking with people as lived in the same coort, and I tould how I was helping Tim. And two Englishmen came to find four men as they wanted for work, and ould Ragin (Regan) tould them what I was working for. And one of 'em said, I was 'a b—— Irish fool,' and ould Ragin said so, and words came on, and thin there was a fight, and the pelleece came, and thin the fight was harder. I was taken to the station, and had a month. I had two black eyes next morning, but was willin' to forget and forgive. No, I'm not fond of fightin'. I'm a paceable man, glory be to God, and I think I was put on. Oh, yis, and indeed thin, your honour, it was a fair fight."

I inquired of an English rubbish-carter as to these fair fights. He knew nothing of the one in question, but had seen such fights. They were usually among the Irish themselves, but sometimes Englishmen were " drawn into them." " Fair fights! sir," he said, " why the Irishes don't stand up to you like men. They don't fight like Christians, sir; not a bit of it. They kick, and scratch, and bite, and tear, like devils, or cats, or women. They're soon settled if you can get an honest knock at them, but it isn't easy."

"I sarved my month," continued my Irish informant, "and it ain't a bad place at all, the prison. I tould the gintleman that had charge of us, that I was a Roman Catholic, God be praised, and couldn't go to his prayers. 'O very well, Pat,' says he. And next day the praste came, and we were shown in to him, and very angry he was, and said our conduc' was a disgrace to religion, and to our counthry, and to him. Do I think he was right, sir? God knows he was, or he wouldn't have said so.

"I hadn't been out of prison two hours before I was hired for a job, at 10*s*. a week. It was in the city, and I carried old bricks and rubbish along planks, from the inside of a place as was pulled down; but the outside, all but the roof, was standin' until the windor frames, and the door posts, and what other timbers there was, was sould. It was dreadful hard work, carrying the basket of rubbish on your back to the cart. The dust came through, and stuck to my neck, for I was wet all over wid sweatin' so. Every man was allowed a pint of beer a day, and I thought nivver anything was so sweet. I don't know who gave it. The masther, I suppose. Will, thin, sir, I don't know who was the masther; it was John Riley as ingaged me, but *he's* no masther. Yis, thin, and I've been workin' that way ivver since. I've sometimes had 14*s*. a week, and sometimes 10*s*., and sometimes 12*s*. A man like me must take what he can get, and I will take it. I've been out of work sometimes, but not so much as some, for I'm young and strong. No, I can't save no money, and I have nothing just now to save it for. When I'm out of work, I sell fruit in the streets."

This statement, then, as regards the Irish labourers, shows the quality of the class employed. The English labourers, working on the same terms, are of the usual class of men so working,—broken-down men, unable, or accounting themselves unable, to "do better," and so accepting any offer affording the means of their daily bread.

OF THE LONDON CHIMNEY-SWEEPERS.

CHIMNEY-SWEEPERS are a consequence of two things—chimneys and the use of coals as fuel; and these are both commodities of comparatively recent introduction.

It is generally admitted that the earliest mention of *chimneys* is in an Italian MS., preserved in Venice, in which it is recorded that chimneys were thrown down in that city from the shock of an earthquake in 1347. In England, down even to the commencement of the reign of Elizabeth, the greater part of the houses in our towns had no chimneys; the fire was kindled on a hearthstone on the floor, or on a raised grate against the wall or in the centre of the apartment, and the smoke found its way out of the doors, windows, or casements.

During the long, and—as regards civil strife—generally peaceful, reign of Elizabeth, the use of chimneys increased. In a Discourse prefixed to an edition of Holinshed's "Chronicles," in 1577, Harrison, the writer, complains, among other things, "marvellously altered for the worse in England," of the multitude of chimneys erected of late. "Now we have many chimneys," he says, "and our tenderlings complain of rheums, catarrhs, and poses. Then we had none but *reredoses*, and our heads did never ache."* He demurs, too, to the change in the material of which the houses were constructed: " Houses were once builded of willow, then we had oaken men; but now houses are made of oak, and our men not only become willow, but a great many altogether of straw, which is a sore alteration."

* " Reredos, dossel (*retable*, Fr.; *postergule*, Ital.)," according to Parker's Glossary of Architecture, was " the wall or screen at the back of an altar, seat, &c.; it was usually ornamented with panelling, &c., especially behind an altar, and sometimes was enriched with a profusion of niches, buttresses, pinnacles, statues, and other decorations, which were often painted with brilliant colours.

" The open fire-hearth, frequently used in ancient domestic halls, was likewise called a reredos.

" In the description of Britain prefixed to Holinshed's ' Chronicles,' we are told that formerly, before chimneys were common in mean houses, ' each man made his fire against a reredosse in the hall, where he dined and dressed his meat.'"

The original word would appear to be *dosel* or *reredosel*; for Kelham, in his " Norman Dictionary," explains the word *doser* or *dosel* to signify a hanging or canopy of silk, silver, or gold work, under which kings or great personages sit; also the back of a chair of state (the word being probably a derivative of the Latin *dorsum*, the back. *Dos*, in slang, means a *bed*, a "dossing crib" being a sleeping-place, and has clearly the same origin). A *rere-dos* or *rere-dosel* would thus appear to have been a

In Shakespeare's time, the chimney-sweepers seem to have become a recognised class of public cleansers, for in "Cymbeline" the poet says—

> "Fear no more the heat o' the sun,
>   Nor the furious winter's rages;
> Thou thy worldly task hast done,
>   Home art gone, and ta'en thy wages:
> Golden lads and girls all must,
>   *As chimney-sweepers* come to dust."

In this beautiful passage there is an intimation, by the "chimney-sweepers" being contrasted with the "golden lads and girls," that their employment was regarded as of the meanest, a repute it bears to the present day.

But chimneys seem, like the "sweeps" or "sweepers," to have been a necessity of a change of fuel. In the days of "rere-dosses," our ancestors burnt only wood, so that they were not subjected to so great an inconvenience as we should be were our fires kindled without the vent of the chimney. Our fuel is coal, which produces a greater quantity of soot, and of black smoke, which is the result of imperfect combustion, than any other fuel, the smoke from wood being thin and pure in comparison.

The first mention of the use of coal as fuel occurs in a charter of Henry III., granting licence to the burgesses of Newcastle to dig for coal. In 1281 Newcastle is said to have had some slight trade in this article. Shortly afterwards coal began to be imported into London for the use of smiths, brewers, dyers, soap-boilers, &c. In 1316, during the reign of Edward I., its use in London was prohibited because of the supposed injurious influence of the smoke. In 1600 the use of coal in the metropolis became universal; about 200 vessels were employed in the London trade, and about 200,000 chaldrons annually imported.

In 1848, however, there were, besides the railway-borne coals, 12,267 cargoes imported, or 3,418,340 tons. The London coal trade now employs 2700 vessels and 21,600 seamen, and constitutes one-fourth of the whole general trade of the Thames.

To understand the *necessity* for chimney-sweepers, and the extent of the work for them to do, that is to say, the quantity of soot deposited in our chimneys during the combustion of the three and a half millions of tons of coals that are now annually consumed in London, we must first comprehend the conditions upon which the evolution of soot depends, soot being simply the fine carbonaceous particles condensed from the smoke of coal fuel, and deposited against the sides of the chimneys during its ascent between the walls to the tops of our houses. These conditions appear to have been determined somewhat accurately during the investigations of the Smoke Prevention Committee.

There are two kinds of smoke from the ordinary materials of combustion—(A) *Opaque*, or black smoke; (B) *Transparent*, or invisible smoke.

A. The *Opaque* smoke, though the most offensive and annoying from its dirtying properties, is, like the muddiest water, the least injurious to animal or vegetable health. It consists of the particles of unconsumed carbon which have not been deposited in the form of soot in the flue or chimney. This is the black smoke which will be further described.

B. *Transparent* smoke is composed of gases which are for the most part invisible, such as carbonic acid and carbonic oxide; also of sulphurous acid, but smokes with that component are both visible and invisible. The sulphurous acid is said by Professor Brande to destroy vegetation, for it has long been a cause of wonder why vegetation in towns did not flourish, since carbonic acid (which is so largely produced from the action of our fires) is the vital air of trees, shrubs, and plants*.

* It has been notorious for many years, that flowers will not bloom in any natural luxuriance, and that fruit will not properly ripen, in the heart of the city. Whilst this is an unquestionable fact, it is also a fact, that greatly as suburban dwellings have increased, and truly as London may be said to have "gone into the country," the greater quantity of the large, excellent, unfailing, and cheap supply of the fruits and vegetables in the London "green" markets are grown within a circle of from ten to twelve miles from St. Paul's. In the course of my inquiries in the series of letters on Labour and the Poor in the *Morning Chronicle*) into the supply, &c., to the "green markets" of the metropolis, I was told by an experienced market-gardener, who had friends and connections in several of the suburbs, that he fancied, and others in the trade were of the same opinion, that no gardening could be anything but a failure if attempted within "where the fogs went." My informant explained to me that the fogs, so peculiar to London, did not usually extend beyond three or four miles from the heart of the city. He was satisfied, he said, that within half a mile or so of this reach of fog the gardener's labours might be crowned with success. He knew nothing of any scientific reason for his opinion, but as far as a purely London fog extended (without regard to any mist pervading the whole country as well as the neighbourhood of the capital), he thought it was the boundary within which there could be no proper growth of fruit or flowers. That the London fog has its *limits* as regards the manifestation of its greatest density, there can be no doubt. My informant was frequently asked, when on his way home, by omnibus drivers and others whom he knew, and met on their way to town a few miles from it: "How's the fog, sir? *How far?*"

The extent of the London fog, then, if the information I have cited be correct, may be considered as indicating that portion of the metropolis where the population, and consequently the smoke, is the thickest, and within which agricultural and horticultural labours cannot meet with success. "The nuisance of a November fog in London," Mr. Booth stated to the Smoke Committee, "is most assuredly increased by the smoke of the town, arising from furnaces and private fires. It is vapour saturated with particles of carbon which causes all that uneasiness and pain in the lungs, and the uneasy sensations which we experience in our heads. I have no doubt of the density of these fogs arising from this carbonaceous matter."

The loss from the impossibility of promoting vegetation in the district most subjected to the fog is nothing, as the whole ground is already occupied for the thousand purposes of a great commercial city. The matter is, however, highly curious, as a result of the London smoke.

Concerning the frequency of fogs in the district of the immediate neighbourhood of the metropolis, it is stated in Weale's "London," that fogs "appear to be owing, 1st,

screen placed *behind* anything. I am told, that in the old houses in the north of England, erections at the back of the fire may, to this day, occasionally be seen, with an aperture behind for the insertion of plates, and such other things as may require warming.

A correspondent says there is "a 'reredos,' or open fire-hearth, now to be seen in the extensive and beautiful ruins of the Abbey of St. Agatha, in the North Riding of Yorkshire. The ivy now hangs over and partially conceals this reredos; but its form is tolerably perfect, and the stones are still coloured by the action of the fire, which was extinguished, I need hardly say, by the cold water thrown on such places by Henry VIII."

I may here observe, that several of the scientific men who gave the results of years of observation and study in their evidence to the Committee of the House of Commons, remarked on the popular misunderstanding of what smoke was, it being generally regarded as something *visible*. But in the composition of smoke, it appears, one product may be visible, and another invisible, and both offensive; while "occasionally you may have from the same materials varieties of products, all invisible, according to the manner to which they are supplied with air."

The Committee requested Dr. Reid to prepare a definition of "smoke," and more especially of "black smoke." The following is the substance of the doctor's definition, or rather description:—

1. *Black Smoke* consists essentially of carbon separated by heat from coal or other combustible bodies. If this smoke be produced at a very high temperature, the carbon forms a loose and powdery soot, comparatively free from other substances; while the lower the temperature at which black soot is formed, the larger is the amount of other substances with which it is mingled, among which are the following:—carbon, water, resin, oily and other inflammable products of various volatilities, ammonia, and carbonate of ammonia.

When the carbon, oils, resin, and water are associated together in certain proportions, they constitute *tar*. *Soft pitch* is produced if the tar be so far heated that the water is expelled; and *hard pitch* (resin blackened by carbon) when the oils are volatilized.

In all cases of ordinary combustion, carbonic acid is formed by the red-hot cinders, or by gases or other compounds containing carbon, acting on the oxygen of the air. This carbonic acid is discharged in general as an *invisible* gas. If the carbonic acid pass through red-hot cinders, or any carbonaceous smoke at a high temperature, it loses one particle of oxygen, and becomes carbonic oxide gas. The lost oxygen, uniting with carbon, forms an additional amount of carbonic oxide gas, which passes to the external atmosphere as an invisible gas, unless kindled in its progress, or at the top of the chimney, when its temperature is sufficiently elevated by the action of air. Carbonic oxide gas burns with a blue flame, and produces carbonic acid gas.

Black smoke is always associated with carburetted hydrogen gases. These may be mechanically blended with the oils and resins, but must be carefully distinguished from them. They form more essentially, when in a state of combustion, the inflammable matters that constitute flame.

2. *Smoke from Charcoal, Coke, and Anthracite*, is always invisible if the material be dry. A flame may appear, however, if carbonic oxide be formed.

3. *Wood or Pyroligneous Smoke* is rarely black. Water and carbonic acid are the products of the full combustion of wood, omitting the consideration of the ash that remains.

4. *Sulphurous Smokes*. Tons of sulphur are annually evolved in various conditions from copperworks. Offensive sulphurous smokes are often evolved from various chemical works, as gas-works, acid-works, &c.

5. *Hydrochloric Acid Smoke* is evolved in general in large quantities from alkali works.

6. *Metallic Smokes*—when ores of lead, copper, arsenic, &c., are used—often contain offensive matter in a minute state of division, and suspended in the smoke evolved from the furnaces.

7. *Putrescent Smokes*, loaded with the products of decayed animal and vegetable matter, are evolved at times from drains in visible vapours, more especially in damp weather. The foetid particles, when associated with moisture in this smoke, are entirely decomposed when subjected to heat.

Dr. Ure says, speaking of the cause of the ordinary black smoke above described, "The inevitable conversion of atmospheric air into carbonic acid has been hitherto the radical defect of almost all furnaces. The consequence is, that this gaseous matter is mixed with an atmosphere containing far too little oxygen, and instead of burning the carbon and hydrogen, which constitute the coal gases, the carbon is deposited partly in a pulverized form, constituting smoke or soot, and a great deal of the carbon gets half-burnt, and forms what is well known under the name of carbonic oxide, which is half-burnt charcoal."

"The ordinary smoke," Professor Faraday said, in his examination before the Committee, "is the visible black part of the products, the unburnt portions of the carbon. If you prevent the production of carbonic oxide or carbonic acid, you increase the production of smoke. You must with coal fuel either have carbonic acid or oxide, or else black smoke.

"Which is the least noxious?" he was asked, and answered, "As far as regards health, carbonic acid and carbonic oxide are most noxious to health; but it is not so much a question of health as of cleanliness and comfort, because I

---

to the presence of the river; and, 2ndly, to the fact that the superior temperature of the town produces results precisely similar to those we find to occur upon rivers and lakes. The cold damp currents of the atmosphere, which cannot act upon the air of the country districts, owing to the equality of their specific gravity, when they encounter the warmer and lighter strata over the town, displace the latter, intermixing with it and condensing the moisture. Fogs thus are often to be observed in London, whilst the surrounding country is entirely free from them. The peculiar colour of the London fogs appears to be owing to the fact that, during their prevalence, the ascent of the coal smoke is impeded, and that it is thus mixed with the condensed moisture of the atmosphere. As is well known, they are often so dense as to require the gas to be lighted in midday, and they cover the town with a most dingy and depressing pall. They also frequently exhibit the peculiarity of increasing density after their first formation, which appears to be owing to the descent of fresh currents of cold air towards the lighter regions of the atmosphere.

"They do not occur when the wind is in a dry quarter, as for instance when it is in the east; notwithstanding that there may be very considerable difference in the temperature of the air and of the water or the ground. The peculiar odour which attends the London fogs has not yet been satisfactorily explained; although the uniformity of its recurrence, and its very marked character, would appear to challenge elaborate examination."

believe that this town is as healthy as other places where there are not these fires.

"It is partly the impure coal gas evolved after the fresh charge of coal which originates the smokes, when not properly supplied with air; but it is a very mixed question. When a fresh charge of coal is put upon the fire, a great quantity of evaporable matter, which would be called impure coal gas according to the language of the question, is produced; and as that matter travels on in the heated place, if there be a sufficient supply of air, both the hydrogen and the carbon are entirely burnt. But if there be an insufficient supply of air, the hydrogen is taken possession of first, and the carbon is set free in its black and solid form; and if that goes into the cool part of the chimney before fresh air gets to it, that carbon is so carried out into the atmosphere and is the smoke in question. Generally speaking, the great rush of smoke is when coal is first put on the fire; and that from the want of a sufficient supply of oxygen at the right time, because the carbon is cooled so low as not to take fire."

This eminent chemist stated also that there was no difference in the ultimate chemical effect upon the air between a wood fire and a coal fire, but with wood there was not so much smoke set free in the heated place, which caused a difference in the gaseous products of wood combustion and of coal combustion. He thought that perhaps wood was the fuel which would be most favourable to health as affecting the atmosphere, inasmuch as it produced more water, and less carbonic acid, as the product of combustion.

What may be called the *peculiarities* of a smoky and sooty atmosphere are of course more strongly developed in London than elsewhere, as the following curious statements show:—

Dr. Reid, in describing metropolitan smoke, spoke of "those black portions of soot that every one is familiar with, which annoy us, for instance, at the Houses of Parliament to such an extent that I have been under the necessity of putting up a veil, about 40 feet long and 12 feet deep, on which, on a single evening, taking the worst kind of weather for the production of soot, we can count occasionally 200,000 visible portions of soot excluded at a single sitting. We count with the naked eye the number of pieces entangled upon a square inch. I have examined the amount deposited on different occasions in different parts of London at the tops of some houses; and on one occasion at the Horse Guards the amount of soot deposited was so great, that it formed a complete and continuous film, so that when I walked upon it I saw the impression of my foot left as distinctly on that occasion as when snow lies upon the ground. The film was exceedingly thin, but I could discover no want of continuity. On other occasions I have noticed in London that the quantity that escapes into individual houses is so great that in a single night I have observed a mixture of soot and of hoar frost collecting at the edge of the door, and forming a stripe three-quarters of an inch in breadth, and bearing an exact resemblance to a pepper and salt grey cloth. Those that I refer to are extreme occasions."

Mr. Booth mentioned, that one of the gardeners of the Botanic Garden in the Regent's-park, could tell the number of days sheep had been in the park from the blackness of their wool, its oleaginous power retaining the black.

Dr. Ure informed the Committee that a column of smoke might be seen extending in different directions round London, according to the way of the wind, for a distance of from 20 to 30 miles; and that Sir William Herschel had told him that when the wind blew from London he could not use his great telescope at Slough.

It was stated, moreover, that when a respirator is washed, the water is rendered dirty by the particles of soot adhering to the wire gauze, and which, but for this, would have entered the mouth.

Professor Brande said, on the subject of the public health being affected by smoke, "I cannot say that my opinion is that smoke produces any unhealthiness in London; it is a great nuisance certainly; but I do not think we have any good evidence that it produces disease of any kind."

"This Committee," said Mr. Beckett, "have been told that, by the mechanical effects of smoke upon the chest and lungs, disease takes place; that is, by swallowing a certain quantity of smoke the respiratory organs are injured; can you give any opinion upon that?"—"One would conceive," replied the Professor, "that that is the case; but when we compare the health of London with that of any other town or place where they are comparatively free or quite free from smoke, we do not find that difference which we should expect in regard to health."

Mr. E. Solly, lecturer on chemistry at the Royal Institution, expressed his opinion of the effect of smoke upon the health of towns:—

"My impression is," he said, "that it produces decided evil in two or three ways: first, mechanically; the solid black carbonaceous matter produces a great deal of disease; it occasions dirt amongst the lower orders, and, if they will not take pains to remove it, it engenders disease. If we could do away the smoke nuisance, I believe a great deal of that disease would be put an end to. But there is another point, and that is, the bad effects produced by the gases, sulphurous acid and other compounds of that nature, which are given out. If we do away with smoke, we shall still have those gases; and I have no doubt that those gases produce a great part of the disease that is produced by smoke."

On the other hand Dr. Reid thought that smoke was more injurious from the dirt it created than from causing impurity in the atmosphere, although "it was obvious enough that the inspiration of a sooty atmosphere must be injurious to persons of a delicate constitution." Dr. Ure pronounced smoke, in the common sense of visible black smoke, unwholesome, but "not so eminently as the French imagine."

Many witnesses stated their conviction that where poor people resided amongst smoke, they felt it impossible to preserve cleanliness in their persons or their dwellings, and that made them careless of their homes and indifferent to a decency of appearance, so that the public-house, and places where cleanliness and propriety were in no great estimation, became places of frequent resort, on the plain principle that if a man's home were uncomfortable, he was not likely to stay in it.

"I think," said Mr. Booth, "one great effect of the evil of smoke is upon the dwellings of the poor; it renders them less attentive to their personal appearance, and, in consequence, to their social condition."

It was also stated that there were "certain districts inhabited by the poor, where they will not hang out their clothes to be cleansed; they say it is of no use to do it, they will become dirty as before, and consequently they do not have their clothes washed." The districts specified as presenting this characteristic are St. George's-in-the East and the neighbourhood of Old-street, St. Luke's.

It must not be lost sight of, that whatever evils, moral or physical, without regarding merely pecuniary losses, are inflicted by the excess of smoke, they fall upon the poor, and almost solely on the poor. It is the poor who must reside, as was said, and with a literality not often applicable to popular phrases, "in the thick of it," and consequently there must either be increased washing or increased dirt.

To effect the mitigation of the nuisance of smoke, two points were considered:—

A. The substitution of some other material, containing less bituminous matter, for the "Newcastle coal."

B. The combustion of the smoke, before its emission into the atmospheric air, by means of mechanical contrivances founded on scientific principles.

As regards the first consideration (A) it was recommended that anthracite, or stone Welsh coal, which is a smokeless fuel, should be used instead of the Newcastle coal. This coal is almost the sole fuel in Philadelphia, a city of Quaker neatness beyond any in the United States of North America, and sometimes represented as the cleanest in the world. The anthracite coal is somewhat dearer than Newcastle coal in London, but only in a small degree.

Coke was also recommended as a substitute for coal in private dwellings.

"Are you of opinion," Dr. Reid was asked, "that smoke may be in a great measure prevented by extending the use of gas and coke?" He answered, "In numerous cities, where large quantities of gas are produced, coke is very frequently the principal fuel of the poor, and the difficulty of lighting that coke, and the difficulty of having heat developed by it in sufficient quantity, necessarily led me to look at the construction of the fire-places adapted for it. And on a general review of the question, I do entertain the opinion, that if education were more extended amongst the humblest classes with respect to the economy of their own fireside (I mean, literally, the fire-place, at present), and if gas were greatly extended, so that they did not drain the coal of the gas-works of the last dregs of gaseous matter, which are of very little use as gas, and more to be considered as adding to the bulk for sale than as valuable gas, that a coke might be left which would be easily accendible, which would be economical, and which, if introduced into fire-places where an open fire is desired, would *entirely remove the necessity of sweeping chimneys even with machines,* and would at the same time give as economical a fire as any ordinary fire-place can produce, for an ordinary coal fire rarely is powerful in its calorific emanations till the mass of gas has been expelled, and we see the cherry-red fire. The amount of gas that has escaped previously to the production or coking of the fire, is the gas that is valuable in a manufactory, and if therefore the individual consumer could have, not the hard-burnt stony coke, but the soft coke, in the condition that would give at once a cherry-red fire, we should attain the two great objects—of economising gas, and at the same time of having a lively cheerful fire. Then this led me to look particularly at the price of a gas lamp for a poor man. In a poor man's family, where the breakfast, the tea and dinner, require the principal attention, and he has some plain cooking utensils, in the heat of summer I believe that he will produce as much heat as he wants for those purposes from a single burner, which can be turned on and left all day, which shall not risk any boiling over, and by having this pure heat directed to the object to be warmed, instead of having a heavy iron grate, this plan would, if gas were generally introduced even into the humblest apartments, prove a great source of economy in summer."

Dr. Reid also told the Committee that there was a great prejudice against the use of coke, many persons considering that it produced a sulphurous smell; but as all ordinary coal coked itself, or became coke in an open fire, and was never powerfully calorific till it became coke, the prejudice would die away.

Very little is said in the Report about the smoke of private houses; an allusion, however, is made to that portion of the investigation:—"Your Committee have received the most gratifying assurances of the confident hope entertained by several of the highest scientific authorities examined by them, that the black smoke proceeding from fires in private dwellings, and all other places, may eventually be entirely prevented, either by the adoption of stoves and grates formed for a perfect combustion of the common bituminous coal, or by the use of coke, or of anthracite; but they are of opinion that the present knowledge on that subject is not such as to justify any legislative interference with these smaller fires."

"I should, in prospect," Professor Faraday said to the Committee, "look forward to the possibility of a great reduction of the smoke from coal fires in houses; but my impression is, that, in the present state of things, it would be tyrannical to determine that that must be done which at present we do not know can be done. Still, I think there is reason to believe that it can be effected in a very high degree."

Dr. Ure also thought that to extend any smoke enactment to private dwellings might be tyrannical in the present state of the chimneys, but he had no doubt that smoke might be consumed in fires in private dwellings.

Such, then, are the causes and remedies for smoke, and consequently of soot, for smoke, or rather opaque smoke, consists, as we have seen, of merely the gases of combustion with minute particles of carbon diffused throughout them; and as smoke is the result of the imperfect burning of our coals, it follows that chimney-sweepers are but a consequence of our ignorance, and that, as we grow wiser in the art of economising our fuel, we shall be gradually displacing this branch of labourers—the means of preventing smoke being simply the mode of displacing the chimney-sweepers—and this is another of the many facts to teach us that not only are we doubling our population in forty years, but we are likewise learning every year how to do our work with a less number of workers, either by inventing some piece of mechanism that will enable one "hand" to do as much as one hundred, or else doing away with some branch of labour altogether. Here lies the great difficulty of the time. A new element—science, with its offspring, steam—has been introduced into our society within the last century, decreasing labour at a time when the number of our labourers has been increasing at a rate unexampled in history; and the problem is, how to reconcile the new social element with the old social institutions, doing as little injury as possible to the community.

Suppose, for instance, the "smoke nuisance" entirely prevented, and that Professor Faraday's prophecy as to the great reduction of the smoke from coal fires in houses were fulfilled, and that the expectations of the sanguine and intense Committee, who tell us that they have "received *the most gratifying* assurances of the *confident* hope entertained by several of *the highest scientific* authorities, that the black smoke proceeding from fires in private dwellings and all other places may be eventually *entirely* prevented,"—suppose that these expectations, I say, be realized (and there appears to be little doubt of the matter), what is to become of the 1000 to 1500 "sweeps" who live, as it were, upon this very smoke? Surely the whole community should not suffer for them, it will be said. True; but unfortunately the same argument is being applied to each particular section of the labouring class,—and the labourers make up by far the greater part of the community. If we are daily displacing a thousand labourers by the annihilation of this process, and another thousand by the improvement of that, what is to be the fate of those we put on one side? and where shall we find employment for the hundred thousand new "hands" that are daily coming into existence among us? This is the great problem for earnest thoughtful men to work out!

But we have to deal here with the chimney-sweepers as they are, and not as they may be in a more scientific age. And, first, as to *the quantity of soot* annually deposited at present in the London chimneys.

The quantity of soot produced in the metropolis every year may be ascertained in the following manner:—

The larger houses are swept in some instances once a month, but generally once in three months, and yield on an average six bushels of soot per year. A moderate-sized house, belonging to the "middle class," is usually swept four times a year, and gives about five bushels of soot per annum; while houses occupied by the working and poorer classes are seldom swept more than twice, and sometimes only once, in the twelve-month, and yield about two bushels of soot annually.

The larger houses—the residences of noblemen and the more wealthy gentry—may, then, be said to produce an average of six bushels of soot annually; the houses of the more prosperous tradesmen, about five bushels; while those of the humbler classes appear to yield only two bushels of soot per annum. There are, according to the last returns, in round numbers, 300,000 inhabited houses at present in the metropolis, and these, from the "reports" of the income and property tax, may be said to consist, as regards the average rentals, of the proportions given in the next page.

Here we see that the number of houses whose average rental is above 50*l*. is 53,840; while those whose average rental is above 30*l*., and below 50*l*., are 90,002 in number; and those whose rental is below 30*l*. are as many as 163,880; the average rental for all London, 40*l*. Now, adopting the estimate before given as to the proportionate yield of soot from each of these three classes of houses, we have the following items:—

	Bushels of Soot per Annum.
53,840 houses at a yearly rental above 50*l*., producing 6 bushels of soot each per annum . . .	323,040
90,002 houses at a yearly rental above 30*l*. and below 50*l*., producing 5 bushels of soot each per annum .	450,010
163,880 houses at a yearly rental below 30*l*., producing 2 bushels of soot each per annum . . .	327,760
Total number of bushels of soot annually produced throughout London .	1,100,810

This calculation will be found to be nearly correct if tried by another mode. The quantity of soot depends greatly upon the amount of volatile or bituminous matter in the coals used. By a table given at p. 169 of the second volume of this work it will be seen that the proportion of volatile matter contained in the several kinds of coal are as follows:—

Cannel or gas coals contain 40 to 60 per cent. of volatile matter.

TABLE SHOWING THE NUMBER OF HOUSES, AT DIFFERENT AVERAGE RENTALS, THROUGHOUT THE METROPOLIS.

Number of Houses whose Average Rental is above £50.			Number of Houses whose Average Rental is above £30 and below £50.			Number of Houses whose Average Rental is below £30.		
	Average Rental (£)	Number of Houses		Average Rental (£)	Number of Houses		Average Rental (£)	Number of Houses
Hanover-square, May Fair	150	8,795	Poplar	44	6,882	Chelsea	29	7,629
St. James's	128	3,460	Pancras	41	18,731	Wandsworth	29	8,290
St. Martin's	119	2,323	Hampstead	40	1,719	St. Luke's	28	6,421
London City	117	7,329	Kensington	40	17,292	Lambeth	28	20,520
Marylebone	71	15,955	Clerkenwell	38	7,259	Lewisham	27	5,936
Strand	66	3,938	East London	38	4,785	Whitechapel	26	8,832
West London	65	2,745	St. Saviour's	36	4,613	Hackney	25	9,861
St. Giles's	60	4,778	Westminster	36	6,647	Camberwell	25	9,417
Holborn	52	4,517	St. Olave's	35	2,365	Rotherhithe	23	2,834
		53,840	Islington	35	13,558	St. George's, Southwark	22	7,005
			St. George's-in-the-East	32	6,151	Newington	22	10,468
					90,002	Greenwich	22	14,423
						Shoreditch	20	15,433
						Stepney	20	16,346
						Bermondsey	18	7,095
						Bethnal Green	9	13,370
								163,880

Newcastle or "house" coals, about 37 per cent.

Lancashire and Yorkshire coals, 35 to 40 per cent.

South Welsh or "steam" coals, 11 to 15 per cent.

Anthracite or "stone" coals, none.

The house coals are those chiefly used throughout London, so that every ton of such coals contains about 800 lbs. of volatile matter, a considerable proportion of which appears in the form of smoke; but what proportion and what is the weight of the carbonaceous particles or soot evolved in a given quantity of smoke, I know of no means of judging. I am informed, however, by those practically acquainted with the subject, that a ton of ordinary house coals will produce between a fourth and a half of a bushel of soot*. Now there are, say, 3,500,000 tons of coal consumed annually in London; but a large proportion of this quantity is used for the purposes of gas, for factories, breweries, chemical works, and steam-boats. The consumption of coal for the making of gas in London, in 1849, was 380,000 tons; so that, including the quantity used in factories, breweries, &c., we may, perhaps, estimate the domestic consumption of the metropolis at 2,500,000 tons yearly, which, for 300,000 houses, would give eight tons per house. And when we remember the amount used in large houses and in hotels, as well as by the smaller houses, where each room often contains a different family, this does not appear to be too high an average. Mr. M'Culloch estimates the domestic consumption at one ton per head, men, women, and children; and since the number of persons to each house in London is 7·5, this would give nearly the same result. Estimating the yield of soot to be three-eighths of a bushel per ton, we have, in round numbers, 1,000,000 bushels of soot as the gross quantity deposited in the metropolitan chimneys every year.

Or, to check the estimate another way, there are 350 master sweepers throughout London. A master sweeper in a "large way of business" collects, I am informed, one day with another, from 30 to 40 bushels of soot; on the other hand, small master, or "single-handed" chimney-sweeper is able to gather only about 5 bushels, and scarcely that. One master sweeper said that about 10 bushels a day would, he thought, be a fair average quantity for all the masters, reckoning one day with another; so that at this rate we should have 1,095,500 bushels for the gross quantity of soot annually collected throughout the metropolis.

We may therefore assume the aggregate yield of soot throughout London to be 1,000,000 bushels per annum. Now what is done with this immense mass of refuse matter? Of what use is it?

The soot is purchased from the masters, whose

---

* The quantity of soot deposited depends greatly on the length, draught, and irregular surface of the chimney. The kitchen flue yields by far the most soot for an equal quantity of coals burnt, because it is of greater length. The quantity above cited is the average yield from the several chimneys of a house. It will be seen hereafter that the quantity collected is only 800,000 bushels; a great proportion of the chimneys of the poor being seldom swept, and some cleansed by themselves.

perquisite it is, by the farmers and dealers. It is used by them principally for meadow land, and frequently for land where wheat is grown; not so much, I understand, as a manure, as for some quality in it which destroys slugs and other insects injurious to the crops*. Lincolnshire is one of the great marts for the London soot, whither it is transported by railway. In Hertfordshire, Cambridge, Norfolk, Suffolk, Essex, and Kent, however, and many other parts, London soot is used in large quantities; there are persons who have large stores for its reception, who purchase it from the master sweepers, and afterwards sell it to the farmers and send it as per order, to its destination. These are generally the manure-merchants, of whom the Post-Office Directory gives 26 names, eight being marked as dealers in guano. I was told by a sweeper in a large way of business that he thought these men bought from a half to three-quarters of the soot; the remainder being bought by the land-cultivators in the neighbourhood of London. Soot is often used by gardeners to keep down the insects which infest their gardens.

The value of the Soot collected throughout London is the next subject to engage our attention. Many sweepers have represented it as a very curious fact, and one for which they could advance no sufficient reason, that the price of a bushel of soot was regulated by the price of the quartern loaf, so that you had only to know that the quartern loaf was 5*d.* to know that such was the price of a bushel of soot. This, however, is hardly the case at present; the price of the quartern loaf (not regarding the "seconds," or inferior bread), is now, at the end of December, 1851, 5*d.* to 6*d.* according to quality. The price of soot per bushel is but 5*d.*, and sometimes but 4½*d.*, but 5*d.* may be taken as an average.

Now 1,000,000 bushels of soot, at 5*d.*, will be found to yield 20,833*l.* 6*s.* 8*d.* per annum. But the whole of this quantity is not collected by the chimney-sweepers, for many of the poorer persons seldom have their chimneys swept; and by the table given in another place, it will be seen that not more than 800,000 bushels are obtained in the course of the year by the London "sweeps." Hence we may say, that there are 800,000 bushels of soot annually collected from the London chimneys, and that this is worth not less than 16,500*l.* per annum.

The next question is, how many people are employed in collecting this quantity of refuse matter, and how do they collect it, and what do they get, individually and collectively, for so doing?

To begin with the number of master and journeymen sweepers employed in removing these 800,000 bushels of soot from our chimneys: according to the Census returns, the number of "sweeps" in the metropolis in the years 1841 and 1831 were as follows:—

* Soot of coal is said, by Dr. Ure, in his admirable Dictionary of Arts and Manufactures, to contain "sulphate and carbonate of ammonia along with bituminous matter."

Chimney-sweepers.	1841.	1831.	Increase in ten years.
Males, 20 years and upwards	619	421	198
,, under 20 years	370	no returns.	
Females, 20 years & upwards	44	,,	
	1033		

But these returns, such as they are, include both employers and employed, in one confused mass. To disentangle the economical knot, we must endeavour to separate the number of master sweepers from the journeymen. According to the Post-Office Directory the master sweepers amount to no more than 32, and thus there would be one more than 1000 for the number of the metropolitan journeymen sweepers; these statements, however, appear to be very wide of the truth.

In 1816 it was represented to the House of Commons, that there were within the bills of mortality, 200 masters, all—except the "great gentlemen," as one witness described them, who were about 20 in number—themselves working at the business, and that they had 150 journeymen and upwards of 500 apprentices, so that there must then have been 850 working sweepers altogether, young and old.

These numbers, it must be borne in mind, were comprised in the limits of the bills of mortality 34 years ago. The parishes in the old bills of mortality were 148; there are now in the metropolis proper 176, and, as a whole, the area is much more densely covered with dwelling-houses. Taking but the last ten years, 1841 to 1851, the inhabited houses have increased from 262,737 to 307,722, or, in round numbers, 45,000.

Now in 1811 the number of inhabited houses in the metropolis was 146,019, and in 1821 it was 164,948; hence in 1816 we may assume the inhabited houses to have been about 155,000; and since this number required 850 working sweepers to cleanse the London chimneys, it is but a rule of three sum to find how many would have been required for the same purpose in 1841, when the inhabited houses had increased to 262,737; this, according to Cocker, is about 1400; so that we must come to the conclusion either that the number of working sweepers had not kept pace with the increase of houses, or that the returns of the census were as defective in this respect as we have found them to be concerning the street-sellers, dustmen, and scavagers. Were we to pursue the same mode of calculation, we should find that if 850 sweepers were required to cleanse the chimneys of 155,000 houses, there should be 1687 such labourers in London now that the houses are 307,722 in number.

But it will be seen that in 1816 more than one-half (or 500 out of 850) of the working chimney-sweepers were apprentices, and in 1841 the chimney-sweepers under 20 years of age, if we are to believe the census, constituted more than one-third of the whole body (or 370 out of 1033). Now as the use of climbing boys was prohibited in 1842, of course this large proportion of the trade has been rendered useless; so that, estimating the master and journeymen sweepers at 250 in 1816, it would appear that about 500 would be required to sweep the chimneys of the metropolis at present. To these, of course, must be added the extra number of journeymen necessary for managing the machines. And considering the journeymen to have increased threefold since the abolition of the climbing boys, we must add 300 to the above number, which will make the sum total of the individuals employed in this trade to amount to very nearly 800.

By inquiries throughout the several districts of the metropolis, I find that there are altogether 350 master sweepers at present in London; 106 of these are large masters, who seldom go out on a round, but work to order, having a regular custom among the more wealthy classes; while the other 244 consist of 92 small masters and 152 "single-handed" masters, who travel on various rounds, both in London and the suburbs, seeking custom. Of the whole number, 19 reside within the City boundaries; from 90 to 100 live on the Surrey side, and 235 on the Middlesex side of the Thames (without the City boundaries). A large master employs from 2 to 10 men, and 2 boys; and a small one only 2 men or sometimes 1 man and a boy, while a single-handed master employs no men nor boys at all, but does all the work himself.

The 198 masters employ among them 12 foremen, 399 journeymen, and 62 boys, or 473 hands, and adding to them the single-handed master-men who work at the business themselves, we have 823 working men in all; so that, on the whole, there are not less than between 800 and 900 persons employed in cleansing the London chimneys of their soot.

The next point that presents itself in due order to the mind is, as to the *mode of working among the chimney-sweepers*; that is to say, how are the 800,000 bushels of soot collected from the 300,000 houses by these 820 working sweepers? But this involves a short history of the trade.

Of the Sweepers of Old, and the Climbing Boys.

FORMERLY the chimneys used to be cleansed by the house servants, for a person could easily stand erect in the huge old-fashioned constructions, and thrust up a broom as far as his strength would permit. Sometimes, however, straw was kindled at the mouth of the chimney, and in that way the soot was consumed or brought down to the ground by the action of the fire. But that there were also regular chimney-sweepers in the latter part of the sixteenth century is unquestionable; for in the days of the First James and Charles, poor Piedmontese, and more especially Savoyards, resorted to England for the express purpose. How long they laboured in this vocation is unknown. The Savoyards, indeed, were then the general showmen and sweeps of Europe, and so they are still in some of the cities of Italy and France.

As regards the first introduction of English children into chimneys—the establishment of the use of climbing boys—nothing appears, according to the representations made to Parliament on several occasions, to be known; and little attention seems to have been paid to the condition of these infants—some were but little better—until about 1780, when the benevolent Jonas Hanway, who is said, but not uncontradictedly, to have been the first person who regularly used an umbrella in the streets of London, called public attention to the matter. In 1788 Mr. Hanway and others brought a bill into Parliament for the better protection of the climbing boys, requiring, among other provisions, all master sweepers to be licensed, and the names and ages of all their apprentices registered. The House of Lords, however, rejected this bill, and the 28th George III., c. 48, was passed in preference. The chief alterations sought to be effected by the new Act were, that no sweeper should have more than six apprentices, and that no boy should be apprenticed at a tenderer age than eight years. Previously there were no restrictions in either of those respects.

These provisions were, however, very generally violated. By one of those "flaws" or omissions, so very common and so little creditable to our legislation, it was found that there was no prohibition to a sweeper's employing his own children at what age he pleased; and "some," or "several," for I find both words used, employed their sons, and occasionally their daughters, in chimney climbing at the ages of six, five, and even between four and five years! The children of others, too, were continually being apprenticed at illegal ages, for no inquiry was made into the lad's age beyond the statement of his parents, or, in the case of parish apprentices, beyond the (in those days) not more trustworthy word of the overseers. Thus boys of six were apprenticed—for apprenticeship was almost universal—as boys of eight, by their parents; while parish officers and magistrates consigned the workhouse orphans, as a thing of course, to the starvation and tyranny which they must have known were very often in store for them when apprenticed to sweepers.

The following evidence was adduced before Parliament on the subject of infant labour in this trade:—

Mr. John Cook, a master sweeper, then of Great Windmill-street and Kentish-town, the first who persevered in the use of the machine years before its use was compulsory, stated that it was common for parents in the business to employ their own children, under the age of seven, in climbing; and that as far as he knew, he himself was only between six and seven when he "came to it;" and that almost all master sweepers had got it in their bills that they kept "small boys for register-stoves, and such like as that."

Mr. T. Allen, another master sweeper, was between four and five when articled to an uncle.

Mr. B. M. Forster, a private gentleman, a member of the "Committee to promote the Superseding of Climbing Boys," said, "Some are put to the

THE LONDON SWEEP.

[*From a Daguerreotype by* BEARD.]

ONE OF THE FEW REMAINING CLIMBING SWEEPS.

[*From a Daguerreotype by* BEARD.]

employment very young; one instance of which occurred to a child in the neighbourhood of Shoreditch, who was put to the trade at four and a quarter years, or thereabouts. The father of a child in Whitechapel told me last week, that his son began climbing when he was four years and eight months old. I have heard of some still younger, but only from vague report."

This sufficiently proves at what infantine years children were exposed to toils of exceeding painfulness. The smaller and the more slenderly formed the child, the more valuable was he for the sweeping of flues, the interior of some of them, to be ascended and swept, being but seven inches square.

I have mentioned the employment of female children in the very unsuitable labour of climbing chimneys. The following is all the information given on the subject.

Mr. Tooke was asked, "Have you ever heard of female children being so employed?" and replied, "I have heard of cases at Hadley, Barnet, Windsor, and Uxbridge; and I know a case at Witham, near Colchester, of that sort."

Mr. B. M. Foster said, "Another circumstance, which has not been mentioned to the Committee, is, that there are several little girls employed; there are two of the name of Morgan at Windsor, daughters of the chimney-sweeper *who is employed to sweep the chimneys of the Castle;* another instance at Uxbridge, and at Brighton, and at Whitechapel (which was some years ago), and at Headley near Barnet, and Witham in Essex, and elsewhere." He then stated, on being asked, "Do you not think that girls were employed from their physical form being smaller and thinner than boys, and therefore could get up narrower flues?" "The reason that I have understood was, because their parents had not a sufficient number of boys to bring up to the business." Mr. Foster did not know the ages of these girls.

The inquiry by a Committee of the House of Commons, which led more than any other to the prohibition of this infant and yet painful labour in chimney-sweeping, was held in 1817, and they recommended the "preventing the further use of climbing boys in sweeping of chimneys;" a recommendation not carried into effect until 1832. The matter was during the interval frequently agitated in Parliament, but there were no later investigations by Committees.

I will adduce, specifically, the grievances, according to the Report of 1817, of the climbing boys; but will first present the following extract from the evidence of Mr. W. Tooke, a gentleman who, in accordance with the Hon. Henry Grey Bennet, M.P., and others, exerted himself on the behoof of the climbing boys. When he gave his evidence, Mr. Tooke was the secretary to a society whose object was to supersede the necessity of employing climbing boys. He said:—

"In the year 1800, the Society for Bettering the Condition of the Poor took up the subject, but little or nothing appears to have been done upon that occasion, except that the most respectable master chimney-sweepers entered into an association and subscription for promoting the cleanliness and health of the boys in their respective services. The Institution of which I am treasurer, and which is now existing, was formed in February, 1803. In consequence of an anonymous advertisement, a large meeting was held at the London Coffee House, and the Society was established; immediate steps were then taken to ascertain the state of the trade; inspectors were appointed to give an account of all the master chimney-sweepers within the bills of mortality, their general character, their conduct towards their apprentices, and the number of those apprentices. It was ascertained, that the total number of master chimney-sweepers, within the bills of mortality, might be estimated at 200, who had among them 500 apprentices; that not above 20 of those masters were reputable tradesmen in easy circumstances, who appeared generally to conform to the provisions of the Act; and which 20 had, upon an average, from four to five apprentices each. We found about 90 of an inferior class of master chimney-sweepers who averaged three apprentices each, and who were extremely negligent both of the health, morals, and education of those apprentices; and about 90, the remainder of the 200 masters, were a class of chimney-sweepers recently journeymen, who took up the trade because they had no other resource; they picked up boys as they could, who lodged with themselves in huts, sheds, and cellars, in the outskirts of the town, occasionally wandering into the villages round, where they slept on soot-bags, and lived in the grossest filth."

The grievances I have spoken of were thus summed up by the Parliamentary Committee. After referring to the ill-usage and hardships sustained by the climbing boys (the figures being now introduced for the sake of distinctness) it is stated:—

"It is in evidence that (1) they are stolen from" [and sold by] "their parents, and inveigled out of workhouses; (2) that in order to conquer the natural repugnance of the infants to ascend the narrow and dangerous chimneys to clean which their labour is required, blows are used; that pins are forced into their feet by the boy that follows them up the chimney, in order to compel them to ascend it, and that lighted straw has been applied for that purpose; (3) that the children are subject to sores and bruises, and wounds and burns on their thighs, knees, and elbows; and that it will require many months before the extremities of the elbows and knees become sufficiently hard to resist the excoriations to which they are at first subject."

1. With regard to the *stealing or kidnapping of children*—for there was often a difficulty in procuring climbing boys—I find mention in the evidence, as of a matter, but not a very frequent matter, of notoriety. One stolen child was sold to a master sweeper for 8*l*. 8*s*. Mr. G. Revely said:—

"I wish to state to the Committee that case in particular, because it comes home to the better sort of persons in higher life. It seems that the child, upon being asked various questions, had been taken away: the child was questioned how he came into that situation; he said all that he could recollect was (as I heard it told at that time) that he and his sister, with another brother, were together somewhere, but he could not tell where; but not being able to run so well as the other two, he was caught by a woman and carried away and was sold, and came afterwards into the hands of a chimney-sweeper. He was not afterwards restored to his family, and the mystery was never unravelled; but he was advertised, and a lady took charge of him.

"This child, in 1804, was forced up a chimney at Bridlington in Yorkshire, by a big boy, the younger boy being apparently but four years old. He fell and bruised his legs terribly against the grate. The Misses Auckland of Boynton, who had heard of the child, and went to see him, became interested by his manners, and they took him home with them; the chimney-sweeper, who perhaps got alarmed, being glad to part with him. "Soon after he got to Boynton, the seat of Sir George Strickland, a plate with something to eat was brought him; on seeing a silver fork he was quite delighted, and said, 'Papa had such forks as those.' He also said the carpet in the drawing-room was like papa's; the housekeeper showed him a silver watch, he asked what sort it was—'Papa's was a gold watch;' he then pressed the handle and said, 'Papa's watch rings, why does not yours?' Sir George Strickland, on being told this circumstance, showed him a gold repeater, the little boy pressed the spring, and when it struck, he jumped about the room, saying, 'Papa's watch rings so.' At night, when he was going to bed, he said he could not go to bed until he had said his prayers; he then repeated the Lord's Prayer, almost perfectly. The account he gave of himself was that he was gathering flowers in his mamma's garden, and that the woman who sold him to the sweeper, came in and asked him if he liked riding? He said, 'Yes,' and she told him he should ride with her. She put him on a horse, after which they got into a vessel, and the sails were put up, 'and away we went.' He had no recollection of his name, or where he lived, and was too young to think his father could have any other name than that of papa. He started whenever he heard a servant in the family at Boynton called George, and looked as if he expected to see somebody he knew; on inquiry, he said he had an uncle George, whom he loved dearly. He says his mamma is dead, and it is thought his father may be abroad. From many things he says, he seems to have lived chiefly with an uncle and aunt, whom he invariably says were called Mr. and Mrs. Flembrough. From various circumstances, it is thought impossible he should be the child of the woman who sold him, his manners being 'very civilized,' quite those of a child well educated; his dialect is good, and that of the south of England. This little boy, when first discovered, was conjectured to be about four years old, and is described as having beautiful black eyes and eyelashes, a high nose, and a delicate soft skin."

Mr. J. Harding, a master sweeper, had a fellow apprentice who had been enticed away from his parents. "It is a case of common occurrence," he said, "for children stolen, to be employed in this way. Yes, and children in particular are enticed out of workhouses: there are a great many who come out of workhouses."

The following cases were also submitted to the Committee:—

"A poor woman had been obliged by sickness to go into an hospital, and while she was there her child was stolen from her house, taken into Staffordshire, and there apprenticed to a chimney-sweeper. By some happy circumstance she learned his fate; she followed him, and succeeded in rescuing him from his forlorn situation. Another child, who was an orphan, was tricked into following the same wretched employment by a chimney-sweeper, who gave him a shilling, and made him believe that by receiving it he became his apprentice; the poor boy, either discovering or suspecting that he had been deceived, anxiously endeavoured to speak to a magistrate who happened to come to the house in which he was sweeping chimneys, but his master watched him so closely that he could not succeed. He at last contrived to tell his story to a blind soldier, who determined to right the poor boy, and by *great exertions* succeeded in procuring him his liberty."

It was in country places, however, that the stealing and kidnapping of children was the most frequent, and the threat of "the sweeps will get you," was often held out, to deter children from wandering. These stolen infants, it is stated, were usually conveyed to some distance by the vagrants who had secured them, and sold to some master sweeper, being apprenticed as the child of the vendors, for it was difficult for sweepers in thinly-peopled places to get a supply of climbing boys. It was shown about the time of the Parliamentary inquiry, in the course of a trial at the Lancaster assizes, that a boy had been apprenticed to a sweeper by two travelling tinkers, man and woman, who informed him that the child was stolen from another "traveller," 80 miles away, who was "too fond of it to make it a sweep." The *price* of the child was not mentioned.

Respecting the sale of children to be apprentices to sweepers, Mr. Tooke was able to state that, although in 1816, the practice had very much diminished of late, parents in many instances still *sold their children for three, four, or five guineas.* This sum was generally paid under the guise of an apprentice fee, but it was known to be and was called a "sale," for the parents, real or nominal, never interfered with the master subsequently, but left the infant to its fate.

2. I find the following account of the *means resorted to, in order to induce, or more frequently compel, these wretched infants to work.*

The boy in the first instance went for a month, or any term agreed upon, "on trial," or "to see how he would suit for the business." During this period of probation he was usually well treated and well fed (whatever the character of the master), with little to do beyond running errands, and observing the mode of work of the experienced climbers. When, however, he was "bound" as an apprentice, he was put with another lad who had been for some time at the business. The new boy was sent first up the chimney, and immediately followed by the other, who instructed him how to ascend. This was accomplished by the pressure of the knees and the elbows against the sides of the flue. By pressing the knees tightly the child managed to raise his arms somewhat higher, and then by pressing his elbows in like manner he contrived to draw up his legs, and so on. The inside of the flue presented a smooth surface, and there were no inequalities where the fingers or toes could be inserted. Should the young beginner fall, he was sure to light on the shoulders of the boy beneath him, who always kept himself firmly fixed in expectation of such a mishap, and then the novice had to commence anew; in this manner the twain reached the top by degrees, sweeping down the soot, and descended by the same method. This practice was very severe, especially on new boys, whose knees and elbows were torn by the pressure and the slipping down continually—the skin being stripped off, and frequently breaking out in frightful sores, from the constant abrasions, and from the soot and dirt getting into them.

In his evidence before Parliament in 1817 (for there had been previous inquiries), Mr. Cook gave an account of the training of these boys, and on being asked:—"Do the elbows and knees of the boys, when they first begin the business, become very sore, and afterwards get callous, and are those boys employed in sweeping chimneys during the soreness of those parts?" answered, "It depends upon the sort of master they have got; some are obliged to put them to work sooner than others; you must keep them a little at it, or they will never learn their business, even during the sores." He stated further, that the skin broke generally, and that the boys could not ascend chimneys during the sores without *very* great pain. The way that I learn boys is," he continued, "to put some cloths over their elbows and over their knees till they get the nature of the chimney—till they get a little used to it: we call it *padding* them, and then we take them off, and they get very little grazed indeed after they have got the art; but very few will take that trouble. Some boys' flesh is far worse than others, and it takes more time to harden them." He was then asked:—"Do those persons still continue to employ them to climb chimneys?" and the answer was: "Some do; it depends upon the character of the master. None of them of that class keep them till they get well; none. They are obliged to climb with those sores upon them. I never had one of my own apprentices do that." This system of padding, however, was but little practised; but in what proportion it *was* practised, unless by the respectable masters, who were then but few in number, the Parliamentary papers, the only information on the subject now attainable, do not state. The inference is, that the majority, out of but 20 of these masters, with some 80 or 100 apprentices, did treat them well, and what was so accounted. The customary way of training these boys, then, was such as I have described; some even of the better masters, whose boys were in the comparison well lodged and fed, and "sent to the Sunday school" (which seems to have comprised all needful education), considered "padding and such like" to be "new-fangled nonsense."

I may add also, that although the boy carried up a brush with him, it was used but occasionally, only when there were "turns" or defects in the chimney, the soot being brought down by the action of the shoulders and limbs. The climber wore a cap to protect his eyes and mouth from the soot, and a sort of flannel tunic, his feet, legs, and arms being bare. Some of these lads were surprisingly quick. One man told me that, when in his prime as a climbing boy, he could reach the top of a chimney about as quickly as a person could go up stairs to the attics.

The following is from the evidence of Mr. Cook, frequently cited as an excellent master :—

" What mode do you adopt to get the boy to go up the chimney in the first instance ?—We persuade him as well as we can; we generally practise him in one of our own chimneys first; one of the boys who knows the trade goes up behind him, and when he has practised it perhaps ten times, though some will require twenty times, they generally can manage it. The boy goes up with him to keep him from falling; after that, the boy will manage to go up with himself, after going up and down several times with one under him: we do this, because if he happens to make a slip he will be caught by the other.

" Do you find many boys show repugnance to go up at first?—Yes, most of them.

" And if they resist and reject, in what way do you force them up?—By telling them we must take them back again to their father and mother, and give them up again; and their parents are generally people who cannot maintain them.

" So that they are afraid of going back to their parents for fear of being starved?—Yes; they go through a deal of hardship before they come to our trade.

" Did you use any more violent means?—Sometimes a rod.

" Did you ever hear of straw being lighted under them?—Never.

" You never heard of any means being made use of, except being beat and being sent home?—No; no other.

" You are aware, of course, that those means being gentle or harsh must depend very much upon the character of the individual master?—It does.

" Of course you must know that there are persons of harsh and cruel disposition; have you not often heard of masters treating their apprentices with great cruelty, particularly the little boys, in forcing them to go up those small flues, which the boys were unwilling to ascend?—Yes; I have forced up many a one myself.

" By what means?—By threatenings, and by giving them a kick or a slap."

It was also stated that the journeymen used the boys with greater cruelty than did the masters —indeed a delegated tyranny is often the worst— that for very little faults they kicked and slapped the children, and sometimes flogged them with a cat, " made of rope, hard at each end, and as thick as your thumb."

Mr. John Fisher, a master chimney-sweeper, said:—" Many masters, are very severe with their children. To make them go up the chimneys I have seen them make them strip themselves naked; I have been obliged myself to go up a chimney naked."

As respects the cruelties of driving boys up chimneys by kindling straw beneath their feet, or thrusting pins into the soles of their feet, I find the following statements given on the authority of B. M. Forster, Esq., a private gentleman residing in Walthamstow:—

" A lad was ordered to sweep a chimney at Wandsworth; he came down after endeavouring to ascend, and this occurred several times before he gave up the point; at last the journeyman took some straw or hay, and lighted it under him to drive him up: when he endeavoured to get up the last time, he found there was a bar across the chimney, which he could not pass; he was obliged in consequence to come down, and the journeyman beat him so cruelly, to use his own expression, that he could not stand for a fortnight.

" In the whole city of Norwich I could find only nine climbing boys, two of whom I questioned on many particulars; one was with respect to the manner in which they are taught to climb; they both agreed in that particular, that a larger boy was sent up behind them to prick their feet, if they did not climb properly. I purposely avoided mentioning about pricking them with pins, but asked them how they did it; they said that they thrust the pins into the soles of their feet. A third instance occurred at Walthamstow; a man told me that some he knew had been taught in the same way; I believe it to be common, but I cannot state any more instances from authority."

3. On the subject of the *sores, bruises, wounds, burns, and diseases*, to which chimney-sweepers in their apprenticeships were not only exposed, but, as it were, condemned, Mr. R. Wright, a surgeon, on being examined before the Committee, said, " I shall begin with *Deformity*. I am well persuaded that the deformity of the spine, legs, arms, &c., of chimney-sweepers, generally, if not wholly, proceeds from the circumstance of their being obliged not only to go up chimneys at an age when their bones are in a soft and growing state, but likewise from their being compelled by their too merciless masters and mistresses to carry bags of soot (and those very frequently for a great length of distance and time) by far too heavy for their tender years and limbs. The knees and ancle joints mostly become deformed, in the first instance, from the position they are obliged to put them in, in order to support themselves, not only while climbing up the chimney, but more particularly so in that of coming down, when they rest solely on the lower extremities.

" *Sore eyes and eyelids*, are the next to be considered. Chimney-sweepers are very subject to inflammation of the eyelids, and not unfrequently weakness of sight, in consequence of such inflammation. This I attribute to the circumstance of the soot lodging on the eyelids, which first produces irritability of the part, and the constantly rubbing them with their dirty hands, instead of alleviating, increases the disease; for I have observed in a number of cases, when the patient has ceased for a time to follow the business, and of course the original cause has been removed, that with washing and keeping clean they were soon got well.

" *Sores*, for the same reasons, are generally a long time in healing.

" *Cancer* is another and a most formidable disease, which chimney-sweepers in particular are liable to, especially that of the scrotum; from which circumstance, by way of distinction, it is called the ' chimney-sweeper's cancer.' Of this sort of cancer I have seen several instances, some of which have been operated on; but, in general, they are apt to let them go too far before they apply for relief. Cancers of the lips are not so general as cancers of the scrotum. I never saw but two instances of the former, and several of the latter."

The "chimney-sweep's cancer" was always lectured upon as a separate disease at Guy's and Bartholomew's Hospitals, and on the question being put to Mr. Wright: " Do the physicians who are intrusted with the care and management of those hospitals think that disease of such common occurrence, that it is necessary to make it a part of surgical education ?"—he replied: " Most assuredly; I remember Mr. Cline and Mr. Cooper were particular on that subject; and having one or two cases of the kind in the hospital, it struck my mind very forcibly. With the permission of the Committee I will relate a case that occurred lately, which I had from one of the pupils of St. Thomas's Hospital; he informed me that they recently had a case of a chimney-sweeper's cancer, which was to have been operated on that week, but the man ' brushed' (to use their expression) or rather walked off; he would not submit to the operation: similar instances of which I have known myself. They dread so much the knife, in consequence of foolish persons telling them it is so formidable an operation, and that they will die under it. I conceive without the operation it is death; for cancers are of that nature that unless you extricate them entirely they will never be cured."

Of the chimney-sweeper's cancer, the following statement is given in the Report: " Mr. Cline informed your Committee by letter, that this disease is rarely seen in any other persons than chimney-sweepers, and in them cannot be considered as frequent; for during his practice in St. Thomas's hospital, for more than 40 years, the number of those could not exceed 20. But your Committee have been informed that the dread of the operation which it is necessary to perform, deters many from submitting to it; and from the evidence of persons engaged in the trade, it appears to be much more common than Mr. Cline seems to be aware of.

"*Cough and Asthma.*—Chimney-sweepers are, from their being out at all hours and in all weathers, very liable to cough and inflammation of the chest.

"*Burns.*—They are very subject to burns, from their being forced up chimneys while on fire, or soon after they have been on fire, and while overheated; and however they may cry out, their inhuman masters pay not the least attention, but compel them, too often with horrid imprecations, to proceed.

"*Stunted growth*, in this unfortunate race of the community, is attributed, in a great measure, to their being brought into the business at a very early age."

To *accidents* they were frequently liable in the pursuit of their callings, and sometimes these accidents were the being jammed or fixed, or, as it was called in the trade, "stuck," in narrow and heated flues, sometimes for hours, and until death.

Among these hapless lads were indeed many deaths from accidents, cruelty, privation, and exhaustion, but it does not appear that the number was ever ascertained. There were also many narrow escapes from dreadful deaths. I give instances of each:—

"On Monday morning, the 29th of March, 1813, a chimney-sweeper of the name of Griggs, attended to sweep a small chimney in the brewhouse of Messrs. Calvert and Co., in Upper Thames-street; he was accompanied by one of his boys, a lad of about eight years of age, of the name of Thomas Pitt. The fire had been lighted as early as two o'clock the same morning, and was burning on the arrival of Griggs and his little boy at eight; the fire-place was small, and an iron pipe projected from the grate some little distance, into the flue; this the master was acquainted with (having swept the chimneys in the brewhouse for some years) and therefore had a tile or two taken from the roof, in order that the boy might descend the chimney. He had no sooner extinguished the fire than he suffered the lad to go down; and the consequence, as might be expected, was his almost immediate death, in a state, no doubt, of inexpressible agony. The flue was of the narrowest description, and must have retained heat sufficient to have prevented the child's return to the top, even supposing he had not approached the pipe belonging to the grate, which must have been nearly red-hot; this, however, was not clearly ascertained on the inquest, though the appearance of the body would induce an opinion that he had been unavoidably pressed against the pipe. Soon after his descent, the master, who remained on the top, was apprehensive that something had happened, and therefore desired him to come up; the answer of the boy was, 'I cannot come up, master; I must die here.' An alarm was given in the brewhouse, immediately, that he had stuck in the chimney, and a bricklayer who was at work near the spot attended, and after knocking down part of the brickwork of the chimney, just above the fire-place, made a hole sufficiently large to draw him through. A surgeon attended, but all attempts to restore life were ineffectual. On inspecting the body, various burns appeared; the fleshy part of the legs, and a great part of the feet more particularly, were injured; those parts, too, by which climbing boys most effectually ascend or descend chimneys, viz., the elbows and knees, seemed burnt to the bone; from which it must be evident that the unhappy sufferer made some attempts to return as soon as the horrors of his situation became apparent."

"In the improvement made some years since by the Bank of England, in Lothbury, a chimney, belonging to a Mr. Mildrum, a baker, was taken down, but before he began to bake, in order to see that the rest of the flue was clear, a boy was sent up, and after remaining some time, and not answering to the call of his master, another boy was ordered to descend from the top of the flue and to meet him half-way; but this being found impracticable, they opened the brickwork in the lower part of the flue, and found the first-mentioned boy dead. In the mean time the boy in the upper part of the flue called out for relief, saying, he was completely jammed in the rubbish and was unable to extricate himself. Upon this a bricklayer was employed with the utmost expedition, but he succeeded only in obtaining a lifeless body. The bodies were sent to St. Margaret's Church, Lothbury, and a coroner's inquest, which sat upon them, returned the verdict—Accidental Death."

"In the beginning of the year 1808, a chimney-sweeper's boy being employed to sweep a chimney in Marsh-street, Walthamstow, in the house of Mr. Jeffery, carpenter, unfortunately, in his attempt to get down, stuck in the flue and was unable to extricate himself. Mr. Jeffery, being within hearing of the boy, immediately procured assistance. As the chimney was low, and the top of it easily accessible from without, the boy was taken out in about ten minutes, the chimney-pot and several rows of bricks having been previously removed; if he had remained in that dreadful situation many minutes longer, he must have died. His master was sent for, and he arrived soon after the boy had been released; he abused him for the accident, and, after striking him, sent him with a bag of soot to sweep another chimney. The child appeared so very weak when taken out that he could scarcely stand, and yet this wretched being, who had been up ever since three o'clock, had before been sent by his master to Wanstead, which with his walk to Marsh-street made about five miles."

"In May, 1817, a boy employed in sweeping a chimney in Sheffield got wedged fast in one of the flues, and remained in that situation near two hours before he could be extricated, which was at length accomplished by pulling down part of the chimney."

On one occasion a child remained above two hours in some danger in a chimney, rather than venture down and encounter his master's anger. The man was held to bail, which he could not procure.

As in the cases I have described (at Messrs. Calvert's, and in Lothbury), the verdict was usually "Accidental Death," or something equivalent.

It was otherwise, however, where wilful cruelty was proven.

The following case was a subject of frequent comment at the time:—

"On Friday, 31st May, 1816, William Moles and Sarah his wife, were tried at the Old Bailey for the wilful murder of John Hewley, alias Haseley, a boy about six years of age, in the month of April last, by cruelly beating him. Under the direction of the learned judge, they were acquitted of the crime of murder, but the husband was detained to take his trial as for a misdemeanor, of which he was convicted upon the fullest evidence, and sentenced to two years' imprisonment. The facts, as proved in this case, are too shocking in detail to relate: the substance of them is, that he was forced up the chimney on the shoulder of a bigger boy, and afterwards violently pulled down again by the leg and dashed upon a marble hearth; his leg was thus broken, and death ensued in a few hours, and on his body and knees were found scars arising from wounds of a much older date."

This long-continued system of cruelties, of violations of public and private duties, bore and ripened its natural fruits. The climbing boys grew up to be unhealthy, vicious, ignorant, and idle men, for during their apprenticeships their labour was over early in the day, and they often passed away their leisure in gambling in the streets with one another and other children of their stamp, as they frequently had halfpence given to them. They played also at "chuck and toss" with the journeymen, and of course were stripped of every farthing. Thus they became indolent and fond of excitement. When a lad ceased to be an apprentice, although he might be but 16, he was too big to climb, and even if he got employment as a journeyman, his remuneration was wretched, only 2s. a week, with his board and lodging. There were, however, far fewer complaints of being insufficiently fed than might have been expected, but the sleeping places were execrable: "They sleep in different places," it was stated, "sometimes in sheds, and sometimes in places which we call barracks (large rooms), or in the cellar (where the soot was kept); some never sleep upon anything that can be called a bed; some do."

Mr. T. Allen, a master sweep for 22 years, gave the Committee the following account of *the men's earnings and* (what may be called) *the General Perquisites of the trade* under the exploded system:—

"If a man be 25 years of age, he has no more than 2s. a week; he is not clothed, only fed and lodged in the same manner as the boys. The 2s. a week is not sufficient to find him clothes and other necessaries, certainly not; it is hardly enough to find him with shoe-leather, for they walk over a deal of ground in going about the streets. The journeyman is able to live upon those wages, for he gets halfpence given him: supposing he is 16 or 20 years of age, he gets the boys' pence from them and keeps it; and if he happens to get a job for which he receives a 1s., he gets 6d. of that, and his master the other 6d. The boys' pence are what the boys get after they have been doing their master's work; they get a 1d. or so, and the journeyman takes it from them, and 'licks' them if they do not give it up." [These "jobs," after the master's work had been done, were chance jobs, as when a journeyman on his round was called on by a stranger, and unexpectedly, to sweep a chimney. Sometimes, by arrangement of the journeyman and the lad, the proceeds never reached the master's pocket. Sometimes, but rarely, such jobs were the journeyman's rightful perquisite.] "Men," proceeds Mr. Allen, "who are 22 and 23 years of age will play with the young boys and win their money. That is, they get half the money from them by force, and the rest by fraud. They are driven to this course from the low wages which the masters give them, because they have no other means to get anything for themselves, not even the few necessaries which they may want; for even what they want to wash with they must get themselves. As to what becomes of the money the boys get on May-day, when they are in want of clothes, the master will buy them, as check shirts or handkerchiefs. These masters get a share of the money which the boys collect on May-day. The boys have about 1s. or 1s. 6d.; the journeyman has also his share; then the master takes the remainder, which is to buy the boys' clothes and other necessaries, as they say. I cannot exactly tell what the average amount is that a boy will get on the May-day; the most that my boy ever got was 5s. But I think that the boys get more than that; I should think they get as much as 9s. or 10s. apiece. The Christmas-boxes are generally, I believe, divided among themselves (among the boys); but I cannot say rightly. It is spent in buying silk handkerchiefs, or Sunday shoes, I believe; but I am not perfectly sure."

Of the condition and lot of the operatives who were too big to go up chimneys, Mr. J. Fisher, a master-sweeper, gave the following account:—

"*They get into a roving way, and go about from one master to another, and they often come to no good end at last.* They sometimes go into the country, and after staying there some time, they come back again; I took a boy of that sort very lately and kept him like my own, and let him go to school; he asked me one Sunday to let him go to school, and I was glad to let him go, and I gave him leave; he accordingly went, and I have seen nothing of him since; before he went he asked me if I would let him come home to see my child buried; I told him to ask his schoolmaster, but he did not come back again. I cannot tell what has become of him; he was to have served me for twelve months. I did not take him from the parish; he came to me. He said his parents were dead. *The effect of the roving habit of the large boys when they become too large to climb, is, that they get one with another and learn bad habits from one another; they never will stop long in any one place.* They frequently go into the country and get various places; perhaps they stop a month at each; some try to get masters themselves, and some will get into bad company, which very often happens. *Then they turn thieves, they get lazy, they won't work, and people do not like to employ them lest they should take anything out of their houses. The generality of them never settle in any steady business.* They generally turn loose characters, and people will not employ them lest they should take anything out of the house."

The criminal annals of the kingdom bear out the foregoing account. Some of these boys, indeed, when they attained man's estate, became, in a great measure, through their skill in climbing, expert and enterprising burglars, breaking into places where few men would have cared to venture. One of the most daring feats ever attempted and accomplished was the escape from Newgate by a sweeper about 15 years ago. He climbed by the aid of his knees and elbows a height of nearly 80 feet, though the walls, in the corner of the prison-yard, where this was done, were nearly of an even surface; the slightest slip could not have failed to have precipitated the sweeper to the bottom. He was then under sentence of death for highway robbery.

"His name was Whitehead, and he done a more wonderfuller thing nor that," remarked an informant, who had been his master. "We was sweeping the bilers in a sugar-house, and he went from the biler up the flue of the chimney, it was nearly as high as the Monument, that chimney; I should say it was 30 or 40 feet higher nor the sugar-house. He got out at the top, and slid down the bare brickwork on the outside, on to the roof of the house, got through an attic window in the roof, and managed to get off without any one knowing what became of him. That was the most wonderfullest thing I ever knowed in my life. I don't know how he escaped from being killed, but he was always an oudacious feller. It was nearly three months after afore we found him in the country. I don't know where they sent him to after he was brought back to Newgate, but I hear they made him a turnkey in a prison somewhere, and that he's doing very well now." The feat at the sugar-house could be only to escape from his apprenticeship.

In the course of the whole Parliamentary evidence the sweepers, reared under the old climbing system, are spoken of as a "short-lived" race, but no statistics could be given. Some died old men in middle age, in the workhouses. *Many were mere vagrants at the time of their death.*

I took the statement of a man who had been what he called a "climbing" in his childhood, but as he is now a master-sweeper, and has indeed gone through all grades of the business, I shall give it in my account of the present condition of the sweepers.

Climbing is still occasionally resorted to, especially when repairs are required, "but the climbing boys," I was told, "are now men." These are slight dwarfish men, whose services are often in considerable request, and cannot at all times be commanded, as there are only about twenty of them in London, so effectually has climbing been suppressed. These little men, I was told, did pretty well, not unfrequently getting 2s. or 2s. 6d. for a single job.

As regards the *labour question*, during the existence of the climbing boys, we find in the Report the following results:—

The *nominal* wages to the journeymen were 2s. a week, with board and lodging. The apprentices received no wages, their masters being only required to feed, lodge, and clothe them.

The *actual* wages were the same as the nominal, with the addition of 1s. as perquisites in money. There were other perquisites in liquor or broken meat.

In the Reports are no accounts of the duration of labour throughout the year, nor can I obtain from master-sweepers, who were in the business during the old mode, any sufficient data upon which to found any calculations. The employment, however, seems to have been generally *continuous*, running through the year; though in the course of the twelvemonth one master would have four and another six different journeymen, but only one at a time. The vagrant propensities of the class is a means of accounting for this.

The *nominal* wages of those journeymen who resided in their own apartments were generally 14s. a week, and their *actual* about 2s. 6d. extra in the form of perquisites. Others resided "on the premises," having the care of the boys, with board and lodgings and 5s. a week in money *nominally*, and 7s. 6d. *actually*, the perquisites being worth 2s. 6d.

Concerning the *general* or average wages of the whole trade, I can only present the following computation.

Mr. Tooke, in his evidence before the House of Commons, stated that the Committee, of which he was a member, had ascertained that one boy on an average swept about four chimneys daily, at prices varying from 6d. to 1s. 6d., or a medium return of about 10d. per chimney, exclusive of the soot, then worth 8d. or 9d. a bushel. "It appears," he said, "from a datum I have here, that those chimney-sweepers who keep six boys (the greatest number allowed by law) gain, on an average, nearly 270l.; five boys, 225l.; four boys, 180l.; three boys, 135l.; two boys, 90l.; and one boy 45l. (yearly), exclusive of the soot, which is, I should suppose, upon an average, from half a bushel to a bushel every time the chimney is swept."

"Out of the profits you mention," he was then asked, "the master has to maintain the boys?"— "Yes," was the answer, "and when the expenses of house and cellar rent, and the wages of journeymen, and the maintenance of apprentices, are taken into the account, the number of master chimney-sweepers is not only more than the trade will support, but exceeds, by above one-third, what the public exigency requires. The Committee also ascertained that the 200 master chimney-sweepers in the metropolis were supposed to have in their employment 150 journeymen and 500 boys."

The matter may be reduced to a tabular form, expressing the amount in money—for it is not asserted that the masters generally gained on the charge for their journeymen's board and lodging—as follows:—

EXPENDITURE OF MASTER CHIMNEY-SWEEPERS UNDER THE CLIMBING-BOY SYSTEM.

	Yearly.
20 journeymen at individual wages, 14s. each weekly	£780
30 ditto, say 12s. weekly	936
100 ditto, 10s. ditto	2,600
Board, Lodging, and Clothing of 500 boys, 4s. 6d. weekly	5,850
Rent, 20 large traders, 10s.	520
Do. 30 others, 7s.	546
Do. 150 do., 3s. 6d.	1,365
20 horses (keep), 10s.	520
General wear and tear	200
	£13,317

It appears that about 180 of the master chimney-sweepers were themselves working men, in the same way as their journeymen.

The following, then, may be taken as the—

YEARLY RECEIPTS OF THE MASTER SWEEPERS UNDER THE CLIMBING-BOY SYSTEM.

	Yearly.
Payment for sweeping 624,000 chimneys (4 daily, according to evidence before Parliament, by each of 500 boys), 10d. per chimney, or yearly	£26,000
Soot (according to same account), say 5d. per chimney	13,000
Total	£39,000
Yearly expenditure	13,317
Yearly profit	£25,683

This yielded, then, according to the information submitted to the House of Commons Select Committee, as the profits of the trade prior to 1817, an individual yearly gain to each master sweeper of 128l.; but, taking Mr. Tooke's average yearly profit for the six classes of tradesmen, 270l., 225l., 180l., 135l., 90l., and 45l. respectively, the individual profit averages above 157l.

The capital, I am informed, would not average above two guineas per master sweeper, nothing being wanted beyond a few common sacks, made by the sweepers' wives, and a few brushes. Only about 20 had horses, but barrows were occasionally hired at a busy time.

In the foregoing estimates I have not included any sums for apprentice fees, as I believe there would be something like a balance in the matter, the masters sometimes paying parents such premiums for the use of their children as they received from the parishes for the *tuition* and maintenance of others.

Of the *morals, education, religion, marriage*, &c., of sweepers, under the two systems, I shall speak in another place.

It may be somewhat curious to conclude with a word of the extent of chimneys swept by a climbing boy. One respectable master-sweeper told me that for eleven years he had climbed five or six days weekly. During this period he thought he had swept fifteen chimneys as a week's average, each chimney being at least 40 feet in height; so traversing, in ascending and descending, 686,400 feet, or 130 miles of a world of soot. This, however, is little to what has been done by a climber of 30 years' standing, one of the little men of whom I have spoken. My informant entertained no doubt that this man had, for the first 22 years of his career, climbed half as much again as he himself had; or had traversed 2,059,200 feet of the interior of chimneys, or 390 miles. Since the new Act this man had of course climbed less, but had still been a good deal employed; so that, adding his progresses for the last 9 years to the 22 preceding, he must have swept about 456 miles of chimney interiors.

OF THE CHIMNEY-SWEEPERS OF THE PRESENT DAY.

THE chimney-sweepers of the present day are distinguished from those of old by the use of machines instead of climbing boys, for the purpose of removing the soot from the flues of houses.

The chimney-sweeping machines were first used in this country in the year 1803. They were the invention of Mr. Smart, a carpenter, residing at the foot of Westminster-bridge, Surrey. On the earlier trials of the machine (which was similar to that used at present, and which I shall shortly describe), it was pronounced successful in 99 cases out of 100, according to some accounts, but failing where sharp angles occurred in the flue, which arrested its progress.

"Means have been suggested," said Mr. Tooke, formerly mentioned, in his evidence before a Committee of the House of Commons, "for obviating that difficulty by fixed apparatus at the top of the flue with a jack-chain and pulley, by which a brush could be worked up and down, or it could be done as is customary abroad, as I have repeatedly seen it at Petersburgh, and heard of its being done universally on the Continent, by letting down a bullet with a brush attached to it from the top; but to obviate the inconvenience, which is considerable, from persons going upon the roof of a house, Mr. John White, junior, an eminent surveyor, has suggested the expediency of putting iron shutters or registers to each flue, in the roof or cockloft of each house; by opening which, and working the machine upwards and downwards, or letting down the bullet, which is the most compendious manner, the chimney will be most effectually cleansed; and, by its aperture at bottom being kept well closed, it would be done with the least possible dirt and inconvenience to the family."

The society for the supersedence of the labour of climbing boys promoted the adoption of the machines by all the means in their power, presenting the new instrument gratuitously to several master sweepers who were too poor to purchase it. Experiments were made and duly published as to the effectual manner in which the chimneys at Guildhall, the Mansion House, the then new Custom House, Dulwich College, and in other public edifices, had been cleansed by the machine. But these statements seem to have produced little effect. People thought, perhaps, that the mechanical means which might very well cleanse the chimneys of large public buildings—and it was said that the chimneys of the Custom House were built with a view to the use of the machine—might not be so serviceable for the same purposes in small private dwellings. Experiments continued to be made, often in the presence of architects, of the more respectable sweepers, and of ladies and gentlemen who took a philanthropic interest in the question, between the years 1803 and 1817, but with little influence upon the general public, for in 1817 Mr. Smart supposed that there were but 50 or 60 machines in general use in the metropolis, and those, it appeared from the evidence of several master sweepers, were used chiefly in gentlemen's houses, many of those gentlemen having to be authoritative with their servants, who, if not controlled, always preferred the services of the climbing boys. Most servants had perquisites from the master sweepers, in the largest and most profitable ways of business, and they seemed to fear the loss of those perquisites if any change took place.

The opposition in Parliament, and in the general indifference of the people, to the efforts of "the friends of the climbing boy" to supersede his painful labours by the use of machinery, was formidable enough, but that of the servants appears to have been more formidable still. Mr. Smart showed this in his explanations to the Committee. The whole result of his experience was that servants set their faces against the introduction of the machine, grumbling if there were not even the appearance of dirt on the furniture after its use. "The first winter I went out with this machine," said Mr. Smart, "I went to Mr. Burke's in Tokenhouse Yard, who was a friend of mine, with a man to sweep the chimneys, and after waiting above an hour in a cold morning, the housekeeper came down quite in a rage, that we should presume to ring the bell or knock at the door; and when we got admittance, she swore she wished the machine and the inventor at the devil; she did not know me. We swept all the chimneys, and when we had done I asked her what objection she had to it now; she said, a very serious one, that if there was a thing by which a servant could get any emolument, some d——d invention was sure to take it away from them, for that she received perquisites."

This avowal of Mr. Burke's housekeeper, as brusque as it was honest, is typical of the feelings of the whole class of servants.

The opposition in Parliament, as I have intimated, continued. One noble lord informed the House of Peers that he had been indisposed of late and had sought the aid of calomel, the curative influence of which had pervaded every portion of his frame; and that it as far surpassed the less searching powers of other medicines, as the brush of the climbing boy in cleansing every nook and corner of the chimney, surpassed all the power of the machinery, which left the soot unpurged from those nooks and corners.

The House of Commons, however, had expressed its conviction that as long as master chimney-sweepers were permitted to employ climbing boys, the natural result of that permission would be the continuance of those miseries which the Legislature had sought, but which it had failed, to put an end to; and they therefore recommended that the use of climbing boys should be prohibited altogether; and that the age at which the apprenticeship should commence should be extended from eight to fourteen, putting this trade upon the same footing as others which took apprentices at that age.

This resolution became law in 1829. The employment of climbing boys in any manner in the interior of chimneys was prohibited under penalties of fine and imprisonment; and it was enacted that the new measure should be carried into effect in three years, so giving the master sweepers that period of time to complete their arrangements. During the course of the experiments and inquiry, the sweepers, as a body, seem to have thrown no obstacles, or very few and slight obstacles, in the way of the "Committee to promote the Superseding of the Labour of Climbing Boys;" while the most respectable of the class, or the majority of the respectable, aided the efforts of the Committee.

This manifestation of public feeling probably modified the opposition of the sweepers, and unquestionably influenced the votes of members of Parliament. The change in the operations of the chimney-sweeping business took place in 1832, as quietly and unnoticedly as if it were no change at all.

The machine now in use differs little from that invented by Mr. Smart, the first introduced, but lighter materials are now used in its manufacture. It has not been found necessary, however, to complicate its use with the jack-chain and pulley, and bullet with a brush attached, and the iron shutters or registers in the roof or cockloft, of which Mr. Tooke spoke.

The machine is formed of a series of hollow rods, made of a supple cane, bending and not breaking in any sinuosity of the flues. This cane is made of the same material as gentlemen's walking-sticks. The first machines were made of wood, and were liable to be broken; and to enable the sweeps on such occasions to recover the broken part, a strong line ran from bottom to top through the centre of the sticks, which were bored for the purpose, and strung on this cord. The cane machine, however, speedily and effectually superseded these imperfect instruments; and there are now none of them to be met with. To the top tube of the machine is attached the "brush," called technically "the head," of elastic whalebone spikes, which "give" and bend, in accordance with the up or down motion communicated by the man working the machine, so sweeping what was described to me as "both ways," up and down.

Some of these rods, which fit into one another by means of brass screws, are 4 feet 6 inches long, and diminish in diameter to suit their adjustment. Some rods are but 3 feet 6 inches long, and 4 feet is the full average length; while the average price at the machine maker's is 2s. 6d. a rod, if bought separately. The head costs 10s., on an average, if bought separately. It is seldom that a machine is required to number beyond 17 rods (extending 68 feet), and the better class of sweepers are generally provided with 17 rods. The cost of the entire machine, for every kind of chimney-work, when purchased new, as a whole, is, when of good quality, from 30s. to 5l., according to the number of rods, duplicate rods, &c. Mr. Smart stated, in 1817, that the average price of one of his machines was then 2l. 3s.

The sweepers who labour chiefly in the poorer localities—and several told me how indifferent many people in those parts were as to their chimneys being swept at all—rarely use a machine to extend beyond 40 feet, or one composed of 10 or 11 rods; but some of the inferior class of sweepers buy of those in a superior way of trade worn machines, at from a third to a half of the prime cost. These machines they trim up themselves. One portion of the work, however, they cannot repair or renew—the broken or worn-out brass screws of the rods, which they call the "ferules." These, when new, are 1s. each. There were, when the machine-work was novel, I was informed, street-artizans who went about repairing these screws or ferules; but their work did not please the chimney-sweepers, and this street-trade did not last above a year or two.

The rods of the machine, when carefully attended to, last a long time. One man told me that he was still working some rods which he had worked since 1842 (nine years), with occasional renewal of the ferules. The head is either injured or worn down in about two years; if not well made at first, in a year. The diameter of this head or brush is, on the average, 18 inches. One of my informants had himself swept a chimney of 80 feet, and one of his fellow-workers had said that he once swept a chimney of 120 feet high; in both cases by means of the machine. My informant, however, thought such a feat as the 120-feet sweep was hardly possible, as only one man's strength can be applied to the machine; and he was of opinion that no man's muscular powers would be sufficient to work a machine at a height of 120 feet. The labour is sometimes very severe; "enough," one strongly-built man told me, "to make your arms, head, and heart ache."

The old-fashioned chimneys are generally 12 by 14 inches in their dimensions in the interior; and for the thorough sweeping of such chimneys— the opinion of all the sweepers I saw according on the subject—a head (it is rarely called brush in the trade) of 18 inches diameter is insufficient, yet they are seldom used larger. One intelligent master sweeper, speaking from his own knowledge, told me that in the neighbourhood where he worked numbers of houses had been built since the introduction of the machines, and the chimneys were only 9 inches square, as regards the interior; the smaller flues are sometimes but 7. These 9-inch chimneys, he told me, were frequent in "scamped" houses, houses got up at the lowest possible rate by speculating builders. This was done because the brickwork of the chimneys costs more than the other portions of the masonry, and so the smaller the dimensions of the chimneys the less the cost of the edifice. The machines are sometimes as much crippled in this circumscribed space as they are found of insufficient dimensions in the old-fashioned chimneys; and so the "scamped" chimney, unless by a master having many "heads," is not so cleanly swept as it might be. Chimneys not built in this manner are now usually 9 inches by 14.

In cleansing a chimney with the machine the sweep stands by, or rather in, the fire-place, having first attached a sort of curtain to the mantle to confine the soot to one spot, the operator standing inside this curtain. He first introduces the "head," attached to its proper rod, into the chimney, "driving" it forward, then screws on the next rod, and so on, until the head has been driven to the top of the chimney. The soot which has fallen upon the hearth, within the curtain, is collected into a sack or sacks, and is carried away on the men's backs, and occasionally in carts. The whalebone spikes of the head are made to extend in every direction, so that when it is moved no part of the chimney, if the surface be even, escapes contact with these spikes, if the work be carefully done, as indeed it generally is; for the cleaner the chimney is swept of course the greater amount of soot adds to the profit of the sweeper. One man told me that he thought he had seen in some old big chimneys, a long time unswept, more soot brought down by the machine than, under similar circumstances as to the time the chimney had remained uncleansed, would have been done by the climbing boy.

All the master sweepers I saw concurred in the opinion that the machine was *not* in all respects so effective a sweeper as the climbing boy, as it does not reach the recesses, nooks, crannies, or holes in the chimney, where the soot remains little disturbed by the present process. This want is felt the most in the cleansing of the old-fashioned chimneys, especially in the country.

Mr. Cook, in 1817, stated to the Committee that the cleansing of a chimney by a boy or by a machine occupied the same space of time; but I find the general opinion of the sweepers now to be that it is only the small and straight chimneys which can be swept with as great celerity by a machine as by a climber; in all others the lad was quicker by about 5 minutes in 30, or in that proportion.

I heard sweepers represent that the passing of the Act of Parliament not only deprived them in many instances of the unexpired term of a boy's apprenticeship in his services as a climber, but "threw open the business to any one." The business, however, it seems, was always "open to any one." There was no art nor mystery in it, as regarded the functions of the master; any one could send a boy up a chimney, and collect and carry away the soot he brought down, quite as readily and far more easily than he can work a machine. Nevertheless, men under the old system could hardly (and some say they were forbidden to) embark in this trade unless they had been apprenticed to it; for they were at a loss how to possess themselves of climbing boys, and how to make a connection. When the machines were introduced, however, a good many persons who were able to "raise the price" of one started in the line on their own account. These men have been called by the old hands "leeks" or "green 'uns," to distinguish them from the regularly-trained men, who pride themselves not a little on the fact of their having served seven or eight years, "duly and truly," as they never fail to express it. This increase of fresh hands tended to lower the earnings of the class; and some masters, who were described to me as formerly very "comfortable," and some, comparatively speaking, rich, were considerably reduced by it. The number of "leeks" in 1832 I heard stated, with the exaggeration to which I have been accustomed when uninformed men, ignorant of the relative value of numbers, have expressed their opinions, as 1000!

The several classes in the chimney-sweeping trade may be arranged as follows:—

The *Master Chimney-Sweepers*, called sometimes "Governors" by the journeymen, are divisible into three kinds:—

The "large" or "high masters," who employ from 2 to 10 men and 2 boys, and keep sometimes 2 horses and a cart, not particularly for the conveyance of the soot, but to go into the country to a gentleman's house to fulfil orders.

The "small" or "low masters," who employ, on an average, two men, and sometimes but one man and a boy, without either horse or cart.

The "single-handed master-men," who employ neither men nor boys, but do all the work themselves.

Of these three classes of masters there are two subdivisions.

The "leeks" or "green-uns," that is to say, those who have not regularly served their time to the trade.

The "knullers" or "queriers," that is to say, those who solicit custom in an irregular manner, by knocking at the doors of houses and such like.

Of the competition of capitalists in this trade there are, I am told, no instances. "We have our own stations," one master sweeper said, "and if I contract to sweep a genelman's house, here in Pancras, for 25s. a year, or 10s., or anythink, my nearest neighbour, as has men and machines fit, is in Marrybun; and it wouldn't pay to send his men a mile and a half, or on to two mile, and work at what I can—let alone less. No, sir, I've known bisness nigh 20 year, and there's nothink in the way of that underworking. The poor creeturs as keeps theirselves with a machine, and nothing to give them a lift beyond it, *they'd* undertake work at any figure, but nobody employs or can trust to them, but on chance." The contracts, I am told, for a year's chimney-sweeping in any mansion are on the same terms with one master as with another.

As regards the *Journeymen Chimney-Sweepers* there are also three kinds:—

The "foreman" or "first journeyman" sweeper, who accompanies the men to their work, superintends their labours, and receives the money, when paid immediately after sweeping.

The "journeyman" sweeper, whose duty it is to work the machine, and (where no under-journeyman, or boy, is kept) to carry the machine and take home the soot.

The "under-journeyman" or "boy," who has to carry the machine, take home the soot, and work the machine up the lower-class flues.

There are, besides these, some 20 climbing men, who ascend such flues as the machines cannot cleanse effectually, and, it must, I regret to say, be added, some 20 to 30 climbing boys, mostly under eleven years of age, who are still used for the same purpose "on the sly." Many of the masters, indeed, lament the change to machine-sweeping, saying that their children, who are now useless, would, in "the good old times," have been worth a pound a week to them. It is in the suburbs that these climbing children are mostly employed.

The *hours of labour* are from the earliest morning till about midday, and sometimes later.

There are *no Houses of Call*, trade societies, or regulations among these operatives, but there are low public-houses to which they resort, and where they can always be heard of.

When a chimney-sweeper is out of work he merely inquires of others in the same line of business, who, if they know of any one that wants a journeyman, direct their brother sweeper to call and see the master; but though the chimney-sweepers have no trade societies, some of the better class belong to sick, and others to burial, funds. The lower class of sweepers, however, seem to have no resource in sickness, or in their utmost need, but the parish. There are sweepers, I am told, in every workhouse in London.

There are three *modes of payment* common among the sweepers:—

1, in money;

2, partly in money and partly in kind; and

3, by perquisites.

The great majority of the masters pay the men they employ from 2s. to 3s., and a few 4s. and 6s. per week, together with their board and lodging. It may seem that 3s. per week is a small sum, but it was remarked to me that there are few working men who, after supporting themselves, are able to save that sum weekly, while the sweepers have many perquisites of one sort or other, which sometimes bring them in 1s., 2s., 3s., 4s., and occasionally 5s. or 6s., a week additional—a sufficient sum to pay for clothes and washing. The journeymen, when lodged in the house of the master, are single men, and if constantly employed might, perhaps, do well, but they are often unemployed, especially in the summer, when there are not so many fires kept burning. As soon as one of them gets married, or what among them is synonymous, "takes up with a woman," which they commonly do when they are able to purchase some sort of a machine, they set up for themselves, and thus a great number of the men get to be masters on their own account, without being able to employ any extra hands. These are generally reckoned among the "knullers;" they do but little business at first, for the masters long established in a neighbourhood, who are known to the people, and have some standing, are almost always preferred to those who are strangers or mere beginners.

It was very common, but perhaps more common in country towns than in London, for the journeymen, as well as apprentices, in this and many other trades to live at the master's table. But the board and lodging supplied, in lieu of money-wages, to the journeymen sweepers, seems to be one of the few existing instances of such a practice in London. Among slop-working tailors and shoemakers, some unfortunate workmen are boarded and lodged by their employers, but these employers are merely middlemen, who gain their living by serving such masters as " do not like to drive their negroes themselves." But among the sweepers there are no middlemen.

It is not all the journeymen sweepers, however, who are remunerated after this manner, for many receive 12s., and some 14s., and not a few 18s. weekly, besides perquisites, but reside at their own homes.

Apprenticeship is now not at all common among the sweepers, as no training to the business is needed. Lord Shaftesbury, however, in July last, gave notice of his intention to bring in a bill to prevent persons who had not been duly apprenticed to the business establishing themselves as sweepers.

The Perquisites of the journeymen sweepers are for measuring, arranging, and putting the soot sold into the purchasers' sacks, or carts; for this is considered extra work. The payment of this perquisite seems to be on no fixed scale, some having 1s. for 50, and some for 100 bushels. When a chimney is on fire and a journeyman sweeper is employed to extinguish it, he receives from 1s. 6d. to 5s. according to the extent of time consumed and the risk of being injured. "Chance sweeping," or the sweeping of a chimney not belonging to a customer, when a journeyman has completed his regular round, ensures him 3d. in some employments, but in fewer than was once the case. The beer-money given by any customer to a journeyman is also his perquisite. Where a foreman is kept, the " brieze," or cinders collected from the grate, belong to him, and the ashes belong to the journeyman; but where there is no foreman, the brieze and ashes belong to the journeyman solely. These they sell to the poor at the rate of 6d. a bushel. I am told by experienced men that, all these matters considered, it may be stated that one-half of the journeymen in London have perquisites of 1s. 6d., the other half of 2s. 6d. a week.

The Nominal Wages to the journeymen, then, are from 12s. to 18s. weekly, without board and lodging, or from 2s. to 6s. in money, with board and lodging, represented as equal to 7s.

The Actual Wages are 2s. 6d. a week more in the form of perquisites, and perhaps 4d. daily in beer or gin.

The wages to the boys are mostly 1s. a week, but many masters pay 1s. 6d. to 2s., with board and lodging. These boys have no perquisites, except such bits of broken victuals as are given to them at houses where they go to sweep.

The wages of the foreman are generally 18s. per week, but some receive 14s. and some 20s. without board and lodging. In one case, where the foreman is kept by the master, only 2s. 6d. in money is given to him weekly. The perquisites of these men average from 4s. to 5s. a week.

The work in the chimney-sweeping trade is more regular than might at first be supposed. The sweepers whose circumstances enable them to employ journeymen send them on regular rounds, and do not engage "chance" hands. If business is brisk, the men and the master, when a working man himself, work later than ordinary, and sometimes another hand is put on and paid the customary amount, by the week, until the briskness ceases; but this is a rare occurrence. There are, however, strong lads, or journeymen out of work, who are *occasionally* employed in "*jobbing,*" helping to carry the soot and such like.

The labour of the journeymen, as regards the payment by their masters, is *continuous*, but the men are often discharged for drunkenness, or for endeavouring to "form a connection of their own" among their employers' customers, and new hands are then put on. " Chimneys won't wait, you know, sir," was said to me, "and if I quit a hand this week, there's another in his place next. If I discharge a hand for three months in a slack time, I have two on when it's a busy time." Perhaps the average employment of the whole body of operatives may be taken at nine months' work in the year. When out of employment the chief resource of these men is in night-work; some turn street-sellers and bricklayers' labourers.

I am told that a considerable sum of money was left for the purpose of supplying every climbing-boy who called on the first of May at a certain place, with a shilling and some refreshment, but I have not been able to ascertain by whom it was left, or where it was distributed; none of the sweepers with whom I conversed knew anything about it. I also heard, that since the passing of the Act, the money has been invested in some securities or other, and is now accumulating, but to what purpose it is intended to be applied I have no means of learning.

Let us now endeavour to estimate the gross yearly income of the operative sweepers.

There are, then, 399 men employed as journeymen, and of them 147 receive a money wage weekly from their masters, and reside with their parents or at their own places. The remaining 252 are boarded and lodged. This board and lodging are generally computed, as under the old system, to represent 8s., being 1s. a day for board and 1s. a week for lodging. But, on the average, the board does not cost the masters 7s. a week, but, as I shall afterwards show, barely 6s.

The men and boys may be said to be all fully employed for nine months in the year; some, of course, are at work all the year through, but others get only six months' employment in the twelve months; so that taking nine months as the average, we have the following table of

WAGES PAID TO THE OPERATIVE SWEEPERS OF LONDON.

							Money wages for nine months.					
	JOURNEYMEN. *Without board and lodging.*						£	s.	d.			
30	Journeymen employed by	3 masters, at	18s. per week				1053	0	0			
14	,,	,,	5	,,	16s.	,,	436	16	0			
6	,,	,,	3	,,	15s.	,,	175	10	0			
27	,,	,,	8	,,	14s.	,,	737	2	0			
63	,,	,,	23	,,	12s.	,,	1474	4	0			
7	,,	,,	3	,,	10s.	,,	136	10	0	Value of board and lodging for nine months estimated at 7s. a week.		
147		45					4013	2	0			
	With board and lodging.									£	s.	d.
3	Journeymen employed by	1 master, at	8s. 0d. per week				46	16	0	40	19	0
17	,,	,,	5	,,	6s. 0d.	,,	198	18	0	232	1	0
1	,,	,,	1	,,	5s. 0d.	,,	9	15	0	13	13	0
41	,,	,,	14	,,	4s. 0d.	,,	319	16	0	559	13	0
3	,,	,,	1	,,	3s. 6d.	,,	20	9	6	40	19	0
80	,,	,,	39	,,	3s. 0d.	,,	468	0	0	1092	0	0
53	,,	,,	26	,,	2s. 6d.	,,	258	7	6	723	9	0
44	,,	,,	31	,,	2s. 0d.	,,	171	12	0	600	9	8
8	,,	,,	4	,,	1s. 6d.	,,	234	0	0	109	4	0
2	,,	,,	1	,,	1s. 0d.	,,	3	18	0	27	6	0
252		123					1731	12	0	3439	13	8
	FOREMEN. *Without board and lodging.*											
2	Foremen employed by	1 master, at	20s. per week				78	0	0			
6	,,	,,	4	,,	18s.	,,	210	12	0			
1	,,	,,	1	,,	16s.	,,	31	4	0			
2	,,	,,	2	,,	14s.	,,	54	12	0			
11		8					374	8	0			
	With board and lodging.											
1	,,	,,	1	,,	2s. 6d.	,,	4	17	6	13	13	0
	BOYS. *Without board and lodging.*											
2	Boys employed by	1 master, at	10s. per week				39	0	0	Board and lodging estimated at 6s. a week.		
	With board and lodging.											
1	,,	,,	1	,,	3s. 0d.	,,	5	17	0	11	14	0
1	,,	,,	1	,,	2s. 6d.	,,	4	17	6	11	14	0
9	,,	,,	8	,,	2s. 0d.	,,	35	2	0	105	6	0
14	,,	,,	14	,,	1s. 6d.	,,	40	19	0	163	16	0
30	,,	,,	28	,,	1s. 0d.	,,	58	10	0	351	0	0
1	,,	,,	1	,,	0s. 9d.	,,	1	9	3	11	14	0
4	,,	,,	2	,,	0s. 0d.	,,				46	16	0
62		54					146	14	9	702	0	0
	Total earnings						6309	14	3			
	Total for board, lodging, &c. . . .						4155	6	8			
	Grand Total						10,465	0	11			

Thus we find that the *constant* or *average casual* wages of the several classes of operative chimney-sweepers may be taken as follows:—

	s.	d.
Journeymen without board and lodging, and with perquisites averaging 2s. a week	12	6
Journeymen with board and lodging and 2s. a week perquisites	9	10½
Foreman, without board and lodging, at 2s. 6d. a week perquisites	15	7
Boys, with board and lodging	5	3

The *general* wages of the trade, including foreman, journeymen, and boys, and calculating the perquisites to average 2s. weekly, will be 10s. 6d. a week, the same as the cotton factory operatives.

But if 10,500l. be the income of the operatives, what do the employers receive who have to pay this sum?

The charge for sweeping one of the lofty chimneys in the public and official edifices, and in the great houses in the aristocratic streets and squares, is 2s. 6d. and 3s. 6d.

The chimneys of moderate-sized houses are swept at 1s. to 1s. 6d. each, and those of the poorer classes are charged generally 6d.; some, however, are swept at 3d. and 4d.; and when soot realized a higher price (some of the present master sweepers *have* sold it at 1s. a bushel), the chimneys of poor persons were swept by the poorer class of sweeps merely for the perquisite of the soot. This is sometimes done even now, but to a very small extent, by a sweeper, "on his own hook," and in want of a job, but generally with an injunction to the person whose chimney has been cleansed on such easy terms, not to mention it, as it "couldn't be made a practice on."

Estimating the number of houses belonging to the wealthy classes of society to be 54,000, and these to be swept eight times a year, and the charge for sweeping to be 2s. 6d. each time; and the number of houses belonging to the middle classes to be 90,000, and each to be swept four times a year, at 1s. 6d. each time; and the dwellings of the poor and labouring classes to be swept once a year at 6d. each time, and the number of such dwellings to be 165,000, we find that the total sum paid to the master chimney-sweepers of London is, in round numbers, 85,000l.

The sum obtained for 800,000 bushels of soot collected by the master-sweepers from the houses of London, at 5d. per bushel, is 16,500l.

Thus the total annual income of the master-sweepers of London is 100,000l.

Out of this 100,000l. per annum, the expenses of the masters would appear to be as follows:—

Yearly Expenditure of the Master-Sweepers.

Sum paid in wages to 473 journeymen	£10,500
Rent, &c., of 350 houses or lodgings, at 12l. yearly each	4,200
Wear and tear of 1000 machines, 1l. each yearly	1,000
Ditto 2000 sacks, at 1s. each yearly	100
Keep of 25 horses, 7s. weekly each	£455
Wear and tear of 25 carts and harness, 1l. each	25
Interest on capital at 10 per cent.	450
Total yearly expenditure of master-sweepers employing journeymen	£16,736

The rent here given may seem low at 12l. a year, but many of the chimney-sweepers live in parlours, with cellars below, in old out-of-the-way places, at a low rental, in Stepney, Shadwell, Wapping, Bethnal-green, Hoxton, Lock's-fields, Walworth, Newington, Islington, Somers-town, Paddington, &c. The better sort of master-sweepers at the West-end often live in a mews.

The gains, then, of the master sweepers are as under:—

Annual income for cleansing chimneys and soot	£100,000
Expenditure for wages, rent, wear, and tear, keep of horses, &c., say	20,000
Annual profit of master chimney-sweepers of London	£80,000

This amount of profit, divided among 350 masters, gives about 230l. per annum to each individual; it is only by a few, however, that such a sum is realized, as in the 100,000l. paid by the London public to the sweepers' trade, is included the sum received by the men who work single-handed, "on their own hook," as they say, employing no journeymen. Of these men's earnings, the accounts I heard from themselves and the other master sweepers were all accordant, that they barely made journeymen's wages. They have the very worst-paid portion of the trade, receiving neither for their sweeping nor their soot the prices obtained by the better masters; indeed they very frequently sell their soot to their more prosperous brethren. Their general statement is, that they make "eighteen pence a day, and all told." Their receipts then, and they have no perquisites as have the journeymen, are, in a slack time, about 1s. a day (and some days they do not get a job); but in the winter they are busier, as it is then that sweepers are employed by the poor; and at that period the "master-men" may make from 15s. to 20s. a week each; so that, I am assured, the average of their weekly takings may be estimated at 12s. 6d.

Now, deducting the expenditure from the receipts of 100,000l. (for sweeping and soot), the balance, as we have seen, is 80,000l., an amount of profit which, if equally divided among the three classes of the trade, will give the following sums:—

	Yearly, each.		Yearly, total.
	£	s.	£
Profits of 150 single-handed master-men	32	10	4,940
Do. 92 small masters	200	0	18,400
Do. 106 large masters	500	0	53,000
			£76,340

Nor is this estimate of the masters' profits, I

am assured, extravagant. One of the smaller sweepers, but a prosperous man in his way, told me that he knew a master sweeper who was "as rich as Crœser, had bought houses, and could not write his own name."

We have now but to estimate the amount of capital invested in the chimney-sweepers' trade, and then to proceed to the characteristics of the men.

	£
1200 machines, 2l. 10s. each (present average value)	3000
3000 sacks, 2s. 6d. each	385
25 horses, 20l. each	500
25 sets of harness, 2l. each	50
25 carts, 12l. each	300
	£4235

It may be thought that the sweepers will require the services of more than 25 horses, but I am assured that such is not the case as regards the soot business, for the soot is carted away from the sweepers' premises by the farmer or other purchaser.

It would appear, then, that the facts of the chimney-sweepers' trade are briefly as under :—

The gross quantity of soot collected yearly throughout London is 800,000 bushels. The value of this, sold as manure, at 5d. per bushel, is 16,500l.

There are 800 to 900 people employed in the trade, 200 of whom are masters employing journeymen, 150 single-handed master-men, and 470 journeymen and under journeymen.

The annual income of the entire number of journeymen is 10,500l. without perquisites, or 13,000l. with, which gives an average weekly wage to the operatives of 10s. 6d.

The annual income of the masters and leeks is, for sweeping and soot, 100,000l.

The annual expenditure of the masters for rent, keep of horses, wear and tear, and wages, is 20,000l.

The gross annual profit of the 350 masters is 80,000l., which is at the rate of about 35l. per annum to each of the single-handed men, 200l. to each of the smaller masters employing journeymen, and 500l. to each of the larger masters.

The capital of the trade is about 5000l.

The price charged by the "high master sweepers" for cleaning the flues of a house rented at 150l. a year and upwards, is from 1s. to 3s. 6d. (the higher price being paid for sweeping those chimneys which have a hot plate affixed). A small master, on the other hand, will charge from 1s. to 3s. for the same kind of work, while a single-handed man seldom gets above "a 2s. job," and that not very often. The charge for sweeping the flues of a house rented at from 50l. to 150l. a year, is from 9d. to 2s. 6d. by a large master, and from 8d. to 2s. by a small master, while a single-handed man will take the job at from 6d. to 1s. 6d. The price charged per flue for a house rented at from 20l. a year up to 50l. a year, will average 6d. a flue, charged by large masters, 4d. by small masters, and from 2d. to 3d. by the single-handed sweepers in some cases; indeed, the poorest class will sweep a flue for the soot only. But the prices charged for sweeping chimneys differ in the different parts of the metropolis. I subjoin a list of the maximum and minimum charge for the several districts.

	d.		s.	d.		d.		s.	d.
Kensington and Hammersmith	4	to	3	0	London City	6	to	2	6
Westminster	3	,,	2	0	Shoreditch	3	,,	1	0
Chelsea	4	,,	2	6	Bethnal Green	3	,,	1	0
St. George's, Hanover-sq.	6	,,	3	6	Whitechapel	4	,,	1	6
St. Martin's and St. Ann's	4	,,	2	6	St. George's in the East and Limehouse	3	,,	1	0
St. James's, Westminster	3	,,	2	6	Stepney	3	,,	1	6
Marylebone	4	,,	2	6	Poplar	4	,,	2	0
Paddington	3	,,	2	0	St. George's, St. Olave's, and St. Saviour's, Southwark	3	,,	1	6
Hampstead	3	,,	1	6	Bermondsey	3	,,	0	9
St. Pancras	4	,,	3	0	Walworth and Newington	4	,,	1	6
Islington	3	,,	1	6	Wandsworth	4	,,	1	6
Hackney and Homerton	3	,,	2	0	Lambeth	3	,,	1	0
St. Giles's and St. George's, Bloomsbury	3	,,	3	0	Camberwell	4	,,	2	0
Strand	4	,,	2	6	Clapham, Brixton, and Tooting	4	,,	2	6
Holborn	4	,,	2	6					
Clerkenwell	3	,,	1	6	Rotherhithe	3	,,	1	6
St. Luke's	3	,,	1	0	Greenwich	3	,,	1	6
East London	3	,,	1	6	Woolwich	3	,,	2	6
West London	4	,,	2	6	Lewisham	6	,,	3	0

N.B.—The single-handed and the knullers generally charge a penny less than the prices above given.

There are three different kinds of soot:—the best is produced purely from coal; the next in value is that which proceeds from the combustion of vegetable refuse along with the coal, as in cases where potato peelings, cabbage leaves, and the like, are burnt in the fires of the poorer classes; while the soot produced from wood fires is, I am told, scarcely worth carriage. Wood-soot, however, is generally mixed with that from coal, and sold as the superior kind.

Not only is there a difference in value in the various kinds of soot, but there is also a vast difference in the weight. A bushel of pure coal soot will not weigh above four pounds; that produced from the combustion of coal and vegetable refuse will weigh nearly thrice as much; while that from wood fires is, I am assured, nearly ten times heavier than from coal.

I have not heard that the introduction of free trade has had any influence on the value of soot, or in reducing the wages of the operatives. The same wages are paid to the operatives whether soot sells at a high or low price.

OF THE GENERAL CHARACTERISTICS OF THE WORKING CHIMNEY-SWEEPERS.

THERE are many reasons why the chimney-sweepers have ever been a distinct and peculiar class. They have long been looked down upon as the lowest order of workers, and treated with contumely by those who were but little better than themselves. The peculiar nature of their work giving them not only a filthy appearance, but an offensive smell, of itself, in a manner, prohibited them from associating with other working men; and the natural effect of such proscrip-

A TABLE SHOWING THE NUMBER OF MASTER CHIMNEY SWEEPERS RESIDING IN THE SEVERAL DISTRICTS OF THE METROPOLIS, THE NUMBER OF FOREMEN, OF JOURNEYMEN, AND UNDER JOURNEYMEN EMPLOYED IN EACH DISTRICT DURING THE YEAR, AS WELL AS THE WEEKLY WAGES OF EACH CLASS.

DISTRICTS.	No. of Master Sweepers in each District.	No. of Foremen employed.	No. of Journeymen employed in the brisk season.	No. of Journeymen employed in the slack season.	No. of Under Journeymen, or Boys, employed.	No. of Bushels of Soot collected Weekly.	Weekly Wages of each Foreman.	Weekly Wages of each Journeyman.	Weekly Wages of each Under Journeyman.
WEST DISTRICTS.									
Kensington and Hammersmith.	11	2	25	16	2	695	18s.	7 at 16s. 6 ,, 15s. 10 ,, 14s. 1 ,, 12s.	10s.
Westminster	13	1	26	18	1	735	14s.	5 at 18s. 10 ,, 12s. 3 ,, 4s. 4 ,, 3s. }b 4 ,, 2s.	3s. b
Chelsea	22	...	23	11	2	670	...	1 ,, 16s. 3 ,, 12s. 4 ,, 10s. 3 ,, 3s. 1 ,, 2s. 6d }b 1 ,, 2s.	1 at 2s. b 1 e
St. George's, Hanover-sq.	10	5	27	25	...	890	4 at 18s. 1 ,, 16s.	5 at 18s. 3 ,, 16s. 2 ,, 15s. 9 ,, 14s. 7 ,, 12s. 1 ,, 6s. b	......
St. Martin's and St. Ann's	9	...	16	15	1	415	...	7 at 6s. 6 ,, 4s. }b 2 ,, 3s.	2s. b
St. James's, Westminster	7	1	9	6	...	355	14s.	5 at 12s. 1 ,, 10s. 1 at 3s. 6d. b	......
NORTH DISTRICTS.									
Marylebone	18	...	21	16	...	775	...	18s.	......
Paddington	10	1	17	10	3	495	18s.	1 at 14s. 1 ,, 10s. 2 ,, 4s. 8 ,, 3s. 6d }b 1 ,, 2s. 6d 2 ,, 1s.	2 at 2s. 1 ,, 1s. 6d }b
Hampstead	2	...	2	2	2	60	...	1 at 3s. }b 1 ,, 2s.	1 at 1s. 6d }b 1 ,, 1s.
Islington	9	...	13	12	3	425	...	3 at 4s. }b 2 ,, 3s.	1s. 6d. b
St. Pancras	18	...	33	21	6	920	...	2 at 14s. 6 ,, 12s. 4 ,, 10s. 6 ,, 4s. 3 ,, 3s 6d 11 ,, 3s. }b 3 ,, 2s 6d 1 ,, 2s.	3 at 2s. 2 ,, 1s. 6d }b 1 ,, 1s.
Hackney and Homerton	13	...	3	3	4	290	...	2s. b	1s. 6d. b

Districts.	No. of Master Sweepers in each District.	No. of Foremen employed.	No. of Journeymen employed in the brisk season.	No. of Journeymen employed in the slack season.	No. of Under Journeymen, or Boys, employed.	No. of Bushels of Soot collected Weekly.	Weekly Wages of each Foreman.	Weekly Wages of each Journeyman.	Weekly Wages of each Under Journeyman.
Central Districts.									
St. Giles's and St. George's, Bloomsbury.	12	...	9	7	5	435	...	8 at 12s. 1 ,, 3s. b	1s. b
Strand	5	...	11	8	2	350	...	4s. b	1 at 2s. 1 ,, 1s. } b
Holborn	6	2	11	10	...	435	20s.	2 at 18s. 3 ,, 8s. 4 ,, 4s. } b 2 ,, 3s.	......
Clerkenwell	6	...	9	9	1	310	...	8 at 3s. 1 ,, 2s 6d. } b	1s. b
St. Luke's	6	...	4	3	2	175	...	2s. b	1s. b
East London	8	...	10	8	...	455	...	3s. b	......
West London	5	...	9	6	...	205	...	3 at 4s. 6 ,, 3s. } b	......
London City	6	...	12	10	2	415	...	6 at 6s. 6 ,, 4s. } b	2s. b
East Districts.									
Shoreditch	13	...	6	5	1	380	...	2s. b	1s. b
Bethnal Green	6	...	2	2	...	150	...	1 at 5s. 1 ,, 2s. b	......
Whitechapel	11	...	1	1	3	330	...	2s. b	3s. e
St. George's-in-the-East and Limehouse.	14	...	14	10	3	650	...	3 at 3s. 4 ,, 2s. 6d } b 7 ,, 2s.	1 at 1s. 6d 2 ,, 1s. } b
Stepney	9	...	3	2	...	275	...	3s. b	......
Poplar	4	...	1	...	1	110	...	2s. b	1s. 6d. b
South Districts.									
Southwark	17	...	...	...	...	385	...	......	......
Bermondsey	8	...	4	4	1	220	...	2s. b	1s. b
Walworth and Newington	9	...	6	4	4	330	...	2s. b	1s. b
Wandsworth	6	...	6	5	1	240	...	3 at 3s. 3 ,, 2s. 6d } b	1s. b
Lambeth	16	...	9	9	5	560	...	3 at 3s. 6 ,, 2s. 6d } b	1 at 1s. 6d 4 ,, 1s. } b
Camberwell	8	...	8	7	1	315	...	2s. 6d. b	1s. b
Clapton, Brixton, and Tooting	11	...	13	7	1	410	...	2s. 6d. b	1s. b
Rotherhithe	7	...	2	2	...	170	...	2s. b	......
Greenwich	6	...	4	4	1	195	...	1s. 6d. b	1s. b
Woolwich	7	...	17	12	3	515	...	13 at 2s. 6d. 4 ,, 1s. 6d.	2 at 1s. 1 ,, 9d. } b
Lewisham	2	...	5	5	1	160	...	2s. b	1s. b
Ramoneur Company	...	...	18	18	...	450	...	18s.	......
Total	350	12	399	313	62	15350			

Note.—*b* means board and lodging as well as money, or part money and part kind; *e* stands for everything found or paid all in kind.

These returns have been collected by personal visits to each district:—the name of each master throughout London, together with the number of Foremen, Journeymen, and Under Journeymen employed, and the Wages received by each, as well as the quantity of soot collected, have been likewise obtained; but the names of the masters are here omitted for want of space, and the results alone are given.

tion has been to compel them to herd together apart from others, and to acquire habits and peculiarities of their own widely differing from the characteristics of the rest of the labouring classes.

Sweepers, however, have not from this cause generally been an hereditary race—that is, they have not become sweepers from father to son for many generations. Their numbers were, in the days of the climbing boys, in most intances increased by parish apprentices, the parishes usually adopting that mode as the cheapest and easiest of freeing themselves from a part of the burden of juvenile pauperism. The climbing boys, but more especially the unfortunate parish apprentices, were almost always cruelly used, starved, beaten, and over-worked by their masters, and treated as outcasts by all with whom they came in contact: there can be no wonder, then, that, driven in this manner from all other society, they gladly availed themselves of the companionship of their fellow-sufferers; quickly imbibed all their habits and peculiarities; and, perhaps, ended by becoming themselves the most tyrannical masters to those who might happen to be placed under their charge.

Notwithstanding the disrepute in which sweepers have ever been held, there are many classes of workers beneath them in intelligence. All the tribe of finders and collectors (with the exception of the dredgermen, who are an observant race, and the sewer-hunters, who, from the danger of their employment, are compelled to exercise their intellects) are far inferior to them in this respect; and they are clever fellows compared to many of the dustmen and scavagers. The great mass of the agricultural labourers are known to be almost as ignorant as the beasts they drive; but the sweepers, from whatever cause it may arise, are known, in many instances, to be shrewd, intelligent, and active.

But there is much room for improvement among the operative chimney-sweepers. Speaking of the men generally, I am assured that there is scarcely one out of ten who can either read or write. One man in Chelsea informed me that some ladies, in connection with the Rev. Mr. Cadman's church, made an attempt to instruct the sweepers of the neighbourhood in reading and writing; but the master sweepers grew jealous, and became afraid lest their men should get too knowing for them. When the time came, therefore, for the men to prepare for the school, the masters always managed to find out some job which prevented them from attending at the appointed time, and the consequence was that the benevolent designs of the ladies were frustrated.

The sweepers, as a class, in almost all their habits, bear a strong resemblance to the costermongers. The habit of going about in search of their employment has, of itself, implanted in many of them the wandering propensity peculiar to street people. Many of the better-class costermongers have risen into coal-shed men and greengrocers, and become settled in life; in like manner the better-class sweepers have risen to be masters, and, becoming settled in a locality, have gradually obtained the trade of the neighbourhood; then, as their circumstances improved, they have been able to get horses and carts, and become nightmen; and there are many of them at this moment men of wealth, comparatively speaking. The great body of them, however, retain in all their force their original characteristics; the masters themselves, although shrewd and sensible men, often betray their want of education, and are in no way particular as to their expressions, their language being made up, in a great measure, of the terms peculiar to the costermongers, especially the denominations of the various sorts of money. I met with some sweepers, however, whose language was that in ordinary use, and their manners not vulgar. I might specify one, who, although a workhouse orphan and apprentice, a harshly-treated climbing-boy, is now prospering as a sweeper and nightman, is a regular attendant at all meetings to promote the good of the poor, and a zealous ragged-school teacher, and teetotaller.

When such men are met with, perhaps the class cannot be looked upon as utterly cast away, although the need of reformation in the habits of the working sweepers is extreme, and especially in respect of drinking, gambling, and dirt. The journeymen (who have often a good deal of leisure) and the single-handed men are—in the great majority of cases at least—addicted to drinking, beer being their favourite beverage, either because it is the cheapest or that they fancy it the most suitable for washing away the sooty particles which find their way to their throats. These men gamble also, but with this proviso—they seldom play for money; but when they meet in their usual houses of resort—two famous ones are in Back C—— lane and S—— street, Whitechapel—they spend their time and what money they may have in tossing for beer, till they are either drunk or penniless. Such men present the appearance of having just come out of a chimney. There seems never to have been any attempt made by them to wash the soot off their faces. I am informed that there is scarcely one of them who has a second shirt or any change of clothes, and that they wear their garments night and day till they literally rot, and drop in fragments from their backs. Those who are not employed as journeymen by the masters are frequently whole days without food, especially in summer, when the work is slack; and it usually happens that those who are what is called "knocking about on their own account" seldom or never have a farthing in their pockets in the morning, and may, perhaps, have to travel till evening before they get a threepenny or sixpenny chimney to sweep. When night comes, and they meet their companions, the tossing and drinking again commences; they again get drunk; roll home to wherever it may be, to go through the same routine on the morrow; and this is the usual tenour of their lives, whether earning 5s. or 20s. a week.

The chimney-sweepers generally are fond of drink; indeed their calling, like that of dustmen, is one of those which naturally lead to it. The men declare they are ordered to drink gin and smoke as much as they can, in order to rid the stomach of the soot they may have swallowed during their work.

Washing among chimney-sweepers seems to be much more frequent than it was. In the evidence before Parliament it was stated that some of the climbing-boys were washed once in six months, some once a week, some once in two or three months. I do not find it anywhere stated that any of these children were never washed at all; but from the tenour of the evidence it may be reasonably concluded that such was the case.

A master sweeper, who was in the habit of bathing at the Marylebone baths once and sometimes twice a week, assured me that, although many now eat and drink and sleep sooty, washing is more common among his class than when he himself was a climbing-boy. He used then to be stripped, and compelled to step into a tub, and into water sometimes too hot and sometimes too cold, while his mistress, to use his own word, *scoured* him. Judging from what he had seen and heard, my informant was satisfied that, from 30 to 40 years ago, climbing-boys, with a very few exceptions, were but seldom washed; and then it was looked upon by them as a most disagreeable operation, often, indeed, as a species of punishment. Some of the climbing-boys used to be taken by their masters to bathe in the Serpentine many years ago; but one boy was unfortunately drowned, so that the children could hardly be coerced to go into the water afterwards.

The washing among the chimney-sweepers of the present day, when there are scarcely any climbing-boys, is so much an individual matter that it is not possible to speak with any great degree of certainty on the subject, but that it increases may be concluded from the fact that the number of sweeps who resort to the public baths increases.

The first public baths and washhouses opened in London were in the "north-west district," and situated in George-street, Euston-square, near the Hampstead-road. This establishment was founded by voluntary contribution in 1846, and is now self-supporting.

There are three more public baths: one in Goulston-street, Whitechapel (on the same principle as that first established); another in St. Martin's, near the National Gallery, which are parochial; and the last in Marylebone, near the Yorkshire Stingo tavern, New-road, also parochial. The charge for a cold bath, each being secluded from the others, is 1*d*., with the use of a towel; a warm bath is 2*d*. in the third class. The following is the return of the number of bathers at the north-west district baths, the establishment most frequented:—

	1847.	1848.	1849.	1850.
Bathers	110,940	111,788	96,726	86,597
Washers, Dryers, Ironers, &c.	39,418	61,690	65,934	73,023
Individuals Washed for	137,672	246,760	263,736	292,092

I endeavoured to ascertain the proportion of sweepers, with other working men, who availed themselves of these baths; but there are unfortunately no data for instituting a comparison as to the relative cleanliness of the several trades. When the baths were first opened an endeavour was made to obtain such a return; but it was found to be distasteful to the bathers, and so was discontinued. We find, then, that in four years there have been 406,051 bathers. The following gives the proportion between the sexes, a portion of 1846 being included:—

Bathers—Males	.	.	.	417,424
,, Females	.	.	.	47,114
Total bathers	.	.	.	464,538

The falling off in the number of bathers at this establishment is, I am told, attributable to the opening of new baths, the people, of course, resorting to the nearest.

I have given the return of washers, &c., as I endeavoured to ascertain the proportion of washing by the chimney-sweeper's wives; but there is no specification of the trades of the persons using this branch of the establishment any more than there is of those frequenting the baths, and for the same reason as prevented its being done among the bathers. One of the attendants at these washhouses told me that he had no doubt the sweepers' wives did wash there, for he had more than once seen a sweeper waiting to carry home the clothes his wife had cleansed. As no questions concerning their situation in life are asked of the poor women who resort to these very excellent institutions (for such they appear to be on a cursory glance) of course no data can be supplied. This is to be somewhat regretted; but a regard to the feelings, and in some respects to the small prejudices, of the industrious poor is to be commended rather than otherwise, and the managers of these baths certainly seem to have manifested such a regard.

I am informed, however, by the secretary of the north-west district institution, that in some weeks of the summer 80 chimney-sweepers bathed there; always having, he believed, warm baths, which are more effective in removing soot or dirt from the skin than cold. Summer, it must be remembered, is the sweep's "brisk" season. In a winter week as few as 25 or 20 have bathed, but the weekly average of sweeper-bathers, the year through, is about 50; and the number of sweeper-bathers, he thought, had increased since the opening of the baths about 10 per cent. yearly. As in 1850 the average number of bathers of all classes did not exceed 1646 per week, the proportion of sweepers, 50, is high. The number of female bathers is about one-ninth, so that the males would be about 1480; and the 50 sweepers a week constitute about a thirtieth part of the whole of the third-class bathers. The number of sweep-bathers was known because a sweep is known by his appearance.

I was told by the secretary that the sweepers, the majority bathing on Saturday nights, usually carried a bundle to the bath; this contained their "clean things." After bathing they assumed their "Sunday clothes;" and from the change in their appearance between ingress and egress, they were hardly recognisable as the same individuals.

In the other baths, where also there is no specification of the bathers, I am told, that of sweepers bathing the number (on computation) is 30 at Marylebone, 25 at Goulston-street, and 15 (at the least) at St. Martin's, as a weekly average. In all, 120 sweepers bathe weekly, or about a seventh of the entire working body. The increase at the three baths last mentioned, in sweepers bathing, is from 5 to 10 per cent.

Among the lower-class sweepers there are but few who wash themselves even once throughout the year. They eat, drink, and sleep in the same state of filth and dirt as when engaged in their daily avocation. Others, however, among the better class are more cleanly in their habits, and wash themselves every night.

Between *the appearance of the sweepers* in the streets at the present time and before the abolition of the system of climbing there is a marked difference. Charles Lamb said (in 1823):—

"I like to meet a sweep—understand me, not a grown sweeper—old chimney-sweepers are by no means attractive—but one of those tender novices blooming through their first nigritude, the maternal washings not quite effaced from the cheek—such as come forth with the dawn, or somewhat earlier, with their little professional notes sounding like the *peep peep* of a young sparrow; or liker to the matin lark should I pronounce them, in their aerial ascents not seldom anticipating the sunrise?"

Throughout his essay, Elia throws the halo of poetry over the child-sweepers, calling them "dim specks," "poor blots," "innocent blacknesses," "young Africans of our own growth;" the natural kindliness of the writer shines out through all. He counsels his reader to give the young innocent 2*d*., or, if the weather were starving, "let the demand on thy humanity rise to a tester" (6*d*.).

The appearance of the little children-sweepers, as they trotted along at the master's or the journeyman's heels, or waited at "rich men's doors" on a cold morning, was pitiable in the extreme. If it snowed, there was a strange contrast between the black sootiness of the sweeper's dress and the white flakes of snow which adhered to it. The boy-sweeper trotted listlessly along; a sack to contain the soot thrown over his shoulder, or disposed round his neck, like a cape or shawl. One master sweeper tells me that in his apprenticeship days he had to wait at the great mansions in and about Grosvenor-square, on some bitter wintry mornings, until he felt as if his feet, although he had both stockings and shoes—and many young climbers were barefoot—felt as if frozen to the pavement. When the door was opened, he told me, the matter was not really mended. The rooms were often large and cold, and being lighted only with a candle or two, no doubt looked very dreary, while there was not a fire in the whole house, and no one up but a yawning servant or two, often very cross at having been disturbed. The servants, however, in noblemen's houses, he also told me, were frequently kind to him, giving him bread and butter, and sometimes bread and jam; and as his master generally had a glass of raw spirit handed to him, the boy usually had a sip when his employer had "knocked off his glass." His employer, indeed, sometimes said, "O, *he's* better without it; it'll only larn him to drink, like it did me;" but the servant usually answered, "O, here, just a thimblefull for him."

The usual dress of the climbing-boy—as I have learned from those who had worn it themselves, and, when masters, had provided it for their boys—was made of a sort of strong flannel, which many years ago was called chimney-sweepers' cloth; but my informant was not certain whether this was a common name for it or not, he only remembered having heard it called so. He remembered, also, accompanying his master to do something to the flues in a church, then (1817) hung with black cloth, as a part of the national mourning for the Princess Charlotte of Wales, and he thought it seemed very like the chimney-sweepers' cloth, which was dark coloured when new. The child-sweep wore a pair of cloth trowsers, and over that a sort of tunic, or tight fitting shirt with sleeves; sometimes a little waistcoat and jacket. This, it must be borne in mind, was only the practice among the best masters (who always had to find their apprentices in clothes); and was the practice among them more and more in the later period of the climbing process, for householders began to inquire as to what sort of trim the boys employed on their premises appeared in. The poorer or the less well-disposed masters clad the urchins who climbed for them in any old rags which their wives could piece together, or in any low-priced garment "picked up" in such places as Rosemary-lane. The fit was no object at all. These ill-clad lads were, moreover, at one time the great majority. The clothes were usually made "at home" by the women, and in the same style, as regarded the seams, &c., as the sacks for soot; but sometimes the work was beyond the art of the sweeper's wife, and then the aid of some poor neighbour better skilled in the use of her scissors and needle, or of some poor tailor, was called in, on the well-known terms of "a shilling (or 1*s*. 6*d*.) a day, and the grub."

The cost of a climbing-boy's dress, I was informed, varied, when new, according to the material of which it was made, from 3*s*. 6*d*. to 6*s*. 6*d*. independently of the cost of making, which, in the hands of a tailor who "whipped the cat" (or went out to work at his customer's houses), would occupy a day, at easy labour, at a cost of 1*s*. 6*d*. (or less) in money, and the "whip-cat's" meals, perhaps another 1*s*. 6*d*., beer included. As to the cost of a sweeper's second-hand clothing it is useless to inquire; but I was informed by a now thriving master, that when he was about twelve years old his mistress bought him a "werry tidy jacket, as seemed made for a gen'leman's son," in Petticoat-lane, one Sunday morning, for 1s. 6d.; while other things, he said, were "in proportionate." Shoes and stockings are not included in the cost of the little sweeper's apparel; and they were, perhaps, always bought second-hand. A few of the best masters (or of those wishing to stand best in their customers' regards), who sent their boys to church or to Sunday schools, had then a non-working attire for them; either a sweeper's dress of jacket and trowsers, unsoiled by soot, or the ordinary dress of a poor lad.

The street appearance of the present race of sweepers, all adults, may every here and there bear out Charles Lamb's dictum, that grown sweepers are by no means attractive. Some of them are broad-shouldered and strongly-built men, who, as they traverse the streets, sometimes look as grim as they are dingy. The chimney-scavager carries the implement of his calling propped on his shoulder, in the way shown in the daguerreotype which I have given. His dress is usually a jacket, waistcoat, and trowsers of dark-coloured corduroy; or instead of a jacket a waistcoat with sleeves. Over this when at work the sweeper often wears a sort of blouse or short smock-frock of coarse strong calico or canvas, which protects the corduroy suit from the soot. In this description of the sweeper's garb I can but speak of those whose means enable them to attain the comfort of warm apparel in the winter; the poorer part of the trade often shiver shirtless under a blouse which half covers a pair of threadbare trowsers. The cost of the corduroy suit I have mentioned varies, I was told by a sweeper, who put it tersely enough, "from 20s. *slop,* to 40s. *slap.*" The average runs, I believe, from 28s. to 33s., as regards the better class of the sweepers.

The *diet of the journeymen sweepers and the apprentices,* and sometimes of their working employer, was described to me as generally after the following fashion. My informant, a journeyman, calculated what his food "stood his master," as he had once "kept hisself."

	Daily.	
	s.	d.
Bread and butter and coffee for breakfast	0	2
A saveloy and potatoes, or cabbage; or a "fagot," with the same vegetables; or fried fish (but not often); or pudding, from a pudding-shop; or soup (a twopenny plate) from a cheap eating-house; average from 2d. to 3d.	0	2½
Tea, same as breakfast	0	2
	0	6½

On Sundays the fare was better. They then sometimes had a bit of "prime fat mutton" taken to the oven, with "taturs to bake along with it;" or a "fry of liver, if the old 'oman was in a good humour," and always a pint of beer apiece. Hence, as some give their men beer, the average amount of 5s. or 6s. weekly, which I have given as the cost of the "board" to the masters, is made up. The drunken single-handed mastermen, I am told, live on beer and "a bite of anything they can get." I believe there are few complaints of inefficient food.

The food provided by the large or high master sweepers is generally of the same kind as the master and his family partake of; among this class the journeymen are tolerably well provided for.

In the lower-class sweepers, however, the food is not so plentiful nor so good in kind as that provided by the high master sweepers. The expense of keeping a man employed by a large master sometimes ranges as high as 8s. a week, but the average, I am told, is about 6s. per week; while those employed by the low-class sweepers average about 5s. a week. The cost of their lodging may be taken at from 1s. to 2s. a week extra.

The sweepers in general are, I am assured, fond of oleaginous food; fat broth, fagots, and what is often called "greasy" meat.

They are considered *a short-lived people,* and among the journeymen, the masters "on their own hook," &c., few old men are to be met with. In one of the reports of the Board of Health, out of 4312 deaths among males, of the age of 15 and upwards, the mortality among the sweepers, masters and men, was 9, or one in 109 of the whole trade. As the calculation was formed, however, from data supplied by the census of 1841, and on the Post Office Directory, it supplies no reliable information, as I shall show when I come to treat of the nightmen. Many of these men still suffer, I am told, from the chimney-sweeper's cancer, which is said to arise mainly from uncleanly habits. Some sweepers assure me that they have vomited balls of soot.

As to the abodes of the master sweepers, I can supply the following account of two. The soot, I should observe, is seldom kept long, rarely a month, on the premises of a sweeper, and is in the best "concerns" kept in cellars.

The localities in which many of the sweepers reside are the "lowest" places in the district. Many of the houses in which I found the lower class of sweepers were in a ruinous and filthy condition. The "high-class" sweepers, on the other hand, live in respectable localities, often having back premises sufficiently large to stow away their soot.

I had occasion to visit the house of one of the persons from whom I obtained much information. He is a master in a small way, a sensible man, and was one of the few who are teetotallers. His habitation, though small—being a low house only one story high—was substantially furnished with massive mahogany chairs, table, chests of drawers, &c., while on each side of the fire-place, which was distinctly visible from the street over a hall door, were two buffets, with glass doors, well filled with glass and china vessels. It was a wet night, and a fire burned brightly in the stove, by the light of which might be seen the master of the establishment sitting on one side, while his wife and daughter occupied the other; a neighbour sat before the fire with his back to the door, and altogether it struck me as a comfortable-looking evening party. They were resting and chatting quietly together after the labour of the day, and everything betokened the comfortable circumstances in which the man, by sobriety and industry, had been able to place himself. Yet this man had been a climbing-boy, and one of the unfortunates who had lost his parents when a child, and was apprenticed by the parish to this business. From him I learned that his was not a solitary instance of teetotalism (I have before spoken of another); that, in fact, there were some more, and one in particular, named Brown, who was a good speaker, and devoted himself during his leisure hours at night in advocating the principles which by experience he had found to effect such great good to himself; but he also informed me that the majority of the others were a drunken and dissipated crew, sunk to the lowest degree of misery, yet recklessly spending every farthing they could earn in the public-house.

Different in every respect was another house which I visited in the course of my inquiries, in the neighbourhood of H——street, Bethnal-green. The house was rented by a sweeper, a master on his own account, and every room in the place was let to sweepers and their wives or women, which, with these men, often signify one and the same thing. The inside of the house looked as dark as a coal-pit; there was an insufferable smell of soot, always offensive to those unaccustomed to it; and every person and every thing which met the eye, even to the caps and gowns of the women, seemed as if they had just been steeped in Indian ink. In one room was a sweep and his woman quarrelling. As I opened the door I caught the words, "I'm d——d if I has it any longer. I'd see you b——y well d——d first, and you knows it." The savage was intoxicated, for his red eyes flashed through his sooty mask with drunken excitement, and his matted hair, which looked as if it had never known a comb, stood out from his head like the whalebone ribs of his own machine. "B——y Bet," as he called her, did not seem a whit more sober than her man; and the shrill treble of her voice was distinctly audible till I turned the corner of the street, whither I was accompanied by the master of the house, to whom I had been recommended by one of the fraternity as an intelligent man, and one who knew "a thing or two." "You see," he said, as we turned the corner, "there isn't no use a talkin' to them ere fellows—they're all tosticated now, and they doesn't care nothink for nobody; but they'll be quiet enough to-morrow, 'cept they yarns somethink, and if they do then they'll be just as bad to-morrow night. They're a awful lot, and nobody ill niver do anythink with them." This man was not by any means in such easy circumstances as the master first mentioned. He was merely a man working for himself, and unable to employ any one else in the business; as is customary with some of these people, he had taken the house he had shown me to let to lodgers of his own class, making something by so doing; though, if his own account be correct, I'm at a loss to imagine how he contrived even to get his rent. From him I obtained the following statement:—

"Yes, I was a climbing-boy, and sarved a rigler printiceship for seven years. I was out on my printiceship when I was fourteen. Father was a silk-weaver, and did all he knew to keep me from being a sweep, but I would be a sweep, and nothink else." [This is not so very uncommon a predilection, strange as it may seem.] "So father, when he saw it was no use, got me bound printice. Father's alive now, and near 90 years of age. I don't know why I wished to be a sweep, 'cept it was this—there was sweeps always lived about here, and I used to see the boys with lots of money a tossin' and gamblin', and wished to have money too. You see they got money where they swept the chimneys; they used to get 2d. or 3d. for theirselves in a day, and sometimes 6d. from the people of the house, and that's the way they always had plenty of money. I niver thought anythink of the climbing; it wasn't so bad at all as some people would make you believe. There are two or three ways of climbing. In wide flues you climb with your elbows and your legs spread out, your feet pressing against the sides of the flue; but in narrow flues, such as nine-inch ones, you must slant it; you must have your sides in the angles, it's wider there, and go up just that way." [Here he threw himself into position—placing one arm close to his side, with the palm of the hand turned outwards, as if pressing the side of the flue, and extending the other arm high above his head, the hand apparently pressing in the same manner.] "There," he continued, "that's slantin'. You just put yourself in that way, and see how small you make yourself. I niver got to say stuck myself, but a many of them did; yes, and were taken out dead. They were smothered for want of air, and the fright, and a stayin' so long in the flue; you see the waistband of their trowsers sometimes got turned down in the climbing, and in narrow flues, when not able to get it up, then they stuck. I had a boy once—we were called to sweep a chimney down at Poplar. When we went in he looked up the flues, 'Well, what is it like?' I said. 'Very narrow,' says he, 'don't think I can get up there;' so after some time we gets on top of the house, and takes off the chimney-pot, and has a look down—it was wider a' top, and I thought as how he could go down. 'You had better buff it, Jim,' says I. I suppose you know what that means; but Jim wouldn't do it, and kept his trowsers on. So down he goes, and gets on very well till he comes to the shoulder of the flue, and then he couldn't stir. He shouts down, 'I'm stuck.' I shouts up and tells him what to do. 'Can't move,' says he, 'I'm stuck hard and fast.' Well, the people of the house got fretted like, but I says to them, 'Now my boy's stuck, but for Heaven's sake don't make a word of noise; don't say a word, good or bad, and I'll see what I can do.' So I locks the door, and buffs it, and forces myself up till I could reach him with my hand, and as soon as he got his foot on my hand he begins to prize himself up, and gets loosened, and comes out at the top again. I was stuck myself, but I was stronger nor he, and I manages to get out again. Now I'll be bound to say if there was another master there as would kick up a row and a-worrited, that ere boy 'ud a niver come out o' that ere flue alive. There was a many o' them lost their lives in that way. Most all the printices used to come from the 'House' (workhouse.) There was nobody to care for them, and some masters used them very bad. I was out of my time at fourteen, and began to get too stout to go up the flues; so after knockin' about for a year or so, as I could do nothink else, I goes to sea on board a man-o'-war, and was away four year. Many of the boys, when they got too big and useless, used to go to sea in them days—they couldn't do nothink else. Yes, many of them went for sodgers; and I know some who went for Gipsies, and others who went for play-actors, and a many who got on to be swell-mobsmen, and thieves, and housebreakers, and the like o' that ere. There ain't nothink o' that sort a-goin' on now since the Ack of Parliament. When I got back from sea father asked me to larn his business; so I takes to the silk-weaving and larned it, and then married a weaveress, and worked with father for a long time. Father was very well off—well off and comfortable for a poor man—but trade was good then. But it got bad afterwards, and none on us was able to live at it; so I takes to the chimney-sweeping again. *A man might manage to live somehow at the sweeping, but the weaving was o' no use.* It was the furrin silks as beat us all up, that's the whole truth. Yet they tells us as how they was a-doin' the country good; but they may tell that to the marines—the sailors won't believe it—not a word on it. I've stuck to the sweeping ever since, and sometimes done very fair at it; but since the Ack there's so many leeks come to it that I don't know how they live—they must be eatin' one another up.

"Well, since you ask then, I can tell you that our people don't care much about law; they don't understand anythink about politics much; they don't mind things o' that ere kind. They only minds to get drunk when they can. Some on them fellows as you seed in there niver cleans theirselves from one year's end to the other. They 'll kick up a row soon enough, with Chartists or anybody else. I thinks them Chartists are a weak-minded set; they was too much a frightened at nothink,—a hundred o' them would run away from one blue-coat, and that wasn't like men. I was often at Chartist meetings, and if they'd only do all they said there was a plenty to stick to them, for there's a somethink wants to be done very bad, for everythink is a-gettin' worser and worser every day. I used to do a good trade, but now I don't yarn a shilling a day all through the year (?). I may walk at this time three or four miles and not get a chimney to sweep, and then get only a sixpence or threepence, and sometimes nothink. It's a starvin', that's what it is; there's so much 'querying' a-goin' on. Querying? that's what we calls under-working*. If they'd all fix a riglar price we might do very well still. I'm 50 years of age, or thereabouts. I don't know much about the story of Mrs. Montague; it was afore my time. I heard of it though. I heard my mother talk about it; she used to read it out of books; she was a great reader—none on 'em could stand afore her for that. I was often at the dinner—the masters' dinner—that was for the boys; but that's all done away long ago, since the Ack of Parliament. I can't tell how many there was at it, but there's such a lot it's impossible to tell. How could any one tell all the sweeps as is in London? I'm sure I can't, and I'm sure nobody else can."

Some years back the sweepers' houses were often indicated by an elaborate sign, highly coloured. A sweeper, accompanied by a "chummy" (once a common name for the climbing-boy, being a corruption of chimney), was depicted on his way to a red brick house, from the chimneys of which bright yellow flames were streaming. Below was the detail of the things undertaken by the sweep, such as the extinction of fires in chimneys, the cleaning of smoke-jacks, &c., &c. A few of these signs, greatly faded, may be seen still. A sweeper, who is settled in what is accounted a "genteel neighbourhood," has now another way of making his calling known. He leaves a card whenever he hears of a new comer, a tape being attached, so that it can be hung up in the kitchen, and thus the servants are always in possession of his address. The following is a customary style :—

"Chimneys swept by the improved machine, much patronized by the Humane Society.

"W. H., Chimney Sweeper and Nightman, 1, —— Mews, in returning thanks to the inhabitants of the surrounding neighbourhood for the patronage he has hitherto received, begs to inform them that he sweeps all kinds of chimneys and flues in the best manner.

"W. H., attending to the business himself, cleans smoke-jacks, cures smoky coppers, and extinguishes chimneys when on fire, with the greatest care and safety; and, by giving the strictest personal attendance to business, performs what he undertakes with cleanliness and punctuality, whereby he hopes to ensure a continuance of their favours and recommendations.

"Clean cloths for upper apartments. Soot-doors to any size fixed. Observe the address, 1, —— Mews, near ——."

At the top of this card is an engraving of the machine; at the foot a rude sketch of a nightman's cart, with men at work. All the cards I saw reiterated the address, so that no mistake might lead the customer to a rival tradesman.

As to their politics, the sweepers are somewhat

---

* Querying means literally inquiring or asking for work at the different houses. The "queriers" among the sweeps are a kind of pedlar operatives.

similar to the dustmen and costermongers. A fixed hatred to all constituted authority, which they appear to regard as the police and the "beaks," seems to be the sum total of their principles. Indeed, it almost assumes the character of a fixed law, that persons and classes of persons who are themselves disorderly, and to a certain extent lawless, always manifest the most supreme contempt for the conservators of law and order in every degree. The police are therefore hated heartily, magistrates are feared and abominated, and Queen, Lords, and Commons, and every one in authority, if known anything about, are considered as natural enemies. A costermonger who happened to be present while I was making inquiries on this subject, broke in with this remark, "The costers is the chaps—the government can't do nothink with them—they allus licks the government." The sweepers have a sovereign contempt for all Acts of Parliament, because the only Act that had any reference to themselves "threw open," as they call it, their business to all who were needy enough and who had the capability of availing themselves of it. Like the "dusties" they are, I am informed, in their proper element in times of riot and confusion; but, unlike them, they are, to a man, Chartists, understanding it too, and approving of it, not because it would be calculated to establish a new order of things, but in the hope that, in the transition from one system to the other, there might be plenty of noise and riot, and in the vague idea that in some indefinable manner good must necessarily accrue to themselves from any change that might take place. This I believe to be in perfect keeping with the sentiments of similar classes of people in every country in the world.

The journeymen lay by no money when in work, as a fund to keep them when incapacitated by sickness, accident, or old age. There are, however, a few exceptions to the general improvidence of the class; some few belong to sick and benefit societies, others are members of burial clubs. Where, however, this is not the case, and a sweeper becomes unable, through illness, to continue his work, the mode usually adopted is to make a raffle for the benefit of the sufferer; the same means are resorted to at the death of a member of the trade. When a chimney-sweeper becomes infirm through age, he has mostly, if not invariably, no refuge but the workhouse.

The chimney-sweepers generally are regardless of the marriage ceremony, and when they do live with a woman it is in a state of concubinage. These women are always among the lowest of the street-girls—such as lucifer-match and orange girls, some of the very poorest of the coster girls, and girls brought up among the sweepers. They are treated badly by them, and often enough left without any remorse. The women are equally as careless in these matters as the men, and exchange one paramour for another with the same levity, so that there is a promiscuous intercourse continually going on among them. I am informed that, among the worst class of sweepers living with women, not one in 50 is married. To these couples very few children are born; but I am not able to state the proportion as compared with other classes.

There are some curious customs among the London sweepers which deserve notice. Their May-day festival is among the best known. The most intelligent of the masters tell me that they have taken this "from the milkmen's garland" (of which an engraving has been given). Formerly, say they, on the first of May the milkmen of London went through the streets, performing a sort of dance, for which they received gratuities from their customers. The music to which they danced was simply brass plates mounted on poles, from the circumference of which plates depended numerous bells of different tones, according to size; these poles were adorned with leaves and flowers, indicative of the season, and may have been a relic of one of the ancient pageants or mummeries.

The sweepers, however, by adapting themselves more to the rude taste of the people, appear to have completely supplanted the milkmen, who are now never seen in pageantry. In Strutt's "Sports and Pastimes of the People of England," I find the following with reference to the milk-people:—

"It is at this time," that is in May, says the author of one of the papers in the *Spectator*, "we see brisk young wenches in the country parishes dancing round the Maypole. It is likewise on the first day of this month that we see the ruddy milkmaid exerting herself in a most sprightly manner under a pyramid of silver tankards, and, like the Virgin Tarpeia, oppressed by the costly ornaments which her benefactors lay upon her. These decorations of silver cups, tankards, and salvers, were borrowed for the purpose, and hung round the milk-pails, with the addition of flowers and ribands, which the maidens carried upon their heads when they went to the houses of their customers, and danced in order to obtain a small gratuity from each of them. In a set of prints, called 'Tempest's Cries of London,' there is one called the 'Merry Milkmaid,' whose proper name was Kate Smith. She is dancing with the milk-pail, decorated as above mentioned, upon her head. Of late years the plate, with the other decorations, were placed in a pyramidical form, and carried by two chairmen upon a wooden horse. The maidens walked before it, and performed the dance without any incumbrance. I really cannot discover what analogy the silver tankards and salvers can have to the business of the milkmaids. I have seen them act with much more propriety upon this occasion, when, in place of these superfluous ornaments, they substituted a cow. The animal had her horns gilt, and was nearly covered with ribands of various colours formed into bows and roses, and interspersed with green oaken leaves and bunches of flowers."

With reference to the May-day festival of the sweepers the same author says:—"The chimney-sweepers of London have also singled out the first of May for their festival, at which time they parade the streets in companies, disguised in various manners. Their dresses are usually deco-

THE MILKMAID'S GARLAND.

THE ORIGINAL OF THE SWEEP'S MAY-DAY EXHIBITION.

THE SWEEPS' HOME.

(*From a sketch taken on the spot.*)

rated with gilt paper and other mock fineries; they have their shovels and brushes in their hands, which they rattle one upon the other; and to this rough music they jump about in imitation of dancing. Some of the larger companies have a fiddler with them, and a Jack in the Green, as well as a Lord and Lady of the May, who follow the minstrel with great stateliness, and dance as occasion requires. The Jack in the Green is a piece of pageantry consisting of a hollow frame of wood or wicker-work, made in the form of a sugar-loaf, but open at the bottom, and sufficiently large and high to receive a man. The frame is covered with green leaves and bunches of flowers, interwoven with each other, so that the man within may be completely concealed, who dances with his companions; and the populace are mightily pleased with the oddity of the moving pyramid."

Since the date of the above, the sweepers have greatly improved on their pageant, substituting for the fiddle the more noisy and appropriate music of the street-showman's drum and pipes, and adding to their party several diminutive imps, no doubt as representatives of the climbing-boys, clothed in caps, jackets, and trowsers, thickly covered with party-coloured shreds. These still make a show of rattling their shovels and brushes, but the clatter is unheard alongside the thunders of the drum. In this manner they go through the various streets for three days, obtaining money at various places, and on the third night hold a feast at one of their favourite public-houses, where all the sooty tribes resort, and, in company with their wives or girls, keep up their festivity till the next morning. I find that this festival is beginning to disappear in many parts of London, but it still holds its ground, and is as highly enjoyed as ever, in all the eastern localities of the metropolis.

It is but seldom that any of the large masters go out on May-day; this custom is generally confined to the little masters and their men. The time usually spent on these occasions is four days, during which as much as from 2*l*. to 4*l*. a day is collected; the sums obtained on the three first days are divided according to the several kinds of work performed. But the proceeds of the fourth day are devoted to a supper. The average gains of the several performers on these occasions are as follows :—

My lady, who acts as Columbine,
  and receives . . . . . 2s. per day.
My lord, who is often the master
  himself, but usually one of the
  journeymen . . . . . 3s. „
Clown . . . . . . 3s. „
Drummer . . . . . . 4s. „
Jack in the green, who is often an
  individual acquaintance, and
  does not belong to the trade . 3s. „
And the boys, who have no term
  term applied to them, receive
  from . . . . . 1s. to 1s. 6d. „

The share accruing to the boys is often spent in purchasing some article of clothing for them, but the money got by the other individuals is mostly spent in drink.

The sweepers, however, not only go out on May-day, but likewise on the 5th of November. On the last Guy-Fawkes day, I am informed, some of them received not only pence from the public, but silver and gold. "It was quite a harvest," they say. One of this class, who got up a gigantic Guy Fawkes and figure of the Pope on the 5th of November, 1850, cleared, I am informed, 10*l*. over and above all expenses.

For many years, also, the sweepers were in the habit of partaking of a public dinner on the 1st of May, provided for every climbing-boy who thought proper to attend, at the expense of the Hon. Mrs. Montagu. The romantic origin of this custom, from all I could learn on the subject, is this:—The lady referred to, at the time a widow, lost her son, then a boy of tender years. Inquiries were set on foot, and all London heard of the mysterious disappearance of the child, but no clue could be found to trace him out. It was supposed that he was kidnapped, and the search at length was given up in despair. A long time afterwards a sweeper was employed to cleanse the chimneys of Mrs. Montagu's house, by Portman-square, and for this purpose, as was usual at the time, sent a climbing-boy up the chimney, who from that moment was lost to him. The child did not return the way he went up, but it is supposed that in his descent he got into a wrong flue, and found himself, on getting out of the chimney, in one of the bedrooms. Wearied with his labour, it is said that he mechanically crept between the sheets, all black and sooty as he was. In this state he was found fast asleep by the housekeeper. The delicacy of his features and the soft tones of his voice interested the woman. She acquainted the family with the strange circumstance, and, when introduced to them with a clean face, his voice and appearance reminded them of their lost child. It may have been that the hardships he endured at so early an age had impaired his memory, for he could give no account of himself; but it was evident, from his manners and from the ease which he exhibited, that he was no stranger to such places, and at length, it is said, the Hon. Mrs. Montagu recognised in him her long-lost son. The identity, it was understood, was proved beyond doubt. He was restored to his rank in society, and in order the better to commemorate this singular restoration, and the fact of his having been a climbing-boy, his mother annually provided an entertainment on the 1st of May, at White Conduit House, for all the climbing-boys of London who thought proper to partake of it. This annual feast was kept up during the lifetime of the lady, and, as might be expected, was numerously attended, for since there were no question asked and no document required to prove any of the guests to be climbing-boys, very many of the precocious urchins of the metropolis used to blacken their faces for this special occasion. This annual feast continued, as I have said, as long as the lady lived. Her son continued it only for three or four years afterwards, and then, I am told, left the country, and paid no further attention to the matter.

Of the story of the young Montagu, Charles Lamb has given the following account:—

"In one of the state-beds at Arundel Castle, a few years since—under a ducal canopy (that seat of the Howards is an object of curiosity to visitors, chiefly for its beds, in which the late duke was especially a connoisseur)—encircled with curtains of delicatest crimson, with starry coronets interwoven—folded between a pair of sheets whiter and softer than the lap where Venus lulled Ascanius—was discovered by chance, after all methods of search had failed, at noon-day, fast asleep, a lost chimney-sweeper. The little creature having somehow confounded his passage among the intricacies of those lordly chimneys, by some unknown aperture had alighted upon this magnificent chamber, and, tired with his tedious explorations, was unable to resist the delicious invitement to repose, which he there saw exhibited; so, creeping between the sheets very quietly, he laid his black head on the pillow and slept like a young Howard." .... "A high instinct," adds Lamb, "was at work in the case, or I am greatly mistaken. Is it probable that a poor child of that description, with whatever weariness he might be visited, would have ventured under such a penalty as he would be taught to expect, to uncover the sheets of a duke's bed, and deliberately to lay himself down between them, when the rug or the carpet presented an obvious couch still far above his pretensions?—is this probable, I would ask, if the great power of nature, which I contend for, had not been manifested within him, prompting to the adventure? Doubtless, this young nobleman (for such my mind misgives me he must be) was allured by some memory not amounting to full consciousness of his condition in infancy, when he was used to be lapt by his mother or his nurse in just such sheets as he there found, into which he was now but creeping back as into his proper incubation (*incunabula*) and resting place. By no other theory than by his sentiment of a pre-existent state (as I may call it) can I explain a deed so venturous."

There is a strong strain of romance throughout the stories of the lost and found young Montagu. I conversed with some sweepers on the subject. The majority had not so much as heard of the occurrence, but two who had heard of it—both climbing-boys in their childhood—had heard that the little fellow was found in his mother's house. In a small work, the "Chimney-Sweepers' Friend," got up in aid of the Society for the Supersedence of Climbing Boys, by some benevolent Quaker ladies and others (the Quakers having been among the warmest supporters of the suppression of climbers), and "arranged" (the word "edited" not being used) by J. Montgomery, the case of the little Montagu is not mentioned, excepting in two or three vague poetical allusions.

The account given by Lamb (although pronounced apocryphal by some) appears to be the more probable version; and to the minds of many is shown to be conclusively authentic, as I understand that, when Arundel Castle is shown to visitors, the bed in which the child was found is pointed out; nor is it likely that in such a place the story of the ducal bed and the little climbing-boy would be *invented*.

The following account was given by the wife of a respectable man (now a middle-aged woman) and she had often heard it from her mother, who passed a long life in the neighbourhood of Mrs. Montagu's residence:—

"Lady M. had a son of tender years, who was supposed to have been stolen for the sake of his clothes. Some time after, there was an occasion when the sweeps were necessary at Montagu House. A servant noticed one of the boys, being at first attracted by his superior manner, and her curiosity being excited fancied a resemblance in him to the lost child. She questioned his master respecting him, who represented that he had found him crying and without a home, and thereupon took him in, and brought him up to his trade. The boy was questioned apart from his master, as to the treatment he received; his answers were favourable; and the consequence was, a compensation was given to the man, and the boy was retained. All doubt was removed as to his identity."

The annual feast at "White Condick," so agreeable to the black fraternity, was afterwards continued in another form, and was the origin of a well-known society among the master sweepers, which continued in existence till the abolition of the climbing-boys by Act of Parliament. The masters and the better class of men paid a certain sum yearly, for the purpose of binding the children of the contributors to other trades. In order to increase the funds of this institution, as the dinner to the boys at White Conduit House was an established thing, the masters continued it, and the boys of every master who belonged to the society went in a sort of state to the usual place of entertainment every 1st of May, where they were regaled as formerly. Many persons were in the habit of flocking on this day to White Conduit House to witness the festivities of the sweepers on this occasion, and usually contributed something towards the society. As soon, however, as the Act passed, this also was discontinued, and it is now one of the legends connected with the class.

SWEEPING OF THE CHIMNEYS OF STEAM-VESSELS.

THE sweeping of the flues in the boilers of steamboats, in the Port of London, and also of land boilers in manufactories, is altogether a distinct process, as the machine cannot be used until such time as the parties who are engaged in this business travel a long way through the flues, and reach the lower part of the chimney or funnel where it communicates with the boilers and receives the smoke in its passage to the upper air. The boilers in the large sea-going steamers are of curious construction; in some large steamers there are four separate boilers with three furnaces in each, the flues of each boiler uniting in one beneath the funnel; immediately beyond the end of the furnace, which is marked by a little wall constructed of firebrick to prevent the coals and fire from running off the firebars, there is a large open space very high and wide, and which space after a month's steaming is generally filled up with soot, somewhat resembling a snow drift collected in a hollow, were it not for its colour and the fact that it is sometimes in a state of ignition; it is, at times, so deep, that a man sinks to his middle in it the moment he steps across the firebridge. Above his head, and immediately over the end of the furnace, he may perceive an opening in what otherwise would appear to be a solid mass of iron; up to this opening, which resembles a doorway, the sweeper must clamber the best way he can, and when he succeeds in this he finds himself in a narrow passage completely dark, but with so strong a current of air rushing through it from the furnaces beneath towards the funnel overhead that it is with difficulty the wick lamp which he carries in his hand can be kept burning. This passage, between the iron walls on either side, is lofty enough for a tall man to stand upright in, but does not seem at first of any great extent; as he goes on, however, to what appears the end, he finds out his mistake, by coming to a sharp turn which conducts him back again towards the open space in the centre of the boiler, but which is now hid from him by the hollow iron walls which on every side surround him, and within which the waters boil and seethe as the living flames issuing from the furnaces rush and roar through these winding passages; another sharp turn leads back to the front of the boilers, and so on for seven or eight turns, backwards and forwards, like the windings in a maze, till at the last turn a light suddenly breaks upon him, and, looking up, he perceives the hollow tube of the funnel, black and ragged with the adhering soot.

Here, then, the labour of the sweeper commences: he is armed with a brush and shovel, and laying down his lamp in a space from which he has previously shovelled away the soot, which in many parts of the passage is knee deep, he brushes down the soot from the sides and roof of the passage, which being done he shovels it before him into the next winding; this process he repeats till he reaches, by degrees, the opening where he ascended. Whenever the accumulation of soot is so great that it is likely to block up the passage in the progress of his work, he wades through and shovels as much as he thinks necessary out of the opening into the large space behind the furnaces, then resumes his work, brushing and shovelling by turns, till the flues are cleared; when this is accomplished, he descends, and the fire bars being previously removed, he shovels the soot, now all collected together, over the firebridge and into the ashpit of the furnace; other persons stand ready in the stoke-hole armed with long iron rakes, with which they drag out the soot from the ashpits; and others shovel it into sacks, which they make fast to tackle secured to the upper deck, by which they "bowse" it up out of the engine-room,

and either discharge it overboard or put it into boats preparatory to being taken ashore. In this manner an immense quantity of soot is removed from the boilers of a large foreign-going steamer when she gets into port, after a month or six weeks' steaming, having burned in that time perhaps 700 or 800 tons of coal: this work is always performed by the stokers and coal-trimmers in the foreign ports, who seldom, if ever, get anything extra for it, although it is no uncommon thing for some of them to be ill for a week after it.

In the port of London, however, the sweeper comes into requisition, who, besides going through the process already described, brings his machine with him, and is thus enabled to cleanse the funnel, and to increase the quantity of soot. Some of the master sweepers, who have the cleansing of the steam-boats in the river, and the sweeping of boiler flues are obliged to employ a good many men, and make a great deal of money by their business. The use of anthracite coals, however, and some modern improvements, by which air at a certain temperature is admitted to certain parts of the furnace, have in many instances greatly lessened, if they have not altogether prevented, the accumulation of soot, by the prevention of smoke; and it seems quite possible, from the statements made by many eminent scientific and practical men who were examined before a select committee of the House of Commons, presided over by Mr. Mackinnon, in 1843, that by having properly-constructed stoves, and a sufficient quantity of pure air properly admitted, not only less fuel might be burned, and produce a greater amount of heat, but soot would cease to accumulate, so that the necessity for sweepers would be no longer felt, and there would be no fear of fires from the ignition of soot in the flues of chimneys; blacks and smoke, moreover, would take their departure together; and with them the celebrated London fog might also, in a great measure, disappear.

The funnels of steamers are generally swept at from 8d. to 1s. 6d. per funnel. The Chelsea steamers are swept by Mr. Allbrook, of Chelsea; the Continental, by Mr. Hawsey, of Rosemary-lane; and the Irish and Scotch steamers, by Mr. Tuff, who resides in the East London district.

Of the "Ramoneur" Company.

The Patent Ramoneur Company demands, perhaps, a special notice. It was formed between four and five years ago, and has now four stations: one in Little Harcourt-street, Bryanstone-square; another in New-road, Sloane-street; a third in Charles-place, Euston-square; and the fourth in William-street, Portland-town.

"This Company has been formed," the prospectus stated, "for the purpose of cleansing chimneys with the Patent Ramoneur Machine, and introducing various other improvements in the business of chimney sweeping. Chimneys are daily swept with this machine where others have failed."

The Company charge the usual prices, and all

the men employed have been brought up as sweepers. The patent machine is thus described:—

"The Patent Ramoneur Machine consists of four brushes, forming a square head, which, by means of elastic springs, contracts or expands, according to the space it moves in; the rods attached to this head or brush are supplied at intervals with a universal spring-joint, capable of turning even a right angle, and the whole is surmounted with a double revolving ball, having also a universal spring-joint, which leads the brush with certainty into every corner, cleansing its route most perfectly."

The recommendation held out to the public is, that the patented chimney-machine sweeps cleaner than that in general use, and for the reasons assigned; and that, being constructed with more and better springs, it is capable of "turning even a right angle," which the common machine often leaves unswept. This was and is commonly said of the difference between the cleansing of the chimney by a climbing-boy and that effected by the present mechanical appliances in general use—the boy was "better round a corner."

The patent machines now worked in London are fifteen in number, and fifteen men are thus employed. Each man receives as a weekly wage, always in money, 14s., besides a suit of clothes yearly. The suit consists of a jacket, waistcoat, and trousers, of dark-coloured corduroy; also a "frock" or blouse, to wear when at work, and a cap; the whole being worth from 35s. to 40s. This payment is about equivalent to that received weekly by the journeymen in the regular or honourable trade; for although higher in nominal amount as a weekly remuneration, the Ramoneur operatives are not allowed any perquisites whatever. The resident or manager at each station is also a working chimney-sweeper for the Company, and at the same rate as the others, his advantage being that he lives rent-free. At one station which I visited, the resident had two comfortable-looking up-stairs'-rooms (the stations being all in small streets), where he and his wife lived; while the "cellar," which was indeed but the ground floor, although somewhat lower than the doorstep, was devoted to business purposes, the soot being stored there. It was boarded off into separate compartments, one being at the time quite full of soot. All seemed as clean and orderly as possible. The rent of those two rooms, unfurnished, would not be less than 4s. or 5s. a week, so that the resident's payment may be put at about 50l. a year. The patent-machine operatives sweep, on an average, the same number of chimneys each, as a master chimney-sweeper's men in a good way of business in the ordinary trade.

Of the Brisk and Slack Seasons, and the Casual Trade among the Chimney-Sweepers.

As among the rubbish-carters in the unskilled, and the tailors and shoemakers of the skilled trades, the sweepers' trade also has its slackness and its briskness, and from the same cause—the difference in the *seasons*. The seasons affecting the sweepers' trade are, however, the *natural* seasons of the year, the recurring summer and winter, while the seasons influencing the employment of West-end tailors are the *arbitrary* seasons of fashion.

The chimney-sweepers' *brisk* season is in the winter, and especially at what may be in the respective households the periods of the resumption and discontinuance of sitting-room fires.

The sweepers' seasons of briskness and slackness, indeed, may be said then to be ruled by the thermometer, for the temperature causes the increase or diminution of the number of fires, and consequently of the production of soot. The thermometrical period for fires appears to be from October to the following April, both inclusive (seven months), for during that season the temperature is below 50°. I have seen it stated, and I believe it is merely a statement of a fact, that at one time, and even now in some houses, it was customary enough for what were called "great families" to have a fixed day (generally Michaelmas-day, Sept. 29) on which to commence fires in the sitting-rooms, and another stated day (often May-day, May 1) on which to discontinue them, no matter what might be the mean temperature, whether too warm for the enjoyment of a fire, or too cold comfortably to dispense with it. Some wealthy persons now, I am told—such as call themselves "economists," while their servants and dependants apply the epithet "mean"—defer fires until the temperature descends to 42°, or from November to March, both inclusive, a season of only five months.

As this question of the range of the thermometer evidently influences the seasons, and therefore, the casual labour of the sweepers, I will give the following interesting account of the changing temperature of the metropolis, month by month, the information being derived from the observations of 25 years (1805 to 1830), by Mr. Luke Howard. The average temperature appears to be :—

	Degrees.		Degrees.
January	35·1	July	63·1
February	38·9	August	57·1
March	42·0	September	50·1
April	47·5	October	42·4
May	54·9	November	41·9
June	59·6	December	38·3

London, I may further state, is 2½ degrees warmer than the country, especially in winter, owing to the shelter of buildings and the multiplicity of the fires in the houses and factories. In the summer the metropolis is about 1¼ degree hotter than the country, owing to want of free air in London, and to a cause little thought about—the reverberations from narrow streets. In spring and autumn, however, the temperature of both town and country is nearly equal.

In London, moreover, the nights are 11·3 degrees colder than the days; in the country they are 15·4 degrees colder. The extreme ranges of the temperature in the day, in the capital, are from 20° to 90°. The thermometer *has* fallen below zero in the night time, but not frequently.

In London the hottest months are 28 degrees warmer than the coldest; the temperature of July, which is the hottest month, being 63·1; and that of January, the coldest month, 35·1 degrees.

The month in which there are the greatest number of extremes of heat and cold is January. In February and December there are (generally speaking) only two such extreme variations, and five in July; through the other months, however, the extremes are more diffused, and there are only two spring and two autumn months (April and June—September and November), which are not exposed to great differences of temperature.

The mean temperature assumes a rate of increase in the different months, which may be represented by a curve nearly equal and parallel with one representing the progress of the sun in declination.

Hoar-frosts occur when the thermometer is about 39°, and the dense yellow fogs, so peculiar to London, are the most frequent in the months of November, December, and January, whilst the temperature ranges below 40°.

The busy season in the chimney-sweepers' trade commences at the beginning of November, and continues up to the month of May; during the remainder of the year the trade is "slack." When the slack season has set in nearly 100 men are thrown out of employment. These, as well as many of the single-handed masters, resort to other kinds of employment. Some turn costermongers, others tinkers, knife-grinders, &c., and others migrate to the country and get a job at hay-making, or any other kind of unskilled labour. Even during the brisk season there are upwards of 50 men out of employment; some of these occasionally contrive to get a machine of their own, and go about "knulling,"—getting a job where they can.

Many of the master sweepers employ in the summer months only two journeymen, whereas they require three in the winter months; but this, I am informed, is not the general average, and that it will be more correct to compute it for the whole trade, in the proportion of two and a half to two. We may, then, calculate that one-fourth of the entire trade is displaced during the slack season.

This, then, may be taken as the extent of casual labour, with all the sufferings it entails upon imprudent, and even upon careful working-men.

A youth casually employed as a sweeper gave the following account:—"I jobs for the sweeps sometimes, sir, as I'd job for anybody else, and if you have any herrands to go, and will send me, I'll be unkimmon thankful. I haven't no father and don't remember one, and mother might do well but for the ruin (gin). I calls it 'ruin' out of spite. No, I don't care for it myself. I like beer ten to a farthing to it. "She's a ironer, sir, a stunning good one, but I don't like to talk about her, for she might yarn a hatful of browns—3s. 6d. a day; and when she has pulled up for a month or more it's stunning is the difference. I'd rather not be asked more about that. Her great fault against me is as I won't settle. I was one time put to a woman's shoe-maker as worked for a ware'us. He was a relation, and I was to go prentice if it suited. But I couldn't stand his confining ways, and I'm sartain sure that he only wanted me for some tin mother said she'd spring if all was square. He was bad off, and we lived bad, but he always pretended he was going to be stunning busy. So I hooked it. I'd other places—a pot-boy's was one, but no go. None suited.

"Well, I can keep myself now by jobbing, leastways I can partly, for I have a crib in a corner of mother's room, and my rent's nothing, and when she's all right *I'm* all right, and she gets better as I grows bigger, I think. Well, I don't know what I'd like to be; something like a lamp-lighter, I think. Well, I look out for sweep jobs among others, and get them sometimes. I don't know how often. Sometimes three mornings a week for one week; then none for a month. Can any one live by jobbing that way for the sweeps? No, sir, nor get a quarter of a living; but it's a help. I know some very tidy sweeps now. I'm sure I don't know what they are in the way of trade. O, yes, now you ask that, I think they're masters. I've had 6d. and half-a-pint of beer for a morning's work, jobbing like. I carry soot for them, and I'm lent a sort of jacket, or a wrap about me, to keep it off my clothes—though a Jew wouldn't sometimes look at 'em—and there's worser people nor sweeps. Sometimes I'll get only 2d. or 3d. a day for helping that way, a carrying soot. I don't know nothing about weights or bushels, but I know I've found it —— heavy.

"The way, you see, sir, is this here: I meets a sweep as knows me by sight, and he says, ' Come along, Tom's not at work, and I want you. I have to go it harder, so you carry the soot to our place to save my time, and join me again at No. 39.' That's just the ticket of it. Well, no; I wouldn't mind being a sweep for myself with my own machine; but I'd rather be a lamp-lighter. How many help sweeps as I do? I can't at all say. No, I don't know whether it's 10, or 20, or 100, or 1000. I'm no scholard, sir, that's one thing. But it's very seldom such as me's wanted by them. I can't tell what I get for jobbing for sweeps in a year. I can't guess at it, but it's not so much, I think, as from other kinds of jobbing. Yes, sir, I haven't no doubt that the t'others as jobs for sweeps is in the same way as me. I think I may do as much as any of 'em that way, quite as much."

Of the "Leeks" among the Chimney-Sweepers.

The *Leeks* are men who have not been brought up to the trade of chimney sweeping, but have adopted it as a speculation, and are so called from their entering *green*, or inexperienced, into the business. There are I find as many as 200 leeks altogether among the master chimney-sweepers of the metropolis. Of the "high masters" the greater portion are leeks—no less than 92 out of 106. I was informed that one of this class was formerly a solicitor, others had been ladies' shoemakers, and others master builders and bricklayers. Among the lower-class sweepers who have taken to this trade, there are dustmen, scavagers, bricklayers' labourers, soldiers, costermongers, tinkers, and various other unskilled labourers.

The leeks are regarded with considerable dislike by the class of masters who have been regularly brought up to the business, and served their apprenticeships as climbing-boys. These look upon the leeks as men who intrude upon, or interfere with, their natural and, as they account it, legal rights—declaring that only such as have been brought up to the business should be allowed to establish themselves in it as masters. The chimney-sweepers, as far as I can learn, have never possessed any guild, or any especial trade regulations, and this opinion of their rights being invaded by the leeks arises most probably from their knowledge that during the climbing-boy system every lad so employed, unless the son of his employer, was obliged to be apprenticed.

This jealousy towards the leeks does not at all affect the operative sweepers, as some of these leeks are good masters, and among them, perhaps, is to be found the majority of the capitalists of the chimney-sweeping trade, paying the best wages, and finding their journeymen proper food and lodging. Into whatever district I travelled I heard the operative chimney-sweepers speak highly in favour of some of the leeks.

Many of the small masters, however, said "it were a shame" for persons who had never known the horrors of climbing to come into the trade and take the bread out of the mouths of those who had undergone the drudgery of the climbing system; and there appears to be some little justice in their remarks.

Since the introduction of machines into the chimney-sweeping trade the masters have increased considerably. In 1816 there were 200 masters, and now there are 350. Before the machines were introduced, the high master sweepers or "great gentlemen," as they were called, numbered only about 20; their present number is 106. The lower-class and master-men sweepers, on the other hand, were, under the climbing system, from 150 to 180 in number; but at present there are as many as 240 odd. The majority of these fresh hands are "leeks," not having been bred to the business.

Of the Inferior Chimney-Sweepers—the "Knullers" and "Queriers."

The majority of occupations in all civilized communities are divisible into two distinct classes, the employers and the employed. The employers are necessarily capitalists to a greater or less extent, providing generally the materials and implements necessary for the work, as well as the subsistence of the workmen, in the form of wages and appropriating the proceeds of the labour, while the employed are those who, for the sake of the present subsistence supplied to them, undertake to do the requisite work for the employer. In some few trades these two functions are found to be united in the same individuals. The class known as peasant proprietors among the cultivators of the soil are at once the labourers and the owners of the land and stock. The cottiers, on the other hand, though renting the land of the proprietor, are, so to speak, peasant farmers, tilling the land for themselves rather than doing so at wages for some capitalist tenant. In handicrafts and manufactures the same combination of functions is found to prevail. In the clothing districts the domestic workers are generally their own masters, and so again in many other branches of production. These trading operatives are known by different names in different trades. In the shoe trade, for instance, they are called "chamber-masters," in the "cabinet trade" they are termed "garret-masters," and in "the cooper's trade" the name for them is "small trading-masters." Some style them "master-men," and others, "single-handed masters." In all occupations, however, the master-men are found to be especially injurious to the interests of the entire body of both capitalists and operatives, for, owing to the limited extent of their resources, they are obliged to find a market for their work, no matter at what the sacrifice, and hence by their excessive competitions they serve to lower the prices of the trade to a most unprecedented extent. I have as yet met with no occupation in which the existence of a class of master-men has worked well for the interest of the trade, and I have found many which they have reduced to a state of abject wretchedness. It is a peculiar circumstance in connection with the master-men that they abound only in those callings which require a small amount of capital, and which, consequently, render it easy for the operative immediately on the least disagreement between him and his employer to pass from the condition of an operative into that of a trading workmen. When among the fancy cabinet-makers I had a statement from a gentleman, in Aldersgate-street, who supplied the materials to these men, that a fancy cabinet-maker, the manufacturer of writing-desks, tea-caddies, ladies' work-boxes, &c., could begin, and did begin, business on less than 3s. 6d. A youth had just then bought materials of him for 2s. 6d. to "begin on a small desk," stepping at once out of the trammels of apprenticeship into the character of a master-man. Now this facility to commence business on a man's own account is far greater in the chimney-sweepers' trade than even in the desk-makers,' for the one needs no previous training, while the other does.

Thus when other trades, skilled or unskilled, are depressed, when casual labour is with a mass of workpeople more general than constant labour, they naturally inquire if they "cannot do better at something else," and often resort to such trades as the chimney-sweepers'. It is open to all, skilled and unskilled alike. Distress, a desire of change, a vagabond spirit, a hope to "better themselves," all tend to swell the ranks of the single-handed master chimney-sweepers; even though these men, from the casualties of the trade in the way of "seasons," &c., are often exposed to great privations.

There are in all 147 single-handed masters, who are thus distributed throughout the metropolis:—

Southwark (17), Chelsea (11), Marylebone, Shoreditch, and Whitechapel (each 9), Hackney, Stepney, and Lambeth (each 8), St. George's-in-the-East (7), Rotherhithe (6), St. Giles' and East London (each 5), Bethnal-green, Bermondsey, Camberwell, and Clapham (each 4), St. Pancras, Islington, Walworth, and Greenwich (each 3), St. James's (Westminster), Holborn, Clerkenwell, St. Luke's, Poplar, Westminster, West London, City, Wandsworth, and Woolwich (each 1); in all, 147.

Thus we perceive, that the single-handed masters abound in the suburbs and poorer districts; and it is generally in those parts where the lower rate of wages is paid that these men are found to prevail. Their existence appears to be at once the cause and the consequence of the depreciation of the labour.

Of the single-handed masters there is a sub-class known by the name of "knullers" or "queriers."

The *knullers* were formerly, it is probable, known as knellers. The Saxon word *Cnyllan* is to knell (to knull properly), or sound a bell, and the name "knuller" accordingly implies the sounder of a bell, which has been done, there can be no doubt, by the London chimney-sweepers as well as the dustmen, to announce their presence, and as still done in some country parts. One informant has known this to be the practice at the town of Hungerford in Berkshire. The bell was in size between that of the muffin-man and the dustman.

The knuller is also styled a "*querier,*" a name derived from his making *inquiries* at the doors of the houses as to whether his services are required or are likely to be soon required, calling even where they know that a regular resident chimney-sweeper is employed. The men go along calling "sweep," more especially in the suburbs, and if asked "Are you Mr. So-and-So's man?" answer in the affirmative, and may then be called in to sweep the chimneys, or instructed to come in the morning. Thus they receive the full charge of an established master, who, for the sake of his character and the continuance of his custom, must do his work properly; while if such work be done by the knuller, it will be hurriedly and therefore badly done, as all work is, in a general way, when done under false pretences.

Some of the sharpest of these men, I am told, have been reared up as sweepers; but it appears, although it is a matter difficult to ascertain with precision, the majority have been brought up to some generally unskilled calling, as scavagers, costermongers, tinkers, bricklayers' labourers, soldiers, &c. The knullers or queriers are almost all to be found among the lower class chimney-sweepers. There are, from the best information to be obtained, from 150 to 200 of them. Not only do they scheme for employment in the way I have described, but some of them call at the houses of both rich and poor, boldly stating that they had been *sent* by Mr. —— to sweep the flues. I was informed by several of the master sweepers, that many of the fires which happen in the metropolis are owing to persons employing these "knullers," "for," say the high masters, "they scamp the work, and leave a quantity of soot lodged in the chimney, which, in the event of a large fire being kept in the range or grate, ignites." This opinion as to the fires in the chimneys being caused by the scamped work of the knullers must be taken with some allowance. Tradesmen, whose established business is thus, as they account it, usurped, are naturally angry with the usurpers.

There is another evil, so say the regular masters, resulting from the employment of the knullers—the losses accruing to persons employing them, as "they take anything they can lay their hands upon."

This, also, is a charge easy to make, but not easy to refute, or even to sift. One master chimney-sweeper told me that when chimneys are swept in rich men's houses there is almost always some servant in attendance to watch the sweepers. If the rich, I am told, be watchful under these circumstances, the poor are more vigilant.

The distribution of the knullers or queriers is as follows:—Southwark (17), Chelsea and St. Giles' (11 each), Shoreditch and Whitechapel (10 each), Lambeth (9), Marylebone, Stepney and Walworth (8 each), St. George's in the East and Woolwich (7 each), Islington and Hackney (6 each), East London, Rotherhithe, and Greenwich (5 each), Paddington, St. Pancras, East London, Retherhithe and Greenwich (5 each), Paddington, St. Pancras, Bethnal Green, Bermondsey, and Clapham (4 each), Westminster, St. Martin's, Holborn, St. Luke's, West London, Poplar, and Camberwell (3 each); St. James's (Westminster), Clerkenwell, City of London, and Wandsworth (2 each), Kensington (1); in all, 183.

Like the single-handed men the knullers abound in the suburbs. I endeavoured to find a knuller who had been a skilled labourer, and was referred to one who, I was told, had been a working plumber, and a "good hand at spouts." I found him a doggedly ignorant man; he saw no good, he said, in books or newspapers, and "wouldn't say nothing to me, as I'd told him it would be printed. He wasn't a going to make a holy-show [so I understood him] of *his*-self."

Another knuller (to whom I was referred by a master who occasionally employed him as a journeyman) gave me the following account. He was "doing just middling" when I saw him, he said, but his look was that of a man who had known privations, and the soot actually seemed to bring out his wrinkles more fully, although he told me he was only between 40 and 50 years old; he believed he was not 46.

"I was hard brought up, sir," he said; "ay, them as 'll read your book—I mean them readers as is well to do—cannot fancy how hard. Mother was a widow; father was nobody knew where; and, poor woman, she was sometimes distracted that a daughter she had before her marriage, went all wrong. She was a washerwoman, and slaved herself to death. She died in the house [workhouse] in Birmingham. I can read and write a little. I was sent to a charity school, and when I was big enough I was put 'prentice to a gunsmith at Birmingham. I'm master of the business generally, but my perticler part is a gun lock-filer. No, sir, I can't say as ever I liked it; nothing but file file all day. I used to wish I was like the free bits o' boys that used to beg steel filings of me for their fifth of November fireworks. I never could bear confinement. It's made me look older than I ought, I know, but what can a poor man do? No, I never cared much about drinking. I worked in an iron-foundry when I was out of my time. I had a relation that was foreman there. Perhaps it might be that, among all the dust and heat and smoke and stuff, that made me a sweep at last, for I was then almost or quite as black as a sweep.

"Then I come up to London; ay, that must be more nor 20 years back. O, I came up to better myself, but I couldn't get work either at the gun-makers—and I fancy the London masters don't like Birmingham hands—nor at the iron-foundries, and the iron-foundries is nothing in London to what they is in Staffordshire and Warwickshire; nothing at all, they may say what they like. Well, sir, I soon got very bad off. My togs was hardly to call togs. One night—and it was a coldish night, too—I slept in the park, and was all stiff and shivery next morning. As I was wandering about near the park, I walked up a street near the Abbey—King-street, I think it is—and there was a picture outside a public-house, and a writing of men wanted for the East India Company's Service. I went there again in the evening, and there was soldiers smoking and drinking up and down, and I 'listed at once. I was to have my full bounty when I got to the depôt—Southampton I think they called it. Somehow I began to rue what I'd done. Well, I hardly can tell you why. O, no; I don't say I was badly used; not at all. But I had heard of snakes and things in the parts I was going to, and I gently hooked it. I was a navvy on different rails after that, but I never was strong enough for that there work, and at last I couldn't get any more work to do. I came back to London; well, sir, I can't say, as you ask, why I came to London 'stead of Birmingham. I seemed to go natural like. I could get nothing to do, and Lord! what I suffered! I once fell down in the Cut from hunger, and I was lifted into Watchorn's, and he said to his men, 'Give the poor fellow a little drop of brandy, and after that a biscuit; the best things he can have.' He saved my life, sir. The people at the bar—they see'd it was no humbug—gathered 7½d. for me. A penny a-piece from some of Maudslay's men, and a halfpenny from a gent that hadn't no other change, and a poor woman as I was going away slipt a couple of trotters into my hand.

"I slept at a lodging-house, then, in Baldwin's-gardens when I had money, and one day in Gray's inn-lane I picked up an old gent that fell in the middle of the street, and might have been run over. After he'd felt in all his pockets, and found he was all right, he gave me 5s. I knew a sweep, for I sometimes slept in the same house, in King-street, Drury-lane; and he was sick, and was going to the big house. And he told me all about his machines, that's six or seven years back, and said if I'd pay 2s. 6d. down, and 2s. 6d. a week, if I couldn't pay more, I might have his machine for 20s. I took it at 17s. 6d., and paid him every farthing. That just kept him out of the house, but he died soon after.

"Yes, I've been a sweep ever since. I've had to shift as well as I could I don't know that I'm what you call a Nuller, or a Querier. Well, if I'm asked if I'm anybody's man, I don't like to say 'no,' and I don't like to say 'yes;' so I says nothing if I can help it. Yes, I call at houses to ask if anything's wanted. I've got a job that way sometimes. If they took me for anybody's man, I can't help that. I lodge with another sweep which is better off nor I am, and pay him 2s. 9d. a week for a little stair-head place with a bed in it. I think I clear 7s. a week, one week with another, but that's the outside. I never go to church or chapel. I've never got into the way of it. Besides, I wouldn't be let in, I s'pose, in my togs. I've only myself. I can't say I much like what I'm doing, but what can a poor man do?"

OF THE FIRES OF LONDON.

CONNECTED with the subject of chimney sweeping is one which attracts far less of the attention of the legislature and the public than its importance would seem to demand : I mean the fires in the metropolis, with their long train of calamities, such as the loss of life and of property. These calamities, too, especially as regards the loss of property, are almost all endured by the poor, the destruction of whose furniture is often the destruction of their whole property, as insurances are rarely effected by them; while the wealthier classes, in the case of fires, are not exposed to the evils of houselessness, and may be actually gainers by the conflagration, through the sum for which the property was insured.

"The daily occurrence of fires in the metropolis," say the Board of Health, "their extent, the number of persons who perish by them, the enormous loss of property they occasion, the prevalence of incendiarism, the apparent apathy with which such calamities are regarded, and the rapidity with which they are forgotten, will hereafter be referred to as evidence of a very low social condition and defective administrative organization. These fires, it was shown nearly a century ago, when the subject of insurance was debated in Parliament, were frequently caused from not having chimneys swept in proper time." I am informed that a chimney may be on fire for many days, unknown to the inmates of the house, and finally break out in the body of the building by its getting into contact with some beam or wood-work. The recent burning of Limehouse Church was occasioned by the soot collected in the flue taking fire, and becoming red hot, when it ignited the wood-work in the roof. The flue, or pipe, was of iron.

From a return made by Mr. Braidwood of the houses and properties destroyed in the metropolis in the three years ending in 1849 inclusive, it appears that the total number was 1111: of contents destroyed (which, being generally insured separately, should be kept distinct) there were 1013. The subjoined table gives the particulars as to the proportion insured and uninsured:—

	Insured.	Uninsured.	Total.
Houses	914	197	1111
Contents	609	404	1013
	1523	601	2124

"The proportion per cent. of the uninsured to the insured, would be—

		Insured. Per Cent.	Uninsured. Per Cent.	Total.
Houses	1111	82·3	17·7	100
Contents	1013	60·1	39·9	100
	2124	71·7	28·3	100

The following table gives the total number of fires in the metropolis during a series of years:

ABSTRACT OF CAUSES OF FIRE IN THE METROPOLIS, FROM 1833 TO 1849, INCLUSIVE. COMPILED BY W. BADDELEY.

	1833	1834	1835	1836	1837	1838	1839	1840	1841	1842	1843	1844	1845	1846	1847	1848	1849	Total	Average
Accidents of various kinds, for the most part unavoidable	83	40	14	13	17	36	25	26	26	44	19	11	17	29	20	19	13	452	27
Apparel ignited on the person	..	..	..	7	7	5	3	12	5	9	5	4	3	3	3	1	2	69	4
Candles, various accidents with	56	146	110	157	125	132	128	169	184	189	166	205	165	229	237	237	241	2876	169
Carelessness, palpable instances of	28	..	19	18	7	17	14	24	25	19	27	15	14	15	20	23	24	309	18
Children playing with fire or candles	..	..	5	6	18	5	12	21	18	16	20	23	19	25	16	19	15	238	14
Drunkenness	..	2	3	..	2	4	6	5	5	11	6	9	7	9	5	3	7	84	5
Fire-heat, application of, to various hazardous manufacturing processes	31	24	39	34	22	40	26	29	16	36	14	21	22	25	16	22	23	440	26
Fire-sparks	..	..	..	7	10	12	9	17	13	23	17	27	24	32	65	63	40	359	21
Fire-works	..	..	3	..	5	3	5	1	4	7	5	3	10	9	6	1	8	70	4
Fires kindled on hearths and other improper places	7	..	9	5	5	15	8	7	8	9	9	8	12	7	3	4	4	120	7
Flues, foul, defective, &c.	71	65	69	72	53	58	58	89	83	90	105	84	78	86	78	56	78	1273	75
Fumigation, incautious	..	3	7	5	2	1	5	3	2	2	1	1	3	4	4	4	2	49	3
Furnaces, kilns, &c., defective or over-heated	..	11	2	9	12	15	20	15	12	23	19	17	29	28	14	16	21	263	16
Gas	20	25	39	38	31	42	72	48	48	52	40	33	54	53	63	65	57	780	46¼
Gunpowder	3	3	..	1	3	1	2	..	..	3	1	..	1	..	2	..	2	22	1⅓
Hearths, defective, &c.	..	..	..	..	..	..	..	..	..	3	5	2	..	4	3	4	3	24	1½
Hot cinders put away	..	..	..	..	..	..	..	..	3	3	7	10	8	9	5	11	..	56	3
Lamps	..	..	..	2	3	9	4	3	5	2	2	6	11	7	2	3	17	76	5
Lime, slaking of	..	3	4	3	..	4	2	2	5	4	2	3	9	7	5	5	3	61	4
Linen, drying, airing, &c.	..	..	22	31	48	32	26	25	27	41	33	45	30	39	34	36	40	509	30
Lucifer-matches	..	..	..	..	8	9	17	18	16	17	14	19	12	14	9	23	12	188	11
Ovens	6	..	..	6	3	11	4	13	13	13	10	10	8	8	8	2	2	117	7
Reading, working, or smoking in bed	..	3	..	..	..	1	2	..	5	2	3	..	..	3	1	1	1	22	1⅓
Shavings, loose, ignited	..	6	9	13	8	17	8	27	35	22	31	18	25	35	37	27	21	339	20
Spontaneous combustion	7	2	5	4	4	5	13	11	22	20	23	34	19	18	15	7	19	228	13
Stoves, defective, over-heated, &c.	18	20	11	28	36	31	24	48	54	32	58	44	51	43	37	48	43	626	37
Tobacco smoking	..	6	4	1	3	4	11	9	22	17	14	21	19	29	18	37	24	239	14
Suspicious	..	..	..	..	7	8	6	11	7	9	16	7	9	7	17	11	10	125	7
Wilful	3	9	6	8	5	6	7	9	13	19	21	11	14	19	17	25	19	211	12
Unknown	125	114	91	96	57	45	67	39	23	32	60	74	32	39	72	38	76	1080	63

Here, then, we perceive that there are, upon an average of 17 years, no less than 770 "fires" per annum, that is to say, 29 houses in every 10,000 are discovered to be on fire every year; and about one-fourth of these are uninsured. In the year 1833 the total number of fires was only 458, or 20 in every 10,000 inhabited houses, whilst, in 1849, the number had gradually progressed to 838, or 28 in every 10,000 houses.

We have here, however, to deal more particularly with the causes of these fires, of which the following table gives the result of many years' valuable experience:—

TABULAR EPITOME OF METROPOLITAN FIRES, FROM 1833 to 1849.
By W. Baddeley, 29, Alfred Street, Islington.

	1833	1834	1835	1836	1837	1838	1839	1840	1841	1842	1843	1844	1845	1846	1847	1848	1849	Total.	Average
Slightly damaged	292	338	315	397	357	383	402	451	438	521	489	502	431	576	536	509	582	6,574	470
Seriously damaged	135	116	125	134	122	152	165	204	234	224	231	237	244	238	273	269	228	2,955	211
Totally destroyed	31	28	31	33	22	33	17	26	24	24	29	23	32	20	27	27	28	365	26
Total No. of Fires	458	482	471	564	501	568	584	681	696	769	749	762	707	834	836	805	838	9,894	770
False Alarms	59	63	66	66	89	80	70	84	67	61	79	70	81	119	88	120	76	1,150	82
Alarms from Chimneys on Fire	75	106	106	126	127	107	101	98	92	82	83	94	87	69	66	86	89	1,307	94
Total No. of Calls	592	651	643	756	717	755	755	863	855	912	911	926	875	1022	990	1011	1003	12,351	882
Insuran. on Building and Contents	..	..	..	169	173	161	169	237	343	321	276	313	313	302	263	310	368	3,718	266
Insurances on Building only	..	..	..	73	47	59	58	92	149	116	124	138	107	137	125	120	163	1,508	108
Insurances on Contents only	..	..	..	104	76	128	115	104	52	112	107	94	73	125	157	134	72	1,453	104
Uninsured	..	..	..	218	205	220	242	248	152	220	242	217	214	270	291	241	235	3,215	230

Thus we perceive that, out of an average of 665 fires per annum, the information being derived from 17 years' experience, the following were the number of fires produced by different causes:—

	Average No. of Fires per Annum.
Candles, various accidents with	169
Flues, foul, defective, &c.	75
Unknown	63
Gas	46
Stoves over-heated	37
Linen, drying, airing, &c.	30
Accidents of various kinds, for the most part unavoidable	27
Fire heat, application of, to various hazardous manufacturing processes	26
Fire sparks	21
Shavings, loose, ignited	20
Carelessness, palpable instances of	18
Furnaces, kilns, &c., defective or over-heated	16
Children playing with fire or candles	14
Tobacco smoking	14
Spontaneous combustion	13
Wilful	12
Lucifer-matches	11
Ovens	7
Fires, kindled on hearths and other improper places	7
Suspicious	7
Lamps	5
Drunkenness	5
Lime, slaking of	4
Apparel, ignited on the person	4
Fireworks	4
Hot cinders put away	3
Incautious fumigation	3
Reading, working, or smoking in bed	1·33
Hearths defective	1·25
	665

Here, then, we find that while the greatest proportion of fires are caused by accidents with candles, about one-ninth of the fires above mentioned arise from foul flues, or 75 out of 665, a circumstance which teaches us the usefulness of the class of labourers of whom we have been lately treating.

It would seem that a much larger proportion of the fires are wilfully produced than appear in the above table.

The Board of Health, in speaking of incendiarism in connection with insurance, report:—

"Inquiries connected with measures for the improvement of the population have developed the operation of insurances, in engendering crimes and calamities; negatively, by weakening natural responsibilities and motives to care and forethought; positively, by temptations held out to the commission of crime in the facility with which insurance money is usually obtainable.

"The *steady increase* in the number of fires in the metropolis, whilst our advance in the arts gives means for their diminution, is ascribable mainly to the operation of these two causes, and to the division and weakening of administrative authority. From information on which we can rely, we feel assured that the crime of incendiarism for the sake of insurance money exists to a far greater extent than the public are aware of."

Mr. Braidwood has expressed his opinion that only one-half of the property in the metropolis is insured, not as to numbers of property, but as to value; but the proportion of insured and uninsured houses could not be ascertained.

Mr. Baddeley, the inspector to the Society for the Protection of Life from Fire, who had given attention to the subject for the last 30 years, gave the Board the following account of the increase of fires:—

	Fires per Annum of Houses and Properties.	Of which were Totally Uninsured.	Proportion per Cent. of Insured Houses and Properties Burnt.
In the first seven years there were on an average	623	215	65·15
In the second seven years	790	244	69·3

During this period there has been a great increase in the number of dwellings, but this has been chiefly in suburban places, where fires rarely occur.

" The frequency of fires," it is further stated, "led Mr. Payne, the coroner of the City of London, to revive the exercise of the coroner's function of inquiring into the causes of fires; most usefully. Out of 58 inquests held by him (in the City of London and the borough of Southwark, which comprise only one-eighteenth of the houses of the metropolis) since 1845, it appears that, 8 were proved to be wilful; 27 apparently accidental; and 23 from causes unknown, including suspicious causes. The proportion of ascertained wilful fires was, therefore, 23 per cent.; which gives strong confirmation to the indications presented by the statistical returns as to the excess of insured property burnt above uninsured."

The at once mean and reckless criminality of arson, by which a man exposes his neighbours to the risk of a dreadful death, which he himself takes measures to avoid, has long, and on many occasions, gone unpunished in London. The insurance companies, when a demand is made upon them for a loss through fire, institute an inquiry, carried on quietly by their own people. The claimant is informed, if sufficient reasons for such a step appear, that from suspicious circumstances, which had come to the knowledge of the company, the demand would not be complied with, and that the company would resist any action for the recovery of the money. The criminal becomes alarmed, he is afraid of committing himself, and so the matter drops, and the insurance companies, not being required to pay the indemnification, are satisfied to save their money, and let the incendiarism remain unnoticed or unpunished. Mr. Payne, the coroner, has on some occasions strongly commented on this practice as one which showed the want of a public prosecutor.

A few words as regards the means of extinction and help at fires.

Upwards of two years ago the Commissioners of Police instructed their officers to note the time which elapsed between the earliest alarm of fire and the arrival of the first engine. Seventeen fires were noted, and the average duration of time before the fire-brigade or any parochial or local fire-engine, reached the spot, was 36 minutes. Two or three of these fires were in the suburbs; so that in this crowded city, so densely packed with houses and people, fifteen fires raged unchecked for more than half-an-hour.

There are in the metropolis, not including the more distant suburbs, 150 public fire stations, with engines provided under the management of the parochial authorities. The fire-brigade has but seventeen stations on land, and two on the river, which are, indeed, floating engines, one being usually moored near Southwark-bridge, the other having no stated place, being changed in its locality, as may be considered best. In the course of three years, the term of the official inquiry, the engines of the fire-brigade reached on the average the place where a fire was raging *thirty-five* times as the earliest means of assistance, when the parochial engines did the same only in the proportion of *two* to the thirty-five.

Mr. Braidwood, the director of the fire-brigade, stated, when questioned on the subject with a view to a report to be laid before Parliament, that "the average time of an engine turning out with horses was from three to seven minutes." The engines are driven at the rate of ten miles an hour along the streets, which, in the old coaching days, was considered the "best royal mail pace." Indeed, there have been frequent complaints of the rapidity with which the fire-engines are driven, and if the drivers were not skilful and alert, it would really amount to recklessness.

"Information of the breaking out of a fire," it is stated in the report, "will be conveyed to the station of the brigade at the rate of about five miles an hour: thus in the case of the occurrence of a fire within a mile of the station, the intelligence may be conveyed to the station in about twelve minutes; the horses will be put to, and the engine got out into the street in about five minutes on the average; it traverses the mile in about six minutes; and the water has to be got into the engine, which will occupy about five minutes, making, under the most favourable circumstances for such a distance, 28 minutes, or for a half-mile distance, an average of not less than 20 minutes."

The average distance of the occurring fires from a brigade station were, however, during a period of three years, terminating in 1850, upwards of a mile. One was five miles, several four miles, more were two miles, and a mile and a half, while the most destructive fires were at an average distance of a mile and three quarters. Thus it was impossible for a fire-brigade to give assistance as soon as assistance was needed, and, under other circumstances, might have been rendered. And all this damage may and does very often result from what seems so trifling a neglect as the non-sweeping of a chimney.

Mr. W. Baddeley, an engineer, and a high authority on this subject, has stated that he had attended fires for 30 years in London, and that, of 838 fires which took place in 1849, two-thirds might have been easily extinguished had there been an immediate application of water. In some places, he said, delay originated from the turn-cocks being at wide intervals, and some of the companies objecting to let any but their own servants have the command of the main-cocks.

The Board of Health have recommended the formation of a series of street-water plugs within short distances of each other, the water to be constantly on at high pressure night and day, and the whole to be under the charge of a trained body of men such as compose the present fire-brigade, provided at appointed stations with every necessary appliance in the way of hose, pipes, ladders, &c. "The hose should be within the reach," it is urged in the report, "fixed, and applied on an average of not more than five minutes from the time of the alarm being given; that is to say, in less than one-fourth of the time within which fire-engines are brought to bear under existing arrangements, and with a still greater proportionate diminution of risks and serious accidents."

Nor is this mode of extinguishing fires a mere experiment. It is successfully practised in some of the American cities, Philadelphia among the number, and in some of our own manufacturing towns. Mr. Emmott, the engineer and manager of the Oldham Water-works, has described the practice in that town on the occurrence of fires:—

"In five cases out of six, the hose is pushed into a water-plug, and the water thrown upon a building on fire, for the average pressure of water in this town is 146 feet; by this means our fires are generally extinguished even before the heavy engine arrives at the spot. The hose is much preferred to the engine, on account of the speed with which it is applied, and the readiness with which it is used, for one man can manage a hose, and throw as much water on the building on fire as an engine worked by many men. On this account we very rarely indeed use the engines, as they possess no advantage whatever over the hose."

When the city of Hamburgh was rebuilt two or three years back, after its destruction by fire, it was rebuilt chiefly under the direction of Mr. W. Lindley, the engineer, and, as far as Mr. Lindley could accomplish, on sanitary principles, such as the abolition of cesspools. The arrangements for the surface cleansing of the streets by means of the hose and jet and the water-plugs, are made available for the extinction of fires, and with the following results, as communicated by Mr. Lindley:—

"Have there been fires in buildings in Hamburgh in the portion of the town rebuilt?—Yes, repeatedly. They have all, however, been put out at once. If they had had to wait the usual time for engines and water, say 20 minutes or half an hour, these might all have led to extensive conflagrations.

"What has been the effect on insurance?—The effect of the rapid extinction of fires has brought to light to the citizens of Hamburgh, the fact that the greater proportion of their fires are the work of incendiaries, for the sake of the insurance money. A person is absent; smoke is seen to exude; the alarm of fire is given, and the door is forced open, the jet applied, and the fire extinguished immediately. Case after case has occurred, where, upon the fire being extinguished, the arrangements for the spread of the fire are found and made manifest. Several of this class of incendiaries for the insurance money are now in prison. The saving of money alone, by the prevention of fires, would be worth the whole expense of the like arrangement in London, where it is well known that similar practices prevail extensively."

The following statement was given by Mr. Quick, an engineer, on this subject:—

"After the destruction of the terminus of the South Western Railway by fire, I recommended them to have a 9-inch main, with 3-inch outlets leading to six stand-pipes, with joining screws for hose-pipes to be attached, and that they should carry a 3-inch pipe of the same description up into each floor, so that a hose might be attached in any room where the fire commenced.

"In how many minutes may the hose be attached?—There is only the time of attaching the hose, which need be nothing like a minute. I have indeed recommended that a short length of hose with a short nozzle or branch should be kept attached to the cock, so that the cock has only to be turned, which is done in an instant.

"It appears that fire-engines require 26 men to work each engine of two 7-inch barrels, to produce a jet of about 50 feet high. The arrangement carried out, at your recommendation, with six jets, is equivalent to keeping six such engines, and the power of 156 men, in readiness to act at all times, night and day, at about a minute's notice, for the extinction of fires?—It will give a power more than equal to that number of men; for the jets given off from a 20-inch main will be much more regular and powerful, and will deliver more water than could be delivered by any engine. The jets at that place would be 70 feet high."

The system of roof-cisterns, which was at one time popular as a means of extinction, has been found, it appears, on account of their leakage and diffusion of damp, to be but sorry contrivances, and have very generally been discontinued. Mr. Holme, a builder in Liverpool, gives the following, even under the circumstances, amusing account of a fire where such a cistern was provided:—

"The owner of a cotton kiln, which had been repeatedly burnt, took it into his head to erect a large tank in the roof. His idea was, that when a fire occurred, they should have water at hand; and when the fire ascended, it would burn the wooden tank, and the whole of the contents being discharged on the fire like a cataract, it would at once extinguish it. Well, the kiln again took fire; the smoke was so suffocating, that nobody could get at the internal pipe, and the whole building was again destroyed. But what became of the tank? It could not burn, because it was filled with water; consequently, it boiled most admirably. No hole was singed in its side or bottom; it looked very picturesque, but it was utterly useless."

The necessity of almost immediate help is

shown in the following statement by Mr. Braidwood, when consulted on the subject of fire-escapes, which under the present system are not considered sufficiently effective :—

"Taking London to be six miles long and three miles broad, to have anything like an efficient system of fire-escapes, it would be necessary to have one with a man to attend it within a quarter of a mile of each house, as assistance, to be *of any use, must generally be rendered within five minutes after the alarm is given.* To do this the stations must be within a quarter of a mile of each other (as the escapes must be taken round the angles of the streets): 253 stations would thus be required and as many men.

"At present scaling ladders are kept at all the engine stations, and canvas sheets also at some of them; several lives have been saved by them; but the distance of the stations from each other renders them applicable only in a limited number of instances."

The engines of the fire-brigade throw up about 90 gallons a minute. Their number is about 100. The cost of a fire-engine is from 60*l.* to 100*l.*, and the hose, buckets, and general apparatus, cost nearly the same amount.

Of the Sewermen and Nightmen of London.

We now come to the consideration of the last of the several classes of labourers engaged in the removal of the species of refuse from the metropolis. I have before said that the public refuse of a town consists of two kinds :—
I. The street-refuse.
II. The house-refuse.

Of each of these kinds there are two species :—
A. The dry.
B. The wet.

The dry street-refuse consists, as we have seen, of the refuse earth, bricks, mortar, oyster-shells, potsherds, and pansherds.

And the dry house-refuse of the soot and ashes of our fires.

The wet street-refuse consists, on the other hand, of the mud, slop, and surface water of our public thoroughfares.

And the wet house-refuse, of what is familiarly known as the "slops" of our residences, and the liquid refuse of our factories and slaughter-houses.

We have already collected the facts in connection with the three first of these subjects. We have ascertained the total amount of each of these species of refuse which have to be annually removed from the capital. We have set forth the aggregate number of labourers who are engaged in the removal of it, as well as the gross sum that is paid for so doing, showing the individual earnings of each of the workmen, and arriving, as near as possible, at the profits of their employers, as well as the condition of the employed. This has been done, it is believed, for the first time in this country; and if the subject has led us into longer discussions than usual, the importance of the matter, considered in a sanitary point of view, is such that a moment's reflection will convince us of the value of the inquiry—especially in connection with a work which aspires to embrace the whole of the offices performed by the labourers of the capital of the British Empire.

It now but remains for us to complete this novel and vast inquiry by settling the condition and earnings of the men engaged in the removal of the last species of public refuse. I shall consider, first, the aggregate quantity of wet house-refuse that has to be annually removed; secondly, the means adopted for the removal of it; thirdly, the cost of so doing; and lastly, the number of men engaged in this kind of work, as well as the wages paid to them, and the physical, intellectual, and moral condition in which they exist, or, more properly speaking, are allowed to remain.

Of the Wet House-Refuse of London.

All house-refuse of a liquid or semi-liquid character is *wet* refuse. It may be called semi-liquid when it has become mingled with any solid substance, though not so fully as to have lost its property of fluidity, its natural power to flow along a suitable inclination.

Wet house-refuse consists of the "slops" of a household. It consists, indeed, of *all* waste water, whether from the supply of the water companies, or from the rain-fall collected on the roofs or yards of the houses; of the "suds" of the washerwomen, and the water used in every department of scouring, cleansing, or cooking. It consists, moreover, of the refuse proceeds from the several factories, dye-houses, &c.; of the blood and other refuse (not devoted to Prussian blue manufacture or sugar refining) from the butchers' slaughter-houses and the knackers' (horse slaughterers') yards; as well as the refuse fluid from all chemical processes, quantities of chemically impregnated water, for example, being pumped, as soon as exhausted, from the tan-pits of Bermondsey into the drains and sewers. From the great hat-manufactories (chiefly also in Bermondsey and other parts of the Borough) there is a constant flow of water mixed with dyes and other substances, to add to the wet refuse of London.

It is evident, then, that *all* the water consumed or wasted in the metropolis must form a portion of the total sum of the wet refuse.

There is, however, the exception of what is used for the watering of gardens, which is absorbed at once by the soil and its vegetable products; we must also exclude such portion of water as is applied to the laying of the road and street dust on dry summer days, and which forms a part of the street mud or "mac" of the scavager's cart, rather than of the sewerage; and we must further deduct the water derived from the street plugs for the supply of the fire-engines, which is consumed or absorbed in the extinction of the flames; as well as the water required for the victualling of ships on the eve of a voyage, when such supply is not derived immediately from the Thames.

The quantity of water required for the diet, or beverage, or general use of the population; the quantity consumed by the maltsters, distillers, brewers, ginger-beer and soda-water makers, and manufacturing chemists; for the making of tea, coffee, or cocoa'; and for drinking at meals (which is often derived from pumps, and not from the supplies of the water companies);—the water which is thus consumed, in a prepared or in a simple state, passes into the wet refuse of the metropolis in another form.

Now, according to reports submitted to Parliament when an improved system of water-supply was under consideration, the daily supply of water to the metropolis is as follows:—

	Gallons.
From the Water Companies	44,383,329
„ „ Artesian Wells	8,000,000
„ „ land spring pumps	3,000,000
	55,383,329

The yearly rain-fall throughout the area of the metropolis is 172,053,477 tons, or 33,589,972,120 gallons, 2 feet deep of rain falling on every square inch of London in the course of the year. The yearly total of the water pumped or falling into the metropolis is as follows:—

	Gallons.
Yearly mechanical supply	19,215,000,000
„ natural ditto	38,539,972,122
	57,754,972,122

The reader will find the details of this subject at p. 203 of the present volume. I recapitulate the results here to save the trouble of reference, and briefly to present the question under one head.

Of course the rain which ultimately forms a portion of the gross wet refuse of London, can be only such as falls on that part of the metropolitan area which is occupied by buildings or streets. What falls upon fields, gardens, and all open ground, is absorbed by the soil. But a large proportion of the rain falling upon the streets, is either absorbed by the dry dust, or retained in the form of mud; hence that only which falls on the house-tops and yards can be said to contribute largely to the gross quantity of wet refuse poured into the sewers. The streets of London appear to occupy one-tenth of the entire metropolitan area, and the houses (estimating 300,000 as occupying upon an average 100 square yards each *) another tithe of the surface. The remaining 92 square miles out of the 115 now included in the Registrar-General's limits (which extend, it should be remembered, to Wandsworth, Lewisham, Bow, and Hampstead), may be said to be made up of suburban gardens, fields, parks, &c., where the

* In East and West London there are rather more than 32 houses to the acre, which gives an average of 151 square yards to each dwelling, so that, allowing the streets here to occupy one-third of the area, we have 100 square yards for the space covered by each house. In Lewisham, Hampstead, and Wandsworth, there is not one house to the acre. The average number of houses per acre throughout London is 4.

rain-water would soak into the earth. We have, then, only two-tenths of the gross rain-fall, or 7,700,000,000 gallons, that could possibly appear in the sewers, and calculating one-third of this to be absorbed by the mud and dust of the streets, we come to the conclusion that the total quantity of rain-water entering the sewers is, in round numbers, 5,000,000,000 gallons per annum.

Reckoning, therefore, 5,000,000,000 gallons to be derived from the annual rain-fall, it appears that the yearly supply of water, from all sources, to be accounted for among the wet house-refuse is, in round numbers, 24,000,000,000 gallons.

The refuse water from the factories need not be calculated separately, as its supply is included in the water mechanically supplied, and the loss from evaporation in boiling, &c., would be perfectly insignificant if deducted from the vast annual supply, but 350,000,000 gallons have been allowed for this and other losses.

There is still another source of the supply of wet house-refuse unconnected either with the rain-fall or the mechanical supply of water—I mean such proportion of the blood or other refuse from the butchers' and knackers' premises as is washed into the sewers.

Official returns show that the yearly quantity of animals sold in Smithfield is—

Horned cattle	224,000
Sheep	1,550,000
Calves	27,300
Pigs	40,000
	1,841,300

The blood flowing from a slaughtered bullock, whether killed according to the Christian or the Jewish fashion, amounts, on an average, to 20 quarts; from a sheep, to 6 or 7 quarts; from a pig, 5 quarts; and the same quantity from a calf. The blood from a horse slaughtered in a knackers' yard is about the same as that from a bullock. This blood used to bring far higher prices to the butcher than can be now realized.

In the evidence taken by a Select Committee of the House of Commons in 1849, concerning Smithfield-market, Mr. Wyld, of the Fox and Knot-yard, Smithfield, stated that he slaughtered about 180 cattle weekly. "We have a sort of well made in the slaughterhouse," he said, "which receives the blood. I receive about 1*l.* a week for it; it goes twice a day to Mr. Ton's, at Bow Common. We used to receive a good deal more for it." Even the market for blood at Mr. Ton's, is, I am informed, now done away with. He was a manufacturer of artificial manure, a preparation of night-soil, blood, &c., baked in what may be called "cakes," and exported chiefly to our sugar-growing colonies, for manure. His manure yard has been suppressed.

I am assured, on the authority of experienced butchers, that at the present time fully three-fourths of the blood from the animals slaughtered in London becomes a component part of the wet refuse I treat of, being washed into the sewers.

The more wholesale slaughterers, now that blood is of little value (9 gallons in Whitechapel-market, the blood of two beasts—less by a gallon—can be bought for 3d.), send this animal refuse down the drains of their premises in far greater quantities than was formerly their custom.

Now, reckoning only three-fourths of the blood from the cattle slaughtered in the metropolis, to find its way into the sewers, we have, according to the numbers above given, the following yearly supply:—

	Gallons.
From horned cattle	840,000
„ sheep	1,743,000
„ pigs	37,500
„ calves	25,590
	2,646,090

This is merely the blood from the animals sold in Smithfield-market, the lambs not being included in the return; while a great many pigs and calves are slaughtered by the London tradesmen, without their having been shown in Smithfield.

The ordure from a slaughtered bullock is, on an average, from ½ to ¾ cwt. Many beasts yield one cwt.; and cows "killed full of grass," as much as two cwt. Of this excrementitious matter, I am informed, about a fourth part is washed into the sewers. In sheep, calves, and pigs, however, there is very little ordure when slaughtered, only 3 or 4 lbs. in each as an average.

Of the number of horses killed there is no official or published account. One man familiar with the subject calculated it at 100 weekly. *All* the blood from the knackers' yards is, I am told, washed into the sewers; consequently its yearly amount will be 26,000 gallons.

But even this is not the whole of the wet house-refuse of London.

There are, in addition, the excreta of the inhabitants of the houses. These are said to average ¼ lb. daily per head, including men, women, and children.

It is estimated by Bousingault, and confirmed by Liebig, that each individual produces ¼ lb. of solid excrement and 1¼ lb. of liquid excrement per day, making 1½ lb. each, or 150 lbs. per 100 individuals, of semi-liquid refuse from the water-closet. "But," says the Surveyor of the Metropolitan Commission of Sewers, "there is other refuse resulting from culinary operations, to be conveyed through the drains, and the whole may be about 250 lbs. for 100 persons."

The more fluid part of this refuse, however, is included in the quantity of water before given, so that there remains only the more solid excrementitious matter to add to the previous total. This, then, is ¼ lb. daily and individually; or from the metropolitan population of nearly 2,500,000 a daily supply of 600,000 lbs., rather more than 267 tons; and a yearly aggregate for the whole metropolis of 219,000,000 lbs., or very nearly about 100,000 tons.

From the foregoing account, then, the following is shown to be

The Gross Quantity of the Wet House-Refuse of the Metropolis.

	Gallons.	Lbs.
"Slops" and unabsorbed rain-water....	24,000,000,000 =	240,000,000,000
Blood of beasts....	2,646,000 =	26,460,000
„ horses....	26,000 =	260,000
Excreta		219,000,000
Dung of slaughtered cattle		17,400,000
Total	24,002,657,000 =	240,263,120,000

Hence we may conclude that the more fluid portion of the wet house-refuse of London amounts to 24,000,000,000 gallons per annum; and that altogether it weighs, in round numbers, about 240,000,000,000 lbs., or 100,000,000 tons.

As these refuse products are not so much matters of trade or sale as other commodities, of course less attention has been given to them, in the commercial attributes of weight and admeasurement. I will endeavour, however, to present an uniform table of the whole great mass of metropolitan wet house-refuse in cubic inches.

The imperial standard gallon is of the capacity of 277·274 cubic inches; and estimating the solid excrement spoken of as the ordinary weight of earth, or of the soil of the land, at 18 cubic feet the ton, we have the following result, calculating in round numbers:—

Wet House-Refuse of the Metropolis.

Liquid .. 24,000,000,000 gal. = 6,600,000,000,000 cub. in.
Solid.... 100,000 tons = 3,110,400,000 „

Thus, by this process of admeasurement, we find the

Wet House-Refuse of London........ } = 6,603,110,400,000 cubic in., or 3,820,000,000 cubic feet.

Figures best show the extent of this refuse, "inexpressible" to common appreciation "by numbers that have name."

Of the Means of Removing the Wet House-refuse.

Whether this mass of filth be, zymotically, the cause of cholera, or whether it be (as cannot be be questioned) a means of agricultural fertility, and therefore of national wealth, it *must* be removed. I need not dilate, in explaining a necessity which is obvious to every man with uncorrupted physical senses, and with the common moral sense of decency.

"Dr. Paley," it is said, in a recent Report to the Metropolitan Commission of Sewers, "gave to Burckhardt and other travellers a set of instructions as to points of observation of the manners and conditions of the populations amongst whom they travelled. One of the leading instructions was to observe how they disposed of their excreta, for what they did with that showed him what men were; he also inquired what structure they had to answer the purpose of a privy, and what were their habits in respect to it. This information Dr. Paley desired, not for popular use, but for himself, for he was accustomed to say, that the facts connected with that topic gave him more information as to the real condition and civilisation of a population than most persons would be aware of. It would inform him of their real habits of cleanliness, of real decency, self-respect, and connected moral habits of high social importance. It would inform him of the real state of police, and of local administration, and much of the general government.

"The human ordure which defiles the churches, the bases of public edifices and works of art in Rome and Naples, and the Italian cities, gives more sure indications of the real moral and social position of the Italian population than any impressions derived from the edifices and works of art themselves.

"The subject, in relation to which the Jewish lawgiver gave most particular directions, is one on which the serious attention and labour of public administrators may be claimed."

The next question, is — *How* is the wet house-refuse to be removed?

There are two ways:—

1. One is, to transport it to a river, or some powerfully current stream by a series of ducts.
2. The other is, to dig a hole in the neighbourhood of the house, there collect the wet refuse of the household, and when the hole or pit becomes full, remove the contents to some other part.

In London the most obvious means of getting rid of a nuisance is to convey it into the Thames. Nor has this been done in London only. In Paris the Seine is the receptacle of the sewage, but, comparatively, to a much smaller extent than in London. The fæcal deposits accumulated in the houses of the French capital are drained into "fixed" and "moveable" cesspools. The contents of both these descriptions of cesspools (of which I shall give an account when I treat of the cesspool system) are removed periodically, under the direction of the government, to large receptacles, called *voiries*, at Montfaucon, and the Forest of Bondy, where such refuse is made into portable manure. The evils of this system are not a few; but the river is spared the greater pollution of the Thames. Neither is the Seine swayed by the tide as is the Thames, for in London the very sewers are affected by the tidal influence, and are not to be entered until some time before or after high-water. I need not do more, for my present inquiry, than allude to the Liffy, the Clyde, the Humber, and others of the rivers of the United Kingdom, being used for purposes of sewerage, as channels to carry off that of which the law prohibits the retention.

Of the folly, not to say wickedness, of this principle, there can be no doubt. The vegetation which gives, demands food. The grass will wither without its fitting nutriment of manure, as the sheep would perish without the pasturage of the grass. Nature, in temperate and moist climates, is, so to speak, her own manurer, her own restorer. The sheep, which are as wild and active as goats, manure the Cumberland fells in which they feed. In the more cultivated sheep-walks (or, indeed, in the general pasturage) of the northern and some of the midland counties, women, with a wooden implement, may be continually seen in the later autumn, or earlier and milder winter, distributing the "stercoraceous treasure," as Cowper calls it, which the animals, to use the North Yorkshire word, have "dropped," as well as any extraneous manure which may have been spread for the purpose. As population and the demand for bread increase, the need of extraneous manures also increases; and Nature in her beneficence has provided that the greater the consumption of food, the greater shall be the promoters of its reproduction by what is loathsome to man, but demanded by vegetation. Liebig, as I shall afterwards show more fully, contends that many an arid and desolate region in the East, brown and burnt with barrenness, became a desolation because men understood not the restoration which all nature demands for the land. He declares that the now desolate regions of the East had been made desolate, because "the inhabitants did not understand the art of restoring exhausted soil." It would be hopeless now to form, or attempt to form, the "hanging gardens," or to display the rich florescence "round about Babylon," to be seen when Alexander the Great died in that city. The Tigris and Euphrates, before and after their junction, Liebig maintains, have carried, and, to a circumscribed degree, still carry, into the sea "a sufficient amount of manure for the reproduction of food for millions of human beings." It is said that, "could that matter only be arrested in its progress, and converted into bread and wine, fruit and beef, mutton and wool, linen and cotton, then cities might flourish once more in the desert, where men are now digging for the relics of primitive civilization, and discovering the symbols of luxury and ease beneath the barren sand and the sunburnt clay."

This is one great evil; but in our metropolis there is a greater, a far greater, beyond all in degree, even if the same abuse exist elsewhere. What society with one consent pronounces filth—the evacuations of the human body—is not only washed into the Thames, and the land so deprived of a vast amount of nutriment, but the tide washes these evacuations back again, with other abominations. The water we use is derived almost entirely from the Thames, and therefore the water in which we boil our vegetables and our meat, the water for our coffee and tea, the water brewed for our consumption, comes to us, and is imbibed by us, impregnated over and over again with our own animal offal. We import guano, and drink a solution of our own fæces: a manure which might be made far more valuable than the foreign guano.

Such are a few of the evils of making a common sewer of the neighbouring river.

The other mode of removal is, to convey the wet house-refuse, by drains, to a hole near the house where it is produced, and empty it periodically when full.

The house-drainage throughout London has two characteristics. By one system all excrementitious and slop refuse generally is carried usually along brick drains from the water-closets, privies, sinks, lavatories, &c., of the houses into the cesspools, where it accumulates until its removal (by manual labour) becomes necessary, which is not, as an average, more than once in two years. By the other, and the newer system, all the house-refuse is drained into the public sewer, the cesspool system being thereby abolished. All the houses built or rebuilt since 1848 are constructed on the last-mentioned principle of drainage.

The first of these modes is cesspoolage.
The second is sewerage.

I shall first deal with the sewerage of the metropolis.

OF THE QUANTITY OF METROPOLITAN SEWAGE.

HAVING estimated the gross quantity of wet house-refuse produced throughout London in the course of the year, and explained the two modes of removing it from the immediate vicinity of the house, I will now proceed to set forth the *quantity* of wet house-refuse matter which it has been *ascertained* is removed with the contents of London sewers.

An experiment was made on the average discharge of sewage from the outlets of Church-lane and Smith-street, Chelsea, Ranelagh, King's Scholar's-pond, Grosvenor-wharf, Horseferry-road, Wood-street, King-street, Northumberland-street, Durham-yard, Norfolk-street, and Essex-street (the four last-mentioned places running from the Strand). The experiments were made "under ordinary and extraordinary circumstances," in the months of May, June, and July, 1844, but the system is still the same, so that the result in the investigation as to the sewage of the year 1844 may be taken as a near criterion of the present, as regards the localities specified and the general quantity.

The surface drained into the outlets before enumerated covers, in its total area, about 7000 acres, of which nearly 3500 may be classed as urban. The observations, moreover, were made generally during fine weather.

I cannot do better by way of showing the reader the minuteness with which these observations were made, than by quoting the two following results, being those of the fullest and smallest discharges of twelve issues into the river. I must premise that these experiments were made on seven occasions, from May 4 to July 12 inclusive, and made at different times, but generally about eight hours after high water. In the Northumberland-street sewer, from which was the largest issue, the width of the sewer at the outlet was five feet. In the King-street sewer (the smallest discharge, as given in the second table) the width of the sewer was four feet. The width, however, does not affect the question, as there was a greater issue from the Norfolk-street sewer of two feet, than from the King-street sewer of four feet in width.

NORTHUMBERLAND STREET.

Date.	Velocity per second.	Quantity discharged per second.
	Feet.	Cubic Feet.
May 4 .	4·600	10·511000
,, 9 .	4·000	6·800000
June 5 .	4·000	6·800000
,, 10 .	4·600	10·350000
,, 11 .	4·920	12·300000
,, 16 .	3·600	5·940000
July 12 .	2·760	3·394800
		56·095800
Being Mean Discharge per second		8·013685
Ditto per 24 hours . .		692382·

KING STREET.

May 4 .	·147	·021756
,, 9 .	·333	·079920
June 5 .	·170	·020400
,, 10 .	·311	·064688
,, 11 .	·300	·048000
,, 16 .	·101	·004040
July 12 .	·103	·008240
		·247044
Mean Discharge per second .		·035292
Ditto per 24 hours		3049·

Here we find that the mean discharge per second was, from the Northumberland-street sewer, 692,382· cubic feet per 24 hours, and from the King-street sewer, 3049 cubic feet per 24 hours.

The discharge from the principal outlets in the Westminster district "being the mean of seven observations taken during the summer," was 1,798,094 cubic feet in 24 hours; the number of acres drained was 7006. *The mean discharge per acre, in the course of 24 hours, was found to be about 256 cubic feet, comprising the urban and suburban parts.*

The sewage, from the discharge of which this calculation was derived—and the dryness of the weather must not be lost sight of—may be fairly assumed as derived (in a dry season) almost entirely from artificial sources or house drainage, as there was no rain-fall, or but little. "*Supposing, therefore,*" the Report states, "*the entire surface to be urban, we have 540 cubic feet as the mean daily discharge per acre.* If, however, the average be taken of the first eight outlets, viz., from Essex-street to Grosvenor-wharf inclusive, which drain a surface wholly urban, the result is 1260 cubic feet per acre in the 24 hours. This excess may be attributed to the number of manufactories, and the densely-populated nature of the locality drained; but, as indicative of the general amount of sewage due to ordinary urban districts, the former ought perhaps to be considered the fairer average."

It is then assumed—I may say officially—that the average discharge of the urban and suburban sewage from the several districts included within an area of 58 square miles, is equal to 256 cubic feet per acre.

	Sq. Miles.
The extent of the jurisdiction included within this area is, on the north side of the Thames	43
And on the Surrey and Kent side	15

	Cubic Feet.
The ordinary *daily* amount of sewage discharged into the river on the north side is, therefore	7,045,120
And on the south side	2,457,600
Making a total of	9,502,720

Or a quantity equivalent to a surface of more than 36 acres in extent, and 6 feet in depth.

This mass of sewage, it must be borne in mind, is but the *daily* product of the sewage of the more populous part of the districts included within the jurisdiction of the two commissions of sewers.

The foregoing observations, calculations, and deductions have supplied the basis of many scientific and commercial speculations, but it must be remembered that they were taken between seven and eight years ago. The observations were made, moreover, during fine summer weather, generally, while the greatest discharge is during rainy weather. There has been, also, an increase of sewers in the metropolis, because an increase of streets and inhabited houses. The approximate proportion of the increase of sewers (and there is no precise account of it) is pretty nearly that of the streets, lineally. Another mattter has too, of late years, added to the amount of sewage— the abolition of cesspoolage in a considerable degreee, owing to the late Building and Sanitary Acts, so that fœcal and culinary matters, which were drained into the cesspool (to be removed by the nightmen), are now drained into the sewer. Altogether, I am assured, on good authority, the daily discharge of the sewers extending over 58 square miles of the metropolis may be now put at 10,000,000 cubic feet, instead of rather more than nine and a half millions. And this gives, as

	Cubic Feet.
The annual amount of discharge from the sewers	3,650,000,000
The total amount of wet house-refuse, according to the calculation before given, is	3,820,000,000
Hence there remains	170,000,000

	Sq. Miles.
Now it will be seen that the total area from which this amount of sewage is said to be drained is	58
But the area of London, according to the Registrar-General's limits, is	115

So that the 3,650,000,000 cubic feet of sewage annually removed from 58 square miles of the metropolis refer to only one-half of the entire area of the *true* metropolis; but it refers, at the same time, to that part of London which is the most crowded with houses, and since, in the suburbs, the buildings average about 2 to the acre, and, in the densest parts of London, about 30, it is but fair to assume that the refuse would be, at least, in the same proportion, and this is very nearly the fact; for if we suppose the 58 miles of the suburban districts to yield twenty times less sewage than the 58 miles of the urban districts, we shall have 182,500,000 cubic feet to add to the 3,650,000,000 cubic feet before given, or 3,832,500,000 for the sewage of the entire metropolis.

It does not appear that the sewage has ever been weighed so as to give any definite result, but calculating from the weight of water (a gallon, or 10 lbs. of water, comprising 277·274 cubic inches, and 1 ton of liquid comprising 36 cubic feet) the total, from the returns of the investigation in 1844, would be

	Tons.
Quantity of sewage *daily* emptied into the Thames	278,000
Ditto Annually	101,390,000

In September, 1849, Mr. Banfield, at one time a Commissioner of Sewers, put the yearly quantity of sewage discharged into the Thames at 45,000,000 tons; but this is widely at variance with the returns as to quantity.

OF ANCIENT SEWERS.

THE traverser of the London streets rarely thinks, perhaps, of the far extended subterranean architecture below his feet; yet such is indeed the case, for the sewers of London, with all their imperfections, irregularities, and even absurdities, are still a great work; certainly not equal, in all respects, to what once must have existed in Rome, but second, perhaps, only to the giant works of sewerage in the eternal city.

The origin of these Roman sewers seems to be wrapped in as great a mystery as the foundation of the city itself. The statement of the Roman historians is that these sewers were the works of the elder Tarquin, the fifth (apocryphal) king of Rome. Tarquin's dominions, from the same accounts, did not in any direction extend above sixteen miles, and his subjects could be but banditti, foragers, and shepherds. One conjecture is, that Rome stands on the site of a more ancient city, and that to its earlier possessors may be attributed the work of the sewers. To attribute them to the rudeness and small population of Tarquin's day, it is contended, is as feasible as it would be to attribute the ruins of ancient Jerusalem, or any others in Asia Minor, to the Turks, or the ruins of Palmyra to the Arabs, because these people enjoy the privilege of possession.

The main sewer of Rome, the Cloaca Maxima, is said to have been lofty and wide enough for a waggon load of hay to pass clear along it. Another, and more probable account, however, states that it was proposed to *enlarge* the great sewer to these dimensions, but it does not appear to have been so enlarged. Indeed, when Augustus "made

THE SEWER-HUNTER.

[*From a Daguerreotype by* BEARD.]

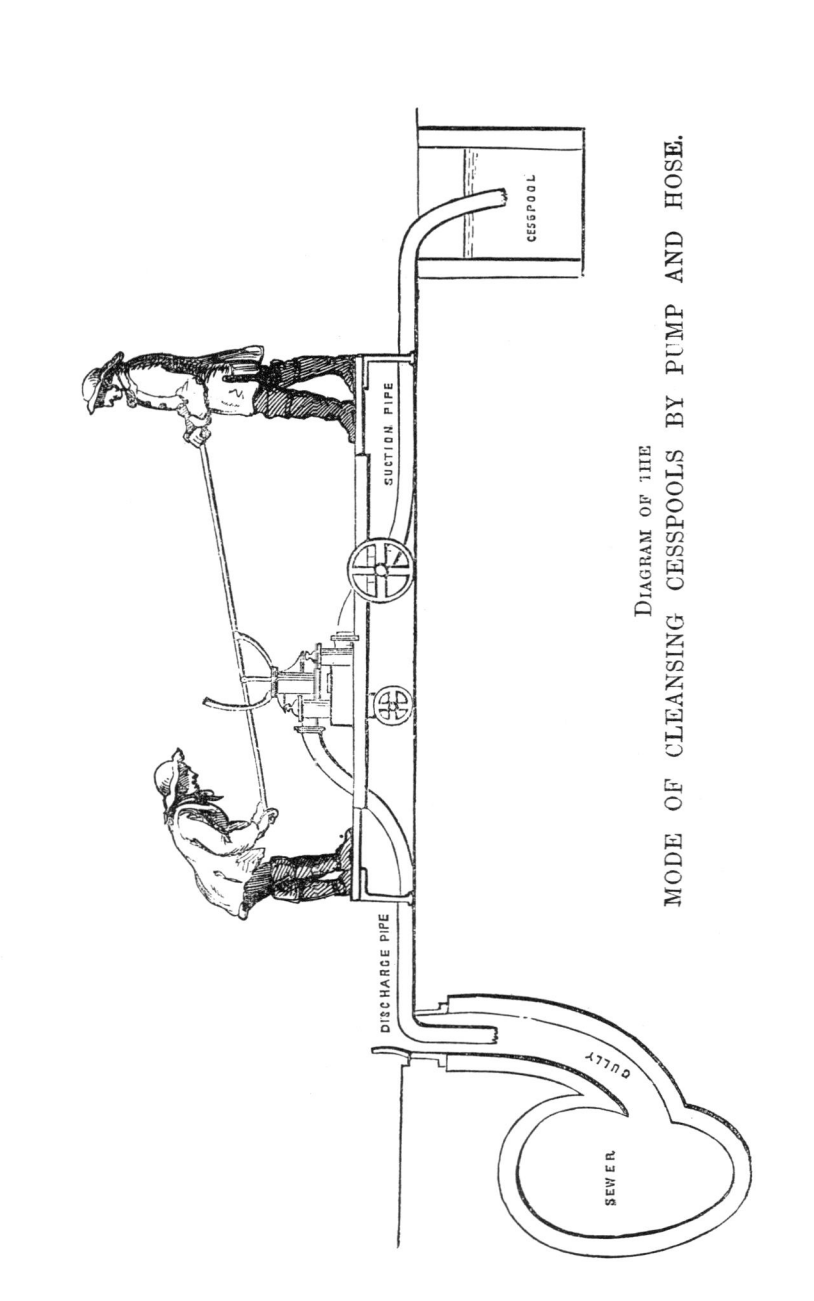

Diagram of the Mode of Cleansing Cesspools by Pump and Hose.

Rome marble," it was one of his great works also, under the direction of Agrippa, to reconstruct, improve, and enlarge the sewers. It was a project in the days of Rome's greatness to turn seven navigable rivers into vast subterraneous passages, larger sewers, along which barges might pass, carrying on the traffic of Imperial Rome. In one year the cost of cleansing, renewing, and repairing the sewers is stated to have been 1000 talents of gold, or upwards of 192,000*l*. Of the *average* yearly cost we have no information. Some accounts represent these sewers as having been rebuilt after the irruption of the Gauls. In Livy's time they were pronounced not to be accommodated to the plan of Rome. Some portions of these ancient structures are still extant, but they seem to have attracted small notice even from professed antiquarians; their subterranean character, however, renders such notice little possible. In two places they are still kept in repair, and for their original purpose, to carry off the filth of the city, but only to a small extent.

Our legislative enactments on the subject of sewers are ancient and numerous. The oldest is that of 9 Henry III., and the principal is that of 23 Henry VIII., commonly called the "Statute of Sewers." These and many subsequent statutes, however, relate only to watercourses, and are silent as regards my present topic—the Refuse of London.

It is remarkable how little is said in the London historians of the *sewers*. In the two folio volumes of the most searching and indefatigable of all the antiquarians who have described the old metropolis, John Stow, the tailor, there is no account of what we now consider sewers, inclosed and subterranean channels for the conveyance of the refuse filth of the metropolis to its destination—the Thames. Had covered sewers been known, or at any rate been at all common, in Stow's day, and he died full of years in 1604, and had one of them presented but a crumbling stone with some heraldic, or apparently heraldic, device at its outlet, Stow's industry would certainly have ferreted out some details. Such, however, is not the case.

This absence of information I hold to be owing to the fact that no such sewers then existed. Our present system of sewerage, like our present system of street-lighting, is a modern work; but it is not, like our gas-lamps, an *original* English work. We have but followed, as regards our arched and subterraneous sewerage, in the wake of Rome.

As I have said, the early *laws* of sewers relate to watercourses, navigable communications, dams, ditches, and such like; there is no doubt, however, that in the heart of the great towns the filth of the houses was, by rude contrivances in the way of drainage, or natural fall, emptied into such places. Even in the accounts of the sewers of ancient Rome, historians have stated that it is not easy, and sometimes not possible, to distinguish between the *sewers* and the *aqueducts*; and Dr. Lemon, in his English Etymology, speaks of sewers as a species of aqueducts. So, in some of our earlier Acts of Parliament, it is hardly possible to distinguish whether the provisions to be applied to the management of a sewer relate to a ditch to which house-filth was carried—to a channel of water for general purposes—or to an open channel being a receptacle of filth and a navigable stream at the same time.

That the ditches were not sewers for the conveyance of the filth from the houses to any very great, or rather any very general extent, may very well be concluded, because (as I have shown in my account of the early scavagers) the excrementitious matter was deposited during the night in the street, and removed by the proper functionaries in the morning, or as soon as suited their convenience. Though this was the case generally, it is evident that the filth, or a portion of it, from the houses which were built on the banks of the Fleet River (as it was then called, as well as the Fleet Ditch), and on the banks of the other " brooks," drained into the current stream. The Corporation accounts contain very frequent mention of the cleansing, purifying, and " thorough" cleansing of the Fleet Ditch, the Old Bourne (Holborn Brook), the Wall Brook, &c.

Of all these streams the most remarkable was Fleet Ditch, which was perhaps the first main sewer of London. I give from Stow the following curious account of its origin. It is now open, but only for a short distance, offending the air of Clerkenwell. At one period it was to afford a defence to the City! as the Tower-moat was a defence to the Tower, and fortress.

" The Ditch, which partly now remaineth and compassed the Wall of the City, was begun to be made by the *Londoners*, in the year 1211, and finished 1213, the 15th of K. *John*. This Ditch being then made of 200 foot broad, caused no small hindrance to the Canons of the Holy *Trinity*, whose Church stood near *Ealdgate*, for that the said Ditch passed through their Ground from the *Tower* unto *Bishopsgate*.

" The first Occasion of making a Ditch about the City seems to have been this: *William*, Bishop of *Ely*, Chancellor of *England*, in the Reign of King *Richard* I., made a great Ditch round about the *Tower*, for the better Defence of it against *John* the King's Brother, the King being then out of the Realm. Then did the City also begin a Ditch to encompass and strengthen their Walls [which happened between the Years 1190 and 1193.] So the Book *Dunthorn*. Yet the Register of *Bermondsey* writes that the Ditch was begun, Oct. 15, 1213, which was in the Reign of King *John* that succeeded to *Richard*.

" This Ditch being originally made for the Defence of the City, was also a long time together carefully cleansed and maintained, as Need required; but now of late neglected, and forced either to a very narrow, and the same a filthy Channel.

" In the Year of *Christ*, 1354, 28 *Ed.* 3, the Ditch of this City flowing over the Bank into the *Tower-ditch*, the King commanded the said Ditch of the City to be cleansed, and so ordered, that the overflowing thereof should not force any Filth into the *Tower-ditch*.

" *Anno*, 1379, John Philpot, Maior of *London*,

caused this Ditch to be cleansed, and every Houshold to pay 5*d.*, which was a Day's Work toward the Charges thereof.

"*Ralph Joseline*, Maior, 1477, caused the whole Ditch to be cast and cleansed...... In 1519, the 10th of Henry 8, for cleansing and scouring the common Ditch, between *Aldgate*, and the Postern next the *Tower-ditch;* the chief Ditcher had by the day 7*d.*, the Second Ditcher, 6*d*, the other Ditchers, 5*d.* And every Vagabond (for as they were then termed) 1*d.* the Day, Meat and Drink, at the Charges of the City. Sum 95*l.* 3*s.* 4*d.*

"Fleet Ditch was again cleansed in the Year 1549," Stow continues, "*Henry Ancoates* being Maior, at the Charges of the Companies. And again 1569, the 11th of Queen *Elizabeth;* for cleansing the same Ditch between *Ealdgate* and the *Postern*, and making a new Sewer and Wharf of Timber, from the Head of the *Postern* into the *Tower-ditch*, 814*l.* 15*s.* 8*d.* (was disbursed). Before the which Time the said Ditch lay open, without either Wall or Pall, having therein great Store of very good Fish, of divers Sorts, as many men yet living, who have taken and tasted them, can well witness. But now no such matter, the Charge of Cleansing is spared, and great Profit made by letting out the Banks, with the Spoil of the whole Ditch."

The above information appeared, but I am unable to specify the year (for Stow's works went through several editions, though it is to be feared he died very poor) between 1582 and 1590. So did the following :—

"At this Day there be no Ditches or Boggs in the City except the said *Fleet-ditch*, but instead thereof large common *Dreins* and *Sewers*, made to carry away the water from the *Postern-Gate*, between the two *Tower-hills* to *Fleet-bridge* without *Ludgate*."

Great, indeed, is the change in the character of the capital of England, from the times when the Fleet Ditch was a defence to the city (which was then the entire capital) ; and from the later era, when "great store of very good fish of divers sorts," rewarded the skill or the patience of the anglers or netters ; but this, it is evident, was in the parts near the river (the Tower postern, &c.), and at that time, or about that time, there was salmon-fishing in the Thames, at least as far up as Hungerford Wharf.

The Fleet Ditch seems always to have had a *sewery* character. It was described, in 1728, as

"The king of dykes! than whom no sluice of mud
  With deeper sable blots the silver flood—"

the *silver* flood being, in Queen Anne's and the First George's days, the London Thames. This silver has been much alloyed since that time.

Until within these 40 or 50 years, open sewer-ditches, into which drains were emptied, and ordure and refuse thrown, were frequent, especially in the remoter parts of Lambeth and Newington, and some exist to this day ; one especially, open for a considerable distance, flowing along the back of the houses in the Westminster-road, on the right-hand side towards the bridge, into which the neighbouring houses are drained. The "Black Ditch," a filthy sewer, until lately was open near the Broadwall, and other vicinities of the Blackfriars-road. The open ditch-sewers of Norwood and Wandsworth have often been spoken of in Sanitary Reports. Indeed, some of our present sewers, in addition to Fleet River and Wall Brook, are merely ditches rudely arched over.

The first covered and continuous street sewer was erected in London—I think, without doubt—when Wren rebuilt the capital, after the great fire of 1666. Perhaps there is no direct evidence of the fact, for, although the statutes and Privy Council and municipal enactments, consequent on the rebuilding of the capital, required, more or less peremptorily, "fair sewers, and drains, and watercourses," it is not defined in these enactments what was meant by a "sewer;" nor were they carried out.

I may mention, as a further proof that open ditches, often enough stagnant ditches also, were the first London sewers, that, after 1666, a plan, originally projected, it appears, by Sir Leonard Halliday, Maior, 60 years previously, and strenuously supported at that time by Nic Leate, "a worthy and grave citizen," was revived and reconsidered. This project, for which Sir Leonard and Nic Leate "laboured much," was "for a river to be brought on the north of the city into it, for the cleansing the sewers and ditches, and for the better keeping London wholesome, sweet, and clean." An admirable *intention;* and it is not impossible nor improbable that in less than two centuries hence, we, of the present sanitary era, may be accounted, for our sanitary measures, as senseless as we now account good Sir Leonard Halliday and the worthy and grave Nic Leate. These gentlemen cared not to brook filth in their houses, nor to be annoyed by it in the nightly pollution of the streets, but they advocated its injection into running water, and into water often running slowly and difficultly, and continually under the eyes and noses of the citizens. *We*, I apprehend, go a little further. We drink, and use for the preparation of our meals, the befouled water, which they did not ; for, more than seven-eighths of our water-supply from the companies is drawn from the Thames, the main sewer of the greatest city in the world, ancient or modern, into which millions of tons of every description of refuse are swept yearly.

OF THE KINDS AND CHARACTERISTICS OF SEWERS.

THE sewers of London may be arranged into two distinct groups—according to the side of the Thames on which they are situate.

Now the essential difference between these two classes of sewers lies in the elevation of the several localities whence the sewers carry the refuse to the Thames.

The chief differences in the circumstances of the people north and south of the river are shown in the annexed table from the Registrar-General's returns :—

	London.	North side of the River.	South side of the River.
Elevation of the ground, in feet, above Trinity high-water mark	39	51	5
Density, or number of persons to an acre, 1849	30	52	14
Deaths from Cholera to 10,000 persons living, in 60 weeks, ending Nov. 24, 1849	66	44	127
Deaths from all causes annually to 10,000 persons (5000 males, 5000 females) living, during the 7 years, 1838–44	252	251	257

Here, it will be seen, that while the houses on the north side of the river stand, on an average, 51 feet above the high-water mark of the Thames, those on the south side are only 5 feet above it. The effect of this is shown most particularly in the deaths from cholera in 1849, which were nearly three times as many on the south as on the north side of the Thames. It is said, officially, that "of the 15 square miles of the Urban district on the south side of the river Thames, *three* miles are from six to seven feet below high-water mark, so that the locality may be said to be drained only for four hours out of the twelve, and during these four hours very imperfectly . . . . . When the tide rises above the orifices of the sewers, the whole drainage of the district is stopped until the tide recedes again, rendering the whole system of sewers in Kent and Surrey only an *articulation of cesspools*."

That this is but the fact, the following table of the elevation in feet above the Trinity high-water mark, as regards the several districts on the Surrey side of the Thames, may be cited as evidence.

	Elevation.		Elevation.
Lewisham	28	St. Olave	2
Wandsworth	22	Bermondsey	0
Greenwich	8	Rotherhithe	0
Camberwell	4	St. George's (Southwark)	0
Lambeth	3		
St. Saviour (Southwark)	2	Newington (below high water)	2

From these returns, made by Capt. Dawson, R.E., the difficulty, to use no stronger word, attending the sewerage of the Surrey district is shown at once. There is no flow to be had, or—the word more generally used, no *run* for the sewage. In parts of the north of England it used to be a general, and still is a partial, saying among country-people who are figuratively describing what they account impossible. " Ay, when? *When* water runs up bank." This is a homely expression of the difficulties attending the Surrey sewerage.

There is, as regards these Surrey, more than the Kent, sewers, another evil which promotes the "articulation of cesspools." Some of these sewers have "dead-ends," like places which in the streets (a parallel case enough) are known as "no thoroughfare," and in these sewers it is seldom, in any state of the tide, that flushing can be resorted to; consequently these cesspool-like sewers remain uncleansed, or have to be cleansed by manual labour, the matter being drawn up into the street or road.

The refuse conduits of the metropolis are of two kinds :—
1. Sewers.
2. Drains.

These two classes of refuse-charts are often confounded, even in some official papers, the sewer being there designated the "main drain." All sewerage is undoubtedly drainage, but there is a manifest distinction between a sewer and a drain.

The First-Class Sewers, which are generally termed "main sewers," and run along the centres of the first-class streets (first-class alike from the extent or populousness of such streets), may be looked upon as underground rivers of refuse, to which the drains are tributary rivulets. No sewer exists unconnected with the drains from the streets and houses; but many house-drains are constructed apart from the sewers, communicating only with the cesspools. Even where houses are built in close contiguity to a public sewer, and built after the new mode without cesspools, there is always a drain to the sewer; no house so situated can get rid of its refuse except by means of a drain; unless, indeed, the house be not drained at all, and its filth be flung down a gully-hole, or got rid of in some other way.

These drains, all with a like determination, differ only in their forms. They are barrel-shaped, made of rounded bricks, or earthenware pipeage, and of an interior between a round and an oval, with a diameter of from 2 to 6 inches, although only a few private houses, comparatively, are so drained. The barrel drain of larger dimensions, is used in the newer public buildings and larger public mansions, when it represents a sort of house or interior sewer as well as a house main drain, for smaller drains find their issue into the barrel-drain. There is the barrel-drain in the new Houses of Parliament, and in large places which cover the site of, and are required for the purposes of several houses or offices. The tubular drain is simply piping, of which I have spoken fully in my account of the present compulsory mode of house drainage. The third drain, one more used to carry refuse to the cesspool than the sewer, but still carrying such refuse to the sewers, is the old-fashioned brick drain, generally 9 inches square.

I shall first deal with the sewerage, and then with the house and street drainage.

The sewer is a twofold receptacle of refuse; into it are conveyed the wet refuse not only of many of the houses, but of all the streets.

The slop or surface water of the streets is conveyed to the sewer by means of smaller sewers or street-drains running from the "kennel" or channel to the larger sewers.

In the streets, at such uncertain distances as the traffic and circumstances of the locality may require, are gully-holes. These are openings into the sewer, and were formerly called, as they were, simply gratings, a sort of iron trap-doors of grated bars, clumsily made, and placed almost at random. On each side of the street was, even into the present century, a very formidable channel, or kennel, as it was formerly written, into which, in heavy rains, the badly-scavaged street dirt was swept, often demanding a good leap from one who wished to cross in a hurry. These "kennels" emptied themselves into the gratings, which were not unfrequently choked up, and the kennel was then an utter nuisance. At the present time the channel is simply a series of stone work at the edge of the footpaths, blocks of granite being sloped to meet more or less at right angles, and the flow from the inclination from the centre of the street to the channel is carried along without impediment or nuisance into the gully-hole.

The gully-hole opens into a drain, running, with a rapid slope, into the sewer, and so the wet refuse of the streets find its vent.

In many courts, alleys, lanes, &c., inhabited by the poor, where there is imperfect or no drainage to the houses, all the slops from the houses are thrown down the gully-holes, and frequently enough blood and offal are poured from butchers' premises, which might choke the house drain. There have, indeed, been instances of worthless street dirt (slop) collected into a scavager's vehicle being shot down a gully-hole.

The sewers, as distinct from the drains, are to be divided principally into three classes, all devoted to the same purpose—the conveyance of the underground filth of the capital to the Thames—and all connected by a series of drains, afterwards to be described, with the dwelling-houses.

The *first-class sewers* are found in the main streets, and flow at their outlets into the river.

The *second-class sewers* run along the second-class streets, discharging their contents into a first-class sewer; and

The *third-class sewers* are for the reception of the sewage from the smaller streets, and always communicate, for the voidance of their contents, with a sewer of the second or first description.

As regards the destination of the sewers, there is no difference between the Middlesex and Surrey portions of the metropolis. The sewage is *all* floated into the river.

The first-class sewers of the modern build rarely exceed 50 inches by 30 in internal dimensions; the second class, 40 inches by 24; the third, 30 inches by 18.

Smaller class or branch sewers, from No. 4 to No. 8 inclusive, also form part of the great subterranean filth-channels of the metropolis. It is only, however, the three first-mentioned classes which can be described as in any way principal *sewers;* the others are in the capacity of branch sewers, the ramifications being in many places very extensive, while pipes are often used. The dimensions of these smaller sewers, when pipes are not used, are—No. 4, 20 inches by 12; No. 5, $17\frac{1}{2}$ inches by $10\frac{1}{2}$; No. 6, 15 inches by 9; No. 7, 12 inches by $7\frac{1}{2}$; and No. 8, 9 inches by 6.

These branch sewers may, from their circumscribed dimensions, be looked upon as mere channels of connection with the larger descriptions; but they present, as I have intimated, an important part of the general system. This may be shown by the fact, that in the estimates for building sewers for the improvement of the drainage of the city of Westminster (a plan, however, not carried out), the estimated, or indeed surveyed, run of the first class was to be 8118 feet; of the second class, 4524 feet; of the third, but 2086 feet; while of the No. 5 and No. 6 description, it was, respectively, 18,709 and 53,284 feet. The branch sewers may, perhaps, be represented in many instances as public drains connecting the sewer of the street with the issue from the houses, but I give the appellation I find in the reports.

The dimensions I have cited are not to be taken as an average size of the existing sewers of the metropolis on either side of the Thames, for no average size and no uniformity of shape can be adduced, as there has been no uniformity observed. The sewers are of all sizes and shapes, and of all depths from the surface of the streets. I was informed by an engineering authority that he had often seen it asserted that the naval authorities of the kingdom could not build a war-steamer, and it might very well be said that the sanitary authorities of the metropolis could not build a sewer, as none of the present sewers could be cited as in all respects properly fulfilling all the functions required. But it must be remembered that the present engineers have to contend with great difficulties, the whole matter being so complicated by the blunderings and mismanagement of the past.

The dimensions I have cited (because they appear officially) exceed the medium size of the *newer* sewerage, the average height of the first class being in such sewers about 3 feet 9 inches.

Of the width of the sewers, as of the height, no precise average can be drawn. Perhaps that of the New Palace main, or first-class sewer, 3 feet 6 inches, may be nearest the average, while the smaller classes diminish in their width in the proportions I have shown. The sewers of the older constructions nearly all widen and deepen as they near the outlet, and this at no definite distance from the river, but from a quarter of a mile or somewhat less to a mile and more. Some such sewers are then 14 feet in width; some 20 feet, and no doubt of proportionate height, but I do not find that the height has been ascertained. For flushing purposes there are recesses of greater or less width, according to the capacity of the sewer, where sluice-gates, &c., can be fixed, and water accumulated.

Under the head of "Subterranean Survey of

the Sewers," will be found some account of the different dimensions of the sewers.

The form of the interior of the sewers (as shown in the illustrations I have given) is irregularly elliptical. They are arched at the summits, and more or less hollowed or curved, internally, at the bottom. The bottom of the sewer is called the "invert," from a general resemblance in the construction to an "inverted" arch. The *best* form of invert is a matter which has attracted great engineering attention. It is, indeed, the important part of the sewer, as the part along which there is the flow of sewage; and the superior or inferior formation of the invert, of course, facilitates or retards the transmission of the contents.

A few years back, the building of egg-shaped, or "oviform" sewers, was strongly advocated. It was urged that the flow of the sewage and the sewer-water was accelerated by the invert (especially) being oviform, as the matter was more condensed when such was the shape adopted, while the more the matter was diffused, as in some of the inverts of the more usual form of sewers, the less rapid was its flow, and consequently the greater its deposit.

What extent of egg-shaped sewers are now, so to speak, at work, I could not ascertain. One informant thought it might be somewhere about 50 miles.

The following interesting account of the velocities of streams, with a relativeness to sewers, is extracted from the evidence of Mr. Phillips:—

"The area of surface that a sewer will drain, and the quantity of water that it will discharge in a given time, will be greater or less in proportion as the channel is inclined from a horizontal to a vertical position. The ordinary or common run of water in each sewer, due from house drainage alone, and irrespective of rain, should have sufficient velocity to prevent the usual matter discharged into the sewer from depositing. For this purpose, it is necessary that there should be in each sewer a contant velocity of current equal to $2\frac{1}{2}$ feet per second, or $1\frac{3}{4}$ mile per hour." Mr. Phillips then states that the inclinations of all rivulets, &c., diminish as they progress to their outfalls. "If the force of the waters of the river Rhone," he has said, "were not absorbed by the operation of some constant retardation in its course, the stream would have shot into the Bay of Marseilles with the tremendous velocity of 164 miles every hour. Even if the Thames met with no system of impediments in its course, the stream would have rushed into the sea with a velocity of 80 feet per second, or $54\frac{1}{2}$ miles in an hour. . . . . The inclinations of the sewers of a natural district should be made to diminish from their heads to their outfalls in a corresponding ratio of progression, so that as the body of water is increased at each confluence, one and the same velocity and force of current may be kept up throughout the whole of them."

Mr. Phillips advocates a tubular system of sewerage and drainage.

The main sewer, which has lately called forth the most public attention and professional controversy, is that connected with the new Houses of Parliament, or as they are called in divers reports and correspondence, the "New Palace at Westminster."

The workmanship in the building of the sewers is of every quality. The material of which some of the older sewers are constructed is a porous sort of brick, which is often found crumbling and broken, and saturated with damp and rottenness, from the exhalations and contact of their contents. The sewers erected, however, within the last twenty, and more especially within the last ten years, are sometimes of granite, but generally of the best brick, with an interior coating of enduring cement, and generally with concrete on their exterior, to protect them from the dampness and decaying qualities of the superincumbent or lateral soil.

The depth of the sewers—I mean from the top of the sewer to the surface of the street—seems to vary as everything else varies about them. Some are found forty feet below the street, some *two* feet, some almost level! These, however, are exceptions; and the average depth of the sewers on the Middlesex side is from twelve to fourteen feet; on the Surrey side, from six to eight feet. The reason is that the north shores of the metropolis are above the tide level, the south shores are below it.

An authority on the subject has said, "The Surrey sewers are bad, owing principally to the land being below tide level. They were the most expensively constructed, because, *perhaps*, in that Commission the surveyors were paid by percentage on the cost of works. When it was proposed, in the Westminster Commission, to effect a reduction of four-fifths in the cost, it was like a proposition to return the officers' salaries to that extent, if they had been paid in that way."

The reader may have observed that the official intelligence I have given all, or nearly all, refers to the "Westminster and part of Middlesex" Commission, and to that of the "Surrey and Kent." This is easily accounted for. In the metropolitan districts, up to 1847, the only Commission which published its papers was the Westminster, of which Mr. L. C. Hertslet had the charge as clerk; when the Commissions were consolidated in 1847, he printed the Westminster and Surrey only, the others being of minor importance.

I may observe that one of the engineers, in showing the difficulty or impossibility of giving any description of a *system* of sewerage, as to points of agreement or difference, represents the whole mass as but a "detached parcel of sewers."

The course of the sewers is in no direct or uniform line, with the exception of one characteristic—all their bearings are towards the river as regards the main sewers (first-class), and all the bearings of the second-class sewers are towards the main sewers in the main streets. The smaller classes of sewers fill up the great area of London sewerage with a perfect network of intersection and connection, and even this network is increased manyfold by its connection with the house-drains.

There is no map of the general sewerage of the metropolis, merely "sections" and "plans" of improvements making or suggested, in the reports of the surveyors, &c., to the Commissioners; but did a map of subterranean London exist, with its lines of every class of sewerage and of the drainage which feeds the sewers; with its course, moreover, of gas-pipes and water-pipes, with their connection with the houses, the streets, the courts, &c., it would be the most curious and skeleton-like map in the world.

Of the Subterranean Character of the Sewers.

In my inquiries among that curious body of men, the "Sewer Hunters," I found them make light of any danger, their principal fear being from the attacks of rats in case they became isolated from the gang with whom they searched in common, while they represented the odour as a mere nothing in the way of unpleasantness. But these men pursued only known and (by them) beaten tracks at low water, avoiding any deviation, and so becoming but partially acquainted with the character and direction of the sewers. And had it been otherwise, they are not a class competent to describe what they saw, however keen-eyed after silver spoons.

The following account is derived chiefly from official sources. I may premise that where the deposit is found the greatest, the sewer is in the worst state. This deposit, I find it repeatedly stated, is of a most miscellaneous character. Some of the sewers, indeed, are represented as the dust-bins and dung-hills of the immediate neighbourhood. The deposit has been found to comprise all the ingredients from the breweries, the gas-works, and the several chemical and mineral manufactories; dead dogs, cats, kittens, and rats; offal from slaughter-houses, sometimes even including the entrails of the animals; street-pavement dirt of every variety; vegetable refuse; stable-dung; the refuse of pig-styes; night-soil; ashes; tin kettles and pans (pansherds); broken stoneware, as jars, pitchers, flower-pots, &c.; bricks; pieces of wood; rotten mortar and rubbish of different kinds; and even rags. Our criminal annals of the previous century show that often enough the bodies of murdered men were thrown into the Fleet and other ditches, then the open sewers of the metropolis, and if found washed into the Thames, they were so stained and disfigured by the foulness of the contents of these ditches, that recognition was often impossible, so that there could be but one verdict returned—"Found drowned." Clothes stripped from a murdered person have been, it was authenticated on several occasions in Old Bailey evidence, thrown into the open sewer ditches, when torn and defaced, so that they might not supply evidence of identity. So close is the connection between physical filthiness in public matters and moral wickedness.

The following particulars show the characteristics of the underground London of the sewers. The subterranean surveys were made after the commissions were consolidated.

"An old sewer, running between Great Smith-street and St. Ann-street (Westminster), is a curiosity among sewers, although it is probably only one instance out of many similar constructions that will be discovered in the course of the subterranean survey. The bottom is formed of planks laid upon transverse timbers, 6 inches by 6 inches, about 3 feet apart. The size of the sewer varies in width from 2 to 6 feet, and from 4 to 5 feet in height. The inclination of the bottom is very irregular: there are jumps up at two or three places, and it contains a deposit of filth averaging 9 inches in depth, the sickening smell from which escapes into the houses and yards that drain into it. In many places the side walls have given way for lengths of 10 and 15 feet. Across this sewer timbers have been laid, upon which the external wall of a workshop has been built; the timbers are in a decaying state, and should they give way, the wall will fall into the sewer."

From the further accounts of this survey, I find that a sewer from the Westminster Workhouse, which was of all shapes and sizes, was in so wretched a condition that the leveller could scarcely work for the thick scum that covered the glasses of the spirit-level in a few minutes after being wiped. "At the outfall into the Dean-street sewer, it is 3 feet 6 inches by 2 feet 8 inches for a short length. From the end of this, a wide sewer branches in each direction at right angles, 5 feet 8 inches by 5 feet 5 inches. Proceeding to the eastward about 30 feet, a chamber is reached about 30 feet in length, from the roof of which hangings of putrid matter *like stalactites* descend *three feet in length*. At the end of this chamber, the sewer passes under the public privies, the ceilings of which can be seen from it. Beyond this it is not possible to go."

"In the Lucas-street sewer, where a portion of new work begins and the old terminates, a space of about 10 feet has been covered with boards, which, having broken, a dangerous chasm has been caused immediately under the road."

"The West-street sewer had one foot of deposit. It was flushed while the levelling party was at work there, and the stream was so rapid that it nearly washed them away, instrument and all."

There are further accounts of "deposit," or of "stagnant filth," in other sewers, varying from 6 to 14 inches, but that is insignificant compared to what follows.

The foregoing, then, is the pith of the first authentic account which has appeared in print of the actually surveyed condition of the subterranean ways, over which the super-terranean tides of traffic are daily flowing.

The account I have just given relates to the (former) Westminster and part of Middlesex district on the north bank of the Thames, as ascertained under the Metropolitan Commission. I now give some extracts concerning a similar survey on the south bank, in different and distant directions in the district, once the "Surrey and Kent." The Westminster, &c., survey took place in 1848; the Kent and Surrey in 1849. In the one case, 72 miles of sewers were surveyed; in the other, 69⅛ miles.

"The surveyors (in the Surrey and Kent sewers) find great difficulty in levelling the sewers of this district (I give the words of the Report); for, in the first place, the deposit is *usually* about two feet in depth, and in some cases it amounts to nearly *five feet* of putrid matter. The smell is usually of the most horrible description, the air being so foul that explosion and choke damp are very frequent. On the 12th January we were very nearly losing a whole party by choke damp, the last man being dragged out on his back (through two feet of black fœtid deposits) in a state of insensibility. . . . . Two men of one party had also a narrow escape from drowning in the Alscot-road sewer, Rotherhithe.

"The sewers on the Surrey side are very irregular; even where they are inverted they frequently have a number of steps and inclinations the reverse way, causing the deposit to accumulate in *elongated cesspools*.

"It must be considered very fortunate that the subterranean parties did not first commence on the Surrey side, for if such had been the case, we should most undoubtedly have broken down. When compared with Westminster, the sewers are smaller and more full of deposit; and, bad as the smell is in the sewers in Westminster, it is infinitely worse on the Surrey side."

Several details are then given, but they are only particulars of the general facts I have stated.

The following, however, are distinct facts concerning this branch of the subject.

In my inquiries among the working scavagers I often heard of their emptying street slop into sewers, and the following extract shows that I was not misinformed:—

"The detritus from the macadamized roads frequently forms a kind of grouting in the sewers so hard that it cannot be removed without hand labour.

"One of the sewers in Whitehall and another in Spring-gardens have from three to four feet of this sort of deposit; and another in Eaton-square was found filled up within a few inches of the 'soffit,' but it is supposed that the scavengers (scavagers) emptied the road-sweepings down the gully-grate in this instance;" and in other instances, too, there is no doubt—especially at Charing Cross, and the Regent Circus, Piccadilly.

Concerning the sewerage of the most aristocratic parts of the city of Westminster, and of the fashionable squares, &c., to the north of Oxford-street, I glean the following particulars (reported in 1849). They show, at any rate, that the patrician quarters have not been unduly favoured; that there has been no partiality in the construction of the sewerage. In the Belgrave and Eaton-square districts there are many faulty places in the sewers which abound with noxious matter, in many instances stopping up the house drains and "smelling horribly." It is much the same in the Grosvenor, Hanover, and Berkeley-square localities (the houses in the squares themselves included). Also in the neighbourhood of Covent-garden, Clare-market, Soho and Fitzroy-squares; while north of Oxford-street, in and about Cavendish, Bryanstone, Manchester, and Portman-squares, there is so much rottenness and decay that there is no security for the sewers standing from day to day, and to flush them for the removal of their "most loathsome deposit" might be "to bring some of them down altogether."

One of the accounts of a subterranean survey concludes with the following rather curious statement:—"Throughout the new Paddington district the neighbourhood of Hyde Park Gardens, and the costly squares and streets adjacent, the sewers abound with the foulest deposit, from which the most disgusting effluvium arises; indeed, amidst the whole of the Westminster District of Sewers the *only* little spot which can be mentioned as being in at all a satisfactory state is the Seven Dials."

I may point out also that these very curious and authenticated accounts by no means bear out the zymotic doctrine of the Board of Health as to the cause of cholera; for where the zymotic influences from the sewers were the worst, in the patrician squares of what has been called Belgravia and Tyburnia, the cholera was the least destructive. This, however, is no reason whatever why the stench should not be stifled.

Of the House-Drainage of the Metropolis as connected with the Sewers.

EVERY house built or rebuilt since the passing of the Metropolitan Sewers Act in 1848, must be drained, with an exception, which I shall specify, into a sewer. The law, indeed, divested of its technicalities is this: the owner of a newly-erected house must drain it to a sewer, without the intervention of a cesspool, if there be a sewer within 100 feet of the site of the house; and, if necessary, in places but partially built over, such owner must continue the sewer along the premises, and make the necessary drain into it; all being done under the approval of the proper officer under the Commissioners. If there be, however, an established sewer, along the side, front, or back of any house, a covered drain must be made into that at the cost of the owner of the premises to be drained. "Where a sewer," says the 46th section of the Act, "shall already be made, and a drain only shall be required, the party is to pay a contribution towards the original expense of the sewer, if it shall have been made within thirty-five years before the 4th of September, 1848, the contribution to be paid to the builder of the sewer." . . . . . . "In cases where there shall be no sewer into which a drain could be made, the party must make a covered drain to lead into a cesspool or other place (not under a house) as the Commissioners may direct. If the parties infringe this rule, the Commissioners may do the work and throw the cost on them in the nature of an improvement rate, or as charges for default, and levy the amount by distress."

I mention these circumstances more particularly to show the extent, and the far-continued ramification, of the subterranean metropolis. I am assured by one of the largest builders in the western district of the capital that the new regulations (as to the dispensing with cesspools) are readily complied with, as it is a recommendation which a house agent, or any one letting new premises, is never slow to advance ("and when it's the truth," he said, "they do it with a better grace"), that there will be in the course of occupancy no annoyance and no expense incurred in the clearing away of cesspoolage.

I shall at present describe only the house-drainage, which is connected with the public sewerage. The old mode of draining a house separately into the cesspool of the premises will, of course, be described under the head of cesspoolage, and that old system is still very prevalent.

At the times of passing both general and local Acts concerning buildings, town improvements and extensions, the erection of new streets and the removal of old, much has been said and written concerning better systems of ventilating, warming, and draining dwelling-houses; but until after the first outbreak of cholera in England, in 1832, little public attention was given to the great drainage of all the sewers. However, on the passing of the Building and Sanitary Acts generally, the authorities made many experiments, not so much to improve the system of sewerage as of house-drainage, so as to make the dwelling-houses more wholesome and sweet.

To effect this, the great object was the abolition of the cesspool system, under which filth must accumulate, and where, from scamped buildings or other causes, evaporation took place, the effects of the system were found to be vile and offensive, and have been pronounced miasmatic. Having just alluded to these matters, I proceed to describe the modernly-adopted connection of house-drainage and street-sewerage.

Experiments, as I have said, were set on foot under the auspices of public bodies, and the opinions of eminent engineers, architects, and surveyors were also taken. Their opinions seem really to be concentrated in the advocacy of *one* remedy—improved house-drainage; and they appear to have agreed that the system which is at present adopted is, under the circumstances, the best that can be adopted.

I was told also by an eminent practical builder, perfectly unconnected with any official or public body, and, indeed, often at issue with surveyors, &c., that the new system was unquestionably a great improvement in every respect, and that some years before its adoption as at present he had abetted such a system, and had carried it into effect when he could properly do so.

I will first show the mode and then the cost of the new system.

I find it designated "back," "front," "tubular," and "pipe" house-drainage, and all with the object of carrying off all fæces, soil water, cesspool matter, &c., before it has had time to accumulate. It is not by brick or other drains of masonry that the system is carried out or is recommended to be carried out, but by means of tubular earthenware pipes; and for any efficient carrying out of the projected improvement a system of *constant*, and not as at present *intermittent*, supply of water from the several companies would be best. These pipes communicate with the nearest sewer. The pipes in the tubular drainage are of red earthenware or stoneware (pot).

The use of earthenware, clay, or pot pipes for the conveyance of liquids is very ancient. Mr. Stirrat, a bleacher in Paisley, in a statement to the Board of Health, mentioned that clay pipes were used in ancient times. King Hezekiah (2nd Book of Kings, chap. 20, and 2nd Book of Chronicles, chap. 32) brought in water from Jerusalem. "His pool and conduit," said Mr. Stirrat, "are still to be seen. The conduit is three feet square inside, built of freestone, strongly cemented; the stone, fifteen inches thick, evidently intended to sustain a considerable pressure; and I have seen pipes of clay, taken by a friend from a house in the ruins of the ancient city, of one inch bore, and about seven inches in diameter, proving evidently, to my mind, that ancient Jerusalem was supplied with water on the principle of gravitation. The pools or reservoirs are also at this day in tolerably good order, one of them still filled with water; the other broken down in the centre, no doubt by some besieging enemy, to cut off the supply to the city."

The new system to supply the place of the cesspools is a *combined*, while the old is principally a *separate*, system of house-drainage; but the new system is equally available for such separate drainage.

As regards the success of this system the reports say experiments have been tried in so large a number of houses, under such varied and, in many cases, disadvantageous circumstances, that no doubts whatsoever can remain in the minds of competent and disinterested persons as to the efficient self-cleansing action of well-adjusted tubular drains and sewers, even without any additional supplies of water.

Mr. Lovick said :—

"A great number of small 4-inch tubular drains have been laid down in the several districts, some for considerable periods. They have been found to keep themselves clear by the ordinary soil and drainage waters of the houses. I have no doubt that pipes of this kind will keep themselves clear by the ordinary discharge of house-drainage; assuming, of course, a supply of water, pipes of good form, and materials properly laid, and with fair usage."

"One of the earliest illustrations of the tubular system," it is stated in a Report of the Board of Health, "was given in the improved drainage of a block of houses in the cloisters of Westminster, which had been the seat of a severe epidemic fever. The cesspools and the old drains were filled up, and an entire system of tubular drainage and sewerage substituted for the service of that block of houses.

"The Dean of Westminster, in a letter on the state of this drainage, says, 'I beg to report to the Commissioners that the success of the entire new pipe-drainage laid down in St. Peter's College during the last twelve months has been complete. I consider this experiment on drainage and sewage of about fifteen houses to afford a triumphant proof of the efficacy of draining by pipes, and of the facility of *dispensing entirely with cesspools and brick sewers*.' Up to this time they have acted, and continue to act, perfectly.

"Mr. Morris, a surveyor attached to the Metropolitan Sewers Commission, gives the following account of the action of trial works of improved house-drainage:—

"'I have introduced the new 4-inch tubular house-drains into some houses for the trustees of the parish of Poplar, with water-closets, and have received no just cause of complaint. In every instance where I have applied it, I found the system answer extremely well, if a sufficient quantity of water has been used.

"'The answer of the householders as to the effect of the new drainage has invariably been that they and their families have been better in health; that they were formerly annoyed with smells and effluvia, from which they are now quite free.

"'Since the new drainage has been laid down there has been only occasion to go on the ground to examine it once for the whole year, and that was from the inefficiency of the water service. It was found that rags had been thrown down and had got into the pipe; and further, that very little water had been used, so that the stoppage was the fault of the tenant, not of the system.'"

Mr. Gotto, the engineer, having stated that in a plan for the improvement of Goulston-street, Whitechapel, not only was the removal of all cesspools contemplated, but also the substitution of water-closet apparatus, gave the following estimate of *the cost*, provided the pipes were made and the work done by contract under the Commissioners of Sewers:—

Water-closet Apparatus, &c.

	£	s.	d.
Emptying, &c., cesspool	0	12	0
Digging, &c., for 8-feet pipe drain, at 4d.	0	2	8
Making good to walls and floor of water-closet over drain, at 3d.	0	2	0
8 feet run of 4-inch pipe, at 3d.	0	2	0
Laying ditto, at 2d.	0	1	4
Extra for junction	0	0	4
Fixing ditto	0	0	2
Water-closet apparatus, with stool cock	0	10	0
Fixing ditto	0	2	0
Contingencies (10 per cent.)	0	3	6
	1	16	0

	£	s.	d.
Brought forward	1	16	0
The yard sink and drain would cost	0	11	2
Kitchen sink and drain	0	15	7½
So that the cost of *back* draining one house, including water-closet, would be	3	2	9½

The *front* tubular drainage of a similar house (with fifteen yards of carriage-way to be paved) would cost 6l. 2s. 7½d.; or the drainage would cost, according to the old system, 11l. 13s. 11d.

"The engineering witnesses who have given their special attention to the subject," state the Board of Health, in commenting on the information I have just cited, "affirm that upon the improved system of combined works the expense of the apparatus in substitution of cesspools would *not greatly exceed one-half the expense* of cleaning the cesspools."

The engineers have calculated — stating the difficulty of coming to a nice calculation — that the present system of cesspools entailed an average expenditure, for cleansing and repairs, of 4d. a week on each householder; and that by the new system it would be but 1¾d. The Board of Health's calculations, however, are, I regret to say, always dubious.

The subjoined scale of the difference in cost was prepared at the instance of the Board.

Mr. Grant took four blocks of houses for examination, and the results are given as a guide to what would be the general expenditure if the change took place:—

"In one block of 44 houses—
The length of drains by back drainage was 1544 feet.
Cost (exclusive of pans, traps, and water in both cases) of back drainage, 83l. 12s., or 1l. 18s. per house.
Cost of separate tubular drainage, 467l. 9s. 6d., or 10l. 12s. 6d. per house.
Cost of separate brick drains, 910l. 19s., or 20l. 14s. 1d. per house.

"In another block of 23 houses—
The length of back drains was 783 feet.
Of separate drains, 1437 feet.
The cost of back tubular drains, 45l. 12s. 6d., or 1l. 19s. 8d. per house.
Of separate tubular drains, 131l. 13s. 6d., or 5l. 14s. 6d. per house.
Of separate brick drains, 305l.7s., or 13l. 5s. 6d. per house.

"In another block of 46 houses—
The length of back drainage, 1143 feet.
Ditto by separate ditto, 1892 feet.
The cost of back tubular drainage, 66l. 5s. 2d., or 1l. 8s. 9¾d. per house.
Ditto of separate ditto ditto, 178l. 19s. 8d., or 3l. 17s. 10d. per house.
Ditto of separate brick ditto, 390l. 4s., or 8l. 9s. 8d. per house.

" In a fourth block of 46 houses—
  The length of back drains, 985 feet.
  Ditto of separate ditto, 2913 feet.
  Cost of back tubular drainage, 66*l*. 8*s*. 2*d*., or 1*l*. 8*s*. 10½*d*. per house.
  Ditto of separate ditto ditto, 262*l*. 11*s*. 7*d*., or 5*l*. 14*s*. 2*d*. per house.
  Ditto of separate brick ditto, 614*l*. 16*s*. 3*d*., or 13*l*. 7*s*. 3¾*d*. per house."

I have mentioned the diversity of opinion as to the best form, and even material, for a sewer; and there is the same diversity as to the material, &c., for house and gully or street-drainage, more especially in the *pipes* of the larger volume. The pipe-drainage of any description is far less in favour than it was. One reason is that it does not promote *subsoil drainage;* another is the difficulty of repairs if the joints or fittings of pipes require mending; and then the combination of the noxious gases is most offensive in its exhalations, and difficult to overcome.

I was informed by a nightman, used to the cleansing of drains and to night-work generally, that when there was any escape from one of the tubular pipes the stench was more intense than any he had ever before experienced from any drains on the old system.

Of the London Street-Drains.

We have as yet dealt only with the means of removing the liquid refuse from the houses of the metropolis. This, as was pointed out at the commencement of the present subject, consists principally of the 19,000,000,000 gallons of water that are annually supplied to the London residences by mechanical means. But there still remain the 5,000,000,000 gallons of surface or rain-water to be carried off from the 1760 miles of streets, and the roofs and yards of the 300,000 houses which now form the British metropolis. If this immense volume of liquid were not immediately removed from our thoroughfares as fast as it fell, many of our streets would not only be transformed into canals at certain periods of the year, but perhaps at all times (except during drought) they would be, if not impassable, at least unpleasant and unhealthy, from the puddles or small pools of stagnant water that would be continually rotting them. Were such the case, the roads and streets that we now pride ourselves so highly upon would have their foundations soddened. " If the surface of a road be not kept clean so as to admit of its becoming dry between showers of rain," said Lord Congleton, the great road authority, " it will be rapidly worn away." Indeed the immediate removal of rain-water, so as to prevent its percolating through the surface of the road, and thereby impairing the foundation, appears to be one of the main essentials of road-making.

The means of removing this surface water, especially from the streets of a city where the rain falls at least every other day throughout the year, and reaches an aggregate depth of 24 feet in the course of the twelvemonth, is a matter of considerable moment. In Paris, and indeed almost all of the French towns, a channel is formed in the middle of each thoroughfare, and down this the water from the streets and houses is continually coursing, to the imminent peril of all pedestrians, for the wheels of every vehicle distribute, as it goes, a muddy shower on either side of the way.

We, however, have not only removed the channels from the middle to the sides of our streets, but instituted a distinct system of drainage for the conveyance of the wet refuse of our houses to the sewers—so that there are no longer (excepting in a very small portion of the suburbs) open sewers, meandering through our highways; the consequence is, the surface-water being carried off from our thoroughfares almost as fast as it falls, our streets are generally dry and clean. That there are exceptions to this rule, which are a glaring disgrace to us, it must be candidly admitted ; but we must at the same time allow, when we think of the vast extent of the roadways of the metropolis (1760 miles !— nearly one-half the radius of the earth itself), the deluge of water that annually descends upon every inch of the ground which we call London (38,000,000,000 gallons !—a quantity which is almost sufficient for the formation of an American lake), and the vast amount of traffic, over the greater part of the capital—the 13,000 vehicles that daily cross London Bridge, the 11,000 conveyances that traverse Cheapside in the course of twelve hours, the 7700 that go through Temple Bar, and the 6900 that ascend and descend Holborn Hill between nine in the morning and nine at night, the 1500 omnibuses and the 3000 cabriolets that are continually hurrying from one part of the town to another, and the 10,000 private carriage, job, and cart horses that incessantly *perviate* the metropolis—when we reflect, I say, on this vast amount of traffic—this deluge of rain—and the wilderness of streets, it cannot but be allowed that the cleansing and draining of the London thoroughfares is most admirably conducted.

The mode of street drainage is by means of what is called a gully-hole and a gully-drain.

The Gully-hole[*] is the opening from the surface of the street (and is seen generally on each side of the way), into which all the fluid refuse of the public thoroughfares runs on its course to the sewer.

The Gully-drain is a drain generally of earthenware piping, curving from the side of the street to an opening in the top or side of the sewer, and is the means of communication between the sewer and the gully-hole.

The gully-hole is indicated by an iron grate being fitted into the surface of the side of a footpath, where the road slopes gradually from its centre to the edge of the footpath, and down this grate the water runs into the channel contrived

---

[*] *Gully* here is a corruption of the word *Gullet*, or throat; the Norman is *guelle* (Lat. *gula*), and the French, *goulet;* from this the word *gully* appears to be directly derived. A *gully*-drain is literally a *gullet*-drain, that is, a drain serving the purposes of a gullet or channel for liquids, and a gully-hole the mouth, orifice, or opening to the *gullet* or gully-drain.

for it in the construction of the streets. These gully-grates, the observant pedestrian—if there be a man in this hive of London who, without professional attraction to the matter, regards for a few minutes the peculiarities of the street (apart from the houses) which he is traversing—an observant pedestrian, I say, would be struck at the constantly-recurring grates in a given space in some streets, and their paucity in others. In Drury-lane there is no gully-grate, as you walk down from Holborn to where Drury-lane becomes Wych-street; whilst in some streets, not a tenth of the length of Drury-lane, there may be three, four, five, or six grates. The reason is this:— There is no sewer running down Drury-lane; a contiguous sewer, however, runs down Great Wyld-street, draining, where there are drains, the hundred courts and nooks of the poor, between Drury-lane and Lincoln's-inn-fields, as well as the more open places leading down towards the proximity of Temple Bar. This Great Wyld-street sewer, moreover, in its course to Fleet Bridge, is made available for the drainage (very grievously deficient, according to some of the reports of the Board of Health) of Clare-market. Grates would of course be required in such a place as Drury-lane, only the street is thought to be sufficiently on the descent to convey the surface-water to the grate in Wych-street.

The parts in which the gully-grates will be found the most numerous are where the main streets are most intersected by other main streets, or by smaller off-streets, and indeed wherever the streets, of whatever size, continually intersect each other, as they do off nearly all the great street-thoroughfares in the City. Although the sewers may not be according to the plan of the streets, the gully-grates must nevertheless be found at the street intersections, whether the nearest point to the sewer or not, or else the water would not be quickly carried off, and would form a nuisance.

I am informed, on good authority, both as regards the City and Metropolitan Commissions, that the average distance of the gully-grates is thirty yards one from another, including both sides of the way. Their number does not depend upon population, but simply on the local characteristics of the highways; for of course the rain falls into all the streets in proportion to their size, whether populous or half-empty localities. As, however, the more distant roads have not such an approximation of grates, and the law which requires their formation is by no means—and perhaps, without unnecessary interference, cannot be—very definite, I am informed that it may fairly be represented, that, of the 1760 miles of London public ways, more than two-thirds, " or " remarked one informant, " say 1200 miles, are grated on *each* side of the street or road, at distances of sixty yards." This would give 59 gully-holes in every one of the 1200 miles of street said to be so supplied. Hence the total number throughout the metropolis will be 70,800.

The gully-drain, which is the street-drain, always presents now a sloping curve, describing, more or less, part of a circle. This drain starts, so to speak, from the side of the street, while its course to the sewer, in order to economize space, is made by any most appropriate curve, to include the reception of as great a quantity of wet street-refuse as possible; for if the gully-drains were formed in a direct, or even a not-very-indirect line, from the street sides to the sewers, they would not only be more costly, more numerous, but would, in fact, as I was told, " choke the under-ground " of London, for now the subterranean capital is so complicated with gas, water, and drain-pipes, that such a system as will allow room for each is indispensable. The new system is, moreover, more economical. In the City the gully-drains are nearly all of nine-inch diameter in tubular pipeage. In the metropolitan jurisdiction they are the same, but not to the same extent, some being only six inches.

Fifty, or even thirty years ago, the old street channels for gully drainage were costly constructions, for they were made so as to suit sewers which were cleansed by the street being taken " up," and the offensive deposit, thick and even indurated as it often was in those days, drawn to the surface. Some few were three and even four feet square; some two feet six inches wide, and three or four feet high; all of brick. I am assured that of the extent or cost of these old contrivances no accounts have been preserved, but that they were more than twice as costly as the present method.

In all the reports I have seen, metropolitan or city—the statements of the flushermen being to the same purport—there are complaints as to the uses to which the gully-holes are put in many parts, every kind of refuse admissible through the bars of the grate being stealthily emptied down them. The paviours, if they have an opportunity, sweep their surplus grout into the gullies, and so do the scavagers with their refuse occasionally, though this is generally done in the less-frequented parts, to get rid of the "slop," which is valueless.

In a report, published in 1851, Mr. Haywood points out the prevalence of the practice of using the gully-gratings as dustbins! A sewer under Billingsgate accumulated in a few months many cart-loads, composed almost wholly of fish-shells; and 114 cart-loads of fish-shells, cinders, and rubbish were removed from the sewers in the vicinity of Middlesex-street (Petticoat-lane); these had accumulated in about twelve months. "Reconstructing the gullies," he says, "so as to intercept improper substances (which has been recently done at Billingsgate), might prevent this material reaching the sewers, but it would still have to be removed from the gullies, and would thus still cause perpetual expense. Indeed, I feel convinced that nothing but making public example by convicting and punishing some offenders, under clause 69 of 'The City of London Sewers' Act,' will stop the practice, so universal in the poorer localities, of using the gullies as dustbins."

The Gully-holes are now trapped—with very few exceptions, one report states, while another report intimates that gully-trapping has no exception at all. The trap is resorted to so that the effluvium from a gully-drain may not infect the air of the public ways; but among engineers and medical sanitary inquirers, there is much difference of opinion as to whether the system of trapping is desirable or not. The general opinion seems to be, however, that all gullies should be trapped.

Of the City gully-traps, Mr. Haywood, in a report for the year 1851, says, as regards the period of their introduction:—

"About seventeen years ago your then surveyor (Mr. Kelsey) applied the first traps to sewer gullies, and from that date to the present the trapping of gullies has been adopted as a principle, and the city of London is still, I believe, the only metropolitan area in which the gullies are all trapped. The traps first constructed have since been (as all first inventions or adaptations ever have or will be) improved upon, and are rapidly being displaced by those of more improved construction.

"Now, of the incompatible conditions required of gully-traps, of the difficulty of obtaining such mechanical appliances so effective and perfect as can *theoretically* be devised, but yet of the extreme desirability of obtaining them as perfect as modern science could produce, your honourable court has, at least, for as long as I have had the honour of holding office under you, been fully alive to; no prejudice has opposed impediment to the introduction of novelties; your court has been always open to inventors, and, at the present time, there are sixteen different traps or modes of trapping gullies under trial within your jurisdiction.

"Nor has the provision of the means of excluding effluvium from the atmosphere been your only care; but the cleanliness of the sewers, and the prevention of accumulation of decomposing refuse, both by regulated cleansings, and by constructing the sewage upon the most improved principles, have also been your aim and that of your officers; and I do not hesitate to assert, that the offensiveness of the escape from the gullies has been of late years much diminished by the care bestowed upon the condition of the sewers.

"374 gullies have been retrapped in the City upon improved principles during the last year."

The gully-traps are on the principle of self-acting valves, but it is stated in several reports, that these valves often remain permanently open, partly from the street refuse (especially if mixed with the débris from new or removed buildings) not being sufficiently liquified to pass through them, and partly from the hinges getting rusted, and so becoming fixed.

OF THE LENGTH OF THE LONDON SEWERS AND DRAINS.

THERE is no official account precisely defining the length of the London sewerage; but the information acquired on the subject leaves no doubt as to the accuracy of the following facts.

About 900 miles of sewers of the metropolis may be said to have been surveyed; and it is known that from 100 to 150 miles more constitute a portion of the metropolitan sewerage; this, too, independently of that of the City, which is 50 miles. Altogether I am assured that the sewers of the urban part of London, included within the 58 square miles before mentioned, measure 1100 miles.

The classes of sewers comprised in this long extent are pretty equally apportioned, each a third, or 366 miles, of the first, second, and third classes respectively. Of this extent about 200 miles are still, in the year 1852, *open* sewers!—to say nothing of the great open sewer, the Thames. The open sewers are found principally in the Surrey districts, in Brixton, Lewisham, Tooting, and places at the like distance from the more central parts of the Commissioners' jurisdiction. These open sewers, however, are disappearing, and it is intended that in time no such places shall exist; as it is, some miles of them are inclosed yearly. The open sewers in what may be considered more of the heart of the metropolis are a portion of the Fleet-ditch in Clerkenwell, and places in Lambeth and Bermondsey, or about 20 miles in the interior to 180 miles in the exterior portion of the capital. These are national disgraces.

The 1100 miles above-mentioned, however, include only the sewers, comprising neither the house nor gully-drains. According to the present laws, all newly-built houses must be drained into the sewers; and in 1850 there were 5000 applications from the western districts alone to the Commissioners, for the promotion of the drainage of that number of old and new houses into the sewers, the old houses having been previously drained into cesspools.

I am assured, on good authority, that fully one-half of the houses in the metropolis are at the present time drained into the sewers. In one street, about a century old, containing in the portion surveyed for an official purpose, on the two sides of the way, 76 houses, the number was found to be equally divided—half the drainage being into sewers and half into cesspools. The number of houses in the metropolis proper, of 115 square miles area, is 307,722. The majority, as far as is officially known, are now drained into the public sewers, or into private or branch sewers communicating with the larger public receptacles, so that—allowing 200,000 houses to be included in the 58 square miles of the urban sewerage, and admitting that some wretched dwelling-places are not drained at all—it is reasonable to assume that at least 100,000 houses within this area are drained into the sewers.

The average length of the house-drains is, I learn from the best sources, 50 feet per house. The builder of a new house is now required by law to drain it, at the proprietor's cost, 100 feet, if necessary, to a sewer. In some instances, in detached houses, where the owners object to the cesspool system, a house drain has been carried 230 feet to a sewer, and sometimes even farther; but in narrow or moderately wide streets, from 18 to 26 feet across, and in alleys and narrow places (in case there is sewerage) the house drains may be but from 12 to 20 feet. Both these lengths of drainage are exceptions, and there is no question that the average length may be put at 50 feet. In some squares, for example, the sewer runs along the centre, so that the house-drains here are in excess of the 50 feet average.

The length of the house-drainage of the more central part of London, assuming 100,000 houses to be drained into the sewers, and each of such drains to be on the average 50 feet long, is, then, 5,000,000 feet, or about 2840 miles.

But there are still the street or gully-drains for the surface-water to be estimated. In the Holborn and Finsbury division alone, the length of the "main covered sewers" is said to be 83 miles; the length of "smaller sewers" to carry off the surface-water from the streets 16 miles; the length of drains leading from houses to the main sewers, 264.

Now, if there be 16 miles of gully-drains to 83 miles of main covered sewers, and the same proportion hold good throughout the 58 square miles over which the sewers extend, it follows that there would be about 200 miles of gully-drains to the gross 1100 miles of sewers.

But this is only an approximate result. The length and character of the gully-drains I find to vary very considerably. If the streets where the gully-grates are found have no sewer in a line with the thoroughfare, still the water must be drained off and conveyed to the nearest sewer, of any class, large or small, and consequently at much greater length than if there were a sewer running down the street. Neither is the number of the gully-holes any sure criterion of the measurement of the gully-drains, for where the intersections are, and consequently the gully-holes frequent, a number, sometimes amounting to ten, are made to empty their contents into the same gully-drain. Neither do the returns of yearly expenditure, presented to Parliament by the Metropolitan Court of Sewers, supply information. But even if the exact length, and the exact price paid for the formation of that length, were given, it would supply but *the year's* outlay as regards the additions or repairs that had been made to the gully-drains, and certainly not furnish us with the original cost of the whole.

One experienced informant told me—but let me premise that I heard from all the gentlemen whom I consulted, a statement that they could only compute by analogy with other facts bearing upon the subject—was confident, that taking only 1200 miles of public way as gully-drained, that extent might be considered as the length of the gully-drains themselves. Even calculating such drains to run from each side of the public way, which is generally the case, I am told that, considering the economy of underground space which is now necessary, the length of 1200 miles is as fair an estimate for gully-drainage (apart from other drainage) as for the length of the streets so gullied.

Hence we have, for the gross extent of the whole sewers and drains of the metropolis, the following result,—

	Miles.
Main covered sewers . . .	1100
House-drains	2840
Gully-drains for surface-water of streets	1200
Total length of the sewers and drains of the metropolis . .	5140

The island of Great Britain, I may observe, is, at its extreme points, 550 miles from north to south, and 290 from east to west. It would, therefore, appear that the main sewers of the capital are just double the length of the whole island, from the English Channel to John-o'-Groats, and nearly three times longer than the greatest width of the country. But this is the extent of the sewerage alone. The drainage of London is about equal in length to the diameter of the earth itself!

OF THE COST OF CONSTRUCTING THE SEWERS AND DRAINS OF THE METROPOLIS.

THE money actually expended in constructing the 1100 miles of sewers and 4000 miles of drains, even if we were only to date from Jan. 1, 1800, is not and never can be known. They have been built at intervals, as the metropolis, so to speak, *grew*. They were built also in many sizes and forms, and at many variations of price, according to the depth from the surface, the good or bad management, or the greater or lesser extent of jobbery or "patronage" in the several independent commissions. Accounts were either not presented in "the good old times," or not preserved.

Had the 1100 miles of sewers to be constructed anew, they would be, according to the present prices paid by the Commissioners—not including digging or such extraneous labour, but the cost of the sewer only—as follows:—

366 miles of sewers of the first class, or 1,932,480 feet, at 15s. per foot	£1,449,360
366 miles, or 1,932,480 feet of the second class, at 11s. per foot .	1,062,864
Same length of third class, at 9s. per foot	869,616
Total cost of the sewers of the metropolis	£3,381,840

As this is a lower charge than was paid for the construction of more than three-fourths of the sewers, we may fairly assume that their cost amounted to from three millions and a half to four millions of pounds sterling.

The majority of the house-drains running into the sewers are brick, and seldom less than 9 inches square; sometimes, in the old brick drains, they are some inches larger, and in the very old drains, and in some 100 years old, wooden planks were often used instead of a brick or stone construction, for the sake of reducing cost, and replaced when rotted. The wood, in many cases, soon decayed, and since 1847 no wooden sewers have been allowed to be formed, nor any old ones to be repaired with new wood; the work must be of stone or brick, if not pipeage. About two-thirds of the drains running from the houses to the sewers are brick; the remaining third tubular, or earthenware pipes. The cost, if now to be formed, would be somewhat as follows :—

1893⅓ miles of brick drains, 5s. per foot, as average of sizes . . £2,499,200
945⅔ feet of tubular drains, average of sizes 2s. 6d. . . . 624,800

Total cost of the house-drains of London £3,124,000

The cost of the street or gully drains have still to be estimated.

The present cost of the 9-inch gully-pipe drains is about 3s. 6d. a foot; of the 6-inch, 2s. 6d. Of the proportionate lengths of these two classes of street-drains I have not been able to gain any account, for, I believe, it has never been ascertained in any way approaching to a total return. Taking 1200 miles, however, as quite within the full length of the gully-drains, and calculating at the low average of 3s. the foot for the whole, the total cost of the street-drains of the metropolis would be 950,400l., or, I am assured, one might say a million sterling, and this, even if all were done at the present low prices; the original cost would, of course, have been much greater.

Hence, according to the above calculations, we have the following

Gross Estimate of the Cost of the Sewers and Drains of the Metropolis.

	£
1100 miles of main covered sewers	3,500,000
2840 miles of house-drains . .	3,000,000
1200 miles of gully or street drains	1,000,000
5140 miles of sewers and drainage =	7,500,000

Of the Uses of Sewers as a Means of Subsoil Drainage.

There is one other purpose toward which a sewer is available—a purpose, too, which I do not remember to have seen specified in the Metropolitan Reports.

"The first, and perhaps most important purpose of sewers, as respects health," says the Report of Messrs. Walker, Cubitt, and Brunel (1848), "is, *as under-drains to the surrounding earth*. They answer this purpose so effectually and quietly, and have done it so long, that their importance in this respect is overlooked. In the Sanitary Commissioners' Reports we do not find it once noticed, and the recommendation of the substitution of stone or earthenware pipes for the larger brick sewers, seems to show, that any provision for the *under-drainage* was thought unnecessary, although such a provision is in our opinion most important.

"Under the artificial ground, the collection of ages, which in the City of London, as in most ancient towns, forms the upper surface, is a considerable thickness of clean gravel, and under the gravel is the London clay. The present houses are founded chiefly on the artificial or 'made ground,' while the sewers are made through the gravel; and it is known practically, that however charged with water the gravel of a district may be, the springs for a considerable distance round are drawn down by making a sewer, and the wells that had water within a few feet of the surface have again to be sunk below the bottom of the sewer to reach the water. Every interstice between the stones of the gravel acts as an under-drain to conduct the water to the sewer, through the sides of which it finds its way, even if mortar be used in the construction.

"Hence the salubrity of a gravel foundation, if the water be drawn out of it by sewers or other means, as is the case with the City and with Westminster. A proof of this principle was afforded by the result of a reference to physicians and engineers in 1838, to inquire into the state of drainage and smells in and near Buckingham Palace, as to which there had been complaints, though none so heavy as Mr. Phillips now makes, when he says, 'that the drainage of Buckingham Palace is extremely defective, and that its precincts are reeking with filth and pestilential odours from the absence of proper sewerage!'"

The Report then shows the pains that were taken to ensure dryness in the Palace. Pits were dug in the garden 14 feet below the surface, and 3½ feet below high-water mark in the river, and they were found dry to the bottom. The kitchens and yard of the palace are, however, only 18 inches above Trinity high-water mark in the Thames, and therefore 18 inches below a very high tide. The physician, Sir James Clarke, and the engineers, Messrs. Simpson and Walker, in a separate Report, spoke in terms of commendation of the drainage of the Palace in 1838, as promotive of dryness. Since that time a connecting chain has been made from the Palace drains into the canal in St. James's-park, to prevent the wet from rising as formerly during heavy rains. "The Palace," it is stated in the Report of the three engineers, "should not be classed with the low part of Pimlico, where the drainage is, we believe, very defective, and to which, for anything we know to the contrary, the character given by Mr. Phillips may be applicable."

Unfortunately, however, for this array of opinions of high authority, and despite the advantages of a gravel bed for the substratum of the palatial sewerage, the drainage and sewerage about Buckingham Palace is more frequently than that of any other public place under repair, and is always requiring attention. It was only a few days ago, before the court left Windsor Castle for London, that men were employed night and day, on the drains and cesspoolage channels, to make, as one of them described it to me—and such working-men's descriptions are often forcible—"the place *decent*. I was hardly ever," he added, "in such a set of stinks as I've been in the sewers and underground parts of the palace."

Of the City Sewerage.

As yet I have spoken only of the sewers of London* "without the City;" but the sewers within the City, though connected, for the general public drainage and sewerage of the capital, with the works under the control of the Metropolitan Commissioners, are in a distinct and strictly defined jurisdiction, superintended by City Commissioners, and managed by City officers, and consequently demand a special notice.

* Of the derivation of the word *Sewer* there have been many conjectures, but no approximation to the truth. One of the earliest instances I have met with of any detailed mention of sewers, is in an address delivered by a "Coroner," whose name does not appear, to "a jury of sewers." This address was delivered somewhere between the years 1660 and 1670. The coroner having first spoken of the importance of "Navigation and Drayning" (draining), then came to the question of sewers.

"Sewars," he said, "are to be accounted your grand Issuers of Water, from whence I conceive they carry their name (*Sewars quasi Issuers*). I shall take his opinion who delivers them to be Currents of Water, kept in on both sides with banks, and, in some sense, they may be called a certain kind of a little or small river. But as for the derivation of the word Sewar, from two of our English words, *Sea* and *Were*, or, as others will have it, *Sea* and *Ward*, give me leave, now I have mentioned it, to—leave it to your judgments.

"However, this word *Sewar* is very famous amongst us, both for giving the title of the Commission of Sewars itself, and for being the ordinary name of most of your common water-courses, for Drayning, and therefore, I presume, there are none of you of these juries but both know—

"1. What Sewars signify, and also, in particular,

"2. What they are; and of a thing so generally known, and of such general use."

The Rev. Dr. Lemon, who gave the world a work on "English Etymology," from the Greek and Latin, and from the Saxon and Norman, was regarded as a high authority during the latter part of the last century, when his quarto first appeared. The following is his account, under the head "Sewers":—

"Skinn. rejects Minsh's. deriv. of 'olim scriptum fuisse *seward* à sea-ward, quod versus mare factæ sunt: longè verisimilius à Fr. Gall. *eauier;* sentina; *incile*, supple. aquarum:'—then why did not the Dr. trace this Fr. Gall. *eauier?* if he had, he would have found it distorted ab 'Υδωρ, *aqua; sewers* being a species of *aqueduct:*—Lye, in his Add., gives another deriv., viz. ' ab Iceland. *sua, colare;* ut existimo; ad quod referre vellem *sewer; cloaca;* per *sordes* urbis ejiciuntur:'—the very word *sordes* gives me a hint that *sewer* may be derived à 'Σαιρω, vel Σαροω, *verro:* nempe quia *sordes*, quæ *everruntur* è domo, in unum locum *accumulantur;* R. Σωρος, *cumulus:* Voss.'—*a collection of sweepings, slop, dirt, &c.*"

But these are the follies of learning. Had our lexicographers known that the vulgar were, as Dr. Latham says, "the conservators of the Saxon language" with us, they would have sought information from the word "shore," which the uneducated, and, consequently, unperverted, invariably use in the place of the more polite "sewer"—the common *sewer* is always termed by them "the common *shore*." Now the word *shore*, in Saxon, is written *score* and *scor* (for *c = h*), and means not only a bank, the land immediately next to the sea, but a *score*, a tally—for they are both substantives, made from the verb *sceran* (p. *scear, scær*, pp. *scoren, gescoren*), to *shear*, cut off, *share*, divide; and hence they meant, in the one case, the division of the land from the sea; and in the other, a division cut in a piece of wood, with a view to counting. The substantive *scar* has the same origin; as well as the verb to *score*, to cut, to gash. The Scandinavian cognates for the Saxon *scor* may be cited as proofs of what is here asserted. They are, Icel., *skor*, a notch; Swed., *skåra*, a notch; and Dan., *skaar* and *skure*, a notch, an incision. It would seem, therefore, that the word *shore*, in the sense of *sewer* (Dan., *skure;* Anglice, *shure*, for *k = h*), originally meant merely a *score* or incision made in the ground, a *ditch* sunk with the view of carrying off the refuse-water, a watercourse, and consequently a drain. A sewer is now a covered ditch, or channel for refuse water.

The account of the City sewers, however, may be given with a comparative brevity, for the modes of their construction, as well as their general management, do not differ from what I have described as pertaining to the extra-civic metropolis. There are, nevertheless, a few distinctions which it is proper to point out.

The City sewers are the oldest in the capital, for the very plain reason that the City itself, in its site, if not now in its public and private buildings, is the oldest part of London, as regards the abode of a congregated body of people.

The ages (so to speak) of these sewers, vary, for the most part, according to the dates of the City's rebuilding after the Great Fire, and according to the dates of the many alterations, improvements, removal or rebuilding of new streets, markets, &c., which have been effected since that period. Before the Great Fire of 1666, all drainage seems, with a few exceptions, to have been fortuitous, unconnected, and superficial.

The *first* public sewer built after this important epoch in the history of London was in Ludgate-street and hill. This was the laudable work of the Dean and Chapter of St. Paul's, and was constructed at the instance, it is said, and after the plans, of Sir Christopher Wren. There is, perhaps, no official or documentary proof of this, for the proclamations from the King in council, the Acts of Parliament, and the resolutions of the Corporation of the City of London at that important period, are so vague and so contradictory, and were so frequently altered or abrogated, and so frequently disregarded, that it is more impossible than difficult to get at the truth. Of the fact which I have just mentioned, however, there need be no doubt; nor that the *second* public City sewer was in Fleet-street, commenced in 1668, the second year after the fire.

There are, nevertheless, older sewers than this, but the dates of their construction are not known; we have proof merely that they existed in old London, or as it was described by an anonymous writer (quoted, if I remember rightly, in Maitland's "History of London"), London "*ante ignem*"—London before the fire. These sewers, or rather portions of sewers, are severally near Newgate, St. Bartholomew's Hospital sewer, and that of the Irongate by the Tower.

The sewer, however, which may be pointed out as the most remarkable is that of Little Moorgate, London-wall. It is formed of red tiles; and from such being its materials, and from the circumstance of some Roman coins having been found near it, it is supposed by some to be of Roman construction, and of course coeval with that people's possession of the country. This sewer has a flat bottom, upright sides, and a circular arch at its top; it is about 5 feet by 3 feet. The other older sewers present much about the same form; and an Act in the reign of Charles II. directs that sewers shall be so built, but that the bottom shall have a circular curve.

I am informed by a City gentleman—one taking an interest in such matters—that this sewer has troubled the repose of a few civic antiquaries, some thinking that it was a Roman sewer, while others scouted such a notion, arguing that the Romans were not in the habit of doing their work by halves; and that if they had sewered London, great and enduring remains would have been discovered, for their main sewer would have been a solid construction, and directed to the Thames, as was and is the Cloaca Maxima, in the Eternal City, to the Tiber. Others have said that the sewer in question was merely built of Roman materials, perhaps first discovered about the time, having originally formed a reservoir, tank, or even a bath, and were keenly appropriated by some economical or scheming builder or City official.

"That the Britons," says Tacitus in his "Life of Agricola," "who led a roaming life, and were easily incited to war, might contract a love for peace, by being accustomed to a pleasanter mode of life, Agricola assisted them to build houses, temples, and market-places. By praising the diligent and upbraiding the idle, he excited such emulation among the Britons, that, after they had erected all those necessary buildings in their towns, they built others for pleasure and ornament, as porticoes, galleries, *baths*, and banqueting-houses."

The sewers of the city of London are, then, a comparatively modern work. Indeed, three-fourths of them may be called modern. The earlier sewers were—as I have described under the general head—ditches, which in time were arched over, but only gradually and partially, as suited the convenience or the profit of the owners of property alongside those open channels, some of which thus presented the appearance of a series of small uncouth-looking bridges. When these bridges had to be connected so as to form the summit of a continuous sewer, they presented every variety of arch, both at their outer and under sides; those too near the surface had to be lowered. Some of these sewers, however, were in the first instances connected, despite difference of size and irregularity of form. The result may be judged from the account I have given of the strange construction of some of the Westminster sewers, under the head of "subterranean survey."

How modern the City sewers are may best be estimated from the following table of what may be called the dates of their construction. The periods are given decennially as to the progress of the formation of *new* sewers:—

	Feet.		Feet.
1707 to 1717	2,805	1777 to 1787	8,693
1717 „ 1727	2,110	1787 „ 1797	3,118
1727 „ 1737	2,763	1797 „ 1807	5,116
1737 „ 1747	1,238	1807 „ 1817	5,097
1747 „ 1757	3,736	1817 „ 1827	7,847
1757 „ 1767	3,736		
1767 „ 1777	7,597		52,810
1827 to 1837	. . .	39,072 feet.	
1837 to 1847	. . .	88,363 „	
		127,435	

Thus the length made in the 20 years previous to 1847 was more than double all that was made during the preceding 120 years; while in the ten years from 1837 to 1847, the addition to the lineal extent of sewerage was very nearly equal to all that had been made in 130 years previously.

This addition of 127,435 feet, or rather more than 24 miles, seems but a small matter when "London" is thought of; but the reader must be reminded that only a small portion (comparatively) of the metropolis is here spoken of, and the entire length of the City sewerage, at the close of 1847, was but 44 miles; so that the additions I have specified as having been made since 1837, were more than one-half of the whole. The *re*-constructions are not included in the metage I have given, for, as the new sewers generally occupied the same site as the old, they did not add to the length of the whole.

The total length of the City sewerage was, on the 31st December, 1851, no less than 49 miles; while the entire public way was at the same recent period, 51 miles (containing about 1000 separate and distinct streets, lanes, courts, alleys, &c., &c.); and I am assured that in another year or so, not a furlong of the whole City will be unsewered.

"The more ancient sewers usually have upright walls, a flat or slightly-curved invert, and a semi-circular or gothic arch. The form of such as have been built apparently more than 20 years ago, is that of two semicircles, of which the upper has a greater radius, connected by sloping side walls; those of recent construction are egg-shaped. The main lines are not unfrequently elliptic; in the case of the Fleet, and other ancient affluents of the Thames, the forms and dimensions vary considerably. Instances occur of sewers built entirely of stone; but the material is almost invariably brick, most commonly 9 inches in substance; the larger sewers 14, and sometimes 18 inches.

The falls or inclinations in the course of the City sewerage vary greatly, as much as from 1 in 240 to 1 in 24, or, in the first case, from a fall of 22 feet, in the latter, of course, to ten times such fall, or 220 feet per mile. There are, moreover, a few cases in which the inclination is as small as 1 in 960; others where it is as high as 1 in 14. This irregularity is to be accounted for, partly by the want of system in the old times, and partly from the natural levels of the ground. The want of system and the indifference shown to providing a proper fall, even where it was not difficult, was more excusable a few years back than it would be at the present time, for when some of these sewers were built, the drainage of the house-refuse into them was not contemplated.

The number of houses drained into the City sewers is, as precisely as such a matter can be ascertained, 11,209; the number drained into the cesspools is 5030. This shows a preponderance of drainage into the sewers of 6179. The length of the house-drains in the City, at an average of 50 feet to each house, may be estimated at upwards of 106 miles. These City drains are included in the general computation of the metropolis.

The gully-drains in the City are more frequent than in other parts of the metropolis, owing to the continual intersection of streets, &c., and perhaps from a closer care of the sewerage and all matters connected with it. The general average of the gully-drains I have shown to be 59 for every mile of street. I am assured that in the City the street-drains may be safely estimated at 65 to the mile. Estimating the streets gullied within the City, then, at an average of 50 miles, or about a mile more than the sewers, the number of gully-drains is 3250, and the length of them about 50 miles; but these, like the house-drains, have been already included in the metropolitan enumeration.

The actual sum expended yearly upon the construction, and repairs, and improvements of the City sewers cannot be cited as a distinct item, because the Court makes the return of the aggregate annual expenditure, as regards pavement, cleansing, and the matters specified as the general expenditure under the Court of Commissioners of the City Sewers. The cost, however, of the construction of sewers comprised within the civic boundaries is included in the general metropolitan estimate before given.

Of the Outlets, Ramifications, etc., of the Sewers.

In this enumeration I speak only of the *public* outlets into the river, controlled and regulated by public officers.

The orifices or mouths of the sewers where they discharge themselves into the Thames, beginning from their eastern, and following them seriatim to their western extremity, are as follows:—

Limehouse Hole.	Bridge-street, Westminster.
Irongate Wharf.	
Ratcliffe Cross.	Pimlico.
Fox-lane, Shadwell.	Cubitt's (also in Pimlico).
London Dock.	Chelsea Bridge.
St. Katharine's Dock.	Fulham Bridge.
The eleven City outlets, which I shall specify hereafter.	Hammersmith Bridge.
	Sandford Bridge (into a sort of creek of the Thames), or near the four bridges.
Essex-street, Strand.	
Norfolk-street, Strand.	
Durham Hill (or Adelphi).	Twickenham.
	Hampton.
Northumberland-street.	In all, 32.
Scotland-yard.	

It might only weary the reader to enumerate the outlets on the Surrey side of the Thames, which are 28 in number, so that the public sewer outlets of the whole metropolis are 60 in all.

The public sewer outlets from the City of London into the Thames are, as I have said, eleven in number, or rather they are usually represented as eleven, though in reality there are twelve such orifices—the "Upper" and "Eastern" Custom-House Sewers (which are distinct) being computed as one. These outlets, generally speaking the most ancient in the whole metropolis, are—

London Bridge.	Tower Dock.
Ancient Walbrook.	Pool Quay.
Paul's Wharf.	Custom House.
The Fleet-street Sewer at Blackfriars Bridge.	New Walbrook.
	Dowgate Dock.
(I mention these four first, because they are the largest outlets).	Hamburg Wharf.
	Puddle Dock.

Until recently, there was also Whitefriars Docks, but this is now attached to the Fleet Sewer outlet.

The Fleet Sewer is the oldest in London. No portion of the ditch or river composing it is now uncovered within the jurisdiction of the City; but until a little more than eleven years ago a portion of it, north of Holborn, was uncovered, and had been uncovered for years. Indeed, as I have before intimated, barges and small craft were employed on the Fleet River, and the City determined to "encourage its navigation." Even the "polite" Earl of Chesterfield, a century ago (for his lordship was born in 1694, and died in 1773), when asked by a Frenchman in Paris, if there was in London a river to compare to the Seine? replied that there certainly was, and it was called Fleet Ditch! This is now the sewer; but it was not a covered sewer until 1765, when the Corporation ordered it to be built over.

The next oldest sewer outlet is that at London Bridge, and London antiquaries are not agreed as to whether it or the Fleet is the oldest.

The Fleet Sewer at Blackfriars Bridge is 18 feet high; between Tudor-street and Fleet Bridge (about the foot of Ludgate-hill), 14 feet 3 inches high; at Holborn Bridge, 13 feet; and in its continuation in the long-unfinished Victoria-street, 12 feet 3 inches. In all these localities it is 12 feet wide.

The New London Bridge Sewer, built or rebuilt, wholly or partly, in 1830, is 10 feet by 8 at its outlet; decreasing to the south end of King William-street, where it is 9 feet by 7; while it is 8 feet by 7 in Moorgate-street.

Paul's Wharf sewer is 7 feet 6 inches by 5 feet 6 inches near the outlet.

With the one exception of the Fleet River, none of the City sewer outlets are covered, the Fleet outlet being covered even at low water. The issue from the others runs in open channels upon the shore.

Mr. Haywood (February 12, 1850), in a report of the City Sewer Transactions and Works, observes,—"During the year (1849) the outlet sewers at Billingsgate and Whitefriars, two of the outlets of main sewers which discharged at the line of the River Wall, have been diverted (times of storm excepted); there remain, therefore, but eleven main outlets within the jurisdiction of this commission, which discharge their waters at the line of the River Wall.

"As a temporary measure, it is expedient to convey the sewage of the whole of the outlets within the City by covered culverts, below low-water mark; this subject has been under the consideration both of this Commission and the Navigation Committee."

Whether the covered culvert is better than the open run, is a matter disputed among engineers (as are very many other matters connected with sewerage), and one into which I need not enter.

Mr. Haywood says further:—"The Fleet sewer already discharges its average flow, by a culvert, below low-water mark; with one exception only, I believe, none of the numerous outlets, which, for a length of many miles, discharge at intervals into the Thames at the line of the River Wall, both within and without your jurisdiction, discharge by culverts in a similar manner."

These eleven outlets are far from being the whole number which give their contents into "the silver bosom of the Thames," along the bank-line of the City jurisdiction. There are (including the 11) 182 outlets; but these are not under the control (unless in cases of alteration, nuisance, &c.) of the Court of Sewers. They are the outlets from the drainage of the wharfs, public buildings, or manufactories (such as gas-works, &c.) on the banks of the river; and the right to form such outlets having been obtained from the Navigation Committee, who, under the Lord Mayor, are conservators of the Thames, the care of them is regarded as a private matter, and therefore does not require further notice in this work. The officers of the City Court of Sewers observe these outlets in their rounds of inspection, but interfere only on application from any party concerned, unless a nuisance be in existence.

To convey a more definite notion of the extent and ramified sweep of the sewers, I will now describe (for the first time in print) some of the chief *Sewer Ramifications*, and then show the proportionate or average number of public ways, of inhabited houses, and of the population to each great main sewer, distinguishing, in this instance, those as *great main sewers* which have an outlet into the Thames.

The reader should peruse the following accounts with the assistance of a map of the environs, for, thus aided, he will be better able to form a definite notion of the curiously-mixed and blended extent of the sewerage already spoken of.

First, then, as to the ramifications of the great and ancient Fleet outlet. From its mouth, so to speak, near Blackfriars Bridge, its course is not parallel with any public way, but, running somewhat obliquely, it crosses below Tudor-street into Bridge-street, Blackfriars, then occupies the centre of Farringdon-street, and that street's prolongation or intended prolongation into the New Victoria-street (the houses in this locality having been pulled down long ago, and the spot being now popularly known as "the ruins"), and continues until the City portion of the Fleet Sewer meets the Metropolitan jurisdiction between Saffron and Mutton hills, the junction, so to call it, being "under the houses"* (a common phrase among flush-

* This outlet is known to the flushermen, &c., as "below the backs of houses," from its devious course *under the houses* without pursuing any direct line parallel with the open part of the streets.

ermen). A little farther on it connects itself with an open part of the Fleet Ditch, running at the back of Turnmill-street, Clerkenwell. In its City course, the sewer receives the issue from 150 public ways (including streets, alleys, courts, lanes, &c.), which are emptied into it from the second, third, or smaller class sewers, from Ludgate-hill and its proximate streets, the St. Paul's locality, Fleet-street and its adjacent communications in public ways, with a series of sewers running down from parts of Smithfield, &c. The *greatest* accession of sewage, however, which the Fleet receives from *one* issue, is a few yards beyond where the City has merged into the Metropolitan jurisdiction; this accession is from a first-class sewer, known as "the Whitecross-street sewer," because running from that street, and carrying into the Fleet the contributions of 60 crowded streets.

After the junction of the covered City sewer with the uncovered ditch in Clerkenwell, the Fleet-river sewer (again covered) skirts round Cold Bath Fields Prison (the Middlesex House of Correction), runs through Clerkenwell-green into the Bagnigge Wells-road, so on to Battle-bridge and King's-cross; then along the Old Saint Pancras-road, and thence to the King's-road (a name now almost extinct), where the St. Pancras Workhouse stands close by the turnpike-gate. Along Upper College-street (Camden-town) is then the direction of this great sewer, and running *under* the canal at the higher part of Camden-town, near the bridge by the terminus of the Great North Western Railway, it branches into the highways and thoroughfares of Kentish-town, of Highgate, and of Hampstead, respectively, and then, at what one informant described as "the outside" of those places, receives the open ditches, which form the further sewerage, under the control of the Commissioners, who cause them to be cleansed regularly.

In order to show more consecutively the direction, from place to place, in straight, devious, or angular course, of this the most remarkable sewer of the world, considering the extent of the drainage into it, I have refrained from giving beyond the Whitecross-street connection with the Fleet, an account of the number of streets sewered into this old civic stream. I now proceed to supply the deficiency.

From a large outlet at Clerkenwell-green (a very thickly-built neighbourhood) flows the connected sewage of 100 streets. At Maiden-lane, beyond King's-cross, a district which is now being built upon for the purposes of the Great Northern Railway, the sewage of 10 streets is poured into it. In the course of this sewer along Camden-town, it receives the issue of some 20 branches, or 40 streets, &c. About 15 other issues are received before the open ditches of Kentish-town, Highgate, and Hampstead are encountered.

It is not, however, merely the sewage collected in the precincts of the City proper, which is "outletted" (as I heard a flusherman call it) into the Thames. Other districts are drained into the large City outlets nearing the river. "Many of your works," says Mr. Haywood, the City surveyer, in a report addressed to the City Commissioners, Oct. 23, 1849," have been beneficially felt by districts some miles distant from the City. Twenty-nine outlets have been provided by you for the sewage of the County of Middlesex; the high land of and about Hampstead, drains through the Fleet sewer; Holloway and a portion of Islington can now be drained by the London Bridge sewer; Norton Folgate and the densely-populated districts adjacent are also relieved by it."

On the other hand, the Irongate sewer (one of the most important), which has its outlet in the Tower Hamlets, drains a portion of the City.

The reader must bear in mind, also, that were he to traverse the Fleet sewer in the direction described—for all the men I conversed with on the subject, if asked to show the course of sewerage with which they were familiar, began *from* the outlet into the Thames—the reader, I say, must remember that he would be advancing all the way *against* the stream, in a direction in which he would find the sewage flowing onward to its mouth, while his course would be towards its sources.

On the left-hand side (for the account before given refers only to the right-hand side) proceeding in the same direction, after passing the underground precincts of the City proper, there is another addition near Saffron-hill, of the sewage of 30 streets; then at Gray's-inn-road is added the sewage of 100 streets; New-road (at King's-cross), 20 more streets; from the whole of Somers-town, a populous locality, the sewerage concentrating all the busy and crowded places round about "the Brill," &c., the sewage of 120 streets is received; and at Pratt-street, Camden-town, 12 other streets.

Thus into this sewage-current, directed to one final outlet, are drained the refuse of 517 streets, including, of course, a variety of minor thoroughfares, courts, alleys, &c., &c., as in the neighbourhoods of Gray's-inn-road, in Clerkenwell, Somers-town, &c. Some of these tributaries to the efflux of the sewage are "barrel-drains," but perform the function of sewers along small courts, where there is "no thoroughfare" either *upon* or *below* the surface.

The London Bridge sewer runs up King William-street to Moorgate-street, along Finsbury-square into the City-road, diverging near the Wharf-road, which it crosses *under* the canal near the Wenlock basin, and thence along the Lower-road, Islington, by Cock-lane, through Highbury-vale; after this, at the extremity of Holloway, the open ditches, as in the former instance, carry on the conveyance of sewage from the outer suburbs.

The King's Scholars' Pond Sewer—which seems to have given the Commissioners more trouble than any other, in its connection with Buckingham Palace, St. James's Park, and the new Houses of Parliament—runs from Chelsea-bridge past Cubitt's workshops, and along the King's-road to Eaton-square, the whole of which is drained into it; then "turning round," as one man described it, it approaches Buckingham Palace, which, with its grounds, as well as a portion of St. James's and the Green parks, is drained into this sewer; then branching away for the reception of the sewage from the houses and gardens of Chelsea, it drains Sloane-street, and, crossing the Knightsbridge-road, runs through or across Hyde-park to the Swan at Bayswater, whence its course is by the Westbourne District and under the canal, along Paddington, until it attains the open country, or rather the grounds, in that quarter, which have been very extensively and are now still being built over, and where new sewers are constructed simultaneously with new streets.

Thus in the "reach," as I heard it happily enough designated, of each of these great sewers, the reader will see from a map the extent of the subterranean metropolis traversed, alike along crowded streets ringing with the sounds of traffic, among palatial and aristocratic domains, and along the parks which adorn London, as well as winding their ramifying course among the courts, alleys, and teeming streets, the resorts of misery, poverty, and vice.

Estimating, then, the number of sewers from the number of their river outlets, and regarding all the rest as the branches, or tributaries, to each of these superior streams, we have, adopting the area before specified as being drained by the metropolitan sewers, viz., 58 square miles, the following results:—

Each of the 60 sewers having an outlet into the Thames drains 618 statute acres.

And assuming the number of houses included within these 58 square miles to be 200,000, and the population to amount to 1,500,000, or two-thirds of the houses and people included in the Registrar-General's Metropolis, we may say that each of the 60 sewers would carry into the Thames the refuse from 25,000 individuals and 3333 inhabited houses. This, however, is partly prevented by the cesspoolage system, which supplies receptacles for a proportion of the refuse that, were London to be rebuilt according to the provisions of the present Building and Sanitary Acts, would *all* be carried, without any interception, into the river Thames by the media of the sewers.

In my account of cesspoolage I shall endeavour to show the extent of fæcal refuse, &c., contained in places not communicating with the sewers, and to be removed by the labour of men and horses, as well as the amount of fæcal refuse carried into the sewerage.

OF THE QUALITIES, ETC., OF THE SEWAGE.

THE question of the value, the uses, and the best means of collecting for use, the great mass of the sewage of the metropolis, seems to have become complicated by the statements which have been of late years put forth by rival projectors and rival companies. In our smaller country towns, the neighbourhood of many being remarkable for fertility and for a green beauty of meadow-land and pasturage, the refuse of the towns, whether sewage or cesspoolage (if not washed into a current, stream, or river), is purchased by the farmers, and carted by them to spread upon the land.

By *sewage*, I mean the contents of the *sewerage*, or of the series of sewers; which neither at present nor, I believe, at any former period, has been applied to any useful or profitable purpose by the metropolitan authorities. The readiest mode to get rid of it, without any care about ultimate consequences, has always been resorted to, and that mode has been to convey it into the Thames, and leave the rest to the current of the stream. But the Thames has its ebbs as well as its flow, and the consequence is the sewage is *never* got rid of.

The most eminent of our engineers have agreed that it is a very important consideration how this sewage should be not only innocuously but profitably disposed of; and if not profitably, in an immediate money return, to those who may be considered its owners (the municipal authorities of the kingdom), at least profitably in a national point of view, by its use in the restoration or enrichment of the fertility of the soil, and the consequent increase of the food of man and beast.

Sir George Staunton has pronounced some of the tea-growing parts of China to be as blooming as an English nobleman's flower-garden. Every jot of manure, human ordure, and all else, is minutely collected, even by the poorest.

I have already given a popular account of the composition of the metropolitan sewage, &c. (under the head of Wet Refuse), and I now give its scientific analysis.

In some districts the sewage is more or less liquid—in what proportion has not been ascertained—and I give, in the first place, an analysis of the sewage of the King's Scholars' Pond Sewer, Westminster, the result having been laid before a Committee of the House of Commons. As the contents of the great majority of sewers *must* be the same, because resulting from the same natural or universally domestic causes (as in the refuse of cookery, washing, surface-water, &c.), the analysis of the sewage of the King's Scholars' Pond Sewer may be accepted as one of sewer-matter generally.

Evidence was given before the committee as to the proportion of "land-drainage *water*" to what was really *manure*, in the matter derived from the sewer in question. A produce of 140 grains of manure was derived from a gallon of sewer-water. Messrs. Brande and Cooper, the analyzers, also state that one gallon (10 lbs.?) of the liquid portion of the sewage, evaporated to dryness, gave 85·3 grains of solid matter, 74·8 grains of which was again soluble, and contained—

Ammonia	3·29
Sulphuric acid . . .	0·62
Phosphate of lime . .	0·29
Lime	6·25
Chlorine	10·00

"and potass and soda, with a large quantity of soluble and vegetable matter, and 10·54 insoluble."

This insoluble portion consisted of

Phosphate of lime . . .	2·32
Carbonate of lime . . .	1·94
Silica	6·28
	10·54

The deposit from another gallon weighed 55 grains, of which 21·22 were combustible, being composed of animal matter "rich in nitrogen," some vegetable matter, and a quantity of fat. Of this matter 33·75 grains consisted of

Phosphate of lime . . .	6·81
Oxide of iron	2·01
Carbonate of lime . . .	1·75
Sulphate of lime . . .	1·53
Earthy matter and sand .	21·65
	33·75

Other Reports and other evidence show that what is described as "earthy matter and sand" is the mac, mud, and the mortar or concrete used in pavement, washed from the surface of the streets into the sewers by heavy rains; otherwise for the most part the proper load of the scavager's cart.

Further analyses might be adduced, but with merely such variation in the result as is inevitable from the state of the weather when the sewage is drawn forth for examination; whether the day on which this is done happens to be dry or wet*.

It has been ascertained, but the exact proportion is not, and perhaps cannot be, given, that the extent of covered to uncovered surface in the district drained by the King's Scholars' Pond Sewer was as 3 to 1, while that of the Ranelagh Sewer, not far distant, was as 1 to 3, at the time of the inquiry (1848).

"It could not be expected, therefore," says the Report, "that the Ranelagh Sewer (which, moreover, is open to the admission of the tide at its mouth), in the quantity or quality of the manure produced, could bear any proportion to the King's Scholars' Pond Sewer."

Mr. Smith, of Deanston, stated in evidence, that the average quantity of rain falling into King's Scholars' Pond Sewer was 139,934,586 cubic feet in a year, and he assumes 6,000,000 tons as the amount of average minimum quantity of drainage (yearly), yielding 4 cwt. of solid matter in each 100 tons = 1 in 500.

* The following is the analysis of a gallon of sewage, also dried to evaporation, by Professor Miller:—

Ammonia	3·26
Phosphoric acid	0·44
Potash	1·02
Silica	0·54
Lime	7·54
Magnesia	1·87
Common salt	13·66
Sulphuric acid	7·04
Carbonic acid	4·41
Combustible matter, containing 0·34 nitrogen	5·80
Traces of oxide of iron.	
Making in solution . . .	45·58
Matters in suspension, consisting of combustible matters, sand, lime, and oxide of iron . .	44·50

Dr. Granville said, on the same inquiry, that he should be sorry to receive on his land 500 tons of diluted sewer water (such as that from the uncovered Ranelagh Sewer) for 1 ton of really fertilizing sewage, such as that to be derived from the King's Scholars' Pond Sewer.

I could easily multiply these analyses, and give further parliamentary or official statements, but, as the results are the same, I will merely give some extracts from the evidence of Dr. Arthur Hassall, as to the microscopic constituents of sewage-water:—

"I have examined," he said, "the sewer-water of several of the principal sewers of London. I found in it, amongst many other things, much decomposing vegetable matter, portions of the husks and the hairs of the down of wheat, the cells of the potato, cabbage, and other vegetables, while I detected but few forms of animal life, those encountered for the most part being a kind of worm or anælid, and a certain species of animalcule of the genus monas."

"How do you account," the Doctor was asked, "for the comparative absence of animal life in the water of most sewers?" "It is, doubtless, to be attributed," he replied, "in a great measure, to the large quantity of sulphuretted hydrogen contained in sewer-water, and which is continually being evolved by the decomposing substances included in it."

"Have you any evidence to show that sewer-water does contain sulphuretted hydrogen in such large quantity as to be prejudicial and even fatal to animal life?" "With a view of determining this question, I made the following experiments:— A given quantity of Thames water, known to contain living infusoria, was added to an equal quantity of sewer-water; examined a few minutes afterwards, the animalculæ were found to be either dead or deprived of locomotive power and in a dying state. A small fish, placed in a wine glass of sewer-water, immediately gave signs of distress, and, after struggling violently, floated on its side, and would have perished in a few seconds, had it not been removed and placed in fresh water. A bird placed in a glass bell-jar, into which the gas evolved by the sewer-water was allowed to pass, after struggling a good deal, and showing other symptoms of the action of the gas, suddenly fell on its side, and, although immediately removed into fresh air, was found to be dead. These experiments were made, in the first instance, with the sewer water of the Friar-street sewer (near the Blackfriars-road); they were afterwards repeated with the water of six other sewers on the Middlesex side, and with the same result, as respects the animalculæ and fish, but not the bird; this, although evidently much affected by the noxious emanations of the sewer-water, yet survived the experiment."

"Would you infer from these experiments that sewer-water, as contained in the Thames near to London, is prejudicial to health?" "I would, most decidedly; and regard the Thames in the neighbourhood of the metropolis as nothing less than diluted sewer-water."

"You have just stated that you found sewer-water to contain much vegetable matter, and but few forms of animal life; the vegetable matter you recognised, I presume, by the character of the cells composing the several vegetable tissues?" "Yes, as also by the action of iodine on the starch of the vegetable matter."

"In what way do you suppose these various vegetable cells, the husks of wheat, &c., reach the sewers?" "They doubtless proceed from the fæcal matter contained in sewage, and not in general from the ordinary refuse of the kitchen, which usually finds its way into the dust-bin."

"Sewer-water, then, although containing but few forms of animal life, yet contains, in large quantities, the food upon which most animalculæ feed?" "Yes; and it is this circumstance which explains the vast abundance of infusorial life in the water of the Thames within a few miles of London."

The same gentleman (a fellow of the Linnæan Society, and the author of "A History of the British Fresh-water Algæ," or water-weeds considered popularly), in answer to the following inquiries in connection with this subject, also said:—

"What species of infusoria represent the *highest* degree of impurity in water?" "The several species of the genera *Oxytricha* and *Paramecium*."

"What species is most abundant in the Thames from Kew Bridge to Woolwich?" "The *Paramecium Chrysalis* of Ehrenberg; this occurs in all seasons of the year, and in all conditions of the river, in vast and incalculable numbers; so much so, that a quart bottle of Thames water, obtained in any condition of the tide, is sure to be found, on examination with the microscope, to contain these creatures in great quantity."

"Do you find that the infusorium of which you have spoken varies in number in the different parts of the river between Kew Bridge and Woolwich?" "I find that it is most abundant in the neighbourhood of the bridges." [Where the outlet of the sewers is common.]

"Then the order of impurity of Thames water, in your view, would be the order in which it approaches the centre of London?" "Yes."

"You find then, in Thames water, about the bridges, things decidedly connected with the *sewer water*, as vegetable and animal matter in a state of decomposition?" "I do; about the bridges, and in the neighbourhood of London, there is very little living vegetable matter on which animalculæ could live; the only source of supply which they have is *the organic matter contained in sewer-water*, and which is to be regarded as the food of these creatures. Where infusoria abound, under circumstances *not* connected with sewage, vegetable matter in a living condition is certain to be met with."

Respecting the *uses of the sewage*, I may add the following brief observations. Without wishing in any way to prejudice the question (indeed the reader will bear in mind that I have all along spoken reprovingly of the waste of sewage), I am bound to say that the opinions I heard during my inquiry from gentlemen scientifically and, in some instances, practically familiar with the subject, concurred in the conclusion that the sewage of the metropolis cannot, with all the applications of scientific skill and apparatus, be made either sufficiently portable or efficacious for the purposes of manure to assure a proper pecuniary return. In this matter, perhaps, speculators have not traced a sufficient distinction between the liquid manure of the sewers and the "*poudrette*," or dry manure, manufactured from the more solid excrementitious matter of the cesspools, not only in Paris, but, until lately, even in London, where the business was chiefly in the hands of Frenchmen. The staple of the French "*poudrette*" is *not* "*sewage*," that is, the outpourings of the sewers—for this is carried into the Seine, and washed away with little convenience, as the tide hardly affects that river in Paris; but it is altogether "*cesspoolage*," that is, the deposit of the cesspools, collected in fixed and moveable utensils, regulated by the "universal" police of Paris, and conveyed by Government labourers to the Voirées, which are huge reservoirs of nightsoil at Montfauçon, about five miles, and in the Forest of Bondy, about ten miles, from the centre of Paris. The London-made manure also was all of cesspoolage; the contents of the nightman's cart being "shot" in the manufacturer's yard; and when so manufactured was, I believe, without exception, sent to the sugar-growing colonies, the farmers in the provinces pronouncing it "too hot" for the ground. The same complaint, I may observe, has been made of the French manufactured cesspool manure. I heard, on the other hand, opinions from scientific and practical gentlemen, that the sewer-water of London was so diluted, it was not profitably serviceable for the irrigation of land. All, however, agreed that the sewage of the metropolis ought not to be wasted, as it was certain that perseverance in experiment (and perhaps a large outlay) were certain to make sewage of value.

The following results, which the Board of Health have just issued in a Report, containing "Minutes of Information attested on the Application of Sewer-water and Town Manures to Agricultural Production," supply the latest information on this subject. The Report says first, that "to be told that the average yield of a county is 30 bushels of wheat per acre, or that the average weight of the turnip crop is 15 tons per acre, means very little, and there is little to be learned from such intelligence; but if it is shown that a certain farm under the usual mode of culture yielded certain weights per acre, and that the same land, by improved applications of the same manure, by the use of machinery, and by *employing double the number of hands, at increased wages*, is made to yield *fourfold* the weight of crop and of *better quality* than was previously obtained, a lesson is set before us worth learning."

It then proceeds to cite the following statements, on the authority of the Hon. Dudley Fortescue, as to the efficiency of sewage-water as a liquid manure applied to land.

"The first farm we visited was that of Craigentinney, situated about one mile and a half south-east of Edinburgh, of which 260 Scotch acres" (a Scotch acre is one-fourth more than any English acre) "receive a considerable proportion of such sewerage as, under an imperfect system of house-drainage, is at present derived from half the city. The meadows of which it chiefly consists have been put under irrigation at various times, the most recent addition being nearly 50 acres laid out in the course of last year and the year previous, which, lying above the level of the rest, are irrigated by means of a steam-engine. The meadows first laid out are watered by contour channels following the inequalities of the ground, after the fashion commonly adopted in Devonshire; but in the more recent parts the ground is disposed in 'panes' of half an acre, served by their respective feeders, a plan which, though somewhat more expensive at the outset, is found preferable in practice. The whole 260 acres take about 44 days to irrigate; the men charged with the duty of shifting the water from one pane to another give to each plot about two hours' irrigation at a time; and the engine serves its 50 acres in ten days, working day and night, and employing one man at the engine and another to shift the water. The produce of the meadows is sold by auction on the ground, 'rouped,' as it is termed, to the cow-feeders of Edinburgh, the purchaser cutting and carrying off all he can during the course of the letting, which extends from about the middle of April to October, when the meadows are shut up, but the irrigation is continued through the winter. The lettings average somewhat over 20*l*. the acre; the highest last year having brought 31*l*., and the lowest 9*l*.; these last were of very limited extent, on land recently denuded in laying out the ground, and consequently much below its natural level of productiveness. There are four cuttings in the year, and the collective weight of grass cut in parts was stated at the extraordinary amount of 80 tons the imperial acre. The only cost of maintaining these meadows, except those to which the water is pumped by the engine, consists in the employment of two hands to turn on and off the water, and in the expense of clearing out the channels, which was contracted for last year at 29*l*., and the value of the refuse obtained was considered fully equal to that sum, being applied in manuring parts of the land for a crop of turnips, which with only this dressing in addition to irrigation with the sewage-water presented the most luxuriant appearance. The crop, from present indications, was estimated at from 30 to 40 tons the acre, and was expected to realize 15*s*. the ton sold on the land. From calculations made on the spot we estimated the produce of the meadows during the eight months of cutting at the keep of ten cows per acre, exclusive of the distillery refuse they consume in addition, at a cost of 1*s*. to 1*s*. 6*d*. per head per week. The sea-meadows present a particularly striking example of the effects of the irrigation; these, comprising between 20 and 30 acres skirting the shores between Leith and Musselburgh, were laid down in 1826 at a cost of about 700*l*.; the land consisted formerly of a bare sandy tract, yielding almost absolutely nothing; it is now covered with luxuriant vegetation extending close down to highwater mark, and lets at an average of 20*l*. per acre at least. From the above statement it will be seen how enormously profitable has been the application in this case of town refuse in the liquid form; and I have no hesitation in stating that, great as its advantages have been, they might be extended four or five fold by greater dilution of the fluid. Four or five times the extent of land might, I believe, be brought into equally productive cultivation under an improved system of drainage in the city, and a more abundant use of water. Besides these Craigentinney meadows, there are others on this and on the west side of Edinburgh, which we did not visit, similarly laid out, and I believe realizing still larger profits, from their closer proximity to the town, and their lying within the toll-gates."*

Such, then, are said to be the results of a practical application of sewer-water. The preliminary remark of the Board of Health, however, applies somewhat to the statement above given; for we are not told what the *same land* produced before the liquid manure was applied; nor are we informed as to the peculiar condition and quantity of the land near Craigentinney, and how it differs from the land near London.

The other returns are of liquid manures, of which sewer-water formed no part, and, therefore, require no special notice of them. The following observations are, however, worthy of attention:—

" The cases above detailed furnish some measure of the possible results attainable in cultivation, especially corroborated as they are by others which did not on this occasion come under our personal observation, but one of which I may mention, having recently examined into it, that of Mr. Dickinson, at Willesden, who estimates his yield of Italian rye-grass at from 80 to 100 tons an acre, and gets 8 or 10 cuttings, according to the season; and as there is no peculiar advantage of soil or climate (the former ranging from almost pure sands to cold and tenacious clays, and the latter being inferior to that of a large proportion of England) to prevent the same system being almost universally adopted, they give some idea of the degree to which the productiveness of land may be raised by a judicious appliance of the means within our reach. When it is considered that such results may, in the vicinity of towns and villages, be most effectually brought about by the instant removal of all those matters which, when allowed to remain in them, are among the most fruitful sources of social degradation, disease, and death, one cannot but earnestly desire the furtherance of such measures as will ensure this double result of purifying the town and enriching the country; and as the facts I have stated came at the same time under the notice of the gentleman I mentioned above, under whose able superintendence the arrangements for the water-supply and drainage of several towns are now in course of execution, I trust it will not be long before this most advantageous mode of disposing of the refuse of towns may be brought into practical operation in various parts of the country.

" I have, &c.,
" D. F. FORTESCUE.
" General Board of Health."

OF THE NEW PLAN OF SEWERAGE.

THIS branch of the subject hardly forms part of my present inquiry, but, having pointed out the defects of the sewers, it seems but reasonable and right to say a few words on the measures determined upon for their improvement. It is only necessary for me, however, to indicate the principal characteristics of the new, or rather intended, mode of sewerage, as the work may be said to have been but commenced, or hardly commenced in earnest, the Report of Mr. Frank Forster (the engineer) bearing the date of Jan. 30, 1851.

In the carrying out of the engineer's plan—which from its magnitude, and, in all human probability, from its cost, when completed, would be *national* in other countries, but is here only *metropolitan*—in the carrying out of this scheme, I say, two remarkable changes will be found. The one is the employment of the power of steam in sewerage; the other is the diversion of the sewage from the current of the Thames. The ultimate uses of this sewage, agriculturally or otherwise, form no part of the present consideration.

I should, however, first enumerate the general principles on which the best authorities have agreed that the London sewers should be constructed so as to ensure a proper disposal of the sewage, for these principles are said to be at the basis of Mr. Forster's plan.

I condense under the following heads the substance of a mass of Reports, Committee Meetings, Suggestions, Plans, &c.:—

1. The channels, or pipeage, or other means of conveying away house-refuse, should be so made that the removal will be *immediate*, more especially of any refuse or filth capable of suspension in water, since its immediate carrying off, it is said, would leave no time for the generation of miasma.

2. Means should be provided for such disposal of sewage as would prevent its tainting any stream, well, or pool, or, by its stagnation or obstruction, in any way poisoning the atmosphere. And, as a natural and legitimate result, it should be *so collected that it could be applied to the cultivation of the land* at the most economical rate.

* The following note appears in Mr. Fortescue's statement:—" In some trial works near the metropolis sewer water was applied to land, on the condition that the value of half the extra crop should be taken as payment. The dressings were only single dressings. The officer making the valuation reported, that there was at the least one sack of wheat and one load of straw per acre extra from its application on one breadth of land; in another, full one quarter of wheat more, and one load of straw extra per acre. The reports of the effects of sewer-water in increasing the yield of oats as well as of wheat were equally good. It is stated by Captain Vetch that in South America irrigation is used with great advantage for wheat."

3. In the providing works of deposit or storage in low districts, or "of discharge where the natural outlets are free," such works should be provided as would not subject any place, or any man's property, to the risk of inundation, or any other evil consequence; while in the construction of the drainage of the substratum, the works should be at such a depth below the foundation of all buildings that tenements should not be exposed to that continued damage from exhalation and dampness which leads to the dry rot in timber, and to an immature decay of materials and a general unhealthiness.

There are other points insisted upon in many Reports to which I need but allude, such as

(*a.*) The channels containing sewage should be of enduring and impermeable material, so as to prevent all soakage.

(*b.*) There should be throughout the channels of the subterranean metropolis a fall or inclination which would suffice to prevent the accumulation of any sewage deposit, with its deleterious influence and ultimate costliness.

(*c.*) Similar provisions should be used were it but to prevent the creation of the noxious gases which now permeate many houses (especially in the quarters inhabited by the poor) and escape into many streets, courts, and alleys, for until improvements are effected the pent-up sewage and the saturated brickwork of the sewers and older drains must generate such gases.

(*d.*) No tidal stream should ever receive a flow of sewage, because then the cause of evil is never absent, for the filth comes back with the tide; and as the Thames water constitutes the grand fount of metropolitan consumption, the water companies, with very trifling exceptions, give us back much of our own excrement, mixed with every conceivable, and sometimes noxious, nastiness, with which we may brew, cook, and wash—and drink, if we can. Filtering remedies but a portion of the evil.

Now it would appear that not one of these requirements, the necessity of which is unquestioned and unquestionable, is fully carried out by the present system of sewerage, and hence the need of some new plan in which the defects may be remedied, and the proper principles carried out.

The instructions given by the Court were to the following effect:—

A. The Thames should be kept free from sewage whatever the state of the tide.

B. There should be intercepting drains to carry off the sewage (so keeping the Thames unsoiled by it) wherever practicable.

C. The sewage should be raised by artificial means into a main channel for removal.

D. The intercepting sewers should be so constructed as to secure the largest amount of effective drainage without artificial appliances.

In preparing his plan, Mr. Forster had the advice and assistance of Mr. Haywood, of the City Court of Sewers.

The metropolis is divided into two portions— "the northern portion of the metropolis," or rather that portion of the metropolis which is on the north or Middlesex bank of the Thames; and the southern portion, or that which is on the south or Surrey side of the river.

The northern portion is in the new plan considered to "divide itself into two separate areas," and to these two areas different modes of sewerage are to be applied:

"1. The interception of the drainage of that district, which, from its elevation above the level of the outlet, is capable of having its sewage and rainfall carried off by gravitation.

"2. The interception of the drainage of that district, which, from its low lying position, will require its sewage, and in most localities its rainfall, to be lifted by steam-power to a proper level for discharge."

The first district runs from Holsden-green (beyond the better-known Kensall-green) in the west, to the Tower Hamlets in the east. Its form is irregular, but not very much so, merely narrowing from Westbourn-green to its western extremity, the country then becoming rural or woodland. Its highest reaches to the north are to Highgate and Stamford-hill. The nearest approach to the south is to a portion of the Strand, between Charing-cross and Drury-lane. Care has evidently been taken to skirt this district, so to speak, by the canals and the railroads. This division of the northern portion is described as "the district for natural drainage."

The area of this division is about $25\frac{1}{3}$ square miles.

The second division meets the first at the highway separating Kensington-gardens from Bayswater; and runs on, bordering the river, all the way to the West India Dock. Its shape is irregular, but, abating the roundness, presents somewhat of that sort of figure seen in the instrument known as a dumb-bell, the narrowest or hand-part being that between Charing-cross and Drury-lane, skirting the river as its southern bound. At its eastern end this second district widens abruptly, taking in Victoria-park, Stratford, and Bromley.

The area of this division of the northern portion is $16\frac{1}{3}$ square miles.

There are, moreover, two small tracts, comprising the southern part of the Isle of Dogs, and a narrow slip on the west side of the river Lea, which are intended to allow the rainfall to run into the Thames and the Lea respectively.

The area of the two is $1\frac{3}{4}$ square mile.

The area to be drained by natural outfall comprises, then, $25\frac{1}{6}$ square miles as regards rainfall, and the same extent as regards sewage; while the area to the drainage of which steam power is to be applied comprises $14\frac{1}{3}$ square miles of rainfall, and $16\frac{1}{6}$ square miles of sewage; the two united areas of rainfall and sewage respectively being $39\frac{1}{2}$ and $41\frac{1}{3}$ square miles.

The length of the great "high-level sewerage" will be, as regards the main sewer, 19 miles and 106 yards; that of the "low-level sewerage," 14 miles and 1501 yards.

I will now describe the course of each of these constructions.

On the eastern bank of the Lea the sewage of both districts is to be concentrated. The high-level sewer will commence and *cross* the Lea near the "Four Mills." It is then to proceed "in a westerly direction under the East and West India Dock Railway and the Blackwall Extension Railway, beneath the Regent's-canal, to the east end of the Bethnal-green-road, at the crossing of the Cambridge-heath-road, at which point it will be joined by the proposed northern division of the Hackney-brook, which drains an extensive district up to the watershed line north of London, including Hackney, Stoke Newington and Holloway, and part of Highgate and Hampstead; from thence the main sewer proceeds along the Bethnal-green-road, Church-street, Old-street, Wilderness-row (where a short branch from Coppice-row will join) to Brook-street-hill; from thence to Little Saffron-hill, where a distance of about 100 yards is proposed to be carried by an aqueduct over the Fleet-valley; thence along Liquorpond-street, at the end of which it will receive a branch from Piccadilly, on the south side, and a diversion of the Fleet-river, on the north side; thence along Theobald's-road, Bloomsbury- square, Hart-street, New Oxford-street, to Rathbone-place (where it will receive a diversion of the Regent-street sewer from Park-crescent), along Oxford-street, and extending thence across Regent-circus to South Molton-lane (where it will intercept the King's Scholars' Pond sewer), continuing still along Oxford-street to Bayswater-place, Grand Junction-road, Uxbridge-road, where it is joined by the Ranelagh sewer, the sewage of which it is capable of receiving, and at this point it terminates."

It is difficult to convey to a reader, especially to a reader who may not be familiar with the localities of London generally, any adequate notion of the largeness, speaking merely of extent, of this undertaking. Even a map conveys no sufficient idea of it.

Perhaps I may best be able to suggest to a reader's mind a knowledge of this largeness, when I state that in the district I have just described, which is but *one* portion (although the greatest) of the sewerage of but *one* side of the Thames, more than half a million of persons, and nearly 100,000 houses are, so to speak, to be sewered.

The low-level tract sewerage, also, concentrates on the Lea, "near to Four Mill's distillery, taking the north-western bank of the Limehouse Cut, at which point it receives the branch intended to intercept the sewage of the Isle of Dogs; thence continuing along the bank of Limehouse Cut, through a portion of the Commercial-road, Brook-street, and beneath the Sun Tavern Fields, into High-street, or Upper Shadwell; thence along Ratcliffe-highway and Upper East Smithfield, across Tower-hill, through Little and Great Tower-streets, Eastcheap, Cannon-street, Little and Great St. Thomas Apostle, Trinity-lane, Old Fish-street, and Little Knight Rider-street; thence beneath houses in Wardrobe-terrace, and on the eastern side of St. Andrew's-hill, along Earl-street to Blackfriars - road. From Blackfriars Bridge it is proposed to construct the sewer along the river shore to the junction of the Victoria-street sewer at Percy-wharf; which sewer between Percy-wharf and Shaftesbury-terrace, Pimlico, becomes thus an integral portion of the intercepting line; at Bridge-street, Westminster, a branch from the Victoria-street sewer is intended to proceed along Abingdon and Millbank-streets, as far as and for the purpose of taking up the King's Scholars' Pond and other sewers at their outlets into the Thames. From Shaftesbury-terrace the Victoria-street sewer is proposed to be extended through Eaton-square and along the King's-road, Chelsea, to Park-walk, intercepting all the sewers along its line, and terminating at a point where the drainage of Kensington may be brought into it without pumping."

The lines of sewerage thus described are, then, all to the *west* of the Lea, and all, whether from the shore of the Thames, or the northern reaches in Highgate and Hampstead, converging to a pumping station or sewage-concentration, on the *east* bank of the Lea, in West Ham. By this new plan, then, the high-level sewer is to *cross* the Lea, but that arrangement is impossible as respects the second district described, which is *below* the level of the Lea, so that its course is to be *beneath* that river, a little below where it is crossed by the high-level line. To dispose of the sewage, therefore, conveyed from the low-level tract, there will be a sewer of a "depth of *forty-seven* feet *below*" the invert of the high-level sewer. This sewer, then, at the depth of 47 feet, will run to the point of concentration containing the low-level sewage.

At this point of the works, in order that the sewage may be collected, so as to be disposed of ultimately in one mass, it has to be *lifted* from the low to the high-level sewer. The invert of the high-level sewer will at the lifting or pumping station be 20 feet *above* the ordnance datum, while that of the low-level sewer will be 27 feet *below* the same standard. Thus a great body of metropolitan sewage, comprising among other districts the refuse of the whole City of London, must be lifted no less than 47 feet, in order to be got rid of along with what has been carried to the same focus by its natural flow.

The lifting is to be effected by means of steam, and the pumping power required has been computed at 1100-horse power. To supply this great mechanical and scientific force, there are to be provided two engines, each of 550-horse power, with a third engine of equal capacity, to be available in case of accident, or while either of the other engines might require repairs of some duration.

The northern sewage of London (or that of the Middlesex bank of the Thames, covered by that division of the capital) having been thus brought to a sort of central reservoir, or meeting point, will be conveyed in two parallel lines of sewerage to the bank of the river Roding, being the eastern extremity of Gallion's Reach (which is below Woolwich Reach), in the Thames. The Roding flows into the Thames at Barking Creek mouth. The length of this line will be four miles.

"At this point," it is stated in the Report,

"the level of the inverts of the parallel sewers will be eight feet below high-water mark, and here it is intended to collect the sewage into a reservoir during the flood-tide, and discharge the same with the ebb-tide immediately after high-water; and, as it is estimated that the reservoir will be completely emptied during the first three hours of the ebb, it may be safely anticipated that no portion of the sewage will be returned, with the flood-tide, to within the bounds of the metropolis."

The whole of the sewage and rainfall, then, will be thus diverted to *one* destination, instead of being issued into the river through a multiplicity of outlets in every part of the northern shore where the population is dense, and will be carried into the Thames at Barking Creek, unless, as I have intimated, a market be found for the sewage; when it may be disposed of as is most advantageous. The only exceptions to this carrying off will be upon the occurrence of long-continued and heavy rains or violent storms, when the surplus water will be carried off by some of the present outlets into the river; but even on such occasions, the *first scour* or cleansings of the sewerage will be conveyed to the main outlet at the river Roding.

The inclination which has been assigned to the whole of the lines of sewers I have described, is, with some unimportant exceptions, 4 feet per mile, or 1 in 1320. These new sewers are, or rather will be, calculated to carry off a fall of rain, equal to $\frac{1}{4}$ inch in 24 hours, in addition to the average daily flow of sewage.

Mr. Forster concludes his Report:—" I am only able to submit approximately that I estimate the cost of the whole of the lines of sewers, the pumping engines, and station, the reservoir, tidal gates, and other apparatus, at one million and eighty thousand pounds (1,080,000*l.*). This estimate does not include the sums required for the purchase of land and houses, which may be needed for the site of the pumping engine-house, or compensation for certain portions of the lines of sewers."

As regards the improvements in the sewerage on the south side of the Thames (the great fever district of the metropolis, and consequently the most important of all, and where the drainage is of the worst kind), I can be very brief, as nothing has been positively determined.

A somewhat similar system will be adopted on the south side of the Thames, where it is proposed to form one main intercepting sewer; but, owing to the physical configuration of this part of the town, none of the water will flow away entirely by gravitation. There will be a pumping station on the banks of the Ravensbourne, to raise the water about 25 feet; and a second pumping station to raise the water from the continued sewer in the reservoir, in Woolwich Marsh, which is to receive it during the intervals of the tides. The waters are to be discharged into the river at the last-named point. The main sewer on the south side will be of nearly equally colossal proportions; for its total length is proposed to be about 13 miles 3 furlongs, including the main trunk drain of about 2 miles long, and the respective branches. The area to be relieved is about proportionate to the length of the drain; but the steam power employed will be proportionally greater upon the southern than upon the northern side.

There are divers opinions, of course, as to the practicability and ultimate good working of this plan; speculations into which it is not necessary for me to enter. Mr. Forster has, moreover, resigned his office, adding another to the many changes among the engineers, surveyors, and other employés under the Metropolitan Commission; a fact little creditable to the management of the Commissioners, who, with one exception, may be looked upon as irresponsible.

OF THE MANAGEMENT OF THE SEWERS AND THE LATE COMMISSIONS.

THE Corporation of the City of London may be regarded as the first Commission of Sewers in the exercise of authority over such places as regards the removal of the filth of towns. In time, but at what time there is no account, the business was consigned to the management of a committee, as are now the markets of the City (Markets Committee), and even what may be called the management of the Thames (Navigation Committee). It is not at all necessary that the members of these committees should understand anything about the matters upon which they have to determine. A staff of officers, clerks, secretaries, solicitors, and surveyors, save the members the trouble of thought or inquiry; they have merely to vote and determine. It was stated in evidence before a Select Committee of the House of Commons on the subject of the Thames steamers, that at that period the Chairman of the *Navigation* Committee was a bread and biscuit baker, but "a very-firm-minded man." In time, but again I can find no note of the precise date, the *Committee* became a *Court* of Sewers, and so it remains to the present time. Commissions of sewers have been issued by the Crown since the 25th year of the reign of Henry VIII., except during the era of the Commonwealth, when there seems to have been no attention paid to the matter.

As the metropolis increased rapidly in size since the close of the last century, the public sewers of course increased in proportion, and so did Commissions of Sewers in the newly-built districts. Up to 1847 these Commissions or Court of Sewers were *eight* in number, the metropolis being divided into that number of districts.

The districts were as follows:—

1. The City.
2. The Tower Hamlets.
3. St. Katherine.
4. Poplar and Blackwall.
5. Holborn and Finsbury.
6. Westminster and part of Middlesex.
7. Surrey and Kent.
8. Greenwich.

Each of these eight Commissions had its own Act of Parliament; its own distinct, often irregular and generally uncontrolled plan of management; each had its own officers; and each had its own patronage. Each district court—with almost unlimited powers of taxation—pursued its own plans of sewerage, little regardful of the plans of its neighbour Commission. This wretched system—the great recommendation of which, to its promoters and supporters, seems to have been patronage—has given us a sewerage unconnected and varying to the present day in almost every district; varying in the dimensions, form, and inclination of the structures.

The eight commission districts, I may observe, had each their sub-districts, though the general control was in the hands of the particular Court or Board of Commissioners for the entire locality. These subdivisions were chiefly for the facilities of rate-collecting, and were usually "western," "eastern," and "central."

The consequence of this immethodical system has been that, until the surveys and works now in progress are completed, the precise character, and even the precise length, of the sewers must be unknown, though a sufficient approximation may be deduced in the interim.

To show the conflicting character of the sewerage, I may here observe that in some of the old sewers have been found walls and arches crumbling to pieces. Some old sewers were found to be not only of ample proportions, but to contain subterranean chambers, not to say halls, filled with filth, into which no man could venture. While in a sewer in the newly-built district of St. John's-wood, Mr. Morton, the Clerk of Works, could only advance stooping half double, could not turn round when he had completed his examination, but had most painfully—for a long time feeling the effects—to back out along the sewer, stooping, or doubled up, as he entered it. Why the sewer was constructed in this manner is not stated, but the work appears, inferentially, to have been *scamped*, which, had there been a proper supervision, could hardly have been done with a modern public sewer, down a thoroughfare of some length (the Woronzow-road).

But the conflicting and disjointed system of sewerage was not the sole evil of the various Commissions. The mismanagement and jobbery, not to say peculation, of the public moneys, appear to have been enormous. For instance, in the "Accountant's Report" (February, 1848), prepared by Mr. W. H. Grey, 48, Lincoln's-inn-fields, I find the following statements relative to the *Book-keeping* of the several Commissions:—

"The *Westminster* plan is full of unnecessary repetition. It is deficient in those real general accounts which concentrate the information most needed by the Commissioners, and it contains *fictions* which are very inconsistent with any sound system of book-keeping.

"The ledger of the Westminster Commission does not give a true account of the actual receipt and expenditure of each district.

"The *Holborn and Finsbury* books are still more defective than those of the Westminster Commission. . . . . . There are the same kind of *fictions*. . . . . . But the extraordinary defect in these books consists in the utter want of system throughout them, by keeping one-sided accounts only in the ledger, with respect to the different sewers in each district, showing only the amount *expended* on each.

"The *Tower Hamlets* books have been kept on a regular system, though by no means one conveying much general information."

"With respect to the *Surrey and Kent* accounts," says Mr. Grey, "the books produced are the most incomplete and unsatisfactory that ever came under my observation. The ledger is always thought to be a *sine quâ non* in book-keeping; but here it has been dispensed with altogether, for that which is so marked is no ledger at all."

Under these circumstances, the Report continues, "It cannot be wondered at that debts should have been incurred, or that they should have swollen to the amount of 54,000*l*., carrying a yearly interest of 2360*l*., besides annuities granted to the amount of 1125*l*. a year.

"The *Poplar and Greenwich* accounts (I quote the official Report), confined as they are to mere cash books, offer no subjects for remark. . . . . . .

"No books of account have been produced with respect to the *St. Katherine's* Commission."

On the 16th December, 1847, the new Commissioners ordered all the books to be sent to the office in Greek-street; but it was not until the 21st February, 1848, that all the minute-books were produced. There were no indexes for many years even to the proceedings of the Courts; and the account-books of one of the local Courts, if they might be so called, were in such a state that the book called "ledger" had for several years been cast up in pencil only.

This refers to what may be characterised, with more or less propriety, as *mismanagement* or *neglect;* though in such mismanagement it is hardly possible to escape *one* inference. I now come to what are direct imputations of *Jobbery,* and where *that* is flourishing or easy, no system can be other than vicious.

In a paper " printed for use of Commissioners" (Sept. 7, 1848), entitled "Draft Report on the Surrey Accounts," emanating from a "General Purposes' Committee," I find the following, concerning the parliamentary expenses of obtaining an Act which it was "found necessary to repeal." The cost was, altogether, upwards of 1800*l*., which of course had to be defrayed out of the taxes.

"This Act," says the Report, "authorized an almost unlimited borrowing of money; and *immediately upon its passing,* in July, 1847, notices were issued for works estimated to amount to 100,000*l*.; and others, we understand, were projected for early execution to the amount of 300,000*l*. . . . . . Considering the general character of the works executed, and from them judging of those projected, it may confidently be averred that the *whole sum* of 300,000*l*., the progressive expenditure of which was stayed by the 'supersedeas' of the old Commission, would have been *expended in waste.*" [The *Italics* are not those of the Reports.]

The Report continues, "It is to be observed that each of the district surveyors would have participated in the sum of 15,000*l.* percentage on the expenditure for the extension of the Surrey works. Thus the surveyors, with their percentages on the works executed, and the clerk, by the fees on contracts, &c., had *a direct interest in a large expenditure.*"

Instances of the same dishonest kind might be multiplied to almost any extent.

After the above evidences of the incompetency and dishonesty of the several district Commissions —and the Reports from which they are copied contain many more examples of a similar and even worse description—it is not to be wondered at that in the year 1847 the district courts were, with the exception of the City, superseded by the authority of the Crown, and formed into one body, the present Metropolitan Commission of Sewers, of the constitution and powers of which I shall now proceed to speak.

OF THE POWERS AND AUTHORITY OF THE PRESENT COMMISSIONS OF SEWERS.

IN 1847 the eight separate Commissions of Sewers were abolished, and the whole condensed, by the Government, into *one* Commission, with the exception of the City, which seems to supply an exception in most public matters.

The Act does not fix the number of the Commissioners. To the Metropolitan Commissioners, five City Commissioners are added (the Lord Mayor for the year being one *ex officio*); these have a right to act as members of the Metropolitan Board, but their powers in this capacity are loosely defined by the Act, and they rarely attend, or perhaps never attend, unless the business in some way or other affects their distinct jurisdiction.

The Commissioners (of whom twelve form a quorum) are unpaid, with the exception of the chairman, Mr. E. Lawes, a barrister, who has 1000*l.* a year. They are appointed for the term of two years, revocable at pleasure.

The authority of the City Commission, as distinct from the Metropolitan, for there are two separate Acts, seems to be more strongly defined than that of the others, but the principle is the same throughout. The Metropolitan Act bears date September 4, 1848; and the City Act, September 5, 1848.

The Metropolitan Commissioners have the control over "the sewers, drains, watercourses, weirs, dams, banks, defences, gratings, pipes, conduits, culverts, sinks, vaults, cesspools, rivers, reservoirs, engines, sluices, penstocks, and other works and apparatus for the collection and discharge of rainwater, surplus land or spring-water, waste water, or filth, or fluid, or semi-fluid refuse of all descriptions, and for the protection of land from floods or inundation within the limits of the Commission." Ample as these powers seem to be, the Commissioners' authority does not extend over the Thames, which is in the jurisdiction of the Lord Mayor and Corporation of the City of London; and it appears childish to give men control over "rivers," and to empower them to take measures "for the protection of land from floods or inundation," while over the great metropolitan stream itself, from Yantlet Creek, below Gravesend, to Oxford, they have no power whatever.

The Commissioners (City as well as Metropolitan) are empowered to enforce proper house-drainage wherever needed; to regulate the building of new houses, in respect of water-closets, cesspools, &c.; to order any street, staircase, or passage not effectually cleansed to be effectually cleansed; to remedy all nuisances having insanitary tendencies; to erect *public* water-closets and urinals, free from any charge to the public; to order houses and rooms to be whitewashed; to erect places for depositing the bodies of poor persons deceased until interment; and to regulate the cleanliness, ventilation, and even accommodation of low lodging-houses.

The jurisdiction of the Metropolitan Commissioners of Sewers extends over "all such places or parts in the counties of Middlesex, Surrey, Essex, and Kent, or any of them *not more than twelve miles distant in a straight line from St. Paul's Cathedral, in the City of London,* but not being within the City of London or the liberties thereof."

This, it must be confessed, is an exceedingly broad definition of the extent of the jurisdiction of the *Metropolitan* Commission, giving the Commissioners an extraordinary amount of *latitude.*

In our days there are many Londons. There is the London (or the metropolitan apportionment of the capital) as defined by the Registrar-General. This, as we have seen, has an area of 115 square miles, and therefore may be said to comprise as nearly as possible all those places which are rather more than *five miles* distant from the Post Office.

There is the *Metropolis* as defined by the Post-Office functionaries, or the limits assigned to what is termed the "London District Post." This London District Post seems, however, to have three different metropolises :—First, there is the Central Metropolis, throughout which there is an hourly delivery of letters after mid-day, and which deliveries are said to be confined to "London." Then there is the six-delivery *Metropolis*, or that throughout which the letters are despatched and received six times per day; this is said to extend to such of the "environs" as are included within a circle of *three miles* from the General Post Office. Then there is the *six-mile Metropolis* with special privileges. And lastly, the *twelve-mile Metropolis*, which, being the extreme range of the London District Post, may be said to constitute the metropolis of the General Post Office.

There is, again, the metropolis of the Metropolitan Commissioners of Police, before the region of rural police and country and parish constables is attained; a jurisdiction which covers 96 square miles, as I have shown at pp. 163-166 of the present volume, and reaches—generally speaking—to such places as are included within a circle of *five miles and a half* from the General Post Office.

There is, moreover, the metropolis, as defined by the Hackney-Carriage Act, which comprises all such places as are within *five miles* of the General Post Office.

And further, there is the Metropolis of the London City Mission, which extends to *eight miles* from the Post Office, and the Metropolis, again, of the London Ragged Schools, which reaches to about *three miles* from the Post Office.

This, however, is not all, for there are divers districts for the registration and exercise of votes, parliamentary, or municipal; there are ecclesiastical and educational districts; there is a thorough complication of parochial, extra-parochial, and chartered districts; there is a world of subdivisions and of sub-subdivisions, so ramified here and so closely blended there, and often with such preposterous and arbitrary distinctions, that to describe them would occupy more than a whole Number.

My present business, however, is the extent of the jurisdiction of the Metropolitan Commissioners of Sewers, or rather to ascertain the boundaries of that *metropolis* over which the Metropolitan Commissioners are allowed to have sway.

The many discrepancies and differences I have explained make it difficult to *define* any district for the London sewerage; and in the Reports, &c., which are presented to Parliament, or prepared by public bodies, little or no care seems to be taken to observe any distinctiveness in this respect.

For instance: The jurisdiction of the Metropolitan Commission of Sewers, which is said to extend to all such places as are not more than 12 miles distant in a straight line from St. Paul's Cathedral, in the City of London, comprises an area of 452 square miles; the metropolis, that of the Registrar-General, presenting a radius of 6 miles (with a fractional addition), contains 115 square miles; yet in official documents 58 square miles, or a circle of about $4\frac{1}{2}$ miles radius, are given as the extent of the *metropolis* sewered by the Metropolitan Commission. By what calculations this 58 miles are arrived at, whether it has been the *arbitrium* of the authorities to consider the sewers, &c., as occupying *the half* of the area of the Registrar-General's metropolis, or what other reason has induced the computation, I am unable to say.

The boundaries of the several metropolises may be indicated as follows:—

The *Three-Mile Circle* includes Camberwell; skirts Peckham; seems to divide Deptford (irregularly); touches the West India Dock; includes portions of Limehouse, Stepney, Bromley, Stratford-le-Bow, and about the half of Victoria-park, Hackney. It likewise comprises a part of Lower Clapton, Dalston, and a portion of Stoke Newington; and closely touching upon or containing small portions of Lower Holloway, and Kentish-town, sweeps through the Regent's and Hyde parks, includes a moiety of Chelsea, and crossing the river at the Red-house, Battersea, completes the circle. This is the six-delivery district of the General Post Office.

In this three-mile district are chiefly condensed the population, commerce, and wealth of the greatest and richest city in the world.

The *Six-Mile Circle* runs from Streatham (on the south); just excludes Sydenham; contains within its exterior line Lewisham, Greenwich, and a part of Woolwich; also, wholly or partially, East Ham, Laytonstone, Walthamstow, Tottenham, Hornsey, Highgate, Hampstead, Kensall-green, Hammersmith, Fulham, Wandsworth, and Upper Tooting. The portion without the three-mile circle, and within the six, is the *suburban* portion or the immediate environs of the metropolis, and still presents rural and woodland beauties in different localities. This may be termed the metropolis of the Registrar-General and Commissioners of Metropolitan Police.

The *Twelve-Mile Circle*, or the extent of the jurisdiction of the *Metropolitan* Commissioners of Sewers, as well as the "*London* District Post," includes Croydon, Wickham, Paul's Cray, Foot's Cray, North Cray, and Bexley; crosses the river at the Erith-reach; proceeds across the Rainham-marshes; comprises Dagenham; skirts Romford; includes Henhault-forest and the greater portion of Epping-forest; touches Waltham-abbey and Cheshunt; comprehends Enfield and Chipping-Barnet; runs through Elstre and Stanmore; comprehends Harrow-on-the-Hill, Norwood, and Hounslow; embraces Twickenham and Teddington; seems to divide somewhat equally the domains of Bushey-park and of Hampton-court Palace; then, crossing the river about midway between Thames Ditton and Kingston, the boundary line passes between Cheam and Ewell, and completes the circuit.

Over this large district, then, the jurisdiction of the Metropolitan Commissioners of Sewers is said to extend, and one of the outlets of the *London* sewers has already been spoken of as being situate at Hampton. The district yielding the amount of sewage which is assumed as being the gross wet house-refuse of the metropolis is, as we have seen, taken at 58 square miles, and is comprised within a circle of about $4\frac{1}{2}$ miles radius; this reaches only to Brixton, Dulwich, Greenwich, East India Docks, Layton, Highgate, Hampstead, Bayswater, Kensington, Brompton, and Battersea. The actual jurisdiction of the Commissioners is, then, nearly eight times larger than the portion to which the estimated amount of the sewage of the metropolis refers.

The metropolitan district is still distinguished by the old divisions of the Tower Hamlets, Poplar and Blackwall, Holborn and Finsbury, Westminster, &c.; but many of these divisions are now incorporated into one district; of which there would appear to be but four at present; or five, inclusive of the City.

These are as follows:—

1. Fulham and Hammersmith, Counter's Creek and Ranelagh districts.
2. Westminster (Eastern and Western), Regent-street, and Holborn.
3. Finsbury, Tower Hamlets, Poplar, and Blackwall.
4. Districts south of the Thames, Eastern and Western.
5. City.

The practical part or working of the Commission of Sewers is much less complicated at present than it was in the times of the independent districts and independent commissions.

The orders for all work to be done emanate from the court in Greek-street, but the several surveyors, &c. (whose salaries, numbers, &c., are given below), can and do order on their responsibility any repair of a temporary character which is evidently pressing, and report it at the next court day. The Court meets weekly and monthly, and what may be styled the heavier portion of the business, as regards expenditure on great works, is more usually transacted at the monthly meetings, when the attendance is generally fuller; but the Court can, and sometimes does, meet much more frequently, and sometimes has adjourned from day to day.

Any private individual or any public body may make a communication or suggestion to the Court of Sewers, which, if it be in accordance with their functions, is taken into consideration at the next accruing court day, or as soon after as convenient. The Court in these cases either comes to a decision of adoption or rejection of any proposition, or refers it to one of their engineers or surveyors for a report, or to a committee of the Commissioners, appointed by the Court; if the proposition be professional, as to defects, or alleged and recommended improvements in the local sewers, &c., it is referred to a professional gentleman for his opinion; if it be more general, as to the extension of sewerage to some new undertaking or meditated undertaking in the way of building new markets, streets, or any places, large and public; or in applications for the use and appropriation by enterprising men of sewage manure, it is referred to a committee.

On receiving such reports the Court makes an order according to its discretion. If the work to be done be extensive, it is entrusted to the chief engineer, and perhaps to a principal surveyor acting in accordance with him; if the work be more local, it is consigned to a surveyor. One or other of these officers provides, or causes to be prepared, a plan and a description of the work to be done, and instructs the clerk of the works to procure estimates of the cost at which a contractor will undertake to execute this work, or, as it is often called by the labouring class, to "complete the *job*" (a word at one time singularly applicable). The estimates are sent by the competing builders, architects, general speculators, or by any one wishing to contract, to the court house (without the intervention of any person, officially or otherwise) and they are submitted to the Board by their clerk. The lowest contract, as the sum total of the work, is most generally adopted, and when a contract has been accepted, the matter seems settled and done with, as regards the management of the Commissioners; for the contractor at once becomes responsible for the fulfilment of his contract, and may and does employ whom he pleases *and at what rates he pleases*, without fear of any control or interference from the Court. The work, however, is superintended by the surveyors, to ensure its execution according to the provisions of the agreement. The contractor is paid by direct order of the Court.

The surveyors and clerks of works are mostly limited as to their labours to the several districts; but the superior officers are employed in all parts, and so, if necessary, are the subordinate officers when the work requires an extra staff.

According to the Returns, the following functionaries appear to be connected with the undermentioned districts:—

Fulham, Hammersmith, Counter's Creek, and Ranelagh.
1 Surveyor.
3 Clerks of the Works.
1 Inspector of Flushing.

Eastern and Western Divisions of Westminster and Regent-street.
1 Surveyor, who has also the Holborn division to attend to.
2 Clerks of the Works.
6 Flap and Sluice keepers.

Holborn.
2 Clerks of the Works.
1 Inspector of Flushing.

Finsbury.
1 Clerk of the Works.
1 Inspector of Flushing.

Tower Hamlets, and Poplar and Blackwall.
1 Surveyor, who has also the Finsbury division included in his district.
2 Clerks of the Works.
2 Inspectors of Flushing.

South of the Thames. Western Districts.
1 Surveyor.
2 Clerks of the Works.
2 Inspectors of Flushing.

Eastern Districts.
1 Surveyor.
2 Clerks of the Works.
2 Inspectors of Flushing.

What may be called the working staff of the Metropolitan Commissioners consists of the following functionaries, receiving the following salaries:—

	£	s.
Chairman, with a yearly salary of	1,000	0
Secretary, with a yearly salary of (besides an allowance of £100, in lieu of apartments)	800	0
Clerk of minutes	350	0
Two clerks of do., (each with a salary of £150)	300	0
One do., with a salary of	120	0
One do. do.	105	0
One do. do.	95	0
One do. do.	90	0
Accountant do.	350	0
Accountant's clerk do.	150	0
Do do.	80	0
Clerk of surveyors' and contractors' accounts	200	0
Do. do.	125	0
Do. do.	110	0
Clerk of rates	250	0
Another do.	180	0
Do. do.	110	0
Do. do.	90	0
Engineer	1,000	0
For travelling expenses	200	0
Surveyor for Fulham and Hammersmith, Counter's Creek, and Ranelagh districts	350	0
Clerk of works (Hammersmith)	150	0
Do. (Counter's Creek)	150	0
Do. (Ranelagh)	150	0
Inspector of flushing	80	0
Surveyor of eastern and western divisions of Westminster, and of Regent-st. and Holborn divisions	300	0
Two clerks of works (eastern and western and Regent - street), with a salary of £300 each	600	0
Two do. (Holborn), with a salary of £150 each	300	0
Inspector of flushing	80	0
Surveyor of Finsbury, Tower Hamlets, and Poplar and Blackwall	300	0
Clerk of works (Finsbury)	150	0
Inspector of flushing	80	0
Two clerks of works (Tower Hamlets, and Poplar and Blackwall), with a salary of £150 each	300	0
Two inspectors of flushings with a salary of £80 each	160	0
One marsh bailiff	65	0

	£	s.		£	s.
Surveyor of the western districts south of the Thames	300	0	Surveyor (of the surveying and drawing staff)	250	0
Do., eastern do.	250	0	Drawing clerk	150	0
Clerk of works (eastern portion)	164	0	Two do., with a salary of £130 each	260	0
Two inspectors of flushing, £80 each	160	0	Five do., with a salary of £105 each	525	0
One wallreeve	22	8	One do.	50	0
Clerk of works (western portion)	164	0	Six surveyors, with a salary of £100 each	600	0
Do. do.	150	0	Six chainmen,18s. a week each	280	0
Two inspectors of flushing, with a salary of £80 each	160	0	Office-keeper and crier (general service)	120	0
Two engineer's clerks, with a salary of £150 each	300	0	Bailiff, &c.	100	0
			Strong-room keeper	80	0
One do.	150	0	One messenger	70	0
One do.	100	0	Two do.,£40 each	80	0
One do.	80	0	Three errand-boys, £32 each	96	0
One by-law clerk	150	0	Housekeeper	150	0
Twenty-two flap and sluice keepers	892	12	Yearly total	£13,874	0

This is called a "reduced" staff, and the reduction of salaries is certainly very considerable.

If we consider the yearly emoluments of tradesmen in businesses requiring no great extent of education or general intelligence, the salaries of the surveyors, clerk of the works, &c., must appear very far from extravagant; and when we consider their responsibility and what may be called their removability, some of the salaries may be pronounced mean; for I think it must be generally admitted by all, except the narrow-minded, who look merely at the immediate outlay as the be-all and the end-all of every expenditure, that if the surveyors, clerks of works, inspectors of flushing, &c., be the best men who could be procured (as they ought to be), or at any rate be thorough masters of their craft, they are rather underpaid than overpaid.

The above statement may be analysed in the following manner:—

	£	s.	£
Chairman			1,000
Secretary and 7 clerks	1860	0	
Accountant and 5 clerks	1015	0	
Clerk of rates and 3 clerks	630	0	
			3,505
Engineer and 5 clerks	1830	0	
7 surveyors, of surveying and drawing staff, with 6 chainmen and 9 drawing clerks	2125	0	
5 district surveyors	1500	0	
12 clerks of works	2278	0	
9 inspectors of flushing	720	0	
22 flap and sluice keepers	892	12	
Bailiff, marsh-bailliff, and wallreeve	187	8	
			9,533

	£	s.	£
Office keeper, strong-room keeper, and housekeeper	350	0	
3 messengers and 3 errand-boys	246	0	
			596
			£14,634

The cost of rent, taxes, stationery, and office incidentals, is now 4440l., which makes the total yearly outlay amount to upwards of 19,000l. The annual cost of the staff in the secretary's department is said to have been reduced from 3962l. 4s. to 3605l.; in the engineers' department from 16,437l. 3s. to 8973l. 16s. In the general service there has been an increase from 606l. 16s. to 696l.

A deputation who waited lately upon Lord John Russell is said to have declared the expenses of the Commissioners' office to be at the rate of from 25 to 30 per cent. on the amount of rate collected. The sum collected in the year 1850 averaged 89,341l. The cost of management in that year was 23,465l.; this, it will be seen, is 26 per cent of the gross income.

The annual statement of the receipts and expenditure under the Commission for the year 1851 has just been published, but not *officially;* from this it appears that in February, 1851—

	£	s.	d.
The balance of cash in hand was	5,750	9	11
The total receipts during the year have amounted to	129,000	0	9
Making together	134,750	10	8

The expenditure, as returned under the general head, is—

	£	s.	d.
For work	£95,539	19	3

(This item includes the cost of supervision and compensation for damages.)

	£	s.	d.
The cost of surveys has been	6,332	19	9
Management	16,430	9	2
Loans	10,442	10	2
Contingencies	2,749	1	1
Total payments	131,494	19	5
Balance in hand	£3,355	11	3

As an instance of the mismanagement of the sewers work of the metropolis, it is but right that the subjoined document should be published.

I need not offer any comment on the following "Return to an Address of the Honourable the House of Commons, dated 28th July, 1851," except that I was told early in January, on good authority, that the matter was now worse than it was when reported as follows:—

"*Privy Gardens, Whitehall Yard, Scotland Yard, &c., Public Sewer.*

"With reference to the two orders of the Commissioners of Her Majesty's Woods, &c., I have the honour to state that, since the 15th of November (when I last sent in a memorandum), I have frequently visited the several Crown buildings affected by the building of the main public sewer for draining Westminster; viz., the Earl of Malmsbury's, the Exchequer Bill Office, the United Service Museum, Lord Liverpool's, Mr. Vertue's, Mr. Alderman Thompson's, and Messrs. Dalgleish's.

"All these buildings have been more or less damaged by the construction of the sewer; the Exchequer Bill Office, the United Service Museum, and Mr. Vertue's, in a manner that, in my opinion, can *never be effectually repaired*.

"At Lord Malmsbury's, the party wall next to the Exchequer Bill Office has *moved*, as shown by some cracks in the staircase; but for this house it may not be necessary to require more to be done than stopping and painting.

"At the Exchequer Bill Office, the old Gothic groins have been cracked in several places, and several settlements have taken place in the walls over and near to where the sewer passes under the building. The shores are still standing against this building, but it would now be better to remove them; the cracks in the groins and walls *can never be repaired* to render the building so substantial as it was before. The cracks in the basement still from month to month show a very slight movement; those in the staircase and roof also appear to increase. As respects this building, I would submit to the Commissioners of Woods that it *would not be advisable to permit the surveyors of the Commissioners of Sewers to enter and make only a surface repair of plaster and paint;* but I would suggest that a careful survey be made by surveyors appointed respectively by the Board of Woods and the Commissioners of Sewers, and that a thorough repair of the building be made (so far as it is susceptible of repair), under the Board of Woods; the Commissioners of Sewers paying such proportion of the cost thereof as may fairly be deemed to have been occasioned by their proceedings.

"At the United Service Museum, the settlements on the side next the sewer appear to me very serious.

"The house occupied by Lord Liverpool, as also Mr. Vertue's house, of which his Lordship is Crown lessee, were both affected, the former to some extent, but not seriously; of the latter, the west front sunk, and pulled over the whole house with it; but as respects these two houses the interference of the Board is, I believe, unnecessary, Mr. Hardwicke (one of the Sewer Commissioners) having, as architect for Lord Liverpool, caused both to be repaired.

"A like repair has also been made in the kitchen offices of Mr. Alderman Thompson's house, where alone any cracks appeared.

"At Messrs. Dalgleish and Taylor's, very serious injury has been done to both their buildings and their trade. The Commissioners of Sewers have a steam-engine still at work on those premises, and have not yet concluded their operations there. Some of the sheds which entirely fell down they have rebuilt; and others, which appear in a very defective if not dangerous state, it is understood they propose to repair or rebuild; but as eventually Messrs. Dalgleish and Taylor will have a very heavy claim against them for interference with business, and as the extent of damage to the buildings which has been done, or may hereafter arise, cannot at present be fully ascertained, it would probably be advisable to postpone this part of the subject, giving notice, however, to the Commissioners of Sewers that it must hereafter come under consideration.

(Signed) "JAMES PENNETHORNE.
"10th May, 1851."

"*Sewer, Whitehall Yard, &c.*
"Under the order of the Commissioners of Her Majesty's Woods, &c., of yesterday's date, endorsed on a letter from Mr. Tonna, I have inspected the United Service Institution in Whitehall Yard, and find most of the cracks have moved.

"The movement, though slight, and not showing immediate danger, is more than I had anticipated would occur within so short a period when I reported on the 10th instant. It tends to confirm the opinion therein given, and shows the necessity for immediate precaution, and for a thorough repair.

(Signed) "JAMES PENNETHORNE.
"16th May, 1851.

"SEYMOUR,
"CHARLES GORE,
⎰ Commissioners of Her Majesty's Woods, Forests, Land Revenues, Works, and Buildings.

"Office of Woods, &c.
"5th August, 1851."

OF THE SEWERS RATE.

HAVING shown the expenditure of the Commission of Sewers, we now come to consider its income.

The funds available for the sewerage and drainage of the several towns throughout the kingdom, are raised by means of a particular property tax, termed the Sewers Rate. This forms part of what are designated the *Local* Taxes of England and Wales.

Local taxes are of two classes:—

I. Rates raised upon property in *defined* districts, as parishes, jurisdictions, counties, &c.

II. Tolls, dues, and fees charged for particular services on particular occasions, as turnpike tolls, harbour dues, &c., &c.

The rates or sums raised upon the property lying within a certain circumscribed locality, admit of being subdivided into two orders—

1. The rates of *independent* districts, or those which, being required for a particular district (as the parish or some equivalent territorial limit), are not only levied within the bounds of that district, but expended for the purposes of it alone; as is the case with the poor rate.

2. The rates of *aggregate* districts, or those which, though required to be expended for the purposes of a given district (such as the county), are raised in detail in the several inferior districts (such as the various parishes) which compose the larger one, and which contribute the sums thus levied to one common fund; such is the case with the county rate.

But the rates of independent districts may be further distinguished into two orders, viz.—

i. Those which are levied on the same classes of persons, the same kinds of property, and the same principles of valuation as the poor rate; such are the highway rate, the lighting and watching, and the militia rate among the independent rates; and the police, borough, and county rates among the aggregate rates.

ii. Those which are *not* levied on the same basis as the poor rate. The church and sewers rates are familiar instances of this peculiarity.

The sewers rate, then, is a local tax required for an *independent* rather than an *aggregate* district, and is *not* levied upon the basis of the poor law.

The assessment of the poor rate, for instance, includes tithes of every kind, that of the sewers rate extends only to such tithes only as are in the hands of laymen. Again, the sewers rate embraces some incorporeal hereditaments to which the poor rate does not extend; but stock in trade, which of late years has been specially exempted from the poor rate, was never subject to the sewers rate.

A sewers rate, however, was known as early as the sixth year of Henry VI. (1427), though "commissions" were not instituted till the time of Henry VIII. The Act which now regulates the collection of the funds required for the cleansing, building, repairs, and improvements of the sewers, is 4 and 5 Vict. (1841). This statute gives the "Courts" or "Commissions" of Sewers, power "to tax in the gross" in each parish, &c., all lands, &c., within the jurisdiction of such courts, for the requirements of the public sewerage. This impost is not periodically levied, nor at any stated or even regularly recurring term, but "as occasion requires:" perhaps once in two or three years. It is (with some exceptions, which require no notice) what is commonly called "a landlord's tax" in the metropolis, that is, the sewers-rate collector must be paid by the occupier of the premises, who, on the production of the collector's receipt, can deduct the amount from his rent. If this arrangement were meant to convey a notion to the public that the sewers tax was a tax on property—on the capitalist who owns, and not on the tenant who merely occupies—it is a shallow device, for every one must know that the more sewers rate a tenant pays *for* his landlord, the more rent he must pay *to* him.

The sewers rate is levied according to the rateable value put upon property by the surveyors and assessors appointed by the Commissioners, who may make the rate "by such ways and means, and in such manner and form, as to them may seem most convenient." It seems a question yet to be determined whether or not there is a right of appeal against the sewers rate, but the general opinion is that there is *no appeal*. The rate can be mortgaged by the Commissioners if an advance of money is considered desirable. The maximum of 1s. in the pound on the net annual value of the property was fixed by the Act. The Commissioners have also the power to levy a "special rate" on any district not connected with the general system of sewerage, but which it has been resolved should be so connected; also an "improvement rate." at a maximum of 10 per cent. on the rack rent, "in respect of works they may judge to be of private benefit," a provision which has called forth some comments.

The metropolitan sewers rate is now collected in nine districts.

There are at present 42 Commissions or Courts of Sewers throughout England and Wales.

The only return which has yet been prepared of the annual amount assessed and collected under the authority of the Metropolitan Commission of Sewers, is one presented to the House of Commons in 1843. It includes the sum assessed in four of the eight districts within the jurisdiction of the Metropolitan Commissioners from 1831 to 1840 inclusive.

Districts.	Total in the 10 years.	Annual Average.
	£	£
Westminster	235,397	23,539$\frac{7}{10}$
Holborn and Finsbury	123,317	12,331$\frac{7}{10}$
Tower Hamlets	82,468	8,246$\frac{8}{10}$
From East Moulsey, in Surrey, to Ravensbourne, in Kent	175,137	17,513$\frac{7}{10}$
	616,319	61,631$\frac{9}{10}$

The following amounts were returned to Parliament as that expended in two other of the metropolitan districts in the year 1833:—

In the City . . . . £17,718$\frac{2}{10}$
Poplar district . . . . 2,746$\frac{9}{10}$

£20,465$\frac{1}{10}$

Annual average of the four above-mentioned districts . . . 61,631$\frac{9}{10}$

Yearly total £82,097

The two districts excluded from the above total are the minor ones of St. Katherine and Greenwich, so that altogether the gross sum levied within the jurisdiction of the Metropolitan Commissioners must have been between 85,000*l*. and 90,000*l*.

The annual amount of the local rates in England and Wales is, according to a work on the subject ("The Local Taxes of the United Kingdom"), published "under the direction of the Poor Law Commissioners" in 1846, 8,801,838*l*.* In this large sum only the average annual outlay on the six districts of the sewers of the metropolis is included (82,097*l*.), and it is stated that not even an approximate average could be arrived at as regards the expenditure on sewers in the country districts. Such absence of statistical knowledge,—and it is a want continually observable—is little creditable to the legislative, executive, and administrative powers of the State.

I shall now proceed to show, from the best data at my command, the present outlay on the metropolitan sewers.

* The following statement may, according to the work above alluded to, be presented as an approximate

According to the present law, the Commissioners are required to submit to Parliament yearly returns of the money collected on account of, and expended in, the sewerage of the metropolis.

I need only state, that in the latest and, indeed, the sole returns upon the subject, the rates in 1845-6-7, under the former separate commissions, were 1d. and 2d. in the pound on land, and from 3d. (Ranelagh and Westminster) to 1s. 10d. (Greenwich) on houses.

The rates made under the combined and consolidated Commissions, from 30th Nov., 1847, to 8th Oct., 1849, were all 6d., excepting the Western division of Westminster sewers, which were 3d., and a part of the Surrey and Kent district, 8d.

The rates under the present Metropolitan Commission, from 8th October, 1849, to 31st July, 1851, are all 6d., with a similar exception in Surrey and Kent. The following are the only further returns bearing immediately on the subject:—

RETURN OF THE PERCENTAGE ON THE TOTAL RATEABLE ANNUAL VALUE OF THE PROPERTY ASSESSED, to which the Rates collected under the separate COMMISSIONS, between January, 1845, and November, 1847, amounted; SIMILAR RETURN as to the combined and consolidated COMMISSIONS, from November, 1847, to October, 1849; and as to the present COMMISSION, from October, 1849, to July 31, 1851.

	Total Rateable Annual Value of the Districts on November 30, 1847, and October 8, 1849, and July 31, 1851, respectively.	Average Amount collected for One Year.	Amount of the Percentage of the Rates collected on the Rateable Annual Value.
	£ s. d.	£ s. d.	£ s. d.
Under the old separate Commissions of Sewers, between January, 1845, and November 30, 1847	6,683,896 0 0	81,738 11 0	1 4 5 or 2¾d. ·72 in the pound per annum.
Under the combined and consolidated Commissions, from November 30, 1847, to October 8, 1849 (including first Metropolitan Commission)	7,128,111 0 0	67,707 16 3	0 18 11¾ or 2¼d. ·11 in the pound per annum.
Under the present Metropolitan Commission of Sewers, from October 8, 1849, to July 21, 1851	8,185,090* 0 0 8,820,325† 0 0	89,341 16 0	1 1 11 or 2½d. ·52 in the pound per annum. 1 0 3 or 2¼d. ·72 in the pound per annum.

* Rental of the districts now rated.
† Rental of the districts within the active jurisdiction in which expenses have been incurred, and which are about to be rated.

AUGUST, 1851.

THOMAS COGGIN,
Clerk of Rates and Collections.

---

return of the present annual amount of the local rates in England and Wales.

I. RATES.
A. RATES OF INDEPENDENT DISTRICTS.
1. *On the basis of the poor rate.*
The poor rate, including the purposes of—
The workhouse building rate }
The survey and valuation rate }
Relief of the poor £4,976,093
Other objects 567,567
Contributions to county and borough rates (see below).
Jail fees rate . . . }
Constables rate . . . } unknown
Highway rates 1,312,312
Lighting and watching rate . . unknown
Militia rate . . . . . not needed
2. *Not on the basis of the poor rate.*
Church rates 506,812
Sewers rate—
General sewers tax—
In the metropolis . . . 82,097
In the rest of the country . unknown
Drainage and inclosure rates . }
Inclosure rate . . . . } unknown
Regulated pasture rate . . }
B. RATES OF AGGREGATE DISTRICTS.
County rates . { Contributed }
Hundred rate . { from the } 1,356,457
Borough rates . { poor rate. }

Total rates of England and Wales . £8,801,834

The amount of the taxation in the shape of tolls, dues, and fees is as follows:—
II. TOLLS, DUES, AND FEES.
Turnpike tolls £1,348,085
Borough tolls and dues . £172,911
City of London . . . 205,100
—————— 378,011
Light dues 257,776
Port dues 554,645
Church dues and fees . }
Marriage fees . . . }
Registration fees . . } unknown
Justiciary fees—
Clerks of the Peace . £11,057
Justices' clerks . . 57,668
—————— 68,725

Total tolls, dues, and fees of England and Wales . . . £2,607,241

The subjoined, then adds the same work, founded on the preceding details, may be regarded as exhibiting an approximate estimate of the present amount of the local taxes in England and Wales, being, however, obviously below the actual total.
Rates £8,801,838
Tolls, dues, and fees . 2,607,241
—————— £11,409,079

"The annual amount of the local taxation of England and Wales may at the present time be stated, in round numbers, at not less than £12,000,000;" or we may say that the local taxation of the country is one-fourth of the amount of the general taxation.

RETURN OF THE COST OF MANAGEMENT PER ANNUM ON THE TOTAL RATEABLE ANNUAL VALUE OF THE DISTRICTS.

YEARS.	Total Rateable Annual Value of the Districts.			Cost of Management per Annum.			Rate per Cent. per Annum of Cost of Management on the Rateable Annual Value of the Districts.		
	£	s.	d.	£	s.	d.	£	s.	d.
1845	6,320,331	0	0	18,591	4	3	0	5	10½
1846	6,423,909	0	0	18,097	5	1	0	5	7½
1847	6,683,896	0	0	24,371	16	9	0	7	3½
1848	6,783,111	0	0	20,008	7	10	0	5	10¾
1849	8,077,591	0	0	20,005	7	6	0	4	11¼
1850	8,791,967	0	0	23,465	18	7	0	5	4

August 7, 1851.

G. S. HATTON,
Accountant.

Of the Cleansing of the Sewers—Ventilation.

There are two modes of purifying the sewers; the one consists in removing the foul air, the other in removing the solid deposits. I shall deal first with that mode of purification which consists in the mechanical removal or chemical decomposition of the noxious gases engendered within the sewers.

This is what is termed the Ventilation of the Sewers, and forms a very important branch of the inquiry into the character and working of the underground refuse-channels, for it relates to the risk of explosions and the consequent risk of destruction to men's lives; while, if the sewer be ill-ventilated, the surrounding atmosphere is often prejudicially affected by the escape of impure air from the subterranean channels.

A survey as to the ventilation, &c., of the sewers was made by Mr. Hawkins, Assistant-Surveyor, and Mr. Jenkins, Clerk of the Works. Four examinations took place of sewers; of those in Bloomsbury; those from Tottenham-court-road to Norfolk-street, Strand; from the Guard-room in Buckingham Palace to the Horseferry-road, Millbank; and in Grosvenor-square and the streets adjacent. There were difficulties attending the experiment. From Castle-street to Museum-street there was a drop of 4 feet in the levels, so that the examiners had to advance on their hands and knees, and it was difficult to make observations. In some places in Westminster also the water and silt were knee deep, and the lamps (three were used) splashed all over. In Bloomsbury the sewers gave no token of the presence of any gas, but in the other places its presence was very perceptible, especially in a sewer on the west side of Grosvenor-square, a very low one, in which the gas was ignited within the wire shade of one of the lamps, but without producing any effect beyond that of immediately extinguishing the light. There was also during the route, in the neighbourhood of Sir Henry Meux's brewery and of an adjoining distillery in Vine-street, a considerable quantity of steam in the sewer, but it had no material effect upon the light.

The examiners came to the conclusion that where there was any liability to an explosion from the presence of carburetted hydrogen, or other causes, the Improved Davy Lamp afforded an almost certain protection.

The attention of the Commissioners seems to have been chiefly given of late, as regards ventilation and indeed general improvement, to the sewers on the Surrey side of the metropolis. Among these a new sewer along Friar-street, running from the Blackfriars to the Southwark-bridge-road, is one of the most noticeable.

Friar-street is one of the smaller off thoroughfares, the character of which is, perhaps, little suspected by those who pass along the open Blackfriars-road. As you turn out of that road to the left hand, advancing from the bridge, almost opposite the Magdalen Hospital, is Friar-street. On its left hand, as you proceed along it, are gas-works, and the factories, or work places, of tradesmen in the soap-boiling, tallow-melting, cat and other gut manufacturing, bone-boiling, and other noisome callings. On the right hand are a series of short and often neatly-built streets, but the majority of them have the look of unmistakable squalor or poverty, though *not* of the poverty of the industrious. Across Flint-street, Green-street, and other ways, few of them horse thoroughfares, hang, on a fair day, lines of washed clothes to dry. Yellow-looking chemises and petticoats are affixed alongside men's trowsers and waistcoats; coarse-featured and brazen-looking women, with necks and faces reddened, as if with brick-dust, from exposure to the weather, stand at their doors and beckon to the passers by. Perhaps in no part of the metropolis is there a more marked manifestation of moral obsceneness on the one hand, and physical obsceneness on the other. With the low prostitution of this locality is mixed the low and the bold crime of the metropolis. Some of the off-shoots from Friar-street communicate with places of as nefarious a character. Hackett, whom his newspaper admirers seem to wish to elevate into the fame of a second Jack Sheppard, resided in this quarter. The gang who were last winter repulsed in their burglarious attack on Mr. Holford's villa in the Regent's-park favoured the same locality, and were arrested in their old haunts. Public-houses may be seen here and there—houses, perhaps, not greatly discouraged by the police—which are at once the rendezvous and the trap of offenders, for to and from such resorts they can be readily traced. And all over this place of moral degradation extends the stench of offensive manufactures and ill-ventilated sewers. Certainly there is now an improvement, but it is still bad enough.

A Report of the 21st September, 1848, shows that a new sewer, 1500 feet in length, had been "put in along Friar-street, with a fall of 15 inches from the level of the sewer in Blackfriars-road to Suffolk-street. The sewer," states the Report, "with which it communicates at its upper end in the Blackfriars-road contains nearly 2 feet in depth of soil; it in consequence has silted up to that level with semi-fluid black filth, principally from the factories, of the most poisonous and sickening description, forming an *elongated cesspool* 1500 feet in length, the filth at its lower end being upwards of 3 feet in depth. Since the building of this sewer, the foul matter so discharged into it has been in a state of decomposition, constantly giving off pestilential and poisonous gases, which have spread into and filled the adjoining sewers; thence they are being drawn into the houses by the house-drains, and into the streets by the street-drains, to such a fearful extent as to infect the whole atmosphere of the neighbourhood, and so to cause the very offensive odour so generally complained of there. Sulphuretted hydrogen is present in these sewers in large quantities, as metals, silver and copper, are attacked and blackened by it; and the smell from it is so sickening as to be almost unbearable."

On the question of how best to deal with sewers such as the Friar-street, Messrs. John Roe and John Phillips (surveyors) and Mr. Henry Austin (consulting engineer) have agreed in the following opinion:—

"The most simple and convenient method would be by placing large strong fires in shafts directly over the crown of the sewers. The expense of each furnace, with the inclosure around it, will be about 20*l*. The fires would be fed almost constantly, by which little smoke would be generated. The heat to be produced from these fires would rarefy the air so much as to create rapidly ascending currents in the shafts, and strong draughts through the sewers, the foul air in which would then be drawn to the fires and there consumed; and as it was being destroyed fresh air would be drawn in at all the existing inlets of house and street drains, pushing forward and supplying the place of the foul air."

Concerning the explosions of, or deaths in, the sewers from the impure gases, there is, I believe, no statistical account. The most remarkable catastrophe of this kind was the death of five persons in a sewer in Pimlico, in October, 1849; of these, three were regular sewer-men, and the others were a policeman and Mr. Wells, a surgeon, who went into the sewer in the hopes of giving assistance. Mr. Phillips, the then chief surveyor of the Commission of Sewers, stated that the cause of these deaths in the sewers was entirely an exceptional case, and the gas which had caused the accident inquired into was not a sewer gas. "There is often," he said, "a great escape of gas from the mains, which found its way into the sewers. The gas, however, which has done the mischief in the present instance would not explode."

Dr. Ure's opinion was, that the deceased men died from asphyxia, caused by inhaling sulphuretted hydrogen and carbonic acid gas in mixture with prussic vapour, and that these noxious emanations were derived from the refuse lime of gas-works thrown in with other rubbish to make up the road above the sewer. Other scientific gentlemen attributed the five deaths to the action of sulphuretted hydrogen gas, or, according to Dr. Lyon Playfair, to be chemically correct, hydro-sulphate of ammonia. The coroner (Mr. Bedford), in summing up, said that Mr. Phillips wished it to be supposed that gas lime was the cause of the foul gas; and Dr. Ure said that gas lime had to do with the calamity. But Dr. Miller, Mr. Richard Phillips, Mr. Campbell, and Dr. Playfair, more especially the latter, were perfectly sure that lime had nothing to do with it. The verdict was the following:— "We find that Daniel Pert, Thomas Gee, and John Attwood died from the inhalation of noxious gas generated in a neglected and unventilated sewer in Kenilworth-street. And we find that Henry Wells and John Walsh met their deaths from the same cause, in their laudable endeavours to save the lives of the first three sufferers. The jury unanimously consider the commissioners and officers of the Metropolitan Sewers are much to blame for having neglected to avail themselves of the unusual advantages offered, from the local situation of the Grosvenor-canal, for the purpose of flushing the sewers in this district."

OF "FLUSHING" AND "PLONGING," AND OTHER MODES OF WASHING THE SEWERS.

THE next step in our inquiry—and that which at present concerns us more than any other—is the mode of removing the solid deposits from the sewers, as well as the condition of the workmen connected with that particular branch of labour. The sewers are the means by which a larger proportion of the wet refuse of the metropolis is removed from our houses, and we have now to consider the means by which the more solid part of this refuse is removed from the sewers themselves. The latter operation is quite as essential to health and cleanliness as the former; for to allow the filth to collect in the channels which are intended to remove it, and there to remain decomposing and vitiating the atmosphere of the metropolis, is manifestly as bad as not to remove it at all; and since the more solid portions of the sewage *will* collect and form hard deposits at the bottom of each duct, it becomes necessary that some means should be devised for the periodical purgation of the sewers themselves.

There have been two modes of effecting this object. The one has been the *carting* away of the more solid refuse, and the other the *washing* of it away, or, as it is termed, *flushing* in the case

FLUSHING THE SEWERS.

(Partly from a Daguerreotype by Beard, *and partly from a Sketch kindly lent by* Mr. Whiting.*)*

THE RAT-CATCHERS OF THE SEWERS.

[*From a Daguerreotype by* BEARD.]

of the *covered* sewers, and *plonging* in the case of the *open* ones. Under both systems, whether the refuse be carted or flushed away, the hard deposit has to be first loosened by manual labourers—the difference consisting principally in the means of after-removal.

The first of these systems—viz., the cartage method—was that which prevailed in the metropolis till the year 1847. I shall therefore give a brief description of this mode of cleansing the sewers before proceeding to treat of the now more general mode of "flushing."

Under the old system, the clearing away of the deposit was a "nightman's" work, differing little, except in being more toilsome, offensive to the public, and difficult. A hole was made from the street down into the sewer where the deposit was thickest, and the deposit was raised by means of a tub, filled below, drawn up to the street, and emptied into a cart, or spread in mounds in the road to be shovelled into some vehicle. A nightman told me that this mode of work was sometimes a great injury to his trade, because "when it was begun on a night many of the householders sleeping in the neighbourhood used to say to themselves, or to their missusses, as they turned in their beds, 'It's them ere cussed cesspools again! I wish they was done away with.' An' all the time, sir, the cesspools was as hinnocent and as sweet as a hangel."

This clumsy and filthy process is now but occasionally resorted to. A man who had superintended a labour of this kind in a narrow, but busy thoroughfare in Southwark, told me that these sewer labourers were the worst abused men in London. No one had a good word for them.

But there have been other modes of removing the indurated sewage, besides that of cartage; and which, though not exactly flushing, certainly consisted in allowing the deposit to be washed away. Some of these contrivances were curious enough.

I learn from a Report printed in 1849, that the King's Scholars' Pond Sewer, in the city of Westminster, running near the Abbey, contained a continuous bed of deposit, of soil, sand, and filth, from 10 to 30 inches in depth, and this for a mile and a half next the river—the first mile yielding more than 6000 loads of matter. This sewer was to be cleansed.

"We first used a machine," says Mr. J. Lysander Hale, "in the form of a plough and harrow combined; a horse dragged it through the deposit in the sewer; one man attended the horse, and another guided the plough. The work done by this machine, in cutting a channel through the soil and causing the water to move through it quickly, was effectual to remove the deposit; but as the sewer is a tidal sewer, and its sole entrance for a horse being its outlet, the machine could only be used for a small part of any day. Sometimes with a strong breeze up the river, the tide would not recede sufficiently to permit the horse to get in at all (and it did not appear advisable to incur the expense of 50*l*. to build a sideway entrance for the animal); so that under these circumstances we were obliged to discontinue the use of the horse and plough; which, under other circumstances, would have been very effective." From this time, I understand, the sewers of London have remained unploughed by means of horse labour.

But the plough was not altogether abandoned, and as horse-power was not found very easily applicable, water-power was resorted to. The plough and harrow were attached to a barge, which was introduced into the sewer. The sluice gates were kept shut until the ebb of the tide made the difference of level between the contents of the sewer and the surface of the Thames equal to some eight feet. "The gates were then suddenly opened, and the rapid and deep current of water following, was then sufficient to bring the barge and plough down the sewer with a force equal to five or six horse-power."

This last-mentioned method was also soon abandoned. We now come to the more approved plan of "flushing."

"The term '*flushing* sewers' implies," says Mr. Haywood, in his Report, "cleansing by the application of *bodies* of water in the sewers; this is periodically effected, varying in intervals according to the necessities of the sewerage or other circumstances."

The flushing system has a two-fold object, viz., to remove old deposits and prevent the accumulation of new. When the deposit is not allowed to accumulate and harden, "flushing consists," says Mr. Haywood, "simply in heading back and letting off *flush at once*" (hence the origin of the term) "that which has been delivered into the sewers in a certain number of hours by the various houses draining into them, diluted with large quantities of water specially employed for the purpose."

Though the operation of "flushing" is one of modern introduction, as regards the metropolis—one, indeed, which may be said to have originated in the modern demand for improved sanitary regulations—it has been practised in some country parts since the days of Henry VIII.

Flushing was practised also by those able engineers, the ancient Romans. One of the grand architectural remains of that people, the best showing their system of flushing, is in the Amphitheatre at Nismes, in France. The site of the ruined amphitheatre presents a large elliptical area, 114,251 superficial feet comprising its extent. Around the arena ran a large sewer 3 feet 6 inches in width, and 4 feet 9 inches in height. With this sewer, elliptical in shape, 348 pipes communicated, carrying into it the rain-fall and the refuse caused by the resort of 23,000 persons, for the seats alone contained that number. "The system of flushing, practised here," says Mr. Cresy, "with such advantage, deserves to be noticed, there being means of driving through this elliptical sewer a volume of water at pleasure, with such force that no solid matter could by any possibility remain within any of the drains or sewers. An aqueduct, 2 feet 8 inches in width, and 6 feet in height, brought this water from the reservoirs of Nismes, not only to fill but to purge the whole of these sewers; after traversing the arena, it deviated a little to the south-west, where it was carried out at the sixth arcade, east of the southern entrance. Man-holes and steps to descend into this capacious vaulted aqueduct were introduced in several places; and there can be no doubt that by directing for some hours such a stream of water through it, the greatest cleanliness was preserved throughout all the sewers of the building."

The flushing of sewers appears to have been introduced into the metropolis by Mr. John Roe in the year 1847, but did not come into general use till some years later. There used to be a partial flushing of the London sewers twelve years ago. The mode of flushing as at present practised is as follows:—

In the first instance the inspector examines and reports the condition of the sewer, and receives and issues his orders accordingly. When the sewer is ordered to be flushed—and there is no periodical or regular observance of time in the operation—the men enter the sewers and rake up the deposit, loosening it everywhere, so as to render the whole easy to be swept along by the power of the volume of water. The sewers generally are, in their widest part, provided with grooves, or, as the men style them, "framings." Into these framings are fitted, or permanently attached, what I heard described as "penstocks," but which are spoken of in some of the reports as "traps," "gates," or "sluice gates." They are made both of wood and iron. By a series of bolts and adjustments, the penstocks can be fixed ready for use when the tide is highest in the sewer, and the volume of water the greatest. They then, of course, are in the nature of dams, the water having accumulated in consequence of the stoppage. The deposit having been loosened, the bolts are withdrawn, when the gates suddenly fly back, and the accumulated water and stirred-up sewage sweeps along impetuously, while the men retreat into some side recesses adapted for the purpose. The same is done with each penstock until the matter is swept through the outlet. The men always follow the course of this sewage-current when the sewer is of sufficient capacity to enable them to do so, throwing or pushing forward any more solid matter with their shovels.

"To flush we generally go and draw a slide up and let a flush of water down," said one man to me, "and then we have iron rakers to loosen the stuff. We have got another way that we do it as well; one man stands here, when the flush of water's coming down, with a large board; then he lets the water rise to the top of this board, and then there's two or three of us on ahead, with shovels, loosening the stuff—then he ups with this board and lets a good heavy flush of water come down. Precious hard work it is, I can assure you. I've had many a wet shirt. We stand up to our fork in the water, right to the top of our jack-boots, and sometimes over them."

"Ah, I should think you often get over the top of yours, for you come home with your stockings wet enough, goodness knows," exclaimed his wife, who was present. "When there's a good flush of water coming down," he resumed, "we're obligated to put our heads fast up against the crown of the sewer, and bear upon our shovels, so that we may not be carried away, and taken bang into the Thames. You see there's nothing for us to lay hold on. Why, there was one chap went and lifted a slide right up, when he ought to have had it up only 9 or 10 inches at the furthest, and he nearly swamped three of us. If we should be taken off our legs there's a heavy fall—about 3 feet—just before you comes to the mouth of the sewer, and if we was to get there, the water is so rapid nothing could save us. When we goes to work we nails our lanterns up to the crown of the sewer. When the slide is lifted up the rush is very great, and takes all before it. It roars away like a wild beast. We're always obliged to work according to tide, both above and below ground. When we have got no water in the sewer we shovels the dirt up into a bank on both sides, so that when the flush of water comes down the loosened dirt is all carried away by it. After flushing, the bottom of the sewer is as clean as this floor, but in a couple of months the soil is a foot to 15 inches deep, and middling hard."

"Flushing-gates," an engineer has reported, "are chiefly of use in sewers badly constructed and without falls, but containing plenty of water; and they are of very little use where the gate has to be shut 24 hours and longer, before a head of water has accumulated; but where intermittent flushing is practised, strong smells are often caused *solely* by the stagnation of the water or sewage while accumulating behind the gate."

The most general mode of flushing at present adopted is not to keep in the water, &c., which has flowed into the sewer from the streets and houses, as well as the tide of the river, but to convey the flushing water from the plugs of the water companies into the kennels, and so into the sewers. I find in one of the Reports acknowledgments of the liberal supplies granted for flushing by the several companies. The water of the Surrey Canal has been placed, for the same object, at the disposal of the Sewer Commissioners.

It is impossible to "flush" at all where a sewer has a "dead-end;" that is, where there is a "block," as in the case of the Kenilworth-street sewer, Pimlico, in which five persons lost their lives in 1848.

There is no difference in the system of flushing in the Metropolitan and City jurisdictions, except that for the greater facilities of the process, the City provides water-tanks in Newgate-market, where the heads of three sewers meet, and where the accumulation of animal garbage, and the fierceness and numbers of the rats attracted thereby, were at one time frightful; at Leadenhall-market, and elsewhere, such tanks were also provided to the number of ten, the largest being the Newgate-market tank, which is a brick cistern of 8000 gallons capacity. Of these tanks, however, only four are now kept filled, for this collection of water is found unnecessary, the regular system of flushing answering the purpose without them; and I understand that in a little time there will be no tanks at all. The tank is filled, when required, by a water company, and the penstocks being opened, the water rushes into the sewers with great force. There is also another point peculiar to the City—in it all the sewers are flushed regularly twice a week; in the metropolitan sewers, only when the inspector pronounces flushing to be required. The City plan appears the best to prevent the accumulation of deposit.

There still remains to be described the system of "*plonging,*" or mode of cleansing the open sewers, as contradistinguished from "*flushing,*" or the cleansing of the covered sewers.

"When we go plonging," one man said, "we has long poles with a piece of wood at the end of them, and we stirs up the mud at the bottom of the ditches while the tide's a going down. We has got slides at the end of the ditches, and we pulls these up and lets out the water, mud, and all, into the Thames." "Yes, for the people to drink," said a companion drily. "We're in the water a great deal," continued the man. "We can't walk along the sides of all of 'em."

The difference of cost between the old method of removal and the new, that is to say, between carting and flushing, is very extraordinary. This cartage work was done chiefly by contract and according to a Report of the surveyors to the Commissioners (Aug. 31, 1848), the usual cost for such work (almost always done during the night) was 7s. the cubic yard; that is, 7s. for the removal of a cubic yard of sewage by manual labour and horse and cart. In February, 1849 (the date of another Report on the subject), the cost of removing a cubic yard by the operation of flushing, was but 8d. This gives the following result, but in what particular time, instance, or locality, is not mentioned:—

79,483 cubic yards of deposit removed by the contract flushing system, at 8d. per cubic yard £2,649
Same quantity by the old system of casting and cartage, 7s. per cubic yard . 27,819

Difference . . . £25,170

"It appears, therefore," says Mr. Lovick, "that by the adoption of the contract flushing system, a saving has been effected within the comparatively short period of its operation over the filthy and clumsy system formerly practised, of 25,170*l.*, showing the cost of this system to be ten and a half times greater than the cost of flushing by contract."

An official Report states: "When the accumulations of years had to be removed from the sewers, the rate of cost per lineal mile has varied from about 40*l.* to 58*l.*, or from 6*d.* to 8*d.* per lineal yard. The works in these cases (excepting those in the City) have not exceeded nine lineal miles."

"On an average of weeks," says Mr. Lovick, in his Report on flushing operations, a few months after the introduction of the contract system, in Sept., 1848, "under present arrangements, about 62 miles of sewers are passed through each week, and deposit prevented from accumulating in them by periodic (weekly) flushing. The average cost per lineal mile per week is about 2*l.* 10*s.*

"The nature of the agreements with the contractors or gangers are now for the prevention of accumulations of deposit in a district. For this purpose the large districts are subdivided, each subdivision being let to one man. In the Westminster district there are four, in the Holborn and Finsbury two, in the Surrey and Kent, seven subdivisions.

"The Tower Hamlets and Poplar districts are each let to one man.

"In the Tower Hamlets it will be perceived that a reduction of 8*l.* has been effected for the performance of precisely the same work as that heretofore performed; the rates of charge standing thus:—

"Under the day-work system 23*l.* per week.
 ,, contract ,, 15*l.* ,,

"In those portions specially contracted for, the work has been let by the lineal measure of the sewer, in preference to the amount of deposit removed.

"In the Surrey and Kent districts the open ditches have been cleansed thrice as often as formerly.

"A large proportion of the deposit removed is from the open ditches; in these the accumulations are rapid and continuous, caused chiefly by their being the receptacles for the ashes and refuse of the houses, the refuse of manufactories, and the sweepings of the roads.

"In the covered sewers one of the chief sources of accumulation is the detritus and mud from the streets, swept into the sewers.

"The accumulations from these sources will not, I think, be over-estimated at two-thirds of the whole amount of deposit removed.

"The contracts in operation, February, 1849, with the districts which they embrace, are as follows:—

"Table No. I.

Districts.	Sewers let for Prevention of Accumulations of Deposit.	Average Rate of Work performed in Sewers passed through each Week.	Contract Charge per Week.
	Lineal Feet.	Lineal Feet.	£ s. d.
Westminster	485,795	150,615	40 0 0
Holborn & Finsbury	355,085	118,000	23 0 0
Tower Hamlets	223,738	30,000	15 0 0
Surrey and Kent ..	440,642	40,000	75 0 0
Poplar	26,000	2,000	6 16 0
	1,531,260	340,615	159 16 0
Westminster—Attendance on Flaps, &c.			4 0 0
			£163 16 0

"The weekly cost prior to the contract system was in the several districts as follows:—

"Table No. II.

	£	s.	d.
In the Westminster District	78	10	0
,, Holborn and Finsbury do.	24	17	0
,, Tower Hamlets do.	23	0	0
,, Surrey and Kent do.	56	8	0
,, Poplar do.	6	13	0
	189	8	0

Hence there would appear to have been a saving of 25*l.* 12*s.* effected. But by what means was this brought about? It is the old story, I regret to say — a reduction of the wages of the labouring men. But this, indeed, is the invariable effect of the contract system. The wages of the flushermen previous to Sept., 1848, were 24*s.* to 27*s.* a week; under the present system they are 21*s.* to 22*s.* Here is a reduction of 4*s.* per week per man, at the least; and as there were about 150 hands employed at this period, it follows that the gross weekly saving must have been equal to 30*l.*, so that, according to the above account, there would have been about 5*l.* left for the contractors or middlemen. It is unworthy of *gentlemen* to make a parade of economy obtained by such ignoble means.

The engineers, however, speak of flushing as what is popularly understood as but "a makeshift"—as a system imperfect in itself, but advantageously resorted to because obviating the evils of a worse system still.

"With respect to these operations," says Mr. Lovick, in a Report on the subject, in February, 1849, "I may be permitted to state that, although I do not approve of the flushing as an ultimate system, or as a system to be adopted in the future permanent works of sewerage, or that its use should be contemplated with regulated sizes of sewers, regulated supplies of water, and proper falls, it appears to be the most efficacious and economical for the purpose to which it is adapted of any yet introduced."

A gentleman who was at one time connected professionally with the management of the public sewerage, said to me,—

"Mr. John Roe commenced the general system of flushing sewers in London in 1847. It is, however, but a clumsy expedient, and quite incompatible with a perfect system of sewerage. It has, nevertheless, been usefully applied as an auxiliary to the existing system, though the cost is frightful."

Of the Working Flushermen.

When the system of sewer cleansing first became general, as I have detailed, the number of flushermen employed, I am assured, on good authority, was about 500. The sewers were, when this process was first resorted to, full of deposit, often what might be called "coagulated" deposit, which could not be affected except by constantly repeated efforts. There are now only about 100 flushermen, for the more regularly flushing is repeated, the easier becomes the operation.

Until about 18 months ago, the flushermen were employed directly by the Court of Sewers, and were paid ("in Mr. Roe's time," one man said, with a sigh) from 24*s.* to 27*s.* a week; now the work is *all done by contract*. There are some six or seven contractors, all builders, who undertake or are responsible for the whole work of flushing in the metropolitan districts (I do not speak of the City), and they pay the working flushermen 21*s.* a week, and the gangers 22*s.* This wage is always paid in money, without drawbacks, and without the intervention of any other middleman than the contractor middleman. The flushermen have no perquisites except what they may chance to find in a sewer. Their time of labour is $6\frac{1}{2}$ hours daily.

The state of the tide, however, sometimes, as a matter of course, compels the flushermen to work at every hour of the day and night. At all times they carry lights, common oil lamps, with cotton wicks; only the inspectors carry Davy's safety-lamp. I met no man who could assign any reason for this distinction, except that "the Davy" gave "such a bad light."

The flushermen wear, when at work, strong blue overcoats, waterproofed (but not so much as used to be the case, the men then complaining of the perspiration induced by them), buttoned close over the chest, and descending almost to the knees, where it is met by huge leather boots, covering a part of the thigh, such as are worn by the fishermen on many of our coasts. Their hats are fan-tailed, like the dustmen's. The flushermen are well-conducted men generally, and, for the most part, fine stalwart good-looking specimens of the English labourer; were they not known or believed to be temperate, they would not be employed. They have, as a body, no benefit or sick clubs, but a third of them, I was told, or perhaps nearly a third, were members of general benefit societies. I found several intelligent men among them. They are engaged by the contractors, upon whom they call to solicit work.

"Since Mr. Roe's time," and Mr. Roe is evidently the popular man among the flushermen, or somewhat less than four years ago, the flushermen have had to provide their own dresses, and even their own shovels to stir up the deposit. To contractors, the comforts or health of the labouring men must necessarily be a secondary consideration to the realization of a profit. New men can always be found; safe investments cannot.

The wages of the flushermen therefore have been not only decreased, but their expenses increased. A pair of flushing-boots, covering a part of the thigh, similar to those worn by sea-side fishermen, costs 30*s.* as a low price, and a flusherman wears out three pairs in two years. Boot stockings cost 2*s.* 6*d.* The jacket worn by the men at their work in the sewers, in the shape of a pilot-jacket, but fitting less loosely, is 7*s.* 6*d.*; a blue smock, of coarse common cloth (generally), worn over the dress, costs 2*s.* 6*d.*; a shovel is 2*s.* 6*d.* "Ay, sir," said one man, who was greatly dissatisfied with this change, "they'll make soldiers find their own regimentals next; and, may be, their own guns, a'cause they can always get rucks of men for soldiers or labourers. I know there's plenty would work for less than we get, but what of that? There always is. There's hundreds would do the work for half what the surveyors and inspectors gets; but it's all right among the nobs."

Nor is the labour of the flushermen at all times so easy or of such circumscribed hours as I have stated it to be in the regular way of flushing. When small branch-sewers have to be flushed, the deposit must first be loosened, or the water, instead of sweeping it away, would flow over it, and in many of these sewers (most frequent in the Tower Hamlets) the height is not more than 3 feet. Some of the flushermen are tall, bulky, strong fellows, and cannot stand upright in less than from 5 feet 8 inches to 6 feet, and in loosening the deposit in low narrow sewers, "we go to work," said one of them, "on our bellies, like frogs, with a rake between our legs. I've been blinded by steam in such sewers near Whitechapel Church from the brewhouses; I couldn't see for steam; it was a regular London fog. You must get out again into a main sewer on your belly; that's what makes it harder about the togs, they get worn so."

The division of labour among the flushermen appears to be as follows :—

The *Inspector*, whose duty it is to go round the several sewers and see which require to be flushed.

The *Ganger*, or head of the working gang, who receives his orders from the inspector, and directs the men accordingly.

The *Lock-keeper*, or man who goes round to the sewers which are about to be flushed, and fixes the "penstocks" for retaining the water.

The *Gang*, which consists of from three to four men, who loosen the deposit from the bottom of the sewer. Among these there is generally a "for'ard man," whose duty it is to remove the penstocks.

The ganger gets 1s. a week over and above the wages of the men.

TABLE SHOWING THE DISTRICTS UNDER THE MANAGEMENT OF THE COMMISSIONERS OF SEWERS; ALSO THE NUMBER AND SALARIES OF THE CLERKS OF THE WORKS, ASSISTANT CLERKS OF THE WORKS, AND INSPECTORS OF FLUSHING, PAID BY THE COMMISSIONERS, AND THE NUMBER AND WAGES PAID TO THE FLUSHERMEN BY THE GENERAL CONTRACTORS.

DISTRICTS.	Paid by the Commissioners of Sewers.									Paid by Contractors.				
	Clerks of Works.		Assist. Clerks of Works *.		Inspectors of Flushings.		Flap & Sluice Keepers.		Aggregate Total.	Gangers.		Flushers.		Aggregate Total.
	No.	Annual Salary of the whole.	No.	Rate of Annual Salary.	No.	Annual Salary of the whole.	No.	Yearly Wages of the whole.		No.	Weekly Wage of each.	No.	Weekly Wage of each.	
		£		£		£		£	£		s.			£ s.
Fulham and Hammersmith.—Counter's Creek and Ranelagh Districts	3	450	4	400	1	120	..	..	970	2	22	13	21	824 4
Westminster Sewers.—Western Division, Eastern Division, Regent-street District, Holborn Division	4	600	3	300	1	80	6	390	1370	3	22	30	21	1809 12
Finsbury Division.—Tower Hamlets Levels, and Poplar and Blackwall Districts	3	450	2	200	3	280	1	70	1000	3	22	27	21	1645 16
Districts south of the Thames	3	450	6	600	4	320	12	374	1744	2	22	22	21	1315 12
Total	13	1950	15	1500	9	800	19	834	5084	10	..	92	..	5595 4
CITY	..	..	..	..	1	80	3	148	228	1	22	9	21	548 12

Total cost of flushing the sewers . . . . . £12,000 per annum.

* These officers are paid only during the period of service, and are chiefly engaged on special works.

The corresponding officers for London are under the City Commissioners.

⁎ The above division of districts is the one adopted by the Commissioners of Sewers, but the districts of the Flushermen are more numerous than those above given, being as follows :—

	Ganger.	Flushermen.	
Fulham and Hammersmith	employing 1	and 6	⎫ 1st District of Commissioners.
Counter's Creek and Ranelagh Districts	,, 1	,, 7	⎭
Westminster (Western Division)	,, 1	,, 10	⎫
Ditto (Eastern Division)	,, 1	,, 12	⎬ 2nd District of Commissioners.
Holborn Division	,, 1	,, 8	⎭
Finsbury Division	,, 1	,, 9	
Tower Hamlets Levels	,, 1	,, 10	⎫ 3rd District of Commissioners.
Poplar and Blackwall	,, 1	,, 8	⎭
Districts south of the Thames	,, 2	,, 22	4th District of Commissioners.
City	,, 1	,, 9	

Holborn and Finsbury districts are under one contractor, and so are the two divisions of Westminster. The same men who flush Holborn flush the Finsbury district also, 17 being the average number employed; but the Finsbury district requires rather more men than the Holborn; and the same men who work on the western division of Westminster flush also the eastern, the number of flushers in the western district being more, on account of its being the larger division.

The inspector receives 80*l*. per annum.

The table on p. 429 shows the number of clerks of the works, inspectors of flushing, flap and sluice keepers, gangers, and flushermen employed in the several districts throughout the metropolis, as well as the salaries and wages of each and the whole.

None of the flushermen can be said to have been "brought up to the business," for boys are never employed in the sewers. Neither had the labourers been confined in their youth to any branch of trade in particular, which would appear to be consonant to such employment. There are now among the flushermen men who have been accustomed to "all sorts of ground work:" tailors, pot-boys, painters, one jeweller (some time ago there was also one gentleman), and shoemakers. "You see, sir," said one informant, "many of such like mechanics can't live above ground, so they tries to get their bread underneath it. There used to be a great many pensioners flushermen, which weren't right," said one man, "when so many honest working men haven't a penny, and don't know which way to turn theirselves; but pensioners have often good friends and good interest. I don't hear any complaints that way now."

Among the flushermen are some ten or twelve men who have been engaged in sewer-work of one kind or another between 20 and 30 years. The cholera, I heard from several quarters, did not (in 1848) attack any of the flushermen. The answer to an inquiry on the subject generally was, "Not one that I know of."

"It is a somewhat singular circumstance," says Mr. Haywood, the City Surveyor, in his Report, dated February, 1850, "*that none of the men employed in the City sewers in flushing and cleansing, have been attacked with, or have died of, cholera during the past year; this was also the case in* 1832–3. I do not state this to prove that the atmosphere of the sewers is not unhealthy—I by no means believe an impure atmosphere is healthy—but I state the naked fact, as it appears to me a somewhat singular circumstance, and leave it to pathologists to argue upon."

"I don't think flushing work disagrees with my husband," said a flusherman's wife to me, "for he eats about as much again at that work as he did at the other." "The smell underground is sometimes very bad," said the man, "but then we generally take a drop of rum first, and something to eat. It wouldn't do to go into it on an empty stomach, 'cause it would get into our inside. But in some sewers there's scarcely any smell at all. *Most of the men are healthy who are engaged in it; and when the cholera was about many used to ask us how it was we escaped.*"

The following statement contains the history of an individual flusherman:—

"I was brought up to the sea," he said, "and served on board a man-of-war, the *Racer*, a 16-gun brig, laying off Cuba, in the West Indies, and thereaway, watching the slavers. I served seven years. We were paid off in '43 at Portsmouth, and a friend got me into the *shores*. It was a great change from the open sea to a close *shore*—great; and I didn't like it at all at first. But it suits a married man, as I am now, with a family, much better than being a seaman, for a man aboard a ship can hardly do his children justice in their schooling and such like. Well, I didn't much admire going down the man-hole at first—the 'man-hole' is a sort of iron trap-door that you unlock and pull up; it leads to a lot of steps, and so you get into the *shore*—but one soon gets accustomed to anything. I've been at flushing and *shore* work now since '43, all but eleven weeks, which was before I got engaged.

"We work in gangs from three to five men." [Here I had an account of the process of flushing, such as I have given.] "I've been carried off my feet sometimes in the flush of a *shore*. Why, to-day," (a very rainy and windy day, Feb. 4,) "it came down Baker-street, when we flushed it, 4 foot plomb. It would have done for a mill-dam. One couldn't smoke or do anything. Oh, yes, we can have a pipe and a chat now and then in the *shore*. The tobacco checks the smell. No, I can't say I felt the smell very bad when I first was in a *shore*. I've felt it worse since. I've been made innocent drunk like in a *shore* by a drain from a distiller's. That happened me first in Vine-street *shore*, St. Giles's, from Mr. Rickett's distillery. It came into the *shore* like steam. No, I can't say it tasted like gin when you breathed it— only intoxicating like. It was the same in Whitechapel from Smith's distillery. One night I was forced to leave off there, the steam had such an effect. I was falling on my back, when a mate caught me. The breweries have something of the same effect, but nothing like so strong as the distilleries. It comes into the *shore* from the brewers' places in steam. I've known such a steam followed by bushels of grains; ay, sir, cart-loads washed into the *shore*.

"Well, I never found anything in a *shore* worth picking up but once a half-crown. That was in the Buckingham Palace sewer. Another time I found 16*s*. 6*d*., and thought that *was* a haul; but every bit of it, every coin, shillings and sixpences and joeys, was bad—all smashers. Yes, of course it was a disappointment, naturally so. That happened in Brick-lane *shore*, Whitechapel. O, somebody or other had got frightened, I suppose, and had shied the coins down into the drains. I found them just by the chapel there."

A second man gave me the following account of his experience in flushing :—

"You remember, sir, that great storm on the 1st August, 1848. I was in three *shores* that fell in —Conduit-street and Foubert's-passage, Regent-street. There was then a risk of being drowned in the *shores*, but no lives were lost. All the house-drains were blocked about Carnaby-market —that's the Foubert's-passage *shore*—and the poor people was what you might call houseless. We got in up to the neck in water in some places, 'cause we had to stoop, and knocked about the rubbish as well as we could, to give a way to the water. The police put up barriers to prevent any carts or carriages going that way along the streets. No, there was no lives lost in the *shores*. One man was so overcome that he was falling off into a sort of sleep in Milford-lane *shore*, but was pulled out. I helped to pull him. He was as heavy as lead with one thing or other—wet, and all that. Another time, six or seven year ago, Whitechapel High-street *shore* was almost choked with butchers' offal, and we had a great deal of trouble with it."

Of the Rats in the Sewers.

I will now state what I have learned from long-experienced men, as to the characteristics of the rats in the sewers. To arrive even at a conjecture as to the numbers of these creatures—now, as it were, the population of the sewers—I found impossible, for no statistical observations have been made on the subject; but all my informants agreed that the number of the animals had been greatly diminished within these four or five years.

In the better-constructed sewers there are no rats. In the old sewers they abound. The sewer rat is the ordinary house or brown rat, excepting at the outlets near the river, and here the water-rat is seen.

The sewer-rat is the common brown or Hanoverian rat, said by the Jacobites to have come in with the first George, and established itself after the fashion of his royal family; and undoubtedly such was about the era of their appearance. One man, who had worked twelve years in the sewers before flushing was general, told me he had never seen but *two* black (or old English) rats; another man, of ten years' experience, had seen but one; others had noted no difference in the rats. I may observe that in my inquiries as to the sale of rats (as a part of the live animals dealt in by a class in the metropolis), I ascertained that in the older granaries, where there were series of floors, there were black as well as brown rats. "Great black fellows," said one man who managed a Bermondsey granary, "as would frighten a lady into asterisks to see of a sudden."

The rat is the only animal found in the sewers. I met with no flusherman or other sewer-worker who had ever seen a lizard, toad, or frog there, although the existence of these creatures, in such circumstances, has been presumed. A few live cats find their way into the subterranean channels when a house-drain is being built, or is opened for repairs, or for any purpose, and have been seen by the flushermen, &c., wandering about, looking lost, mewing as if in misery, and avoiding any contact with the sewage. The rats also—for they are not of the water-rat breed—are exceedingly averse to wetting their feet, and "take to the sewage," as it was worded to me, only in prospect of danger; that is, they then swim across or along the current to escape with their lives. It is said that when a luckless cat has ventured into the sewers, she is sometimes literally worried by the rats. I could not hear of such an attack having been witnessed by any one; but one intelligent and trustworthy man said, that a few years back (he believed about eight years) he had in one week found the skeletons of two cats in a particular part of an old sewer, 21 feet wide, and in the drains opening into it were perfect colonies of rats, raging with hunger, he had no doubt, because a system of trapping, newly resorted to, had prevented their usual ingress into the houses up the drains. A portion of their fur adhered to the two cats, but the flesh had been eaten from their bones. About that time a troop of rats flew at the feet of another of my informants, and would no doubt have maimed him seriously, "but my boots," said he, "stopped the devils." "The sewers generally swarms with rats," said another man. "I runs away from 'em; I don't like 'em. They in general gets away from us; but in case we comes to a stunt end where there's a wall and no place for 'em to get away, and we goes to touch 'em, they fly at us. They're some of 'em as big as good-sized kittens. One of our men caught hold of one the other day by the tail, and he found it trying to release itself, and the tail slipping through his fingers; so he put up his left hand to stop it, and the rat caught hold of his finger, and the man's got an arm now as big as his thigh." I heard from several that there had been occasionally battles among the rats, one with another.

"Why, sir," said one flusherman, "as to the number of rats, it ain't possible to say. There hasn't been a census (laughing) taken of them. But I can tell you this—I was one of the first flushermen when flushing came in general—I think it was before Christmas, 1847, under Mr. Roe—and there was cart-loads and cart-loads of drowned rats carried into the Thames. It was in a West Strand *shore* that I saw the most. I don't exactly remember which, but I think Northumberland-street. By a block or a hitch of some sort, there was, I should say, just a bushel of drowned rats stopped at the corner of one of the gates, which I swept into the next stream. I see far fewer drowned rats now than before the *shores* was flushed. They're not so plenty, that's one thing. Perhaps, too, they may have got to understand about flushing, they're that 'cute, and manage to keep out of the way. About Newgate-market was at one time the worst for rats. Men couldn't venture into the sewers then, on account of the varmint. It's bad enough still, I hear, but I haven't worked in the City for a few years."

The rats, from the best information at my command, do not derive much of their sustenance from the matter in the sewers, or only in particular localities. These localities are the sewers neighbouring a connected series of slaughter-houses, as in Newgate-market, Whitechapel, Clare-market, parts adjoining Smithfield-market, &c. There, animal offal being (and having been to a much greater extent five or six years ago) swept into the drains and sewers, the rats find their food. In the sewers, generally, there is little food for them, and none at all in the best-constructed sewers, where there is a regular and sometimes rapid flow, and little or no deposit.

The sewers are these animals' breeding grounds. In them the broods are usually safe from the molestation of men, dogs, or cats. These "breeding grounds" are sometimes in the holes (excavated by the industry of the rats into caves) which have been formed in the old sewers by a crumbled brick having fallen out. Their nests, however, are in some parts even more frequent in places where old rotting large house-drains or smaller sewers, empty themselves into a first-class sewer. Here, then, the rats breed, and, in spite of precautions, find their way up the drains or pipes, even through the openings into water-closets, into the houses for their food, and almost always at night. Of this fact, builders, and those best informed, are confident, and it is proved indirectly by what I have stated as to the deficiency of food for a voracious creature in all the sewers except a few. One man, long in the service of the Commissioners of Sewers, and in different capacities, gave me the following account of what may be called a rat settlement. The statement I found confirmed by other working men, and by superior officers under the same employment.

"Why, sir, in the Milford-lane sewer, a goodish bit before you get to the river, or to the Strand—I can't say how far, a few hundred yards perhaps—I've seen, and reported, what was a regular chamber of rats. If a brick didn't fall out from being rotted, the rats would get it out, and send it among other rubbish into the sewer, for this place was just the corner of a big drain. I couldn't get into the rat-hole, of course not, but I've brought my lamp to the opening, and—as well as others—have seen it plain. It was an open place like a lot of tunnels, one over another. Like a lot of rabbit burrows in the country—as I've known to be—or like the partitions in the pigeon-houses: one here and another there. The rat-holes, as far as I could tell, were worked one after another. I should say, in moderation, that it was the size of a small room; well, say about 6 yards by 4. I can't say about the height from the lowest tunnel to the highest. I don't see that any one could. Bless you, sir, I've sometimes heerd the rats fighting and squeaking there, like a parcel of drunken Irishmen—I have indeed. Some of them were rare big fellows. If you threw the light of your lamp on them sudden, they'd be off like a shot. Well, I should say, there was 100 pair of rats there—there might be more, besides all their young-uns. If a poor cat strayed into that sewer, she dursn't tackle the rats, not she. There's lots of such places, sir, here, and there, and everywhere."

"I believe rats," says a late enthusiastic writer on the subject, under the cognomen of Uncle James, "to be one of the most fertile causes of national and universal distress, and their attendants, misery and starvation."

From the author's inquiries among practical men, and from his own study of the natural history of the rat, he shows that these animals will have six, seven, or eight nests of young in the year, for three or four years together; that they have from twelve to twenty-three at a litter, and breed at three months old; and that there are more female than male rats, by ten to six.

The author seems somewhat of an enthusiast about rats, and as the sewerage is often the headquarters of these animals—their "breeding-ground" indeed—I extract the following curious matter. He says:—

"Now, I propose to lay down my calculations at something less than one-half. In the first place, I say four litters in the year, beginning and ending with a litter, so making thirteen litters in three years; secondly to have eight young ones at a birth, half male and half female; thirdly, the young ones to have a litter at six months old.

"At this calculation, I will take one pair of rats; and at the expiration of three years what do you suppose will be the amount of living rats? Why no less a number than 646,808.

"Mr. Shaw's little dog 'Tiny,' under six pounds weight, has destroyed 2525 pairs of rats, which, had they been permitted to live, would, at the same calculation and in the same time, have produced 1,633,190,200 living rats!

"And the rats destroyed by Messrs. Shaw and Sabin in one year, amounting to 17,000 pairs, would, had they been permitted to live, have produced, at the above calculation and in the same time, no less a number than 10,995,736,000 living rats!

"Now, let us calculate the amount of human food that these rats would destroy. In the first place, my informants tell me that six rats will consume day by day as much food as a man; secondly, that the thing has been tested, and that the estimate given was, that eight rats would consume more than an ordinary man.

"Now, I—to place the thing beyond the smallest shadow of a doubt—will set down ten rats to eat as much as a man, not a child; nor will I say anything about what rats waste. And what shall we find to be the alarming result? Why, that the first pair of rats, with their three years' progeny, would consume in the night more food than 64,680 men the year round, and leaving eight rats to spare!"

The author then puts forth the following curious statement:—

"And now for the vermin destroyed by Messrs. Shaw and Sabin—34,000 yearly! Taken at the same calculation, with their three years' progeny—can you believe it?—they would consume more food than the whole population of the earth? Yes, if Omnipotence would raise up 29,573,600 more people, these rats would consume as much food as them all! You may wonder, but I will prove it to you:—The population of the earth, including men, women, and children, is estimated to be 970,000,000 souls; and the 17,000 rats in three years would produce 10,995,736,000: consequently, at ten rats per man, there would be sufficient rats to eat as much food as all the people on the earth, and leaving 1,295,736,000. So that if the human family were increased to 1,099,573,600, instead of 970,000,000, there would be rats enough to eat the food of them all! Now, sirs, is not this a most appalling thing, to think that there are at the present time in the British Empire thousands—nay, millions—of human beings in a state of utter starvation, while rats are consuming that which would place them and their families in a state of affluence and comfort? I ask this simple question: Has not Parliament, ere now, been summoned upon matters of far less importance to the empire? I think it has."

The author then advocates the repeal of the "rat-tax," that is, the tax on what he calls the "true friend of man and remorseless destroyer of rats," the well-bred terrier dog. "Take the tax off rat-killing dogs" he says, "and give a legality to rat-killing, and let there be in each parish a man who will pay a reward per head for dead rats, which are valuable for manure (as was done in the case of wolves in the old days), and then rats would be extinguished for ever!" Uncle James seems to be a perfect Malthus among rats. The over-population and over-rat theories are about equal in reason.

OF THE CESSPOOLAGE AND NIGHTMEN OF THE METROPOLIS.

I HAVE already shown—it may be necessary to remind the reader—that there are two modes of removing the wet refuse of the metropolis: the one by carrying it off by means of sewers, or, as it is designated, *sewerage;* and the other by depositing it in some neighbouring cesspool, or what is termed *cesspoolage.*

The object of sewerage is " to transport the wet refuse of a town to a river, or some powerfully current stream, by a series of ducts." By the system of cesspoolage, the wet refuse of the household is collected in an adjacent tank, and when the reservoir is full, the contents are removed to some other part.

The gross quantity of wet refuse annually produced in the metropolis, and which consequently has to be removed by one or other of the above means, is, as we have seen,—liquid, 24,000,000,000 gallons; solid, 100,000 tons; or altogether, by admeasurement, 3,820,000,000 cubic feet.

The quantity of this wet refuse which finds its way into the sewers by street and house-drainage is, according to the experiments of the Commissioners of Sewers (as detailed at p. 388), 10,000,000 cubic feet per day, or 3,650,000,000 cubic feet per annum, so that there remain about 170,000,000 cubic feet to be accounted for. But, as we have before seen, the extent of surface from which the amount of so-called *Metropolitan* sewage was *removed* was only 58 square miles, whereas that from which the calculation was made concerning the gross quantity of wet refuse *produced* throughout the metropolis was 115 square miles, or double the size. The 58 miles measured by the Commissioners, however, was by far the denser moiety of the town, and that in which the houses and streets were as 15 to 1; so that, allowing the remaining 58 miles of the suburban districts to have produced 20 times less sewage than the urban half of the metropolis, the extra yield would have been about 180,500,000 cubic feet. But the greater proportion, if not the whole, of the latter quantity of wet house-refuse would be drained into open ditches, where a considerable amount of evaporation and absorption is continually going on, so that a large allowance must be made for loss by these means. Perhaps, if we estimate the quantity of sewage thus absorbed and evaporated at between 10 and 20 per cent of the whole, we shall not be wide of the truth, so that we shall have to reduce the 182,000,000 cubic feet of suburban sewage to somewhere about 150,000,000 cubic feet.

This gives us the quantity of wet refuse carried off by the sewers (covered and open) of the metropolis, and deducted from the gross quantity of wet house-refuse, annually *produced* (3,820,000,000 cubic feet), leaves 20,000,000 cubic feet for the gross quantity carried off by other means than the sewers; that is to say, the 20,000,000 cubic feet, if the calculation be right, should be about the quantity deposited every year in the London cesspools. Let us see whether this approximates to anything like the real quantity.

To ascertain the absolute quantity of wet refuse annually conveyed into the metropolitan cesspools, we must first ascertain the number and capacity of the cesspools themselves.

Of the city of London, where the sewer-cesspool details are given with a minuteness highly commendable, as affording statistical data of great value, Mr. Heywood gives us the following returns:—

" HOUSE-DRAINAGE OF THE CITY.

" The total number of premises drained during the year was .. 310
" The approximate number of premises drained at the expiration of the year 1850 was 10,923
" The total number of premises which may now therefore be said to be drained is 11,233
" And undrained 5,067

" I am induced," adds Mr. Heywood, " to believe, from the reports of the district inspectors, that a very far larger number of houses are already drained than are herein given. Indeed my impression is, that as many as 3000 might be deducted from the 5067 houses as to the drainage of which you have no information.

" Now, until the inspectors have completed their survey of the whole of the houses within the city," continues the City surveyor, " precise information cannot be given as to the number of houses yet undrained; such information appears to me very important to obtain speedily, and I beg to recommend that instructions be given to the inspectors to proceed with their survey as rapidly as possible."

Hence it appears, that out of the 16,299 houses comprised within the boundaries of the City, rather less than one-third are *reported to* have cesspools. Concerning the number of cesspools without the City, the Board of Health, in a Report on the cholera in 1849, put forward one of its usual *extraordinary* statements.

"At the last census in 1841," runs the Report, "there were 270,859 houses in the metropolis. *It is* KNOWN *that there is scarcely a house without a cesspool under it, and that a large number have two, three, four, and* MORE *under them;* so that the number of such receptacles in the metropolis may be taken at 300,000. The exposed surface of each cesspool measures on an average 9 feet, and the mean depth of the whole is about 6½ feet; so that each contains 58½ cubic feet of fermenting filth of the most poisonous, noisome, and disgusting nature. The exhaling surface of all the cesspools (300,000 × 9) = 2,700,000 feet, or equal to 62 acres nearly; and the total quantity of foul matter contained within them (300,000 × 58½) = 17,550,000 cubic feet; or equal to one enormous elongated stagnant cesspool 50 feet in width, 6 feet 6 inches in depth, and extending through London from the Broadway at Hammersmith to Bow-bridge, a length of 10 miles.

"This," say the Metropolitan Sanitary Commissioners, a body of functionaries so intimately connected with the Board, that the one is ever ready to swear to what the other asserts, "there is reason to believe is an *under estimate!*"

Let us now compare this statement, which declares it to be *known* that there is scarcely a house in London without a cesspool, and that many have two, three, four, and even more under them—let us compare this, I say, with the facts which were elicited by the same functionaries by means of a house-to-house inquiry in three different parishes—a poor, a middle-class, and a rich one—the average rental of each being 22*l.*, 119*l.*, and 128*l.*

RESULTS OF A HOUSE-TO-HOUSE INQUIRY IN THE PARISHES OF ST. GEORGE THE MARTYR, SOUTHWARK, ST. ANNE'S, SOHO, AND ST. JAMES'S, AS TO THE STATE OF THE WORKS OF WATER SUPPLY AND DRAINAGE.

CONDITION OF THE HOUSES.		PARISHES.		
		St. George the Martyr, Southwark.	St. Anne's, Soho.	St. James's.
From which replies have been received	(Number)	5,713	1,339	2,960
With supply of Water—				
To the house or premises	(Per cent)	80·97	95·56	96·48
Near the privy	"	48·87	38·99	43·42
Butts or cisterns, covered	(Number)	1,879	776	1,621
" " uncovered	"	2,074	294	393
With a sink	(Per cent)	48·31	89·29	86·70
With a Well—				
On or near premises	"	5·32	13·97	13·85
Well tainted or foul	"	46·92	3·71	7·36
Houses damp in lower parts	"	52·13	30·90	26·67
Houses with stagnant water on premises	"	18·54	7·95	2·95
Houses flooded in times of storm	"	18·15	5·04	4·05
Houses with Drain—				
To premises	"	87·56	97·12	96·42
Houses with drains emitting offensive smells	"	45·11	37·62	21·41
Houses with drains stopped at times	"	22·37	28·50	13·97
Houses with dust-bin	"	42·69	92·34	89·80
Houses receiving offensive smells from adjoining premises	"	27·82	22·54	16·74
Houses with privy	"	97·03	70·63	62·53
Houses with cesspool	"	82·12	47·27	36·62
Houses with water-closet	"	10·06	45·99	65·86

In this minute and searching investigation there is not only an official guide to an estimation of the number of cesspools in London, but a curious indication of the character of the houses in the respective parishes. In the poorer parish of St. George the Martyr, Southwark, the cesspools were to every 100 houses as 82·12; in the aristocratic parish of St. James, Westminster, as only 36·62; while in what may be represented, perhaps, as the middle-class parish of St. Anne, Soho, the cesspools were 47·27 per cent. The number of wells on or near the premises, and the proportion of those tainted; the ratio of the dampness of the lower parts of the houses, of the stagnant water on the premises, and of the flooding of the houses on occasions of storms, are all significant indications of the difference in the circumstances of the inhabitants of these parishes — of the difference between the abodes of the rich and the poor, the capitalists and the labouring classes. But more significant still, perhaps, of the domestic wants or comforts of these dwellings, is the proportion of water-closets to the houses in the poor parish and the rich; in the one they were but 10·06 per cent; in the other 65·86 per cent.

These returns are sufficient to show the extravagance of the Board's previous statement, that there is "scarcely a house in London without a cesspool under it," while "a large number have two, three, four, and more," for we find that even in the poorer parishes there are only 82 cesspools to 100 houses. Moreover, the engineers, after an official examination and inquiry, reported that in the "fever-nest, known as Jacob's-island, Bermondsey," there were 1317 dwelling-houses and 648 cesspools, or not quite 50 cesspools to 100 houses.

In rich, middle-class, and poor parishes, the proportion of cesspools, then, it appears from the *inquiries* of the Board of Health (their *guesses* are of no earthly value), gives us an average of something between 50 or 60 cesspools to every 100 houses. A subordinate officer whom I saw, and who was engaged in the cleansing and the filling-up of cesspools when condemned, or when the houses are to be drained anew into the sewers and the cesspools abolished, thought from his own experience, the number of cesspools to be less than one-half, but others thought it more.

On the other hand, a nightman told me he was confident that every two houses in three throughout London had cesspools; in the City, however, we perceive that there is, at the utmost, only one house in every three undrained. It will, therefore, be safest to adopt a middle course, and assume 50 per cent of the houses of the metropolis to be still without drainage into the sewers.

Now the number of houses being 300,000, it follows that the number of cesspools within the area of the metropolis are about 150,000; consequently the next step in the investigation is to ascertain the average capacity of each, and so arrive at the gross quantity of wet house-refuse annually deposited in cesspools throughout London.

The average size of the cesspools throughout the metropolis is said, by the Board of Health, to be 9 feet by $6\frac{1}{2}$, which gives a capacity of $58\frac{1}{2}$ cubic feet, and this for 150,000 houses = 8,775,000 cubic feet. But according to all accounts these cesspools require on an average two years to fill, so that the gross quantity of wet refuse annually deposited in such places can be taken at only half the above quantity, viz. in round numbers, 4,500,000 cubic feet. This by weight, at the rate of 35·9 cubic feet to the ton, gives 125,345 tons. This, however, would appear to be of a piece with the generality of the statistics of the Board of Health, and as wide of the truth as was the statement that there was scarcely a house in London without a cesspool, while many had *three, four, and even more*. But I am credibly informed that the average size of a cesspool is rather more than 5 feet square and $6\frac{1}{2}$ deep, so that the ordinary capacity would be $5\frac{3}{4} \times 5\frac{1}{4} \times 6\frac{1}{2} = 197$ cubic feet, and this multiplied by 150,000 gives an aggregate capacity of 29,550,000 cubit feet. But as the cesspools, according to all accounts, become full only once in two years, it follows that the gross quantity of cesspoolage annually deposited throughout the metropolis must be only one-half that quantity, or about 14,775,000 cubic feet.

The calculation may be made another way, viz. by the experience of the nightmen and the sewer-cesspoolmen as to the average quantity of refuse removed from the London cesspools whenever emptied, as well as the average number emptied yearly.

The contents of a cesspool are never estimated for any purpose of sale or labour by the weight, but always, as regards the nightmen's work, by the load. Each night-cart load of soil is considered, on an average, a ton in weight, so that the nightmen readily estimate the number of tons by the number of cart-loads obtained. The men employed in the cleansing of the cesspools by the new system of pumping agree with the nightmen as to the average contents of a cesspool.

As a general rule, a cesspool is filled every two years, and holds, when full, about five tons. One man, who had been upwards of 30 years in the nightman's business, who had worked at it more or less all that time himself, and who is now foreman to a parish contractor and master-nightman in a large way, spoke positively on the subject. The cesspools, he declared, were emptied, as an average, by nightmen, once in two years, and their average contents were five loads of night-soil, it having been always understood in the trade that a night-cartload was about a ton.* The total of the cesspool matter is not affected by the frequency or paucity of the cleansing away of the filth, for if one cesspool be emptied yearly, another is emptied every second, third, fourth, or fifth year, and, according to the size, the fair average is five tons of cesspoolage emptied from each every other year. One master-nightman had emptied as much as

* In one of their Reports the Board of Health has spoken of the yearly cleansing of the cesspools; but a cesspool, I am assured, is rarely emptied by manual labour, unless it be full, for as the process is generally regarded as a nuisance, it is resorted to as seldom as possible. It may, perhaps, be different with the cesspool-emptying by the hydraulic process, which is *not* a nuisance.

fourteen tons of night-soil from a cesspool or soil-tank, and a contractor's man had once emptied as many as eighteen tons, but both agreed as to the average of five tons every two years from all. Neither knew the period of the accumulation of the fourteen or the eighteen tons, but supposed to be about five or six years.

According to this mode of estimate, the quantity of wet house-refuse deposited in cesspools would be equal to 150,000 × 5, or 750,000 tons every two years. This, by admeasurement, at the rate of 35·9 cubic feet to the ton, gives 26,925,000 cubic feet; and as this is the accumulation of two years, it follows that 13,462,500 cubic feet is the quantity of cesspoolage deposited yearly.

There is still another mode of checking this estimate.

I have already given (see p. 385, *ante*) the average production of each individual to the wet refuse of the metropolis. According to the experiments of Boussingault, confirmed by Liebig, this, as I have stated, amounted to ¼ lb. of solid and 1¼ lb. of liquid excrement from each individual per diem (= 150 lbs. for every 100 persons), while, including the wet refuse from culinary operations, the average yield, according to the surveyor of the Commissioners of Sewers, was equal to about 250 lbs. for every 100 individuals daily. I may add that this calculation was made officially, with engineering minuteness, with a view to ascertain what quantity of water, and what inclination in its flow, would be required for the effective working of a system of drainage to supersede the cesspools.* Now the census of 1841 shows us that the average number of inhabitants to each house throughout the metropolis was 7·6, and this for 150,000 houses would give 1,140,000 people; consequently the gross quantity of wet refuse proceeding from this number of persons, at the rate of 250 lbs. to every 100 people daily, would be 464,400 tons per annum; or, by admeasurement, at the rate of 35·9 cubic feet to the ton, it would be equal to 16,670,950 cubic feet.

A small proportion of this amount of cesspoolage ultimately makes its appearance in the sewers, being pumped into them directly from the cesspools when full by means of a special apparatus, and thus tends not only to swell the bulk of sewage, but to decrease in a like proportion the aggregate quantity of wet house-refuse, which is removed by cartage; but though the proportion of cesspoolage which finally appears as sewage is daily increasing, still it is but trifling compared with the quantity removed by cartage.

Here, then, we have three different estimates as to the gross quantity of the London cesspoolage, each slightly varying from the other two.

* It was ascertained that 3 gallons (half a cubic foot) of water would carry off 1 lb. of the more solid excrementitious matter through a 6-inch pipe, with an inclination of 1 in 10.

	Cubic Feet.
The first, drawn from the average capacity of the London cesspools, makes the gross annual amount of cesspoolage	14,775,000
The second, deduced from the average quantity removed from each cesspool	13,462,500
And the third, calculated from the individual production of wet refuse	16,670,950

The mean of these three results is, in round numbers, 15,000,000 cubic feet, so that the statement would stand thus:—

The quantity of wet house-refuse annually carried off by sewers (chiefly covered) from the urban moiety of the metropolis is (in cubic feet)	3,650,000,000
The quantity annually carried off by sewers (principally open) from the suburban moiety of the metropolis	150,000,000
The total amount of wet house-refuse annually carried off by the sewers of the metropolis	3,800,000,000
The gross amount of wet house-refuse annually deposited in cesspools throughout the metropolis	15,000,000
The total amount of sewage and cesspoolage of the metropolis	3,815,000,000

Thus we perceive that the total quantity of wet house-refuse annually *removed*, corresponds so closely with the gross quantity of wet house-refuse annually *produced*, that we may briefly conclude the gross sewage of London to be equal to 3,800,000,000 cubic feet, and the gross cesspoolage to be equal to 15,000,000 cubic feet.

The accuracy of the above conclusion may be tested by another process; for, unless the Board of Health's conjectural mode of getting at *facts* be adopted, it is absolutely necessary that statistics not only upon this, but indeed any subject, be checked by all the different modes there may be of arriving at the same conclusion. False facts are worse than no facts at all.

The number of nightmen may be summed up as follows:—

Masters	521
Labourers	200,000

The number of cesspools emptied during the past year by these men may be estimated at 50,692; and the quantity of soil removed, 253,460 loads, or tons, and this at the rate of 35.9 cubic ft. to the ton gives a total of 6,099,214 cubic ft.

It might, perhaps, be expected, that from the quantity of fæcal refuse proceeding from the inhabitants of the metropolis, a greater quantity would be found in the existent cesspools; but there are many reasons for the contrary.

One prime cause of the dispersion of cesspoolage is, that a considerable quantity of the night-soil does not find its way into the cesspools at all, but is, when the inhabitants have no privies to their dwellings, thrown into streets, and courts, and waste places.

I cannot show this better than by a few extracts from Dr. Hector Gavin's work, published in 1848, entitled, "Sanitary Ramblings; being Sketches and Illustrations of Bethnal Green, &c."

"*Digby-walk, Globe-road.*—Part of this place is private property, and the landlord of the new houses has built a cesspool, into which to drain his houses, but he will not permit the other houses to drain into this cesspool, unless the parish pay to him 1*l.*, a sum which it will not pay." Of course the inhabitants throw their garbage and filth into the street or the by-places.

"*Whisker's-gardens.*—This is a very extensive piece of ground, which is laid out in neat plots, as gardens. The choicest flowers are frequently raised here, and great taste and considerable refinement are evidently possessed by those who cultivate them. Now, among the cultivators are the poor, even the very poor, of Bethnal-green. . . . Attached to all these little plots of ground are summer-houses. In the generality of cases they are mere wooden sheds, cabins, or huts. It is very greatly to be regretted that the proprietors of these gardens should permit the slight and fragile sheds in them to be converted into abodes for human beings. . . . Sometimes they are divided into rooms; they are planted on the damp undrained ground. The privies are sheds erected over holes in the ground; the *soil itself* is removed from these holes and is *dug into the ground* to promote its fertility.

"*Three Colt-lane.*—A deep ditch has been dug on either side of the Eastern Counties Railway by the Company. These ditches were dug by the Company to prevent the foundations of the arches being endangered, and are in no way to be considered as having been dug to promote the health of the neighbourhood. The double privies attached to the new houses (22 in number) are immediately contiguous to this ditch, and are constructed so that the night-soil shall drain into it. For this purpose the cesspools are small, and the bottoms are above the level of the ditch."

It would be easy to multiply such proofs of night-soil not finding its way into the cesspools, but the subject need not be further pursued, important as in many respects it may be. I need but say, that in the several reports of the Board of Health are similar accounts of other localities. The same deficiency of cesspoolage is found in Paris, and from the same cause.

What may be the quantity of night-soil which becomes part of the contents of the street scavenger's instead of the nightman's cart, no steps have been taken, or perhaps can be taken, by the public sanitary bodies to ascertain. Many of the worst of the nuisances (such as that in Digby-street) have been abolished, but they are still too characteristic of the very poor districts. The fault, however, appears to be with the owners of property, and it is seldom *they* are coerced into doing their duty. The doubt of its "paying" a capitalist landlord to improve the unwholesome dwellings of the poor seems to be regarded as a far more sacred right, than the right of the people to be delivered from the foul air and vile stenches to which their poverty may condemn them.

There is, moreover, the great but unascertained waste from cesspool evaporation, and it must be recollected that of the $2\frac{1}{2}$lbs. of cesspool refuse, calculated as the daily produce of each individual, $2\frac{1}{4}$lbs. are liquid.

The gross cesspoolage of Paris should amount to upwards of 600,000 cubic mètres, or more than 21,000,000 cubic feet, at the estimate of three pints daily per head. The quantity actually collected, however, amounts to only 230,000 cubic mètres, or rather more than 8,000,000 cubic feet, which is 13,000,000 cubic feet less than the amount produced.

In London, the cesspoolage of 150,000 *undrained* houses should, at the rate of $2\frac{1}{2}$lbs. to each individual and 15 inhabitants to every two houses, amount to 16,500,000 cubic feet, or about 460,000 loads, whereas the quantity collected amounts to but little more than 250,000 loads, or about 9,000,000 cubic feet. Hence, the deficiency is 210,000 loads, or 7,500,000 cubic feet, which is nearly half of the entire quantity.

In Paris, then, it would appear that only 38 per cent of the refuse which is not removed by sewers is collected in the cesspools, whereas in London about $54\frac{1}{4}$ per cent is so collected. The remainder in both cases is part deposited in by-places and removed by the scavenger's cart, part lost in evaporation, whereas a large proportion of the deficiency arises from a less quantity of water than the amount stated being used by the very poor.

We have now to see the means by which this 15,000,000 cubic feet of cesspoolage is annually removed, as well as to ascertain the condition and incomes of the labourers engaged in the removal of it.

OF THE CESSPOOL SYSTEM OF LONDON.

A CESSPOOL, or some equivalent contrivance, has long existed in connexion with the structure of the better class of houses in the metropolis, and there seems every reason to believe—though I am assured, on good authority, that there is no public or official record of the matter known to exist—that their use became more and more general, as in the case of the sewers, after the rebuilding of the City, consequent upon the great fire of 1665.

The older cesspools were of two kinds— "soil-tanks" and "bog-holes."

"Soil-tanks" were the filth receptacles of

the larger houses, and sometimes works of solid masonry; they were almost every size and depth, but always perhaps much deeper than the modern cesspools, which present an average depth of 6 feet to 6½ feet.

The "bog-hole" was, and is, a cavity dug into the earth, having less masonry than the soil-tank, and sometimes no masonry at all, being in like manner the receptacle for the wet refuse from the house.

The difference between these old contrivances and the present mode is principally in the following respect: the soil-tank or bog-hole formed a receptacle immediately under the privy (the floor of which has usually to be removed for purposes of cleansing), whereas the refuse is now more frequently carried into the modern cesspool by a system of drainage. Sometimes the soil-tank was, when the nature of the situation of the premises permitted, in some outer place, such as an obscure part of the garden or court-yard; and perhaps two or more bog-holes were drained into it, while often enough, by means of a grate or a trap-door, any kind of refuse to be got rid of was thrown into it.

I am informed that the average contents of a bog-hole (such as now exist) are a cubic yard of matter; some are round, some oblong, for there is, or was, great variation.

Of the few remaining soil-tanks the varying sizes prevent any average being computable.

What the old system of cesspoolage *was* may be judged from the fact, that until somewhere about 1830 no cesspool matter could, without an indictable offence being committed, be drained into a sewer! *Now*, no new house can be erected, but it is an indictable offence if the cesspool (or rather water-closet) matter be drained anywhere else than into the sewer! The law, at the period specified, required most strangely, so that "the drains and sewers might not be choked," that cesspools should "be not only periodically emptied, but *made* by nightmen."

The principal means of effecting the change from cesspoolage to sewerage was the introduction of Bramah's water-closets, patented in 1808, but not brought into general use for some twenty years or more after that date. The houses of the rich, owing to the refuse being drained away from the premises, improved both in wholesomeness and agreeableness, and so the law was relaxed.

There are two kinds of cesspools, viz. *public* and *private*.

The *public cesspools* are those situated in courts, alleys, and places, which, though often packed thickly with inhabitants, are not horse-thoroughfares, or thoroughfares at all; and in such places one, two, or more cesspools receive the refuse from all the houses. I do not know that any official account of public cesspools has been published as to their number, character, &c., but their number is insignificant when compared with those connected with private houses. The public cesspools are cleansed, and, where possible, filled up by order of the Commissioners of Sewers, the cost being then defrayed out of the rate.

The *private cesspools* are cleansed at the expense of the occupiers of the houses.

OF THE CESSPOOL AND SEWER SYSTEM OF PARIS.

As the Court of Sewers have recently adopted some of the French regulations concerning cesspoolage, I will now give an account of the cesspool system of France.

When after the ravages of the epidemic cholera of 1848–9, sanitary commissioners under the authority of the legislature pursued their inquiries, it was deemed essential to report upon the cesspool system of Paris, as that capital had also been ravaged by the epidemic. The task was entrusted to Mr. T. W. Rammell, C.E.

Even in what the French delight to designate —and in some respects justly—the most refined city in the world, a filthy and indolent custom, once common, as I have shown, in England, still prevails. In Paris, the kitchen and *dry* house-refuse (and formerly it was the fæcal refuse also) is deposited in the dark of the night in the streets, and removed, as soon as the morning light permits, by the public scavengers. But the refuse is not removed unexamined before being thrown into the cart of the proper functionary. There is in Paris a large and peculiar class, the chiffonniers (literally, in Anglo-Saxon rendering, the *raggers*, or rag-finders). These men nightly traverse the streets, each provided with a lantern, and generally with a basket strapped to the back; the poorer sort, however—for poverty, like rank, has its gradations—make a bag answer the purpose; they have also a pole with an iron hook to its end; and a small shovel. The dirt-heaps or mounds of dry house-refuse are carefully turned over by these men; for their morrow's bread, as in the case of our own street-finders, depends upon *something* saleable being acquired. Their prizes are bones (which sometimes they are seen to gnaw); bits of bread; wasted potatoes; broken pots, bottles, and glass; old pans and odd pieces of old metal; cigar-ends; waste-paper, and rags. Although these people are known as rag-pickers, rags are, perhaps, the very thing of which they pick the least, because the Parisians are least apt to throw them away. In some of the criminal trials in the French capital, the chiffonniers have given evidence (but not much of late) of what they have found in a certain locality, and supplied a link, sometimes an important one, to the evidence against a criminal. With these refuse heaps is still sometimes mixed matter which should have found its way into the cesspools, although this is an offence punishable, and occasionally punished.

Before the habits of the Parisians are too freely condemned, let it be borne in mind that the houses of the French capital are much larger than in London, and that each floor is often the dwelling-place of a family. Such is generally the case in London in the poorer districts, but in Paris it pervades almost all districts. There, some of the houses contain 70, not fugitive but permanent, inmates. The average number of inhabitants to each house, according to the last census, was upwards of *twenty-four* (in London the average is 7·6), the extremes being eleven to each house in St. Giles's and between five and six in the immediate suburbs (see p. 165, *ante*). Persons who are circumstanced then, as are the Parisians, can hardly have at their command the proper means and appliances for a sufficient cleanliness, and for the promotion of what we consider—but the two words are unknown to the French language—the *comforts* of a *home*.

"The greater portion of the liquid refuse," writes Mr. Rammell, " including water, which has been used in culinary or cleansing processes, is got rid of by means of open channels laid across the court-yards and the foot pavements to the street gutters, along which it flows until it falls through the nearest gully into the sewers, and ultimately into the Seine. If produced in the upper part of a house, this description of refuse is first poured into an external shoot branching out of the rainwater pipe, with one of which every floor is usually provided. Iron pipes have been lately much introduced in place of the open channels across the foot pavements; these are laid level with the surface, and are cast with an open slit, about one inch in width, at the top, to afford facility for cleansing. During the busy parts of the day there are constant streams of such fluids running through most of the streets of Paris, the smell arising from which is by no means agreeable. In hot weather it is the practice to turn on the public stand pipes for an hour or two, to dilute the matter and accelerate its flow."

"With respect to fæcal refuse," says Mr. Rammell, " and much of the house-slops, particularly those of bed-chambers, the *cesspool* is universally adopted in Paris as the immediate receptacle."

By far the greater proportion of the wet house-refuse of Paris, therefore, is deposited in cesspools.

I shall, then, immediately proceed to show the quantity of matter thus collected yearly, as well as the means by which it is removed.

The aggregate *quantity* of the cesspool matter of Paris has greatly increased in quantity within the present century, though this might have been expected, as well from the increase of population as from the improved construction of cesspools (preventing leakage), and the increased supply of water in the French metropolis.

The following figures show both the aggregate quantity and the increase that has taken place in the cesspoolage of Paris, from 1810 to the present time:—

	Cub. Mètres.	Cub. Feet.
In 1810 the total quantity of refuse matter deposited in the basins at Montfaucon amounted to	50,151 =	1,770,330
In 1811 the quantity was	49,545 =	1,748,938
In 1812	49,235 =	1,737,995
Giving an average for the three years of .	49·877 =	1,760,658
The quantity at present conveyed to Montfaucon and Bondy amounts, according to M. Héloin (a very good authority), to from 600 to 700 cubic mètres daily, giving, in round numbers, an annual quantity of . . .	230,000 =	8,119,000

This shows an increase in 36 years of very nearly 400 per cent, but still it constitutes little more than one-half the cesspoolage of London.

The quantity of refuse matter which is daily drawn from the cesspools, Mr. Rammell states —and he had every assistance from the authorities in prosecuting his inquiries—at "between 600 and 700 cubic mètres; (21,180 and 24,710 cubic feet), giving, in round numbers, the annual quantity of 230,000 cubic mètres.

"Dividing this annual quantity at 230,000 cubic mètres (or 8,000,000 cubic feet) by the number of the population of Paris (94,721 individuals, according to the last census), we have 243 litres only as the annual produce from each individual. The daily quantity of matter (including water necessary for cleanliness) passing from each person into the cesspool in the better class of houses is stated to be 1¾ litre (3·08 pints), or 638 litres annually. The discrepancy between these two quantities, wide as it is, must be accounted for by the fact of a large proportion of the lower orders in Paris rarely or ever using any privy at all, and by allowing for the small quantity of water made use of in the inferior class of houses. There can be no doubt that this latter quantity of 1¾ litre daily is very nearly correct, and not above the average quantity used in houses where a moderate degree of cleanliness is observed. This proportion was ascertained to hold good in the case of some barracks in Paris, where the contents of the cesspools were accurately measured, the total quantity divided by the number of men occupying the barracks, and the quotient by the number of days since the cesspools had been last emptied; the result showing a daily quantity of 1¾ litre from each individual.

"The average charge per cubic mètre for extraction and transport of the cesspoolage is nine francs, giving a gross annual charge of 2,070,000 francs (82,800*l.* sterling), which sum, it would appear, is paid every year by the house-proprietors of Paris for the extraction of the matter from their cesspools, and its transport to the Voirie."

Mr. Rammell says that, were a tubular system of house-drainage, such as has been described under the proper head, adopted in Paris, in lieu of the present mode, it would cost less than one-tenth of the expense now incurred.

The principal place of deposit for the general refuse of Paris has long been at Montfaucon. A French writer, M. Jules Garnier, in a recent work, "A Visit to Montfaucon," says:—"For more than nine hundred years Montfaucon has been devoted to this purpose. There the citizens of Paris deposited their filth before the walls of the capital extended beyond what is now the central quarter. The distance between Paris and Montfaucon was then more than a mile and a half." Thus it appears that Montfaucon was devoted to its present purposes, of course in a much more limited degree, as early as the reign of King Charles the Simple.

This deposit of cesspool matter is the property of the commune (as in the city of London it would be said to belong to the "corporation"), and it is farmed out, for terms of nine years, to the highest bidders. The amount received by the commune has greatly increased, as the following returns, which are official, will show:—

A.D.		Francs		£
1808	the cesspoolage fetched	97,000,	abt.	3,880
1817	,,	75,000,	,,	3,000
1834	,,	165,000,	,,	7,000
1843	,,	525,000,	,,	21,000

It is here that the "*poudrette*,"* of which I

* Mr. Rammell supplies the following note on the use of "Poudrette."

"In connexion with this subject," he says, "a few observations upon the application of poudrette in agricultural process may not be without interest.

"With regard to the fertilizing properties of this preparation, M. Maxime Paulet, in his work entitled 'Théorie et Pratique des Engrais,' gives a table of the fertilizing qualities of various descriptions of manure, the value of each being determined by the quantity of nitrogen it contains. Taking for a standard good farm-yard dung, which contains on an average 4 per 1000 of nitrogen, and assuming that 10,000 kilogrammes (about 22,000 lbs. English) of this manure (containing 40 kilogrammes of nitrogen) are necessary to manure one hectare (2½ acres nearly) of land, the quantities of poudrette and of some other animal manures required to produce a similar effect would be as follows:—

	Kilogr.
"Good farm-yard dung, the quantity usually spread upon one hectare of land	10,000
Equivalent quantities of human urine, not having undergone fermentation	5,600
Equivalent quantities of poudrette of Montfaucon	2,550
Equivalent quantities of mixed human excrements (this quantity I have calculated from data given in the same work)	1,333

have spoken elsewhere, is prepared. Besides this branch of commerce, Montfaucon has establishments for the extracting of ammonia from the cesspool matter, and the right of doing so is now farmed out for 80,000 francs a-year (3200*l*).

Montfaucon is on the north side of Paris, and the place of refuse deposit is known as

	Kilogr.
"Equivalent quantities of liquid blood of the abattoirs	1,333
Equivalent quantities of bones	650
Equivalent quantities of average of guano (two specimens are given)	512
Equivalent quantities of urine of the public urinals in fermentation, and incompletely dried	233

"M. Paulett estimates the loss of the ammoniacal products contained in the fæcal matters when they are withdrawn from the cesspools, by the time they have been ultimately reduced into poudrette, at from 80 to 90 per cent.

"I have not been able to meet with an analysis of the matters found in the fixed and movable cesspools of Paris, but in the 'Cours d'Agriculture,' of M. le Comte de Gasparin, I find an analysis by MM. Payen and Boussingault of some matter taken from the cesspools of Lille, and in the state in which it is ordinarily used in the suburbs of that city as manure. This matter was found to contain on the average 0·205 per cent of nitrogen, and thus by the rule observed in drawing up the above table, 19·512 kilogrammes of it would be necessary to produce the same effect upon one hectare of land as the other manures there mentioned. The wide difference between this quantity and that (1333 kilogrammes) stated for the mixed human excrements in their undiluted state, would lead to the conclusion that a very large proportion of water was present in the matter sent from Lille, unless we are to attribute a portion of the difference to the accidental circumstance of the bad quality of this matter. It appears that this is very variable, according to the style of living of the persons producing it. 'Upon this subject,' M. Paulet says, 'the case of an agriculturist in the neighbourhood of Paris is cited, who bought the contents of the cesspools of one of the fashionable restaurants of the Palais Royal. Making a profitable speculation of it, he purchased the matter of the cesspools of several barracks. This bargain, however, resulted in a loss, for the produce from this last matter came very short of that given by the first.'

"Poudrette weighs 70 kilogrammes the hectolitre (154 lbs. per 22 gallons), and the quantity usually spread upon one hectare of land (2½ acres nearly) is 1750 kilogrammes, being at the rate of about 1540 lbs. per acre English measure. It is cast upon the land by the hand, in the manner that corn is sown.

"Poudrette packed in sacks very soon destroys them. This is always the case, whether it is whole or has been newly prepared.

"A serious accident occurred in 1818, on board a vessel named the *Arthur*, which sailed from Rouen with a cargo of poudrette for Guadaloupe. During the voyage a disease broke out on board which carried off half the crew, and left the remainder in a deplorable state of health when they reached their destination. It attacked also the men who landed the cargo; they all suffered in a greater or less degree. The poudrette was proved to have been shipped during a wet season, and to have been exposed before and during shipment, in a manner to allow it to absorb a considerable quantity of moisture. The accident appears to have been due to the subsequent fermentation of the mass in the hold—increased to an intense degree by the moisture it had acquired, and by the heat of a tropical climate.

"M. Parent du Châtelet, to whom the matter was referred, recommended that to guard against similar accidents in future, the poudrette intended for exportation, in order to deprive it entirely of humidity, should be mixed with an absorbent powder, such as quicklime, and that it should be packed in casks to protect it from moisture during the voyage."

the Voirie. The following account of it, and of the manufacture of poudrette, is curious in many respects:—

"The area, which is about 40 acres in extent, is divided into three irregular compartments:—

"1. The system of basins.

"2. The ground used for spreading and drying the matter.

"3. The place where the matter is heaped up after having been dried.

"The basins, standing for the most part in gradations, one above another, by reason of the slope of the ground, are six in number. The two upper ones, which are upon a level, first receive the soil upon its arrival at the Voirie; the four others are receptacles for the more liquid portion as it gradually flows off from the upper basins.

"There is a great difference in the character of the soil brought; that taken from the upper part of the cesspools, and amounting to a large proportion of the whole, being entirely liquid; while the remainder is more or less solid, according to the depth at which it is taken. The whole, however, during winter or rainy weather, is indiscriminately deposited in the upper basins; but in dry weather, the nearly solid portion is at once thrown upon the drying-ground." *

* "It is in the upper basins," adds the Reports, "that the first separation of the liquids and solids takes place, the latter falling to the bottom, and the former gradually flowing off through a sluice into the lower basins. This first separation, however, is by no means complete, a considerable deposit taking place in the lower basins. The mass in the upper basins, after three or four years, then appears like a thick mud, half liquid, half solid; it is of depth varying from 12 to 15 feet. In order entirely to get rid of the liquids, deep channels are then cut across the mass, by which they are drained off, when the deposit soon becomes sufficiently stiff to permit of its being dug out and spread upon the drying-ground, where, to assist the desiccation, it is turned over two or three times a-day by means of a harrow drawn by a horse.

"The time necessary for the requisite desiccation varies a good deal, according to the season of the year, the temperature, and the dry or moist state of the atmosphere. Ere yet it is entirely deprived of humidity, the matter is collected into heaps, varying in size usually from 8 to 10 yards high, and from 60 to 80 yards long, by 25 or 30 yards wide. These heaps or mounds generally remain a twelvemonth untouched, sometimes even for two or three years; but as fast as the material is required, they are worked from one of the sides by means of pickaxes, shovels, and rakes; the pieces separated are then easily broken and reduced to powder, foreign substances being carefully excluded. This operation, which is the last the matter undergoes, is performed by women. The poudrette then appears like a mould of a grey-black colour, light, greasy to the touch, finely grained, and giving out a particular faint and nauseous odour.

"The finer particles of matter carried by the liquids into the lower basins, and there more gradually deposited in combination with a precipitate from the urine, yield a variety of poudrette, preferred, by the farmers, for its superior fertilizing properties. In this case the drying process is conducted more slowly and with more difficulty than in the other, but more completely.

"In general the poudrette is dried with great difficulty; it appears to have an extreme affinity for

"The quantity of poudrette sold in 1818 was:—

At the Voirie . . . . 50,000 setiers *
Sent into the departments 20,000 „

Total sale . . . . . 70,000 „
at prices of 7, 8, and 9 francs the setier.

"This is equal, at the average price of 8 francs, to 22,400*l.* sterling.

"The refuse liquids, as fast as they overflow the basins, or are passed through the chemical works, are conducted into the public sewers, and through them into the Seine, nearly opposite the Jardin des Plantes. *They thus fall into the river at the very commencement of its course through Paris, and pollute its waters before they have reached the various works lower down and near the centre of the city, where they are raised and distributed for household purposes, for the supply of baths, and for the public fountains.*

"Rats are found by thousands in the Voirie, and their voracity is such, that I have often known them, during a single night, convert into skeletons the carcasses of twenty horses which had been brought thither the evening before. The bones are burnt to heat the coppers, or to get rid of them.

"Speaking of the disgusting practices at the Voirie, Mr. Gisquet says, 'I have seen men stark naked, passing entire days in the midst of the basins, seeking for any objects of value they might contain. I have seen others fishing for the rotten fish the market inspectors had caused to be thrown into the basins. Two cartloads of spoilt and stinking mackerel were thrown into the largest of the basins; two hours afterwards all the fish had disappeared.'

"The emanations from the Voirie are, as may well be supposed, most powerfully offensive. To a stranger unaccustomed to the atmosphere surrounding them it would be almost impossible to make the tour of the basins without being more or less affected with a disposition to nausea. Large and numerous bubbles of gas are seen constantly rising from a lake of urine and water, while evaporation of the most foul description is going on from many acres of surrounding ground, upon which the solid matter is spread to dry."

The late M. Parent du Châtelet, a high authority on this matter, stated (in 1833)

water; few substances give out moisture more slowly, or absorb it more greedily from the air.

"A good deal of heat is generated in the heaps of desiccated matter. This is always sensible to the touch, and sometimes results in spontaneous combustion.

"The intensity of this heat is not in proportion to the elevation of temperature of the atmosphere. It is promoted by moisture. The only means of extinguishing the fire when it is once developed is to turn over the mass from top to bottom, in order to expose it to the air. Water thrown upon it, unless in very large quantities, would only increase its activity."

* 4¼ heaped bushels each, English measure.

that the emanations from the Voirie were insupportable within a circumference of 2000 mètres (about a mile and a quarter, English measure); while the winds carried them sometimes, as was shown when an official inquiry was made as to the ravages and causes of cholera, 2½ miles; and in certain states of the atmosphere, 8 French miles (not quite 5 English miles). The same high authority has also stated, that in addition to the emanations from the cesspool matter at the Voirie the greater part of the carcasses of about 12,000 horses, and between 25,000 and 30,000 smaller animals, were allowed to rot upon the ground there.

To abate this nuisance a new Voirie was, more than 20 years since, formed in the forest of Bondy, 8 miles from Paris. It consists of eight basins, four on each side of the Canal de l'Ourcq, arranged like those at Montfaucon. The area of these basins is little short of 96,000 square yards, and their collective capacity upwards of 261,000 cubic yards. The expectations of the relief that would be experienced from the establishment of the new Voirie in the forest have not been realized. The movable cesspools only have been conveyed there, by boats on the canal, to be emptied; the empty casks being conveyed back by the same boats. The basins are not yet full; for the conveyance by the Canal de l'Ourcq is costly, and in winter its traffic is sometimes suspended by its being frozen. In one year the cost of conveying these movable cesspools to Bondy was little short of 1500*l.*

In the latest Report on this subject (1835) the Commissioners, of whom M. Parent du Châtelet was one, recommend that all the cesspool matter at the Voiries should be disinfected. M. Salmon, after a course of chemical experiments (the Report of the Commission states), disinfected and carbonized a mass of mud and filth, containing much organic matter, deposited (from a sewer) on the banks of the Seine.

The Commissioners say, " The discovery of M. Salmon awakened the attention of the contractors of Montfaucon, who employed one of our most skilful chemists to find for them a means of disinfection other than that for which M. Salmon had taken out a patent. M. Sanson and some other persons made similar researches, and from their joint investigations it resulted that disinfection might be equally well produced with turf ashes, with carbonized turf, and with the simple *débris* of this very abundant substance; and that the same success might be obtained with sawdust, with the refuse matter of the tan-yards, with garden mould, so abundant in the environs of Paris, and with many other substances. A curious experiment has even shown, that after mixing with a clayey earth a portion of fæcal matter, it was only necessary to carbonize this mixture to obtain a perfect disinfectant powder. Theory had already indicated the result.

This disinfection, however, has not been carried out in the Voiries, nor in the manufacture of poudrette.

From the account of the general refuse depositories of Paris we pass to the particular receptacles or cesspools of the French capital.

The Parisian cesspools are of two sorts:—
1. Fixed or excavated cesspools.
2. Movable cesspools.

" In early times the *excavated cesspools* or pits were constructed in the rudest manner, and cleaned out more or less frequently, or utterly neglected, at the discretion of their owners. As the city increased in size, however, and as the permeations necessarily taking place into the soil accumulated in the lapse of centuries, the evil resulting was found to be of grave magnitude, calling for prompt and vigorous interference on the part of the authorities. It appears certain that prior to the year 1819 (when a strict *ordonnance* was issued on the subject) the cesspools were very carelessly constructed. For the most part they were far from water-tight, and very probably were not intended to be otherwise. Consequently, nearly the whole of the fluid matter within them drained into the springs beneath the substratum, or became absorbed by the surrounding soil. Nor was this the only evil: the basement walls of the houses became saturated with the offensive permeations, and the atmosphere, more particularly in the interior of the dwellings, tainted with their exhalations.

" The *movable cesspools*, for the most part, consist simply of tanks or barrels, which, when full, are removed to some convenient spot for the purpose of their contents being discharged. This form of cesspool, though not leading to that contamination of the substratum which is naturally induced by the fixed or excavated cesspool, may occasion many offensive nuisances from carelessness in overfilling, or in the process of emptying."

"The movable cesspools are of two kinds; the one," says Mr. Rammell, " extremely simple and primitive in construction, the other more complicated. The former retains all the refuse, both liquid and solid, passed into it; the latter retains only the solid matter, the liquid being separated by a sort of strainer, and running off into another receptacle.

" The advantage of this separating apparatus is, that those cesspools provided with it require to be emptied less frequently than the others; the solid matter being alone retained in the movable part. The liquid portion is withdrawn from the tank into which it is received by pumping.

" The other kind of movable cesspool consists simply of a wooden cask set on end, and having its top pierced to admit the soil-pipe. It is intended to retain both solid and liquid matter. When full, it is detached, and the aperture in the top having been closed by a tight-fitting lid secured by an iron bar placed across, it is removed, and an empty one immediately substituted for it.

"The movable cesspool last described is much more generally used than the other kind; very few are furnished with the separating apparatus. But the use of either sort, I am told, is not on the increase. The movable cesspools are found, on the whole, to be more expensive than the fixed, besides entailing many inconveniences, one of which is the frequent entrance of workmen upon the premises for the purpose of removing them, which sometimes has to be done every second or third day. Moreover, if the cask becomes in the slightest degree overcharged, there is an overflow of matter."

Indeed, the movable system of cesspools (it appears from further accounts) seems to be now adopted only in those places where fixed cesspools could not be altered in accordance with the ordonnance, or where it is desired to avoid the first cost of a fixed cesspool.

An ordonnance of 1819 enacts peremptorily that *all* cesspools, fixed or excavated, then existing, shall be altered in accordance with its provisions upon the first subsequent emptying after the date of the enactment, " or if that be found impracticable, they shall be filled up." This full delegation of power to a centralised authority was the example prompting our late stringent enactments as to buildings and sewerage.

The French ordonnance provides also that the walls, arches, and bottoms of the cesspools, shall be constructed of a very hard description of stone, known as " pierres meulières" (millstone); the mortar used is to be hydraulic lime and clean river sand. Each arch is to be 30 to 35 centimètres (12 to 14 inches) in thickness, and the walls 45 to 50 centimètres (18 to 20 inches); the interior height not to be less than 2 mètres (2 yards 6 inches). A soil-pipe is always to be placed in the middle of the cesspool; its interior diameter is not to be less than 9⅜ inches in pottery-ware piping, or 7⅞ inches in cast iron. A vent-pipe, not less than 9⅜ inches in diameter, is to be carried up to the level of the chimney-tops, or to that of the chimneys of the adjoining houses. This is, if possible, to divert the smell from the house to which the cesspool is attached.

"A principal object of the *ordonnance*," it is stated in the Reports, "was to ensure the cesspools being thenceforth made water-tight; so that further pollution of the substratum and springs might be prevented; and the provisions for its attainment have been very strictly enforced by the police. The present cesspools are, in fact, water-tight constructions, retaining the whole of the liquids passed into them until the same are withdrawn by artificial means. The advantage has its attendant inconveniences, and, moreover, has been dearly paid for; for, independently of the cost of the alterations and the increased cost of making the cesspools in the outset—the liquids no longer draining away by natural permeation —the constant expense of emptying them has enormously increased. In the better class of houses, where water is more freely used, the operation has now to be repeated every three, four, or five months, whereas formerly the cesspool was emptied every eighteen months or two years. An increased water supply has added to the evil, moderate even now as the extent of that supply is."

"It is estimated that, in the better class of houses, the daily quantity of matter, including the water necessary for cleanliness and to ensure the passage of the solids through the soil-pipe, passing into the cesspool from each individual, amounts to 1¾ litre (3·08 English pints). Foreign substances are found in great abundance in the cesspools; the large soil-pipes permitting their easy introduction; so that the cesspool becomes the common receptacle for a great variety of articles that it is desired secretly to get rid of. Article 19 of the Police Regulations directs that nightmen finding any articles in the cesspools, especially such as lead to the suspicion of a crime or misdemeanor, shall make a declaration of the fact the same day to a Commissary of Police."

In all such matters the police regulations of France are far more stringent and exacting than those of England.

"The cesspools vary considerably in foulness," continues the Report; "and *it is remarkable that those containing the greatest proportion of water are the most foul and dangerous.* This is accounted for by the increased quantity of sulphuretted hydrogen gas evolved: and is more particularly the case where, from their large size, or from the small number of people using them, much time is allowed for the matter to stagnate and decompose in them. Soap-suds are said to add materially to their offensive and dangerous condition. *The* FOULNESS *of the cesspools, therefore, would appear to be in direct proportion to the* CLEANLY *habits of the inmates of the houses to which they respectively belong.* Where urine predominates ammoniacal vapours are given off in considerable quantities, and although these affect the eyes of those exposed to them—and the nightmen suffer much from inflammation of these organs—no danger to life results. The inflammation, however, is often sufficiently acute to produce temporary blindness, and from this cause the men are at times thrown out of work for days together." *

* I did not hear any of the London nightmen or sewermen complain of inflammation in the eyes, and no such effect was visible; nor that they suffered from temporary blindness, or were, indeed, thrown out of work from any such cause; they merely remarked that they were first dazzled, or "*dazed*," with the soil. But the labour of the Parisian is far more continuous and regular than the London nightman, owing in a great degree to the system of *movable cesspools* in Paris.

The *emptying of the cesspools* is the next point to be considered.

No cesspool is allowed to be emptied in Paris, and no nightman's cart, containing soil, is allowed to be in the streets from 8 A.M. to 10 P.M. from October 1st to March 31st, nor from 6 A.M. to 11 P.M. from April 1st to September 30th. In the winter season the hours of labour permitted by law are ten, and in the summer season seven, out of the twenty-four; while in London the hours of night-work are limited to five, without any distinction of season. These hours, however, only relate to the cleansing of the fixed cesspools of Paris.

Fixed or excavated cesspools are emptied into carts, which are driven to the receptacles. As far as regards the removal of night-soil along the streets, there are far more frequent complaints of stench and annoyance in Paris than in London. None of these cesspools can be emptied without authority from the police, and the police exercise a vigilant supervision over the whole arrangements; neither can any cesspool, after being emptied, be closed without a written authority, after inspection, by the Director of Health; nor can a cesspool, if found defective when emptied, be repaired without such authority.

"With regard to the movable cesspool," it is reported, "the process of emptying is very simple, though undoubtedly demanding a considerable expenditure of labour. The tank or barrel, when filled, is disconnected from the soil-pipe, an empty one being immediately substituted in its place, and the bung-hole being securely closed, it is conveyed away on a vehicle, somewhat resembling a brewer's dray (which holds about eight or ten of them), to the spot appointed as the depository of its discharged contents. The removal of movable cesspools is allowed to take place during the day."

In opening a cesspool in Paris, precautions are always taken to prevent accidents which might result from the escape or ignition of the gases.

The general, not to say universal, mode of emptying the fixed or excavated cesspools is to pump the contents into closed carts for transport.

"This operation is," says Mr. Rammell, "performed with two descriptions of pumps, one working on what may be called the *hydraulic* principle, the other on the *pneumatic*. In the former, the valves are placed in the pipe communicating between the cesspool and the cart, and the matter itself is pumped. In the latter, the valves are placed beyond the cart, and the air being pumped out of the cart, the matter flows into it to fill up the vacuum so occasioned. The real principle is of course the same in both cases, the matter being forced up by atmospheric pressure. One advantage of the pneumatic system is, that there are no valves to impede the free passage of matter through the suction-pipe; another, that it permits the use of a pipe of larger diameter.

"The cart employed for the pneumatic system consists of an iron cylinder, mounted sometimes upon four, but generally upon two wheels, the latter arrangement being found to be the more convenient. Previous to use at the cesspool, the carts are drawn to a branch establishment, situate just within the Barrière du Combat, where they are exhausted of air with an air-pump, worked by steam power. A 12-horse engine erected there is capable of exhausting five carts at the same time; the vacuum produced being equal to $28\frac{3}{4}$ inches (72 centimètres) of mercury. A cart (in good repair, and upon two wheels) will preserve a practical vacuum for 48 hours after exhaustion."

The total weight of one of these carts when full is about 3 tons and 8 cwt. This is somewhat more than the weight of the contents of a London waggon employed in night-soil carriage. Three horses are attached to each cart.

When an opening into the cesspool has been effected, a suction-pipe on the pneumatic principle is laid from the cesspool to the cart. This pipe is $3\frac{15}{16}$ inches in diameter, and is in separate pieces of about 10 feet each, with others shorter (down even to 1 foot), to make up any exact length required. Two kinds are commonly used; one made of leather, having iron wire wound spirally inside to prevent collapse, the other of copper. The leather pipe is used where a certain degree of pliability is required; the copper for the straight parts of the line, and for determined curves; pieces struck from various radii being made for the purpose.

Gutta-percha has been tried as a substitute for leather in the piping, but was pronounced liable to split, and its use was abandoned. So with India-rubber in London.

The communication between the suction-pipe and the vehicle used by the nightmen is opened by withdrawing a plug by means of a forked rod into the "recess" (hollow) of the machine, an operation tasking the muscular powers of two men. This done, the cesspool contents rush into the cart, being forced up by the weight of the atmosphere to occupy the existing vacuum; this occupies about three minutes. The cart, however, is then but three-fourths filled with matter, the remaining fourth being occupied by the rarefied air previously in the cart, and by the air contained in the suction-pipe. This air is next withdrawn by the action of a small air-pump, worked usually by two, but sometimes by one man. The air-pump is placed on the ground at a little distance from the cesspool cart, and communicates with it by a flexible India-rubber tube, an inch in diameter. The air, as fast as it is pumped out, is forced through another India-rubber tube of similar dimensions, which communicates with a furnace, also placed on the ground at a little distance from the air-pump, the pump occupying the middle space between the cart and the furnace, the furnace and the pump being portable. To ascertain when the vehicle is full, a short glass tube is inserted in the end of the air-pipe (the end being of brass), and through this, with the help of a small lantern, the matter is seen to rise.

"The number of carts required for each operation," states Mr. Rammell, "of course varies according to the size of the cesspool to be emptied; but as these contain on the average about five cart-loads, that is the number usually sent.*

"In addition to the carts for the transport of the night-soil, a light-covered spring van drawn by one horse is used to carry the tools, &c., required in the process.

"These tools consist of—

"1. An air-pump when the work is to be done on the pneumatic system, and of an hydraulic pump when it is to be done on the hydraulic system.

"2. About 50 mètres of suction-pipe of various forms and lengths.

"3. A furnace for the purpose of burning the gases.

"4. Wooden hods for the removal of the solid night-soil.

"5. Pails, a ladder, pincers, levers, hammers, and other articles."

I have hitherto spoken of the *Pneumatic* System of emptying the Parisian cesspools. The results of the *Hydraulic* System are so similar, as regards time, &c., that only a brief notice is required. The hydraulic pump is worked by four men; it is placed on the ground in the place most convenient for the operation, and the cart is filled in the space of from three to five minutes.

A furnace is used.

"The furnace," says the Report, "consists of a sheet-iron cylinder, about nine inches in diameter, pierced with small holes, and covered with a conical cap to prevent the flame spreading. The vent-pipe first communicates underneath with a small reservoir, intended to contain the matter in case the operation should be carried too far. A piece is inserted in the bottom of this reservoir, by unscrewing which it may be emptied. The furnace is sometimes fixed upon a plank, which rests upon two projecting pieces behind the cart."

An indicator is also used to show the advancement of the filling of the cart; a glass tube and a cork float are the chief portions of the apparatus of the indicator.

"Towards the end of the operation, when the quantity of matter remaining in the cesspool, although sufficiently fluid, is too shallow for pumping, it is scooped into a large pail; and, the end of the suction-pipe being introduced, drawn up into the cart. When the matter is in too solid a state to pass through the pipe, it is carried to the cart in hods, unless it is in considerable quantity. In that case it is removed in vessels called *tinettes*, in the shape of a truncated cone, holding each about $3\frac{1}{2}$ cubic feet. These vessels are closed with a lid, and are lifted into an open waggon for transport."

Of these two systems the pneumatic is the more costly, and is likely to be supplanted by the hydraulic. Each system, according to Mr. Rammell, is still a nuisance, as, in spite of every precaution, the gases escape the moment the cesspool emptying is commenced, and vitiate the atmosphere. They force their way very often through the joints of the pipes, and are insufficiently consumed in the furnaces. Mr. Rammell mentions his having twice, after witnessing two of these operations, suffered from attacks of illness. On the first occasion, the men omitted to burn the foul air, and the atmosphere being heavy with moisture, the odour was so intense that it was smelt from the Rue du Port Mahon to the Rue Menars, more than 400 yards distant.

The emptying of the cesspools is let by contract, the commune acting in the light of a proprietor. To obtain a contract, a man must have license or permission from the prefect of police, and such license is only granted after proof that the applicant is provided with the necessary apparatus, carts, &c., and also with a suitable dépôt for the reception of the pumps, carts, &c., when not in use. The stock-in-trade of a contractor is inspected at least twice a-year, and if found inadequate or out of repair the license is commonly withdrawn. The "gangs" of nightmen employed by the contractors are fixed by the law at four men each (the number employed in London), but without any legal provision on the subject. The terms of these contracts are not stated, but they appear to have ceased to be undertakings by individual capitalists, being all in the hands of companies, known as *compagnies de vidanges* (filth companies). There are now eight companies in Paris carrying on these operations. More than half of the whole work, however, is accomplished by one company, the "*Compagnie Richer*." The capital invested in their working stock is said to exceed 4,800,000 francs (200,000*l*.). They now require the labour of 350 horses, and the use of 120 vehicles of different descriptions.

The construction of a cesspool in Paris costs about 18*l*. as an average. The houses containing from 30 to 70 inmates may have two, and occasionally more, cesspools. Taking the average at one and a half, the capital sunk in a cesspool is 27*l*. Mr. Rammell says:—

"Adopting these calculations of the number of cesspools to each house, and their cost, and allowing only the small quantity of $1\frac{3}{4}$ litre (3·08

---

* It must be recollected, to account for the greater quantity of matter between the cesspools of Paris and London, that the French fixed cesspool, from the greater average of inmates to each house, must necessarily contain about three times and a half as much as that of a London cesspool. If the dwellers in a Parisian house, instead of averaging twenty-four, averaged between seven and eight, as in London, the cesspool contents in Paris would, at the above rate, be between four and five tons (as it is in London) for the average of each house.

pints) of matter to each individual, the annual expense of the cesspool system in Paris, per house containing 24 persons, will be,—

"For interest, at 5 per cent upon capital sunk in works of construction, 1*l.* 7*s.*

"For extraction and removal of matter, 5*l.* 11*s.*

"Total, 6*l.* 18*s.*

"The annual expense per inhabitant will be 5*s.* 9*d.*

"The latter, then, may be taken as the average yearly sum per head actually paid by that portion of the inhabitants of Paris who use the cesspools."

The following, among others before shown, are the conclusions arrived at by Mr. Rammell:—

1. "That with the most perfect regulations, and the application of machines constructed upon scientific principles, the operation of emptying cesspools is still a nuisance, not only to the inmates of the house to which it belongs, but to those of the neighbouring houses, and to persons passing in the street.

2. "That the cesspool system of Paris presents an obstacle to the proper extension of the water supply, and consequently represses the growth of habits of personal and domestic cleanliness, with their immense moral results; and that in this respect it may be said to be inconsistent with a high degree of civilization of the masses of any community.

3. "That, compared with a tubular system of refuse drainage, it is an exceedingly expensive mode of disposing of the fæcal refuse of a town."

OF THE EMPTYING OF THE LONDON CESSPOOLS BY PUMP AND HOSE.

HAVING now ascertained the quantity of wet house-refuse annually deposited in the cesspools of the metropolis, the next step is to show the means by which these 15,000,000 cubic feet of cesspoolage are removed, and whence they are conveyed, as well as the condition of the labourers engaged in the business.

There are two methods of removing the soil from the tanks :—

1. By pump and hose, or the hydraulic method;

2. By shovel and tube, or manual labour.

The first of these is the new French mode, and the other the old English method of performing the work. The distinctive feature between the two is, that in the one case the refuse is discharged by means of pipes into the sewers, and in the other that it is conveyed by means of carts to some distant night-yard.

According to the French method, therefore, the cesspoolage ultimately becomes sewage; the refuse being deposited in a cesspool for a greater or a less space of time, and finally discharged into the sewers; so that it is a kind of intermediate process between the cesspool system and the sewer system of defecating a town, being, as it were, a compound of the two.

The great advantage of the sewer system, as contradistinguished from the cesspool system of defecation, is, that it admits of the wet refuse being removed from the neighbourhood of the house as soon as it is produced; while the advantage of the cesspool system, as contradistinguished from the sewer system, is, that it prevents the contamination of the river whence the town draws its principal supply of water. The cesspool system of defecation remedies the main evil of the sewer system, and the sewer system the main evil of the cesspool system. The French mode of emptying cesspools, however, appears to have the peculiar property of combining the ill effects of both systems without the advantages of either. The refuse of the house not only remains rotting and seething for months under the noses of the household, but it is ultimately—that is, after more than a year's decomposition—washed into the stream from which the inhabitants are supplied with water, and so returned to them diluted in the form of *aqua pura*, for washing, cooking, or drinking. The sole benefit accruing from the French mode of nightmanship is, that it performs a noisome operation in a comparatively cleanly manner; but surely this is a small compensation for the evils attendant upon it. The noses of those who prefer stagnant cesspools to rapid sewers cannot be so particularly sensitive, that for the sake of avoiding the smell of the nightman's cart they would rather that its contents should be discharged into the water that they use for household purposes.

The hydraulic or pump-and hose method of emptying the cesspools is now practised by the Court of Sewers, who introduced the process into London in the winter of 1847. The apparatus used in this country consists of an hydraulic pump, which is generally placed six or eight feet distant from, but sometimes close to, the cesspool—indeed, on its edge. It is worked by two men, "just up and down," as one of the labourers described it to me, "like a fire-engine." A suction-pipe, with an iron nozzle, is placed in the cesspool, into which is first introduced a deodorising fluid, in the proportion, as well as can be estimated, of a pint to a square yard of matter, and diluted with water from the fire-plugs.

The pipes are of leather, the suction-pipes being wrapped with spring-iron wire at the joints. India-rubber pipes were used, and "answered very tidy," one of the gangers told me, but they were too expensive, the material being soon worn out: they were only tried five or six months. The pipes now employed differ in no respect of size or appearance from the leathern fire-engine pipes; and as the work is always done in the daytime, and no smell arises from it, the neighbourhood is often alarmed, and people begin to ask where the fire is. One outsideman said, "Why, that's always asked. I've been asked—ay, I dare say a hundred times in a day—'Where's the fire? where's the fire?'" A cesspool, by this process, has been emptied into a sewer at 300 yards distant. The pipe is placed within the nearest gullyhole, down which the matter is washed into the sewer. When the cesspool is emptied, it is well sluiced with water; the water is pumped into the sewer, and then the work is complete.

The pumping is occasionally very hard work, making the shoulders and back ache grievously; indeed, some cesspools have been found so long neglected, and so choked with rags and rubbish, that manual labour had to be resorted to, and the matter dug and tubbed out, after the old mode of the nightmen. A square yard of cesspoolage is cleared out, under ordinary circumstances, in an hour; while an average duration of time for the cleansing of a regularly-sized cesspool is from three to four hours.

A pneumatic pump, with an iron cart, drawn by two horses (similar to the French invention), was tried as an experiment, but discontinued in a fortnight.

For the hydraulic method of emptying cesspools, a gang of four men, under the direction of a ganger, who makes a fifth, is required.

The *division of labour* is as follows:—

1. The pumpmen, who, as their name implies, work the engine or pumps.
2. The holeman, who goes into the cesspool and stirs up the matter, so as to make it as fluid as possible.
3. The outsideman, whose business it is to attend to the pipe, which reaches from the cesspool, along the surface of the street, or other place, to the gullyhole.
4. The ganger, who is the superintendent of the whole, and is only sometimes present at the operation; he is not unfrequently engaged, while one cesspool is being emptied, in making an examination or any necessary arrangement for the opening of another. He also gives notice (acting under the instruction of the clerk of the works) to the water company of the district, that the pumps will be at work in this or that place, a notice generally given a day in advance, and the water is supplied gratuitously, from a street fire-plug, and used at discretion, some cesspool contents requiring three times more water than others to liquefy them sufficient for pumping.

The cesspool-pumping gangs are six in number, each consisting of five men, although the "outsideman" is sometimes a strong youth of seventeen or eighteen. The whole work is done by a contractor, who makes an agreement with the Court of Sewers, and finds the necessary apparatus, appointing his own labourers. All the present labourers, however, have been selected as trusty men from among the flushermen, the contractor concurring in the recommendation of the clerk of the works, or the inspector. The cesspool-sewermen work in six districts. Two divisions (east and west) of Westminster; Finsbury and Holborn; Surrey and Kent; Tower Hamlets (now including Poplar); and the City. The districts vary in size, but there is usually a gang devoted to each: in case of emergency, however, a gang from another district (as among the flushermen) is sent to expedite any pressing work. All the men are paid by the job, the payment being 2s. each per job, to the pumpmen and holeman, and 3s. to the ganger; but in addition to the 2s. per job, the holeman has 6d. a-day extra; and the outsideman has 6d. a-day *deducted* from the 4s. he would earn in two jobs, which is a frequent day's work. The men told me that they had four or four and a-half days' work (or eight or nine jobs) every week; but such was the case more particularly when the householders were less cognizant of the work, and did not think of resorting to it; now, I am assured, the men's average employment may be put at five days a week, or ten jobs.

The perquisites of these workmen are none, except the householder sends them some refreshment on his own accord. There may be a perquisite, but very rarely, occurring to the holeman, should he find anything in the soil; but the finding is far less common than among the nightmen, with whom the process goes through different stages. I did not hear among cesspool-sewermen of anything being found by them or by their comrades; of course, when the soil is once absorbed into the pipe, it is unseen on its course of deposit down the gullyhole.

The men have no trade societies, and no arrangements of any equivalent nature; no benefit clubs or sick clubs, for which their number, indeed, is too small; or, as my informant sometimes wound up in a climax, "No, nothing that way, sir." They are sober and industrious men, chiefly married, and with families. Into further statistics, however, of diet, rent, &c., I need not enter, concerning so small a body; they are the same as among other well-conducted labourers.

The men find their own dresses, which are of the same cost, form, and material as I have described to pertain to the flushermen; also their own "picks" and shovels, costing respectively 2s. 6d. and 2s. 3d. each.

One cesspool-sewerman told me, that when he was first a member of one of those gangs he was "awful abused" by the "regular nightmen," if he came across any of them " as was beery, poor fellows;" but that had all passed over now.

The total sum paid to the six gangs of labourers in the course of the year would, at the rate of ten cesspools emptied per week, amount to the following:—

	Yearly Total.
12 pumpmen, 10 jobs a-week each, 20s. per week, or 52l. per year, each .	£624
6 holemen, ditto, ditto, with 2s. 6d. a-week extra	351
6 outsidemen, 20s. a-week, less by 6d. a-day, or 2s. 6d. a-week, 45l. 10s. a-year	296
Carried forward . .	£1271

	Yearly Total.
Brought forward	£1271
6 gangers, 30s. a-week each, or 78l. per year	468
	£1739

Any householder, &c., who applies to the Court of Sewers, or to any officer of the court whom he may know, has his cesspool cleansed by the hydraulic method, in the same way as he might employ any tradesman to do any description of work proper to his calling. The charge (by the Court of Sewers) is 5s. or 6s. per square yard, according to pipeage, &c. required; a cesspool emptied by this system costs from 20s. to 30s. The charges of the nightman, who have to employ horses, &c., are necessarily higher.

Estimating that throughout London 60 cesspools are emptied by the hydraulic method every week, or 3120 every year, and the charge for each to be on an average 25s., we have for the gross receipts . . 3120 × 25s. = £3900
And deducting from this the sum paid for labour 1739

It shows a profit of £2161

This is upwards of 123 per cent; but out of this, interest on capital and wear and tear of machinery have to be paid.

During the year 1851, I am credibly informed that as many as 3000 sewers were emptied by the hydraulic process; and calculating each to have contained the average quantity of refuse, viz. five tons or loads, or about 180 cubic feet, we have an aggregate of 540,000 cubic feet of cesspoolage ultimately carried off by the sewers. This, however, is only a twenty-seventh of the entire quantity.

The sum paid in wages to the men engaged in emptying these 3000 cesspools by the hydraulic process would, at the rate of 2s. per man to the four members of the gang, and 3s. to the ganger, or 11s. in all for each cesspool, amount to 1650l., which is 139l. and 250 cesspools less than the amount above given.

Statement of a Cesspool-Sewerman.

I give the following brief and characteristic statement, which is peculiar in showing the habitual *restlessness* of the mere labourer. My informant was a stout, hale-looking man, who had rarely known illness. All these sort of labourers (nightmen included) scout the notion of the cholera attacking *them!*

"Work, sir? Well, I think I *do* know what work is, and has known it since I was a child; and then I was set to help at the weaving. My friends were weavers at Norwich, and 20 years ago, until steam pulled working men down from being well paid and well off, it was a capital trade. Why, my father could sometimes earn 3l. at his work as a working weaver; there was money for ever then; now 12s. a-week is, I believe, the tip-top earnings of his trade. But *I didn't like the confinement or the close air in the factories*, and so, when I grew big enough, I went to ground-work in the city (so he frequently called Norwich); I call ground-work such as digging drains and the like. Then I 'listed into the Marines. *Oh, I hardly know what made me;* men does foolish things and don't know why; it's human natur. I'm sure it wasn't the bounty of 3l. that tempted me, for I was doing middling, and sometimes had night-work as well as ground-work to do. I was then sent to Sheerness and put on board the *Thunderer* man-of-war, carrying 84 guns, as a marine. She sailed through the Straits (of Gibraltar), and was three years and three months blockading the Dardanelles, and cruising among the islands. I never saw anything like such fortifications as at the Dardanelles; why, there was mortars there as would throw a ton weight. No, I never heard of their having been fired. Yes, we sometimes got leave for a party to go ashore on one of the islands. They called them Greek islands, but I fancy as how it was Turks near the Dardanelles. O yes, the men on the islands was civil enough to us; they never spoke to us, and we never spoke to them. The sailors sometimes, and indeed the lot of us, would have bits of larks with them, laughing at 'em and taking sights at 'em and such like. Why, I've seen a fine-dressed Turk, one of their grand gentlemen there, when a couple of sailors has each been taking a sight at him, and dancing the shuffle along with it, make each on 'em a low bow, as solemn as could be. Perhaps he thought it was a way of being civil in our country! I've seen some of the head ones stuck over with so many knives, and cutlasses, and belts, and pistols, and things, that he looked like a cutler's shop-window. We were ordered home at last, and after being some months in barracks, which I didn't relish at all, were paid off at Plymouth. Oh, a barrack life's anything but pleasant, but I've done with it. After that I was eight years and a quarter a gentleman's servant, coachman, or anything (in Norwich), and then got tired of that and came to London, and got to ground and new sewer-work, and have been on the sewers above five years. Yes, I prefer the sewers to the Greek islands. I was one of the first set as worked a pump. There was a great many spectators; I dare say as there was 40 skientific gentlemen. I've been on the sewers, flushing and pumping, ever since. The houses we clean out, all says it's far the best plan, ours is. 'Never no more nightmen,' they say. You see, sir, our plan's far less trouble to the people in the house, and there's no smell—least I never found no smell, and it's cheap, too. In time the nightmen 'll disappear; in course they must, there's so many new dodges comes up, always some one of the working classes is a being ruined. If it ain't steam, it's something else as knocks the bread out of their mouths quite as quick."

Of the Present Disposal of the Night-Soil.

It would appear, according to the previous calculations, that of the 15,000,000 cubic feet of house-refuse annually deposited in the cesspools of the metropolis, about 500,000 cubic feet are pumped by the French process into the sewers; consequently there still remains about 14,500,000 cubic feet, or about 404,000 loads, to be disposed of by other means. I shall now proceed to explain how the cesspoolage proper, that is to say, that which is removed by cartage rather than by being discharged into the sewers, is ultimately got rid of.

Until about twenty months ago, when the new sanitary regulations concerning the disposal of night-soil came into operation, the cesspool matter was "shot" in a night-yard, generally also a dust-yard. These were the yards of the parish contractors, and were situate in Maiden-lane, Paddington, &c., &c. Any sweeper-nightman, or any nightman, was permitted by the proprietor of one of these places to deposit his night-soil there. For this the depositor received no payment, the privilege of having "a shoot" being accounted sufficient.

There were, till within these six or eight years, I was informed, 60 places where cesspool manure could be shot. These included the nightmen's yards and the wharves of manure dealers (some of the small coasting vessels taking it as ballast); but as regards the cesspool filth, there are now none of these places of deposit, though some little, I was told, might be done by stealth.

Of one of these night-yard factories Dr. Gavin gave, in 1848, the following account:—

"On the western side of Spitalfields workhouse, and entering from a street called Queen-street, is a nightman's yard. A heap of dung and refuse of every description, about the size of a tolerably large house, lies piled to the left of the yard; to the right is an artificial pond, into which the contents of cesspools are thrown. The contents are allowed to desiccate in the open air; and they are frequently stirred for that purpose. The odour which was given off when the contents were raked up, to give me an assurance that there was nothing so very bad in the alleged nuisance, drove me from the place with the utmost speed.

"On two sides of this horrid collection of excremental matter was a patent manure manufactory. To the right in this yard was a large accumulation of dung, &c., but to the left there was an extensive layer of a compost of blood, ashes, and nitric acid, which gave out the most horrid, offensive, and disgusting concentration of putrescent odours it has ever been my lot to be the victim of. The whole place presented a most foul and filthy aspect, and an example of the enormous outrages which are perpetrated in London against society.

"It is a curious fact, that the parties who had charge of these two premises were each dead to the foulness of their own most pestilential nuisances. The nightman's servant accused the premises of the manure manufacturer as the source of perpetual foul smells, but thought his yard free from any particular cause of complaint; while the servant of the patent manure manufacturer diligently and earnestly asserted the perfect freedom of his master's yard from foul exhalations; but considered that the raking up of the drying night-soil on the other side of the wall was 'quite awful, and enough to kill anybody.'

"Immediately adjoining the patent manure manufactory is the establishment of a bottle merchant. He complained to me in the strongest terms of the expenses and annoyances he had been put to through the emanations which floated in the atmosphere having caused his bottles to spoil the wine which was placed in such as had not been *very* recently washed. He was compelled frequently to change his straw, and frequently to wash his bottles, and considered that unless the nuisance could be suppressed, he would be compelled to leave his present premises."

This and similar places were suppressed soon after the passing of the sanitary measures of September, 1848.

The cesspool refuse, which was disposed of for manure, was at that time first shot into recesses in the night-yard, where it was mixed with exhausted hops procured from the brewhouses, which were said to absorb the liquid portions, when stirred up with the matter, and to add not only to the consistency of the mass, but to its readier portability for land manure or for stowage in a barge. It was also mixed with littered straw from the mews, and with stable manure generally. An old man who had worked many years—he did not know how many—in one of these yards, told me that when this night-soil was "fresh shot and first mixed" (with the hops, &c.), the stench was often dreadful. "How we stood it," he said, "I don't know; but we did stand it."

In one of the night-and-dust-yards, I ascertained that as many as 50 loads, half of them waggon-loads, have been shot from the proprietor's own carts, and from the carts of the nightmen "using" the yard, in one morning, but the average "shoot" was about ten loads (half a waggon) a-day for six days in the week.

Of the mode of manufacture of this manure, a full account has been given in the details of the cesspool system of Paris, for the process was the same in London, although on a much smaller scale; and indeed the manufacture here was chiefly in the hands of Frenchmen.

The manure was, after it had been deposited for periods varying from one month to five or six, sold to farmers and gardeners at from 4s. to 5s. the cart-load, although 4s., I was informed, might have been the general average. The cesspool matter, considered *per se*, was not worth, of late years, I am told, above 2s. a ton (or a load, which is sometimes rather more and sometimes less than a ton). It was when mixed that the price was 4s. to 5s. a ton. This cesspool filth was shot on the premises of the manufacturer gratuitously, as it was in any of the night-yards. It was not until it had been kept some time, and had been mixed (generally) with other manures, and sometimes with road-sweepings, that this manure was used in gardens; for it was said that if this had not been done, its ammoniacal vapours would have been absorbed and retained by the leaves of the fruit-trees.

This night-soil manure was devoted to two purposes—to the manufacture of deodorized and portable manure for exportation (chiefly to our sugar-growing colonies), and to the fertilization of the land around London.

When manufactured into manure it was shipped—in new casks generally, the manure casks of the outward voyage being transformed into the brown sugar casks of the homeward-bound vessels. I was told by a seaman who some years ago sailed to the West Indies, that these manure casks in damp weather gave out an unpleasant odour.

It was only to the home cultivators who resided at no great distance from a night-yard, from five to six miles or a little more, that this manure was sold to be carted away; their attendance at the markets with carts, waggons, and horses, giving them facilities of conveying the manure at a cheap rate. But upwards of three-fourths of the whole was sent in barges into the more distant country parts, having a ready water communication either by the Thames or by canal.

The purchaser nearer home conveyed it away in his own cart, and with his own horses, which had perhaps come up to town laden with cabbages to Covent Garden, or hay to Cumberland-market, the cart being made watertight for the purpose. The " legal hours " to be observed in the cleansing of cesspools, and the transport of the contents upon such cleansing, not being required to be observed in this second transport of the cesspool manure, it was carted away at any hour, as stable dung now is.

It is not possible at the present time, when night-yards are no longer permitted to exist in London, and the manufacture of the night-soil manure is consequently suppressed, to ascertain the precise quantities disposed of commercially, in a former state of things.

The money returns to the master-nightman for the manure he now collects need no figures. The law requires him to refrain from shooting this soil in his own yard, or in *any* inhabited part of the metropolis, and it is shot on the nearest farm to which he has access, merely for the privilege of shooting it, the farmer paying nothing for the deposit, with which he does what he pleases. It is mixed with other refuse, I was told, at present, and kept as compost, or used on the land, but the change is too recent for the establishment of any systematic traffic in the article.

OF THE WORKING NIGHTMEN AND THE MODE OF WORK.

NIGHTWORK, by the provisions of the Police Act, is not to be commenced before twelve at night, nor continued beyond five in the morning, winter and summer alike. This regulation is known among the nightmen as the " legal hours," and tends, in a measure, to account for the heterogeneous class of labourers who still seek nightwork; for strong men think little of devoting a part of the night, as well as the working hours of the day, to toil. A rubbish-carter, a very powerfully-built man, told me he was partial to nightwork, and always looked out for it, even when in daily employ, as " it was sometimes like found money." The scavengers, sweeps, dustmen, and labourers known as ground-workers, are anxious to obtain night-work when out of regular employment; and, ten years and more since, it was often an available and remunerative resource.

Night-work is, then, essentially, and perhaps necessarily, extra-work, rather than a distinct calling followed by a separate class of workers. The generality of nightmen are scavengers, or dustmen, or chimney-sweepers, or rubbish-carters, or pipe-layers, or ground-workers, or coal-porters, carmen or stablemen, or men working for the market-gardeners round London—all either in or out of employment. Perhaps there is not at the present time in the whole metropolis a working nightman who is *solely* a working nightman.

It is almost the same with the master-nightmen. They are generally master-chimney-sweepers, scavengers, rubbish-carters, and builders. Some of the contractors for the public street scavengery, and the house-dust-bin emptying, are (or have been) among the largest employers of nightmen, but only in their individual trading capacity, for they have no contracts with the parishes concerning the emptying of cesspools; indeed the parish or district corporations have nothing to do with the matter. I have already shown, that among the best-patronised master-nightmen are now the Commissioners of the Court of Sewers.

For how long a period the master and working chimney-sweepers and scavengers have been the master and labouring nightmen I am unable to discover, but it may be reasonable to assume that this connexion, as a matter of trade, existed in the metropolis at the commencement of the eighteenth century.

The police of Paris, as I have shown, have full control over cesspool cleansing, but the police of London are instructed merely to prevent night-work being carried on at a later or earlier period than "the legal hours;" still a few minutes either way are not regarded, and the legal hours, I am told, are almost always adhered to.

Nightwork is carried on—and has been so carried on, within the memory of the oldest men in the trade, who had never heard their predecessors speak of any other system—after this method:—A gang of four men (exclusive of those who have the care of the horses, and who drive the night-carts to and from the scenes of the men's labours at the cesspools) are set to work. The labour of the gang is divided, though not with any individual or especial strictness, as follows:—

1. The *holeman*, who goes into the cesspool and fills the tub.
2. The *ropeman*, who raises the tub when filled.
3. The *tubmen* (of whom there are two), who carry away the tub when raised, and empty it into the cart.

The mode of work may be thus briefly described:—Within a foot, or even less sometimes, though often as much as three feet, below the surface of the ground (when the cesspool is away from the house) is what is called the "main hole." This is the opening of the cesspool, and is covered with flag-stones, removable, wholly or partially, by means of the pickaxe. If the cesspool be immediately under the privy, the flooring, &c., is displaced. Should the soil be near enough to the surface, the tub is dipped into it, drawn out, the filth scraped from its exterior with a shovel, or swept off with a besom, or washed off by water flung against it with sufficient force. This done, the tubmen insert the pole through the handles of the tub, and bear it on their shoulders to the cart. The mode of carriage and the form of the tub have been already shown in an illustration, which I was assured by a nightman who had seen it in a shopwindow (for he could not read), was "as nat'ral as life, tub and all."

Thus far, the ropeman and the holeman generally aid in filling the tub, but as the soil becomes lower, the vessel is let down and drawn up full by the ropeman. When the soil becomes lower still, a ladder is usually planted inside the cesspool; the "holeman," who is generally the strongest person in the gang, descends, shovels the tub full, having stirred up the refuse to loosen it, and the contents, being drawn up by the ropeman, are carried away as before described.

The labour is sometimes severe. The tub when filled, though it is never quite filled, weighs rarely less than eight stone, and sometimes more; "but that, you see, sir," a nightman said to me, "depends on the nature of the sile."

Beer, and bread and cheese, are given to the nightmen, and frequently gin, while at their work; but as the bestowal of the spirit is voluntary, some householders from motives of economy, or from being real or pretended members or admirers of the total-abstinence principles, refuse to give any strong liquor, and in that case—if such a determination to withhold the drink be known beforehand—the employers sometimes supply the men with a glass or two; and the men, when "nothing better can be done," club their own money, and send to some night-house, often at a distance, to purchase a small quantity on their own account. One master-nightman said, he thought his men worked best, indeed he was sure of it, "with a drop to keep them up;" another thought it did them neither good nor harm, "in a moderate way of taking it." Both these informants were themselves temperate men, one rarely tasting spirits. It is commonly enough said, that if the nightmen have no "allowance," they will work neither as quickly nor as carefully as if accorded the customary gin "perquisite." One man, certainly a very strong active person, whose services where quickness in the work was indispensable might be valuable (and he had work as a rubbish-carter also), told me that he for one would not work for any man at nightwork if there was not a fair allowance of drink, "to keep up his strength," and he knew others of the same mind. On my asking him what he considered a "fair" allowance, he told me that at least a bottle of gin among the gang of four was "looked for, and mostly had, over a gentleman's cesspool. And little enough, too," the man said, "among four of us; what it holds if it's public-house gin is uncertain: for you must know, sir, that some bottles has great 'kicks' at their bottoms. But I should say that there's been a bottle of gin drunk at the clearing of every two, ay, and more than every two, out of three cesspools emptied in London; and now that I come to think on it, I should say that's been the case with three out of every four."

Some master-nightmen, and more especially the sweeper-nightmen, work at the cesspools themselves, although many of them are men "well to do in the world." One master I met with, who had the reputation of being "warm," spoke of his own manual labour in shovelling filth in the same self-complacent tone that we may imagine might be used by a grocer, worth his "plum," who quietly intimates that he will serve a washerwoman with her half ounce of tea, and weigh it for her himself, as politely as he would serve a duchess; for *he* wasn't above his business: neither was the nightman.

On one occasion I went to see a gang of nightmen at work. Large horn lanterns (for the night was dark, though at intervals the stars shone brilliantly) were placed at the edges of the cesspool. Two poles also were temporarily fixed in the ground, to which lanterns were hung, but this is not always the case. The work went rapidly on, with little noise and no confusion.

The scene was peculiar enough. The artificial light, shining into the dark filthy-looking cavern or cesspool, threw the adjacent houses into a deep shade. All around was perfectly still, and there was not an incident to interrupt the labour, except that at one time the window of a neighbouring house was thrown up, a nightcapped head was protruded, and then down was banged the sash with an impatient curse. It appeared as if a gentleman's slumbers had been disturbed, though the nightmen laughed and declared it was a lady's voice! The smell, although the air was frosty, was for some little time, perhaps ten minutes, literally sickening; after that period the chief sensation experienced was a slight headache; the unpleasantness of the odour still continuing, though without any sickening effect. The nightmen, however, pronounced the stench "nothing at all;" and one even declared it was refreshing!

The cesspool in this case was so situated that the cart or rather waggon could be placed about three yards from its edge; sometimes, however, the soil has to be carried through a garden and through the house, to the excessive annoyance of the inmates. The nightmen whom I saw evidently enjoyed a bottle of gin, which had been provided for them by the master of the house, as well as some bread and cheese, and two pots of beer. When the waggon was full, two horses were brought from a stable on the premises (an arrangement which can only be occasionally carried out) and yoked to the vehicle, which was at once driven away; a smaller cart and one horse being used to carry off the residue.

TABLE SHOWING THE NUMBER OF MASTER-SWEEPS, DUST, AND OTHER CONTRACTORS, AND MASTER-BRICKLAYERS, THROUGHOUT THE METROPOLIS, ENGAGED IN NIGHT-WORK, AS WELL AS THE NUMBER OF CESSPOOLS EMPTIED, AND QUANTITY OF SOIL COLLECTED YEARLY. ALSO THE PRICE PAID TO EACH OPERATIVE PER LOAD, OR PER NIGHT, AND THE TOTAL AMOUNT ANNUALLY PAID TO THE MASTER-NIGHTMEN.

	SWEEPS EMPLOYED AS NIGHTMEN.	Number of Cesspools emptied during the year.	Quantity of Night-soil collected annually.	Number of operative Nightmen employed to empty each Cesspool.	Total number of times the working Nightmen are employed during the year.	Sum paid to each operative Nightman engaged in removing soil from Cesspools.	Total Amount paid to the operative Nightmen during the year.			Total Amount paid to Master-Nightmen during the year for emptying Cesspools, at 10s. per load.
			Loads.			Pence.	£	s.	d.	£.
KENSINGTON.	Hurd	8	48	3	24	6	1	4	0	24
	Francis	12	72	4	48	6	1	16	0	36
	Russell	8	48	3	24	6	1	4	0	24
	Hough	20	120	4	80	7	3	10	0	60
CHELSEA.	Burns	12	72	3	36	6	1	16	0	36
	Clements	10	60	3	30	6	1	10	0	30
	Groves	18	108	3	54	6	2	14	0	54
	Clayton	20	120	3	60	6	3	0	0	60
	Sheppard	14	84	4	56	6	2	2	0	32
	Nie	16	96	3	48	6	2	8	0	48
	Haddox	20	120	3	60	6	3	0	0	60
	Albrook	30	180	4	120	7	5	5	0	90
WESTMINSTER.	Peacock	60	360	4	240	7	10	10	0	180
	Reiley	40	240	4	160	7	6	13	4	120
	White	20	120	3	60	6	3	0	0	60
	Ramsbottom	12	72	3	36	6	1	16	0	36
	Ness	12	72	3	36	6	1	16	0	36
	Porter	10	60	3	30	6	1	10	4	30
	Edwards	8	48	3	24	6	1	4	0	24
	Andrews	8	48	3	24	6	1	4	0	24
	Foreman	10	60	3	30	6	1	10	4	30
ST. MARTIN'S.	Wakefield	8	48	3	24	6	1	4	0	24
	Whateley	6	36	3	18	6	0	18	0	18
	Templeton	10	60	3	30	6	1	10	0	30
	Pearce	10	60	3	30	6	1	10	0	30

LONDON LABOUR AND THE LONDON POOR.

District	Name							
MARYLEBONE.	Effery	12	72	3	36	6d.	£1 16 0	£36
	Brigham	10	60	3	30	6	1 10 0	30
	Ballard	8	48	3	24	6	1 4 0	24
	Pottle	25	150	4	100	7	3 15 0	75
	Shadwick	20	120	3	60	6	3 0 0	60
	Wilson	20	120	3	60	6	3 0 0	60
	Lewis	10	60	3	30	6	1 10 0	30
	Cuss	30	180	4	120	7	4 10 0	90
	Wood	20	120	3	60	6	3 0 0	60
PADDINGTON.	Prichard	20	120	3	60	6	3 0 0	60
	Randall	25	150	3	75	6	3 15 0	75
	Brown	10	60	3	30	6	1 10 0	30
	Lamb	20	120	3	60	6	3 0 0	60
	Bolton	10	60	3	30	6	1 10 0	30
	Davis	8	48	3	24	6	1 4 0	24
	Rickwood	8	48	3	24	6	1 4 0	4
HAMPSTEAD.	Elkins	6	36	3	18	6	0 18 0	18
	Kippin	8	48	3	24	6	1 4 0	24
	Bowden	8	48	3	24	6	1 4 0	24
ISLINGTON.	Hughes	25	150	3	75	6	3 15 0	75
	Boven	20	120	3	60	6	3 0 0	60
	Chilcott	25	150	3	75	6	3 15 0	75
	Baker	12	72	3	36	6	1 16 0	36
	Burrows	20	120	3	60	6	3 0 0	60
ST. PANCRAS.	Justo	8	48	3	24	6	1 4 0	24
	Neill	8	48	3	24	6	1 4 0	24
	Robinson	12	72	3	36	6	1 16 0	36
	Marriage	20	120	3	60	6	3 0 0	60
	Rose	12	72	3	36	6	1 16 0	36
	Hall	20	120	3	60	6	3 0 0	60
	Jenkins	12	72	3	36	6	1 16 0	36
	Steel	4	24	3	12	6	0 12 0	12
	Lake	60	360	4	240	7	10 10 0	180
	Hewlett	10	60	3	30	6	1 10 0	30
	Snell	10	60	3	30	6	1 10 0	30
	McDonald	30	180	4	120	7	5 5 0	90
HACKNEY.	Mason	20	120	3	60	6	3 0 0	60
	Clark	12	72	3	36	6	1 16 0	36
	Starkey	25	150	4	100	6	3 15 0	75
	Attewell	20	120	4	80	7	3 10 0	60
	Brown	12	72	3	36	6	1 16 0	36
ST. GILES AND ST. GEORGE'S, BLOOMSBURY.	Store	20	120	3	60	6	3 0 0	60
	Richards	20	120	3	60	6	3 0 0	60
	Norris	12	72	3	36	6	3 16 0	36
	Eldridge	8	48	3	24	6	1 4 0	24
	Davis	10	60	3	30	6	1 10 0	30
	Francis	10	60	3	30	6	1 10 0	30
	Tiney	12	72	3	36	6	1 16 0	36
	Johnson	8	48	3	24	6	1 4 0	24
	Tinsey	8	48	3	24	6	1 4 0	24
	Randall	4	24	3	12	6	0 12 0	12
STRAND.	Day	60	360	4	240	7	10 10 0	180
	Catlin	10	60	3	30	6	1 10 0	30
	Richards	8	48	3	24	6	1 4 0	24
	Hutchins	8	48	3	24	6	1 4 0	24
	Barker	4	24	3	12	6	0 12 0	12
HOLBORN.	Duck	30	180	4	120	7	5 5 0	90
	Eagle	20	120	4	80	7	3 10 0	60
	Froome	12	72	3	36	6	1 16 0	36
	Smith	12	72	3	36	6	1 16 0	36
CLERKENWELL.	Davis	30	180	3	90	6	4 10 0	90
	Brown	20	120	4	80	7	3 10 0	60
	Day	12	72	3	36	6	1 16 0	36
	Hawkins	8	48	3	24	6	1 4 0	24
	Grant	8	48	3	24	6	1 4 0	24

Area	Name							
St. Luke's	Brown	20	120	4	80	7d.	£3 0 0	£60
	Mawley	20	120	4	80	7	3 0 0	60
	Stevens	12	72	3	36	6	1 16 0	36
	Badger	8	48	3	24	6	1 4 0	24
	Lewis	8	48	3	24	6	1 4 0	24
East London	Crozier	30	180	4	120	7	5 5 0	90
	James	20	120	4	80	7	3 10 0	60
	Dawson	8	48	3	24	6	1 4 0	24
	Newell	20	120	4	80	7	3 10 0	60
	Lumley	8	48	3	24	6	1 4 0	24
	Harvey	6	36	3	18	6	0 18 0	18
West London	Rayment	20	120	4	80	6	3 0 0	60
	Clarke	20	120	4	80	7	3 0 0	60
	Watson	12	72	3	36	6	1 16 0	36
	Desater	12	72	3	36	6	1 16 0	36
London, City	Tyler and Tyso	30	180	4	120	7	5 5 0	90
	Burgess	20	120	4	80	7	3 10 0	60
	Wilson	20	120	4	80	7	3 10 0	60
	Potter	10	60	3	30	6	1 10 0	30
	Wright	8	48	3	24	6	1 4 0	24
Shoreditch	Wells	20	120	4	80	6	3 0 0	60
	Whittle	20	120	4	80	6	3 0 0	60
	Collins	15	90	3	45	6	2 5 0	45
	Crew	12	72	3	36	6	1 16 0	36
	Atwood	12	72	3	36	6	1 16 0	36
	Conroy	10	60	3	30	6	1 10 0	30
	Pusey	6	36	3	18	6	0 18 0	18
Bethnal Green	Pedrick	8	48	3	24	6	1 4 0	24
	Crosby	8	48	3	24	6	1 4 0	24
	Mull	12	72	3	36	6	1 16 0	36
	Darby	20	120	4	80	6	3 0 0	60
	Hall	20	120	4	80	6	3 0 0	60
Whitechapel	Collins	12	72	3	36	6	1 16 0	36
	Brazier	10	60	3	30	6	1 10 0	30
	Harrison	20	120	3	60	6	3 0 0	60
	Harris	16	96	3	48	6	2 8 0	48
	Mantz	8	48	3	24	6	1 4 0	24
St. George-in-the-East	Whitehead	20	120	4	80	6	3 0 0	60
	Rawton	20	120	4	80	6	3 0 0	60
	Wrotham	20	120	4	80	6	3 0 0	60
	Harewood	20	120	3	60	6	3 0 0	60
	Rawthorn	25	150	4	100	6	3 15 0	75
	Darling	20	120	4	80	6	3 0 0	60
	Jones	15	90	3	45	6	2 5 0	45
	Johnson	12	72	3	36	6	1 16 0	36
Bermondsey	Simpson	15	90	3	45	6	2 5 0	45
	Wilkinson	12	72	3	36	6	1 16 0	36
	Goring	10	60	3	30	6	1 10 0	36
	Lively	8	48	3	24	6	2 4 0	30
	Stone	9	54	3	27	6	1 7 0	24
	Ward	6	36	3	18	6	0 18 0	24
Walworth and Newington	Kingsbury	6	36	3	18	6	0 18 0	27
	Goodge	4	24	3	12	6	0 12 0	18
	Wells	15	90	3	45	6	2 5 0	18
	Wilks	12	72	3	36	6	1 16 0	12
	James	10	60	3	30	6	1 10 0	45
	Morgan	8	48	3	24	6	1 4 0	36
	Croney	8	48	3	24	6	1 4 0	30
	Holmes	8	48	3	24	6	1 4 0	24
Stepney	Newell	10	60	3	30	6	1 10 0	30
	Fleming	20	120	3	60	6	3 0 0	60
	Tuff	20	120	3	60	6	3 0 0	60
	Hillingsworth	12	72	3	36	6	1 16 0	36
	Smith	10	60	3	30	6	1 10 0	30
	Field	8	48	3	24	6	1 4 0	24

Region	Name									
POPLAR.	Weaver	18	108	3	54	6d.	£2	14	0	£54
	Strawson	12	72	3	36	6	1	16	0	36
	Culloder	8	48	3	24	6	1	4	0	24
	Ward	10	60	3	30	6	1	10	0	30
ST. OLAVE'S, ST. SAVIOUR'S, AND ST. GEORGE'S, SOUTHWARK.	Vines	12	72	3	36	6	1	16	0	36
	Humfry	15	90	3	45	6	2	5	0	45
	Young	10	60	3	30	6	1	10	0	30
	James	12	72	3	36	6	1	16	0	36
	Penn	10	60	3	30	6	1	10	0	30
	Holliday	8	48	3	24	6	1	4	0	24
	Muggeridge	15	90	3	45	6	2	5	0	45
	Alcorn	12	72	3	36	6	1	16	0	36
	Fisher	12	72	3	36	6	1	16	0	36
	Goode	10	60	3	30	6	1	10	0	30
	Smith	8	48	3	24	6	1	4	6	24
	Roberts	8	48	3	24	6	1	4	0	24
	Pilkington	9	54	3	27	6	1	7	0	27
	Lindsey	6	36	3	18	6	0	18	0	18
	Daycock	6	36	3	18	6	0	18	0	18
	Moulton	4	24	3	12	6	0	12	0	12
LAMBETH.	Roberts	25	150	4	100	7	4	7	6	75
	Holland	12	72	3	36	6	1	16	0	36
	Ballard	12	72	3	36	6	1	16	0	36
	Brown	8	48	3	24	6	1	4	0	24
	Mills	10	60	3	30	6	1	10	0	30
	Giles	6	36	3	18	6	0	18	0	18
	Spooner	6	36	3	18	6	0	18	0	18
	Green	4	24	3	12	6	0	12	0	12
	Barnham	4	24	3	12	6	0	12	0	12
	Price	4	24	3	12	6	0	12	0	12
WANDSWORTH CHRISTCHURCH, & BATTERSEA. LAMBETH.	Plummer	18	108	3	54	6	2	14	0	54
	Steers	12	72	3	36	6	1	16	0	36
	Clare	10	60	3	30	6	1	10	0	30
	Garlick	8	48	3	24	6	1	4	0	24
	Hudson	6	36	3	18	6	0	18	0	18
	Jones	4	24	3	12	6	0	12	0	12
	Foreman	15	90	3	45	6	2	5	0	45
	Smith	10	60	3	30	6	1	10	0	30
	Giles	8	48	3	24	6	1	4	0	24
	Davis	6	36	3	18	6	0	18	0	18
	Flushman	4	24	3	12	6	0	12	0	12
ROTHER-HITHE.	Shelley	6	36	3	18	6	0	18	0	18
	Richardson	20	120	4	80	6	3	0	0	60
	Norris	8	48	3	24	6	1	4	0	24
	Smith	12	72	3	36	6	1	16	0	36
	Dyer	8	48	3	24	6	1	4	0	24
GREENWICH & DEPTFORD.	Manning	30	180	4	120	6	4	10	0	90
	Vines	20	120	4	80	6	3	0	0	60
	Roseworthy	20	120	4	80	6	3	0	0	60
	Tyler	12	72	3	36	6	1	16	0	36
	Munshin	12	72	3	36	6	1	16	0	36
WOOLWICH.	Pearce	30	180	4	120	6	4	10	0	90
	Fiddeman	12	72	3	36	6	1	16	0	36
	Sims	12	72	3	36	6	1	16	0	36
	Smithers	12	72	3	36	6	1	16	0	36
	Rooke	8	48	3	24	6	1	4	0	24
	James	8	48	3	24	6	1	4	0	24
LEWIS HAM.	Ridgeway	20	120	4	80	6	3	0	0	60
	Binney	10	60	3	30	6	1	10	0	30
	Total for Sweep-nightmen	2992	14960	3 & 4	10,062	6&7d.	455	15	0	£7480

DUST AND OTHER CONTRACTORS ENGAGED AS NIGHTMEN.

		Loads.			Pence.	£	s.	d.	£	s.
Darke	50	300	4	200	8	10	0	0	157	10
Cooper	300	1800	4	1200	8	60	0	0	945	0
Dodd	300	1800	4	1200	8	60	0	0	945	0
Starkey	250	1500	4	1000	8	50	0	0	787	10
Williams	200	1200	4	800	8	40	0	0	630	0
Boyer	150	900	4	600	8	30	0	0	472	10
Gore	200	1200	4	800	8	40	0	0	630	0
Limpus	200	1200	4	800	8	40	0	0	630	0
Emmerson	150	900	4	600	8	30	0	0	472	10
Duggins	360	2160	4	1440	8	72	0	0	1134	0
Bugbee	250	1500	4	1000	8	50	0	0	787	10
Gould	200	1200	4	800	8	40	0	0	630	0
Reddin	200	1200	4	800	8	40	0	0	630	0
Newman	200	1200	4	800	8	40	0	0	630	0
Tame	300	1800	4	1200	8	60	0	0	945	0
Sinnot	200	1200	4	800	8	40	0	0	630	0
Tomkins	200	1200	4	800	8	40	0	0	630	0
Cordroy	150	900	4	600	8	30	0	0	472	10
Samuels	150	900	4	600	8	30	0	0	472	10
Robinson	100	600	4	400	8	20	0	0	315	0
Bird	100	600	4	400	8	20	0	0	315	0
Clarke	100	600	4	400	8	20	0	0	315	0
Brown	100	600	4	400	8	20	0	0	315	0
Bonner	150	900	4	600	8	30	0	0	472	10
Guess	100	600	4	400	8	20	0	0	315	0
Jeffries	200	1200	4	800	8	40	0	0	630	0
Ryan	60	360	4	240	8	12	0	0	189	0
Hewitt	100	600	4	400	8	20	0	0	315	0
Leimming	50	300	4	200	8	10	0	0	157	10
Ellis	100	600	4	400	8	20	0	0	315	0
Monk	150	900	4	600	8	30	0	0	472	10
Phillips	250	1000	4	1000	8	33	6	8	525	0
Porter	200	1200	4	800	8	40	0	0	630	0
Dubbins	150	900	4	600	8	30	0	0	472	10
Taylor	100	600	4	400	8	20	0	0	315	0
Nicholls	250	1000	4	1000	8	33	6	8	525	0
Freeman	100	600	4	400	8	20	0	0	315	0
Pattison	200	1200	4	800	8	40	0	0	630	0
Rawlins	150	900	4	600	8	30	0	0	472	10
Watkins	200	1200	4	800	8	40	0	0	630	0
Liddiard	100	600	4	400	8	20	0	0	315	0
Farmer	250	1500	4	1000	8	50	0	0	787	10
Francis	150	900	4	600	8	30	0	0	472	10
Chadwick	200	1200	4	800	8	40	0	0	630	0
Perkins	80	480	4	320	8	16	0	0	252	0
Culverwell	100	600	4	400	8	20	0	0	315	0
Rutty	150	900	4	600	8	30	0	0	472	10
Crook	100	600	4	400	8	20	0	0	315	0
M'Carthy	50	300	4	200	8	10	0	0	157	10
Bateman	100	600	4	400	8	20	0	0	315	0
Boothe	250	1500	4	1000	8	50	0	0	787	10
Wood	100	600	4	400	8	20	0	0	315	0
Calvert	150	900	4	600	8	30	0	0	472	10
Tilley	200	1200	4	800	8	40	0	0	630	0
Abbott	100	600	4	400	8	20	0	0	315	0
Potter	250	1500	4	1000	8	50	0	0	787	10
Church	100	600	4	400	8	20	0	0	315	0
Humphries	200	1200	4	800	8	40	0	0	630	0
Jackson	100	600	4	400	8	20	0	0	315	0
Batterbury	50	300	4	200	8	10	0	0	157	10

LONDON LABOUR AND THE LONDON POOR.

Smith	50	300	4	200	8d.	£10	0	0	£157	10
Perkins	200	1200	4	800	8	40	0	0	630	0
Rose	50	300	4	200	8	10	0	0	157	10
Croot	150	900	4	600	8	30	0	0	472	10
Speller	50	300	4	200	8	10	0	0	157	10
Piper	50	300	4	200	8	10	0	0	157	10
North	100	600	4	400	8	20	0	0	315	0
Crooker	150	900	4	600	8	30	0	0	472	10
Tingey	100	600	4	400	8	20	0	0	315	0
Jones	200	1200	4	800	8	40	0	0	630	0
Whitten	300	1800	4	1200	8	60	0	0	945	0
Webbon	150	900	4	600	8	30	0	0	472	10
Ryder	100	600	4	400	8	30	0	0	315	0
Wright	150	900	4	600	8	30	0	0	472	10
Duckett	300	1800	4	1200	8	60	0	0	945	0
Elworthy	200	1200	4	800	8	40	0	0	630	0
Slee	200	1200	4	800	8	40	0	0	630	0
Adams	150	900	4	600	8	30	0	0	472	10
Gutteris	50	300	4	200	8	10	0	0	157	10
Martainbody	200	1200	4	800	8	40	0	0	630	0
Nicholson	100	600	4	400	8	20	0	0	315	0
Mears	100	600	4	400	8	20	0	0	315	0
Parsons	150	900	4	600	8	30	0	0	472	10
Kenning	200	1200	4	800	8	40	0	0	630	0
Hooke	250	1500	4	1000	8	50	0	0	787	10
Michell	100	600	4	400	8	20	0	0	315	0
Walton	200	1200	4	800	8	40	0	0	630	0
Evans	50	300	4	200	8	10	0	6	157	10
Walker	90	540	4	360	8	18	0	0	283	10
Hobman	200	1200	4	800	8	40	0	0	630	0
Stevens	250	1500	4	1000	8	50	0	0	787	10
Jeffry	150	900	4	600	8	30	0	0	472	10
Hiscock	200	1200	4	800	8	40	0	0	630	0
Allen	100	600	4	400	8	20	0	0	315	0
Connall	100	600	4	400	8	20	0	0	315	0
Waller	50	300	4	200	8	10	0	0	157	10
Mullard	50	300	4	200	8	10	0	0	157	10
Miller	100	600	4	400	8	20	0	0	315	0
Barnes	150	900	4	600	8	30	0	0	472	10
Sharpe	100	600	4	400	8	20	0	0	315	0
Graham	150	900	4	600	8	30	0	0	472	10
Wellard	100	600	4	400	8	20	0	0	315	0
Hollis	50	300	4	200	8	10	0	0	157	10
Fletcher	150	900	4	600	8	30	0	0	472	10
Hearne	100	600	4	400	8	20	0	0	315	0
Stapleton	50	300	4	200	8	10	0	0	157	10
Martin	200	1200	4	800	8	40	0	0	630	0
Prett and Sewell	300	1800	4	1200	8	60	0	0	945	0
Jenkins	200	1200	4	800	8	40	0	0	630	0
Westley	150	900	4	600	8	30	0	0	472	10
Bird	100	600	4	400	8	20	0	0	315	0
Gale	200	1200	4	800	8	40	0	0	630	0
Porter	100	600	4	400	8	20	0	0	315	0
Wells	200	1200	4	800	8	40	0	0	630	0
Hall	250	1500	4	1000	8	50	0	0	787	10
Kitchener	150	900	4	600	8	30	0	0	472	10
Wickham	100	600	4	400	8	20	0	0	315	0
Walker	200	1200	4	800	8	40	0	0	630	0
Bindy	100	600	4	400	8	20	0	0	315	0
Styles	250	1500	4	1000	8	50	0	0	787	10
Kirtland	100	600	4	400	8	20	0	0	315	0
Kingston	100	600	4	400	8	20	0	0	315	0
Eldred	150	900	4	600	8	30	0	0	472	10
Rumball	250	1500	4	1000	8	50	0	0	787	10
Mildwater	60	360	4	240	8	12	0	0	189	0
Lovell	100	600	4	400	8	20	0	0	315	0

Clarkson	150	900	4	600	8d.	£30	0	0	£472	10
Rhodes	100	600	4	400	8	20	0	0	315	0
Pine	200	1200	4	800	8	40	0	0	630	0
Monk	250	1500	4	1000	8	50	0	0	787	10
Gabriel	100	600	4	400	8	20	0	0	315	0
Packer	200	1200	4	800	8	40	0	0	630	0
Crawley	250	1500	4	1000	8	50	0	0	787	10
Easton	150	900	4	600	8	30	0	0	472	10
Marsland	150	900	4	600	8	30	0	0	472	10
East	100	600	4	400	8	20	0	0	315	0
Turtle	200	1200	4	800	8	40	0	0	630	0
Fuller	200	1200	4	800	8	40	0	0	630	0
Taylor	100	600	4	400	8	20	0	0	315	0
Ginnow	150	900	4	600	8	30	0	0	472	10
Peakes	150	900	4	600	8	30	0	0	472	10
Fleckell	50	300	4	200	8	60	0	0	157	10
Cook	50	300	4	200	8	10	0	0	157	10
Stewart	100	600	4	400	8	20	0	0	315	0
Cooper	100	600	4	400	8	20	0	0	315	0
Bentley	200	1200	4	800	8	40	0	0	630	0
Harford	200	1200	4	800	8	40	0	0	630	0
Litten	100	600	4	400	8	20	0	0	315	0
Mills	150	900	4	600	8	30	0	0	472	10
Voy	100	600	4	400	8	20	0	0	315	0
Cortman	50	300	4	200	8	10	0	0	157	10
Forster	100	600	4	400	8	20	0	0	315	0
Davison	150	900	4	600	8	30	0	0	472	10
Williams	250	1500	4	1000	8	50	0	0	787	10
Draper	200	1200	4	800	8	40	0	0	630	0
Claxton	100	600	4	400	8	20	0	0	315	0
Robertson	50	300	4	200	8	10	0	0	157	10
Cornwall	100	600	4	400	8	20	0	0	315	0
Price	150	900	4	600	8	30	0	0	472	10
Milligan	200	1200	4	800	8	40	0	0	630	0
West	250	1500	4	1000	8	50	0	0	787	10
Wilson	100	600	4	400	8	20	0	0	315	0
Lawn	100	600	4	400	8	20	0	0	315	0
Oakes	50	300	4	200	8	10	0	0	157	10
Joliffe	150	900	4	600	8	30	0	0	472	10
Liley	100	600	4	400	8	20	0	0	313	0
Treagle	120	720	4	480	8	24	0	0	378	0
Coleman	50	300	4	200	8	10	0	0	157	10
Brooker	200	1200	4	800	8	40	0	0	630	0
Dignam	200	1200	4	800	8	40	0	0	630	0
Hillier	150	900	4	600	8	30	0	0	472	10
Simmonds	150	900	4	600	8	30	0	0	472	10
Penrose	100	600	4	400	8	20	0	0	315	0
Jordan	200	1200	4	800	8	40	0	0	630	0
Macey	100	600	4	400	8	20	0	0	315	0
Williams	150	900	4	600	8	30	0	0	472	10
Palmer	200	1200	4	800	8	40	0	0	650	0
Anderson	100	600	4	400	8	20	0	0	315	0
George	200	1200	4	800	8	40	0	0	630	0
Hasleton	50	300	4	200	8	10	0	0	157	10
Willis	250	1500	4	1000	8	50	0	0	787	10
Farringdon	50	300	4	200	8	10	0	0	157	10
Doyle	100	600	4	400	8	20	0	0	315	0
Lamb	100	600	4	400	8	20	0	0	315	0
Bolton	200	1200	4	800	8	40	0	0	630	0
Lovelock	250	1500	4	1000	8	50	0	0	787	10
Ashfield	50	300	4	200	8	10	0	0	157	10
Braithwaite	100	600	4	400	8	20	0	0	315	0
Total for Dust and other Contractors engaged as Nightmen	27,820	139,100	4	101,240	8d.	£5596	13	4	£73,027	10

MASTER-BRICKLAYERS ENGAGED AS NIGHTMEN.

		Loads.			Average 2 Cesspools a Night.	£	s.	d.	£	s.
Albon	100	600	4	400	5s. ea.	12	10	0	315	0
Danver	150	900	4	600	,,	18	15	0	472	10
Buck	90	540	4	360	,,	11	5	0	283	10
Aldred	150	900	4	600	,,	18	15	0	472	10
Bowler	150	900	4	600	,,	18	15	0	472	10
Deacon	250	1500	4	1000	,,	31	5	0	787	10
Barrett	200	1200	4	800	,,	25	0	0	630	0
Elmes	90	540	4	360	,,	11	5	0	283	10
Gray	100	600	4	400	,,	12	10	0	315	0
Emmerton	150	900	4	600	,,	18	15	0	472	10
Coleman	100	600	4	400	,,	12	10	0	315	0
Belchier	250	1500	4	1000	,,	31	5	0	787	0
Wade	200	1200	4	800	,,	25	0	0	630	0
Turner	100	600	4	400	,,	12	10	0	315	0
Sutton	150	900	4	600	,,	18	15	0	472	10
Cutmore	200	1200	4	800	,,	25	0	0	630	0
Plowman	150	900	4	600	,,	18	15	0	472	10
Brockwell	200	1200	4	800	,,	25	0	0	630	0
Bellamy	200	1200	4	800	,,	25	0	0	630	0
Janes	50	300	4	200	,,	6	5	0	157	10
Higgs	50	300	4	200	,,	6	5	0	157	10
Avery	100	600	4	400	,,	12	10	0	315	0
Bailey	150	900	4	600	,,	18	15	0	472	10
Pitman	200	1200	4	800	,,	25	0	0	630	0
Hosier	150	900	4	600	,,	18	15	0	472	10
Chambers	150	900	4	600	,,	18	15	0	472	10
Turner	100	600	4	400	,,	12	10	0	315	0
Sutton	150	900	4	600	,,	18	15	0	472	10
Phenix	80	480	4	320	,,	10	0	0	252	0
Elsden	50	300	4	200	,,	6	5	0	157	10
Fuller	200	1200	4	800	,,	25	0	0	630	0
Heath	200	1200	4	800	,,	25	0	0	630	0
Beach	80	480	4	320	,,	10	0	0	252	0
Jones	100	600	4	400	,,	12	10	0	315	0
Gilbert	250	1500	4	1000	,,	31	5	0	787	10
Green	100	600	4	400	,,	12	10	0	315	0
King	250	1500	4	1000	,,	31	5	0	787	10
Parker	150	900	4	600	,,	18	15	0	472	10
Kelsey	200	1200	4	800	,,	25	0	0	630	0
Palmer	250	1500	4	1000	,,	31	5	0	787	10
Sinclair	100	600	4	400	,,	12	10	0	315	0
Peck	200	1200	4	800	,,	25	0	0	630	0
Young	50	300	4	200	,,	6	5	0	157	10
Winter	100	600	4	400	,,	12	10	0	315	0
Wolfe	90	540	4	360	,,	11	5	0	283	10
Taber	50	300	4	200	,,	6	5	0	157	10
Kellow	100	600	4	400	,,	12	10	0	315	0
Mercer	150	900	4	600	,,	18	15	0	472	10
Oswell	250	1500	4	1000	,,	31	5	0	787	10
Mallett	90	540	4	360	,,	11	5	0	283	10
Handley	180	1080	4	720	,,	22	10	0	567	0
Bull	150	900	4	600	,,	18	15	0	472	10
Atkinson	200	1200	4	800	,,	25	0	0	630	0
Dennis	250	1500	4	1000	,,	31	5	0	787	10
Fordham	100	600	4	400	,,	12	10	0	315	0
Wigmore	150	900	4	600	,,	18	15	0	472	10

Ricketts	300	1800	4	1200	5s. ea.	£37	10	0	£945	0
Linnegar	250	1500	4	1000	,,	31	5	0	787	10
Price	100	600	4	400	,,	12	10	0	315	0
James	300	1800	4	1200	,,	37	10	0	945	0
Wills	180	1080	4	720	,,	22	10	0	567	0
Templar	100	600	4	400	,,	12	10	0	315	0
Tolley	50	300	4	200	,,	6	5	0	157	10
Smallman	100	600	4	400	,,	12	10	0	315	0
Macey	150	900	4	600	,,	18	15	0	472	10
Livermore	250	1500	4	1000	,,	31	5	0	787	10
Oakham	250	1500	4	1000	,,	31	5	0	787	10
Rudd	100	600	4	400	,,	12	10	0	315	0
Kerridge	150	900	4	600	,,	18	15	0	472	10
Perrin	150	900	4	600	,,	18	15	0	472	10
Thomas	300	1800	4	1200	,,	37	10	0	945	0
Moore	150	900	4	600	,,	18	15	0	472	10
Reeves	200	1200	4	800	,,	25	0	0	630	0
Pearson	100	600	4	400	,,	12	10	0	315	0
Stollery	50	300	4	200	,,	6	5	0	157	10
Connew	250	1500	4	1000	,,	31	5	0	787	10
Floyd	100	600	4	400	,,	12	10	0	315	0
Girling	300	1800	4	1200	,,	37	10	0	945	0
Gilbert	150	900	4	600	,,	18	15	0	742	10
Carter	250	1500	4	1000	,,	31	5	0	787	10
Clayden	200	1200	4	800	,,	25	0	0	630	0
Bibbing	50	300	4	200	,,	6	5	0	157	10
Dunn	100	600	4	400	,,	12	10	0	315	0
Howell	100	600	4	400	,,	12	10	0	315	0
Fursey	100	600	4	400	,,	12	10	0	315	0
Archer	250	1500	4	1000	,,	31	5	0	787	10
Hart	300	1800	4	1200	,,	37	10	0	945	0
Cole	100	600	4	400	,,	12	10	0	315	0
Essex	250	1500	4	1000	,,	31	5	0	787	10
Hinton	100	600	4	400	,,	12	10	0	315	0
Wiseman	150	900	4	600	,,	18	15	0	472	10
Tepner	200	1200	4	800	,,	25	0	0	630	0
Unwin	250	1500	4	1000	,,	31	5	0	787	10
Treharne	300	1800	4	1200	,,	37	10	0	945	0
Havenny	50	300	4	200	,,	6	5	0	157	10
Williams	100	600	4	400	,,	12	10	0	315	0
Plant	200	1200	4	800	,,	25	0	0	630	0
Linfield	250	1500	4	1000	,,	31	5	0	787	10
Morris	150	900	4	600	,,	18	15	0	472	10
Jenkins	300	1800	4	1200	,,	37	10	0	945	0
Buck	200	1200	4	800	,,	25	0	0	630	0
Hadnutt	150	900	4	600	,,	18	15	0	472	10
Cuming	200	1200	4	800	,,	25	0	0	630	0
Douglas	100	600	4	400	,,	12	10	0	315	0
Hogden	300	1800	4	1200	,,	37	10	0	945	0
M'Currey	300	1800	4	1200	,,	37	10	0	945	0
Warne	50	300	4	200	,,	6	5	0	157	10
Whitechurch	200	1200	4	800	,,	25	0	0	630	0
Stevenson	150	900	4	600	,,	18	15	0	472	10
Izard	300	1800	4	1200	,,	37	10	0	945	0
Jones	250	1500	4	1000	,,	31	5	0	787	10
Rutley	100	600	4	400	,,	12	10	0	315	0
Prichard	200	1200	4	800	,,	25	0	0	630	0
Watts	250	1500	4	1000	,,	31	5	0	787	10
Woodcock	150	900	4	600	,,	18	15	0	472	10
Osborn	300	1800	4	1200	,,	37	10	0	945	0
Morland	250	1500	4	1000	,,	31	5	0	787	10
Brown	300	1800	4	1200	,,	37	10	0	945	0
Hughes	150	900	4	600	,,	18	15	0	472	10
Total for Master-Bricklayers engaged as Nightmen	19,880	99,400	4	59,520	5s.	£2,485	0		£52,185	0

SUMMARY OF THE ABOVE TABLE.

MASTER-SWEEPS EMPLOYED AS NIGHTMEN IN	Number of Masters employed as Nightmen.	Number of Cesspools emptied during the year.	Quantity of Night-soil collected annually.	Number of working Nightmen employed to each Cesspool.	Sum per load paid to each operative Nightman engaged in removing soil from Cesspools.	Total Amount paid to Master-Nightmen during the Year for emptying Cesspools.		
			Loads.		Pence.	£	s.	d.
Kensington	4	48	240	3 & 4	6 & 7	120	0	0
Chelsea	8	140	700	3 & 4	6 & 7	350	0	0
Westminster	9	180	900	3	6	450	0	0
St. Martin's	4	34	170	3	6	85	0	0
Marylebone	9	155	775	3 & 4	6 & 7	387	10	0
Paddington	8	107	535	3	6	267	10	0
Hampstead	2	16	80	3	6	40	0	0
Islington	4	82	410	3	6	205	0	0
St. Pancras	13	226	1,130	3 & 4	6 & 7	565	0	0
Hackney	5	89	445	3 & 4	6 & 7	222	10	0
St. Giles's and St. George's, Bloomsbury	11	172	860	3 & 4	6 & 7	430	0	0
Strand	4	30	150	3	6	75	0	0
Holborn	4	74	370	3 & 4	6 & 7	185	0	0
Clerkenwell	5	78	390	3 & 4	6 & 7	195	0	0
St. Luke's	5	68	340	3 & 4	6 & 7	170	0	0
East London	6	92	460	3 & 4	6 & 7	230	0	0
West London	4	64	320	3 & 4	6 & 7	160	0	0
London, City	5	88	440	3 & 4	6 & 7	220	0	0
Shoreditch	7	95	475	3 & 4	6	237	10	0
Bethnal-green	5	68	340	3 & 4	6	170	0	0
Whitechapel	5	66	330	3	6	165	0	0
St. George's-in-the-East	8	152	760	3 & 4	6	380	0	0
Stepney	6	80	400	3	6	200	0	0
Poplar	4	48	240	3	6	120	0	0
St. Olave's, St. Saviour's, and St. George's, Southwark	16	157	785	3	6	392	10	0
Bermondsey	6	60	300	3	6	150	0	0
Walworth and Newington	8	71	355	3	6	177	10	0
Lambeth	10	91	455	3 & 4	6 & 7	227	10	0
Christchurch, Lambeth	6	58	290	3	6	145	0	0
Wandsworth and Battersea	5	43	215	3	6	107	10	0
Rotherhithe	5	54	270	3 & 4	6	135	0	0
Greenwich and Deptford	5	94	470	3 & 4	6 & 7	235	0	0
Woolwich	6	82	410	3 & 4	6	205	0	0
Lewisham	2	30	150	3 & 4	6	75	0	0
Total for Sweeps employed as Nightmen	214	2,992	14,960	3 & 4	6 & 7	7,480	0	0
Total for Dust and other Contractors employed as Nightmen	188	27,820	139,000	4	8	72,027	0	0
Total for Bricklayers employed as Nightmen	119	19,880	99,400	4	5s. a night	52,185	0	0
Gross Total	521	50,692	253,960	3 & 4	6d. 7d. & 8d. per ld. & 5s. per night.	131,692	10	0

A TABLE SHOWING THE QUANTITY OF REFUSE BOUGHT, COLLECTED, OR FOUND, IN THE STREETS OF LONDON.

Articles bought, collected, or found.	Annual gross quantity.	Average Number of Buyers, and quantity sold Daily or Weekly.	Obtained of the Street Buyers.	Price per pound weight, &c.	Average Yearly Money Value. £	s.	d.	Parties to whom sold.
REFUSE METAL.								
Copper	291,600 lbs.	200 buyers ¼ cwt. each weekly	1-500th	6*d*. per lb.	7,290	0	0	Sold to brass-founders and pewterers.
Brass	291,600 „	200 do. ¼ „ do.	„	4*d*. „	4,860	6	8	Do. do.
Iron	2,329,600 „	200 do. 2 „ do.	1-200th	½*d*. „	2,426	13	4	Do. to iron-founders and manufacturers.
Steel	62,400 „	200 do. 6 lbs. do.	none	1*d*. „	260	0	0	Do. to manufacturers.
Lead	1,164,800 „	200 do. 1 cwt. do.	1-500th	1½*d*. „	7,280	0	0	Do. to brass-founders and pewterers.
Pewter	291,600 „	200 do. ¼ „ do.	„	5*d*. „	6,075	13	4	Do. do.
					28,192	13	4	
HORSE & CARRIAGE FURNITURE.								
Carriages	120 „	4 do. 30 sets yearly	none	11*l*. each	1,320	0	0	Sold to Jew dealers.
Wheels (4, from coach-builders)	600 sets	100 do. 8 do.	„	25*s*. a set	750	0	0	Do. to costers and small tradesmen.
Wheels, in pairs for carts & trucks	600 pairs	50 do. 12 pairs yearly	„	7*s*. a pair	210	0	0	Do. do.
Springs for trucks and small carts	780 „	5 do. 3 „ weekly	„	6*s*. per pair	234	0	0	Do. to costers and others.
Lace, from coach-builders	1,344 lbs.	12 do. 112 lbs. yearly	„	1*d*. per lb.	5	12	0	Do. to cab-masters and to Jews.
Fringe and tassels, from ditto	2,688 „	12 do. 224 „ do.	„	½*d*. „	5	12	0	Do. to Jews.
Coach & carriage linings, singly	156	12 do. 13 yearly	„	25*s*. each	195	0	0	Do. to cab-masters.
Harness (carriage pairs)	60 pairs	10 do. 6 pairs do.	„	3*l*. per pair	180	0	0	Do. to omnibus proprietors.
Ditto (single sets)	144 sets	12 do. 12 sets do.	„	30*s*. per set	216	0	0	Do, to cab-masters.
Ditto (sets of donkey and pony)	41,600 „	100 do. 8 sets weekly	harness makers	4*s*. a set	8,320	0	0	Do. to little master harness-makers.
Saddles	1,040 „	10 do. 2 „ do.	none	4*s*. „	203	0	0	Do. do.
Collars	2,080 „	10 do. 4 „ do.	„	9*d*. „	78	0	0	Do. do. and marine stores.
Bridles	4,160 „	10 do. 6 „ do.	„	8*d*. „	138	13	4	Do. do. do.
Pads	2,080 „	10 do. 4 „ do.	„	6*d*. „	52	0	0	Do. do.
Bits	4,160 „	10 do. 3 „ do.	„	2*d*. „	34	13	4	Do. do. do.
Leather (new cuttings from coach-builders)	58,136 lbs.	24 do. 22 cwt. yearly	„	4*d*. „	985	12	0	Do. to Jews and also to gunsmiths.
Ditto (morocco cuttings from do.)	960 „	20 do. 48 „ do.	„	1*s*. 6*d*. „	72	0	0	Do. to tailors' trimming-sellers.
Old leather (waste from ditto)	53,760 „	12 do. 20 „ do.	„	2½*d*. „	560	0	0	Do. to Jews.
					13,560	2	8	
REFUSE LINEN, COTTON, &c.								
Rags (woollen, consisting of tailors' shreds, old flannel drugget, carpet, and moreen)	4,659,200 lbs.	200 do. 4 „ weekly	1-1000th	½*d*. per lb.	9,706	13	4	Sold for manure and to nail up fruit-trees.
Ditto (coloured cotton)	2,912,000 „	200 do. 2½ „ do.	1-500th	½*d*. „	6,066	13	4	Do. to paper-makers and for quilts.
Ditto (white)	1,164,800 „	200 do. 1 „ do.	1-1000th	2*d*. „	9,706	13	4	Do. to paper-makers.
Canvas	44,800 „	200 do. 2 „ yearly	none	1*d*. „	186	13	4	Do. to chance customers.
Rope and sacking	291,200 „	200 do. ¼ „ weekly	1-500th	½*d*. „	606	13	4	Do. for oakum and sacking to mend old sacks.
					36,898	13	4	
PAPER.								
Waste paper	1,397,760 „	60 colls. each disposing of 4 cwt. weekly	all	18*s*. per cwt.	11,232	0	0	Do. to shopkeepers.
GLASS AND CROCKERYWARE.								
Bottles (common and doctors')	62,400 doz.	200 buyers, 24 weekly	1-100th	2*d*. per doz.	520	0	0	Do. to doctors and chemists.
Ditto (wine)	31,200 „	200 do. 12 do.	1-200th	6*d*. „	780	0	0	Do. to Brit. wine merchants & ale stores.
Ditto (porter and stout)	4,800 „	200 do. 24 dozen yearly	none	6*d*. „	120	0	0	Do. to ale and porter stores.
Flint glass	15,600 lbs.	200 do. 1½ lbs. weekly	1-1000th	¼*d*. per lb.	16	5	0	Do. to glass manufacturers.
Pickling jars	7,200 „	200 do. 36 yearly	none	¾*d*. each	22	10	0	Do. to Italian warehouses, &c.
Gallipots	20,800 doz.	200 do. 24 weekly	„	2*d*. per doz.	173	6	8	Do. do.
					1,632	1	8	

Item	Quantity	Rate of collection	Bought of	Price	Total £ s. d.	Sold to
REFUSE APPAREL.						
Coats	624,000	300 colls each, purchasing 8 coats daily	bt. of old clo' men	6s. each	187,200 0 0	Sold to old clo' men and wholesale dealers.
Trousers	312,000 pairs	300 do. do. 4 pr. trousers do.	"	3s. 3d. per pr.	50,700 0 0	Do. do.
Waistcoats	312,000	300 do. do. 3 waistcoats do.	"	7d. each	9,100 0 0	Do. do.
Under-waistcoats	46,800	300 do. do. 3 weekly	"	2d. "	390 0 0	Do. to wholesale and wardrobe dealers.
Breeches and gaiters	15,600 pairs	300 do. do. 1 pair weekly	"	2s. per pair	1,560 0 0	Do. to old clo' men and wholesale dealers.
Dressing-gowns	3,000	100 do. do. 30 yearly	"	4s. 2d. each	625 0 0	Do. to wholesale and wardrobe dealers.
Cloaks (men's)	1,000	100 do. do. 10 cloaks yearly	"	10s. "	500 0 0	Do. to wholesale dealers.
Boots and shoes	1,560,000 pairs	100 do. do. 60 pairs daily	"	7d. per pair	45,500 0 0	Do. to wardrobe dealers and second-hand boot and shoe makers.
Boot and shoe soles	648,000 dz. pr	100 do. each collecting 30 dz. pr. daily	none	1s. per dz. pr.	32,400 0 0	Do. to Jews and gunsmiths to temper gun-barrels.
Boot legs	520,000 " "	200 do. do. 50 " weekly	"	5s. "	130,000 0 0	Do. to translators.
Hats	1,879,000	300 colls, each purchasing 24 hats daily	bt. of old clo' men	4d. each	31,200 0 0	Do. to dealers and master hatters.
Boys' suits	3,600	300 do. do. 12 suits yearly	"	3s. a suit	540 0 0	Do. Jew dealers.
Shirts and chemises	626,400	300 do. do. 8 daily	"	4d. each	10,400 0 0	Do. to old clo' men and wholesale dealers.
Stockings of all kinds	783,000 pairs	100 do. do. 30 pair daily	"	1d. per pair	3,272 10 0	Do. to wholesale and wardrobe dealers.
Drawers (men's and women's)	93,600 "	300 do. do. 6 " weekly	"	3d. "	1,170 0 0	Do. do.
Women's dresses of all kinds	496,800	300 do. do. 6 dresses daily	"	1s. 9d. each	41,107 10 0	Do. do.
Petticoats	939,600	300 do. do. 12 daily	"	7d. "	27,405 0 0	Do. do.
Women's stays	261,000 pairs	300 do. do. 10 pair do.	"	5d. per pair	5,437 10 0	Do. do.
Children's shirts	187,920	60 do. do. 12 daily	"	3d. a doz.	195 15 0	Do. do.
Ditto petticoats	261,000	200 do. do. 5 do.	"	1½d. each	1,639 11 8	Do. do.
Ditto frocks	522,000	200 do. do. 10 do.	"	4d. "	8,700 0 0	Do. do.
Cloaks (women's), capes, visites, &c	5,200	20 do. do. 5 cloaks weekly	"	4s. "	1,040 0 0	Do. to wholesale dealers.
Bonnets	1,409,400	150 do. do. 3 doz. daily	"	6d. "	35,235 0 0	Do. do.
Shawls of all kinds	469,800	300 do. do. 6 daily	"	1s. 2d. "	27,405 0 0	Do. to wholesale and wardrobe dealers.
Fur boas and victorines	261,000	100 do. do. 10 do.	"	1s. 2d. "	15,220 0 0	Do. do.
Fur tippets and muffs	130,500	100 do. do. 5 do.	"	1s. 2d. "	7,612 10 0	Do. do.
Umbrella and parasol frames	518,400	200 do., each collecting 12 daily	all	5d. "	10,300 0 0	Do. to Jews and old umbrella menders.
					675,555 6 8	
HOUSEHOLD REFUSE.						
Tea-leaves	78,000 lbs.	.... do. .... 2 lbs. weekly for 6 months.	costers and fishmongers	2½d. per lb.	812 10 0	Do. to merchants to re-make into tea.
Fish-skins	3,900 "	25 do. do. 50 weekly	all	1d. "	16 5 0	Do. to brewers to fine their ale.
Hare-skins	80,000	50 do. do. 6 lbs. weekly	none	1s. a doz.	333 6 8	Do. to Jews, hatters, and furriers.
Kitchen-stuff	62,400 lbs.	200 do. do. 5 " do.	"	1½d. per lb.	390 0 0	Do. at marine stores.
Dripping	52,000 "	200 buyers 3 cwt. weekly	1-1000th	3d. "	650 0 0	Do. do.
Bones	3,494,400 "	200 do., each purchasing 40 gal. daily	all	¾d. "	105,625 0 0	Do. for manure, knife-handles, &c.
Hogwash	2,504,000 gals.		none	1d. per gallon	10,433 6 8	Do. to pig-dealers.
Dust (from houses)	900,000 loads		"	2s. 6d. per ld.	112,500 0 0	Do. for manure and to brickmakers.
Soot	800,000 bush.	800 colls. each collectg. 19 bush. weekly	"	5d. per bushel	16,666 13 4	Do. to farmers, graziers, and gardeners.
Soil (from cesspools)	750,000 loads	....		10s. per load	375,000 0 0	Do. for manure.
					622,427 1 8	
STREET REFUSE.						
Street sweepings (scavengers')	140,983 "	444 do. the whole " 452 lds. daily	"	3s. "	21,147 9 0	Do. do.
Ditto (street orderlies')	2,817 "	546 do. do. " 9 " do.	"	2s. 6d. "	2,352 2 6	Do. do.
Coal and coke (mudlarks')	64,656 cwt.	550 do., each collecting 42 lbs. do.	"	8d. per cwt.	2,151 17 4	Do. to the poor.
"Pure"	52,000 pails	200 do. do. 5 pails weekly	"	1s. per pail	2,600 0 0	Do. to tanners and leather-dressers.
Cigar ends	2,240 lbs.	50 do. do. 8½ lbs. do.	street-finders	8d. per lb.	74 13 4	Do. to Jews in Rosemary-lane.
					28,326 2 2	
				Gross Total...	1,406,592 1 6	

Curious and ample as this Table of Refuse is—one, moreover, perfectly original—it is not sufficient, by the mere range of figures, to convey to the mind of the reader a full comprehension of the ramified vastness of the Second-Hand trade of the metropolis. Indeed tables are for reference more than for the current information to be yielded by a history or a narrative.

I will, therefore, offer a few explanations in elucidation, as it were, of the tabular return.

I must, as indeed I have done in the accompanying remarks, depart from the order of the details of the table to point out, in the first instance, the particulars of the greatest of the Second-Hand trades—that in Clothing. In this table the reader will find included every indispensable article of man's, woman's, and child's apparel, as well as those articles which add to the ornament or comfort of the person of the wearer; such as boas and victorines for the use of one sex, and dressing-gowns for the use of the other. The articles used to protect us from the rain, or the too-powerful rays of the sun, are also included—umbrellas and parasols. The whole of these articles exceed, when taken in round numbers, twelve millions and a quarter, and that reckoning the "pairs," as in boots and shoes, &c., as but one article. This, still pursuing the round-number system, would supply nearly *five* articles of refuse apparel to every man, woman, and child in this, the greatest metropolis of the world.

I will put this matter in another light. There are about 35,000 Jews in England, nearly half of whom reside in the metropolis. 12,000, it is further stated on good authority, reside within the City of London. Now at one time the trade in old clothes was almost entirely in the hands of the City Jews, the others prosecuting the same calling in different parts of London having been "Wardrobe Dealers," chiefly women, (who had not unfrequently been the servants of the aristocracy); and even these wardrobe dealers sold much that was worn, and (as one old clothes-dealer told me) much that was "not, for their fine customers, because the fashion had gone by," to the "Old Clo" Jews, or to those to whom the street-buyers carried their stock, and who were able to purchase on a larger scale than the general itinerants. Now, supposing that even one twelfth of these 12,000 Israelites were engaged in the old-clothes trade (which is far beyond the mark), each man would have *twelve hundred and twenty-five* articles to dispose of yearly, all second-hand!

Perhaps the most curious trade is that in waste paper, or as it is called by the street collectors, in "waste," comprising every kind of used or useless periodical, and books in all tongues. I may call the attention of my readers, by way of illustrating the extent of this business in what is proverbially refuse "waste paper," to their experience of the penny postage. Three or four sheets of note paper, according to the stouter or thinner texture, and an envelope with a seal or a glutinous and stamped fastening, will not exceed half-an-ounce, and is conveyed to the Orkneys and the further isles of Shetland, the Hebrides, the Scilly and Channel Islands, the isles of Achill and Cape Clear, off the western and southern coasts of Ireland, or indeed to and from the most extreme points of the United Kingdom, and no matter what distance, provided the letter be posted within the United Kingdom, for a penny. The weight of waste or refuse paper annually disposed of to the street collectors, or rather buyers, is 1,397,760 lbs. Were this tonnage, as I may call it, for it comprises 12,480 tons yearly, to be distributed in half-ounce letters, it would supply material, as respects weight, for *forty-four millions, seven hundred and twenty-eight thousand, four hundred and thirty* letters on business, love, or friendship.

I will next direct attention to what may be, by perhaps not over-straining a figure of speech, called "the crumbs which fall from the rich man's table;" or, according to the quality of the commodity of refuse, of the tables of the *comparatively* rich, and that down to a low degree of the scale. These are not, however, unappropriated crumbs, to be swept away uncared for; but are objects of keen traffic and bargains between the possessors or their servants and the indefatigable street-folk. Among them are such things as champagne and other wine bottles, porter and ale bottles, and, including the establishments of all the rich and the comparative rich, kitchen-stuff, dripping, hog-wash, hare-skins, and tea-leaves. Lastly come the very lowest grades of the street-folk—the *finders;* men who will quarrel, and have been seen to quarrel, with a hungry cur for a street-found bone; not to pick or gnaw, although Eugène Sue has seen that done in Paris; and I once, very early on a summer's morning, saw some apparently houseless Irish children contend with a dog and with each other for bones thrown out of a house in King William-street, City—as if after a very late supper—not to pick or gnaw, I was saying, but to *sell* for manure. Some of these finders have "seen better days;" others, in intellect, are little elevated above the animals whose bones they gather, or whose ordure ("pure"), they scrape into their baskets.

I do not know that the other articles in the arrangement of the table of street refuse, &c., require any further comment. Broken metal, &c., can only be disposed of according to its quality or weight, and I have lately shown the extent of the trade in such refuse as street-sweepings, soot, and night-soil.

The gross total, or average yearly money value, is 1,406,592*l.* for the second-hand commodities I have described in the foregoing pages; or as something like a minimum is given, both as to the number of the goods and the price, we may fairly put this total at a million and a half of pounds sterling!

CROSSING-SWEEPERS.

That portion of the London street-folk who earn a scanty living by sweeping crossings constitute a large class of the Metropolitan poor. We can scarcely walk along a street of any extent, or pass through a square of the least pretensions to "gentility," without meeting one or more of these private scavengers. Crossing-sweeping seems to be one of those occupations which are resorted to as an excuse for begging; and, indeed, as many expressed it to me, "it was the last chance left of obtaining an honest crust."

The advantages of crossing-sweeping as a means of livelihood seem to be:

1st, the smallness of the capital required in order to commence the business;

2ndly, the excuse the apparent occupation it affords for soliciting gratuities without being considered in the light of a street-beggar;

And 3rdly, the benefits arising from being constantly seen in the same place, and thus exciting the sympathy of the neighbouring householders, till small weekly allowances or "pensions" are obtained.

The first curious point in connexion with this subject is what constitutes the "*property*," so to speak, in a crossing, or the *right* to sweep a pathway across a certain thoroughfare. A nobleman, who has been one of her Majesty's Ministers, whilst conversing with me on the subject of crossing-sweepers, expressed to me the curiosity he felt on the subject, saying that he had noticed some of the sweepers in the same place for years. "What were the rights of property," he asked, "in such cases, and what constituted the title that such a man had to a particular crossing? Why did not the stronger sweeper supplant the weaker? Could a man bequeath a crossing to a son, or present it to a friend? How did he first obtain the spot?"

The answer is, that crossing-sweepers are, in a measure, under the protection of the police. If the accommodation afforded by a well-swept pathway is evident, the policeman on that district will protect the original sweeper of the crossing from the intrusion of a rival. I have, indeed, met with instances of men who, before taking to a crossing, have asked for and obtained permission of the police; and one sweeper, who gave me his statement, had even solicited the authority of the inhabitants before he applied to the inspector at the station-house.

If a crossing have been vacant for some time, another sweeper may take to it; but should the original proprietor again make his appearance, the officer on duty will generally re-establish him. One man to whom I spoke, had fixed himself on a crossing which for years another sweeper had kept clean on the Sunday morning only. A dispute ensued; the one claimant pleading his long Sabbath possession, and the other his continuous everyday service. The quarrel was referred to the police, who decided that he who was oftener on the ground was the rightful owner; and the option was given to the former possessor, that if he would sweep there every day the crossing should be his.

I believe there is only one crossing in London which is in the gift of a householder, and this proprietorship originated in a tradesman having, at his own expense, caused a paved footway to be laid down over the Macadamized road in front of his shop, so that his customers might run less chance of dirtying their boots when they crossed over to give their orders.

Some bankers, however, keep a crossing-sweeper, not only to sweep a clean path for the "clients" visiting their house, but to open and shut the doors of the carriages calling at the house.

Concerning the *causes which lead or drive* people to this occupation, they are various. People take to crossing-sweeping either on account of their bodily afflictions, depriving them of the power of performing ruder work, or because the occupation is the last resource left open to them of earning a living, and they considered even the scanty subsistence it yields preferable to that of the workhouse. The greater proportion of crossing-sweepers are those who, from some bodily infirmity or injury, are prevented from a more laborious mode of obtaining their living. Among the bodily infirmities the chief are old age, asthma, and rheumatism; and the injuries mostly consist of loss of limbs. Many of the rheumatic sweepers have been bricklayers' labourers.

The classification of crossing-sweepers is not very complex. They may be divided into the *casual* and the *regular*.

By the casual I mean such as pursue the occupation only on certain days in the week, as, for instance, those who make their appearance on the Sunday morning, as well as the boys who, broom in hand, travel about the streets, sweeping before the foot-passengers or stopping an hour at one place, and then, if not fortunate, moving on to another.

The regular crossing-sweepers are those who have taken up their posts at the corners of streets or squares; and I have met with some who have kept to the same spot for more than forty years.

The crossing-sweepers in the squares may be reckoned among the most fortunate of the class. With them the crossing is a kind of stand, where any one requiring their services knows they may be found. These sweepers are often employed by the butlers and servants in the neighbouring mansions for running errands, posting letters, and occasionally helping in the packing-up and removal of furniture or boxes when the family goes out of town. I have met with other sweepers who, from being known for years to the inhabitants, have at last got to be regularly employed at some of the houses to clean knives, boots, windows, &c.

It is not at all an unfrequent circumstance, however, for a sweeper to be in receipt of a weekly sum from some of the inhabitants in the district. The crossing itself is in these cases but of little value for chance customers, for were it not for the regular charity of the householders, it would be deserted. Broken victuals and old clothes also form part of a sweeper's means of living; nor are the clothes always old ones, for one or two of this class have for years been in the habit of having new suits presented to them by the neighbours at Christmas.

The irregular sweepers mostly consist of boys and girls who have formed themselves into a kind of company, and come to an agreement to work together on the same crossings. The principal resort of these is about Trafalgar-square, where they have seized upon some three or four crossings, which they visit from time to time in the course of the day.

One of these gangs I found had appointed its king and captain, though the titles were more honorary than privileged. They had framed their own laws respecting each one's right to the money he took, and the obedience to these laws was enforced by the strength of the little fraternity.

One or two girls whom I questioned, told me that they mixed up ballad-singing or lace-selling with crossing-sweeping, taking to the broom only when the streets were wet and muddy. These children are usually sent out by their parents, and have to carry home at night their earnings. A few of them are orphans with a lodging-house for a home.

Taken as a class, crossing-sweepers are among the most honest of the London poor. They all tell you that, without a good character and "the respect of the neighbourhood," there is not a living to be got out of the broom. Indeed, those whom I found best-to-do in the world were those who had been longest at their posts.

Among them are many who have been servants until sickness or accident deprived them of their situations, and nearly all of them have had their minds so subdued by affliction, that they have been tamed so as to be incapable of mischief.

The *earnings*, or rather "*takings*," of crossing-sweepers are difficult to estimate — generally speaking — that is, to strike the average for the entire class. An erroneous idea prevails that crossing-sweeping is a lucrative employment. All whom I have spoken with agree in saying, that some thirty years back it was a good living; but they bewail piteously the spirit of the present generation. I have met with some who, in former days, took their 3l. weekly; and there are but few I have spoken to who would not, at one period, have considered fifteen shillings a bad week's work. But now "the takings" are very much reduced. The man who was known to this class as having been the most prosperous of all — for from one nobleman alone he received an allowance of seven shillings and sixpence weekly — assured me that twelve shillings a-week was the average of his present gains, taking the year round; whilst the majority of the sweepers agree that a shilling is a good day's earnings.

A shilling a-day is the very limit of the average incomes of the London sweepers, and this is rather an over than an under calculation; for, although a few of the more fortunate, who are to be found in the squares or main thoroughfares or opposite the public buildings, may earn their twelve or fifteen shillings a-week, yet there are hundreds who are daily to be found in the by-streets of the metropolis who assert that eightpence a-day is their average taking; and, indeed, in proof of their poverty, they refer you to the workhouse authorities, who allow them certain quartern-loaves weekly. The old stories of delicate suppers and stockings full of money have in the present day no foundation of truth.

The black crossing-sweeper, who bequeathed 500l. to Miss Waithman, would almost seem to be the last of the class whose earnings were above his positive necessities.

Lastly, concerning the *numbers* belonging to this large class, we may add that it is difficult to reckon up the number of crossing-sweepers in London. There are few squares without a couple of these pathway scavengers; and in the more respectable squares, such as Cavendish or Portman, every corner has been seized upon. Again, in the principal thoroughfares, nearly every street has its crossing and attendant.

I.—OF THE ADULT CROSSING-SWEEPERS.

A. *The Able-Bodied Sweepers.*

The elder portion of the London crossing-sweepers admit, as we have before said, of being arranged, for the sake of perspicuity, into several classes. I shall begin with the *Able-bodied Males;* then proceed to the *Females* of the same class; and afterwards deal with the *Able-bodied Irish* (male and female), who take to the London causeways for a living. This done, I shall then, in due order, take up the *Afflicted* or *Crippled* class; and finally treat of the *Juveniles* belonging to the same calling.

1. The Able-Bodied Male Crossing-Sweepers.

The "Aristocratic" Crossing-Sweeper.

"Billy" is the popular name of the man who for many years has swept the long crossing that cuts off one corner of Cavendish-square, making a "short cut" from Old Cavendish-street to the Duke of Portland's mansion.

Billy is a merry, good-tempered kind of man, with a face as red as a love-apple, and cheeks streaked with little veins.

"His hair is white, and his eyes are as black and bright as a terrier's. He can hardly speak a sentence without finishing it off with a moist chuckle.

His clothes have that peculiar look which arises from being often wet through, but still they are decent, and far above what his class usually wear. The hat is limp in the brim, from being continually touched.

The day when I saw Billy was a wet one, and he had taken refuge from a shower under the Duke of Portland's stone gateway. His tweed coat, torn and darned, was black about the shoulders with the rain-drops, and his boots grey with mud, but, he told me, "It was no good trying to keep clean shoes such a day as that, 'cause the blacking come off in the puddles."

Billy is "well up" in the *Court Guide.* He continually stopped in his statement to tell whom my Lord B. married, or where my Lady C. had gone to spend the summer, or what was the title of the Marquis So-and-So's eldest boy.

He was very grateful, moreover, to all who had assisted him, and *would* stop looking up at the ceiling, and God-blessing them all with a species of religious fervour.

His regret that the good old times had passed, when he made "hats full of money," was unmistakably sincere; and when he had occasion to allude to them, he always delivered his opinion upon the late war, calling it "a-cut-and run affair," and saying that it was "nothing at all put alongside with the old war, when the halfpence and silver coin were twice as big and twenty times more plentiful" than during the late campaign.

Without the least hesitation he furnished me with the following particulars of his life and calling:—

"I was born in London, in Cavendish-square, and (he added, laughing) I ought to have a title, for I first came into the world at No. 3, which was Lord Bessborough's then. My mother went there to do her work, for she chaired there, and she was took sudden and couldn't go no further. She couldn't have chosen a better place, could she? You see I was born in Cavendish-square, and I've *worked* in Cavendish-square—sweeping a crossing—for now near upon fifty year.

" Until I was nineteen—I'm sixty-nine now —I used to sell water-creases, but they felled off and then I dropped it. Both mother and myself sold water-creases after my Lord Bessborough died; for whilst he lived she wouldn't leave him not for nothing.

"We used to do uncommon well at one time; there wasn't nobody about then as there is now. I've sold flowers, too; they was very good then; they was mostly show carnations and moss roses, and such-like, but no common flowers—it wouldn't have done for me to sell common things at the houses I used to go to.

"The reason why I took to a crossing was, I had an old father and I didn't want him to go to the workus. I didn't wish too to do anything bad myself, and I never would—no, sir, for I've got as good a charackter as the first nobleman in the land, and that's a fine thing, ain't it? So as water-creases had fell off till they wasn't a living to me, I had to do summat else to help me to live.

" I saw the crossing-sweepers in Westminster making a deal of money, so I thought to myself *I'll* do that, and I fixed upon Cavendish-square, because, I said to myself, I'm known there; it's where I was born, and there I set to work.

"The very first day I was at work I took ten shillings. I never asked nobody; I only bowed my head and put my hand to my hat, and they knowed what it meant.

" By jingo, when I took that there I thought to myself, What a fool I've been to stop at water-creases!

"For the first ten year I did uncommon well. Give me the old-fashioned way; they were good times then; I like the old-fashioned way. Give me the old penny pieces, and then the eighteen-penny pieces, and the three-shilling pieces, and the seven-shilling pieces—give me them, I says. The day the old halfpence and silver was cried down, that is, the old coin was called in to change the currency, my hat wouldn't hold the old silver and halfpence I was give that afternoon. I had *such a* lot, upon my word, they broke my pocket. I didn't know the money was altered, but a fishmonger says to me, 'Have you got any old silver?' I said 'Yes, I've got a hat full;' and then says he, 'Take 'em down to Couttseses and change 'em.' I went, and I was nearly squeeged to death.

"That was the first time I was like to be killed, but I was nigh killed again when Queen Caroline passed through Cavendish-square after her trial. They took the horses out of her carriage and pulled her along. She kept a chucking money out of the carriage, and I went and scrambled for it, and I got five-and-twenty shillin, but my hand was a nigh smashed through it; and, says a friend of mine, before I went, 'Billy,' says he, 'don't you go;' and I was sorry after I did. She was a good woman, *she* was. The Yallers, that is, the king's party, was agin her, and pulled up the paving-stones when her funeral passed; but the Blues was for her.

"I can remember, too, the mob at the time of the Lord Castlereagh riots. They went to Portman-square and broke all the winders in the house. They pulled up all the rails to purtect theirselves with. I went to the Bishop of Durham's, and hid myself in the coal-cellar then. My mother chaired there, too. The Bishop of Durham and Lord Harcourt opened their gates and hurrah'd the mob, so they had nothing of their's touched; but whether they did it through fear or not I can't say. The mob was carrying a quartern loaf dipped in bullock's blood, and when I saw it I thought it was a man's head; so that frightened me, and I run off.

"I remember, too, when Lady Pembroke's house was burnt to the ground. That's about eighteen year ago. It was very lucky the family wasn't in town. The housekeeper was a nigh killed, and they had to get her out over the stables; and when her ladyship heard she was all right, she said she didn't care for the fire since the old dame was saved, for she had lived along with the family for many years. No, bless you, sir! I didn't help at the fire; I'm too much of a coward to do that.

"All the time the Duke of Portland was alive he used to allow me 7s. 6d. a-week, which was 1s. a-day and 1s. 6d. for Sundays. He was a little short man, and a very good man he was too, for it warn't only me as he gave money to, but to plenty others. He was the best man in England for that.

"Lord George Bentinck, too, was a good friend to me. He was a great racer, he was, and then he turned to be member of parliament, and then he made a good man they tell me; but he never comed over my crossing without giving me something. He was at the corner of Holly Street, he was, and he never put foot on my crossing without giving me a sovereign. Perhaps he wouldn't cross more than once or twice a month, but when he comed my way *that* was his money. Ah! he was a nice feller, he was. When he give it he always put it in my hand and never let nobody see it, and that's the way I like to have *my* fee give me.

"There's Mrs. D——, too, as lived at No. 6; she was a good friend of mine, and always allowed me a suit of clothes a-year; but she's dead, good lady, now.

"Dr. C—— and his lady, they, likewise, was very kind friends of mine, and gave me every year clothes, and new shoes, and blankets, aye, and a bed, too, if I had wanted it; but now they are all dead, down to the coachman. The doctor's old butler, Mr. K——, he gave me twenty-five shillings the day of the funeral, and, says he, 'Bill, I'm afraid this will be the last.' Poor good friends they was all of them, and I did feel cut up when I see the hearse going off.

"There was another gentleman, Mr. W. T——, who lives in Harley-street; he never come by me without giving me half-a-crown. He was a real good gentleman; but I haven't seen him for a long time now, and perhaps he's dead too.

"All my friends is dropping off. I'm fifty-five, and they was men when I was a boy. All the good gentlemen's gone, only the bad ones stop.

"Another friend of mine is Lord B——. He always drops me a shilling when he come by; and, says he, 'You don't know me, but I knows you, Billy.' But I *do* know him, for my mother worked for the family many a year, and, considering I was born in the house, I think to myself, 'If I don't know you, why I ought.' He's a handsome, stout young chap, and as nice a gentleman as any in the land.

"One of the best friends I had was Prince E——, as lived there in Chandos-street, the bottom house yonder. I had five sovereigns give me the day as he was married to his beautiful wife. Don't you remember what a talk there was about her diamonds, sir? They say she was kivered in 'em. He used to put his hand in his pocket and give me two or three shillings every time he crossed. He was a gentleman as was uncommon fond of the gals, sir. He'd go and talk to all the maid-servants round about, if they was only good-looking. I used to go and ring the hairy bells for him, and tell the gals to go and meet him in Chapel-street. God bless him! I says, he was a pleasant gentleman, and a regular good 'un for a bit of fun, and always looking lively and smiling. I see he's got his old coachman yet, though the Prince don't live in England at present, but his son does, and he always gives me a half-crown when he comes by too.

"I gets a pretty fine lot of Christmas boxes, but nothing like what I had in the old times. Prince E—— always gives me half a crown, and I goes to the butler for it. Pretty near all my friends gives me a box, them as knows me, and they say, 'Here's a Christmas box, Billy.'

"Last Christmas-day I took 36s., and that was pretty fair; but, bless you, in the old times I've had my full of money. I tells you again I've have had as much as 5l. in old times, all in old silver and halfpence; that was in the old war, and not this runaway shabby affair.

"Every Sunday I have sixpence regular from Lord H——, whether he's in town or not. I goes and fetches it. Mrs. D——, of Harley-street, she gives me a shilling every Sunday when she's in town; and the parents as knows me give halfpence to their little girls to give me. Some of the little ladies says, 'Here, that will do you good.' No, it's only pennies (for sixpences is out of fashion); and thank God for the coppers, though they are little.

"I generally, when the people's out of town, take about 2s. or 2s. 6d. on the Sunday. Last Sunday I only took 1s. 3d., but then, you see, it come on to rain and I didn't stop. When the town's full three people alone gives me more than that. In the season I take 5s. safe on a Sunday, or perhaps 6s.—for you see it's all like a lottery.

"I should like you to mention Lady Mildmay in Grosvenor-square, sir. Whenever I goes to see her—but you know I don't go often—I'm safe for 5s., and at Christmas I have my regular salary, a guinea. She's a very old lady, and I've knowed her for many and many years. When I goes to my lady she always comes out to speak to me at the door, and says she, 'Oh, 'tis Willy! and how do you do, Willy?' and she always shakes hands with me and laughs away. Ah! she's a good kind creetur'; there's no pride in her whatsumever—and she never sacks her servants.

"My crossing has been a good living to me and mine. It's kept the whole of us. Ah! in the old time I dare say I've made as much as 3l. a week reg'lar by it. Besides, I used to have lots of broken vittals, and I can tell you I know'd where to take 'em to. Ah! I've had as much food as I could carry away, and reg'lar good stuff—chicken, and some things I couldn't guess the name of, they was so Frenchified. When the fam'lies is in town I gets a good lot of food given me, but you know when the nobility and gentlemen are away the servants is on board wages, and cuss them board wages, I says.

"I buried my father and mother as a son ought to. Mother was seventy-three and father was sixty-five,—good round ages, ain't they, sir? I shall never live to be that. They are lying in St. John's Wood cemetery along with many of my brothers and sisters, which I have buried as well. I've only two brothers living now; and, poor fellows, they're not very well to do. It cost me a good bit of money. I pay 2s. 6d. a-year for keeping up the graves of each of my parents, and 1s. 2d. for my brothers.

"There was the Earl of Gainsborough as I should like you to mention as well, please sir. He lived in Chandos-street, and was a particular nice man and very religious. He always gave me a shilling and a tract. Well, you see, I did often read the tract; they was all religious, and about where your souls was to go to—very good, you know, what there was, very good; and he used to buy 'em wholesale at a little shop, corner of High-street, Marrabun. He was a very good, kind gentleman, and gave away such a deal of money that he got reg'lar known, and the little beggar girls follered him at such a rate that he was at last forced to ride about in a cab to get away from 'em. He's many a time said to me, when he's stopped to give me my shilling, 'Billy, is any of 'em a follering me?' He was safe to give to every body as asked him, but you see it worried his soul out—and it was a kind soul, too—to be follered about by a mob.

"When all the fam'lies is in town I has 14s. a-week reg'lar as clock-work from my friends as lives round the square, and when they're away I don't get 6d. a-day, and sometimes I don't get 1d. a-day, and that's less. You see some of 'em, like my Lord B——, is out eight months in the year; and some of 'em, such as my Lord H——, is only three. Then Mrs. D——, she's away three months, and she always gives 1s. a-week reg'lar when she's up in London.

"I don't take 4s. a-week on the crossing. Ah! I wish you'd give me 4s. for what I take. No, I make up by going of errands. I runs for the fam'lies, and the servants, and any of 'em. Sometimes they sends me to a banker's with a cheque. Bless you! they'd trust me with anythink, if it was a hatfull. I've had a lot of money trusted to me at times. At one time I had as much as 83l. to carry for the Duke of Portland.

"Aye, that was a go—that was! You see the hall-porter had had it give to him to carry to the bank, and he gets me to do it for him; but the vallet heerd of it, so he wanted to have a bit of fun, and he wanted to put the hall-porter in a funk. I met the vallet in Holborn, and says he, 'Bill, I want to have a lark,' so he kept me back, and I did not get back till one o'clock. The hall-porter offered 5l. reward for me, and sends the police; but Mr. Freebrother, Lord George's vallet, he says, 'I'll make it all right, Billy.' They sent up to my poor old people, and says father, 'Billy wouldn't rob anybody of a nightcap, much more 80l.' I met the policeman in Holborn, and says he, 'I want you, Billy,' and says I, 'All right, here I am.' When I got home the hall-porter, says he, 'Oh, I am a dead man; where's the money?' and says I, 'It's lost.' 'Oh! it's the Duke's, not mine,' says he. Then I pulls it out; and says the porter, 'It's a lark of Freebrother's.' So he gave me 2l.

to make it all right. That *was* a game, and the hall-porter, says he, 'I really thought you was gone, Billy;' but, says I, 'If everybody carried as good a face as I do, everybody would be as honest as any in Cavendish-square.'

"I had another lark at the Bishop of Durham's. I was a cleaning the knives, and a swellmobsman, with a green-baize bag, come down the steps, and says he to me, 'Is Mr. Lewis, the butler, in?'—he'd got the name off quite pat. 'No,' says I, 'he's up-stairs;' then says he, 'Can I step into the pantry?' 'Oh, yes,' says I, and shows him in. Bless you! he was so well-dressed, I thought he was a master-shoemaker or something; but as all the plate was there, thinks I, I'll just lock the door to make safe. So I fastens him in tight, and keeps him there till Mr. Lewis comes. No, he didn't take none of the plate, for Mr. Lewis come down, and then, as he didn't know nothink about him, we had in a policeman, when we finds his bag was stuffed with silver tea-pots and all sorts of things from my Lord Musgrave's. Says Mr. Lewis, 'You did quite right, Billy.' It wasn't a likely thing I was going to let anybody into a pantry crammed with silver.

"There was another chap who had prigged a lot of plate. He was an old man, and had a bag crammed with silver, and was a cutting away, with lots of people after him. So I puts my broom across his legs and tumbles him, and when he got up he cut away and left the bag. Ah! I've seen a good many games in my time—that I have. The butler of the house the plate had been stole from give me 2*l.* for doing him that turn.

"Once a gentleman called me, and says he, 'My man, how long have you been in this square?' Says I, 'I'm Billy, and been here a'most all my life.' Then he says, 'Can I trust you to take a cheque to Scott, the banker?' and I answers, 'That's as you like,' for I wasn't going to press him. It was a heavy cheque, for Mr. Scott, as knows me well—aye, well, he do—says 'Billy, I can't give you all in notes, you must stop a bit.' It nearly filled the bag I had with me. I took it all safe back, and says he, 'Ah! I knowed it would be all right,' and he give me a half-sovereign. I should like you to put these things down, 'cos it's a fine thing for my charackter, and I can show my face with any man for being honest, that's one good thing.

"I pays 4*s.* a-week for two rooms, one up and one down, for I couldn't live in one room. I come to work always near eight o'clock, for you see it takes me some time to clean the knives and boots at Lord B——'s. I get sometimes 1*s.* and sometimes 1*s.* 6*d.* a-week for doing that, and glad I am to have it. It's only for the servants I does it, not for the quality.

"When I does anythink for the servants, it's either cleaning boots and knives, or putting letters in the post—that's it—anythink of that kind. They gives me just what they can, 1*d.* or 2*d.* or half a pint of beer when they ha'n't got any coppers.

"Sometimes I gets a few left-off clothes, but very seldom. I have two suits a-year give me reg'lar, and I goes to a first-rate tailor for 'em, though they don't make the prime—of course not, yet they're very good. Now this coat I liked very well when it was new, it was so clean and tidy. No, the tailor don't show me the pattern-books and that sort of thing: he knows what's wanted. I won't never have none of them washing duck breeches; that's the only thing as I refuses, and the tailor knows that. I looks very nice after Christmas, I can tell you, and I've always got a good tidy suit for Sundays, and God bless them as gives 'em to me.

"Every Sunday I gets a hot dinner at Lord B——'s, whether he's out of town or in town—that's summat. I gets bits, too, give me, so that I don't buy a dinner, no, not once a-week. I pays 4*s.* a-week rent, and I dare say my food, morning and night, costs me a 1*s.* a-day—aye, I'm sure it does, morning and night. At present I don't make 12*s.* a-week; but take the year round, one week with another, it might come to 13*s.* or 14*s.* a-week I gets. Yes, I'll own to that.

"Christmas is my best time; then I gets more than 1*l.* a-week: now I don't take 4*s.* a-week on my crossing. Many's the time I've made my breakfast on a pen'orth of coffee and a halfpenny slice of bread and butter. What do you think of that?

"Wet weather does all the harm to me. People, you see, don't like to come out. I think I've got the best side of the square, and you see my crossing is a long one, and saves people a deal of ground, for it cuts off the corner. It used to be a famous crossing in its time—hah! but that's gone.

"I always uses what they calls the brush-brooms; that's them with a flat head like a house-broom. I can't abide them others; they don't look well, and they wears out ten times as quick as mine. I general buys the eights, that's 10*d.* a-piece, and finds my own handles. A broom won't last me more than a fortnight, it's such a long crossing; but when it was paved, afore this mucky-dam (macadamising) was turned up, a broom would last me a full three months. I can't abide this muckydam—can you, sir? it's sloppy stuff, and goes so bad in holes. Give me the good solid stones as used to be.

"I does a good business round the square when the snow's on the ground. I general does each house at so much a-week whilst it snows. Hardwicks give me a shilling. I does only my side, and that next Oxford-street. I don't go to the others, unless somebody comes and orders me—for fair play *is* fair play—and they belongs to

THE BEARDED CROSSING-SWEEPER AT THE EXCHANGE.

[*From a Photograph.*]

THE CROSSING-SWEEPER THAT HAS BEEN A MAID-SERVANT.

[*From a Photograph.*]

the other sweepers. I does my part and they does theirs.

"It's seldom as I has a shop to sweep out, and I don't do nothink with shutters. I'm getting too old now for to be called in to carry boxes up gentlemen's houses, but when I was young I found plenty to do that way. There's a man at the corner of Chandos-street, and he does the most of that kind of work."

THE BEARDED CROSSING-SWEEPER AT THE EXCHANGE.

SINCE the destruction by fire of the Royal Exchange in 1838, there has been added to the curiosities of Cornhill a thickset, sturdy, and hirsute crossing-sweeper—a man who is as civil by habit as he is independent by nature. He has a long flowing beard, grey as wood smoke, and a pair of fierce moustaches, giving a patriarchal air of importance to a marked and observant face, which often serves as a painter's model. After half-an-hour's conversation, you are forced to admit that his looks do not all belie him, and that the old mariner (for such was his profession formerly) is worthy in some measure of his beard.

He wears an old felt hat—very battered and discoloured; around his neck, which is bared in accordance with sailor custom, he has a thick blue cotton neckerchief tied in a sailor's knot; his long iron-grey beard is accompanied by a healthy and almost ruddy face. He stands against the post all day, saying nothing, and taking what he can get without solicitation.

When I first spoke to him, he wanted to know to what purpose I intended applying the information that he was prepared to afford, and it was not until I agreed to walk with him as far as St. Mary-Axe that I was enabled to obtain his statement, as follows:—

"I've had this crossing ever since '38. The Exchange was burnt down in that year. Why, sir, I was wandering about trying to get a crust, and it was very sloppy, so I took and got a broom; and while I kept a clean crossing, I used to get ha'pence and pence. I got a dockman's wages—that's half-a-crown a-day; sometimes only a shilling, and sometimes more. I have taken a crown—but that's very rare. The best customers I had is dead. I used to make a good Christmas, but I don't now. I have taken a pound or thirty shillings then in the old times.

"I smoke, sir; I *will* have tobacco, if I can't get grub. My old woman takes cares that I have tobacco.

"I have been a sailor, and the first ship as ever I was in was the Old Colossus, 74, but we was only cruising about the Channel then, and took two prizes. I went aboard the Old Remewa guardship — we were turned over to her—and from her I was drafted over to the Escramander frigate. We went out chasing Boney, but he gived himself up to the Old Impregnable. I was at the taking of Algiers, in 1816, in the Superb. I was in the Rochfort, 74, up the Mediterranean (they call it up the Mediterranean, but it was the Malta station) three years, ten months, and twenty days, until the ship was paid off.

"Then I went to work at the Dockyard. I had a misfortune soon after that. I fell out of a garret window, three stories high, and that kept me from going to the Docks again. I lost all my top teeth by that fall. I've got a scar here, one on my chin; but I warn't in the hospital more than two weeks.

"I was afeard of being taken up solicitin' charity, and I knew that sweeping was a safe game; they couldn't take me up for sweeping a crossing.

"Sometimes I get insulted, only in words; sometimes I get chaffed by sober people. Drunken men I don't care for; I never listen to 'em, unless they handle me, and then, although I am sixty-three this very day, sir, I think I could show them something. I *do* carry my age well; and if you could ha' seen how I have lived this last winter through, sometimes one pound of bread between two of us, you'd say I was a strong man to be as I am.

"Those who think that sweepin' a crossing is idle work, make a great mistake. In wet weather, the traffic that makes it gets sloppy as soon as it's cleaned. Cabs, and 'busses, and carriages continually going over the crossing must scatter the mud on it, and you must look precious sharp to keep it clean; but when I once get in the road, I never jump out of it. I keeps my eye both ways, and if I gets in too close quarters, I slips round the wheels. I've had them almost touch me.

"No, sir, I never got knocked down. In foggy weather, of course, it's no use sweeping at all.

"Parcels! it's very few parcels I get to carry now; I don't think I get a parcel to carry once in a month: there's 'busses and railways so cheap. A man would charge as much for a distance as a cab would take them.

"I don't come to the same crossing on Sundays; I go to the corner of Finch-lane. As to regular customers, I've none—to say regular; some give me sixpence now and then. All those who used to give me regular are dead.

"I was a-bed when the Exchange was burnt down.

"I have had this beard five years. I grew it to sit to artists when I got the chance; but it don't pay expenses—for I have to walk four or five miles, and only get a shilling an hour: besides, I'm often kept nearly two hours, and I get nothing for going and nothing for coming, but just for the time I am there.

"Afore I wore it, I had a pair of large whiskers. I went to a gentleman then, an artist, and he *did* pay me well. He advised me to grow mustarshers and the beard, but he hasn't employed me since.

"They call me 'Old Jack' on the crossing, that's all they call me. I get more chaff from the boys than any one else. "They only say, 'Why don't you get shaved?' but I take no notice on 'em.

"Old Bill, in Lombard Street! I knows him; he used to make a good thing of it, but I don't think he makes much now.

"My wife — I am married, sir — doesn't do anything. I live in a lodging-house, and I pay three shillings a-week.

"I tell you what we has, now, when I go home. We has a pound of bread, a quarter of an ounce of tea, and perhaps a red herring.

"I've had a weakness in my legs for two year; the veins comes down, but I keep a bandage in my pocket, and when I feels 'em coming down, I puts the bandage on 'till the veins goes up again—it's through being on my legs so long (because I had very strong legs when young) and want of good food. When you only have a bit of bread and a cup of tea — no meat, no vegetables — you find it out; but I'm as upright as a dart, and as lissom as ever I was.

"I gives threepence for my brooms. I wears out three in a week in the wet weather. I always lean very hard on my broom, 'specially when the mud is sticky — as it is after the roads is watered. I am very particular about my brooms; I gives 'em away to be burned when many another would use them."

THE SWEEPER IN PORTMAN SQUARE, WHO GOT PERMISSION FROM THE POLICE.

A WILD-LOOKING man, with long straggling grey hair, which stood out from his head as if he brushed it the wrong way; and whiskers so thick and curling that they reminded one of the wool round a sheep's face, gave me the accompanying history.

He was very fond of making use of the term "honest crust," and each time he did so, he, Irish-like, pronounced it "currust." He seemed a kind-hearted, innocent creature, half scared by want and old age.

"I'm blest if I can tell which is the best crossing in London; but mine ain't no great shakes, for I don't take three shilling a-week not with persons going across, take one week with another; but I thought I could get a honest currust (crust) at it, for I've got a crippled hand, which comed of its own accord, and I was in St. George's Hospital seven weeks. When I comed out it was a cripple with me, and I thought the crossing was better than going into the workhouse — for I likes my liberty.

"I've been on this crossing since last Christmas was a twelvemonth. Before that I was a bricklayer and plasterer. I've been thirty-two years in London. I can get as good a character as any one anywhere, please God; for as to drunkards, and all that, I was none of them. I was earning eighteen shilling a-week, and sometimes with my overtime I've had twenty shilling, or even twenty-three shilling. Bricklayers is paid according to all the hours they works beyond ten, for that's the bricklayer's day.

"I was among the lime, and the sand, and the bricks, and then my hand come like this (he held out a hand with all the fingers drawn up towards the middle, like the claw of a dead bird). All the sinews have gone, as you see yourself, sir, so that I can't bend it or straighten it, for the fingers are like bits of stick, and you can't bend 'em without breaking them.

"When I couldn't lay hold of anything, nor lift it up, I showed it to master, and he sent me to his doctor, who gived me something to rub over it, for it was swelled up like, and then I went to St. George's Hospital, and they cut it over, and asked me if I could come in doors as in-door patient? and I said Yes, for I wanted to get it over sooner, and go back to my work, and earn an honest currust. Then they scarred it again, cut it seven times, and I was there many long weeks; and when I comed out I could not hold any tool, so I was forced to keep on pawning and pledging to keep an honest currust in my mouth, and sometimes I'd only just be with a morsel to eat, and sometimes I'd be hungry, and that's the truth.

"What put me up to crossing-sweeping was this — I had no other thing open to me but the workhouse; but of course I'd sooner be out on my liberty, though I was entitled to go into the house, of course, but I'd sooner keep out of it if I could earn an honest currust.

"One of my neighbours persuaded me that I should pick up a good currust at a crossing. The man who had been on my crossing was gone dead, and as it was empty, I went down to the police-office, in Marylebone Lane, and they told me I might take it, and give me liberty to stop. I was told the man who had been there before me had been on it fourteen years, and them was good times for gentle and simple and all — and it was reported that this man had made a good bit of money, at least so it was said.

"I thought I could make a living out of it, or an honest currust, but it's a very poor living, I can assure you. When I went to it first, I done pretty fair for a currust; but it's only three shillings to me now. My missus has such bad health, or she used to help me with her needle. I can assure you, sir, it's only one day a week as I have a bit of dinner, and I often go without breakfast and supper, too.

"I haven't got any regular customers that

allow me anything. When the families is in town sometimes they give me half-a-crown, or sixpence, now and then, perhaps once a fortnight, or a month. They've got footmen and servant-maids, so they never wants no parcels taken—they make *them* do it; but sometimes I get a penny for posting a letter from one of the maids, or something like that.

"The best day for us is Sunday. Sometimes I get a shilling, and when the families is in town eighteen pence. But when the families is away, and the weather so fine there's no mud, and only working-people going to the chapels, they never looks at me, and then I'll only get a shilling."

Another who got Permission to Sweep.

An old Irishman, who comes from Cork, was spoken of to us as a crossing-sweeper who had formally obtained permission before exercising his calling; but I found, upon questioning him, that it was but little more than a true Hibernian piece of conciliation on his part; and, indeed, that out of fear of competition, he had asked leave of the servants and policeman in the neighbourhood.

It seems somewhat curious, as illustrative of the rights of property among crossing-sweepers, that three or four "intending" sweepers, when they found themselves forestalled by the old man in question, had no idea of supplanting the Irishman, and merely remarked,—

"Well, you're lucky to get it so soon, for we meant to take it."

In reply to our questions, the man said,—

"I came here in January last: I knew the old man was did who used to keep the crossin', and I thought I would like the kind of worruk, for I am getting blind, and hard of hearing likewise. I've got no parish; since the passing of the last Act, I've niver lived long enough in any one parish for that. I applied to Marabone, and they offered to sind me back to Ireland, but I'd got no one to go to, no friends or relations, or if I have, they're as poor there as I am mysilf, sir.

"There was an ould man here before me. He used to have a stool to rest himsilf on, and whin he died, last Christmas, a man as knew him and me asked me whither I would take it or no, and I said I would. His broom and stool were in the coal-cellar at this corner house, Mr. ——'s, where he used to leave them at night times, and they gave them up to me; but I didn't use the stool, sir, it might be an obsthruction to the passers-by; and, sir, it looks as if it was infirrumity. But, plaise the Lord, I'll git and make a stool for myself against the hard winter, I will, bein' a carpenter by thrade.

"I didn't ask the gintlefolks' permission to come here, but I asked the police and the servants, and such as that. I asked the servants at the corner-house. I don't know whither they could have kept me away if I had not asked. Soon after I came here the gintlefolks—some of them—stopped and spoke to me. 'So,' says they, 'you've taken the place of the old man that's did?' 'Yes, I have,' says I. 'Very will,' says they, and they give me a ha'penny. That was all that occurred upon my takin' to the crossin'.

"But there were some others who would have taken it if I had not; they tould me I was lucky in gettin' it so soon, or they would have had it, but I don't know who they are.

"I am seventy-three years ould the 2d of June last. My wife is about the same age, and very much afflicted with the rheumatis, and she injured hersilf, too, years ago, by fallin' off a chair while she was takin' some clothes off the line.

"Not to desave you, sir, I get a shillin' a-week from one of my childer and ninepence from another, and a little hilp from some of the others. I have siven childer livin', and have had tin. They are very much scattered: two are abroad; one is in the tinth Hussars— he is kind to me. The one who allows me ninepence is a basket-maker at Reading; and the shillin' I get from my daughter, a servant, sir. One of my sons died in the Crimmy; he was in the 13th Light Dragoons, and died at Scutari, on the 25th of May. They could not hilp me more than they thry to do, sir.

"I only make about two shilling a-week here, sir; and sometimes I don't take three ha'pence a day. On Sundays I take about sivenpence, ninepence, or tinpence, 'cordin' as I see the people who give rigular.

"Weather makes no difference to me—for, though the sum is small, I am a rigular pinsioner like of theirs. I go to Somer's-town Chapel, being a Catholic, for I'm not ashamed to own my religion before any man. When I go, it is at siven in the evening. Sometimes I go to St. Pathrick's Chapel, Soho-square. I have not been to confission for two or three years—the last time was to Mr. Stanton, at St. Pathrick's.

"There's a poor woman, sir, who goes past here every Friday to get her pay from the parish, and, as sure as she comes back again, she gives me a ha'penny—she does, indeed. Sometimes the baker or the greengrocer gives me a ha'penny for minding their baskets.

"I'm perfectly satisfied; it's no use to grumble, and I might be worrus off, sir. Yes, I go of arrinds some times; fitch water now and then, and post letters; but I do no odd jobs, such as hilping the servants to clean the knives, or such-like. No: they wouldn't let me behint the shadow of their doors."

A Third who asked Leave.

This one was a mild and rather intelligent man, in a well-worn black dress-coat and waistcoat, a pair of "moleskin" trousers, and a blue-and-white cotton neckerchief. I found him sweeping the crossing at the end of —— place, opposite the church.

He every now and then regaled himself with a pinch of snuff, which seemed to light up his careworn face. He seemed very willing to afford me information. He said:—

"I have been on this crossing four years. I am a bricklayer by trade; but you see how my fingers have gone: it's all rheumatics, sir. I took a great many colds. I had a great deal of underground work, and that tries a man very much.

"How did I get the crossing? Well, I took it—I came as a cas'alty. No one ever interfered with me. If one man leaves a crossing, well, another takes it.

"Yes, some crossings is worth a good deal of money. There was a black in Regent-street, at the corner of Conduit-street, I think, who had two or three houses—at least, I've heard so; and I know for a certainty that the man in Cavendish-square used to get so much a week from the Duke of Portland—he got a shilling a-day, and eighteenpence on Sundays. I don't know why he got more on Sundays. I don't know whether he gets it since the old Duke's death.

"The boys worry me. I mean the little boys with brooms; they are an abusive set, and give me a good deal of annoyance; they are so very cheeky; they watch the police away; but if they see the police coming, they bolt like a shot. There are a great many Irish lads among them. There were not nearly so many boys about a few years ago.

"I once made eighteenpence in one day, that was the best day I ever made: it was very bad weather: but, take the year through, I don't make more than sixpence a-day.

"I haven't worked at bricklaying for a matter of six year. What did I do for the two years before I took to crossing-sweeping? Why, sir, I had saved a little money, and managed to get on somehow. Yes, I have had my troubles, but I never had what I call great ones, excepting my wife's blindness. She was blind, sir, for eleven year, and so I had to fight for everything: she has been dead two year, come September.

"I have seven children, five boys and two girls; they are all grown up and got families. Yes, they ought, amongst them, to do something for me; but if you have to trust to children, you will soon find out what *that* is. If they want anything of you, they know where to find you; but if you want anything of them, it's no go.

"I think I made more money when first I swept this crossing than I do now; it's not a *good* crossing, sir. Oh, no; but it's handy home, you see. When a shower of rain comes on, I can run home, and needn't go into a public-house; but it's a poor neighbourhood.

"Oh yes, indeed sir, I am always here. Certainly; I am laid up sometimes for a day with my feet. I am subject to the rheumatic gout, you see. Well, I don't know whether so much standing has anything to do with it.

"Yes, sir, I *have* heard of what you call 'shutting-up shop.' I never heard it called by that name before, though; but there's lots of sweepers as sweep back the dirt before leaving at night. I know they do, some of them. I never did it myself—I don't care about it; I always think there's the trouble of sweeping it back in the morning.

"People liberal? No, sir, I don't think there are many liberal people about; if people were liberal I should make a good deal of money.

"Sometimes, after I get home, I read a book, if I can borrow one. What do I read? Well, novels, when I can get them. What did I read last night? Well, *Reynolds's Miscellany*; before that I read the *Pilgrim's Progress*. I have read it three times over; but there's always something new in it.

"Well, weather makes very little difference in this neighbourhood. My rent is two-and-sixpence a-week. I have a little relief from the parish. How much? Two-and-sixpence. How much does my living cost? Well, I am forced to live on what I can get. I manage as well as I can; if I have a good week, I spend it—I get more nourishment then, that's all.

"I used to smoke, sir, a great deal, but I haven't touched a pipe for a matter of forty year. Yes, sir, I take snuff, Scotch and Rappee, mixed. If I go without a meal of victuals, I must have my snuff. I take an ounce a-week, sir; it costs fourpence—that there is the only luxury I get, unless somebody gives me a half pint of beer.

"I very rarely get an odd job, this is not the neighbourhood for them things.

"Yes, sir, I go to church on Sunday; I go to All Souls', in Langham-place, the church with the sharp spire. I go in the morning; once a day is quite enough for me. In the afternoon, I generally take a walk in the Park, or I go to see one of my young ones; they won't come to the old crossing-sweeper, so I go to them."

A REGENT-STREET CROSSING-SWEEPER.

A MAN who had stationed himself at the end of Regent-street, near the County Fire Office, gave me the following particulars.

He was a man far superior to the ordinary run of sweepers, and, as will be seen, had formerly been a gentleman's servant. His costume was of that peculiar miscellaneous description which showed that it had from time to time been given to him in charity. A dress-coat so marvellously tight that the stitches were stretching open, a waistcoat with a remnant of embroidery, and a pair of trousers which wrinkled like a groom's top-boot, had all evidently been part of the wardrobe of the gentlemen whose errands he had run. His boots were the most curious portion of his toilette, for they were large enough for a fisherman, and the portion unoccupied by the foot had gone flat and turned up like a Turkish slipper.

He spoke with a tone and manner which showed some education. Once or twice whilst I was listening to his statement he insisted upon removing some dirt from my shoulder, and, on leaving, he by force seized my hat and brushed it — all which habits of attention he had contracted whilst in service.

I was surprised to see stuck in the wristband of his coat-sleeve a row of pins, arranged as neatly as in the papers sold at the mercers'.

"Since the Irish have come so much — the boys, I mean — my crossing has been completely cut up," he said; "and yet it is in as good a spot as could well be, from the County Fire Office (Mr. Beaumont as owns it) to Swan and Edgar's. It ought to be one of the fust crossings in the kingdom, but these Irish have spiled it.

"I should think, as far as I can guess, I've been on it eight year, if not better; but it was some time before I got known. You see, it does a feller good to be some time on a crossing; but it all depends, of course, whether you are honest or not, for it's according to your honesty as you gets rewarded. By rewarded, I means, you gets a character given to you by word of mouth. For instance, a party wants me to go do a job for 'em, and they says, 'Can you get any lady or gentleman to speak for you?' And I says, 'Yes;' and I gets my character by word of mouth — that's what I calls being rewarded.

"Before ever I took a broom in hand, the good times had gone for crossings and sweepers. The good times was thirty year back. In the regular season, when *they* (the gentry) are in town, I *have* taken from one and sixpence to two shillings a-day; but every day's not alike, for people stop at home in wet days. But, you see, in winter-time the crossings ain't no good, and then we turn off to shovelling snow; so that, you see, a shilling a-day is even too high for us to take regular all the year round. Now, I ain't taken a shilling, no, nor a blessed bit of silver, for these three days. All the quality's out of town.

"It ain't what a man gets on a crossing as keeps him; *that* ain't worth mentioning. I don't think I takes sixpence a-day regular — all the year round, mind — on the crossing. No, I'd take my solemn oath I don't! If you was to put down fourpence it would be nearer the mark. I'll tell you the use of a crossing to such as me and my likes. It's our shop, and it ain't what we gets a-sweeping, but it's a place like for us to stand, and then people as wants us, comes and fetches us.

"In the summer I do a good deal in jobs. I do anything in the portering line, or if I'm called to do boots and shoes, or clean knives and forks, then I does that. But that's only when people's busy; for I've only got one regular place I goes to, and that's in A—— street, Piccadilly. I goes messages, parcels, letters, and anything that's required, either for the master of the hotel or the gents that uses there. Now, there's one party at Swan and Edgar's, and I goes to take parcels for him sometimes; and he won't trust anybody but me, for you see I'm know'd to be trustworthy, and then they reckons me as safe as the Bank, — there, that's just it.

"I got to the hotel only lately. You see, when the peace was on and the soldiers was coming home from the Crimmy, then the governor he was exceeding busy, so he give me two shillings a-day and my board; but that wasn't reg'lar, for as he wants me he comes and fetches me. It's a-nigh impossible to say what I makes, it don't turn out reg'lar; Sunday's a shilling or one-and-sixpence, other days nothing at all — not salt to my porridge. You see, when I helps the party at the hotel, I gets my food, and that's a lift. I've never put down what I made in the course of the year, but I've got enough to find food and raiment for myself and family. Sir, I think I may say I gets about six shillings a-week, but it ain't more.

"I've been abroad a good deal. I was in Cape Town, Table Bay, one-and-twenty miles from Simons' Town — for you see the French mans-of-war comes in at Cape Town, and the English mans-of-war comes in at Simons' Town. I was a gentleman's servant over there, and a very good place it was; and if anybody was to have told me years back that I was to have come to what I am now, I could never have credited it; but misfortunes has brought me to what I am.

"I come to England thinking to better myself, if so be it was the opportunity; besides, I was tired of Africy, and anxious to see my native land.

"I was very hard up — ay, very hard up indeed — before I took to the cross, and, in preference to turning out dishonest, I says, I'll buy a broom and go and sweep and get a honest livelihood.

"There was a Jewish lady and her husband used to live in the Suckus, and I knowed them and the family — very fine sons they was — and I went into the shop to ask them to let me work before the shop, and they give me their permission so to do, and, says she, 'I'll allow you threepence a-week.' They've been good friends to me, and send me a messages; and wherever they be, may they do well, I says.

"I sometimes gets clothes give to me, but it's only at Christmas times, or after its over; and that helps me along — it does so, indeed.

"Whenever I sees a pin or a needle, I picks it up; sometimes I finds as many as a dozen a-day, and I always sticks them either in my cuff or in my waistcoat. Very often a lady sees 'em, and then they comes to me and says, 'Can you oblige me with a pin?' and I says, 'Oh yes, marm; a couple, or three, if you requires them;' but it turns out very rare that I gets a trifle for anything like that. I only does it to be obliging—besides, it makes you friends, like.

"I can't tell who's got the best crossing in London. I'm no judge of that; it isn't a broom as can keep a man now. They're going out of town so fast, all the harristocracy; though it's middling classes—such as is in a middling way like—as is the best friends to me."

A TRADESMAN'S CROSSING-SWEEPER.

A MAN who had worked at crossing-sweeping as a boy when he first came to London, and again when he grew too old to do his work as a labourer in a coal-yard, gave me a statement of the kind of life he led, and the earnings he made. He was an old man, with a forehead so wrinkled that the dark, waved lines reminded me of the grain of oak. His thick hair was, despite his great age — which was nearly seventy—still dark; and as he conversed with me, he was continually taking off his hat, and wiping his face with what appeared to be a piece of flannel, about a foot square.

His costume was of what might be called "the all-sorts" kind, and, from constant wear, it had lost its original colour, and had turned into a sort of dirty green-grey hue. It consisted of a waistcoat of tweed, fastened together with buttons of glass, metal, and bone; a tail-coat, turned brown with weather, a pair of trousers repaired here and there with big stitches, like the teeth of a comb, and these formed the extent of his wardrobe. Around the collar of the coat and waistcoat, and on the thighs of the pantaloons, the layers of grease were so thick that the fibre of the cloth was choked up, and it looked as if it had been pieced with bits of leather.

Rubbing his unshorn chin, whereon the bristles stood up like the pegs in the barrel of a musical-box—until it made a noise like a hair-brush, he began his story :—

"I'm known all about in Parliament-street —ay, every bit about them parts,—for more than thirty year. Ay, I'm as well known as the statty itself, all about them parts at Charing-cross. Afore I took to crossing-sweeping I was at coal-work. The coal-work I did was backing and filling, and anythink in that way. I worked at Wood's, and Penny's, and Douglas's. They were good masters, Mr. Wood 'specially; but the work was too much for me as I got old. There was plenty of coal work in them times; indeed, I've yearned as much as nine shillings of a day. That was the time as the meters was on. Now men can hardly earn a living at coal-work. I left the coal-work because I was took ill with a fever, as was brought on by sweating — over-exaction they called it. It left me so weak I wasn't able to do nothink in the yards.

"I know Mr. G——, the fishmonger, and Mr. J——, the publican. I should think Mr. J—— has knowed me this eight-and-thirty-year, and they put me on to the crossing. You see, when I was odd man at a coal job, I'd go and do whatever there was to be done in the neighbourhood. If there was anythink as Mr. G——'s men couldn't do—such as carrying fish home to a customer, when the other men were busy—I was sent for. Or Mr. J—— would send me with sperrits—a gallon, or half a gallon, or anythink of that sort—a long journey. In fact, I'd get anythink as come handy.

"I had done crossing-sweeping as a boy, before I took to coal-work, when I first come out of the country. My own head first put me up to the notion, and that's more than fifty year ago—ay, more than that; but I can't call to mind exactly, for I've had no parents ever since I was eight year old, and now I'm nigh seventy; but it's as close as I can remember. I was about thirteen at that time. There was no police on then, and I saw a good bit of road as was dirty, and says I, 'That's a good spot to keep clean,' and I took it. I used to go up to the tops of the houses to throw over the snow, and I've often been obliged to get men to help me. I suppose I was about the first person as ever swept a crossing in Charing-cross; (here, as if proud of the fact, he gave a kind of moist chuckle, which ended in a fit of coughing). I used to make a good bit of money then; but it ain't worth nothink, now.

"After I left coal-backing, I went back to the old crossing opposite the Adm'ralty gates, and I stopped there until Mr. G—— give me the one I'm on now, and thank him for it, I says. Mr. G—— had the crossing paved, as leads to his shop, to accommodate the customers. He had a German there to sweep it afore me. He used to sweep in the day—come about ten or eleven o'clock in the morning, and then at night he turned watchman; for when there was any wenson, as Mr. G—— deals in, hanging out, he was put to watch it. This German worked there, I reckon, about seven year, and when he died I took the crossing.

"The crossing ain't much of a living for any body—that is, what I takes on it. But then I've got regular customers as gives me money. There's Mr. G——, he gives a shilling a-week; and there's Captain R——, of the Adm'ralty, he gives me sixpence a fortnight; and another captain, of the name of R——, he gives me fourpence every Sunday. Ah! I'd forgot Mr. O——, the Secretary at the Adm'ralty; he gives me sixpence now and then. Besides, I do a lot of odd jobs for different people; they knows where to come and find me when they wants me. They gets me to carry letters, or a parcel, or a box, or anythink of that there. I has a bit of vittals, too, give me every now and then; but as for money, it's very little as I get on the crossings—perhaps seven or eight shilling a-week, reg'lar customers and all.

"I never heard of anybody as was leaving a crossing selling it; no, never. My crossing ain't a reg'lar one as anybody could have. If I was to leave, it depends upon whether Mr. G—— would like to have the party, as to who gets it. There's no such thing as turning a reg'lar sweeper out, the police stops that. I've been known to them for years, and they are very kind to me. As they come's by they says, 'Jimmy, how are you?' You see, my crossing comes handy for them, for it's agin Scotland-yard; and when they turns out in their clean boots it saves their blacking.

"Lord G—— used to be at the Adm'ralty, but he ain't there now; I don't know why he left, but he's gone. He used to give me six-pence every now and then when he come over. I was near to my crossing when Mr. Drummond was shot, but I wasn't near enough to hear the pistol; but I didn't see nothink. I know'd the late Sir Robert Peel, oh, certainly, but he seldom crossed over my crossing, though whenever he did, he'd give me some-think. The present Sir Robert goes over to the chapel in Spring-gardens when he's in town, but he keeps on the other side of the way; so I never had anythink from him. He's the very picture of his father, and I knows him from that, only his father were rather stouter than he is. I don't know none of the members of parliament, they most on 'em keeps on shifting so, that I hasn't no time to recognise 'em.

"The watering-carts ain't no friends of our'n. They makes dirt and no pay for cleaning it. There's so much traffic with coaches and carts going right over my crossing that a fine or wet day don't make much difference to me, for people are afraid to cross for fear of being run over. I'm forced to have my eyes about me and dodge the wehicles. I never heerd, as I can tell on, of a crossing-sweeper being run over."

2. The Able-bodied Female Crossing-Sweepers.

The Old Woman "over the Water."

She is the widow of a sweep—" as respectable and 'dustrious a man," I was told, " as any in the neighbourhood of the 'Borough;' he was a short man, sir,—very short," said my informant, " and had a weakness for top-boots, white hats, and leather breeches," and in that unsweeplike costume he would parade himself up and down the Dover and New Kent-roads." He had a capital connexion (or, as his widow terms it, " seat of business"), and left behind him a good name and reputation that would have kept the " seat of business" together, if it had not been for the misconduct of the children, two of whom (sons) have been transported, while a daughter " went wrong," though she, wretched creature, paid a fearful penalty, I learnt, for her frailties, having been burnt to death in the middle of the night, through a careless habit of smoking in bed.

The old sweeper herself, eighty years of age, and almost beyond labour, very deaf, and rather feeble to all appearance, yet manages to get out every morning between four and five, so as to catch the workmen and " time-keepers" on their way to the factories. She has the true obsequious curtsey, but is said to be very strong in her " likes and dislikes."

She bears a good character, though sometimes inclining, I was informed, towards " the other half-pint," but never guilty of any excess. She is somewhat profuse in her scriptural ejaculations and professions of gratitude. Her statement was as follows:—

"Fifteen years I've been on the crossing, come next Christmas. My husband died in Guy's Hospital, of the cholera, three days after he got in, and I took to the crossing some time after. I had nothing to do. I am eighty years of age, and I couldn't do hard work. I have nothing but what the great God above pleases to give me. The poor woman who had the crossing before me was killed, and so I took it. The gentleman who was the foreman of the road, gave me the grant to take it. I didn't ask him, for poor people as wants a bit of bread they goes on the crossings as they likes, but he never interfered with me. The first day I took sixpence; but them good times is all gone, they'll never come back again. The best times I used to take a shilling a-day, and now I don't take but a few pence. The winter is as bad as the summer, for poor people haven't got it to give, and gentlefolks get very near now. People are not so liberal as they used to be, and they never will be again.

"To do a hard day's washing, I couldn't. I used to go to a lady's house to do a bit of washing when I had my strength, but I can't do it now.

"People going to their offices at six or seven in the morning gives me a ha'penny or a penny; if they don't, I must go without it. I go at five, and stand there till eleven or twelve, till I find it is no use being there any longer. Oh, the gentlemen give me the most, I'm sure; the ladies don't give me nothing.

"At Christmas I get a few things—a gentleman gave me these boots I've got on, and a ticket for a half-quartern loaf and a hundred of coals. I have got as much as five shillings at Christmas—but those times will never come back again. I get no more than two shillings and sixpence at Christmas now.

" My husband, Thomas —— was his name, was a chimley-sweep. He did a very good business—it was all done by his sons. We had a boy with us, too, just as a friendly boy. I was a mother and a mistress to him. I've had eleven children. I'm grandmother to fifteen, and a great-grandmother, too. They won't give me a bite of bread, though, any of 'em, I've got four children living, as far as I know, two abroad and two home here with families. I never go among 'em. It is not in my power to assist 'em, so I never go to distress 'em.

"I get two shilling a-week from the parish, and I have to pay out of that for a quartern loaf, a quartern of sugar, and an ounce of tea. The parish forces it on me, so I must take it, and that only leaves me one shilling and fourpence. A shilling of it goes for my lodging. I lodge with people who knew my family and me, and took a liking to me; they let me come there instead of wandering about the streets.

"I stand on my crossing till I'm like to drop over my broom with tiredness. Yes, sir, I go to church at St. George's in the Borough. I go there every Sunday morning, after I leave my roads. They've taken the organ and charity children away that used to be there when I was a girl, so it's not a church now, it's a chapel. There's nothing but the preacher and the gentlefolks, and they sings their own psalms. There are gatherings at that church, but whether it's for the poor or not I don't know. I don't get any of it.

"It was a great loss to me when my husband died; I went all to ruin then. My father belonged to Scotland, at Edinboro'. My mother came from Yorkshire. I don't know where Scotland is no more than the dead. My father was a gentleman's gardener and watchman. My mother used to go out a-chairing, and she was drowned just by Horsemonger Lane. She was coming through the Halfpenny Hatch, that used to be just facing the Crown and Anchor, in the New Kent-road; there was an open ditch there, sir. She took the left-hand turning instead of the right, and was drowned. My father died in St. Martin's Workhouse. He died of apoplexy fit.

"I used to mind my father's place till mother died. His housekeeper I was—God help me! a fine one too. Thank the Lord, my husband was a clever man; he had a good seat of business. I lost my right hand when he died. I couldn't carry it on. There was my two sons went for sogers, and the others were above their business. He left a seat of business worth a hundred pound; he served all up the New Kent-road. He was beloved by all his people. He used to climb himself when I first had him, but he left it off when he got children. I had my husband when I was fifteen, and kept him forty years. Ah! he was well-beloved by all around, except his children, and they behaved shameful. I said to his eldest son, when he lay in the hospital, (asking your pardon, sir, for mentioning it)—I says to his eldest son, 'Billy,' says I, 'your father's very bad—why don't you go to see him?' 'Oh,' says he, 'he's all right, he's gettin' better;' and he was never the one to go and see him once; and he never come to the funeral.

"Billy thought I should come upon him after his death, but I never troubled him for as much as a crumb of bread.

"I never get spoken to on my roads, only some people say, 'Good morning,' 'There you are, old lady.' They never asks me no questions whatsomever. I never get run over, though I am very hard of hearing; but I am forced to have my eyes here, there, and everywhere, to keep out of the way of the carts and coaches.

"Some days I goes to my crossing, and earns nothink at all: other days it's sometimes fourpence, sometimes sixpence. I earned fourpence to-day, and I had a bit of snuff out of it. Why, I believe I did yearn fivepence yesterday —I won't tell no story. I got ninepence on Sunday—that was a good day; but, God knows, that didn't go far. I yearned so much I couldn't bring it home on Saturday—it almost makes me laugh,—I yearned sixpence.

"I goes every morning, winter or summer, frost or snow; and at the same hour (five o'clock); people certainly don't think of giving so much in fine weather. Nobody ever mislested me, and I never mislested nobody. If they gives me a penny, I thanks 'em; and if they gives me nothing, I thanks 'em all the same.

"If I was to go into the House, I shouldn't live three days. It's not that I eat much—a very little is enough for me; but it's the air I should miss: to be shut up like a thief, I couldn't live long, I know."

The Old Woman Crossing-Sweeper who had a Pensioner.

This old dame is remarkable from the fact of being the chief support of a poor deaf cripple, who is as much poorer than the crossing-sweeper as she is poorer than Mrs. ——, in —— street, who allows the sweeper sixpence a-week. The crossing-sweeper is a rather stout old woman, with a carneying tone, and constant curtsey. She complains, in common with most of her class, of the present hard times, and reverts longingly to the good old days when people were more liberal than they are now, and had more to give. She says:—

"I was on my crossing before the police was made, for I am not able to work, and only get helped by the people who knows me. Mr. ——, in the square, gives me a shilling a-week; Mrs. ——, in —— street, gives me sixpence; (she has gone in the country now, but she has left it at the oil-shop for me); that's what I depinds upon, darlin', to help pay my rent, which is half-a-crown. My rent was three shillings, till the landlord didn't wish me to go, 'cause I was so punctual with my money. I give a corner of my room to a poor cretur, who's deaf as a beadle; she works at the soldiers' coats, and is a very good hand at it, and would earn a good deal of money if she had constant work. She owed as good as twelve shillings and sixpence for rent, poor thing, where she was last, and the landlord took all her goods except her bed; she's got that, so I give her a corner of my room for charity's sake. We must look to one another: she's as poor as a church mouse. I thought she would be company for me, still a deaf person is but poor company to one. She had that heavy sickness they call the cholera about five years ago, and it fell in her side and in the side of her head too—that made her deaf. Oh! she's a poor object. She has been with me since the month of February. I've lent her money out of my own pocket. I give her a cup of tea or a slice of bread when I see she hasn't got any. Then the people up-stairs are kind to her, and give her a bite and a sup.

"My husband was a soldier; he fought at the battle of Waterloo. His pension was ninepence a-day. All my family are dead, except my grandson, what's in New Orleans. I expect him back this very month that now we have: he gave me four pounds before he went, to carry me over the last winter.

"If the Almighty God pleases to send him back, he'll be a great help to me. He's all I've got left. I never had but two children in all my life.

"I worked in noblemen's houses before I was married to my husband, who is dead; but he came to be poor, and I had to leave my houses where I used to work.

"I took twopence-halfpenny yesterday, and threepence to-day; the day before yesterday I didn't take a penny. I never come out on Sunday; I goes to Rosomon-street Chapel. Last Saturday I made one shilling and sixpence; on Friday, sixpence. I dare say I make three shillings and sixpence a-week, besides the one shilling and sixpence I gets allowed me. I am forced to make a do of it somehow, but I've no more strength left in me than this ould broom."

The Crossing-Sweeper who had been a Servant-Maid.

She is to be found any day between eight in the morning and seven in the evening, sweeping away in a convulsive, jerky sort of manner, close to —— square, near the Foundling. She may be known by her pinched-up straw bonnet, with a broad, faded, almost colourless ribbon. She has weak eyes, and wears over them a brownish shade. Her face is tied up, because of a gathering which she has on her head. She wears a small, old plaid cloak, a clean checked apron, and a tidy printed gown.

She is rather shy at first, but willing and obliging enough withal; and she lives down Little —— Yard, in Great —— street. The "yard" that is made like a mousetrap—small at the entrance, but amazingly large inside, and dilapidated though extensive.

Here are stables and a couple of blind alleys, nameless, or bearing the same name as the yard itself, and wherein are huddled more people than one could count in a quarter of an hour, and more children than one likes to remember,—dirty children, listlessly trailing an old tin baking-dish, or a worn-out shoe, tied to a piece of string; sullen children, who turn away in a fit of sleepy anger if spoken to; screaming children, setting all the parents in the "yard" at defiance; and quiet children, who are arranging banquets of dirt in the reeking gutters.

The "yard" is devoted principally to costermongers.

The crossing-sweeper lives in the top-room of a two-storied house, in the very depth of the blind alley at the end of the yard. She has not even a room to herself, but pays one shilling a-week for the privilege of sleeping with a woman who gets her living by selling tapes in the streets.

"Ah!" says the sweeper, "poor woman, she *has* a hard time of it; her husband is in the hospital with a bad leg—in fact, he's scarcely ever out. If you could hear that woman cough, you'd never forget it. She would have had to starve to-day if it hadn't been for a person who actually lent her a gown to pledge to raise her stock-money, poor thing."

The room in which these people live has a sloping roof, and a small-paned window on each side. For furniture, there were two chairs and a shaky, three-legged stool, a deal table, and a bed rolled up against the wall—nothing else. In one corner of the room lay the last lump remaining of the seven pounds of coals. In another corner there were herbs in pans, and two water-bottles without their noses. The most striking thing in that little room was some crockery, the woman had managed to save from the wreck of her things; among this, curiously enough, was a soup-tureen, with its lid not even cracked.

There *was* a piece of looking-glass—a small three-cornered piece—forming an almost equilateral triangle,—and the oldest, and most rubbed and worn-out piece of a mirror that ever escaped the dust-bin.

The fireplace was a very small one, and on the table were two or three potatoes and about one-fifth of a red herring, which the poor street-seller had saved out of her breakfast to serve for her supper. "Take my solemn word for it, sir," said the sweeper, " and I wouldn't deceive you, that is all she will get besides a cup of weak tea when she comes home tired at night."

The statement of this old sweeper is as follows:—

"My name is Mary ——. I live in —— yard. I live with a person of the name of ——, in the back attic; she gets her living by selling flowers in pots in the street, but she is now doing badly. I pay her a shilling a-week.

"My parents were Welsh. I was in service, or maid-of-all-work, till I got married. My husband was a seafaring man when I married him. After we were married, he got his living by selling memorandum-almanack books, and the like, about the streets. He was driven to that because he had no trade in his hand, and he was obliged to do something for a living. He did not make much, and over-exertion, with want of nourishment, brought on a paralytic stroke. He had the first fit about two years before he had the second; the third fit, which was the last, he had on the Monday, and died on the Wednesday week. I have two children still living. One of them is married to a poor man, who gets his living in the streets; but as far as lays in his power he makes a good husband and father. My other daughter is living with a niece of mine, for I can't keep her, sir; she minds the children.

"My father was a journeyman shoemaker. He was killed; but I cannot remember how—I was too young. I can't recollect my mother. I was brought up by an uncle and aunt till I was able to go to service. I went out to service at five, to mind children under a nurse, and I was in service till I got married. I had a great many situations; you see, sir, I was forced to keep in place, because I had nowhere to go to, my uncle and aunt not being able to keep me. I was never in noblemen's families, only tradespeople's. Service was very hard, sir, and so I believe it continues.

"I am fifty-five years of age, and I have been on the crossing fourteen years; but just now it is very poor work indeed. Well, if I wishes for bad weather, I'm only like other people, I suppose. I have no regular customers at all; the only one I had left has lost his senses, sir. Mr. H——, he used to allow us sixpence a-week; but he went mad, and we don't get it now. By us, I mean the three crossing-sweepers in the square where I work.

"Indeed, I like the winter-time, for the families is in. Though the weather is more severe, yet you *do* get a few more ha'pence. I take more from the staid elderly people than from the young. At Christmas, I think I took about eleven shillings, but certainly not more. The most I ever made at that season was fourteen shillings. The worst about Christmas is, that those who give much then generally hold their hand for a week or two.

"A shilling a-day would be as much as I want, sir. I have stood in the square all day for a ha'penny, and I have stood here for nothing. One week with another, I make two shillings in the seven days, after paying for my broom. I have taken threppence ha'penny to-day. Yesterday—let me see—well, it was threppence ha'penny, too; Monday I don't remember; but Sunday I recollect—it was fippence ha'penny. Years ago I made a great deal more—nearly three times as much.

"I come about eight o'clock in the morning, and go away about six or seven; I am here every day. The boys used to come at one time with their brooms, but they're not allowed here now by the police.

"I should not think crossings worth purchasing, unless people made a better living on them than I do."

I gave the poor creature a small piece of silver for her trouble, and asked her if that, with the threepence halfpenny, made a good day. She answered heartily—

"I should like to see such another day to-morrow, sir.

"Yes, winter is very much better than summer, only for the trial of standing in the frost and snow, but we certainly *do* get more then. The families won't be in town for three months to come yet. Ah! this neighbourhood is nothing to what it was. By God's removal, and by their own removal, the good families are all gone. The present families are not so liberal nor so wealthy. It is not the richest people that give the most. Tradespeople, and 'specially gentlefolks who have situations, are better to me than the nobleman who rides in his carriage.

"I always go to Trinity Church, Gray's-inn-road, about two doors from the Welsh School—the Rev. Dr. Witherington preaches there. I always go on Sunday afternoon and evening, for I can't go in the morning; I can't get away from my crossing in time. I never omit a day in coming here, unless I'm ill, or the snow is too heavy, or the weather too bad, and then I'm obligated to resign.

"I have no friends, sir, only my children; my uncle and aunt have been dead a long time. I go to see my children on Sunday, or in the evening, when I leave here.

"After I leave I have a cup of tea, and after that I go to bed; very frequently I'm in bed at nine o'clock. I have my cup of tea if I can anyway get it; but I'm forced to go without *that* sometimes.

"When my sight was better, I used to be very partial to reading; but I can't see the print, sir, now. I used to read the Bible, and the newspaper. Story-books I have read, too, but not many novels. Yes, *Robinson Crusoe* I know, but not the *Pilgrim's Progress*. I've heard of it; they tell me it is a very interesting book to read, but I never had it. We never have any ladies or Scripture-readers come to our lodgings; you see, we're so out, they might come a dozen times and not find us at home.

"I wear out three brooms in a-week; but in the summer one will last a fortnight. I give threepence ha'penny for them; there are twopenny-ha'penny brooms, but they are not so good, they are liable to have their handles come out. It is very fatiguing standing so many hours; my legs aches with pain, and swells. I was once in Middlesex Hospital for sixteen weeks with my legs. My eyes have been weak from a child. I have got a gathering in my head from catching cold standing on the crossing. I had the fever this time twelvemonth. I laid a fortnight and four days at home, and seven weeks in the hospital. I took the diarrhœa after that, and was six weeks under the

THE IRISH CROSSING-SWEEPER.

[*From a Photograph.*]

THE ONE-LEGGED SWEEPER AT CHANCERY-LANE.

[*From a Photograph.*]

doctor's hands. I used to do odd jobs, but my health won't permit me now. I used to make two or three shillings a-week by 'em, and get scraps and things. But I get no broken victuals now.

"I never get anything from servants; they don't get more than they know what to do with.

"I don't get a drop of beer once in a month.

"I don't know but what this being out may be the best thing, after all; for if I was at home all my time, it would not agree with me."

STATEMENT OF "OLD JOHN," THE WATERMAN AT THE FARRINGDON-STREET CAB-STAND, CONCERNING THE OLD BLACK CROSSING-SWEEPER WHO LEFT £800 TO MISS WAITHMAN.

"YES, sir, I knew him for many year, though I never spoke to him in all my life. He was a stoutish, thickset man, about my build, and used to walk with his broom up and down — so."

Here "Old John" imitated the halt and stoop of an old man.

"He used to touch his hat continually," he went on. "'Please remember the poor black man,' was his cry, never anything else. Oh yes, he made a great deal of money. People gave more then than they do now. Where they give one sixpence now, they *used* to give ten. It's just the same by our calling. Lived humbly? Yes, I think he did; at all events, he seemed to do so when he was on his crossing. He got plenty of odds-and-ends from the corner *there*—Alderman Waithman's, I mean; he was a very sober, quiet sort of man. No, sir, nothing peculiar in his dress. Some blacks are peculiar in their dress; but he would wear anything he could get give him. They used to call him Romeo, I think. Curous name, sir; but the best man I ever knew was called Romeo, and he was a black.

"The crossing-sweeper had his regular customers; he knew their times, and was there to the moment. Oh yes, he was always. Hail, rain, or snow, he never missed. I don't know how long he had the crossing. I remember him ever since I was a postboy in Doctors' Commons; I knew him when I lived in Holborn, and I haven't been away from this neighbourhood since 1809.

"No, sir, there's no doubt about his leaving the money to Miss Waithman. Everybody round about here knows it; just ask them, sir. Miss Waithman (an old maid she were, sir) used to be very kind to him. He used to sweep from Alderman Waithman's (it's the *Sunday Times* now) across to the opposite side of the way.

"When he died, an old man, as had been a soldier, took possession of the crossing. How did he get it? Why, I say, he *took it*. First come, first sarved, sir; that's their way. They never sell crossings. Sometimes (for a lark) they shift, and then one stands treat—a gallon of beer, or something of that sort. The perlice interfered with the soldier—you know the sweepers is all forced to go if the perlice interfere; now with us, sir, we are licensed, and they can't make us move on. They interfered, I say, with the old soldier, because he used to get so drunk. Why, at a public-house close at hand, he would spent seven, eight, and ten shillings on a night, three or four days together. He used to gather so many blackguards round the crossing, they were forced to move him at last. A young man has got it now; he has had it three year. He is not always here, sometimes away for a week at a stretch; but, you see, he knows the best times to come, and then he is *sure* to be here. The little boys come with their brooms now and then, but the perlice always drive them away."

3. THE ABLE-BODIED IRISH CROSSING-SWEEPER.

THE OLD IRISH CROSSING-SWEEPER.

THIS man, a native of "County Corruk," has been in England only two years and a half. He wears a close-fitting black cloth cap over a shock of reddish hair; round his neck he has a coloured cotton kerchief, of the sort advertised as "Imitation Silk." His black coat is much torn, and his broom is at present remarkably stumpy. He waits quietly at the post opposite St. ——'s Church, to receive whatever is offered him. He is unassuming enough in his manner, and, as will be seen, not even bearing any malice against his two enemies, "The Swatestuff Man" and "The Switzer." He says:—

"I've been at this crossin' near upon two year. Whin I first come over to England (about two years and a half ago), I wint a haymakin', but, you see, I couldn't get any work; and afther thrampin' about a good bit, why my eyesight gettin' very wake, and I not knowin' what to do, I took this crossin'.

"How did I get it?—Will, sir, I wint walkin' about and saw it, and nobody on it. So one mornin' I brought a broom wid me and stood here. Yes, sir, I *was* intherfered wid. The man with one arm—a Switzer they calls him—he had had the crossin' on Sundays for a long while gone, and he didn't like my bein' here at all, at all. 'B——y Irish' he used to call me, and other scandalizin' names; and he and the swatestuff man opposite, who was a friend of his, tried everythin' they could to git me off the crossin'. But sure I niver harrumed them at all, at all.

"Yis, sir, I have my rigular custhomers: there's Mr. ——, he's gone to Sydenham; he's very kind, sir. He gives me a shilling a-month. He left worrud with the sarvint while he's away to give me a shilling on the first day in every month. He gave me a letter to the Eye Hospital, in Goulden Square, because of the wakeness of my eyesight; but they'll niver cure it at all, at all, sir, for wake eyes runs in my family. My sister, sir, has wake eyes; she is working at Croydon.

"Oh no, indeed, and it isn't the gintlefolks that thry to get me off the crossin'; they'd rather shupport me, sir. But the poor payple it is that don't like me.

"Eighteenpince I've made in a day, and more: niver more than two shillings, and sometimes not sixpence. Will, sir, I am not like the others; I don't run afther the ladies and gintlemen—I don't persevere. Yesterday I took sixpence, by chance, for takin' some luggage for a lady. The day before yesterday I took three ha'pence; but I think I got somethin' else for a bit of worruk thin.

"Yes, winther is better than summer. I don't know which people is the most liberal. Sure, sir, I don't think there's much difference. Oh yes, sir, young men are very liberal sometimes, and so are young ladies. Perhaps old ladies or old gintlemen give the most at a time,—sometimes sixpence,—perhaps more; but thin, sir, you don't git anything else for a long time.

"The boy-sweepers annoy me very much, indeed; they use such scandalizin' worruds to me, and throw dirrut, they do. They know whin the police is out of the way, so I git no purtiction.

"Sure, sir, and I think it right that ivery person should attind the worruship to which he belongs. I am a Catholic, sir, and attind mass at St. Pathrick's, near St. Giles's, ivery Sunday, and I thry to be at confission wonst a month.

"Whin first I took to the crossin', I was rather irrigular; but that was because of the Switzer man—that's the man with the one arm; he used to say he would lock me up, and iverything. But I have been rigular since.

"I come in the morruning just before eight, in time to catch the gintlefolks going into prayers; and I leave at half-past seven to eight at night. I wait so late because I have to bring a gintleman wather for his flowers, and that I do the last thing.

"I live, sir, in —— lane, behind St. Giles's Church, in the first-flure front, sir; and I pay one-and-threepence a-week. There are three bids in the room. In one bid, a man, his wife, his mother, and their little girl—Julia, they call her—sleep; in the other bid, there's a man and his wife and child. Yes, I am single, and have the third bid to myself. I come from County Corruk; the others in the room are all Irish, and come from County Corruk too. They sill fruit in the sthreet; in the winther they sill onions, and sometimes oranges.

"There a Scotch gintleman as brings me my breakfast every morning; indeed, yes, and he brings it himself, he does. He has gone to Scotland now, but he will be back in a week. He brings me some bread and mate, and a pinny for a half pint of beer, sir. He has done it almost all the time I have been here.

"The Switzer man, sir, took out boards for the *Polytickner*, or some place like that. He got fifteen shillings a-week, and used to come here on Sundays. Yes, sir, *I* come here on Sundays; but it is not better than other days. Some people says to me, they would rather I went to church; but I tells 'em I do; and sure, sir, afther mass, there's no harrum in a little sweepin' between whiles.

"No, sir, there's not a crossin'-sweeper in Ould Ireland. Well, sir, I niver was in Dublin; but I've been in Corruk, sir, and they don't have any crossin' sweepers there.

"Whin I git home of a night, sir, I am very tired; but I always offer up my devotions before sleepin'. Ah, sir, I should niver have swipt crossin's if a friend of mine hadn't died; he was collector of tolls in Clarnykilts, and I used to be with him. He lost his situation, and so I came to England.

"The Switzer man, I think he used to sweep at eight o'clock, just as the people were goin' to prayers. Oh, sir, he was always blackgeyardin' me. 'Go back to your own counthry,' says he—a furriner himsilf, too.

"Will, yes sir, I do wish for bad weather; a good wit day, and a dry day afther, is the best.

"Sure and they can't turn me off my crossin' only for my bad conduct, and I thry to be quiet and take no notice.

"Yis, sir, I have always been a church-goer, and I am seventy-five. I used to have some good rigular customers, but somehow I haven't seen anythin' of them for this last twelve-month. Ah! it's in the betther neighbourhoods that people give rigularly. I niver get any broken victuals. Three-and-sixpence is the outside of my earnings, taking one week with the other.

"What is the laste I ever took? Will, sir, for three days I haven't taken a farthin'. The worust week I iver had was thirteen or fourteen pence altogether; the best week I iver had was the winter before last—that harrud winter, sir, I remember takin' seven shillings thin; but the man at Portman-square makes the most.

"Well, sir, I belave there's some of every nation in the world as sweeps crossin's in London."

THE FEMALE IRISH CROSSING-SWEEPER.

IN a street not far from Gordon-square and the New-road, I found this poor old woman resting from her daily labour. She was sitting on the stone ledge of the iron railings at the corner of the street, huddled up in the way seemingly natural to old Irishwomen, her broom hidden as much as possible under her petticoats. Her shawl was as tidy as possible for its age. She was sixty-seven years, and had buried two husbands and five children, fractured her ribs, and injured her groin, and had nothing left to comfort her but her crossing, her ha'porth of snuff, and her "drop of biled wather," by which name she indicated her "tay."

She was very civil and intelligent, and answered my inquiries very readily, and with rather less circumlocution than the Irish generally display. She seemed much hurt at the closing of the Old St. Pancras churchyard. "They buried my child where they'll never bury me, sir," she cried.

She told the story of her accident with many involuntary movements of her hand towards the injured part, and took a sparing pinch of snuff from a little black snuff-box, inlaid with mother-of-pearl, for which she said she had given a penny. She proceeded thus:—"I'm an Irishwoman, sir, and it's from Kinsale I come, twelve miles beyant Corruk, to the left-hand side, a seaport town, and a great place for fish. It's fifty years the sixteenth of last June since I came in St. Giles's parish, and there my ildest child wint did. Buried she is in Ould St. Pancras churchyarrud, where they'll never bury me, sir, for they've done away with burying in churchyarruds. That girl was forty-one year of age the seventeenth of last February, born in Stratford, below Bow, in Essex. Ah! I was comfortable there; I lived there three year and abouts. I was in sarvice at Mr. ——'s, a Frinch gintleman he was, and kept a school, where they taught Frinch and English both; but I dare say they are all gone did years ago. He was a very ould gintleman, and so was his lady; she was a North-of-England lady, but very stout, and had no children but a son and daughter. I was quite young when my aunt brought me over. My uncle was three year here before my aunt, and he died at Whitechapel. I was bechuxt sixteen and seventeen when I come over, and I reckon meself at sixty-seven come next Christmas, as well as I can guess. I never had a mother, sir; she died when I was only six months old. My father, sir, was maltster to Mr. Walker the distiller, in Corruk. Ah! indeed, and my father was well to do wonst. Early or late, wit or dry, he had a guinea a-week, but he worruked day and night; he was to attind to the corun, and he would have four min, or five or six, undther him, according as busy they might be. My father has been did four-and-twinty year, and I wouldn't know a crature if I wint home. Father come over, sir, and wanted me to go back very bad, but I wouldn't. I was married thin, and had buried some of my childer in St. Pancras; and for what should I lave England?

"Oh! sir, I buried three in eight months, —two sons and their father. My husband was two year and tin months keeping his bed; he has been did fifteen years to the eighth of last March; but I've been married again.

"Siven childer I've had, and ounly two alive, and they've got enough to do to manage for thimsilves. The boy, he follers the market, and my daughter, she is along with her husband; sure he sills in the streets, sir. I see very little of her,—she lives over in the Borough.

"I think I'll be afther going down to Kent, beyant Maidstone, a hop-picking, if I can git as much as to take me down the road.

"My daughter's husband and me don't agree, so I'm bitter not to see them.

"Ivery day, sir—ivery day in the week I am here. This morunning I was here at eight —that was earlier than usual, but I came out because I had not broke my fast with anything but a drop of wather, and that I had two tumblers of it from the house at the corrunner. I intind to go home and take two hirrings, and have a drop of biled wather—tay, I mane, sir.

"I come here at about half-past nine to half-past ten, but I'm gitting a very bad leg. I goes home about five or six.

"I have taken two ha'pennies this morning; thruppence I took yisterday; the day before I took, I think, fourpence ha'penny; that was my taking on Monday; on Sunday I mustered a shilling; on Saturday—I declare, sir, I forgit —fourpence or thruppence, I suppose, but my frinds is out of town very much. They gives me a penny rigular every Sunday, or a ha'penny, and some tuppence. Of a Sunday in the good time I may take eighteenpence or sixteenpence.

"Oh, yes, of Christmas it's better, it is— four or five shillings on a Christmas-day.

"On the Monday fortnight, before last Christmas twelvemonth, I had two ribs broke, and one fractured, and my grine (groin) bone injured. Oh! the pains that I feel even now, sir. I lived then in Phillip's-gardens, up there in the New-road. The policeman took me to the hospital. It was eighteen days I niver got off my bid. I came out in the morunning of the Christmas-day. I hild on by the railings as I wint along, and I thought I niver should git home. How I was knocked down was by a cart; I had my eye bad thin, the lift one, and had a cloth over it. I was just comin' out of the archway of the courrut (close by the beer-shop) away from Mr. ——'s house, when crossing to the green-grocer's to git two pound of praties for my supper, I didn't see the cart comin'. I was knocked down by the shaft. They called, and they called, and he wouldn't stop, and it wint over me, it did. It was loaded with cloth; I don't know if it wasn't a Shoolbred's cart, but the boy said to the hospital-doctor and to the policeman it was heavily loaded. The boy gave me a shilling, and that was all the money I received. For a twelvemonth I couldn't hardly walk.

"On that Christmas-day I took four-and-tinpence, but I owed it all for rint and things; and I'm sure it's a good man that let me run it the score.

"Is it a shillin' I iver git? Well, thin, sir, there's one gintleman, but he's out of town — Sir George Hewitt — niver passes without givin me a shillin'.

"I have taken one-and-ninepence on a Sunday, and I've taken two shillin's. Upon my sowl, I've often gone home with three ha'pence and tuppence. For this month past, put ivery day together, I haven't taken three shilling a-week.

"I wear two brooms out in a week in bad wither, and thin p'rhaps I take four to five shillin', Sunday included; but for the three year since here I've been on this crossin', I niver took tin shillin', sir, niver.

"Yes, there was a man here before me: he had bad eyes, and he was obligated to lave and go into the worrukhouse; he lost the sight of one of his eyes when he came back again. I knew him sweepin' here a long time. When he come back, I said, 'Father,' says I, 'I wint on your crossin'.' 'Ah,' says he, 'you've got a bad crossin', poor woman; I wouldn't go on it again, I wouldn't;' and I niver seen him since. I don't know whether he is living or not.

"A wit day makes fourpence or fippence difference sometimes.

"Indeed, I have heard of crossin'-sweepers makin' so much and so much. I hear people talkin' about it, but, for my parrut, I wouldn't give heed to what they say. In Oxford-street, towards the Parruks, there was a man, years ago, they say, by all accounts left a dale of money.

"I am niver annoyed by boys. I don't spake to none of them. I was in sarvice till I got married, thin I used to sill fruit through Kentish Town, Highgate, and Hampstead; but I niver sould in the streets, sir, and had my rigular customers like any greengrocer. I had a good connixion, I had; but, by gitting old and feeble, and sick, and not being able to go about, I was forrussed to give it up, I was. I couldn't carry twelve pound upon my hid — no, not if I was to get a sov'rin a-day for it, now.

"I niver lave the crossin'. I haven't got a frind; nor a day's pleasure I niver take.

"Oh, yes, sir, I must have a pinch — this is my snuff-box. I take a ha'porth a-day, and that's the only comforrut I've got — that and a cup of tay; for I can't dthrink cocoa or coffee-tay.

"My feeding is a bit of brid and butther. I haven't bought a bit of mate these three months. I used to git two penn'orth of bones and mate at Mrs. Baker's, down there; but mate is so dear, that they don't have 'em now, and it's ashamed I am of botherin' thim so often. I frequintly have a hirrin'. Oh dear! no sir. Wather is my dthrink. I can't afforrud no beer. Sometimes I have a penn'orth of gin and could water, and I find it do me a worruld of good. Sometimes I git enough to eat, but lately, indeed, I can't git that. I declare I don't know which people give the most; the gintlemen give me more in wit wither, for then the ladies, you see, can't let their dresses out of their hands.

"I am a Catholic, sir. I go to St. Pathrick's sometimes, or I go to Gordon-street Churruch. I don't care which I go to — it's all the same to me; but I haven't been to churruch for months. I've nothing to charge mysilf wid; and, indeed, I haven't been to confission for some year.

"Tradespeople are very kind, indeed they are.

"Yes, I think I'll go to Kint a hop-pickin'; and as for my crossin', I lave it, sir, just as it is. I go five miles beyant Maidstone. I worruked fifteen years at Mr. ——; he was a pole-puller and binsman in the hop-ground.

"I've not been down there since the year before last. I was too poorly after that accident. We make about eighteenpence, two shillin's, or one shillin', 'cording as the hops is good. No lodging nor fire to pay; and we git plinty of good milk chape there. I manage thin to save a little money to hilp us in the winther.

"I live in —— street, Siven Dials; but I'm going to lave my son — we can't agree. We live in the two-pair back. I pay nothing a-week, only bring home ivery ha'penny to hilp thim. Sometimes I spind a pinny or tuppence out on mysilf.

"My son is doin' very badly. He sills fruit in the sthreets; but he's niver been used to it before; and he has pains in his limbs with so much walking. He has no connixion, and with the sthrawbirries now he's forrused to walk about of a night as well as a day, for they won't keep till the morrunning; they all go mouldy and bad. My son has been used to the bricklaying, sir: he can lit in a stove or a copper, or do a bit of plasther or lath, or the like. His wife is a very just, clane, sober woman, and he has got three good childer; there is Catherine, who is named afther me, she is nearly five; Illen, two years and six months, named after her mother; and Margaret, the baby, six months ould — and she is called afther my daughter, who is did."

4. The Occasional Crossing-Sweepers.

The Sunday Crossing-Sweeper.

"I'm a Sunday crossing-sweeper," said an oyster-stall keeper, in answer to my inquiries. "I mean by that, I only sweep a crossing on a Sunday. I pitch in the Lorrimore-road, Newington, with a few oysters on week-days, and I does jobs for the people about there, sich as cleaning a few knives and forks, or shoes and boots, and windows. I've been in the habit of sweeping a crossing about four or five years.

"I never knowed my father, he died when I was a baby. He was a 'terpreter, and spoke seven different languages. My father used to go with Bonaparte's army, and used to 'terpret for him. He died in the South of France. I had a brother, but he died quite a child, and my mother supported me and a sister by being cook in a gentleman's family: we was put out to nurse. My mother couldn't afford to put me to school, and so I can't read nor write. I'm forty-one years old.

"The fust work I ever did was being boy at a pork-butcher's. I used to take out the meat wot was ordered. At last my master got broke up, and I was discharged from my place, and I took to sellin' a few sprats. I had no thoughts of taking to a crossing then. I was ten year old. I remember I give two shillings for a 'shallow;' that's a flat basket with two handles; they put 'em a top of 'well-baskets,' them as can carry a good load. A well-basket's almost like a coffin; it's a long un like a shallow, on'y it's a good deal deeper—about as deep as a washin' tub. I done very fair with my sprats till they got dear and come up very small, so then I was obliged to get a few plaice, and then I got a few baked 'taters and sold them. I hadn't money enough to buy a tin—I could a got one for eight shillings—so I put 'em in a cross-handle basket, and carried 'em round the streets, and into public-houses, and cried "Baked taters, all hot!" I used only to do this of a night, and it brought me about four or five shillings a-week. I used to fill up the day by going round to gentlemen's houses where I was known, to run for errands and clean knives and boots, and that brought me sich a thing as four shillings a-week more altogether.

"I never had no idea then of sweeping a crossing of a Sunday; but at last I was obliged to push to it. I kept on like this for many years, and at last a gentleman named Mr. Jackson promised to buy me a tin, but he died. My mother went blind through a blight; that was the cause of my fust going out to work, and so I had to keep her; but I didn't mind that: I thought it was my duty so to do.

"About ten years ago I got married; my wife used to go out washing and ironing. I thought two of us would get on better than one, and she didn't mind helpin' me to keep my mother, for I was determined my mother shouldn't go into the workhouse so long as I could help it.

"A year or two after I got married, I found I must do something more to help to keep home, and then I fust thought of sweepin' a crossing on Sundays; so I bought a heath broom for twopence-ha'penny, and I pitched agin' the Canterbury Arms, Kennington; it was between a baker's shop and a public-house and butcher's; they told me they'd all give me something if I'd sweep the crossing reg'lar.

"The best places is in front of chapels and churches, 'cause you can take more money in front of a church or a chapel than wot you can in a private road, 'cos they look at it more, and a good many thinks when you sweeps in front of a public-house that you go and spend your money inside in waste.

"The first Sunday I went at it, I took eighteenpence. I began at nine o'clock in the morning and stopped till four in the afternoon. The publican give fourpence, and the baker sixpence, and the butcher threepence, so that altogether I got above a half-crown. I stopped at this crossing a year, and I always knocked up about two shillings or a half-crown on the Sunday. I very seldom got anythink from the ladies; it was most all give by the gentlemen. Little children used sometimes to give me ha'pence, but it was when their father give it to 'em; the little children like to do that sort of thing.

"The way I come to leave this crossing was this here: the road was being repaired, and they shot down a lot of stones, so then I couldn't sweep no crossing. I looked out for another place, and I went opposite the Duke of Sutherland public-house in the Lorrimore-road. I swept there one Sunday, and I got about one-and-sixpence. While I was sweeping this crossing, a gentleman comes up to me, and he axes me if I ever goes to chapel or church; and I tells him, 'Yes;' I goes to church, wot I'd been brought up to; and then he says, 'You let me see you at St. Michael's Church, Brixton, and I'll 'courage you, and you'll do better if you come up and sweep in front there of a Sunday instead of where you are; you'll be sure to get more money, and get better 'couraged. It don't matter what you do,' he says, 'as long as it brings you in a honest crust; anythink's better than thieving.' And then the gent gives me sixpence and goes away.

"As soon as he'd gone I started off to his church, and got there just after the people was all in. I left my broom in the churchyard. When I got inside the church, I could see him a-sitten jest agin the communion table, so I walks to the free seats and sets down right close again the communion table myself, for his pew was on my right, and he saw me directly and looked and smiled at me. As he was coming out of the church he says, says he, 'As long as I live, if you comes here on a Sunday reg'lar I shall always 'courage you.'

"The next Sunday I went up to the church and swept the crossing, and he see me there, but he didn't give me nothink till the church was over, and then he gave me a shilling, and the other people give me about one-and-sixpence; so I got about two-and-sixpence altogether, and I thought that was a good beginning.

"The next Sunday the gen'elman was ill, but he didn't forget me. He sent me sixpence by his servant, and I got from the other people about two shillings more. I never see that gentleman, after for he died on the Saturday. His wife sent for me on the Sunday; she was ill a-bed, and I see one of the daughters, and she gave me sixpence, and said I was to be there on Monday morning. I went on the Monday, and the lady was much worse, and I see the daughter again. She gave me a couple of shirts, and told me to come on the Friday, and when I went on that day I found the old lady was dead. The daughter gave me a coat, and trousers, and waistcoat.

"After the daughters had buried the father and mother they moved. I kept on sweeping at the church, till at last things got so bad that I come away, for nobody give me nothink. The houses about there was so damp that people wouldn't live in 'em.

"So then I come up into Lorrimore-road, and there I've been ever since. I don't get on wonderful well there. Sometimes I don't get above sixpence all day, but it's mostly a shilling or so. The most I've took is about one-and-sixpence. The reason why I stop there is, because I'm known there, you see. I stands there all the week selling nighsters, and the people about there give me a good many jobs. Besides, the road is rather bad there, and they like to have a clean crossing of a Sunday.

"I don't get any more money in the winter (though it's muddier) than I do in the summer; the reason is, 'cause there isn't so many people stirring about in the winter as there is in the summer.

"One broom will carry me over three Sundays, and I gives twopence-ha'penny a-piece for 'em. Sometimes the people brings me out at my crossing—'specially in cold weather—a mug of hot tea and some bread and butter, or a bit of meat. I don't know any other crossing-sweeper; I never 'sociates with nobody. I always keeps my own counsel, and likes my own company the best.

"My wife's been dead five months, and my mother six months; but I've got a little boy seven year old; he stops at school all day till I go home at night, and then I fetches him home. I mean to do something better with him than give him a broom: a good many people would set him on a crossing; but I mean to keep him at school. I want to see him read and write well, because he'll suit for a place then.

"There's some art in sweeping a crossing even. That is, you mustn't sweep too hard, 'cos if you do, you wears a hole right in the road, and then the water hangs in it. It's the same as sweeping a path; if you sweeps too hard you wears up the stones.

"To do it properly, you must put the end of the broom-handle in the palm of your right hand, and lay hold of it with your left, about half way down; then you takes half your crossing, and sweeps on one side till you gets over the road; then you turns round and comes back doing the other half. Some people holds the broom before 'em, and keeps swaying it back-'ards and for'ards to sweep the width of the crossing all in one stroke, but that ain't sich a good plan, 'cause you're apt to splash people that's coming by; and besides, it wears the road in holes and wears out the broom so quick. I always use my broom steady. I never splash nobody.

"I never tried myself, but I've seen some crossin'-sweepers as could do all manner of things in mud, sich as diamonds, and stars, and the moon, and letters of the alphabet; and once in Oxford-street I see our Saviour on his cross in mud, and it was done well, too. The figure wasn't done with the broom, it was done with a pointed piece of stick; it was a boy as I see doin' it, about fifteen. He didn't seem to take much money while I was a-looking at him.

"I don't think I should a took to crossin' sweeping if I hadn't got married; but when I'd got a couple of children (for I've had a girl die; if she'd lived she'd a been eight year old now,) I found I must do a somethin', and so I took to the broom."

B. *The Afflicted Crossing-Sweepers.*

THE WOODEN-LEGGED SWEEPER.

THIS man lives up a little court running out of a wide, second-rate street. It is a small court, consisting of some half-dozen houses, all of them what are called by courtesy "private."

I inquired at No. 3 for John ——; "The first-floor back, if you please, sir;" and to the first-floor back I went.

Here I was answered by a good-looking and intelligent young woman, with a baby, who said her husband had not yet come home, but would I walk in and wait? I did so; and found myself in a very small, close room, with a little furniture, which the man called "his few sticks," and presently discovered another child—a little girl. The girl was very shy in her manner, being only two years and two months old, and as her mother said, very ailing from the difficulty of cutting her teeth, though the true cause seemed to be want of proper nourishment and fresh air. The baby was a boy—a fine, cheerful, good-tempered little fellow, but rather pale, and with an unnaturally large forehead. The mantelpiece of the room was filled with little ornaments of various sorts, such as bead-baskets, and over them hung a series of black profiles—not portraits of either the crossing-sweeper or any of his family, but an odd lot of heads, which had lost their owners many a year, and served, in company with a little red, green, and yellow scripture-piece, to keep the wall from looking bare. Over the door (inside the room) was nailed a horse-shoe, which, the wife told me, had been put there by her husband, for luck.

A bed, two deal tables, a couple of boxes, and three chairs, formed the entire furniture of the room, and nearly filled it. On the window-frame was hung a small shaving-glass; and on the two boxes stood a wicker-work apology for a perambulator, in which I learnt the poor crippled man took out his only daughter at half-past four in the morning.

"If some people was to see that, sir," said the sweeper, when he entered and saw me looking at it, "they would, and in fact they *do* say, 'Why, you can't be in want.' Ah! little they know how we starved and pinched ourselves before we could get it."

There was a fire in the room, notwithstanding the day was very hot; but the window was wide open, and the place tolerably ventilated, though oppressive. I have been in many poor people's "places," but never remember one so poor in its appointments and yet so free from effluvia.

The crossing-sweeper himself was a very civil sort of man, and in answer to my inquiries said:—

"I know that I do as I ought to, and so I don't feel hurt at standing at my crossing. I have been there four years. I found the place vacant. My wife, though she looks very well, will never be able to do any hard work; so we sold our mangle, and I took to the crossing: but we're not in debt, and nobody can't say nothing to us. I like to go along the streets free of such remarks as is made by people to whom you owes money. I had a mangle in —— Yard, but through my wife's weakness I was forced to part with it. I was on the crossing a short time before that, for I knew that if I parted with my mangle and things before I knew whether I could get a living at the crossing I couldn't get my mangle back again.

"We sold the mangle only for a sovereign, and we gave two-pound-ten for it; we sold it to the same man that we bought it of. About six months ago I managed for to screw and save enough to buy that little wicker chaise, for I can't carry the children because of my one leg, and of course the mother can't carry them both out together. There was a man had the crossing I've got; he died three or four years before I took it; but he didn't depend on the crossing—he did things for the tradespeople about, such as carpet-beating, messages, and so on.

"When I first took the crossing I did very well. It happened to be a very nasty, dirty season, and I took a good deal of money. Sweepers are not always civil, sir.

"I wish I had gone to one of the squares, though. But I think after —— street is paved with stone I shall do better. I am certain I never taste a bit of meat from one week's end to the other. The best day I ever made was five-and-sixpence or six shillings; it was the winter before last. If you remember, the snow laid very thick on the ground, and the sudden thaw made walking so uncomfortable, that I did very well. I have taken as little as sixpence, fourpence, and even twopence. Last Thursday I took two ha'pence all day. Take one week with the other, seven or eight shillings is the very outside.

"I don't know how it is, but some people who used to give me a penny, don't now. The boys who come in wet weather earn a great deal more than I do. I once lost a good chance, sir, at the corner of the street leading to Cavendish-square. There's a bank, and they pay a man seven shillings a-week to sweep the crossing: a butcher in Oxford Market spoke for me; but when I went up, it unfortunately turned out that I was not fit, from the loss of my leg. The last man they had there they were obliged to turn away—he was so given to drink.

"I think there are some rich crossing-sweepers in the city, about the Exchange; but you won't find them now during this dry weather, except in by-places. In wet weather, there are two or three boys who sweep near my crossing, and take all my earnings away. There's a great able-bodied man besides—a fellow strong enough to follow the plough. I said to the policeman, 'Now, ain't this a shame? and the policeman said, 'Well, *he* must get his living as well as you.' I'm always civil to the police, and they're always civil to me—in fact, I think sometimes I'm too civil—I'm not rough enough with people.

"You soon tell whether to have any hopes of people coming across. I can tell a gentleman directly I see him.

"Where I stand, sir, I could get people in trouble everlasting; there's all sorts of thieving going on. I saw the other day two or three respectable persons take a purse out of an old lady's pocket before the baker's shop at the corner; but I can't say a word, or they would come and throw me into the road. If a gentleman gives me sixpence, he don't give me any more for three weeks or a month; but I don't think I've more than three or four gentlemen as gives me that. Well, you can scarcely tell the gentleman from the clerk, the clerks are such great swells now.

"Lawyers themselves dress very plain; those great men who don't come every day, because they've clerks to do their business for them, they give most. People hardly ever stop to speak unless it is to ask you where places are —you might be occupied at that all day. I manage to pay my rent out of what I take on Sunday, but not lately—this weather religious people go pleasuring.

"No, I don't go now—the fact is, I'd like to go to church, if I could, but when I come home I am tired; but I've got books here, and they do as well, sir. I read a little and write a little.

"I lost my leg through a swelling—there

was no chloroform then. I was in the hospital three years and a half, and was about fifteen or sixteen when I had it off. I always feel the sensation of the foot, and more so at change of weather. I feel my toes moving about, and everything; sometimes, it's just as if the calf of my leg was itching. I *feel* the rain coming; when I see a cloud coming my leg shoots, and I know we shall have rain.

"My mother was a laundress—my father has been dead nineteen years my last birthday. My mother was subject to fits, so I was forced to stop at home to take care of the business.

"I don't want to get on better, but I always think, if sickness or anything comes on——

"I am at my crossing at half-past eight; at half-past eleven I come home to dinner. I go back at one or two till seven.

"Sometimes I mind horses and carts, but the boys get all that business. One of these little customers got sixpence the other day for only opening the door of a cab. I don't know how it is they let these little boys be about; if I was the police, I wouldn't allow it.

"I think it's a blessing, having children—(referring to his little girl)—that child wants the gravy of meat, or an egg beaten up, but she can't get it. I take her out every morning round Euston-square and those open places. I get out about half-past four. It is early, but if it benefits her, that's no odds."

ONE-LEGGED SWEEPER AT CHANCERY-LANE.

"I DON'T know what induced me to take that crossing, except it was that no one was there, and the traffic was so good—fact is, the traffic is too good, and people won't stop as they cross over, they're very glad to get out of the way of the cabs and the omnibuses.

"Tradespeople never give me anything—not even a bit of bread. The only thing I get is a few cuttings, such as crusts of sandwiches and remains of cheese, from the public-house at the corner of the court. The tradespeople are as distant to me now as they were when I came, but if I should pitch up a tale I should soon get acquainted with them.

"We have lived in this lodging two years and a half, and we pay one-and-ninepence a-week, as you may see from the rent-book, and that I manage to earn on Sundays. We owe four weeks now, and, thank God, it's no more.

"I was born, sir, in —— street, Berkeley-square, at Lord ———'s house, when my mother was minding the house. I have been used to London all my life, but not to this part; I have always been at the west-end, which is what I call the best end.

"I did not like the idea of crossing-sweeping at first, till I reasoned with myself, Why should I mind? I'm not doing any hurt to anybody. I don't care at all now—I know I'm doing what I ought to do.

"A man had better be killed out of the way than be disabled. It's not pleasant to know that my wife is suckling that great child, and, though she is so weakly, she can't get no meat.

"I've been knocked down twice, sir—both times by cabs. The last time it was a fortnight before I could get about comfortably again. The fool of a fellow was coming along, not looking at his horse, but talking to somebody on the cab-rank. The place was as free as this room, if he had only been looking before him. Nobody hollered till I was down, but plenty hollered then. Ah, I often notice such carelessness—it's really shameful. I don't think those 'shofuls' (Hansoms) should be allowed—the fact is, if the driver is not a tall man he can't see his horse's head.

"A nasty place is end of —— street: it narrows so suddenly. There's more confusion and more bother about it than any place in London. When two cabs gets in at once, one one way and one the other, there's sure to be a row to know which was the first in."

THE MOST SEVERELY-AFFLICTED OF ALL THE CROSSING-SWEEPERS.

PASSING the dreary portico of the Queen's Theatre, and turning to the right down Tottenham Mews, we came upon a flight of steps leading up to what is called "The Gallery," where an old man, gasping from the effects of a lung disease, and feebly polishing some old harness, proclaimed himself the father of the sweeper I was in search of, and ushered me into the room where he lay a-bed, having had a "very bad night."

The room itself was large and of a low pitch, stretching over some stables; it was very old and creaky (the sweeper called it "an old wilderness"), and contained, in addition to two turn-up bedsteads, that curious medley of articles which, in the course of years, an old and poor couple always manage to gather up. There was a large lithograph of a horse, dear to the remembrance of the old man from an indication of a dog in the corner. "The very spit of the one I had for years; it's a real portrait, sir, for Mr. Hanbart, the printer, met me one day and sketched him." There was an etching of Hogarth's in a black frame; a stuffed bird in a wooden case, with a glass before it; a piece of painted glass, hanging in a place of honour, but for which no name could be remembered, excepting that it was "of the old-fashioned sort." There were the odd remnants, too, of old china ornaments, but very little furniture; and, finally, a kitten.

The father, worn out and consumptive, had been groom to Lord Combermere. "I was with him, sir, when he took Bonyparte's house at Malmasong. I could have had a pension then if I'd a liked, but I was young and foolish, and had plenty of money, and we never know what we may come to."

The sweeper, although a middle-aged man,

had all the appearance of a boy—his raw-looking eyes, which he was always wiping with a piece of linen rag, gave him a forbidding expression, which his shapeless, short, bridgeless nose tended to increase. But his manners and habits were as simple in their character as those of a child; and he spoke of his father's being angry with him for not getting up before, as if he were a little boy talking of his nurse.

He walks, with great difficulty, by the help of a crutch; and the sight of his weak eyes, his withered limb, and his broken shoulder (his old helpless mother, and his gasping, almost inaudible father,) form a most painful subject for compassion.

The crossing-sweeper gave me, with no little meekness and some slight intelligence, the following statement:—

"I very seldom go out on a crossin' o' Sundays. I didn't do much good at it. I used to go to church of a Sunday—in fact, I do now when I'm well enough.

"It's fifteen year next January since I left Regent-street. I was there three years, and then I went on Sundays occasionally. Sometimes I used to get a shilling, but I have given it up now—it didn't answer; besides, a lady who was kind to me found me out, and said she wouldn't do any more for me if I went out on Sundays. She's been dead these three or four years now.

"When I was at Regent-street I might have made twelve shillings a-week, or something thereabout.

"I am seven-and-thirty the 26th day of last month, and I have been lame six-and-twenty years. My eyes have been bad ever since my birth. The scrofulous disease it was that lamed me—it come with a swelling on the knee, and the outside wound broke about the size of a crown piece, and a piece of bone come from it; then it gathered in the inside and at the top. I didn't go into the hospital then, but I was an out-patient, for the doctor said a close confined place wouldn't do me no good. He said that the seaside would, though; but my parents couldn't afford to send me, and that's how it is. I *did* go to Brighton and Margate nine years after my leg was bad, but it was too late then.

"I have been in Middlesex Hospital, with a broken collar-bone, when I was knocked down by a cab. I was in a fortnight there, and I was in again when I hurt my leg. I was sweeping my crossin' when the top came off my crutch. I fell back'ards, and my leg doubled under me. They had to carry me there.

"I went into the Middlesex Hospital for my eyes and leg. I was in a month, but they wouldn't keep me long, there's no cure for me.

"My leg is very painful, 'specially at change of weather. Sometimes I don't get an hour's sleep of a night—it was daylight this morning before I closed my eyes.

"I went on the crossing first because my parents couldn't keep me, not being able to keep theirselves. I thought it was the best thing I could do, but it's like all other things, it's got very bad now. I used to manage to rub along at first—the streets have got shockin' bad of late.

"To tell the truth, I was turned away from Regent-street by Mr. Cook, the furrier, corner of Argyle Street. I'll tell you as far as I was told. He called me into his passage one night, and said I must look out for another crossin', for a lady, who was a very good customer of his, refused to come while I was there; my heavy afflictions was such that she didn't like the look of me. I said, 'Very well;' but because I come there next day and the day after that, he got the policeman to turn me away. Certainly the policeman acted very kindly, but he said the gentleman wanted me removed, and I must find another crossing.

"Then I went down Charlotte-street, opposite Percy Chapel, at the corner of Windmill-street. After that I went to Wells-street, by getting permission of the doctor at the corner. He thought that it would be better for me than Charlotte-street, so he let me come.

"Ah! there ain't so many crossing-sweepers as there was; I think they've done away with a great many of them.

"When I first went to Wells-street, I did pretty well, because there was a dress-maker's at the corner, and I used to get a good deal from the carriages that stopped before the door. I used to take five or six shillings in a day then, and I don't take so much in a week now. I tell you what I made this week. I've made one-and-fourpence, but it's been so wet, and people are out of town; but, of course, it's not always alike—sometimes I get three-and-sixpence or four shillings. Some people gives me a sixpence or a fourpenny-bit; I reckons that all in.

"I am dreadful tired when I comes home of a night. Thank God my other leg's all right! I wish the t'other was as strong, but it never will be now.

"The police never try to turn me away; they're very friendly, they'll pass the time of day with me, or that, from knowing me so long in Oxford-street.

"My broom sometimes serves me a month; of course, they don't last long now it's showery weather. I give twopence-halfpenny a piece for 'em, or threepence.

"I don't know who gives me the most; my eyes are so bad I can't see. I think, though, upon an average, the gentlemen give most.

"Often I hear the children, as they are going by, ask their mothers for something to give to me; but they only say, 'Come along—come along!' It's very rare that they lets the children have a ha'penny to give me.

"My mother is seventy the week before next Christmas. She can't do much now; she does though go out on Wednesdays or Saturdays, but that's to people she's known for years who is attached to her. She does her work there just as she likes.

"Sometimes she gets a little washing—sometimes not. This week she had a little, and was forced to dry it indoors; but that makes 'em half dirty again.

"My father's breath is so bad that he can't do anything except little odd jobs for people down here; but they've got the knack now, a good many on 'em, of doin' their own.

"We have lived here fifteen years next September; it's a long time to live in such an old wilderness, but my old mother is a sort of woman as don't like movin' about, and I don't like it. Some people are everlasting on the move.

"When I'm not on my crossin' I sit poking at home, or make a job of mending my clothes. I mended these trousers in two or three places.

"It's all done by feel, sir. My mother says it's a good thing we've got our feeling at least, if we haven't got our eyesight."

THE NEGRO CROSSING-SWEEPER, WHO HAD LOST BOTH HIS LEGS.

THIS man sweeps a crossing in a principal and central thoroughfare when the weather is cold enough to let him walk; the colder the better, he says, as it "numbs his stumps like." He is unable to follow this occupation in warm weather, as his legs feel "just like corns," and he cannot walk more than a mile a day. Under these circumstances he takes to begging, which he thinks he has a perfect right to do, as he has been left destitute in what is to him almost a strange country, and has been denied what he terms "his rights." He generally sits while begging, dressed in a sailor shirt and trousers, with a black neckerchief round his neck, tied in the usual nautical knot. He places before him the placard which is given beneath, and never moves a muscle for the purpose of soliciting charity. He always appears scrupulously clean.

I went to see him at his home early one morning—in fact, at half-past eight, but he was not then up. I went again at nine, and found him prepared for my visit in a little parlour, in a dirty and rather disreputable alley running out of a court in a street near Brunswick-square. The negro's parlour was scantily furnished with two chairs, a turn-up bedstead, and a sea-chest. A few odds and ends of crockery stood on the sideboard, and a kettle was singing over a cheerful bit of fire. The little man was seated on a chair, with his stumps of legs sticking straight out. He showed some amount of intelligence in answering my questions. We were quite alone, for he sent his wife and child—the former a pleasant-looking "half-caste," and the latter the cheeriest little crowing, smiling "piccaninny" I have ever seen—he sent them out into the alley, while I conversed with himself.

His life is embittered by the idea that he has never yet had "his rights"—that the owners of the ship in which his legs were burnt off have not paid him his wages (of which, indeed, he says, he never received any but the five pounds which he had in advance before starting), and that he has been robbed of 42*l*. by a grocer in Glasgow. How true these statements may be it is almost impossible to say, but from what he says, some injustice seems to have been done him by the canny Scotchman, who refuses him his "pay," without which he is determined "never to leave the country."

"I was on that crossing," he said, "almost the whole of last winter. It was very cold, and I had nothing at all to do; so, as I passed there, I asked the gentleman at the baccer-shop, as well as the gentleman at the office, and I asked at the boot-shop, too, if they would let me sweep there. The policeman wanted to turn me away, but I went to the gentleman inside the office, and he told the policeman to leave me alone. The policeman said first, 'You must go away,' but I said, 'I couldn't do anything else, and he ought to think it a charity to let me stop.'

"I don't stop in London very long, though, at a time; I go to Glasgow, in Scotland, where the owners of the ship in which my legs were burnt off live. I served nine years in the merchant service and the navy. I was born in Kingston, in Jamaica; it is an English place, sir, so I am counted as not a foreigner. I'm different from them Lascars. I went to sea when I was only nine years old. The owners is in London who had that ship. I was cabin-boy; and after I had served my time I became cook, or when I couldn't get the place of cook I went before the mast. I went as head cook in 1851, in the *Madeira* barque; she used to be a West Indy trader, and to trade out when I belonged to her. We got down to 69 south of Cape Horn; and there we got almost froze and perished to death. That is the book what I sell."

The "Book" (as he calls it) consists of eight pages, printed on paper the size of a sheet of note paper; it is entitled—

"BRIEF SKETCH OF THE LIFE OF

EDWARD ALBERT!

A native of Kingston, Jamaica.

Showing the hardships he underwent and the sufferings he endured in having both legs amputated.

HULL:

W. HOWE, PRINTER."

It is embellished with a portrait of a black man, which has evidently been in its time a comic "nigger" of the Jim-Crow tobacco-paper kind, as is evidenced by the traces of a tobacco-pipe, which has been unskilfully erased.

The "Book" itself is concocted from an

LONDON LABOUR AND THE LONDON POOR. 491

affidavit made by Edward Albert before "P. Mackinlay, Esq., one of Her Majesty's Justices of the Peace for the country (so it is printed) of Lanark."

I have seen the affidavit, and it is almost identical with the statement in the "book," excepting in the matter of grammar, which has rather suffered on its road to Mr. Howe, the printer.

The following will give an idea of the matter of which it is composed:—

"In February, 1851, I engaged to serve as cook on board the barque *Madeira*, of Glasgow, Captain J. Douglas, on her voyage from Glasgow to California, thence to China, and thence home to a port of discharge in the United Kingdom. I signed articles, and delivered up my register-ticket as a British seaman, as required by law. I entered the service on board the said vessel, under the said engagement, and sailed with that vessel on the 18th of February, 1851. I discharged my duty as cook on board the said vessel, from the date of its having left the Clyde, until June the same year, in which month the vessed rounded Cape Horne, at that time my legs became frost bitten, and I became in consequence unfit for duty.

"In the course of the next day after my limbs became affected, the master of the vessel, and mate, took me to the ship's oven, in order, as they said, to cure me; the oven was hot at the time, a fowl that was roasting therein having been removed in order to make room for my feet, which was put into the oven; in consequence of the treatment, my feet burst through the intense swelling, and mortification ensued.

"The vessel called, six weeks after, at Valpariso, and I was there taken to an hospital, where I remained five months and a half. Both my legs were amputated three inches below my knees soon after I went to the hospital at Valpariso. I asked my master for my wages due to me, for my service on board the vessel, and demanded my register-ticket; when the captain told me I should not recover, that the vessel could not wait for me, and that I was a dead man, and that he could not discharge a dead man; and that he also said, that as I had no friends there to get my money, he would only put a little money into the hands of the consul, which would be applied in burying me. On being discharged from the hospital I called on the consul, and was informed by him that master had not left any money.

"I was afterwards taken on board one of her Majesty's ships, the *Driver*, Captain Charles Johnston, and landed at Portsmouth; from thence I got a passage to Glasgow, ware I remained three months. Upon supplication to the register-office for seamen, in London, my register-ticket has been forwarded to the Collector of Customs, Glasgow; and he his ready to deliver it to me upon obtaining the authority of the Justices of the Peace, and I recovered the same under the 22nd section of the General Merchant Seaman's Act. Declares I cannot write.
  "(Signed) DAVID MACKINLAY, J. P.

"The Justices having considered the foregoing information and declaration, finds that Edward Albert, therein named the last-register ticket, sought to be covered under circumstances which, so far as he was concerned, were unavoidable, and that no fraud was intended or committed by him in reference thereto, therefore authorised the Collector and Comptroller of Customs at the port of Glasgow to deliver to the said Edward Albert the register-ticket, sought to be recovered by him all in terms of 22nd section of the General Merchant Seamen's Act.
  "(Signed) DAVID MACKINLAY, J. P.
"Glasgow, Oct. 6th, 1852.
"Register Ticket, No. 512, 652, age 25 years."

"I could make a large book of my sufferings, sir, if I liked," he said, "and I will disgrace the owners of that ship as long as they don't give me what they owe me.

"I will never leave England or Scotland until I get my rights; but they says money makes money, and if I had money I could get it. If they would only give me what they owe me, I wouldn't ask anybody for a farthing, God knows, sir. I don't know why the master put my feet in the oven; he said to cure me: the agony of pain I was in was such, he said, that it must be done.

"The loss of my limbs is bad enough, but it's still worse when you can't get what is your rights, nor anything for the sweat that they worked out of me.

"After I went down to Glasgow for my money I opened a little coffee-house; it was called 'Uncle Tom's Cabin.' I did very well. The man who sold me tea and coffee said he would get me on, and I had better give my money to him to keep safe, and he used to put it away in a tin box which I had given four-and-sixpence for. He advertised my place in the papers, and I did a good business. I had the place open a month, when he kept all my savings — two-and-forty pounds — and shut up the place, and denied me of it, and I never got a farthing.

"I declare to you I can't describe the agony I felt when my legs were burst; I fainted away over and over again. There was four men came; I was lying in my hammock, and they moved the fowl that was roasting, and put my legs in the oven. There they held me for ten minutes. They said it would take the cold out; but after I came out the cold caught 'em again, and the next day they swole up as big round as a pillar, and burst, and then like water come out. No man but God knows what I have suffered and went through.

"By the order of the doctor at Valparaiso, the sick patients had to come out of the room I went into; the smell was so bad I couldn't bear it myself — it was all mortification — they had to use chloride o' zinc to keep the smell down. They tried to save one leg, but the mortification was getting up into my body. I got better after my legs were off.

"I was three months good before I could turn, or able to lift up my hand to my head. I was glad to move after that time, it was a regular relief to me; if it wasn't for good attendance, I should not have lived. You know they don't allow tobaccer in a hospital, but I had it; it was the only thing I cared for. The Reverend Mr. Armstrong used to bring me a pound a fortnight; he used to bring it regular. I never used to smoke before; they said I never should recover, but after I got the tobaccer it seemed to soothe me. I was five months and a half in that place.

"Admiral Moseley, of the *Thetis* frigate, sent me home; and the reason why he sent me home was, that after I came well, I called on Mr. Rouse, the English consul, and he sent me to the boarding-house, till such time as he could find a ship to send me home in. I was there about two months, and the boarding-master, Jan Pace, sent me to the consul.

"I used to get about a little, with two small crutches, and I also had a little cart before that, on three wheels; it was made by a man in the hospital. I used to lash myself down in it. That was the best thing I ever had—I could get about best in that.

"Well, I went to the consul, and when I went to him, he says, 'I can't pay your board; you must beg and pay for it;' so I went and told Jan Pace, and he said, 'If you had stopped here a hundred years, I would not turn you out;' and then I asked Pace to tell me where the Admiral lived. 'What do you want with him?' says he. I said, 'I think the Admiral must be higher than the consul.' Pace slapped me on the back. Says he, 'I'm glad to see you've got the pluck to complain to the Admiral.'

"I went down at nine o'clock the next morning, to see the Admiral. He said, 'Well, Prince Albert, how are you getting on?' So I told him I was getting on very bad; and then I told him all about the consul; and he said, as long as he stopped he would see me righted, and took me on board his ship, the *Thetis*; and he wrote to the consul, and said to me, 'If the consul sends for you, don't you go to him; tell him you have no legs to walk, and he must walk to you.'

"The consul wanted to send me back in a merchant ship, but the Admiral wouldn't have it, so I came in the *Driver*, one of Her Majesty's vessels. It was the 8th of May, 1852, when I got to Portsmouth.

"I stopped a little while—about a week—in Portsmouth. I went to the Admiral of the dockyard, and he told me I must go to the Lord Mayor of London. So I paid my passage to London, saw the Lord Mayor, who sent me to Mr. Yardley, the magistrate, and he advertised the case for me, and I got four pounds fifteen shillings, besides my passage to Glasgow. After I got there, I went to Mr. Symee a Custom-house officer (he'd been in the same ship with me to California); he said, 'Oh, gracious, Edward, how have you lost your limbs!' and I burst out a crying. I told him all about it. He advised me to go to the owner. I went there; but the policeman in London had put my name down as Robert Thorpe, which was the man I lodged with; so they denied me.

"I went to the shipping office, where they reckonised me; and I went to Mr. Symee again, and he told me to go before the Lord Mayor (a Lord Provost they call him in Scotland), and make an affidavit; and so, when they found my story was right, they sent to London for my seaman's ticket; but they couldn't do anything, because the captain was not there.

"When I got back to London, I commenced sweeping the crossin', sir. I only sweep it in the winter, because I can't stand in the summer. Oh, yes, I feel my feet still: it is just as if I had them sitting on the floor, now. I feel my toes moving, like as if I had 'em. I could count them, the whole ten, whenever I work my knees. I had a corn on one of my toes, and I can feel it still, particularly at the change of weather.

"Sometimes I might get two shillings a-day at my crossing, sometimes one shilling and sixpence, sometimes I don't take above sixpence. The most I ever made in one day was three shillings and sixpence, but that's very seldom.

"I am a very steady man. I don't drink what money I get; and if I had the means to get something to do, I'd keep off the streets.

"When I offered to go to the parish, they told me to go to Scotland, to spite the men who owed me my wages.

"Many people tell me I ought to go to my country; but I tell them it's very hard—I didn't come here without my legs—I lost them, as it were, in this country; but if I had lost them in my own country, I should have been better off. I should have gone down to the magistrate every Friday, and have taken my ten shillings.

"I went to the Merchant Seaman's Fund, and they said that those who got hurted before 1852 have been getting the funds, but those who were hurted after 1852 couldn't get nothing —it was stopped in '51, and the merchants wouldn't pay any more, and don't pay any more.

"That's scandalous, because, whether you're willing or not, you must pay two shillings a-month (one shilling a-month for the hospital fees, and one shilling a-month to the Merchant Seaman's Fund), out of your pay.

"I am married: my wife is the same colour as me, but an Englishwoman. I've been married two years. I married her from where she belonged, in Leeds. I couldn't get on to do anything without her. Sometimes she goes out and sells things—fruit, and so on—but she don't make much. With the assistance of my wife, if I could get my money, I would set up in the same line of business as before, in a coffee-shop. If I had three pounds I could do it: it took well in Scotland. I am not a common cook, either; I am a pastrycook. I used to make all the sorts of cakes they have in the shops. I bought the shapes, and tins, and things to make them proper.

"I'll tell you how I did—there was a kind of apparatus; it boils water and coffee, and the milk and the tea, in different departments; but you couldn't see the divisions—the pipes all ran into one tap, like. I've had a sixpence and a shilling for people to look at it: it cost me two pound ten.

"Even if I had a coffee-stall down at Coventgarden, I should do; and, besides, I understand the making of eel-soup. I have one child,—it is just three months and a week old. It is a boy, and we call it James Edward Albert. James is after my grandfather, who was a slave.

"I was a little boy when the slaves in Jamaica got their freedom: the people were very glad to be free; they do better since, I know, because some of them have got property, and send their children to school. There's more Christianity there than there is here. The public-house is close shut on Saturday night, and not opened till Monday morning. No fruit is allowed to be sold in the street. I am a Protestant. I don't know the name of the church, but I goes down to a new-built church, near King's-cross. I never go in, because of my legs; but I just go inside the door; and sometimes when I don't go, I read the Testament I've got here: in all my sickness I took care of that.

"There are a great many Irish in this place. I would like to get away from it, for it is a very disgraceful place,—it is an awful, awful place altogether. I haven't been in it very long, and I want to get out of it; it is not fit.

"I pay one-and-sixpence rent. If you don't go out and drink and carouse with them, they don't like it; they make use of bad language—they chaff me about my misfortune—they call me 'Cripple;' some says 'Uncle Tom,' and some says 'Nigger;' but I never takes no notice of 'em at all."

The following is a verbatim copy of the placard which the poor fellow places before him when he begs. He carries it, when not in use, in a little calico bag which hangs round his neck:—

KIND CHRISTIAN FRIENDS

THE UNFORTUNATE

EDWARD ALBERT

WAS COOK ON BOARD THE BARQUE MADEIRA OF GLASGOW CAPTAIN J. DOUGLAS IN FEBRUARY 1851 WHEN AFTER ROUNDING CAPE HORNE HE HAD HIS LEGS AND FEET FROST BITTEN WHEN in that state the master and mate put my Legs and Feet into the Oven as they said to cure me the Oven being hot at the time a fowl was roasting was took away to make room for my feet and legs in consequence of this my feet and legs swelled and burst——Mortification then Ensued after which my legs were amputated Three Inches below the knees soon after my entering the Hospital at Valpariso.

AS I HAVE NO OTHER MEANS TO GET A LIVELYHOOD BUT BY APPEALING TO

A GENEROUS PUBLIC

YOUR KIND DONATIONS WILL BE MOST THANKFULLY RECEIVED.

THE MAIMED IRISH CROSSING-SWEEPER.

HE stands at the corner of —— street, where the yellow omnibuses stop, and refers to himself every now and then as the "poor lame man." He has no especial mode of addressing the passers-by, except that of hobbling a step or two towards them and sweeping away an imaginary accumulation of mud. He has lost one leg (from the knee) by a fall from a scaffold, while working as a bricklayer's labourer in Wales, some six years ago; and speaks bitterly of the hard time he had of it when he first came to London, and hobbled about selling matches. He says he is thirty-six, but looks more than fifty; and his face has the ghastly expression of death. He wears the ordinary close cloth street-cap and corduroy trousers. Even during the warm weather he wears an upper coat—a rough thick garment, fit for the Arctic regions. It was very difficult to make him understand my object in getting information from him: he thought that he had nothing to tell, and laid great stress upon the fact of his never keeping " count" of anything.

He accounted for his miserably small income by stating that he was an invalid—"now and thin continually." He said—

"I can't say how long I have been on this crossin'; I think about five year. When I came on it there had been no one here before. No one interferes with me at all, at all. I niver hard of a crossin' bein' sould; but I don't know any other sweepers. I makes no fraydom with no one, and I always keeps my own mind.

"I dunno how much I earn a-day— p'rhaps I may git a shilling, and p'rhaps sixpence. I didn't git much yesterday (Sunday)—only sixpence. I was not out on Saturday; I was ill in bed, and I was at home on Friday. Indeed, I did not get much on Thursday, only tuppence ha'penny. The largest day? I dunno. Why, about a shilling. Well, sure, I might git as much as two shillings, if I got a shillin' from a lady. Some gintlemen are good—such a gintleman as you, now, might give me a shilling.

"Well, as to weather, I likes half dry and half wit; of course I wish for the bad wither. Every one must be glad of what brings good to him; and, there's one thing, I can't make the wither—I can't make a fine day nor a wit one. I don't think anybody would interfere with me; certainly, if I was a blaggya'rd I should not be left here; no, nor if I was a thief; but if any other man was to come on to my crossing, I can't say whether the police *would* interfere to protect me—p'rhaps they might.

"What is it I say to shabby people? Well, by J——, they're all shabby, I think. I don't see any difference; but what can I do? I can't insult thim, and I was niver insulted mysilf, since here I've been, nor, for the matter of that, ever had an angry worrud spoken to me.

"Well, sure, I dunno who's the most liberal; if I got a fourpinny bit from a moll I'd take it. Some of the ladies are very liberal; a good lady will give a sixpence. I never hard of sweepin' the mud back again; and as for the boys annoying me, I has no coleaguein' with boys, and they wouldn't be allowed to interfere with me — the police wouldn't allow it.

"After I came from Wales, where I was on one leg, selling matches, then it was I took to sweep the crossin'. A poor divil must put up with anything, good or bad. Well, I was a laborin' man, a bricklayer's labourer, and I've been away from Ireland these sixteen year. When I came from Ireland I went to Wales. I was there a long time; and the way I broke my leg was, I fell off a scaffold. I am not married; a lame man wouldn't get any woman to have him in London at all, at all. I don't know what age I am. I am not fifty, nor forty; I think about thirty-six. No, by J——, it's not mysilf that iver knew a well-off crossin'-sweeper. I don't dale in them at all.

"I got a dale of friends in London assist me (but only now and thin). If I depinded on the few ha'pence I get, I wouldn't live on 'em; what money I get here wouldn't buy a pound of mate; and I wouldn't live, only for my frinds. You see, sir, I can't be out always. Iam laid up nows and thins continually. Oh, it's a poor trade to big on the crossin' from morning till night, and not get sixpence. I couldn't do with it, I know.

"Yes, sir, I smoke; it's a comfort, it is. I like any kind I'd get to smoke. I'd like the best if I got it.

"I am a Roman Catholic, and I go to St. Patrick's, in St. Giles's; a many people from my neighbourhood go there. I go every Sunday, and to Confession just once a-year — that saves me.

"By the Lord's mercy! I don't get broken victuals, nor broken mate, not as much as you might put on the tip of a forruk; they'd chuck it out in the dust-bin before they'd give it to me. I suppose they're all alike.

"The divil an odd job I iver got, master, nor knives to clane. If I got their knives to clane, p'rhaps I might clane them.

"My brooms cost threepence ha'penny; they are very good. I wear them down to a stump, and they last three weeks, this fine wither. I niver got any ould clothes — not but I want a coat very bad, sir.

"I come from Dublin; my father and mother died there of cholera; and when they died, I come to England, and that was the cause of my coming.

"By my oath it didn't stand me in more than eighteenpence that I took here last week.

"I live in —— lane, St. Giles's Church, on the second landing, and I pay eightpence a week. I haven't a room to myself, for there's a family lives in it wid me.

"When I goes home I just smokes a pipe, and goes to bid, that's all."

II.—JUVENILE CROSSING-SWEEPERS

A. The Boy Crossing-Sweepers.

BOY CROSSING-SWEEPERS AND TUMBLERS.

A REMARKABLY intelligent lad, who, on being spoken to, at once consented to give all the information in his power, told me the following story of his life.

It will be seen from this boy's account, and the one or two following, that a kind of partnership exists among some of these young sweepers. They have associated themselves together, appropriated several crossings to their use, and appointed a captain over them. They have their forms of trial, and "jury-house" for the settlement of disputes; laws have been framed, which govern their commercial proceedings, and a kind of language adopted by the society for its better protection from its arch-enemy, the policeman.

I found the lad who first gave me an insight into the proceedings of the associated crossing-sweepers crouched on the stone steps of a door in Adelaide-street, Strand; and when I spoke to him he was preparing to settle down in a corner and go to sleep — his legs and body being curled round almost as closely as those of a cat on a hearth.

The moment he heard my voice he was upon his feet, asking me to "give a halfpenny to poor little Jack."

He was a good-looking lad, with a pair of large mild eyes, which he took good care to turn up with an expression of supplication as he moaned for his halfpenny.

A cap, or more properly a stuff bag, covered a crop of hair which had matted itself into the form of so many paint-brushes, while his face, from its roundness of feature and the complexion of dirt, had an almost Indian look about it; the colour of his hands, too, was such that you could imagine he had been shelling walnuts.

He ran before me, treading cautiously with his naked feet, until I reached a convenient spot to take down his statement, which was as follows :—

"I've got no mother or father; mother has been dead for two years, and father's been gone more than that — more nigh five years — he died at Ipswich, in Suffolk. He was a perfumer by trade, and used to make hair-dye, and scent, and pomatum, and all kinds of scents. He didn't keep a shop himself, but he used to serve them as did; he didn't hawk his goods about, neether, but had regular customers, what used to send him a letter, and then he'd take them what they wanted. Yes, he used to serve some good shops: there was H——'s, of London Bridge, what's a large chemist's. He used to make a good deal of money, but he lost it betting; and so his brother, my uncle, did all his. He used to go up to High Park, and then go round by the Hospital, and then turn up a yard, where all the men are who play for money [Tattersall's]; and there he'd lose his money, or sometimes win,—but that wasn't often. I remember he used to come home tipsy, and say he'd lost on this or that horse, naming wot one he'd laid on; and then mother would coax him to bed, and afterwards sit down and begin to cry.

"I was not with father when he died (but I was when he was dying), for I was sent up along with eldest sister to London with a letter to uncle, who was head servant at a doctor's. In this letter, mother asked uncle to pay back some money wot he owed, and wot father lent him, and she asked him if he'd like to come down and see father before he died. I recollect I went back again to mother by the Orwell steamer. I was well dressed then, and had good clothes on, and I was given to the care of the captain—Mr. King his name was. But when I got back to Ipswich, father was dead.

"Mother took on dreadful; she was ill for three months afterwards, confined to her bed. She hardly eat anything: only beaf-tea—I think they call it—and eggs. All the while she kept on crying.

"Mother kept a servant; yes, sir, we always had a servant, as long as I can recollect; and she and the woman as was there—Anna they called her, an old lady—used to take care of me and sister. Sister was fourteen years old (she's married to a young man now, and they've gone to America; she went from a place in the East India Docks, and I saw her off). I used, when I was with mother, to go to school in the morning, and go at nine and come home at twelve to dinner, then go again at two and leave off at half-past four,—that is, if I behaved myself and did all my lessons right; for if I did not I was kept back till I *did* them so. Mother used to pay one shilling a-week, and extra for the copy-books and things. I can read and write—oh, yes, I mean read and write well—read anything, even old English; and I write pretty fair,—though I don't get much reading now, unless it's a penny paper—I've got one in my pocket now—it's the *London Journal*—there's a tale in it now about two brothers, and one of them steals the child away and puts another in his place, and then he gets found out, and all that, and he's just been falling off a bridge now.

"After mother got better, she sold all the furniture and goods and came up to London;—poor mother! She let a man of the name of Hayes have the greater part, and he left Ipswich soon after, and never gave mother the money. We came up to London, and mother took two rooms in Westminster, and I and sister lived along with her. She used to make hair-nets, and sister helped her, and used to take 'em to the hair-dressers to sell. She made these nets for two or three years, though she was suffering with a bad breast;—she died of that—poor thing!—for she had what doctors calls cancer—perhaps you've heard of 'em, sir,—and they had to cut all round here (making motions with his hands from the shoulder to the bosom). Sister saw it, though I didn't.

"Ah! she was a very good, kind mother, and very fond of both of us; though father wasn't, for he'd always have a noise with mother when he come home, only he was seldom with us when he was making his goods.

"After mother died, sister still kept on making nets, and I lived with her for some time, until she told me she couldn't afford to keep me no longer, though she seemed to have a pretty good lot to do; but she would never let me go with her to the shops, though I could crochet, which she'd learned me, and used to run and get her all her silks and things what she wanted. But she was keeping company with a young man, and one day they went out, and came back and said they'd been and got married. It was him as got rid of me.

"He was kind to me for the first two or three months, while he was keeping her company; but before he was married he got a little cross, and after he was married he begun to get more cross, and used to send me to play in the streets, and tell me not to come home again till night. One day he hit me, and I said I wouldn't be hit about by him, and then at tea that night sister gave me three shillings, and told me I must go and get my own living. So I bought a box and brushes (they cost me just the money) and went cleaning boots, and I done pretty well with them, till my box was stole from me by a boy where I was lodging. He's in prison now—got six calendar for picking pockets.

"Sister kept all my clothes. When I asked her for 'em, she said they was disposed of along with all mother's goods; but she gave me some shirts and stockings, and such-like, and I had very good clothes, only they was all worn out. I saw sister after I left her, many times. I asked her many times to take me back, but she used to say, 'It was not her likes, but her husband's, or she'd have had me back;' and I think it was true, for until he came she was a kind-hearted girl; but he said he'd enough to do to look after his own living; he was a fancy-baker by trade.

"I was fifteen the 24th of last May, sir, and I've been sweeping crossings now near upon two years. There's a party of six of us, and we have the crossings from St. Martin's Church as far as Pall Mall. I always go along with them as lodges in the same place as I do. In the daytime, if it's dry, we do anythink what we can—open cabs, or anythink; but if it's wet, we separate, and I and another gets a crossing—those who gets on it first, keeps it,—and we stand on each side and take our chance.

"We do it in this way:—if I was to see two gentlemen coming, I should cry out, 'Two toffs!' and then they are mine; and whether they give me anythink or not they are mine, and my mate is bound not to follow them; for if he did he would get a hiding from the whole lot of us. If we both cry out together, then we share. If it's a lady and gentleman, then we cries, 'A toff and a doll!' Sometimes we are caught out in this way. Perhaps it is a lady and gentleman and a child; and if I was to see them, and only say, 'A toff and a doll,' and leave out the child, then my mate can add the child; and as he is right and I wrong, then it's his party.

"If there's a policeman close at hand we mustn't ask for money; but we are always on the look-out for the policemen, and if we see one, then we calls out 'Phillup!' for that's our signal. One of the policemen at St. Martin's Church—Bandy, we calls him—knows what Phillup means, for he's up to us; so we had to change the word. (At the request of the young crossing-sweeper the present signal is omitted.)

"Yesterday on the crossing I got threepence halfpenny, but when it's dry like to-day I do nothink, for I haven't got a penny yet. We never carries no pockets, for if the policemen find us we generally pass the money to our mates, for if money's found on us we have fourteen days in prison.

"If I was to reckon all the year round, that is, one day with another, I think we make fourpence every day. and if we were to stick to it we should make more, for on a very muddy day we do better. One day, the best I ever had, from nine o'clock in the morning till seven o'clock at night, I made seven shillings and sixpence, and got not one bit of silver money among it. Every shilling I got I went and left at a shop near where my crossing is, for fear I might get into any harm. The shop's kept by a woman we deals with for what we wants—tea and butter, or sugar, or brooms— anythink we wants. Saturday night week I made two-and-sixpence; that's what I took altogether up to six o'clock.

"When we see the rain we say together, 'Oh! there's a jolly good rain! we'll have a good day to-morrow.' If a shower comes on, and we are at our room, which we general are about three o'clock, to get somethink to eat— besides, we general go there to see how much each other's taken in the day—why, out we run with our brooms.

"We're always sure to make money if there's mud—that's to say, if we look for our money, and ask; of course, if we stand still we don't. Now, there's Lord Fitzhardinge, he's a good gentleman, what lives in Spring-gardens, in a large house. He's got a lot of servants and carriages. Every time he crosses the Charing-cross crossing he always gives the girl half a sovereign." (This statement was taken in June 1856.) "He doesn't cross often, because, hang it, he's got such a lot of carriages, but when he's on foot he always does. If they asks him he doesn't give nothink, but if they touches their caps he does. The housekeeper at his house is very kind to us. We run errands for her, and when she wants any of her own letters taken to the post then she calls, and if we are on the crossing we takes them for her. She's a very nice lady, and gives us broken victuals. I've got a share in that crossing,—there are three of us, and when he gives the half sovereign he always gives it to the girl, and those that are in it shares it. She would do us out of it if she could, but we all takes good care of that, for we are all cheats.

"At night-time we tumbles—that is, if the policemen ain't nigh. We goes general to Waterloo-place when the Opera's on. We sends on one of us ahead, as a looker-out, to look for the policeman, and then we follows. It's no good tumbling to gentlemen *going* to the Opera; it's when they're coming back they gives us money. When they've got a young lady on their arm they laugh at us tumbling; some will give us a penny, others threepence, sometimes a sixpence or a shilling, and sometimes a halfpenny. We either do the cat'unwheel, or else we keep before the gentleman and lady, turning head-over-heels, putting our broom on the ground and then turning over it.

"I work a good deal fetching cabs after the Opera is over; we general open the doors of those what draw up at the side of the pavement for people to get into as have walked a little down the Haymarket looking for a cab. We gets a month in prison if we touch the others by the columns. I once had half a sovereign give me by a gentleman; it was raining awful, and I run all about for a cab, and at last I got one. The gentleman knew it was half a sovereign, because he said—'Here, my little man, here's half a sovereign for your trouble.' He had three ladies with him, beautiful ones, with nothink on their heads, and only capes on their bare shoulders; and he had white kids on, and his regular Opera togs, too. I liked him very much, and as he was going to give me somethink the ladies says—'Oh, give him somethink extra!' It was pouring with rain, and they couldn't get a cab; they were all engaged, but I jumped on the box of one as was driving along the line. Last Saturday Opera night I made fifteen pence by the gentlemen coming from the Opera.

"After the Opera we go into the Haymarket, where all the women are who walk the streets all night. They don't give us no money, but they tell the gentlemen to. Sometimes, when they are talking to the gentlemen, they say, 'Go away, you young rascal!' and if they are saucy, then we say to them, 'We're not talking to you, my doxy, we're talking to the gentleman,'— but that's only if they're rude, for if they speak civil we always goes. They knows what 'doxy' means. What is it? Why that they are no better than us! If we are on the crossing, and we says to them as they go by, 'Good luck to you!' they always give us somethink either that night or the next. There are two with bloomer bonnets, who always give us somethink if we says 'Good luck.' Sometimes a gentleman will tell us to go and get them a young lady, and then we goes, and they general gives us sixpence for that. If the gents is dressed finely we gets them a handsome girl; if they're dressed middling, then we gets them a middling-dressed one; but we usual prefers giving a turn to girls that have been kind to us, and they are sure to give us somethink the next night. If we don't find any girls walking, we knows where to get them in the houses in the streets round about.

"We always meet at St. Martin's steps—the 'jury house,' we calls 'em—at three o'clock in the morning, that's always our hour. We reckons up what we've taken, but we don't divide. Sometimes, if we owe anythink where we lodge, the women of the house will be waiting on the steps for us: then, if we've got it, we pay them; if we haven't, why it can't be helped, and it goes on. We gets into debt, because sometimes the women where we live gets lushy; then we don't give them anythink, because they'd forget it, so we spends it ourselves. We can't lodge at what's called model lodging-houses, as our hours don't suit them folks. We pays threepence a-night for lodging. Food, if we get plenty of money, we buys for ourselves. We buys a pound of bread, that's twopence farthing—best seconds, and a farthing's worth of dripping—that's enough for a pound of bread—and we gets a ha'porth of tea and a ha'porth of sugar; or if we're hard up, we gets only a penn'orth of bread. We make our own tea at home; they lends us a kittle, teapot, and cups and saucers, and all that.

"Once or twice a-week we gets meat. We all club together, and go into Newgate Market and gets some pieces cheap, and biles them at home. We tosses up who shall have the biggest bit, and we divide the broth, a cupful in each basin, until it's lasted out. If any of us has been unlucky we each gives the unlucky one one or two halfpence. Some of us is obliged at times to sleep out all night; and sometimes, if any of us gets nothink, then the others gives him a penny or two, and *he* does the same for us when *we* are out of luck.

"Besides, there's our clothes: I'm paying for a pair of boots now. I paid a shilling off Saturday night.

"When we gets home at half-past three in the morning, whoever cries out 'first wash' has it. First of all we washes our feet, and we all uses the same water. Then we washes our faces and hands, and necks, and whoever fetches the fresh water up has first wash; and if the second don't like to go and get fresh, why he uses the dirty. Whenever we come in the landlady makes us wash our feet. Very often the stones cuts our feet and makes them bleed; then we bind a bit of rag round them. We like to put on boots and shoes in the day-time, but at night-time we can't, because it stops the tumbling.

"On the Sunday we all have a clean shirt put on before we go out, and then we go and tumble after the omnibuses. Sometimes we do very well on a fine Sunday, when there's plenty of people out on the roofs of the busses. We never do anythink on a wet day, but only when it's been raining and then dried up. I have run after a Cremorne bus, when they've thrown us money, as far as from Charing-cross right up to Piccadilly, but if they don't throw us nothink we don't run very far. I should think we gets at that work, taking one Sunday with another, eightpence all the year round.

"When there's snow on the ground we puts our money together, and goes and buys an old shovel, and then, about seven o'clock in the morning, we goes to the shops and asks them if we shall scrape the snow away. We general gets twopence every house, but some gives sixpence, for it's very hard to clean the snow away, particular when it's been on the ground some time. It's awful cold, and gives us chilblains on our feet; but we don't mind it when we're working, for we soon gets hot then.

"Before winter comes, we general save up our money and buys a pair of shoes. Sometimes we makes a very big snowball and rolls it up to the hotels, and then the gentlemen laughs and throws us money; or else we pelt each other with snowballs, and then they scrambles money between us. We always go to Morley's Hotel, at Charing-cross. The police in winter times is kinder to us than in summer, and they only laughs at us;—p'rhaps it is because there is not so many of us about then,—only them as is obligated to find a living for themselves; for many of the boys has fathers and mothers as sends them out in summer, but keeps them at home in winter when it's piercing cold.

"I have been to the station-house, because the police always takes us up if we are out at night; but we're only locked up till morning,—that is, if we behaves ourselves when we're taken before the gentleman. Mr. Hall, at Bow-street, only says, 'Poor boy, let him go.' But it's only when we've done nothink but stop out that he says that. He's a kind old gentleman; but mind, it's only when you have been before him two or three times he says so, because if it's a many times, he'll send you for fourteen days.

"But we don't mind the police much at night-time, because we jumps over the walls round the place at Trafalgar-square, and they don't like to follow us at that game, and only stands looking at you over the parrypit. There was one tried to jump the wall, but he split his trousers all to bits, and now they're afraid. That was Old Bandy as bust his breeches; and we all hate him, as well as another we calls Black Diamond, what's general along with the Red Liners, as we calls the Mendicity officers, who goes about in disguise as gentlemen, to take up poor boys caught begging.

"When we are talking together we always talk in a kind of slang. Each policeman we gives a regular name—there's 'Bull's Head,' 'Bandy Shanks,' and 'Old Cherry Legs,' and 'Dot-and-carry-one;' they all knows their names as well as us. We never talks of crossings, but 'fakes.' We don't make no slang of our own, but uses the regular one.

"A broom doesn't last us more than a week in wet weather, and they costs us twopence halfpenny each; but in dry weather they are good for a fortnight."

Young Mike's Statement.

The next lad I examined was called Mike. He was a short, stout-set youth, with a face like an old man's, for the features were hard and defined, and the hollows had got filled up with dirt till his countenance was brown as an old wood carving. I have seldom seen so dirty a face, for the boy had been in a perspiration, and then wiped his cheeks with his muddy hands, until they were marbled, like the covering to a copy-book.

The old lady of the house in which the boy lived seemed to be hurt by the unwashed appearance of her lodger. "You ought to be ashamed of yourself—and that's God's truth—not to go and sluice yourself afore spaking to the jintlemin," she cried, looking alternately at me and the lad, as if asking me to witness her indignation.

Mike wore no shoes, but his feet were as black as if cased in gloves with short fingers. His coat had been a man's, and the tails reached to his ankles; one of the sleeves was wanting, and a dirty rag had been wound round the arm in its stead. His hair spread about like a tuft of grass where a rabbit has been squatting.

He said, "I haven't got neither no father nor no mother,—never had, sir; for father's been dead these two year, and mother getting on for eight. They was both Irish people, please sir, and father was a bricklayer. When father was at work in the country, mother used to get work carrying loads at Coventgarden Market. I lived with father till he died, and that was from a complaint in his chest. After that I lived along with my big brother, what's 'listed in the Marines now. He used to sweep a crossing in Camden-town, opposite the Southampting Harms, near the toll-gate.

"He did pretty well up there sometimes, such as on Christmas-day, where he has took as much as six shillings sometimes, and never less than one and sixpence. All the gentlements knowed him thereabouts, and one or two used to give him a shilling a-week regular.

"It was he as first of all put me up to sweep a crossing, and I used to take my stand at St. Martin's Church.

"I didn't see anybody working there, so I planted myself on it. After a time some other boys come up. They come up and wanted to turn me off, and began hitting me with their brooms,—they hit me regular hard with the old stumps; there was five or six of them; so I couldn't defend myself, but told the policeman, and he turned them all away except me, because he saw me on first, sir. Now we are all friends, and work together, and all that we earns ourself we has.

"On a good day, when it's poured o' rain and then leave off sudden, and made it nice and muddy, I've took as much as ninepence; but it's too dry now, and we don't do more than fourpence.

"At night, I go along with the others tumbling. I does the cat'en-wheel [probably a contraction of Catherine-wheel]; I throws myself over sideways on my hands with my legs in the air. I can't do it more than four times running, because it makes the blood to the head, and then all the things seems to turn round. Sometimes a chap will give me a lick with a stick just as I'm going over—sometimes a reg'lar good hard whack; but it ain't often, and we general gets a halfpenny or a penny by it.

"The boys as runs after the busses was the first to do these here cat'en-wheels. I know the boy as was the very first to do it. His name is Gander, so we calls him the Goose.

"There's about nine or ten of us in our gang, and as is reg'lar; we lodges at different places, and we has our reg'lar hours for meeting, but we all comes and goes when we likes, only we keeps together, so as not to let any others come on the crossings but ourselves.

"If another boy tries to come on we cries out, 'Here's a Rooshian,' and then if he won't go away, we all sets on him and gives him a drubbing; and if he still comes down the next day, we pays him out twice as much, and harder.

"There's never been one down there yet as can lick us all together.

"If we sees one of our pals being pitched into by other boys, we goes up and helps him. Gander's the leader of our gang, 'cause he can tumble back'ards (no, that ain't the cat'enwheel, that's tumbling); so he gets more tin give him, and that's why he makes him cap'an.

"After twelve at night we goes to the Regent's Circus, and we tumbles there to the gentlemen and ladies. The most I ever got was sixpence at a time. The French ladies never give us nothink, but they all says, 'Chit, chit, chit,' like hissing at us, for they can't understand us, and we're as bad off with them.

"If it's a wet night we leaves off work about twelve o'clock, and don't bother with the Haymarket.

"The first as gets to the crossing does the

sweeping away of the mud. Then they has in return all the halfpence they can take. When it's been wet every day, a broom gets down to stump in about four days. We either burns the old brooms, or, if we can, we sells 'em for a ha'penny to some other boy, if he's flat enough to buy 'em."

GANDER—THE "CAPTAIN" OF THE BOY CROSSING-SWEEPERS.

GANDER, the captain of the gang of boy crossing-sweepers, was a big lad of sixteen, with a face devoid of all expression, until he laughed, when the cheeks, mouth, and forehead instantly became crumpled up with a wonderful quantity of lines and dimples. His hair was cut short, and stood up in all directions, like the bristles of a hearth-broom, and was a light dust tint, matching with the hue of his complexion, which also, from an absence of washing, had turned to a decided drab, or what house-painters term a stone-colour.

He spoke with a lisp, occasioned by the loss of two of his large front teeth, which allowed the tongue as he talked to appear through the opening in a round nob like a raspberry.

The boy's clothing was in a shocking condition. He had no coat, and his blue-striped shirt was as dirty as a French-polisher's rags, and so tattered, that the shoulder was completely bare, while the sleeve hung down over the hand like a big bag.

From the fish-scales on the sleeves of his coat, it had evidently once belonged to some coster in the herring line. The nap was all worn off, so that the lines of the web were showing like a coarse carpet; and instead of buttons, string had been passed through holes pierced at the side.

Of course he had no shoes on, and his black trousers, which, with the grease on them, were gradually assuming a tarpaulin look, were fastened over one shoulder by means of a brace and bits of string.

During his statement, he illustrated his account of the tumbling backwards—the "catenwheeling"— with different specimens of the art, throwing himself about on the floor with an ease and almost grace, and taking up so small a space of the ground for the performance, that his limbs seemed to bend as though his bones were flexible like cane.

"To tell you the blessed truth, I can't say the last shilling I handled."

"Don't you go a-believing on him," whispered another lad in my ear, whilst Gander's head was turned: "he took thirteenpence last night, he did."

It was perfectly impossible to obtain from this lad any account of his average earnings. The other boys in the gang told me that he made more than any of them. But Gander, who is a thorough street-beggar, and speaks with a peculiar whine, and who, directly you look at him, puts on an expression of deep distress, seemed to have made up his mind, that if he made himself out to be in great want I should most likely relieve him—so he would not budge an inch from his twopence a-day, declaring it to be the maximum of his daily earnings.

"Ah," he continued, with a persecuted tone of voice, " if I had only got a little money, I'd be a bright youth! The first chance as I get of earning a few halfpence, I'll buy myself a coat, and be off to the country, and I'll lay something I'd soon be a gentleman then, and come home with a couple of pounds in my pocket, instead of never having ne'er a farthing, as now."

One of the other lads here exclaimed, "Don't go on like that there, Goose; you're making us out all liars to the gentleman."

The old woman also interfered. She lost all patience with Gander, and reproached him for making a false return of his income. She tried to shame him into truthfulness, by saying,—

"Look at my Johnny—my grandson, sir, he's not a quarther the Goose's size, and yet he'll bring me home his shilling, or perhaps eighteenpence or two shillings—for shame on you, Gander! Now, did you make six shillings last week?—now, speak God's truth!"

"What! six shillings?" cried the Goose— "six shillings!" and he began to look up at the ceiling, and shake his hands. "Why, I never heard of sich a sum. I did once *see* a halfcrown; but I don't know as I ever touched e'er a one."

"Thin," added the old woman, indignantly, "it's because you're idle, Gander, and you don't study when you're on the crossing; but lets the gintlefolk go by without ever a word. That's what it is, sir."

The Goose seemed to feel the truth of this reproach, for he said with a sigh, "I knows I am fickle-minded."

He then continued his statement,—

"I can't tell how many brooms I use; for as fast as I gets one, it is took from me. God help me! They watch me put it away, and then up they comes and takes it. What kinds of brooms is the best? Why, as far as I am concerned, I would sooner have a stump on a dry day — it's lighter and handier to carry; but on a wet day, give me a new un.

"I'm sixteen, your honour, and my name's George Gandea, and the boys calls me 'the Goose' in consequence; for it's a nickname they gives me, though my name ain't spelt with a *har* at the end, but with a *h'ay*, so that I ain't Gand*er* after all, but Gand*ea*, which is a sell for 'em.

"God knows what I am — whether I'm h'Irish or h'*I*talian, or what; but I was christened here in London, and that's all about it.

"Father was a bookbinder. I'm sixteen now, and father turned me away when I was nine year old, for mother had been dead before that. I was told my right name by my brother-in-law, who had my register. He's a sweep, sir, by trade, and I wanted to know about my real name when I was going down to the *Waterloo*—that's a ship as I wanted to get aboard as a cabin-boy.

"I remember the fust night I slept out after father got rid of me. I slept on a gentleman's door-step, in the winter, on the 15th January. I packed my shirt and coat, which was a pretty good one, right over my ears, and then scrunched myself into a doorway, and the policeman passed by four or five times without seeing on me.

"I had a mother-in-law at the time; but father used to drink, or else I should never have been as I am; and he came home one night, and says he, 'Go out and get me a few ha'pence for breakfast,' and I said I had never been in the streets in my life, and couldn't; and, says he, 'Go out, and never let me see you no more,' and I took him to his word, and have never been near him since.

"Father lived in Barbican at that time, and after leaving him, I used to go to the Royal Exchange, and there I met a boy of the name of Michael, and he first learnt me to beg, and made me run after people, saying, 'Poor boy, sir—please give us a ha'penny to get a mossel of bread.' But as fast as I got anythink, he used to take it away, and knock me about shameful; so I left him, and then I picked up with a chap as taught me tumbling. I soon larnt how to do it, and then I used to go tumbling after busses. That was my notion all along, and I hadn't picked up the way of doing it half an hour before I was after that game.

"I took to crossings about eight year ago, and the very fust person as I asked, I had a fourpenny-piece give to me. I said to him, 'Poor little Jack, yer honour,' and, fust of all, says he, 'I haven't got no coppers,' and then he turns back and give me a fourpenny-bit. I thought I was made for life when I got that.

"I wasn't working in a gang then, but all by myself, and I used to do well, making about a shilling or ninepence a-day. I lodged in Churchlane at that time.

"It was at the time of the Shibition year (1851) as these gangs come up. There was lots of boys that came out sweeping, and that's how they picked up the tumbling off me, seeing me do it up in the Park, going along to the Shibition.

"The crossing at St. Martin's Church was mine fust of all; and when the other lads come to it I didn't take no heed of 'em—only for that I'd have been a bright boy by now, but they carried me over like; for when I tried to turn 'em off they'd say, in a carrying way, 'Oh, let us stay on,' so I never took no heed of 'em.

"There was about thirteen of 'em in my gang at that time.

"They made me cap'an over the lot—I suppose because they thought I was the best tumbler of 'em. They obeyed me a little. If I told 'em not to go to any gentleman, they wouldn't, and leave him to me. There was only one feller as used to give me a share of his money, and that was for larning him to tumble—he'd give a penny or twopence, just as he yearnt a little or a lot. I taught 'em all to tumble, and we used to do it near the crossing, and at night along the streets.

"We used to be sometimes together of a day, some a-running after one gentleman, and some after another; but we seldom kept together more than three or four at a time.

"I was the fust to introduce tumbling backards, and I'm proud of it—yes, sir, I'm proud of it. There's another little chap as I'm larning to do it; but he ain't got strength enough in his arms like. ('Ah!' exclaimed a lad in the room, 'he *is* a one to tumble, is Johnny—go along the streets like anythink.')

"He is the King of the Tumblers," continued Gander—"King, and I'm Cap'an."

The old grandmother here joined in. "He was taught by a furreign gintleman, sir, whose wife rode at a circus. He used to come here twice a-day and give him lessons in this here very room, sir. That's how he got it, sir."

"Ah," added another lad, in an admiring tone, "see him and the Goose have a race! Away they goes, but Jacky will leave him a mile behind."

The history then continued:—"People liked the tumbling backards and forards, and it got a good bit of money at fust, but they is getting tired with it, and I'm growing too hold, I fancy. It hurt me awful at fust. I tried it fust under a railway arch of the Blackwall Railway; and when I goes backards, I thought it'd cut my head open. It hurts me if I've got a thin cap on.

"The man as taught me tumbling has gone on the stage. Fust he went about with swords, fencing, in public-houses, and then he got engaged. Me and him once tumbled all round the circus at the Rotunda one night wot was a benefit, and got one-and-eightpence a-piece, and all for only five hours and a half—from six to half-past eleven, and we acting and tumbling, and all that. We had plenty of beer, too. We was wery much applauded when we did it.

"I was the fust boy as ever did ornamental work in the mud of my crossings. I used to be at the crossing at the corner of Regent-suckus; and that's the wery place where I fust did it. The wery fust thing as I did was a hanker (anchor)—a regular one, with turn-up sides and a rope down the centre, and all. I sweeped it away clean in the mud in the shape of the drawing I'd seen. It paid well, for I took one-and-ninepence on it. The next thing I tried was writing 'God save the Queen;' and that, too, paid capital, for I think I got two bob. After that I tried We Har (V. R.) and a star, and that was a sweep too. I never did no flowers, but I've done imitations of laurels, and put them all round the crossing, and very pretty it looked, too, at night. I'd buy a farthing candle and stick it over it, and make it nice and comfortable, so that the people could look at it easy. Whenever I see a carriage coming I used to douse the glim and run away with it, but the wheels would regularly spile the drawings, and then we'd have all the trouble to put it to rights again, and that we used to do with our hands.

"I fust learnt drawing in the mud from a man in Adelaide-street, Strand; he kept a crossing, but he only used to draw 'em close to the kerb-stone. He used to keep some soft mud there, and when a carriage come up to the Lowther Arcade, after he'd opened the door and let the lady out, he would set to work, and by the time she come back he'd have some flowers, or a We Har, or whatever he liked, done in the mud, and underneath he'd write, 'Please to remember honnest hindustry.'

"I used to stand by and see him do it, until I'd learnt, and when I knowed, I went off and did it at my crossing.

"I was the fust to light up at night though, and now I wish I'd never done it, for it was that which got me turned off my crossing, and a capital one it was. I thought the gentlemen coming from the play would like it, for it looked very pretty. The policeman said I was destructing (obstructing) the thoroughfare, and making too much row there, for the people used to stop in the crossing to look, it were so pretty. He took me in charge three times on one night, cause I wouldn't go away; but he let me go again, till at last I thought he would lock me up for the night, so I hooked it.

"It was after this as I went to St. Martin's Church, and I haven't done half as well there. Last night I took three-ha'pence; but I was larking, or I might have had more."

As a proof of the very small expense which is required for the toilette of a crossing-sweeper, I may mention, that within a few minutes after Master Gander had finished his statement, he was in possession of a coat, for which he had paid the sum of fivepence.

When he brought it into the room, all the boys and the women crowded round to see the purchase.

"It's a very good un," said the Goose. "It only wants just taking up here and there; and this cuff putting to rights." And as he spoke he pointed to tears large enough for a head to be thrust through.

"I've seen that coat before, sum'ares," said one of the women; "where did you get it?"

"At the chandly-shop," answered the Goose.

THE "KING" OF THE TUMBLING-BOY CROSSING-SWEEPERS.

THE young sweeper who had been styled by his companions the "King" was a pretty-looking boy, only tall enough to rest his chin comfortably on the mantel-piece as he talked to me, and with a pair of grey eyes that were as bright and clear as drops of sea-water. He was clad in a style in no way agreeing with his royal title; for he had on a kind of dirt-coloured shooting-coat of tweed, which was fraying into a kind of cobweb at the edges and elbows. His trousers too, were rather faulty, for there was a pink-wrinkled dot of flesh at one of the knees; while their length was too great for his majesty's short legs, so that they had to be rolled up at the end like a washer-woman's sleeves.

His royal highness was of a restless disposition, and, whilst talking, lifted up, one after another, the different ornaments on the mantel-piece, frowning and looking at them sideways, as he pondered over the replies he should make to my questions.

When I arrived at the grandmother's apartment the "king" was absent, his majesty having been sent with a pitcher to fetch some spring-water.

The "king" also was kind enough to favour me with samples of his wondrous tumbling powers. He could bend his little legs round till they curved like the long German sausages we see in the ham-and-beef shops; and when he turned head over heels, he curled up his tiny body as closely as a wood-louse, and then rolled along, wabbling like an egg.

"The boys call me Johnny," he said; "and I'm getting on for eleven, and I goes along with the Goose and Harry, a-sweeping at St. Martin's Church, and about there. I used, too, to go to the crossing where the statute is, sir, at the bottom of the Haymarket. I went along with the others; sometimes there were three or four of us, or sometimes one, sir. I never used to sweep unless it was wet. I don't go out not before twelve or one in the day; it ain't no use going before that; and beside, I couldn't get up before that, I'm too sleepy. I don't stop out so late as the other boys; they sometimes stop all night, but I don't like that. The Goose was out all night along with Martin; they went all along up Piccirilly, and there they climbed over the Park railings and went a birding all by themselves, and then they went to sleep for an hour on the grass— so they says. I likes better to come home to my bed. It kills me for the next day when I do stop out all night. The Goose is always out all night; he likes it.

"Neither father nor mother's alive, sir, but I lives along with grandmother and aunt, as owns this room, and I always gives them all I gets.

"Sometimes I makes a shilling, sometimes sixpence, and sometimes less. I can never take nothink of a day, only of a night, because I can't tumble of a day, and I can of a night.

"The Gander taught me tumbling, and he was the first as did it along the crossings. I can tumble quite as well as the Goose; I can turn a caten-wheel, and he can't, and I can go further on forards than him, but I can't tumble backards as he can. I can't do a handspring, though. Why, a handspring's pitching yourself forards on both hands, turning over in front, and lighting on your feet; that's very difficult, and very few can do it. There's one little chap, but he's very clever, and can tie himself up in a knot a'most. I'm best at caten-wheels; I can do 'em twelve or fourteen times running —keep on at it. It just *does* tire you, that's all. When I gets up I feels quite giddy. I can tumble about forty times over head and heels. I does the most of that, and I thinks it's the most difficult, but I can't say which gentlemen likes best. You see they are anigh sick of the head-and-heels tumbling, and then werry few of the boys can do caten-wheels on the crossings—only two or three besides me.

"When I see anybody coming, I says, 'Please, sir, give me a halfpenny,' and touches my hair, and then I throws a caten-wheel, and has a look at 'em, and if I sees they are laughing, then I goes on and throws more of 'em. Perhaps one in ten will give a chap something. Some of 'em will give you a threepenny-bit or p'rhaps sixpence, and others only give you a kick. Well, sir, I should say they likes tumbling over head and heels; if you can keep it up twenty times then they begins laughing, but if you only does it once, some of 'em will say, 'Oh, I could do that myself,' and then they don't give nothink.

"I know they calls me the King of Tumblers, and I think I can tumble the best of them; none of them is so good as me, only the Goose at tumbling backards.

"We don't crab one another when we are sweeping; if we was to crab one another, we'd get to fighting and giving slaps of the jaw to one another. So when we sees anybody coming, we cries, 'My gentleman and lady coming here;' 'My lady;' 'My two gentlemens;' and if any other chap gets the money, then we says, 'I named them, now I'll have halves.' And if he won't give it, then we'll smug his broom or his cap. I'm the littlest chap among our lot, but if a fellow like the Goose was to take my naming then I'd smug somethink. I shouldn't mind his licking me, I'd smug his money and get his halfpence or somethink. If a chap as can't tumble sees a sporting gent coming and names him, he says to one of us tumblers, 'Now, then, who'll give us halves?' and then we goes and tumbles and shares. The sporting gentlemens likes tumbling; they kicks up more row laughing than a dozen others.

"Sometimes at night we goes down to Covent Garden, to where Hevans's is, but not till all the plays is over, cause Hevans's don't shut afore two or three. When the people comes out we gets tumbling afore them. Some of the drunken gentlemens is shocking spiteful, and runs after a chap and gives us a cut with the cane; some of the others will give us money, and some will buy our broom off us for sixpence. Me and Jemmy sold the two of our brooms for a shilling to two drunken gentlemens, and they began kicking up a row, and going before other gentlemens and pretending to sweep, and taking off their hats begging, like a mocking of us. They danced about with the brooms, flourishing 'em in the air, and knocking off people's hats; and at last they got into a cab, and chucked the brooms away. The drunken gentlemens is always either jolly or spiteful.

"But I goes only to the Haymarket, and about Pall Mall, now. I used to be going up to Hevans's every night, but I can't take my money up there now. I stands at the top of the Haymarket by Windmill-street, and when I sees a lady and gentleman coming out of the Argyle, then I begs of them as they comes across. I says—'Can't you give me a ha'penny, sir, poor little Jack? I'll stand on my nose for a penny;'—and then they laughs at that.

"Goose can stand on his nose as well as me; we puts the face flat down on the ground, instead of standing on our heads. There's Duckey Dunnovan, and the Stuttering Baboon, too, and two others as well, as can do it; but the Stuttering Baboon's getting too big and fat to do it well; he's a very awkward tumbler. It don't hurt, only at larning; cos you bears more on your hands than your nose.

"Sometimes they says—'Well, let us see you do it,' and then p'raps they'll search in their pockets, and say—'O, I haven't got any coppers:' so then we'll force 'em, and p'raps they'll pull out their purse and gives us a little bit of silver.

"Ah, we works hard for what we gets, and then there's the policemen birching us. Some of 'em is so spiteful, they takes up their belt what they uses round the waist to keep their coat tight, and 'll hit us with the buckle; but we generally gives 'em the lucky dodge and gets out of their way.

"One night, two gentlemen, officers they was, was standing in the Haymarket, and a drunken man passed by. There was snow on the ground, and we'd been begging of 'em, and says one of them—'I'll give you a shilling if you'll knock that drunken man over.' We was three of us; so we set on him, and soon had him down. After he got up he went and told the policemen, but we all cut round different ways and got off, and then met again. We didn't get the shilling, though, cos a boy crabbed us. He went up to the gentleman, and says he—'Give it me, sir, I'm the boy;' and then we says—'No, sir, it's us.' So, says the officer—'I sharn't give it to none of you,' and puts it back again in his pockets. We broke a broom over the boy as crabbed us, and then we cut down Waterloo-place, and afterwards we come up to the Haymarket again, and there we met the officers again. I did a caten-wheel, and then says I—'Then won't you give me un now?' and they says—'Go and sweep some mud on that woman.' So I went and did it, and then they takes me in a pastry-shop at the corner, and they tells me to tumble on the tables in the shop. I nearly broke one of 'em, they were so delicate. They gived me a fourpenny meat-pie and two penny sponge-cakes, which I puts in my pocket, cos there was another sharing with me. The lady of the shop kept on screaming—'Go and fetch me a police—take the dirty boy out,' cos I was standing on the tables in my muddy feet, and the officers was a bursting their sides with laughing; and says they, 'No, he sharn't stir.'

"I was frightened, cos if the police had come they'd been safe and sure to have took me. They made me tumble from the door to the end of the shop, and back again, and then I turned 'em a caten-wheel, and was near knocking down all the things as was on the counter.

"They didn't give me no money, only pies; but I got a shilling another time for tumbling to some French ladies and gentlemen in a pastry-cook's shop under the Colonnade. I often goes into a shop like that; I've done it a good many times.

"There was a gentleman once as belonged to a 'suckus,' (circus) as wanted to take me with him abroad, and teach me tumbling. He had a little mustache, and used to belong to Drury-lane play-house, riding on horses. I went to his place, and stopped there some time. He taught me to put my leg round my neck, and I was just getting along nicely with the splits (going down on the ground with both legs extended), when I left him. They (the splits) used to hurt worst of all; very bad for the thighs. I used, too, to hang with my leg round his neck. When I did anythink he liked, he used to be clapping me on the back. He wasn't so very stunning well off, for he never had what I calls a good dinner—grandmother used to have a better dinner than he,—perhaps only a bit of scrag of mutton between three of us. I don't like meat nor butter, but I likes dripping, and they never had none there. The wife used to drink—ay, very much, on the sly. She used when he was out to send me round with a bottle and sixpence to get a quartern of gin for her, and she'd take it with three or four oysters. Grandmother didn't like the notion of my going away, so she went down one day, and says she—'I wants my child;' and the wife says—'That's according to the master's likings;' and then grandmother says—'What, not my own child?' And then grandmother began talking, and at last, when the master come home, he says to me—'Which will you do, stop here, or go home with your grandmother?' So I come along with her.

"I've been sweeping the crossings getting on for two years. Before that I used to go caten-wheeling after the busses. I don't like the sweeping, and I don't think there's e'er a one of us wot likes it. In the winter we has to be out in the cold, and then in summer we have to sleep out all night, or go asleep on the church-steps, reg'lar tired out.

"One of us 'll say at night—'Oh, I'm sleepy now, who's game for a doss? I'm for a doss;' —and then we go eight or ten of us into a doorway of the church, where they keep the dead in a kind of airy-like underneath, and there we go to sleep. The most of the boys has got no homes. Perhaps they've got the price of a lodging, but they're hungry, and they eats the money, and then they must lay out. There's some of 'em will stop out in the wet for perhaps the sake of a halfpenny, and get themselves sopping wet. I think all our chaps would like to get out of the work if they could; I'm sure Goose would, and so would I.

"All the boys call me the King, because I tumbles so well, and some calls me 'Pluck,' and some 'Judy.' I'm called 'Pluck,' cause I'm so plucked a going at the gentlemen! Tommy Dunnovan—'Tipperty Tight'—we calls him, cos his trousers is so tight he can hardly move in them sometimes,—he was the first as called me 'Judy.' Dunnovan once swallowed a pill for a shilling. A gentleman in the Haymarket says—'If you'll swallow this here pill I'll give you a shilling;' and Jimmy says, 'All right, sir;' and he puts it in his mouth, and went to the water-pails near the cab-stand and swallowed it.

"All the chaps in our gang likes me, and we all likes one another. We always shows what we gets given to us to eat.

"Sometimes we gets one another up wild, and then that fetches up a fight, but that isn't often. When two of us fights, the others stands round and sees fair play. There was a fight last night between 'Broke his Bones'—as we calls Antony Hones—and Neddy Hall—the 'Sparrow,' or 'Spider,' we calls him,—something about the root of a pineapple, as we was aiming with at one another, and that called up a fight. We all stood round and saw them at it, but neither of 'em licked, for they gived in for to-day, and they're to finish it to-night. We makes 'em fight fair. We all of us likes to see a fight, but not to fight ourselves. Hones is sure to beat, as Spider is as thin as a wafer, and all bones. I can lick the Spider, though he's twice my size."

THE STREET WHERE THE BOY-SWEEPERS LODGED.

I WAS anxious to see the room in which the gang of boy crossing-sweepers lived, so that I might judge of their peculiar style of housekeeping, and form some notion of their principles of domestic economy.

I asked young Harry and "the Goose" to conduct me to their lodgings, and they at once consented, "the Goose" prefacing his compliance with the remark, that "it wern't such as genilmen had been accustomed to, but then I must take 'em as they was."

The boys led me in the direction of Drury-lane; and before entering one of the narrow streets which branch off like the side-bones of a fish's spine from that long thoroughfare, they thought fit to caution me that I was not to be frightened, as nobody would touch me, for all was very civil.

The locality consisted of one of those narrow streets which, were it not for the paved cartway in the centre would be called a court. Seated on the pavement at each side of the entrance was a costerwoman with her basket before her, and her legs tucked up mysteriously under her gown into a round ball, so that her figure resembled in shape the plaster tumblers sold by the Italians. These women remained as inanimate as if they had been carved images, and it was only when a passenger went by that they gave signs of life, by calling out in a low voice, like talking to themselves, "Two for three haarpence—herrens," — "Fine hinguns."

The street itself is like the description given of thoroughfares in the East. Opposite neighbours could not exactly shake hands out of window, but they could talk together very comfortably; and, indeed, as I passed along, I observed several women with their arms folded up like a cat's paws on the sill, and chatting with their friends over the way.

Nearly all the inhabitants were costermongers, and, indeed, the narrow cartway seemed to have been made just wide enough for a truck to wheel down it. A beershop and a general store, together with a couple of sweeps,—whose residences were distinguished by a broom over the door, — formed the only exceptions to the street-selling class of inhabitants.

As I entered the place, it gave me the notion that it belonged to a distinct coster colony, and formed one large hawkers' home; for everybody seemed to be doing just as he liked, and I was stared at as if condered an intruder. Women were seated on the pavement, knitting, and repairing their linen; the doorways were filled up with bonnetless girls, who wore their shawls over their head, as the Spanish women do their mantillas; and the youths in corduroy and brass buttons, who were chatting with them, leant against the walls as they smoked their pipes, and blocked up the pavement, as if they were the proprietors of the place. Little children formed a convenient bench out of the kerbstone; and a party of four men were seated on the footway, playing with cards which had turned to the colour of brown paper from long usage, and marking the points with chalk upon the flags.

The parlour-windows of the houses had all of them wooden shutters, as thick and clumsy-looking as a kitchen flap-table, the paint of which had turned to the dull dirt-colour of an old slate. Some of these shutters were evidently never used as a security for the dwelling, but served only as tables on which to chalk the accounts of the day's sales.

Before most of the doors were costermongers' trucks—some standing ready to be wheeled off, and others stained and muddy with the day's work. A few of the costers were dressing up their barrows, arranging the sieves of waxy-looking potatoes—and others taking the stiff herrings, browned like a meerschaum with the smoke they had been dried in, from the barrels beside them, and spacing them out in pennyworths on their trays.

You might guess what each costermonger had taken out that day by the heap of refuse swept into the street before the doors. One house had a blue mound of mussel-shells in front of it—another, a pile of the outside leaves of broccoli and cabbages, turning yellow and slimy with bruises and moisture.

Hanging up beside some of the doors were bundles of old strawberry pottles, stained red with the fruit. Over the trap-doors to the cellars were piles of market-gardeners' sieves, ruddled like a sheep's back with big red letters. In fact, everything that met the eye seemed to be in some way connected with the coster's trade.

From the windows poles stretched out, on which blankets, petticoats, and linen were drying; and so numerous were they, that they reminded me of the flags hung out at a Paris fête. Some of the sheets had patches as big as trap-doors let into their centres; and the blankets were—many of them—as full of holes as a pigeon-house.

As I entered the court, a "row" was going on; and from a first-floor window a lady, whose hair sadly wanted brushing, was haranguing a crowd beneath, throwing her arms about like a drowning man, and in her excitement thrusting her body half out of her temporary rostrum as energetically as I have seen Punch lean over his theatre.

"The willin dragged her," she shouted, " by the hair of her head, at least three yards into the court—the willin! and then he kicked her, and the blood was on his boot."

It was a sweep who had been behaving in this cowardly manner; but still he had his defenders in the women around him. One with very shiny hair, and an Indian kerchief round her neck, answered the lady in the window, by calling her a "d——d old cat;" whilst the sweep's wife rushed about, clapping her hands together as quickly as if she was applauding at a theatre, and styled somebody or other "an old wagabones as she wouldn't dirty her hands to fight with."

This "row" had the effect of drawing all the lodgers to the windows—their heads popping out as suddenly as dogs from their kennels in a fancier's yard.

The Boy-Sweepers' Room.

The room where the boys lodged was scarcely bigger than a coach-house; and so low was the ceiling, that a fly-paper suspended from a clothes-line was on a level with my head, and had to be carefully avoided when I moved about.

One corner of the apartment was completely filled up by a big four-post bedstead, which fitted into a kind of recess as perfectly as if it had been built to order.

The old woman who kept this lodging had endeavoured to give it a homely look of comfort, by hanging little black-framed pictures, scarcely bigger than pocket-books, on the walls. Most of these were sacred subjects, with large yellow glories round the heads; though between the drawing representing the bleeding heart of Christ, and the Saviour bearing the Cross, was an illustration of a red-waistcoated sailor smoking his pipe. The Adoration of the Shepherds, again, was matched on the other side of the fireplace by a portrait of Daniel O'Connell.

A chest of drawers was covered over with a green baize cloth, on which books, shelves, and clean glasses were tidily set out.

Where so many persons (for there were about eight of them, including the landlady, her daughter, and grandson) could all sleep, puzzled me extremely.

The landlady wore a frilled nightcap, which fitted so closely to the skull, that it was evident she had lost her hair. One of her eyes was slowly recovering from a blow, which, to use her own words, "a blackgeyard gave her." Her lip, too, had suffered in the encounter, for it was swollen and cut.

"I've a nice flock-bid for the boys," she said, when I inquired into the accommodation of her lodging-house, "where three of them can slape aisy and comfortable."

"It's a large bed, sir," said one of the boys, "and a warm covering over us; and you see it's better than a regular lodging-house; for, if you want a knife or a cup, you don't have to leave something on it till it's returned."

The old woman spoke up for her lodgers, telling me that they were good boys, and very honest; "for," she added, "they pays me rig'lar ivery night, which is threepence."

The only youth as to whose morals she seemed to be at all doubtful was "the Goose," "for he kept late hours, and sometimes came home without a penny in his pocket."

B. *The Girl Crossing-Sweepers.*

The Girl Crossing-Sweeper sent out by her Father.

A LITTLE girl, who worked by herself at her own crossing, gave me some curious information on the subject.

This child had a peculiarly flat face, with a button of a nose, while her mouth was scarcely larger than a button-hole. When she spoke, there was not the slightest expression visible in her features; indeed, one might have fancied she wore a mask and was talking behind it; but her eyes were shining the while as brightly as those of a person in a fever, and kept moving about, restless with her timidity. The green frock she wore was fastened close to the neck, and was turning into a kind of mouldy tint; she also wore a black stuff apron, stained with big patches of gruel, "from feeding baby at home, as she said." Her hair was tidily dressed, being drawn tightly back from the forehead, like the buy-a-broom girls; and as she stood with her hands thrust up her sleeves, she curtseyed each time before answering, bobbing down like a float, as though the floor under her had suddenly given way.

"I'm twelve years old, please sir, and my name is Margaret R——, and I sweep a crossing in New Oxford-street, by Dunn's-passage, just facing Moses and Sons', sir; by the Catholic school, sir. Mother's been dead these two year, sir, and father's a working cutler, sir; and I lives with him, but he don't get much to do, and so I'm obligated to help him, doing what I can, sir. Since mother's been dead, I've had to mind my little brother and sister, so that I haven't been to school; but when I goes a crossing-sweeping I takes them along with me, and they sits on the steps close by, sir. If it's wet I has to stop at home and take care of them, for father depends upon me for looking after them. Sister's three and a-half year old, and brother's five year, so he's just beginning to help me, sir. I hope he'll get something better than a crossing when he grows up.

"First of all I used to go singing songs in the streets, sir. It was when father had no work, so he stopped at home and looked after the children. I used to sing the 'Red, White, and Blue,' and 'Mother, is the Battle over?' and 'The Gipsy Girl,' and sometimes I'd get fourpence or fivepence, and sometimes I'd have a chance of making ninepence, sir. Sometimes, though, I'd take a shilling of a Saturday night in the markets.

"At last the songs grew so stale people wouldn't listen to them, and, as I carn't read, I couldn't learn any more, sir. My big brother and father used to learn me some, but I never could get enough out of them for the streets; besides, father was out of work still, and we couldn't get money enough to buy ballads with, and it's no good singing without having them to sell. We live over there, sir, (pointing to a window on the other side of the narrow street).

"The notion come into my head all of itself to sweep crossings, sir. As I used to go up Regent-street I used to see men and women, and girls and boys, sweeping, and the people giving them money, so I thought I'd do the same thing. That's how it come about. Just now the weather is so dry, I don't go to my crossing, but goes out singing. I've learnt some new songs, such as 'The Queen of the Navy for ever,' and 'The Widow's Last

Prayer,' which is about the wars. I only go sweeping in wet weather, because then's the best time. When I am there, there's some ladies and gentlemen as gives to me regular. I knows them by sight; and there's a beer-shop where they give me some bread and cheese whenever I go.

"I generally takes about sixpence, or seven-pence, or eightpence on the crossing, from about nine o'clock in the morning till four in the evening, when I come home. I don't stop out at nights because father won't let me, and I'm got to be home to see to baby.

"My broom costs me twopence ha'penny, and in wet weather it lasts a week, but in dry weather we seldom uses it.

"When I sees the busses and carriages coming I stands on the side, for I'm afeard of being runned over. In winter I goes out and cleans ladies' doors, general about Lincoln's-inn, for the housekeepers. I gets twopence a door, but it takes a long time when the ice is hardened, so that I carn't do only about two or three.

"I carn't tell whether I shall always stop at sweeping, but I've no clothes, and so I carn't get a situation; for, though I'm small and young, yet I could do housework, such as cleaning.

"No, sir, there's no gang on my crossing— I'm all alone. If another girl or a boy was to come and take it when I'm not there, I should stop on it as well as him or her, and go shares with 'em."

GIRL CROSSING-SWEEPER.

I WAS told that a little girl formed one of the association of young sweepers, and at my request one of the boys went to fetch her.

She was a clean-washed little thing, with a pretty, expressive countenance, and each time she was asked a question she frowned, like a baby in its sleep, while thinking of the answer. In her ears she wore instead of rings loops of string, "which the doctor had put there because her sight was wrong." A cotton velvet bonnet, scarcely larger than the sun-shades worn at the sea-side, hung on her shoulders, leaving exposed her head, with the hair as rough as tow. Her green stuff gown was hanging in tatters, with long three-cornered rents as large as penny kites, showing the grey lining underneath; and her mantle was separated into so many pieces, that it was only held together by the braiding at the edge.

As she conversed with me, she played with the strings of her bonnet, rolling them up as if curling them, on her singularly small and also singularly dirty fingers.

"I'll be fourteen, sir, a fortnight before next Christmas. I was born in Liquorpond-street, Gray's Inn-lane. Father come over from Ireland, and was a bricklayer. He had pains in his limbs and wasn't strong enough, so he give it over. He's dead now—been dead a long time, sir. I was a littler girl then than I am now, for I wasn't above eleven at that time. I lived with mother after father died. She used to sell things in the streets—yes, sir, she was a coster. About a twelvemonth after father's death, mother was taken bad with the cholera, and died. I then went along with both grandmother and grandfather, who was a porter in Newgate Market; I stopped there until I got a place as servant of all-work. I was only turned, just turned, eleven then. I worked along with a French lady and gentleman in Hatton Garden, who used to give me a shilling a-week and my tea. I used to go home to grandmother's to dinner every day. I hadn't to do any work, only just to clean the room and nuss the child. It was a nice little thing. I couldn't understand what the French people used to say, but there was a boy working there, and he used to explain to me what they meant.

"I left them because they was going to a place called Italy—perhaps you may have heerd tell of it, sir. Well, I suppose they must have been Italians, but we calls everybody, whose talk we don't understand, French. I went back to grandmother's, but, after grandfather died, she couldn't keep me, and so I went out begging—she sent me. I carried lucifer-matches and stay-laces fust. I used to carry about a dozen laces, and perhaps I'd sell six out of them. I suppose I used to make about sixpence a-day, and I used to take it home to grandmother, who kept and fed me.

"At last, finding I didn't get much at begging, I thought I'd go crossing-sweeping. I saw other children doing it. I says to myself, 'I'll go and buy a broom,' and I spoke to another little girl, who was sweeping up Holborn, who told me what I was to do. 'But,' says she, 'don't come and cut up me.'

"I went fust to Holborn, near to home, at the end of Red Lion-street. Then I was frightened of the cabs and carriages, but I'd get there early, about eight o'clock, and sweep the crossing clean, and I'd stand at the side on the pavement, and speak to the gentlemen and ladies before they crossed.

"There was a couple of boys, sweepers at the same crossing before I went there. I went to them and asked if I might come and sweep there too, and they said Yes, if I would give them some of the halfpence I got. These was boys about as old as I was, and they said, if I earned sixpence, I was to give them twopence a-piece; but they never give me nothink of theirs. I never took more than sixpence, and out of that I had to give fourpence, so that I did not do so well as with the laces.

"The crossings made my hands sore with the sweeping, and, as I got so little, I thought I'd try somewhere else. Then I got right down to the Fountings in Trafalgar-square, by the crossing at the statey on 'orseback. There were a good many boys and girls on that crossing at the time—five of them; so I went along with them. When I fust went they said, 'Here's another fresh 'un.' They come up to me and says, 'Are you going to sweep here?' and I says, 'Yes;' and they says, 'You mustn't come here, there's too many;' and I says, 'They're different ones every day,'—for they're not regular there, but shift about, sometimes one lot of boys and girls, and the next day another. They didn't say another word to me, and so I stopped.

"It's a capital crossing, but there's so many of us, it spiles it. I seldom gets more than sevenpence a-day, which I always takes home to grandmother.

"I've been on that crossing about three months. They always calls me Ellen, my regular name, and behaves very well to me. If I see anybody coming, I call them out as the boys does, and then they are mine.

"There's a boy and myself, and another strange girl, works on our side of the statey, and another lot of boys and girls on the other.

"I like Saturdays the best day of the week, because that's the time as gentlemen as has been at work has their money, and then they are more generous. I gets more then, perhaps ninepence, but not quite a shilling, on the Saturday.

"I've had a threepenny-bit give to me, but never sixpence. It was a gentleman, and I should know him again. Ladies gives me less than gentlemen. I foller 'em, saying, 'If you please, sir, give a poor girl a halfpenny;' but if the police are looking, I stop still.

"I never goes out on Sunday, but stops at home with grandmother. I don't stop out at nights like the boys, but I gets home by ten at latest."

THE BOY CROSSING-SWEEPERS.

[*From a Daguerreotype by* BEARD.]

INDEX.

	PAGE
Articles for amusement, second-hand sellers of	16
Bear-baiting	54
Bedding, &c., second-hand sellers of	15
Bird-catchers who are street sellers	64
—— duffers, tricks of	69
—— street-seller, the crippled	66
Birds'-nests, sellers of	72
—————————— life of a	74
Birds, stuffed, sellers of	23
—— live, sellers of	58
—— foreign, sellers of	70
Bone-grubbers	139
———————— narrative of a	141
Boots and shoes, second-hand, sellers of	42
Boy crossing-sweepers' room	504
Brisk and slack seasons	297
Brushes, second-hand, sellers of	22
Burnt linen or calico	13
Cabinet-ware, second-hand, sellers of	22
Casual labour in general	297
———————— brisk and slack seasons	297
———————— among the chimney-sweeps	374
Carpeting, &c., second-hand, sellers of	14
Cesspool emptying by trunk and hose	447
Cesspool system of London	437
———————— of Paris	438
Cesspool-sewerman, statement of a	448
Cesspoolage and nightmen	433
Chimney-sweepers, the London	339
———————— of old, and climbing-boys	346
———————— stealing children	347
———————— sores and diseases	350
———————— accidents	351
———————— cruelties towards	352
———————— of the present day	354

	PAGE
Chimney-sweepers, work and wages	357
———————— general characteristics of	365
———————— dress and diet	366
———————— abodes	367
———————— festival at May-day	371
———————— "leeks"	375
———————— knullers and queriers	376
Cigar-end finders	145
Clocks, second-hand, sellers of	23
Clothes worn in town and country, table showing comparative cost of	192
Coal, consumption of	169
—— sellers of	81
Coke, sellers of	85
Commissioners of Sewers, powers of	416
"Coshar" meat killed for the Jews	121
Criminals, number of, in England and Wales	320
Crossing-sweeper, the aristocratic	467
———————— the bearded	471
———————— a Regent-Street	474
———————— a tradesman's	476
———————— "old woman over the water"	477
———————— old woman who had been a pensioner	478
———————— one who had been a servant-maid	479
———————— the female Irish	482
———————— the Sunday	484
———————— the wooden-legged	486
———————— the one-legged	488
———————— the most severely afflicted	488
———————— the negro who lost both his legs	490
———————— the maimed Irish	493

INDEX.

	PAGE
Crossing-sweeper, Mike's statement	498
——— Gander the captain	499
——— the king of the tumbling-boy crossing-sweepers	501
——— the girl sweeper sent out by her father	505
Crossing-sweepers	465
——— able-bodied male	467
——— who have got permission from the police, narratives of	472
——— able-bodied Irish	481
——— the occasional	484
——— the afflicted	486
——— boy, and tumblers	494
——— where they lodge	503
——— their room	504
——— girl	505
Curiosities, second-hand, sellers of	21
Curtains, second-hand, sellers of	14
Dog "finder's" career, a	51
Dog-finders, stealers, and restorers, the former	48
——— extent of their trade	49
Dogs, sellers of	52
——— sporting, sellers of	54
"Dolly" business, the	108
Dredgers, the, or river-finders	147
Dust-contractors	168
Dust-heap, composition of a	171
——— separation of	172
Dustmen, the	166
——— "filler" and "carrier"	175
——— their general character	177
Dustmen, sweeps, and nightmen	159
——— number of	162
Employers, "cutting," varieties of	232
——— "drivers"	233
——— "grinders"	233
Fires of London	378
——— abstract of causes of	379
——— extinction of	381
Flushermen, the working	428
——— history of an individual	430
Furs, second-hand, sellers of	45
Gander, the "captain" of the boy sweepers	499
Garret workmen, labour of	302
Glass and crockery, second-hand, sellers of	15

	PAGE
Gold and silver fish, sellers of	78
Hare and rabbit-skins, buyers of	111
Harness, second-hand, sellers of	23
Hill men and women	173
Hogs'-wash, buyers of	132
Home work	313
Horse, food consumed by, and excretions in twenty-four hours	194
Horse-dung of the streets of London	193
——— gross annual weight of	195
House-drainage, as connected with the sewers	395
Iron Jack	11
Jew old clothes-men	119
——— street-seller, life of a	122
——— boy street-sellers	122
——— their pursuits, traffic, &c.	123
——— girl street-sellers	124
——— sellers of accordions, &c.	131
Jews, the street	115
——— history of	117
——— trades and localities	117
——— habits and diet	121
——— synagogues and religion	125
——— politics, literature, and amusements	126
——— charities, schools, and education	127
——— funeral ceremonies, fasts, and customs	131
Jewesses, street, the	124
Kitchen-stuff, grease, and dripping, buyers of	111
Knullers and queriers	376
Labour, economy of	307
Lasts, second-hand, sellers of	23
"Leeks," the	375
Leverets, wild rabbits, &c., sellers of	77
Linen, second-hand, sellers of	13
Live animals, sellers of	47
London street drains	398
——— extent of	400
——— order of	401
——— outlets, ramifications, &c., of	405
Low wages, remedies for	254
"Lurker's," a, career	51
Marine-store shops	108
May-day	370

INDEX.

	PAGE
May-day, sweeps' festival	371
Men's second-hand clothes, sellers of	40
Metal trays, second-hand, sellers of	12
Metropolitan police district, the	159
———— inhabited houses	164
———— population	165
"Middleman" system of work	329
Monmouth-street, Dickens's description of	36
Mud-larks	155
———— story of a reclaimed	158
Mineral productions and natural curiosities, sellers of	81
Music "duffers"	19
Musical instruments, second-hand, sellers of	18
Night-soil, present disposal of	448
Nightmen, the, working and mode of work	450
Offal, how disposed of	7
Old Clothes Exchange, the	26
———— wholesale business at the	27
Old clothes-men	119
Old hats, sellers of	43
Old John, the waterman, statement of	480
Old woman "over the water," the	477
Old wood gatherers	146
Paris, cesspool and sewer system of	439
——— rag-gatherers of	141
Paupers, street-sweeping, narratives of	245
——— number of, in England and Wales	320
Petticoat-lane, street-sellers of	36
"Pure" finders	143
———— narrative of a female	144
Purl-men, the	93
"Rag and bottle" shops	108
Rag-gatherers	139
Rags, broken metal, bottles, glass, and bone, buyers of	106
"Ramoneur Company," the	373
Rat-killing	56
River beer-sellers	93
River finders	147
Rosemary-lane, street sellers of	39
Rubbish-carters, the	281, 289
———— wages and perquisites of	292

	PAGE
Rubbish-carters, social characteristics of	295
———— casual labourers among	323
———— scurf trade among	327
Salt, sellers of	89
Sand, sellers of	90
Scavenger, statement of a "regular"	224
Scavengers, master, of former times	205
———— oath of	206
———— working	216
———— labour and rates of payment	219
———— "casual hands"	220
———— habits and diet	226
———— influence of free trade on their earnings	228
———— worse paid, the	232
Scavengery, contractors for	210
———— regulations of	211
———— premises of	216
Scavenging, jet and hose system of	275
Scurf-labourers	236
Second-hand apparel, sellers of	25
———— articles, sellers of	5
———— experience of a dealer in	11
———— articles, live animals, productions, &c., street-sellers of, their numbers, capital, and income	97
———— garments, uses of	29
———— ———— varieties of	32
———— store-shops	24
Seven-dials, Dickens's description of	35
Sewage, metropolitan, quantity of	387
———— qualities and uses of	407
Sewerage, the City	403
———— new plan of	411
Sewerage and scavengery, London, history of	179
Sewers, ancient	388
———— kinds and characteristics of	390
———— subterranean character of	394
———— house-drainage in connection with	395
———— ventilation of	423
———— flushing and plunging	424
———— rats in the	431
———— management of the, and the late Commission	414
———— Commissioners, powers of	416
———— rate	420
Sewer-hunters	150
———— numbers of	152
———— strange tale of	154

INDEX. 511

	PAGE
Sewermen and nightmen of London	383
Shells, sellers of	91
Shoddy mills	30
———— fever	31
Smithfield market, second-hand sellers at	46
Smoke, evils of	339
———————— scientific opinions upon	340
Squirrels, sellers of	77
"Strapping" system, the, illustration of	304
Street-buyers, the, varieties of	103
Street-cleansing, modes and characteristics of	207
———————— men and carts employed in	213
———————— pauper labour employed in	243
———————— narratives of individuals	245
Street-finders or collectors, varieties of	136
Street-folk, census of	1
———————— capital and trade	2
———————— proscription of	3
———————— rate of increase	5
Street-muck, or "mac"	198
———————— uses of	198
———————— value of	199
Street Jews, the	115
Street-orderlies, the	253
———————— condition of	261
———————— expenditure of	265
———————— earnings of	266
———————— City surveyor's report of	271
Street-sweeping, employers	209
———————— parishes	209
Street-sweeping, philanthropists	209
Street-sweeping machines	208
———————— hands employed	238
Streets of London, how paved	181
———————— traffic of	184
———————— dust and dirt of	185
———————— loss and injury from	185
———————— mud of the	200
———————— cost and traffic of	278
Sweeping chimneys of steam-vessels	372
Surface-water of the streets of London	202
———————— analysis of	205
Tan-turf, sellers of	87
Tea-leaves, buyers of	133
Telescopes and pocket-glasses, second-hand, sellers of	22
"Translators" of old shoes	34
———————— extent of the trade	35
Tumbling boy-sweepers, king of the	501
Umbrellas and parasols, buyers of	115
Washing expenses in London	190
Waste-paper, buyers of	113
Water, daily supply of the metropolis	203
Watermen's Company, form of license	95
Weapons, second-hand, sellers of	21
Wet house-refuse	383
———————— means of removing	385
Women's second-hand apparel, sellers of	44
Wrappers or "bale-stuff"	13
Young Mike the crossing-sweeper	498